Special Interest Group Profiles *for Students*

(...)

Special Interest Group Profiles *for Students*

Kelle S. Sisung, *Senior Editor*

GALE GROUP

Detroit
San Francisco
London
Boston
Woodbridge CT

Special Interest Group Profiles for Students

Gale Group Staff

Editorial: Kelle S. Sisung, *Project Manager/Series Editor*; Gerda Ann Raffaelle, *Associate Editor*; Bernard Grunow, *Associate Editor*; John F. McCoy, *Assistant Editor*; Talitha A. Jean, *Assistant Editor*

Graphic Services: Barbara J. Yarrow, *Graphic Services Manager*; Randy Bassett, *Image Database Supervisor*; Robert Duncan, Mike Logusz, *Imaging Specialists*; Pamela A. Reed, *Imaging Coordinator*; Christine O'Bryan, *Desktop Publisher*

Permissions: Maria Franklin, *Permissions Manager*; Margaret Chamberlain, *Permissions Specialist*; Shalice Shah-Caldwell, *Permissions Specialist*

Product Design: Cynthia Baldwin, *Product Design Manager*; Pamela A. E. Galbreath, *Senior Art Director*

Production: Mary Beth Trimper, *Production Director*; Evi Seoud, *Assistant Production Manager*; Cindy Range, *Production Assistant*

Graphics Creator: Eric E. Wisniewski

Indexer: Nancy Fulton

Copyright Notice

Library of Congress Cataloging-in-Publication Data

Special interest group profiles for students / Kelle S. Sisung, senior editor.
    p.   cm.
    Includes bibliographic references and index.
    ISBN 0-7876-2794-1 (hard)
    1. Pressure groups—United States.   I. Sisung, Kelle.
JK1118.S688 1999
3249.490973—dc21   99-28056
                                                                  CIP

ISBN 0-7876-2794-1
Printed in the United States of America
10 9 8 7 6 5 4 3 2

Table of Contents

Table of Contents by Type of Special Interest Group

Economic Interest Groups

Single-Issue Groups

Social-Action Groups

Advisors and Contributors

Advisory Board

A nine-member advisory board consisting of teachers, media specialists, and other experts on U.S. government was consulted to help determine the scope and content of *Special Interest Group Profiles for Students.*

Howard Ball: Professor of Political Science, University of Vermont

Marion J. Cannon: Library Media Specialist, Winter Park High School, Winter Park, Florida

Catherine Chauvette: Library Media Specialist, Fairfax County Public Library, Alexandria, Virgina

Fran Cohen: Library Media Specialist (retired), Conestoga High School, Berwyn, Pennsylvania

Michael D. Leahy, Ph.D.: Library Media Specialist (retired), Eastern High School, Bristol, Connecticut

Frank J. Orfei: History Department, Pelham Memorial High School, Pelham, New York

Harriet B. Sawyer: Social Studies Department Chair, Franklin High School, Livonia, Michigan

Jay A. Sigler, Ph.D.: Professor of Public Policy and Administration, Rutgers University

Lavonna Brown Williams: Educator, Minot Public School District, Minot, North Dakota; Bonneville Joint School District, Bonneville, Idaho

Contributors

Many writers contributed to the text of *Special Interest Group Profiles for Students.* An asterisk (*) indicates an author was a primary contributor.

Howard Baker

Sheree L. Beaudry*

Matthew Berglind

Kari Bethel

Gerald E. Brennan*

Andrea Bewick Collins

R. Craig Collins*

Gloria Cooksey*

Julie Davis

Howard Distelzweig

Thomas D. Faulkner

Krister Friday

Daniel C. Holly

Cathy Dybiec Holm*

Christopher C. Hunt

Paul S. Kobel

Michael Robertson

Tracy Roof

Preface

Special Interest Group Profiles for Students (SIGS) is the second volume in the U.S. Government for Students series, preceded by *Federal Agency Profiles for Students,* and followed by *Presidential Administration Profiles for Students.* The purpose of the series is to provide an overall view of the workings of the United States government geared specifically to meet the curriculum needs of high school students, undergraduate college students, and their teachers. Each profile in a U.S. Government for Students volume will cover not only the basic facts found in directories such as the United States Government Manual but will include the historical and political context, or the how and why. Furthermore, the series focuses on the relevancy and immediacy of government, explaining how an agency, a special interest group, or a presidential administration can impact the life of an average citizen and, in some cases, how a citizen can become actively involved in the federal government. While the series was designed to reflect curriculum standards, the general reader and researcher will also be able to find answers to their questions about the U.S. government.

SIGS includes profiles of 150 special interest groups. The term "special interest group" is used to describe any organized group of individuals, united together for a common cause, that attempts to influence public policy. Individuals and groups unite for a variety of reasons. An association may be composed of individuals within the same occupation, another organization may draw together individuals who share the same belief system. Regardless, all special interest groups share several common characteristics: they have an organizational structure; they act on behalf of group members; they broadcast the organization's message to the public; and, most important, they strive to effect political change.

The majority of special interest groups fall under three broad categories: economic interest groups, social-action groups, and single-issue groups. *SIGS* includes profiles of:

- *Agricultural Groups,* such as the National Grange and the American Farm Bureau Federation, which serve the interest of agriculture. (Economic Interest)

- *Animal Rights Groups,* which promote the welfare of animals. Such well-known groups include People for the Ethical Treatment of Animals. (Social Action)

- *Business and Trade Associations,* which are formed to promote and protect business interests. Some of the most well-known groups include the National Association of Manufacturing and the United States Chamber of Commerce. (Economic Interest)

- *Civil Rights Groups,* which attempt to establish, uphold, protect, and extend the rights guaranteed to all Americans under the U.S. Constitution. Such groups may be organized along ethnic or gender lines or may represent particular segments of the U.S. population. Civil Rights Groups include the NAACP, the American Association of Retired Persons, and Lambda. (Social Action)

- *Environmental Protection Groups,* such as the Sierra Club, which work for the conservation and preservation of the global environment. (Social Action)

- *Labor Unions,* including the United Mine Workers and the AFL-CIO, which are composed of workers who have the same sort of job or work within the same industry. Such organizations present a unified voice that can speak for worker benefits and other job-related issues. (Economic Interest)

- *Professional Associations,* which are groups composed of professionals–individuals in occupations that traditionally require specialized training. Examples include the American Medical Association and the American Bar Association. (Economic Interest)

- *Public Interest Groups,* which fight for causes that are believed to benefit not only the members of a particular organization, but all members of society. Public Interest Groups include Common Cause and the Center for Responsive Politics. (Social Action)

- *Religious Groups,* such as the Christian Coalition and the American Jewish Congress, which are composed of members who are aligned along religious beliefs and attempt to influence legislation and policy that reflect these beliefs. (Social Action)

- *Single-Issue Groups,* which are groups that focus all energies on one certain issue, such as abortion. Such issues are usually highly controversial with one group advocating for a particular viewpoint with another taking the opposing side.

- *Veterans' Rights Groups,* which represent the interest of men and women who have served in the U.S. armed forces. (Social Action)

Selection Criteria

Not surprisingly, selecting which special interest groups to profile in *SIGS* was a daunting task as there are virtually thousands of groups in the United States representing millions of Americans. Gale editors began by surveying high school civics and government sources including top-rated textbooks and the *National Standards for Civics and Government.* We also relied on course curriculu supplied by our advisors that represented various school districts across the United States. We further consulted such lists as *Fortune* magazine's *Washington's Power 25,* which is an annual survey of the pressure groups that wield the greatest influence on public policy, and the Center for Responsive Politic's *Open Secrets: The Encyclopedia of Congressional Money and Politics,* that details which groups spent what in congressional elections. We eventually narrowed the list down to approximately 400. A core list soon emerged that included 60 special interest groups that were widely known, studied, and considered extremely influential. Our advisory board, consisting of high school teachers, media specialists, and subject experts, helped sort through and pare down the remaining list based on their knowledge of common classroom assignments.

How Each Profile is Organized

Profiles are arranged in alphabetical order, according to the official name of the special interest group as presented in group literature or if communication with the organization was not made available, we deferred to Gale's *Encyclopedia of Associations.* Each profile heading also includes the organization's acronym or other

variant names. For additional access, readers should refer to the subject index for alternative name representations and the two tables of content: one is in book order, the second is based on type of special interest group. The following elements may be contained in each profile:

- **Established:** Generally refers to the date that the organization as we know it today was established. Because many of the SIGS went through multiple incarnations, the profile's "History" section outlines the SIG's progression over time.

- **Employees:** Includes the number of employees retained by the national organization based on 1998 figures. If figures are based on non-1998 information, the date is included in parentheses. The number of employees is an approximate figure as the structure of an organization can often be quite complicated. In addition, many of the SIGS are partially, or sometimes wholly, staffed by volunteers.

- **Members:** Includes the number of members who belong to the organization based on 1998 figures. If figures are based on non-1998 information, the date is included in parentheses. The number of members is an approximate figure as the structure of an organization can often be scattered. For example, Amnesty is an international organization, but only the U.S. affiliate is profiled in *SIGS.*

- **PACs:** Includes the name of the political action committee (PAC) maintained by the organization. Not all groups retain a PAC, which is the organization's arm responsible for collecting and administering funds for political purposes. For instance, an organization that has been granted 501(c)(3) tax-exempt status by the Internal Revenue Service (IRS) is considered a charitable organization. Part of the restrictions of 501(c)(3) status is the fact that a group may not influence legislation as a substantial part of its activities and may not be involved in political campaign activity.

- **Contact Information:** General mailing address, telephone number, toll free telephone number, TDD number, fax number, E-mail, and URL.

- **SIG Heads:** Limited to the inclusion of the organization's top officials. These individuals shift positions frequently, depending on the group's bylaws, which usually indicate how frequently a president or board member may remain in office.

- **What is Its Mission?:** The mission usually contains a quote directly from the SIG being profiled, which encapsulates the organization's primary motivation. Information was taken directly from published statements released by the SIG administrator or from annual reports. In some instances authors attempted to further define the mission if the statement required clarification.

- **How is it Structured?:** Outlines the general structure of each SIG. The section begins by defining the type of SIG (e.g., labor union, professional association, fraternal organization) and continues by outlining the internal administrative organization at the national level progressing all the way down to the regional and local branches.

- **Primary Functions:** This is the action center of the profile that offers a broad brush look at what a special interest group does. What are its primary responsibilities? Does it lobby Congress, attempt to influence elections, litigate, conduct research, hold public protests? How does it interact with government regulatory agencies or other special interest groups? Authors made a particular effort to stress the connection between special interest groups and U.S. government bodies to underscore that the formation of public policy is truly a collaborative enterprise.

- **Programs:** Offers a general overview of the number and type of programs the organization administers. The section also profiles one or two of the organizations's most notable or newsworthy. For instance, the profile of Mothers Against Drunk Driving includes a description of the Red Ribbon Campaign.

- **Budget Information:** Budget information is based on 1998 actual or 1999 estimated figures. The section details where SIG revenues come from and how resources are allocated. Figures are based on information supplied directly from the special interest group. If a group is considered by law to be a public charity or private foundation, it is required under section 6104(b) of the Internal Revenue Code to make the most current annual Form 990 available to the public. Reports are also available from the National Charities Information Bureau and the Council of Better Business Bureaus.

- A budget graphic accompanies most profiles, which illustrates the organization's revenue and expenses. It is sometimes quite dramatic to see how very much, or very little, of an organization's dollars are spent on a particular initiative.

- **History:** This section details the history of the special interest group, including key events, administrations, people, and legislation. The narrative usually includes history that pre-dates the organization's formation explaining why it was necessary for this particular organization to be established.

- **Political Issue:** The political issue section serves as the nerve center of the profile. It begins with a brief introduction that outlines the organization's current concerns and the controversies surrounding them. A case study is then highlighted to illuminate a particular issue. Authors were careful to include all sides of the story by relating how the organization is involved with the issue, how the public was impacted by the event, how the public feels about the organization, and how other special interest groups, government agencies, or other countries responded.

- **Successes and Failures:** A variety of indicators determines a success or a failure, however such indicators are usually subjective. A failure is apparent when a special interest group establishes a benchmark for success, such as passage of a particular piece of legislation. For example, the National Organization for Women (NOW) has worked for 30 years to enact the passage of the Equal Rights Amendment (ERA). The fact that it has never passed may be viewed by NOW members as a failure. However, defeat of the ERA is considered a success for a group like the Eagle Forum, which has spent considerable time blocking the amendment. Authors were careful to include events that would invite analysis by *SIGS* readers.

- **Future Directions:** Where is the organization headed? What challenges does it face? What are the organization's projected goals for the future? Information for this section was gleaned from reports submitted by SIG administrators.

- **Group Resources:** Resources refers to hot lines, Web sites, information clearinghouses and centers, dockets, libraries, databases, document repositories, and archives. Authors tried to highlight information available to the average consumer or general researcher, although many organizations have members-only access. The section includes how to tap into the information whether via mail, E-mail, telephone, or Internet.

- **Group Publications:** The section provides information about the number and type of publications the organization makes available to both members and non members. Representative pamphlets, newsletters, and other publications are included along with contact information on how an interested party can access them.

- **Bibliography:** An alphabetical list of sources, including books and current periodicals quoted in the profile, with full bibliographic information. Also lists other critical sources that may prove helpful for the student and researcher.

In addition, a *SIGS* profile may contain one or more of the following supplementary sidebars:

- **Fast Facts:** At-a-glance facts that are current and reflect how the organization impacts the daily lives of all citizens. Facts may reflect the workings of the SIG being profiled or might illustrate the issues that have been discussed throughout the essay. Each fact is fully cited.

- **Biography:** An individual who was pivotal to an organization's history is profiled in a biography sidebar that includes birth and death dates, identifier, a brief sketch, and a thumbnail photo.

Additional Features

In an attempt to create a comprehensive, one-stop reference tool for the study of the U.S. federal government, *SIGS* also includes:

- Illustrations that depict historic events, notable individuals, and current issues along with graphics and maps.

- A chronology of over 900 key events in U.S. history that allows students to place each special interest group in an historical context.

- A glossary containing over 450 political terms used throughout the profiles.

- A subject index for easy access to special interest groups, people, places, and events.

Acknowledgments

It is important for Gale to acknowledge the bounty of materials available to all researchers through the United States government. Specifically, the *United States Government Manual* was a much-thumbed, constant source of information that helped untangle the vast web known as the federal government. It is a valuable first-stop directory that is held by most libraries and is available for purchase at U.S. government bookstores. It is also available on-line at http://www.access.gpo.gov/ nara/nara001.html. The Government Printing Office (GPO) is the United States' preeminent publisher that offers a plethora of information resources on every facet of government. Catalogs may be requested by writing to

732 N. Capitol St. NW, Washington, DC 20401 or visit the GPO Web site at http://www.access.gpo.gov/#info.

We must also recognize the contribution made by each of the special interest groups profiled. SIG Web sites made good launching pads for beginning research. To further guarantee accuracy of information and to gather as much information as possible, our industrious researchers and authors undertook a mail, fax, and E-mail blitz for over two months. Organization representatives were sent questionnaires to fill in and sample profiles to review. Our authors were often rewarded for their efforts thanks to helpful special interest group members.

Special thanks must be extended to our advisory board who continue to serve as the backbone of the U.S. Government for Students series. Their input was invaluable from the genesis of the series and remains constant through each volume. In addition, we must mention our various contributors, many of whom are former teachers. Their classroom experience led to the creation of well-researched, thoughtful, and enjoyable profiles that hopefully will stimulate students' interest in U.S. government.

We Welcome Your Suggestions

The editor of *Special Interest Group Profiles for Students* welcomes your comments and suggestions. Please direct all correspondence to:

Editor
Special Interest Group Profiles for Students
The Gale Group
27500 Drake Rd.
Farmington Hills, MI 48331-3535

Chronology

1492: Columbus discovers the Americas.

1565: St. Augustine, Florida, is founded by the Spanish.

1607: Over 140 men and boys form a settlement at Jamestown, Virginia; approximately one-half die before the end of the year. Jamestown becomes the second oldest town in North America, after St. Augustine, and the first permanent British settlement.

1614: Dutch found the colony of New Amsterdam.

1619: Martial law in Virginia is replaced by a general assembly of twenty-two burgesses, the first representative assembly in America.

1620: Off of present-day Cape Cod, Massachusetts, 41 male passengers on the *Mayflower* sign the Mayflower Compact, establishing a preliminary civil body politic and the authority to legislate laws as necessary. The people who debark are known as the Pilgrims.

1629: The Massachusetts Bay Company is formed by English Puritans allowing the company to have governmental autonomy once on the American mainland.

1630: English Puritans, sponsored by the Massachusetts Bay Company, found Boston and ten other settlements in Massachusetts.

1643: Massachusetts, Connecticut, New Haven, and Plymouth form a confederation called the United Colonies of New England.

1647: Rhode Island adopts its first constitution which declares separation of church and state and freedom of religious expression.

1660: Parliament passes the first of the Navigation Acts, which restricts the trade of New England merchants to England and the British West Indies by imposing taxes and duties on goods traded with other countries.

1675: King Philip's War begins and pits the New England Confederation against American Indian tribes led by Chief Philip of the Wampanoags. The two-year conflict results in great loss and destruction for both sides. Twelve New England towns are leveled, and for every 16 white men of fighting age, one loses his life.

1682: William Penn establishes his Frame of Government which allows for the creation of an assembly, council, and governor's office in Pennsylvania.

1685: The Dominion of New England is formed, and the following year Sir Edmund Andros is appointed governor.

1696: William III commissions the Board of Trade to oversee commercial (trade and fishing) and political (powers of appointment and legislative review) concerns in the American colonies.

1702: As part of the War of the Spanish Succession (1702–1713), known as Queen Anne's War in America, James Moore, the English governor of South Carolina, attacks Saint Augustine, Florida, burning outposts and missions in Apalachee, or northern Florida.

1754–1763: The French and Indian War results in the British and Indian allies capturing Quebec and defeating the French.

August 17, 1754: The Albany Plan, formulated by Benjamin Franklin, is rejected. It would have joined the colonies in a defense against the French and would have established an intercolonial council to handle relations with the American Indians.

1763: The Treaty of Paris is signed, concluding the French and Indian War; Britain is given Canada and all French territory east of the Mississippi River and Florida.

1763: The Proclamation of 1763 prohibits colonists from settling west of the Appalachian mountains beyond the reach of British authorities. It is also issued to pacify the American Indians.

April 5, 1764: Parliament passes the Sugar Act, reducing the tariff on molasses imported into North America. However, it also sends custom agents and collectors to the colonies to strictly enforce the remaining laws in effect.

1765: Britain imposes the Stamp Act. This is the first internal tax levied on the colonies. Requiring the purchase of stamps to be affixed to a number of official documents, it affects mostly lawyers, clergymen, and printers.

October 7–25, 1765: Nine colonies represented at the Stamp Act Congress in New York protest Parliament's taxation of the colonies.

March 17, 1766: Parliament rescinds the stamp tax but insists it has the power to tax the colonies.

1767: The Townshend Acts, which impose a tax on goods imported into the American colonies, are passed by the British Parliament and contribute to a revolt against British rule.

May 16, 1769: After Virginia's House of Burgesses rejects Parliament's right to tax the colonies, the governor dissolves the assembly, which continues to meet privately, agreeing not to import British goods.

January 19–20, 1770: The Battle of Golden Hill, New York, results in one death as the Sons of Liberty skirmish with British soldiers trying to remove liberty poles from Golden Hill, Manhattan.

April 12, 1770: Parliament repeals all the Townshend duties except the one on tea.

November 2, 1772: The Boston town meeting creates a 21-member committee of correspondence to communicate with other towns in the colony and to defend the rights of colonists "as Men, as Christians, and as Subjects."

December 16, 1773: In the act that came to be known as the Boston Tea Party, a mob dumps a cargo of tea into Boston Harbor to protest Great Britain's tea tax.

May 20, 1774: The Massachusetts Government Act suspends the colony's charter.

May 27, 1774: A call for a Continental Congress goes out to consolidate action and support economic pressure to force Great Britain to rescind the Massachusetts Government Act.

September 5–October 16, 1774: The First Continental Congress meets in Philadelphia to work out constitutional issues; each state has one vote in this body.

October 18, 1774: The Continental Congress adopts the Continental Association, pledging to cease imports from Great Britain after December 1, 1774.

1775–1783: The American Revolution.

February 9, 1775: The king declares Massachusetts to be in rebellion.

May 5, 1775: The Second Continental Congress convenes for the purpose of uniting the colonies for military action.

June 14, 1775: The Department of the Army is founded as the Continental Army by the Second Continental Congress; George Washington is appointed its first commander in chief.

October 13, 1775: The Department of the Navy is founded; it is commissioned by the Continental Congress and plays a decisive role in the British decision to abandon the American colonies.

November 10, 1775: The U.S. Marine Corps is founded when two battalions of "marines" are authorized by the Continental Congress to serve in the Revolutionary War against Great Britain.

July 2, 1776: The Continental Congress votes unanimously that "these thirteen colonies are, and of right, ought to be, free and independent states."

July 4, 1776: The Declaration of Independence is adopted.

November 15, 1777: The Continental Congress adopts the Articles of Confederation and Perpetual Union; it requires the endorsement of all the state legislatures to take effect.

July 9, 1778: Delegates from 8 of the 10 states that have ratified the Articles of Confederation sign them.

May 18, 1779: The U.S. Army Corps of Engineers is founded to provide engineering, management, and technical support to the United States in peace and war.

September 13, 1779: John Jay, president of the Continental Congress, asks the states to collect taxes in order to pay requisitions to the federal treasury.

January 10, 1781: The Continental Congress creates a ministry for foreign affairs.

May 26, 1781: The Pennsylvania legislature charters the Bank of North America.

April 18, 1783: The Continental Congress proposes a revenue system as a way of paying the national debt.

September 3, 1783: The Treaty of Paris, which recognizes American independence, is signed by British and American negotiators.

December 23, 1783: George Washington resigns his commission as commander in chief of the Continental Army.

January 14, 1784: The Continental Congress ratifies the Treaty of Paris.

January 11, 1785: The Continental Congress moves from Philadelphia to New York City.

May 20, 1785: The Continental Congress passes the Land Ordinance of 1785, revamping the system for settling western areas and setting aside land and revenue to support public education.

May 25–September 17, 1787: The Constitutional Convention meets in Philadelphia with delegates from all states except Rhode Island present.

May 29, 1787: Edmund Randolph submits the Virginia Plan to the Constitutional Convention, proposing a bicameral legislature based on proportional representation, a national executive and judiciary, and a congressional veto of state laws.

May 31, 1787: The Constitutional Convention votes that the people should directly elect members to what will be the House of Representatives.

June 15, 1787: William Paterson presents the New Jersey Plan to the Convention, proposing to retain the unicameral national legislature (with each state having an equal vote) and to expand congressional control over trade and revenue.

July 11, 1787: The Constitutional Convention votes to count three-fifths of the slave population for taxation and representation purposes.

July 13, 1787: The Continental Congress passes the Northwest Ordinance, establishing the Northwest Territory (present-day Illinois, Indiana, Ohio, Michigan, Wisconsin, and parts of Minnesota). The Ordinance defines the steps for the creation and admission of new states and bars slavery in the area.

July 16, 1787: The Constitutional Convention approves the "Great Compromise," granting proportional representation in the House of Representatives and equal state representation in the Senate.

August 29, 1787: The Convention gives the Continental Congress power to pass navigation acts, approves a fugitive slave clause, and forbids Congress from regulating the slave trade before 1808.

December 7, 1787: Delaware is the first of the original 13 states to ratify the Constitution.

December 12, 1787: Pennsylvania is the second of the original 13 states to ratify the Constitution.

December 18, 1787: New Jersey is the third of the original 13 states to ratify the Constitution.

January 2, 1788: Georgia is the fourth of the original 13 states to ratify the Constitution.

January 9, 1788: Connecticut is the fifth of the 13 original states to ratify the Constitution.

February 6, 1788: Massachusetts is the sixth of the original 13 states to ratify the Constitution.

April 28, 1788: Maryland is the seventh of the original 13 states to ratify the Constitution.

May 23, 1788: South Carolina is the eighth of the original 13 states to ratify the Constitution.

June 21, 1788: New Hampshire is the ninth of the original 13 states to ratify the Constitution.

June 25, 1788: Virginia is the tenth of the original 13 states to ratify the Constitution.

July 26, 1788: New York is the eleventh of the original 13 states to ratify the Constitution.

March 4, 1789: The first Congress to meet under the Constitution convenes in New York City.

April 30, 1789: George Washington and John Adams are inaugurated as the first president and vice president of the United States.

May 11, 1789: The Office of the Vice President is founded; the two mandates of the vice presidency under the original Constitution are to preside over the Senate and to succeed to the presidency in time of emergency.

July 4, 1789: The Continental Congress, led by James Madison, passes the Tariff Act of 1789, creating a source of revenue for the federal government.

July 27, 1789: The Department of State is founded with the appointment of Thomas Jefferson as the first secretary of state; its highest concern is the protection of American interests at home and abroad.

July 31, 1789: The U.S. Customs Service is founded to collect the taxes on imported and exported goods, to document data relating to cargo and passenger ships, and to fine people or companies that defy the newly instituted laws.

September 1789: The Office of Attorney General is established.

September 2, 1789: The Department of the Treasury is founded to not only manage the nation's finances but also to provide leadership in setting its fiscal policy in order to plan the country's financial future.

September 11, 1789: Alexander Hamilton is appointed the first secretary of the Treasury.

September 24, 1789: Congress passes the Judiciary Act of 1789, creating a federal court system and giving the Supreme Court the right to review the constitutionality of state laws.

September 25, 1789: Congress, led by James Madison, submits the first ten constitutional amendments (later known as the Bill of Rights) to the states.

September 26, 1789: John Jay is appointed the first chief justice of the United States Supreme Court.

November 10, 1789: The U.S. Marshals Service is created by Congress by the Judiciary Act of 1789.

November 21, 1789: North Carolina is the twelfth of the original 13 states to ratify the Constitution.

November 26, 1789: President George Washington consults department heads on foreign and military affairs, establishing the practice of regular cabinet meetings.

February 2, 1790: The Supreme Court of the United States convenes for the first time with the responsibility of applying the Constitution and laws in deciding cases.

May 29, 1790: Rhode Island is the thirteenth of the original 13 states to ratify the Constitution.

July 1, 1790: Congress approves a site on the Potomac River (Washington, D.C.) as the future capital of the United States.

July 26, 1790: Congress passes Secretary of the Treasury Alexander Hamilton's program for assuming the states' debts; his program for funding the national debt by issuing interest-bearing securities is passed on August 4.

February 25, 1791: President George Washington signs a bill creating the First Bank of the United States after receiving conflicting opinions regarding the bank's constitutionality from Secretary of the Treasury Alexander Hamilton and Secretary of State Thomas Jefferson.

March 3, 1791: Congress passes an excise, or internal, tax on whiskey.

March 4, 1791: Vermont becomes the 14th state.

December 12, 1791: The First Bank of the United States opens in Philadelphia with branches in other cities.

December 15, 1791: The Bill of Rights becomes part of the Constitution. These ten amendments are intended to protect of freedom of religion, speech, and the press.

March 1, 1792: Congress passes the Presidential Succession Act. In case of the death or disability of the president and vice president, power will pass to the president pro tempore of the Senate followed by the Speaker of the House.

April 2, 1792: The U.S. Mint is founded by the Mint Act of 1792, which among other duties determines the materials, denominations, and inscriptions to be used in making U.S. coins.

June 1, 1792: Kentucky becomes the 15th state.

October 13, 1792: The cornerstone of the new executive mansion is laid in Washington, D.C.

February 12, 1793: Congress passes the first Fugitive Slave Law, enforcing part of Article IV, Section 2, of the Constitution, which specifies that a person fleeing a state in which they are charged, must be returned to the state having jurisdiction of the crime.

February 13, 1793: In *Chisholm v. Georgia* the Supreme Court rules that states can be sued in federal court by citizens of other states.

March 4, 1793: President George Washington and Vice President John Adams are inaugurated for a second term.

April 22, 1793: Determined to keep the United States out of the war between France and Great Britain, President Washington issues the Proclamation of Neutrality.

September 18, 1793: President George Washington lays the cornerstone for the Capitol building in Washington, D.C.

July–November 1794: Farmers in Pennsylvania resist officials trying to collect the whiskey tax. President George Washington and Secretary of the Treasury Alexander Hamilton lead a militia to enforce the law, but what became known as the Whiskey Rebellion is over by the time they arrive.

November 19, 1794: Jay's Treaty is signed in London, England. Terms include Great Britain's evacuation of posts in the Northwest Territory by 1796 and limited U.S. trade in the West Indies.

August 3, 1795: The United States and 12 Indian tribes in the Northwest sign the Treaty of Greenville, opening much of present-day Ohio to white settlement.

October 27, 1795: The United States and Spain sign the Pinckney Treaty, recognizing the 31st parallel as the southern boundary of the United States and granting Americans free navigation of the Mississippi River.

March 7, 1796: In *Ware v. Hylton* the U.S. Supreme Court declares a state law unconstitutional for the first time.

March 8, 1796: In *Hylton v. United States* the Supreme Court upholds the constitutionality of an act of Congress for the first time.

June 1, 1796: Tennessee becomes the 16th state.

March 4, 1797: President John Adams and Vice President Thomas Jefferson are inaugurated.

May 16, 1797: President John Adams recommends that Congress approve a three-man diplomatic mission to France, arm merchant vessels, create a navy, fortify harbors, and enlarge the army.

1798: The United States and France begin the "Quasi-War," an undeclared naval conflict in the Caribbean.

January 8, 1798: The Eleventh Amendment is ratified. It declares that states cannot be sued by citizens of another state or foreign country in federal court.

May–July 1798: Congress revokes all treaties with France and approves an enlarged army, a new Navy Department, harbor defenses, and the seizure of all French vessels interfering with U.S. shipping.

June 18, 1798: Congress passes the Naturalization Act, the first of four Alien and Sedition Acts, limiting freedom of speech and the press and the rights of foreigners. The act also increases the residency period required for citizenship to 14 years.

July 9, 1798: Congress passes a direct tax on land, houses, and slaves to pay for the Quasi-War with France.

July 14, 1798: Congress passes the Act for the Punishment of Certain Crimes (the Sedition Act) by a vote of 44 to 41. The act imposes heavy fines and imprisonment on anyone convicted of writing, publishing, or speaking anything of "a false scandalous and malicious nature" against the government and its officers.

November 16, 1798: The Kentucky Resolutions, drafted by Thomas Jefferson and passed by the Kentucky state legislature, declare that states can judge the constitutionality of federal laws, and that the Alien and Sedition Acts are unconstitutional and thus "void and of no force."

November 22, 1799: The Kentucky state legislature passes resolutions reaffirming nullification as a proper constitutional solution.

1800: The Virginia state legislature passes a resolution proposing that freed slaves be resettled in Africa.

January 2, 1800: Free African Americans petition Congress in opposition to slavery and the slave trade. By a vote of 85 to 1, Congress refuses to accept the petition.

April 24, 1800: The Library of Congress is established by the "Act to Make Provision for the Removal and Accommodation of the Government of the U.S." While originally only members of Congress and other government officials are allowed to use the facilities, it later opens its doors to the public.

September 30, 1800: The United States and France sign an agreement ending the Quasi-War.

November 17, 1800: Congress convenes in Washington, D.C., for the first time. John Adams becomes the first president to live in the new Executive Mansion.

January 20, 1801: John Marshall is appointed chief justice of the United States, serving until his death in 1835.

February 13, 1801: Congress passes the Judiciary Act of 1801, reducing the number of Supreme Court justices from six to five, establishing sixteen circuit courts, and increasing the number of judicial officers.

March 4, 1801: Thomas Jefferson is the first president to be inaugurated in Washington, D.C. His vice president is Aaron Burr.

April 6, 1802: Congress abolishes all internal taxes, including the unpopular whiskey tax.

April 29, 1802: After repealing the Judiciary Act of 1801, Congress passes a new Judiciary Act. It authorizes six Supreme Court justices, one session a year for the Supreme Court, and six circuit courts, each presided over by a Supreme Court justice.

August 1, 1802: The U.S. Military Academy is founded to serve as a training facility for military engineers.

August 25, 1802: The Patent and Trademark Office is founded with the mission of administering laws relating to patents and trademarks and advising the government on patent, trademark, and copyright protection.

February 24, 1803: In *Marbury v. Madison* the Supreme Court declares an act of Congress (the Judiciary Act of 1789) unconstitutional for the first time and expands its power of judicial review.

March 1, 1803: Ohio becomes the 17th state in the Union and the first to outlaw slavery from the beginning of statehood.

April 30, 1803: The United States purchases the Louisiana Territory from France for $15 million.

February 25, 1804: In the first congressional caucus Democratic-Republicans unanimously nominate President Thomas Jefferson for a second term and nominate George Clinton for vice president.

March 26, 1804: In the Louisiana Territory Act, the federal government declares for the first time that its intention is to move Indians living east of the Mississippi River to the West.

September 25, 1804: The Twelfth Amendment to the Constitution is ratified, providing separate ballots for president and vice president.

March 4, 1805: President Thomas Jefferson is inaugurated for a second term. His vice president is George Clinton.

March 29, 1806: Congress authorizes the construction of the National Road, connecting Cumberland, Maryland, with Wheeling, Virginia.

April 18, 1806: Congress passes a Non-Importation Act, prohibiting the importation of British goods in protest against the British seizure of American ships and sailors.

March 2, 1807: Congress decides to prohibit the African slave trade and importation of slaves into the United States as of January 1, 1808.

March 4, 1809: President James Madison is inaugurated with George Clinton as vice president.

July 2, 1809: The Shawnee tribal leader Tecumseh begins forming a confederacy of Native American tribes.

September 30, 1809: William Henry Harrison, governor of Indiana Territory, signs a treaty at Fort Wayne by which Amerian Indian tribes cede three tracts of land along the Wabash River.

March 4, 1811: After the Senate votes against rechartering the Bank of the United States, its charter expires.

November 7, 1811: American Indians under Tecumseh's brother, the Prophet, attack Governor William Henry Harrison's (president in 1841) army in the Battle of Tippecanoe; they are repulsed and Prophet's Town is burned. As a result Tecumseh and his followers cross into Canada, later joining British forces in the War of 1812.

November 20, 1811: Construction begins on the National Road, increasing the flow of settlers to the West.

December 24, 1811: Congress authorizes the completion of enlistments in the regular army, the enlistment of 25,000 additional regulars for five years' service and 50,000 volunteers for one year's service, and the call-up of one hundred thousand militia for six months' service at the president's request, and approves additional funds for the navy.

April 30, 1812: Louisiana becomes the 18th state in the Union.

June 18, 1812: After sending a war message to Congress, President James Madison signs the declaration of war against Great Britain, citing impressment, violations of American trade, and the incitement of American Indian warfare as the causes for hostilities with England.

March 4, 1813: President Madison is inaugurated for a second term.

September 13, 1814: As he watches the British attack on Fort McHenry at Baltimore, Maryland, Francis Scott Key composes the "Star Spangled Banner."

December 24, 1814: The United States and Great Britain sign a peace treaty at Ghent. There are no territorial changes, and all other issues are unresolved or postponed.

January 5, 1815: The Hartford Convention, a forum for delegates to discuss ways and means of sectional defense and to take steps to revise the Constitution, ends with hints of secession. The delegates uphold a state's right to nullify federal law and propose constitutional amendments to limit the power of the federal government. After the signing of the Treaty of Ghent, these delegates come to be regarded as treasonous for opposing the war.

December 5, 1815: President James Madison urges Congress to approve a national bank, protective tariffs, and a program of national funding for transportation and education.

1816: The first postwar Congress charters the Second Bank of the United States and passes an internal improvements bill and the Tariff of 1816.

December 11, 1816: Indiana is admitted to the Union as the 19th state.

March 4, 1817: James Monroe is inaugurated as president with Daniel D. Tompkins as vice president.

November 20, 1817: Settlers attack American Indians in Florida, igniting the First Seminole War. Spain is believed to support the Seminoles during the year-long conflict.

December 10, 1817: Mississippi is admitted as the 20th state of the Union.

1818: The Convention of 1818 between the United States and Great Britain sets the border between the United States and Canada at the forty-ninth parallel and establishes joint occupation of Oregon.

December 3, 1818: Illinois is the 21st state admitted to the Union.

1819: Under the Adams-Onis Treaty, Spain cedes Florida to the United States.

December 14, 1819: Alabama is admitted to the Union as the 22nd state.

March 2, 1820: As part of the Missouri Compromise, Congress prohibits slavery in the Louisiana Purchase north of 36°30' but, as part of the compromise, agrees to admit Missouri as a slave state.

March 15, 1820: Maine is admitted as the 23rd state of the Union.

March 4, 1821: James Monroe begins his second term as president.

August 10, 1821: Missouri becomes the 24th state of the Union.

December 2, 1823: President James Monroe delivers a message to Congress, warning European countries not to colonize or interfere with the Western Hemisphere. This policy comes to be known as the Monroe Doctrine.

March 30, 1824: Speaker of the U.S. House of Representatives Henry Clay defines his "American System" in a speech supporting a protective tariff that would generate revenue to fund internal improvements that would in turn expand the American colony.

August 29, 1824: The Bureau of Indian Affairs is founded with the primary functions of acquiring American Indian lands and containing the American Indian people and their culture.

November 1824: John Quincy Adams, Andrew Jackson, Henry Clay, and William Crawford run for the presidency. Jackson wins the popular and electoral votes but fails to secure an electoral majority, requiring the House of Representatives to determine the winner.

1825: President James Monroe calls for the voluntary removal of Americans Indians from the East to lands west of the Mississippi River.

March 4, 1825: After the House selects John Quincy Adams as president, he is inaugurated with John Caldwell Calhoun as his vice president.

May 19, 1828: President John Quincy Adams signs the "Tariff of Abominations" into law that provides extremely high rates on imports of raw materials and manufactured goods. Southerners call it a "hateful law."

March 4, 1829: Andrew Jackson is inaugurated as president. His vice president is John Caldwell Calhoun.

April 13, 1830: At the annual Jefferson Day Dinner, in John C. Calhoun's presence, Andrew Jackson clearly warns against nullification of the 1828 Tariff of Abominations with his toast, "Our Federal Union, it must be preserved."

May 28, 1830: Jackson signs the Indian Removal Act to provide money to purchase land from the Creeks, Seminoles, Cherokees, Chickasaws, and Choctaws and to relocate them in present-day Oklahoma and Arkansas.

May 31, 1831: Congress adjourns before President Andrew Jackson acts on several improvement bills. Jackson thus institutes the concept of "pocket veto" by refusing to sign legislation before the end of the congressional session.

July 10, 1832: Jackson vetoes the charter for the Second Bank of the United States, claiming the bank is a "monster" because of its exclusive power.

November 1832: South Carolina nullifies the tariffs of 1828 and 1832 with the *Ordinance of Nullification.* Subsequently, a more moderate tariff is passed but it does not offer much relief for the southern agricultural economy.

December 1832: At President Jackson's request Congress passes the Force Bill to compel South Carolina to abide by federal tariffs.

March 1, 1833: The Compromise Tariff of 1833 and Force Bill are signed into law.

March 4, 1833: Andrew Jackson is inaugurated for a second term. His vice president is Martin Van Buren.

November 1835–1842: The Second Seminole War is fought in Florida when some Seminole Indians, led by Osceola, refuse to leave their land in defiance of an 1832 treaty.

June 15, 1836: Arkansas is admitted to the Union as the 25th state.

1837: The Panic of 1837 is the first real and lasting economic crisis the United States faces. Land speculation, a failed wheat crop, a 50 percent reduction in the price of cotton, and a crisis in several European banks combine to cause a widespread financial panic.

January 26, 1837: Michigan is admitted as the 26th state of the Union.

March 4, 1837: Martin Van Buren is inaugurated as president with Richard Johnson as vice president.

1838: The forced march of the entire Cherokee nation from Georgia along the Trail of Tears to Oklahoma, ordered by President Andrew Jackson, is carried out during the Van Buren administration.

March 4, 1841: William Henry Harrison is inaugurated as president with John Tyler as vice president.

April 4, 1841: President William Henry Harrison dies of pneumonia, and John Tyler assumes the presidency.

1842: The Webster-Ashburton Treaty settles the border between the United States and Canada in the Northeast.

March 3, 1845: Florida is admitted to the Union as the 27th state.

March 4, 1845: James Polk is inaugurated as president with Henry Clay as vice president.

October 10, 1845: The U.S. Naval Academy is founded to replace the U.S. Navy's former practice of relying on at-sea apprenticeships for midshipmen.

December 29, 1845: Texas is admitted as the 28th state of the Union.

May 13, 1846: The United States declares war on Mexico. The Senate votes 40 to 2 and the House votes 174 to 14 in favor of war.

June 15, 1846: The Senate ratifies a treaty with Britain fixing the Oregon Territory border at the forty-ninth parallel.

August 10, 1846: The Smithsonian Institution is established with funds bequeathed to the United States by English scientist and inventor James Smithson for "the increase and diffusion of knowledge."

May 7, 1847: The American Medical Association is founded in Philadelphia, Pennsylvania, as the national organization for traditionally educated physicians who adopted a code of ethics and passed resolutions for improving medical education.

February 2, 1848: American diplomat Nicholas Trist signs the Treaty of Guadalupe Hidalgo with Mexico. The United States receives California, New Mexico (including modern Arizona and Nevada), and Texas to the Rio Grande for $15 million.

March 10, 1848: The Senate ratifies the peace treaty with Mexico, 38 to 14.

May 29, 1848: Wisconsin is admitted to the Union as the 30th state.

March 3, 1849: The Department of the Interior is founded to manage the sale and lease of federal lands; its focus later shifts to the conservation and protection of U.S. natural resources.

March 4, 1849: Zachary Taylor is inaugurated as president. His vice president is Millard Fillmore.

January 29, 1850: The Compromise of 1850 is introduced by Senator Henry Clay, admitting California as a free state, allowing the territorial legislatures of New Mexico and Utah to settle the slavery issue on their own, exacting a stronger fugitive slave law, outlawing the slave trade in the District of Columbia, and giving Texas $10 million to abandon its claims to territory in New Mexico.

July 9, 1850: President Zachary Taylor, an opponent of Henry Clay's compromise to end the conflict over slavery in the territory won from Mexico, dies. Vice President Millard Fillmore, who favors the compromise, becomes president.

September 9, 1850: California is the 31st state admitted to the union.

December 24, 1851: A fire at the Library of Congress in Washington, D.C., destroys two-thirds of its collection.

March 4, 1853: Franklin Pierce is inaugurated president. William Rufus De Vane King is vice president.

March 31, 1854: Commodore Matthew C. Perry signs the Treaty of Kanagawa, opening Japanese ports to American trade.

May 30, 1854: The Kansas-Nebraska bill is signed into law by President Franklin Pierce.

January 15, 1856: A free state governor and legislature are elected in Kansas, which now has two governments.

1857: The National Teachers Association is founded as a national organization for teachers that serves primarily as a debating society. The group changes its name to the National Education Association when it changes its focus to creating a public education system controlled by professional educators rather than politicians.

March 4, 1857: James Buchanan is inaugurated as president with John C. Breckinridge as vice president.

May 11, 1858: Minnesota is the 32nd state admitted to the union.

June 16, 1858: Abraham Lincoln, nominated for the Senate by Illinois Republicans, delivers his "House Divided" speech.

February 14, 1859: Oregon becomes the 33rd state.

August 1859: The American Dental Association comes into existence in Niagara Falls, New York, as a professional society to improve communication regarding advances in dental technology, offer support among dentists, and improve the consistency of care dental patients receive.

June 23, 1860: The Government Printing Office is founded by Joint Resolution 25 to provide printing services to the U.S. government that are efficient, reliable, and not vulnerable to corruption.

December 20, 1860: South Carolina secedes from the Union. Florida, Alabama, Georgia, Mississippi, Louisiana, and Texas soon follow.

1861–1865: American Civil War.

January 29, 1861: Kansas is admitted to the Union as the 34th state.

February 9, 1861: Jefferson Davis is elected president of the Confederate States of America.

March 4, 1861: Abraham Lincoln is inaugurated as president of the United States. Hannibal Hamlin is vice president.

April 17–May 20, 1861: Virginia, Arkansas, Tennessee, and North Carolina secede from the Union.

May 15, 1862: The Department of Agriculture is founded to enhance the quality of life for Americans by supporting the production of agriculture.

July 1, 1862: The Internal Revenue Service is founded; initially named the Bureau of Internal Revenue, it is created in response to the need for increased revenue to fund the War Department during the American Civil War.

August 29, 1862: The Bureau of Engraving and Printing is founded to produce paper currency as part of the U.S. Department of Treasury's plan to finance the American Civil War; it later becomes the sole manufacturer of the nation's currency and postage stamps.

January 1, 1863: The Emancipation Proclamation is declared in effect.

February 25, 1863: Congress creates a national banking system.

March 3, 1863: Congress passes the Conscription Act.

March 3, 1863: The National Academy of Sciences is created as a private, autonomous organization to objectively and scientifically evaluate the many ideas for new weaponry and inventions proposed during the Civil War.

June 20, 1863: West Virginia is admitted as the 35th state.

November 19, 1863: Lincoln delivers the Gettysburg Address.

October 31, 1864: Nevada becomes the 36th state.

1865: The Thirteenth Amendment abolishing slavery is ratified.

March 4, 1865: Abraham Lincoln is inaugurated for a second term with Andrew Johnson as vice president.

April 9, 1865: Robert E. Lee surrenders the Confederate Army at Appomattox Courthouse, Virginia.

April 15, 1865: Lincoln is assassinated at Ford's Theater by John Wilkes Booth; Andrew Johnson becomes president.

July 5, 1865: The U.S. Secret Service is founded with the mission of protecting U.S. leaders, visiting world leaders, and the integrity of U.S. financial systems.

April 9, 1866: A civil rights act is passed over President Johnson's veto.

April 10, 1866: The American Society for the Prevention of Cruelty to Animals is founded to promote the humane treatment of animals through public education and legislation.

June 13, 1866: Congress approves the Fourteenth Amendment to the Constitution which gives African Americans citizenship and guarantees all persons due process of law.

March 1, 1867: Nebraska becomes the 37th state.

December 4, 1867: The National Grange is founded to represent farmers and their concerns such as establishing fair market values for their products and coping with exorbitantly high railroad shipping rates.

February 24, 1868: The House of Representatives impeaches President Johnson.

May 16, 1868: President Johnson is acquitted of violating the Tenure of Office Act.

November 6, 1868: Red Cloud and other Lakota tribal leaders sign a treaty with U.S. government officials at Fort Laramie, Wyoming, establishing a reservation in nearly all of present South Dakota west of the Missouri River. This area includes the sacred Black Hills.

March 4, 1869: Ulysses S. Grant is inaugurated as the 18th president with Schuyler Colfax as vice president.

September 24, 1869: Black Friday on Wall Street occurs when financiers drive up the price of gold.

March 30, 1870: The Fifteenth Amendment, stating a right to vote regardless of race, color, or previous status of servitude, is declared to be in effect.

May 31, 1870: Congress passes the Enforcement Act to protect African American voters.

June 22, 1870: The Department of Justice is founded during the administration of Ulysses S. Grant and is officially charged with the supervision of all federal law officers and attorneys, the control of immigration, and the investigation of federal crimes.

1871: The National Rifle Association of America is founded to establish gun training programs and competitions both within and outside of the military and to help train future soldiers.

March 4, 1873: Ulysses S. Grant begins his second term as president. Henry Wilson is vice president.

September 18, 1873: Beginning of the financial panic of 1873.

March 1, 1875: Congress passes the Civil Rights Act; key provisions are held unconstitutional in the *Civil Rights* cases of 1883.

July 22, 1875: The American Bankers Association is founded in Saratoga, New York, to coordinate and discuss the future of the United States banking industry.

1876: The American Library Association is founded to represent libraries and the professionals that work in libraries.

August 1, 1876: Colorado is admitted as the 38th state.

March 4, 1877: Rutherford B. Hayes is inaugurated as president with William A. Wheeler as vice president.

August 21, 1878: The American Bar Association is formed in Saratoga Springs, New York, to provide a forum for discussing the increasingly complex legal profession.

March 3, 1879: The U.S. Geological Survey is founded with a combination of responsibilities, including "classification of the public lands, and examination of geological structure, mineral resources, and products of the national domain."

November 17, 1880: The United States and China sign a treaty that allows the United States to "regulate, limit, and suspend" Chinese immigration but not to ban it outright.

March 4, 1881: James Garfield is inaugurated as president. Chester A. Arthur is vice president.

1882: The Knights of Columbus is founded as a fraternal organization to form a unified voice against anti-Catholic sentiment and to provide insurance benefits and social programs to Catholics.

May 6, 1882: Congress passes the Chinese Exclusion Act, suspending Chinese immigration to the United States for 10 years.

September 19, 1882: President James Garfield dies of complications from the wounds he sustained in July when he was shot by Charles Guiteau, who was angry that Garfield had not granted him a federal job under the "spoils system." Garfield is succeeded by Vice President Arthur the next day.

January 16, 1883: Congress passes the Pendleton Civil Service Reform Act, an attempt to depoliticize appointments of federal employees engaged in governmental operations and end the "spoils system." Signed into law by President Arthur, the act establishes a Civil Service Commission and specifies rules for a merit system based on competitive exams.

March 4, 1885: Grover Cleveland is inaugurated as president. Thomas A. Hendricks is vice president.

January 19, 1886: Congress passes a Presidential Succession Act; if both the president and vice president are unable to serve, they are succeeded by members of the cabinet in the order that their departments were created.

October 25, 1886: In *Wabash, St. Louis & Pacific Railway v. Illinois*, the Supreme Court rules that only the federal government, not the individual states, may regulate interstate railway rates.

November 1886: Samuel Gompers establishes the American Federation of Labor which emphasizes "bread and butter" unionism.

February 4, 1887: Congress passes the Interstate Commerce Act establishing the Interstate Commerce Commission, the first national regulatory commission, in an attempt to curb price fixing and other abuses by interstate railroads.

February 8, 1887: Congress passes the Dawes Act, which provides for the division of tribal lands among individual American Indians and the sale of "surplus" land to non-Indians.

September 20, 1887: The American Institute of Certified Public Accountants is founded as the American Association of Public Accountants to establish a professional examination and a distinctive title. The organization changed its name in 1957 after merging with a related group.

May 5, 1888: The International Association of Machinists and Aerospace Workers is organized as the Order of United Machinists and Mechanical Engineers to strengthen solidarity and skills within the trade and to provide its members with insurance. The organization changed its name in the 1960s when new trades are admitted.

March 4, 1889: Benjamin Harrison is inaugurated as president. Levi P. Morton is vice president.

August 30, 1889: The National Association of Letter Carriers is formed as a result of the struggle of letter carriers to work an eight hour day. The group will strive to improve working conditions for letter carriers.

November 2, 1889: North Dakota and South Dakota become states, followed by Montana on November 8 and Washington on November 11, becoming the 39th through 42nd states of the Union, respectively.

January 25, 1890: The United Mine Workers of America is organized to fight against the long hours, low wages, and dangerous working conditions endured by mine workers and to advocate for their rights.

April 14, 1890: At a conference that began in Washington, D.C., on October 2, 1889, Western Hemisphere nations form the Pan-American Union.

June 18, 1890: The National Association of Life Underwriters is founded to promote high standards of conduct in the insurance industry and serve as a credible voice for the industry.

July 3, 1890: Idaho becomes the 43rd state.

July 10, 1890: Wyoming becomes the 44th state.

March 3, 1891: The Immigration and Naturalization Service is created by the Immigration Act of 1891; originally called the Bureau of Immigration, it is the first federal agency in charge of enforcing immigration laws and standards.

June 18, 1891: The International Brotherhood of Electrical Workers is formed to address the deplorable working conditions in the light and power industry.

June 4, 1892: The Sierra Club is founded to explore and enjoy the mountains of the Pacific coast and make them more accessible to the public.

March 4, 1893: Grover Cleveland is inaugurated to a second term as president. Adlai E. Stevenson is vice president.

May 5, 1893: Stock prices on Wall Street drop. More than 600 banks close their doors in June as the United States enters a financial depression that lasts four years.

October 3, 1893: Following a meeting of the National League for Good Roads, a lobbying group dedicated to the passage of national road legislation, the Federal Highway Administration is founded as the Office of Road Inquiry, an agency in the Department of Agriculture.

June 26–August 3, 1894: Supporting the Pullman strikers, the American Railway Union, led by Eugene V. Debs, strikes against most railroads. President Cleveland sends in federal troops to break up the strike, based on a court injunction prohibiting workers from interfering with the delivery of mail.

January 1895: The National Association of Manufacturers is founded as a vehicle for helping United States manufacturers locate new markets for their products in foreign countries.

May 20, 1895: The Supreme Court in *Pollock v. Farmers' Loan and Trust Company* rules that the federal income tax provision of the Wilson-Gorman Tariff Act is unconstitutional.

January 4, 1896: Utah becomes the 45th state.

September 29, 1896: Independent Insurance Agents of America is organized as the National Association of Local Fire Insurance Agents to work on insurance related legislation. The group changed its name in 1975.

1897: The American Nurses Association is formed to promote state licensing for nurses, improve industry standards, and provide a forum for professional exchanges.

February 17, 1897: The National Congress of Parents and Teachers is founded to lobby for legislation to protect children and improve education.

March 4, 1897: William McKinley is inaugurated as president with Garret A. Hobart as vice president.

1898: The National Cattleman's Beef Association is founded as the National Livestock Growers Association to meet annually and discuss issues affecting their business such as rapid and humane rail transportation of stock and state livestock inspections. The organization changed its name in 1966.

April 24, 1898: Spain declares war on the United States.

July 7, 1898: Recognizing the strategic military value of its base at Pearl Harbor, Congress approves the annexation of Hawaii by joint resolution.

1899: The expansion of the federal government makes it one of the leading U.S. employers, reaching close to 250,000 by 1899.

1899: Secretary of State John Hay convinces Great Britain, France, Russia, Germany, Italy, and Japan to agree to an "Open Door" policy to assure all nations equal trading rights with China.

1899: The Veterans of Foreign Wars is founded as the American Veterans of Foreign Service to fight for the specific needs of veterans including pensions, health care benefits, and employment assistance. The organization changed its name in 1913 when it joined with other similar groups to form a national organization.

January 9, 1899: Congress ratifies the treaty with Spain, which is signed by President McKinley on February 10. The United States acquires Puerto Rico and Guam, and Spain grants independence to Cuba. The United States buys Spanish holdings in the Philippines, gaining virtual control over the islands.

September 1899: The American Hospital Association is founded in Cleveland, Ohio, as the Association of Hospital Superintendents to address issues of hospital management, economics, procedure, and inspections. The organization changed its name in 1906 when it broadened its membership.

April 13, 1900: For the fourth time in eight years the House of Representatives adopts a resolution favoring a constitutional amendment for the election of U.S. senators by direct vote of the people instead of by state legislatures. The Senate finally concurs in 1911.

September 18, 1900: The first direct primary in the United States is held in Hennepin County, Minnesota.

March 3, 1901: The National Institute of Standards and Technology is founded to provide better measurements and more uniformity, precision, and control in laboratory and factory activities.

March 4, 1901: William McKinley is inaugurated for a second term as president; Theodore Roosevelt is sworn in as vice president.

September 14, 1901: After being shot by an anarchist seven days earlier, President McKinley dies. Theodore Roosevelt becomes president.

November 1901: Alabama adopts a new constitution that effectively disenfranchises African Americans (and some poor whites) by including literacy and property tests, as well as a measure known as the "grandfather" clause, which states that a person cannot vote if his grandfather was ineligible. It also denies suffrage to individuals convicted of certain "criminal" acts.

December 3, 1901: In his first State of the Union message to Congress, President Roosevelt calls for the regulation of business trusts "within reasonable limits" and becomes the first president to advocate the conservation of natural resources on public land.

March 6, 1902: The Bureau of the Census is founded, responsible for collecting information regarding the U.S. population and its economic and social institutions.

March 10, 1902: At President Roosevelt's instigation, Attorney General Philander C. Knox files to dissolve the Northern Securities Company under the Sherman Antitrust Act.

July 8, 1902: The Bureau of Reclamation is founded to study, locate, and construct large-scale irrigation projects in the West.

1903: The International Brotherhood of Teamsters is founded as the Team Drivers International Union to address the poor working conditions and salaries of drivers of horse-drawn vehicles. The organization changed its name to reflect its growing membership including drivers of motor vehicles and workers from other industries.

April 13, 1903: The Laborer's International Union is created as the International Hod Carriers and Building Laborer's Union to protect construction of American workers against hazardous working conditions, low wages, and forced unlimited workdays. The union changed its name in 1965 as it diversified its membership beyond the construction trade.

April 27, 1903: The Supreme Court upholds the clauses in the Alabama constitution which effectively deny African Americans the right to vote.

November 18, 1903: The United States and Panama sign the Hay-Bunau-Varilla Treaty giving the United States permanent rights to a ten-mile-wide canal zone in return for $10 million and an annual payment of $250,000 after nine years.

March 14, 1904: The Supreme Court upholds the Sherman Anti-Trust Act in *Northern Securities Company v. United States*.

January 5, 1905: The National Audubon Society is created to protect wild birds and their eggs and is named after the great bird painter John James Audubon.

January 20, 1905: President Roosevelt invokes the Roosevelt Corollary (asserting the right of the United States to intervene in Latin American internal affairs) for the first time, as the United States begins to supervise the payment of national and international debts owed by the Dominican Republic.

February 1, 1905: The Department of Forestry, created in 1881, is renamed the Forest Service; it is charged with studying forest conditions, disseminating forest information, and protecting and managing the national forests.

March 4, 1905: Theodore Roosevelt is inaugurated as president for a second term. He is the youngest elected president to date. His vice president is Charles Warren Fairbanks.

June 29, 1906: Congress passes the Hepburn Act, which puts teeth in the Interstate Commerce Act by permitting regulation of rates charged by railroads, pipelines, and terminals. President Roosevelt has strongly endorsed the act and helped guide it through Congress.

June 30, 1906: The Federal Food and Drug Act is passed.

September 29, 1906: The United States invokes the Platt Amendment (an amendment to Cuba's constitution allowing the United States to intervene to maintain order) and assumes military control of Cuba. The United States continues to govern Cuba until January 1909.

June 14, 1907: The National Council on Crime and Delinquency is formed as a professional association for probation officers to share information and advocate for reform of the criminal justice system.

October 1, 1907: A downturn in the stock market touches off the Panic of 1907. At the request of the federal government J. Pierpont Morgan and fellow bankers bring $100 million in gold from Europe to restore confidence in the economy and end the currency panic that has caused runs on banks.

November 16, 1907: Oklahoma becomes the 46th state.

1908: The National Governors' Association is created by President Theodore Roosevelt to convince the state governors to support his conservation policies and evolves into a forum for governors to discuss and act on common issues and federal-state activities.

May 12, 1908: The National Association of Realtors is organized to unite the real estate men of the United States to influence matters of interest to the real estate industry.

June 8, 1908: At the urging of Gifford Pinchot, head of the U.S. Forest Service, President Roosevelt appoints a 57-member National Commission for the Conservation of Natural Resources, naming Pinchot as chairman. The commission's job is to compile the first list of all American natural resources.

July 26, 1908: The Federal Bureau of Investigation is created by Attorney General Charles J. Bonaparte as a corps of special agents to serve as the investigative arm of the Department of Justice.

March 4, 1909: William Howard Taft is inaugurated as the twenty-seventh president of the United States. James S. Sherman is vice president.

July 12, 1909: Congress proposes the Sixteenth Amendment, which authorizes a federal income tax. It is ratified by the states in 1913.

1910: The Carnegie Endowment for International Peace is founded with a gift from steel magnate Andrew Carnegie. The endowment will fund projects that foster peace.

1910: The National Urban League is formed as a collaboration between social welfare groups to train African American social workers to work among African American immigrants who had come from the South to live in northern cities.

March 17, 1910: Congressman George W. Norris (R-Neb.) introduces a resolution to limit the power of speaker of the house during Joseph G. Cannon's dictatorial speakership. The measure passes, indicating the growing strength of progressive Republicans.

June 18, 1910: Congress passes the Mann-Elkins Act, which extends jurisdiction of the Interstate Commerce Commission (ICC) to include telephone, telegraph, cable, and wireless companies. It also augments ICC regulation of railroads, and it establishes a Commerce Court (which is abolished in 1913).

June 25, 1910: Congress passes the Publicity Act, which requires members of Congress to report campaign contributions.

1911: The National Association for the Advancement of Colored People is established by a group of prominent African Americans and whites as a multiracial organization to address racial inequities in the United States.

January 21, 1911: The National Progressive Republican League, founded by Sen. Robert M. La Follette of Wisconsin and other insurgent Republicans, issues its platform, which calls for direct election of U.S. senators, the initiative, the referendum, the recall, and other reforms.

July 24, 1911: The United States renews its commercial treaty with Japan. Among its provisions, the treaty reaffirms the "Gentlemen's Agreement" of 1907, in which President Theodore Roosevelt pledged to see that Japanese residents of the United States were well treated if Japan voluntarily prevented Japanese laborers from immigrating to the United States.

1912: The Council of Better Business Bureaus is founded to promote and monitor honesty in regional and national advertising.

1912: The United States Chamber of Commerce is formed to present a unified voice on national issues and represent the interests of business.

January 6, 1912: New Mexico becomes the 47th state.

February 14, 1912: Arizona is admitted as the 48th state.

August 2, 1912: Sen. Henry Cabot Lodge (R-Mass.) introduces a resolution—subsequently known as the Lodge Corollary—extending the Monroe Doctrine to pertain to foreign companies and non-European nations.

March 4, 1913: Woodrow Wilson takes the oath of office and becomes the twenty-eighth president of the United States with Thomas R. Marshall as vice president.

March 4, 1913: The Department of Labor becomes a separate department from the Department of Commerce "to foster, promote, and develop the welfare of working people, to improve their working conditions, and to enhance their opportunities for profitable employment."

March 4, 1913: The Bureau of Labor Statistics is founded as part of the Department of Labor with the goal of protecting workers and improving their working conditions by providing accurate statistics.

May 31, 1913: The Seventeenth Amendment to the Constitution, providing for the direct election of U.S. senators, is officially adopted following ratification by thirty-six states. Previously senators were selected by state legislatures.

December 23, 1913: The Federal Reserve System is established by the Federal Reserve Act of 1913 to counter financial disruptions by coordinating the Federal Reserve banks and by controlling the "discount rate," or interest rate at which banks could lend each other money.

August 1914: World War I begins.

August 3, 1914: The Panama Canal opens.

September 1, 1914: The Federal Trade Commission is created and granted an unprecedented authority by the Federal Trade Commission Act of 1914 to investigate, publicize, and prohibit all unfair methods of business competition.

1915: The Fraternal Order of Police is created to seek better working conditions for police officers. The organization declares it is not a labor union and denounces the use of strikes by police officers.

April 28, 1915: The U.S. Coast Guard is founded; over the years it becomes responsible for, among other things, patrolling U.S. shores for icebergs, performing lifesaving operations, and enforcing Prohibition laws and drug control policies.

May 7, 1915: The *Lusitania,* a British passenger liner, is sunk off the Irish coast by a German submarine. The dead include 128 Americans.

1916: The American Jewish Congress is founded to represent Jewish interests in negotiations to end World War I. It becomes a permanent institution in 1920 to promote the establishment of a Jewish state and fight anti-Semitism.

1916: The Planned Parenthood Federation of American is founded by birth control advocate Margaret Sanger as the Birth Control Federation of America. The federation provides contraceptive information, advice, and devices to women.

April 1916: The American Federation of Teachers is founded by three Chicago, Illinois, teachers' unions and a nearby Gary, Indiana, teachers' union to address teachers' grievances.

June 3, 1916: Congress passes the National Defense Act, which provides for the expansion of the regular army to 220,000, authorizes a National Guard of 450,000 men, establishes the Reserve Officers Training Corps (ROTC) at colleges and universities, and makes provisions for industrial preparedness.

August 25, 1916: The National Park Service is founded to promote and regulate the use of national parks and monuments.

September 7, 1916: Congress passes the Shipping Act, which authorizes the creation of the U.S. Shipping Board to oversee the requisition of ships through the Emergency Fleet Corporation.

September 7, 1916: Congress passes the Workmen's Compensation Act, which offers coverage to half a million federal employees.

September 8, 1916: The U.S. International Trade Commission is founded as the United State Tariff Commission and is charged with the duty of providing Congress with trade information and statistics that would help members of Congress make rational decisions regarding tariff revisions.

1917: Jeannette Rankin is elected to the House of Representatives. She is the first woman elected to Congress.

1917: The National Automobile Dealers Association is formed to represent dealers' interests in Congress and provide members with services such as insurance and credit.

March 5, 1917: President Wilson is inaugurated for his second term in office.

April 4, 1917: The United States declares war on Germany.

July 24, 1917: Congress appropriates $640 million to develop an army air force. The goal is to build forty-five hundred planes by the spring of 1918.

November 6, 1917: An amendment to the New York State constitution gives women the right to vote in state elections.

January 8, 1918: In an address before Congress President Wilson puts forward his proposal for peace (the Fourteen Points).

March 19, 1918: To conserve energy during the war, Congress passes legislation that puts daylight saving time into effect.

1919: The Eighteenth Amendment, known as the Prohibition amendment, is ratified.

1919: The National Restaurant Association is formed to discuss and work for the interest of the restaurant industry.

February 14, 1919: President Wilson delivers his proposal for a League of Nations to the Paris Peace Conference.

March 1919: The American Legion is formed by World War I veterans to address veterans' needs such as health care and employment.

June 28, 1919: The Treaty of Versailles is signed, officially ending World War I.

September 25, 1919: After making his fortieth speech in support of the League of Nations, President Wilson collapses in Pueblo, Colorado, and is forced to return to the White House, where he suffers an incapacitating stroke from which he never fully recovers.

October 1919: The Volstead Act is passed to provide for the enforcement of the Eighteenth Amendment (the Prohibition Amendment).

November 12, 1919: The American Farm Bureau Administration was founded in Chicago to promote the economic welfare of commercial farmers.

1920: The Nineteenth Amendment, which grants women the right to vote, passes.

1920: The American Civil Liberties Union is founded to uphold the freedoms guaranteed by the Bill of Rights.

1920: Disabled American Veterans is organized from a coalition of veterans groups to help veterans overcome their physical and emotional wounds, navigate the confusing government system of benefits, and advocate for legislation to assist veterans.

February 14, 1920: The League of Women Voters is formed six months before women attain the right to vote to prepare women to use their political power to influence and shape public policy.

March 19, 1920: In a victory for opponents of the Treaty of Versailles, the Senate rejects U.S. membership in the League of Nations.

1921: The Council on Foreign Relations is formed to promote positive relations between the United States and other countries. The council intends to promote alternatives to the popular idea that the United States should isolate itself from international issues.

March 4, 1921: Warren G. Harding is inaugurated as twenty-ninth president of the United States. Calvin Coolidge is vice president.

April 23, 1921: The Service Employees International Union is chartered as the Building Services Employees International Union to work for better wages and working conditions for janitors. In 1968, the union changed its name to reflect its broader membership including hospital workers and maintenance workers.

May 19, 1921: Harding signs the Emergency Immigration Act, restricting immigration to the United States from any European country to 3 percent of the individuals of that nationality in the United States at the time of the 1910 census. The act also creates an annual ceiling of 355,000 immigrants.

September 1, 1921: The General Accounting Office is founded and given the authority to interpret any laws concerning government payments, to investigate receipt and use of public funds, to recommend to Congress ways of making government expenditures more economical and efficient, and to standardize accounting systems, forms, and procedures among all government agencies.

1922: The Association on American Indian Affairs is formed to oppose the Bursum Bill which proposed that non-Indians should acquire legal rights to Pueblo Indian lands. The association resolves to preserve Indian culture and territory.

1922: The Motion Picture Association of America is formed as the Motion Picture Producers and Distributors of America to unify the interests and opinions of the industry and regulate the amount of violence, sex, and lawlessness shown on movie screens. The organization changed its name in 1945.

October 3, 1922: Rebecca Felton of Georgia becomes the first female U.S. senator. Her term, to which the governor of Georgia appointed her following the death of Sen. Thomas Watson, lasts only one day.

April 9, 1923: The U.S. Supreme Court rules the minimum-wage law for women and children in Washington, D.C., to be unconstitutional in *Adkins v. Children's Hospital.*

April 26, 1923: The National Association of Broadcasters is founded to create its own library of music and music licensing bureau to compete with the American Society for Copyright and Artist Protection's recent decision to revoke all radio station licenses for broadcasting popular music.

August 2, 1923: President Harding dies in San Francisco on a goodwill tour of the country that took him all the way to Alaska.

August 3, 1923: Calvin Coolidge is sworn in as the thirtieth president of the United States.

May 17, 1924: Congress overrides President Coolidge's veto of the Veterans' Bonus Bill, which allocates $2 billion for veterans of World War I.

May 24, 1924: The United States decides that it must become more involved in international affairs after the tremendous loss of life in Word War I (1914–18); the Foreign Service is thus created by the Rogers Act of 1924 to better represent the country's political and economic interests abroad.

March 4, 1925: Calvin Coolidge is inaugurated and begins his first elected term as president. Charles G. Dawes is vice president.

March 4, 1929: Herbert Hoover is inaugurated as the thirty-first president of the United States. Charles Curtis is his vice president.

April 6, 1929: The Japanese American Citizens League is founded as a group to serve the needs of the Japanese American community of Los Angeles. Soon, other chapters of the league form all along the Pacific coast to work against anti-Japanese American sentiment and legislation.

June 18, 1929: President Hoover signs the reapportionment bill, which gives the president the authority to reapportion Congress after each decennial census if Congress fails to act. Hoover finds this legislation necessary because Congress has so far refused to reapportion congressional districts on the basis of the 1920 census.

October 29, 1929: Prices on the New York Stock Exchange collapse and the United State enters the Great Depression which will last into World War II (1939–45).

May 14, 1930: The Bureau of Prisons is founded under an act of Congress to consolidate the operations of all federal prisons.

May 26, 1930: The National Institutes of Health is founded; it is originally a federal laboratory dedicated to the research of diseases, navigable stream pollution, and information dissemination.

July 21, 1930: President Hoover signs into law an act establishing the Veterans Administration.

July 26, 1930: The Food and Drug Administration is founded to enforce the regulations set out in the Food and Drug Act of 1906 and the Meat Inspection Act, establishing federal food standards and prohibiting the misbranding and adulteration of food and drugs.

1931: The Air Line Pilots Association International is founded in Chicago, Illinois, to protest pay cuts, poor working conditions, and arbitrary management practices.

September–October 1931: Hoarding of gold increases as the economic depression worsens; banks are failing in great numbers (522 close during October alone), and their depositors, uninsured by the government, lose most of their savings.

February 2, 1932: On the recommendation of President Hoover, Congress establishes the Reconstruction Finance Corporation, giving it wide-ranging power to extend credit to private banks and businesses.

February 27, 1932: Congress passes the Glass-Steagall Credit Expansion Act, making $750 million of the government gold reserve available for industrial and business needs.

August 17, 1932: The American Federation of Government Employees is founded to protect the rights of and improve the working conditions and benefits of government workers.

February 6, 1933: The Twentieth Amendment to the U.S. Constitution, the "lame duck" amendment, is ratified. It moves the date of the presidential inauguration from March 4 to January 20 and sets the beginning of terms for senators and congressmen as January 3, which is also established as the first day of the new session.

March 4, 1933: Franklin D. Roosevelt is inaugurated president of the United States. John N. Garner is vice president.

March 5–13, 1933: Because bank runs and closings continue to sweep the country, President Roosevelt declares a "bank holiday," suspending regular bank business to provide a cooling-off period.

March 9–June 16, 1933: Congress convenes to deal with the banking crisis, beginning the "First Hundred Days" of the "First New Deal." Many emergency bills are passed, such as the National Industrial Recovery Act, the Emergency Banking Relief Act, the Agricultural Administration Act, and the Farm Credit Act.

May 18, 1933: The Tennessee Valley Authority is founded; originally established to provide flood control, navigation, and electric power to the people in the Tennessee Valley area, it grows to become the United States's largest electric power producing company.

June 12– July 27, 1933: At the London Economic Conference, European nations and the United States are unable to develop a plan for international cooperation in ending the wide fluctuation of exchange rates and reducing trade barriers.

July 26, 1933: The Farm Credit Administration is founded.

November 16, 1933: The United States formally recognizes the Soviet Union, sixteen years after the Bolshevik Revolution of 1917.

December 5, 1933: The Twenty-first Amendment repealing Prohibition is ratified.

1934: Congress passes the National Housing Act, which establishes the Federal Housing Administration (FHA).

1934: The Credit Union National Association and Affiliates is founded to represent credit unions' interest in legislative matters and establish industry standards.

1934: The Transport Workers Union of America is founded to protect transit workers from poor wages, long hours, and poor working conditions.

January 1, 1934: The Federal Deposit Insurance Corporation (FDIC) is established to help restore the country's confidence in its banking system as a result of the bank failures of the Great Depression.

February 2, 1934: The Export-Import Bank of the United States is founded; it is inspired by the economic conditions of the 1930s when exports are seen as a desperately needed stimulus for the economy of the Great Depression.

June 21, 1934: The National Mediation Board is founded to handle disputes that often arise between labor and management.

July 2, 1934: The Securities and Exchange Commission is founded to administer federal securities laws that curb fraudulent stock and investment practices.

July 26, 1934: The Federal Communications Commission (FCC) is founded to combine the functions of the Federal Radio Commission (regulating airwave use and radio licenses) with the telephone and telegraph policies previously regulated by the Interstate Commerce Commission and the Postmaster General.

1935: The Wilderness Society is founded to preserve wilderness areas through legislative action and citizen participation.

January 4, 1935: The "Second New Deal" begins as President Roosevelt outlines a program for social reform that will benefit laborers and small farmers.

July 5, 1935: The National Labor Relations Board is founded by the Wagner Act, a response to an appeal by President Roosevelt for a greater degree of "industrial peace" so that economic recovery from the Great Depression could be achieved.

August 14, 1935: The Social Security Administration is founded to promote the security of the U.S. economy by managing the nation's new social security system.

August 26, 1935: The United Automobile, Aerospace, and Agricultural Implement Workers of America is founded to gain and protect the rights of autoworkers in the burgeoning automobile industry.

January 1, 1936: The Rural Utilities Service is founded to provide assistance to rural areas of the United States in establishing electricity, water, and telecommunications.

February 1936: The Consumer's Union of the United States is formed as an extension of the labor movement to improve the quality and safety of products and increase public awareness of unfair labor practices.

June 1936: The United Steelworkers of America is founded to organize both skilled and unskilled workers in mass production industries such as steel and autos.

September 1936: The American Federation of State, County, and Municipal Employees becomes an independent, international union representing the interests of government employees.

1937: National Small Business United is founded to demand that the government stay out of private business affairs, that Social Security and other taxes be simplified, and to promote other business interests.

January 20, 1937: President Roosevelt begins his second term, declaring, "I see one-third of a nation ill-housed, ill-clad, ill-nourished." John N. Garner is his vice president.

February 5, 1937: President Roosevelt requests that Congress pass legislation to increase the number of justices on the U.S. Supreme Court to as many as fifteen. His proposal is decried as "court packing" and fails.

August 5, 1937: The National Cancer Institute is founded by legislation providing for federal involvement in the prevention and control of cancer.

September 2, 1937: President Roosevelt signs the National Housing Act, creating the U.S. Housing Authority.

December 12, 1937: Japanese planes bomb and sink the U.S. gunboat *Panay* on the Yangtze River in China; two American sailors are killed. Two days later Japan formally apologizes for the incident, but relations between Japan and the United States are further strained.

1938: Communications Workers of America is founded as the National Federation of Telephone Workers to protect the rights and improve the benefits and working conditions of telephone company employees. The organization absorbed many smaller unions and changed its name to its present one in 1947.

1938: The National Wildlife Federation is organized by melding conservation groups into a national organization to protect U.S. resources and wildlife.

February 16, 1938: President Roosevelt signs the second Agricultural Administration Act, replacing the first AAA, which had been declared unconstitutional in 1936.

November 1938: The National Cotton Council of America is founded to represent the needs of all segments of the cotton production industry through public relations and legislation.

February 27, 1939: The U.S. Supreme Court rules wildcat strikes (strikes in violation of a contract) to be illegal.

May 16, 1939: The U.S. Department of Agriculture introduces food stamps, which needy people can redeem for surplus agricultural goods.

July 1, 1939: The Office of Management and Budget is founded with the responsibility of assisting the president in overseeing the preparation of the federal budget and supervising its administration in executive branch agencies.

August 7, 1939: The Administrative Office of the U.S. Courts is founded to handle all administrative duties for the federal courts and to continually study, research, and make recommendations for running the court system.

September 3, 1939: Responding to the German invasion of Poland on September 1, Great Britain and France declare war on Germany. On the same day 30 Americans are killed when Germany sinks a British passenger ship; President Roosevelt restates U.S. neutrality.

September 8, 1939: The White House Office is founded; early staff positions involve mostly clerical duties. By the twentieth century, the office grows to include more advisory and political positions.

September 8, 1939: Due to the conflict in Europe, President Roosevelt declares a limited state of emergency that gives him the ability to act quickly if needed.

October 11, 1939: The NAACP Legal Defense and Education Fund is organized and pledges an all-out fight against discrimination.

1940: The National Federation of the Blind is founded to advocate for scientific and educational advances to benefit the blind as well as supportive legislation.

January 26, 1940: The 1911 U.S.-Japan Treaty of Commerce expires, and Secretary of State Cordell Hull informs the Japanese government that trade will continue only on a day-to-day basis.

May 25, 1940: President Roosevelt establishes the Office of Emergency Management.

June 30, 1940: The Bureau of the Public Debt is founded to borrow money needed to operate the government by issuing Treasury bills, notes, and bonds, guaranteeing repayment of the value plus interest to the owner.

September 1, 1940: The U.S. Fish and Wildlife Service is founded to study the abundance, distribution, and habits of fish and wildlife and to manage national wildlife refuge sites.

September 27, 1940: The Tripartite Pact, a ten-year military and economic alliance among Germany, Italy, and Japan, is formalized. The three Axis powers pledge mutual assistance to one another in case of attack by any nation not already at war with another member. Observers see this pact as a clear warning to the United States.

October 29, 1940: Secretary of War Henry Stimson draws the first number in the Selective Service lottery, initiating the first peacetime draft in American history.

January 6, 1941: In his State of the Union Address, President Roosevelt asks Congress to support the Lend-Lease program by lending or leasing war supplies to Great Britain. He also outlines the "four essential freedoms" for which the Allies are fighting: freedom of speech, freedom of worship, freedom from want, and freedom from fear.

January 20, 1941: Franklin D. Roosevelt and Henry A. Wallace are inaugurated as president and vice-president. Roosevelt becomes the first three-term president.

February 3, 1941: The U.S. Supreme Court rules in *United States v. Darby Lumber Co.* that the Fair Labor Standards Act of 1938 is constitutional.

June 28, 1941: The Office of Scientific Research and Development (OSRD) is set up by executive order, with Dr. Vannevar Bush as chairman. The OSRD will coordinate the development of radar, sonar, and the first stages of the atomic bomb.

August 14, 1941: President Roosevelt and British prime minister Winston Churchill meet to discuss the Atlantic Charter, which becomes the blueprint for the United Nations.

November 17, 1941: In Washington, D.C., Japanese ambassador Nomura Kichisaburo and special envoy Kurusu Saburo suggest that war could result if the United States does not remove its economic embargo and refrain from interfering with Japanese activities in China and the Pacific.

December 7, 1941: Japan attacks Pearl Harbor, Hawaii, as well as U.S. bases in Thailand, Malaya, Singapore, the Philippines, Guam, Wake Island, and Hong Kong.

December 8, 1941: Calling the Japanese attack "a date which will live in infamy," President Roosevelt asks Congress for a declaration of war against Japan. Only one member fails to vote for the declaration: Representative Jeannette Rankin (R-Mont.), a committed pacifist who was against American involvement in World War I.

December 11, 1941: Germany declares war on the United States, with Italy following suit.

1942: The National Association of Home Builders is founded to develop ways to tackle housing shortages created by the increased number of workers moving near industrial plants during World War II.

January 12, 1942: The National War Labor Board is established to settle labor disputes.

June 13, 1942: The Office of Strategic Services (OSS), the forerunner of the Central Intelligence Agency, is established with Maj. Gen. William "Wild Bill" Donovan as director.

November 8, 1942: Operation Torch begins with four hundred thousand Allied troops landing in Algeria and Morocco in northern Africa under the command of Gen. Eisenhower.

1943: The United Nations Association of the United States of America is founded to educate America about the United Nations, global issues, and the importance of the United States' active participation in the work of the United Nations.

January 14, 1943: The Casablanca Conference begins. President Roosevelt and Prime Minister Winston Churchill decide to demand unconditional surrender from the Axis powers of Germany, Italy, and Japan.

May 1, 1943: In the name of "national security," President Roosevelt seizes all bituminous-coal mines in the eastern United States in response to wildcat strikes that threaten war production.

May 20, 1943: The National Federation of Independent Business is founded as the National Federation of Small Business to champion small business interests in Congress. The organization changed its name in 1949 to distinguish itself from the National Small Business Association.

June 10, 1943: The Current Tax Payment Act takes effect, requiring the withholding of federal income taxes from individual paychecks on a regular basis. This act revolutionizes the collecting of taxes and gives government more power to spend than before.

December 17, 1943: Congress repeals all Chinese Exclusion Acts enacted throughout the century.

January 22, 1944: President Roosevelt creates the War Refugee Board to help resettle millions of refugees after the war.

March 29, 1944: Congress authorizes $1.35 billion to seed the United Nations Relief and Rehabilitation Fund, initiating a massive program to aid Europe's displaced millions.

April 3, 1944: In *Smith v. Allwright* the U.S. Supreme Court rules that African Americans cannot be denied the right to vote in the Texas Democratic primary.

June 6, 1944: The long-planned "Operation Overlord," the invasion of Nazi-occupied France, begins on D-Day on the beaches of Normandy in northern France. By day's end 150,000 troops successfully land, catching the Germans off guard. Within a week more than 350,000 troops are moving toward Germany.

June 20, 1944: The Battle of the Philippine Sea ends with the decisive defeat of Japanese forces.

July 22, 1944: The Bretton Woods Conference in New Hampshire, begun July 1, ends. Representatives of 44 nations, not including the Soviet Union, establish the International Monetary Fund (IMF) and the International Bank for Reconstruction and Development (the World Bank).

August–October 1944: The Dumbarton Oaks conference is convened by President Roosevelt, with delegates from Great Britain, China, and Russia in attendance, to work out proposals that will serve as a basis for the United Nations charter.

November 1944: The National Congress of American Indians is formed to promote Indian tribal survival and the preservation of Indian culture and spirituality. The group also demands the same civil rights for Indians as those enjoyed by citizens including veteran's benefits and voting rights.

December 9, 1944: The American Veterans of World War II, Korea, and Vietnam is founded in Kansas City, Missouri, to provide emotional support, assistance with benefits, and political action on behalf of World War II veterans. The names of later wars were added as veterans from each conflict joined the organization.

January 20, 1945: Franklin D. Roosevelt is inaugurated for an unprecedented fourth term as president, with Harry S. Truman as vice president.

February 11, 1945: The Yalta Conference ends with President Roosevelt, Winston Churchill of Great Britain, and Joseph Stalin of Russia agreeing on the postwar division of Europe and Asia, on the treatment of war criminals, and on holding the first meeting of the United Nations to discuss further issues.

March 27, 1945: The National Technical Information Service is founded as a result of the government's attempts to deal with the release of thousands of war-related documents to U.S. industry following World War II.

April 12, 1945: President Roosevelt dies of a cerebral hemorrhage. Truman is sworn in as president.

May 8, 1945: Germany surrenders, ending the European war. Victory in Europe (V-E) Day is declared in the United States as massive celebrations erupt.

August 6, 1945: The United States drops an atomic bomb on Hiroshima, Japan. The resulting devastation amazes even the scientists who created it. More than 50,000 people perish in seconds, and four square miles of the city are reduced to rubble.

August 9, 1945: An atomic bomb is dropped on Nagasaki in southern Japan, killing 40,000 Japanese civilians immediately. Tokyo announces its intention to surrender.

August 27, 1945: The Allies begin to divide Korea, with the Soviets occupying the territory north of the 38th parallel and the Americans the southern half of the peninsula.

September 2, 1945: Japan signs a formal surrender onboard the *U.S.S. Missouri* in Tokyo Bay.

September 6, 1945: President Truman announces his economic recovery plan to Congress. Later known as the "Fair Deal," the program promises full employment, a substantial raise in the minimum wage, the extension of Social Security, national health insurance, federal aid to education, and government-sponsored housing for the poor.

December 14, 1945: General Marshall is named special ambassador to China to make peace between the communist forces of Mao Tse-tung and the nationalist forces of Chiang Kai-shek.

December 31, 1945: President Truman dismantles the War Labor Board, replacing it with the Wage Stabilization Board in an effort to slow the pace of rapidly growing labor unrest.

1946: The Association of Trial Lawyers of America is founded to train attorneys to represent injured workers and to provide a forum for attorneys to exchange ideas.

January 10, 1946: The first General Assembly of the United Nations meets in London. Heading the American delegation are Secretary of State James F. Byrnes and former first lady Eleanor Roosevelt.

January 21, 1946: The United Steelworkers close down the nation's steel plants in a dispute over wage contracts.

February 20, 1946: The Employment Act of 1946 is passed by Congress, establishing the Council of Economic Advisers to help the nation's economy change from a high-production wartime economy to a civilian economy without a loss in stability or employment.

April 29, 1946: The U.S. Department of Agriculture reports that farm prices, and hence the cost of food, are at record highs, underscoring the need for higher wages among workers.

June 3, 1946: The U.S. Supreme Court rules in *Morgan v. Commonwealth of Virginia* that segregated seating on interstate buses is unconstitutional.

July 1, 1946: The Centers for Disease Control and Prevention is founded to eradicate communicable diseases; it later expands its activities beyond the bounds of infectious disease to include areas such as nutrition, chronic disease, and occupational and environmental health.

July 4, 1946: The United States grants political independence to the Philippines, but maintains the right to station ships and planes on Philippine territory at Subic Bay and Clark Air Base.

July 16, 1946: The Bureau of Land Management is founded with the responsibility for managing public land use by focusing on the extraction of livestock forage, timber, and energy and mineral commodities.

August 1, 1946: Under the McMahon Act, the U.S. Atomic Energy Commission (AEC) is established to provide civilian control over military and nonmilitary atomic-energy development.

August 2, 1946: Congress passes the Legislative Reorganization Act, which requires registration of political lobbyists and the reporting of expenses.

November 9, 1946: Responding to pressures from business and conservatives, President Truman lifts price controls on most consumer goods even though recently enacted legislation is supposed to safeguard against this for six more months.

December 5, 1946: Despite conservative opposition, especially in the South, President Truman issues Executive Order 9809, creating the Committee on Civil Rights to investigate the treatment of African Americans in the United States—the first time in American history that a president focuses on civil liberties for racial minorities.

January 1, 1947: The Federal Mediation and Conciliation Service is founded to minimize interruptions of business that grow out of labor disputes and to settle labor and management disputes through conciliation and mediation.

March 12, 1947: Announcing his "containment policy," President Truman declares that the United States will provide $400 million to Greece and Turkey to fight communism. The Truman Doctrine will commit the United States to becoming a global anticommunist policeman.

June 23, 1947: Over President Truman's veto, Congress passes the Taft-Hartley Act (Labor Management Relations Act), which bans the closed shop by which only union members may be hired and which permits employers to sue unions for damages incurred in strikes. The act also allows the government to enforce an 80-day cooling-off period, forbids political contributions by unions, and requires union leaders to swear they are not communists.

July 18, 1947: The Presidential Succession Act is passed, making the speaker of the House of Representatives next in line for the presidency after the vice president. Following the speaker is the president pro tempore of the Senate and cabinet members according to rank.

July 26, 1947: The National Security Council is founded "to advise the president with respect to the integration of domestic, foreign, and military policies relating to the national security."

September 2, 1947: President Truman flies to Brazil to sign the Inter-American Treaty of Reciprocal Assistance (Rio Pact), in which nineteen American nations commit themselves to "collective defense against aggression."

September 8, 1947: The Joint Chiefs of Staff is founded as a collaboration of operations among the nation's military branches.

September 18, 1947: The Central Intelligence Agency is founded to gather and analyze intelligence information and to document the activities of foreign governments in order to better protect national security interests.

September 18, 1947: The Department of the Air Force is founded as its own agency, replacing the Army Air Force.

October 18, 1947: The House Un-American Activities Committee (HUAC) launches an extensive investigation into Communist activities in the movie industry.

1948: The National Committee for an Effective Congress is founded by Eleanor Roosevelt and a group of friends as a nonpartisan group to raise funds to elect candidates to Congress who recognized the United States's new role as the leader of the free world.

March 8, 1948: The U.S. Supreme Court rules in *McCollum v. Board of Education* that religious training in public schools is unconstitutional.

April 30, 1948: The International Conference of American States, with twenty-one members in attendance at Bogota, Colombia, establishes the Organization of American States (OAS).

May 14, 1948: Israel declares its independence from Britain as a sovereign state. The United States becomes the first nation to recognize the new country.

June 11, 1948: The Vandenberg Resolution passes in the Senate, allowing the United States to enter into collective security alliances outside the western hemisphere.

June 26, 1948: In response to the Soviet shutdown of all traffic from the West into Berlin on June 24, the United States initiates the Berlin airlift. For the next year nearly 275,000 flights will provide Berliners with 2.3 million tons of food and fuel.

August 3, 1948: Former communist Whittaker Chambers accuses Alger Hiss, a high-ranking State Department diplomat, of membership in the Communist Party, lending credence to right-wing charges that subversives have infiltrated the government.

November 1, 1948: The National Institute of Allergy and Infectious Diseases is founded as a division of the National Institutes of Health to establish federal research in the areas of allergy and infectious diseases.

1949: The National Trust for Historic Preservation is established as a nationwide organization to acquire, restore, and protect historic properties.

January 20, 1949: President Truman is inaugurated for his second term with Alben W. Barkley as vice president. In his speech Truman emphasizes the importance of foreign aid.

March 2, 1949: To prove that the United States possesses intercontinental air-strike capabilities, the U.S. Air Force's B-50 bomber circumnavigates the globe.

April 15, 1949: The National Institute of Mental Health, founded after World War II, brings mental illness to public attention as numerous men were either rejected for military service or medically discharged because of mental illness; the institute is created to address the critical lack of knowledge about mental illness and a lack of mental health professionals.

July 1, 1949: The General Services Administration is founded with the responsibility for all of the federal government's purchases; it is later redefined in the 1990s when it opens itself up to competition from the private sector.

July 21, 1949: The Senate ratifies the North Atlantic Treaty creating the North Atlantic Treaty Organization (NATO). The United States has never before concluded an alliance treaty with any European power during peacetime.

August 10, 1949: President Truman signs an amendment to the National Security Act of 1947, placing defense secretaries under the authority of the Department of Defense.

August 10, 1949: The Department of Defense is founded to create a command and interservice cooperation of land, sea, and air forces, both at home and in foreign countries where U.S. armed forces are stationed.

September 1949: The American Health Care Association holds its first organizational meeting and establishes its objectives of improving the standards of service and administration in nursing homes and promote education and legislation on long-term care issues.

October 1, 1949: Mao Tse-tung announces the creation of the People's Republic of China. The United States does not recognize the new government.

October 26, 1949: The Fair Labor Standards Act is amended to raise the minimum wage from 40 cents to 75 cents an hour.

May 10, 1950: The National Science Foundation is founded, establishing the U.S. government's role in promoting and sponsoring scientific discoveries and projects.

May 24, 1950: The Maritime Administration is founded to regulate the maritime industry, determine subsidies, and oversee federal Merchant Marine programs associated with the Department of Commerce.

June 1950–July 1953: The Korean War is fought.

1951: The Twenty-second Amendment, limiting the president's service to two terms, is ratified.

1952: The National Cable Television Association is founded as the National Community Television Association to link cable television systems providing services to customers unable to receive direct transmissions from local broadcast antennas because of surrounding high terrain. The organization changed its name in 1969 to reflect the growth in the industry.

October 24, 1952: The National Security Agency is founded with the responsibility for the signals intelligence and communications security activities of the U.S. government.

January 20, 1953: Dwight David Eisenhower is inaugurated president and Richard Nixon as vice president.

July 27, 1953: An armistice is concluded in Korea that leaves that country divided. The United States guarantees economic aid and military security.

August 1, 1953: The U.S. Information Agency is founded to consolidate all of the United States's overseas information and cultural programs into one centralized agency to make them more efficient.

August 2, 1953: The Foreign Agricultural Service is founded to increase exports, to administer import quotas on foreign agricultural goods, and to provide the government with information for trade negotiations.

October 1, 1953: The Small Business Administration is founded to provide financial, technical, and management assistance to small business owners.

1954: The American Israel Public Affairs Committee is founded to advocate for continuing United States aid to Israel.

May 17, 1954: In *Brown v. Board of Education* the U.S. Supreme Court rules that racial segregation in public schools is unconstitutional.

May 18, 1954: The U.S. Air Force Academy is legislated by Congress and signed into law by President Eisenhower; its construction near Colorado Springs, Colorado, is completed in 1958.

November 22, 1954: The Humane Society of the United States is founded to eliminate animal abuse and neglect by promoting humane treatment of farm and domestic animals.

1955: The United States opposes the entry of additional communist nations, especially "Red" China, into the United Nations.

1955: The eighty-fourth Congress has a record 18 women (16 in the House of Representatives, one in the Senate, and one nonvoting delegate from Hawaii).

1955: The National Right to Work Committee is created to establish right-to-work laws that prohibit labor unions from requiring employees to pay dues if they do not choose to belong to a particular union.

September 1, 1955: The Indian Health Service is founded, creating the staff, facilities, and programs necessary to provide treatment and preventative care for American Indians.

December 5, 1955: The American Federation of Labor-Congress of Industrial Organizations is formed when the two organizations merge to improve workers' conditions through pressure on employers and legislation.

1956: The Health Insurance Association of America is formed by the merger of the Bureau of Accident and Health Underwriters and the Health and Accident Underwriters Conference. The association is the voice of traditional fee-for-service health insurers.

1956: The Knights of the Ku Klux Klan is organized in its modern form to promote white supremacy and oppose racial integration. The group united with other Klan organizations in 1961.

1957: Peace Action is founded as the National Committee for a Sane Nuclear Policy to lobby against the testing and use of nuclear weapons. The group changed its name in 1993 to reflect its broad mission of eliminating the causes of war.

January 20, 1957: Dwight David Eisenhower is inaugurated for his second term as president with Richard Nixon as vice president.

May 18, 1957: The United States Commission on Civil Rights is founded with the mission of reporting to the president and Congress about all forms of discrimination throughout the United States.

September 24, 1957: President Eisenhower orders U.S. Army paratroopers to prevent interference with racial integration at Central High School in Little Rock, Arkansas.

April 1, 1958: The National Aeronautics and Space Administration is founded; it becomes the principal operating agency for manned space flight, space science, and launch-vehicle development, as well as a significant research-and-development source for space-flight technology and aeronautics.

July 1, 1958: The American Association of Retired Persons is formed in Washington, D.C., to improve the lives of aging Americans through increased benefits and services and favorable legislation.

August 2, 1958: The Federal Aviation Administration is founded with roots in the Air Commerce Act of 1926 which provides for the regulation of pilots and aircraft, for setting up a system of airways and navigational aids, and for fostering air commerce in general.

December 9, 1958: The John Birch Society is created as a nonpartisan organization to promote an aggressive agenda of anticommunist education and action in response to communist advances around the world.

January 3, 1959: Alaska becomes the 49th state.

August 21, 1959: Hawaii becomes the 50th state.

November 16, 1959: The Department of Justice initiates a lawsuit in U.S. District Court to end "white primaries" in Tennessee, where blacks had been prohibited from voting.

December 31, 1959: The Bureau of International Labor Affairs is created to focus on international economic and labor issues and to exchange information with other countries about labor issues.

May 5, 1960: The Soviet Union shoots down an American U-2 spy plane and captures the pilot, Francis Gary Powers. A conference between President Eisenhower and Soviet premier Nikita Khrushchev is consequently canceled.

June 10, 1960: The National Center for Atmospheric Research is founded to support meteorological research at universities and to support the education and training required to carry on an expanded program of atmospheric research.

1961: The Twenty-third Amendment grants voting rights in presidential elections to citizens who reside in Washington, D.C.

1961: Amnesty International USA is founded to join the international organization's efforts to protect human rights, particularly those of political prisoners, worldwide.

January 1, 1961: The Federal Maritime Commission is established to ensure that U.S. goods shipped overseas receive fair treatment and that foreign goods shipped to the United States are fairly tariffed.

January 20, 1961: John F. Kennedy is inaugurated president with Lyndon B. Johnson as vice president.

March 1, 1961: President Kennedy establishes the Peace Corps by executive order.

March 15, 1961: The U.S. Arms Control and Disarmament Agency is founded to deal with arms control and the threat of nuclear proliferation.

April 17, 1961: Cuban exiles backed by the CIA invade Fidel Castro's Cuba at the Bay of Pigs. Cuba defeats the invaders by April 20, and the surviving members of the force are captured and imprisoned.

May 4, 1961: The Freedom Riders begin their bus travels to various southern cities, seeking to eliminate segregation in interstate transportation.

May 5, 1961: Slightly more than three weeks after Soviet cosmonaut Yuri Gagarin became the first human to fly in space, American astronaut Alan B. Shepard is launched in the *Freedom 7* spacecraft into space.

May 18, 1961: The Agency for International Development is founded to provide foreign assistance and humanitarian aid to advance the political and economic interests of the United States.

August 13, 1961: East Germany closes its borders with West Berlin and begins construction of the Berlin Wall.

November 3, 1961: Gen. Maxwell Taylor and State Department official Walt Rostow return from a fact-finding trip to South Vietnam and recommend quick military action.

December 1961: The World Wildlife Fund (WWF) is established as an affiliate of the international WWF to mount a global conservation effort beginning with a campaign to save endangered animals and their habitats.

1962: The Center for Strategic and International Studies is founded to research the growth of the United States as a world power, discover how it uses that power, and learn how its findings affect government policy.

February 19, 1962: John Glenn, a lieutenant colonel in the U.S. Marine Corps and pilot of the *Friendship 7* spacecraft who later becomes a senator from Ohio, is the first American to orbit Earth. He does so three times.

October 14, 1962: The United States discovers Soviet offensive missiles in Cuba and issues an ultimatum demanding their removal. Cuba is quarantined and placed under a U.S. naval blockade. After several days of tense confrontation, the Soviets agree to remove their missiles from Cuba on October 28.

October 17, 1962: The National Institute of Child Health and Human Development is founded by Public Law 87-838, which allows for the establishment of an institute committed to maternal health, child health, and human development.

January 15, 1963: The Office of the U.S. Trade Representative is created and given responsibility and authority to negotiate all international trade agreement programs that had been authorized under the Tariff Act of 1930 and the Trade Expansion Act of 1962.

August 28, 1963: Civil rights supporters march on Washington, D.C., and listen to Dr. Martin Luther King, Jr.'s now-famous "I have a dream" speech.

November 22, 1963: President Kennedy is assassinated while riding in a motorcade in Dallas, Texas. Lee Harvey Oswald is later charged with the murder. Subsequently, Lyndon B. Johnson is sworn in as president of the United States onboard Air Force One en route from Dallas to Washington, D.C.

1964: The Twenty-fourth Amendment passes. It bans the poll tax, which had been used to prevent many African Americans from voting.

June 10, 1964: The Senate invokes the cloture rule, ending a southern filibuster designed to prevent a vote on a civil rights bill—the first time cloture has successfully been invoked on civil rights legislation.

July 2, 1964: President Johnson signs the Civil Rights Act of 1964, the most extensive and far-reaching civil rights act since the Reconstruction.

August 3, 1964: U.S. ships are attacked in the Gulf of Tonkin by North Vietnamese patrol boats, prompting a retaliation by the United States and passage of the Tonkin Gulf Resolution, giving President Johnson congressional approval for all future actions he takes regarding the war.

August 20, 1964: President Johnson signs the War on Poverty Bill.

December 21, 1964: The American Conservative Union is created to lay plans for promoting and advancing the cause of modern conservatism through public education and political action.

January 20, 1965: Lyndon B. Johnson is inaugurated for a second term. Hubert H. Humphrey is vice president.

March 2, 1965: U.S. aircraft begin bombing North Vietnam.

March 8, 1965: The first U.S. combat troops are sent to Vietnam; earlier forces had consisted primarily of military advisers and support personnel.

April 28, 1965: The United States invades the Dominican Republic, ostensibly to prevent a Communist takeover.

July 2, 1965: The Equal Employment Opportunity Commission is established under Title VII of the Civil Rights Act of 1964 to investigate and conciliate all claims of discrimination in the workplace on the basis of race, color, national origin, sex, and religion.

August 6, 1965: President Johnson signs the Voting Rights Act of 1965.

August 7, 1965: The Administration on Aging is founded to carry out the provisions of the Older Americans Act, the first comprehensive plan for social services for aging citizens.

August 10, 1965: The Economic Development Administration is founded under the terms of the Public Works and Economic Development Act to target federal resources to economically distressed areas and to help develop local economies in the United States.

September 25, 1965: The National Endowment for the Humanities is founded after advocates of the humanities in the United States see the large investments being made for improvements in the sciences and argue that improving the disciplines of the humanities is equally important to the country's interests.

September 29, 1965: The National Endowment for the Arts is founded; since its creation, it has sponsored thousands of individual and organizational arts projects, supported the establishment of arts councils in every state, and worked to make the arts in America excellent and accessible.

November 9, 1965: The Department of Housing and Urban Development is founded to form an integrated approach to addressing housing and community development needs, taking into consideration the social, physical, and economic conditions that help communities thrive.

1966: The National Conference of Catholic Bishops is created to focus on internal church matters that affect the financial well being of the Church, aid to Catholic schools, funding of Catholic social services and social justice issues.

June 30, 1966: The National Organization for Women forms in an effort to end discrimination against women in almost every aspect of life in the United States through demonstrations, grassroots activism, media coverage, and political lobbying.

August 22, 1966: The United Farm Workers of America is formed when the National Farm Workers Association and the Agriculture Workers Organizing Committee merge. The organization's purpose is to protect and represent the interest of Mexican and Mexican American farm workers in the United States.

September 9, 1966: President Johnson signs a bill authorizing the establishment of federal automobile safety standards.

October 15, 1966: The Department of Transportation is founded as a cabinet-level agency responsible for creating and regulating policy for the entire transportation industry in the United States.

October 15, 1966: The Federal Railroad Administration is founded to enforce laws concerning railroad safety issues, such as hours of service, accident reporting, signals, and locomotive inspections, that were previously enforced by the Interstate Commerce Commission.

November 1, 1966: The National Institute of Environmental Health Sciences is founded as a division of the National Institutes of Health to be a national center dedicated to environmental health problems.

1967: The Twenty-fifth Amendment is ratified, whereby the vice president assumes the presidency if the president dies or becomes disabled.

1967: Action on Smoking and Health is founded to protect the rights of nonsmokers in the workplace and other public places.

1967: Morality in Media is begun by a Catholic priest, an Orthodox Jewish rabbi, a Lutheran pastor, and a Greek Orthodox priest to research the problem of pornography and the law and share information about this research with the public.

April 1, 1967: The National Transportation Safety Board is founded to investigate transportation accidents and to recommend ways of preventing future accidents.

April 14, 1967: The Federal Judicial Center is founded to study and analyze the methods and procedures used in the court systems and to educate court members in their duties.

November 1967: The Consumer Federation of America is established to advocate for new legislation to protect consumers. Participants in the federation includes consumer advocacy and education organizations, cooperatives, and trade unions.

1968: The National Council of La Raza is founded in Arizona as the Southwest Council of La Raza to address issues facing U.S. Hispanics and advocate for this growing community. The organization changed its name in 1972 to reflect its national membership and focus.

March 31, 1968: President Johnson announces to a national television audience that he is halting the bombing of North Vietnam; he invites North Vietnam to begin peace negotiations and announces he will not run for reelection.

April 4, 1968: Civil rights leader Martin Luther King, Jr., is murdered in Memphis, Tennessee. Riots occur in many U.S. cities.

April 11, 1968: President Johnson signs the Civil Rights Act of 1968, directed at reducing racial discrimination practices in housing.

June 5, 1968: New York senator Robert F. Kennedy, brother of slain president John Kennedy, is shot and killed hours after winning the California Democratic presidential primary.

July 1968: The American Indian Movement is founded in Minneapolis, Minnesota, to promote American Indian cultural awareness and speak out against discrimination.

July 1, 1968: The Federal Transit Administration is established by the Urban Mass Transportation Act of 1964 (now known as the Federal Transit Act) to provide programs for matching grants, technical assistance, and research on mass transit to be funded by the federal government.

July 1, 1968: The Nuclear Non-Proliferation Treaty is signed by the United States, the Soviet Union, and many other nations.

August 1968: The Center for Study of Responsive Law is formed to work on behalf of consumers by safeguarding and protecting the public interest through investigative task forces.

1969: The Congressional Black Caucus is formed to increase the power and influence of black members of Congress to lobby for economic programs to benefit all poor people and strengthen and enforce civil rights laws.

1969: The National Abortion and Reproductive Action League is created to legalize abortion and ensure a woman's right to make her own reproductive choices.

1969: The National Taxpayers Union is founded to defend taxpayers against exorbitant government taxation by working for changes in tax laws.

Jaunary 1, 1969: The United Transportation Union is founded when four smaller unions merge to represent the interests of and fight for the rights of railroad workers.

January 20, 1969: Richard M. Nixon is inaugurated president with Spiro Agnew as vice president.

March 5, 1969: The Minority Business Development Agency is founded to "stimulate those enterprises that can give members of minority groups confidence that avenues of opportunity are neither closed nor limited."

July 20, 1969: American astronauts Neil Armstrong and Edwin Aldrin are the first people to walk on the moon.

August 8, 1969: The Food and Nutrition Service is founded to oversee the U.S. Department of Agriculture's (USDA) food assistance programs, ensuring that every American family has sufficient and nutritious food.

September 1, 1969: The Inter-American Foundation is founded to provide for a mutually beneficial alliance among the Americas.

November 15, 1969: Over 250,000 march in Washington, D.C., to protest the Vietnam War. American opinion is deeply divided over the war effort; "hawks" call for increased military action while "doves" want to reduce military activity.

1970: The National Organization for the Reform of Marijuana Laws is founded to function as a national lobby for legal reform of laws governing the possession and use of marijuana.

January 1, 1970: The Council on Environmental Quality is founded as part of the National Environmental Policy Act of 1969 to provide for systematic reorganization of environmental control activities.

January 1, 1970: The Occupational Safety and Health Administration is founded with the goal of preventing injuries and deaths in the workplace and protecting the health of U.S. workers.

March 19, 1970: The National Highway Traffic Safety Administration is founded by the National Traffic and Motor Vehicles Act of 1966 that made auto design and manufacturing subject to federal regulation.

May 14, 1970: The Congressional Research Service is founded to provide a full range of research and information services to Congress and its committee members.

June 15, 1970: In *Welsh v. United States* the U.S. Supreme Court rules that the claim of conscientious-objector status can be argued on the basis of moral objection to war rather than long-standing religious belief alone.

August 1970: Common Cause is founded to lobby in the public interest at all levels of government, especially federal. The organization will press for the revitalization of the public process by encouraging citizens to become involved in political issues.

August 1970: The Gray Panthers group is founded to redefine the role of senior citizens in U.S. society and to unite older and younger Americans for social change.

August 1, 1970: The Postal Rate Commission is founded by the Postal Reorganization Act of 1970 to review postal rate and mail classification changes requested by the U.S. Postal Service.

August 5, 1970: The National Credit Union Administration is founded with responsibility for administrating the National Credit Union Insurance Fund (NCUIF) and regulating U.S. credit unions.

August 12, 1970: The U.S. Postal Service is founded with the mandate to provide prompt, reliable, and efficient postal services to the people of the United States.

September 22, 1970: President Nixon signs a bill authorizing a nonvoting congressional representative to the House of Representatives for the District of Columbia, the first since 1875.

October 3, 1970: The National Oceanic and Atmospheric Administration is founded as a response to what President Nixon described as an urgent need for better protection of life and property from natural hazards, as well as a need for exploration and development leading to the intelligent use of marine resources.

December 2, 1970: The Environmental Protection Agency is founded as a coordinated and inclusive effort to control pollution in all its forms.

December 31, 1970: The National Institute on Alcohol Abuse and Alcoholism is founded to develop health, education, training, research, and planning programs for alcohol-related problems.

1971: The Twenty-sixth amendment lowers the voting age to 18.

1971: The Citizens Committee for the Right to Keep and Bear Arms is founded by students at the University of Tennessee to advocate for the rights of gun owners.

1971: Greenpeace USA is created with the purpose of creating an environmentally safe and peaceful world.

February 11, 1971: The United States, the Soviet Union, and sixty-one other nations sign the Seabed Arms Control Treaty, banning nuclear weapons from the ocean floor.

April 7, 1971: The Supreme Court upholds court-ordered busing to achieve racial balance.

July 7, 1971: The National Women's Political Caucus is founded to fight sexism, racism, institutional violence, and poverty through reforming major political parties and electing women candidates to office.

October 25, 1971: With the support of the United States, members of the United Nations vote to admit the People's Republic of China and expel Nationalist China (Taiwan).

1972: Eagle Forum is founded by conservative author and lawyer Phyllis Schlafly to advocate traditional pro-family values and defeat the proposed Equal Rights Amendment.

January 1, 1972: The Bureau of Economic Analysis is founded to gather information about the nation's economy in order to predict and avoid further national financial disasters; its predecessor, the Bureau of Foreign and Domestic Commerce, was created during the 1940s to measure the effect of World War II on the U.S. economy.

January 22, 1972: In *Roe v. Wade* the Supreme Court decides that states cannot prevent a woman from obtaining an abortion during the first trimester of pregnancy.

February 14, 1972: President Nixon announces that he will take steps to limit the scope of court-ordered busing.

March 22, 1972: The Twenty-seventh Amendment to the Constitution, prohibiting discrimination on the basis of gender, is passed by Congress and sent to the states for ratification. By the end of 1972, twenty-two of the necessary 38 states have ratified the amendment, also known as the Equal Rights Amendment.

April 1, 1972: The Center for Defense Information is founded to express opposition to the nuclear arms race and United States military spending.

April 7, 1972: The Federal Election Campaign Act goes into effect. The law sets limits and requires disclosures on personal contributions to political candidates.

May 22–30, 1972: President Nixon becomes the first American president to visit Moscow. While in the Soviet Union he signs treaties on antiballistic missiles and other strategic weapons.

July 1, 1972: The Bureau of Alcohol, Tobacco, and Firearms is founded as a distinct division of the Department of the Treasury for the regulation of alcohol, tobacco, and firearms.

September 12, 1972: The Senate approves President Nixon's $33.5-billion revenue-sharing plan that will disburse federal funds to state and local governments over a five-year period.

November 27–30, 1972: Following a full collapse in the Paris peace talks, Nixon orders massive bombing raids against the North Vietnamese cities of Hanoi and Haiphong. The campaign continues for 11 days, pausing only for Christmas.

December 2, 1972: The Employment Standards Administration is founded as one of the major divisions of the Department of Labor (DOL), sharing the DOL's primary mission to improve and monitor the U.S. workplace.

1973: The Children's Defense Fund is created as a research and public education program that addresses issues related to the well being of children. The organization later broadens its activities to include political activism on behalf of children.

1973: Lambda Legal Defense and Education Fund is organized to attain equal rights for gays and lesbians through the courts and public relations campaigns.

1973: The National Gay and Lesbian Task Force is organized to advocate for civil, social, and employment rights for gays and lesbians.

1973: The National Right-to-Life Committee is founded to serve as a national organization to speak for the pro-life movement that opposes legalized abortion.

1973: The Organization of Chinese Americans is founded to provide a unified voice for the Chinese American community that will push for and monitor legislation related to their needs.

January 20, 1973: Richard M. Nixon begins a second term as president.

January 30, 1973: Former Nixon campaign members James W. McCord and G. Gordon Liddy are convicted of breaking into and illegally wiretapping the Democratic party headquarters at the Watergate office complex.

February 27–May 8, 1973: Members of the American Indian Movement (AIM) exchange gunfire with federal agents in Wounded Knee, South Dakota. They seize a church and post office and hold them for 73 days to call attention to grievances they have against the federal government and tribal management.

April 30, 1973: In the wake of the Watergate scandal, H. R. Haldeman, White House chief of staff; John Ehrlichman, domestic policy assistant; John Dean, presidential counsel; and Richard Kleindienst, attorney general, all resign their offices. In a televised address President Nixon denies any involvement in the Watergate break-in or cover-up.

May 14, 1973: The Consumer Product Safety Commission is created under the Consumer Product Safety Act and is charged with regulating consumer products, enforcing compliance with manufacturing safety standards, and developing a widespread consumer information system.

July 1, 1973: The Drug Enforcement Administration is founded to fight illegal drug use and trafficking.

July 31, 1973: Representative Robert F. Drinan (D-Mass.) introduces a resolution calling for President Nixon's impeachment on four grounds: the bombing of Cambodia; the unauthorized taping of conversations; the refusal to spend impounded funds; and the establishment of a "supersecret security force within the White House."

October 10, 1973: Agnew resigns the vice presidency and pleads nolo contendere (no contest) to income-tax evasion in return for the dropping of other criminal charges. He receives a three-year suspended sentence and a $10,000 fine. Gerald Ford is sworn in as vice president on December 6.

November 7, 1973: Over President Nixon's veto Congress passes the War Powers Act, requiring congressional approval for any commitment of U.S. forces abroad beyond 60 days.

1974: Handgun Control Inc. is founded as a citizens' gun control lobbying organization. The organization intends to work for handgun control through public education and legislative efforts.

January 1, 1974: The Commodity Futures Trading Commission is founded to organize forward markets, allowing farmers to space deliveries throughout the year without worrying about seasonal price fluctuations and guaranteeing buyers a solid price, thus reducing financial risk for both parties.

January 2, 1974: President Nixon signs into law a bill that requires states to lower speed limits to 55 miles per hour in order to receive federal highway funds. The bill is designed to help conserve energy.

April 24, 1974: The Legal Services Corporation is founded by Congress under the Nixon administration as a bipartisan nonprofit federal corporation to ensure equal access to legal services under the law for all Americans.

May 31, 1974: The National Institute on Aging is founded after the federal government recognizes the need for a separate institute on aging at the 1971 White House Conference on Aging.

July 24, 1974: The Supreme Court rules, in *United States v. Richard M. Nixon,* that the White House has no claim to "executive privilege" in withholding the Watergate tapes from Special Prosecutor Jaworski. President Nixon turns over the tapes on July 30 and August 5.

August 8, 1974: In a televised address Richard Nixon announces his resignation from the presidency, effective at noon on August 9. He becomes the first president in American history to resign.

August 9, 1974: Gerald R. Ford is inaugurated as the thirty-eighth president of the United States.

August 20, 1974: President Ford nominates former New York governor Nelson A. Rockefeller for vice president. He is confirmed in December.

August 25, 1974: The Pension Benefit Guaranty Corporation is founded to ensure pension benefit payments to private sector employees who are in a defined pension program.

September 8, 1974: President Ford grants Nixon "a full, free, and absolute pardon" for any crimes he might have committed while in office. In opinion polls Ford's popularity drops from 71 percent to 49 percent.

October 10, 1974: Congress passes legislation providing for public funding of presidential primaries and elections.

October 17, 1974: The National Institute on Drug Abuse is established in response to the growing national concern over the rapid rise of casual drug use and the abuse of some prescription medications.

November 21, 1974: Over President Ford's veto Congress passes the Freedom of Information Act, increasing public access to government files.

January 19, 1975: The Nuclear Regulatory Commission is founded; its predecessor, the Atomic Energy Commission, was established in 1946 and charged with the responsibility of promoting the potential of nuclear power as an energy source and regulating its use.

February 24, 1975: The Congressional Budget Office is founded to give Congress more control over the nation's finances and to counter growing presidential power in budgeting.

April 14, 1975: The Federal Election Commission is founded, charged with enforcing the Federal Election Campaign Act of 1971, which had provisions requiring full reporting of campaign contributions and expenditures, limiting advertising in the media, and allowing corporations and labor unions to form Political Action Committees (PACs) through which they could solicit contributions.

May 2, 1975: The Labor Department announces an unemployment rate of 8.9 percent in April, the highest since 1941.

November 15, 1975: The Manpower Administration is renamed the Employment and Training Administration; its mandate is to help administer unemployment payments and to provide workers with the access and training to available jobs.

1976: *Viking I* and *Viking II* space probes land on Mars and send detailed information back to Earth about that planet's surface.

January 30, 1976: The Supreme Court upholds the provisions of the 1974 Campaign Financing Reform Act. It also requires that members of the Federal Election Commission be appointed by the president, not Congress.

May 11, 1976: The Office of Science and Technology Policy is founded to provide support and counsel to the president in matters of science and technology.

July 2, 1976: The Supreme Court upholds the death penalty laws of Georgia, Florida, and Texas. It strikes down death penalties in North Carolina and Louisiana.

1977: The American Family Association is formed as the National Federation for Decency to protest against the violence and sexual content of television programs. The organization changed its name in 1988.

1977: Consumer Alert is founded to offer policymakers and the public an alternative approach to consumer protection by advocating a reduced number of government regulations and regulatory agencies.

January 19, 1977: The Mine Safety and Health Administration is founded; recognizing the need for setting and maintaining safety standards in mining operations, it is charged with inspecting and enforcing standards in all mines and establishing financial and criminal penalties for violation.

January 20, 1977: Jimmy Carter is inaugurated president of the United States. Walter Mondale takes the oath of office as vice president.

March 9, 1977: The Health Care Financing Administration is founded to more effectively coordinate Medicare and Medicaid and to address the issues created by escalating health care costs and the growing number of beneficiaries.

August 3, 1977: The Office of Surface Mining Reclamation and Enforcement is founded to encourage environmentally sound methods of surface coal mining and to ensure that when mined land is abandoned it is reclaimed.

October 1, 1977: The Department of Energy is founded to oversee energy-related activities and programs and to incorporate nuclear technology as an alternative energy source within the United States.

October 1, 1977: The Federal Energy Regulatory Commission is created by the Department of Energy Organization Act of 1977 to establish and oversee U.S. energy policy.

1978: The National Coalition Against Domestic Violence is created during hearings by the United States Commission on Civil Rights on battered women. The purpose of the coalition is to create and maintain communications between agencies dedicated to helping battered women and their children, and help agencies locate funding sources.

March 27, 1978: The National Telecommunications and Information Administration is founded as part of the Department of Commerce as the government's adviser on domestic and international telecommunications and information technology issues.

April 18, 1978: The Senate ratifies a Panama Canal treaty that will turn control of the waterway over to Panama in 1999.

June 10, 1978: The National Council on Disability is founded as an advisory board within the Department of Education to address educational issues affecting the disabled.

June 28, 1978: The Supreme Court hands down the Bakke decision; it upholds a reverse discrimination ruling made after Allen Bakke was rejected twice for admission to California Medical School at Davis, because a special-admissions minority program reduced the number of positions available for whites.

October 6, 1978: The Senate votes to extend the deadline for ratification of the Equal Rights Amendment to June 30, 1982. Thirty-five states have approved the amendment, three short of the necessary thirty-eight.

1979: Citizens for Tax Justice is created to protest California's passage of the real estate tax measure known as Proposition 13.

1979: Concerned Women for America is founded in response to the proposed Equal Rights Amendment (ERA). The founders do not completely disagree with segments of the ERA, but feel that Judeo-Christian women need representation of their own and that their agenda doesn't necessarily match the militancy of United States feminists.

1979: The United Food and Commercial Workers International Union is formed when the Retail Clerks Union and the Amalgamated Meat Cutters Union merge. The union's purpose is to represent the rights of workers in changing economic times.

January 1, 1979: The Federal Labor Relations Authority is created under Title VII of the Civil Service Reform Act, to oversee the certification of federal employees' bargaining units and to handle labor-management issues.

January 1, 1979: The Office of Special Counsel is founded; its responsibilities focus specifically on the investigation and prosecution of Prohibited Personnel Practices (PPPs) and violations of the Hatch Act, which poses restrictions on the ability of certain government employees to participate in political activities.

January 1, 1979: The United States recognizes the People's Republic of China and terminates its mutual defense treaty with Taiwan.

March 26, 1979: Egyptian president Anwar Sadat and Israeli prime minister Menachem Begin sign a for-

mal peace treaty between their two nations in a ceremony held at the White House. The peace treaty, ending thirty-one years of warfare, was based upon negotiations mediated by U.S. president Jimmy Carter at Camp David in 1978.

March 31, 1979: The Federal Emergency Management Agency is founded with the primary mission to help the United States recover in the event of a nuclear attack; helping people recover from disasters is its secondary function. By the 1990s, however, the agency is transformed from a national defense-oriented agency to one that proactively assists people to recover from all types of disasters.

June 18, 1979: In Vienna the SALT II Accord, limiting production of nuclear weapons, is signed by President Carter and Soviet president Brezhnev.

June 27, 1979: The Supreme Court upholds the affirmative action program by ruling that an employer can establish voluntary programs to eliminate racial imbalance.

November 4, 1979: In Tehran several hundred Iranian militants storm the U.S. embassy and seize the diplomatic personnel. The militants announce they will release the hostages when the United States returns the shah, who is recovering from medical treatments in a New York hospital, to Iran to stand trial. President Carter declares he will not extradite the shah.

1980: The Human Rights Campaign is founded to advocate for gay civil rights and fight HIV related discrimination and discrimination against gays in the workplace.

1980: People for the Ethical Treatment of Animals is established as an information hub to educate people about the cruel treatment animals are subjected to by the medical and fashion industries, as well as in zoos and circuses.

1980: People for the American Way is organized by television producer Norman Lear to counteract the influence of the conservative religious movement by advocating respect for diversity and freedom of religion and expression.

January 1, 1980: The International Trade Administration is founded with the task of promoting and developing commerce and industry in the United States.

January 4, 1980: President Jimmy Carter reacts to the Soviet invasion of Afghanistan on December 29, 1979, by withdrawing the SALT II arms-control treaty from consideration by the U.S. Senate. He also places an embargo on the sale of grain and some types of electronic equipment to the Soviet Union.

February 2, 1980: The news media report the results of a two-year sting operation (code name: Abscam) in which an FBI agent posing as a wealthy Arab offered bribes to elected officials. Among those arrested and eventually convicted on bribery or related charges are Sen. Harrison Williams Jr. (D-N.J.) and Representatives John W. Jenrette, Jr. (D-S.C.), Richard Kelly (R-Fla.), Raymond Lederer (D-Pa.), John M. Murphy (D-N.Y.), Michael Myers (D-Pa.), and Frank Thompson, Jr. (D-N.J.).

April 18, 1980: The African Development Foundation is founded to raise the standard of living in developing African countries through a unique program of grants and aid.

May 1980: Mothers Against Drunk Driving is founded by Candy Lightner whose daughter Cari was killed by a drunk driver in a hit-and-run accident. The purpose of the organization is to find ways to create and enforce stricter penalties for drunk driving.

May 4, 1980: The Department of Education is founded; its predecessor was created by Congress in 1867 to collect information on schools and teaching that would help the states establish more effective school systems.

May 4, 1980: The Department of Health and Human Services is founded; its roots go back to the earliest days of the nation when the first marine hospital was established in 1798 to care for sailors.

June 14, 1980: The Agency for Toxic Substances and Disease Registry is founded by Congress to implement the health-related sections of the Comprehensive Environmental Response, Compensation, and Liability Act (CERCLA) that protect the public from hazardous wastes and environmental spills of hazardous substances.

July 1, 1980: The Trade and Development Agency is founded as an operating unit within the U.S. Agency for International Development to promote economic growth in developing countries while broadening the market for U.S. firms.

August 20, 1980: The Defense Department announces the development of the Stealth aircraft, which can elude detection by radar.

October 3, 1980: The U.S. Holocaust Memorial Museum is founded as a memorial for victims of the Holocaust of World War II.

January 20, 1981: The Iran hostages are freed on the same day that Reagan is inaugurated as president and George Bush is inaugurated as vice president.

March 1981: President Reagan directs the CIA to assist "Contra" guerrilla forces opposed to the Marxist Sandinista government of Nicaragua.

April 11, 1981: President Reagan returns to the White House and a restricted work schedule after surgery and eleven days of hospitalization resulting from a March 30 assassination attempt.

June 17, 1981: The Food Safety and Inspection Service is founded to focus attention on the problem of quality and purity of food products sold to the public.

September 29, 1981: President Reagan orders the U.S. Coast Guard to turn back boatloads of Haitian refugees fleeing their country without proper immigration papers.

1982: Because three-fourths of the states have failed to ratify the Twenty-seventh (Equal Rights) Amendment, even after an extension, it dies.

1982: Co-Op America is formed to provide consumers with information on companies that sell socially and environmentally responsible products and to link the companies for increased competitive advantages.

1982: The National Coalition for the Homeless is founded to link advocates for the homeless nationwide and lobby for supportive policy initiatives.

1982: The National Committee to Preserve Social Security and Medicare is founded to explore ways to strengthen and preserve these economically troubled programs.

1982: The National Organization on Disability is established as an all-purpose advocacy group for the disabled.

1982: The Rutherford Institute is formed to propose conservative answers to modern issues such as home schooling, prayer in public school, and abortion.

January 19, 1982: The Minerals Management Service is founded to support the leasing of mineral rights to the energy industry while overseeing the industry's accountability for its financial and environmental activities.

September 1, 1982: The Health Resources and Services Administration is founded when two previous agencies of the Public Health Service—the Health Resources Administration and the Health Services Administration—are merged with the goal of meeting the health needs of minority and low-income Americans.

October 1, 1982: The House of Representatives votes down a proposed constitutional amendment requiring a balanced federal budget.

December 8, 1982: Congressman Edward Boland (D-Mass.) successfully sponsors legislation making it illegal to use U.S. funds to overthrow the Sandinista government of Nicaragua. Congress renews the amendment in 1983, 1984, and 1985, extending it through the 1986 fiscal year.

1983: The Center for Responsive Politics is created as a nonprofit, nonpartisan attempt to improve the quality of the American political system, examine its problems, and explore possibilities for change.

1983: The Family Research Council is founded as a conservative organization to advocate for pro-family public policies.

1983: U.S. English is founded by ex-Senator S. I. Hayakawa to promote English as the official language of the United States.

March 23, 1983: President Reagan proposes the development of a defense shield—at least partly based in space—to intercept incoming missiles. Formally called the Strategic Defense Initiative (SDI), this proposal is popularly known as "Star Wars."

April 1983: The American public learns that the CIA assisted a Contra attack on Nicaraguan oil terminals.

October 25, 1983: U.S. troops invade Grenada after the assassination of Grenadan prime minister Maurice Bishop during a coup led by militant leftist Gen. Hudson Austin.

1984: AIDS Action is founded to advocate for a supportive federal AIDS policy and to coordinate AIDS advocacy groups nationwide.

1984: The United States Public Interest Research group is founded to investigate issues of concern to the American public and propose solutions and legislation to address these issues.

April 9, 1984: Nicaragua asks the International Court of Justice to rule that U.S. aid to the Contra rebels and its role in mining Nicaraguan harbors is illegal. On May 10 the court orders the United States to pay reparations to Nicaragua and to refrain from further involvement with the Contras. The United States contends that the court has no jurisdiction on the matter.

July 17, 1984: Congress passes a bill that will cut federal highway funding for states that fail to raise their minimum drinking age to twenty-one.

August 1, 1984: The U.S. Institute of Peace is founded; its first president, Richard Solomon, describes the new agency as "a complement to the military academies, which train for war fighting. We were set up to wrestle with ways to manage conflict with peaceful means."

September 26, 1984: Congress passes a law requiring tougher health warnings on cigarette packages.

October 1, 1984: The Office of Justice Programs is founded to help the nation's justice system become more effective in preventing and controlling crime by dispensing federal aid and providing assistance to law enforcement agencies.

November 26, 1984: The United States and Iraq resume diplomatic ties, severed since 1967.

1985: Israeli intelligence tells the United States that Shiite Muslims will exchange western hostages for arms for Iran.

1985: The American Foundation for AIDS Research is founded when the AIDS Medical Foundation and the National AIDS Research Foundation merge. The purpose of the organization is to raise funds for AIDS research.

1985: EMILY's List is founded by a grassroots coalition of pro-choice activists to provide campaign funds for pro-choice Democratic women candidates.

January 20, 1985: President Reagan takes the oath of office marking the beginning of his second term; George Bush becomes vice president. Because of the bitter cold, public ceremonies are postponed until January 21.

March 12, 1985: The United States and the Soviet Union reopen formal arms-control talks in Geneva.

April 1, 1985: The National Archives and Records Administration is founded to preserve U.S. history by overseeing the management of federal records.

October 10, 1985: The U.S. Sentencing Commission is founded as a permanent independent agency for formulating national sentencing guidelines that strictly define judges' actions.

1986: The national debt soars to over $2 trillion. The trade deficit worsens as does the budget deficit.

1986: The Council on Competitiveness is founded to create a concerted national response to economic realities that threaten the booming economy. The council's goal is to increase the economic competitiveness of the United States.

January 1, 1986: The Pension and Welfare Benefits Administration is founded to prevent abuse and mismanagement of funds collected from employees in the private sector as part of pension and benefit plans.

January 7, 1986: President Reagan declares a state of emergency between the United States and Libya, ordering U.S. oil companies out of Libya and ending trade and transportation between the two nations.

January 28, 1986: All seven astronauts aboard the U.S. space shuttle *Challenger* perish when their craft explodes. It is the worst accident in the history of the U.S. space program.

February 25, 1986: The United States recognizes the Philippine government of Corazon Aquino after the Reagan administration at first refused to acknowledge that outgoing president Ferdinand Marcos had attempted to prevent her election victory through vote fraud.

June 25, 1986: The U.S. House of Representatives approves $100 million in humanitarian and economic aid to the Contras.

July 7, 1986: The Supreme Court declares unconstitutional a key provision of the Gramm-Rudman Act that would allow the comptroller general to decide precise spending cuts in each federal department.

September 27, 1986: Congress passes the most sweeping tax-reform bill since the 1940s.

October 2, 1986: Congress overrides President Reagan's veto of the Comprehensive Anti-Apartheid Act, which condemns racial separation in South Africa, institutes an embargo on most South African imports, and bans most American investment in that nation.

November 13, 1986: President Reagan says the United States has sent Iran a few defensive weapons and spare parts, but he denies any attempt to exchange weapons for hostages.

1987: Operation Rescue National is founded to aggressively represent the anti-abortion movement by staging demonstrations and protests at medical facilities where abortions are performed.

February 4, 1987: Congress overrides President Reagan's veto of a $20 billion Clean Water Act. It is identical to an act he vetoed successfully in 1986.

February 26, 1987: The Tower Commission report places chief blame for the Iran-Contra affair on National Security Council director Robert McFarlane, Lt. Col. Oliver North, Adm. John Poindexter, and former CIA director William Casey. It also criticizes the president for remaining too distant from the planning process.

April 2, 1987: Congress overrides President Reagan's veto of an $87.5 billion highway and transit bill that also allows states to raise speed limits to 65 MPH on interstate highways in sparsely populated areas.

October 1, 1987: The Bureau of Export Administration is founded to curtail exports to enemy nations who might become powerful through trade in materials that would benefit their strategic effort.

October 19, 1987: Black Monday. The stock market plunges a record 508 points during one session.

November 18, 1987: In its final report on the Iran-Contra hearings Congress criticizes those involved in the operation for "secrecy, deception and disdain for the law."

December 8–10, 1987: During a summit meeting in Washington, D.C., President Reagan and Premier Gorbachev sign the Intermediate Nuclear Forces (INF) Treaty, agreeing to eliminate intermediate-range weapons from their nuclear arsenals.

March 22, 1988: Congress overrides President Reagan's veto of the Civil Rights Restoration Act, which extends federal anti-bias laws to an entire school or other organization if any of its programs receive federal funding.

May 11, 1988: The Office of Technology Policy is founded to develop policies that maximize technology's contribution to U.S. economic growth, the creation of high-wage jobs, and improvements in quality of life.

September 13, 1988: President Reagan signs a bill extending the Fair Housing Act of 1968 to protect the disabled and families with children.

September 29, 1988: The Defense Nuclear Facilities Safety Board is founded to serve as an independent oversight organization within the executive branch and is charged with advising the secretary of energy on nuclear safety issues.

October 22, 1988: Congress passes a Taxpayer's Bill of Rights.

1989: The Communist party in Poland loses power in the national elections. New governments replace the Communist regimes in Romania, Bulgaria, and Czechoslavakia.

1989: Advocates for Highway and Auto Safety is created to coordinate efforts among associations groups concerned with road safety.

1989: The Christian Coalition is founded by televangelist and 1988 presidential candidate Pat Robertson to promote conservative Christian values.

1989: The Families and Work Institute is founded by two researchers from the fields of family and employment studies who saw a need for information on how these fields impact each other. The institute is created to be a consulting and research organization.

January 20, 1989: George Bush is inaugurated president with Dan Quayle as vice president.

January 23, 1989: The Supreme Court invalidates a Richmond, Virginia, affirmative action program calling it reverse discrimination.

January 29, 1989: The Office of National Drug Control Policy is founded to establish policies for the nation's drug control program with the goal of reducing drug abuse, manufacturing, and trafficking; drug-related crime and violence; and drug-related health consequences.

October 1, 1989: The Office of Government Ethics is founded to ensure that employees of the executive branch of government perform their public duties in an ethical manner.

June 11, 1990: A constitutional amendment proposing to make the desecration of the American flag a crime is overturned by the House of Representatives.

July 1990: The Electronic Frontier Foundation is founded to help support legal actions on behalf of computer software publishers and bulletin board system operators whose First Amendment rights are challenged.

July 26, 1990: The Americans with Disabilities Act is signed into law prohibiting discrimination on the basis of disability in employment, programs, or services provided by the government.

August 2, 1990: Iraqi forces, on the order of dictator Saddam Hussein, invade Kuwait; in response, President George Bush dispatches American military forces to the Persian Gulf.

October 22, 1990: President George Bush vetoes the Civil Rights Act of 1990 on the basis that the act would create "quotas" in the workplace.

November 15, 1990: The Clean Air Act is signed by President Bush, setting restrictions on automobile and utility emissions and the use of chlorofluoro-carbons.

November 21, 1990: The Cold War is formally brought to an end with the signing of the Charter of Paris by the leaders of 34 North American and European nations.

1991: Forces from 34 nations, including the United States, overwhelm troops in Iraq and occupy Kuwait in Operation Desert Storm. On February 27, President Bush's popularity soars to 89 percent when he declares to Congress, "Kuwait is liberated."

1991: Choice in Dying is founded when several right-to-die organizations merge to improve the implementation of living wills in each state.

April 18, 1991: The Administration for Children and Families is founded as part of a reorganization effort that merges former Department of Health and Human Services (HHS) agencies to deliver more comprehensive and cost-efficient services to families and to address increasing concerns over children's issues.

July 31, 1991: The Strategic Arms Reduction Treaty is signed between the United States and the Soviet Union to reduce and limit strategic offensive weaponry.

October 23, 1991: After televised Senate Judiciary Committee hearings into charges of sexual harassment made against Clarence Thomas, a federal appeals court judge, by former colleague Anita F. Hill, Thomas is sworn as Court Justice of the Supreme Court of the United States.

November 1, 1991: The National Institute for Literacy is founded as part of the National Literacy Act with the goal of ensuring 100 percent literacy for all adults in the United States by the year 2000.

December 21, 1991: Following continued economic and political deterioration, Soviet republics with the exception of Georgia sign a pact establishing the Commonwealth of Independent States. President Gorbachev resigns on December 25, heralding the official end of the Union of Soviet Socialist Republics (U.S.S.R.).

1992: Navy Secretary H. Lawrence Grant III is forced to resign after scandal erupts from the 1991 Tailhook Association convention in Las Vegas, Nevada, where women were assaulted by members of the navy. Three navy admirals are disciplined as a result of the incident.

1992: The WISH List is formed to raise money to finance the campaigns of pro-choice Republican women candidates to state and national offices.

March 1992: Project Vote Smart launches its operations to provide a politically disillusioned public with an alternative to sensationalistic and biased campaigns through objective assessments of candidates and issues.

May 7, 1992: The Twenty-seventh Amendment to the Constitution is ratified barring pay raises for members of Congress between terms.

October 1, 1992: The Substance Abuse and Mental Health Services Administration is founded to provide federal research and service activities in the areas of substance abuse and mental health.

December 9, 1992: Twenty-eight thousand U.S. troops are sent to Somalia in Operation Restore Hope, an effort to stem widespread famine and restore order among warring clans.

December 17, 1992: The North American Free Trade Agreement (NAFTA) is signed by the leaders of the United States, Canada, and Mexico to abolish most restrictions on trade between the countries.

January 20, 1993: Bill Clinton is inaugurated president with Al Gore as vice president.

January 25, 1993: The National Economic Council is founded by President Bill Clinton as an advisory council to help formulate and coordinate economic policy throughout the government in both domestic and international arenas.

February 5, 1993: The Family and Medical Leave Act is enacted, entitling eligible employees to take up to 12 weeks of unpaid, job-protected leave for specific family or medical reasons.

March 3, 1993: The National Partnership for Reinventing Government is founded when President Bill Clinton appoints Vice President Al Gore head of the National Performance Review; Gore is given six months to study the problems associated with the federal government and then report recommendations for improvement.

March 12, 1993: Janet Reno is sworn in as the first woman attorney general of the United States.

September 21, 1993: The Corporation for National and Community Service is founded as a fulfillment of a campaign promise by President Bill Clinton to institute and revitalize America's long-standing commitment to community service.

November 30, 1993: President Clinton signs the Brady Bill, which requires a five-day waiting period for hand gun purchases. The bill is named after President Ronald Reagan's press secretary who was wounded while protecting the president in an assassination attempt.

May 6, 1994: A unprecedented sexual-harassment suit is filed against President Bill Clinton by a former Arkansas state employee, Paula Jones.

July 26–August 5, 1994: Congressional hearings take place concerning the Whitewater affair, questionable financial dealings that took place in the 1980s linked to President Bill Clinton and First Lady Hillary Rodham Clinton.

July 30, 1994: In *Madsen v. Women's Health Center, Inc.* the Supreme Court rules to inhibit pro-life activists from blocking public access of abortion clinics and from physically abusing persons entering or leaving the clinic.

August 28, 1994: U.S. Forces occupy Haiti and force General C,dras to step down, restoring President Jean-Bertand Aristide to power.

October 15, 1994: The Farm Service Agency is created by the secretary of agriculture to centralize the U.S. government's farm programs, assuming functions of the Agricultural Stabilization and Conservation Service, the Farmers Home Administration, and the Federal Crop Insurance Corporation.

December 7, 1994: The National Resources Conservation Service is founded to study and treat the growing problem of resource erosion and depletion.

June 5, 1995: The White House Office for Women's Initiatives and Outreach is founded to serve as a liaison between the White House and women's groups around the country and to ensure that the concerns of women are heard by the administration.

November 1995: Serbs, Muslims, and Croats of Bosnia sign a U.N.-brokered peace accord after the United States conducts limited air raids on the country, which led the warring parties to the negotiation table.

December 31, 1995: The Agency for Health Care Policy and Research is founded to establish new research initiatives in all areas of health care, including technology and information dissemination, serving not only policymakers but also consumers, health care providers, researchers, and health plan purchasers.

1996: The American Association of Health Plans (AAHP) is created when the Group Health Association of America merges with the American Managed Care and Review Association. The AAHP is designed to give the managed health care industry a unified voice.

February 8, 1996: The Telecommunications Act is signed by President Bill Clinton; its objectives include allowing all Americans access to the Information Superhighway and developing technology that will allow parents to have more control over the type of television programming watched by their children.

April 9, 1996: President Bill Clinton signs a bill permitting line item veto, or the veto of specific spending or taxing provisions of legislation, modifying past stipulations that allowed a president to veto an entire bill only.

May 20, 1996: In *Romer v. Evans* the Supreme Court rules to overturn an amendment to the Colorado constitution that prohibits extending legal protection from discrimination to homosexuals, stating it violates the Fourteenth Amendment's equal protection clause.

June 13, 1996: The Supreme Court rules in *Shaw v. Hunt* that a redistricting plan in North Carolina assigning voters to a district based mainly on their race is unconstitutional, violating the Fourteenth Amendment.

June 26, 1996: The case of *United States v. Virginia* is decided by the Supreme Court, finding the male-only admission policy of the Virginia Military Institute (a public institute of higher learning) to be unconstitutional.

August 22, 1996: President Bill Clinton signs into law the Personal Responsibility and Work Opportunity Reconciliation Act, replacing previous welfare programs with one requiring work in exchange for monetary assistance.

September 1996: The Rainbow/PUSH Coalition is founded when Operation PUSH and the National Rainbow Coalition merge. Both groups were founded by civil rights leader, Reverend Jesse Jackson to work for economic and political equity for low income citizens. The coalitions' purpose is to found chapters in every state to continue the fight for economic and political support for low income and minority citizens.

1997: Congress passes a bill reducing funds for Medicare by $115 billion over five years.

January 20, 1997: Bill Clinton begins a second term in office.

May 27, 1997: Denying an attempt by President Bill Clinton to delay a sexual harassment lawsuit initiated by former employee Paula Jones, the Supreme Court decides in *Clinton v. Jones* that a serving president is not entitled to immunity for actions previous to or outside of office responsibilities.

June 26, 1997: Two Supreme Court cases challenging the ban against physician-assisted suicide are overturned. In *Vacco v. Quill* and *Washington v. Glucksberg*, the court rules that states may continue denying terminally-ill patients the right to a doctor's assistance in ending their lives.

June 26, 1997: The Supreme Court rules in *Reno v. American Civil Liberties Union* that a 1996 law prohibiting "indecent" material from being displayed on the Internet is unconstitutional, violating the First Amendment right of free speech.

June 27, 1997: In *Printz v. United States* the Supreme Court overturns a provision of gun control legislation (Brady Bill) requiring local law enforcement officers to perform background checks on potential handgun purchasers.

August 5, 1997: President Bill Clinton signs a federal budget bill promising to balance the budget by 2002.

January 16, 1998: Tobacco companies, sued by the state of Texas for Medicare funds lost treating individuals for smoking-related diseases, decide to settle for $15.3 billion over 25 years.

January 21, 1998: Reports of an alleged sexual relationship between President Bill Clinton and former White House intern Monica S. Lewinsky surface. President Clinton denies the allegations.

March 4, 1998: The Supreme Court rules that sexual discrimination in the workplace extends to include same-sex sexual harassment in *Oncale v. Sundowner Offshore Services, Inc.*

May 22, 1998: The White House attempts to protect aides from testifying in accusations against the president by citing executive privilege; Federal judge Norma Holloway Johnson rules that the Secret Service must testify before the grand jury.

June 25, 1998: The Supreme Court rules in *Bragdon v. Abbott* that individuals with HIV, even if they are not suffering from symptoms of AIDS, are protected from discrimination under the Americans with Disabilities Act.

June 25, 1998: In *Clinton v. New York City* the Supreme Court strikes down the line-item veto law, stating that giving the president power to veto specific items in spending bills is unconstitutional and disrupts the balance of power.

September 9, 1998: Independent Counsel Kenneth Starr submits to Congress a 445-page report documenting evidence collected during an investigation of President Clinton, triggering the first impeachment review against a president since Watergate.

October 29, 1998: Seventy-seven-year-old John Glenn and six fellow astronauts take off aboard the space shuttle *Discovery*. Glenn was the first American to orbit the earth in 1962. The launch, the 123rd in the U.S. space program, makes Glenn the oldest person to go into space. NASA plans extensive medical studies on Glenn to determine how space travel affects older people.

November 1998: The House Judiciary Committee begins hearings on whether or not to recommend impeachment of President Clinton to the House of Representatives.

December 16, 1998: A U.S. and British air campaign against Iraq, called "Operation Desert Fox," is initiated in order to severely degrade Sadaam Hussein's ability to make weapons of mass destruction.

December 19, 1998: Accusing him of perjury and obstruction of justice, the U.S. House of Representatives vote along party lines to impeach President Clinton.

February 6, 1999: President Clinton is acquitted by the Senate, which cannot muster a majority to convict the President—much less the two-thirds vote needed to unseat Clinton. Only a handful of Democrats in the House, and none in the Senate, vote for conviction.

March 24, 1999: After months of peace talks with Serbian leaders and attempts to establish peacekeeping forces in Kosovo, NATO launches massive airstrikes against Yugoslavia.

Action on Smoking and Health (ASH)

WHAT IS ITS MISSION?

Action on Smoking and Health (ASH) is a national nonprofit organization dedicated to increasing public awareness about the many dangers of cigarette smoking and protecting the rights of nonsmokers against second-hand smoke. ASH functions both as a collective voice for those concerned with the problems of smoking and a vehicle for legal action intended to reduce the dangers smoking poses to society. Using scientific and educational resources along with its legal expertise, ASH fights the war against smoking through public awareness campaigns, legal actions, and the assistance it offers during the drafting of congressional legislation.

HOW IS IT STRUCTURED?

ASH is a nonprofit organization with 501(c)(3) status. John F. Banzhaf III is both the organization's executive officer and founder, and he acts as the head of ASH. The national headquarters is located in Washington, D.C.; a governing board made up of eight members meets at ASH's headquarters four times per year and serves as the collective voice directing the organization. Individuals across the country may join ASH as members by making an annual tax-deductible contribution of at least $25. In return they receive various educational, promotional, and legal materials, including a one-year subscription to ASH's newsletter, information packets on the dangers of secondhand smoke, legislative issues, an explanation of nonsmokers' rights, and legal forms to help them file complaints against workplaces and businesses that do not protect nonsmokers.

ESTABLISHED: 1967
EMPLOYEES: 10 (1996)
MEMBERS: Not made available
PAC: None

Contact Information:

ADDRESS: 2013 H St. NW
    Washington, DC 20006
PHONE: (202) 659-4310
URL: http://www.ash.org
EXECUTIVE DIRECTOR: John F. Banzhaf, III

Vice President Al Gore speaks against tobacco advertising aimed at children in 1996. (Photograph by Rogelio Solis, AP/Wide World Photo)

PRIMARY FUNCTIONS

In its fight to protect nonsmokers from the dangers of smoking and secondhand smoke, ASH pursues a number of avenues, including public education, legislative monitoring and reform, and legal action.

ASH's educational initiative can be divided into three areas. First, the organization educates people about the dangers of smoking and secondhand smoke. For example, ASH makes available an informational booklet titled, "Taking Action to Protect You and Your Family from Tobacco Smoke." Second, ASH educates nonsmokers on their legal rights and provides supporting legal help. To this end it makes available copies of an Occupational Safety and Health Administration (OSHA) complaint form that nonsmokers can use to file complaints against smoking in the workplace. The form, provided by ASH, contains the correct legal language so that, by law, OSHA must investigate the complaint. Finally, ASH educates the public on legislation. The ASH Web site is updated daily with press releases, relevant news stories, and commentary on legislative events and organization business.

In addition to the Internet, ASH uses many mediums to promote its educational campaign. Education information is disseminated via a bimonthly newsletter, educational booklets and materials, and media interviews and press releases. ASH founder Banzhaf has appeared frequently on talk, news, and debate shows, including

MacNeil-Lehrer, Today, Good Morning America, CBS This Morning, Crossfire, Nightline, Face the Nation, and *Larry King Live.*

ASH spends considerable energy working to inform and educate members of Congress concerning technical, medical, statistical, and legal aspects of issues as they relate to cigarette smoking. The organization gives input on pending legislation and suggests reforms. ASH also strongly encourages its members and visitors to put pressure on congressional members through phone calls, E-mails, and letters.

Because ASH has defended the rights of nonsmokers on countless fronts, it can claim at least partial credit for almost every major victory in the U.S. anti-smoking campaign. ASH has brought and participated in many legal actions related to smoking, including: *Banzhaf v. Federal Communications Commission* (1968), which upheld the FCC ruling that television and radio stations must provide substantial free time for anti-smoking messages; *ASH v. Civil Aeronautics Board* (1983), which resulted in mandatory nonsmoking sections on airplanes and was eventually adapted into a ban on smoking on almost all domestic flights; and *ASH v. Lujan,* which forced the U.S. Park Service to discontinue allowing tobacco company promotions in parks under its control.

On May 26, 1977, ASH filed a petition with the Food and Drug Administration (FDA) to regulate tobacco in cigarettes, and later appealed the FDA's denial of its petition. *ASH v. Harris* (1980) provided the legal grounds used by the FDA in its decision to regulate nicotine levels in cigarettes. When tobacco companies attempted to reverse the FDA decision, ASH's threat to sue the FDA became a major factor in the administrative agency's decision to hold its ground. Associate FDA Commissioner Ronald G. Chesemore confirmed in a May 16, 1997, letter that the agency's decision to regulate cigarettes was strongly influenced by ASH's petition. Many more such victories are documented throughout ASH's history.

PROGRAMS

ASH sponsors a number of programs that target such goals as public awareness, legislative reform, and legal issues. For example, ASH is a member of the anti-smoking coalition Save Lives, Not Tobacco, which is made up of more than 300 organizations. Coalition members, including ASH, work to present a united front against the powerful tobacco lobby. ASH is also a founding member of the Advisory Committee on Tobacco Policy and Public Health, an organization that publishes written opinions on pending legislation.

In August of 1997, ASH played a major role in that year's World Conference on Tobacco or Health held in Beijing, China. Banzhaf presented five papers to the conference, including "Thirty Years Proves Legal Action against Smoking Works," "Shedding Light on Evil: The Power of Publicity and How to Get It," and "Attacking Drug Pushers by Regulating Nicotine as a Drug." Throughout the conference ASH posted updates to its Web site, issued press releases, and sent messages to members of Congress.

BUDGET INFORMATION

For the fiscal year ending 1996 ASH had total expenditures amounting to $1,211,904. Of that total, $962,934 went to program services, $81,171 went to administration, and $167,799 to fundraising. Total revenue equaled $1,417,685, representing an increase of approximately five percent in total operating revenue over the previous five years. ASH collected $1,303,965 in contributions and earned $92,672 through interest and investments. Contributions reflect a seven percent increase over the previous five years. Interest on investments represents a five percent decrease over the previous five years.

HISTORY

Attorney John Banzhaf founded ASH in 1967 and has acted as executive director during its entire existence.

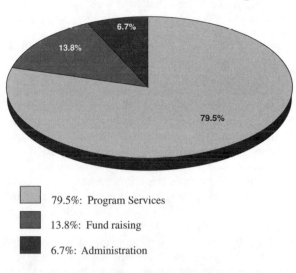

BUDGET:
1996 ASH Expenses

6.7%

13.8%

79.5%

- 79.5%: Program Services
- 13.8%: Fund raising
- 6.7%: Administration

He was joined by physicians, attorneys, and other prominent citizens in creating ASH as a nonprofit organization dedicated to protecting the rights of nonsmokers. Banzhaf first began making his mark in the smoking wars in 1966 when he started a campaign for free television airtime for anti-smoking messages. He petitioned the Federal Commerce Commission, citing that the "Fairness Doctrine" which allowed for opposing viewpoints in matters of public concern and interest applied to cigarette commercials. Thus, if radio and television stations accepted hundreds of millions of dollars worth of cigarette advertisements, they should also be required to devote the same amount of broadcast time to anti-smoking messages. In 1969 ASH filed a complaint charging that several tobacco companies were knowingly misleading consumers by promoting filter cigarettes. That same year Banzhaf's initial anti-smoking crusade proved victorious when the U.S. Supreme Court upheld the Fairness Doctrine ruling.

ASH in the 1970s

In 1972, under the leadership of ASH trustee Betty Carnes, Arizona became the first state to pass laws aimed at protecting nonsmokers. Beginning on January 2, 1972, cigarette manufacturers, with an eye to the Supreme Court's Fairness Doctrine decision, agreed to withdraw cigarette commercials from radio and television. Concurrent with its battle over television airtime, ASH had also been working to ensure the rights of nonsmoking airline passengers, and in 1971, in response to a request made by ASH, United Airlines became the first carrier to provide "smoking" and "nonsmoking" seating. By

1973 a petition ASH had filed with the Civil Aeronautics Board resulted in the adoption of a ruling mandating nonsmoking sections on all airlines. ASH entered the work arena in 1976, assisting an office worker allergic to cigarette smoke in obtaining an injunction prohibiting smoking in her office. That same year ASH petitioned the Interstate Commerce Commission to restrict smoking on trains.

ASH in the 1980s

Carried by its strong momentum built during the 1970s, the 1980s found ASH riding a swelling tide of activities promoting the rights of nonsmokers across the United States. The organization petitioned the Federal Aviation Administration (FAA) to require smoke detectors in airplane lavatories, worked with health insurance companies to increase rates for smokers, and helped states enact nonsmoking legislation for workplaces and public areas. In 1983 ASH won a ruling by the U.S. Court of Appeals that required the Civil Aeronautics Board to reinstate three anti-smoking regulations it had rescinded in 1981. Two years later ASH held the first World Conference on Nonsmokers' Rights in Washington, D.C. In 1987 it joined the American Public Health Association, the Public Citizen Health Research Group, and other organizations in asking OSHA to ban smoking in common workplaces. In 1989 ASH worked to persuade Congress to ban smoking on all domestic flights. The ban went into effect in 1990.

ASH in the 1990s

In 1993 the *Journal of the American Medical Association* released a study that showed smoke levels in non-smoking sections of restaurants to be significantly higher than in office workplaces or homes with one or more smokers. After this report, ASH stepped up its efforts to create totally smoke-free environments. Responding to pressure from ASH, many fast-food restaurants eliminated smoking from their establishments, among them McDonald's, Chuck E. Cheese, Arby's, Taco Bell, Dairy Queen, and Dunkin' Donuts.

Throughout its history, ASH has worked diligently to inform nonsmokers of the dangers of tobacco smoke. Perhaps even more importantly, it established the legal basis for the right of nonsmokers to be free from exposure to tobacco smoke, thus opening the door to increased pressure and legal action against tobacco manufacturers. In 1997 the tobacco industry reached a settlement agreement with a consortium of state attorneys general that had sued the industry for the medical costs of treating health problems related to smoking. However, the settlement, which proposed no price increase and afforded the industry immunity from class-action and similar lawsuits in the future, was denounced by ASH as being too weak to significantly impact the use of tobacco in the United States.

CURRENT POLITICAL ISSUES

ASH continues to monitor the regulations governing smoking in the workplace and restaurants, on buses, trains, and planes, and in other public places. The growing popularity of cigars has also become an issue for the organization. In addition, ASH has entered into the debate over smoking as a deciding factor in determining child custody arrangements when a child is severely medically affected by smoke due to allergies, asthma, or smoke sensitivity.

With teenage smoking on the rise, and as more and more questions emerge regarding efforts by tobacco companies to suppress information on the hazardous health effects of smoking and the addictive nature of nicotine, ASH found itself in the midst of one of the hottest issues of the late 1990s—working to reform legislation regarding tobacco companies.

Case Study: The McCain Bill

During the 1990s tobacco companies found themselves increasingly involved in litigation against individuals whose health had been adversely affected by smoking. Many of these lawsuits were class action suits—a suit brought collectively by many people making the same allegation. State attorneys general began filing suits demanding millions of dollars in damages, arguing that their states were incurring enormous expenses caring for people whose health had been adversely affected by the use of cigarettes.

In the late 1990s public pressure for the federal government to intercede via some form of legislation continued to grow. Finally, in 1998 tobacco legislation began making its way through Congress. One important proposal was dubbed the "McCain Bill" after its primary sponsor, Senator John McCain (R-Ariz.), chairperson of the Senate Commerce Committee. Using all its public awareness and influence channels, ASH worked to ensure that the bill was passed in a form that could alter the future of smoking in the United States.

The McCain Bill proposed placing a per-pack fee on cigarettes, starting at 65 cents in 1999 and rising to $1.10 by 2003. Other provisions of the bill gave the Food and Drug Administration (FDA) broad authority in the regulation of tobacco products and set an annual limit of $6.5 billion on tobacco company payouts in damages from liability cases. Finally, the bill proposed establishing restrictions on tobacco advertising and marketing strategies attractive to young people. Billboard advertisements, stadium signs, T-shirts and other promotional giveaways, and the use of human and cartoon figures in tobacco product ads would be banned under the bill.

While the McCain Bill was a significant step forward in the implementation of federal regulation of tobacco products and companies, ASH was critical of the bill. Specifically, the organization felt the bill did not go far enough in the areas of price increases and regulation, and the cap on liability payments was viewed as favorable to tobacco companies.

ASH promoted the need for a significant price hike, citing numerous studies showing price to be the biggest deterrent to teen smoking and citing the lack of solid evidence showing restricted advertising to carry the same results. In a 1998 CNN interview, Banzhaf stated, "The tax increase is far less than the entire public health community and the National Academy of Sciences believes is necessary to really significantly reduce teen smoking. We're looking for a two-dollar-a-pack tax increase. That will help shock the kids out of smoking."

In April 1998, shortly after the McCain Bill cleared the Senate Commerce Committee by a vote of 19 to 1, R. J. Reynolds threatened to withdraw from negotiations and was quickly joined by other tobacco companies. At issue was the constitutionality of certain aspects of the bill, including marketing and advertising restrictions and penalties for failure to bring down youth smoking rates. The tobacco industry was also deeply concerned about losing the liability cap. Without setting a limit on the damages that could be awarded in any one court case, they argued, excessive litigation could put their companies out of business. Although it was not legally required, Congress hoped to come to an agreement with the tobacco industry, thereby avoiding potential legal battles over the industry's constitutional rights.

Despite ASH's criticisms, the McCain Bill was seen by many as the best chance to enact national tobacco legislation. However, on June 17, 1998, the Senate defeated a move for cloture—an attempt to end debate and put the McCain Bill to a vote. The bill was dealt a final blow when the Senate voted to return it to the Commerce Committee for more study. Opponents of the bill said that too many amendments—including one for tax cuts and one establishing drug abuse programs—had made the bill more about taxing and spending than about tobacco. Supporters of the bill claimed that pressure from tobacco companies had doomed the bill.

Public Impact

After the McCain Bill was essentially killed in the Senate, its opponents rushed to defend their stand on a tax-and-spend bill while its supporters predicted that those who opposed it would hear from angry voters in the fall elections. The public response was lukewarm. While many voters agreed that federal tobacco legislation was necessary, they also agreed the bill had too many unrelated amendments. And while some Republican seats in Congress were lost in the November 1998 elections, tobacco issues did not seem to be a factor in those elections. Nonetheless, ASH and other public health groups decried the defeat of the McCain Bill and vowed to continue their efforts to create national tobacco legislation.

Although ASH's hopes for the McCain Bill may have seemed unrealistic, the efforts by it and other anti-smoking groups in support of the bill resulted in one of the most effective public-awareness and health-issue campaigns ever launched. While the McCain Bill essentially disappeared, strong feelings that remain on all sides of the tobacco issue guarantee that public debate and activism will continue into the future.

FUTURE DIRECTIONS

ASH continues to establish new fronts on which to fight its anti-smoking battles. The organization is offering a $25,000 reward through its Web site for any information leading to the arrest and conviction of a current or former tobacco industry executive. ASH hopes to find information implicating tobacco executives in industry-related felonies such as perjury, obstruction of justice, false swearing, or conspiracy. In addition, ASH has filed a petition with the Federal Trade Commission (FTC) requesting a warning label similar to that on cigarettes be placed on cigars. If the FTC does not comply with ASH's request, Banzhaf has already indicated that ASH will pursue legal action against the FTC. Third, ASH is stepping up a campaign to protect children from parents who smoke. ASH has developed legal theories under which smoking can be used as a determining factor in child custody and child abuse cases, child neglect, and endangerment. This would apply in situations where smoke poses a serious health risk to children with asthma, hay fever, and allergies.

GROUP RESOURCES

ASH maintains a comprehensive Web site that can be accessed at http://www.ash.org. On a daily basis, ASH posts an average of four to five new articles relevant to smoking gleaned from newspapers, magazines, and interviews, along with ASH press releases, information, and analysis. This makes their site one of the most current and comprehensive sources available regarding the anti-smoking campaign.

The Web site features a kids' page with over 15 links to pages with anti-smoking information and activities for children and teens. Visitors to the site can also access information on the dangers of secondhand smoke, find E-mail addresses for members of Congress, and link to tobacco companies' home pages. ASH also posts upcoming radio and television programs that feature issues related to smoking. The ASH home page can be accessed in three languages besides English. The information is periodically translated into French, German, and Spanish.

GROUP PUBLICATIONS

To its members, ASH provides a bimonthly newsletter, *ASH Smoking and Health Review*. The eight-page newsletter contains analyses of many issues surrounding the smoking debate, updates on ASH's activities in the anti-smoking campaign, and information on pending legislation. The newsletter also regularly features a page titled "News You Should Know," which highlights anti-smoking activities around the United States and supplies brief facts and statistical data about smoking. Each issue also contains an "Executive Director's Report," contributed by founder John Banzhaf.

Numerous materials covering a broad range of issues related to the anti-smoking campaign are available from ASH for a small charge. Booklets, such as "Taking Action to Protect Yourself from Tobacco Smoke in Public Places" and "Custody Information Package" are offered. A wide range of papers is also available, such as "Addiction to Nicotine," "State Smoking Laws," and "Raising Taxes on Tobacco." Other materials available include "Thank You for Not Smoking" decals and an airline complaint kit that includes forms for filing a complaint. Materials may be purchased by writing to ASH at 2013 H St. NW, Washington, DC 20006.

BIBLIOGRAPHY

Berkowitz, Harry. "Tobacco Bill Gains." *Newsday,* 2 April 1998.

Connolly, Ceci. "Tobacco Bill Clears Senate Panel." *Washington Post*, 2 April 1998.

"FTC Mulls Cigar Warning Labels." *Baltimore Sun,* 14 April 1998.

Rosenbaum, David E. "Procedural Votes Kill Tobacco Bill in Senate." *Rocky Mountain News,* 18 June 1998.

———. "Teen Smoking Curbs Scrapped." *Denver Post,* 18 June 1998.

"Snuff out Poor Tobacco Deal." *USA Today,* 2 April 1998.

Stout, David. "Gringrich Says Bill on Tobacco Has Little Hope." *Washington Post,* 18 April 1998.

Weinstein, Henry. "Tobacco Firms Threaten Assault on Cigarette Bill." *Los Angeles Times,* 4 April 1998.

Advocates for Highway and Auto Safety (Advocates)

WHAT IS ITS MISSION?

Advocates for Highway and Auto Safety, often simply referred to as Advocates, is a national alliance of insurance companies and consumer, health, and safety organizations. Its core mission is to save lives and reduce injuries on U.S. roads and highways—a goal sought primarily through lobbying for the adoption of federal and state laws, policies, and programs. A secondary goal is the reduction of financial burdens—property loss, medical and emergency bills, productivity loss, and other costs—placed on insurers and public agencies as a result of road accidents. Advocates also recruits other groups and agencies to participate in its efforts. In this way, it hopes both to maximize the effects of its actions and avoid duplicating the efforts of the nation's various public policy groups.

ESTABLISHED: 1989
EMPLOYEES: 9
MEMBERS: 22 member groups
PAC: None

Contact Information:

ADDRESS: 750 First St. NE, Ste. 901
     Washington, DC 20002
PHONE: (202) 408-1711
TOLL FREE: (800) 659-2247
FAX: (202) 408-1699
E-MAIL: advocates@saferoads.org
URL: http://www.saferoads.org
PRESIDENT: Judith Lee Stone

HOW IS IT STRUCTURED?

Based in Washington, D.C., Advocates is an organization composed of equal numbers of insurance organizations and consumer, health, and safety organizations, each of which has at least one member serving on the organization's board of directors. Non-insurer groups include Mothers Against Drunk Driving (MADD), the Emergency Nurses Association, the Police Foundation, and the Consumer Federation of America. Insurance organizations on the board include private companies such as State Farm, Prudential, Kemper, and Liberty Mutual, as well as agent organizations such as the Alliance of American Insurers and the National Association of Professional Insurance Agents. The insurers pro-

Pennsylvania first lady Michele Ridge helps demonstrate bicycle safety during National "Safe Kids" week in 1996. The Advocates for Highway and Auto Safety promote events such as "Safe Kids" week and other awareness programs. (Photograph by Kalim A. Bhatti, AP/Wide World Photo)

vide virtually all of Advocates' financial resources, but all member organizations participate equally in establishing program and policy priorities; it is for this reason that Advocates is careful to balance each funding group with a non-funding group. If the board cannot establish consensus on an issue, the issue is dropped from consideration.

The president of Advocates is elected periodically by the board (since the group's formation in 1989, there has been only one president, Judith Lee Stone). The president conducts the board's program and policy-making activities, but also oversees the activities of Advocates' small professional staff and its corps of consultants. The president pays the group's bills, administrates salary and payroll, and serves as its primary spokesperson.

The professional staff is divided into Advocates' three major areas of interest. One group deals with federal laws and policies that affect highway safety; an example is Advocates' effort to promote stricter standards nationwide for the blood-alcohol content that constitutes "drunk driving." Another group works with issues and laws at the state level, such as licensing laws, while a third group focuses on regulatory issues.

In the states of California, Connecticut, and New York, state coalitions have been formed with strong ties to the national organization. To reduce traveling and research expenses, Advocates maintains a number of con-

sultants in these states. Consultants monitor issues of interest to Advocates in their prospective states, report such happenings to the national organization, and lobby state legislators and regulators according to the program and policy guidelines of the group.

PRIMARY FUNCTIONS

Advocates pursues its goals through a number of specific strategies. Each year, the board of directors establishes a program plan to identify opportunities for affecting national laws and policies. After identifying these opportunities, the board establishes its priorities and determines how its resources will be distributed. Because of its modest budget, Advocates does not contribute directly to the campaigns of specific political candidates; the group spends money primarily on the activities and products of its staff. In the early stages of an Advocates' policy effort, the staff is responsible for tracking legislation, researching and analyzing issues, and composing reports for the board's consideration.

Once a program plan has been established, the staff develops a strategy for the group's efforts, and may attempt to influence policy in a number of ways. Staff members participate in coalitions that may already exist for the promotion of a specific policy, or they organize new ones as needed. They also lobby federal and state legislatures for new or different laws or regulations, and file technical comments on regulatory actions that affect road and highway safety. One of the group's most high-profile methods for influencing legislators and regulators is the formal petition, submitted on a particular issue. An example is the petition submitted to the National Highway Traffic Safety Administration, requesting a revision of the Federal Motor Vehicle Safety Standards (FMVSS) regarding side-impact protection for automobile passengers.

In addition to maintaining close ties at the legislative level, Advocates also attempts to reach out to the public, primarily through media relations. The group also publishes a newsletter and various fact sheets, all of which are available to the public. To make sure Advocates has the greatest possible impact at the local level, the staff maintains a database of grassroots activists who are interested in highway safety issues, and who may be recruited for a particular campaign.

PROGRAMS

There are no formal, ongoing education or training programs operated by Advocates; its programs are formulated in response to areas of current interest to both its members and the general public, and its efforts are organized appropriately. According to the group's fact sheet, "About Advocates," the group's current efforts include, but are not limited to vehicle occupant safety and drunk driving.

As part of its efforts to increase vehicle occupant safety, the organization targets three areas: the use of passenger restraints; safe automobile design; and safe driving. Advocates promotes laws and regulations concerning the manufacture and use of safety belts, child safety seats, air bags, and motorcycle helmets. The group also encourages improved head injury and side-impact crash protection; improved safety standards for light trucks and vans; rollover standards for high-centered vehicles, including sport utility vehicles; and protection standards for pedestrians and child passengers. As part of its efforts to decrease the number of highway accidents, Advocates promotes reasonable speed limits and increased enforcement, as well as voluntary restraints on the part of the automobile industry in portraying excessive speed in its advertisements.

Impaired driving remains one of the organization's biggest concerns. Advocates seeks a uniform .08% blood alcohol content (BAC) as the drunk-driving standard law in all states; a lowered BAC tolerance for young drivers; and the administration of sobriety checkpoints by local law enforcement. In conjunction with these lobbying efforts, Advocates participates in a few programs that involve a number of other organizations. For example, Advocates participates in the National Drunk and

Drugged Driving (3D) Prevention Month Coalition, which stages its 3D Month every December as a means of educating younger drivers. The 3D Month coalition involves over 50 member organizations, including policy groups such as Advocates, automobile manufacturers, law enforcement groups, and federal agencies such as the National Highway Traffic Safety Administration and the National Transportation Safety Board.

BUDGET INFORMATION

Advocates for Highway and Auto Safety is funded entirely by its member insurance companies, which are required to pay a minimum annual installment of $100,000. Because some of the 11 member companies pay slightly more, however, Advocates' annual budget is currently about $1.4 million.

HISTORY

Highway safety has been a high priority in the United States since the advent of the gasoline-powered automobile, but in the early twentieth century it was a cause that was championed by groups that were either small in size or that had only a peripheral association with the issue of road and auto safety. In addition, these groups did not have long-term evidence about the effects of unsafe road conditions, insufficient regulations, and weak law enforcement.

This situation changed dramatically in the mid-1980s, when a team of public-health professionals from the nation's most prestigious institutions wrote and published a study called *Cost of Injury in the United States: A Report to Congress*. The report clearly showed that the leading cause of injury in the United States was the motor vehicle accident. The real and measurable costs of these accidents were set forth in black and white for U.S. lawmakers to see.

Using this study as a keystone, the highway safety movement was then able to encourage legislative action by reminding the public that road safety is an issue with a financial effect on virtually every U.S. citizen, and that delaying public policy changes to reduce these injuries could not be justified. In 1988 the various groups with an interest in highway safety began to discuss a stronger, more unified organization. These insurance and consumer groups recognized the need to look past their differences and to formalize their relationship in order to strengthen the movement. In 1989 Advocates for Highway and Auto Safety was formally created, and by the following year had secured office space on Capitol Hill and hired its professional staff. According to 1992 statistics the highway safety movement made an impact within its first four years of formalization: the nation's highway death toll dropped 5.5 percent in that year, to 39,250—the lowest death rate in 30 years.

Many of Advocates' early efforts were focused on building and expanding its associations with other groups. In 1994 it developed a specific program, the Grassroots Outreach Project, to engage large national organizations in their causes. Through these efforts, Advocates has formed new alliances with powerful, high-profile groups such as the National Parent Teacher Association (PTA) and the Epilepsy Foundation. In 1995, due to the efforts of Advocates at the local level, the first state coalitions began to form. Permanent state coalitions exist today in California, New York, and Connecticut.

In the second half of the 1990s, Advocates began placing particular emphasis on the role of alcohol and drugs in motor vehicle accidents, and on the disproportionate amount of younger drivers who are involved in such incidents. In pushing for a national standard on permissible blood-alcohol content (BAC) and tougher state licensing laws for younger drivers, Advocates has begun to shape the way in which the federal and state governments deal with drunk drivers and those teenagers who lack experience behind the wheel.

CURRENT POLITICAL ISSUES

Petitions and lobbying efforts on the part of Advocates and other groups are often the first step toward the passage of new laws, and when an ordinance, law, or regulation concerning vehicle or highway safety is under consideration somewhere in the United States, the organization is almost sure to be involved. In March of 1998, for example, after years of lobbying on the part of Advocates and other groups, Congress established a national mandate on state laws governing legal blood alcohol levels for drivers. The standard was attached as a rider to a federal highway spending bill. According to the bill, any state that did not establish a .08 percent maximum blood-alcohol content (BAC) for drunk driving would lose its federal highway funds. Other issues, including truck safety, impact standards, child restraint standards, and lower BAC tolerances for younger drivers, continue to be important issues that Advocates attempts to keep in the public eye.

Case Study: Graduated Licensing

In the late 1990s one of Advocates' most fervent battles was fought in the area of licensing teenage drivers. Citing a National Highway Traffic Safety Administration (NHTSA) statistic that approximately 35 percent of all deaths for young people ages 15 to 20 are the result of motor vehicle crashes, and that the crash rate for that age group is four times as high as for adults over the age of 21, Advocates and other groups such as the American Automobile Association (AAA) began to pro-

mote the concept of graduated licensing—a system designed to phase young drivers into acquiring full driving privileges as they mature and develop their driving skills and attitudes. Because the death rate among younger drivers has been perceived to result from both a lack of experience and a greater tendency toward risky behavior, the point of graduated licensing is to ensure that early driving experience is accumulated under low-risk conditions.

In the slightly more than 20 U.S. states in which graduated licensing laws have been adopted, the particulars of the system have differed, but the idea remains the same: young drivers first receive a learner's permit, and then move on to an intermediate license, a period in which the drivers' activities are restricted. State laws vary: most limit the number of passengers allowed in a car driven by an intermediate driver; some require that the driver be accompanied by an adult; and some allow no driving at all after dark. In nearly all states the intermediate license involves zero tolerance for the use of alcohol. After this intermediate period has been passed without an accident or traffic violation, the driver can take another examination to receive a full license with adult provisions.

Graduated licensing systems are fairly new in the United States, and few statistics have yet been collected to support them. According to a 1991 study in New Zealand, whose experiments in graduated licensing first inspired Advocates to take up the cause, vehicle crashes and fatalities dropped by nearly one-third, only six months after its graduated licensing laws went into effect.

While few young drivers, or their parents, openly disagree with the concept of graduated licensing, the fact remains that as of 1999 only about half the states had adopted such laws. The reason most often mentioned for states being slow to adopt the laws is convenience: although teenagers do not have a lot of political clout, parents may resent the lack of flexibility and freedom involved in having a teenager who can drive anywhere at any time. State lawmakers are generally hesitant to pass unpopular laws that restrict an activity as universal as driving.

An example of initial resistance to graduated licensing occurred during the summer of 1998 in California, shortly after that state passed one of the strictest graduated licensing laws in the nation. Some parents, expressing annoyance with the state's attempt to dictate when and with whom their children could drive, vowed to ignore some of the provisions of the law, especially the one that required 50 hours of parent-supervised driving practice. In spite of these objections, most parents—and many teens—remain supportive of the principles behind graduated licensing laws, and the trend toward the states' adoption of them seems likely to continue.

SUCCESSES AND FAILURES

Because of the common perception that government laws and regulations impacting both the nation's highways and auto safety constitute a burdensome interference into the lives of private citizens, the efforts of Advocates sometimes fail to influence legislation it considers to be harmful. In recent years perhaps the most notable example was the 1995 repeal of the national 55 miles-per-hour speed limit, included as part of a highway spending bill. After the bill was signed into law by a reluctant President Bill Clinton (who did not want political squabbling to delay highway funds from reaching the states), several states increased highway speed limits to 65 mph or more. Through the urging of the president, as well as groups such as Advocates, many state legislatures decided to keep the 55 mph speed limit in place.

In any given year, however, Advocates scores numerous victories that have a huge national impact, such as the national drunk-driving standard established in the spring of 1998 that imposes a .08 percent BAC for drunk driving. The group also cites smaller achievements that, while infrequently make headlines, have a lasting effect on drivers. In November of 1998, for example, the group announced that the NHTSA had granted its petition for improving the level of protection for auto passengers injured when the vehicle in which they were riding was struck from the side. The agency planned to do this by developing stricter manufacturing standards for equipping vehicles with side-impact air bags or other dynamic safety technologies. As part of its convincing argument, Advocates cited both statistics (more than one-third of the serious-to-severe injuries suffered in passenger vehicle crashes in the preceding 12-month period were the result of side impacts) and public opinion (81 percent of the American people wanted the government and auto manufacturers to upgrade side-impact protection, according to a Harris poll.

FUTURE DIRECTIONS

One of the areas in which Advocates believes there is still much work to be done is in the passage of motorcycle helmet laws nationwide. As of 1999 only 25 states had laws requiring motorcycle riders to wear helmets, a situation due largely, Advocates maintains, to the circulation of myths about the use of helmets by those who simply do not want to wear them. This will be a battle in which Advocates will play a major role in the first years of the twenty-first century.

Advocates also points out that the use of bicycles is becoming increasingly more than merely a recreational activity in the United States; it is a serious mode of transportation—especially in urban areas—that should be considered part of the traffic mix. The education of bicyclists and those who share the roadway with cyclists, the

FAST FACTS

According to the National Highway Traffic Safety Administration, motor vehicle crashes claim nearly 42,000 lives each year, and cost Americans over $150 billion.

(Source: Advocates for Highway and Auto Safety. "About Advocates," 1999.)

promotion of bicycle helmet laws, and roadway and trail improvements to accommodate cyclists are all planned priorities for Advocates for 2000.

GROUP RESOURCES

The best source of information about Advocates is the group's Web site at http://www.saferoads.org. The site contains general information about the group, as well as press releases, fact sheets, policy statements, special reports, texts of recent petitions and testimonials, and links to its member organizations. The site also contains numerous links to other safety-related sites.

Specific requests for information can be directed to the manager of public affairs for Advocates, who can be reached by telephone at (202) 408-1711; fax (202) 408-1699, or E-mail chickey@saferoads.org.

GROUP PUBLICATIONS

Advocates' newsletter, *Safety Advocate*, is published three to four times per year, primarily as an update of the group's policy efforts and of issues that are a growing concern. In addition, the group publishes a number of fact sheets and press releases, many of which are organized by topic on the Advocates' Web site. For further information about publications, contact the public affairs manager.

BIBLIOGRAPHY

Abrams, Jim. "Lobbyists Score in Fight Over National Drinking Standards." *Seattle Times*, 6 April 1998.

Eastman, Joel W. *Styling vs. Safety: the American Automobile Industry and the Development of Automotive Safety, 1900–1966.* Lanham, Md.: University Press of America, 1984.

Hazleton, Leslie. "Fear is Increasing on the Roads, But That May Not Be a Bad Thing." *New York Times*, 16 October 1997.

Set Up a Simple Highway Safety Program and Save. National Highway Traffic Safety Administration, 1997.

Wald, Matthew. "Balancing Costs and Benefits of Highway Improvements." *New York Times*, 27 March 1998.

————. "Preaching Caution, Officials Allow Cutoff Switches for Airbags." *New York Times*, 19 November 1997.

————. "Reduce Risk in Crash: Front or Back, Use Belt." *New York Times*, 7 September 1997.

————. "Where Every Day They Hit the Wall." *New York Times*, 21 October 1998.

Wilson, Marshall. "Higher Speed Limits, Lower Death Rates: Statistics Surprise Many Observers of State's Highways." *San Francisco Chronicle*, 2 November 1998.

AIDS Action (AAC)

ESTABLISHED: 1984
EMPLOYEES: 20
MEMBERS: 3,200 community-based organizations

Contact Information:

ADDRESS: 1875 Connecticut Ave. NW #700
    Washington, DC 20009
PHONE: (202) 986-1300
TDD (HEARING IMPAIRED): (202) 332-9614
FAX: (202) 986-1345
E-MAIL: aidsaction@aidsaction.org
URL: http://www.aidsaction.org
EXECUTIVE DIRECTOR: Daniel Zingale

WHAT IS ITS MISSION?

According to the organization, "Aids Action is dedicated to defeating the AIDS epidemic and improving the quality of life for hundreds of thousands of HIV-infected Americans." Founded in 1984, AIDS Action advocates, at the federal level, for more effective AIDS policy, legislation, and funding. Nearly one million Americans are believed to be infected with HIV.

HOW IS IT STRUCTURED?

AIDS Action is the union of AIDS Action Council, a 501(c)(4) organization and the AIDS Action Foundation, a tax-exempt 501(c)(3) organization. The organization is split as such because of federal laws that restrict the activities of tax-exempt and taxable organizations. Therefore, AIDS Action Council (AAC) advocates for a comprehensive federal AIDS policy, and AIDS Action Foundation supports the work of the council through policy research, media advocacy, information dissemination, grassroots outreach, and education. AIDS Action is a network of over 3,200 community-based organizations and represents the diversity of people affected by HIV/AIDS in the United States. Member organizations include AIDS service providers, public clinics, state and local health departments, university and hospital departments and programs, and other AIDS advocates such as the Gay Men's Health Crisis of New York City; the Samaritan Housing Project of Fort Worth, Texas; the Alaskan AIDS Assistance Association of Anchorage; and the Mountain State AIDS Network of Morgantown, West Virginia.

AIDS Action is headquartered in Washington, D.C., and has no branches or chapters. It is headed by an executive director and two deputy executive directors, one for operations and development and one for programs. Also at headquarters reside four major departments: Government Affairs, which monitors policy and lobbies; Communications, which creates press releases, other communications, and acts as a liaison to the media; Operations and Development, which supports the structure of the organization and pursues fund raising and membership; and Finance and Administration, which provides accounting and administrative services.

AIDS Action Council is governed by a 30-member board of directors; a 13-member board of directors heads AIDS Action Foundation. Member organizations appoint representatives to the AIDS Action Council Board and to the AIDS Action Public Policy Committee.

PRIMARY FUNCTIONS

The main function of AIDS Action is to advocate at the federal level for effective AIDS policy, legislation, and funding, with special emphasis on the research and development of new treatments for AIDS. Up until the early 1990s, when AIDS Action began treatment-advocacy projects, few AIDS organizations focused on issues of drug development, science, or management of treatment. Instead, efforts were focused on funding, prevention, and services.

To this end, AAC works to educate policymakers about the needs of HIV/AIDS carriers in relation to: access to sufficient drug and health care treatments; coordinated research needs and opportunities; federal funding needs; discrimination; and education and prevention efforts. AAC is active through the entire policy development process. Staff monitor policy, testify at hearings, create press releases, write position statements, and continuously organize at the grassroots level to shape AAC's agenda. Specifically, AAC administers a community outreach program that works with organizations on the local level to help them lobby for funding and to effectively communicate with federal agencies.

Other efforts focus on fighting HIV/AIDS-based discrimination. According to AIDS Action, AIDS/HIV carriers are at risk of losing their homes, jobs, military careers, health insurance, and families. The organization works to improve this situation by acting as a watchdog and monitoring legislative, judicial, and regulatory developments in the civil rights arena. The organization interprets new policies or court decisions for the public and the media.

To garner support for its initiatives, AIDS Action builds coalitions between both member and nonmember organizations. An example of such a coalition is the National Organizations Responding to AIDS (NORA), a group of more than 175 national health care groups, civil liberties groups, women's groups, minority groups, and gay groups. NORA formulates long-range strategy regarding AIDS and advocates for and monitors AIDS-related federal legislation. AIDS Action also coordinates the Patient's Coalition (a group of chronic-disease organizations and activists) and the AIDS Drug Assistance Program (ADAP) Working Group, a coalition of AIDS activists and organizations, pharmaceutical companies, and government officials that work together on treatment-accessibility issues.

AIDS Action produces a number of educational and informational resources including: brochures, fact sheets, question-and-answer sheets, reports, and monographs. These are available to community organizations or individuals. A large information initiative is the AIDS Action Network, which is a national link for 1,400 community-based organizations (although not necessarily AIDS Action members) who are involved in AIDS advocacy efforts at the federal level. AIDS Action provides the AIDS Action Network with weekly Action Alerts that not only detail the current status of AIDS legislation and congressional votes, but also suggest action for the network organizations, their clients, staff, and peers. AIDS Action Network organizations are also informed of relevant funding opportunities and deadlines for applying.

PROGRAMS

Among the AAC's various programs and inititiatives is the Treatment and Research Advocacy Program, which is dedicated to finding effective treatments for AIDS that will cure and halt the progression of HIV. Through this program AIDS Action works with Congress, the National Institutes of Health, the Food and Drug Administration (FDA), and pharmaceutical companies to coordinate research agendas, secure funding, get treatments to those who need them, and pursue the development of effective drugs.

AIDS Action manages the Pedro Zamora Public Policy Fellowship Program, which provides young adults, particularly those of color, with an opportunity to learn about and participate in the development of federal HIV/AIDS policy. Specifically, the fellowship program focuses on education and prevention, opposes legislative efforts to restrict the content of HIV-prevention materials, supports access to condoms for young men and prisoners, advocates for community needle-exchange programs to prevent the spread of HIV/AIDS, and seeks increased funding for federal Centers for Disease Control (CDC) and prevention. The program is named for Pedro Zamora, an advocate for AIDS education and a highly publicized member of the AIDS Action Board, who died of AIDS in 1994.

BIOGRAPHY:
Pedro Zamora

AIDS Activist (1972–1994)   After the death of Pedro Zamora at the age of twenty-two, President Bill Clinton commented on the effect he'd had on the people he left behind saying, "In his short life, Pedro enriched and enlightened our nation. He taught all of us that AIDS is a disease with a human face and one that affects every American, indeed, every citizen of the world. And he taught people living with AIDS how to fight for their rights and live with dignity." Zamora began his campaign to educate the world about AIDS and how to avoid contracting the disease after learning he had AIDS as a seventeen-year-old high school student. The attractive, eloquent speaker spoke in frank, non-clinical terms to rooms full of kids his age, stressing the fact that unprotected sex was a sure way to earn a place beside him. Zamora was called to testify before Congress in order to help shape public health policy for teens. As director of the AIDS Action Foundation, Zamora lobbied for increased government funding for AIDS research. Near the end of his life, Zamora's influence skyrocketed when he signed on as a cast member of MTV's popular show, "The Real World." Millions of mostly young Americans

listened through sixteen episodes as Zamora explained his life-style, his illness, and the effects of both on the world around him. In an *NBC News* interview, Zamora spoke of the stigma the disease carried, "It's very hard to come out and tell people that you're HIV positive. It's not who you are that gives you the disease, it's what you do."

BUDGET INFORMATION

AIDS Action funding comes from organizations, individuals, and foundations; the organization receives no federal donations. For tax purposes, budgets for AIDS Action Council and AIDS Action Foundation are separate entities.

For the foundation, contributions and grants make up the largest source of revenue. In 1996, AIDS Action Foundation brought in $1,151,039. Of that figure, $509,546 came in the form of contributions, and $408,338 was supplied in grants. The foundation also received revenues of $57,912 in 1996 which were specifically designated to the Pedro Zamora Memorial Fund. Foundation expenses in 1996 totaled $1,264,037. Eighty-one percent of that went toward program expenses.

AIDS Action Council has a relatively smaller revenue and expense budget. In 1996 the council had revenues of $814,897 and expenses of $757,329. The council's largest source of revenues came from memberships ($758,291) and the largest expenses were program costs ($629,895).

HISTORY

AIDS Action was founded in 1984 by activists who were concerned with what they perceived as the U.S. government's indifference to the rising AIDS epidemic.

Three years after news of the epidemic was released, the number of AIDS cases in the nation had increased to over 4,000. The founders of AIDS Action believed that a federal AIDS policy needed to be directed and that a supportive policy needed to be advocated for. Also, these advocates saw a need for better coordination of AIDS advocates everywhere.

In the 1990s, several events helped shape the direction of an AIDS policy. Ryan White, a teenager with AIDS who attracted much media coverage, died in April of 1990. AIDS-advocate groups, including AIDS Action, used the opportunity to lobby for, and successfully pass, the Ryan White Care Act of 1990. The legislation provided emergency monies to communities and programs impacted by AIDS. AIDS Action and other groups were also successful in achieving a reauthorization of the bill on May 1, 1996.

The 1990s also brought a focus on treatment programs. According to the AAC, research and development of new treatments was proceeding at a fast pace, but the U.S. government was slow in making these treatments available. AIDS Action and the Human Rights Campaign Fund (a gay rights group) advocated for the use of these progressive new treatments, and worked to convince policymakers that the will and the dollars were available to bring treatments to the public.

In 1992 AIDS Action turned its attention toward improving its grassroots organizing, and started a Community Organizing and Education department. The department worked with local organizations to teach

FAST FACTS

Since its identification in 1981, AIDS incidence has doubled each year, bringing total reported AIDS cases in the United States to 548,102 and deaths to 343,000 (as of June 1996).

(Source: "HIV/AIDS in the United States; Profile of the Epidemic." AIDS Action, 1997.)

them the intricacies of lobbying policymakers and dealing with federal agencies. Particular cities with large AIDS populations, such as Cleveland, Ohio, and San Diego, California, were targeted first.

AIDS Action continued to advocate on a number of AIDS-related fronts during the 1990s. During the 1996 legislative session, AIDS Action was successful in several of its endeavors. The organization aided in the repeal of a military HIV ban that was part of a provision sponsored by Rep. Robert Dornan (R-Calif.) in the 1996 $265 billion defense authorization bill. The provision would have resulted in the discharge of 1,049 HIV-positive members of the U.S. Armed Services. AIDS Action also succeeded in keeping the legislature from eliminating established AIDS Education & Training Centers (AETCs).

On October 18, 1996, Daniel Zingale became executive director of AIDS Action. Zingale had served as political director of the Human Rights Campaign, the largest lesbian and gay political organization in the United States. In his new position, Zingale defined his first challenges as forging partnerships with traditional civil rights groups. By doing so, Zingale believed that AIDS Action could better address underserved communities and help them gain access to promising, yet expensive HIV treatments.

Another strategic move was the October 2, 1997, appointment of Jeff Jacobs to the legislative director position. Jacobs, a leading public health expert, had been a senior lobbyist to Congress during the Clinton administration on issues including: Medicaid, Medicare, FDA, child health, and AIDS. By hiring a health expert, the organization attempted to end the perception that AIDS and public health policy were at odds.

CURRENT POLITICAL ISSUES

The various initiatives of AIDS Action help shape federal policy to improve the lives of those with HIV/AIDS. Many efforts relate to health care access, such as the fight to retain Medicaid coverage for HIV/AIDS treatments, which was threatened as part of federal health care reform initiatives. In 1997 AIDS Action and other advocacy groups were successful in their efforts to prevent a restructuring of the Medicaid program. The restructuring would have included funding cuts as well as a per capita cap that would have been easily exceeded by HIV/AIDS patients because of the high cost connected with HIV/AIDS treatment. Also, in 1997 AIDS Action worked with the Clinton administration to put a "Medicaid expansion initiative" into place. This measure expanded coverage to HIV/AIDS people who were formerly not eligible for Medicaid benefits.

Another concern is AIDS/HIV testing. AIDS Action argues that mandatory testing in health care settings would allow providers to refuse treatment to infected people in need. Additionally, mandatory testing would allow health care providers to maintain a database of those who tested positive, raising personal-privacy issues. The HIV Prevention Act of 1997, which provides for mandatory testing, was authored by Representative Tom Coburn (also a doctor) and endorsed by the American Medical Association. AIDS Action was successful in getting Coburn to delay action on the bill that, according to AIDS Action, would mandate a database of people with HIV without a good reason and would allow doctors to refuse treatment to those who had not been tested.

AIDS Action considers prevention and education the strongest weapons in the fight against HIV/AIDS. AIDS Action maintains that one of the most effective prevention techniques is needle-exchange programs, which allow intravenous drug users to trade in used needles for clean ones. AIDS advocacy groups, and some health providers say needle exchanges reduce HIV infection among intravenous drug users without increasing drug use. According to AIDS Action, needle-exchange programs have the support of the American Medical Association, the American Public Health Association, and the American Bar Association. A February 1997 Department of Health and Human Services report supported these claims that syringe-exchange programs reduce HIV transmission among intravenous drug users, their sexual partners, and their children, without encouraging drug use.

Case Study: Federal Funding of Needle Exchanges

In 1998 more than one hundred needle-exchange programs existed in approximately half of the United States, however they are funded by the few cities, states, or private foundations that wish to support such a controversial prevention method. No federal funding has ever been provided for such programs.

In September 1997, AIDS advocate groups were alarmed as a legislative amendment to the FY 1998

Labor/Health and Human Services (HHS) appropriations bill was initiated by Rep. Tom Coburn (R-Okla.) and sponsored by Reps. Dennis Hastert (R-Ill.) and Roger Wicker (R-Miss.). The legislation, if passed, would repeal the authority of the secretary of HHS to permit federal funding for needle-exchange programs.

AIDS Action monitored the process of the legislation, including tracking which congressional members would be serving on conference committees that would be discussing House and Senate versions of the appropriations bill. The organization made committee member names known to AIDS Action members, so that members could contact their representatives and request that the amendment be dropped. AIDS Action also carried out a media blitz, detailing the status of the legislation through press releases. The organization also worked with Miss America Kate Shindle to convince her to publicly support needle-exchange programs. However, in a blow to AIDS advocacy groups, the amendment was attached to the FY 1998 Appropriations bill, which passed in the House by a vote of 266 to 158. The bill was passed with the provision that Donna Shalala, secretary of HHS, make a decision by March 31, 1998, on whether to ban federal funding for needle-exchange programs.

AIDS groups lost their second chance for victory on the issue when Shalala decided not to fund the programs with federal money. Additionally, in April 1998 President Bill Clinton angered AIDS advocacy groups by stating that he continued to support needle-exchange programs but would not federally fund them.

Public Impact

Needle-exchange programs address the largest identifiable subset of people at risk of contracting HIV/AIDS—intravenous drug users. Among men, intravenous drug use is the second-largest cause of transmission; the first is sexual contact. Among women it ranks first. While the opposition disagrees, AIDS Action holds that such programs decrease the rate of the spread of HIV/AIDS among intravenous-drug users as well as their spouses, partners, and unborn children. If this is true, federal funding would make more needle-exchange programs possible and decrease the spread of HIV/AIDS. Needle exchanges paired with drug rehabilitation referral programs may even help decrease levels of drug use.

Additionally, AIDS organizations claim needle-exchange programs are cost effective and cite an average annual cost of $20,000 to $100,000 for a local program, as opposed to $120,000 to treat one person with HIV/AIDS. However, if needle exchanges were federally funded, opponents would surely be vocal in their opposition to where their tax dollars are being spent. A Family Research Council survey showed 62 percent of respondents oppose needle-exchange programs.

FAST FACTS

AIDS treatments are expensive: one year's worth of protease inhibitors can cost between $10,000 and $15,000. This does not include the cost of numerous other drugs often taken to prevent other related diseases.

(Source: Elizabeth Neus. "Expensive New AIDS Drugs Drain State Funds." *Gannett News Service*, July 10, 1997.)

FUTURE DIRECTIONS

According to the organization, one of the challenges AIDS Action faces is dispelling the general perception that "AIDS is over." In particular the organization has the goal of "reinventing" the current Medicaid system. According to AIDS Action, new drug therapies that may possibly prevent the onset of full-blown AIDS have given hope to the one million Americans who are HIV-positive. However, Medicaid, the health care program for the economically disadvantaged, does not provide access to the health care and drugs that prevent full-blown AIDS until one develops full-blown AIDS.

To address this, AIDS Action has begun working with other advocacy groups to develop ways to expand Medicaid and allow more low-income Americans with HIV to access care and therapies. This initiative, endorsed by Vice President Al Gore, will be headed by a collaboration among AIDS Action, community-based service organizations, the Health Care Financing Administration, and the Office of Management and Budget. Some strategies already identified, but not implemented, include: developing a process that expands Medicaid eligibility, taking into account the unique environment of individual states; soliciting ongoing input from stakeholders on improving the Medicaid program; and developing databases to measure costs and projections.

GROUP RESOURCES

A broad range of information, including an archive of articles, press releases, and state-specific AIDS/HIV information can be accessed from AIDS Action's Web site at http://www.aidsaction.org. AIDS Action publications (including the *AIDS Action Quarterly* newsletter) may be ordered by mail or e-mail (accessible from the Internet site), at aidsaction@aidsaction.org. Public inquiry is also fielded from AIDS Action headquarters at (202) 986-1300.

GROUP PUBLICATIONS

Through AIDS Action, more than a dozen fact sheets, question-and-answer sheets, reports, monographs, and brochures are available; among these are the "AIDS Fact Book," "Blueprint for Reforming Federal AIDS Prevention Programs," and "Housing: Meeting the Needs of People with HIV/AIDS." For material availability and pricing, contact AIDS Action Publications, 1875 Connecticut Ave. NW, #700, Washington, DC 20009; (202) 986-1300.

BIBLIOGRAPHY

Connole, Patrick. "Lawmakers Urge End to Ban on Needle Exchange Funds." *Reuters*, 27 March 1998.

Gallagher, John. "At Last, A Compromise Kept? (Federal AIDS Funding in America)." *The Advocate*, 16 November 1993.

————. "The New Crisis Facing AIDS Organizations: Adapt or Die." *The Advocate*, 27 May 1997.

Horowitz, Craig. "Has AIDS Won?" *New York*, 20 February 1995.

Kocieniewski, David. "Hard Line on Needle Exchanges." *New York Times*, 2 February 1999.

Merson, Michael H. "Returning Home: Reflections on the USA's Response to the HIV/AIDS Epidemic." *The Lancet*, 15 June 1996.

Moss, J. Jennings. "Weak Medicine; First National Plan to Battle AIDS Lacks Substance." *The Advocate*, 4 February 1997.

Rogers, David E., and June E. Osborn. "AIDS Policy: Two Divisive Issues." *JAMA, The Journal of the American Medical Association* , 28 July 1993.

Air Line Pilots Association, International (ALPA)

WHAT IS ITS MISSION?

According to the organization, the mission of the Air Line Pilots Association (ALPA) is to "promote and champion all aspects of aviation safety throughout all segments of the aviation community; to represent, in both specific and general respects, the collective interests of all pilots in commercial aviation; to assist in collective bargaining activities on behalf of all pilots represented by the association; to promote the health and welfare of the members of the association before all government agencies; to be a strong, forceful advocate of the airline piloting profession, through all forms of media, and with the public at large; and to be the ultimate guardian and defender of the rights and privileges of the professional pilots who are members of the association."

HOW IS IT STRUCTURED?

The ALPA's national headquarters are divided between two offices, one in Washington, D.C., and one in Herndon, Virginia. It is governed by a board of directors, which meets twice per year to set overall policy for the association. The board is composed of local council representatives from all pilot groups. The ALPA is also headed by an executive board and executive council that provide interim guidance between board of director biennial meetings. Day-to-day policies are administered by four national officers—president, vice president, secretary, and treasurer.

The ALPA is divided into "pilot groups." Each group consists of all the pilots at a particular airline.

ESTABLISHED: 1931
EMPLOYEES: 260
MEMBERS: 53,000 at 51 airlines in the U.S. and Canada
PAC: Air Line Pilots Association Political Action
      Committee

Contact Information:

ADDRESS: 1625 Massachusetts Ave. NW
      Washington, DC 20036
PHONE: (202) 797-4600
FAX: (202) 797-4052
URL: http://www.alpa.org
PRESIDENT: Duane E. Woerth

FAST FACTS

Although spectacular air crashes get a significant amount of media coverage, air travel remains one of the safest forms of travel. In 1997 there were only two passenger fatalities aboard major U.S. carriers.

(Source: "U.S. Airline Deaths, Injuries Drop in 1997." *Air Line Pilot,* April 1998.)

Although the pilot groups get substantial help from the ALPA national office, they negotiate their own labor contracts and have considerable autonomy over their internal affairs. Each pilot group is governed by a Master Executive Council, which is composed of two or three elected representatives from each of the pilots' local councils. Local councils are located at individual airline headquarters.

PRIMARY FUNCTIONS

The ALPA functions both as a member organization and a public safety advocate and enforcer. To achieve its goals along both fronts, the ALPA undertakes a variety of initiatives. In order to protect its members' interests in Washington the ALPA is at the fore in lobbying members of Congress and government regulatory agencies, particularly the Federal Aviation Administration. The ALPA is especially concerned with matters such as flight safety, aircraft performance standards, and anti-terrorism measures. In addition, the ALPA's PAC wields a strong presence in congressional campaigns: in the 1995–96 election cycle, its PAC contributed $822,000 in campaign contributions ($633,000 to Democrats and $189,000 to Republicans).

The ALPA provides a wide range of services to its members including legal advice, representation in labor disputes and collective bargaining, education, and training. Specifically, the association's representation department has administrators that help local groups negotiate contracts.

Airline safety is a major goal of the ALPA; it devotes more than 20 percent of its dues income to support aviation safety. Approximately 600 pilots serve on national and local safety committees; they are assisted by a staff of aeronautics engineers and safety experts. The ALPA is usually granted "interested party" status in most major

airline accidents, which means ALPA accident investigators assist National Transportation Safety Board staff in on-site accident investigations and participate in public hearings.

PROGRAMS

Most of the ALPA's programs focus on member support services, with a particular emphasis placed on training and education. For example the association has an annual negotiations training seminar for pilot negotiators. The seminar covers such topics as bargaining tactics and procedures, language drafting and preparation of proposals, and help with economic and legal issues relating to the collective bargaining process.

Other ALPA training programs include the Basic Safety School, the Basic Accident Investigation Course, and the Advanced Accident Investigation Course. The Critical Incident Response Program, established in 1994, provides crew members with help from mental health professionals in dealing with catastrophic events and the Human Intervention and Motivation Study, founded in 1974, is the ALPA's alcohol and drug prevention program.

BUDGET INFORMATION

The ALPA has an annual budget of approximately $100 million. The vast majority of its income (about 84 percent of the revenue in 1996) comes from membership dues. About half its expenditures in 1996 went for office and administrative expenses and salaries, with another 18 percent allocated to professional services and fees.

HISTORY

According to the *Almanac of Federal PACs,* the Air Line Pilots Association was founded in 1931 by David Behncke in Chicago, Illinois. Behncke, a Boeing Air Transport pilot, formed the group to protest Depression-era pay cuts, poor working conditions, and arbitrary management practices. The group's first political milestone came in 1933 when Congress extended the Railway Labor Act's job security provisions to airline employees. While this provision has greatly helped the ALPA's efforts to negotiate work agreements with airlines, to this day the association has been unable to negotiate a master contract with all airlines on behalf of all its members. This has led to a discrepancy in wages and working conditions at various airlines, and resulted in the creation of separate air industry labor unions.

After its relationship with the ALPA became particularly contentious, the pilots of American Airlines broke off and formed the Allied Pilots in 1963. That same year, clerical and passenger service employees in the airline industry broke away to form an independent chartered affiliate, the Air Line Employees Association International. In 1973 flight attendants broke off and formed the Association of Flight Attendants.

A turning point for ALPA came after the deregulation of airlines in the late 1970s, which caused severe financial difficulties at some airlines. In 1983 Continental Airlines Chairman Frank Lorenzo filed for Chapter 11 and, in the process, extracted deep wage cuts from his 1,400 pilots. Other carriers began demanding concessions of their own, and the ALPA was spurred into action. The organization drew up collective guidelines designed to stop the down slide of pilot wages. When United Airlines balked in 1984, ALPA members staged a 26-day strike.

In recent years, the ALPA has supported pilot groups involved in a number of contentious contract negotiations, including American and US Airways. In 1997 the association merged with the Canadian Air Line Pilots Association.

CURRENT POLITICAL ISSUES

In many ways the ALPA is a typical labor union, fighting for higher wages and better working conditions for its members. It is unique, however, because it has an equally important responsibility to ensure safety in the airways. To that end it is involved in all aspects of air safety from investigating flight accidents to modernizing the Air Traffic Control System. In many of its efforts, the ALPA works in collaboration with government regulatory bodies like the National Transportation Safety Board and the Federal Aviation Administration. An example is the association's crusade to crack down on disruptive airline passengers.

Case Study: Disruptive Airline Passengers

In 1996 the ALPA became concerned about an upswing in the number of airline passengers getting physically or verbally abusive with airline crews and fellow passengers. While it is illegal for passengers to disrupt the action of flight crew members, according to federal statistics, reports of passengers interfering with crews rose from 96 in 1993 to 174 in 1995. At a meeting of the security committee of the International Federation of ALPA in 1996, members from airlines around the world cited disruptive passengers as a growing threat to air safety.

Observers point to a number of reasons for this growing trend: increased frustration among the public, which was also being manifested on the ground in "road rage"; the elimination of smoking on flights, which may result in agitated passengers who might compensate by

increased alcohol consumption; and overcrowding of flights. Said Capt. Steve Luckey, chairman of ALPA's security committee: "Put a nervous or a stressed-out passenger into a crowded airliner cabin, maybe add a little alcohol—or in some cases a lot—take away the cigarettes and, in some cases, the fear of prosecution, and almost anything can happen."

In April of 1997 the ALPA sponsored an International Conference on Disruptive Airline Passengers in Washington, D.C., to focus public and media attention on this issue. Among those testifying were members of Congress, social scientists, and representatives of several airlines. The conference generated widespread publicity. Part of the reason for the conference was to communicate to the flying public that airlines would have a zero tolerance policy for disruptive behavior. The ALPA was also seeking additional training in confrontation management for airline crews, tough prosecution and sentencing of disruptive passengers, stricter control over deportees being transported aboard airlines, and the creation of a national database to track incidents and perpetrators.

It is difficult to say how much impact the conference will have on public attitudes, but the concerns raised by the ALPA have already had some effect. For instance, the Executive Office of U.S. Attorneys named a deputy director as the point of contact for coordinating cases involving disruptive passengers. In addition, United Airlines started a program called Protect Our Employees, under which flight attendants were given legal advice, paid absences, and other support to help them testify in criminal assault cases. Further, several cases in late 1998 involving disruptive passengers have resulted in heavy fines and imprisonment.

FUTURE DIRECTIONS

One problem the ALPA is grappling with is the fact that its political action committee has been waning during the late 1990s. In fact, according to the 1998 ALPA President's Report, 1997 marked the sixth straight year of decline. A 1998 *Air Line Pilot* article cited that PAC donations from ALPA members had dropped from $800,000 in 1990 to $551,000 in 1996. The article further noted, "A reduced campaign war chest translates into a diminished role for airline pilots in the federal election process and, eventually, a loss of effectiveness . . . we must get our PAC back on track." Initiatives to boost funds include a competition among all pilot groups to post the biggest increase in PAC contributions.

Another pending crises concerns the federal rule requiring commercial airline pilots to retire at age 60. The rule, which has been in place since 1959, has come under strong attack in recent years. The ALPA supports the rule, although some government officials who are against age discrimination want to end it. Many believe the ALPA is more concerned with protecting the interests of its younger members. In the early 1990s the organization prevailed upon Congress to quash a move by the Federal Aviation Administration to end the rule. It is uncertain how long the ALPA will continue to head off the ruling, especially when the trend throughout the rest of society is toward later and later retirements.

GROUP RESOURCES

The group's Web site at http://www.alpa.org was launched in 1997. It is aimed at ALPA members, but does include information of interest to the general public including speeches and testimonies, news releases, facts about the organization, highlights from the group's monthly magazine, and articles covering the latest issues involving the air industry. The site also includes extensive coverage of air safety with links to government regulatory sites.

GROUP PUBLICATIONS

The ALPA publishes *Air Line Pilot,* a glossy, full-color magazine published 10 times per year. The magazine, which has a 70,000 circulation, covers issues of con-

cern to pilots and the airline industry and updates on labor issues. For information, call (703) 481-4468 or view full-length featured articles at the ALPA Web site.

BIBLIOGRAPHY

Babbitt, Randolph. "President's Annual Report for 1997–98."

———. "Retooling for a New Century." *Air Line Pilot,* Fall 1997.

Bryant, Adams. "No Longer Flying in Formation." *New York Times,* 17 January 1997.

Lieber, Ronald. "The Fight to Legislate Incompetence Out of the Cockpit." *Fortune,* 5 February 1996.

Mattlick, Teresa. "International Conference on Disruptive Airline Passengers." *Air Line Pilot,* June/July 1997.

Miles, Gregory, Matt Rothman, William C. Symonds, and Vicky Cahn. "The Pilots are Finally Throwing Their Weight Around." *Business Week,* 28 October 1985.

Pasztor, Andy, and Jeff Cole. "FAA, Industry Plan Campaign on Air Safety.'" *Wall Street Journal,* 11 February 1998.

Rose, Robert. "US Airways Ties Growth Prospects to Cost Concessions from Pilots." *Wall Street Journal,* 18 September 1997.

Zuckerman, Laurence. "Pilot Talks at Northwest Are Stalled." *New York Times,* 18 December 1997.

———. "Pilots Press to End Forced Retirement at 60." *New York Times,* 17 May 1998.

American Association of Health Plans (AAHP)

WHAT IS ITS MISSION?

The American Association of Health Plans (AAHP) represents more than 1,000 health maintenance organizations (HMOs), preferred provider organizations (PPOs), and other health network organizations that, together, provide health care for more than 100 million Americans. The group aims to present a strong, unified voice for the managed care industry and to present a positive image of the industry to the general public.

The group is dedicated to defending and improving managed care, a system in which groups of doctors offer care with tight controls on costs and procedures. This method of providing health care, although increasingly popular, has been criticized for sacrificing quality of care at the expense of cost. The group's "philosophy of care" states: "AAHP believes that comprehensive health care is best provided by networks of health care professionals who are willing to be held accountable for the quality of their services and the satisfaction of their patients."

ESTABLISHED: 1996
EMPLOYEES: 125
MEMBERS: More than 1,000 organizations
PAC: Health Plan Political Action Committee

Contact Information:

ADDRESS: 1129 Twentieth St. NW, Ste. 600
   Washington, DC 20036
PHONE: (202) 778-3200
FAX: (202) 331-7487
E-MAIL: americanassociation@aahp.org
URL: http://www.aahp.org
PRESIDENT; CEO: Karen Ignagni

HOW IS IT STRUCTURED?

The AAHP is a trade organization headquartered in Washington, D.C., headed by a chief executive officer with the oversight of a board of directors. There are seven categories of membership depending upon the type of health care provider. Members range from small local health plans to national chains. There is also an individual membership category.

Members can participate in the formulation of policy through a number of working groups and task forces

FAST FACTS

In 1998 85 percent of Americans with health insurance belonged to some form of managed health care plan, up from 52 percent in 1994.

> (Source: Bill Marvin. "Cut Government Intervention in Choosing Health Care." *San Diego Business Journal*, April 1998.)

on issues such as Medicare and Medicaid. Members also voice opinions through regional membership meetings and at the association's annual meeting, where national policy is formulated.

PRIMARY FUNCTIONS

The AAHP works to both protect the managed health care industry and to ensure the quality of health care for all Americans. In the legislative arena, the association attempts to influence public health care policy through several methods. First, it conducts research on a variety of health issues, and produces studies and reports that support the managed health care industry. These studies are provided to policymakers, government agencies, and the media. The AAHP often conducts clinical research in conjunction with federal health agencies such as the National Institutes of Health and the Centers for Disease Control.

The association is also an effective grassroots organizer, and has had tremendous success mobilizing health care workers and organizations to put pressure on Congress and state legislatures. The AAHP's state affairs staff offers local members how-to manuals designed to help members mobilize a network of activists at the state level. The association's political action committee is also a powerful political force; during the 1995–96 election cycle, the Health Plan PAC contributed approximately $47,000 in political contributions, with a little more than half going to Republican candidates.

As a membership organization, the AAHP also exists to serve the needs of its various members. The association helps members keep abreast of legislative and regulatory changes through a bimonthly magazine, a bulletin on government affairs, research briefs, and other publications; as well as legislative updates, bill analyses and other services. The AAHP also has a legal staff that

provides advice to members, offers referrals, and acts as a clearinghouse on legal issues. Member organizations receive regular communications on new regulations, tax changes, and other legal matters.

PROGRAMS

The AAHP provides several types of education and training opportunities for members, including education forums, conferences, and seminars at which experts provide information on health care issues. In addition, the group has an Executive Leadership Program for administrators and medical directors.

The image the AAHP attempts to project for its member organizations is embodied in Putting Patients First, a set of principles to which all members are required to abide. The self-policing program is viewed by critics of managed care as an attempt by AAHP to head off new state and federal laws and regulations. But, regardless of the sincerity of the AAHP's motives, Putting Patients First requires a high standard of its members. The program's goals, according to AAHP literature, are threefold: "To communicate the facts about how health plans work for the benefit of patients; to make it clear that the AAHP and its member plans are listening to the concerns of patients and physicians and changing when necessary to meet their needs; and to provide a mechanism for member plans to demonstrate their commitment to high standards of accountability."

The AAHP also sponsors a number of programs that support public health initiatives. In association with the American Cancer Society (ACS), the association holds an annual awareness campaign to educate women about breast cancer and the need for regular health screenings. The joint campaign began in 1996 and is held each year on Mother's Day. In 1998 more than 200 television stations ran the public service announcement that provided 500 million viewers with the thoughtful impression that "The best gift for Mother's Day . . . is more Mother's Days."

BUDGET INFORMATION

Not made available.

HISTORY

The AAHP was created in 1996 when the Group Health Association of America merged with the American Managed Care and Review Association. The merger took place gradually; in February, the group's "philosophy of care," outlining its commitment to cost-effective yet high-quality health care was released, and in March the two groups announced that the name of the merged group would be the American Association of Health Plans.

The new association was designed to give the managed health care industry a stronger and more unified voice. At the time, managed care organizations were under heavy criticism for allegations that they encouraged or forced doctors to cut corners on health care in order to keep down costs. Congress was discussing proposals for a variety of mandates on the industry. "We believe that it is time to stand up for this style of health care and face down efforts to undermine it," said George Halvorson, AAHP's chairman of the board, in early 1996.

Since its founding, the group has fought what it considers unnecessary or burdensome state and federal controls and regulations on the managed care industry. Among its tactics are direct lobbying by its officials in the halls of Congress, mobilizing its members around the United States to contact Congress and state governments, and providing studies and reports for its allies within and outside Congress. At the same time, the group has tried to clean up its own house. In December 1996, the AAHP launched Putting Patients First, a set of principles for managed care providers designed to ensure patients that managed care was not cutting corners and was, in fact, providing high-quality care.

For instance, Putting Patients First includes the assertion that "nothing in any health plan policies should be interpreted as prohibiting physicians from discussing treatment options with patients." That item was aimed squarely at allegations that some HMOs had a "gag clause" that prevented doctors from discussing options for treatment with their patients because the treatments may be costly. Some critics, however, questioned AAHP's sincerity. Dr. Jerome Kassirer, writing in the *Journal of the American Medical Association*, claimed that "Putting Patients First amounts to little more than a thinly veiled attempt to ward off state and federal actions to curb the abuses of managed care."

AAHP officials and members defended the program and insisted its goals were to foster better care and were not at all political. In June 1997, AAHP members at the group's annual meeting in Seattle, Washington, voted to make Putting Patients First guidelines a condition of membership. The move was seen as a way of showing critics and, more importantly, the public, that the group was dedicated to providing the best health care possible.

CURRENT POLITICAL ISSUES

Because the health and safety of patients is the primary concern of the AAHP, it becomes involved in almost every piece of health legislation and every health debate that affects the American public. The 1990s found the association involved in controversies over the safety and reliability of air bags, the availability of quality medical services for mothers and children, and women's health care issues such as research into the cause and treatment of menopause.

The AAHP also finds itself embroiled in legislation aimed directly at its system of managed health care. For instance, in 1996, Congress passed a law governing the length of stays in hospital maternity wards after an outcry that some health plans, to limit costs, were sending new mothers home too quickly. The association has fought hard, however, against new regulations, and is always quick to remind Congress of the unpredictable dangers of trying to "micromanage" the complicated health care industry. In particular, the AAHP has helped block the most comprehensive managed care reform proposal in Congress, the Patient Access to Responsible Care Act (PARCA).

Case Study: PARCA

The battle waged over PARCA illustrates how AAHP fights for the interests of the managed care industry, while at the same time trying to guarantee health care policies that have the potential to affect millions of Americans. In early 1998, reform of health maintenance organization (HMO) practices was considered one of the most important issues facing Congress. The HMO industry, although growing in popularity, had been the subject of a number of critical reports in the media and other forums. For instance, in 1996 the *Journal of the American Medical Association,* reported on a four-year study of 2,235 patients, which found that almost twice as many elderly patients had declined in health while under the care of HMOs compared to treatment under traditional, fee-for-service health plans.

Representative Charlie Norwood (R-Geor.) sponsored a bill that would require HMOs to allow patients greater access to medical specialists, require better disclosure of health plan benefits, and make it easier for patients to sue if they believe they were denied proper health care. By February 1998, Representative Norwood's bill had 219 co-sponsors and supporters were optimistic that the bill would pass. But the AAHP was studying the bill's potential impact and publicizing its findings. The association warned that the bill would drive up health insurance premiums and released a study concluding that a one percent increase in premiums would result in 600,000 employees losing insurance. This study led one powerful group, the National Association of Manufacturers, to ask its members to go to Washington in February to fight all new HMO regulations. The AAHP prepared more studies on the legislation's impact and publicized them in regional press conferences.

HMO reform advocates were preparing reports of their own. In February, Patient Access to Responsible

Care Alliance, an organization that supported the PARCA legislation, released a study that claimed the bill would cause only a slight increase in managed care premiums, between 0.7 percent and 2.6 percent. Louise Kertesz, writing for *Modern Healthcare Magazine* complained in March: "This latest debate has cranked up the self-serving research machine. Special-interest groups are starting to flood the halls of Congress with reports on how the proposed legislation would help or hurt consumers (read help or hurt their cause)."

While the conflicting reports may have been confusing for some, the AAHP reports that concluded premiums would rise were apparently beginning to have some effect. For instance, the AAHP released a study projecting that Louisiana families could lose $325 in take-home pay per household in 1999 if wages were cut to offset higher health insurance. *New Orleans City Business Magazine* noted that HMO reforms were fueled by horror stories of managed care organizations withholding authorization of care, sometimes resulting in irreversible injury or death. "But while the public seems to want greater access to health care," the magazine reported, "they may cry foul when the costs rise. The latter is the reason some congressmen withdrew their support for the patients' rights legislation when the reality of the cost sank in."

In March, former House Speaker Newt Gingrich gave a speech strongly opposing the legislation offered by his fellow Georgia Republican. The speech was so favorable to AAHP that even members of the group were stunned. As of late 1998, PARCA's fate was uncertain. The bill was still in committee and the full House had not voted upon it.

FUTURE DIRECTIONS

While the AAHP apparently has held off the Patient Access to Responsibility Act and other legislation that would force comprehensive changes upon the managed care industry, proponents of such legislation intend to keep pushing for them. Karen Ignagni, AAHP president, has said that many such proposals "that might seem necessary today will stifle the ability of the healthcare system to remain innovative and flexible tomorrow." Rick Smith, AAHP director of policy, further added that the additional regulations under consideration could be devastating. If AAHP officials are right about the effect of proposals being considered by Congress, then the organization will have to work hard to protect its members from damaging proposals that at one point had the support of almost half the House and still apparently have a strong residual support among many members of Congress.

GROUP RESOURCES

The AAHP maintains a Web site at http://www.aahp.org that is geared toward members, but does offer extensive information both about the association and the managed health care industry. Especially useful is the AAHP's on-line research library that includes reports and briefs on managed care facts and patient health care choices, along with consumer fact sheets on issues such as women's health care. For more information about the organization, write to the American Association of Health Plans, 1129 Twentieth St. NW, Ste. 600, Washington, DC 20036 or call (202) 778-3200.

GROUP PUBLICATIONS

The group's publications include the *Medical Affairs Issues Report*, the *Childhood Immunization Newsletter*, *An Introduction to Clinical Practice Guidelines*, the *Government Affairs Bulletin*, and *Guide to PPO State Laws and Regulations*. For more information about AAHP publications, E-mail the Customer Action Center at americanassociation@aahp.org, call (202) 778–3269, or write to the American Association of Health Plans, 1129 Twentieth St. NW, Ste. 600, Washington, DC 20036.

BIBLIOGRAPHY

Firshein, Janet. "U.S. Study Raises Questions About HMO Quality of Care." *Lancet,* 12 October 1996.

"GAO Study of 529 HMOs Found None Used Contract ('Gag') Clauses Limiting Commentary." *Insurance Advocate Magazine,* 4 October 1997.

Kertesz, Louise. "Self-Interest Reigns." *Modern Healthcare Magazine,* 16 March 1998.

McGinley, Laurie. "Study Says Patient-Protection Proposals Would Raise Health Costs Moderately." *Wall Street Journal,* 23 April 1998.

"Managed Care Surveys: Something to Talk About." *People's Medical Society Newsletter,* April 1998.

Marvin, Bill. "Cut Government Intervention in Choosing Health Care," *San Diego Business Journal*, April 1998.

Mukherjee, Sougata. "Interests Prep for Managed Care War on Capitol Hill." *Tampa Bay Business Journal,* February 1998.

Pear, Robert. "High Rates Hobble Law to Guarantee Health Insurance." *New York Times,* 17 March 1998.

Serb, Chris. "Religion." *Hospitals & Health Networks Magazine,* 20 February 1998.

"Yes, Virginia, There is no Gag Clause." *Modern Healthcare,* 6 October 1997.

American Association of Retired Persons (AARP)

WHAT IS ITS MISSION?

The American Association of Retired Persons (AARP) describes itself as "a nonprofit, non-partisan membership organization dedicated to addressing the needs and interests of people 50 and older. We seek through education, advocacy and service to enhance the quality of life for all by promoting independence, dignity and purpose." The organization's motto is "To Serve, Not to Be Served," and it holds out as its vision to "excel . . . as a dynamic presence in every community, shaping and enriching the experience of aging for each member and for society." To this end, the AARP informs and advises its members on social, economic, and political issues while also stressing a sense of community among senior citizens and promoting the image of Americans over age 50 as empowered and active.

ESTABLISHED: July 1, 1958
EMPLOYEES: 1,787 (1997)
MEMBERS: 31.5 million (1997)

Contact Information:
ADDRESS: 601 E. St. NW
   Washington, DC 20049
PHONE: (202) 434-2277
TOLL FREE: (800) 424-3410
TDD (HEARING IMPAIRED): (202) 434-6561
FAX: (202) 434-6483
E-MAIL: member@aarp.org
URL: http://www.aarp.org
EXECUTIVE DIRECTOR: Horace B. Deets

HOW IS IT STRUCTURED?

At the head of the AARP is the executive director, who also serves as spokesperson for the organization, and an elected 21-member board of directors. The executive director works collaboratively with the board, particularly the board president, in directing the social and legislative agendas of the organization. Historically, the board has been composed of retired educators and public servants, which critics charge makes them anti-business and pro-subsidy. The AARP is also closely affiliated with the National Retired Teachers Association, reflecting a large segment of members who are or were educators with a history of strong union participation. Similar factors

Volunteers known as "Fraud Fighters" work for the AARP to raise senior citizen awareness of fraudulent mail and telephone schemes. *(Photograph by Patricia McDonnell, AP/Wide World Photo)*

directing AARP's social agenda are the recommendations of its 41-member volunteer National Legislative Council.

Five regional offices, each with a director coordinating grassroots initiatives, provide the foundation for the AARP, although state organizations in popular retirement states like Florida and California are growing in effectiveness. AARP state organizations utilize volunteer task forces, or state legislative committees, which determine policy priorities in their respective states. Certified chapters are authorized to participate in AARP programs and meet at regularly specified times and locations. The chapters address individual community concerns and provide valuable field research to the national organization that is also used in determining the organization's national goals.

The AARP holds a convention every two years to elect new officers and new board members, while bylaw changes and resolutions are decided by a delegate assembly. This convention is a significant political event that attracts those who court support for political candidates or for policies from the AARP's huge membership.

PRIMARY FUNCTIONS

The AARP is best known for its powerful lobbying presence and its efficiency in mobilizing public opinion for or against politicians and policy. Such efforts are often very high profile; in 1989, for example, former House Ways and Means Committee Chair Dan Rostenkowski was confronted by angry seniors demanding the repeal of the Medicare Catastrophic Care Act which had been passed a year earlier to remedy the problem of growing Medicare costs and increased demands on the health care system. Surrounded by protesters, the congressman was intimidated into abandoning his car and leaving a public meeting on foot, an event that was widely reported. The legislative reform was repealed due to the tremendous outpouring of anger from seniors who resented the cost of the bill to them, and the AARP gained even more respect as an effective watchdog group dedicated to preserving entitlements for seniors.

When such large-scale mobilization of the AARP becomes necessary, the organization gears up its grassroots efforts. It can alert its "telephone trees" and spark letter-writing campaigns almost immediately through its volunteer network, cyberspace, media alerts, and especially through mass mailings. The AARP consistently relies on its AARP/VOTE program, a sophisticated network of grassroots activists trained to influence legislators to support AARP positions by applying pressure through demonstrations and rallies, compiling voter guides, and sponsoring public forums.

Recruitment is another major AARP initiative. With the baby boom generation hovering around the age of 50, AARP recruiting efforts have been largely successful. Steady growth has also come about as a result of AARP marketing campaigns, designed to appeal to those who otherwise might be put off by the "retired persons" label. Television and print advertising highlight the organization's strength and scope, and discounts and benefits are available to AARP members for the single small fee of $8 annually (1997).

As a member organization, the AARP fosters solidarity among seniors and offers a range of services and programs. Most programs are staffed by volunteers who often are retired specialists in a variety of fields. By utilizing the abilities of these retired professionals, the organization taps its largest asset.

The AARP also promotes advances in gerontology, a fast-growing specialty that encompasses medicine, psychology, and sociology. Continuing the legacy begun by co-founder Leonard Davis, the organization funds the AARP Andrus Foundation's applied research in U.S. universities, its databases on aging, and its research into global trends in gerontology.

PROGRAMS

AARP benefit programs provide compelling reasons for members to join the organization. The financial programs, in particular, are quite attractive: a range of low-rate credit cards, special mutual funds programs, and an annuity program with generous terms and guaranteed returns. The Pharmacy Service has been very successful, offering reasonable prices on brand name and generic drugs as well as leaflets on approximately 500 prescription medications. Members can order from a mail-order catalog or go to one of the eight AARP pharmacies for counter service. The AARP also has an auto club and travel services, and a variety of insurance programs for home, auto, life, and health insurance.

AARP educational programs, among other things, help seniors manage their money. Aptly titled, "Money after 50" helps members with limited means achieve financial fitness through skill-building programs. The Tax-Aide program, which assists low-income members with tax preparation, is supported financially by the Internal Revenue Service to help defray volunteer costs.

Several AARP programs focus on health issues. Health Advocacy Services has a variety of programs promoting wellness and assisting members in navigating the health care system, as well as contributing to the public debate on health care issues. Women's health is a particular focus; Women's Initiative addresses older women's health, economic, and social concerns. Connections for Independent Living helps members remain in their own homes as long as possible, and the Widowed Persons Service provides the services of mental health, religious, and social-service volunteers for those who have recently lost a spouse.

The AARP Grandparent Information Center specializes in helping surrogate parents and caregivers confronted with raising their grandchildren when parents are absent due to death, illness, or family strife. Additionally the organization provides legal advice and family counseling for members confronted with this situation and other issues related to the changing nature of U.S. families.

BUDGET INFORMATION

In 1997 the AARP generated income of $529,890,000. Membership dues accounted for the largest portion of the organization's income, at $139,460,000. Another $106,960,000 comes to the AARP through its administration of AARP Health Care Options. Federal and other grant programs brought in $80,370,000 in 1997, but the vast majority of these funds funneled directly into community service programs. Royalties and sponsorships generated $77,830,000. Investment income totaled $66,360,000. Advertising in the AARP's publications brought in $57,160,000. Other sources of income totaled $1,750,000 for the year.

The AARP's expenses in 1997 totaled $438,690,000. The cost of producing the AARP's publications was the organization's largest expense, at $104,270,000. Federal and other grant programs totaled $79,830,000. The AARP's own program and field ser-

BUDGET:

1997 AARP Revenue

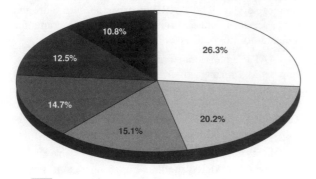

☐   26.3%: Membership dues

☐   20.2%: AARP Health Care Options

☐   15.1%: Federal and other grant programs

☐   14.7%: Royalties and sponsorships

☐   12.5%: Investment income

☐   10.8%: Advertising in the AARP's publications

1997 AARP Expenses

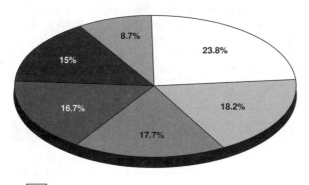

☐   23.8%: Publications

☐   18.2%: Federal and other grant programs

☐   17.7%: Program and field services

☐   16.7%: Member services and recruitment

☐   15%: Administrative costs

☐   8.7%: Legislative, legal, and research activities

vices cost $77,430,000. Member services and recruitment efforts cost the AARP $73,220,000. Administrative costs ran to $43,360,000 in 1997. Expenses for legislative, legal, and research activities were $38,140,000. The costs associated with AARP leadership and headquarters' activities in 1997 were $22,440,000.

HISTORY

The AARP was formed July 1, 1958, in Washington, D.C., by Dr. Ethel Percy Andrus, a woman of vision who pursued her goal of bettering lives for aging Americans. Andrus, the first female school principal in the state of California, was forced to retire at age 65; in response she formed the National Retired Teachers Association (NRTA) in 1947. NRTA, now a division of the AARP, grew rapidly as seniors saw the benefit in Dr. Andrus's social planning (her dream was retirement villages). They particularly clamored for insurance benefits at a time when insurance companies refused to insure people over 65 and Medicare had yet to be established.

Dr. Andrus was able to offer NRTA members group insurance through Leonard Davis, a young executive with Colonial Penn, a mail-order insurance company. This accomplishment was unprecedented, and by 1958 Davis and Dr. Andrus had co-founded AARP as a way to extend much needed insurance benefits to all seniors. The new organization grew and Colonial Penn was rewarded with enormous profits, despite criticism that the insurer was actually running the AARP. Because Davis controlled the membership lists, he could sell members not only insurance (health, life, homeowners, and auto) but also travel services, which he promoted in the pages of AARP's member magazine, *Modern Maturity*. After Dr. Andrus's death in 1967, Davis became the de facto head of the organization.

Davis's personal wealth was enormous and he was a generous philanthropist; he endowed a school of gerontology at the University of Southern California that was named for him and Dr. Andrus. The AARP attracted the attention of the publishers of *Consumer Reports,* which, in 1976, profiled the uncomfortably close relationship between Colonial Penn and the AARP. The furor caused by the article, which showed how Colonial Penn's enormous profits were substantially dependent on AARP members, signaled an end to Davis's involvement.

More trouble followed a 1978 *60 Minutes* segment titled "Super Salesman" that painted Davis as the real power in the organization. Davis "retired" from Colonial Penn in 1983 after avoiding a felony conviction, and the group health insurance that had been so profitable for Colonial Penn was awarded to Prudential Insurance. While the organization continues to venerate the memory of Dr. Andrus, Davis deliberately goes unmentioned in most AARP literature.

The 1980s saw the AARP regain respectability as it renewed its commitment to a socially responsible agenda. However, its very size and influence attracted, and continues to attract, unwelcome attention from its critics, notable among them the iconoclastic former Senator Alan Simpson (R-Wyom.), a long-time foe of the AARP who in 1995 senate hearings lambasted the organization for what he claimed were abuses of its tax-exempt status. One of the sharpest critics of AARP's "liberal" agenda even as the Reagan revolution years gave way to the Democratic Clinton administration, Simpson continued to try and rein in the AARP. Noting the organization's practice of mailing solicitations for AARP products ranging from mutual funds to prescription drugs at reduced postal rates, Simpson pointed to a 1992 $2.8 million settlement with the U.S. Postal Service over the improper use of reduced rates in a health insurance solicitation. He wryly characterized postal employees as burdened by the sheer bulk of AARP mailings, and suggested that AARP member dues funded the comfortable retirements of organization leaders.

An important part of the 1992 hearings concerned a $135 million settlement paid to the IRS to settle a dispute over what constituted taxable income from 1983 to 1993. The AARP claimed Simpson was trying to deflect attention from congressional efforts to cut Medicare and Social Security benefits, a move generally regarded as a Republican reform initiative. AARP executive director Horace Deets refuted Simpson's charges in a presentation before Congress and was able to somewhat deflect Simpson's attack, in large part because the AARP was joined in the spotlight by other mega-nonprofit organizations like the National Rifle Association with regard to questionable tax practices. Simpson was especially irate about the AARP's "liberal" leadership, who, he charged "imposes a policy agenda on an unwilling membership." His campaign affected the organization's operations: in 1996, after Congress began requiring nonprofits receiving federal funding to end lobbying efforts, the AARP transferred its federally funded programs to the AARP Foundation.

The AARP attained more positive prominence throughout the welfare reform debate of 1996, reminding the nation that despite the media image of affluent seniors willing to break the system to serve their own interests, many seniors live in poverty. The situation becomes particularly dire if those seniors are deprived of the safety net provided by Medicare and Medicaid, and AARP aggressively maintained its conservative attitude towards reforming such entitlement programs.

CURRENT POLITICAL ISSUES

As the voice that represents the views and interests of millions of U.S. seniors, the AARP has spoken out on many political issues, including Social Security, health

care, tax reform, and Medicare. In the 1990s the AARP addressed a growing concern over criminal telemarketing frauds with a plan of action that included educating consumers and increasing cooperation with law enforcement agencies.

Case Study: Operation Unload

By the mid-1990s over 140,000 telemarketing firms conducted business within the United States. While most of these firms conducted themselves lawfully, as many as 10 percent were suspected of fraudulent activity. The most popular scams included offering free prizes, illegal sweepstakes, fake investment plans, or exceptional prices on goods if the individual called agreed to send money or provide a bank account or credit card number. These "deals" resulted in victims paying for things they never received or having their credit cards used for unauthorized purchases. More than half the victims of telemarketing scams are people over 50, but in contradiction of the assumption that such victims are confused or isolated older people, senior victims are most often well educated, informed, and financially secure. AARP research found that many seniors have difficulty distinguishing legitimate sales pitches from fraudulent ones and are unable to end calls from high-pressure telemarketers.

The AARP joined with the FBI, the National Association of Attorneys General, and the U.S. Postal Service to fight phone fraud through a program named "Operation Unload." In this program, many approaches are used to educate consumers about telemarketing fraud, among them public service announcements, fact sheets, and other informational materials—even a video to help consumers practice their response to telemarketer calls. "Boiler rooms"—the phone centers from where fraudulent telemarketers conduct their scams—were set up in reverse: a staff of AARP volunteers and law enforcement personnel phoned consumers over the age of 50, warning them about telemarketing fraud and explaining what they could do to protect themselves. Many people were informed that their names appeared on "mooch" lists—lists of known victims who are considered likely to fall for other scams—that are circulated among fraudulent telemarketers. A manual was created and distributed nationwide to law enforcement, aging, and consumer protection agencies explaining the process for conducting reverse boiler rooms in other communities.

Through the AARP, informational materials were provided to local, state, and federal politicians to inform them about the growth and severity of telemarketing fraud. AARP staff gave testimony on the issue to members of Congress. Hot lines were established so consumers could call for information as well as report fraudulent activities and register complaints. These hot lines have been funded through private and government sources and the AARP has encouraged the federal government to expand funding for educational materials and the creation of a national hot line program.

Public Impact

While the AARP continues to advocate for a stronger, more widespread campaign against telemarketing fraud, Operation Unload has had positive results. Since 1997 over a dozen reverse boiler rooms have been organized, delivering warnings about telemarketing fraud to over 9,000 citizens, almost 60 percent of those who have requested more information. An AARP survey found that seniors were receiving fewer telemarketing calls than in the past, a fact that can be attributed to increased consumer awareness that telemarketing fraud is a crime and the more than 1,000 arrests involving fraudulent telemarketing that have resulted from consumer reporting. Nineteen states have introduced legislation to strengthen laws related to telemarketing fraud.

FUTURE DIRECTIONS

As it has in the past, the U.S. Social Security system continues to occupy much of the AARP's attention. With the baby boomer generation becoming eligible for Social Security benefits by the early part of the twenty-first century, and fewer employed Americans contributing to the fund, the stability of Social Security will be of primary concern to seniors. The AARP will continue to represent such interests in the ongoing debate regarding such things as the use of projected federal budget surpluses for Social Security and instituting individual investment options for current and future funds.

Long-term health care will also be a front-burner issue for the AARP. As people live longer, their need for health and personal care increases. Many older people, while unable to safely live alone, cannot pay someone to assist them. And many nursing homes provide substandard care, leaving many Americans with no good options as their health declines. As more and better options for long-term care are developed the AARP will be at the forefront, exploring and evaluating possible solutions such as Medicare coverage for long-term care, national standards of care, and tax credits for family caregivers.

The AARP will also continue to educate the public on the need to develop economic plans for retirement that do not rely solely or too heavily on Social Security benefits. Americans must utilize more forms of pre-retirement savings such as IRA's, contributing to employer retirement plans, and increasing their knowledge of investment options. The AARP has developed numerous educational materials and plans to increase its financial planning materials and services well into the twenty-first century.

GROUP RESOURCES

The AARP has a Web site at http://www.aarp.org that highlights its programs and keeps members up-to-date on relevant legislation, research, and services. From this site users can access the AgeLine Database, a repository of summaries of publications for and about older persons and aging.

The AARP maintains regional, state, and local offices that provide members with information on issues and services. These offices can be located through the Web site or by calling 1-800-424-3410. Information Centers that provide publications, meeting spaces, and phone stations can be located through the Web site or by calling 1-800-424-3410.

The AARP provides members with resources and benefits directly through its programs. AARP Pharmacy Service can be reached at 1-800-456-2277 for information on at-home service and pharmacological questions. Members can also obtain health care information and assistance with services by contacting AARP Health Care Options at 1-800-523-5800. And members can contact AARP Legal Services Network at 1-800-424-3410 for a list of attorneys who work with seniors and offer free half-hour consultations.

GROUP PUBLICATIONS

AARP members receive the bimonthly *Modern Maturity,* which includes news, member information, resources, and articles on lifestyle, finance, and health. A subscription to *Modern Maturity* requires joining the organization as an associate member and paying the membership fee. Subscription information can be obtained by calling 1-800-424-3410.

The *Bulletin* newsletter, published 11 times per year, is sent directly to members. It focuses on up-to-date information on issues that affect people over 50, including Social Security, pensions, workplace regulations, and tax reform. The *Bulletin* also provides information on current legislation related to member interests.

The AARP also distributes to the general public free "Information Publications" on such topics as "Living with Alzheimer's Disease," "How to Stay Employable," "A Woman's Guide to Pension Rights," and "Aging America: Trends and Projections." A complete list of these brochures, fact sheets, and reports can be obtained by calling 1-800-424-3410.

BIBLIOGRAPHY

Carlson, Elliot, and Leah Glasheen. "AARP Denies Simpson's Charges." *AARP Bulletin,* June 1995.

Cooper, Matthew. "White House Watch: Geezers for Grabs." *New Republic,* 6 May 1996.

Frawley, Colette. "Simpson Zeroes in on AARP and Its Tax Exemption." *Congressional Quarterly Weekly Report,* 17 June 1995.

Hess, John L. "A Warm and Fuzzy Gorilla." *Nation,* 26 August/2 September 1996.

Lieberman, Trudy. "Social Insecurity: The Campaign to Take the System Private." *Nation,* 1 January 1997.

Morris, Charles R. *The AARP: America's Most Powerful Lobby and the Clash of Generations.* New York, N.Y.: Times Books/Random House, 1996.

Peterson, Peter G. *Will America Grow up before It Grows Old? How the Coming Social Security Crisis Threatens You, Your Family, and Your Country.* New York, N.Y.: Random House, 1996.

Rosensteil, Thomas. "Buying off the Elderly: As the Revolution Gets Serious, Gingrich Muzzles the AARP." *Newsweek,* 2 October 1995.

"Testimony of Helen Boosalis: Regarding Telemarketing Scams." AARP Testimony before Congress, Washington, D.C., 5 February 1998.

Wittman, Marshall, and Charles P. Griffin. "Browbeating AARP." *Commentary,* 25 October 1995.

American Bankers Association (ABA)

ESTABLISHED: July 22, 1875
EMPLOYEES: 410
MEMBERS: 8,000
PAC: BankPAC

Contact Information:

ADDRESS: 1120 Connecticut Ave. NW
    Washington, DC 20036
PHONE: (202) 663-5000
TOLL FREE: (800) 338–0626
FAX: (202) 663-7533
URL: http://www.aba.com
PRESIDENT: R. Scott Jones
EXECUTIVE VICE PRESIDENT: Don G. Ogilvie

WHAT IS ITS MISSION?

The American Bankers Association's (ABA) purpose is stated in the declaration of its constitution: "To promote the general welfare and usefulness of banks and financial institutions and to secure uniformity of government; to obtain practical benefits to be derived from personal acquaintance and from the discussion of subjects of importance to the banking and commercial interests of the country, and especially in order to obtain the proper consideration of questions regarding the commercial and financial usages, customs and laws that affect the banking interests of the entire country, and for protection against crime." Primarily the ABA works to serve the interests of banks and educate the public about the banking industry.

HOW IS IT STRUCTURED?

The for-profit ABA is headquartered in Washington, D.C., and is led by a president who guides the organization in its day-to-day affairs. Policy and direction for the organization is provided by a board of directors and a general convention that assembles annually. Each member bank may designate a delegate to attend the convention. Between conventions an executive council elected by the delegates acts in their place. The ABA staff is divided into four divisions that represent the four types of functions that it fulfills: national bank, state bank, savings, and trust. Most of the commercial banks in the United States belong to the ABA; in return for dues based on a bank's capital and surplus the ABA provides its membership with its lobby and information dissemination powers.

The ABA has a number of different affiliates that cover a wide range of functions. It sponsors the American Institute of Banking, an adult higher education center that teaches bank employees about the latest innovations in the industry. The Corporation for American Banking is a subsidiary of the ABA established in 1983 that provides products and services to the banking industry that it would not have access to otherwise. Another subsidiary of the ABA is the ABA Securities Association, an organization that specializes in understanding and recommending policy on securities, proprietary mutual funds, and derivatives. The ABAecom seeks to explore the options of banking on-line and find ways of making it cost-effective for both banks and consumers. Finally, the ABA Education Fund is the arm of the organization that works to educate the public and its membership about the banking industry.

PRIMARY FUNCTIONS

The ABA's primary means of serving its membership is through legislative and judicial advocacy. The ABA lobbies Congress on such issues as loan procedures, tax laws, bankruptcy reform, and fraud prevention. In 1995, for example, ABA testified before Congress and regulatory agencies almost two dozen times and filed more than 24 official letters of comment. It works with such federal agencies as the Federal Deposit Insurance Corporation (FDIC) to ensure that federal banking regulations reflect the concerns of commercial banks. The ABA also files *amicus curiae* (friend of the court) briefs and even lawsuits in court where issues affecting the banking industry arise.

The ABA also provides its members with a wide range of services, the most important of them being information dissemination. The ABA keeps its membership up-to-date on the latest banking industry trends and advises them on best practices. It also monitors federal regulations and educates its members on how to satisfy new requirements. In addition the organization also offers a number of different training opportunities to employees of ABA member banks, covering leadership techniques, customer service, or marketing.

The organization also works to educate the public on issues that face its membership. For example, when member banks introduced ATM fees for customers who accessed their accounts at banks other than their own, the ABA put out several press releases explaining why the new fees were necessary.

PROGRAMS

The ABA maintains a number of different programs. Most revolve around serving its membership's customers while some are directed toward its membership directly.

The Personal Economics Program educates schoolchildren and the community on banking, economics, and personal finance. Member banks are given educational materials such as videotapes and brochures and encouraged to hold seminars using this information as a base upon which to build. The ABA estimates that the program has helped more than 14 million children learn more about banking since its inception in 1977.

The ABA's In Charge program seeks to educate young adults about both the benefits and the drawbacks of owning credit cards. Member banks can purchase resource kits that include video presentations, lesson plans, and sample budgeting exercises in order to help young adults deal responsibly with credit. While credit cards represent a safe and convenient way to spend money, the In Charge program also explains how to avoid debt and a bad credit rating through careful budgeting and use.

The ABA sponsors a coin program for its members; it works with the U.S. Mint to obtain commemorative coins for member banks to sell to customers. The ABA allows banks to purchase them in small enough quantities to offer for sale to customers who seek unique gifts. These include such rarities as uncirculated nickels, dimes, and quarters as well as coins never meant for circulation such as American Eagle dollar, 5 dollar, and 10 dollar coins.

BUDGET INFORMATION

The 1997 budget of the ABA was $62 million. Further information was not made available.

HISTORY

The American Bankers Association began in 1875 when some 350 banking representatives from 32 states met in Saratoga, New York, to coordinate and discuss the future of the U.S. banking industry. At the time, trade associations were all but unknown; of the 12,000 in existence today, no more than three predate the ABA. With no models to learn from, the ABA pioneered methods and mechanisms to serve its members. Its early initiatives centered on representing banking views to legislators and members of Congress. The repeal of Civil War taxes on bank transactions was one of its first directives. However affecting legislation was only one of the duties that the ABA took up. It was soon apparent that one of banking's greatest needs and opportunities lay in the upgrading of banking principles and practices. Education, training, and the dissemination of information were soon included in the ABA's general goals.

In its efforts to broaden its education focus, the ABA founded the Stonier Graduate School of Banking (SGSB) in 1935. The school offers advanced study for bankers on the officer level and is conducted by the ABA through Rutgers, The State University, New Brunswick, New Jersey. The SGSB offers a 3-year course with annual two-week resident sessions on the Rutgers campus. Its overall purpose is to give officers a broad education about contemporary economic and social forces and to improve banking services through the field of executive management.

The 1960s saw the ABA enact four educational programs. In 1961 its National Trust School, conducted by the Trust Division at Northwestern University, Evanston, Illinois, was established, which offers both a 3-year advanced course and a one-year basic course. The National Mortgage School held its first resident session on the campus of Ohio State University at Columbus in 1963, seeking to appeal to employees who have had limited experience in mortgage lending or who wish to update their knowledge of mortgage credit operations. The National Installment Credit School held its inaugural session in 1965, in the new Center for Continuing Education on the University of Chicago campus, and was designed to fill a gap in existing educational facilities available to bankers on the technical aspects of installment lending. Finally, The National Automation School was begun at Purdue University, Lafayette, Indiana, with an aim to help bankers better understand current and future applications of electronic data processing on more general banking procedures.

CURRENT POLITICAL ISSUES

The ABA's government-relations team is the largest in the banking industry and works to influence dozens of legislative proposals and scores of regulatory projects each year. The ABA's aggressive lobbying presence on Capitol Hill has grown into one of the strongest operations nationwide, raising and distributing over $2 million in the 1994 election cycle. Among the laws or amendments to law that the ABA is calling for are protection of banking from prosecution under current environmental laws, toughened collections efforts on student loans, changes in currencies to prevent counterfeiting, and bankruptcy reform.

Case Study: ABA Supports Bankruptcy Reform in late-1990s

Beginning in 1997 the American Bankers Association called on Congress to reform U.S. bankruptcy laws in order to reduce the growing number of bankruptcy filings. The ABA joined with other concerned groups such as the America's Community Bankers, the National Retail Federation, and Visa U.S.A., Inc., to form the National Consumer Bankruptcy Coalition (NCBC). The NCBC responded to what it perceived as inadequate congressional recommendations made by the National Bankruptcy Review Commission (NBRC) that, in some cases,

would have made it easier for individuals to be absolved of debt. The ABA and the coalition suggested that Congress enact new bankruptcy laws with "need-based" requirements that would require more people to repay their debts. The ABA argued that dramatic increases in personal bankruptcy filings during a period of general economic well-being showed that old bankruptcy laws were flawed. The organization also believed that a change in attitudes had lessened the social stigma associated with bankruptcy and that an increased number of people used the process as a repeated and sometimes planned form of dealing with debt.

The first debt reform legislative proposal was introduced by Rep. Bill McCollum (R-Fla.) and Rep. Rick Boucher (D-Va.) in 1997. They sought to create a system where a debtor receives only as much bankruptcy relief as he or she requires, and in some cases to eliminate a choice between filing for Chapter 7 or Chapter 13 bankruptcy. Chapter 7 proceedings absolve a debtor of all debts after liquidating non-exempt assets, while Chapter 13 gives individuals relief from creditors while they set up a court-approved payback plan. The proposal eliminated such a choice for debtors who can repay at least 20 percent of their debts.

The reform bills benefited from having the backing of the ABA and other powerful and wealthy organizations. There also was bipartisan agreement that the Depression-era bankruptcy laws needed updating. However the complex legislation involved many details beyond setting criteria for who can file for Chapter 7. Opposition to the bills came from consumer protection organizations who felt that the proposed legislation unfairly advantaged lenders over borrowers. A number of Democrats sought the requirement that credit card companies must tell the consumer how much it would cost in interest to make only the minimum payment on their debt. Protection of child support payments and conflict with state homestead laws created further partisan conflict. Senate and House proposals also took on radically different shapes, with Senate versions proving to be far more conservative. While House and Senate bills were passed in 1998, a compromise bill was not approved by both before the end of the session. Thus, the 1999 congressional session was faced with continued partisan battles, particularly in the Senate where Democrats had killed the compromise bill by threat of filibuster.

FUTURE DIRECTIONS

The ABA has been at legal odds with credit unions over the ways in which they draw their membership. Specifically the ABA took issue with how credit unions could draw membership from outside of the occupation around which a specific credit union was formed. For example, the relatives of a teacher could become members of his or her credit union, even if the teacher subsequently left the credit union. The ABA filed suit against the National Credit Union Association, the federal agency that regulates credit unions, and was victorious before the Supreme Court in February of 1998. However, in August of that year, President Bill Clinton signed a law, the Credit Union Membership Access Act, that allowed credit unions to continue to gain membership as they had previously. In light of the ABA's defeat, one of the ABA's central tasks for the future is to support a legislative reversal of this new law. In March of 1999, the ABA filed an injunction against the institution of the law that was rejected; however, the ABA will seek a summary judgement against this law by June of 1999.

updates. In addition the ABA offers a number of other publications, including *ABA Management Update of Personal Trust and Private Banking, AIB Leader Letter, Bank Compliance Magazine, Bank Insurance and Protection Bulletin, Bank Operations Bulletin, Bank Personnel News*, and *Bankers News*. Many of these publications are available to members only while some may be subscribed to by someone outside of the organization. For information on how to obtain the ABA's publication, write to the American Bankers Association, 1120 Connecticut Ave., Washington, DC 20036 or call (202) 663–5000.

GROUP RESOURCES

The ABA maintains a comprehensive site on the World Wide Web at http://www.aba.com, which is fully keyword searchable: for the non-member, the site offers background information on the ABA; members are provided with banking news and given access to association services, Bankers Mart (access to an on-line electronic mall), and more. In addition, the Center for Banking Information, available on-line at http://www.aba.com/aba/centerforbankinginformation/cbi.asp, offers banks a wealth of resources covering every aspect of the industry. The ABA also maintains American Financial Skylink, a satellite telecommunications network delivering news, information, and training directly into banks via weekly, two-hour telecasts and live, interactive telecasts throughout the year as warranted. For more information about the organization, write to the American Bankers Association, 1120 Connecticut Ave., Washington, DC 20036 or call (202) 663–5000.

GROUP PUBLICATIONS

The ABA's *ABA Banking Journal* is the standard information reference for all commercial banks, containing information on banking trends and legislative

BIBLIOGRAPHY

American Bankers Association. *Banking Terminology* Washington, DC: American Bankers Association, 1981.

"Banking Panel's Leach Pushes to Get Overhaul to Floor." *Congressional Quarterly Weekly Report*, 25 May 1996.

Barancik, Scott. "ABA Plans Suit Challenging NCUA Rule on Membership." *American Banker*, 8 January 1999.

Dean, Virginia. "Some Consumer Trends." *Vital Speeches*, 1 December 1995.

Kostnett, Jeff. "Bankrupt? No Problem. Credit is in the Mail." *Kiplinger's Personal Finance Magazine*, September 1993.

McClellan, Doug. "Desktop Counterfeiting." *Technology Review*, February/March 1995.

Rockwell, Llewellyn H. "Misery Loves Company." *Forbes*, 26 September 1994.

"The Rubber Meets the Road." *Economist*, 16 September 1995.

Stern, Linda. "Credit-Card Fees More than a Nuisance." *Modern Maturity*, February/March 1994.

"The Surge in Bank Charges." *U.S. News and World Report*, 21 August 1995.

Ullmann, Owen. "Banking on Reform." *Business Week*, 19 December 1994.

Zipser, Andy. "Scraping the Bottom." *Barron's*, 1 November 1995.

American Bar Association (ABA)

ESTABLISHED: August 21, 1878
EMPLOYEES: 750
MEMBERS: 392,000
PAC: None

Contact Information:

ADDRESS: 750 N. Lake Shore Dr.
    Chicago, IL 60611
PHONE: (312) 988-5000
FAX: (312) 988–6081
URL: http://www.abanet.org
PRESIDENT: Philip S. Anderson

WHAT IS ITS MISSION?

The mission of the American Bar Association (ABA), as stated on their Web site, is "to be the national representative of the legal profession, serving the public and the profession by promoting justice, professional excellence and respect for the law." The ABA works to improve the justice system and to guarantee that each citizen is able to find strong legal representation regardless of their economic or social status. The ABA also works on behalf of its members to increase public understanding and appreciation of the legal profession and to guarantee the highest standards of professional conduct and competence among lawyers.

HOW IS IT STRUCTURED?

The American Bar Association is a nonprofit, nonpartisan organization. According to its Web site, the ABA is the largest voluntary professional association in the world, representing more than 392,000 members. The organization is governed by the ABA house of delegates, which is responsible for making policy decisions on behalf of the ABA. When the house of delegates takes action on a specific issue, that action then becomes official ABA policy. The house of delegates consists of 525 members, including delegates from state and local bar associations, delegates-at-large, and present and former officers and board members, among others. The house of delegates meets twice each year, at the ABA annual and mid-year meetings.

The ABA board of governors has the authority to act for the ABA when the house of delegates is not in session. All actions taken by the board of governors, however, must be in strict accordance with previous actions of the house of delegates. The board of governors has 37 members and it usually meets five times each year. The board of governors oversees the general operation of the ABA and develops action plans for specific issues.

The president of the ABA is elected at the annual meeting of the house of delegates, and serves a one-year term. The president serves as the official spokesperson for the ABA, with the authority to communicate policy positions as determined by the house of delegates. The president also presides over meetings of the board of governors. He or she has the authority to appoint the chairs and members of standing and special committees of the association and the board.

The ABA is organized into over 2,000 different groups, which vary widely in size, purpose, and organizational structure. The ABA's 23 sections and five divisions combined have thousands of members and contain many sub-committees. They serve to bring together lawyers with similar interests, with sub-groupings such as the Business Law section and the Young Lawyers division. Divisions tend to have a more complicated organization, with separate conferences and their own members, officers, and committees. Many sections, divisions, and even committees have their own publications and programs.

Membership in the ABA is open to any lawyer who has been admitted to practice and is in good standing before the bar of any state or territory of the United States. Also eligible to join the ABA are professionals in law-related fields, such as non-lawyer judges, and federal court executives and law school educators, among others. Specific sections and committees may have additional restrictions on membership.

The headquarters for the ABA are located on the campus of the Northwestern University School of Law at the American Bar Center in Chicago. The ABA also has a Washington, D.C., office, which houses its Governmental Affairs Office (GAO). The GAO serves as the "eyes, ears and voice" of the ABA in the U.S. capitol by providing the association's views on a broad range of political issues to various government offices.

PRIMARY FUNCTIONS

The ABA directs its vast resources and energies into two major areas: upholding the professional image, conduct, and prestige of lawyers and other members of the legal profession; and working on behalf of the justice system itself, to ensure that laws are fairly enacted and enforced and that all citizens' have access to legal representation in the court system.

FAST FACTS

The membership of the ABA represents half of all lawyers in the United States.

(Source: American Bar Association, 1998.)

The ABA develops and enforces standards for the ethical behavior of lawyers. These standards focus mainly on professional regulation, professionalism, and client protection mechanisms. The ABA also works to encourage and maintain communication among the various bar organizations and the agencies responsible for supervising and regulating the professional conduct of lawyers and judges. The association does this by organizing conferences, conducting and publishing legal research and ethics opinions, and developing educational programming and curriculum designed to educate the general public about various aspects of the law and ethical legal behavior.

The ABA publishes several legal journals and sponsors continuing legal education seminars through its various sections, divisions, and forums. These seminars ensure that members of the legal profession are aware of the latest legislation and research regarding their own legal specialty. The ABA also evaluates those members of the legal profession nominated to high levels of public office, often providing its professional opinion to members of House and Senate committees. For example the ABA provides the Senate Judiciary Committee with an evaluation and rating for every lawyer who is nominated to the Supreme Court. Although the ABA's recommendation about a nominee's professional conduct and background is not binding, it does carry some weight in the consideration of the nominee's candidacy.

In addition to policing itself and the members of its profession, the ABA also conducts research and presents opinions regarding nearly every piece of legislation that affects the legal profession or the justice system in general. During the 104th Congress alone, the association's GAO testified at 50 congressional hearings and sent more than 150 letters to congressional members, congressional committees, and officers of the executive branch outlining the ABA's position on countless pieces of legislation. The ABA also operates a State Legislative Clearinghouse, which monitors the activities of state legislatures as well.

U.S. Supreme Court Justice Stephen Breyer (right) discusses First Amendment concepts with Boston high school students as part of Law Day 1996. Law Day is a program sponsored by the American Bar Association that promotes legal education and public service. (Photograph by Susan Walsh, AP/Wide World Photo)

Besides monitoring and providing its opinions on important legislation, the ABA also takes legal action to protect what it considers important constitutional rights. The ABA only becomes involved in those legal cases whose outcomes are "a matter of compelling public interest . . . or a case of special significance to lawyers and the legal profession" (ABA Web page).

Finally the ABA is committed to providing legal aid to all citizens, regardless of their ability to pay for legal services. The ABA works diligently to encourage its members to take on pro bono cases—for which lawyers will not be paid—in areas of civil rights and public rights law, the representation of charitable organizations, and the administration of justice. The ABA has established public service commissions in several areas, and it established a division whose sole purpose is to provide support services to those ABA committees providing free legal care to the public.

PROGRAMS

The American Bar Association sponsors, creates, and manages hundreds of programs to achieve its primary goals. The ABA works to ensure that all Americans, regardless of income, have access to legal repre-

sentation in both criminal and civil cases through a variety of channels. The American Bar Association Center for Pro Bono has developed a directory of local pro bono programs. Pro bono programs match clients with lawyers who will work on their cases for free. Many lawyers who are otherwise employed in the legal profession volunteer their legal services in this way. Although the ABA does not operate these programs directly, it does provide citizens with valuable guidance in locating them. This is especially important, since communities can be served by several legal services programs, and discovering which one is most appropriate for a certain case can be difficult.

The ABA also works to support agencies which secure legal representation for the poor. For example, the Legal Services Corporation, a government-run agency which provides grants to non-profit organizations who, in turn, provide legal services to low-income Americans, has seen its federal funding cut by 33 percent since 1995. By helping to fund such organizations, the ABA helps achieve its goal of ensuring that all citizens have access to legal representation. The ABA also runs a lawyer referral and information service, and it has established standing committees to oversee legal aid for military personnel and indigent defendants, among others.

In an effort to safeguard the independence of the legal profession and encourage the professional excellence of all lawyers, the ABA established the Center for Professional Responsibility. The Center works on behalf of ABA members to promote "discussion and resolution of pressing issues of professional responsibility" (ABA Web page). It also works to create communication among the various bar associations and establish uniform and enforceable standards of professional conduct.

BUDGET INFORMATION

Not made available.

HISTORY

The American Bar Association was formed on August 21, 1878, in Saratoga Springs, New York. It was established by 100 lawyers from 21 states, and its purpose was to provide a forum for discussing the increasingly complex legal profession. Until that time, there was no national code of ethics for lawyers. Individuals studied under a system of apprenticeship, in which people who wished to join the profession simply learned as much as they could from a practicing lawyer. When the ABA formed, its stated purpose was to "advance the science of jurisprudence . . . and promote the administration of justice . . . throughout the country" (ABA Web page).

As the legal profession grew in numbers and prestige, so did the ABA. Between 1878 and the early 1920s, membership in the ABA grew substantially. During this time members also began to articulate their goals for ensuring that all Americans had equal access to legal representation. In 1920 the ABA established the Special Committee on Legal Aid, whose purpose was to help guarantee that any person seeking legal aid or advice could obtain it regardless of their ability to pay for legal services. The organization has since adopted the guarantee of representation as one of its primary goals, and has worked diligently to promote pro bono legal services among its members.

As the legal profession continued to grow and change, the ABA began to articulate national standards of ethical conduct for lawyers. The organization sought to be more than just a network of lawyers—it hoped to serve as a kind of conscience for the profession, holding lawyers to the highest levels of conduct and reminding them of their public and professional responsibilities.

The ABA also began to act as a kind of information clearinghouse, providing a means for lawyers to update their skills and understanding of changing and developing laws. As the organization grew, it gained a greater level of political influence—which it has used to protect the interests of lawyers. In 1957 the ABA established the Governmental Affairs Office in Washington, D.C. The

purpose of the GAO is to monitor all federal legislation which would impact the stated goals and concerns of the ABA. The GAO reports on the status of such legislation, sending information to state and local bar associations when necessary. The GAO also tracks important legislation at the state level.

Although it no longer resembles the small forum for discussing legal issues that formed in the nineteenth century, the ABA has remained committed to its initial goals of providing national standards of ethical conduct and guaranteeing legal representation for all Americans. In 1997 membership in the ABA reached more than 392,000 members. Its concerns, nevertheless, have remained remarkably consistent, despite the growing number and diversity of its membership.

CURRENT POLITICAL ISSUES

As an advocate for lawyers and legal privileges, the ABA sometimes finds itself in the midst of very public battles in which the outcome will have profound effects on basic constitutional rights. The ABA's 1998 fight to protect the attorney-client privilege is a case in point.

Case Study: Attorney-Client Privilege

In 1994 Kenneth Starr was appointed independent counsel to investigate charges against President and Mrs. Clinton concerning a development project named Whitewater. The charges were based on loans and investments made in 1978 while Clinton was still governor of Arkansas. Although Starr's original investigation was very narrow, it eventually expanded to include several other issues, including the president's firing of the White House travel office staff in 1993. As part of his investigation into the travel office firings, Starr subpoenaed notes taken during a meeting between then White House Deputy Counsel Vincent Foster and his lawyer, James Hamilton. That meeting took place in 1993, and nine days later Vincent Foster committed suicide.

Information that is exchanged between lawyers and their clients is protected by something called the attorney-client privilege. This privilege has become almost sacred in the legal profession. It has been effectively defended and protected for centuries. Traditionally the courts have always held that information exchanged between a lawyer and client was absolutely private, which meant that a lawyer could never be asked to testify about their clients. The ABA feels that this privilege is essential to a meaningful lawyer-client relationship, since a client who cannot trust their lawyer may not disclose information vital to a fair legal defense. It helps ensure that clients will feel safe while being absolutely honest with their lawyers, no matter how embarrassing, or even incriminating, their situation may be. Without this privilege, lawyers argue, clients will not be honest with their counsel, out of fear that the information they provide may someday be used against them.

In the case of Vincent Foster, however, Prosecutor Starr argued that the attorney-client privilege ended when Foster died and that the notes taken during the meeting with his attorney should be turned over to Starr to aid in his investigation. In June of 1998, the U.S. District Court of Appeals ruled in Starr's favor. In response to this ruling, the American Bar Association filed a brief urging the Supreme Court to overturn the decision. In its brief the ABA said there were "hundreds of thousands, if not millions of Americans" making plans in case they should die unexpectedly or otherwise. The ABA asserted, "Many of these people undoubtedly have secrets and confidences that, if revealed, would be at the least highly embarrassing to themselves or their friends and loved ones." Disclosing this information after death could have far-reaching negative effects on survivors (*New York Times*, "Lawyer-Client Privilege Faces a Critical Test." June 7, 1998).

In June of 1998, the Supreme Court overturned the decision of the U.S. Court of Appeals, siding with the American Bar Association. In its decision the Supreme Court said, "many clients might be discouraged from seeking legal advice, given their interest in posthumously (after-death) preserving their reputations and protecting their survivors from the intrusion of investigators" (*New York Times*, "Justices Deal Starr a Defeat." June 26, 1998.)

FUTURE DIRECTIONS

As the legal profession continues to grow, the ABA plans to take on more responsibilities in its efforts to maintain and enforce ethical standards of conduct within the legal profession, and in working to ensure that all people are granted access to adequate legal representation in the courts. The role of the Governmental Affairs Office (GAO) will continue to expand, focusing on bills in state legislatures as well as those in Congress. As technology grows more complicated and sophisticated, so will the laws governing its use, providing lawyers with a new legal frontier. The ABA has already established a special forum on Communications Law to begin providing resources to members working within this field.

GROUP RESOURCES

The ABA maintains a Web page at http://www.abanet.org which provides a great deal of information on specific ABA committees, forums, organizations, and boards. The ABA can also be contacted at 750 N. Lake Shore Dr., Chicago, IL 60611. The ABA phone number is (312) 988-5000. The Lawyer Referral Services program, which provides free legal referrals and information services can also be accessed at the ABA Web site. The ABA also manages Legal Help for the Poor and the Center for Pro Bono Programs at its Web site. Information about Pro Bono Programs in different states can be obtained through the links provided by the site. Also the current Directory of Pro Bono Programs can be requested by writing to the Chicago address listed above.

The ABA also provides a great deal of information about the Center for Professional Responsibility, including lawyer's manuals, lawyer assistance programs, client protection and publications. You can contact the center via the ABA Web site or write them at the Center for Professional Responsibility, American Bar Association, 541 N. Fairbanks Ct., Chicago, IL 60611. The center can be reached by telephone at (312) 988-5304 or by E-mail at: ctrprofresp@abanet.org.

GROUP PUBLICATIONS

The ABA calls itself one of the largest publishers in the United States and the largest legal publisher in the world (ABA Web page). It publishes over 60 books a year and over 50 periodicals for ABA sections, divisions, and commissions. Publications include works intended primarily for legal professionals, such as *A Guide to Federal Agency Rulemaking*. Others are intended for a wider audience, including *Finding the Right Lawyer*, *The American Bar Association Family Legal Guide*, and booklets such as *Mediation: A Consumer's Guide*, and *Law and the Courts*. Information about these publications can be found at the ABA Publishing home page at http://www.abanet.org/abapubs/home.html. Publications can be ordered at this Web site, over the phone at 1-800-285-2221, or by mail at ABA Publication Orders, PO Box 10892, Chicago, IL 60610-0892.

BIBLIOGRAPHY

Caytas, Ivo G. *Transnational Legal Practice: Conflicts in Professional Responsibility*. New York: Commonwealth Press, 1992.

Coquillette, Daniel R. *Lawyers and Fundamental Moral Responsibility*. Cincinnati, OH: Anderson Publishing Company, 1995.

"A Crucial Privlege Case." *New York Times (Late New York Edition)*, 9 June 1998.

Garth, Bryant G. *Neighborhood Law Firms for the Poor: A Comparative Study of Recent Developments in Legal Aid and in the Legal Profession*. Rockville, Md.: Sijthoff & Noordhoff, 1980.

Greenhouse, Linda. "Lawyer-Client Privilege Faces a Critical Test." *New York Times*, 7 June 1998.

Labaton, Stephen. "Justices Deal Starr a Defeat." *New York Times*, 26 June 1998.

Lewin, Tamar. "Debate Over Marriage Education for High-School Students." *New York Times*, 14 October 1998.

Lewis, Neil A. "How to Build a Better Independent Counsel." *New York Times*, 17 May 1998.

Luizzi, Vincent. *A Case for Legal Ethics: Legal Ethics as a Source for Universal Ethics*. Albany, N.Y.: State University of New York Press, 1993.

McCue, Howard M. III. "Attorney-Client Privilege: Upheld After the Death of the Client?" *Trust & Estates*, September 1998.

Sinopoli, Richard C. *The Foundations of American Citizenship: Liberalism, the Constitution and Civic Virtue*. New York: Oxford University Press, 1992.

Sunderland, Edson R. *History of the American Bar Association and Its Work*. New York, N.Y.: Random House, 1953.

American Civil Liberties Union (ACLU)

ESTABLISHED: 1920
EMPLOYEES: 150
MEMBERS: 300,000
PAC: None

Contact Information:
ADDRESS: 125 Broad St., 18th Fl.
New York, NY 10004
PHONE: (212) 549-2500
E-MAIL: aclu@aclu.org
URL: http://www.aclu.org
EXECUTIVE DIRECTOR: Ira Glasser
PRESIDENT: Nadine Strossen

WHAT IS ITS MISSION?

The primary mandate of the American Civil Liberties Union (ACLU) is to defend and preserve the Bill of Rights, the amendments to the U.S. Constitution that guarantee individual civil rights to each of the country's citizens. The ACLU, a public interest law firm, works in "courts, legislatures, and communities to defend and preserve the individual rights and liberties guaranteed to all people in this country by the Constitution and laws of the United States." In accordance with that stated purpose, the ACLU expends a significant amount of its effort in the nation's courtrooms defending lawsuits it files against governments, corporations, and individuals suspected of violating the civil rights of U.S. citizens.

HOW IS IT STRUCTURED?

The ACLU's national office in New York City is managed by an eight-member staff. The individual ultimately responsible for the day-to-day operations of the ACLU is the executive director. As top staff member, the executive director reports directly to an 84-member board of directors.

While a national organization, the ACLU maintains a local presence in many communities across the United States. The ACLU has 50 state-based affiliates and 379 local chapters with these offices primarily staffed by volunteers. The organization's state and local chapters operate independently of the national organization. Each of the 50 state affiliates has a representative on the ACLU's board of directors.

A couple holds their adopted 2-year-old son at an ACLU press conference following a 1997 New Jersey court landmark ruling allowing joint adoption of foster care children by gay or unmarried couples. (Photograph by Rich Schultz, AP/Wide World Photos)

The ACLU has 300,000 members nationwide. ACLU members are simply supporters who pay annual dues. Members do not generally get involved with the day-to-day operations of the organization. More active, volunteer members, make up a significant portion of ACLU's work force. Approximately 2,000 volunteer attorneys collaborate with 60 paid staff attorneys to handle an average of 6,000 ACLU cases annually.

Since 1968 the ACLU has administered some of its activities through the ACLU Foundation. Like the ACLU, the foundation litigates, but it does not lobby legislatures. One major initiative created by the ACLU and

the ACLU Foundation in tandem has been a push for increased public education programs. The ACLU and the ACLU Foundation use direct mail to deliver information about civil rights legislation, the institution's activities, and fund raising efforts.

PRIMARY FUNCTIONS

First and foremost, the ACLU is a law firm dedicated to the defense of civil rights. Therefore the organization does most of its work in U.S. courtrooms, representing a wide range of clients on a variety of issues. In fact, the ACLU has argued before the U.S. Supreme Court more than any other organization—apart from the government itself—in its efforts to change local, state, or federal laws or statutes that violate civil liberties. For example, in 1996 the ACLU sued a Mississippi public school system that required students to participate in religious instruction. The ACLU will also defend individual plaintiffs it believes are being prosecuted unfairly by the justice system.

In addition to its work in courts across the United States, the ACLU maintains a presence in Washington, D.C., lobbying Congress to prevent potential civil rights abuses. A prime example of ACLU lobbying efforts is its continued attempt to defeat U.S. flag amendments. The ACLU has historically defended individuals who have used the flag in making political statements, such as citizens who set fire to the stars and stripes in symbolic protest against the government and its policies. There have been movements across the country to add an amendment to the Constitution that would make such acts illegal. The ACLU has consistently fought such movements, maintaining that a flag desecration amendment would severely and unfairly limit free speech.

The ACLU also works to educate the public about issues with the potential to infringe on constitutionally guaranteed rights. It disseminates information to its members and the public at large about how members of Congress, the Supreme Court, and local lawmakers and courts are responding to the civil liberties issues that are presented to them. It also alerts its members when mobilizing supporters to contact legislators who could make a difference.

PROGRAMS

Most of the ACLU's programs have to do with educating the public on various civil rights issues. Others revolve around various legal challenges. Two ACLU programs in particular focus on the rapid dissemination of information. With its Action Alert program, the organization aims to quickly spread word to the public about important civil liberties issues being introduced before Congress. The ACLU sends E-mail on these issues and encourages its members to write to their legislators. The Execution Alert program centers around the ACLU's continuing opposition to the death penalty: its belief that no individual should be put to death by the state, no matter what manner of crime has been committed. The organization keeps track of prisoners on death row and if an execution appears imminent, it sends out E-mail to alert those interested.

The Women's Rights Project is a special division within the ACLU that, since the early 1970s, has fought to ensure equal rights for women. The project has challenged such things as lack of professional advancement for women, and discrimination in the workplace on the basis of pregnancy.

BUDGET INFORMATION

The ACLU and the ACLU Foundation receive no money from the federal government. Rather, the organizations get their operating capital from membership dues, grants, and contributions from private sources. These sources are indeed substantial: the combined 1995 operating budget of both the ACLU and its foundation was approximately $26 million. That figure was for the national organization only, and excluded the operating budget of state affiliates. The 1995 budget breakdown included expenses of $7 million on legal services, $4 million on education, and $5 million on fundraising. The ACLU sent state affiliates almost $6 million in support and spent $1 million on management. It also ran a cash surplus of approximately $3 million.

HISTORY

The ACLU was founded in 1920, the same year the Nineteenth Amendment granting women the right to vote was added to the Constitution. By 1920 the U.S. Supreme Court had yet to uphold any free speech claims that fell under the First Amendment, but that would soon change. Within five years controversial defense attorney Clarence Darrow had joined with the ACLU to defend a Tennessee public school teacher named John Scopes in what would become known as the "Monkey Trial." Scopes had been indicted and prosecuted for teaching the theory of evolution in his class, which was illegal in the state of Tennessee. In a case that would spark national controversy revolving around freedom of religion issues and which was later immortalized in the play *Inherit the Wind*, Darrow defended Scopes's right to teach Darwinian theories despite their irreconcilability with the region's prevailing Christian beliefs.

In 1933 the ACLU helped win the battle over Irish novelist James Joyce's *Ulysses*, a work of fiction considered by many at the time to be pornographic. Published in Europe, the novel was not even allowed to enter the United States until Judge John Woolsey granted general U.S. distribution of *Ulysses* in a historic Supreme Court decision.

Infringements on the Bill of Rights continued into the 1940s as West Coast ACLU affiliates fought the imprisonment of Japanese Americans during World War II (1939–45). Claiming national security interests, the U.S. government relocated 110,000 Japanese Americans into internment camps, causing many of these citizens to lose everything they owned and spend the duration of the war in these camps.

In the 1950s the ACLU was a participant in the legal dispute over desegregation that culminated in the historic U.S. Supreme Court ruling *Brown v. Board of Education*. In the early years of the decade, public school systems like other areas of society were still racially segregated; blacks and whites were not allowed to attend the same schools. In its dedication to help end segregation, ACLU volunteers acted as part of the legal team successfully fighting for desegregation in public schools.

In one of the most controversial cases ever decided by the U.S. Supreme Court, the ACLU helped bring about the ruling in 1973's *Roe v. Wade* that decriminalized abortion. The ACLU was active in the pro-choice movement before *Roe v. Wade* and has been involved in the subsequent debate over abortion legislation. In contrast to advancing a strongly liberal agenda with *Roe v. Wade,* in late 1977 the ACLU supported, defended, and ultimately won the right of members of the U.S. Nazi Party to march in Skokie, Illinois, in support of their conservative beliefs. At the time, 1,000 victims of the Nazi Holocaust lived in Skokie, a suburb of Chicago. The march was considered inflammatory, and the ACLU was resoundingly criticized for its work on behalf of the Nazis.

In 1981, 56 years after the Scopes Monkey Trial, the ACLU fought another evolution versus creationism battle when it contested an Arkansas statute that endorsed the biblical story of creation as a scientific and acceptable alternative to the theory of evolution. The statute called for creationism to be taught in schools. The ACLU sued and the statute was found to be unconstitutional by U.S. District Judge William Overton.

For 51 years the ACLU declined to either endorse or oppose candidates to the U.S. Supreme Court. However, the organization reversed this intentional policy of neutrality in 1987 when it successfully opposed the nomination of Robert Bork, a controversial conservative judge nominated by President Ronald Reagan. A year later Vice President George Bush attempted to fuel his campaign for president by attacking his opponent, former Massachusetts Governor Michael Dukakis, as a "card-carrying member" of the "liberal" ACLU. Bush won the race, but the ACLU's popularity rose and its membership increased by 50,000. The late 1980s also saw the ACLU helping defend Oliver North after his conviction by a federal court of being involved in the Iran-Contra arms-for-hostages scandal. The ACLU successfully defended North by asserting his Fifth Amendment right against self-incrimination. Said North of the organization: "The ACLU has taken some very tough stands on some very tough issues. I'm one of those examples."

The ACLU has not always met with success. In 1990 the organization represented the family of a Missouri woman who had been in a coma, unable to breathe or eat on her own, for more than seven years. The family, believing there to be no hope of recovery, wanted to disconnect the life support system keeping the woman "alive." However, the State of Missouri denied the right of the family to let her die, and their decision was upheld by the U.S. Supreme Court.

The ACLU was involved in other sensational cases in the 1990s. In 1995 it filed a brief on behalf of Mumia Abu-Jamal a death row inmate awaiting his sentence for killing a Philadelphia police officer. Abu-Jamal claimed he was innocent and his case received widespread national attention. In jail he authored *Live from Death Row,* a book that was critical of the Pennsylvania penal system. The ACLU brief supported Abu-Jamal in his lawsuit against members of the penal system Abu-Jamal felt were punishing him. The ACLU would file a similar brief on behalf of Paula Jones in her suit against President Bill Clinton for sexual harassment while he was governor of Arkansas. In 1997 the Supreme Court struck down the 1996 Communications Decency Act (CDA) in *ACLU v. Reno*. The Act prohibited "indecent" speech on the internet. It was a major victory for the ACLU, which saw the CDA as censorship.

CURRENT POLITICAL ISSUES

While the ACLU claims to be nonpartisan, when it takes a particular position it may be involuntarily affiliating itself with a political party. For instance, the ACLU's position on abortion is similar to that of the Democratic Party. The union has also been viewed as "liberal," also an earmark of the Democratic Party. During the presidential campaign of 1988, George Bush attacked the ACLU as a Democratic Party organization with a liberal agenda.

Contributing to the organization's liberal cachet is the fact that the ACLU has been a vocal opponent of the "Religious Right." "Religious Right" is a term used to describe a segment of the Republican Party dedicated to a conservative social agenda that includes anti-gay and anti-abortion legislation. The ACLU not only disagrees with the Religious Right's position on social issues; it opposes the increasing power of the group in a more fundamental way. To the ACLU, politics and religion are poor partners that endanger the constitutionally mandated separation of church and state. Since the ACLU opposes the more conservative elements within the Republican Party, it becomes, in a way an opponent of the party itself.

The ACLU involves itself in numerous issues having to do with personal freedoms as related in the Bill of Rights. These include the right to the freedoms of speech and expression. In the 1990s the ACLU continued to uphold individual rights, often tackling issues that expanded interpretation and always caused controversy. One of the issues the organization would focus on in the late 1990s is the legalization of marijuana for certain purposes.

Case Study: Medical Use of Marijuana

In the 1990s there was a legislative movement in several states to legalize the use of marijuana in medical treatment. Many physicians believe marijuana eases the pressure on the eyes created by the degenerative eye disease glaucoma. Others believe marijuana reduces arthritis-related joint pain. Recently, patients with AIDS claim marijuana is effective in relieving nausea. Marijuana also increases appetite; AIDS patients often lose their appetites because of drug treatment. They begin to suffer from "wasting disease," losing muscle as well as body fat. Proponents assert marijuana builds hunger and helps these patients gain weight. However, the federal government insisted and continues to insist marijuana is a dangerous drug and should not be legalized, even for medical use.

In 1996 initiatives calling for the legalization of marijuana for medical use appeared in California and Arizona. These propositions, numbered 215 in California and 200 in Arizona, were passed by a majority of voters. Billionaire activist George Soros spent $1 million on the California initiative. The Arizona statute, which also allowed heroin in medical use, was approved by a two-to-one margin by voters. The Arizona initiative was bolstered by an endorsement of former conservative Senator Barry Goldwater (R-Ariz.).

In January of 1997, two months after the referenda were approved, the Clinton administration announced its opposition to Propositions 215 and 200. The director of the Office of National Drug Control Policy, Barry McCaffrey, warned doctors not to break the federal law. McCaffrey and U.S. Attorney General Janet Reno said any doctors who attempted to prescribe marijuana for medical use would be prosecuted. Furthermore, the administration threatened to take Medicaid and Medicare funds away from any doctor who recommended marijuana.

Days after it was made public that the government intended to prosecute doctors, the ACLU filed a lawsuit on behalf of doctors, patients, and medical associations. The lawsuit blocked federal government prosecutors from action. For the ACLU, the issue of medical marijuana was more complicated than a simple question of legality; it was a First Amendment and civil liberties issue. ACLU counsel Ann Brick said, "This case is not about whether the government should legalize the medical use of marijuana; it is about whether the government may prevent doctors from providing a patient with an honest medical opinion recommending marijuana." U.S. District Court Judge Fern Smith agreed with the ACLU, issuing a temporary restraining order prohibiting the government from acting on its threat to prosecute. In her ruling Judge Smith said, "The First Amendment allows physicians to discuss and advocate medical marijuana, even though use of marijuana is illegal."

In 1998 the federal government lost ground on its opposition to medical marijuana. Four more states—Washington, Alaska, Oregon, and Nevada—ratified referenda similar to the California and Arizona initiatives. Rep. Barney Frank (D-Mass.) introduced a bill into Congress that called for the legalization of marijuana for medicinal purposes. Further judicial rulings regarding the legalization of marijuana was expected to occur in late 1999.

FUTURE DIRECTIONS

The ACLU has dubbed free speech via the internet and other related issues "cyber-liberties." The internet is a new medium and there are few precedents for free speech judgments as there are in television, radio, and newspapers. Censorship and internet issues will receive significant attention in years to come, precisely because rules for internet free speech have not been written. In 1998 the ACLU helped defeat CDA-type legislation in Georgia and New York. The ACLU expects the proportion of cases involving cyber-liberties to increase at a tremendous rate, and has been fighting a public relations campaign against a widely supported bill introduced in the House of Representatives that calls for actions similar to the CDA. The ACLU calls the legislation "Son of CDA." The ACLU vowed to pursue this issue with diligence, believing free speech on the internet to be of the utmost importance.

GROUP RESOURCES

The ACLU maintains a Web site that reviews its most recent activities and also contains biographies of ACLU executives. In addition it has complete transcriptions of particular ACLU court actions. The Web site is accessible at http://www.aclu.org. Individuals interested in contacting the ACLU may call the organization at (212) 549-2500 or write the American Civil Liberties Union, 125 Broad St., 18th Fl., New York, NY 10004.

GROUP PUBLICATIONS

The ACLU composes briefing papers that are available through the ACLU's Office of Public Education. These briefing papers cover a variety of subjects and may include a history of the ACLU or a summary of the organization's position on a particular issue. The organization's Public Education office also sends out direct mail pieces to donors and potential donors.

BIBLIOGRAPHY

Chowder, Ken. "The ACLU Defends Everybody." *Smithsonian*, January 1998.

Conn, Joseph L. "Armed and Dangerous?" *Church and State*, March 1997.

Donohue, William A. *Twilight of Liberty: The Legacy of the ACLU*. New Brunswick, N.J.: Transaction Publishers, 1994.

Elvin, John. "Can a Political Odd Couple Reconcile Its Differences?" *Insight on the News*, 28 July 1997.

Kirchner, Jake. "When It Comes to the Web, the ACLU Is Clueless." *PC Magazine*, 7 October 1997.

Miller, Greg. "Web Decency Hearing May Alter Landscape." *Los Angeles Times,* 21 January 1999.

Reno, Janet. *Reno v. American Civil Liberties Union*. Bethesda, Md.: University Publications of America, 1998.

Walker, Samuel. *In Defense of American Liberties: A History of the ACLU*. New York: Oxford University Press, 1990.

"When Liberty Is Not So Sweet: Elections and Rights." *Economist*, 4 April 1998.

American Conservative Union (ACU)

ESTABLISHED: December 21, 1964
EMPLOYEES: 5
MEMBERS: 500,000 (1997)
PAC: ACU-PAC

Contact Information:

ADDRESS: 1007 Cameron St.
   Alexandria, VA 22314
PHONE: (703) 836-8602
TOLL FREE: (800) 228-7345
FAX: (703) 836-8608
E-MAIL: acu@conservative.org
URL: http://www.conservative.org
CHAIRMAN: David A. Keene

WHAT IS ITS MISSION?

According to the organization's Statement of Principles drafted in 1964, the American Conservative Union (ACU) supports "capitalism, belief in the doctrine of original intent of the framers of the Constitution, confidence in traditional moral values, and commitment to a strong national defense. . . . ACU is created to realize these ends through the cooperation in responsible political action of all Americans who cherish the principles upon which the Republic was founded."

The ACU describes itself as the nation's oldest grassroots conservative lobbying and public education organization; its purpose is to effectively communicate and advance the goals, issues, and principles of conservatism through a single umbrella organization. Historically, conservatism as represented by the ACU has translated itself into advocacy of lower taxes and a decrease in federal spending, as well as a continuous opposition to extensive federal regulation of the economy, among many other issues.

HOW IS IT STRUCTURED?

The ACU is governed by a 33-member board of directors. From this group, five individuals are elected to serve as an executive committee, comprising a chairman, first and second vice chairmen, a secretary, and a treasurer. All elected officers serve two-year terms. New board members are drawn from among the ranks of conservative activists; they are nominated and voted on by the sitting board. No more than two members of each

house of Congress may serve on the board at any given time, in 1998, for example, senators Jesse Helms (R-N.C.) and Serphin Maltese (R-N.Y.), and representatives Duncan Hunter (R-Calif.) and Louis Jenkins (R-La.) were members.

Similarly, while the first ACU chairman was Representative John Ashbrook of Ohio, the bylaws have since been altered to state that no sitting member of Congress may serve in the capacity of chairman. The board, which meets quarterly, is responsible for the overall direction of the organization and for developing ACU positions on public policy issues. Most importantly, it decides which issues the organization will focus its lobbying efforts on, such efforts being the goal of all the ACU's grassroots activity.

The ACU had 42 state affiliates (state conservative unions) in the 1970s. However, with the advent of fax communications, direct mail, and the Internet, it has become possible for the organization's central headquarters to communicate directly with members. Consequently, the state network has become less active, and the number of state affiliates decreased to half by the late 1990s. State affiliates currently in operation include Alaska, Arizona, Colorado, Florida, Illinois, Indiana, Michigan, New York, Ohio, and Tennessee.

With this smaller collection of state groups to service, headquarters staff has been downsized accordingly. From a staff numbering as many as 30 members, the ACU now employs five full-time positions: directors of legislative, finance, and field activities, an executive director, and an office manager. The ACU actively recruits interns—preferably college juniors and seniors—to supplement office staff, making from 13 to 15 internships available each year. The Union puts the number of members and supporters at more than 500,000.

PRIMARY FUNCTIONS

The ACU sees itself as the grassroots lobby for the entire conservative movement, and as such functions as a policy-making and advocating body. Through its conferences, the organization helps provide direction and policy for the conservative movement. The ACU then advocates these policies at a grassroots level, strengthening the conservative movement by encouraging and coordinating public action. One important aspect of the ACU's activities is the monitoring of a broad spectrum of issues before Congress that are of concern to its conservative constituents. Its focus is on four general areas: Economic and Budget, which includes such areas as tax legislation and attempts to balance the budget; Social and Cultural, which encompasses welfare reform and abortion legislation; Foreign Policy and Defense, including the United Nations and foreign aid; and Institutional Reform, such as campaign finance reform and lobbying reform.

A good example of an ACU grassroots campaign was its push in the 1990s for major tax reform. In 1994, after a Republican majority was established in both houses of Congress for the first time since the 1920s, the ACU began a massive campaign to have the tax system replaced. The ACU's goals included abolishing the Internal Revenue Service (IRS) and replacing it with a simpler and fairer tax system, repeal of the Sixteenth Amendment giving Congress the power to establish an income tax, and termination of the present tax code. "Abolish the IRS" committees were established around the country to coordinate grassroots activity. Throughout the 1990s thousands of petitions were mailed to members, urging them to gather signatures, call talk radio shows, contact their representatives in Congress, write letters to editors, and talk to their neighbors about the importance of tax reform.

PROGRAMS

ACU programs are aimed at stimulating grassroots activity and building coalitions around specific issues, with the ultimate aim of influencing the course of legislation in Congress. One of the ACU's most successful programs is the annual CPAC which, despite its acronym, is not a political action committee. The Conservative Political Action Conference was started by the Union in 1973 as a means of rallying demoralized conservatives in the wake of the Watergate scandal which led to the resignation of President Richard M. Nixon in 1974. The conference became the catalyst for building a grassroots movement, training and motivating talented conservatives for political action.

The three-day event, held in the Washington, D.C., area in late winter and open to the general public, has become the largest annual gathering of conservatives in the nation. It has attracted more than 2,000 participants who meet to debate current issues and policies, see and hear up-and-coming conservative candidates and leaders, and formulate the future conservative agenda. The CPAC attracts key political and media figures as speakers, and has become a popular forum for contenders for upcoming presidential races. The inclusiveness of the ACU umbrella is attested to by the number of conservative groups—a total of 64—that cosponsored the twenty-fifth CPAC in 1998.

An example of the ACU's success at coalition-building is its Committee for a Conservative Platform project, which has developed consensus platform positions for every Republican presidential nominating convention since 1972. More than 50 conservative organizations were able to generate a consensus platform that was ultimately adopted by the Republican Party during its 1996 convention.

The program for which the ACU is perhaps best known is its annual congressional rating, undertaken and published continuously since 1971. The ratings, done on a scale of zero to 100, track a wide range of current issues before Congress in order to provide a reliable and useful gauge of each member's political leaning as well as an overall measurement of conservative strength. The ratings, released every April, have become a fixture in reference guides and political almanacs, and are also available free of charge on-line or in printed form. The organization's stated purpose in issuing its vote ratings is not to influence Congress one way or the other, but to show the public just where individual legislators stand along an absolute ideological spectrum. In addition, the ACU periodically publishes voting indices on specific issue areas, which have included defense, judicial nominations, and pork-barrel spending. In election years, the ACU provides voters with interim ratings of Congress to enable them to track votes in the congressional session preceding the elections.

BUDGET INFORMATION

The ACU's budget of approximately $760,000 annually is raised almost entirely from membership dues and donations. Regular dues are $25 per year, patron membership, $100, Chairman's Club, $1,000. Major expenditures include monies spent to support headquarters operations and paid staff in Alexandria, Virginia, and lobbying, publications, and grassroots activity.

HISTORY

The ACU was created in 1964 during the weeks following the landslide victory of incumbent President Lyndon Johnson over conservative Republican Barry Goldwater. A group of conservative leaders met in Washington, D.C., to lay plans for promoting and advancing the cause of modern conservatism. The organization born of that meeting was dedicated to public education and direct action in the political arena. Early on the ACU took strong stands in favor of decreasing taxes and government spending, developing a strong military, and supporting the Vietnam War (1959–75). It opposed recognition of the People's (Communist) Republic of China and detente with the then-Soviet Union.

In 1968 the ACU supported Richard Nixon's successful campaign for president, but by 1971 had withdrawn its support due to disagreements over foreign and domestic policy issues, Nixon's failure to reduce government spending, the implementation of wage and price controls, the president's initiative to abolish the Electoral College mechanism spelled out in the U.S. Constitution, and his visit to Communist China. In 1972 the ACU formally endorsed the presidential campaign of Congressman John Ashbrook (R-Oh.). While Ashbrook's challenge to Nixon's renomination was unsuccessful, it was a pointed reminder that the support of conservatives was not to be taken for granted.

Some of the ACU's fights during the administration of Jimmy Carter included its opposition to Carter's Panama Canal giveaway (the United States ceded control of the Panama Canal to the nation of Panama under a 1979 treaty), its efforts to ease the regulatory burden placed by the Office of Safety and Health Administration (OSHA) on small businesses, its grassroots opposition to the SALT (Strategic Arms Limitation Talks) II treaty between the United States and the Soviet Union, its support of sending aid to freedom fighters in communist countries, the confirmation of conservative justices to the U.S. Supreme Court, and the never-ending battle to lower taxes.

In 1976 the ACU mounted a massive independent campaign in support of Ronald Reagan's unsuccessful bid for the Republican presidential nomination. Along with thousands of conservative activists, it stuck by Reagan, backing him in his victorious run for the presidency in 1980 and again in 1984. The organization played a strong role in support of Reagan's administration, mobilizing Project One Million—a grassroots effort to push the President's 1981 economic reform plan—supporting his Strategic Defense Initiative (SDI), and mounting a "peace offensive" in opposition to the nuclear freeze movement.

ACU: Born Again

The election of a democratic president in 1992 was a shot in the arm to the conservative movement. "Clinton has touched the hot button of every ilk of conservative," according to *New Republic* commentator Fred Barnes in July of 1993. Barnes claimed, as did many political analysts, that Clinton had done for Republicans what they were unable to do for themselves: namely, united the party and revived the conservative movement beyond its wildest dreams. "Most astonishing is the born-again experience of the American Conservative Union," Barnes wrote. "Underfunded, ACU had been a spent force for years."

CURRENT POLITICAL ISSUES

As a leading lobbying organization for the U.S. conservative movement, the ACU has taken a leading position in many major public policy battles. Some of the so-called Hot Issues tracked by the ACU in the 1990s include educational savings accounts, racial and gender preferences, campaign finance reform, school vouchers, the partial birth abortion ban, the Chemical Weapons treaty, the minimum wage, and health care. This last issue became the focus of major ACU activity after the election of President Bill Clinton in 1992. The ACU took an early lead in challenging the new administration, targeting its showpiece—national health insurance.

Case Study: Health Reform—A Fight to the Finish

The campaign to defeat the newly elected liberal president's proposed reform of the nation's health care system was one of the ACU's most successful efforts. Clinton's proposed legislation, a 1,342-page bill introduced in 1993, was produced after months of meetings by the cabinet-level Task Force on National Health Care Reform presided over by First Lady Hillary Rodham Clinton. The plan called for a comprehensive overhaul of the nation's health care system that the ACU opposed as "allowing for a government take-over of the industry." The organization, responding quickly, led the conservative response to the plan by organizing an opposition coalition—Citizens against Rationing Health (CARH)—to mobilize the grass roots. For the next 18 months, the ACU and CARH sponsored more than 30 town meetings in cities around the country, including Providence, Rhode Island; Philadelphia; Baton Rouge; Macon, Georgia; Birmingham, Alabama; Milwaukee; Livonia, Michigan; Oklahoma City; Phoenix; Seattle; and Sacramento. Physicians in many localities helped to organize the events, which typically featured speeches by experts in health care, while local activists helped to generate crowd turnout and promote media coverage. An effective tool used by speakers was to hold up a copy of the telephone-book-sized health reform bill by way of demonstrating its complexity; a large chart of the complex plan gave graphic expression to the same point.

When, in mid-1994, Mrs. Clinton set out on a "Health Care Express" bus tour to promote the legislation, the ACU countered with a whistlestop bus trip called the "National Health Care Truth Tour" which made a circuit of several states including New Jersey, Pennsylvania, Ohio, Kentucky, Indiana, Illinois, and Missouri. Speakers at each stop made the case against the health plan. The ACU would mount a similar bus tour in California that same year in the fight against Proposition 186, a wide-ranging proposal to overhaul California's health insurance system.

Millions of pieces of direct mail went out to the ACU's database of members and supporters, urging them to call or write their representative in Congress and to write letters to the editor of their local newspapers. A 15-minute video, featuring warnings on the dangers of Clintoncare by experts and congressional leaders from both sides of the aisle, was made available to members. The year-long battle ended in stalemate on September 26, 1994, when Senate Majority Leader George Mitchell (D-Me.) formally pronounced health care reform dead. A few weeks later, California's Proposition 186 went down in defeat in the November 8 election. Keene noted with satisfaction that Hillary Clinton herself credited the skill and tenacity of conservatives and the power of direct mail for the result.

FUTURE DIRECTIONS

The evolution of the ACU from its origins as a network of affiliated state conservative groups to a centralized organization focused on lobbying, communication, and direct action seems likely to continue on its present trend. While the goals of the organization are likely to remain constant for some years to come, its methods of operation are rapidly changing. The ACU is increasingly trying to reach out directly to individuals. Direct mail, once primarily a fund-raising mechanism, has become the union's primary communication tool. On-line communication is also an area of growing interest for the organization; the ACU's InfoNet is expected to grow in importance as a means of disseminating information via fax and E-mail.

GROUP RESOURCES

The ACU maintains a Web page at http://www.conservative.org that offers an ACU history, commentary on issues, access to the annual ratings of Congress archived back to 1971, publications and audiovisual tapes, names of staff and board members, and information on CPAC. For research, the union draws on the product of think tanks like the Cato Institute and the Heritage Foundation; the ACU Education & Research Institute, a vehicle for research, studies, policy analysis and publications on vital issues, was spun off as a separate organization in the 1980s. InfoNet, started in 1997, is a free service available at the Web site offering confidential memos, published commentaries and essays by ACU leaders, news releases, and letters to Congress on key legislation. The site maintains "Legislative Update," a frequently updated list of Hot Issues before Congress, each item on which can be accessed for a news release or further information. Voters are urged to "Keep Your Eye on the Floor," and "Get Involved, send E-mail to your Senators and Representative Now!" With the E-mail address of every House and Senate member listed, doing so requires no more effort than the click of a mouse. Chairman Keene contributes a column twice monthly to *The Hill,* a newspaper about Congress, and Donald Devine, treasurer, writes regular columns for the *Washington Times.* Their columns are available at the Web site.

GROUP PUBLICATIONS

The ACU produces a range of publications aimed at influencing members of Congress on public policy matters and educating members and supporters on the issues before lawmakers. Its legislative guides are used as working manuals primarily by members of Congress and their staffs; one such is *The Clinton Plan: More Power to Gov-*

ernment, documenting the Clinton record. Another is *The 1996 Committee for a Conservative Platform.* Video and audio tapes are also produced by the ACU; recent topics include opposition to the invasion of Haiti and an "informercial" on health care reform. *Battle Line* (originally the *Republican Battle Line*), a newsletter initiated soon after the ACU's founding, lapsed during the 1980s, but has resumed quarterly publication. It is sent to all members. Subscriptions are available to nonmembers free of charge. The annual congressional ratings and other publications are produced in-house and distributed from headquarters. They can be ordered on-line at http://www.conservative.org; by telephone at (703) 836-8602; or by fax at (703) 836-8608. Complete audiovisual tapes of the annual CPAC proceedings are also available; for information, call the CPAC at 1-800-752-4391 or (703) 739-2550.

BIBLIOGRAPHY

Balz, Dan, and John Yang. "Republicans Set Legislative Priorities." *Washington Post,* 7 March 1997.

Barnes, Fred. "Right Back: Born-again Experience of the American Conservative Union." *New Republic,* 5 July 1993.

Broder, David. "Outside the Beltway, the Republicans Reign." *Washington Post,* 26 February 1998.

Crawford, Alan. *Thunder on the Right: The "New Right" and the Politics of Resentment.* New York, N.Y.: Pantheon, 1980.

Grove, Lloyd. "In the Right Place at the Right Time; Conservatives Conspire to Meet and Gloat." *Washington Post,* 30 January 1998.

Heard, Alex. "Brat PAC: Among the Conservative Weenies." *New Republic,* 4 March 1991.

Nash, George H. *The Conservative Intellectual Movement in America since 1945.* New York, N.Y.: Basic Books, 1976.

Ridgeway, James. "IRS R.I.P.? Stand of the American Conservative Union and Other Conservative Groups." *Village Voice,* 1 April 1997.

Seelye, Katharine. "House G.O.P. Is Said to Be United on Keeping Gingrich as Speaker." *New York Times,* 4 January 1997.

Shogan, Robert. "Conservatives Gather, Target Clinton Policies for Counterattack." *Los Angeles Times,* 13 February 1994.

Shogan, Robert. "GOP's Comeback Trail Looms as Long, Bumpy." *Los Angeles Times,* 15 November 1992.

American Dental Association (ADA)

WHAT IS ITS MISSION?

The American Dental Association (ADA) is a professional association of dentists that seeks to serve the profession of dentistry and the public health. The ADA's mission is to promote the oral health of the public by working with member dentists to make quality care available to everyone and to promote the profession of dentistry by monitoring and defining the ethics of the profession, improving patient/dentist relationships, and offering information and resources to its members. Through education, advocacy, research, and the development of standards, the ADA works to accomplish these goals.

HOW IS IT STRUCTURED?

The national headquarters of the ADA is located in Chicago, Illinois. The board of trustees, the organization's administrative body, is composed of a president, president-elect, two vice presidents, and 16 trustees. Each trustee represents one of 16 geographical districts of the United States. The organization's executive director also sits on the board of trustees as an ex-officio member.

The House of Delegates, which acts as the organization's legislative body and convenes once per year, is made up of 423 delegates representing 54 constituent societies, namely ADA state or territorial branch associations. The House of Delegates also contains representatives from five federal dental services and the American Student Dental Association. The speaker of the House of Delegates attends meeting of the board of trustees but does not have voting rights.

ESTABLISHED: August 1859
EMPLOYEES: 400
MEMBERS: 143,000
PAC: American Dental Political Action Committee

Contact Information:
ADDRESS: 211 E. Chicago Ave.
    Chicago, IL 60611
PHONE: (312) 440-2500
FAX: (312) 440-2800
E-MAIL: publicinfo@ada.org
URL: http://www.ada.org
CEO: Dr. John S. Zapp

FAST FACTS

In 1996 only one half of all Americans had dental insurance.

(Source: Doug Gunzler. "Redefining Dental Coverage." *Business and Health,* October 1998.)

The ADA has 16 councils and committees that recommend policy, each representing a particular field of special interest. Their members study issues related to these areas of interest and recommend policy and policy changes to the board of trustees and the House of Delegates. Areas of interest represented by councils and committees include dental practice, ethics, insurance and scientific affairs.

The ADA Health Foundation (ADAHF) was established in 1964 by the board of trustees as a means to provide charitable support. The ADAHF sponsors a variety of research and educational programs, offering student scholarships to dental students and grants to fund research studies. The ADAHF also sponsors national conferences such as the Annual Conference on Special Care Issues in Dentistry and the Dental Research Conference.

PRIMARY FUNCTIONS

The ADA is a multi-faceted organization that assists dentists, as medical professionals, in maintaining a high standard of conduct, ethics, and professionalism in dentistry. It also educates the public regarding oral hygiene and health.

The ADA offers many support services for member dentists. Some of the services most often used by dentists include the publications *Journal of the American Dental Association* (*JADA*) and the *ADA News,* insurance plans, continuing education programs, and ADA's Occupational Safety and Health Administration (OSHA) compliance information. The organization also offers members legislative newsletters, financial services, library resources, and infection control recommendations. Dentists also benefit from the ADA's involvement in the research and development of new technology. The ADA also lobbies Congress on behalf of dental professionals in areas such as Medicare and Medicaid, malpractice law, and health care reform.

To practice dentistry in the United States, one must first receive a license to practice from a state or regional authority. While not an official part of this accreditation process, the standards and tests that the ADA administers are widely used in the licensing process. A degree from an ADA-accredited college is accepted throughout the United States as proof of adequate dental education. The ADA's National Board Dental Examinations are also widely used to measure the skills and knowledge of an applicant for a license. As a condition of membership, every ADA member agrees to abide by the ADA Principle of Ethics and the Code of Professional Conduct (ADA Code). According to the code, members "recognize that continued public trust in the dental profession is based on the commitment of individual dentists to high ethical standards of conduct."

The ADA provides numerous educational tools to the public. Through its award-winning Web site, the organization offers free information on oral hygiene. In addition consumers can access information on topics such as tooth whitening, fluoridation, dental amalgam, bad breath, cleaning teeth and gums, and gum disease. The Web site also offers a Kids' Corner with information geared specifically towards children.

PROGRAMS

The ADA sponsors a number of programs that promote professional growth, patient information, and consumer awareness. Each year at the annual session of the ADA House of Delegates thousands gather not only to consider legislative matters, but also to participate in a plethora of educational experiences. Almost 30,000 dentists, dental assistants, dental hygienists, business assistants, and guests attended the 1997 annual meeting. Attendees were able to interact with almost 8,000 exhibitors and dental dealers during the three-day session. The ADA sponsors and co-sponsors various events geared toward dental professionals, among them the National Conference on the New Dentist, a two-day workshop titled "Dentistry as a Business: Money, Management, Marketing, and You," and a seminar geared towards accreditation in the dental office.

Since its inception in 1964, the ADAHF has held an annual Health Screening Program. Each year member dentists are offered free screenings of basic health tests. During the 1990s the ADA added two new tests to its screenings: latex allergies and HIV. Because dentists use latex gloves during treatment, allergies to latex can cause serious problems. Also dentists come into contact with patients' body fluids and operate with sharp instruments, thus raising their risk of exposure to the HIV virus.

The ADA assists consumers with choosing dental products through its Seal of Acceptance program, which boasts 350 voluntary participants. Publishing its first critique of toothpaste in 1866 and establishing guidelines for testing and advertising in 1930, the first ADA Seal of Acceptance was awarded in 1931. Approximately 1,300 products carry the ADA Seal of Approval; of these, approximately 30 percent are public consumables such as toothpaste, floss, and toothbrushes. The rest, such as antibiotics and dental restorative materials, are used by dentists.

BUDGET INFORMATION

Each year a preliminary budget is drawn up based on all budget requests by a committee consisting of the ADA's president-elect, treasurer, and executive director. The budget is then presented to the board of trustees for approval; once approved, it goes before the House of Delegates for final approval. For 1999 the ADA had a proposed budget of $65.3 million, with revenues anticipated to reach $65.1 million. A dues increase of $82 was proposed to balance the budget, fund renovations to the building housing ADA headquarters, and boost ADA reserves.

HISTORY

The ADA came into existence in August 1859 when 26 dentists met in Niagara Falls, New York, to form a professional society. The association was formed to improve communication regarding advances in technology, offer support and dialogue among dentists, and improve the consistency of care dental patients received. A year later the ADA formalized its newly structured organization by adopting a constitution and bylaws. By 1890 the organization was competing for members with almost 100 other dental societies, and in 1897 merged with the Southern Dental Association to form the National Dental Association (NDA). By 1899, already in existence for 40 years, the NDA had fewer than 250 members. In response, membership policies were revised to attract new members.

1900–1930

In 1908 the NDA published its first patient dental-education pamphlet. In the same year, with membership now growing quickly, the NDA also instituted the beginnings of a tripartite membership structure, in which members belong to a local association, a state or regional association, and the national association. In 1913 the NDA continued to strengthen its structural base by adopting a new constitution and bylaws and by establishing the House of Delegates and board of trustees.

During the early 1900s the NDA developed a relief fund, established group health insurance, and began publication of the *Journal of the National Dental Associa-*

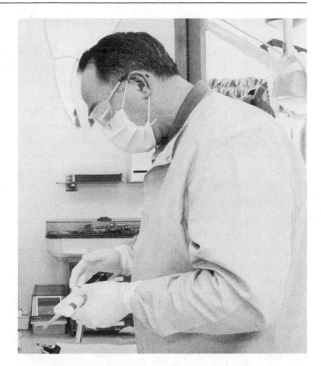

Dentist Robert Bragdon was charged with discrimination when he refused to treat an HIV positive woman outside of a hospital setting. When he appealed, the U.S. Supreme Court ruled that HIV-infected people are protected by the Americans with Disabilities Act. (Photograph by Michael C. York, AP/Wide World Photo)

tion. In 1928 the NDA worked with the National Bureau of Standards (NBS) to establish the National Board of Dental Examiners. The NDA changed its name to the American Dental Association in 1922 and by 1929 the newly renamed organization boasted a membership of 30,000. Its journal, now called the *Journal of the American Dental Association,* was hailed as the leading publication in dental literature.

1930–1960

During the 1930s the ADA's membership increased by 6,000, rising to a total of approximately half of all dentists practicing in the United States. In 1934 it joined the U.S. Public Health Service to give dental exams to 1.5 million children in 26 states. During World War II (1939–1945) the ADA worked to obtain preferential purchase of automobiles, gasoline, and dental supplies for dentists. In so doing, members were able to obtain supplies that were in short supply due to the war and not readily available to the general public. By the close of the 1940s 85 percent of U.S. dentists held membership in the ADA.

In 1950 the ADA lobbied Congress to declare February 6 as National Children's Dental Health Day. In the same year the ADA publicly endorsed the importance of fluoridation in dental health. Fluoride is a natural element that helps prevent tooth decay when consistently ingested or applied topically. In 1955 the ADA successfully lobbied the World Health Organization to establish a dental unit and began developing television advertisements and scripts. The 1950s also saw substantial improvements in dental equipment, with new and more effective X-ray machines and tooth repair materials being introduced into use.

In 1954 an ADA-NBS research team made an important advancement in dental instrumentation with the creation of the turbine contra-angle handpiece. Two years later research teams also developed panoramic X-ray equipment and glass-filled resin composites, the latter an improved substance used in the repair of teeth. Already involved in accreditation of dentists through its affiliation with the NBS, the ADA established accreditation programs in postgraduate training for dental laboratory technicians (1951), dental hygienists (1952), and dental assistants (1962).

1960 to the Present

During the 1960s the ADA stepped up its public health campaign, dedicating one-third of its funds to dental education activities. In 1964 the ADA Health Foundation, formed to support research and education, began its annual health screening program. The organization also became the first nonprofit agency to produce a color public service announcement for television.

In 1965 the ADA relocated within Chicago, Illinois to its new headquarters building on Chicago Avenue. The agency also moved the NBS testing and certification programs into the building. Two floors of the building were dedicated to laboratory facilities for ADA's research arm, the Research Institute. In 1966 the ADA Council on Dental Materials and Devices was established.

In 1970 *ADA News* was published for the first time. The ADA Council on Dental Practice (1978), the Commission on Dental Accreditation (1979), and the Division of Membership and Marketing Services (1980) were established. During the late 1970s the organization began budgeting funds for national print and television test marketing campaigns and discussing the growing interest in creating a branch office in Washington, D.C., which eventually opened in 1984. In 1989 the ADA Publishing Company (ADAPCO) was incorporated as a for-profit subsidiary of ADA. ADAPCO took over all publishing aspects of the ADA, including *JADA* and the *ADA News*.

With the opening of its Washington office, the ADA increased its lobbying efforts during the 1990s. Through legislative and legal means, the ADA aggressively battled the OSHA regulations and the National Practitioners Data Bank. Both agencies advocated laws and regulations that the ADA believed to be detrimental to both dentists in providing quality care and the public in receiving quality care.

CURRENT POLITICAL ISSUES

The ADA has long been involved in advocating for both the public's right to quality dental care and for the profession of dentistry. In the mid-1990s the high cost of health care, along with the complex statutes governing health insurance and health care providers, prompted many calls for reform. Debate raged in Congress and the media, a debate in which the ADA was heavily involved. The ADA has traditionally used its resources to lobby for legislative and regulatory reforms that would benefit member dentists and has often found itself standing against the insurance company lobbyists. While the organization advocates for increasing both the number of dental procedures covered by health insurance and the benefits paid for such procedures, insurance companies struggle to keep escalating health care costs in check by limiting allowable procedures and benefits to patients.

Case Study: The Patient Access to Responsible Care Act

The ADA's long-term health care reform goal, as stated in a February 23, 1998, "action alert" letter to dentists from ADA President David A. Whiston, is to create a "health care system that controls costs, allows patients to choose their own doctors, gives subscribers access to information to make smart choices, and offers appeals when coverage is denied." When Representative Charlie Norwood (R-GA) introduced House Bill 1415 in April of 1997, the ADA immediately moved to support it. This bill, better known as the Patient Access to Responsible Care Act (PARCA), was just what the ADA had been hoping for.

The ADA strongly supported several provisions of PARCA. The most significant changes proposed in the bill were in the area of a medical insurer's accountability to their clients. PARCA would grant patients new rights to appeal treatment decisions that they disagree with and to sue insurance companies for decisions which proved harmful. So-called "gag rules," which allow insurers to restrict medical practitioners from discussing certain treatment options, would also be banned. According to the ADA, these changes would allow patients more choice in treatment and hold insurers responsible for the consequences of their decisions to deny coverage for certain types of medical care. Importantly, the ADA insisted that PARCA could be implemented without major increases in the cost of medical insurance. According to a study sponsored by a pro-PARCA organization, if a patient's insurance premium was $160 per month under the existing laws, the increase in costs caused by PARCA would be no more than $4.16 per month, less than a three percent increase.

PARCA's Opponents

PARCA's opponents were numerous. Both the Health Insurance Association of America and Blue Cross/Blue Shield Association lobbied against its passage. Such organizations as the Self-Insurance Institute of America (SIIA) and the Association of Private Pension and Welfare Plans (APPWP) also joined together to wage a one million dollar advertising campaign against PARCA.

Opponents of PARCA claimed that by making insurance companies subject to many new and costly lawsuits, PARCA would force insurance companies to drastically raise their prices. According to the numbers put forth by PARCA's opponents, the act would increase health insurance premium costs by approximately 23 percent. They further estimated that with such a price increase, nine million people would lose insurance coverage because their employers would no longer be able to afford to pay for insurance benefits. Thus, while SIIA and APPWP both affirmed the need for better patient protection, they viewed PARCA as overly extreme legislation that would do more harm than good.

New Legislation

Eventually, PARCA's opponents won out. In June of 1998 PARCA was effectively abandoned by its sponsor, Representative Norwood. While Norwood supported another patient protection legislation developed by other House Republicans—the ADA criticized the new bill. In a statement released in June of 1998, ADA President David Whiston stated that the new legislation failed to make health insurers liable to their patients, and that the "proposal ignores the need for health plan liability and its patient choice provisions are so weak and riddled with exceptions that millions of Americans will still be denied real choice." Nevertheless, this bill went on to pass the House in July of 1998.

Public Impact

The health care debate continued to loom large on America's political and economic agenda as the nation moved into the twenty-first century, and the ADA still pushed for measures such as those proposed in PARCA. The organization has much to gain from the passage of legislation that impacts patient and provider rights. By working for these new laws, the ADA also works to fulfill its mission. If patients are offered more comprehensive services by insurance companies, dentists will be better able to provide quality services to more people. Also, if insurers covered more medical procedures and treatments, being pushed to do so under the threat of law suits should a patient be adversely affected by treatment being withheld, the profession of dentistry benefits from more patients with more coverage and more choices.

FUTURE DIRECTIONS

The ADA is seeking to serve its members better in a number of areas, including advocacy, practice support, information, and research. In order to become a better advocate for its members, the organization plans to increase its lobbying efforts on such issues as access to care and insurance coverage. In the area of practice support, the ADA has plans to promote education in several areas including dental reimbursement systems and debt management. Access to more information will focus on the use of new technology to increase information available to both member dentists and the public. The ADA also planned to use its research capabilities to push technology in such areas as a vaccine to prevent cavities and the use of lasers rather than drills to repair cavities.

GROUP RESOURCES

The ADA maintains a comprehensive Web site which can be accessed at http://www.ada.org. The site offers a number of informational resources for the consumer, the dental student, and the dental professional. For dentists, ADA Online features the *ADA News Daily,* select articles from *JADA,* legislative newsletters, ADA library information, and an event calendar. Dental students can find dental career fact sheets, information on dental schools and programs, and information on testing and financial planning. Patients and consumers will find numerous topics addressed, including a list of frequently asked questions and a Kids' Corner. Although most services offered at the Web site are available to everyone, some information requires ADA membership and is accessed only with an ADA membership number.

GROUP PUBLICATIONS

All ADA publications are produced and distributed by ADAPCO. *JADA* is the ADA's primary published resource and is distributed monthly to all members. Its mission is to provide dentists with information that will help dentists in practice and science. *JADA* is also published by ADAPCO in Spanish and Portuguese for distribution in Spain and numerous South American countries. The *ADA News* is published 22 times a year, and focuses on socioeconomic and political developments. The *ADA Legal Adviser,* which covers all legal issues affecting dentists, is published in conjunction with the ADA Division of Legal Affairs. It is a monthly newsletter available by subscription. The *ADA Washington Report* discusses the legislative and regulatory activities related to health care. It is distributed to key dental leaders and can be found in its entirety at ADA's Web site. ADAPCO also publishes several guides and pamphlets covering various topics related to dentistry. Information on all ADAPCO publications can be requested on-line at http://www.ada.org/adapco, by E-mailing ADAPCO at adapco@ada.org, or by phone at (312) 440-2867.

BIBLIOGRAPHY

"ADA Budgets Time, Effort to Strategic Planning." *ADA News Daily,* 17 July 1998.

"ADA Reacts to House GOP Patient Protection Proposal." *ADA News Daily,* 25 June 1998.

"Dentistry: Cavity Vaccine." *Discover,* August 1998.

Eisenberg, Anne. "Overbite, Underbite, Megabyte: Dentistry Gets an Upgrade." *New York Times,* September 1998.

"GOP Leadership Attacks Patient Protection Bill." *ADA News Daily,* 7 November 1997.

Gunzler, Doug. "Redefining Dental Coverage." *Business and Health,* October 1998.

Hamilton, Kenall, and Joan Raymond. "More Lasers, Less Lidocaine—Meet Dr. Friendly, D.D.S." *Newsweek,* 13 April 1998.

Norwood, Charlie. "Restoring Responsibility to Managed Care: Proposed Legislation Would Curb Health Care Organizations' Ability to Run Roughshod over the Rights of Patients." *USA Today,* July 1998.

"Public Awareness Campaign Reviewed." *ADA News Daily,* 15 July 1998.

"Radio Spots Promote PARCA Bill." *ADA News Daily,* 18 June 1998.

"Talking Points on PARCA Sent Via Action Alert to Grassroots Dentist." *ADA News Daily,* 26 February 1998.

Wynbrandt, James. *The Excruciating History of Dentistry.* New York, N.Y.: St. Martin's Press, 1998.

American Family Association (AFA)

ESTABLISHED: 1977
EMPLOYEES: 125
MEMBERS: 250 local affiliates
PAC: None

Contact Information:
ADDRESS: PO Drawer 2440
    Tupelo, MS 38803
PHONE: (601) 844-5036
FAX: (601) 844-9176
URL: http://www.afa.net
EXECUTIVE DIRECTOR: Donald E. Wildmon

WHAT IS ITS MISSION?

According to the organization's Web site, the American Family Association (AFA) serves "people who are tired of cursing the darkness and who are ready to light a candle." Founded as a nonprofit organization by Donald Wildmon in 1977, the AFA "stands for traditional family values, focusing primarily on the influence of television and other media—including pornography—on our society."

The agenda of the AFA is driven by a belief that the entertainment industry has done much to contribute to the decay of morals and culture in U.S. society. The organization cites a rise in teen pregnancy, the increase in the incidence of AIDS, and the proliferation of pornography as examples of such decay. It carries out its mission by targeting media or companies that the AFA believes contribute to a decline in what it perceives as family values.

HOW IS IT STRUCTURED?

The AFA structure is set up to facilitate the organization's fight for promoting values of decency in everyday life or in the media. It provides assistance to its regional affiliates, coordinates legal assistance when needed, and carries out watchdog efforts that canvas the government and the media. The AFA's main office in Tupelo, Mississippi, houses the AFA Law Center, which is staffed by six attorneys. Attorneys work with more than 400 AFA affiliate attorneys across the nation to provide legal assistance for Christians who believe their constitutional rights have been violated. The main office also

houses the Office of General Counsel, another legal part of the organization that focuses on corporate legal issues. This office serves not only the AFA and its affiliates, but also American Family Radio, a Christian-sponsored radio station, and the AFA's Office of Governmental Affairs. The organization's Mississippi office also houses the outreach division, which provides help and counseling for sex addicts.

The AFA Office of Governmental Affairs is located in Washington, D.C., and serves to monitor legislation relevant to Christian and Family Values organizations. Staff from this branch of the AFA keeps supporters current on the status of policies relating to family values.

Individuals wishing to support the AFA agenda have the option of forming local AFA affiliates and carrying out activist functions in their communities. Approximately 250 AFA affiliates are linked to the national organization. These function at the local level and are overseen by 21 state directors. The national office provides support and activist/leadership training to affiliate members.

PRIMARY FUNCTIONS

The AFA uses many tactics to fight what it considers the causes of moral decay in U.S. society. Most of these methods involve putting pressure on companies that appear to be violating biblical standards of decency in their advertising or other business practices. The AFA also uses pressure to get advertisers to withdraw financial backing for what the organization considers objectionable entertainment.

Through public awareness campaigns, the AFA helps its supporters know which companies and which aspects of the entertainment industry are contributing to moral degradation, so that supporters can protest to those companies and avoid using their products. For example, in 1996 the AFA publicized a "Dirty Dozen" list of prime-time television advertisers that used what the group considered objectional material in their ads. The organization also undertakes public education efforts to advance its agenda, producing resources that not only describe its work, but provide people tools for dealing with family value or decency issues. For example, in 1994 the AFA produced a "Marriage Savers" video series aimed at helping couples work through differences and avoid divorce. The organization produces the monthly *AFA Journal*, which is sent to 400,000 subscribers. The AFA radio show, *AFA Report*, broadcasts daily from the Washington, D.C., office and allows listeners at over 1,200 local radio stations to hear the latest policy news on family values issues.

Sometimes the AFA takes more direct action, using E-mail alert lists for grassroots mobilization, instructing supporters to write or call their representatives, boycott products, or take other action, depending upon the issue.

The organization organizes on-site boycotts and pickets when an issue is deemed particularly important. For example AFA supporters picketed convenience stores that were owned by the Southland Corporation; as a result, pornographic magazines were pulled from the stores by management. The AFA also provides legal assistance for Christians dealing with family issues at the national and the affiliate level. Legal issues may involve First Amendment Rights, the rights of the unborn child, or instances when individuals have been persecuted for their faith.

PROGRAMS

AFA programs are organized to help supporters become aware of issues of concern to the organization, and to help these supporters institute change by acting at the grassroots level. For example the AFA initiated the annual Pornography Awareness Week in 1982; the event has been held in nationwide locations ever since, beginning the last Sunday in October. Churches and interested groups use the event to carry out discussions on the effects of pornography on society. The AFA provides resources to participating communities, including anti-porn posters. Another program initiated by the AFA is Meet at City Hall, first carried out by the organization in 1992. On this day, the AFA asks Christians to pray together in their towns for 20 minutes at noon on the first Thursday in May. People pray for their town, the nation, the world, and many other concerns.

BUDGET INFORMATION

The AFA is a member of the Evangelical Council for Financial Accountability, which means that all bookkeeping is handled by an independent firm. The organization buys nothing on credit and completely owns all its assets. The AFA is a 501(c)3 non-profit organization.

For the fiscal year beginning in July 1, 1996 and ending June 30, 1997, the organization had total revenue of $10,798,861. Revenue included direct public support ($9,819,406); program service revenue ($827,873); interest on savings ($16,216); dividends from securities ($6,138); gross rents ($44,033); net gain from sale of assets ($51,266); and other revenue ($33,929). Expenses totaled $10,152,679 and included program services ($8,758,156); management and general ($212,405); and fundraising ($1,182,118). In a separate breakdown of expenses, highest expenses included salaries and wages ($2,435,987) and postage/shipping ($1,507,606).

HISTORY

The AFA actually started out as an organization called the National Federation for Decency (NFD), which was founded in 1977. The founder, Donald Wildmon, was an ordained United Methodist Minister. The idea of NFD was born as Wildmon watched television one night and could find nothing among the program selections that did not contain violence or adultery. Disturbed, Wildmon came up with a plan to get members of his church to turn off their televisions for a week. The national media picked up on the event and it began to be implemented across the country as "Turn off the TV Week." The success of the event led Wildmon to form the NFD.

One of the historical highlights of the organization occurred in 1987 with the debut of the movie *The Last Temptation of Christ*. Christians objected to the movie on the grounds that it portrayed Jesus Christ in a negative and sinful light. The AFA worked to mobilize opposition to the movie by presenting its position to the public and encouraging supporters to boycott the film.

In 1988 the NFD changed its name to the American Family Association. The organization began mobilizing opposition to the federal government's National Endowment for the Arts (NEA) in 1989. According to the AFA, the NEA spends taxpayer dollars on artistic endeavors that, in some cases, are pornographic and indecent. The AFA's high profile attacks on the NEA brought it increasing publicity and attention from the public.

The AFA's ideals gained wide acceptance during the late 1980s and early 1990s. Republican presidents Ronald Reagan and George Bush both emphasized family values as part of their political platforms. Though the AFA was disappointed with the election of Democrat Bill Clinton to the presidency in 1992, a Republican majority dominated the Congress throughout the 1990s and was in general sympathetic to the organization's concerns.

Through the 1990s the organization remained active in its multiple functions of appealing to companies, picketing and boycotting, or conducting public awareness campaigns. In May of 1996 the AFA convinced giant soft-drink manufacturer PepsiCo to withdraw its backing of the premier of the *Dana Carvey* show, a television program featuring skits of drug use and gay characters. The show later floundered and was taken off the air. In a collaborative effort with southern Baptist groups, the AFA organized a boycott of Disney World in June 1997. The organization's Disney boycott was launched in opposition to Disney films that the AFA considered anti-Christian and pornographic. The organization also opposed the Disney employee policy that allowed partner benefits to homosexual employees. When Disney sponsored a segment of the television series *Ellen* (April 1997) which featured a lesbian character coming out on television in a supportive environment, the event added fuel to the AFA's campaign against the entertainment

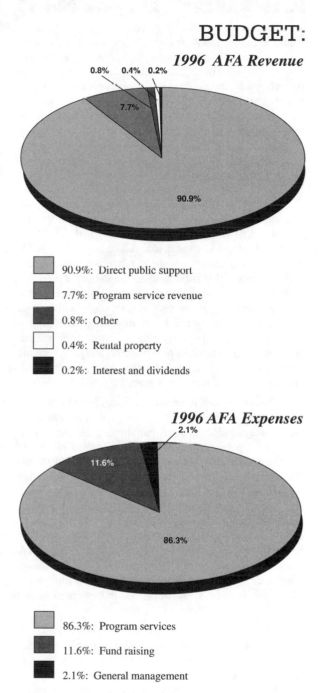

BUDGET:

1996 AFA Revenue

- 90.9%: Direct public support
- 7.7%: Program service revenue
- 0.8%: Other
- 0.4%: Rental property
- 0.2%: Interest and dividends

1996 AFA Expenses

- 86.3%: Program services
- 11.6%: Fund raising
- 2.1%: General management

giant. To aid supporters in their boycott efforts, the AFA produced materials listing what it maintained were Disney's anti-family practices. The organization also published a list of Disney's business holdings. Another AFA-sponsored boycott occurred in January of 1996 and focused on the Circle K convenience store chain since these stores were selling pornographic magazines.

CURRENT POLITICAL ISSUES

The AFA carries out its mission of restoring family values in the United States by focusing on what the organization considers key issues, such as pornography and homosexuality. The organization is concerned by material offered by the entertainment industry that AFA representatives feel violates biblical standards of decency. Of particular concern to the organization is the exploitation of children in pornography.

Case Study: Pornography at Barnes & Noble?

When Barnes & Noble bookstores across the country began selling books that featured nude photography collections of young children, the AFA and other like-minded groups were incensed. According to the AFA, the books in question—*Radiant Identities* and *The Last Day of Summer* by Jock Sturges; *Immediate Family* by Sally Mann; *The Age of Innocence* by David Hamilton— featured preteen girls in provocative poses, children of the same sex holding hands or embracing, and children touching their genitals. Though the books were expensively packaged and didn't look like typical pornographic offerings, the AFA claimed that the books exploited children and were, in fact, pornography.

The AFA asked its members to call local bookstores and request that the books be removed from store shelves. Other like-minded groups participated in the effort, including Operation Rescue National (which pickets in front of stores); the Middle Tennessee Coalition for the Protection of Children and Families, a small group that was one of the first to object to the books and to picket; and Loyal Opposition, which has organized protests across the nation. The organization also called for a boycott of Barnes & Noble bookstores for stocking what the organization considers child pornography. Barnes & Noble refused to pull the books from its shelves, claiming that they were not violating any laws, and while some might consider the works indecent, they were protected by the First Amendment of the Consitution.

The AFA's efforts met with mixed results. In 1997 and 1998 Barnes & Noble was indicted in Alabama and Tennessee respectively for violation of state pornography laws, but in other states, such as Kansas, prosecutors did not feel a case could be made against the bookseller. The indictments drew national attention, and some in the media talked of a landmark legal decision that would set readily enforceable guidelines differentiating art from pornography. Public interest in the issue declined rapidly, however. In May of 1998 the Tennessee case was settled out of court, and charges against Barnes & Noble were dropped. In return, the bookstore agreed to treat the books as "adult," meaning that they could still be sold at the store, but could only be displayed on racks at least five and a half feet tall, with no more than one third of their covers visible.

FUTURE DIRECTIONS

An area of growing concern to the AFA is the Internet, which may provide anybody with a computer and an on-line account access to pornography or sexual material. While conservative groups endeavor to control children's Internet access to pornography using such things as the on-line filters proposed in the Child Online Protection Act in 1998, groups concede that it is difficult to control a medium such as the Internet which grows at the rate of 4,000 sites per day. The AFA is examining the most effective way to reduce the pervasiveness of this particular form of pornography.

GROUP RESOURCES

The AFA maintains a Web site at http://www. afa.net. The site includes a discussion of current organization issues as well as an on-line version of the *AFA Journal* and a section aiding viewers who want to contact their representative. Other materials that can be ordered include anti-porn and sexual addiction posters. For more information abou the organization, contact the AFA by mail at American Family Association, Inc., PO Drawer 2440, Tupelo, MS, 38803; by phone at (601) 844-5036; or by fax at (601) 844-9176.

GROUP PUBLICATIONS

The AFA publishes the monthly *AFA Journal,* available to subscribers by contacting the organization directly or through its Web site at http://www.afa.net. The *Fight Back Book* is a publication that lists contact information and descriptions of all advertisers that sponsor prime-time TV. Other AFA publications include: *Homosexuality in America; Exposing the Myths, Public School Sex Education,* and *Anti-Christian Bias in America.* For more information on AFA publications, contact the organization by mail at American Family Association, Inc., PO Drawer 2440, Tupelo, MS 38803; by phone at (601) 844-5036; or by fax at (601) 842-7798.

BIBLIOGRAPHY

Coatney, Caryn. "When Toddlers Tune in to CNN, Should Parents Worry?" *Christian Science Monitor,* 18 February 1998.

"Conservative Groups Step Up Criticism of Disney." *Reuters Business Report,* 23 July 1997.

Farrell, James M. "The Indecency of Pornography." *University Wire,* 10 February 1998.

Frank, Ariel R. "Homosexuals Urged to Find 'Natural' Identity." *University Wire,* 14 October 1997.

Innerst, Carol. "Some Kindergartners Are Taught about Homosexuality." *Washington Times,* 7 December 1997.

McAllester, Matthew. "Netting Child Pornographers; As Web Smut Replaces Mail Porn, the Vice Squad Goes Online." *Newsday,* 11 February 1998.

Mieses, Stanley. "Singing for Satan vs. the Status Quo." *Newsday,* 30 October 1996.

Mosier, Andrew. "Colorado Churches Divided on Homosexuality Issue." *University Wire,* 27 February 1998.

American Farm Bureau Federation (AFBF)

ESTABLISHED: November 12, 1919
EMPLOYEES: 116
MEMBERS: 4.7 million families
PAC: Farm Bureau PACs are operated by state farm
    bureaus

Contact Information:

ADDRESS: 225 Touhy Ave.
    Park Ridge, IL 60068
PHONE: (847) 685-8600
FAX: (847) 685-8896
E-MAIL: joef@fb.com
URL: http://www.fb.com
PRESIDENT: Dean R. Kleckner

WHAT IS ITS MISSION?

The American Farm Bureau Federation (AFBF or simply "Farm Bureau") is a national affiliation of the more than 2,800 county farm bureaus in the United States. As such, it considers itself to be "the voice of agriculture at the national level." Through their participation in the AFBF, farmers work together to secure the benefits of this united effort—to make the business of farming more profitable; to make agricultural communities better places to live; and to maintain as much autonomy as possible in farming and ranching enterprises.

HOW IS IT STRUCTURED?

The programs and policies of the Farm Bureau begin at the local level, with the members of the county bureaus. County members vote on policies which are then sent to state bureaus, which in turn discuss and vote on the issues and ultimately send delegates to the national meeting of the AFBF. Once these national polices are established, putting them into action is the task of the board and officers of the national Farm Bureau organization.

The president, vice president, and members of the AFBF's board of directors are active farmers or ranchers who are elected at the annual meetings. The president is responsible for directing the daily operations of the Farm Bureau and for acting as the organization's national spokesperson. The board is made up of 22 state farm bureau presidents, who are elected to the board for two-year terms. Four national officers are appointed by the board: the administrator, who directs the staff; the treasurer; the secretary; and the general counsel. In addition to acting as the legal representative of the AFBF, the general counsel's office also serves the important function of pursuing agricultural policy issues in the courts and before government agencies. For example, the general counsel may lead the AFBF's legal challenge to regulations it considers unfair, or defend the labor practices in certain farming sectors.

The staff of the AFBF is generally divided between two offices: a general headquarters in Park Ridge, Illinois, and an office in Washington, D.C., which naturally focuses on government relations and public information. The Governmental Relations Division is staffed mostly by registered lobbyists who are specialists on agricultural issues, and who maintain daily contact with Congress and the regulatory agencies to advocate the interests of farmers and ranchers.

Much of the AFBF's mission is carried out by the Organization Division, which coordinates the bureau's membership activities and policy development process. This is the division which most directly reaches out to local farmers, and which coordinates and operates most of the Farm Bureau's educational and legislative programs. The Organization Division also coordinates national and regional meetings, and provides training for members and staff.

Another important office, the Public Policy Division, provides research, education, and policy support for the AFBF and state farm bureaus. This division is not so much involved in operating programs as in researching and analyzing information that might influence the way in which programs are carried out or policies are adopted.

The AFBF operates two affiliate organizations: the American Farm Bureau Research Foundation and the American Agricultural Insurance Company. The Research Foundation, financed by contributions from individual members and state and county bureaus, is a funding agency which supports private research on important agricultural issues such as pesticide use and livestock nutrient management. The American Agricultural Insurance Company is a reinsurance agency which provides added security to state Farm Bureau casualty and property insurance companies.

PRIMARY FUNCTIONS

The Farm Bureau's mission—making life and business better for farmers—is a simple one, but it involves several areas of operation. To keep its members equipped to take advantage of the increasing technological, economic and legislative changes influencing U.S. agriculture, the Farm Bureau seeks to educate and train its members in areas such as marketing, animal and plant breeding and nutrition, agricultural machinery, and care

FAST FACTS

From its peak of about 33 million in 1910, the U.S. farm population has declined to about 4.6 million people today.

(Source: American Farm Bureau Federation. "Farm Facts," 1999.)

of the environment. These efforts focus not only on practicing farmers, but also on young people in the farming community.

The Farm Bureau's legislative programs serve the overall objective of protecting farmers and ranchers from as many regulatory burdens as possible. Farm Bureau staff monitor pending legislation, consult with government representatives, and keep members informed about the content and probable impact of certain laws and regulations. The Farm Bureau usually publicizes its opinions about certain legislation, and in some cases it may present a legal challenge to laws or regulations which it considers to be unfair to farmers.

On occasion, the Farm Bureau may form a task force to look into certain issues. The organization conducts its own research and analysis on current issues, in order to provide timely support to its members, and it also funds private research on issues which have long-term implications for American farmers.

An important Farm Bureau function is the dissemination of information to its members and the public. AFBF provides news releases, commentaries and reports to newspapers and national and regional news organizations; it publishes background materials on agricultural issues; and it develops brochures and other materials for members and interested public citizens. One of the AFBF's most significant services to farmers is its effort to promote the two-way transfer of information between the national organization and individual farmers.

PROGRAMS

Although most Farm Bureau programs are operated at the local level, they are often variations or subsidiaries of initiatives formed at the national level. For example, most state farm bureaus carry out a program called Agriculture in the Classroom (AITC), as part of a nationwide

A dust storm approaches homes in Springfield, Colorado, during the "Dust Bowl" of the early 1930s. This storm engulfed the town for almost half an hour. (The Library of Congress)

program for educating school children—from kindergarten through 12th grade—about agriculture. Another AFBF education program, the I Care Program, is a nationally-organized effort to promote the understanding of how animals function in agriculture, and to promote their humane and ethical treatment on farms. I Care instructs young people in proper husbandry and showmanship practices, and then requires them to fill out a pledge card outlining their intention to treat their animals with respect and compassion.

Most state farm bureaus operate some kind of program for teaching farmers about the marketing of certain commodities. Market Master, AFBF's national marketing education program, provides the basic structure for many state programs. Many of the AFBF's educational programs target non-farmers. The Adopt-A-Scientist program, for example, is an effort to bring agricultural scientists face-to-face with the daily operations of a working farm. In bringing scientists on to farms, the AFBF seeks to provide those scientists who develop agricultural products—fertilizers, pesticides, and plant cultivars—with the information they need to better understand the population to whom these products are marketed.

The core of the AFBF's legislative initiative is the National Legislative Action Program (NLAP), a nationwide effort to focus and coordinate the Farm Bureau's bid to educate and influence the makers of national agriculture policy. Although the lobbyists of the Governmental Relations Division play a major role in this program,

NLAP relies heavily on local volunteers, who contact members of Congress and regulatory agencies about issues that concern them. Part of NLAP's success is this link between Congress and actual constituents.

One of the most exciting Farm Bureau programs is ACRES, a computerized marketing, news, and weather system available to Farm Bureau member-subscribers. For a fee, ACRES delivers information via satellite to a personal computer in the farmer's home. Another communications initiative, the Farm Bureau Advantage Skynet Satellite Network, provides a data link between the AFBF and state farm bureaus.

BUDGET INFORMATION

Not made available.

HISTORY

The move toward the local organization of farmers began in the early twentieth century, and these local units rapidly expanded to form state groups. In 1919, representatives from 30 states gathered in Chicago and founded the American Farm Bureau Federation, with a primary goal of promoting the economic welfare of commercial farmers. The Farm Bureau's first president was James R. Howard of Iowa, who was instrumental in bringing together farmers from all over the country to formulate a single coherent policy platform to present to the government and the American public.

Because of the structure of the farming industry at the time, the AFBF's early efforts focused on representing the interests of the small family farm. The AFBF initially favored government intervention on behalf of the farmer, especially after the troubles brought on by the Great Depression and the Dust Bowl crisis of the 1930s. After helping to form a powerful bipartisan bloc in Congress, the AFBF was instrumental in influencing the farm policies of President Franklin D. Roosevelt's New Deal Program. In particular, the AFBF helped formulate the landmark Agricultural Adjustment Act of 1933, which gave the federal government responsibility for administering direct economic assistance to farmers. The Agricultural Adjustment Administration, created by this legislation, established the state and county administrative structures used by most present-day farm programs.

Government programs proved effective in re-stabilizing an agricultural system that had been hit hard by a reduction in both supply and demand. The economic boom that occurred after World War II, however, created a new problem for American farmers—a production surplus. As prices fell, farmers who had relied on government support found themselves in trouble. The overproduction of certain commodities threatened to cause dramatic drops in farm income levels. The food needs of war-torn countries in Europe helped absorb some of the surplus, but oversupply continued to be a problem.

The AFBF responded by calling for more a more flexible system that imposed less government control over agricultural production. During the administration of President Dwight Eisenhower, the AFBF argued for a free market system, rather than continued federal subsidies that involved the control of production. Under agricultural secretary Ezra Taft Benson, the government began to lower its price supports, but the later administrations of Presidents John Kennedy and Lyndon Johnson reversed this trend, over the objections of the AFBF.

Government administrations throughout most of the 1970s, at the urging of the AFBF, began to move government policy in a different direction, not only relaxing government control but also attempting to expand agricultural exports—although neither of these efforts was as complete as the AFBF would have liked. The government still had far to go in adapting to the changed conditions of the world's agricultural markets.

The Farm Crisis and the Remaking of Government Agricultural Policy

Throughout the 1980s it was made clear that government policies were not enabling American farmers to compete in international markets. Due to a number of complex factors—including a surplus that caused

grain prices to fall and farmers to default on federal loans—the U.S. agricultural industry fell into what is now referred to as the Farm Crisis of the 1980s. Foreclosure was forced upon many families who had been farming the same land for generations. It was clear to the AFBF, if not other agricultural advocacy groups, that Depression-era policies would do little to help American farmers gain access in an increasingly competitive global market.

Federal legislation and trade agreements negotiated in the early 1990s gave farmers some relief and helped to secure greater access to international export markets. But many crippling farm policies remained in place. The main problem, according to the AFBF and other organizations, was that for 60 years the government s efforts had been focused on managing the supply of agricultural commodities, rather than allowing producers themselves to manage production.

For once, the government appeared to be listening. The Federal Agricultural Improvement and Reform (FAIR) Act of 1996, supported by the AFBF, did away with many of these policies. By allowing producers more flexibility in planting and the opportunity to respond to market signals, the law returned much of the management of agricultural production to the farm community. The FAIR Act replaced Depression-era price supports with fixed-payment Agricultural Market Transition Payments to farmers who were having difficulty adjusting to fewer regulations.

In early 1999, U.S. agriculture hit a rough spot which caused many farmers to call for a repeal of the FAIR Act and a return to the more certain price-support system. The decline of Asian economies, among other factors, was shrinking foreign agricultural markets, and farmers were reminded of the conditions that precipitated the farm crisis of the 1980s. The AFBF, however, publicly urged Congress to stay the course on the FAIR Act and to fulfill the promises made when the FAIR Act was passed—specifically, in exchange for the AFBF's support of the FAIR Act, Congress had agreed to look into farmers' concerns about trade issues affecting market development, regulatory reform, taxes, and risk management. While uncertain about the future of the international agricultural market, the AFBF was reluctant to return control of production to the federal government.

CURRENT POLITICAL ISSUES

Since the Depression era, farming has been the subject of much government involvement, and the range of issues that affect agriculture reflects this fact. Every year, it seems, the AFBF, as the largest farm organization in the country, publicizes its position on a number of issues, from taxation to exports to crop insurance. It also serves as a major force in debating regulations involving such things as environmental quality, food quality, labor and wage practices, and commodity marketing. Often, the Farm Bureau is able to work out a compromise with legislators on certain issues, presenting facts and figures suggesting that a certain law regulatory burden may be too costly to farmers. On rare occasions, the AFBF is able to mount a successful legal challenge to federal actions it considers to be unlawful, or at least unfair to farmers.

Case Study: The Short-Lived Reintroduction of the Yellowstone Wolves

In 1994 the U.S. Fish and Wildlife Service launched a plan to gradually reintroduce gray wolves—animals once native to Yellowstone Park but virtually extinct since the 1920s—into the park and a nearby wilderness area in central Idaho. The wolves were to be trapped from wild areas in Canada. Environmentalists and other proponents of the plan argued that it was the right thing to do, since sheep and cattle ranchers had in the past essentially exterminated gray wolves in these areas. The wolves were natural predators of the deer, elk, and moose populations which, without any natural controls, had reached an all-time high in Yellowstone.

Ranchers in the surrounding area were strongly opposed to the wolf-recovery program. There was no fence around these vast areas, they argued, and it was only a matter of time before the wolves strayed from the park or wilderness, killed sheep or livestock, and perhaps even spread diseases such as rabies or brucellosis. The government recognized this concern and allowed two important concessions: ranchers would be financially compensated for any livestock lost to wolves, and they would be allowed to shoot any tagged wolves (the small native wolf population was protected under the Endangered Species Act), which were actually caught in the act of preying on domestic animals.

But these assurances weren't enough for the ranchers. Before the wolf-recovery plan was under way, the AFBF, in conjunction with the state bureaus of Montana, Wyoming, and Idaho, filed a lawsuit seeking a temporary restraining order against the government's plan. The restraining order was denied by a Wyoming judge, and the first wolves were reintroduced in early 1995.

The wolves were welcomed by much of the American public, but not by many ranchers. By 1997, 12 of the immigrant wolves had been shot, and the Farm Bureau's lawsuit had taken a new turn. A federal district judge in Wyoming found the means by which the wolves had been reintroduced to be unlawful, and ordered the Department of the Interior, the parent agency of the Fish and Wildlife Service, to recapture and remove them from the region. The judge also, however, suspended the enforcement of this order until his decision could be appealed. By 1999, as the appeals process dragged on, immigrant wolves remained in and around Yellowstone and central Idaho.

FUTURE DIRECTIONS

In the coming years, the Farm Bureau's efforts will be focused primarily on the further expansion of exports into foreign agricultural markets. In his 1998 annual address, AFBF President Dean Kleckner pointed out that of the more than 30 bilateral and regional trade agreements operating in the Western Hemisphere, the United States is involved in only one, the North American Free Trade Agreement (NAFTA). "As we debate and deliberate on the merits of just talking with other nations," Kleckner argued, "European and Japanese competitors are signing sweetheart deals with our trading partners in South America." (AFBF press release, January 12, 1998) The AFBF pledges to pursue fast-track negotiating authority for the U.S. president—an authority that has recently been denied by a federal court—in order to speed the process of boosting agricultural exports.

The AFBF also intends to continue lobbying against what it perceives to be unfair burdens on American farmers. A particularly troubling problem in recent years, as land values in many regions of the United States have skyrocketed, is the estate tax levied against families who inherit the assets of deceased parent. Since 99 percent of U.S. farms are owned by individuals, families, or family-owned corporations, the estate tax, which can be as high as 55 percent, hits farmers particularly hard, in many cases forcing the heirs to sell off an entire farm just to meet their tax burden. The AFBF has supported Congress' effort to reduce the estate tax burden in recent years, and argues for the gradual elimination of this death tax.

GROUP RESOURCES

The Farm Bureau's award-winning site on the World Wide Web (http://www.fb.com) is probably the best place to start for information on the national organization. In addition to descriptions of the Farm Bureau's mission and basic functions, the site contains numerous position statements on agricultural issues; a collection of facts about American agriculture; links to other agriculture-related sites; and links to each of the state farm bureaus. For further information about the AFBF, contact the public relations office at (847) 685-8750.

GROUP PUBLICATIONS

In addition to numerous news releases and issue papers, many of which can be viewed on the AFBF's Web site, the AFBF publishes short information brochures such as *This is the Farm Bureau* and *Working for You*. AFBF's Information and Public Relations Division also releases two significant periodicals, *Executive News Watch*, a newsletter providing daily updates on important agricultural issues, and a weekly publication, the *Farm Bureau News*, which is intended to provide county and state leaders with updates on Farm Bureau activities. The Farm Bureau News can be reached by E-mail at fbnews@fb.com.

BIBLIOGRAPHY

Campbell, Christiana McFadyen. *The Farm Bureau and the New Deal: A Study of the Making of National Farm Policy, 1933-40.* Champaign, Ill.: University of Illinois Press, 1962.

Estrada, Richard T. "American Farm Bureau Official Attacks Global-Warming Talks." *Knight-Ridder/Tribune Business News,* 9 December 1997.

"Farm Groups Oppose Railroad Merger." *Los Angeles Times,* 25 May 1996.

Farm Policy: The Politics of Soil, Surpluses, and Subsidies. Washington, D.C.: Congressional Quarterly, 1984.

Howard, Robert P. *James R. Howard and the Farm Bureau.* Ames, Iowa: Iowa State University Press, 1983.

Klintberg, Patricia Peak. "Farm Bureau Backs Off Policies." *Farm Journal,* February 1999.

Middleton, Otesa. "Farms are Growing in Size, Shrinking in Number, According to Farm Bureau." *Knight-Ridder/Tribune Business News,* 4 December 1996.

Richardson, Valerie. "Waging War Over Wolves." *Insight on the News,* 11 January 1999.

Tarrant, John. *Farming and Food.* New York: Oxford University Press, 1991.

American Federation of Government Employees (AFGE)

ESTABLISHED: August 17, 1932
EMPLOYEES: Undetermined
MEMBERS: 600,000
PAC: AFGE-PAC

Contact Information:
ADDRESS: 80 F St. NW
    Washington, DC 20001
PHONE: (202) 737-8700
URL: http://www.afge.org
PRESIDENT: Bobby L. Harnage
WOMEN'S/FAIR PRACTICES DIRECTOR: Kitty Peddicord

WHAT IS ITS MISSION?

The object of the American Federation of Government Employees (AFGE), according to the organization's constitution, is "to promote the general welfare of government employees, promote efficiency, advance plans of improvement and promote the full participation of women and minorities in AFGE activities at all levels throughout the Federation." The AFGE holds itself responsible for ensuring fairness, due process, decent and safe working conditions, fair pay and voice on the job for government employees. It advocates creative and positive solutions to shape the government into a model employer. The union protects and expands those rights through legal representation by its general counsel's office, legislative advocacy, and a labor management department that provides technical expertise and informational services.

HOW IS IT STRUCTURED?

The AFGE is comprised of 12 regional district offices which provide support services to some 1,200 local chapters. Each district office is directed by a national vice president. The national vice presidents and the executive officers, such as the president, secretary-treasurer, and women's/fair practices director, make up the union's National Executive Council, the union's policy-making body. Agencywide bargaining councils and locals are the bodies that bargain collectively with the U.S. government.

The AFGE prides itself on representing diverse employee groups. Members include food inspectors,

nurses, printers, cartographers, lawyers, police officers, census workers, health and safety inspectors, janitors, truck drivers, secretaries, artists, plumbers, immigration inspectors, scientists, doctors, cowboys, botanists, park rangers, computer programmers, foreign service workers, airplane mechanics, environmentalists, writers, and many more.

The AFGE is a member of the American Federation of Labor-Congress of Industrial Organizations (AFL-CIO), and the AFGE president serves on the AFL-CIO executive council. The AFGE's secretary-treasurer and women's/fair practices director also play major roles in AFL-CIO departments and activities.

PRIMARY FUNCTIONS

As a union, the primary function of the AFGE is to secure good wages and working conditions for its members. The AFGE differs from most unions, however, in that all of its employees are employed by the federal government. Thus, the organization's bargaining is conducted under Title VII of the Civil Service Reform Act, and is subject to a number of restrictions and circumstances unique to government employees. For example, pay and benefits for federal employees are established by Congress through the legislative process, rather than by a company's management. Thus the union lobbies and testifies at length on issues relevant to its members and works collaboratively with government agencies to improve working conditions.

In part because of its limited bargaining capabilities, the AFGE coordinates a full-scale legislative and political action program to keep current on issues affecting its members, and influence government policy. For example, the union maintains a presence during congressional debates on issues such as federal employee health care or funding of government programs involving federal workers. On occasion, the AFGE mounts media campaigns or undertakes lawsuits to ensure the rights of its members.

PROGRAMS

The programs of the AFGE consist mainly of benefits for its members. These include: the Union Secured Credit Card for members with no credit history or a damaged credit history; the Union Member Mortgage and Real Estate Program with special rates for members; the Union Privilege Discount Pharmacy Program; and the Union Driver and Traveler Program. The Privileged Loan Program allows members to take out unsecured loans bearing low interest rates from the union. The union's Legal Services Program includes free consultations and document review, and a discount on further assistance if

BUDGET:
1996 AFGE Expenses

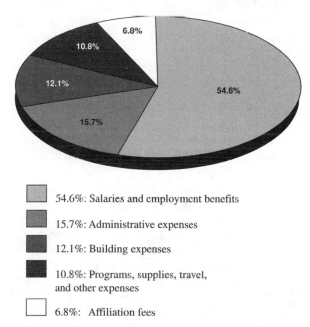

■ 54.6%: Salaries and employment benefits

■ 15.7%: Administrative expenses

■ 12.1%: Building expenses

■ 10.8%: Programs, supplies, travel, and other expenses

□ 6.8%: Affiliation fees

it proves necessary. The union also offers a dental plan, a college financing program, an auto club, and accidental death and dismemberment insurance.

BUDGET INFORMATION

More than 85 percent of AFGE revenue comes from membership dues. The other 14.5 percent comes from rental and other revenues. For 1996 total revenue was $26,143,327. Most was from dues ($21,881,147); the rest was income from death benefits, buildings and garages, interest, sale of supplies, sale of organizing materials, and miscellaneous sources.

Expenditures totaled $23,680,190 and were led by salaries and employment benefits ($12,919,967). Administrative expenses were $3,706,589, followed by building expenses ($2,863,086) and affiliation fees ($1,605,185). Organizing programs and supplies, travel, and other expenses comprised the remainder.

HISTORY

In December of 1931 the National Federation of Federal Employees (NFFE) split from the American

Federation of Labor (AFL) after a leadership conflict over the organization of skilled craft employees. Leaders who sided with the principles and objectives of the AFL formed the Joint Conference on Re-affiliation, which evolved into the American Federation of Government Employees.

Then-AFL president William Green appointed David Glass and Helen McCarty to head up the Joint Conference on Re-affiliation. Glass previously had tried to smooth over differences between NFFE defectors and those wanting to keep ties with the AFL. When that effort failed, the Joint Conference, which represented some 42 lodges, began planning an October founding convention for AFGE. Because so many of the fledgling union's leaders worked in Washington, D.C., the first AFGE office was established in rooms above a bank at 1700 Pennsylvania Avenue.

Several women served in important leadership positions in the union during its early history, making important contributions to the AFGE and paving the way for women to become involved elsewhere in the labor movement. At the AFGE's founding convention in 1932, 14 of the 42 delegates were women, and one, Esther Penn was chosen to serve as a vice president. Helen McCarty became the union's head of organizing activities and led a highly successful membership campaign in the union's early days.

During the Great Depression of the 1930s, the AFGE fought, often unsuccessfully, to protect its member's wages and privileges. In those hard times, forcing government employees into retirement and limiting their pay were easy ways to cut government costs. At the same time, the passage of the Hatch Act strictly limited the ability of government employees to collectively protest against poor working conditions, either through the political process or the traditional weapon of unions, strikes and other work stoppages. The ground-breaking labor legislation of the period, such as the Wagner Act and the Taft-Hartley Act, largely excluded government employees.

As the U.S. economy recovered during World War II (1939–45) private-sector workers saw significant growth in their incomes. While the number of government employees began to increase, their wages remained frozen, resulting in a 15 percent disparity between government- and private-sector wages by the war's end. AFGE lobbying efforts kept the issue before Congress throughout the war, and in 1945 federal employees were granted a 15.9 percent pay raise.

In the 1950s the AFGE began to consolidate after the troubled times of the Depression and World War II. Membership rose steadily throughout the decade from 61,000 to 83,000. AFGE efforts in Congress helped win liberalized retirement benefits, further improvements in the government's payroll system, and federal aid for employee health insurance. In 1962 President John F. Kennedy issued Executive Order 10988, establishing a system under which federal agencies were required to work with the AFGE (or other unions representing government workers) to establish the agencies's working conditions. The union engaged in a massive organizing campaign and by 1972 its membership had soared to 310,000 government employees.

The 1970s were a difficult time for the AFGE due to a poor economy and changes in government philosophy. Many believed that the federal government had grown too large, and throughout the 1970s and 1980s the AFGE lost members due to cuts in government spending. It also saw many jobs formerly filled by government employees contracted out to private businesses. Many more would have been contracted out if not for the AFGE's lobbying efforts in Congress and successful use of the courts to prevent unwarranted elimination of federal jobs. One major gain for the union in the 1970s was the Civil Service Reform Act of 1978. This act expanded the ability of federal workers to organize and collectively bargain with government agencies, and established the Federal Labor Relations Board to govern the relationship between the government and its employees.

During the 1980s the AFGE was hampered by some of the programs enacted by the administration of President Ronald Reagan. For example, 3.5 percent pay raises were imposed at the top of the scale while wages at the bottom were frozen completely. Blue-collar pay became tied to white-collar levels. According to AFGE figures, by 1981 federal employee pay was nearly 26 percent less than in the private sector. The AFGE was, for a time, unable to convince the government to raise wages, and in 1985, federal workers were forced to take a complete pay freeze. The Reagan administration's "War on Drugs" affected the organization in September 1986 by forcing many of its employees to be randomly tested for illegal drug use. Testing continued despite several lawsuits challenging its constitutionality.

The 1990s saw a successful resolution of several long-standing AFGE concerns. In 1991 the passage of the Federal Employees Pay Comparability Act made government pay more in balance with that of non-government workers. Two years later the AFGE rejoiced at the passage of the Hatch Reform Act. With these reforms, restrictions on government employee participation in the political process were lifted after more than 50 years of AFGE opposition. Two years later, however, the AFGE mourned the loss of dozens of members in the bombing of the Alfred P. Murrah Federal Building in Oklahoma City, Oklahoma. In response, the union raised hundreds of thousands of dollars to aid the survivors. This fund would evolve into AFGE's permanent disaster relief fund.

In 1994 the Republican party gained control of Congress. The resulting disputes between Congress and President Bill Clinton, a Democrat, over government budgets and spending policies led to two government shutdowns in 1995. Most government employees were unable to work, while others serving in critical jobs, such as hospital employees, were forced to work without any guarantee they would be paid. Over 50 work days were lost during the two shutdowns, and their impact continued to be felt in 1996 as government workers struggled to catch up with the work that had accumulated in their absence.

CURRENT POLITICAL ISSUES

The AFGE has a particularly strong and active political program due to the fact that such things as pay rates, raises, retirement benefits, and health care benefits for federal employees are all determined by Congress through legislation. Thus, the organization works closely with Congress and the president to protect and enhance the rights of government workers. Union representatives meet with legislators, give testimony to Congress, and provide informational materials on issues to politicians. The AFGE also provides information on issues to members and encourages them to contact lawmakers directly. The president of the AFGE is also a member of the National Partnership Council established by President Clinton to help streamline aspects of the federal government that have grown overly bureaucratic. The AFGE president's participation ensures that the rights and roles of government workers are protected in any government reorganization plans.

As a member of the AFL-CIO, the AFGE also participates in efforts to inform legislators on issues affecting all workers. Such issues have included raising the minimum wage and increasing workplace safety. The future of the Social Security system became a top priority for both the AFL-CIO and the AFGE in the late 1990s.

Case Study: *Reform of the Social Security System*

The U.S. Social Security System is a federal program that provides financial support to retired workers and to the spouses and minor children of deceased workers. Social security funds accumulate through deductions taken from the pay checks of current workers. In 1955 there were 8.6 workers paying into the fund for every one recipient. By 1995 there were only 3.3 workers per recipient. As large numbers of Baby Boomers begin to retire the number of workers contributing to the fund will further decrease, shifting the ration of contributors to recipients. Most experts claim that if things remain as they are, more money will be paid out in benefits than will be coming into the system from taxes. As the point when the number of retirees exceeds the number of workers paying into the social security system comes closer, legislators and workers alike have made fixing the system an important priority.

Since the creation of the program, social security funds have been invested in government bonds. Government bonds are an extremely safe investment, but they do not pay much interest. Some people believed that investing social security funds in the stock market, which posted a higher return on investments than bonds for much of the twentieth century, would increase the funds available for payout. During the 1990s, as the need to reform the social security system became obvious, many people proposed that social security taxes be invested in stocks rather than bonds. Supporters of this proposal even suggested forming private retirement accounts wherein workers could invest all, or a portion, of their social security taxes in the stocks of their choice.

In many ways these stock market and privatization plans were more attractive than other suggestions for saving the social security system. Unlike the proposal for raising the age at which retirees could receive benefits, increasing social security taxes, or decreasing benefits paid out to recipients, the stock market plans claimed that the social security system could be stabilized and maintained without reducing benefits or increasing the cost to taxpayers.

Both the AFL-CIO and the AFGE strongly opposed these proposed solutions to the Social Security problem. The AFGE represents many retirees and soon-to-be retirees who do not want more of their benefits taxed or do not want to have to wait several years longer to begin collecting social security benefits, respectively. The AFGE also rejects the proposal that social security funds be invested in the stock market. Stocks can, and often do, lose money for their investors, and while the stock market has historically performed better than government bonds, there is no guarantee that this would continue. The union has maintained that, as a guaranteed benefit, social security should not be left to chance.

The AFGE supports other ways to resolve the social security issue. These include using surplus government monies to increase social security coffers and raising the cap on the amount of workers' pay subject to social security tax. The federal government was predicted to have budget surpluses totaling over $4 trillion between 2000 and 2014. The AFL-CIO estimated that contributing two-thirds of these surplus funds to social security would ensure that benefits could be paid through 2049. Under the existing system, only the first $72,600 a person earns is taxed for social security. The AFGE feels that this limit should be removed, or raised considerably, as a way of raising additional revenues for the Social Security system.

While many groups discussed possible solutions to the social security problem there were no concrete proposals for government action until President Clinton's State of the Union address in January of 1999. Clinton proposed that most of the budget surplus over the next 15 years be put into social security and that 15 percent of the fund be invested in the stock market. The president's plan was sent to Congress for consideration.

In response, the AFGE joined with other unions and sent a letter to every member of Congress in March of 1999. In the letter the AFGE praised the president for committing budget surpluses to Social Security, but objected to the government investing any funds in the stock market. The AFGE expressed its concerns that investing in the stock market was too risky, that continued economic growth was not a certainty, and that such investments would require that money be paid up front, which could hurt other government programs.

Public Impact

The debate over how to fix the social security system did not end with the president's proposal. Congress was given the task of debating the issue and devising legislation the president would agree to sign. The AFGE and other interested parties planned to continue lobbying lawmakers to draft legislation acceptable to their membership. The impact on the public remains to be seen. Either the system will be repaired or it will continue to be problematic and in danger of failure. Currently, millions of Americans are receiving social security benefits. The benefits of future recipients are at the mercy of politics and unpredictable economic events.

FUTURE DIRECTIONS

One of the AFGE's greatest challenges over the 1980s and 1990s—the loss of federal jobs to the private sector—seems likely to continue. The union will oppose efforts, such as 1998's Freedom from Government Competition Act, to transfer duties from the federal government to private industry through contracting and outsourcing. Not only do such transfers cost some union members their jobs, but the AFGE believes that private industry often provides lower-quality service than government-run operations. At the same time that the AFGE opposes these transfers, however, it will work to ensure that federal employees meet the same productivity standards as private-sector employees.

GROUP RESOURCES

The AFGE maintains a Web site at http://www.afge.org that carries historical and organizational information, along with links for members to various benefits and services. The site also contains news releases and on-line versions of several union publications. For more information on the AFGE, contact the organization by mail at American Federation of Government Employees, 80 F Street NW, Washington, DC 20001; or by phone at (202) 737- 8700.

GROUP PUBLICATIONS

The AFGE publishes two monthly newsletters, the *AFGE Bulletin* and the *Government Standard*, as well as the *AFGE NetWorker* and *An Equal Voice*. Many AFGE publications can be accessed on the organization's Web site, at http://www.afge.org/pubs1/pubs.htm. For more information on AFGE publications, contact the organization by mail at American Federation of Government Employees, 80 F Street NW, Washington, DC 20001; or by phone at (202) 737-8700.

BIBLIOGRAPHY

Eddings, Jerelyn. "The Human Face of Bureaucrats." *U.S. News and World Report*, 15 January 1996.

Gleckman, Howard, and Mike McNamee. "Advantage Clinton." *Business Week*, 1 February 1999.

Greenhouse, Linda. "Court Loosens Muzzle on Government Workers." *New York Times*, 23 February 1995.

Novack, Janet. "Antifreeze." *Forbes*, 12 April 1993.

Stevenson, Richard W. "Clinton Social Security Plan Runs into Opposition." *New York Times*, 20 January 1999.

Wayne, Leslie. "For Interest Groups, Battle Lines Form in Debate over Social Security." *New York Times,* 30 December 1996.

Weiner, Tim. "The Men in the Grey Federal Bureaucracy." *New York Times*, 10 April 1994.

American Federation of Labor-Congress of Industrial Organizations (AFL-CIO)

WHAT IS ITS MISSION?

According to its Web site, the mission of the American Federation of Labor-Congress of Industrial Organizations (AFL-CIO) is "to improve the lives of working families—to bring economic justice to the workplace and social justice to our nation." In representing workers' interests before both the government and the public at large, the AFL-CIO seeks to lead and coordinate the activities of its affiliated unions in political action, organizing new members and bargaining with employers.

HOW IS IT STRUCTURED?

The AFL-CIO is a federation of 78 national unions and 12 international unions; union members typically belong to one of over 35,000 local unions affiliated with a national union member. Some of the largest unions affiliated with the AFL-CIO include the American Federation of State, County, and Municipal Workers, the Service Employees International Union, and the International Brotherhood of Teamsters. The national unions are, in turn, often affiliated according to trade with one of nine AFL-CIO departments: Building and Construction Trades, Food and Allied Service Trades, Professional Employees, Industrial Union, Maritime Trades, Metal Trades, Public Employees, Transportation Trades, or Union Label and Service Trades.

In addition to the local chapters and their national unions, the AFL-CIO also comprises 51 state organizations and approximately 626 local central bodies. The 51 state organizations—which include Puerto Rico—are

ESTABLISHED: December 5, 1955
EMPLOYEES: 300
MEMBERS: 13,600,000
PAC: AFL-CIO Committee on Political Education (COPE)

Contact Information:

ADDRESS: 815 16th St. NW
Washington, DC 20006
PHONE: (202) 637-5000
FAX: (202) 637-5058
URL: http://www.aflcio.org
PRESIDENT: John J. Sweeney
SECRETARY-TREASURER: Richard L. Trumka
EXECUTIVE VICE PRESIDENT: Linda Chavez-
Thompson

composed of different local unions, while local central bodies, or central labor councils, are composed of representatives of unions in a particular community. Central bodies provide the means through which the AFL-CIO handles local, day-to-day business.

The AFL-CIO is headed by an executive council, which includes a president, secretary-treasurer, executive vice president, and 51 vice presidents. The council sets the overall AFL-CIO policy.

PRIMARY FUNCTIONS

While the AFL-CIO does not have direct authority over the activities of its affiliated unions, affiliates generally let the federation take the lead in setting and pursuing organized labor's political agenda. The AFL-CIO's main purpose is and has always been improving workers' wages and benefits. While AFL-CIO-affiliated unions historically used strikes and work stoppages as a primary means of obtaining demands, by the 1980s and 1990s the unions had greatly increased their reliance on congressional lobbying and media relations to further their interests.

The AFL-CIO considers advancing pro-labor legislation to be one of its primary objectives. In 1996 it spent over $35 million supporting congressional candidates who pledged to back pro-labor legislation. Like most public interest groups, the AFL-CIO attempts to influence congressional voting and legislation through a wide variety of activities, including letter writing, lobbying, leafleting, telemarketing, and organizing issue-education programs. Though officially non-partisan, the AFL-CIO traditionally supports Democrats and Democratic initiatives.

In addition to its lobbying efforts, the AFL-CIO organizes boycotts and negative publicity campaigns against corporations and industries it accuses of unfair labor practices. Its Union Label and Service Trades department regularly publishes a list of national boycotts the federation endorses and routinely identifies industries resistant to unionization. While boycotts are often instituted and conducted by specific unions against local employers, to garner official AFL-CIO endorsement they must meet guidelines established by the Executive Council. During boycotts, members of all AFL-CIO affiliated unions are advised of the boycott and encouraged to avoid supporting or patronizing the company in question, while local unions in the employer's area will often picket, distribute leaflets, or hold news conferences promoting the boycott.

PROGRAMS

In additional to the AFL-CIO's extensive political operation it operates several programs designed to strengthen the labor movement, further the interests of workers, reach out to segments of the work force such as women and minorities, and improve organized labor's public image.

Although the federation has historically left the task of organizing up to individual unions, by the early 1990s the AFL-CIO had launched two major programs designed to help affiliated unions reverse the long decline in labor union membership. In 1989 the federation created the Organizing Institute to educate and train union leaders and organizers. In an effort to recruit skilled organizers among rank-and-file union members and community activists, the institute offers intensive, three-day workshops around the country and places graduates in apprenticeships. Paid a modest stipend for living expenses, the apprentices assist in local organizing campaigns and help workers organize unions at their workplaces. Roughly 90 percent of program graduates are eventually offered fulltime jobs with affiliated unions. In an effort to attract young organizers and rebuild interest in social and economic justice on U.S. college campuses, the AFL-CIO launched the first Union Summer program in June of 1996. A 25-day educational internship aimed at college students selected from around the country, program interns are paid a small stipend to help organize drives, educate the public on labor issues, organize picket lines and boycotts, stage demonstrations, and help build coalitions between labor and community organizations. Senior Summer, a similar program for senior citizens that was designed to take advantage of the skill and experience of retired union members, was launched in 1997.

The AFL-CIO makes an effort to reach out to women workers who have historically been marginalized in the labor movement, through its Working Women Department. The federation encourages unions to organize such woman-dominated fields as teaching and health care. Through a survey of women workers titled "Ask a Working Woman," the AFL-CIO has also developed an agenda of issues of particular concern to working women, among them quality child and elder care, family leave, flexible work hours, and equal pay for work of equal skill level. As part of this outreach effort the AFL-CIO has publicized the problem of comparable worth by encouraging women to visit the Web site at www.aflcio.org/women, plug in information about their job and education, and find out how much they lose over a lifetime because they are paid less than men.

In an effort to improve public opinion of organized labor and make the climate more hospitable to union organizing and political success, the AFL-CIO launched a "repositioning" campaign in 1997. The campaign included pilot projects in selected cities consisting of paid and free media coverage, speaker appearances, and community outreach. In the same year the federation introduced a more broad-based community outreach program, Union Cities, designed to rebuild the labor movement at the grassroots and mobilize one percent of all union members as activists. By August of that year over 100 central labor councils earned the title of "union cities" after pledging to mobilize members to participate in "Street Heat" activities wherein teams respond to unionizing-related firings within 24 hours by organizing rallies. These councils also agree to encourage the organization of new workers, sponsor economics education, and endorse diversity in union leadership.

BUDGET INFORMATION

The 1996 budget of $118 million reflected a significant increase over the roughly $70 million budgeted for previous years due to new organizing initiatives and the AFL-CIO pledge to spend $35 million on its "Labor '96" election activities. The AFL-CIO's primary income comes from per capita dues paid by affiliated unions on behalf of their members. It also earns a small income from investments and the sale of publications, supplies, and services. The additional spending in 1996 was funded by a special assessment of 15 cents per member per month for the year, the use of sums held in a reserve fund, and the liquidation of some investments.

A large percentage of the organization's budget goes to salaries and administrative expenses. Other significant expenses include roughly $14 million for "field mobilization"—including grassroots lobbying and political action—over $12 million for political education, over $8 million for organizing, and over $6 million for public affairs.

HISTORY

The AFL-CIO was formed in 1955 due to the merger of the American Federation of Labor (AFL) and the Congress of Industrial Organizations (CIO). The AFL, the older of the two, was formed in 1886 and soon emerged as the major national federation of organized U.S. labor. AFL president Samuel Gompers guided the fledgling federation using the principal of "pure and simple" trade unionism in which the AFL—unlike European labor movements or earlier U.S. movements—would limit its participation in politics and focus on improving workers' conditions through pressure on employers. Although the AFL supported legislation outlawing child labor it opposed proposals restricting the maximum hours in a work week and instituting a minimum wage. Although challenged by some in the labor movement, Gompers's vision of trade unionism dominated until the Great Depression struck in the 1930s.

The AFL Splinters

In 1935 Congress, with the support of Democratic President Franklin Roosevelt, passed the National Labor Relations Act (NLRA) which legally guaranteed workers' rights to organize in unions. It also set up the National Labor Relations Board (NLRB) to handle disputes between unions and employers over organizing and labor law violations. From its formation the AFL had organized workers by craft rather than by industry, and tended to emphasize the unionization of skilled workers. The legions of unskilled or low-skilled factory workers to emerge in the late nineteenth and early twentieth centuries were considered too difficult to organize. The passage of the NLRA, however, presented a new opportunity to organize these workers.

The 1935 AFL convention became a battleground between dissidents wishing to launch major organizing drives of industrial workers and the conservative and traditional AFL leadership. The dissidents soon broke away to form a rival labor federation, the CIO. The CIO differed from the AFL in its dedication to the organization of unskilled factory workers along industrial lines such as steel and auto manufacturing, and its commitment to liberal political activism. A large contributor to Roosevelt's re-election campaign in 1936, the CIO was a key supporter of many of his New Deal legislative initiatives such as the Fair Labor Standards Act, which established a standard work week, overtime pay, and a minimum wage.

The Turbulent 1940s and 1950s

The 1940s and 1950s were a stormy time for organized labor. The unions affiliated with the AFL and the CIO locked in bitter competition with each other over the organization of new workers. Both federations grew considerably as a result of the economic growth associated with World War II (1939–45). However, a post-war wave of strikes resulted in conservative political attacks against the newly powerful unions, and restrictive labor laws were passed at both the state and national level, one of which was the Taft-Hartley Act. The new government role in labor-management relations, as well as the nation's turn toward more conservative politics, caused the AFL to shed its distaste for political action and become more liberal.

In 1952 the AFL made its first presidential endorsement supporting unsuccessful Democratic candidate Adlai Stevenson. It also began cooperating with the CIO in politics. AFL leader George Meany and CIO leader Walter Reuther came to see the merger of their respective organizations as the key to both reversing the attacks on organized labor and promoting liberal legislation. In 1955 the two unions merged and Meany was named president. The new unity of the labor movement was short lived, however; during the 1957 AFL-CIO convention a vote was taken to oust one of the largest unions, the International Brotherhood of Teamsters, for corruption. The vote was not enough to forestall a highly publicized congressional investigation into trade-union corruption that led to the 1959 passage, over the AFL-CIO's strong objections, of the Landrum-Griffin Act, further regulating internal union affairs.

The Law Withdraws

The 1960s saw a rise in political influence of the AFL-CIO. The federation supported Democrat John F. Kennedy's election as president in 1960 and retained significant leverage during the Kennedy administration. The union developed its Committee on Political Education (COPE), which made contributions to candidates and mobilized union members and other Democratic constituencies such as minorities and the elderly on election day. Although the AFL-CIO failed to win repeal of the Taft-Hartley Act, the federation played a central role in passing Johnson's "Great Society" initiatives, which included civil rights legislation, increased federal funding for housing and education, consumer protection legislation, anti-poverty programs, and Medicare and Medicaid.

As the 1960s came to a close, issues associated with the Vietnam War (1959–75) and the social movements of the decade divided the labor movement just as they divided the nation. Reuther, now president of the United Auto Workers (UAW), publicly criticized the AFL-CIO's diehard support of the nation's involvement in Vietnam, its lack of commitment to unionizing more workers, and its failure to keep in touch with the interests and concerns of rank-and-file union members and economically disadvantaged groups. In 1968 Reuther withdrew the UAW, then the largest union in the federation, from the AFL-CIO.

When Meany convinced AFL-CIO leadership not to endorse 1972 Democratic presidential nominee George McGovern because of McGovern's pledge to end the war, Reuther assembled a labor coalition to campaign for McGovern that included the UAW, the National Education Association (NEA), and liberal AFL-CIO-affiliated unions such as the American Federation of State, County, and Municipal Workers (AFSCMW). However, for the first time since the start of election polling in the 1940s, the Democratic presidential candidate received less than 50 percent of the votes of union members and Republican President Richard Nixon easily won reelection.

Challenges in the 1970s and 1980s

Organized labor faced a number of challenges in the 1970s and 1980s. Labor union membership as a percentage of the entire work force declined slowly, from roughly a third of all workers in the mid-1950s to roughly a quarter of all workers by the late 1970s, although the number of union members continued to increase during this period. By the 1980s the absolute number of union members began to decline as well, falling from over 23 million in 1978 to under 17 million in 1989. AFL-CIO-affiliated United Steel Workers lost over half its membership. Unionized U.S. industries faced increasing competition from overseas and many companies began to move production to Third World countries where wages are a fraction of those paid nationally. Faced with a loss of bargaining power, unions accepted significant wage

and benefit cutbacks. Politically organized labor did not fare much better. Conservative Republican Ronald Reagan was elected in 1980 and most of his political agenda, including social spending cutbacks, deregulation, and tax cuts for upper income groups, was strongly opposed by the AFL-CIO.

In ill health, Meany retired in 1979 and Lane Kirkland became president. The change in union leadership, as well as the political attack on unions launched by Reagan and congressional Republicans, encouraged renewed unity in the labor movement. The UAW reaffiliated in 1981, the Teamsters returned in 1987, and the United Mine Workers affiliated in 1989. By the end of the 1980s the NEA was the only major union outside the federation. The AFL-CIO sought to strengthen its influence in Congress and better coordinate the lobbying efforts of its affiliated unions. Although many political pundits had declared labor dead as a political force by the early 1980s, by the decade's close, particularly after the Republicans lost control of the Senate in 1986, labor again enjoyed considerable influence in Congress. In a major victory, the AFL-CIO secured passage of a bill requiring employers to give workers 60 days' advance notification of plant closings.

The Sweeney Years

The AFL-CIO had mixed success in politics in the 1990s. While it supported the candidacy of Democrat Bill Clinton in 1992 and 1996, Clinton would go on to engineer the passage of the North American Free Trade Agreement (NAFTA), which opened up trade between the United States, Canada, and Mexico. Organized labor lobbied heavily against the measure, which was viewed as encouraging manufacturers to move to low-wage Mexico. While this led to initial bad blood between the AFL-CIO and the Clinton administration, that relationship was patched up prior to the ultimately unsuccessful 1993 legislative battle over Clinton's plan to provide health care to all Americans, a plan that labor supported. The election of a Republican majority to the House of Representatives in 1994 for the first time in forty years came as one of the most devastating political blows to the AFL-CIO in recent history. Many newly elected Republicans challenged the programs labor had fought for since the New Deal; talk centered around abolishing the minimum wage, cutting back social programs, and reducing occupational health and safety protections.

Declining union membership and economic strength combined with political defeats such as the passage of NAFTA and the 1994 election results sent ripples of discontent throughout the labor movement, resulting in the first contested election for the presidency of the AFL-CIO in the federation's history. Responding to intense criticism Kirkland retired. Dissidents in the federation coalesced behind the candidacy of Service Employees International Union president John Sweeney, who won the office after a heated campaign. Sweeney pledged that

BIOGRAPHY:
Samuel Gompers

Labor Leader (1850–1924)   During a time when the industrial revolution was transforming the political, social, and economic landscapes of the United States, Samuel Gompers emerged to become one of the most influential labor leaders in history. Weaned on trade union ideals from the time he was a young apprentice cigar maker, Gompers's interest in the welfare of skilled and unskilled workers was undying. In the early 1880s, Gompers lobbied hard for laws that would abolish the tenement sweatshops that were springing up in New York City. At the age of 37, Gompers was instrumental in creating the American Federation of Labor (AF of L) and went on to lead the organization as its president for the remaining 38 years of his life. The AF of L's support of President Woodrow Wilson resulted in the creation of the Department of Labor and passage of important pro-labor legislation. In 1917 President Wilson appointed Gompers to the National War Labor Board. From this position, Gompers negotiated improved work-

ing conditions and relaxed resistance to labor unions. Although great strides were made during World War I (1914–18), they were short-lived. At the time of Gompers's death, anti-union businesses, newspapers, and politicians had painted union ideology with broad, red, socialist strokes that transformed post-war patriotism into strong anti-union sentiment. It is his enduring legacy that the labor federation he so carefully constructed was able to weather this hostile climate for a decade. Only then did the the federal government, under President Franklin Roosevelt, pass legislation with lasting protections for the rights of unions and workers.

---

the federation would take a greater role in organizing new workers into unions and resolved he would reverse the decline in labor's political influence putting economic and social justice back on the agenda. He also promised to strengthen AFL-CIO ties to other liberal groups at the national and local level, including minority, civic, and religious organizations and to put renewed emphasis on organizing low-skilled service sector workers, minorities, and women.

In 1996 the AFL-CIO devoted itself to electing a labor-friendly Congress, spending over $35 million supporting Democratic candidates. While the Republican majority prevailed, their numbers were weakened. The AFL-CIO again placed significant emphasis on electing a labor-friendly Congress in 1998, but with a changed strategy. Rather than spending massive amounts on advertising, the federation and affiliated unions focused on grassroots mobilization and voter education. Labor union members represented 22 percent of the electorate in 1998, as opposed to 14 percent in 1994, and over 70 percent voted for Democrats. Organized labor was credited with significantly helping to reduce the Republican majority to just six seats in the House and with contributing to a number of high-profile Senate wins. The year 1998 also produced the first year of growth in union membership since the 1970s. Membership grew by 100,000 to 16.2 million workers although labor union members as a percentage of the total labor force continued to decline from 14.1 to 13.9 percent.

CURRENT POLITICAL ISSUES

The AFL-CIO has been an adamant supporter of social insurance programs that benefit middle class workers, such as Social Security, Medicare, and subsidized student loans. It also supports programs that benefit the poor, such as public assistance, public housing, and free or reduced-rate school lunches. A long-time supporter of civil rights, it continues to lobby in defense of affirmative action. The AFL-CIO has also been a major proponent of reforms in the health-care system that would offer access to more citizens and improve the quality of care.

The AFL-CIO lobbies for measures such as worker education and training, occupational health and safety regulations, comparable worth legislation ensuring that women are paid the same as men, increases in the minimum wage, regulations to secure pension funds and health care, and laws protecting workers' ability to form and join unions. Because the AFL-CIO represents a wide range of workers—from college professors to electricians to janitors—it lobbies on a variety of issues specific to certain sectors of the work force, such as legislation to restrict the imports of steel or the use of public money to fund private education.

The AFL-CIO also lobbies against measures that threaten its right to participate in politics. Although claiming to support campaign finance reform, the AFL-CIO has repeatedly fought against measures that would

FAST FACTS

According to the U.S. Department of Labor and the U.S. Bureau of Labor Statistics, in 1956 the percentage of workers who belonged to a union peaked at 35 percent and steadily decreased to 14.5 percent by 1996.

(Source: *Nation's Business*, June 1997.)

restrict union PAC activities. It has also fought state proposals such as Proposition 226 in California that would have placed new restrictions on the use of union dues in politics.

Case Study: Proposition 226

Organized labor's aggressive participation in the 1996 elections supporting Democratic congressional candidates—including the AFL-CIO's decision to spend a record $35 million largely on radio and television advertising attacking conservative Republicans—created a backlash. After the Republican Congress failed to pass legislation reining in union participation in politics, conservative forces moved to the state level. One of the most threatening measures was California's Proposition 226. A referendum presented to the voters in the June 1998 primary required that union members provide annual, written authorization for the use of any of their dues money for politics. The effort, started by three disgruntled men who had lost school board races against candidates supported by teachers' unions, quickly attracted support from groups such as the Americans for Tax Reform and the National Rifle Association. It was also backed by national political leaders such as then-Speaker of the House Newt Gingrich and California governor Pete Wilson. Proponents of the initiative called it the "paycheck protection" act and argued it was unfair for union leaders to use dues money without members' permission to help political candidates or policies that members may or may not support.

The AFL-CIO and its California affiliates saw the bill as a major attack on labor's right to participate in the electoral process. The AFL-CIO sent staff to support the California AFL-CIO chapter as well as a host of California and Washington political consultants in directing the anti-Proposition 226 effort. They organized the participation of hundreds of AFL-CIO-affiliated locals and the non-affiliated California Teachers Association, a longtime foe of Governor Wilson.

AFL-CIO supporters gathered signatures for another initiative that would have restricted corporate spending on political campaigns. They agreed not to put this measure on the ballot as long as larger businesses and corporate executives agreed to remain neutral on Proposition 226 and not provide financial support to its backers. As a consequence, opponents of Proposition 226 outspent supporters by as much as three to one in television advertising, running ads claiming that if labor's lobbying was restricted the measure would have the effect of hurting education, undermining patients' rights legislation, weakening Medicare, and sending jobs overseas. Because of the wording of Proposition 226, opponents argued it might even hurt charities by making it difficult for organizations such as United Way to arrange for automatic deductions from voluntary contributors' paychecks.

Supporters of Proposition 226 put it on the primary rather than the general election ballot because voter turnout is typically much lower for primaries, and they assumed that labor unions would have a harder time mobilizing their members. However, thousands of union members became active in the grassroots battle against the initiative. According to AFL-CIO President Sweeney, union activists canvassed over 5,000 voting precincts, visited more than 18,000 work sites to educate employees, and made over 650,000 phone calls to union households to turn out the vote. The campaign against Proposition 226 worked. Although early polls had shown strong support for the proposition, even among union members, by election day opinions had turned against it. The measure failed with union members voting against it by a 71 to 29 percent margin.

FUTURE DIRECTIONS

Building on its success in the 1998 congressional elections, the AFL-CIO announced by 1999 that it planned to spend over $40 million on the 2000 elections during the two-year period preceding election day. The money would come from a special assessment on affiliated unions of $1 per member per year for two years and would not go to candidates or the parties but would be used for grassroots mobilization such as distribution of political literature, phone banks, and voter registration. While the AFL-CIO hoped to return the Congress to Democratic control, it again announced its intention to support moderate, pro-labor Republicans in an effort to strengthen that element within the party. The AFL-CIO, imitating a tactic of the Christian Coalition, also encouraged union members to run for political office and set a goal of putting 2,000 unionists on the ballot in 2000.

GROUP RESOURCES

The AFL-CIO provides a wide variety of information on its current activities and on pending legislative issues, most of which is available on-line through the organization's Web page at http://www.aflcio.org. These resources include an Economic Research Library with articles and statistics of interest to working families; a list of press releases and editorials by the organization; a list of national boycotts sanctioned by the AFL-CIO; and Executive Paywatch, a web program allowing users to compare their salaries with those of corporate CEO's. Executive Paywatch can be accessed directly at http://www.paywatch.org.

GROUP PUBLICATIONS

The AFL-CIO has one publication it issues to subscribing members, *America@Work.* Published monthly, the magazine is aimed at leadership officers and activists of local unions and offers articles and information on building coalitions, organizing, and motivating union members. While geared toward a select audience, the magazine can be ordered by calling the AFL-CIO's Public Affairs Department at (202) 637-5340. In addition, the George Meany Institute publishes the *Labor Heritage Quarterly*, which provides information on the history of the labor movement in general and the AFL-CIO in particular. It can be obtained by calling the institute's customer service department at (301) 431-5457. For more information, visit the AFL-CIO's Web site at http://www.aflcio.org, or write to 815 16th St. NW, Washington, DC 20006.

BIBLIOGRAPHY

Bernstein, Aaron. "Sweeney's Blitz." *Business Week*, 17 February 1997.

Bernstein, Aaron, Amy Borrus, and Steven Brull. "A Bazooka Aimed at Big Labor Backfires on the GOP." *Business Week,* 15 June 1998.

Broder, David S. "Labor Outspent, Out-Organized Foes on Initiative." *Washington Post,* 4 June 1998.

Hornblower, Margot. "Labor's Youth Brigade." *Time*, 15 July 1996.

Lynchseki, John E. "Unions Employ New Growth Strategies." *HR Focus*, September 1996.

Masters, Marick. *Unions at the Crossroads.* New York: Quorum Books, 1997.

Moberg, David. "Can Labor Change?" *Dissent*, winter 1996.

Reynolds, Larry. "Labor's Blueprint Targets Contingent Workers." *HR Focus*, September 1996.

Seal, Kathy. "Unions Seek to Organize via Increased Boycotts." *Hotel & Hotel Management*, 16 September 1996.

Shales, Amity. "Labor's Return." *Commentary*, October 1996.

Sweeney, John J. *America Needs a Raise.* Boston: Houghton Mifflin, 1996.

Worsham, James. "Labor's New Assault." *Nation's Business*, June 1997.

American Federation of State, County and Municipal Employees (AFSCME)

ESTABLISHED: September 1936
EMPLOYEES: 423
MEMBERS: 1,300,000
PAC: Public Employees Organizing to Promote
     Legislative Equality (PEOPLE)

Contact Information:

ADDRESS: 1625 L St. NW
     Washington, DC 20036
PHONE: (202) 429-1000
TDD (HEARING IMPAIRED): (202) 659-0446
FAX: (202) 429-1293
E-MAIL: organize!@afscme.org
URL: http://www.afscme.org
INTERNATIONAL PRESIDENT: Gerald McEntee

WHAT IS ITS MISSION?

The preamble to the American Federation of State, County and Municipal Employee (AFSCME) constitution observes that "for unions, the work place and the polling place are inseparable, and the exercise of the awesome rights and responsibilities of citizenship is equally required in both." AFSCME thus has two major goals: organizing public employees into the union and using collective bargaining to secure them better wages, improved working conditions, and participation in decision making in the workplace; and promoting legislation that benefits both union members and the public.

HOW IS IT STRUCTURED?

AFSCME is composed of roughly 3,400 local unions, most of which are affiliated with one of 63 regional councils. The international headquarters, located in Washington, D.C., works on issues concerning large segments of the membership and assists and coordinates activities of the councils and locals. The international office has eleven departments dealing with politics, legislation, and public policy; training, organizing, and field services; specialized areas such as women's rights; and the Public Employees Organizing to Promote Legislative Equality (PEOPLE) Department which runs AFSCME's political action committee (PAC). The councils further the goals of the international organization by coordinating on a regional basis the activities of the locals in such areas as research, organizing, education, and political action.

AFSCME is one of the more democratic unions. The international office is governed by the international executive board composed of the president, secretary-treasurer, and 31 vice presidents. Officers are elected for four-year terms by local and council delegates to the biennial international convention. The convention sets the organization's priorities and adopts policies and programs. The international office also has a nine-member judicial panel which arbitrates internal union affairs. Locals elect their own officials and have a great deal of autonomy in their local affairs such as collective bargaining.

Members can be employees of state, county or municipal governments, hospitals, schools, universities, and nonprofit agencies in the United States, Panama, and Puerto Rico. Over 325,000 members are employed in the health care industry. Another 325,000 members are clerical and secretarial employees, and about 100,000 members are corrections officers.

AFSCME is affiliated with the American Federation of Labor and Congress of Industrial Organizations (AFL-CIO) and Public Services International (PSI), a worldwide organization of public employees.

PRIMARY FUNCTIONS

To further its public policy goals, AFSCME actively lobbies and campaigns on behalf of its membership. The international office employs several full time lobbyists who advocate the union's positions. They inform elected officials on how policies would affect AFSCME's membership through regular meetings and by testifying at congressional hearings. The international office's computerized telephone operation is capable of placing several thousand calls to members in a single evening encouraging them to vote or contact their representatives on a particular issue. All levels of the union work on developing grassroots (local) lobbies, recruiting volunteers for political activities, orchestrating voter registration and "get out the vote" drives, and distributing campaign literature. The PEOPLE political action committee (PAC) raises and distributes financial contributions to candidates and the Democratic party. In the 1995–96 election cycle PEOPLE was the second largest political contributor among all PACs and private donors.

In the workplace, AFSCME staff assists locals by offering information on organizing union membership and research and collective bargaining resources. They provide training materials and programs for local leaders, sample contracts, budget analysis, and pay studies. The international office has reference materials and can provide expertise on health and safety issues relevant to AFSCME members in contract negotiations. It also helps locals develop strategies to fight privatization (to change a business from public to private control) of government jobs.

The AFSCME public affairs operation creates press releases on political and workplace issues, conducts press conferences, maintains relationships with reporters, and assists locals with public relations activities. It also produces informational, training, and organizing videos for use by the locals and councils. It disseminates reports through its research arm that bolster the union's image. For example, a report entitled "Getting It Right," which found job protection and compensation for public and private employees to be comparable, was released to counter proposals for tax and budget cuts that portrayed public payrolls as inflated.

The union also provides legal assistance to locals and councils, frequently filing lawsuits on its members' behalf to further public policy goals, such as equal pay for women. In 1997 an AFSCME local filed the first sex discrimination lawsuit against Congress over equal pay. AFSCME argued that the Capitol's female custodial staff is paid thousands of dollars less a year than the male laborer crew for similar work.

PROGRAMS

AFSCME participated with other unions in the Labor '96 program, which was designed to educate union members on the politics and voting records of political candidates and to call politicians' attention to issues concerning workers. There was a massive contribution of money, staff, and materials dedicated to political education in preparation for the 1996 elections. At the local level activists talked with fellow members and wrote letters to the editors of their local newspapers on political issues that would affect AFSCME members. Local union leaders arranged for television and radio spots produced by the AFL-CIO on issues such as Medicare to air on local stations. Fearing defeat in the 1996 elections, some Republicans broke from conservative ranks to help pass a minimum wage increase and new regulations on the health insurance industry. Four million more union households voted in 1996 than in 1992 while nationwide turnout decreased. Moreover union households voted overwhelmingly for Democratic congressional candidates. The program fell short of its goal of displacing the Republican majority in Congress but it did narrow the margin and thus the likelihood that there would be significant reductions in workplace protections or welfare state programs would be passed.

AFSCME encourages locals to develop "contract campaigns" designed to build community support and strengthen the union's position in collective bargaining. In this program members are encouraged to contact other workers one-on-one or in small groups to identify issues outside of wages, benefits, and working conditions that will impact the public at large. Thus if a union hopes to fight hospital privatization and the loss of union jobs it may choose to emphasize that such action would be a threat to the quality of patient care. Committees are then established to oversee negotiations with the employer, communications with the membership, and communications with the media and the public. These committees also organize rallies and demonstrations as well as letter writing campaigns and public service announcements.

Through the AFSCME Advantage programs, the union offers its members and their families benefits such as low cost mortgage and real estate programs, life insurance, legal assistance, travel club memberships, and low interest credit. The union also administers a scholarship program.

BUDGET INFORMATION

Not made available.

HISTORY

A small group of Wisconsin employees gathered in Madison in 1932 to form an organization that would soon become the Wisconsin State Employees Association. The organization was founded by workers who feared that with the Great Depression state politicians might abandon Wisconsin's famed competitive civil service system in favor of distributing government jobs as political patronage to friends and supporters. The union became affiliated with the American Federation of Labor (AFL), and with the federation's help, defeated the legislative effort that was underway to dismantle the civil service system.

One of the earliest leaders of the Wisconsin organization, Arnold Zander, hoped to establish a national union of state employees. When the AFL granted national jurisdiction over state, county, and municipal government employees in 1935 to the American Federation of Government Employees (AFGE), a union dominated by federal government workers, Zander quickly convinced its leaders to allow him to form a relatively autonomous union within the AFGE that was to become the American Federation of State, County and Municipal Employees. Intense disputes over the degree of AFSCME's independence from AFGE were resolved when the AFL granted a separate charter to AFSCME allowing it to became an independent international union in 1936. Membership grew rapidly—surpassing fifty thousand members by the end of World War II (1939–45). During this period the primary focus of the union was to lobby for civil service laws that secured the merit system (competitive award of state and local government jobs).

By the 1950s AFSCME's political strategy was shifting. Many states had laws that forbid collective bargaining contracts between public sector workers and their government employers or outlawed strikes by govern-

ment employees. An insurgency within AFSCME, led by New York labor leader Jerry Wurf, encouraged the international leadership to place greater emphasis on securing laws recognizing the rights of public workers to unionize and engage in collective bargaining. Several political events built up momentum for public sector unionization. In 1958 New York City Mayor Robert Wagner, under pressure from AFSCME, recognized public employees' rights to collective bargaining. In 1961 President John F. Kennedy issued an executive order recognizing the rights of federal employees to collective bargaining, contributing to a more favorable climate for the unionization of all public employees.

In 1964 Wurf was elected international president of AFSCME. He stressed aggressive organizing and bargaining as well as reform of the union and the implementation of more democratic procedures. In 1965 AFSCME became the first U.S. union to adopt a bill of rights for its members. By 1966 several states enacted laws favorable to public employee legislation and AFSCME's membership grew to over 250,000.

In the 1960s and 1970s the demand for the employee's right to organize became linked to the demand for other rights and liberal causes. AFSCME developed an alliance with the Civil Rights movement at the national, state, and local levels. In 1968 Dr. Martin Luther King, Jr., was assassinated while visiting Memphis, Tennessee, to support striking AFSCME sanitation workers in their demand for union recognition and an end to discriminatory employment practices. AFSCME also joined traditionally liberal unions such as the United Auto Workers (UAW) in opposition to the Vietnam War. AFSCME, along with the Service Employees International Union (SEIU), led the movement among unions for equal pay for women.

By 1975 the union had over 680,000 members and wielded considerable political influence. While most unions in the private sector were maintaining or declining in membership, public employee unions continued to grow. During the 1970s the leadership of AFSCME increased the emphasis on political action. The PEOPLE political action committee was formed and AFSCME participated in elections at every level of government across the country. In 1981 AFSCME sent the largest delegation of any union to join the Solidarity Day demonstration in Washington, D.C., organized by the AFL-CIO to demonstrate labor's opposition to the policies of the newly elected Republican president Ronald Reagan.

During the 1980s AFSCME often found itself allied with its state and local government employers who opposed cutbacks in federal programs such as welfare, law enforcement assistance, and revenue sharing. Gerald McEntee was elected to head the union in 1981 following Jerry Wurf's death. Under his leadership AFSCME became the second largest union affiliated with the AFL-CIO, with over 1.3 million members. McEntee strengthened the union's ties to the Democratic Party and took a leading role in the 1992 presidential nomination of Bill Clinton through an early endorsement and vigorous campaigning. Clinton and other Democrats have been criticized for failing to take on "big government" because of their close ties to public employee unions such as AFSCME.

McEntee also served as a vice-president of the AFL-CIO, where he has pushed for more aggressive political involvement on the part of the entire labor movement. When he became chair of the federation's PAC, he played a major role in determining the policy direction and political involvement of the labor movement as a whole in which AFSCME became a dominant player. AFSCME members represented one quarter of all AFL-CIO delegates to the 1996 Democratic Convention.

CURRENT POLITICAL ISSUES

AFSCME advocates a range of liberal political issues such as minimum wage increases, maintenance of Medicare and Medicaid, and greater worker protections through the Occupational Safety and Health Administration (OSHA). AFSCME was a key member in the coalition that supported President Clinton's effort to establish universal health insurance and in the wake of the plan's failure to be enacted, AFSCME has endorsed greater regulation of the health care system in alliance with other unions and consumer advocates. AFSCME also supports policies of particular interest to its large number of women members, such as parental leave and child care initiatives. It opposes a balanced budget amendment and efforts to restructure government bureaucracies that result in the loss of public service jobs. It also opposes privatization of government services in which private businesses contract to perform the jobs of government employees.

AFSCME has also been a major opponent of efforts to reform welfare. Over AFSCME leaders' strenuous objections, President Clinton signed into law a welfare reform bill passed by the Republican Congress in 1996 that gave states considerable discretion in how they operate their welfare systems. Since passage of the bill, many states have developed or expanded "workfare" in which welfare recipients are forced to enter work programs run by private employers or to perform services typically done by government employees in exchange for their welfare checks. In order to protect unionized government jobs (many of which are targeted for workfare workers), AFSCME is trying to shape the way these programs are implemented at all levels of government.

Case Study: Workfare

Reformers argue that because workfare participants are "work experience trainees" they should not be subject to federal or state regulations such as minimum wage,

worker's compensation, and workplace health and safety laws. But AFSCME and advocates for the poor argue that the welfare recipients in these programs are workers and that they deserve the full rights of employees. They further argue that workfare programs will put downward pressure on the income, benefits, and working conditions of other unskilled workers. At the federal level, AFSCME pushed the Clinton administration to rule that workfare workers are protected by federal labor law and wage requirements. The union continues to press state governments to apply their own employee protections to workfare workers.

AFSCME participates in the Jobs With Justice Campaign in alliance with other labor groups, community activists, and church leaders in an effort to call attention to changes in welfare in the wake of reform. This campaign publicizes the high level of competition for low-skill, low-wage jobs and focuses on this as the underlying cause of poverty and the need for welfare. This campaign is aimed at convincing the public that workfare programs are an attempt by employers to exploit welfare recipients by using them to perform work for wages far below the minimum wage. Participants in the campaign also criticize the programs for failing to offer participants adequate child care and future training and educational opportunities. In late 1997 the Campaign organized a National Day of Action for Welfare/Workfare Justice with 50 rallies around the country demanding that federal welfare-to-work grants be used by the states to create what they term "living wage" jobs rather than workfare programs.

AFSCME also participates in local coalitions that are active on the workfare issue. In Baltimore, Maryland, AFSCME has joined a very effective grassroots alliance of religious and community activists, Baltimoreans United In Leadership Development (BUILD). BUILD had won a "living wage" ordinance in Baltimore in which city contractors would be required to pay significantly more than the minimum wage to their employees, only to see it undercut by workfare programs. The alliance argued that if companies can get workers for free or sub-minimum wages why would they choose to employ unskilled workers not on welfare at full price? Observers estimated that one thousand low-wage workers were displaced by workfare participants in the first six months of 1997. AFSCME President McEntee argued that this is a cruel form of "musical chairs" in which "people who had a little something will be out and on welfare and welfare workers will be in with below minimum wages."

AFSCME and BUILD arranged protests and demonstrations designed to push Maryland's governor Parris Glendening into modifying the state's workfare program. The governor agreed to subsidize only newly created workfare jobs thus decreasing the chance that workers will be displaced. However, he refused to create significant numbers of long-term government positions to absorb workfare participants. AFSCME and BUILD continued to lobby the state legislature to create public sector jobs for welfare recipients that pay a living wage and to deny tax credits to private employers for hiring workfare workers that displace other workers. These changes are opposed by Work Not Welfare, an organization of corporate employers that have agreed to hire workfare participants and wish to maintain the current system.

AFSCME and BUILD pressured private employers such as the Johns Hopkins University that were considering workfare jobs. At Hopkins they demonstrated with student groups in early 1997 to protest university efforts to cut the hours of unionized employees so that workfare workers could be hired at $1.50 an hour.

Despite regional and local successes, AFSCME was unable to get any legislation passed on a national level to alter the ways in which workfare is administered.

FUTURE DIRECTIONS

In its fight to minimize the negative effects of workfare programs on public employment and wages, AFSCME has declared its intention to organize workfare participants. In New York seven thousand workfare workers have signed cards to join a workfare workers organizing committee. The international organization encourages locals to develop or expand similar efforts. AFSCME also plans to expand its efforts at organizing child care workers—one of the lowest paying occupations in the United States.

GROUP RESOURCES

AFSCME maintains an extensive Web site at http://www.afscme.org that features information from each of its departments, news on upcoming events, updates on ongoing campaigns, and archives of press releases, reports, and publications. The site also contains the organization's constitution and various training manuals. For more information about AFSCME write to the American Federation of State, County and Municipal Employees, 1625 L St. NW, Washington, DC 20036 or contact its public affairs office at (202) 429-1130.

GROUP PUBLICATIONS

In addition to various reports on political and workplace issues AFSCME publishes three internal publications. *The Public Employee* covers general AFSCME news and is sent to all members seven times a year. *The Leader* is a weekly newsletter aimed at local and council leaders with special issues focused on political action and health and safety. *The AFSCME Steward* is a quarterly publication directed to union stewards, officers and staff. Recent issues of all three as well as various other newsletters and reports are available on-line at http://www.afscme.org/publications/content.htm. Locals also distribute their own newsletters. More information about AFSCME's publications can be obtained by writing to the American Federation of State, County and Municipal Employees, 1625 L St. NW, Washington, DC 20036 or calling its public affairs office at (202) 429-1130.

BIBLIOGRAPHY

Barnes, James A. "Unions Mobilize on GOP Agenda." *National Journal,* 29 April 1995.

Clairborne, William. "Unions Fear Job Losses in Welfare Reform." *Washington Post,* 6 January 1994.

Cooper, Marc. "When Push Comes to Shove: Who Is Welfare Reform Really Helping?" *Nation,* 2 June 1997.

Greenhouse, Steven. "Union Seeks to Enlist 35,000 in New York City's Workare Program." *New York Times,* 29 June 1997.

Johnston, Paul. *Success While Others Fail: Social Movement Unionism and the Public Workplace.* Ithaca, New York: ILR Press, 1994.

———. "Labor's Along for the Ride." *National Journal,* 3 May 1997.

Kosterlitz, Julie. "Labor's Pit Bull." *National Journal,* 2 August 1997.

Matlack, Carol. "Unionizing Government." *National Journal,* 10 September 1988.

Mitchell, Chris. "Gang of Three." *Washington Monthly,* September 1992.

Persinos, John F. "Left Jab." *Campaigns and Elections,* July 1995.

Riccucci, Norma M. *Women, Minorities, and Unions in the Public Sector.* New York: Greenwood Press, 1990.

American Federation of Teachers (AFT)

WHAT IS ITS MISSION?

The American Federation of Teachers (AFT) was founded to give teachers an independent, organized voice before school administrators and the public. Its traditional mission as a union is to seek improved pay, benefits, and working conditions for its members through collective bargaining contracts. However, former AFT President Albert Shanker asserted that "it is as much the duty of the union to preserve public education as it is to negotiate a good contract." In the political arena the AFT is an advocate of expanding and improving public education and social programs that benefit children. The AFT describes itself as "a dynamic force for quality education and human services as well as economic and social justice for this and future generations of Americans."

ESTABLISHED: April 1916
EMPLOYEES: 200
MEMBERS: 1,000,000
PAC: American Federation of Teachers Committee on
    Political Education (AFTCOPE)

Contact Information:

ADDRESS: 555 New Jersey Ave. NW
    Washington, DC 20001
PHONE: (202) 879-4561
TOLL FREE: (800) 238-1133
FAX: (202) 879-4537
URL: http://www.aft.org
PRESIDENT: Sandra Feldman

HOW IS IT STRUCTURED?

The AFT is affiliated with the American Federation of Labor and Congress of Industrial Organizations (AFL-CIO). The AFT is governed by an executive council composed of a president, secretary-treasurer, and 38 vice presidents who are elected at biennial conventions of delegates from the roughly 2,100 local unions affiliated with the federation. The convention also establishes the organization's policies and priorities.

The national headquarters represents members before the federal government and the national media, and provides support services to the local unions and state federations. The organization maintains separate departments to handle legislative relations, public affairs, and

organizing, as well as departments to serve particular segments of the membership such as the Higher Education Department and the K-12 Teachers Department. Other departments include the Department of Research, which generates reports on educational and collective bargaining issues; Financial Services, which assists local union treasurers; Human Rights and Community Relations; and International Affairs.

State federations, chartered by the AFT in most states, serve as a communications link among local unions. Working with the national headquarters, they organize political action campaigns, lobby at the state government level, conduct organizing drives for new members, and deliver services to the locals such as help with contract negotiations or leadership training.

Because the American educational system is very decentralized with most policies on pay, teacher standards, and curriculum determined by individual school districts, the local unions are the most important component in the organization's structure. Local unions, typically chartered by the AFL to represent members employed by a common employer, enter contract negotiations with employers over pay, working conditions, and other labor-management issues. They handle member grievances with employers and represent members before their communities and local authorities. While most members are organized through local unions, there is an associate membership program that allows educators with a professional interest in the issues handled by the AFT to join the organization without gaining local representation before employers.

The largest segment of the AFT membership is public and private school teachers of kindergarten through twelfth-grade classes. The union represents many other school-related personnel, from teaching assistants and guidance counselors to janitors and cafeteria workers. The membership also includes over 100,000 faculty and professional staff at colleges and universities. Smaller segments of the AFT's membership include nurses, other health professionals, and state and local government employees.

PRIMARY FUNCTIONS

The main goal of the AFT in the workplace is to obtain fair pay, benefits, and working conditions for its members. Contracts often cover issues such as class size, class loads, and teacher responsibilities. To support local union leaders in their contract negotiations, the national office provides services such as training, financial analysis, evaluation of health insurance and pension plans, and sample contracts. When contract negotiations fail, the union can resort to rallies, demonstrations, and strikes to achieve their goals.

The AFT is very politically active; it lobbies national, state, and local governments and it evaluates, endorses, and makes financial contributions to candidates. The AFT's political action committee (AFTCOPE) contributed $1,619,635 to candidates for federal office in the 1995–96 election cycle, with over 98 percent of these funds going to Democrats. Perhaps a more valuable contribution is comprised by the time and labor of AFT members who are frequent and reliable volunteers in political campaigns and drives to turn out voters. Members are also encouraged to become delegates to the Democratic National Convention where the party platform and nominations for presidential candidates are determined—in 1996 over 100 such delegates were AFT members. Because teachers are an important constituency for the party, Democratic politicians often consult with AFT leaders in the formulation of policy proposals.

The AFT leadership and national office staff try to influence the opinions of the public and policymakers through a continuous public relations effort and the building of ties to other organizations. The AFT runs a weekly essay in the *New York Times*; written by the organization's president, it is entitled "Where We Stand" and explains the union's position on current issues of concern to the AFT, teachers, parents, and children. The AFT frequently issues press releases and reports to publicize its positions. AFT leaders are often appointed by presidents, governors, and mayors to serve on commissions and task forces concerned with education, child welfare, and other social and economic issues. Leaders also maintain ties to civic organizations by serving on their boards. For example, AFT President Sandra Feldman has ties to the National Council of Americans to Prevent Handgun Violence, the National Urban League, the National Association for the Advancement of Colored People, and United Nations Children's Fund.

In keeping with its commitment to preserve public education, the AFT seeks to improve the quality of teaching and public schools through research and teacher training. The AFT analyzes and publicizes other organizations' research on educational issues and conducts its own original research. Reports such as the annual *Making Standards Matter* assess academic standards and student performance across school districts, states, and nations. Other reports and training materials are designed to provide teachers with new, effective teaching tools or techniques and to discourage schools from resorting to methods that have failed. The union has set up task forces to examine educational problems such as the AFT Task Force on Low Performing Schools, which developed a resolution on ways to improve schools that was adopted by the 1998 national convention. The AFT also sponsors conferences and workshops where teachers gain information and training in new teaching methods.

PROGRAMS

The AFT offers a number of training programs. The Educational Research and Dissemination Program

(ER&D) is designed to share research with educators to improve the performance of teachers and students. The program offers a number of short-term courses across the country. The Union Leadership Institute (ULI) is run by the Department of Organization and Field Services to help local unions and state federations develop leaders, organizers, and activists and to educate members about the union's goals and activities. It offers training materials and annual schools for elected leadership and staff.

As part of its public relations effort, the AFT launched an ongoing campaign entitled "Lessons for Life: Responsibility, Respect, Results" with the motto "Other education reforms may work; high standards of conduct and achievement do work—and nothing else can work without them." The campaign is designed to call public attention to proven solutions for improving public schools and to build support for public education. The campaign includes materials to help union locals participate and projects that can be set up on a local level.

As part of its international efforts, the AFT runs the Education for Democracy/International Project which promotes the teaching of democracy and civics throughout the world. In one instance, the AFT participated in a project to reform civics education in Nicaragua. The project has also offered short-term training programs in countries such as Mongolia, Poland, and Romania and cosponsored national civic education conferences in Nicaragua and Russia. The project includes a Classroom-to-Classroom program that links students and teachers to their peers around the world.

BUDGET INFORMATION

Not made available

HISTORY

In the late nineteenth century, teacher salaries were very low, benefits such as pensions were insufficient or nonexistent, and school administrators denied teachers a voice in the way schools were run. In 1897 the Chicago Teachers' Federation (CTF) was founded by elementary school teachers to improve members' work conditions. The leaders hoped to form a national teachers' union that would challenge the National Education Association (NEA), which was dominated by school administrators and college professors and put little emphasis on improving conditions for teachers—even though they were the majority of the membership. In 1902 the CTF joined the local affiliate of the American Federation of Labor (AFL). This move, along with the CTF's support for social welfare causes such as child labor laws, marked a break from the policies of the National Education Association.

The CTF's interests were adopted by the American Federation of Teachers (AFT) when, in 1916, it was founded by three Chicago teachers' unions and a nearby Gary, Indiana union. Within the year local unions from New York, Oklahoma, Pennsylvania, and Washington, D.C. joined the organization. Like the CTF, the AFT promptly affiliated with the AFL and, unlike the NEA, it focused on teachers' grievances. Charles Stillman was elected the AFT's first president. This period marked the beginning of a bitter rivalry between the AFT and the NEA that persisted for decades. The NEA, which considered affiliation with organized labor and involvement in politics to be unprofessional, encouraged local authorities to launch drives against the AFT which hurt the organization's ability to grow and push for change. But the AFT gained a great deal of help from the AFL in organizing and by 1920 its membership stood at 10,000.

Teachers, like other workers, were hurt by the Great Depression of the 1930s. Salaries were lowered and unemployment was high. The AFT had trouble maintaining a stable membership and many locals were not effective in gaining concessions from administrators because often only a minority of teachers in a district were members. Political, ethnic, and religious diversity among the mostly urban local unions made it difficult for the national organization to develop a unified mission. Some locals wanted to focus exclusively on the material needs of teachers while others were more interested in social and political issues. This produced conflicts at the national level and contributed to the short tenure of AFT presidents in the 1930s and 1940s. However, social and political liberals dominated the AFT and the organization was an early advocate of causes such as racial equality and women's rights. The politics surrounding World War II shook up the union and in 1941 the AFT convention voted to expel four locals that were heavily influenced by Communists, causing the AFT to lose almost a third of its membership.

Teachers did not share in the economic prosperity of the post-World War II period. Teachers noted the gains unionized industrial workers were making through strikes and collective bargaining, and interest in these standard union practices developed within the AFT. The 1946 convention called for a study of collective bargaining and a reevaluation of the union's no-strike policy. Although the no-strike pledge was not officially withdrawn until the early 1960s, many AFT local affiliates engaged in strikes in the late 1940s and 1950s. Carl Megel assumed the presidency in 1952 and served until 1965. He brought stability to the organization and worked to improve the administration of the national office. The union's finances improved and it developed a network of state federations with full-time staff and a commitment to organizing new locals.

Events in the early 1960s forever changed the AFT and the American education system. The political environment had historically been hostile to unionization and collective bargaining among public employees such as

FAST FACTS

The November 1998 merger of the Minnesota Education Association with the AFT-affiliated Minnesota Federation of Teachers expanded AFT membership to over a million members and made it one of the five largest AFL-CIO-affiliated unions.

(Source: American Federation of Teachers. "AFT Tops One Million Members," November 19, 1998.)

teachers. But in 1959 Wisconsin passed the first law allowing public employees to bargain collectively, and three years later President John F. Kennedy issued an executive order which allowed federal employees to unionize and engage in collective bargaining. New York City, during the Administration of pro-labor Mayor Robert Wagner, became the focus of AFT activity.

New York's United Federation of Teachers (UFT) gained assistance from the AFT and the AFL-CIO to launch a massive organizing drive in 1960. Following a couple of one-day strikes and highly politicized negotiations, the UFT became the exclusive representative of the city's 40,000-plus teachers. By 1964 the AFT had negotiated a series of contracts that secured measures including sizable salary increases, reductions in class loads, and limits on class size.

After the high-profile events in New York, the AFT quickly gained collective bargaining rights and contracts in a large number of northeastern cities. By 1970 membership exceeded 200,000 and it more than doubled over the following decade. But the AFT failed to move much beyond its existing geographic base into rural and suburban areas or the South and West, where the NEA has traditionally been stronger. At the same time, however, the success of the AFT strategy to behave more like a union and less like a professional association encouraged imitation by the much larger NEA.

Albert Shanker, the longest serving president in the AFT's history, assumed office in 1974. The charismatic Shanker had made a name for himself within the labor movement as one of the UFT leaders that brought collective bargaining and teacher militancy to the AFT. Shanker encouraged teachers to become more politically active and initiated a political activism training program for members. The AFT was an early supporter of winning Democratic presidential candidate Jimmy Carter, who promised more money for public education. Under Shanker's leadership the AFT was critical of Republican

presidents Reagan and Bush, who endorsed cuts in social services and proposals the union viewed as threats to public education such as tax credits for parents who send their children to private and parochial schools.

Faced with growing criticism of the quality of public education in the 1980s and 1990s, Shanker gained notoriety as an outspoken advocate of educational reforms. He had always argued that the standards for teacher certification, which varied from state to state, should be raised and that teachers should be required to take a national examination of basic skills and knowledge in the subjects they taught. By the mid-1990s he advocated changes in many of the procedures unions had once fought for, such as pay based on performance rather than a uniform scale based on years of service and the streamlining of due-process protections in the handling of grievances and the firing of unsatisfactory teachers. Shanker argued that "unless we restore the public's faith in what we do, public education is going to collapse."

The AFT was one of the first and most active of unions to support Bill Clinton in the race for the Democratic presidential nomination in 1992. Clinton endorsed many of the AFT's proposals such as the call for national education standards and the limiting of social promotion in schools in which unprepared children are advanced to the next grade.

Sandra Feldman became AFT president in 1997 after Shanker became ill. She endorsed and expanded on the educational reforms he advocated. In response to the conservative proposal to eliminate tenure in order to make it easier to fire incompetent teachers, Feldman endorsed peer review and intervention in which experienced teachers evaluate the performance of other teachers and work to assist those found lacking in skills.

Feldman's other major focus has been to bring about a merger of the AFT and the NEA—an idea that has been entertained by the two organizations for a generation. The rejection of the merger plan by delegates to the NEA's 1998 summer convention temporarily set back the merger. The AFT convention delegates, however, gave overwhelming support to the merger and negotiations between the two organizations have resumed. Meanwhile, a number of local affiliates of the AFT and the NEA have already merged and at the end of 1998 the Minnesota state affiliates merged into one organization.

CURRENT POLITICAL ISSUES

The AFT often coordinates its political activities with the AFL-CIO and it is a strong supporter of the Democratic Party and liberal causes such as expanded rights for minorities and women. The AFT advocates increased funding for public and higher education and suggested in the early 1990s that the "peace dividend" brought about by the end of the Cold War be spent on education and programs benefiting children. Beginning in the late 1970s the AFT called attention to the rising problem of drugs, crime, and violence in and around schools and it has been a vocal supporter of increased discipline in public schools. Most AFT members teach in urban schools, many of which are attended by disadvantaged children. The union argues that poverty, homelessness, hunger, poor health care, and other social and economic problems make it difficult for these children to learn. Thus the AFT has been a strong advocate of social programs such as Head Start, which provides preschool classes for impoverished children, and President Clinton's failed 1994 proposal to provide universal health care.

Teachers unions have themselves become a controversial political issue. Despite the AFT national leadership's endorsement of educational reforms, critics argue that politically powerful unions continue to be roadblocks to educational reform and improvement. Critics believe union contracts protect incompetent teachers through seniority rules and due-process procedures that make it very difficult to fire bad teachers. Critics further argue that teachers' unions cling to a system where teachers are promoted and paid based on years of service rather than merit and that they protect licensing systems that prevent or discourage bright people without degrees in education from teaching in public schools.

A 1998 Wall Street Journal/NBC poll showed that 41 percent of the public believes unions are part of the problem with public education. Politicians, particularly Republicans, have tried to capitalize on this public sentiment by attacking the AFT and the NEA. In a highly publicized statement that caused teachers' unions to redouble their campaign efforts for Clinton, Republican challenger Bob Dole announced at the 1996 Republican national convention, "To the teachers' unions, I say, when I am President, I will disregard your political power . . . . If education were a war, you would be losing it." The AFT has responded by publicizing research that shows student performance is actually better in states with high levels of unionization.

The AFT argues that in addition to the influence of larger social problems such as single-parent households and income inequality, the real problem with many schools is inadequate funding, poor administration, and insufficient standards. Although the AFT has accepted some reforms, it fiercely resists market-based approaches to school reform such as turning over public schools to private companies. The union is also against voucher programs in which students are given government-issued certificates that pay for attending private schools.

Case Study: School Vouchers

Vouchers have been proposed as a solution to the poor state of public schools, particularly in economically depressed inner cities. Proponents of vouchers argue that the public schools are an education monopoly, free from

FAST FACTS

Average student Scholastic Assessment Test (SAT) scores are 43 points higher in states where more than 90 percent of teachers are unionized than in states where less than 50 percent of teachers participate in some form of collective contract negotiation.

(Source: "Are Teacher Unions Hurting American Education?" *The Institute for Wisconsin's Future*, October 1996.)

the market competition that would force them to adequately educate students or go out of business. They argue that giving students and parents the opportunity to choose schools would increase the flow of resources and students into high performing schools and cause bad schools to either improve or close. Critics of vouchers counter that such programs would only benefit a small minority of students and undermine many public schools by siphoning off money, the best students, and the most dedicated parents—leaving the majority of students isolated in even worse schools. They argue that many poorly performing schools have very troubled students who would not be accepted by private schools and, even if they were, would still do badly. Critics fear that not enough good schools would emerge to meet the demand and that most programs would end up subsidizing well-off students who would have attended private schools anyway.

The AFT and the NEA, advocates of public education in colleges and universities, liberal think tanks, and the federal government have been the major opponents of voucher initiatives. Proponents of school vouchers include free enterprise advocates and organizations from the religious right such as the Christian Coalition, who think vouchers will give parents more control over their children's education and the resources to send their kids to religious schools or to school them at home. Conservative think tanks such as the Heritage Foundation and organizations with the primary goal of advocating school reforms such as the Center for Education Reform support the use of vouchers. Some African American activists have come to support voucher programs as a way of offering poor, inner-city children the same educational choices as more advantaged students.

The AFT joined with the NEA to fight voucher initiatives in a number of states and local political jurisdictions. In a high profile battle in California in 1993, the teachers' unions in alliance with the PTA poured millions of dollars into a successful campaign to defeat a referendum that would have set up a statewide voucher program. The unions stalled the Republican efforts in the Congresses elected in 1994 and 1996 to pass bills creating voucher programs for the District of Columbia. They lobbied AFT supporters in the Senate to threaten a filibuster and President Clinton to veto such proposals. The AFT has also worked to defeat candidates for Congress and state offices that are strong proponents of vouchers.

Only two publicly funded voucher programs have been approved and put into operation—one in Cleveland, Ohio and one in Milwaukee, Wisconsin. Having lost the fight against these initiatives, the AFT is now pursuing a strategy of publicizing their weaknesses and preventing their expansion. The AFT released a report on the Cleveland program in 1997 that argued the program was more expensive than its advocates predicted, that over a quarter of the students who used the vouchers had attended private schools before the program was enacted, and that many students who qualified were not able to participate, perhaps because they were not accepted by the private schools of their choice. The AFT has joined the NEA in filing a lawsuit to prevent the expansion of the program. The program in Milwaukee has been challenged by a lawsuit filed by the American Civil Liberties Union (ACLU) which opposes the voucher system because it gives public funds to religious schools. In 1998 the AFT released a report based on the two voucher experiments that found small class size was more effective in improving student performance than vouchers.

The AFT also seeks to disarm the voucher movement by promoting alternative educational reforms. AFT leaders argue that voucher programs are designed to grab headlines for politicians but that genuine improvements in education will only be achieved through high, uniform standards for teachers and students and ongoing professional development and training. Many local unions have conceded to experiments with merit pay and charter schools where bureaucratic rules including union contract provisions are not enforced. In cities such as Houston, Texas and Newark, New Jersey the AFT has sponsored or helped design charter school programs. The union hopes that by proving its commitment to school reform and improving student performance it can discourage demands for abandoning the public school system through programs such as voucher systems.

FUTURE DIRECTIONS

AFT President Sandra Feldman asserted in a speech at the organization's 1998 convention that "we must do everything within our power to make turning around low-performing schools—improving all schools—the top agenda of every community in this nation!" Encouraging the local unions and rank-and-file members to endorse and demand educational reform as outlined in the resolution on redesigning low-performing schools adopted by the 1998 convention will be a main focus of the AFT in the future.

The AFT will also work to merge the AFT and the NEA. The rivalry between the AFT and the NEA has gradually been replaced by a need for unity in the face of what both unions see as efforts by conservative politicians and organizations to undermine public education. Leaders of the two organizations hope to create a mega-union of 3.3 million members that will have more clout in schools and in politics.

GROUP RESOURCES

The AFT has an extensive Web site at http://www.aft.org which includes information on officers, programs, and educational and political issues as well as recent press releases, reports, and publications. More information about the AFT can be obtained by writing to the American Federation of Teachers, 555 New Jersey Ave. NW, Washington, DC 20001 or by calling the Public Affairs Department at (202) 879-4400.

GROUP PUBLICATIONS

In addition to numerous reports and manuals, the AFT publishes two journals covering educational issues. The *American Teacher* is issued eight times a year and the *American Educator* is published quarterly. Many of the reports are available on-line at http://www.aft.org. Journal subscriptions and publications may be purchased by writing the American Federation of Teachers Order Department, 555 New Jersey Ave. NW, Washington, DC 20001; or by calling 1-800-238-1133.

BIBLIOGRAPHY

Applebome, Peter. "Push for School Safety Led to New Rules on Discipline." *New York Times,* 14 May 1997.

Broder, David. "So Much Talk About Better Education." *Washington Post,* 16 February 1997.

Chaddock, Gail Russell. "Teachers Unions Jump on Bandwagon of School Reform." *The Christian Science Monitor,* 17 October 1997.

Cocco, Marie. "Teachers' Vote—In Disunity There is Strength." *Newsday,* 7 July 1998.

Gleick, Elizabeth. "Mad and Mobilized." *Time,* 9 September 1996.

Lauter, David. "Clinton and Unions Work for Strong Ties." *Los Angeles Times,* 3 October 1993.

Lieberman, Myron. *The Teachers Unions: How the NEA and AFT Sabotage Reform and Hold Students, Parents, and Teachers Hostage to Bureaucracy.* New York: The Free Press, 1997.

Ratnesar, Romesh. "The Bite on Teachers." *Time,* 20 July 1998.

Sanchez, Rene. "Teachers' Union Merger Rejected." *Washington Post,* 6 July 1998.

Toch, Major Garrett Thomas, and Herbert Wray. "Will Teachers Save Public Schools?" *U.S. News and World Report,* 20 July 1998.

Worth, Robert. "Reforming the Teachers' Unions: What the Good Guys Have Accomplished—and What Remains to be Done." *Washington Monthly,* May 1998.

American Foundation for AIDS Research (AmFAR)

ESTABLISHED: 1985
EMPLOYEES: 57
MEMBERS: None
PAC: None

Contact Information:
ADDRESS: 120 Wall St. 13th Flr.
    New York, NY 10005
PHONE: (212) 806-1600
TOLL FREE: (800) 392-6327
FAX: (212) 806-1601
URL: http://www.amfar.org
CHAIRMAN: Mathilde Krim, Ph.D.

WHAT IS ITS MISSION?

According to the group, the mission of the American Foundation for AIDS Research (AmFAR) is "to prevent death and disease associated with HIV/AIDS and to foster sound AIDS-related public policies." AmFAR contends that the HIV/AIDS epidemic is the greatest health crisis of the twentieth century—by 1998 more than 600,000 Americans had been diagnosed with the disease since it was detected in the early 1980s, and at least another one million Americans were believed to be infected. AmFAR carries out its fight against this epidemic by raising funds for AIDS research and by helping to shape AIDS-related legislation.

According to an article about AmFAR in *Frontier* (June 14, 1996), the organization often appears to have a contradictory image. To many people, AmFAR represents glitz and glamour—an organization that makes use of celebrity support and endorsement. However, while actress Elizabeth Taylor does serve as AmFAR's national chairperson, the organization's founder is Dr. Mathilde Krim. For many AIDS activists, AmFAR represents a critical funding source for innovative AIDS research.

HOW IS IT STRUCTURED?

AmFAR is headed by a 31-person board of directors with members that include doctors, pharmacologists, and religious leaders. Committees that function under the board include: Basic Research, Finance, Fund-raising/Development, Prevention/Science, Public Policy, External Relations, Clinical Research, and Global Initiatives. These committees provide guidance to the organization's staff. AmFAR has no membership; funds are solicited through events, fund-raising efforts, and direct mail.

AmFAR has three offices, one in New York City, New York; Los Angeles, California; and Washington, D.C. AmFAR's Washington office is also known as the AmFAR Public Policy Office and was established in 1991 to give the organization a permanent and influential presence in the nation's capital. The office is run by a public policy director, who manages daily operations, and is given overall guidance by the Public Policy Committee of AmFAR's board of directors.

PRIMARY FUNCTIONS

AmFAR carries out its mission by raising funds for AIDS research and conducting advocacy and public information programs. AmFAR holds AIDS fund-raisers on a regular basis—for example, the group planned 12 fund-raisers between the period of October 1997 and June 1998. Fund-raisers are organized at the local and state levels, and make use of a variety of themes and settings to broaden fund-raising opportunities. In July 1997 Honeywell, Inc. (an international corporation based in Minnesota) cosponsored the Twin Cities (Minnesota) Corporate Breakfast. The event included guests from large corporations located throughout the Minneapolis-St. Paul region.

In June of 1997, AmFAR hosted the "Friend for Life" benefit in Beverly Hills, California. The event honored "friend for life" Cristina Saralegui, who has been a journalist for 25 years and was one of the first people to speak out about the threat of AIDS to the Latino community. The event raised more than $500,000 for AIDS research, and featured appearances by a number of celebrities, including Gloria Estefan and Jimmy Smits.

AmFAR is known for its strong use of celebrity support and endorsements in its fund-raising efforts, but it does not restrict its activities to corporate and celebrity fund-raisers. AmFAR supporters have been able to participate in silent auctions by mail, and U.S. federal employees are able to contribute to AmFAR with automatic payroll deduction. Supporters sometimes take the initiative to create unique ways to donate to AmFAR, such as the flight attendants at American Airlines who started an aluminum recycling program and have donated a portion of the proceeds to AmFAR since 1993.

The funding that AmFAR raises has impacted the status of the HIV/AIDS epidemic in a variety of ways. Since 1985 AmFAR has invested more than $140 million in its programs—the majority of this money going as grants to more than 1,700 AIDS research teams. Many of these teams were pursuing research that, at the time, seemed too farfetched for funding from other foundations. AmFAR's support of these teams gave them credibility and allowed them to pursue additional funding from the government, private industry, or other foundations.

AmFAR is also active in educating the public about AIDS. AmFAR sponsors many conferences on AIDS and AIDS-related issues. For example, in September 1997 AmFAR cohosted the Conference on Global Strategies for the Prevention of HIV Transmission From Mothers to Infants. AmFAR also sponsors physician updates in major cities on topics such as "Rational Approaches to Antiretroviral Therapy in the Clinic."

Under the auspices of its public policy program, AmFAR uses strategies to influence public policy. To that aim, AmFAR representatives testify at congressional hearings, work with key policymakers, and build coalitions with members of the medical community on relevant issues. AmFAR also influences policy with its funding directions. The organization funded some of the first studies on AIDS ethics, leading to policy enactment that protects the confidentiality of people (and their medical records) with HIV/AIDS. AmFAR advocated for enactment of policies such as the HOPE Act of 1988 (the first federal law to combat AIDS), the Americans with Disabilities Act of 1990 (which provides certain rights for those with HIV/AIDS and other disabilities), and the Ryan White CARE Act of 1990 (which provides funding for AIDS treatment and prevention).

PROGRAMS

AmFAR designs programs to carry out the organization's mission of reducing the death, disease, and other misfortunes associated with AIDS. The Basic Biomedical Research Program is a major AmFAR research grant program. In contrast to the federal government, which favors established, multiyear projects for funding, AmFAR awards grants for new AIDS research. Often the recipients of AmFAR's awards are researchers new to the AIDS community and are only able to break into AIDS research with the backing of an AmFAR grant. For example, AmFAR-funded researchers have made significant contributions to the field of gene therapy. Gene therapy introduces specific genes into HIV-susceptible cells to make these cells HIV resistant. AmFAR also funds research that has potential to improve the quality of life for those with other diseases such as cancer, heart disease, and autoimmune disorders. For example, AIDS research has led to the use of 3TC—a treatment similar to the AIDS treatment AZT—for treating the hepatitis-B virus.

Another one of AmFAR's grant programs, the Clinical Research and Information Program, establishes and supports AIDS community research and treatment centers, thereby bringing clinical treatment and research into communities heavily impacted by AIDS. Under the Clinical Research Program, AmFAR places a special emphasis on attracting and awarding grants for research that educates and includes women and minorities in community-based clinical trials for HIV/AIDS. Women and minorities have historically been underrepresented in HIV/AIDS community-based trials. AmFAR encourages funding requests from community organizations that urge women and minorities to get involved in community trials and assist them in enrolling in trials.

AmFAR is active in advocating and shaping AIDS public policy through its Sheldon W. Andelson Public Policy Program, which is based in the organization's Washington, D.C., office. Under this program, the organization advocates for policy by influencing key legislators, testifying at congressional hearings, educating the public and the media, and building coalitions with important people in the medical community—some of whom serve on AmFAR's board of directors. Some of the issues that the organization has advocated for under the Public Policy Program include: support of human rights issues for those with HIV/AIDS, support for funding for the National Institute of Health (NIH) Office of AIDS Research, and support for needle-exchange programs for HIV-infected people.

BUDGET INFORMATION

In fiscal year 1996 AmFAR had total revenue of $17,847,303. This included: direct public support ($12,035,277), government contributions/grants ($1,815,000), interest on savings and investments ($30,714), a loss on sales of assets other than inventory (-$65,150), net income from special events ($3,994,360), and other revenue ($37,102). Expenses totaled $14,845,945 and included: program services ($10,916,597), management and general ($824,147), and fund-raising ($3,105,201). In a separate breakdown of expenses, some of the most notable included: grant and allocations paid out ($2,663,112), salaries and wages ($1,932,365), and printing and publications ($2,125,269). AmFAR assets during fiscal year 1996 totaled $10,632,073.

HISTORY

In the early 1980s, the medical community was just beginning to be aware of what would become known as AIDS. In 1981 Dr. Michael Gottlieb and others reported five cases of a new acquired immune deficiency syndrome in the United States. By 1983 a major outbreak of AIDS occurred in Africa and 2,807 cases were reported in the United States. In response, organizations across the country formed to fight the growing epidemic. One of those organizations was the AIDS Medical Foundation (AMF), which was founded by Dr. Mathilde Krim, a sci-

entist with four doctorates including one in biology, who put up $100,000 of her own money. Krim in particular was active in AIDS research through related research that she had carried out with interferons—substances used to treat some viral diseases. Early on, AMF served as a research organization and established a scientific advisory committee.

In the meantime, the National AIDS Research Foundation of Los Angeles (NARF) was formed with a $250,000 donation from actor Rock Hudson, who had been diagnosed with AIDS. NARF and AMF joined forces in 1985 to become AmFAR—cochaired by doctors Krim and Gottlieb. Actress Elizabeth Taylor was appointed as national chairman.

AmFAR has not been without its ups and downs during its relatively short history. The first five years of AmFAR's existence were flush and successful, with Taylor lending the visibility that the organization needed and Krim contributing the scientific credibility and passion of her own for AIDS research. The U.S. public seemed to collectively realize that AIDS was a serious epidemic not to be taken lightly. In 1987 the Reagan administration—who had been closed-mouthed about the AIDS epidemic—broke from tradition when then President Ronald Reagan discussed AIDS for the first time at an AmFAR benefit.

Cochair Gottlieb parted from AmFAR in 1990 over a disagreement about the organization's community-based clinic trial program. The program created a national system of community clinics that provided free medical care and experimental drugs to HIV/AIDS patients. Gottlieb opposed the program, feeling that it would not be sufficiently professional or objective. Established in 1988, the program brought clinical treatment and research directly into 24 communities that were highly impacted by AIDS/HIV during its first 10 years. Government and industry would go on to adopt this method of research as well.

In 1991 AmFAR opened its Washington, D.C., office in order to maintain a presence in the nation's capital and to influence policy regarding AIDS research and AIDS advocacy. The organization reached a turning point in 1991, when Terry Beirn—who had facilitated the merger that created AmFAR and had served as AmFAR's program officer—died of AIDS. Among other accomplishments, Beirn had crafted the Ryan White CARE Act of 1990, a landmark bill which provided substantial federal funding to AIDS treatment centers across the country.

When Krim replaced Beirn with Bob Brown, a heterosexual, white man and a March of Dimes executive, several people on staff left and members of the gay community as well as National Chairman Taylor were infuriated at Krim's decision. Some perceived Brown as sexist and homophobic. Donations plummeted and even though Brown was fired two years after he started, AmFAR faced a significant budget shortfall by 1995. The organization was forced to trim its budget from $20 million to $16 million in order to keep up with grant commitments. During this time, AIDS organizations in general were having a harder time competing for dollars, because of the many AIDS organizations that had sprung into existence.

According to Krim in *Frontier* (June 14, 1996), it seemed that in the early 1990s the sense of public urgency about AIDS began to drop off. AIDS organizations struggled with convincing the public that the AIDS battle still needed to be fought. In addition, AmFAR was snubbed by some of the gay community, who associated the organization with mainstream, heterosexual appeal and celebrity representation and tactics. However, some of the country's foremost gay AIDS activists soon recognized AmFAR as a leader in AIDS research. With the passage of time, AmFAR could take credit for accomplishments such as: funding research in support of needle-exchange programs and funding research that led to the development of protease inhibitors, a treatment that holds much promise for those with HIV/AIDS.

In February 1997 Arthur Ammann, M.D. was named president of AmFAR. Ammann had served on AmFAR's Board of Directors between 1988 and 1994 and was a respected scientist in the field of pediatric immunology. His contributions to the field of AIDS research included being the first to describe cases of HIV transmission from mother to infant and being the first to describe cases of HIV transmission through blood transfusion. With the appointment of influential members of the medical community to its board and staff, AmFAR continued in the 1990s to aggressively pursue the funding of AIDS research and to advocate for research and civil rights-related AIDS issues.

CURRENT POLITICAL ISSUES

In its ongoing effort to fund and promote AIDS research and policy, AmFAR is involved in a number of AIDS related issues. One of these concerns is the FDA approval of drugs for AIDS/HIV. In August 1997, the Clinton administration endorsed the testing of AIDS treatments for children, a move which AmFAR supported. In the past, drugs had been more easily approved for adults than children, since there was little data about the side effects that children might suffer from these drugs. AmFAR lobbied for this reform and continues to push the FDA to move quickly to test and approve the many new drugs proposed for AIDS treatment.

According to AmFAR, needle-exchange programs have been proven to decrease AIDS infection among intravenous drug users, without increasing drug addiction. In late 1997 and early 1998, AmFAR and other AIDS advocate groups pushed hard for federal funding for such programs.

BUDGET:

1996 AmFAR Revenue

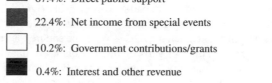

■ 67.4%: Direct public support

■ 22.4%: Net income from special events

□ 10.2%: Government contributions/grants

■ 0.4%: Interest and other revenue

1996 AmFAR Expenses

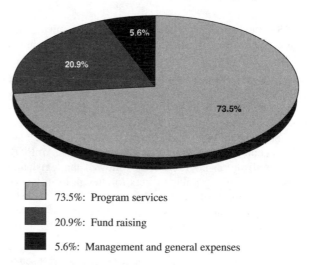

■ 73.5%: Program services

■ 20.9%: Fund raising

■ 5.6%: Management and general expenses

Case Study: Needle-Exchange Programs

According to an article in *The Columbian*, 50 percent of those with HIV get the virus through unsanitary needles used for intravenous drugs, or are the children of infected addicts. AIDS organizations have long advocated for needle-exchange programs that allow drug users to exchange unsanitary needles for clean needles, at no cost to the drug user. In one case, needle users came from a 60-mile distance to take part in such a program south

BIOGRAPHY:
Ryan White

Activist (1971–1990) Thirteen-year-old Ryan White was diagnosed with AIDS in 1984. One unique aspect of his case was that he did not contract AIDS through sexual activity or intravenous drug use; he contracted AIDS when tainted blood was used in a routine transfusion to treat his hemophilia. The teenager's diagnosis came shortly after the disease was first identified, a time when the media was sounding hysterical alarms about the threat of this epidemic. Public ignorance and misunderstanding about how AIDS was transmitted and treated resulted in widespread fear, confusion, and discrimination. White's community in Indiana was so fearful, he was refused the right to attend public school forcing his family to fight a highly publicized court battle to regain his rights. The unsuspecting teenager's bid to be 'normal' made him an overnight spokesman for AIDS. While he endured homophobic jokes, piles of garbage on his front lawn, hate letters, and a bullet fired through his family's living room window, White inspired others to join his cause against

fear and prejudice. Appearing on television and radio programs and speaking to audiences in person, White shared with as many people as possible what he knew about AIDS and what he experienced as an AIDS patient. The 1988 film, *The Ryan White Story,* further broadcast his struggle to a mass audience. White died of AIDS complications two years later at the age of eighteen. His

celebrity helped foster a public awareness that gave rise to the American Foundation for AIDS Research (AmFAR). In his eulogy, Reverend Raymond Probasco summed up the impact White's courage and determination had, "It was Ryan who first humanized the disease called AIDS."

---

of Seattle. In 1998, 110 of these programs operated, without federal support, in approximately half of the United States.

Organizations such as AmFAR have advocated for federal funding for such programs. When in 1997, President Bill Clinton ordered Health and Human Services Secretary Donna Shalala to study the issue and make a recommendation by early 1998, AmFAR lobbied hard for an outcome that would provide the funding. AmFAR, through its Washington office, followed the legislation and met with key policymakers to attempt to influence the decision. AmFAR also launched a massive media campaign in newspapers, aimed at getting an understanding of the issue out to the public.

But in April 1998, Shalala—even while admitting all the benefits of needle-exchange programs—refused to recommend that the federal government fund such programs. The decision angered AIDS advocate groups that claimed it was the first time they had seen the government endorse, but refuse to support, a position.

Public Impact

According to AIDS groups, the cost of needle-exchange programs is actually much less per person than AIDS treatment for people who become infected. While treatment for one person with AIDS from initial diagnosis until death costs about $65,000, a needle-exchange program that serves 250 people would cost $50,000 annu-

ally. Needle-exchange advocates also point to studies that show a decrease in drug use among participants in some needle-exchange programs. Several federally funded studies showed that drug use did not increase for users of needle-exchange programs. While supporters of the programs argue that drug use is not likely to go away completely, opponents feel that the programs send the wrong message to society and that they are akin to providing drug addicts with unlimited, free drugs.

FUTURE DIRECTIONS

Looking to the future, AmFAR is supporting new research that studies the integrase viral enzyme. Successful research findings could lead to integrase inhibitors that could suppress the AIDS virus. More crucial, however, is finding a vaccine for AIDS. According to Krim, "that is the real solution for humanity because people in the Third World will not be able to afford the drugs." Recent research has yielded a possible step toward developing a vaccine that deals with naked DNA fragments. AmFAR has awarded a grant to Dr. Johnston of Southwest Medical Center in Dallas, Texas, who came up with the idea. The process involves extracting DNA from a virus or bacterium, breaking it into pieces, and injecting it into an organism. The injected DNA fragments act as an internal vaccination and produce antibodies against the bacterium.

GROUP RESOURCES

AmFAR maintains a Web site at http://www.amfar. org that covers the organization's programs, current solicitations for funding proposals, publications from previous studies, upcoming fund-raisers and conferences, and current news releases. Persons who are HIV positive may obtain the AmFAR Treatment Directory for free by calling the National AIDS Clearinghouse at 1-800-458-5231.

GROUP PUBLICATIONS

AmFAR has many publications available for the public. For example, AmFAR publishes the *AIDS/HIV Treatment Directory* twice yearly. The directory is a comprehensive listing of approved and experimental treatments for HIV and related disorders, and is available to individuals for $55, and organizations for $125. Other publications include: *The AmFAR Newsletter, Facts about AIDS,* and *HIV/AIDS Educator.* For more information, visit AmFAR's Web page at http://www. amfar.org, or contact AmFAR by mail at 120 Wall St., Thirteenth Flr., New York, NY 10005; by telephone at (212) 806-1600; or by fax at (212) 806-1601.

BIBLIOGRAPHY

Cohen, Jon. "AIDS: A Justifiable Share." *Science,* 18 April 1997.

Gallagher, John. "Experts Agree: An AIDS Vaccine is Doable." *The Advocate,* 18 February 1997.

Garey, Juliann. "Cause Celeb." *Glamour,* August 1996.

Gorman, Christine. "The Odds Grow Longer." *Time,* 24 November 1997.

Ho, David D. "It's AIDS, Not Tuskegee: Inflammatory Comparisons Won't Save Lives in Africa." *Time,* 29 September 1997.

Jacobs, Jr., Andrew. "Can AmFAR Survive AIDS?" *New York,* 8 April 1996.

Lurie, Peter, and Ernest Drucker. "An Opportunity Lost: HIV Infections Associated with Lack of a National Needle Exchange Programme in the USA." *The Lancet,* 1 March 1997.

Marshall, Eliot. "Lobbyists Seek to Reslice NIH's Pie." *Science,* 18 April 1997.

Walker, Paulette V. "Improvements Seen in Federal Effort to Study AIDS." *The Chronicle of Higher Education,* 23 May 1997.

Wurtman, Richard. "Cure All: A New Prescription for Medical Research." *The New Republic,* 10 November 1997.

American Health Care Association (AHCA)

ESTABLISHED: September 1949
EMPLOYEES: 21
MEMBERS: 12,000

Contact Information:

ADDRESS: 1201 L St. NW
    Washington, DC 20005
PHONE: (202) 842-4444
TOLL FREE: (800) 555-9414
FAX: (202) 842-3860
URL: http://www.ahca.org
CHAIRMAN: Daniel D. Mosca
INTERIM PRESIDENT: David Seckman

WHAT IS ITS MISSION?

The American Health Care Association (AHCA) is a federation of 51 state-affiliated associations that represents the interests of the long-term health care community. Long-term care facilities include nursing facilities, subacute care centers, rehabilitation centers, intermediate care facilities for the mentally retarded, residential care facilities, and assisted living facilities. The organization seeks to improve the standards of service and administration of long-term care, and to help quality long-term care facilities secure public trust and approval. The AHCA attempts to achieve its mission by offering educational information to its members and to the public, and by lobbying for regulatory and legislative changes.

HOW IS IT STRUCTURED?

The AHCA is a federation of 51 affiliate associations, with one in each state plus one in Washington, D.C. These state affiliates are grouped together into 13 regions, each of which has its own governing vice president. AHCA membership is granted to long-term care institutions, not individuals. Between all of its affiliate organizations, the AHCA boasted a membership of nearly 12,000 institutions in 1999.

The AHCA has two governing bodies, the House of Delegates and a board of directors. The House of Delegates meets once a year, and the board of directors at least three times a year. Between them, they set the overall policy and goals of the AHCA. The AHCA's Executive Committee is responsible for implementing the decisions of the House of Delegates and board of directors. The national staff is managed by a president, and is composed of four departments: Regulatory Affairs, Legislative Affairs, Administration, and Public Relations/Professional Development.

PRIMARY FUNCTIONS

The AHCA works on behalf of almost 12,000 member facilities, which care for more than one million residents, through several different avenues. One major activity of the AHCA is to help members provide the best possible care to their patients. To this end, the ACHA works to develop and maintain standards of long-term care. The AHCA's many professional publications and educational resources also help maintain high quality care in the industry, by keeping the skills of long-term caretakers current. Through these quality efforts, the ACHA not only ensures that residents in its members' facilities are well cared for, but that the public image of the long-term care industry is maintained.

The AHCA also works on behalf of its members to shape legislation and regulation to benefit the long-term care industry. To do so, the AHCA lobbies members of Congress, testifies before congressional committees and regulatory agencies, and informs both the legislative and executive branches of the impact pending legislative and regulatory reforms may have on the long-term care community. According to AHCA literature, its goal is to develop "necessary and reasonable public policies which balance economic and regulatory principles to support quality care and quality of life."

PROGRAMS

The AHCA maintains few national programs, however AHCA state affiliates all sponsor initiatives of their own. The programs that the ACHA does maintain are primarily educational in nature. Since its inception in 1949, the AHCA has sponsored an annual convention and exposition. This three-day event is designed for professionals in subacute medical care, skilled nursing care, managed care, care for the developmentally disabled and other special populations, adult day care, home-based care, and residential and assisted living. Nurses and nursing home and assisted living administrators can earn up to 20 hours of continuing education credit by participating in a selection of over 60 seminar topics. The convention also features addresses by keynote speakers and a large exposition of companies which serve the long-term care industry. Smaller conferences are also held throughout the year and focus on particular issues of concern to the AHCA.

BUDGET INFORMATION

Not made available.

HISTORY

Nursing facilities first developed in the United States around 1900. They traditionally began when boarding-house operators found themselves caring for their aging boarders. Such residences developed into facilities that specialized in the needs of the disabled and aged. By the 1920s, states began to regulate these facilities by developing licensing programs that were implemented and monitored by state health departments.

On January 15, 1945, nine licensed nursing facility administrators met in Indianapolis, Indiana, to discuss the development of a national organization. Plans were made for a midwestern conference of nursing facilities, which subsequently took place in January 1948 with 103 people in attendance. Another conference was held a year later, at which time the American Association of Nursing Homes was formed. The first organizational meeting was held in September 1949 in Toledo, Ohio. The objectives of the newly founded organization was to improve standards of service and administration of member nursing homes, to secure recognition and approval of the public for the work of nursing homes, and to promote education, legislation, and awareness of long-term care issues.

In November 1952, the *American Association of Nursing Homes Journal* was first published. In 1975 the organization changed its name to the American Health Care Association and the publication was renamed the *American Health Care Journal.* In 1986, the magazine name was changed again to *Provider.*

During its history, the AHCA has grown from a small organization into the largest representative of the long-term care community. Because an incident of abuse, neglect, or mismanagement often receives national media coverage, the AHCA has been dedicated to improving methods of quality control for its member organizations. On the other hand, the AHCA also has worked against what it considers to be over-regulation imposed upon the nursing care industry by government agencies such as the Occupational Safety and Health Administration (OSHA). According to reports released by the Health Care Financing Administration (HCFA) and President Bill Clinton, the quality of care in the nursing facility industry has improved. In the 1990s, "overuse" of anti-psychotics was reduced by 50 percent, inappropriate use of physical restraints was reduced from 38 percent to less than 15 percent, and inappropriate use of urinary catheters was reduced by almost 30 percent. Because of its efforts, the AHCA can claim at least partial credit for these improvements.

CURRENT POLITICAL ISSUES

The long-term care industry has expanded rapidly since the founding of the AHCA, as the need for extended care has increased with an aging population. The AHCA has been involved with the increasingly diverse range of services including nursing facilities, subacute care centers, rehabilitation centers, intermediate care facilities for the mentally retarded, residential care facilities, and assisted living facilities. The AHCA has worked to influence legislation and enact regulatory reforms on behalf of the long-term care community.

According to the Health Care Financing Administration (HCFA), in 1998 approximately 1.5 million people were living in nursing facilities in the United States. The HCFA also reported that Medicaid was the primary payer source for 68 percent of patients, and Medicare was the primary payer source for 9 percent. On average, nursing facility care costs almost $41,000 annually per patient. These numbers add up to an extremely expensive industry in which government funding is a critical component. Thus, AHCA members have an important stake in how and when government funding, namely Medicaid and Medicare, is appropriated.

Case Study: The Medicaid Community Attendant Service Act

With the cost of institutional care rising yearly and the popular movement to allow people with disabilities to live as independently as possible, issues surrounding attendant services in home- and community-based (HCB) settings became increasingly popular in the 1990s. In an effort to save tax dollars and increase the quality of life for people with special needs, legislation to create HCB services emerged in 1997.

The Medicaid Community Attendant Service Act was introduced in the House of Representatives as H.R. 2020 by Speaker Newt Gingrich on June 24, 1997. It was subsequently referred to the House Committee on Commerce. The act called for the creation of a national program of HCB services, which it called attendant services. The intent of the bill was to allow people with disabilities to receive personal care services, household services, mobility services, and other health-related tasks in their homes. Under the Attendant Service Act, any individual eligible for Medicaid funding for a stay in a nursing facility, or an intermediate care facility for the mentally retarded (ICF/MR), would qualify for attendant service funds. They could then use these funds to pay for necessary services at home, or in a community setting such as a school, workplace, or religious facility. The legislation allocated $2 billion over six years to help states transition people from institutional to HCB services.

The main proponent of the act was the organization American Disabled for Attendant Programs Today (ADAPT). This organization represents people with disabilities who wish to be cared for in their homes, rather than in long-term care facilities like nursing homes. Representing much of the U.S. long-term care industry, the AHCA stood to lose many patients and future patients if the Medicaid Community Attendant Service Act passed. The AHCA asserted that HCB care is not a cost-effective substitute for nursing facility care. According to the AHCA, the act was fundamentally flawed, because it was based on mistaken assumptions regarding cost, quality of care, and nursing facility population. The AHCA did not believe that the act would accomplish what it was meant to do, but would only place new burdens on the government and taxpayers.

The AHCA argued that the act underestimated the cost of the proposed new system. Specifically, the AHCA claimed there would be a "woodwork effect." By this, the AHCA meant that if the government were to start paying for HCB, many people who had previously paid for home care themselves, or gone without rather than go into a long-term care facility, would come out of the woodwork and demand HCB aid. This meant that, rather than simply shifting money that had been paid exclusively to long-term care facilities over to HCB services, new funds would have to be found to pay for the increased number of eligible people actually seeking help.

The AHCA also challenged the idea that people who could get by with HCB services were being forced into nursing homes to get federal benefits. According to data compiled by the AHCA, nursing facility residents need much more assistance than the population currently served by HCB care. For example, 56 percent of home health patients, compared to 95 percent of nursing home residents, need help bathing. Only 13 percent of home health patients need help eating whereas 57 percent of nursing home residents need assistance with this activity. Many residential patients have complex medical problems that need the attention of highly trained professionals around the clock. Thus, asserted the AHCA, nursing facility residents are usually poor candidates for at-home care, and would have to remain in long-term care facilities even if the Medicaid Community Attendant Service Act was passed. For these same reasons, the AHCA maintained that enacting the bill would do nothing to reduce the number of people who would have to enter long-term care facilities in the years to come.

Due in part to AHCA efforts, the Medicaid Community Attendant Service Act never came up for vote in the 105th Congress. The AHCA helped convince congressmen that the system laid out by the bill would fail to give long-term care patients new options, while at the same time increase the amount of money the government spends on care for the disabled and elderly. The debate over the bill, however, failed to resolve the question of how home health care can be made practical and affordable for those who could benefit from it.

FUTURE DIRECTIONS

The AHCA is attempting to secure a place for a long-term representative on the Medicare Payment Advisory Commission (MedPAC), which currently has no members with extensive long-term care experience. MedPAC was created by the Balanced Budget Act of 1997 to provide Congress with advice and recommendations on Medicare policy. MedPAC replaced the Physicians Payment Review Commission (PPRC) and the Prospective Payment Assessment Commission (PROPAC). The AHCA will have to push for legislation to increase the number of seats on MedPAC in order to gain representation. The AHCA has partnered with rural health groups who also feel inadequately represented in this forum.

The AHCA will continue to work to reform the accreditation process. The AHCA maintains that the current HCFA inspection focuses too much on structural compliance and process-related activities and has little to do with actual quality of patient care. In addition, claims the AHCA, the ineffective accreditation inspection processes are carried out inconsistently from state to state. The AHCA hopes to see legislation introduced that allows more options and better accrediting processes to be established.

GROUP RESOURCES

The AHCA maintains a variety of current information and resources at its Web site, which can be accessed at http://www.ahca.org. The Web site contains information on the nature of the AHCA, its mission, and its members. Also available are AHCA press releases and statistical reports on long-term care, as well as the "Gazette," a daily electronic abstract of issues and trends in the industry. The AHCA also maintains a toll-free Consumer Information Line for families needing guidance about long-term care services, insurance issues, and tips for evaluating a long-term care facility. The line is open daily from 7 A.M. to 10 P.M., eastern standard time, at 1-800-555-9414.

GROUP PUBLICATIONS

The AHCA's largest and oldest publication is the *Provider,* which is available by subscription to the general public, and is provided free of charge to qualified

FAST FACTS

From 2010 to 2030, the number of people age 65 to 84 will increase by an estimated 80 percent.

(Source: American Health Care Association. "Who We Are," 1999.)

long-term care professionals. The magazine covers trends, legislative and regulatory issues, management and financial issues, and other topics important to the long-term care professional. Selected articles are available at the AHCA Web site. The AHCA sells a variety of source books, brochures, and videos. The *Facts and Trends Sourcebook Series* contains three titles covering nursing facilities and assisted living. These publications are geared toward the long-term care professional whereas others, such as *Helping Hands: The Right Way to Choose a Nursing Home*, are aimed at the consumer. To order materials, write the AHCA at 1201 L St. NW, Washington, DC, 20005, or call (202) 842-4444.

BIBLIOGRAPHY

Health Care Financing Administration. *Health Care Financing Review,* Summer 1995.

McGinn, Daniel, and Julie Edelson Halpert. "Final Farewells." *Newsweek,* 14 December 1998.

McGinley, Laurie. "HMOs Press U.S. to Allow Them to Raise Premiums, Cut Benefits Under Medicare." *Wall Street Journal,* 25 September 1998.

Quinn, Jane Bryant. "Reinventing Medicare." *Newsweek,* 28 September 1998.

Rimer, Sara. "Families Bear a Bigger Share of Caring for the Frail Elderly." *New York Times,* 8 June 1998.

Welch, H. Gilbert, David Wennberg, and W. Pete Welch. "The Use of Medicare Home Health Care Services." *New England Journal of Medicine,* 1 August 1996.

American Hospital Association (AHA)

ESTABLISHED: September 1899
EMPLOYEES: 500
MEMBERS: 45,600
PAC: American Hospital Association Political Action
    Committee

Contact Information:

ADDRESS: One N. Franklin Ave.
    Chicago, IL 60606
PHONE: (312) 422-3000
TOLL FREE: (800) 424-4301
FAX: (312) 422-4796
URL: http://www.aha.org
PRESIDENT: Dick Davidson
CEO: Jack Lord, M.D.

WHAT IS ITS MISSION?

The American Hospital Association (AHA) is a national nonprofit organization that serves the interests of hospitals and health care networks. In doing so, it also improves health care services to patients as well as to the community at large. The mission of the AHA is to improve the health of individuals and raise the standard of health care services in communities nationwide.

HOW IS IT STRUCTURED?

The organization's Chicago office was established as AHA national headquarters in 1920. This office houses the majority of the AHA's programs, including member services and leadership programs, as well as the majority of AHA employees. The AHA's office in Washington, D.C., houses the office of the president and AHA policy, communication, and national advocacy staff. Teams of legislative directors and regional executives are officed throughout the United States.

The AHA Board of Trustees acts as the executive branch of the organization. The board consists of 25 trustees, including a chairperson and chairperson-elect. The speaker of the house and the president also sit on the board. The board of trustees has final policy approval authority. The AHA has a House of Delegates that meets annually and serves as the legislative arm of the AHA. Delegates are apportioned according to the number of institutional and personal members in each state. The speaker of the house presides over each sitting of the House of Delegates. Regional policy boards meet between the sessions of the House of Delegates to debate AHA policy options. State hospital association executives from each region serve as ex officio members of the regional policy boards.

Constituency Sections

In 1983 the AHA added seven constituency sections—committees made up of AHA members from across the United States—as a means to better serve and represent the distinct needs of each of its members. Each constituency section is composed of an average of 22 representatives who meet to discuss economic and political issues of common interest. The seven groups are health care systems, small or rural hospitals, metropolitan hospitals, federal hospitals, long-term care and rehabilitation, psychiatric and substance abuse services, and maternal and child health.

Membership

Membership in the AHA is divided into three categories: institutional, associate, and personal. Institutional members include hospitals, preacute and postacute non-hospital facilities, and hospital-affiliated educational programs. Associate members include organizations ineligible for institutional membership, such as commercial firms, consultants, and suppliers. Personal members include those working in the health care field in either private- or government-sector jobs, students studying hospital administration, and health care executive assistants. The AHA has over 5,000 institutional, 600 associate, and 40,000 personal members. It also maintains partnerships with 52 state associations, including Puerto Rico and the District of Columbia, and over 30 metropolitan associations.

PRIMARY FUNCTIONS

The AHA operates on behalf of both its members and the general public in health care delivery matters. Through advocacy, education and information, and leadership development, the organization seeks to impact the formation of legislation and regulatory policy at the national level, as well as provide services and support at the community level.

Advocacy

The AHA uses its Center for Public Affairs (CPA), based in Washington, D.C., to advocate for legislative and regulatory reform and to influence the executive branch of the federal government. The goal of the CPA is to monitor, evaluate, and influence federal policy making. To this end, the AHA makes its leadership available to aid in CPA lobbying efforts, such as testifying before congressional committees and federal agencies. The

AHA also issues formal comments in response to proposed court and administrative rulings and new government policy.

By monitoring pending legislation affecting health care delivery, the AHA lobbies Congress on issues such as ensuring access to home health services, treatment and health insurance plans, Medicare and Medicaid, affordable care, and care for children. In 1978 the organization established the AHA Political Action Committee to increase pressure on Congress and the executive branch.

Education and Information

Education and information offered by the AHA responds to members' needs to stay abreast of current regulations, policies, and social trends. The AHA also helps members remain in compliance with the many regulatory and statutory requirements of hospital administration. Educational and informational services are available to AHA members in several formats.

The AHA Resource Center provides extensive information services to health care professionals. In existence for over 75 years, the Resource Center houses more than 64,000 volumes of current and historical documents on health care administration. The Resource Center is staffed by trained information specialists who locate and retrieve information in support of management decisions and policies, strategic planning, education, and research. The Resource Center also houses the *HealthSTAR* database and *Hospital and Health Administration Index*. Both resources provide comprehensive information on issues, trends, and developments in all areas of health care delivery, including hospital management and public policy. Another responsibility of the Resource Center is the maintenance of the official Center for Hospital and Healthcare Administration History and the National Information Center for Health Services Administration.

Through its Web site, the AHA is able to continually update its members on developments in legal, regulatory, and legislative arenas. The AHA's on-line Legal Resource Library offers a listing of AHA responses to all pending legal and regulatory actions that affect healthcare delivery in the United States. Complicated new regulations, pending policies, and laws are explained in a way that helps members understand their impact. For example, when the federal budget was approved in 1997 as Public Law 105-33, the AHA responded by posting a summary of major provisions, estimated dollar impact of budget provisions, and explanations of particular subjects such as skilled nursing facilities, medical outpatient services, and private contracting under Medicare. The AHA also offers its members a Regulatory Standards Manual.

Leadership

Ongoing leadership training and support is offered through the AHA's Center for Health Care Leadership. The Center provides AHA-member executives assistance in navigating marketing and management issues. Services include providing current information, resources for building a community-based network, educational and networking opportunities, and forums to bring together executive leaders having common interests and goals. The AHA's Division of Trustee and Community Leadership helps health care trustees, executives, and community leaders make strategic decisions, form community partnerships, and improve local health-care services.

PROGRAMS

The AHA sponsors a wide range of programs for its members. In January 1997, for example, the AHA initiated the New Partnership for Action (PFA). PFA is a legislative and grassroots advocacy program designed to build a team of hospital and health care system advocates called "key contacts." The PFA program is open to anyone—members and nonmembers—in the health care system. Key contacts range from hospital administrators, senior staff, and trustees to volunteers and patients. Through distribution of resources and up-to-date information, the AHA prepares its key contacts to advocate for the hospital and health care system.

In an attempt to bring the issue of health care coverage to the forefront of the public policy agenda, the AHA created its "Campaign for Coverage: A Community Health Challenge" program in 1997. The campaign's goal was to reduce the number of people without health care coverage by four million during 1998. In conjunction with state associations the AHA used the Campaign for Coverage as a forum to increase public awareness, advocate at the state and federal level for legislative actions, and encourage member organizations to expand the number of their own employees covered by health insurance.

The AHA also attempted to address the problem posed by the "millennium bug"—the inability of computer chips to recognize the year 2000. Because hospitals operate seven days a week, 24 hours a day, and are heavily dependent on computer operations to deliver safe, effective care, the AHA formed a task force to study the Y2K problem. The objective of the task force was to educate health care practitioners and patients about the potential problems of the "millennium bug" and press medical device and computer manufacturers to bring equipment into compliance with Year 2000 standards.

BUDGET INFORMATION

Not made available.

HISTORY

The AHA had its origins in the Association of Hospital Superintendents formed in Cleveland, Ohio, in 1899 by eight hospital superintendents. Originally, only superintendents were allowed membership; in 1906 the organization expanded to include other hospital executives as non-voting, associate members, and also changed its name to the American Hospital Association. Institutional membership was incorporated into the AHA structure in 1918.

Upon its formation, the Association of Hospital Superintendents focused on hospital management: procedures and methods, hospital economics, and hospital inspection concerns. As the AHA broadened its membership, its goals also broadened, and by 1937 the organization's focus was the development of outpatient services, professional education, and scientific research. By 1920, shortly after expanding its membership, AHA headquarters was located in Chicago; in 1942, in response to the supply shortage caused by World War II (1939–45), a second office was opened in Washington, D.C. to help members contact federal agencies and obtain needed supplies. The Washington office now serves as the lobbying center for the AHA.

Until a House of Delegates was established in 1938, every AHA member attending the organization's annual convention had a vote. Thus, those members closest to the convention site had a major voting advantage. With the formation of the AHA House of Delegates, proportionate representation from each state created the voting body at annual meetings. In the same year, the AHA formed its first six policy development councils.

In 1968 regional advisory boards (RABs) were created to improve communications between trustees and delegates on the matter of policy issues. With one board representing each of nine regions, RAB members originally discussed policy and relayed concerns, issues, and interests to the Board of Trustees. The AHA underwent further restructuring in 1987, altering its executive and legislative bodies and expanding its mission to stress leadership in public policy, representation and advocacy, and services. In addition, RABs were transformed into regional policy boards authorized to debate policy options. Final policy approval authority was removed from the House of Delegates and given to the Board of Trustees.

Developing the Organization

In the late 1930s health insurance coverage was new and controversial. In 1937 the AHA established the Hospital Service Plan Commission (HSPC) and two years later adopted a blue cross as a logo designating health coverage plans that met certain criteria of this new organization. The HSPC eventually became Blue Cross/Blue Shield, and the AHA retained close ties with it until 1960 when the Blue Cross Association was created. Formal relations between the two were dissolved in 1972.

The AHA was instrumental in creating the Commission on Hospital Care which, in 1946, set forth the recommendations that served as the basis for the Hospital Survey and Construction Act. This act, also known as the Hill-Burton Act, earmarked federal funds for modernizing those hospitals that had postponed updating their facilities during the Great Depression and World War II (1939–45). Beginning in 1946 more than $4.6 billion in grant money, along with $1.5 billion in loans, was distributed to approximately 6,800 health care facilities in more than 4,000 communities. In return for funding, hospitals agreed to provide free or reduced-fee care to persons unable to pay for treatment. AHA contributions to patient welfare continued in 1951 with the establishment of the Commission on Financing of Hospital Services, which focused on health care problems unique to the elderly and led to the creation of Medicare in 1965.

CURRENT POLITICAL ISSUES

Public policy issues surrounding health care delivery are extensive and complex. Much of the AHA's lobbying efforts revolve around interpreting and implementing federal policy, law, and programs such as Medicare. Created in 1965 as part of the Social Security Act, Title XVIII, Medicare is a federally funded health insurance program for Americans 65 years and older and those with special disabilities. Because Medicare directly impacts the economic management of hospitals and health care facilities, the AHA has a vested interest in the formation of Medicare-related policies.

Case Study: The False Claims Act

The False Claims Act authorizes the U.S. Department of Justice to sue any person or company that has submitted a false claim for payment. The law, which had been in existence for several years, was added to the AHA's agenda when the Justice Department began a major investigation of Medicare billing practices at 4,700 hospitals across the United States. With the threat of significant fines and legal costs mounting, the AHA worked to repeal or change the False Claims Act to limit member liability.

The False Claims Act allows the government to recover up to three times the amount of money falsely claimed. For example, if a hospital received $50,000 from Medicare for services not rendered, they could be fined $150,000. Also, the Act imposes a punitive fine of $5,000 to $10,000 for every fraudulent claim made.

The False Claim Act addresses three areas where erroneous billing can result: laboratory "unbundling," the "diagnostic-related group (DRG) three-day window," and "physicians at teaching hospitals" or PATH audits. Penalties are incurred from hospitals submitting bills for individual laboratory tests when tests should be "bun-

dled" and submitted together for a lower reimbursement per test. Second, Medicare's DRG three-day window requiring that hospitals bill inpatients for certain pre-admission services provided within three days of admission is suspect as an avenue for double billing. And finally, the government investigates physicians at teaching hospitals who falsely bill Medicare for services actually performed by medical residents.

In response to the Justice Department probe, the AHA claims hospitals have been unfairly targeted and assumed to be guilty. While acknowledging that billing errors are made, the organization insists that errors do not constitute fraud. Hospitals and health systems submit on average nearly 200,000 Medicare claims each day, totaling approximately 72 million a year. Total compliance requires following 1,800 pages of law, 1,300 pages of regulations interpreting the law, and thousands of additional pages of instructions. Under such a complicated and oftentimes contradictory set of guidelines, errors naturally occur.

The Justice Department's approach to the problem—hospitals under investigation were sent a letter demanding they choose between being penalized for false claims or settling within 20 days for a much smaller amount—was called "heavy-handed" by the AHA. In fact, demand letters with fines and penalties totaling almost $36 million were sent to 22 hospitals in Massachusetts. A survey found that, in a group of over two million bills totaling more than $2.3 billion, only 2,960 claims were in error, the total of the error $450,000. However, rather than face legal costs and the possibility of larger fines, the hospitals settled for approximately $943,000.

Insisting that the Justice Department misused the False Claims Act, the AHA has argued that, although providers make every possible effort to minimize errors, some errors are unavoidable due to confusing, unclear, and contradictory policies and procedures. In an effort to eliminate the fines imposed on what they claim were honest mistakes, the AHA threw its support behind the proposed Health Care Claims Guidance Act of 1998.

The Health Care Claims Guidance Act, designed to amend the False Claims Act to distinguish between fraud and mistakes, would only apply to federally funded health care, namely Medicare and Medicaid. Under the act, fines would be reduced to the amount erroneously billed plus interest, rather than $5,000 to $10,000 per bill; health care claims would only fall under the False Claims Act if the overbilling was greater than a set percentage of the provider's total annual claims; and the Justice Department would be required to show "clear and convincing evidence" of fraud rather than a "preponderance of evidence."

Strong initial support for the Health Care Claims Guidance Act prompted action by the Department of Health and Human Services Office of the Inspector General (OIG). In 1998 the OIG announced new guidelines for investigating hospital fraud, agreeing to establish min-

FAST FACTS

By 2005 nearly 47 million Americans will be uninsured.

(Source: American Hospital Association. "Campaign for Coverage," 1999.)

imum monetary thresholds for billing error investigations. The Justice Department also stated its intention to seek substantial evidence before launching a full investigation.

Public Impact

Although the Health Care Claims Guidance Act did not pass, the AHA considers itself the victor in the battle over false claims: The sentiment represented by the bill forced the government to initiate new policies answering two of the AHA's three demands. However, according to the AHA, the unfair enforcement of the False Claims Act left hospitals and health care systems in a precarious position. Forced to pay settlement costs to avoid legal fees and large-scale penalties wrongly imposed, the health care delivery system is now under siege. While the AHA works vigorously to persuade the government to find a different resolution to honest mistakes, taxpayer groups, such as Taxpayers against Fraud and Citizens against Government Waste, have given voice to a rising concern over the mismanagement and waste of taxpayer money. With health care costs continuing to rise and budget cuts underway, such battles for fiscal responsibility will continue to be waged.

FUTURE DIRECTIONS

The AHA continues to address the False Claims Act and other regulatory and legislative issues affecting the field of medicine. For example, as part of the Balanced Budget Act of 1997 hospitals began to be penalized for releasing patients from treatment earlier than the national average. These hospitals now receive lower reimbursement rates from Medicare, costing those facilities $450 million and undermining their ability to provide cost-effective care. The AHA also suggests that reducing funding for home health care, also a result of the Balanced Budget Act, would jeopardize seriously ill individuals, and supports legislation designed to protect home health agencies' ability to remain financially solvent while caring for their patients.

GROUP RESOURCES

The AHA maintains a Web site at http://www.aha.org that includes current, comprehensive information on organization activities. While select information is only available to members via password, most of the Web site can be accessed by the public. Information available includes updates on pending legislative and regulatory issues, programs such as the Campaign for Coverage and Year 2000, and leadership and educational opportunities. The site also offers compliance resources and access to on-line resources such as the Legal Resource Library and the Resource Center catalog. The Resource Center provides extensive informational services on a fee-for-service basis. The AHA's Washington, D.C. office can be contacted toll-free at 1-800-424-4301.

GROUP PUBLICATIONS

All AHA publications are produced through the AHA-owned American Hospital Publishing, Inc., which puts out five publications. On-line versions and subscription information are available at http://www.amhpi.com. With a paid circulation of over 105,000, *Hospitals & Health Networks* is read primarily by hospital managers and focuses on trends and issues affecting health care delivery. *Materials and Management* is utilized by health care executives responsible for purchasing and managing supplies and equipment and has a paid circulation of over 26,000. *Health Facilities Management* and *Trustee,* both with a paid circulation over 30,000, target facilities management administrators and trustees of local hospitals. The *AHA News,* which has a circulation of almost 25,000, is a weekly newspaper for health care delivery executives that covers federal and state public policy and health care news. The subscription rate is $50 per year for AHA members and $110 per year for nonmembers.

BIBLIOGRAPHY

Annas, George J. *The Rights of Patients: The Basic ACLU Guide to Patient Rights.* Carbondale, Ill.: Southern Illinois University Press, 1989.

"Best Hospital Finder." *U.S. News Online,* http://www.usnews.com.

Chandrasekaran, Rajiv. "Health Coalition Warns of Year 2000 Crisis in Medical Devices." *Washington Post,* 10 July 1998.

Lesparre, Michael, Gail Lovinger, and Kathy Poole. "A Century of the AHA." *Hospitals and Health Networks,* 20 July 1998.

Southwick, Arthur F. *The Law of Hospital and Health Care Administration.* Ann Arbor, Mich.: Health Care Administration Press, 1978.

American Indian Movement (AIM)

WHAT IS ITS MISSION?

The American Indian Movement (AIM) seeks, in broadest terms, to further the political, economic, social, and cultural well-being of American Indians throughout the United States, and to raise public awareness of American Indian issues among both Indians and non-Indians. Throughout the organization's history, AIM has concerned itself with a wide variety of issues in pursuit of its mission. Many of its efforts have centered around promoting American Indian sovereignty and self-determination. These concepts involve the establishment of truly autonomous tribal self-government and greater control of land, economic resources, and educational institutions within Indian communities. AIM also works to better social conditions, both on reservations and in urban areas.

HOW IS IT STRUCTURED?

Since 1993, understanding AIM's structure has posed quite a challenge. In that year, a dispute grew between two major internal factions, and the situation has remained tangled. One faction views AIM as a centralized organization, with local chapters under the control of national headquarters; the other considers AIM to be a confederation of autonomous local chapters. Each side of this internal conflict sees itself as the authentic manifestation of AIM and emphatically denies the legitimacy of the other.

The first faction, calling itself "National AIM," has headquarters in Minneapolis, Minnesota. One leader of this group is Dennis Banks, who acts as National Field

ESTABLISHED: July 1968
EMPLOYEES: Undetermined
MEMBERS: 5,000
PAC: None

Contact Information:
E-MAIL: http://www.dickshovel.com/AIMIntro.html

Director and operates out of Kentucky. Other leaders include Vernon Bellecourt, who heads the Minneapolis office, Vernon's brother Clyde, Carol Standing Elk, and William Means. Banks and Clyde Bellecourt, Ojibwe men from Minnesota reservations and veterans of the Minnesota prison system by their early twenties, helped found AIM in Minneapolis in 1968. Vernon Bellecourt and Means joined the organization later in its history and, like Banks, have remained prominent leaders. Standing Elk became the western regional director of National AIM in the 1990s.

The other faction calls itself the "International Confederation of Autonomous Chapters." It includes over 20 chapters—some regional, some based in individual cities—in all areas of the United States and Canada. The spokespeople of these chapters, such as Ward Churchill of the Colorado chapter, Bobby Castillo of San Francisco, and long-time AIM activist Russell Means, deny the existence of a national headquarters or any centralized decision-making body.

After Russel Means, an Oglala Lakota, joined AIM in 1969, he became one of the organization's best-known and most controversial leaders. He now stands on the opposite side of the AIM divide from his brother, William. Ward Churchill is a prolific writer on American Indian sovereignty, lands, treaties, and environmental concerns, and serves as the director of the American Indian Studies program at the University of Colorado at Boulder.

Committees and Affiliates

Within local AIM chapters—whether they associate themselves with National AIM or consider themselves autonomous—there often exist councils or committees that focus on certain segments of the community they serve. The Arizona chapter, for instance, includes both a Youth Council and an Elders Council.

Over the years, AIM has forged a number of alliances in order to better pursue its various objectives. Today some members of the organization retain close ties to the International Indian Treaty Council (IITC), founded by AIM members in 1974, which acts as a consultant to the United Nations on indigenous issues worldwide. On a local level, grassroots groups such as the Lakota Student Alliance affiliate themselves with AIM chapters as they work to increase public awareness of native issues. AIM representatives have also worked with a great number of tribal entities and reservation communities. Some chapters encourage the formation of local support groups in order to facilitate canvassing or education campaigns.

PRIMARY FUNCTIONS

Given the broad scope of AIM's concerns, and the fractured nature of its structure, its activities have ranged widely. Various factions, chapters, and individuals have employed many types of action ranging from confrontational, physical protests to scholarly publication, from international lobbying to the establishment of local alternative institutions.

Reestablishing Sovereignty

Part of AIM's mission includes the reestablishment of sovereignty and self-determination among Indian people. A central goal is to reinstate and protect treaty rights. Between 1790 and 1870, the U.S. government signed over 350 treaties with American Indian tribes, procuring land and natural resources and paving the way for westward expansion, settlement, and development. In exchange, the treaties promised Indian people various types of compensation, including money, food rations and material goods, reservations safe from further encroachment, and rights to hunt, fish, and gather on homelands relinquished under the agreements. Government representatives, however, sometimes established the treaties by dishonest means. Additionally, the United States government has failed to honor many of these agreements.

Many Indian activists focus on treaties as a means of recovering land and reclaiming resources lost to non-Indian development and environmental destruction. They push to dissolve invalid treaties and demand the rights guaranteed under valid ones. They point out that the treaty-making government considered the Indian tribes sovereign nations and this supports American Indian self-determination. AIM has also pushed for Indian control of political, economic, and educational institutions on reservations.

Reclaiming Culture

Indian-controlled education also helps AIM's goal to strengthen and reclaim American Indian cultural identity. Within Indian communities, AIM speaks out against apathy and defeatism, encourages sobriety, and promotes a return to traditional spirituality. These efforts provide countermeasures against the social ills that plague the American Indian population, which experiences the highest rates of poverty, malnutrition, infant mortality, and teen suicide of any group in the country, as well as disproportionately high rates of alcoholism and unemployment.

AIM's leaders devote energy to changing attitudes in the wider non-Indian society through public speaking engagements as well as protests against stereotypical, racist representations and symbols. For example, some AIM chapters regularly protest annual Columbus Day parades. To many Indian people, Columbus' arrival in the Americas does not represent the beginning of discovery, settlement, and success. Instead, they believe it marks the first step toward centuries of oppression, destruction, and displacement for hundreds of Indian

BIOGRAPHY:

Dennis J. Banks

Activist; Educator; and Author (b. 1932) American Indian Movement (AIM) cofounder Dennis Banks is an American Indian leader, teacher, lecturer, activist, and author. He was born in 1932 on the Leech Lake Indian Reservation in northern Minnesota. Banks was the principal leader of AIM when worldwide media focused on the group in 1973 during a 71-day occupation of Wounded Knee on the Pine Ridge Sioux Reservation. Said Banks of the protest that turned into a forced occupation, "The decision to take Wounded Knee came when Ellen Moves Camp pointed at us and said, 'What are you men going to do about it?' If the women hadn't done that, we'd still be meeting." Convicted of riot and assault charges stemming from a protest that pre-dated the Wounded Knee event, Banks refused his sentence and fled underground. When then California Governor Jerry Brown offered him amnesty, Banks relocated and began to attend the University of California at Davis. He also taught classes at Deganawidah-Quetzecoatl University

(an all-Indian controlled institution) and became their first American Indian university chancellor. In 1985 Banks finally surrendered to South Dakota authorities and served 18 months in prison. Today Banks lectures worldwide and has collaborated and worked on several musical releases and films. In 1994 Banks coauthored, with Duane Champagne, *Native America: Portrait of the*

Peoples. Banks's legacy will best be served by his promotion of the Sacred Run. In 1978 Banks began the annual multicultural, international event as a means of spreading the awareness of the sacredness of all Life and of humankind's relationship to the planet, Mother Earth.

---

tribes. AIM protesters therefore see Columbus Day as an occasion for sorrow, rather than celebration.

PROGRAMS

AIM's specific programs vary among regions and individuals. Some have a national scope; leaders of National AIM organized national conferences throughout the 1980s and 1990s. Other programs operate independently of official AIM sponsorship and focus on local issues, such as the American Indian Opportunities Industrialization Center in Minneapolis. Founded in 1979 by Clyde Bellecourt—one of AIM's founders and a member of National AIM—this organization provides job training for Minneapolis-St. Paul's Indian population.

One of AIM's most unique educational projects has proven to be one of its most enduring. In 1972, some of AIM's founders helped establish the Heart of the Earth survival school in Minneapolis. The school took in Indian students who had left mainstream schools, whether by dropping out or by suspension. Eventually it became an alternative to mainstream education, one that sought to give Indian children pride in their culture and to teach neglected aspects of American Indian history. The Heart of the Earth school still operates under a board of directors composed of Indian community members and par-

ents, and its culture-based approach to education has provided an example for other programs elsewhere in the country.

BUDGET INFORMATION

Not made available.

HISTORY

AIM began in Minneapolis, Minnesota, in the summer of 1968 under the leadership of several individuals, including George Mitchell, Harold Goodsky, Clyde Bellecourt, Eddie Benton Banai, Dennis Banks, and Pat Ballanger. Bellecourt and Benton met while serving time in Stillwater prison, where they began an Indian cultural-awareness program. In the late 1960s and early 1970s, AIM joined other organizations of politically and socially disadvantaged groups—including African Americans, Mexican Americans, women, gays, and lesbians—in asserting their rights and speaking out against discrimination and inequality.

Although AIM began from a wave of general activism, the movement's development also stemmed from factors specific to the American Indian experience. In the 1950s and 1960s, the U.S. government launched a new federal Indian policy of termination and relocation. Under termination, the government targeted tribes it deemed ready for assimilation into mainstream society, and rescinded their federally recognized status. This nullified protection of their reservations and cut them off from government funding and social services. Relocation encouraged Indian people to leave their reservations and tribal communities for urban centers, giving them money to move to a number of designated cities and promising assistance with employment and housing upon their arrival. Although the government intended relocation to transform Indian people from economically dependent reservation communities into assimilated urban dwellers, the policy proved ill-conceived and poorly administered. It left in its wake an underemployed, culturally alienated urban Indian population with insufficient social services.

In response to relocation, AIM began to work on improving urban social conditions for Minneapolis-St. Paul's American Indian population. It created the Indian Patrol, a citizen's patrol formed in response to police mistreatment of Indians in the East Franklin neighborhood of Minneapolis. In addition to the patrol, early AIM activities included the establishment of a legal rights center, a reform program for juvenile offenders, and a survival school for Indian youth.

The Movement Grows

As AIM grew in strength and scope, and as American Indians in other parts of the country began to organize, the group's Minneapolis-based leaders became increasingly involved in broader national issues. They also began to articulate a more philosophical ideology. Members attended meetings of the National Council of Churches in 1969 and the National Conference of Welfare Workers in 1970, trying to bring attention to Indian people's unequal social and political status and to raise money for AIM.

The movement also turned increasingly to high-profile protest, hoping to raise public awareness of Indian issues through symbolism and confrontational rhetoric. Leaders spoke out against racist images and stereotypical representations in popular culture; for instance, they encouraged national demonstrations against the depiction of American Indians in the film *A Man Called Horse* in 1970. AIM also used public protest to raise awareness of Indian land claims and treaty rights, and to challenge the standard version of American history with a more Indian-centered story of colonization, displacement, and government deception. In this vein, AIM staged protests at Mt. Rushmore in 1970 and 1971, on the *Mayflower II* at Plymouth Rock on Thanksgiving, 1970, and in an abandoned building at Fort Snelling in St. Paul for a week in 1971.

During this time, AIM also expanded its organizational network. It recruited charismatic spokespeople such as Russell Means, then director of the Cleveland American Indian center, Carter Camp, and John Trudell. By 1971, AIM had chapters in Minnesota, Ohio, and Kansas. At a conference in the spring of 1971, it elected Means as its first national coordinator.

While AIM increased its political activities and formulated its stance on sovereignty and treaty issues, several of its members displayed a growing interest in traditional culture and spirituality. The AIM leaders began publicly to emphasize the need for American Indians to reconnect with their reservations, their spiritual roots, and the traditions and values of their elders and ancestors. In 1972 Oglala Lakota medicine man Leonard Crow Dog became a spiritual advisor to AIM.

AIM vs. the U.S. Goverment

Beginning in 1972, AIM entered a period of high national media exposure and conflict with the government, particularly the FBI. In October, AIM and other Native American organizations began the Trail of Broken Treaties Caravan from the West Coast to Washington, D.C., stopping at reservations along the way. The caravan of several hundred Indians arrived in Washington in November, just before the presidential election, intending to stage nonviolent demonstrations and to present the government with its Twenty Points of demands. The document focused on the honoring of existing treaties, the reestablishment of a treaty relationship between the government and sovereign Indian nations, and a reorganization of the Bureau of Indian Affairs (BIA). When participants discovered that organizers had not made lodging arrangements as promised, they decided to go to the Bureau of Indian Affairs building. There Interior Department officials worked to find them lodging, while local riot police monitored the situation from nearby.

Unfortunately, this tense but peaceful situation eventually turned violent. As the Indians waited in the BIA lobby, a government miscommunication caused police to burst into the building and demand that the Indians leave. A fight broke out, and the angry Indians pushed the police out of the building and then barricaded themselves inside. They remained there while negotiating with federal officials, and vandalized much of the bureau's interior. Finally, as the protesters grew weary, the government agreed to review the Twenty Points and offered them a monetary settlement, thus ending the six-day occupation. Eventually the Nixon administration virtually dismissed the Twenty Points, which fueled AIM resentment and recalcitrance in later encounters.

After the BIA incident in Washington, AIM's efforts gravitated toward South Dakota, where the organization was to have its widest national impact. Early in 1973, AIM arrived in Custer, South Dakota, to protest the murder of Wesley Bad Heart Bull, an Indian man, by a white resident. The protest resulted in a riot and a violent confrontation with police. Although Indians in the region had long complained of racial violence and unequal legal protection, it was AIM's growing notoriety that brought widespread public attention to this case. In addition, AIM's efforts fostered a sense of solidarity among Indian people and gave them a determination to stand up for themselves.

In February, AIM became even more involved in South Dakota conflicts. Oglala Lakota people of the Pine Ridge Reservation near Custer, frustrated with Tribal Chairman Richard Wilson's alleged corrupt administration, asked AIM for help. Wilson supposedly manipulated elections and used physical intimidation to remain in power. On February 27, in protest of Wilson's tactics and what they saw as his collusion with corrupt federal officials in the BIA, AIM leaders and members of the Oglala Sioux Civil Rights Organization took control of Wounded Knee, a village on the Pine Ridge Reservation and the site of the infamous 1890 massacre of over 300 Lakota men, women and children by government troops. The occupation, which received national media attention lasted 71 days, and inspired a military siege by the army, the FBI, the BIA, and state and local police. It also garnered a good deal of public sympathy for the protesters.

After the occupation ended, a period of accelerated militant confrontation ensued on Pine Ridge between AIM members and supporters and Wilson's police force, accompanied by the constant presence of the FBI. Throughout the mid-1970s the government made a proliferation of arrests and dozens of violent deaths occurred, including over 60 AIM supporters and two FBI agents.

Beyond Wounded Knee

Several AIM leaders became embroiled in lengthy court trials for their participation at Wounded Knee and for alleged implication in the two FBI agents' deaths. Internal solidarity weakened, as both rumored and exposed FBI informants fostered suspicions and accelerated already existing rivalries. By 1979 AIM had dissolved the position of national chair. During the 1980s, several AIM-affiliated representatives became active internationally in the global struggle for indigenous peoples' rights, and others kept some of AIM's initiatives alive through local chapters, but the movement as a nationally organized whole had lost much of its effectiveness.

In the 1990s, factionalism arose between those who tried to resurrect a national headquarters—calling themselves National AIM—and those who prefer local autonomy, and who have organized into the Confederation of Autonomous Chapters. The members of the confederation feel that a centralized bureaucracy compromises the kind of grassroots activism they see as the heart of the movement and furthers only individual political interests. Churchill told the *San Francisco Chronicle* in 1994 that the Banks/Bellecourt faction "considers AIM to be a corporation—a career—but we consider it to be a national

liberation movement." The confederation also condemns Clyde for his 1986 conviction on drug-dealing charges as setting a poor example.

National AIM, on the other hand, challenges Churchill's claims of American Indian heritage, denies him the right to speak for Indian people, and refuses to recognize the Confederation of Autonomous Chapters. Vernon Bellecourt has even gone so far as to accuse Churchill (as well as Russell Means, Bobby Castillo, and others) of working as FBI agents to undermine AIM. These internal conflicts have prompted some to say that AIM no longer exists at all. Others insist that as long as a spirit of stubborn resistance and cultural pride remains strong in Indian communities, AIM too remains alive.

Throughout its history, AIM's tactics and its legacy of militant rhetoric and violent confrontation have sparked controversy in wider American Indian circles. AIM has clashed with more conservative Indian organizations such as the National Congress of American Indians (NCAI). The NCAI, a political lobbying group, has dismissed AIM's radical style as an ineffective means of political and social change, while AIM has criticized the NCAI for working within the mainstream political system. Gerald Vizenor, a well-respected Indian scholar and long an outspoken critic of AIM, has also denounced AIM leaders for their radicalism. Vizenor accuses AIM's most prominent leaders of putting on the trappings of spiritualism and traditional culture only to court white supporters, and challenges their right to speak for reservation issues from an urban context.

CURRENT POLITICAL ISSUES

Despite recent internal squabbling, AIM leaders continue to function as activists for Indian rights. Whether representing National AIM or an autonomous chapter, or acting independently, they address a variety of political issues affecting American Indian people. AIM members promote tribal recovery of land and control over resources and join other environmental activists in condemning overdevelopment of land and industrial pollution. Some of them actively protest the imprisonment of AIM activist Leonard Peltier for the death of two FBI agents. They see him as a political prisoner and lobby for his release. Other AIM representatives work to combat racist attitudes among non-Indians and remove stereotypical representations of Indian people in American culture.

While fighting to replace negative perceptions of American Indians, AIM also works to promote a more realistic understanding of Indian people and cultures. This includes an effort to inject an Indian perspective into the telling of American history. AIM activists say that the story of the United States's founding includes the dispossession of indigenous cultures. To promote that message, AIM activists often turn to national historical symbols as potent sites of protest.

Case Study: Little Bighorn National Monument

One of the United States's most powerful historical symbols, "Custer's Last Stand," is kept alive at Little Bighorn National Monument in Crow Agency, Montana. The battlefield, a popular tourist site, is also a place where AIM has worked to change historical representation of American Indians. Since its creation, the site has marked the 1876 defeat of George Custer's Seventh Cavalry, by Crazy Horse and his Cheyenne and Oglala Sioux warriors, with a 12-foot granite obelisk honoring Custer's men and their Crow scouts. In 1988, though, AIM activists erected their own makeshift memorial, a rough steel plaque dedicated to the Cheyenne and Sioux who fought Custer and died while protecting their homelands, families, and way of life from further white encroachment.

Although the park service removed the plaque within weeks, AIM's action caused the park superintendent to push his superiors to complete plans for an official monument to the Indian warriors. Within two years, Congress passed a bill to that effect, and finally, in the fall of 1997, an Indian memorial received approval. In a 1996 article in the *Bismarck Tribune*, Little Bighorn Park Superintendent Gerard Baker commented that the site ". . . needs balance. What happened here means so many things to so many people, the best way to understand the battle is to let all the stories be told." The addition of the new memorial will help realize AIM's vision of a more complex and complete understanding of Indian-white conflicts.

SUCCESSES AND FAILURES

As evidenced at Little Bighorn National Monument, although AIM frequently inspires controversy the movement has proved successful over the years at raising public awareness of American Indian issues and inserting at least one version of an Indian perspective into mainstream American life. AIM has not proved successful in all of its endeavors. Leonard Peltier's imprisonment offers a case in point. Despite symbolic marches, appeals to the president of the United States, petitions, and international lobbying efforts, the former AIM activist remains in prison. Internal conflicts have surfaced here as well, as members of National and Autonomous AIM disagree over who should head efforts to free Peltier.

FUTURE DIRECTIONS

In the future, AIM's most formidable challenge involves repairing the schisms within its ranks. As long as various factions expend energy fighting each other instead of working toward common goals, the movement's effectiveness remains curtailed. Until its leaders find some way to overcome internal factionalism, AIM most likely will continue to pursue similar goals from apparently opposing fronts in its campaign for American Indian sovereignty, self-determination, equal opportunity, and cultural viability.

GROUP RESOURCES

Various AIM chapters offer a number of resources, including statistics and other research, archives, and educational and social services. Following are ways to access some of these resources:

- AIM web site: The site, maintained by Jordan S. Dill, includes the perspectives of both major AIM factions and offers links to many related sites. Access the site at http://www.dickshovel.com/AIMIntro.html.

- Office of National Field Director of National AIM: Contact Dennis Banks at P.O. Box 315, Newport, KY, 41071; phone: (606) 431-2346; fax: (606) 581-9458.

- American Indian Opportunities Industrialization Community Job Training Center: Contact Vernon Bellecourt at 1915 Chicago Ave., Minneapolis, MN, 55404; phone: (612) 879-8113

- AIM Arizona: Call (602) 668-8926

- Autonomous AIM chapter, Cleveland: 2012 W. 25th St., Rm. 515, Cleveland, OH, 44113; phone: (216) 641-8684; E-mail: acjazz@iserv.net.

- Autonomous AIM chapter, Michigan: 1336 Commonwealth, Ypsilanti, MI, 48198; E-mail: bryanhalf @aol.com.

GROUP PUBLICATIONS

AIM publishes one periodical, *Survival News*, on a quarterly basis.

BIBLIOGRAPHY

Annette, Jaimes M. *The State of Native America: Genocide, Colonization, and Resistance*. Boston: South End Press, 1992.

Bruce, Heather. "Protesters Finish 3000-Mile March Calling for Release of American Indian Leader." *Knight-Ridder/Tribune News Service,* 15 July 1994.

Churchill, Ward. *Struggle for the Land: Indigenous Resistance to Genocide, Ecocide, and Expropriation in Contemporary North America*. Monroe, Maine: Common Courage Press, 1993.

Deloria, Vine Jr. *Behind the Trail of Broken Treaties: An Indian Declaration of Independence*. Austin: University of Texas Press, 1974.

Elvin, John. "Indian Murders Still Beg the Question of Justice." *Washington Times,* 1 July 1996.

Giago, Tim. "Indian Nations Across the U.S. Say They Don't Need Organizations Speaking For Them," *Knight-Ridder/Tribune News Service,* 13 October 1993.

Glier, Ray, and Chuck Murr. "AIM Secures Permits, Plans Series Protests." *USA Today,* 19 October 1995.

Hayes, Jack. "Blood Brothers." *Minneapolis-St. Paul Magazine,* March, 1996.

Pevar, Stephen L. *The Rights of Indians and Tribes: The Basic ACLU Guide to Indian and Tribal Rights.* Carbondale, Ill.: Southern Illinois University Press, 1992.

Reeves, Tracey A. "20 Years After Shooting of Federal Agents, Imprisoned American Indian Has Won Support Around the World." *Knight-Ridder/Tribune News Service,* 28 June 1995.

Salter, Peter. "Past Lives in the Present." *Bismarck Tribune,* 30 June 1996.

Smith, Paul Chaat, and Robert Allen Warrior. *Like a Hurricane: The Indian Movement from Alcatraz to Wounded Knee.* New York: The New Press, 1996.

Vizenor, Gerald. "Separatists Behind the Blinds." *Wordarrows: Indians and Whites in the New Fur Trade.* Minneapolis: University of Minnesota Press, 1978.

American Institute of Certified Public Accountants (AICPA)

ESTABLISHED: September 20, 1887
EMPLOYEES: 750
MEMBERS: 332,335
PAC: American Insitutes of Certified Public
     Accountants Effective Legislation Committee

Contact Information:

ADDRESS: 1211 Avenue of the Americas
     New York, NY 10036
PHONE: (212) 596-6200
TOLL FREE: (888) 777-7077
FAX: (212) 596-6213
E-MAIL: Memsat@aicpa.org
URL: http://www.aicpa.org
CHAIRMAN: Stuart Kessler
PRESIDENT; CEO: Barry C. Melancon

WHAT IS ITS MISSION?

The American Institute of Certified Public Accountants (AICPA) is the national professional organization for all Certified Public Accountants, commonly known as CPAs. The institute's own mission statement claims a single fundamental purpose: "to provide members with the resources, information, and leadership that enable them to provide valuable services in the highest professional manner to benefit the public as well as employers and clients."

To achieve this purpose the AICPA pursues a number of major objectives. To protect and promote its members' interests, it represents all CPAs before government and regulatory bodies. It establishes uniform standards for the certification and licensing of CPAs, in order to protect the "CPA" designation and keep it meaningful. Similarly it establishes professional standards for the work of all CPAs, and monitors the performance of its members. Through its public awareness campaigns, the institute also endeavors to promote confidence in the integrity and professionalism of CPAs.

HOW IS IT STRUCTURED?

The AICPA is a private, nonprofit professional association. Its top leadership is divided into three significant bodies: the Governing Council, the Board of Directors, and the Joint Trial Board. The Governing Council is the policy-making body of the institute, and meets only twice a year to determine programs and policies. It includes 260 members with representatives from every U.S. state

and territory. The Board of Directors, the acting executive committee of the Council, directs the institute's activities between council meetings. The board consists of a chair, vice-chair, immediate past chair, and president; three representatives of the public; and 16 directors. The chair has ultimate authority in board proceedings, while the president is the chief administrative officer of the AICPA staff. The Joint Trial Board enforces professional standards by setting disciplinary charges against state societies and AICPA members.

The work of the AICPA is divided among approximately 135 boards, committees, subcommittees, and teams, which consist mostly of volunteers and which are rounded out by members of the AICPA staff. Some of these are designated "senior" committees by the institute's bylaws because of their importance. Senior committees include the Board of Examiners, which administrates the Uniform CPA Examination, the Information Technology Executive Committee; the Tax Executive Committee, and ten other boards or committees.

Some senior committees are further distinguished as "senior technical" committees and boards, a designation that means they are authorized to make public statements on matters relating to their expertise—without prior clearance from the council or the board of directors. These eight committees include the AICPA Peer Review Board, which aims to improve the quality of services offered by professional accountants, the Professional Ethics Executive Committee; and the Management Consulting Services Executive Committee, which provides guidance to CPAs engaged in consulting work.

The additional committees and teams in the AICPA are divided among five basic functional categories. Technical teams such as the Personal Financial Planning Team develop standards and integrate new technologies; member interest teams such as the Publications Division provide members with resources; self-regulation teams such as the Professional Ethics Team help to maintain professional standards; external relations teams such as Academic and Career Development reach out to members of Congress, the public, and potential CPA candidates. Administrative teams such as the Planning and Research Team help to carry out the programs and policies of the AICPA staff.

PRIMARY FUNCTIONS

One of the AICPA's most important functions is to promote uniform certification and licensing standards for professional accountants. In fact the institute has absolute authority over whether an accountant should be called a CPA. It designs, publishes, administers, and grades the Uniform CPA Examination, which must be passed before an accountant can be granted a CPA license.

In its exclusive authority to develop accounting and auditing standards for every member of its profession, the AICPA enjoys an unusual degree of power for a private organization. The institute's two standard-setting boards, the Financial Accounting Standards Board (FASB) and Governmental Accounting Standards Board (GASB), develop these standards subject to the approval of the Securities and Exchange Commission (SEC), a federal regulatory agency. The SEC's interest in accounting arises from the fact that a company's financial statements are often a primary factor in determining the worth of its stock on the open market.

Once FASB or GASB standards are approved by the SEC, they virtually have the authority of law. In addition to the power of the federal government to enforce these rules, the AICPA has its own Standards Committee, Ethics Committee, Peer Review Board, and Joint Trial Board, which serve to hold its members to the highest standard of ethics and professionalism. The AICPA also provides technical assistance to government and private-sector rulemaking organizations in the areas of taxation, banking, and examination of financial resources.

Besides serving as a watchdog for its members, the AICPA serves a number of functions meant to protect and strengthen the ranks of CPAs in the United States. It recruits highly qualified candidates for the CPA profession, supports the development of academic programs, and provides a vast array of resources—from publications to national conferences and seminars—to help CPAs in their professional development. The Institute also serves as an advocate for its members, representing them before the government and other regulatory bodies. The AICPA's lobbyists in Washington monitor legislation that has a potential impact on accounting or auditing practices, or the business practices of CPAs. Once the AICPA decides where it stands on such legislation, it mounts a strong campaign for passage, amendment, or rejection of pending bills.

PROGRAMS

Among the AICPA's many programs are educational projects and services for the academic community. Because the AICPA believes the future of the profession depends on how accounting students are educated, these programs promote good curriculum development and instruction, and encourage professional interaction. One example is the Industry Field Visit Program, run by the AICPA to give educators the opportunity to get first-hand exposure to current practices and issues occurring in the corporate sector. Educators can visit corporations, hear presentations on new practices, and actually observe operations in progress. The hope is that these visits will foster a better understanding of the types of skills necessary for accountants to succeed in industry.

The AICPA also conducts a number of conferences and seminars designed to help CPAs in specialized fields. Examples from 1998 include the National Real Estate

Conference in Beverly Hills, California, where accountants met to receive an overview of the industry, critical technical updates, and an understanding of the industry's accounting, auditing taxation and technology; and the National Conference on Credit Unions, held in New Orleans. The AICPA also holds one-week training schools, for hands-on, interactive, classroom-style training. Accountants at the schools participate in exercises and simulations that give members a wealth of information and new ideas.

The CPA WebTrust is an AICPA certification program that ensures that the on-line transactions of companies—including accountants or accounting firms—are sound, secure, and encrypted. Authentic WebTrust sites are marked with the CPA WebTrust insignia, and can be verified by viewing a registered digital identification code. By ensuring safe and effective electronic commerce, the institute hopes to preserve and strengthen a growing sector of activity for its members.

BUDGET INFORMATION

The AICPA is a nonprofit organization whose operating revenues are accumulated from a number of income sources. Some 40 percent of the AICPA's money comes from membership dues, and an additional 27 percent is collected from the sale of publications and software authored by the institute. Fees collected for professional development and service conferences, along with the administration of professional examinations, account for about 24 percent of the institute's revenue. About nine percent of AICPA's annual income is interest earned on investments. According to the Institute's 1997–1998 annual report, these revenues amounted to about $143.5 million.

The AICPA's expenses during this period surpassed income, totaling $145.6 million. Major categories of expense included those related to producing publications and software (21 percent); professional development and service conferences (17 percent); general management (12 percent); and technology and technical assistance (13 percent). Other expense categories are regulation and legislation; organizational development, and communications/public relations.

According to the *Almanac of Federal PACS 1996–1997*, the AICPA's Effective Legislation Committee contributed slightly more than $1.7 million to the campaigns of political candidates during the 1993–1994 election cycle; an amount distributed nearly equally among Democratic and Republican candidates.

HISTORY

When the American Association of Public Accountants (AAPA), the AICPA's predecessor, was founded in 1887, the biggest obstacle facing accountants in America was a lack of formal legal recognition of their public practice. Among the first goals of the organization was to establish a professional examination and a distinctive title. However it took a while for many Americans to become interested in the organization. It had been founded and led by a group of British-born New Yorkers and interest was so low that by the turn of the century the association only had about 100 members.

In 1913 as the passage of a significant tax law created tax brackets, and income rather than wealth became the measure of the nation's well-being, the market for accounting services expanded exponentially. The effect on the accounting profession was mixed; while the new law provided security for many practitioners, the demand also attracted unqualified people who had no qualms about calling themselves accountants and tax experts.

The AAPA continued to have trouble influencing state legislation to follow its recommended certification standards, and in the early twentieth century it refused to recognize CPA certificates from several states whose standards did not meet its own. By 1915 the situation had deteriorated to where the AAPA would recognize certificates from only 30 of the 39 states that had CPA certification laws. The AAPA was at a crisis point. In some states, it considered legislation to be inadequate. But when appeals were made for the establishment of one single, national standard, the federal government started to make noise about taking control of the certification process itself. To make matters worse, charges that the association was elitist and exclusionary were hard to disprove. In 1916 only three of 156 candidates were issued CPA certificates in New York.

It was clear that if the association was to survive, the AAPA would have to reorganize. The new AAPA, called the American Institute of Public Accountants after 1917, would have the authority to admit new members on an individual basis, rather than approving the decisions of the separate states. The reorganization did quiet criticism and prevent federal intervention, but its abandonment of the CPA certificate also left the organization open to competition from a rival organization, the American Society of CPAs (ASCPA), a federation of state societies.

After the Securities Acts of 1933 and 1934

The Great Depression and the subsequent Securities Acts of 1933 and 1934, however, soon eliminated any desire for competition between the two rival professional accountancy groups. Establishing a new federal agency, the Securities and Exchange Commission, to regulate the financial reporting process for publicly traded companies, the 1934 act increased the demand for accounting services, conferred upon CPAs the responsibility to help create and uphold investor confidence in the public markets, and threatened the professional autonomy of accountants. The AIPA and ASCPA merged in 1937 and,

in order to protect the status of the profession, limited the new institute's membership to certified public accountants. It was in 1957 that the institute finally adopted its present name, the American Institute of Certified Public Accountants (AICPA).

For the new AICPA, the most important priorities were the standardization of accounting standards among all professionals—a process begun in cooperation with the SEC in 1937—and the strengthening of academic training for CPA candidates. By the 1970s the AICPA had established the university as the setting for the education of most of the nation's CPAs. In 1973 the institute formed the Financial Accounting Standards Board (FASB), a policy-making body that remains one of the most powerful in the private sector.

In the 1980s and 1990s the AICPA faced new challenges. The tasks of accountants were growing increasingly complex, and frequently involved transactions outside the United States. The emergence of the global capital market, along with an expanding role for accountants themselves, led to the ongoing expansion into areas such as education, management consulting, and information technology. The AICPA has done its best to stay current with the rapidly changing profession and accordingly, to develop standards of practice that will ensure professionalism in these growing fields.

CURRENT POLITICAL ISSUES

During the 1990s the AICPA's power to determine accounting rules for all CPAs created controversy among some business owners. While the SEC has had the authority to establish accounting rules and procedures for public companies since 1934, it has since relegated this authority to the AICPA's Financial Accounting Standards Board (FASB). Many members of the business community are uncomfortable with this degree of regulatory power in the hands of a privately-funded organization. Once approved by the SEC, the FASB's rules and standards carry the full force of SEC regulations.

In fact the FASB's power became the subject of federal legislation in early 1998, in the form of the Financial Accounting Fairness Act (FAFA). The primary purpose of FAFA, as it was introduced to the House of Representatives, was to allow companies who were unhappy with an FASB rule to file a grievance in the federal court system. The current system allowed for appeals to be made only to the SEC—the very body which had approved the rules. Some businesses thought this practice was unfair. The AICPA came out strongly against FAFA, stating that it was a push by a "special interest group," unhappy with the results of its appeals, to influence the way accounting rules were made in this country.

BUDGET:
1996 AICPA Revenue

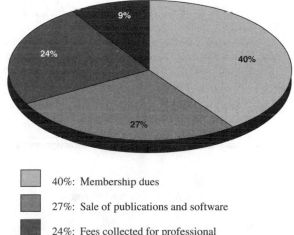

- 40%: Membership dues
- 27%: Sale of publications and software
- 24%: Fees collected for professional development and service conferences, and from administration of professional examinations
- 9%: Interest earned on investments

1996 AICPA Expenses

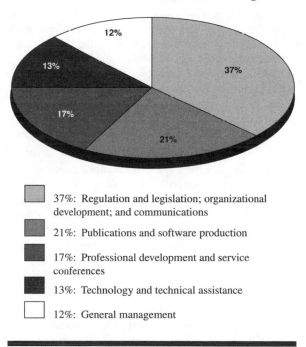

- 37%: Regulation and legislation; organizational development; and communications
- 21%: Publications and software production
- 17%: Professional development and service conferences
- 13%: Technology and technical assistance
- 12%: General management

Case Study: The U.S. Film Industry

The American film industry may well have been the "special interest group" the AICPA was referring to

FAST FACTS

Of the total AICPA membership, 43.9 percent are CPAs in business and industry; 39.6 percent are in public accounting; 4.4 percent are in government; and 2.4 percent are in education.

(Source: *A Future in the Making.* AICPA 1997–1998 Annual Report.)

in its public statement against the Financial Accounting Fairness Act. The bill was introduced on the floor of the House of Representatives less than one month after the FASB announced its intention to change the rules by which accountants in the film industry were operating.

For years many film companies had engaged in somewhat dubious accounting practices. In order to keep investors happy and to downplay films that were not economically successful, accountants would distribute high costs associated with a film project, such as advertising, a number of years into the future. Their justification for this was that even if a film did badly in the United States, it could still make money in the future through foreign releases, video, and sales to television networks. The advertising was an investment in those future profits. Often, after having spent hundreds of millions of dollars for advertising on a film, a company might record only a fraction of these expenses, delaying the remainder for a later time.

On the other hand these same film companies were doing exactly the opposite with their revenues. If the company did sign a contract for the foreign release of a film, for video release, or for television, the full amount of the contract—which could extend years into the future—could be recorded in one lump sum, though many of the profits would not be realized for years.

To the FASB these were deceptive practices, permitting film companies to present certain films to their investors as a success, when clearly they had been box office bombs. Such accounting procedures were not permitted in other businesses, and the FASB and the AICPA set out to level the playing field for film investors. They developed a number of rules that would keep companies from delaying the recording of expenses that had already been incurred, while requiring that profit statements be based on actual income, rather than hopeful projections. The FASB considered such rules to be the only way of

ensuring that film companies weren't duping people into unwise investments. To many of the film companies, however, they were an unfair limitation on the financial picture the companies wanted to give to potential investors.

FUTURE DIRECTIONS

The CPA profession faces several crucial issues in the twenty-first century, including increased competition among its members, a growing concern over the different accounting practices used in international business transactions, and the expansion of the CPA's role into areas such as software consulting. Upon being named chair of the AICPA in October of 1998, Olivia Kirtley called on all CPAs to assume greater responsibility in helping to formulate and adopt international accounting and auditing standards. "It's impossible to have a path to the twenty-first century without reaching beyond our borders," she said.

The AICPA has been concerned enough about future professional implications to coordinate the CPA Vision Project, a grassroots effort to prepare the institute and its members for the future. According to the project's report, *2011 and Beyond*, the CPA profession faces challenges beyond the expansion of the global marketplace and the growth of technology. It must confront increasing competition among its members and a demand for more skills and competencies. As a result, the report predicts, there will be increasing specialization among CPAs in the years to come.

GROUP RESOURCES

An excellent source of information about the AICPA is the institute's Web site at http://www.aicpa.org, which provides information on programs, events, and developments. A series of press releases about current issues and internal events is accessible from this site, along with a list of links to other accounting- and government-related sites. For further information about the AICPA, contact the Communications/Public Relations Team at (212) 596-6236.

GROUP PUBLICATIONS

Each member of the AICPA receives subscriptions to its magazines and newsletters. The *Journal of Accountancy*, a monthly magazine that focuses on the latest accounting-related news and developments, is written for CPAs and other accounting professionals. Other serial publications include the *CPA Letter, The Practicing*

CPA, and *The Tax Adviser*. The AICPA's most widely distributed publications are its book-length information sources for accounting professionals: *AICPA Professional Standards*; *AICPA Audit and Accounting Manual*; *Codification of Statements on Auditing Standards*; and *AICPA Technical Practice Aids*.

AICPA publications are numerous; each board or committee issues its own publications, and nearly all are intended to be read by CPAs. The Professional Ethics Executive Committee, for example, publishes the institute's ethics code and bylaws; the Communications/Public Relations team publishes press releases; and the Accounting Standards Executive Committee publishes the proceeds of its meetings along with advisory publications such as *Improving Business Reporting—A Customer Focus*.

The Institute does publish a small number of brochures that are intended for public consumption, with titles such as "Understanding and Using CPA Services," "How to Choose a CPA," and "Questions and Answers for Business Owners and Individuals." Several of these brochures, along with many of the institute's publications, can be viewed or downloaded from the AICPA's Web site at http://www.aicpa.org.

BIBLIOGRAPHY

"Baker Introduces the Financial Accounting Fairness Act of 1998." (Press release from the House Banking Subcommittee on Capital Markets, Securities and Government Sponsored Enterprises, 5 February 1998).

Edwards, James Don. *History of Public Accounting in the United States*. Tuscaloosa: University of Alabama Press, 1978.

Hansell, Saul. "SEC Crackdown on Technology Write-Offs." *New York Times*, 29 September 1998.

Miller, Karen L. "Good Webkeeping Seals of Approval." *New York Times*, 17 May 1998.

Miller, Paul B. W. *The FASB: the People, the Process, and the Politics*. Irwin Publishing, 1986.

Petersen, Melody. "Accounting Rule Hurts Software Companies' Revenues." *New York Times*, 30 April 1998.

———. "Computer Consulting by Accountants Stirs Concern." *New York Times*, 13 July 1998.

Previts, Gary John, and Barbara Dubis Merino. *A History of Accountancy in the United States: The Cultural Significance of Accounting*. Columbus: Ohio State University Press, 1998.

Van Riper, Robert. *Setting Standards for Financial Reporting: FASB and the Struggle for Control of a Critical Process*. Quorum Books, 1994.

American Israel Public Affairs Committee (AIPAC)

ESTABLISHED: 1954
EMPLOYEES: 115
MEMBERS: 55,000
PAC: None

Contact Information:
ADDRESS: 440 First St. NW, Ste. 600
    Washington, DC 20001
PHONE: (202) 639-5200
FAX: (202) 347-4889
E-MAIL: webmaster@aipac.org
URL: http://www.aipac.org
PRESIDENT: Lionel Kaplan
CHAIRMAN: Melvin A. Dow
EXECUTIVE DIRECTOR: Howard A. Kohr

WHAT IS ITS MISSION?

The American Israel Public Affairs Committee (AIPAC) is an advocacy group devoted to building a strong relationship between the United States and Israel. AIPAC believes that such a relationship is highly beneficial for the United States, and crucial for the safety and well-being of Israel. According to its Web site, the organization considers itself to be "America's pro-Israel lobby," with a mission "to collaborate with Congress and Presidential Administrations to nurture and advance the bilateral relationship between the United States and Israel." Issues of interest to AIPAC range from stopping international terrorism and promoting Israeli technological development to fostering economic and military cooperation between Israel and the United States. As Executive Director Howard Kohr said in an April 1998 interview with *The New York Times*, "We want to make sure that the security and well-being of Israel and the Jews are maintained."

HOW IS IT STRUCTURED?

Headquartered in Washington, D.C., AIPAC has eight U.S. regional offices in California (2), Georgia, Florida, Illinois, Montana, New York, and Texas, plus another in Israel's capital, Jerusalem. In addition, field organizers work with students at over 200 affiliated college campuses in 50 states. Both regional and college groups communicate with state and national legislators, sponsor local seminars, and actively broadcast AIPAC's message.

A board of directors and an executive committee act as AIPAC's primary governing bodies. The board consists of approximately 30 members and convenes monthly, while the 300-member executive committee (consisting of the presidents of 55 major American Jewish organizations as well as leaders from the pro-Israel community and two college students) meets quarterly and ratifies the organization's policy statement at the annual Policy Conference. The executive director, who handles day-to-day operations, works with seven primary departments to devise AIPAC strategies: Legislative, Political Outreach, Research and Information, Foreign Policy, Media, Development and Campus Leadership.

A nonpartisan, domestic lobbying group, AIPAC had approximately 55,000 dues paying members in 1998. Annual dues are $50, or $15 for students. As a registered domestic lobbying group, by law the organization receives no financial aid from Israel or any national or foreign entity. Despite the "PAC" in its name, AIPAC is not a political action committee, and does not contribute to political campaigns.

PRIMARY FUNCTIONS

AIPAC functions primarily as a lobbying group, and is consistently ranked as one of the most effective groups in the United States. AIPAC lobbyists meet with congressmen and key government officials to encourage them to support pro-Israel initiatives. AIPAC's general membership and supporters lobby congressmen through letter-writing campaigns. AIPAC staff also attend congressional hearings and review congressional testimony to keep abreast of pertinent U.S.-Israel legislation. These researchers then track the voting records of U.S. senators and representatives to determine which lawmakers support a strong bilateral relationship.

PROGRAMS

AIPAC's programs exist mainly to complement its primary goal of convincing lawmakers in Washington to support Israel. The AIPAC sponsors numerous conferences throughout each year, where the public can come to hear the latest information on Israel and U.S.-Israeli relations. AIPAC's Political Leadership Development Program teaches college students how to become pro-Israel leaders at the community level. The AIPAC internship program also works with college students. Working in AIPAC offices, interns gain experience in U.S.-Israeli issues and the U.S. political process, which they can then put to use in their community.

BUDGET INFORMATION

In the 1997–98 fiscal year, AIPAC operated from a $14 million budget, all of which came from membership dues and private contributions. Aside from raising approximately $300 per person at the 1998 Policy Conference, AIPAC conducts direct mailing, community activities, and fund-raising dinners to help meet its operating costs.

HISTORY

Although AIPAC was not founded until 1954, the strong relationship between Israel and the United States began in 1948. In that year, the Israeli state was founded as a homeland for the Jewish people. The United States recognized Israel as a nation that same year. The United States continued to support Israel, and in 1951 approved an aid package to assist Israel in the resettling of refugees from the Holocaust. In 1954, the newly founded AIPAC successfully lobbied Congress to prevent the termination of this aid package to Israel. Also in 1954, AIPAC began to push the U.S. Congress to lift the arms embargo on Israel, and limit the sale of weapons to Israel's hostile Arab neighbors.

Israel captured the Egyptian-controlled Sinai Peninsula during the Suez Crisis of 1956, which led to calls by U.S. President Dwight Eisenhower for a unilateral Israeli withdrawal. AIPAC lobbied Congress to support Israel's calls for negotiations against the president's demands. AIPAC, and Israel, would continue to call for direct negotiations between Israel and its Arab neighbors for years.

In 1962, after a 10-year AIPAC campaign, President John F. Kennedy lifted the 13-year-old arms embargo against Israel, thereby opening the path for Israel to purchase sophisticated Hawk surface-to-air missiles. After the Six-Day War (1967) between Israel and Egypt, Syria, and Jordan, AIPAC lobbied for the United States to support Israel's demands for a directly negotiated peace. AIPAC leaders worked with members of Congress the following year to pass legislation allowing the sale of F-4 Phantom jets to Israel. In 1973 Israel suffered a surprise attack by Syria, Egypt, and other Arab nations on Yom Kippur, the holiest day of the year for Jews. President Richard Nixon and the U.S. Congress approved $2.2 billion in emergency and military aid for Israel in response to this attack, the first time the United States gave direct military aid to Israel.

In association with several other Jewish organizations, AIPAC convinced 76 Senators and 288 Representatives to co-sponsor the landmark 1974 Let Our People Go Law. This measure revoked the Soviet Union's trading privileges with the United States until that nation permitted Jews living within its borders to emigrate out of the country. Over one million Jews would eventually emigrate to Israel from the Soviet Union.

A Texas farmer digs irrigation channels in his cornfield in 1996 to combat low rainfall. The American Israeli Public Affairs Committee recommended using Israeli irrigation methods to help farmers contend with drought conditions. (AP/Wide World Photo)

In 1978, after over 25 years of Israeli demands and letter writing campaigns by AIPAC, Egyptian President Anwar Sadat agreed to meet with Israeli leaders and negotiate for peace. President Sadat and Israeli Prime Minister Menachem Begin met at Camp David in the United States, and their face-to-face meetings produced the historic Camp David Accords. Under the 1979 Egyptian-Israeli Peace Treaty, Israel withdrew from the Sinai in exchange for full peace with Egypt. This groundbreaking pact set the stage for subsequent peace agreements based upon direct negotiations. Meanwhile, Congress approved a $4.9 billion aid and loan package to Israel. Congress would continue to provide steady support for Israel in the years that followed; from 1985 on it provided Israel with $3 billion a year in defense grants.

AIPAC lobbied throughout its history for formal military ties between Israel and the United States. It won a major victory in 1983 when President Ronald Reagan and Israeli Prime Minister Yitzhak Shamir initiated formal strategic cooperation between Israel and the United States. In their Memorandum of Understanding, the two leaders committed the United States and Israel to intelligence sharing, joint military exercises, and technology sharing.

The 1984 AIPAC-conceived Texas-Israel Exchange Program—the first such program between Israel and a U.S. state—introduced Israeli irrigation methods to

Texas farmers. By 1999, over 15 states had formed similar cooperative endeavors with Israel. In 1985, AIPAC helped conceptualize and lobby for the passage of the U.S.-Israel Free Trade Agreement, which more than doubled trade between the two nations, resulting in increased sales, profits, and jobs for both American and Israeli firms.

After Israel suffered through 29 Iraqi missile attacks during the 1991 Persian Gulf War, AIPAC successfully appealed to President George Bush for $650 million in emergency military assistance. Cooperation through the exchange of desert warfare tactics demonstrated the strength of the binational friendship. In 1992 AIPAC called upon Congress and helped approve loan guarantees from the U.S. to Israel in order to take in more than 600,000 Russian and Ethiopian immigrants.

The September 1993 Declaration of Principles (otherwise known as the "Oslo Agreement") set the framework for a peace between Israel and the Palestine Liberation Organization (PLO) by requiring Israel to recognize the PLO as the representative of the Palestinian people, while the PLO promised to cease using violence against Israel. Since 1993, AIPAC has been lobbying not only to ensure that U.S. policies promote the landmark agreement, but also to oversee the PLO in fulfilling its promise to combat terrorism. Further agreements between Israel and the PLO have led to ever increasing autonomy for Israel's Palestinian population, including political control over several areas.

CURRENT POLITICAL ISSUES

Throughout its history, AIPAC has worked with Congress to ensure that the U.S.-Israeli relationship is a strong one. AIPAC has successfully lobbied Congress for many years to provide Israel with billions of dollars in financial and military aid. During the long-running negotiations between Israel and Palestinians over a Palestinian homeland, AIPAC has supported Israel's position and urged the United States to remain prepared to combat a return to terrorism. Terrorism is not the only threat to Israel's security, however. There are many nations in the Middle East, such as Libya, Iraq, and Iran, that have been hostile to Israel for many years. Much of AIPAC's efforts are devoted to securing the help of the United States in limiting the ability of these nations to harm Israel.

Case Study: Iran Missile Proliferation Sanctions Act (IMPSA)

Israel has long considered the nation of Iran to be one of its greatest security threats. Iran has been overtly hostile to Israel for many years; it often refers to Israel as the "Little Satan." Iran is widely believed to be the major source of funds for terrorist organizations that have killed many hundreds of people in Israel and around the world.

As Iran does not share a border with Israel, the greatest concern is that Iran will develop long-range missiles, capable of launching chemical and biological weapons already in its possession. Iran is also believed to be developing nuclear weapons, which would pose even greater danger to Israel if fitted to long-range missiles. In light of this fact, Israel and AIPAC pushed for the United States to prevent the sale of any materials or technology to Iran that would assist it in its development of long-range missiles.

In this case, the problem did not so much involve U.S. firms as it did businesses in other countries, such as Russia and China. The situation was further affected by the fact that the relationship between Iran and the United States is no better than that between Israel and Iran (the United States is the "Great Satan" to Israel's "Little Satan"). However, Congress could still react to AIPAC pressure by penalizing foreign countries and businesses that were assisting Iran.

In September of 1997 the U.S. Congress passed the Iran Missiles Proliferation Sanctions Act (IMPSA). This bill called for the United States to impose a number of economic sanctions on any foreign business which was known to be assisting Iran to develop long-range missiles. For example, U.S. loans to such businesses would be stopped, and U.S. firms would not be allowed to do business with sanctioned companies.

President Clinton vetoed IMPSA because he was concerned about the effect it would have on the relationship between the United States and Russia. In addition, with the very poor performance of the Russian economy in the 1990s, many Russian businesses had proved willing to deal with Iran. The Russian government made some attempts to curtail the transactions, but with only limited success. President Clinton was concerned that sanctions, if not used carefully, would worsen the Russian economy even further, making that nation less inclined to cooperate with the United States. When it became apparent that Congress would probably override his veto, however, Clinton acted to implement the bill's provisions. Through an Executive Order, Clinton put most of the policies described in IMPSA into effect, while leaving himself some discretion as to how and when to impose sanctions.

Public Impact

The passage of IMPSA in the U.S. Congress demonstrates the high level of importance that body places on Israel's security. This is due in no small part to the efforts of AIPAC over the course of its 45–year history. As the voice of Israeli interests in the United States, AIPAC has built a lasting relationship with Congress, that has led in turn to bills like IMPSA. While IMPSA was vetoed, AIPAC's goals were still met by Clinton's Executive Order. By 1999 ten Russian firms had been sanctioned by the Clinton administration for their dealings with Iran.

FUTURE DIRECTIONS

The peace process between Israel and Palestine will be one of AIPAC's top priorities for years to come. While AIPAC supports the peace process, it supports it only so long as Israel's needs are met. Thus, the organization opposes efforts to turn Jerusalem into an open city partly under the control of Palestinians. Similarly, AIPAC will push for the United States to fully enforce the agreements as they are written, and deny any attempts by Palestinians to expand their authority or influence at the expense of Israel.

GROUP RESOURCES

AIPAC's Web site can be accessed at http://www.aipac.org. This site includes information on AIPAC's programs, history, and policy stances on topics like terrorism, the peace process, and economic assistance. The site also maintains a video archive. AIPAC's Legislative Alert is a free E-mail subscription system that sends subscribers news briefs on the latest developments in U.S.-Israeli relations. For further information on AIPAC, write to AIPAC, 440 First St. NW, Ste. 600, Washington, DC 20001; or call (202) 639-5200.

GROUP PUBLICATIONS

The *Near East Report* is AIPAC's biweekly official newsletter on U.S. policy toward the Middle East. *Near East Report* is available free of charge to members. There is also limited access to the newsletter via AIPAC's Web site at http://www.aipac.org. For more information on AIPAC publications, contact AIPAC by mail at AIPAC, 440 First St. NW, Ste. 600, Washington, DC 20001; or by phone at (202) 639-5200.

BIBLIOGRAPHY

Eagelton, Thomas F. "Despair Returning to the Middle East." *Journal of Commerce and Commercial*, 24 December 1997.

Fialka, John. "Pro-Israel Lobby: Jewish PACs Emerge as a Powerful Force in U.S. Election Races." *Wall Street Journal*, 26 February 1985.

Greenhouse, Linda. "High Court Lowers Shield of Election Panel; Also Agrees to Hear Deportation Appeal." *New York Times*, 2 June 1998.

Isaacs, Stephen D. *Jews and American Politics*. New York, N.Y.: Doubleday, 1974.

Lelyveld, Michael S. "Pro-Israel Lobby Tones Down Drive for Iran Ban." *Journal of Commerce and Commercial*, 30 March 1998.

————. "Sanctions on Russia Face Veto: Senate Passes Iran Penalties After President Delays Action." *Journal of Commerce and Commercial*, 26 May 1998.

Music, Kimberley. "Court Ruling Could Limit AIPAC Influence on U.S.-Mideast Policy." *The Oil Daily*, 12 December 1996.

"No Surrender: Israel's Supporters." *Economist*, 12 April 1997.

Rosenthal, A. M. "The War Against Bibi." *New York Times*, 17 July 1998.

Tivnan, Edward. *The Lobby: Jewish Political Power and American Foreign Policy*. New York, N.Y.: Simon & Schuster, 1987.

"The Voice Within: America and Israel." *Economist*, 6 June 1998.

American Jewish Congress (AJCongress)

WHAT IS ITS MISSION?

The American Jewish Congress describes itself not as an organization but as a movement "motivated by the need to ensure the creative survival of the Jewish people." Its stated mission is to "protect fundamental constitutional freedoms and American democratic institutions, particularly the civil and religious rights and liberties of all Americans and the separation of church and state; advance the security and posterity of the State of Israel and its democratic institutions, and to support Israel's search for peaceful relations with its neighbors in the region; advance social and economic justice, women's equality, and human rights at home and abroad; remain vigilant against anti-Semitism, racism, and other forms of bigotry, and to celebrate cultural diversity and promote unity in American life, and invigorate and enhance Jewish religious, institutional, communal and cultural life at home and broad, and to seek creative ways to express Jewish identity, ethics and values."

ESTABLISHED: 1916
EMPLOYEES: 40
MEMBERS: 50,000
PAC: None

Contact Information:

ADDRESS: 15 E. 84th St.
New York, NY 10028
PHONE: (212) 879-4500
FAX: (212) 249-3672
E-MAIL: national@ajcongress
URL: http://www.ajcongress.org
PRESIDENT: Jack Rosen
EXECUTIVE DIRECTOR: Phil Baum

HOW IS IT STRUCTURED?

The AJCongress is a nonprofit Jewish coalition with headquarters based in New York City. Day-to-day organizational policy is formulated at regular meetings of a 275-member governing council, and by a smaller executive committee, whose director serves as head of the AJCongress national staff. The AJCongress hosts a convention every two years, at which the membership debates and votes on the group's agenda, and elects national officers to two-year terms. The New York headquarters includes subdivisions with particular areas of

responsibility, such as the Commission on Law and Social Action, the Commission for Women's Equality, and the Bio-Ethics Task Force.

While it employs a "permanent representative" on Capitol Hill, AJCongress does not maintain a political action committee for campaign funding. Regional offices operate in 16 metropolitan areas, largely setting their own priorities for local projects and initiatives, while taking part in national programs. AJCongress also maintains an Israel office, in Jerusalem, which publishes the weekly newsletter *Inside Israel*.

PRIMARY FUNCTIONS

As a political force, AJCongress pursues two main strategies: lobbying (particularly in Washington, D.C.) and litigation. Wherever possible, it forms coalitions with like-minded groups, including other Jewish organizations and a variety of human and civil rights groups, to promote a wide-ranging agenda, mostly of liberal causes and principles, and centered on steadfast support for the state of Israel. AJCongress is also very active in the court system, challenging laws it considers unfair, and defending rights and freedoms from possible erosion. Whether AJCongress attorneys have initiated lawsuits themselves or joined in those brought by others, the group claims to have "participated in virtually every major test case affecting the religion clauses of the First Amendment to come before the United States Supreme Court," as well as many landmark civil and human rights cases.

However, AJCongress' ambitious goals are not limited to U.S. government affairs. Several programs reflect a general commitment to facilitating cross-cultural dialogue, particularly with the Middle East and among its contending factions. AJCongress sponsors travel and exchange programs to Israel, for political leaders and ordinary citizens alike. It also pursues a kind of unofficial diplomacy, while not participating directly in official peace processes. AJCongress delegations have developed contacts with members of Arab governments and sought to open channels of communication with their Israeli counterparts. Similar outreach programs foster communication between American Jews and a number of other communities, including religious and ethnic groups.

AJCongress also promotes scholarship and education in a variety of ways: by sponsoring conferences and seminars, offering scholarship programs, and by underwriting scholarly analyses of selected issues— particularly Mideast social and political circumstances, and various aspects of Jewish culture.

PROGRAMS

AJCongress sponsors programs in both Israel and the United States. They address the needs of individuals, including travelers to Israel, as well as the interests of entire communities. Regional programs in the United States have been formed to impact various issues, including civil rights and health.

AJCongress' International Travel Project offers members a number of tour packages to Israel. The group established the Louis Waterman Youth Hostel in Jerusalem, Israel's largest, in 1954; there it provides training programs for new Israelis, and multicultural forums to bring young Jewish, Moslem, Christian and Druze Israelis together.

Since 1980, AJCongress has sponsored an annual spring Jerusalem Conference of Mayors, offering elected officials from the United States and other countries the opportunity to experience Israeli society first-hand. Over 200 American mayors have participated in the program. The annual America-Israel dialogues, established in 1962, provide a forum for intellectuals and political leaders from the two countries to explore their shared concerns. Another program, the *Hasbara* Interns Project, provides a very specific kind of aid to Israel. Since 1984 it has brought Israeli diplomats to America for training in public relations skills and media management.

Regional chapters have instituted a number of innovative programs. For example, the Northern Pacific Region, centered in San Francisco, founded the Jack Berman Advocacy Center for Violence Reduction, which provides educational programs as well as legal and legislative action. The Boston-based New England Region established the Gene Team, which drafts legislation on such issues as genetic privacy, ethical research, and insurance restrictions.

BUDGET INFORMATION

Not made available.

HISTORY

Founded in 1916, AJCongress was originally intended to be a temporary organization with a single mission: to represent Jewish interests in negotiations to end World War I. Specifically, it sought to influence the U.S. peace delegation to demand full civil rights for previously-disenfranchised Jews (and other minorities) in Europe, and to assert the Zionist claim to a homeland in Palestine, as provided in Britain's 1917 Balfour Declaration. It was also conceived as a *democratic* Jewish organization, in contrast to what founders saw (in the words of an AJCongress pamphlet) as a "benevolent yet self-appointed aristocracy that had been at the helm of American Jewish life since the mid-nineteenth century."

Delegates to its first convention, held in Philadelphia in December 1918, were elected through nationwide

BIOGRAPHY:

Stephen Samuel Wise

Rabbi; Zionist Activist (1874–1949) Stephen Wise was one of the earliest and most successful proponents of Zionism, the worldwide movement to establish an independent state and Jewish homeland in Palestine. Rabbi Wise spent his entire adult life helping to articulate the movement's ideology and to organize a following. He began by rallying his own congregation (a Reform congregation) and founding the New York Federation of Zionist Societies and, in 1898, the nationwide Federation of American Zionists. Swelling membership in these groups was evidence to President Woodrow Wilson that a large majority of American Jews supported Zionist aims. Wise joined U.S. Supreme Court Justice Louis D. Brandeis and Harvard lawyer and eventual Supreme Court Justice Felix Frankfurter in helping to formulate the text of the Balfour Declaration of 1917 on behalf of President Wilson. This declaration of the British government favored the establishment of a Pales-

tine homeland for Jews. Back home, Wise led in the organization of the American Jewish Congress (AJC). This proactive group was conceived to resolve the needs and problems of Jews from a political position. Wise served a leadership role in the AJC from 1921 until his death in 1949. Israel wasn't established until the final year of his life. Until then–to

Jews who argued that Zionism stoked domestic anti-Semitism by suggesting that Jews were divided in their national loyalties—Rabbi Wise responded, "I have been an American all my life, but I have been a Jew for four thousand years."

---

balloting of 350,000 American Jews; the convention then elected a delegation to attend the Versailles peace conference. Although the delegation was not entirely successful at Versailles, enthusiasm for "grassroots" political participation led to the establishment of AJCongress as a permanent institution in 1920. The organization's first president was Rabbi Stephen Wise.

Through the 1920s and 1930s, AJCongress worked to promote the eventual establishment of a Jewish state, and to fight anti-Semitism, both at home and in Europe. The United States saw the rise of the Ku Klux Klan and other nativist groups, widespread discriminatory immigration policies, and many Jewish groups targeted as "un-American" revolutionaries; in Europe, brutal anti-Jewish pogroms were on the rise in Poland, Russia, and Romania, and fascist movements were growing in Spain, Italy, and Germany. In 1933, when Hitler began to solidify his control over Germany, AJCongress staged a massive anti-Nazi rally at New York City's Madison Square Garden, calling for an international boycott of the Nazi regime. In 1936, it organized the World Jewish Congress, and launched a $1 million defense fund to rescue Jewish children orphaned by the Nazis. During and after World War II, AJCongress publicized early reports of the Holocaust. As the level of Jewish victimization was revealed, it pushed harder to gain support for a Jewish state, and for early U.S. recognition of Israel when it was established in 1948.

In the postwar era, AJCongress has expanded its agenda, particularly in domestic affairs, to include "the

goal of full equality in a free society for all Americans." It was an early supporter of the civil rights movement of the 1950s and 1960s, forging coalitions with African American groups and contributing to legal challenges of racial discrimination in housing, schools, and employment. It has also been strongly involved in issues of church and state separation, civil liberties, gun control, reproductive rights and women's equality.

Beyond its efforts on behalf of Israel, AJCongress' international activism has embraced human rights struggles worldwide. For example, in the 1970s and 1980s, it helped pressure the Soviet government to ease restrictions on Jewish emigration, and campaigned to end racial *apartheid* in South Africa. In the mid-1990s, it publicized atrocities in the former Yugoslavia, urging both the United States and European governments to intervene in the conflict, and arguing that the failure to act constituted "acquiesce[nce] in Europe's most grievous calamity since the Holocaust." It has also been active in efforts to combat international terrorism, and has encouraged U.S. administrations in their efforts to advance the Middle East peace process.

CURRENT POLITICAL ISSUES

In 1993, when the term "liberal" had become a common political epithet, AJCongress adopted a mission statement proudly declaring that it was "informed by lib-

---

FAST FACTS

In a 1988 *Los Angeles Times* poll, 75 percent of American Jews reported they felt "close to Israel." When the poll was repeated in 1998, only 58 percent agreed with the statement.

(Source: Alan Abrahamson and Judy Pasternak. "Jews in America: Choosing a Future." *Los Angeles Times,* April 20, 1998.)

eral principles." Its ambitious agenda includes a number of causes and principles traditionally identified as liberal, and traditionally opposed by conservatives. It supports separation of church and state, social welfare programs, reproductive choice (including access to abortion), gun control, women's equality, affirmative action (but not quotas), and universal health care; it is against school prayer, capital punishment, prejudice in all forms, and human rights abuses. AJCongress usually works in coalition with other groups and often serves in a position of fostering dialogue among diverse interests.

Case Study: Religion and Government

Given its founding mission to combat anti-Semitism and secure the rights of Jewish minority populations, issues of religious freedom have always been high priorities for AJCongress. It has taken an active interest in state and federal legislation that affects religious practice, and has joined in legal challenges of laws it opposes. AJCongress embraces the Constitution's First Amendment guarantee of religious freedom, and favors the strict separation of church and state. It has consistently opposed mandatory prayer in public schools, the display of religious symbols on public property, and public funding for religious schools (including recent proposals for "school choice" and "voucher" programs).

The AJCongress fundamental legal position is that the First Amendment, in its provision that "Congress shall make no law respecting an establishment of religion, or prohibiting the free exercise thereof," creates a solid "wall of separation" between the public functions of government and the private practice of religion. At the same time, it protects everyone's right to freely express their faith. Sometimes the public interest seems to conflict with the free exercise of religion: for example, when laws require autopsies to be performed on accident victims, Hmong or Orthodox Jewish family members object

to the procedure on religious grounds. In such instances, AJCongress applies certain "balancing tests" to weigh the government interest against the private liberty. This usually means that government can interfere with religious practice only when it can demonstrate a "compelling public interest" to do so. Similar tests are also traditionally applied in cases involving freedom of speech and of the press.

For many years, Supreme Court rulings tended to follow similar logic, particularly in a series of landmark school-prayer cases that resulted in the 1962 Supreme Court decision in *Engel v. Vitale* that prayer in public schools was unconstitutional. Since then many groups, particularly religious conservatives, have been fighting to get organized prayer back into the schools and to legally guarantee further expressions of religious freedom. During the 1990s, the AJCongress found itself in strong opposition to several pieces of proposed "religious freedom" legislation.

Particularly in the wake of the 1994 mid-term elections, in which Republicans gained majorities in both houses of Congress, several proposals were offered that, in AJCongress' view, went beyond "protection" of religion, and came dangerously close to government sanction of a particular faith. In 1995, Rep. Henry Hyde (R-Ill.) proposed a constitutional amendment, the Religious Equality Amendment (REA), which would have allowed for greater religious expression in public places. Opponents felt it could lead to compulsive religious activities in schools, and to public practices that might offend members of other faiths. Shunning any "major surgery" to the time-tested Constitution, AJCongress characterized the REA as "a radical reworking of a very careful balance struck by the First Amendment," and helped lobby for its eventual defeat.

In 1997, Rep. Ernest Istook (R-Okla.) launched another effort to amend the Constitution, with the backing of Hyde and many conservative Christian organizations. Like REA, the Religious Freedom Amendment (RFA) would have allowed expanded religious expression in public places; but it also addressed school prayer. By allowing "voluntary, self-directed" prayer in public schools, Istook's amendment would have weakened the strict prohibition defined by Supreme Court rulings from the 1960s. Joined by groups such as the American Civil Liberties Union (ACLU) and the National Council of Churches, AJCongress lobbied hard against the RFA, which was defeated in the House in June of 1998.

FUTURE DIRECTIONS

While continuing to pursue its wide-ranging domestic and international agendas, AJCongress has introduced several new initiatives, which it hopes to expand in the future. Women's rights and women's health issues, in particular, have been growing concerns. Research has shown that Askenazi Jewish women may have a genetic predisposition to higher rates of breast and ovarian cancer. AJCongress programs support research and education, and explore legal issues related to genetic information. Another issue that will continue to be targeted is the fight to control terrorism both at home and abroad.

GROUP RESOURCES

The AJCongress Web site at http://www.ajcongress. org includes a 2-year file of press releases, articles from AJCongress publications, and links to Israeli media Web sites. Research requests should be directed to the Public Relations office at the National Headquarters, 15 E. 84th St., New York NY 10028; phone (212) 879-4500.

GROUP PUBLICATIONS

AJCongress publishes several periodicals, both for members and the general public. *Congress Monthly,* "a magazine of Jewish political, social, and cultural comment," and *Judaism,* "a quarterly journal of Jewish life & thought" are provided to members at no cost, and by subscription to non-members. Three other publications provide detailed coverage of developments in the Middle East. *Radical Islamic Fundamentalism Update,* a bimonthly newsletter, monitors social and political developments in the Muslim world; subscriptions are available at $20/year. *Inside Israel,* a weekly newsletter on Israeli politics, is published by AJCongress' Jerusalem office; *Boycott Report,* a monthly newsletter, reports on efforts against the Arab economic boycott of Israel.

In addition, AJCongress publishes and distributes a number of educational pamphlets, as well as the findings of academic studies it has commissioned. Recent examples include *Religion in the Public Schools: A Joint Statement of Current Law* (compiled in conjunction with 37 different religious and civil-rights organizations), *Blacks & Jews in Congress: A House Undivided* (a study of the voting patterns of Black and Jewish legislators), and *American Jews & Middle East Policy: a Survey of the Options.* All publications are available through the Public Relations office at the National Headquarters, 15 E. 84th St., New York NY 10028; phone (212) 879-4500.

BIBLIOGRAPHY

Abrahamson, Alan, and Judy Pasternak. "Jews in America: Choosing a Future." *Los Angeles Times,* 20 April 1998.

Baker, Peter, and Joan Biskupic. "On Workplace Religious Guidelines, Varying Degrees of Faith." *Washington Post,* 15 August 1997.

Flowers, Ronald B. *That Godless Court? Supreme Court Decisions on Church-State Relations.* Nashville, Tenn.: Freedom Forum, 1994.

Jones, Arthur. "Bill in Congress Targets Religious Persecution." *National Catholic Reporter,* 1 August 1997.

Menendez, Albert J. "Church, State, and the 1996 Election." *The Humanist,* November-December 1996.

"Religious Amendment Unveiled." *Christian Century,* 6 December 1995.

Thomas, Oliver, and Bruce Fein. "Is the Religious Freedom Restoration Act Good for America?" *Insight on the News,* 9 December 1996.

Weis, Jeffrey. "Supreme Court Still Struggling with Cases Involving Faith." *Dallas Morning News,* 5 July 1997.

American Legion

ESTABLISHED: March 1919
EMPLOYEES: 300
MEMBERS: 2,900,000
PAC: None

Contact Information:

ADDRESS: 700 North Pennsylvania St.
    P.O. Box 1055
    Indianapolis, IN 46206
PHONE: (317) 630-1200
FAX: (317) 630-1223
URL: http://www.legion.org
NATIONAL COMMANDER: Harold L. Miller

WHAT IS ITS MISSION?

The American Legion is a Veterans Service Organization (VSO) founded in 1919 by U.S. veterans of World War I (1914–18). The organization was created to represent veterans' political concerns to the U.S. Congress and to help them obtain health benefits and pensions from the federal government. The American Legion also provided veterans with a chance to gather together and provide emotional support to one another. This camaraderie helps soldiers readjust to civilian life and overcome the stresses of war after returning home. Since 1919 the American Legion has evolved from being a veterans support group to a sophisticated community service organization.

HOW IS IT STRUCTURED?

The American Legion is led by a national commander, the chief administrative officer of the organization. An 11-member committee, the National Officers, assist the national commander with day-to-day management of the Legion. The organization is further divided into 55 departments representing the fifty states as well as the District of Columbia, Mexico, the Philippines, France, and Puerto Rico.

The Legion's departments are responsible for the administration of approximately 15,000 posts around the country that serve as the local chapters for the organization. Post halls are multi-use facilities where members organize for social activities, participate in fund-raisers such as bingo, and collect goods for the needy. Each of the three million members worldwide belongs to a post. Any military veteran who has been honorably discharged or is presently serving and who saw active duty in any twentieth-century conflict involving the U.S. military—from World War I to the conflict in Bosnia—is eligible for membership in the American Legion.

Each post elects delegates to the American Legion Convention to introduce and pass legislative resolutions that determine the organization's positions on political issues, authorize the expenditure of American Legion funds, and direct congressional lobbying efforts. Convention delegates also elect the national commander and the national officers. The convention is held annually in a different U.S. city every year.

The American Legion's Legislative Division

The Legislative Division of the American Legion is responsible for bringing American Legion resolutions to Congress and attempting to persuade Congress to accept those resolutions. It also analyzes congressional bills and their effect on veterans. In addition, Legislative Division staffers prepare reports and arrange guests for House of Representatives and Senate veterans' committees.

Affiliated Associations

The American Legion has three different associations that help it fulfill its mission. The Women's Auxiliary was formed to give women a voice in the organization. Founded in 1920 and with a current membership of 1 million, the Women's Auxiliary mimics the American Legion in operation and structure. There are 12,000 Women's Auxiliary chapters, called units, open to female members of American Legion members' families or to women fulfilling the American Legion's membership criteria.

The Sons of the American Legion was established in 1932 as an organization for the male descendants, stepsons, or adopted sons of members or deceased eligible members of the American Legion. With a membership of approximately 210,000 in 1998, the affiliate participates in community service projects and provides its membership with the opportunity to be trained in the ideals of the American Legion.

In 1994 the American Legion, with a coalition of VSO's and individual citizens, formed the Citizen's Flag Alliance. More independent than the Women's Auxiliary or Sons of the American Legion, the Citizen's Flag Alliance is a group dedicated to making the desecration of the U.S. flag a crime.

PRIMARY FUNCTIONS

Veterans' rights, benefits, and concerns are the American Legion's primary focus. The Legion lobbies

Congress on behalf of veterans and the Department of Veterans Affairs (VA). It runs job training and placement programs for its members. Through its *American Legion Magazine* and similar forums the organization attempts to raise public consciousness regarding the Gulf War Syndrome, the plight of homeless veterans, and a variety of other political, economic, and social issues affecting U.S. military veterans.

Political power is crucial to implement the American Legion's main objective, which is to represent the interests of veterans to the U.S. government. While the American Legion lobbies Congress, it leverages its large membership base rather than expending large amounts of money to exercise political clout. The thrust of the American Legion's lobbying efforts focus on military and veterans-related issues, which include: increased funding for the VA; support of a constitutional amendment making desecration of the U.S. flag a crime; and support of expansion of the North Atlantic Treaty Organization (NATO), a military alliance of European and North American countries.

Aside from advancing veterans' concerns nationally, the American Legion supports a number of community services, many with an emphasis on youth-oriented programs. The organization offers scholarships to qualified relatives of its membership and promotes scholarship contests with patriotic themes.

PROGRAMS

The American Legion has created, developed, and financed many initiatives during its history, some of which were designed to advance the organization's political agenda. Several programs were created for veterans themselves, while others were designed for young people.

American Legion Baseball

American Legion posts across the country have supported the American Legion Baseball League since its establishment in 1925. Created to help young people develop skills, sportsmanship, and physical fitness, the league has enjoyed the participation of more than eight million children since its inception. During the 1997–98 season, American Legion posts sponsored more than 5,000 Legion baseball teams at a cost of $17 million.

Scholarships and Educational Assistance

The American Legion administers several scholarship programs for relatives of American Legion members. One of the most notable is the *Samsung* American Legion Scholarship. The Korean-based *Samsung* Corporation established a $5 million endowment to provide scholarships for descendants of U.S. war veterans.

The American Legion protested the Smithsonian Institution's planned exhibit of the Enola Gay, *which contained graphic photos and relics from the atomic bombing of Hiroshima, Japan. Veterans feared the exhibit would negatively reflect on the decision to drop the bomb.* (Photograph by Ruth Fremson, AP/Wide World Photo)

In addition the American Legion publishes *Need a Lift?,* a booklet that details scholarships for which veterans and their families might be eligible. This resource also contains information on how to apply for college and financial aid as well as some basic information on colleges and universities located in the United States.

Boys State and Boys Nation

Boys State is a civics education program designed to teach male high school juniors about the workings of state government. Forty-nine departments nationwide run Boys State programs in a variety of different forms; however, all strive to provide young men with an understanding and appreciation of U.S. government from the local and state levels. Those who excel at Boys State are invited to participate in Boys Nation, which educates students about the federal government.

The American Legion Vietnam Rehabilitation Program

Since 1992 the American Legion has developed a humanitarian assistance program for disabled Vietnamese-army veterans. This program raises and donates funds to disabled veterans of Vietnamese nationality for the purposes of job training. Veterans receive this training at a site near Ho Chi Minh City, Vietnam. This initiative was established by the American Legion as a way of creating a dialogue between the two nations and healing the political and emotional gulf between Vietnam and the United States.

BUDGET INFORMATION

Not made available.

HISTORY

The American Legion was formed in the spring of 1919 by veterans returning home from Europe to the United States from service in World War I. The veterans organized because they realized that they needed a national organization to address the special needs that they had, such as health care for those who were wounded and finding suitable jobs. The Legion recognized the necessity of including family members and created the American Legion's Women Auxiliary for the female family members of Legionnaires.

In 1921 the federal government formed the U.S. Veterans Bureau, which later became the Department of Veterans Affairs (VA). This move was in response to the demands of the fledgling American Legion organization, which required a government-sponsored vehicle for administering health care and other benefits to U.S. vets. In 1923 the American Legion's long association with, respect for, and care of the U.S. flag began with the drafting of a protocol for handling the stars and stripes. The protocol, called the *Flag Code,* would be adopted by Congress in 1942. In 1931 the membership of the American Legion surpassed one million for the first time. In 1935 the first of the organization's Boys States would be held in Springfield, Illinois.

As the United States entered World War II (1939–45), the American Legion recognized there would soon be a new class of veterans who would require the same assistance that those of World War I had required. In 1942 the organization amended its charter to accept veterans of World War II as members. In 1943 an American Legion member drafted a bill that would become known as the GI Bill of Rights. This bill, signed into law by President Franklin Delano Roosevelt in 1945, gave veterans low-cost loans for housing and education and improved the quality of veterans' health care. After World War II thousands of returning soldiers took advantage of the benefits awarded them by the GI Bill of Rights by attending college, purchasing their first home, and establishing families.

The Vietnam War presented special challenges to the American Legion. As early as 1966 the Legion began pressing the federal government for the status of those soldiers classified as prisoners of war or missing in action (POW/MIAs). The issue was increasingly politicized due to the difficult relationship between the United States and Vietnam, and its resolution was made nearly impossible.

In 1983 the American Legion began a joint study with Columbia University to determine the effects of exposure to the chemical known as Agent Orange on U.S. veterans of the Vietnam conflict. Agent Orange is a powerful herbicide that was used during the war to kill jungle vegetation and expose the positions of North Vietnamese troops. U.S. soldiers who handled Agent Orange began suffering from mysterious symptoms years after their exposure. The illnesses required special care, and it took the VA years to recognize the effects of Agent Orange.

The American Legion and other VSOs lobbied for years to have the VA changed to a cabinet-level post with special advisory access to the president. In 1989, under President George Bush, the VA was elevated in status to a cabinet-level department. In October of 1995 the American Legion formed an advisory board called the Persian Gulf Task Force to help serve the special health and service needs of veterans of the Gulf War, such as the mysterious Gulf War Syndrome.

CURRENT POLITICAL ISSUES

The American Legion takes an active part in lobbying for its position even in controversial issues. The majority of these issues surround the needs of veterans, or the military itself. For example, the American Legion has long been calling for reform of the VA health care system, on which many veterans depend for medical care. The VA, facing a crisis in funding due to budget cuts in the 1990s, was forced to become more selective in the benefits it offered. The American Legion wants to see full benefits restored for all veterans. It proposed a plan, the GI Bill of Health, that would transform the VA into something resembling a private managed care organization, open to all veterans. This restructuring would be costly but the American Legion insists that costs would be offset by revenues generated by new insurance payers that would have new access to the opened system.

Also in the 1990s, the question of whether or not homosexuals should be allowed to serve in the military became a topic of much debate. The American Legion does not believe homosexuals have a right to serve in the Armed Forces. The Legion believes that the homosexual lifestyle is incompatible with service in the military. Pressure from the American Legion and other veterans groups forced President Clinton to back down from his campaign promise of an unqualified end to the military's ban on homosexuals. Clinton's compromise position became

known as "Don't ask, don't tell," meaning that recruits entering the military would no longer be asked about their sexual orientation. The Legion has opposed this policy since it was instituted in 1993, believing that allowing homosexuals to join the armed forces compromises the strength of the military, and has lobbied for a return to an outright ban on homosexuals.

The list of rules for proper care of the U.S. flag, the *Flag Code*, was devised by the American Legion in 1923. The Legion has always been a champion of laws designed to make desecration of the U.S. flag a federal crime. Thus, the organization was dismayed by a 1989 U.S. Supreme Court ruling that maintained that altering, and even destroying, the U.S. flag was a form of free speech protected by the First Amendment to the U.S. Constitution. Thus, laws which prevented desecration of the flag were unconstitutional.

After the 1989 Supreme Court ruling, the American Legion and other VSOs began putting pressure on Congress to approve a constitutional amendment prohibiting flag desecration. If passed by both houses of Congress and ratified by the states, such an amendment would become part of the Constitution and eliminate the grounds for the 1989 ruling. Flag protection amendment bills passed in the House several times in the 1990s, but had yet to be successful in the Senate.

Case Study: Smithsonian Institution Enola Gay Exhibit

The *Enola Gay* is the U.S. airplane that carried and dropped an atomic bomb on Hiroshima, Japan, at the conclusion of World War II; it marked the first time an atomic weapon was ever used in warfare. The Hiroshima bomb and the atomic bomb that was dropped a few days later on Nagasaki, Japan, are generally thought to have forced the Japanese to surrender.

The *Enola Gay* had fallen into disrepair after the war. It was restored to its original condition in the early 1990s, and the Smithsonian planned to display the restored airplane in June of 1995 to commemorate the fiftieth anniversary of the end of the war. Museum curators wanted to show the restored plane, but they also wanted to show the effects of the bomb it had dropped. In the first room of the exhibit, the curators planned to display the plane's fuselage alongside photos of her smiling crewmen. After walking past a large photo reproduction of a mushroom cloud, viewers would enter a room filled with graphic photos of the burned victims and charred human remains of the residents of Hiroshima. The proposed exhibit also included personal effects of the residents of Hiroshima.

Reports of the planned exhibit appeared in the media months before it was scheduled to open and veterans groups were incensed. The American Legion believed that the exhibit, with its prominent display of the suffering caused by the bombing, implied that the decision to

FAST FACTS

Eight million surviving World War II veterans were aged 70 years or older by the beginning of 1991.

(Source: Judith Waldrop. "27 Million Heroes." *American Demographics.* November 1993.)

drop the bomb was wrong. Controversy among historians over whether or not the use of atomic weapons against civilians was necessary or justifiable has long existed; while the bombings clearly resulted in a quick end to the war, they took thousands of civilian lives, and some historians believe that the United States would have defeated Japan, in time, without using atomic bombs. The American Legion and other VSOs believed otherwise, however. They maintained that the atomic bomb spared the Allied Forces an invasion of Japan that would have lasted for years and cost the lives of thousands, or even hundreds of thousands, of soldiers.

The American Legion joined in a media campaign against the exhibit. Members of the organization wrote editorials assailing the exhibition's curators. *Time* magazine published a lengthy article discussing the decision to drop the bomb. Members wrote letters threatening to lobby Congress to take away Smithsonian funding. In January of 1995 the Smithsonian's curators, bowing to public pressure, announced that the museum would change the exhibit. The *Enola Gay* exhibit was turned into a display dedicated to the manufacture and restoration of the airplane itself.

The American Legion approved of this second version of the exhibit, which it felt celebrated the end of the war while avoiding political commentary. Others, including many museum curators, felt that the original display raised legitimate questions which the American Legion successfully censored. Nevertheless, while polls taken near the time of the 50th anniversary of Hiroshima and Nagasaki showed that over half of Americans believed dropping the atomic bomb was unnecessary, veterans' groups were nonetheless able to change the programming of America's most prominent museum.

FUTURE DIRECTIONS

As the disproportionately large population of Americans known as Baby Boomers grows older, their demand

for medical care will put a heavy strain on the health care system and those organizations that provide health benefits, such as the VA and the American Legion. Economics and population figures may combine to create financial problems for the VA. The American Legion has for many years petitioned the government for changes in the VA and considering the organization's own aging population, this will remain a major concern of the organization in the years to come.

GROUP RESOURCES

The American Legion maintains a 10,000-volume library at its headquarters in Indianapolis, Indiana. It is a private library, but staffers answer requests from researchers, students, and others. Individuals interested in contacting the American Legion Library or the American Legion may phone (317) 630-1223 or write to the American Legion, P.O. Box 1055, Indianapolis, IN 46206. On-line visitors may access the American Legion Web site at http://www.legion.org, which contains basic information on the organization and its activities.

GROUP PUBLICATIONS

The American Legion publishes the *American Legion* monthly magazine; it contains updates on monuments, changes in VA policy, veterans' memorials, and the workings of the organization. The magazine also includes articles and essays about global political events, such as China's takeover of the former British colony of Hong Kong. Recent issues are available for viewing on the Internet at http://www.legion.org/pubs/publica. htm#mag. The *American Legion Dispatch* is another magazine that the American Legion produces. Containing information on national security and foreign relations issues of interest to American Legion members, it is available for viewing via the World Wide Web at http://www.legion.org/pubs/current/dispatch.htm. The American Legion also publishes *Need a Lift?*, a scholarship and financial aid guide for veterans and their families. *Need a Lift?* lists available scholarships, tuition at many universities, and career information. Information on obtaining any of the organization's publications is available by writing to the American Legion, 700 N. Pennsylvania St., P.O. Box 1055, Indianapolis, IN 46206, by calling (317) 630-1200, or by E-mailing at magazine@legion.org.

BIBLIOGRAPHY

Dethlefsen, Merle, and James Canfield. *Transition from Military to Civilian Life.* Harrisburg, Penn.: Stackpole, 1984.

DeWitt, Karen. "Smithsonian Scales Back Exhibit of Plane in A-Bomb Attack." *New York Times*, 31 January 1995.

Gold, Philip. *Evasions: The American Way of Military Service.* New York: Paragon, 1985.

Jordan, Anthony. "Commander's Message." *American Legion Magazine,* January 1998.

McCarthy, Coleman. "Glory Seekers and the Bomb." *Washington Post,* 7 February 1995.

Rumer, Thomas. *The American Legion: An Official History, 1919–1989.* New York: Simon & Schuster, 1990.

"Simpson's Shot at Veterans." *Washington Post,* 3 April 1996.

Snyder, Keith, and Richard O'Dell. *Veterans Benefits.* New York: Harper Collins, 1994.

Waldrop, Judith. "27 Million Heroes." *American Demographics,* November 1993.

American Library Association (ALA)

ESTABLISHED: 1876
EMPLOYEES: 275
MEMBERS: 57,000
PAC: None

Contact Information:

ADDRESS: 50 E. Huron
     Chicago, IL 60611
PHONE: (312) 280-3215
TOLL FREE: (800) 545-2433
TDD (HEARING IMPAIRED): (312) 944-7298
FAX: (312) 440–9374
URL: http://www.ala.org
PRESIDENT: Ann K. Symons

WHAT IS ITS MISSION?

According to the organization, the mission of the American Library Association (ALA) is "to provide leadership for the development, promotion and improvement of library and information services and the profession of librarianship in order to enhance learning and ensure access to information for all." As an organization that represents a variety of libraries including educational, public, state, or special libraries; the ALA is primarily concerned with providing free and equal access to information to library users. The organization advocates for policy that will help it to achieve its mission and directs outreach and educational efforts to help library staff and users better appreciate the abundance of information available through libraries.

HOW IS IT STRUCTURED?

The ALA's main headquarters is in Chicago, Illinois, and includes a number of offices that focus on specific areas such as chapter relations, research, literacy, library personnel, intellectual freedom, information technology, and accreditation. A separate ALA Washington, D.C., office monitors legislation, conducts advocacy efforts, and provides information to the organization and members regarding relevant political issues. Included in the Washington office is the ALA's Office for Information Technology Policy, formed in 1995, to promote and advocate for free and open information across on-line or Internet channels.

Overseeing the ALA is a 175-member council, elected by ALA membership. Council members serve four-year terms and represent either state library associations or function in an at-large representative capacity. The council considers resolutions put forth by membership and votes on them. Immediately under the council is an executive board, which consists of the organization officers as well as eight positions that are elected from the ALA membership by the council (and serve four-year terms). The board implements policies set forth by the council, makes recommendations to the council, and lays out managerial and administrative direction for the organization with the approval of the council.

State chapters include legislative liaisons and are active in influencing and tracking policy as well as disseminating information to members through newsletters. Student chapters are active on many U.S. campuses. Several organizations are also affiliated with the ALA, including specialized library groups like the Urban Libraries Council, Black Caucus of ALA, Chinese American Librarians Association, and Art Libraries Society of North America.

Members may join the ALA as an individual or as an organization. Members work mainly for libraries, but may include anyone (and have included authors and publishers) who supports the organizational mission of access to information that is free of cost and otherwise unimpeded. Members join through one of 11 divisions that represent the various aspects of the library profession, and include representation of school libraries, technical libraries, research libraries, reference libraries, young adult libraries, and more. Members, through their divisions, engage in activities such as developing standards for the work that they do, holding conferences, and publishing material.

PRIMARY FUNCTIONS

As a membership organization, the ALA protects the needs of its members; while as an association of information providers, it works to ensure that all library patrons have access to information. The ALA functions with the overall goal of protecting intellectual freedom, while at the same time providing quality library services throughout the United States.

The ALA assists library professionals on many fronts. It begins by helping to develop criteria to accredit masters programs in library and information studies. The association fosters professional development opportunities for its members, by making information regarding job placement and scholarship opportunities available. The ALA also provides technical support by preserving printed material.

In an advocacy capacity, the Washington office monitors relevant political developments and makes reports to members. The ALA also advocates for funding and policy that will benefit libraries. The ALA Office for Technology Policy (also located in Washington) provides research and factual material to support ALA positions, and also provides technical support to state chapters if needed.

The ALA also monitors cases of censorship and provides assistance to libraries facing such situations with its Office for Intellectual Freedom. The organization created the *Library Bill of Rights,* an interpretation of the First Amendment from a librarian's point of view. The document is used to defend the belief that libraries should be able to stock any number of types of material for public viewing. The ALA works in concert with the Freedom to Read Foundation, an organization that provides legal support for court cases involving threats to intellectual freedom.

The ALA promotes public education and outreach programs, especially in the area of literacy. The ALA researches literacy issues and makes the findings available to its members. As an example, the ALA conducted a research study that identified libraries across the United States that were most in need of resources. The Gates Library Foundation used the findings of the ALA research and additional information from the U.S. Census to fund 1,000 libraries in low income or rural areas in 1997. The libraries received grants ranging from $4,000 to $30,000 for computers, as well as development and technical support.

PROGRAMS

ALA programs benefit both library staff and library patrons. Many of the organization's programs are well-established, annual events, some of which promote library usage; others are developed to address timely issues that are of immediate concern to the nation's libraries. All programs promote activity in the ALA's key action areas of: diversity; education and continuous learning; equity of access; and twenty-first century literacy.

The ALA launched the *America Links Up* campaign in mid-1998 with the goal of ensuring that children learn to use the Internet and have a safe experience doing it. Libraries held teach-ins to coach children on the use of on-line resources and the ALA provided libraries with lesson plans and press materials for the event.

The ALA facilitates annual events that libraries can hold to promote certain aspects of the profession and of the library. Some of these include: Library Card Sign Up Month, which is held in September to encourage people not only to sign up for a library card but to keep returning to the library on a regular basis; Teen Read Week, an October event that includes contests and activities to encourage teenagers to read; and National Library Week, held in April to promote the role of the library in society.

Banned Books Week, which is held at the end of September, promotes the ALA's viewpoint that all books, even those that are considered controversial by some, should be available to whomever wants to read them. The ALA provides libraries with an annual kit to hold activities during the week. Activities include skits, exhibits, and discussions about censorship. Libraries may sell related merchandise or hand out promotional materials such as bookmarks commemorating the event. Also discussed during the week are specific-challenged books, meaning books that groups have attempted to ban. Challenged books that were highlighted in the 1997 Banned Books Week included *I Know Why the Caged Bird Sings* by Maya Angelou and *Of Mice and Men* by John Steinbeck. These two books are not isolated instances; between 1995 and 1996 the ALA was notified of 740 cases where books were challenged.

The ALA holds an annual Library Legislative Day in May. The national office organizes the event that has library staffs across the United States meeting with legislators and discussing the status of libraries and related issues.

BUDGET INFORMATION

The ALA is a nonprofit organization and receives about 80 percent of its revenue from sources like grants, conferences, and ALA publications. The remaining 20 percent of revenue comes from member dues. The organization's 1998 anticipated budget was projected to exceed $37 million.

At the end of fiscal year 1996, the ALA had revenues totaling $35,405,000, which included: membership dues ($6,258,000), publications ($12,122,000), and meetings ($9,434,000). Expenses for fiscal year 1996 included: $916,000 (meetings and conferences), $404,000 (program offices), and $731,000 (grants and awards). Assets for fiscal year 1996 totaled $28,561,000.

HISTORY

The ALA was founded in 1876 when library advocates Melvil Dewey and Justin Winson saw the need for creating an organization that would represent libraries and the professionals that worked in them. Dewey had been active in the library profession; he established the popular Dewey Classification System for library materials and he created a library department at Columbia University. The ALA quickly mobilized and over the next few decades, members worked to advance the cause of librarianship. During World War I (1914–18), the ALA created a library source for enlistees. After the war, members focused their efforts on improving classification systems, creating new libraries, and supporting the growth of existing libraries in the United States and abroad.

In the 1950s, the beginnings of the Cold War and the perceived threat of rising Communism facilitated an increased interest in censorship. The ALA, in line with its mission of promoting free and open access to material, spoke out against censorship in any form. The organization stated its position on the subject in 1939 by creating and publishing the *Library Bill of Rights*, which laid out the ALA's belief that libraries had a right to stock and make available to the public a variety of types of information.

During its history, the ALA has played a role in the advocacy of policy to benefit its mission. The ALA successfully lobbied for legislation in 1956 that first granted federal funds to libraries. Later, in the 1960s, ALA fought for and achieved legislation (Library Services and Construction Act) that provided funding for libraries to expand their services and to offer services such as bookmobiles, computer use, and library branches.

The 1980s and 1990s saw the expansion of information capabilities with the advent of the Internet and the World Wide Web. Although the ALA may not have predicted the tremendous impact of the Internet on the flow of global information, the organization positioned itself to deal with the new issues that on-line media presented. The ALA established an office devoted to dealing with information technology policy and legislation. In particular the Internet raised entirely new issues regarding censorship and access to information. For example, children at home now had instant access to a variety of types of information, simply by signing on to the Internet on their own home computer. Opponents of free and open information access via the Internet argued that children could easily access detrimental material like pornography. The ALA, ever vigilant in its promotion of information access, continued to advocate for open access to Internet resources.

CURRENT POLITICAL ISSUES

In line with its goal of making information easy to access, the ALA advocates for a number of related political issues. For example, the organization advocates for increased funding for library services and programs. The ALA believes that many libraries lack the facilities, such as up-to-date Internet resources or appropriate holdings, to be able to offer extensive, quality information. In 1998 the ALA advocated for increased levels of funding for the Library Services and Technology Act to ensure that libraries across the United States had adequate funding to be able to go on-line, provide job search information, and to promote literacy. Additionally, the ALA advocated for increased funding to update materials in school libraries.

The ALA is involved with promoting literacy in the United States. In 1998 the ALA advocated for the passage of legislation that would fund child literacy programs including the Reading Excellence Act (H.R. 2614, S. 1596, which was sponsored by Sen. P. Coverdell, R-Ga.). The ALA is also concerned with copyright regulations and works to promote laws that will continue to enable fair access to materials. For example, in 1998 the ALA lobbied for copyright legislation that would protect the fair use of the material and would allow for digital preservation.

The ALA is concerned with maintaining telecommunications connections to rural communities, or establishing these connections where they are lacking. Inner-city or rural schools may need these resources to access materials not available to them normally, but the cost of such service can be prohibitive. Particularly in rural areas, the cost of installing and maintaining such networks is relatively high and can include expenses for updating inadequate phone lines. Between 1995 and 1998, the organization pursued and advocated for discounted on-line service to rural and inner-city libraries and school libraries. While the Telecommunications Act of 1996 (S. 652, Public Law 104-104, Snowe-Kerry-Rockefeller-Exon amendment) designated schools and libraries eligible to receive on-line services, the ALA and other advocate groups had a battle ahead of them to achieve the services at a discount.

Case Study: E-Rate Discounts

One of the provisions of the Telecommunications Act was that upon passage, the Federal Communications Commission (FCC) would set up a committee process to determine how newly legislated services would be funded or supported. After the act became law in February 1996, the FCC began a study of implementing the act, including requesting comments from involved stakeholders. The ALA actively participated in the process, forming a coalition, called EdLiNC, with other library and education groups, which jointly filed more than 30 comments between April 1996 and May 1997. During this time period, the ALA and the coalition continued to advocate for library and school discounts using other methods: the ALA president testified before a board of the FCC and EdLiNC carried out a media campaign designed to explain the issues to library and school users, professionals, and policymakers.

The FCC released final recommendations in May 1997, which included a measure for discounts on on-line service for schools and libraries ranging from 20 percent to 80 percent. However, the details about how to implement the subsidies and who would be responsible for them continued to be discussed through 1998. The ALA remained involved in the implementation process and with EdLiNC, worked on an E-Rate Work Group established by the FCC. E-rate is short for education rate. During 1997 the ALA and the coalition were confronted with opponents who attempted to do away with the subsidies and a demand from industry that higher education be made to pay for the discounts. The ALA advocated

against this measure, and the FCC ultimately opposed it.

Through 1997 and 1998 the ALA continued to advocate for the subsidy, asking the FCC to determine funding for the program and requesting that the application process for schools and libraries be simplified. For first-year eligibility, more than 30,000 applications for discounted on line service were received. The group ultimately responsible for the program was established as the Schools and Library Corporation (SLC). The SLC was organized into the Schools and Library Division (SLD) under a directive by the FCC that effective January 1, 1999, "the e-rate program along with its sister program for rural health care providers merge with the Universal Service Administrative Company which administers the larger and long-standing universal service program."

The SLD began sending commitment letters to libraries in November 1998. During its third wave of mailings, which occurred in January 1999, the SLD mailed over 1,300 letters of commitment, which amounted to approximately $8 million. "We congratulate the Schools and Libraries Division for recognizing it is critically important to get the e-rate discounts out to our nation's libraries," said ALA President Ann K. Symons. "This special mailing acknowledges that libraries are a critical player in providing equitable access to the information superhighway."

FUTURE DIRECTIONS

At the end of the 1990s, the ALA focused on building shared values and coalitions among all libraries, particularly in the arena of intellectual freedom. The ALA seeks to create opportunities for dialog and information sharing among libraries and will circulate a twenty-first century intellectual freedom statement, which was drafted in mid-1998. The statement outlines principles that should be encouraged if libraries are to succeed and flourish as a source of free access to information in the future. The ALA will also be making an effort to focus on addressing diversity issues through library services and collections, promoting continuing education for library staff, facilitating equal access to library resources for all, and promoting literacy in the United States.

GROUP RESOURCES

The ALA maintains an on-line library and archives at http://ala.org/library. The site also includes an extensive record of facts pertaining to U.S. libraries, including the number of such institutions, classification, and bibliographies. The main ALA Web site at http://www.ala.org has a great deal of information about the organization, including a current roster of issues relevant to the

ALA, status of pending legislation, and contact information for legislators.

The ALA also hosts dozens of e-mail mailing lists for its members, such as the ALA Advocacy Now! List, the ALA Intellectual Freedom Round Table, and the SRRT Gay, Lesbian & Bisexual Task Force. Those among the general public who are interested in library related issues can also subscribe to these free lists. For more information, visit the ALA's list server Web page at http://www.ala.org/membership/lists.html.

GROUP PUBLICATIONS

The ALA produces hundreds of different publications and supporting materials such as posters, video and audio tapes, and promotional items such as totebags and mugs. There are dozens of ALA periodical publications. Most are available for free to members of the ALA or to members of various ALA committees and task forces. Many of these publications are also avialable to the public through subscriptions. *American Libraries* is a bimonthly publication available for free to ALA members or in a weekly format at the ALA Web site. It is also available through subscription by faxing (312) 944-784. The ALA makes available a free E-mail newsletter on current policy initiatives and actions needed called the *ALA Washington Office Newsline,* which is available by

subscribing through the Web site at http://www.ala.org/washoff/alawopub.html. For more information on these and other ALA publications, visit their Web site at http://www.ala.org/market, or contact the ALA by mail at American Library Association, 50 E. Huron, Chicago, IL 60611.

BIBLIOGRAPHY

Brogan, Pamela. "Summit on Making 'Net Safe for Children to Convene in Washington Next Month." *Gannett News Service,* 20 November 1997.

Chapman, Steve. "On Internet Filters, Who Should Decide?" *Washington Times,* 13 September 1998.

Cieslak, David J. "Literacy Needs New Definition, Prof. Says." *University Wire,* 20 February 1998.

Ferranti, Marc. "FCC Decides to Scale Back Funding for 'E-Rate' Telecom Initiative."*InfoWorld,* 22 June 1998.

Goodman, Ellen. "Saving Curious Kids from X-Rated Net." *Rocky Mountain News,* 27 July 1997.

Miller, Leslie Miller. "Libraries Torn over Censoring Internet's Seamy Side." *USA Today,* 22 April 1997.

Rohde, David. "Federal E-Rate Limps to the Finish Line." *Network World,* 29 March 1999.

Tweet, Margaret. "Taxpayers Support Pornography in Local Libraries." *The Columbian,* 19 February 1998.

American Medical Association (AMA)

WHAT IS ITS MISSION?

According to the American Medical Association (AMA), its goal is to "promote the science and art of medicine and the betterment of public health. We serve physicians and their patients by establishing and promoting ethical, educational, and clinical standards for the medical profession and by advocating for the highest principle of all—the integrity of the patient/physician relationship."

The AMA, a federation of 54 state and territorial medical associations and societies, was founded in 1847 and is the largest and oldest national professional organization for physicians in the United States. Its efforts are directed toward furthering the interests of the medical profession and improving the health of the U.S. public. Membership is open to doctors of medicine (M.D.s), doctors of osteopathy (D.O.s), and medical students. In 1997 about 40 percent of the nation's 700,000 physicians and 55 percent of its medical students belonged to the AMA.

ESTABLISHED: May 7, 1847
EMPLOYEES: 1,100 (1997)
MEMBERS: 297,000 (1997)
PAC: American Medical Political Action Committee (AMPAC)

Contact Information:

ADDRESS: 515 N. State St.
    Chicago, IL 60610
PHONE: (312) 464-5000
FAX: (312) 464-4184
URL: http://www.ama-assn.org
PRESIDENT: Nancy W. Dickey, MD

HOW IS IT STRUCTURED?

The 54 state and territorial medical associations and societies that make up the AMA (formally known as "constituent associations") represent all 50 states, Guam, Puerto Rico, the Virgin Islands, and the District of Columbia. The constituent associations are composed of several hundred county and district medical societies. Most AMA members buy a combined local, state, and national membership package, although it is possible to join the national AMA directly.

AMA policies are set by the organization's 475-member house of delegates, which meets twice per year. Delegates represent various groups: the constituent associations; 95 national medical specialty societies, such as the American College of Surgeons and the American Psychiatric Association; the surgeon general of the United States and a handful of other federal service agencies; and the AMA's six "special sections" representing the interests of medical residents, medical schools, medical students, hospital and clinic physicians, young physicians, and graduates of foreign medical schools.

The board of trustees is an 18-member body charged with handling the general business of the organization and implementing the policies of the house of delegates. The board also serves as the public face of the AMA; its members often deliver the AMA message to medical and nonmedical organizations, government bodies, and the media. Board trustees are elected by the house of delegates with the exception of a medical-student trustee who is elected by the Medical Student Section Assembly. The trustees include a president-elect, a president, and an immediate past president, each of whom holds office for one year before rotating into the next position. All other trustees serve four-year terms, except for two elected to represent medical students and medical residents, who hold office for a shorter period. Board officers include a chair, a vice chair, a secretary-treasurer, and three members who act as an executive committee. Day-to-day management of AMA affairs, however, is the job of a board-appointed executive vice president.

AMA policy is guided, in part, by seven advisory bodies: the Council on Constitution and Bylaws, the Council on Medical Education, the Council on Medical Service, the Council on Ethical and Judicial Affairs, the Council on Long Range Planning and Development, the Council on Legislation, and the Council on Scientific Affairs. A special position is occupied by the nine-member Council on Ethical and Judicial Affairs (CEJA) which, among other things, is responsible for interpreting the AMA's code of ethics, a document that dates back to the AMA's foundation in 1847 and lies at the heart of the AMA's identity as an organization. The CEJA investigates ethical issues as a result of its own initiative or through resolutions by the house of delegates or public complaints about improper medical behavior.

The AMA has three affiliates, all headquartered in Chicago. The American Medical Association Alliance, Inc., founded in 1922 as the Woman's Auxiliary, is an organization of more than 60,000 spouses of AMA members who, through more than 800 local chapters, seek to improve public health. The Accreditation Council for Graduate Medical Education evaluates and certifies medical residency programs in the United States. There is also an Accreditation Council for Continuing Medical Education.

PRIMARY FUNCTIONS

As a professional association, the AMA works to further the interests of its members; as a preeminent health care organization, it also has the goal of improving and ensuring the public's health. The AMA's work includes maintaining a code of medical ethics for its members; setting standards for and helping to finance medical education; producing the *Journal of the American Medical Association* and other publications; sponsoring a political action committee (AMPAC) and lobbying Congress for legislative changes favorable to the medical profession; campaigning against smoking and for other improvements in public health; and making medical information available to the public through the Internet and other media.

The AMA also maintains special-interest groups for medical students, minority physicians, and others. It sponsors practice-related initiatives such as the Doctors Advisory Network, which puts AMA members needing business advice in touch with the appropriate professionals, and Project USA, a program which recruits primary care physicians to serve as short-term volunteer replacements for U.S. Public Health Service physicians in rural areas. The focus of AMA activity is the organization's Chicago headquarters. Lobbying and federal government relations are conducted out of a Washington, D.C., office. Smaller offices in New York and New Jersey look after advertising sales for AMA publications.

The AMA in Washington

AMA Washington staffers monitor federal and state legislation and regulations, work with the Council on Legislation and other AMA bodies to develop new legislative initiatives, testify before Congress, meet with government officials, and engage in other activities intended to further the AMA's political policies.

The AMA's political efforts are spearheaded by AMPAC, which was established in 1961. AMPAC has two main goals: to provide financial and other aid to members of Congress who support AMA positions, and to educate and mobilize physicians and their spouses for participation in the political process. AMPAC's 10-member board (which includes a seat for a physician spouse) is appointed by the AMA's board of trustees from nominations submitted by various AMA groups.

The AMA's Division of Political and Legislative Grassroots works with AMPAC to mobilize a force of more than 100,000 politically committed AMA members. Seminars and workshops on political issues and tactics are offered throughout the United States. The AMA Political Grassroots Conference, held every second year in Washington, is attended by several hundred AMA activists and features leading Republicans and Democrats as speakers. The AMA has been at the forefront to use the Internet and other communications advances for political purposes. For example, the AMA sends "Blast

Faxes" and E-mail alerts to inform members about perceived legislative threats and has a toll-free telephone hot
line system that automatically transfers members' calls
to an appropriate congressional member.

PROGRAMS

The AMA's interests are reflected in the many programs and initiatives it sponsors. For instance, in 1997
the AMA founded an Ethics Institute to investigate the
ethical implications of genetic research, care for the
dying, and other issues; created a National Patient Safety
Foundation to find ways to reduce mistakes in medical
practice; developed a joint initiative with NASA to
examine the health effects of spaceflight; and worked
with universities to develop programs to reduce binge
drinking by students. Two of the AMA's campaigns
have been especially ambitious: its antismoking efforts
since the 1970s, and its creation and promotion of the
American Medical Accreditation Program (AMAP) in
1997–98.

The AMA founded AMAP in 1997 to provide a uni-
versally recognized process for evaluating physicians'
credentials and performance. When physicians join a
hospital or health plan, they must undergo periodic performance reviews to ensure that their medical care meets
the organization's standards. The problem for physicians
is that they are usually affiliated with several hospitals
and health plans at once, each of which has its own performance standards and review procedures. AMAP's
goal is to reduce the costly and time-consuming burden
of multiple performance reviews on physicians and the
U.S. health care system in general by replacing the thousands of privately run accreditation programs with a voluntary, nationwide program under AMA auspices. In
developing and promoting AMAP, the AMA has
enlisted the cooperation of national health and regulatory agencies, state medical associations and societies,
hospital systems, insurance companies, employers'
coalitions, consumer groups, and other organizations
with an interest in how medical care is delivered.
AMAP's success in instituting this national initiative is
far from certain, however, for it still faces two major
challenges: convincing thousands of U.S. hospitals and
health plans to abandon their tried-and-true accreditation procedures in favor of AMAP's, and certifying
700,000 U.S. physicians.

BUDGET INFORMATION

In 1996 the AMA reported operating revenues of
$220.7 million. Membership dues accounted for 31.5 per-
cent of operating revenues, down from 35.8 percent in
1995.

HISTORY

During the 1840s, when the idea for a national medical organization first arose in the United States, a small
number of university-trained physicians competed for
patients with homeopaths, herbalists, midwives, and
other healers who had learned their craft outside the traditional university system. Nationwide medical education standards did not exist and legislative restrictions on
who could practice medicine were few and ineffective.
In the eyes of medical scholar Nathaniel Chapman, the
AMA's first president, the U.S. medical profession was
flooded with inferior practitioners, and urgently in need
of reform. The concerns expressed by Chapman and other
critics prompted 268 physicians from 22 states to meet
in Philadelphia, Pennsylvania, in May 1847 to establish
the AMA as the national organization for traditionally
educated physicians. At that first meeting, delegates
adopted a code of ethics that raised the standards of practice at that time. They also passed resolutions for improving medical education and appointed a committee to promote that effort.

Despite its promising start, however, the AMA languished for more than 50 years and by 1900 only 8,000
physicians belonged to the association. During the first
decade of the twentieth century, the AMA settled its differences with the homeopaths and other opponents and
reformed its organizational structure. As a result, by 1910
it had 70,000 members—half of all U.S. physicians. A
decade later, it represented 60 percent of the profession.
In 1904 the AMA formed a Council on Medical Education to weed out substandard medical schools and within
the space of just a decade or so managed to convince
state licensing boards to certify only those physicians
who were graduates of council-approved schools. Since
the 1940s undergraduate medical programs have been
accredited by the Liaison Committee on Medical Education, a joint effort of the AMA and the Association of
American Medical Colleges.

The early part of the twentieth century also witnessed the beginning of the AMA's long-standing opposition to government-sponsored health insurance plans
and other efforts viewed as limiting physicians' economic freedom. In 1943 the AMA opened its Washington office and formed a Council on Medical Service and
Public Relations to fight Congress's Wagner-Murray-
Dingell bill, which sought to provide medical and hospital insurance for every family receiving Social Security, and would have required physicians treating such
patients to adhere to a fee schedule. A few years later the
AMA opposed President Harry Truman's goal of comprehensive national health insurance, as well as efforts
by Presidents John F. Kennedy and Lyndon Johnson that
led to the passage of Medicare (the national health insurance program for the elderly) in 1965.

After its defeat on Medicare, however, the AMA
developed a more pragmatic approach to the issue of
health care reform. In 1991 it unveiled Health Access

America, a policy supporting universal access to health care through mandatory workplace coverage and enlargement of the scope of Medicare and Medicaid (the national health insurance program for the poor). When Bill Clinton became president in 1992, Health Access America formed the basis of the AMA's reply to President Clinton's ultimately unsuccessful crusade for comprehensive health care reform and a national health insurance plan. Rather than totally rejecting the president's Health Security Act of 1993, as it might have done in the past, the AMA carefully detailed which Clinton proposals were acceptable and which were not, and energetically promoted its own policies for reform.

In the 1990s the AMA had to cope with a steep decline in membership. In the 1960s about 90 percent of U.S. physicians in private practice had been AMA members, but by 1987 only about 50 percent of U.S. physicians belonged to the AMA, and that number dropped to about 40 percent over the following decade. One widely acknowledged reason for the decline was the AMA's refusal to consider alternatives to the traditional fee-for-service approach to compensating physicians. Under this system a physician receives a fee from the patient or the patient's insurer for each service he or she provides, rather than, say, a yearly lump sum from a government insurance plan for each patient in the physician's practice. Many physicians—particularly younger ones—saw the AMA's vigorous defense of the economic status quo as contributing to a national crisis in health care.

Another possible reason for the decline was the AMA's perceived ambivalence toward the large numbers of physicians who had come to the United States from other countries since the 1960s and 1970s. Despite the AMA's attempts to meet the needs of foreign-trained physicians by, for instance, establishing a special section for them in 1996, some detractors still viewed the AMA as hostile or indifferent to their concerns. This may explain why physicians educated outside the United States, who accounted for almost 25 percent of the nation's practitioners in 1997, made up a small proportion of the AMA's membership. The AMA was also less than successful in bringing African American and female physicians into its ranks.

Finally, the AMA's role as a consensus-building institution within the medical profession was being eroded by the rise of health maintenance organizations (HMOs) and other corporate arrangements for the delivery of medical services that were fragmenting a profession that had formerly enjoyed a shared economic identity based on single-physician and small-group medical practices. By the late 1990s the fact remained, however, that in terms of membership numbers, financial power, and political influence, the AMA still eclipsed all other U.S. professional medical organizations.

CURRENT POLITICAL ISSUES

The AMA seeks to influence government policies on a wide range of public health issues. Its vigorous 25-year campaign against the tobacco industry is a case in point. Family violence, children's television programming, and AIDS testing in the prison system are a few of the other issues that the AMA has turned its attention to in recent years. The AMA also intervenes in lawsuits that affect the interests of the medical profession, some of which have broader public policy implications. In 1996 for instance, the AMA submitted an *amicus curiae* (friend of the court) brief to the U.S. Supreme Court opposing physician-assisted suicide.

As a political force, the AMA has always shown a willingness to tackle big issues and take on powerful opponents such as the tobacco industry, but only in 1997 did it become embroiled in what is perhaps the most emotional topic in contemporary U.S. political life—abortion.

Case Study: The Partial-Birth Abortion Debate

In 1973 the U.S. Supreme Court issued its famous decision in *Roe v. Wade,* which declared that a woman has a constitutionally protected right to terminate her pregnancy under certain circumstances. Shortly after, the AMA's house of delegates adopted a resolution stating that abortion is a medical procedure properly carried out only by licensed physicians, but that the decision to perform abortions is a matter of conscience for each physician. After 1973 the AMA supplemented its general policy on abortion with stands on particular issues, such as the availability of the abortion pill RU-486, but for almost 25 years avoided involvement in legislative debates over abortion. The issue that drew the AMA into the abortion conflict in 1997 was the use of a procedure known among physicians as intact dilatation and extraction and popularly referred to as partial-birth abortion.

Because a partial-birth abortion is sometimes performed when a fetus is 20 weeks or older, some opponents of abortion view the procedure as infanticide. Even some pro-choice are bothered by the fact that the procedure is done with fetuses whose physiological development is well underway. Congress first entered the controversy over partial-birth abortion in 1995, when a Republican-sponsored bill to outlaw the procedure passed the House and the Senate but was vetoed by President Clinton in April 1996. An attempt to override the veto failed.

At the December 1996 meeting of the AMA's house of delegates, members were asked to vote on a resolution supporting the criminalization of partial-birth abortion. Instead, they adopted a resolution reaffirming the AMA's existing abortion policy and sent the issue to the board of trustees for further study. The committee submitting the alternative resolution indicated that its recommendations were based on a core tenet of AMA ideology, "the belief that governmental interference into the practice of medicine is inappropriate and ultimately harmful to the patient." A few months later, in mid-May 1997, the AMA confirmed that it did "not support any [abortion] legislative proposals at this time." Yet just a few days later, on May 19, the AMA unexpectedly reversed its position. AMA Executive Vice President P. John Seward sent a letter on behalf of the board of trustees to Republican Senator Rick Santorum, who had recently introduced a bill outlawing partial-birth abortion, stating that the AMA supported Santorum's bill on the basis that partial-birth abortion is "a procedure we all agree is not good medicine."

The unexpectedness and timing of the AMA's action raised suspicions about the organization's motives among pro-choice activists and within the medical profession itself. Timing was an issue because May 19 was also the day that Seward sent 125 congressional leaders an eight-page list of requests concerning upcoming negotiations over Medicare budget cuts that threatened to harm the medical profession's economic position. Kate Michelman, president of the National Abortion and Reproductive Rights Action League, was quoted by Helen Dewar and Judith Havemann in the *Washington Post* as saying that she felt the AMA was attempting to protect physicians's wallets and that "the AMA cares much more about moving their political agenda through a Republican-controlled anti-choice Congress than they do about women's health and women's rights." Both the AMA and Santorum, however, dismissed such claims.

Santorum's bill was approved by the Senate on May 20 and sent to the House for its consideration. In the meantime, controversy continued to build within the AMA over the board of trustees' endorsement. Groups such as the American College of Obstetricians and Gynecologists, and some state medical associations, resented the fact that the board had made such a momentous decision without gaining the support of the house of delegates. Another concern was that the bill, by setting limits on a particular medical procedure, opened the door to widespread government interference in medical decision making. The controversy came to a head at the house of delegates meeting that June, where, after five hours' debate, the members finally voted to support the board's actions.

A June 1997 *Washington Post* article by Abigail Trafford offered a possible explanation for the AMA's decision. AMA's president-elect Nancy W. Dickey observed that since 1995 many states had attempted to pass their own laws against partial-birth abortion, some of which were more strongly worded than the federal bill. The AMA board therefore made a strategic decision to support the federal bill as a way of short circuiting the more restrictive state bills. As Dickey said, "In an ideal world, there would have been no legislation. That was our preference. Unfortunately, it's not an ideal world." Dickey's revelation that the board would have preferred not to support the bill was in keeping with the AMA's

FAST FACTS

During the 1995–96 election cycle, AMPAC gave $2,319,197 to candidates for federal office (80 percent to Republicans), more than double the amount given by any other health care PAC and a sum that placed AMPAC among the top ten federal PACs in terms of contributions.

(Source: Larry Makinson and Joshua Goldstein. *Open Secrets: The Encyclopedia of Congressional Money and Politics.* Washington, D.C.: Congressional Quarterly, 1996.)

traditional aversion to government interference in medical decision making, but her comments undercut Seward, her organization's executive vice president, who only a month before had told the *New York Times* that the AMA supported the federal bill on ethical grounds. Despite the reasoning behind the AMA's decision, the partial-birth abortion bill was quickly vetoed by President Clinton after being approved by the House in October 1997.

FUTURE DIRECTIONS

A pressing problem that the AMA faces is to find a way to reverse the AMA's declining membership. While the percentage of U.S. physicians belonging to the AMA has been falling since the 1960s, the AMA's efforts as a public health advocate have grown more ambitious and costly. A smaller membership base means less revenue to finance the organization's initiatives. At the December 1997 meeting of the house of delegates, according to Mary Chris Jaklevic, writing in *Modern Healthcare,* "declining membership . . . became a rallying cry for nearly every topic on the agenda."

GROUP RESOURCES

A good starting point for information on the AMA is its Web site at http://www.ama-assn.org, which provides, in addition to press releases and descriptions of various AMA activities, a downloadable "PolicyFinder" file that includes a searchable database of the organization's constitution and bylaws, the policies of its house of delegates, and the formal opinions of its Council on Ethical and Judicial Affairs. Although much of the Web site is geared toward physicians and medical students, it also offers an impressive collection of health and fitness resources for consumers, including "AMA Physician Select," a geographically organized database containing information on nearly every MD and DO in the United States.

GROUP PUBLICATIONS

The weekly *Journal of the American Medical Association (JAMA)*, widely considered one of the world's leading medical journals, contains reports of original research as well as articles on ethical, social, and political issues affecting the medical profession. *JAMA*, which can be found in some public libraries, is distributed to every member of the AMA, as is another weekly, the *American Medical News*, a newspaper that concentrates on political, professional, and business matters. The AMA also publishes nine specialized medical journals, available by subscription, and books for physicians and medical students. Since the early 1980s the organization has also promoted a line of well-received consumer publications such as *The American Medical Association Family Medical Guide* and the *American Medical Association Complete Guide to Women's Health*, both published by Random House.

BIBLIOGRAPHY

American Medical Association. *Caring for the Country: A History and Celebration of the First 150 Years of the American Medical Association.* Chicago: American Medical Association, 1997.

Baker, Robert, et al. "Crisis, Ethics, and the American Medical Association: 1847 and 1997." *Journal of the American Medical Association,* 9 July 1997.

Dewar, Helen. "AMA Backs Partial Birth Abortion Curb." *Washington Post,* 20 May 1997.

Gawande, Atul. "Partial Truths in the Partial-Birth-Abortion Debate." *Slate,* 29 January 1998.

Gorman, Christine. "Doctors' Dilemma." *Time,* 25 August 1997.

Havemann, Judith. "AMA Adversaries Question Timing of Abortion Ban Stance, Legislative Requests." *Washington Post,* 30 May 1997.

Jaklevic, Mary Chris. "AMA on Sunbeam Cleanup Mission." *Modern Healthcare,* 15 December 1997.

———. "AMA-Sunbeam Dispute Heads to Court." *Modern Healthcare,* 15 September 15 1997.

Menduno, Michael. "Physician Accrediting: A Credit to Quality?" *Hospitals & Health Networks,* 5 June 1998.

Starr, Paul. *The Social Transformation of American Medicine.* New York: Basic Books, 1982.

Trafford, Abigail. "The Doctors Invite Congress In." *Washington Post,* 30 June 1997.

Zipperer, Lorri A., ed. *The Health Care Almanac: A Resource Guide to the Medical Field.* Chicago: American Medical Association, 1995.

Zuger, Abigail. "After Bad Year for A.M.A., Doctors Debate Its Prognosis." *New York Times,* 2 December 1997.

American Nurses Association (ANA)

ESTABLISHED: 1897
EMPLOYEES: 198 (1997)
MEMBERS: 174,609 (1997)
PAC: American Nurses Association Political Action
Committee (ANA-PAC)

Contact Information:

ADDRESS: 600 Maryland Ave. SW, Ste. 100 W.
Washington, DC 20024-2571
PHONE: (202) 651-7000
TOLL FREE: (800) 274-4262
FAX: (202) 651-7001
URL: http://www.nursingworld.org
PRESIDENT: Beverly L. Malone

WHAT IS ITS MISSION?

According to the American Nurses Association's published statement, its mission is to "advance the nursing profession by fostering high standards of nursing practice, promoting the economic and general welfare of nurses in the workplace, projecting a positive and realistic view of nursing, and by lobbying the Congress and regulatory agencies on health care issues affecting nurses and the general public."

HOW IS IT STRUCTURED?

The American Nurses Association (ANA), a federation of 53 state and territorial nurses associations (SNAs), is the leading professional organization for registered nurses (RNs) in the United States. RNs are nurses who hold a diploma or degree in nursing and have passed a state licensing examination set by the National Council of State Boards of Nursing. RNs automatically become members of the ANA by joining an SNA. The ANA's 53 SNAs, also known as "constituent members," are drawn from each of the 50 states, Guam, the Virgin Islands, and the District of Columbia. The SNAs, in turn, are made up of district and regional associations, of which there were well over 800 in 1998. For individual RNs, SNA membership has been a prerequisite for ANA membership since 1982.

The ANA's general policies and positions are determined by its House of Delegates, which meets annually and comprises representatives elected to two-year terms by the members of each SNA. One of its tasks is to elect

the ANA's 15-member board of directors, which is responsible for implementing House of Delegates' decisions and for conducting the general business of the organization. The board of directors includes five officers—a president, two vice presidents, a secretary, and a treasurer—and ten directors. Officers are elected to two-year terms, directors to four-year terms. The day-to-day running of the ANA is in the hands of an executive director and a Washington staff including RNs, economists, attorneys, lobbyists, and communications officers.

Organizational Structure

The ANA has devised a complex organizational structure for addressing professional and organizational issues and ensuring that the concerns of SNAs and individual members are heard. Two key bodies are the Congress of Nursing Practice and the Congress on Nursing Economics, which advise the House of Delegates and the board of directors. Each congress has 15 members, 9 elected by the House of Delegates and 6 appointed by the board of directors.

The Congress of Nursing Practice is assisted by the Institute of Constituent Members on Nursing Practice, which includes one representative from each SNA. The bylaws also allow the board of directors to establish consultative councils, open to any ANA member, to work with the Congress of Nursing Practice.

The Congress on Nursing Economics receives advice from two bodies, the Institute of Constituent Member Collective Bargaining Programs, whose membership comprises one representative from each of the more than 25 SNAs that act as collective bargaining agents for their nurses, and the Commission on Economic and Professional Security, consisting of eight congressional appointees. Yet another advisory body is the Constituent Assembly, which includes two representatives from each SNA (the president and the chief administrator) and reports to the House of Delegates and board of directors on professional and organizational issues.

Affiliates

The ANA works with three affiliated organizations to advance the cause of nursing. The oldest is the American Nurses Foundation, a nonprofit organization incorporated by the ANA in 1955 to provide financial support for nursing research and education. The American Academy of Nurses, founded by the ANA in 1973, is a self-governing body of prominent nurses who seek to influence American health care policy and oversee research into various issues that affect the nursing profession. The American Nurses Credentialing Center, founded in 1991, grew out of earlier ANA efforts to offer specialist certification in areas such as pediatric and geriatric nursing.

ANA ties with other nursing and health care organizations in the United States are established and maintained through participation in numerous organizations

and cooperative endeavors. Two particularly important institutions are the Nursing Organization Liaison Forum, an ANA-sponsored body whose membership encompasses representatives from more than 70 specialized nursing organizations, and the Tri-Council for Nursing, which initially included the ANA, the National League for Nursing, and the American Association of Colleges of Nursing. A fourth member, the American Organization of Nurse Executives, was added later, but the Tri-Council kept its original name.

PRIMARY FUNCTIONS

The ANA engages in a wide range of activities designed to further the interests of RNs and improve health care for Americans. These include developing standards for nursing education and practice; maintaining a code of ethical conduct for nurses; supporting nursing research; promoting collective bargaining by nurses at the state level; championing nursing issues through the media; seeking to shape national policy on nursing and health care by lobbying members of Congress, sponsoring a political action committee (ANA-PAC), and undertaking other Washington-based efforts; helping SNAs develop state-level political action programs; and forging links with other nursing and health care organizations in the United States and internationally.

The ANA's Legislative and Regulatory Efforts in Washington

ANA political activity at the national level is overseen by two branches of the organization, the Department of Federal Government Relations and the Department of Political and Grassroots Programs. The latter is responsible for assisting ANA-PAC and for directing a grassroots mobilization initiative known as the Nurses Strategic Action Team (N-STAT). ANA-PAC and N-STAT both place a heavy emphasis on educating RNs to play a more effective role in politics at the national and state levels.

The Department of Federal Government Relations uses in-house lobbyists to forward the ANA's legislative agenda by working with members of Congress and their staffs to shepherd legislation through Congress. This includes drafting of bills for presentation by the ANA's congressional allies, obtaining congressional cosponsors, and preparing testimony for delivery to congressional committees and subcommittees. In many cases the department forms alliances with other nursing organizations, labor unions, and consumers', women's, and minority groups. Once a bill becomes law, the department lobbies the relevant federal agencies to ensure that the desired regulations are passed.

The staff of the Department of Political and Grassroots Programs have several responsibilities, one of which is to assist ANA-PAC's board of trustees, which endorses and financially supports congressional and presidential candidates whose platforms meet with ANA approval. ANA-PAC, which was founded in 1974, increased its political presence substantially in the 1990s. During the 1993-94 election cycle, it ranked 30th among more than 4,000 PACs in terms of the size of its monetary contributions to candidates for federal office, and among health care PACs was surpassed only by the American Medical Association and the American Dental Association. ANA-PAC funds are raised for the most part through a mail and telephone campaign directed at ANA members.

N-STAT represents a sophisticated effort by the Department of Political and Grassroots Programs, in cooperation with the SNAs, to mobilize the political potential of the ANA's large membership. Each member of the House and Senate is assigned a nurse who is responsible for bringing the ANA's legislative concerns to the member's attention and for mobilizing ANA political efforts in the member's congressional district or state. These Congressional District Coordinators and Senate Coordinators, as they are called, collectively make up the N-STAT Leadership Team. They are supported by the N-STAT Rapid Response Team, more than 50,000 politically committed rank-and-file ANA members who work on ANA political campaigns and can be called on to write or telephone their legislators en masse in support of particular initiatives.

PROGRAMS

ANA programs and initiatives run the gamut from holding political policy conferences and workshops for RNs, to offering a comprehensive syllabus of continuing education courses, to financially supporting sexual health education efforts in schools through the ANA/Foundations Nurses Campaign to Reduce Adolescent High Risk Behaviors.

Many ANA activities are motivated by a belief that, as Kathleen Canavan writes in the *American Journal of Nursing,* "inadequate RN staffing levels result in higher rates of negative patient outcomes." In the 1990s era of hospital downsizing and restructuring, the ANA has attempted to stave off large-scale cuts in nursing staff and the replacement of RNs with minimally trained and less expensive technicians and nurses' aides. The centerpiece of this campaign is the Nursing Safety and Quality Initiative, launched in 1994 as a multifaceted effort to convince legislators, hospital administrators, and the general public that reductions in RN staffing levels make for unsound fiscal and public health policy.

On the consumer outreach front, the initiative has included a drive to persuade the public that "Every Patient Deserves a Nurse." In 1995-96, the initiative provided funding for six SNAs to develop standards for

quantifying the impact of RN care on patients—a first step in obtaining the hard evidence needed to demonstrate a link between RN staffing levels and patient outcomes.

In the legislative arena, the ANA worked with Representative Maurice Hinchey (D-N.Y.) to introduce a Patient Safety Act in the 104th Congress in April 1996. The act contained three main requirements: that health care institutions collect and publish specific information about staffing and patient outcomes; that "whistleblower" provisions be added to the Medicare law to prevent employer retaliation against nurses who report or express concern about unsafe conditions for patients; and that the U.S. Department of Health and Human Services be given the task of reviewing the health and safety impact on patients of all mergers and acquisitions involving health care institutions, and the authority to halt those judged to be a threat to patients. Although the bill failed to get past the committee stage, it was reintroduced by Hinchey in the 105th Congress in March 1997. According to an ANA board member commenting on the bill's reintroduction, several years might be needed to build public and political support for the bill.

BUDGET INFORMATION

The ANA is a nonprofit organization with federal 501(c)6 filing status. In 1996, the ANA reported total revenues of $24,394,319. These revenues consisted of $13,018,059 in member dues, $5,108689 in program service revenues, $2,618,239 of income from investments, $1,464,456 in government contributions, $358,113 from the sale of assets, $173,000 in direct public support, and $1,653,763 of revenue from other sources, including conference fees, affiliate fees, and advertising.

ANA expenses in 1996 totaled $23,286,549. These expenses included $7,381,014 in employee salaries, $3,735,874 in administrative expenses, $2,076,882 in rent and other occupancy expenses, $1,796,553 in employee benefits and payroll taxes, $1,303,098 is spent on conferences and meetings, $1,199,933 goes towards travel expenses, $1,199,243 goes to professional fees, $1,037,766 is allocated in grants, $950,516 is spent on printing and publications, $797,097 in compensation for officers, and $1,808,663 in other expenses.

HISTORY

The first steps toward establishing the organization later known as the ANA were taken by members of 10 nurses alumnae associations at a meeting held outside New York City in 1896. The following year they founded the Nurses Associated Alumnae of the United States and Canada, which became the ANA in 1911. The ANA's current federated structure came into being in 1982.

BUDGET:

1996 ANA Revenue

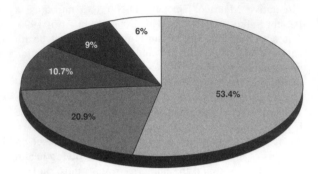

- ■ 53.4%: Member dues
- ■ 20.9%: Program service revenues
- ■ 10.7%: Income from investments
- ■ 9%: From other sources
- ☐ 6%: Government contributions

1996 ANA Expenses

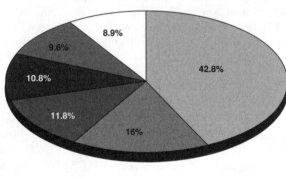

- ■ 42.8%: Salaries, benefits, and compensation for officers
- ■ 16%: Administrative expenses
- ■ 11.8%: Publications and other expenses
- ■ 10.8%: Conferences, meetings, and travel
- ■ 9.6%: Professional fees and grants
- ☐ 8.9%: Rent and other occupancy expenses

During its early years the ANA concentrated on promoting state licensing for nurses, which began in North Carolina in 1903 and was adopted by the last of the then 48 states in 1923. This campaign provided the impetus

for the establishment of SNAs. In the 1940s the ANA turned its attention to collective bargaining, which it endorsed in 1946 (although it maintained a no-strike policy until 1968). The right of nurses in the nonprofit hospital sector to organize and strike, however, was not granted by the National Labor Relations Act until 1974. Today, collective bargaining is the province of the SNAs, although the parent organization retains a keen interest in labor relations issues.

Although the ANA established a Committee on Legislation in 1923 and placed a lobbyist in Washington in 1951, the organization did not embark on an energetic program of political advocacy at the national level until the 1980s. During the first half of the 1990s, two important developments accelerated the ANA's involvement in national politics. One was its 1991 move from Kansas City, Missouri, to Washington, D.C. Lucille Joel, the ANA's president at the time, told Mohammed Hanif of the *Washington Post* that the decision to relocate was made to "give us the visibility and clout we need to increase our effectiveness with the lawmakers, funding agencies and other health-related associations." It was also intended to strengthen the ANA's working relationship with its Washington-based affiliates and with women's organizations, labor unions, and similar groups.

The second development was the ANA's participation in national health care reform efforts from 1991 to 1994. The genesis of this activity was the ANA's 1989 creation of a task force to propose changes to the American health care system. After extensive consultations with the SNAs and other nursing organizations, the ANA produced a document entitled *Nursing's Agenda for Health Care Reform* in 1991, which endorsed universal health care and a revamping of the manner in which medical services were delivered. In time it received the support of 76 nursing and health care organizations in the United States.

From 1992 to 1994 the ANA produced several position papers elaborating on the proposals in *Nursing's Agenda for Health Care Reform*. In conjunction with its political action committee, ANA-PAC, the ANA worked strenuously to promote its ideas on health care reform in Congress and to offer financial and other support to sympathetic legislators. The November 1992 presidential and congressional elections marked a turning point in this process. Presidential candidate Bill Clinton's pledge of sweeping health care reform won over the ANA, which in August became the first group of health professionals to endorse his campaign (he received the ANA's endorsement again in 1996). Eventually the ANA lent its public support to 260 congressional candidates, 76 percent of whom were elected.

Shortly after his inauguration, Clinton put together a health care transition team in Washington, whose work eventually led to the creation of the Health Security Act (HSA). During the months leading up to the introduction of the HSA in September 1993, ANA representatives met with Clinton officials to discuss health care reform on more than 50 occasions. When the HSA finally appeared, it incorporated the fundamental principles that had been proposed in *Nursing's Agenda for Health Care Reform* and further developed at an August 1993 summit of 63 American nursing organizations: "universal benefits; removal of barriers to nursing care; a nursing work force transition plan (monies and opportunities) to the restructured delivery system; a dedicated graduate nursing education (GNE) fund; and nursing inclusion on federal, state, and local health policy boards."

The HSA was one of the most controversial initiatives of the first Clinton administration, and after heated public and legislative debate was rejected by Congress in September 1994. Although this was a great disappointment for the ANA, Virgina Trotter Betts, president of ANA from 1992 to 1996, believes that the ANA's health care reform activities brought the organization to "a new position of strength," including a greatly enhanced public and media presence, vastly improved access to public policymakers, and stronger links with other nursing organizations. Nor has the ANA abandoned the health care reforms that it endorsed in the early 1990s. In 1998 the ANA continues to promote specific changes in nursing and health care policy originally set forth in *Nursing's Agenda for Health Care Reform* in 1991 and refined in 1992-94.

CURRENT POLITICAL ISSUES

Throughout its history the ANA has spearheaded or actively participated in issues involving all aspects of U.S. healthcare. To ensure "patient safety" and "nursing quality" it has advocated for state and federal regulations that affect both patients and caregivers. A specific example is the Health Worker Protection Act of 1997, which the ANA sponsored along with Congressman Pete Stark (D-Calif.). This legislation required health care facilities to use FDA-approved needle devices to prevent workers from being stuck by needles. The ANA became particularly vocal when education for nurses was threatened.

Case Study: The Nurse Education Act

The ANA's cordial relationship with the Democratic Party goes back at least to 1984, when the organization lent its support to the presidential campaign of Walter Mondale. In 1992 and 1996, Bill and Hillary Clinton's backing of health care reform and other ANA-approved causes cemented the relationship. Bill Clinton addressed the ANA's June 1996 annual convention, and in June 1997 Hillary Clinton was the keynote speaker at a luncheon honoring ANA-PAC donors.

As the ANA learned during the health care reform fight of 1993-94, however, the Clintons' good intentions were not always a sufficient guarantee that the RN agenda would easily prevail in Washington. This point was brought home with even greater force in early 1997, when the president slashed funding for the Nurse Education Act (NEA), which provides the bulk of federal monies for nurse education. The NEA is primarily used to support specialized training for nurses beyond the two to four years required before taking the RN examination.

In 1996, Clinton had been applauded by the ANA for adding $7 million to NEA funding, bringing the total to over $63 million for the fiscal year 1997. But in February 1997, as part of his attempt to balance the national budget, Clinton announced that NEA funding would be reduced to a mere $7.7 million for the fiscal year 1998. The ANA pronounced itself "stunned" and "appalled." ANA president Beverly L. Malone, quoted in a press release, repeated the familiar ANA refrain that what is good for RNs is also good for the public: "Without stable funding to support graduate-level education for nurses, we'll enter the 21st century ill-prepared to provide adequate health care to aging baby boomers and their grandchildren."

The ANA responded to Clinton's move with an intense White House and congressional lobbying campaign by its Washington staff and N-STAT. After several months of N-STAT activity, meetings with White House and congressional politicians and staff members, and congressional testimony on the need for graduate-level education for nurses, the president received from Congress and signed into law in November an appropriations bill that, among other things, restored NEA funding to its previous level. In a press release, an ecstatic ANA proclaimed the bill "a huge victory for nursing and a testament to grassroots lobbying efforts."

FUTURE DIRECTIONS

A 1997 ANA publication, *Legislative and Regulatory Initiatives for the 105th Congress,* identifies three major goals for the organization: nurse advocacy, ensuring that the RN "is an essential provider in all practice settings through education, research, collective bargaining, work-place advocacy, legislation and regulation"; access to quality health care for everyone living in the United States, "with particular attention given to proposals that will move towards the goal of 100 percent universal health care coverage for all U.S. citizens and residents"; and ANA/SNA viability, ensuring that the "ANA and the SNAs as multipurpose organizations will continue to be strong and effective at the national and state levels."

GROUP RESOURCES

The ANA's Web site (http://www.nursingworld.org) includes press releases, position statements, and fact sheets on various issues and activities. Information on the ANA can also be obtained by contacting the organization's communications department at 1-800-274-4262. A good way to learn about current ANA political and professional concerns is to consult issues of the monthly *American Journal of Nursing.* Federal government financial data on ANA-PAC and other PACs is provided by the Web site of the Center for Responsive Politics (http://www.crp.org).

GROUP PUBLICATIONS

The ANA's flagship periodical, the *American Journal of Nursing,* is sent monthly to every ANA member and can be found in public as well as medical libraries. It covers clinical, professional, and political topics. *The American Nurse,* also distributed to the entire ANA membership, is a bimonthly newspaper that focuses on political and organizational matters. *Capitol Update* and *Nursing Trends & Issues* are specialized newsletters available by subscription. There is also an *Online Journal of Issues in Nursing.* American Nurses Publishing, the publications arm of the American Nurses Foundation (an ANA affiliate), sells brochures, fact sheets, and books on many aspects of nursing. A catalog is available by telephoning 1-800-637-0323.

BIBLIOGRAPHY

Bullough, Bonnie, and Vern L. Bullough, eds. *Nursing Issues for the Nineties and Beyond.* New York: Springer Publishing, 1994.

Canavan, Kathleen. "Proving Nursing's Value." *American Journal of Nursing,* July 1997.

Hanif, Mohammed. "Nursing Association to Move to D.C." *Washington Post,* 16 September 1997.

Kelly, Lucie Young, and Lucille A. Joel. *Dimensions of Professional Nursing.* New York: McGraw-Hill, 1995.

Lumsdon, Kevin. "Faded Glory: Will Nursing Ever Be the Same?" *Hospitals & Health Networks,* 5 December 1995.

McCloskey, Joanne Comi, and Helen Kennedy Grace, eds. *Current Issues in Nursing,* St. Louis: Mosby, 1994.

Raffel, Marshall W., and Norma K. Raffel. *The U.S. Health System: Origins and Functions.* Albany: Delmar Publishers, 1994.

Ramsay, Craig, ed. *U.S. Health Policy Groups: Institutional Profiles.* Westport, Conn.: Greenwood Press, 1995.

Trotter Betts, Virginia. "Nursing's Agenda for Health Care Reform: Policy, Politics, and Power through Professional Leadership." *Nursing Administration Quarterly,* Spring 1996.

Zerwekh, JoAnn, and Jo Carol Claborn, eds. *Nursing Today: Transition and Trends.* Philadelphia: W.B. Saunders, 1997.

American Society for the Prevention of Cruelty to Animals (ASPCA)

WHAT IS ITS MISSION?

As its name clearly states, the mission of the American Society for the Prevention of Cruelty to Animals (ASPCA) is "to provide effective means for the prevention of cruelty to animals throughout the United States." The ASPCA, in carrying out its mission, deals with numerous animal-related issues, including pet overpopulation and locating homes for abandoned animals; law enforcement; animal experimentation; animal abuse; and standards of animal care. To combat cruelty toward animals, the ASPCA employs such methods as education, advocacy, legal counsel, and outreach.

ESTABLISHED: April 10, 1866
EMPLOYEES: 200
MEMBERS: 425,000
PAC: None

Contact Information:

ADDRESS: 424 East 92nd St.
New York, NY 10128-6804
PHONE: (212) 876-7700
FAX: (212) 860-3435
E-MAIL: press@aspca.org
URL: http://www.aspca.org
PRESIDENT: Dr. Larry Hawk

HOW IS IT STRUCTURED?

The ASPCA's headquarters are located in New York City. An additional office in Washington, D.C., houses the organization's Legislative Affairs Department, which is staffed by three people and works with the federal legislature and administrative agencies having regulatory power over animal-related issues. An additional Legislative Affairs office based in Albany, New York, deals with animal-related issues at the state level. The ASPCA has a regional office in Los Angeles that houses the organization's programming and fundraising departments, and one in Urbana, Illinois, that houses the ASPCA National Animal Poison Control Center. The organization also maintains a Humane Law Enforcement office in Long Island, New York, that administers law enforcement activities within that state as they pertain to animal cruelty.

FAST FACTS

One unaltered cat and her offspring can produce 420,000 cats in seven years, and one unaltered dog and her offspring can produce 67,000 dogs in six years.

(Source: "Thousands of Organizations, Volunteers to Participate in 'Spay Day USA.'" *Business Wire,* February 23, 1998.)

The ASPCA is governed by a 21-member board that sets the broad organizational direction. The ASPCA has no other regional offices—other state and local SPCAs are independent organizations. ASPCA members who have decided to contribute efforts to advocacy are known as the ASPCA Legislative Action Team. Members join the ASPCA at annual rates from $20 to $500 and above, and receive publications, voting privileges at annual meetings (if over age 18), and discounts on veterinary services or training.

PRIMARY FUNCTIONS

The ASPCA advocates for the safety of animals. It has a direct impact on animals by providing homes, improving animal health, and protecting animals from mistreatment. The organization also educates people and offers resources that will make pet-owners better providers for their pets. Finally, the ASPCA works to influence legislation relating to animal welfare and monitors its enforcement.

The ASCPA offers a placement service for animals that need homes. Animals are received from other humane organizations or from owners who can no longer care for them. The ASPCA gives these animal any needed vaccinations and spays or neuters them prior to adoption. When an animal is offered for adoption the ASCPA takes potential owners through a screening process to make sure the adoption will be a good match. It also provides a free medical exam for the animal once it has been adopted. In 1997 alone the ASCPA provided homes for over 1,300 animals through its placement program, charging a $50.00 fee for each animal adoption. The organization's Web site displays a daily roster (with pictures) of cats and dogs available for adoption.

The ASPCA provides community outreach so that the public understands the mission of the organization.

It holds public events like street fairs and bazaars in order to place animals under its temporary care and educate people about the humane treatment of animals. The ASPCA also carries out Humane Education programs in schools and to other targeted audiences.

Adoption and education efforts rely greatly on the support of volunteers who go through a screening and training process. ASPCA volunteers serve in a number of capacities, including: assisting with adoption placement, walking and socializing animals, providing foster care, assisting with legislative initiatives, preparing publications, assisting with community outreach efforts, and providing education programs that teach people how to treat animals humanely. Volunteers receive an ASPCA *Volunteer Newsletter* that addresses upcoming volunteer needs and events.

The ASPCA's Bergh Memorial Animal Hospital in New York City provides services for animals, including spaying and neutering, dental care, biopsies, surgery, and vaccinations. Members get a 10-percent discount on hospital services. A help line is available for medical-related questions.

In addition to its other missions, the ASPCA also functions as a law enforcement body employing licensed peace officers to enforce animal welfare laws. Officers investigate cruelty to animals (such as animal abuse or cockfighting); inspect pet shops, circuses, and movie sets for animal welfare violations; and issue arrests and court summonses when necessary. More than 5,000 animal welfare-related cases are investigated each year and over 300 people are arrested annually for violations. The ASPCA's legal department provides counsel to the organization regarding enforcement of animal welfare laws.

Crucial to carrying out its mission are ASPCA lobbying efforts. The organization lobbies for and tracks legislation at the federal and state level, produces position papers, solicits letters of support, runs political advocacy ads and campaigns, and works with related federal agencies that have regulatory power in animal cruelty issues. Members who join the ASPCA Legislative Action Team are called upon (via action alerts) to contact congressmen on the phone or through letters regarding pending legislation.

PROGRAMS

Many of the ASPCA's programs benefit pets, animals in foster care, and animals chosen for adoption. Other programs are designed to teach individuals of all ages to respect animals and treat them well.

The ASCPA Foster Care Program provides a temporary home for animals that are too sick or aggressive to be offered for adoption. Volunteers give the animals a place to live; the ASCPA provides pet food and other supplies. The ASPCA National Animal Poison Control Center (ASPCA/NAPCC) is a fee-based phone-in resource for animal poison incidents. The center, established in 1978 as the first and only national poison control center for animals in the United States, became part of the ASCPA in 1996. The ASCPA's Animal Population Control Program (APCP) provides low-cost spay/neutering and inoculations for animals adopted in New York State. New York residents have the option of supporting the program by purchasing special license plates.

ASPCA Humane Education programs are extensive and aimed at a variety of issues and audiences. For example, the organization's "Web of Life" and "Extend the Web" materials are kits for use in schools that help provide insight into human and animal interrelationships. The "Adopt a School" program allows individuals to sponsor the introduction of humane education materials into a particular school. Publications are available for teachers that are informational and useful as teaching aids. Humane education programs also include videos, seminars, class pet programs—which place a pet in a classroom and teach children proper behavior and care—and a number of books.

BUDGET INFORMATION

The ASPCA is a nonprofit organization. By the end of 1996 the ASPCA's animal protection budget had increased 67 percent over previous levels. Fortunately, 1996 also saw a huge increase in donors and membership: membership climbed 30 percent that year and donors—those who contribute more than $500—climbed from 220 in 1995 to 750 in 1996.

In 1997 the organization posted total revenues of $24,299,90–$18,209,855 in contributions, $3,609,488 in program service revenue, $721,507 in interest on investments, $43,720 in rental income, $752,459 on sale of assets, $16,389 in special event income, and $946,483 in other revenue—against expenses totaling $21,385,845. The greatest expenses came in the areas of salaries and wages and direct mail costs; in addition the organization donated $34,000 worth of humane education materials to schools and made cash grants to organizations like the Greyhound Project, the Jane Goodall Institute, and local SPCAs.

HISTORY

The ASPCA was founded in 1866 by Henry Bergh who, three years prior, had witnessed a man beating a horse and felt moved to stop the beating. Concerned with the humane treatment of animals, he visited the London Royal Society for the Prevention of Cruelty to Animals, which served as the model when he founded the ASPCA. Bergh's organization was the first humane organization of its sort in North America.

BUDGET:
1997 ASPCA Revenue

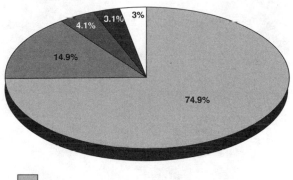

- 74.9%: Contributions
- 14.9%: Program service revenue
- 4.1%: Other including rental income and special event income
- 3.1%: Sale of assets
- 3%: Interest on investments

1997 ASPCA Expenses

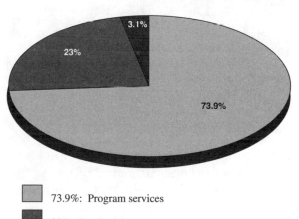

- 73.9%: Program services
- 23%: Fund raising
- 3.1%: Management and general services

Shortly after Bergh founded the ASPCA, he was able to persuade the New York State legislature to pass the nation's first anti-cruelty law and authorize his society to enforce it. By 1867 the society had provided an ambulance—the first of its kind—for injured horses. By 1873, 25 other states and territories had established independent SPCAs modeled after the ASPCA. By the late

The Society for the Prevention of Cruelty to Animals works on behalf of animals like these three beagles, among 40, which the ASPCA saved from animal experimentation in 1997. (Photograph by Daniel Hulshizer)

1990s, 8,000 local and independent SPCAs operated around the United States working to decrease animal cruelty. While not affiliated with these groups, the ASCPA provides outreach services and coordinates information among shelters.

One of the prevailing attitudes the ASCPA had to contend with as early as 1916 was the public's view of animals as property rather than companions. The ASPCA

began Humane Education programs in 1916 and geared these programs toward children in the hope that early learning would help children develop, and keep, an empathetic attitude toward animals. Humane Education has remained a large part of the organization's mission into the 1990s, and includes teachers, parents, and people of all ages.

World Wars I (1914–18) and II (1939–45) drew on the use of animals, and the ASPCA stepped forward to offer expertise. In 1916 the organization raised money to provide care for 934,000 horses serving U.S. forces during World War I. During World War II the organization provided education programs on the care of animals during air raids. In 1944 the ASCPA held its first dog and owner obedience classes.

The society also took an increasing role in inspecting situations for the safe, ethical, and humane treatment of animals. In 1939 the organization inspected all 2,000 animals at the New York World Fair. In 1952 the ASPCA began the first program to conduct voluntary inspections of animal research laboratories. The organization opened the Animalport at Kennedy International Airport to inspect animals entering or leaving the United States. That function was later taken over by the U.S. Department of Agriculture (USDA).

The ASPCA made important inroads into improved veterinary care. The organization performed its first canine open heart surgery in 1961. In 1973 the ASPCA began requiring spay and neutering procedures for all animals adopted out. The organization made its presence more politically visible by opening its Washington, D.C. office in 1985. In 1990 the ASPCA opened an office in Los Angeles to monitor humane issues in western U.S. states. Strategically, the ASPCA increased its focus on education and advocacy in 1995 by declining to renew its 100-year-old animal control contract with the city of New York. A year later the organization acquired the National Animal Poison Control Center, a 24-hour resource for poison information and emergencies.

CURRENT POLITICAL ISSUES

The ASPCA is involved with a variety of political issues at the federal and state level that relate to animal cruelty. According to the organization, cruelty to animals exists in many forms: cockfighting, the sale of animals that can no longer walk, the sale of animals to research labs, trapping, starvation, homelessness, and certain types of hunting are only a few. The organization lobbies for the protection of particular species that may be subject to acts of cruelty. Endangered species such as the rhino or tiger are killed to make products for humans. Bear gallbladders are extremely valuable and used for Asian medicinal purposes, resulting in the killing of bears specifically for that purpose. Reacting to the absence of any consistent federal law protecting bears, the ASPCA lobbied for the passage of 1998's Bear Protection Act (H.R. 619) and sent action alerts to members, requesting them to contact their congressman to urge them to support the bill.

According to the ASPCA, domestic pet population control is a serious issue in the United States, resulting in many homeless pets that die, live with disease, or must be either adopted out or euthanized by the ASPCA and other SPCAs around the country. The ASPCA endorses spay and neutering programs and educates the public about the serious implications of pet overpopulation. The organization in early 1998 opposed the USDA stance on puppy mills—operations that breed animals intensively for pet store sales. Conditions at puppy mills are often substandard, with emphasis on producing quantities of animals rather than professional breeding procedures or sanitary conditions. The USDA's unwillingness to regulate conditions at puppy mills prompted an ASPCA pushed for regulation of these operations beginning in 1998.

Similarly, the ASPCA opposed a program instigated by the Bureau of Land Management (BLM) that allows people to adopt wild horses rounded up by that government agency. Many of these horses are slaughtered to provide meat for overseas markets. The ASPCA alerted members and asked them to contact their representatives and demand a hearing on the issue. The organization also requested members to contact the head of the USDA and urge an end to the killing of these horses.

Trapping methods also concern the ASPCA. Many animals are killed for their fur using a steel-jawed leg-hold trap. The ASPCA considers the trap unreasonably cruel and dangerous to others who may be hurt by it, such as children or other animals. As late as 1998 no consistent federal law existed to ban the trap. The ASPCA lobbied for passage of the Steel Jaw Leg Hold Trap Ban (H.R. 1176), which would prohibit the buying or selling of animals for fur that had been killed using the trap. The organization monitored the legislation, produced position papers, and requested members to contact their congressman, providing a list of points members could include in letters to Congress.

ASPCA legislative initiatives are not limited to the federal level. By early 1998 only 21 states had laws that made animal cruelty a felony rather than a misdemeanor. During the 1998 New York state legislative session, the ASPCA pushed for legislation that would make animal cruelty a felony in New York state.

Case Study: Animal Cruelty Bill Stalled

In New York state, according to the ASPCA, all acts of animal cruelty are punished equally, regardless of the level or type of pain inflicted. All offenses are prosecuted as misdemeanors, or, as the ASPCA put it, by less than the penalty for stealing a car.

During the 1997–98 state legislative session, the ASPCA lobbied for the Felony Cruelty Act (A.2268-C), which if passed would make all acts of cruelty to ani-

mals a felony in New York state. The ASPCA monitored the legislation, ensured media coverage, produced position papers, ran advocacy ads, and urged New York resident members to contact their state representatives, while ASPCA staff traveled daily between Albany and New York City. The hunting, farm, and gun lobbies—normally on the opposite side of issues from the ASPCA—also supported the passage of the bill.

Although the Senate passed the bill and moved it to the general assembly, the bill was stalled when the Speaker attached his own bill to the Felony Cruelty Act. With three days to go in the session, the new bill was required to age three days before it could be acted upon. The stalling tactic caused time to run out during the legislative session and the Felony Cruelty Act did not pass during the 1997–98 New York legislative session.

Had the Felony Cruelty Act passed, offenders would have faced greatly increased punishment for acts of cruelty to animals, including fines up to $2,500 and prison terms up to two years. The act would also have given a court the power to require psychiatric evaluation of offenders and recommend treatment. A felony punishment for animal cruelty, an issue central to the ASPCA, is expected to be advocated for in future state and federal legislative sessions.

FUTURE DIRECTIONS

Due to the large growth in support that ASPCA experienced in 1996, the organization planned to install an ASPCA fellowship at John Hopkins University for the purpose of studying alternatives to animal testing. The society also made plans to improve facilities at the Duke University Primate Center. While the ASPCA continues to try to capitalize on its growth in membership experienced during the late 1990s, it also remains focused on advocacy and education about preventing cruelty to animals.

GROUP RESOURCES

The ASCPA's behavior help line provides answers to callers about animal problems, such as biting, training, spraying, or animal care tips. Calls are taken at (212) 876-7700, ext. 4357, weekday afternoons. Through its Bergh Memorial Animal Hospital, the ASPCA offers a medical help line at (212) 876-7700, extension 4203. The organization's National Animal Poison Control Center, a hot line for poison issues and emergencies, can be reached at 1-800-548-2423, 1-888-426-4435, or 1-900-680-0000. The fee is $30 per call.

GROUP PUBLICATIONS

"Extend the Web" Humane Education resources can be ordered directly from the ASPCA Web site at http://www.ascpa.org.educate/eduform2.htm or by calling the organization directly. Some of the books available include: *I Can Save the Earth* by Anita Holmes and Julian Messner (1993) and the Newbery Award-winning *Shiloh* by Phyllis Reynolds Naylor (1991). The ASPCA also publishes the *Volunteer Newsletter* for its volunteers and the *ASPCA Animal Watch* for members, both which include updates on animal-related news and issues.

BIBLIOGRAPHY

Brand, Rich. "Board Bites Man in SPCA Lawsuit." *Newsday,* 27 December 1995.

Cheng, Mae M. "A Home of Their Own/Animal Haven in Flushing May Be the Last Hope for 170 Dogs and Cats (and One Rabbit)." *Newsday,* 9 June 1996.

Hancock, Shawn Hartley. "A Member of the Family: While We Teach Fido to Fetch, He Teaches Our Kids Lasting Values." *Dallas Morning News,* 3 December 1996.

Moon, Duncan R. "Harlem's Patron Saint of Animals." *Christian Science Monitor,* 13 January 1998.

Newman, Sarah Casey. "Loving, Adaptable Greyhounds Make Good Pets and Companions." *St. Louis Post-Dispatch,* 13 June 1998.

Watson, Catherine. "Traveling and Pets Don't Always Mix." *Star Tribune,* 26 February 1995.

Wells, Jeffrey. "Bug Actors Get Special Treatment on the Set." *Dallas Morning News,* 20 June 1997.

American Veterans of World War II, Korea and Vietnam (AMVETS)

WHAT IS ITS MISSION?

Soliders returning home from World War II (1939—45) created AMVETS in 1944. Initially established to give veterans representation and a collective voice in Washington, D.C., as well as to give aid to impoverished veterans, AMVETS sees itself as "veterans helping veterans." As a community of veterans, the organization allows current and former soldiers to maintain ties with each other, learn about issues of concern to veterans, and effectively represent their views to government.

HOW IS IT STRUCTURED?

AMVETS is a nonprofit organization based in Lanham, Maryland. It is led by a national commander who is assisted by a board of directors. These representatives of the organization are elected at the annual AMVETS national convention. The more than 1,300 posts nationwide elect delegates to attend the convention, which serves to decide the direction and policy of AMVETS. Each post sends a minimum of two delegates (total number of delegates depending on the population of the post) to the convention.

The 250,000 members of AMVETS are organized through the local posts. Anyone who has served in the United States Armed Forces after September 15, 1940, is eligible for membership. While not required to have taken part in combat, members must have received an honorable discharge or still be presently serving in the armed forces.

ESTABLISHED: December 9, 1944
EMPLOYEES: Not made available
MEMBERS: 250,000
PAC: None

Contact Information:

ADDRESS: 4647 Forbes Blvd.
Lanham, MD 20706
PHONE: (301) 459-9600
URL: http://www.amvets.org
NATIONAL COMMANDER: Josephus Vandengoorbergh

The National Service Foundation (NSF) is the development wing of AMVETS, raising money for AMVETS programs. The NSF runs AMVETS thrift stores and sponsors AMVETS clothes drives. It also administers the White Clover Program, a regular fund-raiser meant to raise money for needy veterans.

PRIMARY FUNCTIONS

Nationally, AMVETS attempts to represent the concerns and interests of its members to the federal government. AMVETS advocates for favorable government action on issues of special concern to veterans, such as flag desecration, funding for the Department of Veterans Affairs (VA), health care reform, and expansion of the North Atlantic Treaty Organization (NATO). However AMVETS does not lobby Congress aggressively with contributions; instead, AMVETS relies on active participation by its members. For example, in 1997 Representative and Chairman of the House Transportation and Infrastructure Committee Bud Shuster (R-Pa.) introduced a mass transit funding bill that would have borrowed from other discretionary spending authorizations, including VA health care. Pennsylvania AMVETS members called and wrote members of Congress protesting the action and shortly thereafter, Shuster removed the bill from consideration.

AMVETS works closely with the VA, the branch of the federal government created to provide benefits, medical assistance, and other forms of aid to U.S. service personnel. It keeps members informed on changes in VA policy, acting as a liaison between the VA and veterans. For example the Department of Defense (DoD) and the VA have used AMVETS to contact veterans who might be suffering from Gulf War Syndrome, a mysterious illness affecting some soldiers who served in the Persian Gulf War.

AMVETS also operates on a more personal level for its members. AMVETS local chapters offer camaraderie, a spirit of inclusion to those who share the common bond of service in the armed forces. AMVETS also offers more tangible services to individual members in the form of veterans benefit information and assistance with VA health care claims. The organization also offers member discounts on a variety of services including hotels, rental cars, and eye care. On a broader level, local AMVETS branches maintain a visible presence within their communities, sponsoring activities and acting as a gathering place, wedding hall, or bingo parlor.

Finally AMVETS engages in community activism. AMVETS collects second-hand clothes for the needy, provides student scholarships for children of veterans, gives out AMVETS medals to students excelling in Reserve Officers Training Corps (ROTC) programs, and sponsors patriotic activities such as parades, essays, and poster contests.

PROGRAMS

AMVETS has created and supported many diverse initiatives. There are several themes to the organizations' activities, but youth and community are the dominant ones. AMVETS college scholarship programs provide financial assistance to the children or grandchildren of AMVETS members, or deceased veterans who were eligible to become a member. AMVETS also sponsors poster and essay contests for younger children, who receive prizes for writing on themes such as patriotism or the perils of drug and alcohol abuse.

White Clover

The NSF raises funds for needy veterans through its White Clover program. The white clover, a small plant with white flowers and three-lobed leaves, is a pasture plant and can be found on battlefields worldwide. It is because of this that the organization used the white clover as its symbol. White Clover volunteers go out on the streets on Independence Day, Memorial Day, and Veterans Days each year to sell small fabricated white clovers. Initiated in 1946, the program has been a reliable and consistent source of support for the organization's efforts to help fund its veterans services, such as programs to solve the problems of homeless veterans.

BUDGET INFORMATION

Not made available.

HISTORY

As wounded and discharged U.S. soldiers returned home from World War II, they formed clubs with their fellow veterans. These clubs provided members with a friendship and camaraderie forged by the common experience of war. Beside emotional benefits, the clubs were practical. Veterans confused over benefits could discuss their problems with other veterans. The clubs provided the power and security of collective political action; as more veterans joined, the organization could use its strength to make politicans aware of veteran issues.

By late 1944, nine states had highly organized World War II veterans clubs. In December of that year, those nine groups met in Kansas City, Missouri, and formed the American Veterans of World War II, or AMVETS. The newly formed organization held its first convention in Chicago in October, 1945. In 1946 the organization applied for a national charter with the federal government. The charter, offering official recognition from Congress, was signed by President Harry S Truman in 1947.

The voting power of AMVETS and other veterans service organizations (VSOs) was soon apparent. There were 500 federal laws concerning veterans enacted after World War II, providing them with a wide variety of benefits and protections. One of the earliest and most famous of these new laws was the GI Bill of 1945. The GI Bill made it easy for veterans to get money for education, to buy homes, and gain access to health care. Another significant legislative occurrence for veterans was the 1948 repeal of the so-called Economy Bill. The Economy Bill was a law passed in 1933 that limited financial benefits veterans were eligible to receive.

AMVETS has amended its membership criteria on several occasions, to keep itself a vital and relevant organization. In 1950 U.S. troops participated in the Korean War (1950–53) under the auspices of the United Nations. AMVETS amended its charter to include Korean War veterans. In 1966 while the United States was engaged in the Vietnam War (1959–75), the AMVETS charter was changed again, and qualifications for membership were altered significantly. AMVETS membership was open to "...any person who served in the Armed Forces of The United States of America or any American Citizen who served in the armed forces of an allied nation of the United States is eligible for regular membership in AMVETS, provided such service when terminated by discharge or release from active duty be by honorable discharge or separation."

Until 1984 AMVETS did not accept membership of those who served in the armed forces after the Vietnam War. President Ronald Reagan signed a bill opening up AMVETS membership to service people who had served honorably after the Vietnam War. AMVETS is now open to anyone serving or who has served honorably in the Armed Forces of the United States—including the National Guard and Reserve—anytime after September 15, 1940.

For many years, there was no appeals process for veterans denied benefits by the VA. Often the VA would refuse to even explain why it had denied benefits to a veteran. The only recourse was for the veteran to sue the government and the VA. This was an expensive and untimely way of getting information or securing benefits. AMVETS and other VSOs sought an appeals system that would evaluate the VA's action and force it to explain why a claim may be denied. In 1988 the Court of Veterans Appeals was created to handle these cases. The Court of Veterans Appeals also handles cases of veterans who were also dissatisfied with their treatment by the VA.

In the 1990s the Persian Gulf War (1991) presented a new set of challenges to AMVETS. Some of the veterans returning from this conflict suffered from a mysterious illness known as Gulf War Syndrome. AMVETS encouraged the VA and other federal agencies devoted to health care to examine this issue and suggest methods of treatment. As the 1990s drew to a close, AMVETS worked to get additional federal budget support for the VA as budget surpluses were posted.

CURRENT POLITICAL ISSUES

AMVETS dedicates its political activity to the issues that the organization finds crucial. For instance AMVETS and other VSOs, such as the Veterans of Foreign Wars (VFW), lobby Congress for increased funding for the VA. Not only do the VSOs pursue additional appropriations for the VA, they attempt to change the nature of VA allocations. The VSOs want Congress to remove VA supervision from Veterans Affairs Committees and create a new appropriations committee dedicated solely to the VA.

Another long-standing issue of concern for AMVETS is the fate of U.S. prisoners of war (POWs) and soldiers missing in action (MIAs). AMVETS has put political pressure on the VA, congressional veterans affairs committees, and the presidential administration to continue investigations of the fate of soliders who were captured or reported missing during combat in Korea and Vietnam, with the hope of eventually finding and bringing home all U.S. service personnel.

Case Study: Veterans Employment Opportunities Act

In the late 1990s AMVETS made it a priority to convince Congress to strengthen the Veterans Preference program. During World War II, laws were enacted that gave combat veterans a preference when it came to federal government hiring. While not designed in such a way as to allow unqualified veterans to gain positions in the government, it was intended to give them an advantage over other qualified job applicants. In theory, this preference would prevent veterans, who may not have as much work experience as other job applicants because of the time they spent in the military, from being passed over in federal hiring and promotions.

According to AMVETS, the program has not been applied properly in the years since World War II. Because there was no official enforcement mechanism for it however, it was possible for those doing the hiring to ignore it without suffering any penalty. AMVETS held that because of this, veterans were often passed over for positions that, according to the bill, they should have been hired for.

The Veterans Employment Opportunities Act of 1997 was designed to correct this problem through the establishment of an official system for grievances. The act also proposed a number of other changes that AMVETS supported. It proposed an expansion of veterans preference to include veterans who had served various types of hazardous duty, even if they had not been in an official war. It also created of a new kind of preference; while not extending the advantages of veterans preference to veterans who had not seen combat or other hazardous duty, the act proposed allowing any veterans to apply for any federal job, even jobs that would otherwise only be offered to people who already worked for the agency where the opening existed.

AMVETS, as well as the other major VSOs, were all in favor of the Veterans Employment Opportunities Act of 1997. The organization was particularly excited by the proposed greivance system. As AMVETS saw it, this would finally allow veterans to take advantage of the benefits promised them by Veterans Preference, and end what they considered to be hiring discrimination against veterans.

The Veterans Employment Opportunities Act was signed into law in 1998. While AMVETS saw this victory as an end to discrimination against veterans, others saw it as a victory for discrimination in favor of veterans, and against other qualified applicants. That such a proposal would be enacted in 1998, at the same time that debate raged over affirmative action programs that many claimed were unfairly favoring minority groups, demonstrated the strength of AMVETS and veterans organizations in politics.

FUTURE DIRECTIONS

AMVETS considers the U.S. flag one of the main symbols of the nation and ideals for which its members fought. The organization feels that the flag should be treated with respect, and be legally protected from disfigurement and desecration. Ever since the Supreme Court ruled in 1989 that desecration of the flag, such as burning it, is a form of free speech and is protected by the First Amendment of the Constitution, AMVETS has been working toward the passage of a flag-protection amendment. Its efforts have not been successful; in 1998 proposed flag-protection legislation expired when the 105th session of Congress adjourned. However, working with the Citizens Flag Alliance, of which it is a member, AMVETS plans to continue introducing such legislation until it passes.

GROUP RESOURCES

Those interested in more information on AMVETS may call the organization at (301) 459-9600. Inquiries may be sent to AMVETS National Headquarters, 4647 Forbes Blvd., Lanham, MD 20706. The AMVETS Web site, containing some information about the group and its activities, can be accessed at http://www.amvets.org.

AMVETS sends its scholarship information to nearly all U.S. high schools. Individuals interested in contacting AMVETS about their poster and essay contests or seeking information about AMVETS scholarships may call (301) 459-9600 or write AMVETS National Headquarters, 4647 Forbes Blvd., Lanham, MD 20706.

GROUP PUBLICATIONS

AMVETS publishes many pamphlets available at individual posts designed to help veterans who are seeking benefits from the federal government. The *National AMVET Magazine* is a publication available to AMVETS members. It keeps members apprised of events, updated legislation, and service changes. Nonmembers may obtain information about AMVETS publications by calling (301) 459-9600 or by writing AMVETS National Headquarters, 4647 Forbes Blvd., Lanham, MD 20706.

BIBLIOGRAPHY

Amador, Ronald. "Disabled Vets." *Los Angeles Times*, 26 May 1997.

Crispell, Diane. "Mustering Out." *American Demographics*, November 1993.

Cuhane, Charles. "Veterans Groups Urge Expanded Eligibility for VA Care." *American Medical News*, 10 August 1992.

Dethlefsen, Merle, and James Canfield. *Transition from Military to Civilian Life.* Harrisburg, Pa.: Stackpole, 1984.

Fisher, Ernest. *Guardians of the Republic: A History of Noncommissioned Corps of the United States Army.* New York: Ballantine, 1994.

Gardner, Jonathan. "VA on the Spot: Care Quality, Oversight to be Probed by Congress." *Modern Healthcare.* 2 February 1998.

Gold, Philip. *Evasions: The American Way of Military Service.* New York: Paragon, 1985.

Scharnberg, Ken. "VA and the Aging Veteran." *The American Legion.* March 1993.

Snyder, Keith and Richard O'Dell. *Veterans Benefits.* New York: Harper Collins, 1994.

Waldrop, Judith. "27 Million Heroes." *American Demographics*, November 1993.

Amnesty International USA (AIUSA)

WHAT IS ITS MISSION?

As the U.S. section of the worldwide Amnesty International organization, Amnesty International of the USA (Amnesty USA; AIUSA) works to uphold the organization's statutes. Thus, Amnesty USA opposes "grave violations of the rights of every person freely to hold and to express his or her convictions and to be free from discrimination and of the right of every person to physical and mental integrity."

An international organization, Amnesty International engages in the protection of human rights of people throughout the world. Their work and beliefs are based on the principles set forth in the United Nations Universal Declaration of Human Rights and on related human rights standards adopted by the United Nations (UN). Regardless of the philosophy of the government where perceived human rights violations occur, the organization opposes illegal detention, political imprisonment, torture, and the death penalty. The group works for the immediate and unconditional release of "prisoners of conscience," people detained for political beliefs, color, ethnic origin, language or religion, but who do not use or advocate violence. The organization also works for fair and speedy trials for political prisoners and supports prisoners who are detained without being tried.

AIUSA volunteers, however, would not be found advocating for prisoners in the United States. In order to maintain independence and impartiality, national sections of Amnesty International, such as AIUSA, work on behalf of prisoners of other countries. Thus human rights violations and conditions for prisoners in the United States would be addressed by one of the organization's other national sections.

ESTABLISHED: 1961
EMPLOYEES: 86 (1997)
MEMBERS: 300,000 (1997)

Contact Information:
ADDRESS: 322 Eighth Ave.
New York, NY 10001
PHONE: (212) 807-8400
FAX: (212) 627-1451
E-MAIL: aimember@aiusa.org
URL: http://www.amnesty-usa.org
CHAIRMAN: Morton E. Winston
EXECUTIVE DIRECTOR: William Schulz
SENIOR DEPUTY EXECUTIVE DIRECTOR: Curt Goering

HOW IS IT STRUCTURED?

Amnesty International is a worldwide group of volunteers with over a million members organized into national sections and affiliated groups. With 300,000 members, Amnesty USA is the largest of Amnesty's 54 national organizations. The parent organization's policies are determined by an International Council that meets at least once every two years. Between meetings of the International Council an International Executive Committee of nine members meets at least twice a year and sets direction for the organization. Eight of the Executive Committee members are elected to two-year terms by the International Council; the ninth is a member of the International Secretariat. No more than one person from any section or group of Amnesty can serve on the Executive Committee. The Executive Committee appoints a secretary general who is responsible for day-to-day operations, and that person appoints as many staff members as necessary to complete the work of the International Secretariat, located in London.

AIUSA is supervised by an 18-member board of directors. The board selects an executive director, who runs the organization's staff. Policy is determined at the international level, and interpreted and carried out by the national board and executive director. Headquarters are located in New York City, New York. Amnesty USA also maintains a Washington, D.C., office focused on governmental programs overseas; regional offices in San Francisco, California; Culver City, California; Atlanta, Georgia; Chicago, Illinois; Washington, D.C., and Somerville, Maryland; an Urgent Action office in Nederland, Colorado; a refugee office in San Francisco, and a UN office in New York, New York.

PRIMARY FUNCTIONS

Amnesty International and Amnesty USA use publicity and grassroots political pressure in their efforts to protect the human rights of all peoples. AIUSA mounts many advertising campaigns that bring attention to human rights abuses around the world. For example, in the 1990s AIUSA took part in the Campaign for Women. Based on evidence collected by Amnesty International, AIUSA ran advertisements in the press, issued reports, and gave interviews on the many human rights abuses women are subjected to, oftentime specifically because of their gender. By raising public consciousness of the plight of women, AIUSA hoped to pressure the United States and other governments to take action to protect women. AIUSA members were also encouraged to contact their congressmen and urge them to ratify the UN Convention on the Elimination of All Forms of Discrimination Against Women.

Amnesty International is particularly well known for its efforts on behalf of prisoners. It seeks the release of prisoners who are being held unjustly, such as "prisoners of conscience," or prisoners of any type who are being treated inhumanely. When Amnesty International researchers discover prisoners who need help, they are assigned to one or more local Amnesty groups. The groups "adopt" the prisoners assigned to them. Members of the local groups write appeals to the appropriate public officials including cabinet members and prison officials. They also solicit publicity for their cause and often seek out famous people to endorse these appeals. They correspond with the prisoners' families and send relief parcels. Amnesty staffers or volunteers often visit the offending nation's embassy or trade delegation in their own country.

Amnesty International and AIUSA also at times send observers to political trials to ensure they are conducted fairly. Its members may directly urge governments to give political prisoners a fair trial or may ask for an independent review of trial procedures. The group often calls for legislation to ensure impartial trials and pressures governments to comply with UN standards for humane treatment of prisoners, especially its ban on torture.

As with all Amnesty groups, AIUSA never claims credit for the release of specific prisoners. But AIUSA, with its large numbers and sophisticated Urgent Action Network, clearly has been one of the most effective international organizations. In 1996 it aided in gaining the release of 400 prisoners in Morocco, and was helpful in obtaining the release of Chinese dissidents Tong Yi and Liu Gang.

PROGRAMS

AIUSA has many programs that help it to carry out the overall mission of Amnesty International. Most programs are designed to generate publicity about ongoing human rights abuses, including torture and the use of the death penalty, or to directly aid those who are victims of such abuses. Some of AIUSA's many programs include the Urgent Action Network, the Program to Abolish the Death Penalty, and the Defending the Defenders Program.

The Urgent Action Network was established in 1972 as part of an Amnesty International effort to mobilize opposition to torture. Since then, it has grown into one of AIUSA's best means of generating direct support for prisoners among AIUSA members and the general public. Anyone can subscribe to the Network through mail and, in more recent years, the Internet. The Urgent Action Network publicizes cases of abuse and unjust imprisonment of a particularly urgent nature, directing members and the public as to how they can help—usually by writing letters.

The Program to Abolish the Death Penalty represents Amnesty USA's effort to fulfill one of the major goals of the Amnesty International organization. In the short-term, the program uses education and grassroots political activism to push for a reduction in the use of the death penalty but in the long-term advocates for the elimination of the death sentence from the world's legal systems. The program publishes the *Death Penalty Newsletter* six times annually. Available to both AIUSA members who are leading efforts against the death penalty and to other interested parties, the newsletter details major news events in the fight against the death penalty, focusing primarily on the United States. The newsletter also contains information on upcoming anti-death penalty events and helps to coordinate AIUSA action. The program also manages a Weekly Death Penalty Action, where it describes a case of concern to AIUSA and recommends specific action that AIUSA members and other interested parties can take to help.

Defending the Defenders is a program jointly initiated by AIUSA and the Sierra Club in 1999. Its purpose is to save defenders of the environment from persecution and human rights abuses. AIUSA is concerned by the increasing number of prisoners of conscience who are suffering because they have tried to protect the environment from unscrupulous governments and corporations. Through the Defending the Defenders Program's press releases and letter writing campaigns, AIUSA and the Sierra Club hope to draw attention to this growing problem and protect both the environment and human rights.

BUDGET INFORMATION

AIUSA is funded primarily by donations from members and supporters. It does not accept contributions from any governments or political parties. For the fiscal year ending September 30, 1996, AIUSA reported $19,154,956 in contributions from individuals. It also received $499,842 from foundations; $1,367,461 in bequests; $1,975,610 in donated services (primarily professional help in public service announcements); $287,843 in literature and merchandise sales; $99,870 in rentals of mailing list, and various other items for total revenues of $24,519,147.

AIUSA reported expenses of $23,961,948 for its fiscal year 1996. Of that amount, $7,258,955 was spent on communications and publications; $5,123,412 went to the International Secretariat; $3,772,540 funded campaigns and actions; $3,316,984 was expended on fundraising; $2,960,778 went to membership programs; and $1,529,279 was spent on management and general expenses. As of September 30, 1996, Amnesty USA reported total assets of $10,441,492.

HISTORY

The founder of Amnesty International, British lawyer Peter Benenson, first became active in human rights issues after learning of and joining an organization of lawyers called Justice in 1957. In May of 1961, after reading of the brutal repression of students in Portugal, Benenson decided to start a worldwide group. With other British lawyers and publishers he drafted the "Appeal for Amnesty, 1961," which called for the release of all "prisoners of conscience." The appeal brought more than one thousand offers of support for the idea of an international human rights organization.

The British organizers of Amnesty set up a system of local groups, including neighbors, co-workers, and church members who would "adopt" prisoners and publicize their plight through letter-writing campaigns. A friend of Benenson, Diana Redhouse, designed the organization's symbol—a candle burning in barbed wire.

In July 1961 an assembly of delegates from six nations met in Luxembourg and decided to broaden the appeal into a permanent international campaign. Within 12 months of its founding, Amnesty International had chapters and groups in 21 nations, had taken up 210 cases, and had sent delegations to four countries to lobby for better treatment of prisoners. The U.S. section of Amnesty International was one of the first national sections to be formed. Its cofounder, Ginetta Sagan, brought a few people together in her kitchen in the San Francisco Bay Area of California to launch the group.

Since inception, Amnesty International has encouraged its members to focus on cases outside their own countries, giving the organization a reputation for independence and impartiality.

Growth and Crisis in the 1960s

With the help of Major John McBride, an Irish resistance fighter, Benenson undertook Amnesty's first "missions" to help individual prisoners. One of the first cases the group took up was that of Archbishop Josef Beran of Prague; within a few years he was freed. Early on, the group also "adopted" Nelson Mandela of South Africa, although in later years Amnesty's support of Mandela diminished, because of his advocacy of violent resistance.

In 1964 Benenson traveled to Haiti, where infamous dictator Francois "Papa Doc" Duvalier was conducting a reign of terror. Amnesty issued a report on conditions in Haiti that received worldwide attention. Amnesty International membership grew from 70 groups in 1962 to 360 in 1964. In 1965, when thousands wanted to join who were not affiliated with local groups, Amnesty International began sending action kits to individual members. These kits contained Amnesty International greeting cards and monthly newsletters instructing members on where they should send cards in order to appeal to authorities about inhumane conditions. That same year Amnesty sponsored the UN resolution calling for an end to capital punishment, and issued reports on South Africa, Portugal, and Romania.

Amnesty went through a crisis between 1965 and 1967 when it exposed British atrocities in Aden (at the time a British protectorate between Yemen and Oman). The British government denied the reports. The organization became caught up in political infighting, and Benenson resigned his post. After this crisis, the rule that members would work only on cases outside their country became firmly established.

In 1968 Martin Ennals became Amnesty International's secretary general at a conference in Stockholm, Sweden. Also in 1968, an Amnesty International report embarrassed the new junta in Greece by exposing the military leaders' prison torture techniques and other human rights violations. During the late 1960s members formed local prisoner adoption groups to work on campaigns in specific countries and on grassroots fundraising drives in their own communities.

Gaining Credibility: the 1970s and 1980s

In 1973 Amnesty International issued its first comprehensive report on human rights abuses around the globe, covering the previous decade. Since 1975 when the report was updated, Amnesty International has issued annual reports, which become the most authoritative handbooks for assessing how well governments observe human rights. In 1977 Amnesty International won the Nobel Peace Prize for its work.

During the early 1980s the number of Amnesty USA groups on college campuses increased. Because most of their members were students and therefore transient, these campus-based groups did not adopt prisoners. Instead, they worked on campaigns, organized publicity, and wrote letters on behalf of other groups' adopted prisoners.

Amnesty International, while always strong in Europe and the United States, continued to grow as an international movement throughout the 1980s. Many new sections were added in Africa, the Middle East, Central America, South America, and Asia. Amnesty's "urgent action messages" often brought swift results. When a prominent physician was imprisoned by the Chilean government for accusing the Pinochet regime of torturing dissidents, Amnesty alerted activists in over 50 nations. Their ambassadors' protests pressured Chilean authorities into releasing the doctor within a few days.

During the tenure of Executive Director Jack Healey, from 1981 to 1992, AIUSA's membership grew from 40,000 to 400,000 and its budget grew from $2.5 million to $22 million. Healey also forged strong ties with the music industry. Starting in 1986, benefit concert tours were held regularly to raise money for Amnesty International. The initial 1986 Conspiracy of Hope tour featured U2, Peter Gabriel, the Police, Bryan Adams, Joan Baez, and Jackson Brown. The 1988 Human Rights Now! tour was headlined by Bruce Springsteen, Sting, and Tracy Chapman and played 20 locations on five conti-

nents. In 1991 *Billboard* magazine awarded Amnesty International the first Bill Graham Award for outstanding contributions to the music industry.

The 1990s

With the end of the Cold War, Amnesty International groups quickly sprouted in the former Soviet-occupied countries of eastern Europe and the new republics that emerged from the breakup of the Soviet Union. In 1993 Amnesty was the principal organizer of the UN World Conference on Human Rights in Vienna, Austria, that brought together delegates from 154 nations and two thousand non-governmental organizations. That same year it launched a new campaign against human rights violations in nominally democratic countries, focusing on the counter-insurgency tactics of the governments of Peru, Turkey, and Sri Lanka.

In the United States and abroad, Amnesty International employs public service announcements on television and over the Internet to promote its work, often using television and movie celebrities. Amnesty International became a leader in bringing its message to new audiences through sophisticated use of the media. It remains one of the most prominent human rights organization in the world, and journalists worldwide rely on Amnesty International for information on human rights abuses.

CURRENT POLITICAL ISSUES

The nature of Amnesty International and Amnesty USA's mission involves it in a great deal of controversy. The organization routinely finds itself in conflict with various governments over the use of torture, secret trials, unfair trials where prisoner's cannot choose their own lawyers or defend themselves, and the use of the death penalty. While Amnesty International is not a prison reform group, its mission includes efforts to ensure that prisoners are held in proper conditions, especially prisoners of conscience. It seeks to improve prison conditions when conditions are deemed inhumane.

Case Study: American Use and Export of Stun Guns

In 1997 and 1998, Amnesty International began, for the first time, to systematically study human rights abuses within the United States. The organization's concern arose out of growing sales of U.S.-made stun weapons to both domestic and international consumers. Electro-shock or stun weapons, devices designed to incapacitate a person with a powerful electric shock, are a major concern for Amnesty International. The organization claims that electro-shock devices such as tasers and stun belts are unsafe and often used for torture. The group claims that there has been little scientific study on the long-term effects of the stun weapons or the effects on people suffering from heart or breathing conditions. Because stun weapons are easy to use and leave little physical evidence, Amnesty International fears that they are ideal torture devices for use against prisoners.

In a March 1997 report, Amnesty International listed 100 manufacturers of stun devices. Forty-two of the companies on the list were U.S. companies and many of them enjoyed a healthy export business. Amnesty International reported that U.S. companies had sold stun weapons to repressive regimes in Panama, Yemen, Saudi Arabia, Mexico, Argentina, Ecuador, the Philippines, Thailand, and the United Arab Emirates—all nations where torture is known to have been used.

Although the United States is not generally considered to be a nation where prisoners are at risk of torture, the widespread use of stun weapons disturbed Amnesty International. For the first time, Amnesty International began an in-depth study of possible human rights abuses in the United States, and the organization discovered many instances when electro-shock devices were misused. For example, in 1986 the Los Angles police used a stun gun to force a confession from a 17-year-old boy accused of stealing. In this case the officers involved were prosecuted and a monetary settlement was made with the teenager.

It was learned that in the Phoenix, Arizona, jail system, all jail guards carried stun guns. A U.S. Department of Justice investigation found that the devices were sometimes used to torture the prisoners. Although the Maricopa County Jail disputed the allegations, in 1996 an inmate at the Maricopa jail died while fighting with officers. Examination of his body disclosed 21 electro-shock burns. In August 1997, Amnesty International released details of several more incidents of mistreatment involving stun guns in Phoenix area jails.

Amnesty International was very disturbed by the increasing use of electro-shock belts to maintain order within chain gangs in the state of Wisconsin. Amnesty International already considered chain gangs to be a violation of a prisoner's human rights, and using electro-shock devices only made the practice more degrading and dangerous. When the belt was used on a 17-year-old inmate, Amnesty cited the act as a violation of the international convention on the rights of the child.

Public Impact

Based on the use of electro-shock weapons in the United States and other human rights abuses including inhumane prisons, unjust treatment of asylum seekers, police brutality, and the use of the death penalty, in October 1998 Amnesty International launched a Campaign on the United States. It is important to note that this action was not initiated or directed by the USA section of Amnesty International (a section does not campaign against its home country). However, members of Amnesty International as individuals, including U.S.

members, were encouraged to join in the letter writing campaigns and other efforts to raise public awareness that Amnesty International hopes will lead to reforms in the United States' treatment of prisoners and will limit sales of electro-shock weapons.

FUTURE DIRECTIONS

A future focus for AIUSA and Amnesty International is the establishment of an International Criminal Court, which it first called for in 1993. In the first of a series of position papers published in 1997 and 1998, Amnesty International noted that many nations had failed to call their own leaders to account for atrocities committed in the half century since the Nuremberg and Tokyo tribunals held to try fascist war criminals the end of World War II (1939-45). Amnesty International urged that an International Court should "have jurisdiction over genocide, other crimes against humanity and serious violations of humanitarian law," including widespread murder, forced disappearance, torture, rape, arbitrary deportation, political persecution, and arbitrary imprisonment.

GROUP RESOURCES

Amnesty International USA maintains a Web site at http://www.amnesty-usa.org that contains basic information about the organization as well as detailed summaries of its current campaigns and programs. Amnesty frequently produces press releases and has produced a CD-ROM on its work. Amnesty's Urgent Action Network sends information to members via E-mail and other means, urging them to write appeals to authorities in targeted countries. Additional information about Amnesty International USA can be obtained by writing Amnesty International USA, 322 Eighth Ave., New York, NY 10001 or by calling (212) 807-8400.

GROUP PUBLICATIONS

Amnesty has a 28-page catalogue of publications for sale including: reports on individual countries' human rights records, its annual report on human rights situations worldwide, newsletters, and calendars. Amnesty also maintains an on-line library that contains its annual and country reports at http://www.amnesty.org/ailib/index.html. Amnesty International also publishes *The I.S. Newsletter*, a monthly newsletter. The catalogue and *The I.S. Newsletter* are available by calling (212) 807-8400 or by writing to Amnesty International USA, Publications, 322 Eighth Ave., New York, New York 10001.

BIBLIOGRAPHY

Cage, Mary Crystal. "An Activist Scholar: Amnesty International's New Leader." *Chronicle of Higher Education,* 21 February 1997.

Cusac, Anne-Marie. "Shock Value: U.S. Stun Devices Pose Human-Rights Risk." *Progressive,* September 1997.

Drinan, Robert F. "A Mobilization of Shame." *Commonweal,* 7 October 1994.

Goldrich, Robert. "Amnesty International PSA Enlists Animation." *SHOOT,* 27 January 1995.

Larsen, Egon. *A Flame in Barbed Wire: The Story of Amnesty International.* New York: W.W. Norton and Co., 1979.

Miller, Cindee. "Amnesty International Injects Pizzazz into Its Marketing Approach." *Marketing News,* 17 February 1992.

Newman, Mclinda. "Amnesty Seeks New Chief as Healey Departs." *Billboard,* 2 October 1993.

Pietrucha, Bill. "A Tale of Three Web Sites." *Journal of Business Strategy,* January-February 1996.

Staunton, Marie, Sally Fenn, and Amnesty International USA. *The Amnesty International Handbook.* Claremont, Calif.: Hunter House, 1991.

Stein, M.L. "Rejected Ad Flap." *Editor and Publisher,* 23 March 1996.

Association of Trial Lawyers of America (ATLA)

WHAT IS ITS MISSION?

According to its promotional literature, the Association of Trial Lawyers of America (ATLA) "promotes justice and fairness for injured persons, safeguards victims' rights—particularly the right to trial by jury—and strengthens the civil justice system through education and disclosure of information critical to public health and safety."

Unlike other lawyers' groups (notably the American Bar Association) which seek to represent the profession as a whole, ATLA focuses on the concerns of plaintiffs attorneys: those who represent individuals, or groups of individuals, in civil cases that involve personal or property damages. As a result, its goals often conflict with those of other attorneys—particularly corporate defense lawyers who are often their adversaries. The rights of injured parties, the accountability of wrongdoers, and the institutional guarantees that uphold those principles, are ATLA's constant priorities.

ESTABLISHED: 1946
EMPLOYEES: 165
MEMBERS: 60,000
PAC: ATLA PAC

Contact Information:
ADDRESS: 1050 31st St. NW
     Washington, DC 20007
PHONE: (202) 965-3500
TOLL FREE: (800) 424-2725
FAX: (202) 625-7312
E-MAIL: help@atlahq.org
URL: http://www.atlanet.org
PRESIDENT: Mark S. Mandell

HOW IS IT STRUCTURED?

ATLA defines itself as "a voluntary professional organization governed by the membership." Its leadership consists of two branches: a board of governors that votes on all policy issues, and an executive committee of national officers that administers ATLA's day-to-day operations. Members who sit on the board of governors are elected to three-year terms and represent local associations in each of the 50 states, the Provinces of Canada, the District of Columbia, Puerto Rico, and four other

FAST FACTS

About 9.5 million people per year receive nonfatal injuries in product-related accidents, excluding automobiles. Fewer than five percent of these injuries result in any claim for compensation.

(Source: Paula Mergenhagen. "Product Liability: Who Sues?" *American Demographics*, June 1995.)

countries (Ireland, the United Kingdom, and two seats that alternate among different nations). The executive committee consists of a president, vice president, executive director, secretary, treasurer, parliamentarian, and the president-elect for the coming year. Officers, who serve one-year terms, are elected by the membership at an annual convention and presidents are elected one year before their terms begin.

A Bylaws Committee and a Standing Committee help set board policies; the president is also empowered to appoint a Presidential Committee for specific purposes. State delegates take responsibility for membership recruitment and retention. Sections and Litigation groups concentrate on particular legal specialties—such as employment discrimination and toxic products liability—collect and share information, and organize training programs. An International Section coordinates activities in those countries not represented on the board of governors.

PRIMARY FUNCTIONS

ATLA is best known for its advocacy efforts at the state and federal government levels. It is particularly involved in opposing proposals that, in ATLA's view, would seriously weaken the civil justice system—and the rights of consumers—by unfairly changing the rules under which civil cases are tried. ATLA closely monitors proposed state and federal tort legislation, and joins the debate on several fronts, such as lobbying lawmakers, generating publicity and grassroots pressure, and providing testimony before administrative and regulatory agencies. When possible, ATLA coordinates its lobbying efforts with like-minded organizations, primarily consumers' groups and other lawyers' associations.

As an association of legal professionals, ATLA members take cases before the courts. At the national level, they may act on their own or they may work with state trial lawyer associations in mounting constitutional challenges and test cases of local tort reforms. ATLA staffers often act in an advisory capacity even when they are not actually principally involved in a case. In such instances, ATLA submits amicus curiae (friend of the court) briefs to the Supreme Court and other courts.

As a professional association, ATLA provides a number of services to its members, and sponsors a series of conferences and seminars geared toward continuing legal education. These gatherings provide attorneys, law students, and legal paraprofessionals with training on courtroom skills and techniques, as well as the opportunity to share information on recent developments in such specialized fields as product liability and medical malpractice. To the same end, ATLA maintains an extensive database of documents from thousands of court cases, enabling members to research facts, precedents, and expert testimony, and to communicate with other attorneys who have handled similar cases. Through its foundations, the group also sponsors awards, contests, grants and scholarships to support legal education and grassroots advocacy.

ATLA sponsors many educational programs for the general public, in forums ranging from academic roundtables to state fairs, high schools, and community centers. Informative public outreach programs address such issues as access to legal services, home and workplace safety, the jury system, and knowing one's legal rights. In addition to providing speakers and display materials, ATLA publishes several books and pamphlets on legal issues for the general public. To its members, the association also markets a wide range of journals, books, audio cassettes, and videotapes.

Finally, ATLA is known for its powerful political presence. The association's Political Action Committee (ATLA PAC) contributes generously to the campaigns of candidates who endorse its views and the private political contributions of individual ATLA members amount to millions more. *Fortune* magazine has called ATLA "one of Washington's most formidable lobbies," noting that it is both well-funded and effectively organized.

PROGRAMS

ATLA sponsors a number of initiatives, conferences, caucuses, programs, and opportunities to benefit its members and the public it serves. Such initiatives may be educational in nature or politically motivated.

Training and educational programs for members are offered through ATLA's National College of Advocacy (NCA). For members unable to attend in person, NCA produces and distributes audiotapes of the presentations. Electronic services for members include ATLTA NET, the organization's Web site, and the ATLA Exchange, an extensive database on tort cases nationwide. Through its foundation and the Legal Affairs Department, ATLA maintains an ongoing dialogue with other attorneys' groups and legal scholars.

Long-running ATLA educational programs include "When Justice Is Up to You," a teaching model for junior and senior high schools focusing on the jury system; "Trial by Jury: The Lawyer's Craft," in which attorneys explain and play out the elements of a trial; and "The People's Law School," a seminar series that teaches citizens about their legal rights. ATLA also publishes several books and brochures on topical issues; for example, "The Justice You Deserve" is a handbook on accessing legal and other services in cases of domestic violence.

ATLA supports two foundations. The Civil Justice Foundation, established in 1986, provides grants to tax-exempt grassroots advocacy organizations in three categories: groups of injured consumers, injury-prevention work, and projects to improve the care and treatment of injured consumers. Grants range from $5,000 to $20,000 and more than 80 grants have been awarded, totaling over $1 million. The Roscoe Pound Foundation, named for a former dean of Harvard Law School, sponsors many seminars that promote dialogue among jurists, academics, the media, and public-interest groups, and offers a growing program of scholarships, awards, and contests.

BUDGET INFORMATION

Not made available.

HISTORY

In 1945 two prominent Boston attorneys, Ben Marcus and Sam Horovitz, shared a common concern about the serious disadvantage injured workers faced when litigating their claims against employers and insurance companies. According to Marcus, "We thought we should have a national organization to train attorneys for injured workers and [provide a forum for them] to exchange ideas." The two men gathered together nine others who shared the same goal and in 1946, after each man paid a $1 fee in dues, the National Association of Claimants' Compensation Attorneys (NACCA) was officially established.

While initially conceived as an organization for labor attorneys only, the group slowly began accepting membership from lawyers of other specialties (admiralty, railroad, and personal injury law) who shared similar goals and concerns. By 1964 the Boston-based group had swelled to nearly 20,000 members and represented all personal injury lawyers. To reflect this new, broader representation, the NACCA was renamed the American Trial Lawyers Association (ATLA). Although its focus had broadened, education of its members remained the group's core mission. The organization's flagship publication, *TRIAL,* was first published in 1964 to a circulation that extended beyond members to include state governors, members of Congress, members of the federal judiciary, and members of the state supreme courts. Today the monthly publication boasts 70,000 to 80,000 readers.

Beginning in the late 1960s, the ATLA began its first round of legislative battles. The group rallied to oppose both the advent of no-fault automobile insurance and medical malpractice reform proposals. In mounting these and other defenses against tort reform, the ATLA began spending less time educating its members and more time lobbying for their interests. In 1972 the organization was renamed again. This time the change was subtle and resulted in the name the Association of Trial Lawyers of America (ATLA).

By 1977 the change to the organization's focus was so evident that some members considered moving the headquarters from the educational hub of Boston to the political hub of Washington, D.C. By a slim margin, members voted to relocate to the nation's capitol. The divisive nature of this decision is reflected in the comments of ATLA historian and former *TRIAL* editor Richard Jacobson, "The critical thing was the wisdom of some of the leaders [of that time]. They saw that as much as they loved education, the laws themselves were the predominant force affecting the welfare of the client."

Education is still an integral part of ATLA; information is widely disseminated among members through both group publications and seminar programs run by ATLA's National College of Advocacy. The ATLA is a strong, broad-based, international coalition of attorneys, judges, law professors, paralegals, and law students all committed to preserving the adversary system of justice and protecting every person's right to a trial by jury.

CURRENT POLITICAL ISSUES

ATLA's political activity has centered around a series of proposals to change the civil justice system, collectively known as the tort reform movement. This movement began in the 1960s, when critics diagnosed a growing crisis in the civil justice system and proposed a wide range of reforms to correct it. Disturbing trends include a steady increase in the number of lawsuits filed, excessive amounts of damage awards being granted, and aggressive advertising by attorneys working for contingency fees, meaning there are no fees to the client unless the client wins, in which case the attorney receives a share of the settlement.

The courts, defenders of tort reform say, are so clogged with lawsuits that the system is overworked, and justice is delayed for all. Further, they argue that juries routinely award outrageous and excessive damages to

WHAT IS A TORT?

Generally speaking, a tort is a civil case (as opposed to a crime, or criminal case) in which someone claims to have been harmed by someone else. The alleged harm may take the form of physical impairment, pain and suffering, property damage, or damage to one's reputation. If convicted, defendants are required to compensate the injured parties, usually by paying money damages. Libel cases, claims of medical or professional malpractice, worker's compensation, and injuries caused by unsafe consumer products are only a few of the most common types of tort cases.

plaintiffs and because of this, there is a crisis in the cost of doing business. Small companies may be wiped out by a single lawsuit and larger corporations face mounting costs for legal insurance services, even if they never lose a lawsuit. In turn, critics say that these costs are passed on to the consumer. In particular, the cost of malpractice insurance is cited as a major cause of spiraling health care expenses.

Much of ATLA's activity has consisted of countering the claims and assumptions of tort reform and expressing their views to lawmakers, courts and regulatory agencies, the public, the media, and to the rest of the legal profession. Central to their argument is that the crisis depicted by tort reformers is greatly exaggerated. For example, ATLA publicizes studies showing that tort claims amount to only a small percentage of all civil claims, and that plaintiff win rates have remained relatively constant over the years. The real increase in litigation, ATLA claims, has been in businesses suing each other over contracts, not suits brought by consumers.

Tort reformers claim that attorneys who oppose tort reform do so purely out of self-interest, for attorneys are the ones who profit the most. To that end, ATLA continues to block tort reform and advocates continue to propose remedies in stage legislatures and on Capitol Hill. One of the most frequently mentioned reforms is that of a legislative cap on the total amount of damages that can be awarded.

Case Study: Tort Reform in the States

While tort reform at the federal level receives wide attention, ATLA claims the battle in state houses has been even more intense and has more far-reaching effects since nearly 95 percent of tort cases are tried in state, not fed-

eral, courts. Because of this, trial lawyers give heavily to state political campaigns; one study cites $17.3 million in such contributions, over a four-year period, in the states of California, Texas, and Alabama alone. Since the mid-1980s, a wide range of tort reforms have been enacted by state legislatures, particularly in the wake of Republican gains in the 1994 elections. ATLA's response, working with local organizations, has been to continue the battle in the judicial branch, by challenging the constitutionality of reform measures.

For example, Illinois passed a sweeping reform act in 1995, capping all noneconomic damages at $500,000. In December 1997 the Illinois Supreme Court ruled the law in violation of the state constitution. Similar reversals have occurred in Indiana, Montana, and Ohio; one report claims that courts have struck down damage caps in 25 states. When tort reformers enact ballot initiatives, ATLA has also found success in taking its case to the public. In March 1998 California voters decided against three highly publicized tort reform proposals. According to ATLA, these reform campaigns were marked by attempts to exploit antilawyer sentiment and economic fears. Despite heavy funding from state business interests, the three proposals were soundly defeated.

Public Impact

ATLA insists that some reform proposals are unnecessary because the problems they seek to correct are exaggerated. Other proposals are thought to be dangerous because they would weaken the rights of individuals and the accountability of corporations. Punitive damages, for example, are believed to be necessary and effective in the great majority of cases. They are usually invoked only in the most serious of circumstances—one to two percent of all liability cases—and are believed to have a strong deterrent effect. As one ATLA report notes, "In nearly 80 percent of the products liability cases in which punitive damages were awarded, the manufacturer made a subsequent safety change. Beyond that, just the threat of punitive damages causes safety to be taken into account, thereby resulting in a safer America."

According to ATLA, to cap the amount of compensation victims may receive would be to seriously weaken the deterrent effects of tort law and the consumer benefits that result. ATLA argues that the system already has safeguards against abuse (in the rare cases when juries grant excessive awards, judges can and do reduce them), and that its benefits are far greater than its flaws. Again, ATLA argues that the reform has not been proven necessary, and that its adoption would effectively deny many citizens access to justice. Against charges of self-interest, the trial lawyers portray themselves as defenders of the very rights the civil justice system was meant to ensure. In turn, ATLA describes tort reform as an attempt by business interests to roll back recent gains by consumers, avoid accountability, and increase profits.

FUTURE DIRECTIONS

Because it is essentially a reactive organization, the issues that ATLA becomes involved with are ever changing. Specific events trigger ATLA to take action. One possible area that ATLA may concern itself with is the jury system itself. Controversial jury verdicts in high-profile criminal cases have brought about efforts to have civil cases decided by judges, rather than juries. To this end, ATLA might launch a campaign to oppose the assault on juries. Another issue that ATLA might become involved with is lawyer advertising. ATLA also hopes to increase its involvement in international affairs.

As much as its budget allows, ATLA plans to expand its educational outreach programs, in order to foster greater public awareness of the nature and importance of the civil justice system. To many members, these programs are ATLA's most fundamental purpose, and provide the best hope of its ultimate success, since both the jury system and the political process are presumed to depend on an informed, concerned citizenry.

GROUP RESOURCES

ATLA's public Web site at http://www.atlanet.org provides background on the organization, press releases, and journal articles. It is a useful starting point for research projects. The ATLA Exchange and trial databases are accessible only to members. Research requests, and requests for ATLA publications, should be directed to the public relations office at national headquarters: 1050 31st St. NW, Washington, DC 20007; phone 1-800-424-2725.

GROUP PUBLICATIONS

ATLA publishes several periodicals for its members including *TRIAL,* a monthly legal journal; *The Law Reporter,* a research collection; and *The ATLA Advocate,* ATLA's monthly newsletter. All are provided to members at no cost. Two other journals, the *Professional Negligence Law Reporter* and the *Products Liability Law Reporter* are geared to the specialties indicated by their titles. Each is offered at a subscription rate of $113/year for members, or $195 for nonmembers. The Roscoe Pound Foundation publishes *Civil Justice Digest,* a quarterly of legal news and research, as well as many academic papers and reports. ATLA publications are available through the public relations office at 1-800-424-2725. In concert with the legal publishers the West Group, ATLA has also helped produce and distribute dozens of texts and videotapes for legal professionals; these materials are offered by the West Group at 1-800-221-9428.

BIBLIOGRAPHY

"America's Third Political Party: a Study of Political Contributions by the Plaintiff's Lawyer Industry." *Ohio CPA Journal,* June 1995.

Fisher, Mary Jane. "Tort Bill Gets Wide Support." *National Underwriter, Life & Health,* 1 December 1997.

Kemper, Vicki. "Lawyers on Trial." *Common Cause,* Fall 1993.

Novack, Janet. "Torture by Tort." *Forbes,* 6 November 1995.

Press, Aric. "Are Lawyers Burning America?" *Newsweek,* 20 March 1995.

Smith, Lee. "Trial Lawyers Face a New Change." *Fortune,* 26 August 1991.

Spence, Leslie. "Troubling Days for Trial Lawyers." *Forbes,* 11 June 1990.

Thornburgh, Richard L. "The New Judicial Imperialism: Tort Reform Victories in State Legislatures Are Being Undone in the Courts." *Wall Street Journal,* 18 May 1998.

Association on American Indian Affairs (AAIA)

ESTABLISHED: 1922
EMPLOYEES: 6
MEMBERS: 40,000
PAC: None

Contact Information:
ADDRESS: PO Box 268
    Tekakwitha Complex
    Agency Rd. 7
    Sisseton, SD 57262
PHONE: (605) 698-3998
FAX: (605) 698-3316
EXECUTIVE DIRECTOR: Jerry Flute

WHAT IS ITS MISSION?

The Association on American Indian Affairs (AAIA) is a national, nonprofit, private-citizens' organization that exists to promote the well-being of American Indians and Alaska Natives and to defend their rights. The AAIA works with Indian communities throughout the United States, helping them, in its own words, "to achieve full economic and social equality while preserving their unique culture."

To fulfill its mission, the AAIA pursues a number of goals. The organization works to keep native communities better informed of federal legislation that affects them, while also striving to bring Indian interests more effective representation in federal policy-making processes. The AAIA seeks to reverse the disproportionately high levels of unemployment, poverty, disease, alcoholism, and suicide among Indians, and to improve economic stability and living conditions for Indian people. It also seeks to protect tribal land bases and to increase understanding and protection of American Indian religious beliefs and practices.

HOW IS IT STRUCTURED?

The AAIA consists of a small paid staff led by an executive director, a governing board of directors, and a general membership of about 40,000 individuals. General membership meetings take place once a year. Though each of the organization's structural levels is open to Indians and non-Indians alike, in 1997 every member of the board of directors as well as the executive director had American Indian heritage. While the main office operates out of Sisseton, South Dakota, (where it moved from New York in 1995), the AAIA also has field offices in Washington, D.C., and Concord, California.

The executive director, the AAIA's highest-paid staff member, takes responsibility for leading the organization in its daily operations and acts as the primary spokesperson. Other staff members include an executive secretary, an attorney, a general counsel, and a scholarship coordinator, as well as other part-time staff.

The board of directors includes both office-holding members and general members and meets twice a year. Offices include a president, vice president, secretary, and treasurer. In 1997, 13 directors sat on the board; their backgrounds included the fields of education, law, health, and public service.

In order to pursue its mission of serving American Indian interests on a national level, the AAIA frequently allies itself with like-minded organizations. These affiliates include other national Indian-oriented groups such as the National Congress of American Indians (NCAI) and the Native American Rights Fund (NARF), more localized entities such as individual tribes or organized groups within tribes, and non-Indian organizations such as environmental activist groups.

PRIMARY FUNCTIONS

The AAIA works to improve the lives of American Indians. It tracks federal legislation, keeps members informed of policies that affect Indian communities, lobbies for Indian interests at both the federal and state levels, provides congressional testimony, and drafts legislation. The organization also conducts research on a variety of Indian issues, organizes conferences, and publishes information intended to educate Indian communities, state and federal policymakers, and the general public. Other services offered to tribes and individuals include legal assistance, technical support, grants, and scholarships.

The AAIA's interest in policy formation and implementation frequently requires its representatives to interact with government bodies. These include federal agencies such as the Bureau of Indian Affairs (BIA), the Indian Health Service, and the National Park Service (NPS), as well as state governments and officials. In fact, since its inception, the AAIA has tended to cooperate closely with government agencies, an approach that has sparked criticism from more militant groups such as the American Indian Movement (AIM).

Outside of government, the AAIA also works to build coalitions among Indian advocacy organizations—often involving the NCAI and the NARF—and other groups with compatible agendas. Examples include the Medicine Wheel Coalition and the National Coalition for Religious

Freedom. The Medicine Wheel Coalition brings together AAIA representatives, tribal organizations, and environmentalists seeking to protect sacred sites in the Plains states, while the National Coalition for Religious Freedom includes the AAIA, the NCAI, several tribes, environmentalists, churches, and civil rights groups.

PROGRAMS

Many of the AAIA's initiatives occur on a case-by-case basis, in response to tribes that have asked for help with particular situations. Often the AAIA drafts legislation that addresses tribal concerns. Federally adopted AAIA proposals include the Native American Graves Protection and Repatriation Act (NAGPRA), which protects American Indian burial sites and requires museums to return ceremonial artifacts and human remains to tribes, and the Indian Child Welfare Act (ICWA), which seeks to keep the adoption of Indian children within Indian rather than non-Indian homes.

To combat poor health conditions on reservations, the AAIA played an instrumental role in creating advocacy organizations such as the Association of American Indian Physicians and the Association of American Indian Nurses. It has also organized conferences on such topics as the high rate of diabetes among Indian people. The AAIA provides legal resources and advice to tribes looking to recover land, control resources, and protect sacred sites, and to Indian communities seeking federal recognition. The AAIA has also helped create curriculum guidelines and bibliographic materials for educational purposes.

The AAIA's ongoing programs include the publication of a newsletter called *Indian Affairs* and a scholarship program for American Indians and Alaskan Natives. The AAIA administers a number of scholarships for undergraduate and graduate study, including the Emergency Aid and Health Professions Scholarships, the AAIA/Adolph Van Pelt Special Fund for Indian Scholarships, and the Sequoyah Graduate Fellowships. These scholarships demonstrate the AAIA's interest in education as well as its commitment to developing leadership from within Indian communities.

BUDGET INFORMATION

In 1997, the AAIA had an operating budget of $750,000. Traditionally the AAIA has generated the bulk of its revenue through contributions—including membership dues—and grants; between 1991 and 1995, private contributions and grants (including government grants) constituted an average of 93 percent of total revenue. Other revenue sources include literature sales and investments.

The Taos people secured the return of Blue Lake, a site in New Mexico sacred to their tribe, with the help of the Association on American Indian Affairs. The federal government in 1970 placed the lake in a permanent trust for the tribe. (National Archives and Records Administration)

The AAIA devotes most of its outgoing funds to program expenses, which include legal costs, public education, scholarships and grants, technical assistance, and training. In 1996, 77 percent of total expenses went to such program expenses, up from 59 percent in 1995. Other expenses include fund-raising and administrative costs.

HISTORY

The AAIA formed in 1922 as a regional, single-issue organization dominated by non-Indians. Since then, it has grown into a national entity, governed by Indian leaders and considered one of the major players among American Indian special-interest groups.

The AAIA began in 1922 in response to proposed anti-Indian legislation in the southwestern United States. In the 1920s, prevailing opinion sought to assimilate Indian people into the mainstream culture and thus threatened Indian-held lands, native religious practices, and other cultural traditions. These trends came to a head in the Southwest with the introduction of the Bursum Bill in 1922. In this bill, Senator Holm Bursum of New Mexico proposed that non-Indian squatters should acquire legal rights to appropriate Rio Grande Pueblo lands. A group of non-Indians sympathetic to the Pueblo side of the conflict formed the Eastern Association on Indian Affairs (EAIA)

in opposition to the Bursum Bill, thus founding the first incarnation of the AAIA. In cooperation with the American Indian Defense Association (AIDA) and the New Mexico Association on Indian Affairs (NMAIA), the EAIA launched a national effort to defeat the Bursum Bill, a campaign which proved successful.

The opposition efforts against the Bursum Bill began a pattern for Indian advocacy that continued throughout the 1920s. These forces were led by well-educated white men with both a personal and an academic interest in Indian cultures and issues. In addition to their fight against the Bursum Bill, they also sought to protect southwestern and plains tribes' right to perform religious ceremonies.

New Focus

In the 1930s, the AAIA went through a number of changes. It came under the leadership of Oliver LaFarge, whose influence dominated the organization until 1963. It also grew into a national organization that worked on a broader range of issues. LaFarge, a writer and anthropologist, began his association with the AAIA as board president of the EAIA. During his term, the organization changed its name to the National Association on Indian Affairs (NAIA), to reflect its interest in moving from its southwestern focus to a more national scope. Later in the decade the group became the American Association on

Indian Affairs, and finally settled on the Association of American Indian Affairs (AAIA) in 1946. When John Collier, executive secretary of the AIDA, left that post to become the national commissioner of Indian affairs, LaFarge played an instrumental role in merging with the AIDA, a move that probably saved his organization, which suffered from financial difficulties at the time. Though LaFarge's and Collier's personalities had sometimes clashed over the years, because of their organizations' similar agendas, the merger made sense and proved a success.

Tensions between LaFarge and Collier continued as Collier's national Indian policies took shape. LaFarge became president of the AAIA in 1937, and he disagreed with Collier's proposals to make sweeping changes in the BIA and substantially to revamp the system governing national Indian policy. LaFarge favored a more moderate approach and closer cooperation with the existing BIA. On the other hand, LaFarge and the AAIA did support Collier's denunciation of the government's previously aggressive assimilation policies, and his efforts to preserve American Indian cultures and promote more political autonomy for reservation communities. Collier's anti-assimilationist policies became known as the "Indian New Deal," and the AAIA stood behind them. The AAIA also pursued its own agenda of protecting Indian religions, encouraging Indian arts and crafts, and pushing for improvements in agriculture and health conditions on reservations.

World War II (1939–45) brought a shift in the AAIA's activities and level of influence. During the war, LaFarge left his presidency to serve in the air transport command, and the organization's activities almost came to a halt. After the war, LaFarge resumed leadership and the AAIA underwent a reorganization that left it stronger than ever. LaFarge expanded fund-raising efforts, which enabled him to take on more projects. He also restructured the organization by creating an executive director, a legal committee, and a legal counsel. This restructuring allowed the AAIA to defend Indian civil and constitutional rights in the courts, before administrative bodies, and in congressional committees.

The AAIA also launched a more concerted public education campaign, conducting research and field studies that allowed it to publish reports on such topics as the status of the Navajos and California tribes, American Indians and advanced education, living conditions on southwestern reservations, and adjustment to urban environments. AAIA leaders established institutes on a variety of issues; these consisted of public discussions organized around position papers on topics such as self-government and assimilation. The organization also began producing regular publications. It published a quarterly journal called *The American Indian* from 1943 to 1959, and began publishing its current newsletter, *Indian Affairs*, in 1949.

The AAIA needed its new-found strength, as the postwar period also brought new challenges. The National Congress of American Indians (NCAI), founded in 1944, presented one challenge. Unlike the AAIA, the NCAI began as a national organization created by Indian people concerned with Indian issues. As the new organization gained momentum and strengthened its ties with Indian communities across the country, its American Indian leadership contrasted to the white-dominated AAIA.

Federal Policy

Despite differences between the NCAI and the AAIA, they united in opposition to the AAIA's major challenge of the 1950s: the federal policy of termination. Throughout Collier's term as Indian commissioner, many members of the administration had opposed what they saw as his Indian-friendly policies, and after the war, this opposition developed into a bipartisan resistance. In 1953, Collier's opponents gained sway over federal Indian affairs, launching the official policy of termination, which included provisions to end federally recognized and financially supported Indian tribes and reservations. Termination legislation also included a relocation program that sought to move Indian people from reservation communities into major cities. Though LaFarge initially saw some advantages to termination, he eventually changed his mind, and the AAIA joined the NCAI in fighting the policy, which by 1958, had effectively died.

In the late 1950s and 1960s, the AAIA turned to issues that spanned the country and brought the organization into close cooperation with three American Indian groups. Under the leadership of LaVerne Madigan, the AAIA assisted Alaska natives residing near Point Hope in resisting successfully the placement of a nuclear experimental test site near their communities, and gaining greater protection for their lands, resources, and hunting and fishing rights. The AAIA also joined the Senecas of New York in opposing the Kinzua Dam project, begun in the mid-1950s, which threatened to flood a large portion of a Seneca reservation. The resistance failed, and the dam, completed in 1965, flooded Indian burial sites and forced over 700 Seneca people to relocate. Finally, the AAIA provided support to the Taos Pueblo's efforts to secure the return of sacred Blue Lake. The AAIA's legal and technical assistance and congressional lobbying proved crucial to the success of the Taos people's cause in 1970, when the federal government placed the lake in permanent trust for the tribe.

The late 1960s and 1970s saw Indian activism change dramatically. Frustrated with those organizations that worked for gradual change from within the system, new Indian-led groups such as the National Indian Youth Council (NIYC) and the American Indian Movement (AIM) introduced a more radical voice that rejected the system altogether. Criticizing the tradition of political lobbying and cooperation with government bodies, these activists pursued "Red Power" through militant rhetoric, public protest, and an overall confrontational style that sought to shake the foundations of federal Indian policy and promote "Indian pride." This period also saw the rise of direct litigation as an increasingly sophisticated version of Indian advocacy. Both of these trends threatened the AAIA's authority as an authentic and effective representative of Indian interests.

The AAIA rose to the challenge, however. The 1980s and 1990s saw an increasing amount of Indian control within the organization. By 1997, the entire board of directors, as well as the executive directorship, were comprised of American Indians. The AAIA also began to develop legislative skills more fully and to put an increasing amount of effort into building coalitions with other Indian organizations. By adapting to change, the AAIA managed to survive, and retain its importance within the broad spectrum of Indian advocacy groups.

CURRENT POLITICAL ISSUES

The AAIA's current concerns involve many of the issues it has focused on in the past. AAIA leaders see child welfare and the strengthening of American Indian families as one of its top priorities. The AAIA works to implement the ICWA by helping tribes negotiate agreements with state officials to keep adoption of Indian children within Indian communities. The AAIA also promotes tribal self-government and federal recognition for Indian communities that would benefit from the economic assistance and protection of land and resources that comes with official tribal status. In its ongoing concern with health issues, the AAIA has begun focusing on fetal-alcohol syndrome and the high incidence of diabetes among American Indians.

Finally, the organization devotes much of its energy and resources to promoting and protecting religious freedom for Indian people. By participating in such groups as the National Coalition for Religious Freedom, and supporting legislation like the Native American Cultural Protection and Free Exercise of Religion Act, the AAIA advocates Indian cultures' rights to use peyote and eagle feathers for religious ceremonies, to practice their religions while in prison, and to enjoy access to, and respect for, their sacred sites.

Case Study: The Medicine Wheel Coalition

One of AAIA's highest priorities is protecting American Indian sacred sites. Sacred sites include geological formations, lakes, burial sites, and other areas that play key roles in Indian communities' religious ceremonies, historical consciousness, and understanding of the natural world and their place in it. Many of these sites become threatened by non-Indian development due to resource extraction, road building, settlement, and tourism. In the 1990s, the AAIA frequently responded to

these threats through its participation in the Medicine Wheel Coalition.

The Medicine Wheel Coalition includes AAIA leaders, tribes and tribal organizations, and non-Indian environmental groups interested in protecting sacred sites in the Plains states. The group first formed in response to threats posed to the sacred Medicine Wheel site by tourism and logging enterprises. Located in Wyoming's Bighorn National Forest, the site consists of an ancient, man-made stone circle with spiritual significance for area tribes. The coalition's efforts brought success in 1996, when the Forest Service created a Historic Preservation Plan to protect the site.

As concerned organizations came together to protect the Medicine Wheel site, they decided to expand their scope to include other endangered sacred areas throughout the Plains states. At Devil's Tower in eastern Wyoming, recreational and commercial rock climbing threatened ceremonial use of the area by several Plains tribes. In 1996, the AAIA and other coalition members worked with the NPS to create and implement a Climbing Management Plan, intended to protect the spiritual integrity of the site by placing restrictions on rock climbing there. Specifically, the plan banned commercial climbing during the month of June, when many American Indian tribes gather to celebrate the summer solstice with religious rites.

This ban proved short-lived, however, when a group of commercial climbers challenged the restrictions and went to federal court to fight them. Initial rulings went against the ban, which was found to be a violation of the First Amendment's provision that the government would not favor or establish any religion. The Coalition and NPS appealed the case, and also made the ban voluntary, simply encouraging climbers to stay off of Devil's Tower in June rather than preventing it. In April of 1998, the U.S. District Court of Wyoming ruled that a voluntary ban, made not to benefit, but rather to respect, American Indian religions, was legal and permissible.

The lobbying and educational efforts of American Indian organizations and coalitions have helped raise public awareness of the importance of sacred sites to American Indian cultures, and of the need for greater understanding and protection of Indian religious freedom. In May of 1996, President Bill Clinton issued an executive order calling for federal agencies to respect sacred areas and to allow Indian people ceremonial access to them. Yet as AAIA executive director Jerry Flute pointed out in a 1997 interview in the Minneapolis *Star Tribune*, the president's move remains largely symbolic until Congress passes measures to back it up. While Flute acknowledges such executive orders as "a sign of good intent," he points out that they "don't have the force of law."

FUTURE DIRECTIONS

It seems likely that religious freedom and sacred sites will continue to be a top priority for AAIA. With this, as with other issues, the organization will continue to form coalitions and encourage partnerships in order to reach a broader audience and maintain a vital presence in the policy-making process. AAIA leaders hope to move from encouraging statements of support from the president and other federal and state officials to form legislation and sanctions that will protect native spirituality with the force of law.

GROUP RESOURCES

The AAIA maintains a library with over 200 holdings related to American Indian history and contemporary issues. It also provides mailing lists as well as legal and technical expertise. To access these services, call the national office at (605) 698-3998, or write to PO Box 268, Tekakwitha Complex, Agency Rd. 7, Sisseton, SD 57262.

GROUP PUBLICATIONS

The AAIA publishes a newsletter, *Indian Affairs*, three times a year. The newsletter includes updates on the status of federal and state legislation affecting Indian communities. It also describes recent activities of the AAIA, its leaders and members, and the various coalitions of which it is a part. Finally, the newsletter gives information on upcoming meetings, conferences, and publications of interest, and includes lists of AAIA scholarship recipients.

In addition to its newsletter, the AAIA has also published a number of reference materials and reports in an effort to provide support to Indian communities and to educate the general public. These include the *Economic and Community Development Resource Guide for Native Americans*, the *Tribal Bond Handbook*, the *Arts and Crafts Resource Guide*, the "Proceedings of the National Sacred Sites Caucus," and documents entitled "Sacred Lands and Religious Freedom," the "American Indian Religious Freedom Project," and *Sacred Lands and Religious Freedom*, written by Vine Deloria, Jr., with an introduction by Keith Basso. For more information, contact the organization by mail at Association on American Indian Affairs, PO Box 268, Tekakwitha Complex, Agency Rd. 7, Sisseton, SD, 57262; or by phone at (605) 698-3998.

BIBLIOGRAPHY

"American Indian Religious Freedom Project." New York: Association on American Indian Affairs, 1993.

Champaign, Duane, ed. *The Native North American Almanac.* Detroit: Gale Research, Inc., 1994.

Debo, Angie. *A History of the Indians of the United States.* Norman, Okla.: University of Oklahoma Press, 1970.

Deloria, Vine. "Sacred Lands and Religious Freedom." New York: Association on American Indian Affairs, 1991.

Hecht, Robert A. *Oliver LaFarge and the American Indian: A Biography.* Metuchen, N.J.: The Scarecrow Press, Inc., 1991.

Hirschfelder, Arlene B., and Mary B. Davis, ed. "Association on American Indian Affairs." *Native America in the Twentieth Century: An Encyclopedia.* New York: Garland Publishing, Inc., 1994.

Kelly, Lawrence C. *The Assault on Assimilation: John Collier and the Origins of Indian Policy Reform.* Albuquerque: University of New Mexico Press, 1983.

Klein, Barry T. *Reference Encyclopedia of the American Indian.* 7th ed. East Nyack, N.J.: Todd Publications, 1995.

Mannes, Marc. "Factors and Events Leading to the Passage of the Indian Child Welfare Act." *Child Welfare*, January-February, 1995.

McNickle, D'Arcy. *Indian Man: A Life of Oliver LaFarge.* Bloomington, Ind.: Indiana University Press, 1971.

Utter, Jack. *American Indians: Answers to Today's Questions.* Lake Ann, Mich.: National Woodlands Publishing Co., 1993.

Welsch, Chris. "An Interview with Jerry Flute, Advocate for Indian Sacred Sites." *Minneapolis Star Tribune,* 13 April 1997.

Carnegie Endowment for International Peace (CEIP)

ESTABLISHED: 1910
EMPLOYEES: 115
MEMBERS: None
PAC: None

Contact Information:

ADDRESS: 1779 Massachusetts Ave. NW
　　　Washington, DC 20036-2103
PHONE: (202) 483-7600
FAX: (202) 483-1840
E-MAIL: info@ceip.org
URL: http://www.ceip.org
PRESIDENT: Jessica Tuchman Mathews

WHAT IS ITS MISSION?

According to the organization's Web site, "the Carnegie Endowment for International Peace (CEIP) conducts programs of research, discussion, publication, and education that will increase understanding of international affairs and U.S. foreign policy." The organization is named for its founder, Andrew Carnegie, who endowed CEIP in the early 1900s. CEIP functions as a think tank on foreign policy and devotes time on innovative research and discussion building that addresses a broad range of foreign policy issues. CEIP research is then presented to policymakers to help them make better foreign policy decisions, with the goal of promoting peace.

HOW IS IT STRUCTURED?

CEIP is governed by a 19-member board of directors that serve three-year terms. Directors can be reelected indefinitely until age seventy. Board members come from a variety of backgrounds that complement CEIP's mission including: business, foreign policy, journalism, and government service. The board is responsible for appointing the organization president, who serves an indefinite term at the discretion of the board.

Functioning as the research arm of the CEIP, 35 associates carry out research both at the CEIP's office in Washington, D.C., and the Carnegie Moscow Center (CEIP's Moscow office) on topics including international affairs, global security, ethnicity, and global issues. The administrative staff at CEIP includes: a president and three vice presidents, Moscow Center employees, staff of the CEIP publication *Foreign Policy*, employees who work on specific CEIP programs, and other administrative personnel. The organization has no affiliates and no members.

PRIMARY FUNCTIONS

To carry out its mission, CEIP makes information on international peace available to policymakers and other interested parties. The organization creates ongoing research, which is presented in books, articles, and speeches. Research is carried out by staff and a group of associates, who have diverse backgrounds in law, business, journalism, and public affairs. The purpose of the research is to address the various aspects of international peace. For example, CEIP's 1998 publications covered topics such as: Russia-China relations, nuclear proliferation, Mexican economics, and post-Soviet Union status of arsenals and exports. Much of CEIP research is carried out under formal programs. In addition to publishing research, the organization publishes the quarterly journal *Foreign Policy*. According to CEIP, the journal is read regularly by government and business leaders, world leaders, and students of foreign policy.

The organization also organizes seminars, conferences, and meetings. These assemblies bring key people together to discuss timely issues. There are numerous such gatherings and they take place at a variety of locations around the world or at the CEIP's U.S. conference center, which is located at its Washington, D.C., office.

CEIP is not an activist organization in the traditional sense, that is, it carries out research activities rather than lobbying or testifying at congressional hearings. The views expressed in organizational research or publications have at times been counter to the position of governmental administrations, including the United States's. CEIP maintains its independence because it funds its own research, with additional assistance from private, philanthropic organizations.

PROGRAMS

Much of CEIP's research and discussion-building work is carried out under formal programs that are organized under various geographic and thematic concerns. The Russian and Eurasian Affairs Program, for example, has studied a range of issues including the economy of former Soviet Union countries after the disbanding of the Soviet Union, the state of relations between the United States and Russia, and security policy. One project of the program promoted nuclear nonproliferation in the former Soviet Union and in the United States. To accomplish this, organizers held a number of meetings, including an annual CEIP conference, where participants outlined ways to decrease nuclear proliferation through the use of controlling exports, setting norms, and cooperatively reducing threats.

CEIP's Politics of Economic Reform Program studies the connections that reforming countries have between political and economic arenas. The program creates a network of former policymakers and ministers from countries that have attempted economic market controls in the past in concert with political reform. Participants have hailed from Latin America, the former Soviet Union, and Africa. CEIP organizes these forums to generate ideas and information.

The Democracy Project was founded by CEIP in 1994 to study the effects and impacts of countries that were emerging democracies. The project has publicized findings on the topic, as well as hosted roundtables and study groups. For example, CEIP held a roundtable in mid-1998 that discussed court system reform efforts in Latin America. One publication, *Between Democracy and Personal Rule: The New African Leaders and the Reconstruction of the State*, published in fall 1998, looks at the authoritarian, dictatorial model of government that has been predominant in many African countries. The report shows the strengths and weaknesses of these regimes in contrast to democracy.

Carnegie Endowment's Junior Fellows Program offers job opportunities within the organization to selected graduating college seniors. Junior Fellows have the chance to work with CEIP associates on research or to assist the editorial staff of the *Foreign Policy* quarterly. Up to 12, one-year fellowships are offered annually.

BUDGET INFORMATION

For the fiscal year ending June 1997, CEIP had total revenue of $18,779,125 including $2,268,049 in contributions, gifts, and grants; $7,588 in investment interest; $4,360,829 in investment dividends; $11,518,583 in gain from sale of assets; and $624,076 in other income. Expenses totaled $11,041,356 and included $510,332 in compensation for officers and directors; $3,354,088 in salaries; $1,019,297 in employee benefits; $27,436 in legal fees; $76,068 in accounting fees; $1,481,007 in professional fees; $4,251 in taxes; $144,748 in depreciation; $2,310,734 in occupancy; $754,335 in travel and meetings; $625,709 in printing and publications; and $733,351 in other expenses. The organization had $219,653,283 in assets during fiscal year 1997.

HISTORY

CEIP was founded in 1910 with a gift from Andrew Carnegie. A Scotsman, he earned his wealth after establishing the successful Carnegie Steel Company in Pittsburgh, Pennsylvania. Carnegie believed that the rich had

BUDGET:

1997 CEIP Revenue

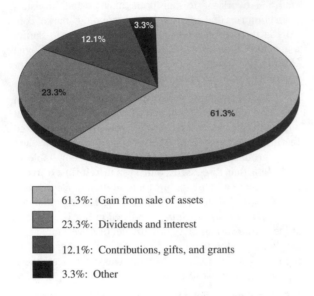

3.3%
12.1%
23.3%
61.3%

■ 61.3%: Gain from sale of assets

■ 23.3%: Dividends and interest

■ 12.1%: Contributions, gifts, and grants

■ 3.3%: Other

1997 CEIP Expenses

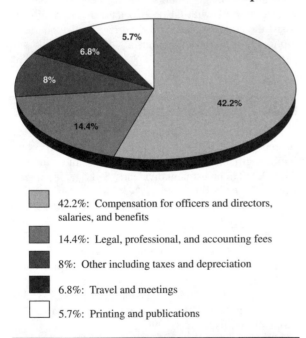

5.7%
6.8%
8%
42.2%
14.4%

■ 42.2%: Compensation for officers and directors, salaries, and benefits

■ 14.4%: Legal, professional, and accounting fees

■ 8%: Other including taxes and depreciation

■ 6.8%: Travel and meetings

□ 5.7%: Printing and publications

an obligation to use their wealth to benefit society. CEIP was only one of many philanthropic establishments and initiatives launched by Carnegie. The largest was the Carnegie Corporation of New York, established with an endowment in the early 1900s of $135,000,000.

Toward the end of his life, Carnegie became convinced that war caused many problems and he wanted to create opportunities to foster peace. For example, he built the Hague Peace Palace in the Netherlands—a location that provides and facilitates arbitration of international issues. But when World War I (1914-18) broke out, Carnegie became discouraged that the war he had tried to prevent had become a reality and retired from public service. He died in 1919.

After Carnegie's death, CEIP continued to evolve as a foreign policy think tank, addressing timely world issues by publishing new research findings and facilitating discussion opportunities among key decision makers. As an organization focused on promoting international peace, CEIP became concerned during the 1950s through the 1970s with nuclear proliferation among Communist countries, such as the Soviet Union, East Germany, and China. Little was known at that time about the status of arms in these countries by outside governments. Additionally, CEIP was concerned about the escalating nuclear arms race between the United States and the Soviet Union.

In 1970, the organization created *Foreign Policy*, its quarterly journal, and in 1992, it won a MediaGuide Award for being one of the most influential publications in the United States. The journal has been praised for its new and cutting-edge perspectives. It has a self-admitted antiestablishment voice when it outlines findings or initiatives that are not aligned with the policies of the United States.

The collapse of the Soviet Union in the 1980s brought an end to the Cold War and a new set of challenges to those involved in the nuclear nonproliferation movement. This historic event meant that the United States and Moscow were no longer pursuing an arms race, and CEIP pursued initiatives to bring an end to or slow nuclear proliferation worldwide. One result of the organization's initiatives, the Comprehensive Test Ban Treaty, was accepted by President Bill Clinton in 1997 and expected to be enacted by September 1998. At a 1997 annual CEIP conference, one keynote speaker likened the treaty as the key to an international structure and set of norms that would, on the international scale, prevent the spread of nuclear, chemical, and biological weapons, according to *U.S. Newswire,* June 9, 1997.

On the other hand, the organization feared that the relaxation of barriers in the former Soviet Union also made the possibilities for nuclear weapons technology and smuggling easier than it had been in the past. CEIP also realized that although Russia was now more willing to cooperate with nonproliferation efforts, other independent states of the former Soviet bloc were pursuing nuclear technology that previously had been difficult to access.

CEIP established its Carnegie Moscow Center in 1993, for the purpose of fostering intellectual collaboration and working relationships between foreign policy specialists in Russia, other post-Soviet states, and the

BIOGRAPHY:

Andrew Carnegie

Industrialist; Philanthropist (1835–1919) For most of his life, Andrew Carnegie's position and stature was a product of the immense amount of money he earned; but it was the immense amount of money that he *gave away* in the last part of his life that secured for him widespread adoration and an enduring legacy. The son of poor Scottish immigrants, Carnegie spent his early teens working long, hard hours in factories while at the same time attending night school. He bought $600 worth of stock at age 21 and, upon the arrival of his first dividend check, legend has it that Carnegie's prophetic response was, "Here's the goose that lays the golden eggs." Both his fortune and interest in other companies multiplied until he cashed-out at the turn of the century. In a deal constructed by investment banker J. P. Morgan, Carnegie realized more than $300 million from the sale of his company, Carnegie Steel. Believing that wealthy men should use their money to advance society, Carnegie set a standard that may never

be matched. He systematically funded more than $50 million to build 2,800 public libraries. Of the estimated $350 million he donated over his lifetime, the largest single chunk, $125 million, was used in 1911 to endow the Carnegie Corporation of New York. The corporation was charged solely with advancing knowledge through the pro-

motion of schools, libraries, research, and publication. Perhaps his most noteworthy accomplishment is that he combined his acquired business-world knowledge with his philanthropic objectives: Andrew Carnegie did not only spend his money generously, but wisely.

United States. Collaborators have included intellectuals, government officials, academics, journalists, and private-sector leaders. The Moscow Center continues to provide the means for such collaboration by functioning like its U.S. counterpart—providing forums and workshops for discussion, encouraging research, publishing findings, and maintaining open international relationships with involved policymakers.

Although nuclear nonproliferation continued to be a concern of the organization, the consistent warfare and humanitarian crises of the 1990s forced the organization to look at the huge displacement of people that occurred during these upheavals. Several research reports were published in the 1990s that addressed issues of human displacement. Report topics included: streamlining the intake of immigrants in the United States, Europe's difficulty in establishing consistent immigration and asylum policy among European countries, and the United States' lack of a cohesive immigrant policy.

During the 1990s, CEIP focused on additional issues such as global warming and organized crime that it felt needed to be addressed on a worldwide basis. The CEIP continued to study world trends that impacted peace—such as the ongoing hostility between Arab and Israeli nations and the previous collapse of the Soviet Union. For example, CEIP published a report in 1998 that studied the impact of a new working relationship between Russia and Communist China. The organization also researched the Ukraine's role and direction as a newly

independent country. Additionally, CEIP tracked world economic trends including: the 1994 Mexico economic collapse; the possibilities for economic reform in Latin American countries by promotion of stronger banking systems; and the role of the United States in offering economic assistance to other countries.

CURRENT POLITICAL ISSUES

As an organization whose main function is to foster research and discussion of issues that relate to world peace, CEIP does not lobby or take other direct action on particular policies in the manner that many special-interest groups do. The organization does, however, focus its research and other activities on areas it considers important. Among these critical topics are nuclear proliferation and the African continent.

CEIP is concerned with global issues—or challenges that are so large that they cannot effectively be dealt with on a national or regional scale. Examples include: environmental issues such as global warming; infectious diseases; international-organized crime; migration; and refugees. According to CEIP, governments are generally ill-equipped to respond to global problems and often do so in a haphazard fashion with no provisions for sharing results. CEIP seeks to facilitate study and learning across borders.

Post-Cold War Nuclear Proliferation

CEIP does much work in the area of nuclear non-proliferation, or the prevention of the spread of nuclear weapons technology. The end of the Cold War signaled a change in nuclear arms strategy around the world as the United States and the former Soviet Union were no longer locked in an arms race. However, CEIP believes that proliferation issues are still vital. While Russia and other former Soviet states now participate in an international agreement to limit arms proliferation, other nations may continue to develop their own arsenals, or receive smuggled weapons across the newly opened borders of former communist countries. CEIP's nonproliferation program tracks the status of this issue around the globe and produces publications such as *Tracking Nuclear Proliferation, 1998*, which outlines proliferation initiatives around the world. The CEIP program also hosts an annual, international nonproliferation conference and sets up discussion roundtables. The group facilitates the flow of up-to-date information by organizing press briefings and distributing regular briefs and updates to a community of experts in the field.

Africa

CEIP devotes a large amount of time and resources to monitoring governmental and policy trends in Africa. According to the organization, the objections of non-African governments, such as the United States, to apartheid in South Africa led to a worldwide withdrawal of resources and interest in the African continent. African foreign policy, according to CEIP, took a low priority to other international issues. In the United States, this led to the American people receiving little information about African policy other than what the media provided.

To create an environment in which the United States could pursue more constructive relations with African nations, the CEIP began an African Policy Initiative in the late 1990s. The initiative launched a National Summit on Africa to promote policy discussion among interested stakeholders—the summit included several regional gatherings and ended with a national summit in late 1999. In addition to public education goals, the initiative also published studies on African policy to help policymakers and leaders make informed decisions about African foreign policy.

FUTURE DIRECTIONS

In CEIP President Jessica T. Mathew's inaugural address in mid-1997, she pointed out that the roles of Nongovernmental Organizations (NGOs) such as CEIP have greatly changed in the late twentieth century. NGOs have taken on much expanded roles, said Mathews, citing the Canadian- and NGO-backed attempt to pursue a global nuclear ban despite opposition by members of the United Nations. Mathews urged CEIP to be prepared to take risks and to respond to a myriad of situations, while still keeping its traditional, nonadvocacy stance on issues.

GROUP RESOURCES

CEIP's on-line library at http://ceip.org/library/library.htm features 8,500 works relating to foreign affairs and includes two hundred periodical subscriptions. An interlibrary loan feature is available for other libraries. Hard copy reports of CEIP research or publications are available by contacting the organization by mailing 1779 Massachusetts Ave. NW, Washington, DC 20036-2103; by telephone at (202) 483-7600; by fax at (202) 483-1840; or by E-mail at info@ceip.org.

GROUP PUBLICATIONS

CEIP publishes the quarterly magazine *Foreign Policy*, which can be viewed in entirety at its Web site at http://www.foreignpolicy.com or ordered by contacting the organization. CEIP publishes research and reports that are available from the Brookings Institute Press; call 1-800-275-1447 for information. Some of these include: *Changing Our Ways: America and the New World* (Carnegie Endowment National Commission on America and the New World, 1992) and *The Price of Peace: Emergency Economic Intervention and U.S. Foreign Policy* (Rothkopf, David J., 1998). Abstracts of publication are located on-line at http://ceip.org/pubs/pubs.htm. To order these publications, contact CEIP by mail at 1779 Massachusetts Ave. NW, Washington, DC 20036-2103; by phone at (202) 483-7600; by fax at (202) 483-1840; or by E-mail at info@ceip.org.

BIBLIOGRAPHY

Abiola, Hafsat. "U.S. Must Help Restore Democracy in Nigeria." *Star Tribune,* 7 November 1996.

Beinart, Peter. "Learning to Live with Nuclear Weapons—Again: The Return of the Bomb." *The New Republic,* 3 August 1998.

Blank, Stephen. "Russia: The Once and Future Hegemon?" *The World & I,* 1 November 1997.

Graff/Davos, James L. "Business: A Global Warning Brace the World Economy Now, Urges TIME's Board of Economists, Before More East Asian Fallout Slams Shut the Window of Opportunity." *TIME International,* 16 February 1998.

Guardiano, John R. "The Politics of Foreign Aid." *The World & I,* 1 May 1995.

Mann, Paul. "Russian Armory Remains Huge." *Aviation Week & Space*, 7 September 1998.

Manning, Robert A. "The Nuclear Age: The Next Chapter." *Foreign Policy,* 1 December 1997.

Marshall, Tyler. "Mutual Loyalty Helps Clinton's 'ABC' Team Tackle ABCs of Foreign Policy; Diplomacy: Secretaries of State and Defense Consult Each Other and National Security Advisor Far More than Many in Past." *Los Angeles Times,* 1 March 1998.

Miller, Judith. "Promotion of Democracy Losing its Charm." *Star Tribune,* 3 March 1996.

Shevtsova, Lilia, and Scott A. Bruckner. "Russian Instability; Heading for Crisis?" *Current,* 1 May 1997

Vesley, Milan. "SA Nuclear Power Worries U. S." *African Business*, July/August 1998.

Center for Defense Information (CDI)

ESTABLISHED: April 1, 1972
EMPLOYEES: 25
MEMBERS: None
PAC: None

Contact Information:

ADDRESS: 1779 Massachusetts Ave. NW
   Washington, DC 20036
PHONE: (202) 332-0600
TOLL FREE: (800) 234-3334
FAX: (202) 462-4559
E-MAIL: info@cdi.org
URL: http://www.cdi.org
PRESIDENT: Rear Adm. Gene R. LaRocque

WHAT IS ITS MISSION?

According to its monthly newsletter, *The Defense Monitor*, "The Center for Defense Information (CDI) believes that strong social, economic, political, and military components and a healthy environment contribute equally to the nation's security. CDI opposes excessive expenditures for weapons and policies that increase the danger of war." As part of its mission to raise public awareness, CDI acts as an independent monitor of the military and defense establishment, collecting and analyzing information, and distributing it to Congress, the media, and the public at large. In line with the organization's focus on military issues, CDI has historically been led by retired senior military officers.

HOW IS IT STRUCTURED?

Headquartered in Washington, D.C., CDI is a nonprofit organization headed by senior retired military officers. These officers draw on their professional experience and knowledge to direct the activities of the center's staff, which includes military and civilian researchers, analysts, TV and radio personnel, an administrative staff, librarian, and assistant librarian. CDI is not a membership organization.

As a nonprofit entity, the center is required by law to have a board of directors and a president, who is the official legal head of the corporation, CDI, Inc. These officers establish general center policy and broadly oversee administration and finances. In addition, CDI has a director who runs the center's activities on a day-to-day basis, with advice from the president and board. An important responsibility of the director is overseeing the development of material for center publications, TV programs, and radio shows.

CDI is divided into three departments. The Administrative Department is responsible for finance, public relations, and general administration and is headed by a director of administrative services. The Research Department is staffed by retired senior military officers and civilians with extensive experience in military analysis. The center's extensive library on military matters is part of the Research Department. The Television and Radio Department produces, edits, and distributes the center's television and radio programming.

CDI's board of advisers is composed of approximately 35 individuals who have made sizable financial contributions to the center. They include former members of the military, corporate executives, and individuals from the arts community. This board does not exert any direct control over the center; they do, however, provide regular advice and suggestions. Center officials meet with members of the board of advisers at least once a year.

The Military Advisory Committee (MAC) is composed of about one hundred retired military personnel who support CDI's goals. MAC members usually first approach CDI and express an interest in the center. CDI then invites those individuals whose point of view is sympathetic to the general principles of CDI to join the MAC.

PRIMARY FUNCTIONS

CDI considers itself to be primarily an educational institution. Its most important function is the research and analysis of topics related to national defense, including the U.S. defense budget, military policy, weapons systems, and nuclear testing. All of the center's data is collected from unclassified sources such as Pentagon press releases, government reports, congressional hearings, and the news media. The findings of the research staff form the basis for all the center's publications, media broadcasts, and public presentations, and are distributed to the media, members of Congress, and the general public.

The most important channels through which CDI publicizes information are its newsletter, *The Defense Monitor*, its television series, *America's Defense Monitor*, and its weekly radio show, *Question of the Week*. In addition, the center publishes two electronic journals on its Web site: *Weekly Defense Monitor* and *Russia Weekly*. The center maintains a media service and speaker's bureau whose members make presentations to interested groups.

All CDI publications and broadcast materials are produced in-house at the CDI offices in Washington, D.C. Facilities are available there for video and radio production editing and distribution. *The Defense Monitor* is sent to everyone who contributes $35 or more to

the center. CDI television programming is distributed free-of-charge to stations across the United States. Approximately 65 Public Broadcasting System stations carry *America's Defense Monitor* on a weekly basis; others broadcast the show on an occasional basis, depending on the particular issue covered or their other particular programming needs. The show has a relatively high profile on cable television. It is shown regularly on the Military Channel and, because it is free, it is carried on a great deal of community cable stations as well. The center sells videos of past shows for a nominal fee for use in college courses or by interested organizations. The center's weekly radio show, *Question of the Week*, is also distributed free-of-charge to public and private radio stations.

Because of its particular nonprofit status, the Center for Defense Information is prohibited from lobbying Congress. Its political impact comes exclusively from the quality of its information and from the ability of the center to reach policymakers via their publications and broadcasts and to motivate the American public to make their concerns known to their individual congressmen.

PROGRAMS

One of the most notable of CDI's initiatives is its internship program. Three times per year, it offers internships to qualified college undergraduate and graduate students. While at CDI headquarters in Washington, interns work full-time at the center and receive hands-on experience in research, computers, and television production. Research interns conduct research for *The Defense Monitor* and other publications, and may at times also write articles. Interns with computer skills help maintain the center's databases and Web site, assist the staff with computer questions, and troubleshoot problems. Television interns learn the full TV production process: editing, interviewing, shooting a show, and distributing videotapes. Internships are paid, although interns may also elect to work part-time without compensation.

BUDGET INFORMATION

CDI has an annual budget of $1.8 million. Funding for the center comes from three sources, including from past contributors, who account for less than half of CDI's total support. Large public foundations, such as the MacArthur Foundation and the Carnegie Foundation, provide another important source of funding. The third source of financing comes from members of CDI's board of advisers, some of whom make contributions of over $100,000 per year.

FAST FACTS

The 1999 proposed U.S. defense budget, which totaled $271 billion, was four times larger than that of the world's next largest spender, Russia.

(Source: Center for Defense Information. "Last of the Big Time Spenders," 1999.)

HISTORY

The Center for Defense Intelligence was founded by Rear Admiral Gene R. LaRocque on April 1, 1972. According to CDI's Deputy Director Eugene Carroll, the CDI "arose in response to the tragic, abortive U.S. action in Vietnam and the costly, dangerous arms race with the USSR." In May of the same year CDI released the first issue of its leading publication, *The Defense Monitor*.

The early days at CDI were difficult ones for Admiral LaRocque. His critical stance toward the U.S. defense establishment won him the enmity of other officers, former colleagues, defense contractors, and the conservative establishment in general. The military, in particular, treated him as something of a traitor. At one point during the mid-1970s several hundred retired admirals took out an ad in the *Washington Times* attacking CDI and Admiral LaRocque. According to Admiral Carroll, *Readers Digest* on occasion portrayed the center as a group of Communist sympathizers.

Undaunted, the center persevered in its independent criticism of the nuclear arms race and military spending. Throughout the 1970s and 1980s it sponsored a number of conferences to study and publicize important issues. Among the most significant were the First Nuclear War Conference held in December 1978 in Washington, D.C.; the Conference on Nuclear War in Europe held in May 1981 in Groningen, the Netherlands; and the National Women's Conference to Prevent Nuclear War that took place in September of 1984 in Washington, D.C.

In 1976 CDI became one of the first organizations to advocate the conclusion of the Panama Canal Treaty. The center worked hard to support the treaty's ratification. Admiral LaRocque met with President Jimmy Carter personally to discuss transfer of the canal to the Republic of Panama.

Between 1987 and 1989 CDI sponsored three historical conferences of retired U.S. and Soviet generals and admirals. Two were held in Washington, D.C., one

in Moscow. Part of the results of the conferences was the release of a statement from the U.S. and Soviet participants calling for an end to development and testing of nuclear weapons by both superpowers and advocating cooperation between the United States and the United Soviet Socialist Republic (USSR) in preventing the spread of nuclear weapons to the rest of the world. The 1980s also saw an increase in CDI's media offerings. In August 1986 the center produced the first edition of "Question of the Week," its weekly radio show. Six months later, in March of 1987, the first installment of its TV series, *America's Defense Monitor,* was produced. By August 1998 CDI had broadcast 602 radio commentaries and 266 TV films.

The collapse of the USSR changed CDI's focus to a degree. The center was able to reinforce the beliefs its members had always proposed: that the defense problem in the United States was not the USSR and it was not lack of American military strength. The problem, CDI continued to maintain, was that the nation needed to find a new approach to security, and it began to stress the economic health of the country, environmental factors, social well-being, and education. The organization now addresses the broader issues of quality of life and stability in the United States.

CURRENT POLITICAL ISSUES

Since its founding CDI has been outspoken about a wide range of issues relating to the military, including: wasteful defense spending, a ban on nuclear testing, the Panama Canal Treaty, scrapping the B2 bomber, strengthening the United Nations, doing away with the land mines that still pose a hazard in former war zones, and the problem of child soldiers throughout the world. Most concerns relate to the relationship between the U.S. military and the rest of the world, although CDI has also been critical of the effect the military has on Americans themselves. A specific case was the center's work publicizing the U.S. military's role as the nation's major polluter.

Case Study: U.S. Military Polluters

In mid-1989 CDI published its first report on the harm the U.S. military had done to the environment. That issue of *The Defense Monitor* was titled "Defending the Environment? The Record of the U.S. Military." The *Monitor* summed up the problem: "The pursuit of military power has gravely undermined another element of overall security: the sound, healthy environment necessary to sustain life on this planet." It went on to document a history of military environmental neglect. And while a few of the cases CDI cited took place at bases overseas, most of them were located in the United States.

Over the years, in different issues of *The Defense Monitor* and on its television program, CDI described the full range of environmental problems attributed to the military; radioactive waste from bomb production; dismantled nuclear weapons; irresponsible transport of nuclear waste and biological weapons; aging stores of biological and chemical weapons; electronic pollution caused by electromagnetic systems designed to defend military communications; and bases so contaminated they could not be converted to civilian use. The center further revealed that the majority of U.S. military facilities did not meet state and federal waste control requirements. By the beginning of the 1990s CDI predicted the cost of clean-up as in excess of $150 billion.

By the mid-1990s CDI reported that a fundamental shift in attitude had taken place. The Defense Department had begun work on many contaminated sites and had identified new ones as well. In all, by 1994 the Defense Department had spent about $7.9 billion cleaning up contamination and had actually completed work on 571 sites. Nonetheless, CDI criticized the government for not attacking the problem with more determination. Congress, the center reported, was concerned that cleanup was proceeding too slowly and that funds were being wasted. In 1995 Congress cut the funds available to the Defense Department for clean-up. Meanwhile the cost, based on some estimates, had grown to $200 billion.

Public Impact

According to CDI, the U.S. military's pollution has been accumulating for more than 40 years, and has already begun to threaten communities. McClellan Air Force Base, located in Sacramento, California, is just one case the organization publicized. At McClellan the military so contaminated the ground water with discarded solvents that it had to provide the local communities with safe drinking water from another source. Nuclear bomb production facilities like Fernald, near Cincinnati, Ohio, released half a million pounds of radioactive and chemical wastes into the environment; the Hanford facilities in the state of Washington released 200 billion gallons. And, according to CDI, the 40-acre Rocky Mountain Arsenal nerve gas production facility is the most polluted square mile on earth; although the pollution around the site was noted as early as 1951 no clean-up was begun until 1988.

Despite the danger posed by radioactive and chemical waste and biological weapons, the U.S. military was able to hide its pollution throughout most of the twentieth century. Its bases and production facilities were restricted; its records were classified. Toxic waste was routinely shipped in unmarked trucks on public highways; the Army shipped deadly germ warfare samples through the U.S. mails. By the 1990s, however, partly due to CDI's efforts to draw public attention to the issue, the military was forced legislatively to become more responsible and began to take tentative steps to remedy this serious problem.

A crater, possibly containing radioactive contamination, was formed by a 1960s nuclear test at the Nevada Test Site in Mercury, Nevada. The Center for Defense Information seeks to educate and increase public awareness about nuclear testing and its effects. (Photograph by Lennox McLendon, AP/Wide World Photo)

FUTURE DIRECTIONS

CDI predicts a number of organizational and policy challenges in the coming years. Within the organization itself, there has been a growing willingness to bring civilians into leadership positions that have been traditionally military. One reason has been a desire by the CDI board to sharpen its political message, directing it more forcefully at policymakers, and giving the center a new level of influence.

Working toward strengthening the United Nation's role in world politics will be a major issue for CDI after 2000. The center believes that, before the next quarter- to half-century have passed, the United States must give up its role as the world's policeman and become a more cooperative member of the community of nations. If the U.S. government does not make this realization, CDI maintains the continuation of the status quo will hurt the nation, economically, socially, and environmentally.

GROUP RESOURCES

CDI has the most comprehensive library on military affairs outside of the Pentagon. The library contains the complete text of military-related congressional hearings and reports from the Government Accounting Office, the Central Intelligence Agency, the Congressional Budget Office, the Pentagon, and the White House. The center's collection also includes other valuable material on video-cassette, including material films, network television programs, interviews with military officers and analysts, and important congressional debates. It is open to the public 9:00 A.M. to 5:00 P.M. Monday through Friday, excluding holidays.

CDI's television series, *America's Defense Monitor*, which presents "critical information on the military's impact on the political system, the economy, the environment, and society as a whole," is featured on PBS and many cable stations. The half-hour programs are also available on video, accompanied by related issues of *The Defense Monitor* and other study aids. A catalog of videos can be obtained by writing to: Center for Defense Information, 1779 Massachusetts Ave. NW, Washington, DC 20036, or by calling 1-800-234-3334. *Question of the Week,* CDI's two-minute radio commentary, assesses national security issues. It airs on public and college radio stations throughout the country.

The CDI Web site located at http://www.cdi.org contains a wealth of information, including electronic versions of *The Defense Monitor*, transcripts of radio commentaries, issue papers, TV transcripts, editorials, and the comprehensive Conventional Arms Trade database.

CDI will provide speakers for groups interested in defense or national security issues. To arrange for a CDI expert to give a talk, contact the CDI Media Office at (202) 332-0600, ext. 111. The Media Office will also arrange interviews with CDI specialists and can supply copies of background information and reports.

Information on the CDI Internship Program can be obtained by writing to the Intern Coordinator, Center for Defense Information, 1779 Massachusetts Ave. NW, Washington, DC 20036. Applicants are required to submit a resume with cover letter, a transcript of all college-level courses, two letters of recommendation, and a three-to-five-page writing sample. Internships are available from January to May, from June to August, and from September to December.

GROUP PUBLICATIONS

The Defense Monitor is CDI's most influential publication. For over 25 years it has provided valuable information about military programs and helped focus the attention of both the public and government officials on critical military issues which might otherwise have remained unknown. A subscription to the *Monitor* is available for a contribution of $35 or more. A sample copy can be obtained for $1.

CDI also has two electronic publications available exclusively on its Web site. *Weekly Defense Monitor* is composed of short articles on military affairs and foreign policy. *Russia Weekly* examines important political, social, and military events in Russia. All publications may be obtained by writing Center for Defense Information, 1779 Massachusetts Ave. NW, Washington, DC 20036, or by calling 1-800-234-3334.

BIBLIOGRAPHY

Carroll, Eugene J., Jr. "NATO Expansion Would Be an Epic 'Fateful Error.'" *Los Angeles Times*, 7 July 1997.

————. "Pentagon Pursues Implausible Scenario." *Newsday*, 22 May 1997.

"The Fiscal 1999 Military Budget." *The Defense Monitor*, vol. XXVII, no. 4.

Isenberg, David. "U.S. Lauds, but Thwarts, Diana's Call for Mine Ban." *Christian Science Monitor*, September 1997.

"The Military and the Environment." *The Defense Monitor*, vol. XXIII, no. 9.

Schoch, Deborah. "No Desirable Options for Cleaning Underground Toxic Plume; Pollution." *Los Angeles Times*, 23 August 1996.

"The Stealth Bomber: Just Say No." *The Defense Monitor*, vol. XIX, no. 9.

Center for Responsive Politics (CRP)

WHAT IS ITS MISSION?

According to the Center for Responsive Politics (CRP), the organization is "a non-partisan, non-profit research group based in Washington D.C. that specializes in the study of Congress and particularly the role that money plays in its elections and actions. The Center conducts computer-based research on campaign finance issues for the news media, academics, activists, and other interested observers of Congress. The Centers' work is aimed at creating a more involved citizenry and a more responsive Congress." Essentially the CRP is a congressional watchdog group, monitoring Congress to make certain its members are acting in the best interest of the nation.

ESTABLISHED: 1983
EMPLOYEES: 14
PAC: None

Contact Information:
ADDRESS: 1320 19th St. NW
    Ste. 620
    Washington, DC 20036
PHONE: (202) 857-0044
FAX: (202) 857-7809
E-MAIL: info@crp.org
URL: http://www.crp.org
EXECUTIVE DIRECTOR: Larry Makinson
CHAIRMAN: Paul S. Hoff

HOW IS IT STRUCTURED?

The nonprofit CRP is based in Washington, DC. An executive director manages the organization's day-to-day operations and is selected by the nine- to ten-member board of directors. The board, led by a chairman, works with the executive director to decide upon the policy and direction of the CRP. In addition to the executive director and the board of directors, the CRP employees 14 staff people in the following positions: deputy director, research director, communications director, IT director, office manager, state database programmer, administrative assistant, webmaster, and six researchers. The CRP has no membership.

FAST FACTS

In the 1996 campaign, 92 percent of House and 88 percent of Senate races were won by candidates that spent the most money.

(Source: Ronald D. Elving. *Congressional Quarterly Weekly Report*, November 29, 1997.)

PRIMARY FUNCTIONS

The CRP's primary activity is the research and publication of reports on the effect of money in American politics. It researches the information that the Federal Election Commission (FEC) amasses on financial contributions to candidates, political parties, and political action committees (PACs). For instance, the CRP's *The Big Picture* is a thorough accounting of congressional contributions in the 1995–96 election cycle. *The Big Picture* tracks how much money political action committees gave to Congress and catalogues how much certain Senators and Representatives received from private industry. *The Big Picture* also included the list of the top 100 contributors to political candidates or political parties.

The CRP makes its research on the records of the millions of campaign and lobbying dollars spent on congressional officeholders and candidates available and accessible to the public through both print and electronic products. The organization encourages voting citizens to examine which special interests may have a hand in deciding which way congressional or presidential candidates may vote. The CRP also acts as an information source for the news media, activist groups, and similar institutions in an effort to expand public awareness of campaign finance and its impact on the legislative process. Occasionally the CRP's reports will be used as testimony in congressional hearings as well.

PROGRAMS

The CRP maintains various programs to achieve its goals. One of these is its Outreach Program. The Outreach Program consists of conferences and seminars created for the media and for various nonprofit organizations. These seminars instruct attendees on the finer points of research techniques.

The Cashing In Project is a program that attempts to expose money-for-influence transactions. The Cashing In Project's staff closely examines government documents, voting records, and other transactions to find evidence of PAC, corporate, and special interest money's influence on Capitol Hill and federal agencies. What makes this program unique is the speed of the reports. These findings are distributed to the public through weekly news releases, radio spots and media reports.

FEC Watch assesses the activities of the Federal Election Commission (FEC), the federal agency that monitors financial behavior of candidates in elections nationwide. FEC Watch checks the FEC's work for errors and oversights. Through Internet research and disclosure reports, FEC Watch looks for any improper activity by legislators. The FEC Watch also tracks the outcomes of lawsuits that affect campaign finance and analyzes campaign finance law.

Another CRP initiative is the Open Secrets Project. The Open Secrets Project uses computer-aided research to follow 200,000 PAC contributions and 800,00 individual contributions. This information is available to any interested parties, who may use the information to monitor patterns and trends that may exist between contributors' agendas and the campaigns to which they give. The Open Secrets Project's findings are available in its supplemental publication, *The Big Picture*.

BUDGET INFORMATION

The CRP has a small payroll with 14 staff members; substantial work is accomplished by interns who may receive a small stipend or may work for free. The CRP annual budget is nearly $1.5 million. The great majority of its funding comes from grants from nonprofit organizations and foundations such as the Carnegie Corporation and the Florence and John Schumann Foundation.

In 1996 the center spent over $600,000 on its program services. Approximately $200,000 of this was spent on consultants' fees. Nearly $6,000 was spent on fundraising and almost $30,000 was spent on general management. A significant portion of the center's budget is spent maintaining and upgrading its extensive computer database.

HISTORY

The CRP was created in 1983 by former senators Frank Church (D-Idaho) and Hugh Scott (R-Penn.) as a nonprofit, nonpartisan attempt to improve the quality of the American political system, examine its problems, and explore possibilities for change. Initially the CRP languished in relative obscurity. However, it was in the mid to late 1980s that the organization developed and refined its research methods to identify the ways in which money affected politics. Soon, the two-person CRP staff gradually grew and so with it its resources and exposure.

The 1990s marked a time of increased public recognition. Acknowledgment of CRP work came in 1991 when Common Cause, another group dedicated to political change, honored CRP's former executive director Kent Cooper with its esteemed Public Service Award. The CRP quickly became a recognized leader in the political scene, but it remained an exclusive organization working primarily with journalists and activists. The organization launched its newsletter, *Capital Eye* in May of 1994, in an attempt to make the results of the organization's research, watchdog, and monitoring activities accessible to all interested individuals.

The battle over campaign finance reform brought even greater visibility to the CRP's work. Although the CRP was involved with the issue for years, public outrage over the huge sums of money spent on political campaigns became louder after the election of 1996. There were allegations of improper fund-raising by the administration of President Bill Clinton after his successful campaign for reelection. The CRP came to the forefront of a burgeoning campaign finance reform movement and its research was frequently the primary source for information on the effect of money on politics.

CURRENT POLITICAL ISSUES

One particular facet of CRP's investigations of campaign finance revolves around "soft money." Campaign finance law limits the amount of money candidates may receive from individuals to $1,000 per election cycle. However there is no limit to the amount of money political parties may give to candidates. Instead of limiting their contribution by giving to individuals, donors instead give to the party, which has no limits imposed on gifts. These contributions are known as soft money and are essentially a circumvention of campaign finance laws. Although both parties used soft money, the administration of President Bill Clinton was particularly criticized in its use of the process. The CRP has worked to reveal the sources of soft money and lobbied to firm up laws regarding this type of contribution.

Campaign donations may take more subtle forms. Donations may be steered to nonprofit organizations rather than specific candidates. These groups, while they do not specifically endorse or denounce candidates, run advertising campaigns promoting causes or issues that may be central to a particular campaign. These causes can easily be linked to candidates who support those issues and causes. There is no limit to the amount spent on this advertising. These organizations are therefore able to contribute significantly more than the $1,000 individual donation limit. Such practices are known as "issue ads."

The CRP also investigates groups set up specifically to help individuals donate as much money to candidates as possible, sometimes skirting campaign finance rules. These organizations help match contributors' money to PACs which in turn pass it on to particular candidates. This is within the bounds of the law as long as money given to PACs for specific candidates is counted as part of an individual's $1,000 limit. Occasionally however, groups attempt to not declare the intent of this money. In 1997 the CRP investigated the activities of one such group, the Triad Management Services.

Case Study: The CRP v. Triad Management Services

During the 1996 election cycle, Triad Management Services assisted the Faith, Family, and Freedom PAC, formed by Representative David McIntosh (R-Ind.), in finding individuals interested in making donations to politically conservative candidates. It produced a video about the PAC and sent it to several wealthy donors in the hope of convincing them to donate money. Many did, as Faith, Family, and Freedom contributed $61,500 to 52 conservative candidates in 1995 and 1996.

The CRP and its publication *Capital Eye* turned up some interesting facts when it analyzed the FEC records of the 1996 election cycle. It found 41 instances in which people who donated the maximum $1,000 to a particular candidate also had the money they donated to Faith, Family, and Freedom donated to that same candidate. While it is possible that this was merely coincidence, the CRP alleged that Triad helped to match these donors to McIntosh's PAC so that individuals could earmark their money for particular candidates. If this was true, campaign finance laws had been violated.

In addition to this charge, the CRP also stated that Triad's use of issue ads may also have been in violation of campaign finance law. Triad used two nonprofit organizations, the Citizens for Reform and the Citizens for the Republic Education Fund, to affect the outcome of elections in favor of Republican candidates. The CRP alleged that Triad coordinated its efforts with the Republican Party and the nonprofit groups in an effort to produce advertisements for particular candidates. As it is illegal for political parties and their candidates to direct nonprofit groups in their actions, including campaign advertising, the CRP accused Triad of again circumventing campaign finance laws.

In 1996–97, the Senate's Governmental Affairs Committee, led by Senator Fred Thompson (R-Tenn.), held hearings that investigated Triad Management Services while examining the allegations of campaign fundraising abuses by the Clinton administration. Senator Thompson's committee investigated Triad and considered reports from groups like the CRP but was unable to uncover enough concrete evidence of wrongdoing. As a result of its investigations, the committee made recommendations to the Senate about changes to campaign finance law reform, however no direct legislative changes have been made as a result of these recommendations. Triad Management Services disregarded the statements made by the CRP in questioning the legality of their actions, stating that it had stayed within the bounds of campaign finance law.

GROUP RESOURCES

The CRP maintains the National Library on Money and Politics. The library acts as an information source for the press, schools, activists, and other groups interested in campaign finance. It has created and continues to build upon an extensive computer database that tracks parallels between congressional voting records and the monetary backing of these elected officials.

The CRP Web site can be accessed via the World Wide Web at http://www.opensecrets.org. The Web site contains a wealth of current information on the CRP's various programs and on issues relating to money in politics. Persons interested in finding out more about the CRP or its library may call the organization at (202) 857-0044 or write to the Center for Responsive Politics, 1320 19th St. NW, Ste. 620, Washington, DC 20036.

GROUP PUBLICATIONS

The CRP's bimonthly newsletter *Capital Eye* is a comprehensive update of campaign finance and money-in-government issues. Recent issues may be viewed via the World Wide Web at http://www.opensecrets.org/ newsletter. The findings of the Open Secrets Project, *Open Secrets*, may be found at some public and university libraries across the country. The CRP reports on

issues ranging from soft money contributions to critiques of the FEC may be found on the CRP's Web site at http://www.opensecrets.org/pubs/index.htm. Information on obtaining any of the organization's publications can be had by writing to the Center for Responsive Politics, 1320 19th St. NW, Ste. 620, Washington, DC 20036 or by calling (202) 857-0044.

BIBLIOGRAPHY

Apple, R.W. "Money, Politics, and Its Suckers." *New York Times*, 9 February 1997.

"Corporations, Not Citizens, Dominate Political Giving." *Tribune News Service*, 18 October 1996.

Elving, Ronald D. "New Study Confirms Big Jump in Campaign Spending." *Congressional Quarterly Report*, 29 November 1997.

Grann, David, and Erica Niedowski. "The Dirty Hill." *New Republic*, 7 April 1997.

"Kindness of Strangers: Congressional Races Fueled Largely By Out-of-State Money." *Barron's*, 28 October 1996.

Makinson, Larry. *Money and Politics: The Price of Admission: An Illustrated Atlas of Campaign Spending in the 1988 Congressional Elections*, Washington, D.C.: The Center for Responsive Politics, 1989.

————. *The Price of Admission: Campaign Spending in The 1990 Elections*, Washington, D.C.: The Center for Responsive Politics, 1991.

"Money and Politics: How Money Impacts Our Political System." *Spectrum: The Journal of State Government*, Summer 1997.

Novak, Viveca, and Michael Weisskopf. "The Secret GOP Campaign." *Time*, 3 November 1997.

Schram, Martin. *Speaking Freely: Former Members of Congress Talk About Money and Politics*. Washington, D.C.: The Center for Responsive Politics, 1995.

Center for Strategic and International Studies (CSIS)

WHAT IS ITS MISSION?

The mission of the Center for Strategic and International Studies (CSIS) "is to inform and shape selected policy decisions in government and the private sector to meet the increasingly complex and difficult challenges that leaders will confront in the next century." Its primary goal is to actively affect U.S. foreign and domestic policy formation. The scope of its research, conferences, and other activities entails the use of every resource at a nation's disposal—political, economic, and military—to influence the actions of other nations. CSIS strategies for change are not limited to government policy; they also include business, the environment, and myriad issues that cross all demographics in the private sector.

HOW IS IT STRUCTURED?

The CSIS is a private, nonprofit, tax-exempt public policy research institute. The board of trustees, headed by a chairman and vice chairman, is responsible for broad policy decisions; the daily operations of the center are run by a president who answers to the board. The president is assisted by a chief executive officer (CEO) who is also a vice president. The center has a number of officers who report directly to the CEO and are responsible for various policy and administrative areas. These include the managing director for Domestic and International Issues; the senior vice president for International Security Affairs; the senior vice president and director of Studies; and vice presidents in the areas of International Finance and Economic Policy, Development and Corporate Security, Finance, and External Relations.

ESTABLISHED: 1962
EMPLOYEES: 300
MEMBERS: None
PAC: None

Contact Information:
ADDRESS: 1800 K St. NW
    Washington, DC 20006
PHONE: (202) 887-0200
FAX: (202) 775-3199
E-MAIL: info@csis.org
URL: http://www.csis.org
PRESIDENT; CEO: Robert B. Zoellick
CHANCELLOR: David Abshire

FAST FACTS

The CSIS International Women's Leadership Forum held in Stockholm in May 1996 brought together six of the world's 16 women prime ministers and presidents to assess the challenges posed by the coming decade and to suggest ways of effectively meeting them.

(Source: *CSIS 1995–1996: Leadership into the 21st Century*. Washington: CSIS, 1996.)

The center's 12 departments are divided along geographic areas—African Studies; Asian Studies; European Studies; Russian and Eurasian Studies; Middle East Studies; and the Americas—and on a functional basis—Domestic Policy Issues, Energy Studies and National Security Studies; International Business and Economics; International Communications; Political-Military Studies; and Preventative Diplomacy. Each department has its own priorities for research and special activities. The center's departments are staffed by approximately 80 research specialists, 80 support staff, and 70 to 100 interns at any given time. Together they generate strategic analyses, analyze policy options, explore contingencies, and make recommendations.

Affiliated with the center are groups of counselors and advisers. CSIS counselors are foreign policy specialists who have formerly held high-level posts in government. Advisers are scholars and academics who contribute to a full range of center projects.

The center sponsors eight "Endowed Chairs" for the work of distinguished scholars. They are the Arleigh A. Burke Chair in Strategy; the Freeman Chair in China Studies; the Japan Chair; the Henry A. Kissinger Chair in International Politics; Diplomatic History and National Security Policy; the William M. Scholl Chair in International Business; the William A. Schreyer Chair in Global Analysis; and the William E. Simon Chair in Political Economy.

The Pacific Forum CSIS in Honolulu, Hawaii, known as the center's "Gateway to Asia," is a semiautonomous institute that specializes in problems and policy affecting Pacific Rim nations. Made up of 20 research institutes around the region, the Pacific Forum has a separate administrative structure, which takes its direction from and answers to the CSIS board in Washington, D.C.

PRIMARY FUNCTIONS

The CSIS is sometimes referred to as a think tank because members are dedicated to research and analysis in the hopes of effecting public policy change. To achieve its mission, members work along three key areas: generating analysis; convening policy members and leaders from academia, business, and the private sector; and building structures for policy action.

First and foremost, the center generates strategic analysis, which includes an examination of military, economic, and political strengths. A staff of expert researchers conducts research not only on the United States, but on all major geographical regions of the world. All CSIS research is nonpartisan and nonproprietary.

CSIS research groups and conferences release regular reports on their findings to the media, members of the government, and the general public. Over the years, the CSIS has become a valuable and respected source of information to the press. In addition, CSIS experts make frequent appearances in the media, and produce thousands of articles each year. The center also publishes a number of periodicals, the primary title being its policy journal, *Washington Quarterly*. Other CSIS periodicals include *Washington Papers*, *CSIS Panel Reports*, and *CSIS Reports*. The CSIS publishes a series of newsletters, including *News@CSIS*, *Euro-Focus*, *Post-Soviet Prospects*, and *Business Alerts*. *Watch*, a digest of the latest political and economic news, is faxed to members of Congress, the executive branch, and corporate executives. The CSIS also publishes books in conjunction with scholarly presses.

Global Policy Networks

An important function of the CSIS is bringing together government officials, corporate executives, and scholars from around the world to examine specific issues of global importance. The center organizes 700 to 800 meetings, seminars, presentations, and conferences every year on topics that include the stability of political institutions in eastern Europe, the future of Asian economies, and the effect of the Year 2000 problem on the world's computers. The Global Organized Crime Commission, for example, considers the implications of the growing threat that narcotics trafficking, financial crime, Russian- and Asian-organized crime, terrorism, and nuclear blackmail present to global stability.

The Global Information Infrastructure Commission encourages corporate leadership in developing information technology, networks, and services. It also fosters cooperation of the public and private sectors in this area. Its 40 members include executives from major corporations, government officials, and representatives of the World Bank. The American-Ukrainian Advisory Committee is an example of a CSIS project group committed to studying a specific part of the world. According to the CSIS, this advisory committee "identifies opportunities for closer political and economic cooperation between the two countries."

Finally, the CSIS attempts to influence national policy through action plans. Specifically, participants in CSIS seminars and conferences may be asked to lobby and consult with government officials or write articles and editorials for magazines and newspapers.

PROGRAMS

The CSIS administers a myriad of programs that study issues from every area of the world. They range from economic and military problems in the emerging Third World, the threat of nuclear and biological sabotage, the future of Europe and Asia, and problems caused by the Year 2000 computer bug. Some of the most important are the Global Strategic Analysis and Global Policy Networks Programs.

The Global Strategic Analysis Program's main components are the Seven Revolutions Project, Global Trends 2002, and Middle East Dynamic Net Assessment. The Seven Revolutions Project attempts to pinpoint and study the most important issues world leaders will face in the year 2020. The project focuses on seven areas of "revolutionary change:" demography, technology, knowledge, finance and economics, conflict, politics, and society. Results of this program, including trends and examples of CSIS contingency thinking about possible future developments, are the subject of a multimedia presentation, which the CSIS has shown groups across the United States.

Global Trends 2002 researchers identify and analyze major world trends and their implications for certain key countries. What differentiates this program from Seven Revolutions is its much shorter time frame, the year 2002 rather than 2020. In addition, global trend analysts study trends and issues in greater depth and the scenarios they develop are specific and focused on individual countries. Middle East Dynamic Net Assessment is an example of a program that studies issues limited to a specific area of the world. It focuses on political and military questions that affect stability and security in the Middle East.

BUDGET INFORMATION

In 1997 the CSIS had an annual budget of approximately $17 million. About 85 percent of those revenues were contributions from more than 300 corporations, foundations, and individuals. The remaining funds came from endowment income, government contracts, and publication sales.

HISTORY

The CSIS was founded in 1962 as the Center for Strategic Studies by David M. Abshire and Admiral Arleigh Burke at Washington, D.C.'s Georgetown University. Their original intention was to research U.S. growth and how and when the United States used its power in the world. That plan was quickly modified when Abshire and Burke proposed that the group go beyond creating reports and become involved in learning how its findings affected government policy. The center also rejected the strict statistical methods of analyzing international situations used by the Department of Defense (DOD) and influential institutions like the Rand Corporation. Instead the center's researchers relied on the knowledge and intuition of its staff in understanding data and using that knowledge to develop analysis.

The Cold War between the United States and the Soviet Union was a major concern of Abshire and Burke. One purpose of forming the center was to better understand the strengths of both the United States and the Soviet Union. Thus the group's focus in its early years was on military resources, military strategy, and the international economics of national security.

The center's first conference in 1963 was dedicated to national defense and economic issues. While conservative in its outlook, the center avoided becoming aligned with any particular political camp. In 1966 the center became an early critic of the way the Johnson administration was financing the Vietnam War (1959–75), maintaining that it would lead to a recession, a prediction that came to pass in the early 1970s. Later in the 1960s, the center recognized the possibility of an energy crisis and the depth of the division between the Russians and Chinese.

The rules under which the center was founded prohibited classified research as well as funding from the DOD or Central Intelligence Agency (CIA). However, during the Vietnam War, many believed the organizations had close links. In response, Admiral Burke, who had refused government funding in order to maintain the center's independence, went so far as to publish a list of its funding sources. The first government money the center accepted were grants from the Environmental Protection Agency (EPA) and the Arms Control and Disarmament Agency. Still, according to a *Macleans* report in 1980, there was a regular exchange of staff between the center and the CIA throughout the 1970s.

In 1968 the center changed its name to the Center for Strategic and International Studies. At the same time, it formed the International Research Council, to expand the range of CSIS interests. The council was composed primarily of prestigious scholars, in contrast to the center's advisory board which was made up of former government officials, congressional members, and corporate executives. In 1972 Burke resigned and Abshire returned from a position he had taken in the State Department to become the center's chairperson.

In the 1970s the CSIS began providing briefings rather than issuing detailed reports. CSIS experts would make 10-minute presentations directly to policymakers. In June 1973 it convened the first Quadrangle Conference, a meeting of the United States, Canada, Japan, and European nations to discuss international trade, monetary issues, energy issues, and Western security. Energy was a dominant topic at that conference. In 1975 the CSIS helped make the public aware of the energy crisis when it contracted with Hanna-Barbera studios for a half-hour long "Flintstones" cartoon on energy, which was shown in late 1976 in about 75 television markets and in schools across the country.

Starting in the late 1970s ex-government officials began joining the CSIS, including Henry Kissinger in 1977. When Kissinger joined, it attracted more attention to the CSIS than any other event in the center's history. Other officials followed, and included James Schlessinger, a former secretary of defense and energy and Zbigniew Brezenski, President Jimmy Carter's national security adviser. In the late 1970s the CSIS was home to many critics of the Carter administration and the election of President Ronald Reagan attracted many CSIS thinkers to the new administration. David Abshire himself was put in charge of Reagan's national security transition team. In all, CSIS people handled the transition for about 27 executive departments and agencies and seven staff members left to take full-time jobs in the Reagan White House.

In the 1980s the CSIS took steps to secure its place as one of the country's most respected think tanks. The volume of reports, books, and other publications had presented problems in that the quality often varied widely from one report to another, which threw the quality of even the best products into question. In the mid-1980s Amos Jordan, who became CSIS president when Abshire took a position in the Reagan administration, introduced more rigorous intellectual standards. The result was a cutback in the number of CSIS publications and a corresponding rise in quality across the board. By the early 1990s, the CSIS could boast that it was, along with the Brookings Institute and the Carnegie Endowment, one of the three top public policy research institutions in the United States.

By the mid-1980s, the CSIS's ties to Georgetown University began to loosen. The CSIS shared less and less of Georgetown's political conservatism, and few university scholars took part in CSIS studies and conferences. In addition, the CSIS realized that having a board of directors independent of the university would make fund-raising easier. In 1987 the two institutions severed all ties by mutual agreement.

During the Clinton administration, the CSIS broadened its outlook, instituting projects to examine domestic issues that could threaten U.S. world leadership. The Strengthening of America Commission, headed by Senators Sam Nunn and Pete Domenici, presented the first proposals for restructuring the federal tax system. In addition, it was the first group to call for a balanced budget by 2002. The National Commission on Retirement Policy released a report that was the first comprehensive bipartisan proposal for Social Security reform. Throughout the 1990s the CSIS actively studied proliferation of nuclear weapons and materials following the collapse of the Soviet Union. The Global Organized Crime Task issued reports on the danger of a black market in nuclear materials; the Nuclear Black Market Report led to legislation designed to halt the spread of nuclear weapons and materials once held by the Soviet Union.

CURRENT POLITICAL ISSUES

The CSIS has been involved in numerous political issues relating to the U.S. leadership role in the world and U.S. national security. Since the 1970s the CSIS has become increasingly aware of the global impact of domestic issues. The state of the U.S. economy or congressional legislation, for example, affects the United States's impact around the world. For instance, if the U.S. government has to repay loans taken out in the 1980s, it will shrink the amount of money available for financial assistance to struggling nations or to mount full-scale military actions overseas. In the 1990s these domestic issues assumed a central position in the CSIS's work.

Case Study: Social Security Reform

The make up of the U.S. population is becoming older as life expectancies are increasing dramatically. Added to this is the fact that the baby boomers, the generation of children born in the 1950s and 1960s, are now reaching retirement age. These two forces, together with the decline in private pension plans available to U.S. workers, will put unprecedented financial pressures on the Social Security system, and the economy in general. As these pressures grow, they could significantly endanger the financial futures of millions of Americans and the financial stability of the country. The CSIS formed the National Commission on Retirement Policy (NCRP) to address these crucial issues and educate the public about them.

The 23-member NCRP was chaired jointly by Senators Judd Gregg and John Breaux; Representatives Jim Kolbe and Charles W. Stenholm; Donald B. Marron of the Paine Webber Group; and Dr. Charles A. Sanders, formerly of Glaxo, Inc. The NCRP set three primary objectives: 1) to educate Americans about the nature and scope of the national retirement problem; 2) to provide a nonpartisan forum for national debate of the Social Security issue; and, 3) to lay the groundwork for a national consensus that will enable Americans to begin making the changes necessary.

The NCRP held conferences, roundtable discussions, and town hall meetings throughout the United

States. It also introduced an aggressive media campaign, as part of its public education program. The NCRP enlisted analysis and testimony from economists, scholars, and retirement policy experts and used that work to formulate practical policy recommendations. They were published in the NCRP's final report, *Can America Afford To Retire?*, released in January 1998.

Using studies that had already been conducted by the government and private groups, the NCRP report concluded that if the current Social Security system remained unchanged, its costs could increase the federal budget deficit by 8 percent by 2030, and that payroll deductions for Social Security might have to be raised to 18 percent in the immediate future to maintain current benefits through 2070. The NCRP articulated for a national retirement policy that will provide Americans with a reasonable standard of living, contribute to long-term growth and prosperity for the country at large, and be financially sound and economically sustainable. Quoting the Congressional Budget Office, the report stated, "shortfalls projected for future years are so large that they could put an end to the upward trend in living standards that the nation has long enjoyed."

The report recommended immediate action if depletion of the Social Security fund by 2029 were to be avoided. Its other main recommendations included: expanding employer-based pensions, which currently provide income to less than one-half of all retirees; that Americans increase their personal savings, which fell from peak of nine percent in 1974 to less than five percent in 1996; and educating Americans fully about these pressing needs.

Not long after the publication of the report, the commission sponsored a conference in Washington, D.C., the first in a series of discussions on the practical mechanics of Social Security reform. That first conference examined the feasibility of introducing individual retirement accounts into the Social Security system. The questions addressed included the cost of such a system, the problems of administering it for over 100 million workers, and the investment options that could be offered to workers. Future discussions will bring policymakers and citizens together to begin working toward the implementation of the NCRP recommendations. At that time, the congressional cochairpersons will also introduce newly proposed legislation.

SUCCESSES AND FAILURES

The CSIS has been particularly successful in assessing the importance of the Middle East and how the forces there could affect U.S. political and business interests. In the late 1960s the CSIS, spurred on by some of its scholars from Great Britain, began stressing the importance of the Persian Gulf area. Awareness of the Persian Gulf was so low in 1968 that when the CSIS sponsored a confer-

ence on the Middle East that year, it had to design its own maps of the area because no suitable ones could be found. Their early attention to the geopolitics of the area led them to warn of the possibility of an energy crisis nearly two years before it happened in 1973. In 1989 CSIS analysts warned that Iraq, strengthened after its war with Iran, could attack one of its oil-producing neighbors. When the invasion actually came a year later, however, it was in Kuwait, not Saudi Arabia as the CSIS predicted.

FUTURE DIRECTIONS

Two of the top items on the CSIS agenda going into the twenty-first century will be the global economy and energy security. The center will continue to examine trends in global finance. More important, it will attempt to understand how the United States can prosper in the global economy. In the CSIS's eyes, a sound energy policy is vital. The CSIS will study energy interdependence in the world and make recommendations about how the United States can decrease its dependence on regions of the world that are politically volatile or unstable. Along these lines, the center hosted a major conference entitled the Strategic Energy Initiative in 1999.

GROUP RESOURCES

The CSIS has a comprehensive Web page that includes information about the center, upcoming conferences, new publications, and contact information. Many CSIS newsletters and research reports are also available at the site. The CSIS Web page can be accessed at http://www.csis.org.

GROUP PUBLICATIONS

Individuals can subscribe to *The Washington Quarterly* for $36 a year. Orders should be sent to Circulation Department, MIT Press Journals, 5 Cambridge Ctr., Cambridge, MA 02142-1407. For information on subscriptions to other CSIS journals, like *Washington Papers*; *Significant Issues Series*; *CSIS Panel Reports*; *CSIS Reports*, or for a list of books published by CSIS write: The CSIS Press, Publications Sales Office, 1800 K St. NW, Washington, DC 20006. Information is available by phone by calling (202) 775-3119.

CSIS publishes a series of informative newsletters, including *News@CSIS*, *Euro-Focus*, *Post-Soviet Prospects*, *Business Alert*, *Capital Markets*, *Domestic Policy*, *Hong Kong Update*, *Briefing Notes on Islam, Society, and Politics*, and *Watch*. For information on subscriptions contact the CSIS Press. Most newsletters are available in electronic form on the CSIS Web site.

BIBLIOGRAPHY

Belt, Bradley D. "Rethinking National Retirement Policy: the Twenty-First Century Retirement Security Plan." *Washington Quarterly*, Winter 1999.

Jordan, Amos A. "CSIS: 25 Years of Shaping the Future." In *America in the World 1962-1987*, ed. Walter Laquer and Brad Roberts. New York: St Martin's Press, 1987.

Kondrake, Morton. "Georgetown's Think Tank on the Potomac." *Change*, September 1978.

Lowther, William. "Academic Cloaks and CIA Daggers." *Macleans*, 24 November 1980.

Newsom, David D. "Reforming US Diplomacy." *Christian Science Monitor,* 25 November 1998.

Potter, E. B. *Admiral Arleigh Burke: A Biography.* New York: Random House, 1990.

Center for Study of Responsive Law

WHAT IS ITS MISSION?

The Center for Study of Responsive Law seeks to raise the public's awareness of consumer issues and to encourage public and private institutions to be more responsive to the needs of citizens and consumers. The center conducts a broad range of research and it supports various educational projects in order to encourage political, economic, and social institutions to be more aware of the needs of citizens. Specifically the Center for Study of Responsive Law works to make government and corporate America accountable to consumers by exposing fraud and other types of abuse, and by publishing a variety of reports on public interest issues. The center also sponsors conferences and litigation related to health and safety issues for consumers and workers.

HOW IS IT STRUCTURED?

The Center for Study of Responsive Law is a nonprofit, nonpartisan organization. Although the center works on behalf of all citizens and consumers, it has no membership and no political action committee (PAC). The center is run by an administrator and a staff of 20 to 25 people. These staff members include participants in the Fellowship Program which grants two-year positions to recent law school graduates. Fellows work on law-related projects that do not involve litigation. The staff also includes social and consumer activists who conduct research and publish studies on various issues, and the attorneys who manage the center's legal activities.

ESTABLISHED: August 1968
EMPLOYEES: 25
MEMBERS: None
PAC: None

Contact Information:

ADDRESS: PO Box 19367
   Washington, DC 20036
PHONE: (202) 387-8030
FAX: (202) 234-5176
E-MAIL: csrl@CSRL.org
URL: http://www.csrl.org
ADMINISTRATOR: John Richard

PRIMARY FUNCTIONS

The Center for Study of Responsive Law works on behalf of consumers through two major channels. The center educates consumers about issues important to their health and well-being by publishing books, sponsoring conferences, and organizing projects. Some of the center's publications include *Getting the Best From Your Doctor* and *Why Women Pay More*.

In addition to educating consumers, the Center for Study of Responsive Law works to make government agencies and corporations accountable to consumers and more responsive to their needs. The center does this by investigating and researching various industries and government services that are widely used by the public. The center then publicizes its results, which often include examples of fraud, mismanagement, unethical activities, or other threats to the public good. For example in 1972 the center published *The Madness Establishment,* a book that exposed the mismanagement and fraud of mental health centers following the passage of the Community Mental Health Centers Act.

In 1972 the Center for Study of Responsive Law also established the Freedom of Information Clearinghouse. The purpose of the clearinghouse is to ensure that the federal government lives up to its responsibilities as outlined in the Freedom of Information Act. That act requires the government to turn over certain types of federal records and information to citizens who request them. The law outlines which types of information the government may keep secret and which types it may not.

The Freedom of Information Clearinghouse clarifies and publicizes information concerning access to federal records so that people will understand how to make freedom of information laws work to their benefit. The clearinghouse has also developed an extensive program of litigation, which it uses to reduce illegal secrecy and to secure favorable judicial interpretations in areas where Freedom of Information Acts are unclear. In other words, the clearinghouse not only uses legal action to ensure that the government does not wrongfully withhold information which citizens are entitled to, it also works to lobby judges to draft broad interpretations of Freedom of Information Act laws.

PROGRAMS

The Center for Study of Responsive Law has developed several programs to help consumers and to guarantee accountability on behalf of government agencies and corporations. In 1995 the center created the Consumer Project on Technology a public education service which monitors issues relating to antitrust cases, telecommunications policy, software and computer products, privacy, and electronic commerce. The Consumer Project on Technology works to make sure that citizens understand their rights in the world of technology, especially their rights to privacy and to information. The project also works to educate consumers about the importance of antitrust cases and it keeps an updated commentary on the implications of major cases as well as major corporate mergers. On its Web page, http://www.cptech.org, the Consumer Project on Technology contains links to related Web sites and it lists the titles and E-mail addresses of government officials who work on antitrust cases.

In addition to working on behalf of American consumers, the Center for Study of Responsive Law also works on behalf of third world workers and consumers. This function has become more important due to the growing global marketplace; increasingly, issues affecting U.S. workers affect the workers of the world. The Center for Study of Responsive Law works to ensure decent standards of working and living conditions worldwide. In its effort to protect all consumers and citizens, the center created the Malaria Project to convince governments throughout the world to increase funding for malaria research. In 1996 the Wellcome Trust reported that funding for malaria research had declined since 1985 and that the total funding from all sources amounted to only $84 million per year, which amounts to 1-50th of what the U.S. government alone spends on cancer research. Especially alarming to the Center for Study of Responsive Law is the fact that this decrease has occurred at a time when malaria has begun a resurgence. According to a report from the Institute of Medicine of the National Academy of Sciences, the disease is a public health problem for more than 40 percent of the world's population.

BUDGET INFORMATION

Not made available.

HISTORY

The Center for Study of Responsive Law was formed by Ralph Nader in 1968 to work on behalf of consumers. Nader formed the organization to help safeguard and protect the public interest after having gained a reputation as a safety watchdog. In 1966 Nader exposed safety problems with the General Motors Corvair automobile in his book *Unsafe at Any Speed.* The book helped trigger a national debate about automobile safety. During U.S. Senate hearings on automobile design and safety in 1967, General Motors admitted that they had hired private investigators to follow Nader during his investigation of the Corvair. This revelation generated even more publicity and support for Nader and his book.

In order to continue his work, Nader assembled a group of investigators. They investigated the Federal

BIOGRAPHY:

Ralph Nader

Consumer Activist; Lawyer (b. 1934) Ralph Nader began his consumer activism while an undergraduate at Princeton University. For over 40 years since then, Ralph Nader has written, spoken, testified, and campaigned for consumer protection issues so successfully that his name has become a household word. His first high-profile crusade began while studying auto injury cases at Harvard Law School. Nader wrote articles supporting his position that the faulty designs of U.S. car makers were responsible for the staggering accident statistics. He became distressed at the automobile industry's indifference, claiming they had the technology to make cars safer. In 1965 he catapulted into the national spotlight with the publication of his stinging indictment of the automobile industry, *Unsafe at Any Speed: The Designed-in Dangers of the American Automobile.* Nader soon had a dedicated team of young people, known as "Nader's Raiders," who increased the scope

of his investigations as they gathered information about all types of industries and government bureaus. In 1969 he organized these efforts into the Center for Study of Responsive Law. Throughout the years Nader continued his dogged pursuit of consumer issues that included industrial hazards, pollution, unsafe consumer products, and government indifference to consumer safety laws. Public interest and awareness in Nader flared again in 1996 when he unsuccessfully ran for president as a member of the Green Party. Said Nader, "You've got to keep the pressure on, even if you lose. The essence of the citizens' movement is persistence."

Trade Commission (FTC), the government agency responsible for protecting consumers from faulty business practice, products, and deceptive advertising. Within the FTC, Nader's group found widespread evidence of bias toward big business and cronyism (providing jobs on the basis of personal relationships rather than qualifications). Nader's report eventually prompted a reorganization of the FTC and its various field offices. After this investigation Nader decided to create the Center for Study of Responsive Law as a means of continuing his advocacy for consumer rights.

In 1969 the center began to hire law students to work on task forces investigating government agencies and exposing social problems that were in danger of being ignored. In 1970 and 1971 alone, the center published reports exposing fraud in the Interstate Commerce Commission and the Food and Drug Administration, and publicized the effects irresponsible business practices were having on the environment.

In 1972, in response to the passage of the Freedom of Information Act, the center established the Freedom of Information Clearinghouse. The clearinghouse soon developed an extensive program of litigation, which it uses to reduce illegal secrecy and to secure favorable judicial interpretations in areas where Freedom of Information Act is unclear. During the 1970s and 1980s the clearinghouse used this program to challenge court decisions that threatened to narrow or reduce the government's responsibility to allow private citizens access to public records. For example, in 1987, the center suc-

cessfully challenged court decisions that would have prevented researchers from gaining access to tax return information. In instances where the disclosure of this information would not threaten the privacy of any individual taxpayer, the center argued, the government has no right to withhold it.

In addition to work done by the clearinghouse, the center continued to research and publish its findings regarding key government agencies and social problems during the 1970s and 1980s. Between 1970 and 1999 the center published reports on issues such as nursing home abuse, fraud in the development of land in California, and water pollution. In 1995, the center published a report on banking violations of the 1969 Truth in Lending Act. Although the law requires banks to disclose key loan terms and other fees, the center found that banks routinely violate the law by hiding the costs of automated teller machine (ATM) transactions and phone transactions. A study conducted by the center found that federal bank regulators discovered over 4,000 violations of the Truth in Lending Act during an investigation into over 5,000 banks.

CURRENT POLITICAL ISSUES

The Center for Study of Responsive Law works to educate consumers and to expose those agencies or institutions who harm consumers, whether it be through fraud, disregard for safety, or exploitation. It has been involved in such issues as antitrust law, nursing home abuse, and automobile safety. In 1994 and 1995, for example, the Center for Study of Responsive Law began an aggressive campaign to expose so-called corporate welfare, at a time when the federal government was working to pass strict limitations on social welfare programs.

Case Study: Corporate vs. Social Welfare

In 1996 Congress and the Clinton administration passed sweeping reforms of the federal welfare system. Welfare is a term often used to describe a variety of benefits that the government provides to the needy, including monetary assistance. These reforms cut $56 billion from welfare spending and gave individual states more direct control over who would qualify for welfare. Critics of these welfare reforms, including Senator Daniel Moynihan (D-N.Y.), claimed that the new laws did not reform welfare programs so much as they abolished them. As Moynihan stated on the Senate floor, "This bill terminates the basic Federal commitment of support for dependent children in hopes of altering the behavior of their mothers" ("From the Senate Debate on Welfare," *New York Times*, August 2, 1996).

Ralph Nader and The Center for Study of Responsive Law also criticized these reforms and particularly disapproved of cuts to Aid For Dependent Children, a federal program which reserved funds for impoverished children. The center found cuts in federal social welfare programs to be particularly unjustified because the government continued to provide large sums to business interests across the country. In a press release from the Center for Study of Responsive Law entitled, "Survey Finds Corporate Welfare Spending Exceeds Social Welfare," Ralph Nader criticized the Clinton administration for ignoring corporate entitlements. The center claimed that the federal government spent almost $30 billion more on "corporate welfare" payments than it did on social welfare payments.

The center's definition of "corporate welfare" is broad and includes subsidies such as those provided by the Agriculture Department's Export Enhancement Program, which provides bonuses to exporters of particular agricultural products grown in the United States in order to encourage the growth of new markets overseas. It also includes federal money given to scientists for research done in the private sector. In essence any federal money granted to profitable corporations in order to encourage research, the growth of new markets, or to offset heavy financial losses, was included under the center's definition of "corporate welfare." Dr. Janice Shields, a staff member at the center and author of, "Aid for Dependent Corporations," stated the center's position in a *New York Times* article: "Why shouldn't the companies be paying? Why does the Government pay for some products and not for others? These huge companies that are on the Fortune 500 [list] with enormous profits, enormous com-

pensation for their top executives—why do they need welfare at the same time that we're talking about not giving a pittance to teen-age mothers so their kids can eat a nutritious meal?"

The center's position on corporate and social welfare is controversial. Critics argue against the concept of corporate welfare by pointing out that federal subsidies are designed to create new markets, keep current markets open, and promote a healthy economy for the good of all consumers and workers. Nevertheless, because of its experienced research staff, the center is able to provide compelling data to the public in a way that is easy to grasp. Instead of simply criticizing the welfare reform laws, the center coined a compelling new term in order to illustrate the contrast between government support for corporations and government support for welfare recipients. While critics argue that corporations cannot be compared to welfare recipients, the center's research capability, combined with its experience at the center of many social policy storms, allows it to capture the attention of the public and the media with simple but powerful messages.

FUTURE DIRECTIONS

As the United States becomes more involved in the development of a global marketplace, the Center for Study of Responsive Law will increase its efforts to expose the growing practice of large corporations to move their operations overseas in order to utilize cheaper sources of labor. The center will continue, and likely heighten, its efforts to expose the growing economic gaps between rich and poor in the United States and abroad. The center also finds itself working to keep up with rapidly changing technologies. In 1995, for example, the center formed the Consumer Project on Technology, which focuses on educating the public about antitrust enforcement issues; telecommunications policy; intellectual property; software and computing; and privacy issues on the Internet.

As common consumer decisions become more and more complex, the center will likely find itself in the position of acting as a kind of translator for the public—explaining issues in terms of legal rights and consequences, and then educating consumers about how to make the best decisions. As marketing strategies become more sophisticated and consumers are given more and more options regarding the use of credit, leasing, and other models for buying and renting products, the Center for Study of Responsive Law will continue to work not only to make corporations and government agencies responsive to consumer needs, but also to make sure consumers understand exactly what they are buying, and how.

GROUP RESOURCES

The Center for Study of Responsive Law maintains a Web site at http://www.csrl.org which provides information about the center's current concerns and activities. The Web site also contains press releases from the center and links to other organizations affiliated with Ralph Nader. The center's E-mail address is csrl@CSRL.org.

GROUP PUBLICATIONS

The center publishes investigative reports and press releases on its Web site at http://www.csrl.org. You can also request these reports by writing to the Center for Study of Responsive Law at PO Box 19367, Washington DC 20036 or by calling (202) 387-8030. The center also publishes a monthly magazine called the *Multinational Monitor* which contains stories about government and corporate mismanagement. The magazine can be obtained by contacting the Web site http://www.csrl.org or writing to PO Box 19367, Washington DC 20036.

BIBLIOGRAPHY

Broder, John. "Big Social Changes Revive the False God of Numbers." *New York Times*, 17 August 1997.

Fitzgerald, Ernest A. *The Pentagonists: An Insider's View of Waste, Mismanagement and Fraud in Defense Spending.* Boston, Mass.: Houghton Mifflin, 1989.

"From the Senate Debate on Welfare." *New York Times* 2 August 1996.

Kilborn, Peter. "Welfare Shift Reflects New Democrat." *New York Times*, 2 August 1996.

Leary, Warren. "Panel Cites Lack of Security on Medical Records." *New York Times*, 6 March 1997.

Melman, Seymour. *The Pentagon and the National Debt: The Consequences of the Global Military Mission of the United States.* Northampton, Mass.: Aletheia Press, 1994.

"A Pittance to Fight Malaria." *Washington Post*, January 1998.

"Resurgence of a Deadly Disease." *Atlantic Monthly*, August 1997.

Roberts, Shawn. *After the Guns Fall Silent.* Atlantic Highlands, N.J.: Humanities Press, 1995.

Children's Defense Fund (CDF)

ESTABLISHED: 1973
EMPLOYEES: 170
PAC: Action Council

Contact Information:

ADDRESS: 25 E St. NW
     Washington, DC 20001
PHONE: (202) 628-8787
FAX: (202) 662-3530
E-MAIL: cdinfo@childrensdefense.org
URL: http://www.childrensdefense.org
PRESIDENT: Marian Wright Edelman

WHAT IS ITS MISSION?

The Children's Defense Fund (CDF) is a national, nonprofit, advocacy organization dedicated to improving the quality of lives of American children. The CDF's main objective is to act as guardian of the health and welfare of children, giving particular attention to the special needs of poor, minority, and disabled children. According to the organization's 1996 Annual Report, "CDF exists to provide a strong and effective voice for all the children of America, who cannot vote, lobby, or speak for themselves."

HOW IS IT STRUCTURED?

General oversight of the CDF, including major management and policy decisions, is conducted by a board of directors. More than fifteen individuals comprise the CDF's board; the majority of members are drawn from the ranks of private enterprise and the board is headed by a president.

Under the supervision of the board of directors, a chief of staff coordinates the daily efforts of the CDF's departments. The CDF's work is conducted by staff managed by a director of programs and policy, director of communications, director of development, director of finance and administration, director of the black community crusade for children, and director of intergovernmental affairs.

The CDF does not have members in the general public. It does solicit contributions from individuals, organizations and businesses but those donors have no technical or managerial input in CDF affairs.

PRIMARY FUNCTIONS

The CDF is primarily an advisory organization. Its staff includes experts and specialists in a number of child welfare fields. These experts deliver testimony to Congress and state legislatures on children's issues. The CDF also conducts studies and drafts reports, which government policymakers and lawmakers can use to understand how their decisions will affect the children of the United States. The CDF offers advice, support and information to other public and private child welfare agencies and the media.

The CDF also considers itself a government and public policy watchdog group. It monitors state and congressional legislation and tracks development and implementation of governmental policies that affect children. If it feels that a particular policy is dangerous for children, the CDF will lobby Congress to change it. It also pursues a child welfare legislative agenda to federal and state governments.

The CDF does not limit its work to government. It trains community and child care leaders to be more effective and responsive caretakers of children's needs. The CDF forms collaborations with community groups and religious congregations to start education programs. It helps communities establish awards ceremonies for "at risk" children who excel at school and develop vaccination strategies.

PROGRAMS

The CDF has created programs to help meet the complicated and demanding needs of children, especially poor, minority, and disabled children. Most of the programs do not engage these "at risk" children directly but instead are designed for community leaders and child care workers. These programs use the child care resources already in place in many communities. They are collaborations with communities, similar child welfare organizations, educators, and religious congregations.

Child Watch

Child Watch is a program designed to directly expose community leaders to child neglect and suffering. Business, political, religious, community, and media leaders visit with children who suffer poverty, abuse, and malnutrition. The CDF calls this experience "visitation" and its goal in running this program is to reveal the effect of poverty on children and the outcome of child welfare policy. Child Watch puts a name and a face on the effects of state and federal policies. It is a collaborative effort

FAST FACTS

Children comprise 27 percent of the American population but comprise 40 percent of the population living in poverty.

(Source: Children's Defense Fund. *CDF Reports*, February 1998.)

with other national organizations such as the National Council of Negro Women and the American Association of Retired Persons.

Black Community Crusade for Children (BCCC)

The CDF created the Black Community Crusade for Children specifically for children in the African American community. The CDF believes that the problems facing children in the African American community are different than those children face in the white community, and thus require unique solutions. The BCCC attempts to train individuals to become leaders in the African American community. These leaders are taught methods in effective community action. It also sponsors Freedom Schools, which are summer retreats for children conducted by community organizations. The BCCC provides critical curriculum and training guides for these Freedom Schools. Twenty-seven Freedom Schools served 2,000 children in 1996.

BUDGET INFORMATION

Funding for the CDF comes from donations from foundations, corporations and individuals. In 1996 the CDF's total revenue was $19.4 million. The organization's total disbursements were approximately $20 million that year. The majority of the CDF funds were spent on programs. Of these programs, the largest amount spent was on the BCCC (16 percent of the CDF's budget) with a total of $3.7 million (19 percent) going toward other programs. The CDF dedicated another $4.3 million (22 percent) to lobbying, government, and community affairs. Other major expenditures for the CDF included $2.6 million (13 percent) to fund-raising, $2.2 million (11 percent) to publications and other forms of public

BUDGET:

1996 CDF Expenses

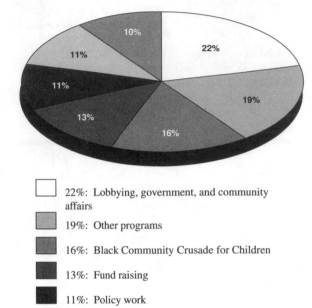

☐ 22%: Lobbying, government, and community affairs

▨ 19%: Other programs

▨ 16%: Black Community Crusade for Children

▨ 13%: Fund raising

■ 11%: Policy work

☐ 11%: Publications and other forms of public education

▨ 10%: Administration

education, $2.1 million (11 percent) to policy work, and $2 million (10 percent) to administration.

HISTORY

The CDF was created by Marian Wright Edelman in 1973. For the first ten years of its existence, the CDF did not actively participate in politics. It was primarily a research and public education group. Early work included investigations into the treatment of problems of children in adult jails and substandard health care and education for underprivileged children. It published these findings to raise public awareness of children's welfare issues.

The CDF eventually decided that simple research and advocacy were inadequate courses of action for the challenges of child welfare. In the early 1980s it broadened the scope of its work and altered its mission. CDF began holding annual conferences for child advocates. It also published the first edition of *The State of America's Children and Children's Defense Budget*, an annual report that investigates how government budget choices and priorities affect children.

Also in the early 1980s, the CDF expanded its collaborations with state and community child care leaders. Child Watch was introduced in 1981 as a research initiative meant to document the impact of President Ronald Reagan's federal budget cuts on children. Child Watch only gradually evolved into a visitation program, with the first visits beginning in 1990.

The 1990s saw a major expansion of CDF activities. In 1990 the CDF began Beat the Odds, a program which celebrates the achievements of children who have overcome difficult situations to succeed in life. On June 1, 1996 the CDF held the first Stand for Children, in collaboration with a number of national, state, and local organizations. Stand for Children called hundreds of thousands of supporters of children's rights together in their communities. These supporters gathered in public places and demonstrated with their numbers the commitment of the public to children's rights. In 1997 and 1998 CDF organized similar stands for Healthy Children and Quality Child Care. The CDF celebrated its twenty-fifth anniversary in 1998 with a gala event that included several Nobel laureates, ambassadors, and royalty, as well as First Lady Hillary Rodham Clinton.

CURRENT POLITICAL ISSUES

There are no issues involving children in the United States that are not a concern for the CDF. The CDF has advocated for reform of the U.S. juvenile justice system, seeking to reverse the trend of placing youths in adult prisons, which it feels puts them at a high risk of abuse without correcting their behavior. Instead the CDF would like the federal government to fund more crime prevention programs and enact laws making it more difficult for children to get guns.

In the 1990s the CDF fought to protect funding for federal programs like Temporary Assistance for Needy Families (TANF) and Food Stamps that provide funds for families to feed and care for their children. The CDF wishes to see federal spending limits eased, so that cuts in children's programs would not be necessary at a time when the federal government is enjoying surplus revenues.

Case Study: The Children's Health Insurance Program

The CDF and other child advocates worked for years to convince Congress that there were children who needed the federal government's help paying their medical bills. The CDF proposed a new program, called the Children's Health Insurance Program (CHIP), which would ensure that no child was denied health care due to lack of funds.

However, many in Congress felt that an expensive new program like CHIP was unnecessary. They believed

One of the events sponsored by the Children's Defense Fund is an annual Children's Day celebration. During Children's Day the CDF publicizes the services and resources available for addressing children's issues. (AP/Wide World Photos)

that those children who truly needed health care assistance were already adequately covered by the Medicaid program. Other congressmen opposed the bill because they thought it would mostly be paying to care for children whose parents had simply chosen not to pay for health insurance for their children. The CDF struggled to demonstrate to these members of Congress that their beliefs were misguided. According to the CDF, the real beneficiaries of a new program would be children whose parents were working, and earning enough money so that they no longer qualified for Medicaid, but still didn't earn enough money to purchase health insurance for their children.

Even if it convinced Congress that there were children who legitimately needed assistance with medical expenses, the CDF needed to convince Congress that there were practical ways in which the federal government could help. Throughout the middle and late 1990s, the organization was working with a Republican controlled Congress that was committed to reducing the size and bureaucracy of the federal government. These lawmakers were unlikely to support the creation of a large and expensive new federal program. Eventually, CHIP's supporters hit upon the idea of a block grant system.

A block grant is a lump allocation of federal government funds to the states. The states are given certain goals that the money is intended to meet, but are allowed to determine exactly how they will put the money to use. Thus, instead of creating more federal bureaucracy to administer a new program, CHIP would direct money to the states, which could then develop children's health programs to meet the needs of their citizens. Congress had already enacted a number of programs that used block grants, and had reformed existing programs to use this system as well.

Having convinced congressmen that there were children with a legitimate need for better health care, and having developed a system to provide that care without creating the kind of large federal program that Republicans disliked, the CDF was able to develop bipartisan support for CHIP. In 1997 Senators Orrin Hatch of Utah, a Republican, and Edward Kennedy of Massachusetts, a Democrat, sponsored a CHIP bill that passed with an 80 to 19 vote. In the House of Representatives, a similar bill passed 346 to 85. Thus CHIP, now the State Children's Health Insurance Program, was enacted, and funded with $48 billion over ten years.

FUTURE DIRECTIONS

With the completion of CHIP's expansion of Medicaid, the CDF has redirected its legislative agenda to its Child Care Now! campaign to increase federal government spending on child care. Getting adequate child care is extremely difficult for low-income families. Child Care Now! calls for financial assistance to needy parents to get quality child care. In the attempt to have similar success, the organization recommends a block grant system similar to CHIP's. The CDF proposes $20 billion over five years for its Child Care Now! initiative.

GROUP RESOURCES

CDF maintains a comprehensive Web site via the World Wide Web at http://www.childrensdefense.org. The Web site contains biographies of CDF leaders, detailed information about government programs like CHIP and child welfare issues such as violence prevention. Individuals interested in finding out more about CDF may send inquiries to Children's Defense Fund, 25 E St. NW, Washington, DC 20001 or call (202) 628-8787.

GROUP PUBLICATIONS

The CDF publishes a monthly magazine called *CDF Reports*. *CDF Reports* contains articles, results of studies, congressional voting records, updates and strategies for child welfare professionals. It is available to the public at a rate of $30 per year.

The CDF releases a large amount of its research, findings and investigations in many separate publications. *The State of America's Children Yearbook* is the CDF's annual report and analysis on the social, health and welfare conditions of children. It also contains raw statistics on problems such as the availability of low-income housing. Additionally the CDF publishes introductory materials for its programs. *Stand for Children! A Parent's Guide to Child Advocacy* was inspired by CDF's Stand for Children event. The CDF also makes its research and analysis of legislation available. *A Summary of the Welfare Bill* was the CDF's attempt to assess the affects of the 1996 Welfare Act on children. Through *CDF Reports*, CDF offers publications from other sources, including government departments such as Education and Social Security.

Information on obtaining any of the CDF's publications is available by contacting the Children's Defense Fund, 25 E St. NW, Washington, DC 20001 or by calling (202) 628-8787. Several of the CDF's publications are available on-line at http://www.childrensdefense.org/publications.html.

BIBLIOGRAPHY

Block, Jean Libman. "A Voice for the Children." *Good Housekeeping,* June 1996.

Dickerson, Debra. "Suffer the Children." *Nation,* 24 June 1996.

Golden, Renny. *Disposable Children: America's Child Welfare System.* Belmont, Calif.: Wadsworth Press, 1997.

Hellwege, Jean. "We Can Do Better." *Trial,* August 1998.

"Standing for Children: 200,000 Demand New Agenda." *Ebony,* August 1996.

Stein, Ruth E.K., ed. *Health Care for Children: What's Right, What's Wrong, What's Next.* New York: United Hospital Fund of New York, 1997.

Thomkins, James R. *Child Advocacy : History, Theory, and Practice.* Durham, N.C.: Carolina Academic Press, 1998.

Wekesser, Carol, ed. *Child Welfare: Opposing Viewpoints.* San Diego, Calif.: Greenhaven Press, 1998.

Choice in Dying (CID)

WHAT IS ITS MISSION?

According to the organization, "Choice In Dying (CID) is a national, not-for-profit organization dedicated to fostering communication about complex end-of-life decisions among individuals, their loved ones and health care professionals. The organization invented living wills in 1967 and has been at the forefront of end-of-life issues ever since."

CID and other right-to-die organizations believe that people have the right to participate fully in decisions about their medical treatment toward the end of their lives. With the creation of the living will, CID ensured that people could make provisions for these rights while they were capable of doing so. The organization also provides resources and support for family members who anticipate or are currently making the difficult decisions that come when a loved one is near death.

HOW IS IT STRUCTURED?

CID is a nonprofit, 501(c)3 organization with two offices. The national office is located in Washington, D.C., where it houses CID's advocacy efforts, media and other outreach activities, membership support, and interorganization relations. The Washington office also provides general administrative support for the organization. CID's program office is located in New York City. This office staffs CID's toll-free phone line, provides educational outreach to the public and to the medical profession, and houses a legal services division. CID publications are handled by an independent clearinghouse in Maryland.

ESTABLISHED: 1991
EMPLOYEES: 20
MEMBERS: 32,000-35,000
PAC: None

Contact Information:

ADDRESS: 1035 30th St. NW
      Washington, DC 20007
PHONE: (202) 338-9790
TOLL FREE: (800) 989-9455
FAX: (202) 338-0242
E-MAIL: cid@choices.org
URL: http://www.choices.org
EXECUTIVE DIRECTOR: Karen Orloff Kaplan, ScD

A 15-member board of directors is composed of individuals who serve two-year terms and are elected by other board members. Board members work closely with an executive director, who creates initiatives for organizational direction. Board members may propose organizational initiatives as well.

CID's members contribute $25 (or $40 for couples) and receive a state-specific advance directive package with updates and revisions if state policy changes. Members also receive the quarterly newsletter *Choices* and a 20 percent discount on CID pamphlets and publications. Members may be asked for input on organization initiatives or relevant issues.

PRIMARY FUNCTIONS

CID carries out its organizational mission to help patients and their families participate in decisions about end-of-life medical care in a number of ways.

CID provides, upon request, state-specific advance directive documents which may include living wills or durable power of attorney documents. The living will allows an individual to state their wishes about medical treatment at the end of their life. Power of Attorney documents allow an individual to appoint a representative to make certain medical or legal decisions, should the individual become unable to do so for themself. Living will and power of attorney laws vary in different states and CID provides assistance specific to technicalities in each state. The organization also provides counseling regarding technical questions about advance directive documents, such as their applicability in particular situations.

CID also works to monitor state and federal policy regarding right-to-die initiatives or issues. The organization tracks related state and federal legislation, consults with policymakers on proposed legislation, and provides lawmakers with relevant information. CID takes a stand on all issues related to end-of-life care except physician-assisted suicide. The organization works, for example, to prevent legislation that would restrict palliative care (such as painkillers) when a person is dying. During 1997 and 1998 the organization continued to work with federal policymakers to enhance and strengthen the Patient Self Determination Act (passed as part of the Omnibus Budget Reconciliation Act of 1990, in October 1990). The act was the first law that ensured that patients were informed of their right to accept or refuse medical care.

The organization also maintains a legal department which attempts to shape policy through the court system. CID's legal department files *amicus curiae* (Friends of the Court) briefs in state and federal courts for cases that concern right-to-die issues. One such case was being tried in January 1997, when CID filed an *amicus curiae* brief for the Supreme Court Case *Vacco v. Quill*. In a previous version of this case (*Quill v. Vacco*, April 1996), a second circuit New York court had ruled that the U.S. Constitution protected the rights of terminally ill patients to receive medications for committing suicide. However, the Supreme Court reversed this decision, making each state responsible for making the decision of whether to ban assisted suicide.

The organization is involved in providing outreach and education about right-to-die issues to the public and to medical and legal professionals. CID works with medical schools to ensure that subjects related to death and dying are included in curricula. The organization publishes the *Right-to-Die Law Digest*, aimed at giving doctors, lawyers, and medical ethicists current material on right-to-die court cases, legislation, and other aspects of death such as withholding treatment and dying at home. According to CID, these issues are discussed by few organizations because of the painful subject matter. The organization also publishes a quarterly newsletter, *Choices*. The organization provides a national toll-free hot line that allows people to call for information or counseling on end-of-life issues. CID receives over 300 such calls each month.

PROGRAMS

CID's programs are created to give the public, as well as professionals, an understanding of right-to-die issues. These issues, which may range from end-of-life care to the legalities of living wills, may be poorly understood by those who have never had to deal with a loved one's death. In the corporate arena, for example, CID has developed a "train the trainer" program, which helps Human Resource professionals become versed in right-to-die issues and offer information to employees. CID also promoted a public television documentary in 1996, titled *WHOSE Death Is It, Anyway?* The organization subsequently won an award for an educational program and video that it created around the documentary, which included discussion formats for use in the community.

In 1997 CID created a national education campaign called *Break the Silence*. The program has two goals: to serve as a public education tool and to help individuals become advocates on right-to-die issues. The program seeks to gather broad-based support for compassionate and humane care at the end of life, including hospice services, dying at home, pain management, and palliative care. Individuals are encouraged to submit a petition to CID to voice their support of such measures. CID provides petition and fact sheets for interested participants, who share fact sheets with friends and return the signed petition to CID. The organization will compile all petitions and present them to policymakers at the states and federal level and to the media.

BUDGET INFORMATION

At the end of fiscal year 1996, CID had revenue totaling $2,482,451. Revenue included direct public support ($2,118,878), program service revenue ($244,933), dividends and interest from securities ($43,268), and net gain from sale of assets ($75,372). Expenses totaled $2,452,946 and included program services ($1,938,442), management and general ($351,706), and fund-raising ($162,798). In a separate breakout, highest expenses included compensation of officers ($396,437) and other salaries and wages ($438,158).

HISTORY

Although CID adopted its current name in 1991, the organization is really the evolution of several like-minded predecessors. The first right-to-die organization in the United States was the Euthanasia Society, founded in 1938. By the 1960s the society had grown to 500 members. In 1967 a conceptual milestone in the movement was realized when the first living will was created by the society. For the first time a document existed that allowed individuals to specify the kind of treatment and decisions that they wanted for their end-of-life care. In 1968 more than 100,000 living wills had circulated in the United States.

During the 1970s more progress was made in establishing participation in end-of-life decisions, an acknowledged patient prerogative. The American Medical Association created the Patient Bill of Rights, which required informed consent for patients and allowed patients to refuse treatment. In the meantime, the Euthanasia Society became the Society for the Right to Die and its complementary organization, The Euthanasia Educational Council, became Concern for Dying. By the late 1980s, these organizations had achieved a combined membership of over 64,000.

In 1976, a precedent setting and news-making Supreme Court case in New Jersey (In Re Quinlan, 70 N.J. 10, 355 A. 2d 647, 1976) established that a patient's wishes regarding the right-to-die were to be placed above the state's mandate to preserve life. The Karen Ann Quinlan case, which was widely publicized in the media, involved a young woman who had been in a coma for several years and who was being kept alive solely through life support machinery. The case did much to expose issues about care at the end of life and state legislation followed on a number of fronts. California enacted the first right-to-die act (California Natural Death Act, California Health and Safety Code Section 7185-7194.5) in September 1976. The following year, treatment refusal laws were passed in several states. By 1984, 22 states recognized advance directives such as living wills and power of attorney provisions as legal documents.

In 1990 another Supreme Court decision (*Cruzan v. Director,* Missouri Department of Health, 497 U.S. 261)

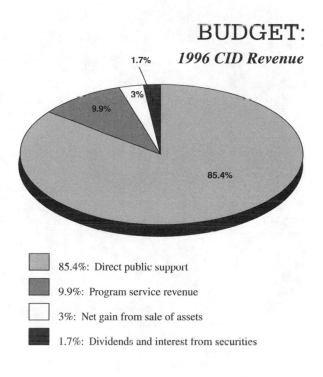

BUDGET:
1996 CID Revenue

1.7%
3%
9.9%
85.4%

- ■ 85.4%: Direct public support
- ■ 9.9%: Program service revenue
- □ 3%: Net gain from sale of assets
- ■ 1.7%: Dividends and interest from securities

1996 CID Expenses

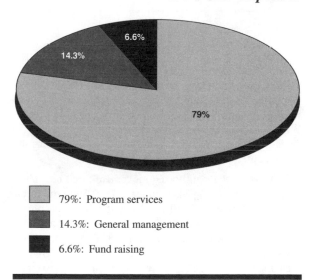

6.6%
14.3%
79%

- ■ 79%: Program services
- ■ 14.3%: General management
- ■ 6.6%: Fund raising

set a precedent by determining that a patient had the constitutional right to refuse medical treatment. This court decision prompted the U.S. Congress to pass legislation (The Patient Self Determination Act, 1990, sponsor S. Levin (D-Mich.)) which formalized a patient's right to make choices about medical care and required that they were notified of that right.

Choice in Dying officially became an organization in 1991 with the merger of Concern for Dying and the Society for the Right to Die. Now that living wills were

Retired pathologist Jack Kevorkian (right) has made news since the early 1990s with his facilitation of assisted suicide. In 1999 a Michigan court sentenced him to 10 to 25 years in prison for second degree murder. (Archive Photos, Inc.)

legal and more and more widely accepted, organization membership dropped, eventually dropping to one-fifth of the size that combined membership had reached during peak years. CID's budget decreased from $9 million to $1 million and CID was forced to redirect its efforts. While pursuing the legality of living wills was no longer an issue, work remained to be done on improving the implementation of living wills in each state.

CID and the right-to-die movement faced new challenges during the 1990s. A January 1997 Supreme Court decision (*Vacco v. Quill*) held that state bans on physician-assisted suicide were not unconstitutional. This essentially put the decision for legalizing physician-assisted suicide in the hands of each state. In a groundbreaking court case, Oregon became the first state to legalize physician-assisted suicide under certain circumstances. At that time, 44 states had laws that criminalized physician-assisted suicide under most circumstances. The Oregon decision (*Lee v. Oregon*, U.S. Court of Appeals, Ninth Circuit; February 1997) may open up possibilities for other states to follow in a similar direction.

CURRENT POLITICAL ISSUES

As an organization that advocates for the rights of people who are dying, the issues that CID is involved

with are usually controversial. Right-to-die stances are opposed by pro-life organizations such as the National Right to Life Committee, which believe that human life should be preserved at all costs. Such organizations oppose euthanasia and the withholding of medical treatment toward the end of life, even if these actions are in accord with the patient's wishes.

CID's battle over right-to-die issues saw a major victory in 1990, when the U.S. Supreme Court decided that a patient has the constitutionally-protected right to refuse medical treatment. Since that time CID's focus has been on educating the public about their rights and making it easier for them to exercise these rights. It has also worked to defend court decisions against pro-life challenges. CID has supported several unsuccessful efforts in Congress to pass an Advanced Planning and Compassionate Care Act. This act would make advanced directives a formal part of medical records and make it easier to transfer advance directives between states.

The most controversial right-to-die issue with which the CID has been involved recently is physician-assisted suicide. According to CID, physician-assisted suicide refers to a situation where a physician provides medications or other interventions to a patient with the knowledge that the patient will use the medications to end their life. This differs from withholding care or otherwise allowing a sick patient to die, because the physician is acting to help end the patient's life, rather than ceasing treatment that might prolong it.

Case Study: Physician-Assisted Suicide in Oregon

The legality and morality of physician-assisted suicide has been hotly debated. CID has advocated for an open discussion of the issue, rather than supporting or opposing the practice. In 1997 the U.S. Supreme Court upheld state laws which made physician-assisted suicide illegal. This effectively left the issue in the hands of state courts and legislatures.

Before 1994 physician-assisted suicide was not legal anywhere in the world. In the Netherlands it enjoyed a quasi-legal status, neither illegal nor legally protected. In other places the practice may have been tolerated despite its illegal status. For example, in Michigan retired pathologist Jack Kevorkian has made news since the early 1990s with his participation in assisted suicides, events where he provides the means (gas mask and carbon monoxide) and the patient removes a clip in order to breathe the poisonous gas. Kevorkian claims to have assisted more than 100 people end their lives. Despite increasingly strict laws against physician-assisted suicide, several attempts to convict Kevorkian failed. Eventually, Kevorkian went so far as to provide the television program *60 Minutes* with tapes of himself injecting lethal chemicals into someone who had asked for his help in commiting suicide. The tapes were later aired in a highly controversial episode. The lawsuit arising out of this incident led to Kevorkian's conviction for second degree murder in 1999.

In November 1994 Oregon voters approved the Oregon Death With Dignity Act (DDA, Ballot measure 16), a referendum which permitted physician-assisted suicide in certain situations. The referendum was challenged in court over the next few years, and the legislature placed another initiative on the 1997 ballot, one which would repeal the DDA if accepted. Opponents to the DDA made a number of arguments in favor of repeal. Some were opposed to the bill on moral grounds, believing that suicide, or assisting another in suicide, is wrong and should be prevented. Others feared that if the DDA were to go into effect, and Oregon became the only state which allowed physician-assisted suicide, many people wishing to die would come to the state in search of assistance. Voters disagreed, however, and the attempt to repeal the DDA failed with 60 percent of the vote against repeal. Faced with clear public support for the measure, the Oregon legislature soon expanded its state Medicare system to cover the costs of physician-assisted suicide for the poor.

Public Impact

Despite dire predictions by its opponents, the implementation of the DDA has not led to a massive immi-

FAST FACTS

Fifty-three percent of surveyed AIDS specialists admitted to writing prescriptions for overdoses to assist AIDS patients in committing suicide, according to survey data from Thomas Mitchell of the University of California, San Francisco.

(Source: Jim Cleaver. "Report Says Many Doctors and Nurses Are Helping Patients Die." *Los Angeles Sentinel,* July 25, 1996.)

gration of the ill and suicidal to Oregon. In 1998 there were 15 cases of physician-assisted suicide reported under the new law. While CID has been careful to avoid taking a strong stand on the issue of physician-assisted suicide, the organization encourages and supports the need for dialogue on the issue and will continue to do so by promoting public outreach around end-of-life issues with programs such as the Break the Silence Campaign. The organization will also monitor relevant legislation and court cases and will be watching closely as the issue plays itself out in the United States.

CID points out that, outside of Oregon, the medical profession and the government have been silent on exploring the options and issues around assisted suicide. While CID has been reluctant to lead the way in an indepth policy discussion on assisted suicide, the organization maintains that patients faced with such issues are often ignored by a medical system that does not know how to respond to their concerns. It is likely that assisted suicide and alternatives such as improved end-of-life care will be more widely discussed as the medical profession, and the nation, struggle to decide how to deal with death and dying.

FUTURE DIRECTIONS

As an advocate for improved end-of-life medical treatment, CID will continue to promote the use of palliative care methods that make the dying process more humane. The use of painkillers, for example, is a palliative measure that CID supports, while opponents argue that such medications can lead to drug addiction. CID will also be working to network with other agencies to improve the effectiveness of living wills. However, the organization realizes that living wills and power of attorney provisions often do not cover the full range of issues that may be faced at the end of life. CID hopes to affect changes that will improve the quality in end-of-life care, thereby providing a viable alternative to assisted suicide.

GROUP RESOURCES

CID maintains a Web site at http://www.choices.org. Included at the site are publications, resources, and videos that the public may purchase by calling CID directly. The organization maintains a toll-free phone line (1-800-989-9455) devoted to offering advice and support for those dealing with end-of-life situations and interpreting advance directives. Legal and program resources as well as publications and membership information are also available through the toll-free phone line. CID offers a free state-specific advance directive packet for callers, when requested.

GROUP PUBLICATIONS

CID members automatically receive the newsletter *Choices*. CID produces a number of other publications and media presentations dealing with right-to-die issues, including the award-winning video *WHOSE Death is it Anyway?* ($24.95). A question-and-answer series of publications ranges in cost from about $3.00 to $6.00 and includes the titles *Q&A: Health Care Agents: Appointing One and Being One* and *Q&A: The Physician-Assisted Suicide Debate: Understanding the Issues.* Guides for professionals include *Advance Directive Protocols and the Patient Self-Determination Act: A Resource Manual for the Development of Institutional*

Protocols ($25.00) and *Advance Directives and Community Education: A Manual for Institutional Caregivers* ($52.00). Publications may be ordered by calling the organization's toll-free number (1-800-989-9455) or writing to CID's publication distributor: Choice In Dying Publications/Membership, 325 East Oliver St., Baltimore, MD 21202; fax: (410) 539-4700.

BIBLIOGRAPHY

"All Sue Rodriguez Wanted Was To Die With Dignity." *Time International,* 28 February 1994.

Cain, Brad. "Judge Delays Ruling on Assisted Suicide Challenge." *The Columbian,* 18 February 1998.

"Catholic Church Alters Tactics on Suicide Law." *Los Angeles Times,* 1 November 1997.

Donnelly, Ann. "Doctor Assisted Suicide Threatens Our Moral Climate." *The Columbian,* 9 November 1997.

Machacek, John. "Advocates Form Group to Push Legislation, Focus Attention on End-of-life Care." *Gannett News Service,* 4 December 1997.

———. "Right-to-die Movement Revives as Oregonians Keep Doctor Assisted Suicide Law." *Gannett News Service,* 5 November 1997.

Thomas, Cal. "We're Walking a Thin Moral Line With the Right-to-die Movement." *Newsday,* 3 March 1998.

Usher, Rod. "Live and Let Die Should a Rational Person Who Chooses Death be Forced to 'Soldier On'?" *Time International,* 26 January 1998.

Wade, Betsy. "Travel With Your Living Will." *Rocky Mountain News,* 26 January 1997.

Christian Coalition (CC)

WHAT IS ITS MISSION?

According to Christian Coalition (CC) literature, the organization was founded on the belief that "faith is not meant to be confined to monasteries or to atrophy behind stained glass windows." Its actions are motivated by the "pledge to use our voices to continue speaking out for families, for children, for free enterprise and for the return of common sense values to the mainstream of American life."

Founded by former presidential candidate Pat Robertson, the CC is a network of Christian grassroots activists united to change public policy. It gets involved in a broad range of issues, ranging from protecting religious freedom to protecting children from pornography on the Internet. What ties the efforts together is the desire to bring a higher sense of morality, as the coalition defines it, to public policy and public affairs.

HOW IS IT STRUCTURED?

The CC is a nonprofit organization based in Chesapeake, Virginia. It is headed by a president who handles the coalition's management, long-term strategy, and day-to-day affairs, and an executive director, who works primarily as a liaison to Capitol Hill and the group's local chapters. The CC also has a government affairs office based in Washington, D.C. Founder Pat Robertson serves as chairman of the board of directors. He concentrates heavily on evangelical efforts around the world.

The CC boasts of an extensive grassroots organization. It has about 2,000 local chapters across the country, and almost 100 full- or part-time staff operating in all 50

ESTABLISHED: 1989
EMPLOYEES: 87
MEMBERS: 1.9 million
PAC: None

Contact Information:

ADDRESS: 1801-L Sara Dr.
　　　　 Chesapeake, VA 23320
PHONE: (757) 424-2630
TOLL FREE: (800) 325-4746
FAX: (757) 424-9068
E-MAIL: coalition@cc.org
URL: http://www.cc.org
PRESIDENT: Donald P. Hodel
EXECUTIVE DIRECTOR: Randy Tate
CHAIRMAN: Pat Robertson

states. The staff helps to recruit and mobilize volunteers who serve as chapter leaders, church liaisons, and neighborhood coordinators. There are also two international affiliates: the Christian Coalition of British Columbia and the Conservative Christian Fellowship of Great Britain.

PRIMARY FUNCTIONS

The CC's primary aim is to have "permanent impact on American public policy" by promoting political, community, and social action for people of faith. While it does not advocate for or against political candidates, it does provide citizens with political information by producing voter guides, voter education materials, and scorecards that highlight the positions of candidates on various issues. For example, the coalition distributed voter guides in 1993 prior to the New York City school board elections highlighting the pro-family candidates; according to the coalition, more than half of those candidates won. In the 1996 elections, the Christian Coalition—working through churches, civic groups, and volunteer networks—distributed 66 million voter guides nationwide.

The coalition boasts of one of the most effective grassroots lobbying networks in the nation, which it uses to attempt to sway elected officials on particular issues. The group also attempts to influence legislation. Its annual report says its grassroots network "can strike at a moment's notice, mobilizing literally thousands of Christian Coalition activists to flood the Capitol with calls and letters." Its grassroots volunteer network uses state-of-the-art communications technology to mobilize members, including "high-speed faxes, computerized automatic dialing equipment, broadcast electronic mail, and a string of satellite dishes that stretches from coast to coast."

The coalition does not simply react to legislative proposals put forth by others; it has put together the Contract with the American Family, an agenda for Congress that the coalition summarizes as a plan to "strengthen the family and restore common-sense values." The plan emerged from a survey of Christian Coalition members and supporters conducted in 1995 as well as consultation with members of Congress and their staffs. The contract includes a constitutional amendment to protect religious liberties, a transfer of funding from the federal level to families and local school boards and mechanisms such as vouchers to allow parents greater choice in choosing schools.

PROGRAMS

The various programs supported by the Christian Coalition are geared toward its mission to involve individuals of faith in political, community, and social activism. As part of its effort to foster empowerment among members and supporters, the coalition has a training program for community activists. Such programs train members in political activism, as well as nonpolitical initiatives aimed at goals such as fostering religious growth and alleviating poverty. By the end of 1996, the coalition had graduated more than 52,000 activists. The programs target state leaders, chapter chairs, church liaisons, and neighborhood coordinators. The coalition also sponsors an annual conference, Road to Victory, at which attendees learn techniques for grassroots activism.

An example of a community outreach program is the Save the Churches Fund, which donates money to black churches that were victims of arson. As of mid-1997, the fund had distributed $850,000 to churches in the South and Midwest.

Another outreach program is The Samaritan Project, which was launched in January 1997. The Samaritan Project is an eight-part plan to fight poverty that involves a collaboration of inner-city churches, community institutions, neighborhoods, and individuals. According to the coalition, it took action because the state and federal government failed to significantly alleviate poverty despite having spent $5.4 trillion on antipoverty programs by the time The Samaritan Project was launched.

BUDGET INFORMATION

In 1996, the last year for which complete figures are available, the coalition had $26.5 million in revenues, including $14.8 million from direct mail solicitations, $5.1 million from member gifts, $4.3 million from telemarketing, and $1.2 million from gifts from major donors. Members must contribute at least $15 to join, but as budget figures indicate, the average member gives much more.

The group spent $27 million in 1996, the largest category of which was $11.9 million for legislative affairs. Other expenditures include $3.1 million for field programs, $2.6 million for education, and $2.2 million for the newsletter.

HISTORY

The Christian Coalition was founded in 1989 by Pat Robertson, a televangelist widely known for his television program, *The 700 Club*. While Robertson ran unsuccessfully for president in 1988, he generated energy and enthusiasm among Christian conservatives. Such support sparked the genesis for a national group united on common ground. From the beginning, however, the group has not been without detractors. The media considered the coalition to be a fringe group of religious fanatics. In 1993 the *Washington Post* described coalition members as "largely poor, uneducated and easy to command."

BIOGRAPHY:

Pat Robertson

Evangelist; Politician (b. 1930)   During the presidential primary elections of 1988, the existing Washington power structure was treated to a political awakening courtesy of then presidential candidate Pat Robertson. Although eventually fading in the wake of mainstream politicians, Robertson's strong showing in early primaries surprised everyone. Before the start of the primaries, the born-again Christian spoke about his political aims in *New York* magazine, "The people who have come into [our] institutions are primarily termites. They are destroying institutions that have been built by Christians, whether it is universities, governments, or our own traditions that we have . . . . The termites are in charge now, and that is not the way it ought to be, and the time has arrived for a godly fumigation." Robertson came to the election as chairman and chief executive officer of the Christian Broadcasting Network (CBN), a cable television channel that carried the televangelist's message to 37 million households. In 1989,

Robertson founded the Christian Coalition built on the strong voter support of the previous year. Today Robertson divides his time among his television network, his writing, and the Coalition. In 1991 critics labeled his book *The New World Order* as anti-Semitic, a charge Robertson denies. To *People* magazine, Robertson plots the path of

his life going forward in the familiar tones of a politician: "My plans are not . . . a flaming crusade, but just some intelligent things that would draw our country to-gether, put [it] on a course for a better way of life, ensure stability of family, ensure jobs and ensure the domestic security of this nation."

Since the early 1990s, the group has grown in members, sophistication, and influence due in large part to the leadership of Ralph Reed, the former executive director, who has often been described as forceful and charismatic. Reed's work was made easier by the fact that millions of Americans, as several polls have shown, were deeply concerned with moral decline in society and were anxious for elected officials to do something about it.

In 1994, the coalition was credited with playing a crucial role in the strong showing by Republicans in congressional elections. Polls showed that Christian conservatives made up 43 percent of voters for Republican candidates, helping to bring about a GOP sweep that brought about the first Republican Congress in 40 years.

By September 1995, the coalition's evolving image was evidenced by a *Wall Street Journal* editorial that called the group "a political powerhouse" that "had earned a place in the political mainstream" and whose goals were "broad-based and decidedly nonfanatical."

When the coalition launched its Contract with the American Family in 1995, among the attendees at the unveiling were House Speaker Newt Gingrich, Senate Majority Whip Trent Lott, Texas Sen. Phil Gramm and more than a dozen other House and Senate Republicans. Reed declared, and media reports treated the claim seriously: "As religious conservatives, we have finally gained what we have always sought: a place at the table, a sense of legitimacy and a voice in the conversation that we call democracy."

The group's growing influence brought it under the spotlight and generated controversy. In 1996 the Federal Elections Commission (FEC) sued the Christian Coalition, charging that it had improperly assisted Republican political candidates. The group's tax-exempt status depends on its activities being nonpartisan, but the FEC charged that the group had conducted election activities "in coordination, cooperation and/or consultation" with Republican candidates. The charges, which coalition officials strongly deny and countercharge as an attempt to stifle free speech, were still pending as of March 1999.

Another debate arose in 1996, this time surrounding coalition efforts to reach out to other constituencies, especially minorities. The CC launched a campaign to help rebuild black Southern churches that had burned as a result of arson. The coalition's efforts were met with cynicism on the part of some African American organizations. The head of the Southern Christian Leadership Council, a black civil rights group, criticized the efforts as an attempt to make inroads among African Americans from a group associated with a conservative agenda that helped foster the climate of hate leading to the church fires. And when Ralph Reed appeared on a Black Entertainment Television news show in 1997, he was on the defensive as panelists questioned sharply the coalition's commitment to minorities.

In 1997 Reed left the group to pursue other ventures. As an indication of how forceful a role he played in advancing the coalition, he was replaced by two people:

Donald Hodel, a former member of President Ronald Reagan's cabinet, and Randy Tate, a former Congressman from Washington state.

The coalition seemed to lose momentum at the end of the 1990s. In early 1999, after strong efforts by the CC and other religious groups failed to influence the removal of President Bill Clinton from office, observers—even some within the "religious right"—were wondering whether efforts of religious conservatives to transform politics had failed. A *New York Times* article in March 1999 described religious conservatives as disillusioned and the movement as "fractured."

CURRENT POLITICAL ISSUES

The CC has successfully acquired widespread support for many of its legislative proposals. In 1996 alone, proposals signed into law included the Defense of Marriage Act, which defined marriage for federal purposes as a union between a woman and a man; a ban on pornography on the Internet; a ban on the sale of pornography in stores on military bases; and the creation of a National Gambling Commission to study the social and economic impact of gambling.

In 1997 the coalition saw two planks of its Contract with the American Family become law: a $500 per child tax credit, which was part of the 1997 Taxpayer Relief Act; and the Balanced Budget Act, which contains comprehensive spending and entitlement reforms the contract advocated.

But the coalition has failed to win support for some of its more controversial or ambitious plans. For instance, it has been unsuccessful in its quest for a constitutional amendment ensuring the right to prayer in public schools. In addition, the group's growing prominence has fueled a government challenge that poses a serious threat.

Case Study: Federal Elections Commission Lawsuit

The Christian Coalition does not have a political action committee that would allow it to legally engage in partisan political activity (and would bring it under a number of federal regulations, including reporting requirements and spending limits). To keep its tax-exempt status, the coalition must remain nonpartisan. Although the group can enlighten voters on candidates' positions, it cannot campaign for or against them.

While purporting to be nonpartisan, the coalition's markedly conservative political agenda is perceived to be more in line with the Republican platform. In the early 1990s the Democratic National Committee began to complain that the CC was favoring Republican candidates. In July 1996 the FEC acted on the complaint and sued the coalition.

According to the FEC the coalition in the early 1990s had "coordinated, cooperated and/or consulted with" the campaigns of Republican candidates, including President George Bush, Vice President Dan Quayle, Senator Jesse Helms, and U.S. senatorial candidate Oliver North. The FEC lawsuit detailed further that the coalition coordinated its efforts—such as distributing voter guides and mounting get-out-the-vote drives and mailings—with the candidate's campaigns.

The coalition's political enemies hailed the move. "The evidence shows everyone that this group is a hardball political operation that has been cloaking itself in religion," Barry Lynn of Americans United for Church and State was quoted as saying in media reports. The lawsuit asked the court to impose fines that could reach hundreds of thousands of dollars, to prevent the coalition from using certain funds to help candidates and to disclose the money it spends on politics.

In response to the lawsuit, coalition officials have pointed out that they never explicitly advocated the election of any candidate, denied there was any collusion, and said their campaign efforts fell under their constitutionally protected rights of free speech and free association. Ralph Reed, then coalition executive director, called the suit "totally baseless" and said he was confident the courts "will affirm that people of faith have every right to be involved as citizens and voters," according to media reports.

In September 1998 the coalition asked a federal judge to dismiss the lawsuit. As of March 1999, the case was pending. The lawsuit has not deterred the coalition. In 1998, for example, it distributed millions of voter guides. But the adverse publicity has caused division within the group. According to a report in the *New York Times* in October 1998, many churches were refusing to distribute the guides because the "coalition and its guides were tainted by a perceived affiliation with the Republican Party."

FUTURE DIRECTIONS

The coalition's emphasis to 2000 and beyond will focus on community outreach with the expansion of its current initiatives and the launching of ambitious new ones. The Families 2000 Strategy is geared toward mobilizing hundreds of thousands of pro-family activists by November of 2000. Specifically, the strategy has the goal of recruiting 100,000 volunteers who will serve as liaisons between community churches and the coalition chapters.

In the hopes of revitalizing distressed urban areas, the coalition plans to create Empowerment Zones in 100 communities through its Samaritan Project. The agenda includes enacting tax-relief legislation to assist small-business developers, and creating job opportunities and better transportation.

GROUP RESOURCES

In addition to the coalition's newsletter and magazine, it has a Web site, at http://www.cc.org, which includes voter guides that detail how elected representatives vote on particular issues, links to elected officials, news and special events announcements, and an E-mail link. In addition, the coalition has a monthly satellite television program, *Christian Coalition Live.* The program, broadcast from Washington, D.C., presents information from the nation's capital, and is used to train and inform religious leaders and activists. Guests have included former House Speaker Newt Gingrich and Senate Majority Whip Don Nickles.

GROUP PUBLICATIONS

The coalition generates a variety of publications including its flagship magazine, *The Christian American,* which features columns by Pat Robertson. *Religious Rights Watch* is a monthly newsletter that tracks incidents of bigotry against people of faith and updates readers on current political issues. Subscriptions are available by contacting the Family Christian Coalition's Resource Center. Archived articles are also available for viewing at the group's Web site.

BIBLIOGRAPHY

Benedetto, Richard. "Poll Points Toward Conservative Electorate." *USA Today,* 22 May 1996.

Berke, Richard L. "From Cabinet to Leadership of Coalition." *New York Times,* 12 June 1997.

Brownstein, Ronald. "Dissatisfied Public May Spell Democratic Losses." *Los Angeles Times,* 28 July 1994.

"Christians Gain a Voice." *Wall Street Journal,* 14 September 1995.

Fletcher, Michael A. "Reed Plans Effort on Church Fires." *Washington Post,* 19 June 1996.

Goldberg, Carey. "In Abortion War, High-Tech Arms." *New York Times,* 9 August 1996.

Goodstein, Laurie. "Church Debate over Voter Guides." *New York Times,* 29 October 1998.

Gvozdas, Susan. "Christian Coalition Broadens Focus." *USA Today,* 27 August 1997.

Niebuhr, Gustav, and Richard Berke. "Unity Is Elusive as Religious Right Ponders 2000 Vote." *New York Times,* 7 March 1999.

Riley, Jason. "Breaking Racial Ranks." *Wall Street Journal,* 7 February 1997.

Sharn, Lori. "New Leaders, New Goals for Christian Coalition." *USA Today,* 12 June 1997.

Citizens Committee for the Right to Keep and Bear Arms (CCRKBA)

ESTABLISHED: 1971
EMPLOYEES: 40
MEMBERS: 650,000
PAC: None

Contact Information:

ADDRESS: James Madison Bldg.
    12500 N.E. Tenth Pl.
    Bellevue, WA 98005
PHONE: (425) 454-4911
TOLL FREE: (800) 426-4302
FAX: (425) 451-3959
E-MAIL: info@ccrkba.org
URL: http://www.ccrkba.org
CHAIRMAN: Alan M. Gottlieb

WHAT IS ITS MISSION?

The Citizens Committee for the Right to Keep and Bear Arms (CCRKBA) is an organization "dedicated to the individual right of all law abiding citizens to privately own and possess firearms." The group opposes all limitations on the constitutional right to keep and bear arms as spelled out by the second amendment. Further, it believes that the maintenance of other constitutional rights is directly linked to gun rights. The CCRKBA, which maintains that the National Rifle Association (NRA) does not go far enough in its defense of gun rights, is considered one of the most radical and uncompromising of the gun activist organizations.

HOW IS IT STRUCTURED?

The Citizens Committee for the Right to Keep and Bear Arms is a nonprofit lobbying organization based in Bellevue, Washington. It has lobbying offices in Washington, D.C., Sacramento, California, and Olympia, Washington and has informal groups in most other states. CCRBKA is headed by an executive director who is responsible for the day-to-day management of the organization. The executive director also gathers information and directs the group's lobbying efforts. A board of directors oversees the group's long-term goals, policies, and finances, and appoints all CCRKBA officers. The Washington office, the center of CCRKBA congressional lobbying efforts, is run by the group's director of public affairs.

In general, membership is open to anyone who pays the $15 annual dues. Members may organize into state or local groups, which are, in the main, informal organizations, and not part of the group's official hierarchy. Where local groups have officers, they are elected by local members. The Second Amendment Foundation, founded by the CCRKBA's founders, is the group's sister organization. Defined in its charter as a lobbying organization, the CCRKBA is very limited in the fundraising it is allowed to do; the Second Amendment Foundation, in contrast, was organized as a fund-raising group. CCRKBA accepts other local groups as affiliates but does not maintain a network of local chapters.

PRIMARY FUNCTIONS

In its work to safeguard the constitutional right to possess firearms, the CCRKBA works extensively at the legislative level. An essential function of the organization is to influence gun legislation. Therefore it lobbies elected officials at all levels of government, working to defeat any legislation that limits the ownership of firearms.

The CCRKBA also works to cultivate a large grassroots following in the United States. It assists local gun rights activists in setting up local chapters and helps local groups to lobby effectively. The group also considers education to be an important initiative. The CCRKBA educates gun owners and nongun owners about gun issues and the political processes that affect gun owners, in particular the legislative process. The group is a clearinghouse of information for members and gun owners; it circulates news about proposed gun legislation and encourages members to express their pro-gun opinions to lawmakers.

The CCRBKA provides pro-gun messages and speakers to the media. The group's extensive grassroots network makes possible the deployment of CCRBKA representatives to the media quickly when antigun legislation is proposed. Its spokespeople have appeared in many national media forums, including *USA Today,* the *Washington Post*, CNN with Larry King, ABC's *20-20*, public broadcasting, and the Nashville Network.

PROGRAMS

CCRBKA's influence on lawmakers comes in large measure from the strength of its grassroots organization. Its ability to affect the course of proposed legislation in states and Congress depends on its ability to mobilize members and gun enthusiasts at large to make their views known to lawmakers and executives who sign legislation into law. The group's Citizen Action Project uses grassroots mobilization. For instance, every month the group posts action alerts on its Web sites to encourage members and supporters to become involved in gun issues. The site offers suggestions on ways to get involved, such

as writing letters to lawmakers about an issue in the news. The site provides clear instructions on how to accomplish this by explaining what kind of letter to write and to whom the letter should be sent. In response to the letter-writing campaign, the group has asked members to forward copies of the replies they receive from public officials to the national CCRBKA office for tracking. At other times, the group has recommended ways to become more effective at grassroots action by taking courses offered by party organizations or reading useful books on a particular subject.

Every year CCRBKA, in cooperation with its sister organization, Second Amendment Foundation, sponsors the Gun Rights Policy Conference, a meeting of activists interested in gun rights from around the country. The 1998 conference was attended by more than 500 individuals from around the United States. The conference, together with dozens of Leadership Training Conferences held regionally every year, is part of the CCRBKA's educational mission. The conferences are free of charge to anyone who wishes to attend.

BUDGET INFORMATION

The CCRBKA has a total annual budget of approximately $3 million per year. Most of its operating funds come from membership dues and donations. As of 1999, members paid $15 annually or $150 for a lifetime membership.

HISTORY

CCRBKA was founded in 1971 by a group of students at the University of Tennessee. Originally called the National Student Citizens Committee for the Right to Keep and Bear Arms, the group was loosely associated with the Young Americans for Freedom. Alan Gottlieb, the group's later chairman, became involved in the organization in 1972. When he moved to Seattle, Washington, around the end of 1973, he spun a group off the Young Americans, renamed it the Citizens Committee for the Right to Keep and Bear Arms, and set up headquarters in Washington state. In the years since the group was founded, its membership has multiplied twenty-fold. Over the years the organization has written or supported a number of pieces of legislation, including the Firearm Owners Protections Act, the Second Amendment Affirmation Act, and the Anti-Drug-Abuse Act of 1986.

CURRENT POLITICAL ISSUES

The right to own and possess firearms has long been a controversial issue in the United States. Opponents to

FAST FACTS

According to CCRBKA 1998 statistics, registered firearms exist in 70 million households in the United States and there are over 200 million privately owned firearms.

(Source: Citizens Committee for the Right to Bear and Keep Arms, 1999.)

gun rights legislation claim that access to firearms contributes to crime and violence in the United States. Defenders say guns are the bedrock of U.S. freedom. According to pro-gun activists guns enable Americans to defend their other constitutional rights. The issue leaps to the forefront of public consciousness whenever the murder rate in the United States or one of its major cities jumps or when shootings are publicized in the news. When it does, the gun control advocates renew their efforts to limit access to guns while proponents of gun rights, in particular the CCRBKA, fight restrictions on gun owners. The CCRBKA consistently maintains that citizens have the right to carry concealed weapons and continues to adamantly oppose all bans on any class of firearms. The depth of the CCRBKA's opposition to gun control was illustrated most starkly in the summer of 1998 following a series of school shootings over the previous twelve months.

Case Study: The 1997–99 School Shootings

Between October 1997 and April 1999, a series of shootings took place in various schools across the United States. Dozens of teachers and students were wounded or killed in Pearl, Mississippi; West Paducah, Kentucky; Jonesboro, Arkansas; Springfield, Oregon; Edinboro, Pennsylvania; and Littleton, Colorado. What was particularly disturbing was the fact that the individuals responsible for the shootings were children. The incidents unleashed a national debate on the availability of weapons in homes, the ease with which children can use guns, and the extent to which parents are responsible for children who kill with firearms.

Gun control advocates immediately renewed their demands for tighter restrictions on firearms. They argued that rifles should be regulated more stringently, as handguns and assault weapons are by the Brady gun control law, which mandates background checks on individuals

buying handguns and assault weapons and a waiting period on gun sales of those types. Others called for gun manufacturers to build locks into new firearms or for laws that would make parents legally responsible for acts their children performed with guns that had been carelessly stored.

The shootings roused nationwide antipathy toward guns. In their wake, the NRA, the leading national organization for gun owners refrained from speaking out against the gun restrictions being proposed. "Given the shock and horror of this tragedy, it transcends any political tit-for-tat," was the NRA spokesperson's comment as reported by Scott Bowles and Gary Fields in *USA Today*.

The CCRBKA, on the other hand, spoke out bluntly in favor of gun rights. It denounced the suggestion that sales of rifles and shotguns—guns whose sale is virtually unrestricted—be subject to a waiting period while a background check is run on the purchaser. A CCRBKA spokesperson quoted in *USA Today* said the effort to control hunting weapons was part of a pattern in the country that began first with the banning of cheap handguns, so-called "Saturday night specials." Later plastic handguns and semiautomatic assault weapons were forbidden. It would follow, the CCRBKA claimed, that rifles would be next, despite the fact that the organization estimated that rifles and shot guns were found at fewer than one percent of crime scenes where guns were a factor. The ultimate aim of gun control advocates, the CCRBKA concluded, was to ban all guns.

In June 1998 Congresswoman Carolyn McCarthy, a Democrat from New York, introduced the Children's Gun Violence Prevention Act in the House. The bill required gun locks on newly manufactured guns and imposed criminal penalties on adults who do not properly store guns and as a result, allow juveniles to obtain and use the weapons. It also funded gun awareness programs in schools and a study of firearms by the Centers for Disease Control.

Alan Gottlieb, chairman of the CCRBKA, said of the bill that it "won't take one criminal off the street." Instead the organization supported an alternative bill (Senate Bill 2169) sponsored by Sen. Ron Wyden (D-Ore.) and Sen. Gordon Smith (R-Ore.). That bill encouraged state legislation to detain students who violated state or federal law by carrying firearms on school premises. Violators would be held, for a period no longer than 72 hours, for psychiatric observation followed by a judge's ruling on the student's potential danger to himself or others. Gottlieb told *USA Today* "This approach is one we strongly support." He said the problem was not firearms, but the failure of society—teachers, parents and other students in this case—to recognize the signals that disturbed students send out before they erupt in violence.

Congress adjourned before the bills could make it out of committee. In the meantime, the effort to impeach President Bill Clinton and the Democratic upset in the 1998 midterm elections pushed the shoot-

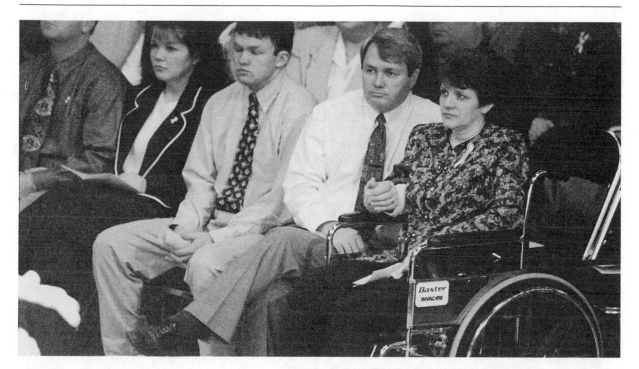

A Jonesboro, Arkansas, teacher wounded in a 1998 school shooting, attends a memorial service for the slain students and teacher. The shooting at Jonesboro, and others like it, unleashed a national debate on the availability of weapons in homes, children's use of guns, and parental responsibility for children who kill with firearms. (AP/Wide World Photo)

ings from public memory. Polls continue to regularly show that most Americans favor gun control as a way of reducing violent crime. And the CCRBKA continues to maintain that gun control is a "divisive and polarizing issue." It believes that cooperative efforts, such as Senate Bill 2169, work for gun owners and non-gun owners alike.

SUCCESSES AND FAILURES

The CCRKA played a key role in the defeat of Initiative 676, a handgun control measure on the ballot in Washington State in November 1997. The proposal would have required that all handgun owners attend an eight-hour, state-run training course and obtain a license issued by the state. Failure to comply would have been a felony offense and violators would have had their guns confiscated. CCRBKA, with other gun rights organizations such as the NRA, organized grassroots movements opposing the measure. The CCRBKA and more than 12,000 activists raised over $3 million to fight the initiative. The proposal was ultimately defeated by a 71 percent margin.

FUTURE DIRECTIONS

The CCRBKA will be looking closely at the implementation of the national instant-check system for gun purchasers that was instituted as part of the Brady law. The law called for the creation of a national computer system that would allow for an instant check of past felonies or records of mental instability for individuals buying handguns. CCRBKA is very concerned about the operative definition of instant in the new system. It will also monitor the system to assure that it does not result in a national database of gun owners. Such a database, the group contends, would be in violation of federal law. On a practical level, the group fears that such a database would be used to keep tabs on all gun owners in the country and could eventually result in harassment or other violations of gun owners' civil rights.

CCRBKA will continue its struggle for the right of gun owners to carry concealed weapons. The group supports the mandatory automatic issuance of a concealed weapons permit to anyone except individuals with felony records, currently under indictment for a felony crime, or who have a history of mental disorders. It is also fighting for passage of a federal law that would require states to recognize, within their borders, concealed weapons permits issued by other states. Some states do not allow private citizens to carry concealed weapons at all.

GROUP RESOURCES

The CCRBKA Web site, available at http://www. ccrbka.org, contains a wealth of information on gun rights and constitutional issues surrounding the second amendment. The site includes Hindsight columns from *Gun Week Magazine,* editorials from the magazine *Women & Guns,* and miscellaneous articles on gun rights that readers have submitted. In 2000, a section on legal issues connected to gun ownership and second amendment rights will be introduced. Publications from its sister organization, the Second Amendment Foundation, such as the *Gottlieb-Tartaro Report, Gun Week, Women and Guns,* and *Gun News Digest,* are posted a month or so after their original publication.

The CCRBKA Web site is a source for books about guns, shooting, and second amendment issues. For example, a full-text version of *How to Defend Your Gun Rights* is available for downloading. A wide variety of books, which are listed at the site, can be ordered directly from the CCRBKA. The Gun Rights Hot Line is maintained by the CCRBKA in cooperation with the Second Amendment Foundation. The hot line is a source of information on gun legislation; it can also be used to report new proposed legislation. The hot line's number is 1-800-426-4302.

GROUP PUBLICATIONS

The CCRBKA publishes a monthly newsletter, *Point Blank.* It contains news, information on pending gun legislation, upcoming CCRBKA events, and opinion articles. A subscription is free with a $15 annual CCRBKA membership. A free sample issue can be obtained by writing CCRBKA at James Madison Bldg., 12500 NE Tenth Place, Bellevue, WA 98005 or calling (425) 454-4911.

BIBLIOGRAPHY

Bill of Rights: Opposing Viewpoints. San Diego, Calif.: Greenhaven Press, 1994.

Bowles, Scott, and Gary Fields. "New Territory for Gun Debate: Hunting Rifles Might Be Drawn In." *USA Today,* 27 March 1998.

Fields, Gary. "New Gun Bill Resulted from School Shootings." *USA Today,* 17 June 1998.

Gottlieb, Alan M. *Gun Rights Fact Book.* Bellevue, Wash.: Merril Press, 1988.

———. *The Rights of Gun Owners: A Second Amendment Foundation Handbook.* Bellevue, Wash.: Merril Press, 1991.

Gun Control: An American Issue. Wylie, Tex.: Information Plus, 1997.

Gun Control: Opposing Viewpoints. San Diego, Calif.: Greenhaven Press, 1997.

Kruschke, Earl R. *Right to Keep and Bear Arms: A Continuing American Dilemma.* Springfield, Ill.: C.C. Thomas, 1985.

Violence Policy Center. "Female Persuasion: A Study of How the Firearms Industry Markets to Women and the Reality of Women and Guns." Contemporary Women's Issues Database, 1998.

Weir, William. *A Well Regulated Militia: The Battle Over Gun Control.* North Haven, Conn.: Archon Books, 1996.

Citizens for Tax Justice (CTJ)

WHAT IS ITS MISSION?

Citizens for Tax Justice (CTJ) addresses perceived inequities in the U.S. federal tax system. The CTJ enumerates its mission clearly on its Web site as a six-fold purpose: to seek equity in taxation for middle- and lower-income taxpayers; to insure that the wealthiest taxpayers are taxed according to their fair share; to eliminate loopholes that favor large corporations; to ensure sufficient funding for government functions and services; to minimize and reduce the federal debt; and to minimize the imbalance of economic markets through equitable taxation.

Fundamentally the CTJ seeks to protect the common person from wealthy special interest groups and corporate lobbies that can overwhelm the legislature with demands for special interests, often to the detriment of the middle class.

HOW IS IT STRUCTURED?

The CTJ is a small, nonprofit organization that operates from a single office in Washington, D.C. A handful of employees maintain CTJ operations. The CTJ office environment is loosely structured in order to operate within the restraints of a comparatively small budget. Under the leadership of the director of the CTJ, every member of the staff is assigned specific responsibilities; however, there is no rigid hierarchy and each member of the CTJ staff reports to every other member. Decisions are finalized through discussion, feedback, and group consultation when necessary.

ESTABLISHED: 1979
EMPLOYEES: 10
MEMBERS: 2,500
PAC: None

Contact Information:

ADDRESS: 1311 L St. NW
    Washington, DC 20005
PHONE: (202) 626-3780
TOLL FREE: (888) 626-2622
E-MAIL: ctj@ctj.org
URL: http://www.ctj.org
DIRECTOR: Robert S. McIntyre

FAST FACTS

Popular proposals for a national sales tax program would require a tax of at least 30 percent to be paid on all transactions, including free checking accounts, free health care, and church services.

(Source: Robert S. McIntyre. "The 23 Percent Solution." *New York Times,* January 23, 1998.)

The CTJ staff encourages citizens nationwide to join the organization by making a $25 contribution sent directly to the office in Washington, D.C. In return for the membership fee, individuals receive a copy of CTJ's newsletter, *CTJ Update,* which is published nine times annually. Members also receive discounts when purchasing other CTJ publications.

The Institute on Taxation and Economic Policy (ITEP) is a research arm of the CTJ. The ITEP is legally independent of the CTJ, although the two groups share a common address. The ITEP utilizes its experts in the field of tax studies to contribute to the research of the CTJ.

Similarly named groups throughout the United States, such as Minnesota Citizens for Tax Justice, are not directly affiliated with the CTJ, except by coincidence of name and perhaps in mission. Despite any overlap of mutual interests between such organizations and the CTJ, there is no official organizational tie. The CTJ does, however, collaborate at times with such groups in the pursuit of a common cause.

PRIMARY FUNCTIONS

CTJ staff members perform research and advocacy to promote the principles of a progressive income tax structure. Progressive income tax exists when citizens and corporations with greater economic means incur a larger tax liability in proportion to their wealth.

The CTJ studies federal and local tax laws to determine their fairness at every level of income. The CTJ staff works and talks with local groups around the country about existing federal, state, and local tax systems, and about the importance of a progressive income tax structure. CTJ employees occasionally write articles and editorials for major media publications such as the *New York Times* and work with labor unions, church groups, and local policymakers to promote progressive taxation. CTJ works with local advocacy groups with a similar focus, such as the Iowa Citizens Action group, to further their mutual goals. The staff also publishes a newsletter, the *CTJ Update,* and responds directly to queries regarding its efforts or general tax law information through a toll-free telephone line.

As a 501(c)4 advocacy organization, the CTJ does not lobby the government and does not maintain a political action committee.

PROGRAMS

The CTJ does not sponsor formal programs or activities. Instead the CTJ aims to spread the message of progressive taxation, to publish related facts, and to encourage legislation that is compatible with CTJ principles.

The CTJ often works in collaboration with the Institute on Taxation and Economic Policy (ITEP) research group. The work of the ITEP is to perform microsimulations using an in-house database representing national, state, and local taxpayer bases. ITEP economists, programmers, and analysts use output from database manipulations to determine the consumption and tax burden within U.S. communities, against specific demographic factors including income. The database reportedly contains nearly one million entries. In addition to microsimulation projects, the ITEP maintains and distributes publications dealing with tax policy.

Good Jobs First

On July 14, 1998 the ITEP formally announced that it would house an organization called Good Jobs First. Like ITEP and CTJ, Good Jobs First is a separate legal entity. Greg LeRoy founded the program with funds he received as the 1998 Public Interest Pioneer Award recipient. The goal of Good Jobs First is to encourage accountability on the part of corporate employers to create "family-wage" jobs—jobs that will actually support a family. LeRoy created the organization to combat unscrupulous employment practices by corporations that collect government and community subsidies in return for creating jobs. Good Jobs First works to ensure that corporate employers will provide appropriate compensations for such jobs, particularly those created using publicly-funded incentives such as subsidies and reduced taxes.

Good Jobs First is a self-described clearinghouse of resources for unions, community groups, and others to access information in order to further the interests of family-wage earners. Good Jobs First has been endorsed by the AFL-CIO and other public interest groups.

BUDGET INFORMATION

The CTJ is a tax-exempt social welfare organization under tax code 501(c)4. As such the group performs research and advocacy work from which no individual or private interest is allowed to profit. In 1998 the CTJ operated on a budget of approximately $400,000. The CTJ collects its operating funds largely from membership dues and sales of research reports and other publications produced by the CTJ staff. The CTJ is also the recipient of (non-tax deductible) donations from individuals, labor unions, and other organizations. The entire CTJ budget goes to staff wages and salaries, office expenses, and miscellaneous cost of operations.

HISTORY

The CTJ is a grassroots organization that originated in California in protest of that state's passage of a real estate tax measure known as Proposition 13. Proposition 13 was passed by a 65 percent majority of California voters on June 6, 1978. The measure placed a "cap" or limit on real estate taxes for property owners. While the concept of limiting taxes was appealing, there were many citizens who viewed the measure as regressive—a tax that penalizes those with proportionally less wealth—because the rate of tax would decrease proportionately for larger landholders. Public interest groups and labor unions came together in protest of the passage of Proposition 13. Membership in this movement was always very informal, and few records remain of the original members of the group. At some point in 1979, however, individuals from that original protest group carried their concerns to Washington D.C., where they expanded the scope of their advocacy movement and established themselves as a 501(c)4 tax entity with an office in the nation's capital. The result was Citizens for Tax Justice.

In the 1980s the organization had several successes. The press and other media acknowledged that, thanks in part to CTJ studies and publications such as *Corporate Taxpayers & Corporate Freeloaders* and *Money for Nothing: The Failure of Corporate Tax Incentives, 1981-1984*, the administration of President Ronald Reagan was prodded into passing the Tax Reform Act of 1986. The Act of 1986 dealt a blow to many so-called "tax shelters" and loopholes that were habitually employed by large businesses as a method of reducing tax liability. The legislation of 1986 eliminated certain deductions for real estate and drastically limited business entertainment expenses that reaped extensive tax savings for corporations while otherwise contributing little or nothing to corporate profits.

The sweeping tax reform of 1986 was followed by expanded debate in the media and in Congress over the issue of "flat" federal taxes. Although a variety of flat tax schemes came under discussion, the underlying principle of every flat tax proposal was that taxpaying persons or entities would be required to pay the exact same percentage in taxes—either in the form of an income tax or in the form of a national sales tax on goods and services. The CTJ quickly spoke out against a flat tax rate in any form and condemned the overall concept as a non-progressive tax scheme. Throughout the 1990s the CTJ reacted with a widespread campaign against flat tax proposals, including testimony before the Joint Economic Committee of Congress on May 17, 1995, by Director Robert S. McIntyre. The CTJ also accelerated its campaign efforts to improve state and local tax schemes for a more equitable distribution of the tax burden, and increased efforts to mandate the accountability of corporate recipients of tax dollars designated for social welfare purposes.

CURRENT POLITICAL ISSUES

Throughout the 1980s and 1990s income tax reform was hotly debated. In 1996 publisher Steve Forbes entered the race for the Republican presidential nomination on a platform distinguished exclusively by tax reform and the "flat" tax issue. By 1998 the issue of tax reform became a nonpartisan issue within the federal legislature. Perhaps the two most commonly proposed methods of reform were the levy of a national sales tax and the implementation of a flat income tax. Each of these solutions received enthusiastic endorsement from members of both houses of Congress. The so-called "flat-tax" proposals were the most popular, according to a 1997 poll conducted for *Money* by ICR Research of Media, Pennsylvania. According to ICR the flat tax proposal received a support rating of 66 percent. ICR further reported that 66 percent of Americans were in favor of drastic tax reform measures and the elimination of the existing income tax system in general. In its efforts to conceive a tax system that is fair to everyone, the CTJ has paid close attention to this debate.

Case Study: Flat Income Tax

Among the most popular flat tax proposals was a system furthered in 1996 and 1997 by House Majority Leader Dick Armey. Under the proposal all federal income tax filing would be accomplished via a postcard-sized form. There would be no "allowable deductions" as with the traditional system, and the tax rate would be 17 percent of all wages, salaries, and retirement income. Individual deductions would be permitted up to $11,000 plus $5,000 for dependent minors. All tax on investment income would be eliminated. Proponents of the flat-rate income tax purported total savings of $147 billion, including the costs to the taxpayers of preparation, plus the costs to the government of printing and mailing forms and the cost of collecting the taxes.

Despite the perceived support for tax reform, the flat tax proposal did not ultimately draw bipartisan support within the federal legislature. In general Republicans in both houses of Congress supported the flat tax proposal, although some favored the levy of a national sales tax—a revenue system deemed "regressive" by others. The sales tax proposal, estimated at a rate of 15 percent, was nonetheless supported by a substantial minority.

During this period President Bill Clinton opposed all flat tax measures. He expressed disapproval of comprehensive tax reform in general and inferred that radical change would bring serious problems. House Minority Leader Richard Gephardt also expressed disapproval of the flat tax noting that the middle class would inevitably experience a substantial tax increase while taxes for the rich would be reduced. Strong public sentiment nonetheless caused Clinton and his administration to rethink this policy, and early in 1997 Clinton made provisions for his advisers to examine the issue of dramatic tax reform in greater depth.

Long before the issue received such exposure in Congress, the CTJ had examined both sides of the flat tax debate. In May of 1995 CTJ director Robert S. McIntyre testified before the Joint Economic Committee of the U.S. Congress regarding a flat tax. McIntyre rejected all flat tax proposals and maintained that they were founded in "supply-side" policies that would place an increased burden on the middle- and lower-income taxpayers while reducing the tax burden on the very rich.

McIntyre noted that the top one percent of income earners paid tax at a rate of 39 percent under the traditional system. The lowest income earners meanwhile generated a negative tax liability called "earned income credit" by which the federal government returned a sum of money to the taxpayer in the form of a tax credit. A proposed flat tax system of 20 percent would decrease the tax liability of those in the 39 percent tax brackets by 19 percent.

Overall, investment income would be exempted from taxation, a fact mostly appealing to wealthy, higher income taxpayers. The tax liability of the lowest income earners would in turn increase to 20 percent and would result in elimination of the earned income refund. Lower-income American families who paid no tax under the traditional tax system would suffer as their so-called "disposable income" would be reduced greatly by a 20 percent flat tax. McIntyre concluded his remarks by stating, "Rather than expanding tax entitlements for corporations and the well off and lowering their tax rates, we should seek *real tax* reform. In our view that means that existing loopholes should be curtailed, tax laws simplified, and graduated tax rates maintained."

The CTJ and the Clinton administration were not the only ones to disagree with flat tax theories. A number of noted economists came forward with words of caution; among them were Roger Brinner, William Gale, and James Poterba. They cited the burden of home ownership that would result from the loss of the home mortgage deduction. The resulting increase in the cost of owning a home would, in turn, drive the value of real estate down. The likelihood that the loss of employee health care payment deductions made by employers would lead to a loss of health care benefits for a large group of working class taxpayers was also contended. Economists further argued that a flat tax rate as originally proposed would ultimately be adjusted upward to a more realistic figure of 23 percent—an amount higher than most middle income Americans pay under the graduated system. The only taxpayers likely to benefit from a flat tax, it was predicted, might be married couples with children—whose incomes exceeded $300,000 annually.

Following McIntyre's statements in 1995, the CTJ published many related articles and studies discussing the implications of both the flat tax and the national sales tax. These included *Rich are Big Winners, Poor are Losers, Who Pays?: A Distributional Analysis of the Tax System of All 50 States Under House Tax Plans*, and *Malcolm S. Forbes, Jr.'s $1.9 Billion Tax Cut—for Himself*. Despite persistent renewal of the arguments on both sides, there was no forward motion on the issues by the end of 1998, and none was anticipated until after 2000.

FUTURE DIRECTIONS

The CTJ is committed to monitoring the actions of federal and state legislatures, not only in matters of tax legislation but in areas of spending as well. The CTJ wants to ensure that tax dollars are spent wisely in funding government services. With the 1998 fiscal year ending in a surplus for the federal government and with surpluses anticipated for future years, the CTJ plans to research the best way to spend these funds.

Director Robert McIntyre warned against the urge to cut taxes in reaction to the federal budget surplus experienced in 1998. The surplus, according to McIntyre, was the direct result of a surplus in the Social Security system. McIntyre went on to further admonish the members of the legislature to shun any tax cut scheme that might serve to aggravate existing imbalances in the tax system. According to McIntyre, this would be any tax agenda that placed a greater burden on lower income wage earners while simultaneously rewarding wealthy taxpayers and corporations benefiting from tax loopholes.

McIntyre also urged Congress to reject any proposals that might result in the conversion of Social Security investment funds from government bonds into riskier higher-yield stock certificates. Such a conversion would create a conflict of interest by increasing government control over corporations, by virtue of excessive stock ownership in those companies. The CTJ will focus resources on understanding these new issues and promoting policies that will result in the fairest distribution of these surplus funds.

GROUP RESOURCES

The CTJ has a toll-free number for its headquarters at 1-888-626-2622. Additionally the CTJ maintains a Web site at http://www.ctj.org. Further information about the CTJ can be obtained by writing to the Citizens for Tax Justice, 1311 L St. NW, Washington, DC 20005 or by calling (202) 626-3780.

GROUP PUBLICATIONS

The numerous CTJ publications, testimonies, reports, fact sheets, and press releases that are available in print fill a small catalog. CTJ publications deal with a wide variety of topics and include publications regarding individual state tax systems, appraisals of various tax reforms and flat tax proposals, and commentary on public policy and current events. Sample titles include *Who Pays?: A Distributional Analysis of the Tax Systems of All 50 States, The Hidden Entitlements, Corporate Taxpayers & Corporate Freeloaders,* and *Social Insecurity.* Additionally, CTJ publishes its newsletter, *CTJ Update,* nine times each year. Queries and orders for publications can be sent in writing to the Citizens for Tax Justice, 1311 L St. NW, Washington, DC 20005 or by calling (202) 626-3780.

A list of CTJ publications appears on the CTJ Web page at http://www.ctj.org/html/ctjpub.htm. Publications can be downloaded at this site free of charge.

BIBLIOGRAPHY

Adams, Charles. *For Good and Evil: The Impact of Taxes on the Course of Civilization.* New York: Madison Books, 1993.

Boskin, Michael. *Frontiers of Tax Reform.* San Diego, Calif.: Hoover Institution Press, 1996.

Chait, Jonathan. "The Flat Tax Scam: What Dick Armey Doesn't Want You to Know." *New Republic,* 15 December 1997.

Graetz, Michael J. *The Decline (and Fall?) of the Income Tax.* New York: W.W. Norton, 1997.

McIntyre, Robert S. "Why Not Tax Reform?" *The Nation,* 27 April 1998.

———. "The 23 Percent Solution." *New York Times,* 23 January 1998.

McIntyre, Robert S., and David Wilhelm. *Unfair Share; The Case Against Federal Sales Taxes.* Washington, DC: Citizens for Tax Justice, 1986.

Seidman, Laurence S. *The USA Tax: A Progressive Consumption Tax.* Cambridge, Mass.: MIT Press, 1997.

Slemrod, Joel, ed. *Tax Progressivity and Income Inequality.* Cambridge, England: Cambridge University Press, 1994.

Co-Op America

ESTABLISHED: 1982
EMPLOYEES: 27
MEMBERS: 50,000 individual; 2,000 business
PAC: None

Contact Information:

ADDRESS: 1612 K Street NW, Ste. 600
     Washington, DC 20006
PHONE: (202) 872-5307
TOLL FREE: (800) 584-7336
FAX: (202) 331-8166
E-MAIL: info@coopamerica.org
URL: http://www.coopamerica.org
EXECUTIVE DIRECTOR: Alisa Gravitz

WHAT IS ITS MISSION?

According to the organization, "Co-Op America, a national nonprofit organization founded in 1982, provides the economic strategies, organizing power, and practical tools for businesses and individuals to address today's social and environmental problems. While many environmental organizations choose to fight important political and legal battles, Co-Op America is the leading force in educating and empowering our nation's people and businesses to make significant improvements through the economic system."

Co-Op America empowers consumers economically and functions in a different fashion than other special interest groups. The organization motivates consumers to make environmentally or socially correct decisions, facilitates information flow, and has a focus that is much broader than the typical special interest group. The organization's focus on encouraging businesses and consumers to make purchasing and manufacturing choices that benefit the world, have led it to cover diverse issues including mutual fund holdings, boycotts, child labor, and sustainable use of natural resources. According to the organization's broad mission, such topics can be significantly impacted by consumer or business economic power.

HOW IS IT STRUCTURED?

Co-Op America has its main office located in Washington, D.C., and an additional one-person office in San Francisco, California, which administers the organization's *Woodwise Consumer Initiative*, a program designed to educate consumers about the state of the world's timber supply and ways to conserve the use of wood and wood products. The Washington office houses departments including business, consumer programs, publications, operations, and accounting.

The organization's strategic direction and operation is supervised by a six-member board of directors, which includes representatives for organization members and personnel in the form of one business representative, two consumer representatives, and three staff members. Board members serve three-year terms and are elected by the group they represent; for example, staff elect staff board members and business members elect business board members. Staff use strategic direction set by the board to carry out policy. The executive director is appointed by the board for an indefinite term of service. The executive director position has a capped salary agreement stating that the executive director can make no more than four times the salary of the lowest paid staff member; in 1998 the executive director made two-and-a-half times as much as the lowest paid worker.

After one year of employment, staff members may apply to become a worker/member. Worker/members are eligible to serve on the board and cannot be fired unless two-thirds of the staff vote to fire them. Management structure at Co-Op America is participatory, and staff members have input into policy decisions. Worker/members also receive the right to vote. The organization has an open financial policy, and records are available to all staff employees.

Members join Co-Op America in one of three categories: individual/family; business; or financial professional/institution. Individual/family members pay dues starting at $15 and receive benefits including socially responsible financial planning assistance, credit card opportunities, and travel discounts. Businesses pay dues starting at $50 and receive a free listing in the on-line *Green Pages*, as well as discounted shipping benefits, credit cards, and telephone service. Financial institutions pay dues starting at $135 and automatically receive joint membership to the Social Investment Forum, a network of socially responsible financial institutions that make investment decisions based on socially and ecologically acceptable criteria. For example, investing in firms that do not pollute or that do not hire child labor. The average individual Co-Op America member is a woman in her fifties, of at least middle class income. Member recruitment is mainly done through mail solicitation.

PRIMARY FUNCTIONS

Co-Op America works to inform the public of how to use consumer buying power to the advantage of the environment and society. The organization believes that economic leveraging can be effective in tackling what the organization considers current social problems, such as environmental destruction or compromised social health, and the organization seeks to give its members the opportunity to use their economic influence in positive ways.

Co-Op America's *National Green Pages* is a listing of environmentally or socially correct businesses that consumers can patronize to leverage their buying power. Businesses are screened by the organization for appropriate ethics and business operations—for example, screening criteria might include assessing whether a business polluted the environment or whether it recycled manufacturing materials.

The organization provides other resources for consumers to focus their buying power, particularly in the investment arena. The organization provides members with financial planning basics, including *Financial Planning Handbook*, which gives guidance on how to invest using socially responsible criteria. The organization offers financial counseling to members in areas including retirement planning, tax savings, choosing a financial advisor, savings, and cooperative strategies such as resource sharing or bartering.

While Co-Op America does not organize boycotting, the organization does provide detailed information on how to carry out this kind of campaign. According to the organization, businesses consider boycotts to be one of the most effective and damaging actions that consumers can take against them. Co-Op America encourages members to use boycotts as an economic leveraging tool. The organization makes an effort to educate members about boycotts that are being organized and gives background information on the reasons for a specific boycott. For example, jeans are commonly manufactured using child labor, and often in substandard working conditions. Co-Op America identifies signs that consumers should look for to avoid buying such products and suggests alternative manufacturers to choose from.

Co-Op America also makes resources available to members wishing to live simpler and more "sustainable" lives. Sustainable living is a concept which includes reducing wasteful consumerism, reducing dependence on non-renewable resources and environmentally damaging products, and recycling and reusing rather than creating unnecessary garbage. According to the organization, sustainable living practiced individually and at home can make just as much of an impact toward improving world conditions as larger companies that adopt similar policies. The organization provides information to members and the public such as home audit tips for improving the energy efficiency of a home, tips on what and what not to shop for, and information on current political controversies. Co-Op American also provides guidelines to businesses that wish to operate in a more sustainable fashion.

In addition to educating consumers about personal economic power, Co-Op America facilitates discussion and information exchange between socially responsible businesses and financial institutions. The organization

FAST FACTS

Two-thirds of investors don't know if their funds hold tobacco stocks.

(Source: Yanklovich Partners survey data cited in: Andrew Leckey. "When Picking Stocks, Follow the Leaders." *St. Louis Post-Dispatch,* May 30, 1997.)

---

believes that consumers are increasingly interested in frequenting socially and environmentally responsible businesses. According to the organization, data show that 76 percent of consumers would switch to a company that is socially or environmentally responsible, given equal price or quality (Ray, Paul H., Institute of Noetic Sciences, Sausalito, CA and Fetzer Institute, Kalamazoo, MI. 1996). The organization's Business Network included 2,000 members in 1998, who used benefits from Co-Op America including targeted customer access, advertising, press coverage, and benefits to cut the cost of business such as reduced shipping or telephone rates. Businesses that are able to list in the *National Green Pages* join the Co-Op America Business Network, a group that shares information and expands customer opportunities.

While financial institutions are a subset of business, the organization believes that these institutions can model socially and environmentally responsible investing by the types of investment vehicles that they offer. Financial institutions that meet socially responsible criteria and are members of the organization receive benefits similar to those of businesses—such as advertising and discounted services.

PROGRAMS

Co-Op America's programs all serve to educate consumers or businesses on environmental and social issues, and to help them incorporate these issues into their criteria for doing business and for consuming goods. Programs focus on sustainable living, business decisions that are good for the environment, and socially and environmentally aware consumer decisions.

The Green Business Program helps businesses get off the ground that are socially and environmentally responsible—organizations that are increasingly described as "green." The organization provides publicity for successful green businesses and helps them increase their customer base by making them more visible to the public through advertising and information such as the *Green Pages*. The organization also provides member businesses with discounts to help them lower the cost of doing business.

The Consumer Education and Empowerment Program educates the public on socially responsible investing by providing members with a number of informational resources, including a handbook, magazine, and links to additional information and resources. Members receive information including recognized socially responsible funds, recognized funds that don't meet social and environmental criteria, and performance records for funds. Members receive information on how to exercise activism as shareholders through submitting and voting on proxy resolutions.

The Corporate Responsibility Program works to educate corporations on becoming socially accountable. The program also coordinates information about boycotts that have been organized against irresponsible companies. Member corporations receive information on selected office equipment that meets environmental and social criteria in its production and use. Resources are also provided to help businesses carry out operations in a sustainable fashion.

The Sustainable Living Program provides interested members with the information on how to lead a more sustainable life—at the community level, at work, and at home. The program also works to influence development overseas by advocating for language that promotes sustainability in United Nations documents for overseas projects. The Sustainable Living Program also works with a Washington, D.C., Sustainable Community Program, which measures how resources move through the D.C. area.

BUDGET INFORMATION

In 1997 Co-Op America had a budget of $2.2 million. Ninety percent of revenues were received from member dues and donations. The other 10 percent of revenue included 5 percent from foundation grants and 5 percent from advertising. Expenses in 1997 included 75 percent in program expenses, and 25 percent toward fund raising and administration.

The organization's 1996 revenues totaled $1,993,038 and included direct public support ($1,138,398), program service revenue ($262,277), membership dues ($446,598), interest on savings ($1,253), other investment income ($3,727), and other revenue ($140,785). Expenses for fiscal year 1996 totaled $1,997,800 and included program services ($1,512,739), management and general expenses ($72,650), and fundraising ($412,411).

HISTORY

The cooperative movement in the United States of America actually started in the nineteenth century among farmers. Cooperatives, which had originated in Great Britain, usually involved people organizing around a common goal, often an economic one. Cooperatives in America came to represent nonprofit enterprises which operated for the benefit of their members. In the United States, farmers organized cooperatives within such organizations as the National Grange. The cooperative movement became more popular among the general public in the 1960s and 1970s, and food cooperatives remained a mainstay in many U.S. locations in the 1990s.

Co-Op America was founded in 1982 by Paul Freundlich. He and other peers were concerned about having the ability to locate and purchase socially and environmentally responsible products. While they were able to locate such companies, a link still didn't exist to bring these companies closer to other customers. Freundlich founded the organization to facilitate that link and to give consumers the power to choose such companies, as well as give the companies an increased competitive advantage.

To help consumers leverage their economic power, the organization started out by producing quarterly catalogues with items that met social and environmentally responsible criteria. The catalogue business quickly expanded, and in 1991 Co-Op America redirected efforts in a larger way towards helping these businesses reach customers when the organization introduced the *National Green Pages*. The *Green Pages* grew quickly from an initial 400 business listings to 2,000 listings by 1998. In June 1998 the *Green Pages* went on-line to reach even greater numbers of American consumers and businesses.

The 1980s were portrayed by the media as a decade of greed where the gap between the rich and poor widened. Evidence from the Federal Reserve showed that many Americans increased their personal wealth during the decade. According to a Federal Reserve study, about 450,000 families who represented wealthy Americans had a growth in total net worth during 1983-1989 from $2.5 trillion to $4.4 trillion (*U.S. News & World Report*, June 1, 1992). During this same period, however, many Americans began considering the concept of investing in socially responsible funds or stocks—investment vehicles which aligned with personal values. Between 1984 and 1994, the amount invested in socially responsible funds increased from $64 billion to $639 billion. By the end of this period, such funds had grown from only three to over 40 offerings (*Los Angeles Times*, April 30, 1996). The trend fit nicely into Co-Op America's mission of aligning consumer dollar power to improve social and environmental conditions, and the organization continued to offer and refine investing resources for members.

The 1990s saw the growth of the voluntary simplicity movement, a small but noticeable trend among young professionals to downscale and live more sustain-

BUDGET:
1996 COA Revenue

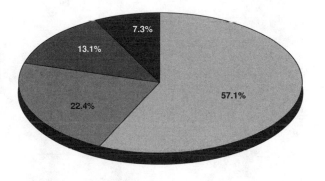

- 57.1%: Direct public support
- 22.4%: Membership dues
- 13.1%: Program service revenue
- 7.3%: Interest on savings, other investment income, and other revenue

1996 COA Expenses

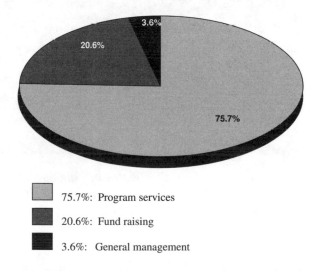

- 75.7%: Program services
- 20.6%: Fund raising
- 3.6%: General management

ably. Many of these people shared the same concerns as the typical Co-Op America member, such as a concern with U.S. consumption of limited resources. According to a publisher of a trends periodical quoted in the *Los Angeles Times,* (July 18, 1996), the voluntary simplicity trend was significant, and 15 percent of young professionals were anticipated to be buying into that lifestyle

A New York State Labor Standards investigator talks with Chinese immigrants employed as collar assemblers in a New York City garment factory. Co-op America works to raise public awareness of unacceptable business practices. (Photograph by Kathy Willens, AP/Wide World Photo)

by 2000. Co-Op America participated in the trend by providing resources to those interested in the voluntary simplicity lifestyle, such as tips on sustainable living and ecologically correct shopping techniques.

CURRENT POLITICAL ISSUES

Co-Op America is not a political organization in the traditional sense; it doesn't lobby for legislation or mobilize members to contact congressional representatives.

Rather, the organization compiles and presents information that allows members and consumers to make socially and environmentally responsible choices. The strategy seeks to impact directly on businesses that can influence the outcome of relevant issues. For example, the organization is concerned with inappropriate use of child labor in the United States and other countries. According to Co-Op America, over 250 million children below legal employment age work in sweatshops all over the world. These children face dangers such as pesticide inhalation and, in some cases, are chained to looms to weave rugs. To combat the problem, the organization publishes steps that individual consumers can take to protest child labor in sweatshops, including providing a letter to manufacturers, informing consumers of labels that indicate fair labor practices, and providing information on contacting other organizations working to end sweatshop labor.

The organization is also concerned with the tobacco industry, an industry that in Co-Op America's opinion, harms the collective health of the human population. According to the Co-Op America executive director (*Star Tribune,* May 19, 1996), most Americans don't smoke and don't wish to invest in smoking-related products. But many investors may be unaware of tobacco investments in their portfolios or lack the time to screen new tobacco additions to mutual funds that they already hold. To educate consumers about tobacco stocks, Co-Op America screened the 15 top performing mutual funds for tobacco holdings, finding that nine of the 15 funds had tobacco-related stock, and that combined tobacco holdings totaled $3 billion.

Rarely does Co-Op America become active in traditional, political advocacy. The organization instead focuses on empowering people and businesses economically. But when the integrity of consumer shareholder power was threatened by the Securities and Exchange Commission (SEC), the organization stepped in and took political action to make members' voices heard.

Case Study: Co-Op America Opposes SEC Restrictions

Traditionally, stockholders have retained the right to vote during annual meetings and proxy votes and to address policy changes or election of governing positions. In September 1997 the SEC proposed to severely limit shareholder rights under the auspices of shareholder reform.

In a departure from its traditional role, Co-Op America waged a political campaign to force the SEC to drop the proposed restrictions. The organization formed a coalition with other like-minded groups. It put together an intensive media campaign to spread information about the upcoming issue. Members and citizens were urged to write letters to the SEC, voicing their opinion about the restrictions. After a multitude of letters, the SEC abandoned the proposal in May 1998.

Public Impact

Shareholder voting rights are often the only way that a stock owner has of voicing an opinion about business management. Co-Op America's success in 1998 allowed all stockholders to keep their economic leverage. Stockholders, for example, retain the right to object by vote if a mutual fund begins to include non-green holdings. Voters may also exercise their preference for stock management by deciding who gets to set policy for stocks or funds.

FUTURE DIRECTIONS

Co-Op America will be working to attract more membership. The organization feels that an untapped segment of the American population—estimated at between 40-50 million people—care deeply about environmental and social issues. If the organization succeeds in representing this segment, the cumulative power of U.S. consumers will become far more effective in pursuing the organization's goal of a better world. Co-Op America hopes to identify more membership through its Woodwise Initiative program in a direct mail campaign.

GROUP RESOURCES

Co-Op America offers a number of resources for members including publications and a Web site at http://www.coopamerica.org. Some of these resources are available to non-members, including the Woodwise Consumer Initiative and the on-line *Green Pages.* Resources can be accessed at the organization Web site or by contacting the organization at 1612 K St. NW, Ste. 600, Washington, DC 20006; by phoning (202) 872-5307 or 1-800-584-7336; or by faxing (202) 331-8166.

GROUP PUBLICATIONS

Co-Op America publishes a number of items including the *National Green Pages,* a directory of socially responsible businesses which is free to members; *Co-Op America Quarterly,* a magazine for members; *Financial Planning Handbook for Responsible Investors,* which gives assistance on socially responsible investing (fee for nonmembers); and *Co-Op America Connections,* which is free to socially responsible businesses and offers information on functioning in the marketplace. Publications can be ordered by contacting the organization directly at 1612 K St. NW, Ste. 600, Washington, DC 20006; by calling (202) 872-5307 or 1-800-584-7336; or by faxing (202) 331-8166.

BIBLIOGRAPHY

Abbott, Charles. "Biotech Foes Boycott Gene-Altered U.S. Corn, Soya." *Reuters,* 7 October 1996.

Anderson, Curt. "Farm Cooperatives on the Rise." *Rocky Mountain News,* 17 August 1997.

Cummins, H. J. "Check Out Charitable Organizations Groups Give Advice on Giving Good Gifts." *Newsday,* 9 December 1993.

Dugas, Christine. "Socially Responsible Mutual Funds Make Their Mark." *Newsday,* 6 February 1994.

Farhan Haq. "Cooperatives-USA: Harlem Group Brings Kwanzaa Spirit to Youth." *Inter Press Service English News Wire*, 18 December 1995.

Knight Ridder Newspapers. "Web Site Makes it Easy to be Green." *The Dallas Morning News*, 29 April 1998.

Maynard, Roberta. "Sprouting Sales With 'Green' Products." *Nation's Business*, 1 May 1996.

Morgan, Jerry. "Social Investing: Sometimes a Screen Can Be a Door That Opens Onto Profit." *Newsday*, 23 February 1997.

Ward, Janet. "Creating Sustainable Communities: Living to Leave a Legacy." *American City and County*, 1 January 1998.

Common Cause (CC)

WHAT IS ITS MISSION?

The mission of Common Cause (CC) "is to ensure government is open, honest and accountable, at the federal, state and local levels." CC and its members fight for good government, for ethics and campaign finance reform, for civil rights protection for all citizens, and for limits on the influence lobbyists and special interests have on legislators. CC is particularly dedicated to the issue of campaign spending. It works toward ending the so-called soft money system, for laws requiring the immediate disclosure of all campaign contributions, and for mandatory free airtime for candidates on television.

HOW IS IT STRUCTURED?

CC is a lobbying organization headquartered in Washington, D.C., with chapters in 46 of the 50 states. The group is headed by a president who manages its day-to-day operations, including overseeing CC programs, finances, and public relations. The president is the organization's chief lobbyist and its main representative on Capitol Hill. The CC president is a leading national expert on government ethics, money in politics, and government accountability and speaks out regularly on these issues. Long-term CC policy and its finances are overseen by the national governing board. Members, who serve without compensation, are elected to three-year terms by the CC membership. Board meetings are held three times per year.

ESTABLISHED: August 1970
EMPLOYEES: 90
MEMBERS: 250,000

Contact Information:
ADDRESS: 1250 Connecticut Ave. NW
    Washington, DC 20036
PHONE: (202) 833-1200
FAX: (202) 659-3716
URL: http://www.commoncause.org
PRESIDENT; CEO: Ann McBride

FAST FACTS

Between January 1997 and June 1998, the Republican and Democratic parties raised $115.8 million in soft-money donations, more than double the $50 million collected in the corresponding period of the 1994 election cycle.

(Source: Common Cause. "U.S. House of Representatives Passes Campaign Finance," August 6, 1998.)

PRIMARY FUNCTIONS

CC is first and foremost an activist organization devoted to effecting change in the political system. The group's main function is lobbying. Its representatives work closely with congressional members and their staffs on legislation dealing with issues such as campaign financing and government ethics. CC sometimes forms ad hoc alliances with other groups to work on specific issues. It does not take part in formal coalitions of special-interest groups in order to avoid being identified with issues it does not deem important.

The organization's lobbying effort relies on CC's 250,000 members throughout the country. Organizers on the state and local level work with members and volunteers to communicate their opinion on different issues to their representatives. Grassroots activists also bring the CC viewpoint to the public by speaking to community groups and writing letters to the editor and opinion pieces for local newspapers. When a bill is up for vote in Congress, CC volunteers voice their opinions to congressional members. To accomplish this, volunteers make telephone calls, visit their representatives' offices, and introduce themselves as CC members when congressional members make public appearances.

CC finances and conducts investigations into issues with which it is involved, and publishes reports of their findings. In 1996 and 1997, for example, CC released studies that were highly critical of the broadcast lobby, the influence of the tobacco industry in Washington, D.C., the special-interest money contributed to then-House Speaker Newt Gingrich, and the relation of large donors to the congressional tax deal in 1997. CC publications are intended to educate Americans on the current political system and to provide the basis for political action.

PROGRAMS

CC is an activist organization that works at a grass-roots level, organizing activists and voters to put pressure on legislators to take action on specific issues. The group focuses its efforts on specific issues that have high priority, in particular campaign finances, government ethics, and accountability in government. It organizes short-term, results-oriented projects. An example of this is Project Independence, conducted in spring and summer 1998, in which 30,000 volunteers gathered one million signatures for campaign finance reform.

CauseNet is an effort by CC to create a network of volunteer activists linked by E-mail. Individuals who are interested in helping in CC campaigns register as a member of CauseNet on the CC Web site. Members are issued a password that allows them access to activist-only information about CC's political activities. CC then contacts members regularly with alerts, legislative updates and other news about important issues. CC includes legislators' fax numbers and E-mail addresses with the CauseNet alerts. Members are then asked by CC to communicate with their congressman on important issues. Members are also asked to participate in other grassroots activities.

BUDGET INFORMATION

CC has an annual budget of approximately $10 million. CC's financing comes primarily from dues paid by members and contributions. About 84 percent of its money comes in increments of $100 or less; about five percent comes from contributions of $1,000 or more. As of 1998, memberships in the organization were $10 for students, $20 for individuals; and $30 for families. Most new members are the result of direct-mail campaigns. CC has an explicit policy of not accepting grants from governments or foundations. It does not accept contributions greater than $100 per year from corporations or labor unions.

HISTORY

CC was founded in summer 1970 by John W. Gardner. Gardner had been secretary of Health, Education and Welfare, head of the Carnegie Institute, and the chairman of a presidential commission on education policy. CC was founded at a time when there was great upheaval in U.S. public life: the war in Vietnam, the growing racial polarization of U.S. cities, the dissatisfaction of many young people and the search for viable alternatives to the status quo. In the nonprofit organization's first public announcement, it described its aims: "Common Cause is a national citizens' lobby. We will lobby in the public interest at all levels of government, but especially at the federal level. We will assist our members to speak and act in behalf of legislation designed to solve the nation's problems. We will press for a reordering of national priorities. We will also press for the revitalization of the public process, to make our political and governmental institutions more responsive to the needs of the nation and the will of its citizens." (Gardner, 42)

In the first six months, 100,000 members joined the new group; by the end of its first year, it had 200,000 members. In its first year, CC worked on a number of legislative issues. Sen. Gaylord Nelson called its contribution to the passage of the Employment and Training Opportunities Act crucial. The group was instrumental in bringing the House of Representatives to its first recorded vote on the Vietnam War (1959–75). It spearheaded the citizens' drive for a constitutional amendment extending the vote to 18-year-olds. Other issues included campaign finance reform, reform of the congressional seniority system, and opposition to funding of the supersonic transport, a controversial aircraft project.

In the first half of the 1970s, CC actively supported the effort to ratify the Equal Rights Amendment (ERA), a movement which ultimately failed. In 1972 CC published the *Manual on Money & Politics,* a guide for citizens interested in enforcing campaign finance laws. In 1973 it launched a daily radio show on Mutual Radio.

CC was involved in most of the crucial reform fights of the 1970s. It released a report detailing the sources of money in President Richard Nixon's 1972 presidential campaign. As the Watergate scandal developed, CC continued to make information about Republican finances public, urged the broadcast of the Watergate hearings, and spoke out publicly for a fair, bipartisan investigation of President Nixon. CC's work on campaign reform eventually led to major new legislation governing presidential campaigns.

Following Nixon's resignation and the end of the war in Vietnam, CC's membership dropped from 260,000 to 220,000 during the years of the administration of President Jimmy Carter. It would rise again during the presidency of Ronald Reagan, when there was an increase in adverse feelings toward government brought on by allegations of corruption in the administration, arms buildups, and the renewed perception of a threat of nuclear war.

Major Successes

By its tenth anniversary, CC could point to two major successes. In 1975 it won passage of the federal Sunshine Law which mandated that most federal meetings must be open to the public. In 1978 Congress passed the Ethics in Government, which regulated the gifts and outside income federal employees could receive, and forbade employees from taking jobs for a year after leaving federal service. However, in other areas, such as legislation to provide public funding for congressional elections and regulation of lobbyists, the group was not successful.

At the same time, the organization went through changes of its own. In April 1977 John Gardner resigned as leader of the organization. Archibald Cox, the Watergate independent prosecutor whom Richard Nixon had fired became the chairman of its board in 1980. "The 1980s can be made a time of renewing our sense of common purpose, reviving our self-confidence, and rekindling the sense of individual personal responsibility for the common enterprise," Cox told the group. In fall 1980, the group's bimonthly magazine *Frontlines* was redesigned and retitled. *Common Cause* magazine was launched that year with an exposé of sex discrimination in Congress.

Between the mid-1970s and the mid-1990s, CC took on political action committees (PACs) and the inordinate influence their money buys in Congress. It came out in favor of scrapping the electoral college system. It criticized the superficial process by which the Senate confirmed presidential nominees. It also called for reform of the filibuster system which allowed a minority of members to block action by the rest of the Senate. Early on, during the Reagan presidency, the national governing board voted to make nuclear arms control CC's top priority. It subsequently devoted most of its resources to fighting the MX missile, Star Wars, and other costly arms programs advocated by the Reagan administration.

When the organization celebrated its twentieth anniversary, the Cold War had ended and the Soviet Union was no longer seen as a nuclear threat. By the 1990s, CC had turned its focus back to the issue of money in politics specifically campaign fund-raising and the millions of dollars available to congressional members from PACs. It fought for and won a comprehensive ban on gifts to representatives and senators with passage of a bill in 1996. Early in the 1990s CC predicted a federal election scandal, which came to pass when millions of dollars in unregulated contributions were misused by candidates Bill Clinton and Robert Dole in their 1996 presidential race.

CURRENT POLITICAL ISSUES

CC has waged a number of hard-fought battles for principles it believed important for the nation. It opposed the Vietnam War, it fought to reform the congressional seniority system, and it worked to cut off funds for the MX missile system. In the 1990s, however, as U.S. society became more divided than ever along income lines, CC returned to one of its oldest crusades: the fight for campaign finance reform.

Case Study: The Soft Money Debate

Following the Watergate scandal in 1974, the Election Reform Act was passed by Congress, in part as a result of CC's efforts. The new laws specified limits on how much money individuals or organizations could con-

FAST FACTS

Federal Election Commission auditors concluded that during the 1996 presidential campaign the Clinton campaign broke a $30 million spending limit by more than $46 million while the Dole campaign spent more than $17 million over the permissible limits.

(Source: U.S. Newswire, December 1, 1998.)

---

tribute to a federal candidate, how much candidates could spend on a campaign, and required candidates to make a public accounting of the sources and amount of their campaign war chests. Almost as soon as the law was passed, however, campaign committees and lobbyists devised ways to stretch the limits of the law.

One of the loopholes around the law is the contribution of soft money. Individuals and labor unions whose contributions to federal candidates are limited, or corporations who are forbidden from giving money to federal candidates can earmark dollars for special Republican or Democratic accounts. While these special accounts are designated as nonfederal, the accounts can be used for activities that can greatly influence a federal election, such as advertising and get-out-the-vote drives. The contributor can make virtually unlimited donations to candidates this way and the political party gets access to money the law would otherwise deny.

CC reported that Amway made the largest single contribution of soft money ever made when it gave $2.5 million a few days before the 1994 congressional elections. The tobacco industry donated more than $5 million in soft money in 1996, according to CC. Common Cause believes soft money is little more than an illegal money laundering operation—the page on its Web site is called "The Soft Money Laundromat." During the 1996 election campaigns the two major parties collected $260 million in soft money, more than triple the amount in the 1992 elections. As a result, CC decided to devote 85 percent of its resources to toughening up campaign finance laws to end the abuse.

In early 1998, with the support of CC and other citizens' action groups, the McCain-Feingold Bill was introduced in the Senate. The bill would have made soft money illegal. It also would have established more restrictions on advertising during campaigns and required candidates to make fuller disclosures of their campaign donors. The proponents of the bill were able to put together a coalition of 52 senators—bare majority enough to pass the bill. Republican opponents, however, used a filibuster to prevent the Senate from voting. The bill's backers needed to muster 60 votes to end the filibuster, and they didn't have the extra eight supporters.

Public Impact

CC was scathing in their criticism of the senators that blocked the majority from passing a piece of legislation to end such obvious abuse. "The . . . obstructionist senators have put their stamps of approval on the scandals and abuses of the 1996 election," CC President Ann McBride told the press, "and have personally endorsed unlimited, unregulated soft money contributions from tobacco companies, corporate polluters, and other special interests." The filibuster showed that members of Congress will effectively block a reform that they believe threatens their ability to raise money. Senator Fred Thompson predicted unprecedented campaign abuses will continue until a law is passed to make soft money contributions illegal. "The loopholes are bigger than the laws," he told the *Christian Science Monitor*. After the defeat Senator John McCain, one of the Senate bill's sponsors, said that reform would not take place until the American people rise up "voicing their displeasure and outrage. We've got to see the mood of the American people."

However in December 1998 auditors of the Federal Election Commission (FEC) spoke on the soft-money question. They suggested to the FEC that the 1996 campaign funds of Bill Clinton and Bob Dole be required to repay millions of dollars of soft-money contributions that were allegedly spent inappropriately. Auditors claimed that so-called "issue ads" run during the campaign were used to promote candidates, in violation of federal law. In a case such as this, the full FEC must consider the auditors' recommendation and then make a ruling on the matter. Even if the FEC rules against the candidates, the matter can be brought on appeal before a federal court.

SUCCESSES AND FAILURES

CC has played a leading role in the legislative successes that have helped make the federal government more open, answerable, and ethical. The group has worked hard to achieve the passage of so-called "sunshine laws"—laws that required that the meetings of most federal offices be open to the public. Other successful legislation supported by CC have helped end many questionable financial practices on Capital Hill. CC successes include: barring members of Congress from accepting large speaking fees from special-interest groups, controlling the amounts and types of gifts lobbyists can give to congressional members, and not allowing members of Congress to keep unused campaign money when they retire from Congress.

FUTURE DIRECTIONS

Although CC wants to especially strengthen presidential campaign finance laws, the group's top priority is campaign finance reform at all levels of government To that aim, during 1997 and 1998, CC helped pass campaign finance laws in Massachusetts, Arizona, and Florida. The group's goal is to have similar legislation passed throughout the United States.

GROUP RESOURCES

The Common Cause Web site, available at http://www.commoncause.org, has an archive of the organization's publications: press releases, campaign finance studies, and corporate welfare studies. There are also databases available. The Soft Money Laundromat presents information about the sources and amounts of soft money that political parties have received through the 1990s. "Know Your Congress" contains information on the voting record of members of Congress, and the campaign contributions they accepted from various PACs. There is also a form that can be used to write a letter of praise or complaint. Various congressional documents including reports, committee hearing transcripts, testimony, and lobbyist disclosure reports are posted regularly on the Web site. Information about membership or contributions to Common Cause can be obtained by writing the organization at 1250 Connecticut Ave., NW #600, Washington, DC 20036, or by calling (202) 659-3716.

GROUP PUBLICATIONS

Common Cause publishes reports regularly that document soft-money contributions from special interests to officials and candidates, campaign expenses, PAC money, and other issues. All CC publications are available to the public free of charge. CC does not print a publications list. Most of the organization's publications, however, are listed and may be ordered from its Web site.

BIBLIOGRAPHY

Chen, Edwin. "Campaign Reform Bill All but Killed for Year." *Los Angeles Times,* 27 February 1998.

"Common Cause, Coalition Calls on Congress to Pass Campaign Finance Reform Legislation." *U.S. Newswire,* 17 February 1998.

Gardner, John W. *In Common Cause.* New York: W.W. Norton, 1972.

Goodrich, Lawrence J. "Campaign-Finance Reform: Still Alive?" *Christian Science Monitor.* 26 March 1998.

McFarland, Andrew S. *Common Cause: Lobbying in the Public Interest.* Chatham, N.J.: Chatham House Publishers, 1984.

Rothenberg, Lawrence S. *Linking Citizens to Government: Interest Group Politics at Common Cause.* New York: Cambridge University Press, 1992.

"U.S. Auditors Seek Clinton/Dole Campaign Repayment" *Reuters,* 1 December 1998.

Communications Workers of America (CWA)

ESTABLISHED: 1938
EMPLOYEES: 520
MEMBERS: 630,000
PAC: CWA Committee on Political Education (CWA-COPE)

Contact Information:
ADDRESS: 501 3rd St. NW
    Washington, DC 20001-2797
PHONE: (202) 434-1100
FAX: (202) 434-1279
E-MAIL: cwaweb@earthlink.net
URL: http://www3.cwa-union.org/home
PRESIDENT: Morton Bahr

WHAT IS ITS MISSION?

According to the organization, "Communications Workers of America (CWA) bargains contracts setting forth wages, benefits and working conditions for our members, along with day-to-day enforcement of these contracts through grievance and arbitration procedures and lawsuits."

While CWA started out as a union that represented telephone industry workers, the organization has evolved to include members in many other communications sectors, including broadcasting, print media, and health care organizations. The organization deals with a number of issues, and as the nature of communications in the world has changed with technological advances such as the Internet and global communications, CWA has attempted to broaden its focus to address trends that affect its members.

HOW IS IT STRUCTURED?

CWA is a union with headquarters in Washington, D.C. The organization is overseen by a 17-member executive board which meets four times a year and develops policy between CWA's annual constitutional conventions. Board members serve for three-year terms and represent each of CWA's eight U.S. geographic sectors. In addition six board members represent groups within CWA's membership, including communications and technologies; telecommunications; public and health care; printing, publishing, and media; the Newspaper

Guild; and broadcast and television. The remaining three board members include the president, executive vice president, and secretary-treasurer.

CWA members belong to more than 1,200 local unions in the United States and Canada and represent about 10,000 communities. Members participate in civic projects and those with an interest in activism work to influence policy at the grassroots level and to elect like-minded political candidates.

PRIMARY FUNCTIONS

CWA's primary concern is bargaining for better working conditions for its members. During its existence, the organization has achieved more than 1,000 collective bargaining agreements that lay out working conditions, wages, and benefits. The agreements may also grant worker demands for vacation and sick leave, education funding, child care, uniform and tool allowances, and bereavement pay. To initiate the collective bargaining process, members first agree upon and vote on contract goals. Members then elect a negotiating committee, but retain rights to determine if the final agreement reached is acceptable.

To address issues which may not require a collective bargaining process, CWA employs stewards who are trained in contract negotiations, legal issues, and related worker concerns. Stewards represent workers at the workplace and attempt to resolve issues between union members and management.

In addition to its work in conflict resolution, CWA follows workplace trends that affect its membership. In the late 1990s the organization was concerned with the use of technology to monitor worker productivity or after-hours behavior. The organization mobilizes its membership to address other workplace issues, such as health care or the right to organize. CWA local unions establish committees to monitor health hazards on the job, such as indoor pollution, the use of poisonous chemicals, and the potential hazards of emissions from computer terminals.

At a local level CWA members may take part in grassroots advocacy, such as contacting legislators regarding labor-related legislation or participating in civic activities. According to the organization CWA members have been instrumental in bringing Internet access to schools and libraries in many areas.

CWA takes part in shaping national policy by monitoring legislation and advocating for policy that benefits its members. The organization supports like-minded political candidates through its PAC and with donations that are partially generated from member dues.

CWA works in concert with similar unions in Asia, the United Kingdom, Europe, and Latin America. All of these unions belong to the 4.5 million member organization Communications International. The organization feels that a global focus correctly reflects the trend toward global business.

PROGRAMS

CWA programs serve members in striving for a better workplace. For example, the CWA Organizing Department helps members organize work-related advocacy efforts. Organizing efforts include forming unions in the workplace. CWA staff assist workers who want to set up unions through the process.

For members or others with on-line access and interested in advocating for CWA issues, CWA offers an Electronic Activist List. The list notifies users of relevant issues and suggests actions to take (such as contacting representatives or key congressional committee members). In 1998, for example, this service advocated to save the E-Rate—a discount that would allow schools and libraries to go on-line at reduced phone rates. CWA also maintains a list of other related Web sites and groups that deal with issues of interest to CWA members.

CWA also offers ongoing news updates (on-line) regarding relevant issues. For example, the FCC approved a merger between MCI and Worldcom in 1998; a merger which CWA opposed. For members and others interested in following the developments, CWA posted an on-line recap of up-to-date news on the subject.

BUDGET INFORMATION

CWA has an annual budget of $42 million. More detailed information was not made available.

HISTORY

CWA's predecessor, the National Federation of Telephone Workers (NFTW), was founded in 1938 both in Chicago and New Orleans. Previously telephone workers had attempted to organize into unions beginning in 1910. The federal government endorsed their right to strike after a 1919 telephone service strike that effectively stopped telephone service in New England and threatened to spread nationwide. After the strike telephone company management attempted to organize management-controlled unions called associations. The associations wiped out older worker unions until 1935, when Congress voted that the company associations were illegal by means of the Wagner Act. The decision was reiterated by the Supreme Court in 1937.

When NFTW formed in 1938 it included 31 telephone organizations and 145,000 members. However it

Members of the Communications Workers of America in Owatonna, Minnesota, protest working conditions during a picket staged outside the U. S. West directory assistance facility in 1998. (*Photograph by The Owatonna Press, Dave Schwarz, AP/Wide World Photo*)

functioned as many independent unions rather than as one unified entity. This proved to be a detriment after World War II (1939–1945). Because wages among many telephone unions had become widely disparate during the war, unions prepared to strike in both 1946 and 1947. While the earlier strike was resolved on an industry-wide basis, the latter was quickly quelled by AT&T, who made wage agreements contingent upon the unions not clearing the agreements in NTFW. The unions fractured and many withdrew from the strike, ending it.

The CWA is Established

Such fracturing was the impetus for the formation of CWA in 1947, which was deliberately created as one unified group, rather than as many autonomous ones. The first national convention of the new union represented 162,000 members and elected Joseph Beirne as president.

The new union got busy politically. In 1950 CWA lobbied successfully for a Senate investigation into the Bell telephone system's labor relations—the investigation found that Bell practices had impeded collective bargaining and had been part of an anti-union initiative by the telephone company. In 1995 CWA launched a 72-day strike against Southern Bell which resulted in a new contract for workers, including higher wages. CWA held its first national strike against the Bell system in 1968 which

lasted 18 days, involved 200,000 strikers, and resulted in a 20 percent increase in wages and benefits for workers.

AT&T continued to face scrutiny by the federal government in 1970, and was charged with discrimination on the basis of race and gender. The charges resulted in large settlements for AT&T women employees and employees of color. In the meantime CWA fought for and received the largest settlement in its history in 1971, when the organization successfully launched a seven-day strike against the Bell system again. This strike enlisted the help of Task Force '71—a group of 50,000 local union leaders who conducted information outreach before and during the strike and prepared strikers with training.

Structural Changes

CWA also went through some structural changes from the 1970s through the 1990s. In 1974 it merged with the Federation of Women Telephone Workers, a southern California group. Also in that year Beirne, the long-standing CWA president, died and was replaced by then-treasurer Glenn Watts. In the beginning of the 1980s, the union expanded to include public workers outside of the field of telecommunications. The union also began responding to the needs of minority members and created leadership conferences and training specifically geared to address minority workers' issues. When AT&T changed its own structure and went through divestiture in the mid-1980s, the union feared for job loss and relocation implications for its members which, in fact, did happen. Collective bargaining faced challenging new logistics, as national bargaining could no longer occur with AT&T, and the union began dealing at 48 AT&T-related bargaining tables. The organization's next president, Morton Bahr, took the helm in the mid-1980s and remained president of the union into the late 1990s. The union gained another sector of workers in the late 1980s, when the International Typographical Union merged with CWA.

Beginning in the late 1980s, the organization placed an increased emphasis on empowering members to mobilize for anticipated bargaining with AT&T. Members unified in a 17-week strike against NYNEX, the New York telephone company. Sadly, one CWA member was killed on the picket line.

Into the 1990s the union continued to grow and to represent wider segments of workers in the communications field, even as total union membership in the United States extended a decline that began in the 1970s. Continuing its bargaining activity, in 1994 CWA successfully prevented NYNEX from laying off 20,000 employees. The union was joined by the National Association of Broadcasting Engineers and Technicians in 1992 and the Newspaper Guild in 1997. The union also broadened its reach into international issues and began working with similar unions in England to address global aspects of telecommunications.

CURRENT POLITICAL ISSUES

CWA advocates for a number of issues that impact the communications industry. In some cases the organization's advocacy work is directed toward government intervention as in CWA's work in stopping FCC approval of an MCI-Worldcom merger in 1998. The organization is also involved in issues that affect all communications workers—such as wages, safety, and health care. For example, the organization has pushed to raise the minimum wage. According to the organization, a full-time worker earning minimum wage would make an annual income of $10,700—almost $3,000 below the poverty marker for a family of three. Purchasing power of those earning minimum wage has also continued to decrease—according to the union—even though the stock market has climbed steadily from the 1960s to the 1990s and corporations have continued to accumulate wealth. CWA advocates for fair wages by entering into collective bargaining processes with management of selected companies, or striking if necessary.

CWA is also concerned with policy that in their opinion, compromises the Occupational Safety and Health Act (OSHA). The Act provides for worker protection on the job but in 1998 the union opposed efforts by Congress to make the workplace safety standards outlined in the law

voluntary. According to CWA, 55,000 U.S. workers regularly die in the workplace and seven million are injured on the job.

CWA also follows health care issues closely—particularly when they impact member workers. The union takes the position that affordable private health care should be available to workers even when they are forced out of jobs. CWA opposed initiatives in Congress that would compromise Medicare and Medicaid coverage for retired or working union members. The union also bargains for improved benefits (including health care) in its collective bargaining endeavors.

Campaign reform issues have also occupied the energies of CWA. The union believes that members should have unimpeded access to support union-friendly candidates for office through the organization's PAC. However, a June 1998 referendum on a California ballot threatened this freedom, according to CWA.

Case Study: CWA Successfully Defeats Proposition 226

In 1997 and 1998 a Republican Congress initiated policy addressing campaign finance reform. One measure that particularly concerned CWA and other unions were initiatives that would have prevented union members from making political contributions. While such legislation was introduced at the federal level as well as in other state congresses, it materialized into a real threat to unions in California, when the measure made it onto the state ballot as a referendum. According to CWA, Proposition 226 had powerful backers including the state's Republican governor Pete Wilson and GOP activist Grover Norquist, who had connections with Republican house speaker Newt Gingrich and who headed a conservative organization named Americans for Tax Reform.

Proposition 226 would have required union members to annually provide written authorization to unions to use portions of their dues toward political contributions. While some opponents found it reasonable for union members to give individual permission for portions of their dues to go to political causes, CWA argued that Republicans had made no real progress in dealing with campaign finance reform and were targeting the wrong culprit. The organization claimed that corporate political spending outweighed union political spending by 11 to 1. The union asserted its right to provide members with a political voice unimpeded by what it called bureaucratic red tape. CWA argued that successful passage of the referendum would shut down the voice of working people in politics—giving an upper hand to influential and wealthy corporations.

To mobilize voters in California, CWA urged all members to register to vote and to go to the polls on June 2, 1998. Additionally CWA asked members to educate co-workers and friends about the issues, to make their view known through the local media, and to volunteer at their California locals. The proposition was defeated; notably, 75 percent of California Latino voters voted against Proposition 226.

SUCCESSES AND FAILURES

One of the union's largest losses politically has involved trade policy. Although CWA and other unions banded together to oppose the original North American Free Trade Agreement (NAFTA), they were unsuccessful. CWA takes the position that NAFTA, which relaxed international trade barriers, not only costs Americans jobs but disempowers workers from all countries and allows corporations to abuse cheap labor and relaxed working standards. CWA attempted to mobilize against the original legislation by using direct mail, member meetings, and publications to get members to generate calls, letters, and E-mail to Congress.

FUTURE DIRECTIONS

CWA is striving to keep its growth in step with the expanding telecommunications industry. The organization wants to create a large information union that will be well-equipped to deal with major media conglomerates. Toward this end, by mid-1998 additional communications sectors had joined the union, including broadcast employees, The Newspaper Guild, the International Typographical Union, and Dow Jones editorial workers.

GROUP RESOURCES

Contact the organization directly by calling (202)-434-1100; or writing 501 3rd St., Washington, DC, 20001-2797. Visit the CWA web site (http://www3.cwa-union.org) for information including: updates on collective bargaining agreements, current news, job bank, links to affiliate and local Web sites, and general information on labor organizing.

GROUP PUBLICATIONS

CWA publications are available either on linc (http://www3.cwaunion.org/aboutcwa/cwapubs/index.htm#page top) or by contacting the organization for a print copy; they include: *CWA News*, a monthly paper; *Sector News*, which provides coverage of the printing sector; and various reports, press releases, and speeches by the CWA president. CWA publications include *CEO Compensation in the Information Industries* (July 1996) and *The Information Superhighway: Exploring Strategies for Workers—Summary of Conference Sessions* (December 1995).

BIBLIOGRAPHY

Becker, Maki. "Outrage Over Overtime Plan: Thousands Protest as State Panel Holds Hearing in L.A. on Proposal to Change the Way Workers are Compensated for Extra Hours." *Los Angeles Times,* 5 April 1997.

Hodges, Jill. "Lines Blur Over Wiring; Communications, Electrical Unions are in a Turf Battle for Similar Work." *Star Tribune,* 7 February 1995.

Joshi, Pradnya. "Labor Clout on Upswing; New Strength for Unions as Aims, Strategy Change with Economy." *Newsday,* 7 August 1998.

Kanell, Michael E. "Stakes High as a Walkout Edges Closer at Bell South." *The Atlanta Journal and Constitution,* 5 August 1998.

Kilborn, Peter T. "Labor's Day; AFL-CIO Charts a New Direction as Unions Gather to Pick New Leader." *Star Tribune,* 24 October 1995.

"Labor Unions Face Hurdles in Organizing Low-Paid Workers." *Gannett News Service,* 23 December 1996.

McCune, Jenny C. "Telecommuting Revisited." *Management Review,* 1 February 1998.

Rachleff, Peter. "Labor Movement Moving into New Era." *Star Tribune,* 4 September 1995.

"UFCW, CWA Unions Begin Discussions About Merger." *Star Tribune,* 19 February 1997.

Worsham, James. "A Course Change at the NLRB (National Labor Relations Board)." *Nation's Business,* 1 February 1998.

Concerned Women for America (CWA)

WHAT IS ITS MISSION?

According to the organization, "the mission of Concerned Women for America (CWA) is to protect and promote biblical values among all citizens—first through prayer, then education, and finally by influencing our society—thereby reversing the decline in moral values in our nation. The vision of CWA is for women and like-minded men, from all walks of life, to come together and restore the family to its traditional purpose and thereby allow each member of the family to realize their God-given potential and be more responsible citizens."

CWA, which calls itself the largest pro-family organization for women in the United States, hopes to serve as a conservative voice for women interested in preserving a Judeo-Christian heritage and promoting the values of a strong family system. To this end the organization attempts to influence policy, publishes material in line with its mission, and forms prayer groups across the nation.

ESTABLISHED: 1979
EMPLOYEES: 35
MEMBERS: 600,000
PAC: None

Contact Information:
ADDRESS: 1015 15th St. NW, Ste. 1100
        Washington, DC 20005
PHONE: (202) 488-7000
FAX: (202) 488-0806
E-MAIL: feedback@www.cwfa.org
URL: http://www.cwfa.org
PRESIDENT: Carmen Pate

HOW IS IT STRUCTURED?

The CWA national office is governed by a 16-member board of directors, each of whom serve three-year terms. The board meets periodically to establish the direction of the organization, and is headed by Beverly LaHaye, CWA founder and chairman of the board. The board also includes the national office president and the CEO.

The national offices are located in Washington, D.C., and include a Field Department, which carries out liaison work with CWA state affiliates. Staff from the

Field Department work with each state affiliate (larger states such as California and Texas have two chapters) to provide assistance, training, and issue updates. The CWA also conducts an annual Leadership Conference for state affiliate directors. State affiliates focus primarily on issues at the state level.

Individuals who join the CWA pay annual dues of $20 or higher and receive legislative updates, information on current issues, and printed resources from the organization. Members who choose to become part of the organization's Citizen Action Program (available at the CWA Web site) receive E-mail updates on current issues and links to contacting Congress. Members also form prayer chapters (several hundred of these exist across the United States) that meet regularly to pray and sometimes conduct advocacy work.

PRIMARY FUNCTIONS

While the CWA attempts to influence policy, the organization devotes an equal amount of attention to outreach and educational efforts. In the policy arena, the CWA tracks relevant legislation, lobbies for initiatives in line with its mission, testifies at hearings, and prepares position papers on current issues. The organization mobilizes members when needed and requests them to contact congressional members. CWA works to influence policy at the state level as well. For example, after President Bill Clinton vetoed the Partial Birth Abortion Ban legislation (H.R. 1122) in late 1997, CWA state affiliates and other state pro-life groups worked to enact legislation banning the procedure in 22 states.

CWA also mobilizes members into taking action beyond contacting representatives. In 1997 members of the organization joined a boycott against Disney. The boycott was in response to objections over certain Disney-sponsored television programs and Disney's gay-friendly employee policy. Boycott participants refused to frequent Disney attractions or purchase Disney entertainment products. The California CWA state affiliate leader organized a protest march at Disney offices and members all over the United States wrote opinion letters to Disney's president.

CWA works extensively to educate the public and its supporters about its mission and position on issues. Organization Chair Beverly LaHaye broadcasts a daily 30-minute radio show. The organization produces a number of publications, pamphlets, issue briefs, and Action Alerts for members and supporters. CWA liaisons regularly with the media; CWA spokespeople frequently appear in public forums, talk shows, or debate settings.

As part of its function, CWA places an emphasis on prayer chapters. The organization believes strongly that the power of prayer can have an impact on society. More than 700 of these groups meet across the nation on a regular basis and focus their prayers on particular issues or societal situations. Prayer chapters sometimes take on advocacy work for the organization.

PROGRAMS

CWA programs work to fulfill the organization's mission of promoting biblical values in the United States through action, education, and prayer. To this end, the CWA Action Network encourages citizens to become involved in the political process. In 1999 the program called on supporters to contact all parties involved in the presidential impeachment trial. Members or supporters could participate in this program through the organization's Web site. People who visited the Web site were provided with E-mail addresses for senators and officials involved in the trial proceedings.

The Action Network also urges supporters to take part in organized humanitarian efforts. For example, CWA mobilized network supporters when Hurricane Mitch devastated Nicaragua and Honduras in late 1998. The organization also used its radio show to announce the need for supplies to be sent to the devastated countries. The first broadcast alone collected 18 truckloads of supplies including food, money, clothing, and medical supplies.

BUDGET INFORMATION

CWA budget information is available to the public only at national headquarters. The information may be reviewed in entirety on-site at CWA offices, but is not mailed to the public.

HISTORY

CWA was founded in 1979 by an Illinois Catholic woman named Beverly LaHaye in response to the proposed Equal Rights Amendment (ERA). LaHaye's incentive for starting the group grew when she watched a television debate featuring National Organization for Women (NOW) leader Betty Friedan, who claimed to speak for all American woman. While LaHaye and her peers didn't completely object to the ERA (they believed, for example, that women should not be considered second-class citizens), LaHaye felt strongly that Judeo-Christian women needed representation of their own, and that their agenda didn't necessarily match the militancy of U.S. feminists.

By 1985 according to *Time* magazine, CWA was the top counterfeminist women's group, with a larger membership than any other like-minded organizations. In fact, CWA's 500,000 members exceeded the combined membership of such well-known feminist groups as the NOW and the League of Women Voters.

By 1994 CWA found sympathetic allies to its cause when increasing numbers of moderate or conservative women were elected to Congress. In the House alone, five Republican women captured seats, bringing the number of Republican women to 17 (out of a total of 47 women in the House). In the Senate, Republican women had three seats, with Democratic women holding down five. In *USA Today* (December 27, 1994) a CWA spokesperson commented that, "We've got women who will not be practicing the doctrine of gender politics." The increased number of Republican women in Congress complemented CWA's focus, which preferred to address a wide variety of issues that affected pro-family values and the Judeo-Christian heritage, rather than focusing strictly on traditional women's issues such as abortion and family leave.

After the 1994 elections however, CWA and other conservative Christian organizations felt that many Republicans—who had run on pro-family issues—sold out and took a more moderate, compromising approach. Conservative religious leader Pat Dobson of the group Focus on the Family was one of the members of the pro-family movement who publicly criticized what he called Republicans lack of courage to take on moral issues. In the late 1990s, CWA continued to look for conservative political allies—whether Democrat or Republican—with a pro-family agenda based on what the group considered appropriate morals. The family value platform failed to get President George Bush reelected in 1992, and successor Bill Clinton promoted causes (such as gay rights) that CWA and others found objectionable. One of these causes was the National Endowment for the Arts (NEA), an organization that CWA believed supported indecent art or pornography. Despite CWA's objections, the NEA was saved from near termination in 1995.

CURRENT POLITICAL ISSUES

CWA is involved with a number of issues related to its mission of preserving family values and Judeo-Christian heritage in the United States. For example, the organization is concerned with issues surrounding the sanctity of life including euthanasia, abortion, and birth control. The group is particularly concerned by the content of education in many of the nation's schools. Specifically, CWA believes that school sex education programs place too much emphasis on safe sex rather then abstinence—thereby sending the message that sex before marriage is acceptable.

The organization opposes the gay rights agenda because, according to CWA, homosexuality is immoral, a sin, and not consistent with family values. CWA opposed a video used in public school systems called *It's Elementary—Talking about Gay and Lesbian Issues in School,* claiming the video encourages school-aged

FAST FACTS

U.S. high-school seniors scored way below the world average in the Third International Mathematics and Science Study. In the advanced math and physics testing, the United States ranked lowest of all participating countries.

(Source: Gail Russell Chaddock. "U.S. 12th-Graders Miss the Mark." *Christian Science Monitor,* February 25, 1998.)

---

children to accept homosexuality as normal. CWA also objected to the fact the video was funded by the NEA and supported in part by taxpayer dollars. The organization made copies of the video available to its members and urged them to work with parents and school boards to ban the video from school use.

CWA also opposes the fight for gay marriage (an ongoing legal battle that originated in Hawaiian courts during the 1990s). CWA believes that allowing same-sex couples to marry will redefine the concept of family in an immoral way. Similarly, CWA opposes the attempts on the part of the gay rights movement to allow same-sex couples other family-type rights such as adoption or domestic-partner benefits. CWA members voice their objection by participating in boycotts against companies, such as Disney, which offer gay-friendly employee policies. In addition, CWA monitors and responds to relevant legislation.

Case Study: Federal Affirmative Action Status

CWA opposes civil rights legislation or policy for the homosexual population. CWA claims that including gays in the civil rights cause is an insult to other minority groups, particularly because CWA believes that the homosexual lifestyle is an immoral one. CWA and other conservative groups were angered in May 1998, when President Clinton signed an executive order that gave homosexuals affirmative action preference and established hiring quotas for gays in federal employment.

When President Clinton signed the order that gave gays the same affirmative action considerations as other minorities for federal employment (Employment Nondiscrimination Act), CWA and other pro-family groups took action immediately. CWA criticized the move publicly and called on members and supporters to voice concerns to their congressional representatives. Under pressure from groups such as CWA, legislation was attached to the Treasury Department appropriations bill (H.R. 2607, District of Columbia Appropriations, Medical Liability Reform, and Education Reform Act of 1998) which prohibited the federal government from funding President Clinton's order. By attaching the legislation to a larger and important funding bill, CWA and pro-family groups hoped that the president would be unwilling to veto the package in its entirety. As of 1999, the measure was still being debated.

SUCCESSES AND FAILURES

In addition to curriculum content, the CWA is also concerned with academic standards in U.S. schools. According to the organization, in early 1998 U.S. high-school seniors ranked 19th out of 21 countries in science and math subjects. CWA claimed that in the late 1990s, the amount of money spent per student had doubled, with no measurable results to show for it in improved education. The organization claims that the solution to poor education in the United States lies in removing education from government control and empowering school boards and parents to take charge. CWA lobbies for legislation that supports that position, such as the A+ Education Accounts Bill (H.R. 2646, S.1133), which, thanks in part to advocacy efforts of CWA, passed the House and the Senate in mid-1998. The bill allows tax-free saving accounts of up to $2,000 for family education expenses, and prohibits voluntary testing in reading and math.

FUTURE DIRECTIONS

CWA will continue to fight for policy that furthers pro-family values such as the Partial Birth Abortion Ban. The CWA lobbied fiercely for the partial-birth abortion ban legislation (H.R. 1122) that passed in 1997. CWA wanted to prohibit the procedure, which takes place in the third trimester of pregnancy and which many people, including those in the pro-choice camp, believe is unnecessarily brutal. The bill, however, was vetoed by President Clinton. Specifically, CWA and other pro-life groups plan to pressure Congress to override the veto of this abortion-related legislation.

In 1998 the group's concerns became global when CWA leaders asked members to focus on the persecution of Christians in countries such as China and Sudan and to become advocates for religious freedom worldwide. To accomplish this, CWA suggested that members write letters to editors, call or write embassies of countries that persecute Christians, petition Congress, and pray.

GROUP RESOURCES

CWA offers a variety of resources to purchase at http://www.cwfa/prg/catalog/catroot.html. Items include videotapes such as *After the Choice* on the topic of abortion, and *Wait for Me*, which covers teen sexuality. The site also sells audio cassettes, bumper stickers, and books. The CWA offers pamphlets on subjects including birth control, sex education, crisis pregnancy, breast cancer, and public education.

GROUP PUBLICATIONS

CWA offers a number of books, which can be purchased through their Web site, that cover topics ranging from family values to societal trends to political activism. The organization also produces the monthly magazine *Family Voice,* which can be purchased in its entirety or read in excerpts at the Web site. Nonmembers can receive three free issues of the magazine by entering order information at http://security.ability.net/cwfa/catalog/orderfree. html. Other free resources that can be ordered through the Web site include booklets on sex education, the RU-486 abortion pill, breast cancer, and issues regarding public education.

BIBLIOGRAPHY

Chaddock, Gail Russell. "U.S. 12th-Graders Miss the Mark." *Christian Science Monitor,* 25 February 1998.

"Decency a Valid Concern for NEA." *Atlanta Journal,* 1 December 1997.

MacLeish, Ron. "Gingrich & Co. Keep Bead on Arts Endowment." *Christian Science Monitor,* 22 April 1997.

Mantilla, Karla. "Workshop: Women and the Religious Right." *Contemporary Women's Issues Database,* 1 August 1997.

Mathis, Deborah. "What Might Hillary's Role be in a Second Clinton Administration?" *Gannett News Service,* 31 October 1996.

Ross, Loretta J. "How to Get the Goods on the Right." *On the Issues,* 1 December 1997.

Savage, David G. "High Court Set to Weigh Reach of Religious Liberty." *Los Angeles Times,* 17 February 1997.

Stan, Adele M. "Power Preying." *Mother Jones,* 21 November 1995.

Weiser, Carl. "New Planned Parenthood Chief Says Opponents Have Problem with Sex for Pleasure." *Gannett News Service,* 6 June 1996.

Congressional Black Caucus (CBC)

WHAT IS ITS MISSION?

The Congressional Black Caucus (CBC) was founded in 1969 in order to coordinate and solidify the influence of African American members of Congress. The caucus, working with its political action committee (PAC) and the Congressional Black Caucus Foundation, has expanded its efforts to increase the influence of African Americans in the political, legislative, and public-policy arenas. Specifically, members of the caucus work "to promote the public welfare through legislation designed to meet the needs of millions of neglected citizens," according to the organization's Web site. The CBC drafts and supports passage of legislation designed to help not only the nation's black population, but the poor in general. Because of its efforts on behalf of the traditionally underrepresented citizens, the CBC sometimes refers to itself as the "conscience of Congress."

ESTABLISHED: 1969
EMPLOYEES: 2
MEMBERS: 38
PAC: Congressional Black Caucus PAC

Contact Information:

ADDRESS: 319 Cannon House Office Bldg.
   Washington, DC 20501-0535
PHONE: (202) 225-2201
URL: http://www.cbcf.org
CHAIRMAN: James Clyburn

HOW IS IT STRUCTURED?

The CBC is a nonprofit, nonpartisan organization independent of Congress but funded by dues from congressional members. Federal law prohibits the CBC, as well as other caucuses, from receiving private funds. CBC members serve in both the House and the Senate; their constituencies span a broad spectrum, from urban to rural and northern to southern regions. During the 106th Congress the CBC had 38 members.

In 1976 members of the caucus established the CBC Foundation. Unlike the caucus, the foundation is able to receive private funding. A nonpartisan, nonprofit

organization dedicated to public policy and educational research, it sponsors several national education programs. The foundation is governed by a board of directors consisting of 33 members from both private and public institutions. In addition to the foundation, the caucus also runs the Congressional Black Congress PAC, whose members work to raise money for political campaigns and lobby members of congress regarding legislation relevant to the caucus.

PRIMARY FUNCTIONS

The CBC works to enhance the political influence of African Americans through a variety of channels. Its most visible role is that of public information center, coordinating and distributing information among the various levels of government and the public. The CBC holds legislative briefings on bills relevant to its constituency, conducts seminars, organizes hearings, and provides testimony and information services. It also organizes and participates in demonstrations and boycotts, promotes letter-writing campaigns, and endorses clemency appeals for political prisoners and their families.

The CBC attempts to influence both domestic and foreign policy. It drafts and supports legislation designed to help poorer citizens—who are also disproportionately African American—and to strengthen and enforce civil rights laws. The caucus also works to ensure that black representatives are appointed to powerful House committees. The 1986 passage of economic sanctions against South Africa and its system of apartheid (or institutionalized racism) was a major victory for the caucus.

Each year the CBC drafts and coordinates its "Alternative Federal Budget." Because it focuses on fair treatment for underrepresented citizens—including the elderly, students, low-income wage earners and minorities—this budget usually differs a great deal from the budget submitted by the president of the United States. Although the CBC budget has never been passed, it helps focus public and political attention on those people most in need.

The CBC Foundation also helps advance the efforts of the caucus by working to "assist leaders of today while helping to prepare a new generation of leaders for tomorrow," according to the foundation's Web site. It achieves it goals through a broad variety of educational programs, including fellowship and intern programs, as well as an Annual Legislative Conference.

PROGRAMS

CBC programs are administered through the CBC Foundation (CBCF), which conducts issue forums and leadership seminars in order to "stimulate dialogue and educate African Americans in the fundamentals of legislative and public policy development." Specifically, the

foundation sponsors several national education programs. The CBC Fellowship program was developed in 1976 in response to a congressional report which found that blacks were seriously under represented in professional positions within Congress. Fellowships last for nine months and are designed to expose African American graduate students to all aspects of the legislative process. Fellows draft legislation and initiatives as members of a congressional staff. They also conduct research, respond to mail, and coordinate testimony for public hearings.

The CBC Internship program, established in 1986, works in much the same way as the Fellowship program. Talented African American undergraduate students are awarded paid internships which expose them to the legislative process. Interns work with CBC members to draft letters, respond to constituents, and perform other office duties. The CBCF has also developed a high school internship program in which students from underprivileged areas are granted eight-week internships in House and Senate offices. They perform a variety of tasks designed to enhance their workplace skills as well as their understanding of the legislative process.

In addition to these programs, the CBCF also sponsors community programs. The CBC Spouses Education Scholarship Fund was established in 1988 to offset some of the effects of federal cuts in education programs. These scholarships are awarded within the congressional districts of every black member of Congress. Scholarships provide tuition assistance to university students. The CBCF also awards Public Health fellowships that allow fellows to "address a wide array of public policy issues of vital concern to the African American community."

Additionally, the CBC Foundation sponsors an Annual Legislative Conference each September that focuses on strategies and solutions to policy problems facing African Americans. The foundation also sponsors regional conferences designed to explore various public policy concerns at the local level.

BUDGET INFORMATION

In 1995 the Republican-led Congress passed a law effectively defunding all legislative service organizations operating within Congress. This law eliminated the funding which organizations like the Congressional Black Caucus, the Women's Caucus, and the Hispanic Caucus relied on. As a result the CBC was forced to relinquish all of its permanent staff and office space, and now operates out of the office of the CBC chairperson. The two staff members employed by the CBC are classified as "shared-staff," which means they work for both the CBC and the congressperson whose office they share. These staff members, therefore, tend to work on issues that most closely parallel the concerns of the congressperson for whom they work. The CBC portion of the staff members' salaries is paid for by a rotation system in which

BIOGRAPHY:
Adam Clayton Powell Jr.

Clergyman; Congressman (1908–1972) For almost 30 years, Adam Clayton Powell, Jr., served as a firebrand politician who used his unrelenting calls for justice to fuel the civil rights movement. As a 33-year-old freshman member of Congress, Powell quickly made a reputation for himself by engaging in heated, passionate debates on the House floor with veteran segregationists. A prolific legislator, Powell sponsored bills advocating federal aid to education, a minimum-wage scale, and greater benefits for the chronically unemployed. He was chairman of the House Committee on Education and Labor and had a hand in the passage of over 48 laws involving a capital outlay of $14 billion dollars. Powell's flamboyant style was effective in calling attention to the disparity between the ideals of American democracy and the reality of American life. Unfortunately, his personal life was characterized by an extravagance and brashness that would eventually be his undoing. Although years of extramarital affairs, a lack of

attendance for key votes, and a tax fraud indictment did not seem to undercut his legislative effectiveness, a 1967 House subcommittee probe into Powell's handling of congressional funds resulted in a 307 to 116 vote by Congress to bar him. While the Supreme Court later ruled this vote unconstitutional, and Powell was reinstated, his

personal behavior and high absenteeism rate eventually resulted in his loss of popular support and his House seat. Powell died a short time later of complications from prostate surgery, but his legacy endures as one of the earliest and most prominent black voices in the American civil rights movement.

each member of the CBC donates the salary for one staff person from his or her office budget that month. Members of the CBC meet during monthly luncheon meetings, rotating responsibility for paying for the lunches provided during these meetings.

HISTORY

Despite the fact that the Congressional Black Caucus was not formed until 1969, African American members of Congress have been working together for many years. Between 1870 and 1991 almost 70 blacks served in Congress—three as senators and 65 as representatives in the House. During the nineteenth century, all African Americans serving in Congress were Republican, in allegiance to Republican President Abraham Lincoln who had freed the slaves and then supported civil rights before his assassination. During the 1890s, however, white Republicans and Democrats began redrafting the election laws that had made it possible for African Americans to gain office. Between 1870 and 1901, 25 black men were elected to, and served in, Congress. But between 1901 and 1929, no African Americans served in Congress.

During the 1930s two blacks were finally elected to Congress: Oscar De Priest, a Republican, and Arthur Mitchell, a Democrat. Between 1942 and 1960, four African Americans were elected to Congress, namely Democrats William Dawson, Adam Clayton Powell,

Charles Diggs, and Robert Nix. Many African Americans began to switch parties, leaving the Republicans and joining the Democrats, during the presidency of Franklin D. Roosevelt, beginning a trend that continued through the end of the century.

During the civil rights movement of the 1960s, several blacks were elected to Congress. This was due, in large part, to the passage of the civil rights amendment in 1964 and the Voting Rights Act in 1965. These laws removed many of the impediments to voting that had been established early in the century, and African Americans were able to vote in unprecedented numbers. It was during this time that black members of Congress, although still a significant minority, began to realize the importance of working together to achieve their political goals. African American members of Congress were not awarded important committee assignments or elected chairmen of any powerful committees. In order to remedy this situation, and to further the interests and needs of their constituencies, African American members formed the Congressional Black Caucus in 1969.

The stated goals of the newly formed CBC were to increase the power and influence of black members of Congress; to lobby for economic programs that would benefit all poor people; and to strengthen and enforce civil rights laws. Soon after the CBC was formed members demanded a meeting with President Richard Nixon. Nixon declined to schedule a meeting for 14 months, finally giving in after the CBC boycotted his State of the Union address. At the meeting, Nixon was presented with several recommendations for action in areas such as community and urban development, and civil rights. Although Nixon's administration took no direct action in response to the CBC recommendations, the meeting did garner national attention for the caucus, establishing it as a legitimate representative of the interests and concerns of African Americans.

In 1972, Barbara Jordan (D-Tex.) and Andrew Young (D-Geor.) were elected to the House of Representatives. They were the first African Americans elected to Congress during the twentieth century from states which had been part of the Confederacy during the Civil War. Throughout the 1970s and 1980s, CBC members who had been elected during the 1960s began to gain seniority in Congress and consolidate their power. Many members gained appointments to the most powerful committees in the House. In 1985, William Gray III, a black Democrat from Pennsylvania, was elected chairman of the Budget Committee, one of the most powerful committees in Congress. Prior to his 1991 retirement, Gray served as Democratic whip, the third most powerful position in the House. His success was viewed as a result, not only of his own talent and ability, but of the increasing power and visibility of the caucus itself.

Another sign of the caucus's increased power was the successful passage of economic sanctions against South Africa in 1986. The South African government operated under a system of apartheid, which forbade black citizens from holding public office and denied them many basic freedoms. The passage of U.S. trade sanctions began a powerful and international outcry against the South African government, which contributed to the end of apartheid policies in that country.

In 1998 there were more than 40 black members of Congress, including both the second black to be elected to the Senate in the twentieth century and the first black woman senator. The influence and power of the CBC has increased as its numbers have increased. African American members of Congress are now routinely appointed to the most powerful and prestigious committees in the House. Furthermore, because its members present such a united front, the caucus has gained a greater share of political visibility. The success of the CBC has inspired other minority groups to form caucuses. For example, in 1977 women in the House of Representatives formed the Women's Caucus.

CURRENT POLITICAL ISSUES

Members of the Congressional Black Caucus claim both a national and an international constituency. Along with the members of their own districts, members of the caucus also represent the interests of African Americans nationwide. The caucus also works to focus attention on regions of the world wherein problems are also directly relevant to African Americans. In 1986, for example, the

CBC successfully lobbied the U.S. government to withdraw its investments from South Africa so long as that nation operated under an apartheid system. This divestiture was a major victory for the CBC, and it inspired governments and companies around the world to also divest their money. In 1990 apartheid was abolished in South Africa.

Members of the CBC represent the interests of African Americans, even when such interests require unpopular positions. In 1991, for instance, the CBC voted against supporting Operation Desert Storm. A disproportionate number of blacks serve in the U.S. military, and members of the CBC felt that the threat to U.S. interests in the Persian Gulf was not strong enough to warrant sending U.S. troops into harm's way. The CBC has also taken positions on issues that have threatened the health and welfare of African Americans. In May of 1998, several members of the CBC called for the resignation of Barry McCaffrey as director of the Office of National Drug Control Policy. A month earlier McCaffrey had convinced President Clinton to enforce a ban on the federal funding of needle exchange programs. Members of the CBC noted that AIDS is the leading killer of black men and women aged 25 to 44, and that in more than half of those deaths, the virus was transmitted by sharing needles to inject drugs. CBC members accused McCaffrey and President Clinton of ignoring scientific evidence that needle exchange programs prevent the spread of AIDS.

Members of the CBC often find themselves embroiled in issues which have profound national implications. The controversy over a series of articles appearing in the *San Jose Mercury News* in 1996 and 1997, claiming a connection between the Central Intelligence Agency (CIA) and the introduction of crack cocaine into African American communities, is a case in point.

Case Study: The Crack Cocaine-CIA Connection

In 1996, the *San Jose Mercury News* ran a series of articles examining the original source of crack cocaine in U.S. cities. The articles alleged that supporters of the Nicaraguan contra rebels, who were supported by the CIA, sold tons of cocaine to a drug dealer in South Central Los Angeles, California, a predominately African American neighborhood, as a way to fund their rebellion. The articles alleged that agents working for the CIA were aware of the connection between the drug-trafficking and funding of the contras and may have even supported it. The implication was that, at best, the CIA had stood idly by while crack cocaine was allowed to flood the streets of South Central Los Angeles, and at worse, had supported and cooperated in the introduction of crack cocaine to South Central Los Angeles.

These articles created a national controversy. Congresswoman Maxine Waters, who represented South Central Los Angeles and was also chair of the CBC, led the public outcry, calling for congressional and federal investigations into the allegations. Members of the CBC soon joined the crusade. Within a few months both the Senate and the House launched investigations, calling hundreds of witnesses to testify. The Director of the CIA, John M. Deutch, appeared before an angry gathering of citizens in South Central Los Angeles, and fielded their questions for hours. Both the Justice Department and the CIA began investigations into the allegations.

In 1999 the CIA published a report claiming that the charges were largely groundless. Several newspapers, including the *Los Angeles Times,* also conducted investigations and found that, while there was evidence to suggest that drug traffickers had contributed money to the contras, there was no proof that CIA operatives had any knowledge of these transactions. The newspapers' findings were consistent with the findings of the House and Senate investigations.

Although the exact nature of CIA involvement in the introduction of crack cocaine onto the streets of South Central Los Angeles remained unclear, the power and influence of the CBC was apparent. Members responded quickly and vigorously to the articles, and their calls for investigations from the House, Senate, and Justice Department were heeded almost at once. Although crack cocaine has had a disproportionate and devastating effect on the black community in the United States, it is a national problem that transcends the boundaries of race. In its work on behalf of African Americans, members of the CBC often find themselves speaking and fighting for the interests of all Americans.

FUTURE DIRECTIONS

As more and more African Americans are elected to congressional office, the CBC will continue to grow in influence, prestige, and power. Although the caucus began with only nine members, in 1998 it had nearly forty members. As its constituency and their interests expand, the CBC's workload will also increase. The CBC will also have to address the growing diversity of opinion among its members. Through the 1990s, members of the CBC displayed an unprecedented unity of purpose and opinion, but as the caucus continues to expand, so will the difficulties in maintaining that unity of opinion. In order to maintain its current level of influence, the CBC will have to work hard to avoid the fate of the Women's Caucus and the Hispanic Caucus, both of which have suffered from a lack of political unity.

GROUP RESOURCES

The CBC Foundation maintains a Web page (http://www.cbcfonline.org) that provides information on specific CBCF programs, events, and activities. The CBCF also provides press releases on political issues. The CBC itself does not maintain a Web page, but its individual member's pages can be reached through the internet site for the U.S. House of Representatives (http://www.house.gov) and the U.S. Senate (http://www.senate.gov). CBC member's Web sites contain information on the organization and those issues important to it, including numerous press releases.

GROUP PUBLICATIONS

The CBCF publishes a quarterly on-line newsletter available at http://www.cbcfonling.org. The foundation also publishes news releases and information about the educational programs it sponsors. This information can be obtained by contacting the CBC Foundation at 1004 Pennsylvania Ave. SE, Washington DC, 20003.

BIBLIOGRAPHY

Bivins, Larry. "Ex-Detroiter at the Forefront in CIA-Drug Furor." *Detroit News,* 22 December 1996.

Christopher, Maurine. *Black Americans in Congress.* New York: Crowell, 1976.

Daerr, Elizabeth. "Clinton Drug Czar May Irk Allies but Gets Things Done." *Wall Street Journal*, 12 May 1998.

Davidson, Roger H., and Walter J. Oleszek. *Congress and Its Members*. Third Edition. Washington, DC: CQ Press, 1990.

McManus, Doyle. "CIA Probe Absolves Agency on L.A. Crack." *Los Angeles Times*, 4 January 1998.

Neal, Terry M. "Drug Policy Chief Is Facing Some New Foes." *Washington Post*, 18 May 1998.

Ragsdale, Bruce, and Joel D. Treese. *Black Americans in Congress, 1870-1989*. Washington, DC: U.S. Government Printing Office, 1990.

Swain, Carol M. *Black Faces, Black Interests: The Representation of African Americans in Congress*. Cambridge, Mass.: Harvard University Press, 1993.

Weiss, Nancy J. *Farewell to the Party of Lincoln: Black Politics in the Age of FDR*. Princeton, N.J.: Princeton University Press, 1983.

Consumer Alert

ESTABLISHED: 1977
EMPLOYEES: 4
MEMBERS: 3,500
PAC: None

Contact Information:

ADDRESS: 1001 Connecticut Ave. NW, Ste. 1128
     Washington, DC 20036
PHONE: (202) 467-5809
FAX: (202) 467-5814
E-MAIL: consumeralert@consumeralert.org
URL: http://www.consumeralert.org
EXECUTIVE DIRECTOR: Frances B. Smith

WHAT IS ITS MISSION?

The published mission of Consumer Alert is to "enhance understanding and appreciation of the consumer benefits of a market economy so that individuals and policymakers rely more on private rather than government approaches to consumer concerns." Consumer Alert is an interest group whose members are tied together by a common philosophy, which is to protect consumer choice and promote economic growth without government interference. Many other consumer groups consider this mission to be a contradiction in terms and accuse the group of being more interested in protecting business than consumers. According to Consumer Alert, however, its supporters and financial contributors include private citizens in all 50 states, as well as foundations and corporations. The group does not do "contract" work for any business or individual.

Consumer Alert is strongly opposed to big government and to expansion of government regulation, a sharp contrast to the type of consumerism pushed by noted consumer advocate Ralph Nader, who believes consumers need strong government regulation of business and industry. Consumer Alert further believes in a "free market" approach to consumer protection and considers "competition as the best regulator of business, and individual choice as the best expression of consumer interest."

HOW IS IT STRUCTURED?

Consumer Alert is a nonprofit organization based in Washington, D.C. It is headed by a nine-member

FAST FACTS

According to the White House Climate Change Task Force, the temperature worldwide in the twentieth century was the warmest in 600 years, and 1997 was the single warmest year on record.

(Source: Charles Pope. "Fresh Focus on Global Warming Does Not Dispel Doubts About Kyoto Treaty's Future." *Congressional Quarterly Weekly,* June 6, 1998.)

in fact a concern. "Consumer Alert was virtually the only consumer group to point out the downside of air bags," Consumer Alert recalled in a 1996 article that appeared in its *Consumer Comments* magazine.

On the flip side of the issue, Ralph Nader was urging the government to mandate air bags as soon as possible, in the interest of saving lives. Nader directly attacked Consumer Alert and other groups who opposed air bags as speaking for the auto industry in the name of American consumers. But Consumer Alert countered Nader and others who shared his approach for proposing "a 'one size fits all' solution that fails to take into account individual judgment and responsibility." By the 1990s, after air bags killed or injured a number of children and small adults and their dangers became apparent, Consumer Alert asserted that their long-standing opposition to the devices had been vindicated. In a January/February 1997 *Consumer Comments'* article, Executive Director Fran Smith urged the National Highway Traffic Safety Administration to reconsider the air bag mandate. The NHTSA eventually adopted a rule that allows some vehicle owners to have dealers install cut-off switches. The regulation went into effect in January of 1998.

Not all of Consumer Alert's positions are so divisive. For instance, on tax reform, Consumer Alert has been an outspoken advocate of lower taxes and a simpler tax code, a goal urged by many grassroots groups. Many groups, along with Consumer Alert, participate in the annual "taxpayer day of outrage" in Washington, D.C. At one such rally on April 15, 1997, Consumer Alert Policy Analyst Rich Zipperer criticized the time-consuming and confusing process of filing tax reforms. "Working for a consumer group, I have heard of hundreds of consumer scams," Zipperer said, "but one look at the current tax system shows that it is one of the biggest consumer rip-offs of all time."

CURRENT POLITICAL ISSUES

Consumer Alert finds itself involved in a wide variety of political issues, with the aim of offering the consumer viewpoint. The various issues include consumer product safety, the environment, personal finance, diet and food safety, privacy and freedom, taxation, and health. Some groups maintain that proposed government regulation in these areas is necessary to prevent dangers and end abuses. Consumer Alert often feels that the same regulation is an interference, is quite often based on unfounded and unsubstantiated fears, and may quite possibly result in unintended harmful consequences.

For instance, in 1998 the group filed comments with the Environmental Protection Agency objecting to a brochure the agency distributed that promoted organic food. The brochure claimed that organic foods are purer and healthier than food on which pesticides are used. Consumer Alert asserted that such comments issued from a government agency may mislead consumers into thinking that organically grown food does not have to be washed thoroughly, which according to the group could lead to very negative health effects. Consumer Alert further faulted the brochure for not putting into perspective the risks posed by pesticides compared to other health risks.

Consumer Alert has been directly involved in many ongoing environmental debates. It specifically followed the international discussions held in the 1990s that focused on global warming.

Case Study: The Kyoto Treaty

The Kyoto treaty was drawn up in Japan in December of 1997 when representatives of 160 nations met to discuss and devise plans to reduce global warming. Responding to environmental concerns, many countries including the United States were committed to reducing pollution by "greenhouse gases," which many scientists blame for producing a gradual warming of the climate. The main greenhouse gases given off by human activity are carbon dioxide, methane, and nitrous oxide. Others, often released during industrial manufacturing processes, are hydrofluorocarbons, perfluorocarbons, and sulfur hexachloride. If the Earth's climate continued to increase, scientists predicted severe flooding, catastrophic rises in sea levels and other dire consequences.

"I think we all have to agree that the potential for serious climate disruption is real," President Bill Clinton said in October 1997. "It would clearly be a mistake to bury our heads in the sand and pretend the issue will go away." Vice President Al Gore attended part of the 11-day conference in Kyoto in December to underscore the administration's commitment.

The treaty resulting from the conference set limits on greenhouse gas emissions for 38 developed nations, and required the nations to reduce emissions of six gases. The United States target was a 7 percent reduction by volunteer board of directors from around the country that meets at least twice per year. A 36-member Advisory Council composed of scientific and economic experts often attends board meetings and offers advice on issues.

Membership is open to anyone who shares the group's philosophy and sends a donation. The group suggests $35 (and provides a free subscription to its magazine for that price), but members can send as much or as little as they want. There is no annual meeting or convention for members.

Although the group has few members, Consumer Alert forged the National Consumer Coalition, a network of 27 like-minded groups, including Americans for Tax Reform, Citizens for a Sound Economy, and the National Center for Policy Analysis. According to Consumer Alert, the collective represents over four million members all of whom share the belief that a market economy free from government intervention is the ultimate benefit to consumers. The coalition consists of various subcommittees that focus on issues such as the environment, health and safety, and transportation. Each subcommittee is headed by a group of specialists who represent the various member organizations. The coalition sponsors educational programs, conducts informational exchanges, and in general attempts to advance the market-oriented approach to consumer protection advocated by Consumer Alert.

PRIMARY FUNCTIONS

Consumer Alert uses a variety of methods in order to promote a free market economy. Members challenge federal and international policy that will potentially harm consumers by testifying before, and providing research, formal comments, and petitions to legislative and regulatory bodies. Consumer Alert doggedly monitors legislation that proposes regulatory changes and will take legal action if necessary. Members are also invited to provide testimony before committees of Congress that will illustrate how proposed legislation might ultimately affect consumers.

Simultaneously Consumer Alert has the goal of directly protecting and educating consumers. It does this through legal action, consumer alerts, and media outreach. Consumer Alert staff also sponsors, investigates, and evaluates consumer health and safety issues. Such information is delivered to the public through media interviews, press releases, public appearances at events covered by the media, and editorial pieces distributed to the media.

At times, investigative research is taken directly to the source. In 1996 another consumer group called the Consumer Federation of America wrote to representatives of baseball and softball leagues advising them to switch to soft-core baseballs because they were safer than traditional baseballs. A Consumer Alert policy analyst wrote to the same representatives and challenged that advice, citing research that the soft-core baseballs might actually be more dangerous.

The group dispenses consumer tips through a Commonsense Consumer Column, which attempts to provide useful information in such areas as taxes, food safety, the environment and financial concerns. Some of the information is also on the group's Web site. Consumer Alert also has three publications that cover consumer issues and offer consumer tips and advice on such topics as managing credit card debt, choosing home improvement contractors, and how to effectively complain about products or services.

BUDGET INFORMATION

Consumer Alert has an annual budget of approximately $250,000. The group's activities are funded through donations from private individuals and grants from corporations and foundations. The group has no government contracts and gets no government grants.

HISTORY

Consumer Alert was founded in 1977 by Barbara Keating-Edh, a conservative California activist concerned about the proliferation of government agencies in the 1970s. Keating-Edh ran unsuccessfully for the state Assembly in California, but is still considered among the conservative leaders in the United States. She is a member of the Council for National Policy, a somewhat secretive group of influential conservatives formed in 1981 to push national policy to the right.

Although Consumer Alert has never become one of the most widely known or powerful groups in Washington, it is an active group and its leaders are widely quoted by or published in the media. The group has been persistent over the years in offering policymakers and the public an alternative approach to consumer protection from typical consumer groups. This alternative approach frequently puts the group at odds with other consumer advocates, who consistently challenge their motives. Consumer Alert's philosophical bent and its relationship to other consumer groups is illustrated by the air bag issue.

In the early 1980s Consumer Alert urged the U.S. federal government not to mandate vehicle manufacturers to install air bags. According to the group, such a mandate amounted to imposing safety measures on consumers rather than letting the free market determine what consumers wanted and were willing to pay for. Besides, the group warned, air bags posed a danger to young children. These warnings came as early as 1981, long before a rash of accidents made it clear that such dangers were

Tax protestors gather in a park near the White House on April 15, 1996, during the third annual Taxpayer Day of Outrage. Groups such as Consumer Alert regularly lobby Congress advocating for tax reform and reduction. (Photograph by Joe Marquette, AP/Wide World Photo)

2012. Under the terms of the treaty, governments had until March 1999 to sign and ratify it. In the United States, the treaty has to be approved by the U.S. Senate. Before the Kyoto conference had even begun, the U.S. Senate passed a resolution stating that it did not intend to sign any agreement that bound the United States to emissions limitations, unless the agreement also restricted the emissions of developing nations. The Kyoto Protocol does not include such restrictions, and many senators urged Clinton not to sign it.

Consumer Alert, anticipating the treaty, began to rally opposition to measures to reduce global warming even before it was drawn up. In May 1997 Consumer Alert formed a subgroup of the National Consumer Coalition called the "Cooler Heads" Coalition, to address the consumer impact of climate change policies. In July 1997, the group established a Web site at http://www.globalwarming.org to serve as a clearinghouse of information and to challenge the fact that global warming posed a serious global environmental threat. The September/October 1997 issue of Consumer Alert's magazine reported New Scientist Online had rated the site as one of the top five sources for information on global climate issues on the Internet.

Consumer Alert spread its message that the scientific community had not reached a consensus that global warming was a serious threat, let alone the type of threat

that would require the drastic economic sacrifices spelled out at the Kyoto conference. The group claimed that sharply reducing emissions would hurt industry, drive up energy costs, and result in the loss of millions of jobs. They also cited statistics that say 98 percent of total global greenhouse gas emissions are natural (mostly water vapor), while only 2 percent are from man-made sources. According to research conducted by Dr. Robert C. Balling at Arizona State University, "man-made emissions have had no more than a minuscule impact on the climate. Although the climate has warmed slightly in the last 100 years, 70 percent of that warming occurred prior to 1940, before the upsurge in greenhouse gas emissions from industrial processes."

When the Clinton administration in October 1997 conducted a "teach in" at Georgetown University in Washington to rally public support for the upcoming treaty, Consumer Alert members showed up outside the university to protest. They shouted such slogans as "Show us the science!" The protest was filmed by CNN and public television. Consumer Alert Executive Director Fran Smith was quoted in a number of publications that explored the topic. For instance, she told Crain's Chicago Business in February 1998: "We are concerned because (the treaty) calls for a drastic energy diet, and there has been no discussion about how consumers and small businesses will be affected."

In April 1998, Consumer Alert member and Virginia homemaker Judy Kent testified before a congressional committee that the treaty, if implemented, would raise her family's electric bill by $1,400 a year and her gasoline bill by $840 a year. These and other efforts by Consumer Alert and other groups helped galvanize public—and congressional—opposition to the treaty.

Despite the protests of Consumer Alert and the Senate President Clinton signed the Kyoto Protocol on November 12, 1998. However, the treaty is not binding until it is ratified by a Senate vote. In light of the strong opposition to the treaty in that body, President Clinton decided not to submit the treaty for a vote until additional restrictions for developing nations would be included. Further points were ironed out at a fourth international session for climate change, held in Buenos Aires from November 2–13, 1998. While Clinton hoped these restrictions would be added in 1999, it remains to be seen if this will be enough to convince the Senate to support it.

GROUP RESOURCES

The Consumer Alert Web site at http://www.consumeralert.org contains information about the group's activities and positions and has links to a number of other conservative or free-market sites. It also links to http://www.globalwarming.org that offers information and arguments challenging the need for strong measures to reduce the emission of greenhouse gases. Consumer Alert offers the Commonsense Consumer Column to newspapers around the country. The column offers consumer tips as well as information that supports its market approach to consumer protection. For more information on the organization, write to Consumer Alert, 1001 Connecticut Ave. NW, Ste. 1128, Washington, DC 20036 or call (202) 467-5809.

GROUP PUBLICATIONS

The group's magazine, *Consumer Comments,* is published bimonthly. It has information about the group's

activities and publishes articles on market-oriented consumer topics. The group began a newsletter called *CPSC Monitor* in 1996 that it makes available on its Web site and by fax. The newsletter monitors the activities of the Consumer Product Safety Commission, which Consumer Alert believes has become overzealous and strayed beyond its mission of protecting consumers from "unreasonable risk of injury." Since 1997 Consumer Alert has offered *On the Plate,* a fax newsletter published "to educate the public on food policy issues." The newsletter attempts to throw light on "food scares" and distinguish "facts from fabrications and exaggerations" on food safety issues. For information on how to obtain the organization's publications, write to Consumer Alert, 1001 Connecticut Ave. NW, Ste. 1128, Washington, DC 20036 or call (202) 467-5809.

BIBLIOGRAPHY

Bergman, B. J. "Copout in Kyoto." *Sierra Club Bulletin,* March/April 1998.

"CA Member Testifies Against Kyoto Protocol." *Consumer Comments,* May/June 1998.

"CA Vindicated on Airbag Concerns." *Consumer Comments,* December 1996.

"EPA/USDA Reassess Pesticide Use." *Consumer Comments,* May/June 1998.

Smith, Frances B. "The Airbag Controversy." *Consumer Comments,* Fall 1996.

Klein, David, Marymae E. Klein, and Douglas D. Walsh. *Getting Unscrewed and Staying That Way: The Sourcebook for Consumer Protection.* New York: Harry Holt and Co., 1993.

"Kyoto's Unfinished Business." *Foreign Affairs,* 1 July 1998.

Miller, William H. "Global Warming: The Game's Afoot." *Industry Week,* 5 January 1998.

———. "The Split Over Global Warming." *Industry Week,* 8 June 1998.

Pope, Charles. "Fresh Focus on Global Warming Does Not Dispel Doubts About Kyoto Treaty's Future." *Congressional Quarterly Weekly,* 6 June 1998.

Consumer Federation
of America
(CFA)

WHAT IS ITS MISSION?

According to the mission statement of the Consumer Federation of America (CFA), the umbrella organization "works to ensure that all consumers, but particularly those who are least able to speak out for themselves, are not ignored by the system." Over the years the organization's goals have shifted in response to consumer needs and abuses. During the late 1960s and early 1970s the CFA was concerned with truth-in-lending and truth-in-packaging issues. By the 1980s many of its efforts were targeted at "big business," especially fighting inflation in the areas of food and energy. More recently, the CFA has been involved in matters concerning the purchase of new and used cars, as well as making sure consumer abuses do not occur on the Internet. But while its specific involvement has changed with the times, its overall mission remains: serving as a watchdog for the U.S. consumer.

ESTABLISHED: November 1967
EMPLOYEES: 20 (1997)
MEMBERS: 240 organizations representing 50 million individuals (1997)
PAC: Consumer Federation of America Political Action Committee

Contact Information:

ADDRESS: 1424 16th St. NW, Ste. 604
    Washington, DC 20036
PHONE: (202) 387-6121
FAX: (202) 265-7989
EXECUTIVE DIRECTOR: Stephen C. Brobeck

HOW IS IT STRUCTURED?

Composed of representatives from over 240 consumer groups and agencies with allied interests, the CFA is governed by a board of directors elected by organization members. The board has the authority to elect officers and other board members and to determine the consumer policies of the organization. The entire membership debates and adopts policy resolutions at CFA annual meetings, which are held in conjunction with a consumer assembly. Policy committees oversee specific issues, including energy, food, health, product safety, communications, antitrust, the disabled,

finances, low income, insurance, transportation, and the environment.

Since the board of directors meets only once a year at the convention, it delegates most of its authority to an elected 10-member executive committee which includes a president, secretary-treasurer, and eight vice presidents representing both national and grassroots organization members. That board, in turn, delegates certain responsibilities to the executive director, who is hired for an indeterminate period, and the CFA staff. Since its creation the CFA has had four executive directors, each appointed after the voluntary departure of his or her predecessor.

Member participation and control has been one of the greatest strengths of the CFA, helping to ensure that policies reflect a broad, grassroots consensus and providing the organization with credibility. Nevertheless, the CFA board extends a great deal of administrative discretion to the executive director, including the hiring of personnel, recommending annual legislative and regulatory priorities, and interpreting policy resolutions.

The CFA seeks to strengthen the consumer movement by building bridges between pro-consumer organizations. Staff members coordinate ongoing communication among hundreds of consumer and community organizations around the country. In addition to working with small groups of both member and non-member organizations on issues before Congress and regulatory agencies, the CFA operates the Coalition for Consumer Health and Safety. This unique alliance of 37 consumer, health, and insurer groups has defined goals and proposed solutions to problems in the areas of motor vehicle safety, home and product safety, indoor air quality, food safety and nutrition, cigarette and alcohol consumption, and AIDS. The coalition works to implement its agenda through legislative, regulatory, and public education initiatives.

The CFA is first and foremost an advocacy organization, working to advance pro-consumer policy on a variety of issues. Its staff works with Congress and regulators to promote policies beneficial to consumers, oppose harmful policies, and engage debate on all issues in which consumers have a stake. It is also an educational organization intent on providing information on consumer issues to the public and the media, as well as to policymakers and other public interest advocates, by means of reports, books, news releases, newsletters, and press conferences. Finally, the CFA is dedicated to supporting national, state, and local organizations committed to the goals of consumer advocacy and protection. Member organizations include grassroots consumer groups, senior citizen organizations, labor unions, and cooperatives.

To achieve its goals and remain effective, the CFA also provides comments and information to Congress, federal agencies, and the courts; conducts surveys on consumer concerns; monitors legislation; lobbies; provides information to the media; and forms coalitions with other local, state and national consumer organizations.

Although their intentions may be the same—to protect consumers—CFA interactions with local and state organizations have not been without conflict. Especially in the organization's early years, CFA representatives at the national level frequently battled with grassroots representatives over control of the organization. Large trade unions and cooperatives felt that they should control the organization since they contributed the largest portion of income and were located in Washington, D.C.; grassroots groups believed that because of their character as consumer organizations, they were entitled to run the federation. A balance was struck by electing board members from both constituencies.

PRIMARY FUNCTIONS

From its inception, the CFA has dedicated itself to representing the interest of U.S. consumers and ensuring them a voice in policy decisions that affect their daily lives. The size and diversity of its membership enables the CFA to represent virtually all consumers on a wide variety of issues. But its special interest always has been advocating on behalf of those with the greatest needs: children, the poor and near poor, and the elderly living on fixed incomes. Before Congress, the courts, and federal regulatory agencies the CFA has pushed for equitable ways to stabilize the U.S. economy and protect consumers by ensuring that the marketplace promotes competition, product safety, protection against fraud and abuse, quality healthcare, and pollution regulations. It has supported deregulation only in economic sectors where meaningful competition exists, such as in the telecommunications industry.

PROGRAMS

Each year the CFA sponsors the Consumer Assembly, a conference addressing consumer issues, needs, and priorities. The assembly provides a unique forum for leading consumer advocates and leaders representing labor, senior citizen, and rural interests to meet and exchange views and information with government, academic, and industry representatives. More than 500 typically attend.

The CFA also sponsors a full schedule of single-issue conferences each year. At these conferences, consumer advocates and representatives of government and industry discuss emerging issues in such areas as telecommunications, financial services, indoor air quality, electric utilities, energy, and marketing. CFA's annual Awards Dinner honors members of government, the media, and public interest organizations with distinguished records in advancing the cause of the U.S. consumer.

BUDGET INFORMATION

Under the leadership of Stephen Brobeck, the CFA has increased its annual income from about $200,000 in 1980 to $2 million in 1997. A reserve fund has been built up to more than $600,000, and membership services have been expanded. Most notably, a state and local grants fund was created. The increased funds were the result of a more diversified financial base. Instead of relying simply on membership dues to run the federation, the CFA began to publish and sell consumer-oriented books and pamphlets, as well as host and charge for workshops and conferences on various issues, such as energy and financial services. These and other projects were funded by a diverse group of institutions, including government agencies, publishers, corporations, trade associations, and CFA members.

HISTORY

The CFA was organized by reform-minded Washington, D.C.-based advocates during the mid-1960s, a time of turbulent change and social protest. Most of these advocates, drawn from organizations established earlier in the century such as the Consumers Union, industrial labor unions, and rural electric cooperatives, thought the time was ripe for new consumer protections and agencies.

In 1964 representatives of several of these groups began meeting informally and planning ways to advance consumer legislation; a year later they organized a national consumer forum. Held for the first time in April of 1966, this consumer assembly was co-sponsored by 30 national organizations representing workers, small farmers, consumer cooperatives, and women, as well as individual consumers. At this meeting White House Consumer Adviser Esther Peterson urged the creation of a federation of state and local groups to press for consumer legislation.

Later in 1966, after a lengthy debate, participants decided that the federation should include not only consumer advocacy and education organizations but also cooperatives, trade unions, and other supporting nonprofit groups. By the next assembly, held in November 1967, the foundation for the organization had been laid, a charter and bylaws prepared, and temporary officers selected.

1968–1973: The Angevine Years

During the federation's first annual meeting, held in April, 1968, 56 charter members elected officers and directors and appointed activist Erma Angevine, a professor of English at the University of Kansas and a member of several cooperatives, as the CFA's first executive director. Angevine's greatest challenge was building the organization from scratch, with minimal funds contributed by members. She also mediated ongoing tension between grassroots consumer organizations and the trade unions

and cooperatives which represented about three-quarters of the federation's membership. This disagreement over representation culminated in the establishment of an offshoot of eight state consumer groups that was called the Conference on Consumer Organizations (COCO).

In addition to building the federation and dealing with internal turmoil, Angevine was expected to take the lead on numerous issues. During her tenure, she involved the CFA in dozens of congressional issues, developing position papers and fact sheets, mobilizing CFA members, and communicating with members of Congress and their staffers. Working closely with other consumer advocates, cooperative and union lobbyists, and a supportive group of Democratic congressional leaders, she helped ensure the passage of key consumer legislation involving truth in lending and truth in packaging.

1973–1980: The Foreman/O'Reilly Years

Angevine's successor, Carol Foreman Tucker, who served as executive director from 1973 to 1977, also faced many challenges in helping the federation grow and evolve. The daughter and granddaughter of Arkansas politicians, Tucker had worked on Capitol Hill, in the executive branch, and at a community-level Planned Parenthood office.

After Tucker left the CFA due to her appointment as assistant secretary in the U.S. Department of Agriculture in 1977, legislative director Kathleen O'Reilly took over the top spot, where she served until 1980. Before joining the CFA in 1975, O'Reilly had practiced law in the District of Columbia, where her corporate and insurance-industry defense litigation work included drafting the first federal no-fault auto insurance legislation. At the CFA, O'Reilly would become known for forceful consumer advocacy. She organized numerous coalitions, testified more than 200 times before congressional and state legislative bodies, and frequently was interviewed by national media. O'Reilly led a successful congressional effort to reduce sugar price supports and to expand protections against credit discrimination.

Despite her political savvy, O'Reilly found herself battling the Carter administration, which, surprisingly for a Democratic administration, seemed to support big business as it organized against consumer initiatives. To encourage the election of a more consumer-friendly Congress, the organization established its political action committee, which endorsed, but did not give financial contributions to, congressional candidates. One of the CFA's top priorities during the Carter presidency of the 1970s was fighting inflation, especially in the areas of food and energy.

The 1980s and Beyond: The Brobeck Years

After O'Reilly's departure to run for Congress, she was replaced by Stephen Brobeck, a social history professor at Case Western Reserve University who had served on the CFA board and executive committee. He became executive director just prior to the election of Ronald Reagan as president. During Reagan's first term, CFA consumer advocates remained almost continuously on the defensive, trying to protect agencies such as the Federal Trade Commission's Bureau of Competition and the Consumer Product Safety Commission from elimination and defending existing consumer protections, such as state ceilings on interest rates, which were under attack.

During the Bush administration, antipathy to consumer efforts lessened; the Clinton administration that followed would be even more supportive, although consumer advocates were unprepared for the overwhelming Republican victory in the 1994 elections. In addition to building the federation's financial base, Brobeck spearheaded efforts to create new organizations such as the Advocates for Auto and Highway Safety, advocacy groups like the Coalition against Insurance Fraud, the Coalition for Consumer Health and Safety, and the Consumer Literacy Consortium, and created the CFA's Tele-Consumer Hotline.

During the 1980s and 1990s the CFA staff established annual single-focus conferences on energy, utilities, and financial services, prepared a half-dozen books and more than a dozen pamphlets, established toll-free hot lines on telephone services and radon, and conducted consumer literacy tests that served as the basis for a new organization, the Consumer Literacy Consortium, which developed and disseminated money-saving tips. These and other projects were funded by a diverse group of institutions including government agencies, publishers, corporations, trade associations, and CFA members.

CURRENT POLITICAL ISSUES

Shifting consumer concerns have always dictated the focus of the CFA. Over the years the organization has followed such concerns as they have arisen; however, it has also raised public awareness regarding problems the average consumer might not be aware of, such as the dangers of formaldehyde, a substance used in furniture, home-building materials, and carpet manufacturing that is suspected of causing allergies and respiratory problems. One of the federation's most recent targets for reform has been the practice of "lemon laundering": dealers' misrepresentation to buyers of the condition of used vehicles.

Case Study: Defective Vehicles

In 1996 the CFA, along with the National Association of Consumer Agency Administrators, co-petitioned the Federal Trade Commission (FTC) to take steps to curb lemon laundering. Deeply concerned about the continuing problems encountered by consumers in connec-

tion with used car-sales and repairs, the CFA conducted surveys of consumer protection agencies concerning consumer complaints. In any given recent year, automobiles—both new and used car-sales and repairs—have been the product consumers complain about most. In listing the top five most frequent categories of complaints received, the survey found that autos comprised three of the four most frequent responses, with "used car sales" topping the list.

CFA representatives told the FTC that auto manufacturers' claims that vehicles are repaired before being marketed should be viewed with skepticism. Often problems are intermittent and may only become apparent under specific road conditions that are not duplicated when the vehicle is tested on the road or in the laboratory. Examples of problems include failure to start in certain climatic conditions, or stalling when there are changes in temperature or altitude. If vehicles with flaws are repurchased and resold to subsequent buyers who lack warranty protection, the vehicles may remain unfixed indefinitely. The CFA called for disclosure, title branding, and public registry of all vehicles repurchased by auto manufacturers and their agents or dealers.

CFA representatives also pointed to the false intentions of many car dealers who claim they will take back a lemon but then refuse to do so when pressed by the buyer or fail to inform customers that a vehicle has a history of known defects or was previously salvaged or rebuilt. Although 37 states and the District of Columbia require this kind of disclosure to buyers, law enforcement records show that manufacturers commonly fail to make such a disclosure, according to the CFA. While state disclosure laws vary in effectiveness, the main problem cited by consumer advocates is noncompliance. The CFA supports federal action to enforce disclosure of vehicle origin and condition as long as such laws do not preempt stronger state statutes.

Public Impact

The impact of lemon laundering on the public is clear. With the price of a new vehicle equalling as much as it once cost to purchase a modest home, many people have resorted to purchasing used cars and trucks as a way to economize. In addition, according to the CFA, more than 52,000 people are stuck with "lemons" each year. The organization contends that the problem of defective automobiles is not only a consumer issue but a safety issue as well. People driving unsafe vehicles endanger many lives, including their own.

FUTURE DIRECTIONS

The CFA and the Center for Media Education (CME) have launched a joint campaign to ensure that the "information superhighway" is built in an efficient and fair manner, filing comments with the Federal Communication Commission and the Department of Justice. "The rhetoric of the information superhighway paints beautiful images of a free-flowing information teletopia, but the reality can degenerate into anti-social, anti-consumer, and anti-competitive programming, pricing, and marketing practices. We intend to prevent that," director of research Dr. Mark Cooper noted in a CME report. The purpose of the campaign is two-fold: to ensure that telephone ratepayers do not bear an unfair share of the burden of the massive build-out of the phone network to provide video and advanced information services, and to ensure that consumers have access to a broad range of programming.

GROUP RESOURCES

All queries or requests for literature or reports should be made to the CFA information center by writing Consumer Federation of America, 1424 16th St. NW, Ste. 604, Washington, DC; or by calling (202) 387-6121. Information concerning specific consumer issues can be obtained by contacting the following CFA-related organizations: Advocates for Auto and Highway Safety at (202) 366-0123; Coalition against Consumer Fraud at (202) 393-7330; Tele-Consumer Hotline at (202) 347-7208 or 1-800-332-1124; and Coalition for Consumer Protection and Quality in Health Care Reform at (202) 789-3606.

GROUP PUBLICATIONS

The CFA's legislative staff conducts original research as a foundation for advocacy work. Often this research becomes the basis for new consumer legislation, and research results are frequently published in report form and made available to the public for a small fee. To obtain a list of available reports contact the CFA at 1424 16th St. NW, Ste. 604, Washington, DC 20036, or call (202) 387-6121.

The CFA publishes several book-length consumer guides, among them *How to Fly, The Bank Book, The Childwise Catalog,* and *The Product Safety Book.* Other consumer information is available in informational pamphlets obtained through a written request accompanied by a self-addressed envelope. Available topics include consumer credit options, indoor air quality, store brands, and dangers associated with formaldehyde.

CFA's most notable book is *The Encyclopedia of the Consumer Movement,* published in 1997 and edited

by Stephen Brobeck and professors Robert N. Mayer and Robert O. Herrmann. The nearly 700-page book is the first comprehensive reference guide to the consumer movement in the United States and worldwide. Its 198 entries cover general topics, special consumer populations, consumer movement activities, consumer organizations, consumer leaders, product protections, and consumer movements.

The organization also publishes three newsletters. *CFAnews* keeps readers up-to-date on organization advocacy efforts, conferences, and publications, is issued eight times a year, and is available by subscription. The *Consumer Health and Safety Update,* providing up-to-date coverage of legislative and regulatory actions regarding home products, auto safety, cigarette and alcohol consumption, food safety, AIDS, and more is issued four times per year to members of the Consumer Coalition for Health and Safety. *Indoor Air News,* also published quarterly, provides legislative and regulatory information related specifically to air pollution. For an annual contribution of $225 individuals can join CFA's Newsletter and Information Service, a comprehensive package of consumer news that includes three newsletters; CFA policy resolutions; CFA testimony before Congress, regulatory agencies, and executive departments (an average of 40 documents); special legislative alerts on issues of concern to consumers; a congressional voting record, including detailed analysis of votes on key consumer issues; pamphlets on consumer topics; and dozens of news releases on events impacting consumers. For more information, contact the CFA at its central address.

BIBLIOGRAPHY

"Airline Ticket Prices." *Consumer Reports,* July 1997.

Fillion, Roger. "FCC to Propose New Cable Programming." *Reuters News Service,* 17 December 1997.

Hall, Jessica. "U.S. Telecommunications Consolidation to Intensify." *Reuters News Service,* 14 December 1997.

"Holiday Excesses Leave Many Americans in Need of Budget." *Business Wire.* 29 December 1997.

Lawsky, David. "Many Used Car Dealers Violate Federal Regulations." *Reuters News Service,* 3 December 1997.

Shanoff, Carolyn. "FTC Reminds Consumers: Know the Rules and Use the Tools During National Consumer Protection Week." *Credit World,* January/February 1999.

Smith, Frances B. "Bank Mergers: Boon or Bane for Consumers?" *Consumers' Research Magazine,* August 1998.

Szekely, Peter. "Group: Bank Tactics Raise Credit-Card Scare." *Reuters News Service,* 17 December 1997.

Consumers Union of the United States (CU)

ESTABLISHED: February 1936
EMPLOYEES: 450
MEMBERS: 216,668
PAC: None

Contact Information:

ADDRESS: 101 Truman Ave.
    Yonkers, NY 10703
PHONE: (914) 378-2948
FAX: (914) 378-2455
URL: http://www.consunion.org
PRESIDENT: Rhonda H. Karpatkin

WHAT IS ITS MISSION?

The Consumers Union (CU) works on behalf of the public to ascertain the value and, in certain instances, the hazards involved in using and producing consumer products. According to the organization's Web site, the "Consumers Union, publisher of *Consumer Reports*, is an independent, nonprofit testing and information organization serving only consumers. We are a comprehensive source for unbiased advice about products and services, personal finance, health and nutrition, and other consumer concerns. Since 1936, our mission has been to test products, inform the public, and protect consumers."

HOW IS IT STRUCTURED?

The CU is a an independent nonprofit 501(c)3 organization and is headquartered in Yonkers, New York. It is governed by a voluntary eight-member board of directors. Six people on the board are elected by CU members to a three-year term and meet quarterly. Nominations for the board of directors are published each August in *Consumer Reports,* and each potential member of the board must receive two letters of recommendation from non-family members in order to be nominated. In order to remain unbiased in its investigations and findings, the CU bylaws prohibit influential members of the business community from serving on its board of directors. The board of directors oversees all major activities, manages property, and approves the budget and all major CU policy decisions. Decisions about which products are tested by the CU are not made by the board of directors; they are made by editorial, technical, and other staff members.

In addition to its headquarters, the CU has three advocacy offices that target consumer issues that affect low-income households. The advocacy offices are located in Washington, D.C.; San Francisco, California; and Austin, Texas.

Members of the CU come from all walks of life but are united in having a concern for the consumer public. There are three ways to become a member of the CU. One can become a member by written request; by voting in a board of directors election; or by nominating someone for a position on the board of directors.

PRIMARY FUNCTIONS

The CU employs a number of strategies to prevent products that are hazardous to consumers and the environment from reaching the market. The primary method is reporting on consumer products in its widely regarded publication, *Consumer Reports*. This magazine gives the results of the numerous product tests that the organization conducts at its facility in Yonkers, New York. Because the CU accepts no advertising in its magazine, it is able to provide nonbiased reporting and, as a result, sometimes create rather powerful enemies.

Another service that the CU provides to the public is access to information about complex consumer products. For instance, for a small fee, one can request CU staff members to research specific new and used automobiles to determine the fair market value of the vehicle. This information is especially helpful because of the high cost of automobiles and the high-pressured sales nature of car buying. For new car purchases, the CU provides information such as the price that a car dealer paid for a particular automobile. Potential retail buyers can then markup from the dealer's cost to determine what to pay for the automobile. The CU also provides information on the value of a used car through the Consumer Reports Used Car Price Service. For $10, the CU will fax a four-page report outlining the value of a used car. And, at a cost of $12, the CU will provide their Consumer Reports Auto Insurance Price Service to consumers needing insurance advice.

A cornerstone of the CU's political activity has been influencing public policy in a way that protects consumers and the environment. The CU has political activists who analyze legislation and inform the public of legislative proposals that may pose a threat to consumer health, safety, and potentially exploitative business practices. The organization has advocacy groups that are regional, national, and international in scope as well as a Consumer Policy Institute whose purpose is to influence policy that promotes consumer rights.

PROGRAMS

The CU operates programs that educate the public on a variety of issues that the organization believes are important. One such issue is the introduction of commercialism in the classroom. School administrators operating on tight budgets are beginning to contract with private industries as a way of increasing funds for school budgets. For example, some schools are beginning to contract with soft drink companies to supply their product in exchange for multimillion dollar contracts. The CU established the Center for the Analysis of Commercialism in Education (CACE) to provide objective information to school administrators, public policymakers, parents, and educators on the impact that commercial activities such as this might have on education. The program is centered in the Department of Curriculum and Instruction at the University of Wisconsin-Milwaukee.

Since 1990 the CACE has produced two studies on commercialism in schools: *Selling America's Kids* (1990) and *Captive Kids* (1995). The CU funds the CACE, which concentrates on five core activities: identifying trends of commercialism in schools; maintaining records on the corporate activities in schools; disseminating its findings to the public; collaborating with other individuals and groups with similar goals and interests; and offering a University of Wisconsin-Milwaukee course on commercialism in the classroom.

Additionally the CU informs the public on matters related to consumers rights and provides services that enable the public to learn how to spend their money wisely. One of the ways it does this is by launching educational campaigns on various subjects. For example, in the spring of 1998 the CU initiated a program on potential dangers of home equity loans. The organization provided brochures in English and Spanish and held seminars for consumers on how to avoid home equity loan frauds.

The CU also sponsors the Colston E. Warne Program, which encourages diverse organizations to get involved in consumer protection activities. The program, whose name honors the first chairman of the board of directors of the CU, was started in 1991 and functions on a budget of $365,000. The budget is used to award grants to national, state, and local consumer organizations.

BUDGET INFORMATION

The CU's income comes from three sources: the sale of *Consumer Reports* magazine and other publications and services; individual contributions; and noncommercial grants. The CU's fiscal year runs from June 1 to May 31. The operating budget for 1997 was $135 million. Seven percent of this operating budget (or $9.5 million) was derived from individual contributions. Total revenue for 1997 was approximately $140 million.

FAST FACTS

The CU tests 2,000 products per year in 66 categories.

(Source: Paula Crawford Squires. "If People Use It, Consumers Union Tests It." *Richmond Times-Dispatch*, 1994.)

HISTORY

When the CU was formed in 1936 the United States was in the middle of its worst economic depression. The CU developed, in large part, as an extension of the labor movement which was growing in popularity at the time. Poor working conditions for laborers in textile, steel, mining, and other industries during the Depression brought attention to some of the side effects of free enterprise. The CU was formed by a group of professors, labor leaders, journalists, and engineers who were determined to improve conditions created by the social and environmental fallout of a largely unregulated capitalist economy.

The nonprofit organization concentrated its resources on scientifically testing consumer products for quality and safety but remained committed at the same time to elevating public awareness to unfair labor practices, social issues, and the national political agenda. Three months after the CU formed, it published a magazine that was the forerunner of *Consumer Reports* magazine. Due to its low-operating budget, the CU was forced to test inexpensive items such as fans, hot-water bottles, and radios. The first issue of the magazine included a report that questioned the effectiveness of Alka Seltzer, a stomach medicine.

In 1942 the CU's magazine became known as *Consumer Reports* in an effort to expand its appeal beyond labor union members. *Consumer Reports* was one of the first to report on the health hazards of cigarette smoking. The consistent testing and reporting on consumer products and their impact on social well-being enabled *Consumer Reports* to win the National Magazine Award on three occasions.

In the 1950s the United States experienced a postwar economic boom causing a radical increase in the demand for consumer products. The demand for consumer products also created a demand for unbiased consumer product information. As a result, subscriptions to

Consumer Reports ballooned to 400,000. The increase in revenues provided by the magazine enabled the CU to open its own testing lab in Mt. Vernon, New York, before it moved to present headquarters in Yonkers, New York.

CU reports have played a role in U.S. economic developments. For instance, in 1965 *Consumer Reports* tested the Toyota Corona and gave it a favorable review. A decade later Toyota became the United States' top imported automobile. The diligent testing of consumer products also had a considerable impact on the formation in 1970 of the National Commission on Product Safety.

The success of *Consumer Reports* magazine enabled the CU to expand its reporting to television in the 1980s and also allowed for expansion to the youth market with *Zillions* magazine (originally *Penny Power*) in 1980. In 1986 the CU purchased its own automobile testing track in Connecticut.

In the mid- to late 1990s, the CU made a concerted effort to use newly available technology to disseminate its information. In 1995 the organization produced a CD-ROM about automobile pricing. Two years later, the CU created a Web site to give easy access to a broad range of its data.

CURRENT POLITICAL ISSUES

There is a misconception that the CU is synonymous with its extremely influential magazine. Apart from reporting on consumer product safety, the CU applies a number of strategies in the public forum to prevent products that are hazardous to consumers and the environment from reaching the market. The CU follows legislation that might have some affect on the consumer public and lobbies Congress in an effort to ensure that pending laws benefit consumers.

For example, in May 1998 CU representatives testified before the Senate's Subcommittee on Antitrust Business Rights and Competition. The CU urged Congress to crack down on the telecommunications industry by prohibiting "monopolistic" mergers that discourage competition and inflate prices for consumers. The CU had issued a warning before the passage of the 1996 Telecommunications Act that the act would open the door for consumer rights violations in the telecommunications industry. The Telecommunications Act was designed to encourage competition by deregulating the industry and, just as the CU had warned, the bill's enactment encouraged companies to merge and ended up increasing consumer prices. Similarly, CU representatives provided testimony concerning the lack of competition in the cable television industry. In their testimony, CU spokespeople noted that the Federal Communication Commission had "virtually abandoned all efforts to police market abuses or challenge inflated cable TV rates."

A 1996 Acura SLX tips over after making a quick turn during an avoidance maneuver test. The Consumers Union of the United States, along with other advocacy groups, alerts citizens to potential defects in automobiles and other products. (Photograph by Consumers Reports, AP/Wide World Photo)

Case Study: Some Rate CU's Rollover Test "Not Acceptable"

Many Americans have come to rely on advice from *Consumer Reports* magazine to determine how to get the most for their money and how to avoid products that are unsafe. Ever since Lawrence Crooks, an independently wealthy businessman with an interest in automobiles, headed up the CU's Auto Test Division in 1936, the organization has been providing important information to consumers about the quality and safety of vehicles. Early on, however, the CU could not afford to purchase vehicles for testing. Crooks tested vehicles he had purchased with his own money or borrowed vehicles from friends to test. The organization now uses an advanced automobile testing facility that tests just about every vehicle that comes off the assembly line and is sold in the United States.

On rare occasions the CU will rate a product "not acceptable," which is a red flag to consumers. This rating is meant to warn the public not to trust the product. In 1988 the CU flagged the Suzuki Samurai with its "not acceptable" rating because of its tendency to roll over. This caused sales of the vehicle to plummet and it was eventually discontinued. In 1997 nearly a decade after *Consumer Reports* rated the Samurai "not acceptable," Suzuki uncovered startling evidence to support their claim that the CU manufactured the test in order to increase magazine sales.

The CU generally uses a standard test to determine whether a vehicle maneuvers safely on the road. The test involves simulating an emergency response in which a vehicle is swerved to the left to avoid an object, then back to the right to regain control. The test is conducted on both long and short courses. The National Highway Traffic Safety Administration (NHTSA) has expressed concern about the legitimacy of the CU's short course test. In 1988 the NHTSA tested the Suzuki Samurai and found that the vehicle was just as stable, if not more stable, than other vehicles of its class.

George Ball, an attorney for Suzuki, presented video footage and an affidavit from a former employee, to support Suzuki's claim that the CU faked the rollover propensity test. The film that Ball entered as evidence captures CU members celebrating after having tipped the Samurai on their forty-seventh attempt. In addition, Suzuki offered the testimony of Ronald L. Denison, an auto technician for the CU from 1979 to 1989, who claimed the organization deliberately falsified its information. Denison claimed that, while he worked for CU, it was "common knowledge that dramatic test results were good for magazine sales." Denison also said that "[I]t was generally understood that the testing we did must be interesting enough to generate publicity to help sell magazines." According to Denison, Irwin Landau, then editorial director of the CU, instructed testers to push the Samurai until it rolled over. The test driver who eventually made the Samurai tip over was Richard Small. Legal counsel for Suzuki also entered as evidence Small's original notes on the Samurai test that concluded that there was "no real problem" with the Samurai and gave the vehicle a rating of a "5 plus," one of the best marks for handling.

Countering that evidence, R. David Pittle, the CU technical director, claimed that Denison was personally motivated to attack the CU because the organization had dismissed him for incompetence. Pittle also noted that, adding to the legitimacy of the CU's tests, "at least 147 deaths have been directly linked to Samurai rollover accidents." In 1996 the CU tested the Isuzu Trooper II and found, like the Samurai, it had a propensity to roll over. In response, Isuzu filed a lawsuit against the CU. However, the CU stands by the testing methods that led to the "not acceptable" rating. No company has ever won a defamation suit against the CU. As of March of 1999, the suit against CU was unresolved.

FUTURE DIRECTIONS

The CU launched a program in March 1999 designed to educate children, parents, and teachers on consumer issues affecting today's youth through an Internet subscription service that will be posted on *Junior Net.* The CU also plans to develop a Web site, accessible at http://www.zillionsedcenter.org, that will outline teaching guidelines for educators and parents. For example, one of the teaching projects offered through the Web site instructs students to collect and monitor the trash they intend to throw out to learn how certain items such as paper are needlessly taking up valuable landfill space. The site offers a log sheet, reading material, and questions and answers for teachers to provide students to guide them through the project. The projects are designed to encourage students to think critically and learn how to protect themselves from some of the pitfalls of consumerism.

Additionally, the CU also plans to make it easier for schools to make *Zillions* magazine available to it students. *Zillions,* an offshoot of *Consumer Reports,* provides consumer protection information for kids. The CU currently offers the magazine to schools at one-fifth the subscription cost. However, because some schools cannot afford to pay even this amount, the plan is to offer free sets of *Zillions* to economically disadvantaged school districts. The program will enable the CU message to reach 47,000 kids in 1999.

GROUP RESOURCES

The CU provides a number of different sources for consumer information. Its Web site, accessible via the World Wide Web at http://www.consumersunion.org,

offers a listing of recent and past press releases. It also offers information on recent research done on consumer products such as automobiles, investments, health products, electronics, and appliances. One can access a data bank of past reports done on consumer products from the Web site and order copies for a small fee. For more information on the organization, write to the Consumers Union, 101 Truman Ave., Yonkers, NY 10703 or call (914) 378-2455.

GROUP PUBLICATIONS

The CU is the publisher of *Consumer Reports.* The magazine provides access to information such as price comparisons and quality assessments on various consumer products, including automobiles, appliances, electronics, office supplies, and leisure items. To order a subscription to *Consumer Reports,* write to Consumer Reports, Subscription Department, PO Box 53029, Boulder, CO 80322-3029 or call 1-800-208-9696. The CU also provides a *Consumer Reports* Web site to which one can subscribe.

The CU also publishes *Consumer Reports On Health,* which is a monthly newsletter devoted to health and well-being issues. Other publications offered by the CU include *Consumer Reports Travel Letter, Zillions For Kids,* and *Zillions School Program.* The CU also publishes a series of annual specialty books such as *Consumer Reports Preview '99* and *Consumer Reports Guide to Baby Products (Fifth Edition).* A number of brochures are also accessible via the organization's Web site at http://www.consumersunion.org. For more information on any CU publications, write to the Consumers Union, 101 Truman Ave., Yonkers, NY 10703 or call (914) 378-2455.

BIBLIOGRAPHY

"Consumers Union Launches Public Education Campaign on Home Equity Lending Dangers." *Business Wire*, 28 April 1998.

"Consumers Union Warns of Pesticide Residues in Fruits and Vegetables." *Chemical Market Reporter*, 22 February 1999.

Crawford Squires, Paula. "If People Use It, Consumers Union Tests It." *Richmond Times-Dispatch*, 1994.

"Isuzu Sues Consumers Union over Trooper Report." *Sacramento Bee*, 8 August 1997.

Karpatkin, Rhonda H. "Memo to Members." *Consumer Reports,* May 1996.

Landler, Mark. "F.C.C. Is Urged to Keep Close Eye on Cable Rates." *New York Times*, 24 September 1997.

Sakson, Steve. "Consumer Reports Seeks Recall of Two Sport-Utility Vehicles." *Seattle Post-Intelligencer*, 21 August 1996.

Stoffer, Harry. "Swerves of Controversy: Test Tries to Simulate Emergency." *Automotive News*, 8 June 1998.

Council of Better Business Bureaus (CBBB)

WHAT IS ITS MISSION?

According to the Council of Better Business Bureaus (CBBB), its mission is "to promote and foster the highest ethical relationship between businesses and the public through voluntary self-regulation, consumer and business education, and service excellence." Ultimately, CBBB seeks to bring about fair and honest relationships between businesses and consumers, consumer confidence, and an ethical business environment. Although this is not an organization with political affiliations or aggressive lobbying efforts, CBBB influences governmental actions by bringing attention to consumer issues—such as fraud in advertising or scams related to automobile sales—which, in turn, may spur governmental action in the form of new regulations.

ESTABLISHED: 1912
EMPLOYEES: 140 (1997)
MEMBERS: 153 regional Better Business Bureaus; 350 member companies (1997)
PAC: None

Contact Information:

ADDRESS: 4200 Wilson Blvd., Ste. 800
    Arlington, VA 22203-1804
PHONE: (703) 276-0100
FAX: (703) 525-8277
E-MAIL: ehasychak@cbbb.bbb.org
URL: http://www.bbb.org
PRESIDENT; CEO: James L. Bast

HOW IS IT STRUCTURED?

The Council of Better Business Bureaus is a private, nonprofit, umbrella organization for the Better Business Bureau (BBB) system of the United States and Canada which claims 230,000 local business members, more than 300 "leading-edge" national corporations, and 137 local Better Business Bureau chapters. The CBBB is headed by a president and CEO (one person) and the 50 elected members who comprise the board of directors: 15 chairmen of local BBB boards, 15 members of local BBB boards, 15 national members-at-large, three Canadian representatives, and two members of the general public. Board members are elected to three-year terms; the president serves an indeterminate length. Together, the president and the board oversee the national organization, set

policy and direction for CBBB and regional BBBs, and manage the daily operations of the council. The national organization maintains two offices, one in Arlington, Virginia, and one in New York.

Main headquarters are located in Virginia, and include the CBBB Foundation, which produces publications and offers training and technical assistance to promote business and consumer education programs. Small and medium-sized businesses and BBB chapters are generally the beneficiaries of the foundation which has recently focused its attention on assisting businesses in complying with the Americans With Disabilities Act (ADA). The CBBB National Advertising Division (NAD) is located in New York, and is in charge of investigating and assessing the truthfulness and accuracy of national ads, for which a complaint has been filed. Most cases are brought to the NAD by product competitors. Recurring issues that provoke complaint include improper use of implied or expressed claims, demonstrations, pricing, product testing, taste and sensory appeals, and testimonials.

There are 137 affiliated BBB chapters across the United States. All chapters must meet the BBB's standards for membership, agree to support the BBB's principles of ethical business practices and voluntary self-regulation, and be invited by the national BBB to join. Chapter members pay a fee to belong to the local BBB, and those membership fees support the local bureau's programs, staff, and activities. In return, the member companies receive representation by the local BBB and the CBBB in governmental affairs affecting business. They also receive publications on business and legislative activities, and may participate in all programs and activities sponsored by the CBBB. In addition, being a BBB member grants a company a certain status within the local community. Because the company must have met certain standards of ethical conduct before being granted membership, consumers assume they are a good company to do business with.

PRIMARY FUNCTIONS

Through its various national divisions and regional membership, the CBBB works to promote fair business practices that are beneficial to both the buyer and seller. It does so by collecting and reporting information to help prospective buyers make informed decisions; developing programs to encourage businesses to regulate their own advertising and selling practices; serving as a neutral third party to help settle marketplace disputes; and influencing public policy and legislation.

The CBBB acts as a watchdog by monitoring advertising and selling practices. Through its Publications Division, it reports on its findings and produces publications for consumers, businesses, and the media. These publications alert consumers to fraudulent and harmful

practices in the marketplace and provide accurate information for making informed buying decisions. The Philanthropic Advisory Service promotes ethical standards within the charitable community by advising public and corporate donors on wise giving. This includes providing information about charities and other organizations seeking donations.

The BBB hears complaints about products and advertising from consumers and businesses and attempts to resolve them outside the courts—through arbitration, mediation, and self-regulation by advertising and business. The BBB encourages self-regulation of advertising through the National Advertising Review Board, which evaluates advertisements for truth and ethical standards. In other industries, the BBB encourages self-regulation by requiring members to promise, when they join BBB, that they will adhere to its standards.

The BBB also serves as a neutral third party in disputes between business members and consumers. Consumers may file a complaint with the BBB about a product or service. The complaint is then taken up with the company involved. Because most businesses care about satisfying their customers, complaints are generally quickly resolved and the matter is closed. However, even after extensive effort, some complaints cannot satisfactorily be resolved. In those cases, the bureau may offer an alternative way to settle the dispute, such as arbitration or mediation. In some cases, the bureau may be unable to get a company to cooperate. A pattern of unanswered or unresolved complaints becomes a part of the firm's record. An unsatisfactory report could lead to the business being asked to leave the BBB. In extreme cases, the BBB may refer its file on the company to a law enforcement agency to determine if further action is necessary.

One of the key functions of the CBBB is to influence the government to bring about consumer protections. Representatives of the agency testify before Congress and in U.S. courts about problems they believe exist which need to be remedied through legislation or court order. The group also works to effect change by working in collaboration with federal agencies such as the Federal Trade Commission.

Although the CBBB puts forth great efforts to aid consumers, there are limitations to its functions. It does not have police powers, and it cannot force a business to do what the consumer wants. It does not give legal advice, make collections, provide credit information, endorse businesses, or pass judgement on the quality of products.

PROGRAMS

CBBB initiatives and programs exist to foster a better business climate across all types of industry. The Auto Line program provides dispute resolution between auto

James L. Bast, president of the Council of Better Business Bureaus, introduces the new BBB OnLine service and the "Care Seal" logo in 1996. The logo appears on the Web sites of companies that have agreed to comply with standards set by the Better Business Bureau. (Photograph by Court Mast, AP/Wide World Photo)

manufacturers and consumers. If, for example, a consumer has a complaint about a car he has purchased and the manufacturer contends there is nothing wrong, Auto Line representatives will step in to help mediate and reach a resolution. One of the largest customer/business out-of-court dispute resolution programs in the United States, this nationwide program closed 32,203 cases in 1996, of which 5,698 cases (18 percent) were resolved through formal arbitration hearings with trained BBB arbitrators.

The Children's Advertising Review Unit seeks to accomplish responsible advertising to children by encouraging voluntary self-regulation. CARU studies advertising aimed at children under the age of 12. When advertising is found to be misleading, inaccurate, or inconsistent with established guidelines, the unit seeks change by first asking the advertisers to voluntarily cooperate. CARU also offers "preclearance" review of proposed advertising throughout the year as a service to advertisers and their agencies. Although this cannot guarantee that the finished advertisement will comply with CARU guidelines, it can spot potential violations and eliminate the need for costly revisions.

Each year this unit's staff attends the American International Toy Fair in New York to view new advertising and alert advertisers to potential conflicts with the unit's guidelines. This preview of new products helps the staff evaluate the advertising it sees throughout the year. In

1996, much of CARU's focus was on the critical importance of the emerging interactive electronic media and its implications for children. In addition to monitoring traditional media, CARU reviewed 60 Web sites for children as part of its jurisdiction over on-line advertising and to become more knowledgeable about the on-line environment and the unique issues it raises for children.

To complement its programs, the CBBB in 1996 established an annual awards program to gain recognition for U.S. companies that maintain a solid commitment to conducting their business practices in an ethical fashion. Each year, three U.S. companies are selected through a nationwide competition to receive the Better Business Bureau Torch Award for Marketplace Ethics. The Torch Award is designed to promote not only the importance of ethical business practices but the willingness and efforts made by outstanding businesses to ensure that the U.S. marketplace remains fair and honorable.

BUDGET INFORMATION

BBBs around the country are organized as nonprofit corporations, financed almost entirely by membership dues or subscriptions paid by businesses and professional firms in the local community. The CBBB is funded in the same way, with almost all of its $1 million annual budget coming from member dues and subscriptions. In 1996, the most recent statistics available, the council's assets grew by $40,000, while its expenses increased by $525,000. The increase in expense was largely due to the start-up costs for technology initiatives of $400,000, which were supported by deferred revenue.

The greatest portion of CBBB's revenue is devoted to financing dispute resolution, financing national membership programs, and paying for general and administrative costs. BBBOnLine, a program launched in 1996 and designed to help consumers identify reliable businesses on the Internet, was funded independently of the rest of the council's activities. It received $1.6 million in pledges at the end of 1996.

HISTORY

As early as the late 1700s, groups were forming to examine deceptive newspaper advertising about goods such as cotton, tobacco, and rum. "Complete sewing machine—25 cents" ran one ad for a single needle worth far less. Despite the long tradition of deception in advertising, however, it took until 1911 before the crusade against false advertising began in earnest.

Sam Dobbs was elected president of the Associated Advertising Clubs of America (AACA) in 1909. He recruited John Irving Romer, publisher of an advertising journal called *Printers' Ink,* who began researching existing laws against fraudulent representations and drawing up a model state law penalizing fraudulent and misleading advertising. A model statute appeared in Romer's magazine in 1911. Recognizing the law he proposed lacked an enforcement mechanism, Romer suggested that members of the AACA set up Vigilance Committees to investigate alleged misrepresentations, eliminate abuses, and create advertising codes and standards. In 1912, Vigilance Committees began springing up in cities around the United States.

Spurred by the success of the local committees, George Coleman, then president of the AACA, decided to form a National Vigilance Committee to focus on regional and national advertising. That led to the birth of the organization which in 1921 became the Better Business Bureau of the Associated Advertising Clubs of the World, and later, simply the National Better Business Bureau.

By the 1920s, the fight for truth and honesty had moved to a new battleground. The stock market was soaring, attracting hordes of investors and an extraordinary number of unscrupulous people. Stock swindling had become such big business that it inevitably attracted the attention of the BBB. The organization undertook a campaign against swindlers, providing the public with printed material on wise investing and bulletins about scam artists and swindlers. The organization also worked with

the post office to convict those sending fraudulent material through the mail.

The 1930s saw a significant change in the role of the BBB. Having become an international organization in 1928, when a bureau was established in Montreal, Canada, BBB was evolving into one of the most respected guardians of the public trust. One measure of the bureau's effectiveness is the fact that many of the unscrupulous characters it targeted tried to intimidate individual bureaus with threats and lawsuits. As the 1930s dawned, 53 lawsuits had been filed against 24 BBBs, with damage claims totaling nearly $15 million. Not a penny of those claims was ever paid.

During this decade, the bureau worked with the American Pharmaceutical Association to create a set of voluntary advertising standards for medicine. The concept of voluntary trade practice spread, and more standards were developed for such diverse products as batteries, hosiery, shirts, and insulation materials. The Federal Trade Commission was later to adopt and enforce many of these standards developed by the bureaus.

By the onset of World War II (1939-45), the BBB was turning its attention to a new scourge being inflicted on American consumers—scare advertising. During the war, Americans were deluged with offers ranging from the far-fetched to the truly outlandish. Some were seemingly innocuous, such as the specially treated sand to be used for extinguishing bombs. Others were exercises in morbidity, as swindlers sought to collect imaginary loans from the families of soldiers whose names appeared on casualty lists. When Congress passed the War Charities Act, requiring that all charitable appeals on behalf of servicemen be cleared by the government, the BBBs were pressed into service to help the overburdened federal government

After the war and throughout the 1950s, the BBB led the fight against increasingly sophisticated schemes involving kickbacks to doctors for prescription drugs, and home repair and improvement scams. At the same time, the bureaus helped to ferret out, publicize, and stop overcharges for automobile insurance, which at that time was being written into the sales contracts for automobiles without the owner's consent, and which may have cost unsuspecting buyers as much as $25 million.

In the 1960s, the bureaus were active in helping consumers with problems such as nondelivery of merchandise, lengthy delays in receiving "guaranteed funds," and failure to service merchandise covered by warranty. At the same time, the organization continued its longstanding efforts against unscrupulous activities. Now, it was puzzle contest promotions, employment offers, correspondence schools, insurance companies, and vendors of unordered merchandise. The 1960s also saw a resurgence of land speculation on a scale unmatched since the 1920s. Although unusable land in the Everglades continued to be sold for unbelievable prices, unethical promoters also were pushing barren, mountainous, or waterlogged plots in the American Southwest, as well as Latin America, the Caribbean, and Brazil.

Another phenomenon of the 1960s and 1970s changed the entire face of business. With the emergence of conglomerates, holding companies, and franchises the direct bond between buyers and sellers slowly dissolved. And as business grew larger and more impersonal, civility between consumers and businesses also waned. Officials of President Richard Nixon's administration turned to the BBB to promote and enhance the relationship between business and consumers, which had become strained.

In July 1970 a watershed event occurred when the National Better Business Bureau and the Association of Better Business Bureaus merged to form the Council of Better Business Bureaus. The merger was prompted in part by the realization that the bureaus needed to redefine their purpose and approach. The council undertook to strengthen the bureau system with new programs and ideas. In the years following, the emphasis of the bureau's efforts changed dramatically, adding new activities to their long and successful efforts to combat fraud and unsavory business practices. The BBB began to devote more resources to correcting customer problems and attempting to preserve consumer confidence in business through information and education.

BBB mobile units began to service impoverished neighborhoods and sponsor seminars to explore the misunderstandings on both sides of the issues which divided businesses and customers. The bureaus began working with government agencies to correct consumer complaints, and they brought the great wealth of knowledge they had accumulated to hearings before Congress and regulatory agencies, where the bureaus testified during consideration of new consumer protection laws and regulations.

Regulatory agencies and the courts began specifying BBB arbitration as a means of settling cases brought before them. Other authorities and companies of all types began using this method to resolve consumer disputes. By 1985, BBB arbitration was considered one of the largest out-of-court dispute settlement programs in the country.

CURRENT POLITICAL ISSUES

Wherever there is a possibility of fraud or incident of unethical business practice, the CBBB is usually somehow involved. In the late 1990s, the CBBB investigated claims of false advertising against such companies as Starkist Tuna, Revlon, Clairol, and Spalding. Since its inception, the CBBB has also worked in collaboration with government and the courts to tackle issues ranging from product quality to consumer protection laws. As business and technology have moved into the twenty-first century, so have the watchdog efforts of the CBBB.

Case Study: Junk Mail Scams

The CBBB, along with the Federal Trade Commission (FTC) and the U.S. Postal Inspection Service, has monitored thousands of pieces of junk E-mail and is keeping track of on-line schemers. The agencies found that there is a great deal of E-mail that appears to be deceptive or fraudulent, which is in violation of the FTC Act and the Postal Statute. Violations of these laws leave offenders open to fines, penalties, or jail.

The largest category of junk mail targeted by the groups was chain letters, which are illegal under state and federal laws. Usually, chain letter schemes urge E-mail recipients to send money to a list of people, remove one name and add their own, and forward the E-mail in bulk to friends and relatives. The scheme is quite similar to traditional mail chain letters. Some chain letters are disguised as legitimate businesses, offering too-good-to-be-true promises of trips and cash rewards. Other categories of E-mail that receive a warning message from the groups are get-rich-quick business opportunities, diet and medical solicitations, credit history scams, and hoax E-mails that contain viruses.

Possibly the worst of these chain letter frauds is the sympathy E-mail. The subject line reads something like, "Little Girl Dying" and goes on to explain that this legitimate E-mail is sponsored by a well-known group like the American Cancer Society. For each E-mail sent, this organization will send three cents to assist little Jessica with her medical bills. Such E-mails prey on consumers, clog E-mail systems, and threaten to damage the reputation of established organizations.

Because it is very difficult to locate and prosecute the originator of the E-mails, the FTC, Postal Service, and the CBBB focus most of their efforts on education. The BBB advises E-mail users not to forward any electronic chain letter. They also suggest that consumers seeking additional information on E-mail hoaxes check with the Computer Incident Advisory Capability (CIAC) located at http://ciac.llnl.gov/ciac/CIACHoaxes.html. This site is sponsored by the U.S. Department of Energy to inform and educate the public. According to the CIAC, if you receive an E-mail chain letter, either delete it or send it to your system administrator, who can investigate and warn users not to pass on the E-mail. Consumers may also forward E-mail they believe may be fraudulent or deceptive to the FTC at uce@ftc.gov.

FUTURE DIRECTIONS

Knowing that technology has trained customers to expect information at the push of a button, CBBB will continue to broaden its outreach through its BBBOnLine service. Designed to protect consumers making purchases on the Internet, the program will provide a means for approved businesses selling a product or service on-line to identify their commitment to ethical business practices. Such businesses will be licensed to display a specially-protected BBBOnLine seal on their advertising only after meeting a strict set of on-line standards, which include a precommitment to advertising review, as well as an agreement by the company to respond quickly to complaints and agree to arbitrate, if necessary.

When consumers click on the BBBOnLine seal, they will reach an on-line BBB company report, which gives immediate information on the company's location, principals, address, and the BBB's conclusions regarding its marketplace record. If a business fails to answer consumer complaints or refuses to comply with BBBOnLine standards, the seal will immediately be withdrawn from the company.

A key strength of the program lies in the nationwide network of BBBs. The ownership and place of business for BBBOnLine participants will have been verified by BBB staff through a visit to the company's physical premises.

GROUP RESOURCES

In addition to print publications, CBBB offers videos such as *Buying a Recreational Vehicle* and *Self Defense for Car Expense*. These and other resources can be obtained by contacting a local Better Business Bureau or the headquarters at 4200 Wilson Blvd., Arlington, VA 22203-1804. Inquiries may also be faxed to (703) 276-0100 or phoned in at (703) 276-0100. Questions and requests can also be sent via electronic mail to ehasychak @cbbb.bbb.org

Company reports are available at CBBB's Web site (www.bbb.org). Bureau reports are based on information in the bureau's files. Generally, a report contains information about the length of time the company has been in business or known to the bureau, a summary of the company's complaint history or other experiences, and information developed through special bureau investigations. Information on nonprofit and charitable organizations is also provided.

GROUP PUBLICATIONS

The CBBB distributes over 700,000 educational booklets and pamphlets on a variety of products and ser-

vices to consumers and businesses. New pamphlets concerning how to avoid frauds and schemes when purchasing products and services on-line are in the works. The council published the revised 1996 edition of *Do's and Don'ts in Advertising*, with new sections covering children's advertising, finance, the environment, international issues, telemarketing, and on-line advertising. This most recent edition of *Do's and Don'ts* is a two-volume set, consisting of more than 1,700 pages of the laws, codes, standards, and rules governing advertising. Plans are underway to publish it in an electronic CD-ROM format and make it available on the Internet.

In a joint venture with the North American Securities Administrators Association (NASAA) and the Benjamin Company, CBBB revised its popular book *Investor Alert! How to Protect Your Business From Schemes, Scams and Frauds,* now retitled *How to Be an Informed Investor: Protect Your Money from Schemes, Scams and Frauds.* The book advises consumers about the workings and warning signs of investment fraud, and provides the informational tools necessary to make wise investment decisions.

The CBBB's Philanthropic Advisory Service continues to publish its quarterly newsletter, *Give But Give Wisely,* which provides tips on making charitable donations, and the CBBB Foundation continues to promote and disseminate the popular *Access Equals Opportunity* guides, which help businesses comply with the Americans With Disabilities Act. These guides cover nine industry areas including retail stores, grocery stores, restaurants and bars, car sales and service, fun and fitness, medical offices, shops and services, professional offices, and tour and travel agents.

BIBLIOGRAPHY

Block, Sandra. "Warning Signs Can Expose Scams." *USA Today,* 15 January 1997.

Case, John. "The Best Places in America to Own a Business." *Inc. Magazine,* August 1992.

Council of Better Business Bureaus. "Tips to Safeguard You Before and After Giving." *USA Today,* 4 November 1997.

Gair, Christina. "Sealing the Deal with BBBOnline." *Home Office Computing,* November 1998.

"A Parent's Guide to Cyberspace." *Consumer Reports,* May 1997.

Whittelsey, Frances Cerra. "Fostering Truth in Advertising." *Nation's Business,* July 1998.

Council on Competitiveness

ESTABLISHED: 1986
EMPLOYEES: 16
MEMBERS: 140
PAC: None

Contact Information:
ADDRESS: 1401 H St. NW, Ste. 650
    Washington, DC 20005
PHONE: (202) 682-4292
FAX: (202) 682-5150
URL: http://www.compete.org/home.html
PRESIDENT: John Yochelson

WHAT IS ITS MISSION?

According to the Web site of the Council on Competitiveness, the organization "sets an action agenda to drive U.S. economic competitiveness and leadership in world markets in order to raise the standard of living for all Americans. We focus on strengthening U.S. innovation, upgrading the workforce, and benchmarking national economic performance."

HOW IS IT STRUCTURED?

Headquartered in Washington, D.C., the agenda of the nonprofit Council on Competitiveness is determined by an executive committee composed of 30 prominent business, university, and labor leaders. Further the council's staff of 16 provides research and operational support and is led by a president and a distinguished fellow.

The council's membership is composed of more than 140 chief executives from business, higher education, and organized labor. In addition the heads of more than 50 prominent research organizations, professional societies, and trade associations serve as national affiliates of the council to help coordinate comprehensive private sector approaches to competitiveness-related issues. These affiliates include organizations such as the American Association for the Advancement of Science, the American Electronics Association, the Association of American Universities, The Brookings Institution, the Center for Strategic and International Studies, and the Information Technology Industry Council.

FAST FACTS

From 1992 to 1996, U.S. technological competitiveness (based on a combination of the number of patents granted and the number of patents cited) was rated at 308,003. The next closest country was Japan with 117,255.

(Source: Council on Competitiveness. "Charting Competitiveness." *Challenges,* January/February 1998.)

PRIMARY FUNCTIONS

Known for its policy recommendations and its international benchmarking of U.S. competitiveness, the Council on Competitiveness is dedicated to mobilizing a concerted national response to the economic realities of the new global marketplace. To achieve this goal the council publishes reports and position statements on a wide range of public policy issues and hosts forums which are developed with the assistance of council members and affiliates. Major reports have addressed technology, trade, and fiscal policies and compared U.S. competitiveness to that of other industrialized nations. Perhaps the best known of these reports is the annual Competitiveness Index which explores U.S. progress in recapturing global market shares, growth of per capita gross domestic product (GDP), budget and deficit reduction, and job creation.

While the council's reports provide policymakers and business leaders with an important base of knowledge and facts, the council's work is not limited to research and analysis. Strategies to bring the council's recommendations to fruition include testimony of council members and staff before congressional committees, consultation with congressional and administration officials, and public education campaigns.

Normally focusing on two major initiatives a year, the council combines policy analysis with the insights of business, academic, and labor leaders. Members and staff assemble data, develop recommendations, and implement follow-up strategies throughout the country.

PROGRAMS

In its efforts to bring key economic policy issues into the public arena, the Council on Competitiveness has launched several programs aimed at engaging members of Congress, administration officials, and council representatives in a dialogue on the future of the U.S. economy.

In 1997 the council took the lead in organizing a National R&D (Research and Development) Dialogue. Using its report on the future of American R&D enterprise *Endless Frontiers, Limited Resources* as a starting point, the council called for a new national consensus on U.S. innovation strategy and organized three regional summits in 1997 and a national summit in 1998.

Another important council program is the Global Innovation Project. Focused on how U.S. leadership in science and technology can be sustained in the new era of R&D globalization, the Global Innovation Project brings together 40 representatives from industry, research universities, and the executive branch. The project's goals include benchmarking global innovation capabilities, examining the internationalization of R&D in five key sectors, and developing policy recommendations with input from a congressional working group.

In the face of what many see as the declining skills and education levels of the American workforce, the Council on Competitiveness has instituted a Workforce Technology Project consisting of more than 50 experts on workers, new technology tools, and challenges facing small and medium-sized enterprises. Through site visits and other research the task force seeks to determine the best ways to strengthen the U.S. workforce and to build consensus on policy options at the federal and state levels.

BUDGET INFORMATION

The Council on Competitiveness is a private, nonprofit 501(c)(3) organization supported through contributions from its members, foundations, and other granting institutions. With a 1996 budget of $1,573,213, the council spent more than two-thirds of its revenues on program services. These included General Programs ($451,676), Research and Development ($151,791), Health Information Infrastructure ($149,198), Workforce and Technology ($133,315), and Globalization of R&D ($117,045). Another $438,152 was spent on management and administrative expenses. The council spent $125,036 on fund-raising.

HISTORY

The Council on Competitiveness was created in 1986 to create a concerted national response to new economic realities that threatened to undermine the booming economy of the mid-1980s. Key industries were losing market share to international competitors, the U.S. position in a host of critical high-technology sectors seemed to be slipping, and the country had shifted from being the world's largest creditor to its largest debtor in just over five years. Fears of "Japan, Inc." were especially prevalent and numerous economists and analysts suggested that the era of U.S. economic dominance had come to an end.

In an increasingly competitive global marketplace, the traditional hands-off approach to economic development no longer seemed to be sufficient. A group of two dozen industrial, university, and labor leaders who shared this concern about the United States' international standing got together and formed the Council on Competitiveness. Their goal was to raise the profile of economic competitiveness and develop strategies that would foster major changes in public policy and public attitudes, as well as improved performance from the private sector. As Council Founding Chairman John Young said, "The basic goal that we established in founding the Council remains the right one for the decade ahead: to unite the nation around an agenda that will raise the living standards of all Americans by improving the ability of U.S. companies and workers to compete in world markets."

The council's diverse membership, rigorous analysis, and balanced approach to economic issues quickly established it as one of the strongest and most respected voices on economic policy. While other business organizations pushed for unrestricted free enterprise and increased deregulation, the council saw the government as a pivotal player in the drive to increase U.S. competitiveness.

One of the council's earliest initiatives was to call for a national strategy to regain U.S. technological leadership. The council also conducted a thorough appraisal of trade policy and began its annual benchmarking of U.S. economic performance with the *Competitiveness Index,* which soon became the definitive competitiveness indicator.

Over the years the council has focused special attention on the importance of science and technology to innovation and economic success. This interest led to the 1988 publication *Picking Up the Pace* and, in 1991, the landmark study *Gaining New Ground* which identified, prioritized, and promoted the development of key generic technologies. Although this form of industrial strategy had played a central role in the development of the Japanese and European economies, *Gaining New Ground* marked the first time such an effort was made in the United States.

The council's emphasis on innovation continued in 1996 with *Endless Frontier, Limited Resources,* which called for a bipartisan consensus regarding the role of the federal government in research and development. This was followed in 1997 by the Global Innovation project, a nationwide campaign to find new ways to increase American innovative capacity. A series of regional summits brought together corporate chief executives, university presidents, governors, members of Congress, and senior administrative officials to hammer out new solutions to the challenge of global innovation. The campaign culminated with a National Innovation Summit at the Massachusetts Institute of Technology in March 1998.

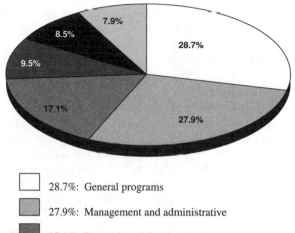

BUDGET:
1996 COC Expenses

- 28.7%: General programs
- 27.9%: Management and administrative
- 17.1%: Research and development
- 9.5%: Health information infrastructure
- 8.5%: Workforce and technology
- 7.9%: Fund raising

CURRENT POLITICAL ISSUES

In its drive to foster national competitiveness, the Council on Competitiveness concentrates on just a few issues that it considers critical. These include technological innovation, education, training, and the benchmarking of U.S. economic performance against other countries.

For more than a decade, innovation has topped the council's list of priorities. With federal support for research and development declining following the end of the Cold War, the council has persistently called on the federal government to play a greater role in encouraging R&D, as well as for industry/government/university partnerships.

An equally important issue from the council's point of view is education. A globally competitive economy can only be supported by a globally competitive workforce. Council members are convinced that the education and skills of the U.S. workforce will be the most critical issue to emerge over the next decade. Pointing out that American schools do not produce enough graduates to meet the needs of a knowledge-driven economy and that the wage gap between high- and low-skilled workers is widening, the Council is working to define a collaborative action agenda for companies, workers, educators, and the public sector.

Case Study: National Innovation Summit

The Council on Competitiveness works to influence government policy by trying to build support within Congress and the administration for specific goals. Since it does not support individual politicians or parties, and makes no attempt to influence legislation, the Council functions more as an advisory group whose advice can be accepted or rejected as officials see fit, rather than a political advocacy group dedicated to advancing the interests of a specific group.

One example of how the council seeks to achieve its goals is the 1998 National Innovation Summit and the preceding regional summits in 1997. Organized by the Council on Competitiveness and hosted by MIT in March 1998, the National Innovation Summit brought together more than 150 of the nation's leading corporate chief executives and university presidents, as well as governors, members of Congress and senior administration officials to devise a strategy to strengthen America's long-term capacity to innovate.

Among the chief findings of the summit was that the United States is living on borrowed time—harvesting the results of past innovations without making adequate efforts to develop a new pool of talent or invest in the infrastructure required to sustain its leadership. To strengthen the U.S. system of innovation, the summit called for "an improved synergy among industry, universities and the federal research apparatus . . . Public policy must grasp the new reality that to innovate is to collaborate."

With participants agreeing that "Congress and the Executive Branch play a pivotal role in innovation," the stage was set for the federal government to apply the council's recommendations to the formulation of investment strategies, as well as fiscal, trade, and regulatory policies. Supportive senators like William Frist (R-Tenn.) worked in Congress to educate their fellow legislators about the importance of partnerships between the government, universities, and corporations, and called for the federal government to play a "stewardship" role to promote focused research with measurable results and funding of research, science, and math education.

SUCCESSES AND FAILURES

Since the Council on Competitiveness does not engage in partisan debate and does not have a well-defined political agenda, it is difficult to characterize its effect on government policy in terms of success or failure. On the one hand, it has succeeded in raising awareness among legislators and administration officials of the importance of investment in research and technology in maintaining America's competitive edge. It has also highlighted the key role of education in building a strong, innovative economy. On the other hand, despite acknowledgment by various members of Congress and President

Clinton that these issues needed to be addressed, the council's major recommendations had still not been translated into policy by 1998.

At the state level, however, several initiatives reflecting council priorities have been put into place. These include California's tax incentives for research and development collaboration, Georgia's Research Alliance, and Indiana's University-Industry Technology Assistance Centers.

FUTURE DIRECTIONS

While the Council on Competitiveness is continuously researching ways to enhance the ability of U.S. businesses to compete in the global marketplace, it has been faced with a challenge in the 1990s due to the burgeoning economy. With so many companies seeing their businesses succeeding with existing resources and technologies, fewer and fewer dollars are being spent on finding innovative practices to further capitalize on their achievements. Recognizing this, the council published a report in March of 1999 entitled "The New Challenge to America's Prosperity: Findings from the Innovation Index," stating that if this trend is not reversed, the economy may decline.

GROUP RESOURCES

The Council on Competitiveness offers a wide range of information resources. These include a Web site at http://www.compete.org/home.html where visitors can learn about the council's policies and programs, as well as read excerpts from some of its recent reports. Information about other council publications is also available. For more information on the organization, write to the Council on Competitiveness, 1401 H St. NW, Ste. 650, Washington, DC 20005 or call (202) 682-4292.

GROUP PUBLICATIONS

To promote public awareness, the Council on Competitiveness publishes a monthly newsletter called *Challenges* that chronicles major trends, policies, and people affecting competitiveness, and which covers competitiveness-related developments in the legislative and executive branches of the federal government. A *Competitiveness Index* comparing U.S. performance to that of its major competitors is also released annually. Major policy reports published by the Council include *Endless Frontier, Limited Resources: U.S. R&D Policy for Competitiveness, Highway to Health: Transforming U.S. Health Care in the Information Age,* and *Vision for a 21st Century Information Infrastructure.* A complete list of publications can be obtained by visiting the council's publications page at its Web site at http://www.compete. org/bookstore/book_index.html. For more information on obtaining the council's publications, write to the Council on Competitiveness, 1401 H St. NW, Ste. 650, Washington, DC 20005 or call (202) 682-4292.

BIBLIOGRAPHY

Anthes, Gary H. "Links Between R&D, Success Remain Elusive." *Computerworld,* 14 November 1994.

Carey, John. "Research: What Price Science?" *Business Week,* 26 May 1997.

Flanigan, James. "Today's Trade Figures Don't Tell Story of Future." *Los Angeles Times,* 15 December 1996.

Lepkowski, Wil. "Good But Never Good Enough: Council on Competitiveness Fears Erosion of U.S. Technological Innovation Puts Global Leadership at Risk." *Chemical and Engineering News,* 21 September 1998.

Maynard, Roberta. "The Heat is On." *Nation's Business,* October 1997.

Miller, William H. "R & D Alert." *Industry Week,* 3 June 1996.

Port, Otis, and John Carey. "Innovation: Getting To Eureka!'" *Business Week,* 10 November 1997.

Yochelson, John. "The Outlook for U.S. Innovation: Bright for How Long?" *Chief Executive,* June 1998.

Council on Foreign Relations (CFR)

ESTABLISHED: 1921
EMPLOYEES: 175
MEMBERS: 3,400
PAC: None

Contact Information:

ADDRESS: 58 E. 68th St.
    New York, NY 10021
PHONE: (212) 434-9400
FAX: (212) 861-1789
E-MAIL: communications@cfr.org
URL: http://www.foreignrelations.org/public
PRESIDENT: Leslie Gelb

WHAT IS ITS MISSION?

According to the mission statement of the Council on Foreign Relations (CFR), the organization is "a non-profit, nonpartisan research and national membership organization dedicated to promoting improved understanding of international affairs and to contributing ideas to U.S. foreign policy." The Council on Foreign Relations' ultimate goal is to ensure that the United States remains an important participant in world affairs. The council believes it is critical for the United States to be invested and engaged in international treaties, conflicts, cultural exchanges and trade agreements.

HOW IS IT STRUCTURED?

The CFR is a research organization with headquarters located in New York City. The day-to-day operations of the council are conducted by the organization's president. Policy and direction for the council are provided by a chairman and board of directors in conjunction with a president. A nominating committee, composed of both council members and officers, help name and elect board members.

The council's research and report work is done by a staff divided into diverse categories. One group of council staff may be directed to research and offer recommendations on an economic crisis in Southeast Asia while another addresses the lingering influence of communism in post-Cold War Russia.

The council has 3,400 members scattered throughout the United States. These members are current and

former government officials, scholars, and other accomplished business and civic leaders. They are chosen by other council members and are united by their dedication, knowledge, and sensitivity to foreign affairs.

PRIMARY FUNCTIONS

The Council on Foreign Relations' primary function is that of a think tank, meaning it is an organization dedicated to research. The council staff, with occasional assistance from scholars and foreign affairs experts, investigate and analyze important and topical international issues. For instance, a 1998 council task force investigated the implications of nuclear weapon tests by India and Pakistan. These evaluations and subsequent reports serve the organization in different ways. Some council reports are presented as testimony before Congress while others are referenced by the media or used by the council as a foundation for public debate.

The council also informs federal foreign policy through its Great Debates and Policy Impact Panels (PIPs). The Great Debates are roundtable discussions, often televised, designed to educate and engage the public. A typical Great Debate of 1998 was an evaluation of efforts to reach a settlement between Israelis and Palestinians over disputed land. PIPs are investigations into important international issues of the day. Council members and journalists hear testimony and ask questions of witnesses in a panel format. PIPs generally attempt to reach conclusions, resolutions, and recommendations for U.S. foreign policy.

Because the CFR recognizes that support for United States foreign policy depends on an informed public, another of its objectives is to educate the public about foreign affairs. Council staff compose editorials and magazine articles and appear on television. The organization works with television networks such as C-SPAN to act as effective forums for the council's public education efforts. Great Debates and PIPS appeared several times on C-SPAN in 1998.

PROGRAMS

The council has developed several programs that help the organization execute its mission. Most revolve around creating forums for debate but some focus on public education.

The Great Debates and PIPs are two of the council's more significant initiatives. The organization created the programs to be multi-functional. The initial purpose of both is to gather information on a particular topic. Secondly, the programs are meant to stimulate discussion and generate ideas to solve problems inherent in the topic. The two programs also serve a vital public education role.

The Great Debates and PIPs are held sporadically throughout the year.

The council's Congress and U.S. Foreign Policy Program was designed with the hope of doing away with partisanship when foreign policy is being formulated. The council brought Democratic and Republican foreign policy staff from Congress together to participate in simple roundtable discussions on issues such as international trade.

The council's Next Generation Fellows is an internship program that places exceptional young scholars on the council staff. The council hopes participation in the organization will encourage interest in foreign policy and affairs.

BUDGET INFORMATION

The Council on Foreign Relations had a total operating budget of approximately $20 million in 1997. The majority of the council's income ($4 million) came from its publications. Other significant sources of income came from individual membership dues ($2.5 million) and corporate membership ($2.7 million). The council spent $13.6 million on programs with $6 million going to its studies programs and $2 million to its meetings programs. The organization spent $5.5 million on support services with the bulk of those outlays ($4 million) spent on management and the rest on fund-raising. Publication of *Foreign Affairs* magazine cost the council $4.1 million. The organization spent approximately $1.5 million on media, book publications, and fellowships.

HISTORY

The Council on Foreign Relations was formed in 1921 at a time when the U.S. political philosophy of isolationism was extremely popular. Concerned bankers, lawyers, and businessmen created the council because they feared that isolationism was a dangerous and unproductive policy. These founders believed that the future prosperity and welfare of the United States could only be achieved through relations with the rest of the world; to maintain a systematic policy of isolation would be foolish.

Once established, the council wanted to provide a forum for its findings, investigations, and analysis. The first issue of its magazine *Foreign Affairs* was published in 1922. The council's first study and research groups dedicated to economic issues were also formed that year. The young council found early prominence in the 1920s, especially due to one of its founders, Henry L. Stimson. Stimson was not only an executive of the council but also President Herbert Hoover's secretary of state. During the 1930s, interest in foreign affairs waned due to the Great

Depression as the minds of the U.S. public turned to their financial strife.

However, by the time of World War II (1939–45), the council once again enjoyed a measure of popularity. Several council studies helped form government policy throughout the war. Members of the organization were brought together with members of the State Department to create the Advisory Committee on Postwar Foreign Policy. President Harry Truman took a council recommendation into consideration when he decided to use the atomic bomb on Hiroshima and Nagasaki in 1945. Additionally, the Marshall Plan (named after Secretary of State George C. Marshall) to rebuild postwar Europe was largely based on an earlier council reconstruction study and report.

The following several decades were dedicated to the study of communist influence throughout the world. It began with the 1947 publication of an influential article in *Foreign Affairs* magazine that became the basis for the U.S. Cold War policy of containment. Containment included the directive to limit the spread of Soviet-style communism through any means. Throughout the Korean and Vietnam wars, the council continued to advocate the policy of containment.

The 1970s and 1980s were a period of transition for the council. It remained influential, with council member Henry Kissinger helping to design the U.S. policy of openness with China. However, the council also began to be viewed as overly elitist and not always effective. It continued to study conflict areas such as Afghanistan and Grenada, but the plans of action it developed were sharply questioned. Critics claimed that the organization's recommendations had become too esoteric to be useful.

In the 1990s newly elected CFR president Leslie Gelb made strides to add real-world meaning to the organization's efforts. Gelb introduced the Great Debates in 1996 and the Congress and U.S. Foreign Policy in 1997. He put a new emphasis on communications, public education, and membership growth. He also worked to improve the quality and number of the organization's study groups.

CURRENT POLITICAL ISSUES

The Council on Foreign Relations addresses many of the same issues that arise for the U.S. State Department. One of the organization's primary focuses throughout the 1990s has been the continuing and bloody conflicts in the former Yugoslavia. The council has researched and produced reports on what it believes to be the best methods of addressing both the massacre and mass exodus of Bosnians and Albanians. Related to this issue is the council's focus on revising the U.S. philosophy of military defense.

Case Study: Council Assessment of U.S. Defense Policy

One priority and concern of the Council on Foreign Relations has been the U.S. defense policy. The council believes that the end of the Cold War, rather than signaling an end to the need for a definitive defense strategy, instead means a new series of challenges and threats to U.S. foreign interests. It has warned that the United States must remain aware of these threats and responsive to such challenges. What is more, the council has been critical of U.S. post-Cold War defense policy as guided by Presidents Bill Clinton and George Bush, claiming that U.S. defense policy has lagged behind global political and military developments. A prime example that the CFR cites was the United States' slow and unsure intervention in the war between the Balkan states of Bosnia and Serbia. In addition the council felt that the Middle East and terrorist acts are also areas in which the U.S. response was not wholly adequate. The council claimed that the United States defense policy had remained unchanged despite radical shifts in world affairs.

In an effort to reverse the trend, the council released a policy initiative in 1998 that recommended a series of changes. It appeared as a report called *Future Visions for U.S. Defense Policy*. The report advised a 10 percent increase in U.S. military spending, suggested a renewed emphasis on the development of military technologies, and recommended a new focus on fighting low-level threats from terrorists and ethnic conflicts. The council presented its findings to an audience of defense experts and journalists in Washington, D.C. To raise awareness of the issue, it also sponsored regional debates in the form of the Policy Initiatives Series. The basis of the series was to allow various foreign affairs experts to voice their opinions about the direction of U.S. policy.

It appeared that the council's reports may have had some affect. When President Clinton announced his proposed budget for 1999, he declared that he planned to increase the U.S. defense budget for the next decade. Clinton proposed that this increased funding would be dedicated toward just such areas as the council suggested: counter-terrorism and Middle East and European conflicts. The council plans to continue its research into the most effective ways in which the federal government could appropriate these newly-designated funds.

SUCCESSES AND FAILURES

The council's most notable success was its contribution to U.S. foreign policy during the Cold War. The organization investigated, analyzed, and composed studies, reports, and strategic plans that helped determine the fate of the entire world.

The council has also made mistakes in the form of referrals and recommendations that did not end as quietly as the Cold War. The council's philosophy of containment led to two very bloody wars: the Korean conflict is still not fully resolved and the Vietnam War ended in defeat for the United States. The atomic bomb that ended World War II killed hundreds of thousands of Japanese citizens and remains a debatable decision in the eyes of many Americans.

Its education mission has also seen somewhat mixed results. The council has succeeded in raising public awareness of foreign affairs, however international issues still remain distant, confusing, and unimportant to many Americans. According to public opinion polls the issue of foreign affairs routinely ranks toward the bottom of American's concerns. To that end, the council still has tremendous strides to make in reaching the general public.

FUTURE DIRECTIONS

The Council on Foreign Relations has laid out immediate and long range goals for its future. In particular, it wants to diversify its membership and dispel the long-held perception that it is an elitist east coast establishment that has little contact with the rest of the United States. CFR plans to spread out its membership geographically and believes such diversification will involve and affect more of the general public.

GROUP RESOURCES

The Web site of the Council on Foreign Relations, available at http://www.foreignrelations.org/public, contains information on the group's mission, publications, functions, and programs. For more information on the organization, write to the Council on Foreign Relations, 58 E. 68th St., New York, NY 10021, call (212) 434-9400, or E-mail communications@cfr.org.

GROUP PUBLICATIONS

The Council on Foreign Relations publishes full-length books on international topics such as *Behind the Open Door: Foreign Enterprises in the Chinese Marketplace*. The council also offers papers, studies, reports, and even transcripts of speeches made to the council. However, most important of all council publications is the *Foreign Affairs* magazine. Issues can be accessed via the World Wide Web at http://foreignrelations.org. For more information on council publications, write to the Council on Foreign Relations, 58 E. 68th St., New York, NY 10021 or call (212) 434-9400.

BIBLIOGRAPHY

The American Encounter: The United States and the Making of the Modern World. New York: Basic Books, 1997.

Brzezinski, Zbigniew. "American Leadership and World Security: New Opportunities." *Current*, November 1996.

Grose, Peter. *Continuing the Inquiry: The Council on Foreign Relations from 1921 to 1996.* New York: The Council on Foreign Relations, 1996.

Hoge, James. "Editor's Note: Seventy Five and Counting." *Foreign Affairs*, January–February 1997.

Huntington, Samuel. "The Erosion of American National Interest." *Foreign Affairs*, September–October 1997.

Kennan, George. "Diplomacy Without Diplomats." *Foreign Affairs*, September–October 1997.

Konigsberg, Eric. "The Park Avenue State Department: The Council on Foreign Relations in New York, New York." *New York*, 7 October 1996.

Lucier, James. "Foreign Policy: Whose Ball is it Anyway?" *Insight on the News*, 29 June 1998.

Schulzinger, Robert. *The Wise Men of Foreign Affairs: The History of the Council on Foreign Relations.* New York: Columbia University Press, 1984.

Credit Union National Association and Affiliates (CUNA)

ESTABLISHED: 1934
EMPLOYEES: 364
MEMBERS: 11,800
PAC: The Credit Union Campaign for Consumer Choice

Contact Information:

ADDRESS: PO Box 431
    Madison, WI 53701–0431
TOLL FREE: (800) 356-9655
FAX: (608) 231-4263
URL: http://www.cuna.org
PRESIDENT: Daniel Mica
CHAIRMAN: Nancy L. Pierce

WHAT IS ITS MISSION?

The Credit Union National Association (CUNA)'s mission is to provide the credit union industry and its members with the services and representation they need to ensure the continuation of the fair-minded, democratic traditions that are at the very core of the industry's philosophy.

HOW IS IT STRUCTURED?

From bases in both Madison, Wisconsin, and Washington, D.C., CUNA is directed by a 24-member board of industry volunteers. The board members are elected by member credit unions from within their geographical region and asset/membership range. State credit union leagues from each region also elect a representative to the board.

As a result of a Renewal Program introduced in the fall of 1996, individual credit unions are no longer represented in CUNA by their state leagues but now belong to both CUNA and their state leagues, enabling them to vote directly for CUNA board members, vote on all matters relating to CUNA's bylaws and dues, and provide direct input on regulatory and legislative issues.

PRIMARY FUNCTIONS

CUNA is a major national trade association serving U.S. credit unions. In partnership with state credit union leagues, CUNA provides a wide variety of services to credit unions. These include legal and governmental representation, which may involve testifying in courts or before Congress regarding issues related to credit unions. For instance, several times in 1998 and 1999, members of CUNA's Y2K subcommittee reported to Congress on the state of credit union readiness for 2000. CUNA also files *amicus curiae* (friend of the court) briefs on behalf of credit unions that have become ensnared in legal battles.

CUNA provides information resources to both its members and to the general public. For instance, the organization produces *Buyer's Guide,* an electronic directory that lists various vendors that credit unions may use. CUNA also publicizes the possible advantages of banking with a credit union instead of a bank.

PROGRAMS

CUNA's programs mainly revolve around internally oriented activities formulated to help its member unions develop and thrive in the marketplace. CUNA offers several educational and support programs designed to help individual credit unions offer new services to strengthen their competitive positions. For instance, the organization runs IRA Supertrain, a program designed to help credit unions understand and further their ability to work with individual retirement accounts (IRAs). Classes for both those just beginning to learn about IRAs and those who are more experienced are offered. These classes give employees a better understanding of their customers' needs enabling them to serve their customers in the same way a bank might.

Through its Center for Professional Development, CUNA offers training to credit union professionals in a variety of subject areas. One such program is the Certified Credit Union Executive (CCUE) program. For those credit union employees interested in pursuing a leadership role, CCUE offers opportunities to learn more about what skills are needed for promotion and to earn certification towards management positions.

The CUNA-run Credit Services Group (CSG) offers individual unions and state leagues a vast array of business tools and services to enhance their competitiveness and customer service. Telecommunications and data transmission services, publicity and marketing materials, forms and stationery, IRS reporting, and short-term investment products are just a few of the services offered by CSG.

BUDGET INFORMATION

Not made available.

HISTORY

The basic premise of the credit union system is the idea that people in a particular location or occupation pool their money and use this pool to make loans to each other based on the strength of their mutual interest, rather than for financial gain. Thus, those without a great deal of money for building a house or starting a business would be able to borrow from their credit union even if they did not have much collateral. This was quite different from banks that looked to make a profit on loans. The first credit union association was established in 1909 after a Massachusetts law was passed allowing its formation.

Initially credit unions were not successful. The 1920s was a period of booming economic growth in the United States and it was not very difficult to borrow money. However, with the onset of the Great Depression a decade later, credit unions with more lenient lending practices than banks were ideal for those who suffered great financial loss. The number of states that passed laws allowing credit unions skyrocketed, and by the mid-1930s there were almost 3,500 credit unions nationwide. It became apparent that there was a need for a national organization to represent credit unions' interests and in 1934, CUNA was established.

World War II (1939–45) was a difficult time for credit unions and growth slowed; however, with the end of the war the movement experienced renewed vigor. In just 20 years, the number of credit unions more than quadrupled to over 16,000 in 1955. This growth continued through the 1960s with the number of credit unions peaking at the end of the decade at more than 23,000.

The 1970s was a period of change for CUNA and its member unions. The number of credit unions declined as a result of smaller unions merging. Despite the smaller number of institutions, membership continued to boom, growing to more than 43 million during this time. Important changes were made in the way that credit unions operated as new services, such as mortgage lending, were added to make them even more competitive with banks.

Increased flexibility coupled with financial failure for some credit unions characterized the 1980s. CUNA helped its member unions expand their membership by relaxing the prerequisites for admission to a credit union. In the mid- to late-1990s, CUNA and all credit unions came under legal and legislative attack. Banking institutions felt threatened by the strength of credit unions and accused the industry of using overly-loose terms for membership which violated the laws that had established them. CUNA was forced to revise its recommended policies for credit union membership. The organization underwent a change in its structure as well. When it was organized in 1934, CUNA was a federation of state leagues with individual credit unions enjoying affiliation with CUNA through their league. In 1996 CUNA conducted a movement-wide study, the Renewal Project, and changed its bylaws to make credit unions members of both CUNA and their state league. The change meant that individual credit unions could participate directly in the election of 18 of the 24 CUNA board members and vote on bylaws and dues.

CURRENT POLITICAL ISSUES

CUNA focuses on a number of political issues, all of which involve the effect of particular pieces of legislation on its member credit unions. Issues include reducing auxiliary fees levied on credit unions, preventing banking fraud through legislation, and guarding credit unions against stifling lending rules. However, by far the biggest issue that CUNA confronted in the 1990s is the assertion by the American Bankers Association (ABA) and other members of the banking industry that the National Credit Union Administration and credit unions' membership policies violated the law.

Case Study: Credit Unions v. the Banking Industry

In 1982 the National Credit Union Administration (NCUA), the federal agency which regulates credit unions, decided to recommend that membership rules be relaxed, based on new interpretations of the laws governing credit unions. Previously credit unions could only sign up members who were employed by a particular company; however, the NCUA changed the rules so that credit unions could accept members from unrelated groups of employees of different companies. By becoming less exclusive, credit unions using the new guidelines allowed their membership to grow. CUNA supported these new rules.

In 1991, after incredible growth in credit union membership, the ABA and other members of the banking industry filed suit against the NCUA, arguing that those credit unions who chose to incorporate under federal law rather than state law should be subject to what it claims were the more restrictive regulations on occupation-based credit union membership. Those credit unions formed to serve the members of a particular occupation or trade must stick to those guidelines, argued the ABA. The ABA claimed that such unions should not be able to extend their services to other groups and form multiple-group unions, and it disputed the NCUA's right to recognize such groupings.

The ABA insisted that its advocacy of the narrow- or single-group interpretation would have very little impact on the credit union industry. CUNA counter-claimed that more than half of all credit unions with federal charters were of the multiple-group kind, most of these occupationally based, and that a judgment in favor of the banking industry would effectively rob the public of the right to choose the financial institution they preferred. CUNA pointed out that many of the states modeled their own incorporation procedures on the federal model, so failure of multi-group recognition at the federal level would inevitably result in the demise of the multi-group state-chartered credit union as well.

CUNA felt as though this was an attempt by traditional banks to destroy their competition, rather than an honest attempt at preventing illegal behavior. CUNA's president and CEO Daniel Mica's remarked in a letter to Donald Ogilvie, Executive Vice President of the ABA: "the ABA has often been a champion of deregulation, freer markets, and more unfettered competition in the financial services industry . . . For the banking industry to embark on a campaign to destroy credit unions through the imposition of stifling layers of court decisions, regulations, and legislation at all levels of government is a departure from what we thought were the first principles of most bankers. Or is it only when reduced regulation serves bankers' interests that bankers favor consumer choice?"

"Consumer choice" has become the catch-phrase for the CUNA campaign against the ABA. Despite support from President Bill Clinton's administration, an injunction was granted on October 26, 1996, forbidding federally chartered credit unions from accepting new members from companies or organizations outside their "core" employee groups. In its 1998 decision of *National Credit Union Administration v. First National Bank & Trust Co.* the Supreme Court ruled 5 to 4 that the NCUA did not have the authority to allow federal credit unions to serve more than one membership group. CUNA was forced to shift its attention from interpreting the law to changing or superseding the law.

Joining forces with the National Association of Federal Credit Unions (NAFCU), CUNA established the Credit Union Campaign for Consumer Choice (CUCCC), a national campaign to coordinate lobbying of both local and national legislators in support of new legislation that would allow the continuation of the broad-membership credit union system that had existed since 1982. The Credit Union Membership Access Act (H.R. 1151) was the legislation that realized the CUCCC's goal. This law, signed by President Clinton on August 7, 1998, enabled NCUA to reinstate its broader membership rules, which in turn enabled CUNA to count on the membership that it had accumulated through the multiple-group employee method.

FUTURE DIRECTIONS

With the success of the Credit Union Membership Act, CUNA recognizes that it must reevaluate its policies and priorities. In early 1999 CUNA called for a forum of the participants in the Credit Union Campaign for Consumer Choice so that the ramifications of the membership act can be discussed and acted upon. CUNA hopes to be able to preserve the new law against attack by the banking industry as well as develop grassroots strategies to ensure success.

GROUP RESOURCES

CUNA maintains an extensive Web site at http://www.cuna.org that contains basic information on the organization, member services, and CUNA policies. For further information about CUNA, write to the Credit Union National Association, PO Box 431, Madison, WI 53701 or call 1-800-356-9655.

GROUP PUBLICATIONS

CUNA has a variety of publications aimed at helping to improve credit union services and to educate members and prospective members. *Credit Union Magazine* is a monthly publication that keeps credit unions abreast of the latest news in the industry. *Home and Family Finance* is a quarterly newsletter aimed at members and covers such topics as credit union services and money management. Many of CUNA's publications can be downloaded at http://www.cuna.org/data/cu/pubs/pubs.html. For more information about CUNA publications, call CUNA Customer Service at 1-800-356-8010 or write

to the Credit Union National Association, PO Box 431, Madison, WI 53701.

BIBLIOGRAPHY

Asseo, Laurie. "Credit Union Expansion Gets Cool Reception From Court." *Rocky Mountain News,* 7 October 1997.

"Bankers File New Suit Against N.C.U.A. in Credit Union Fight." *Business Wire,* 10 May 1997.

Blake, Peter. "Colorado Credit Unions Take It To The Banks." *Rocky Mountain News,* 30 April 1997.

"Credit Unions Need Help." *Rocky Mountain News,* 5 May 1997.

DePass, Dee. "Case May Put Credit Unions on the Ropes." *Star Tribune,* 13 November 1997.

Fouts, Dean. "Cornered Credit Unions Come Out Fighting." *Business Week,* 16 March 1998.

Maynard, Micheline. "Customers, Employees Love Credit Union." *USA Today,* 21 July 1995.

Meredith, Robyn."Checking In On Credit Unions." *USA Today,* 21 July 1995.

Disabled American Veterans (DAV)

ESTABLISHED: 1920
EMPLOYEES: 630
MEMBERS: 1.1 million
PAC: None

Contact Information:

ADDRESS: PO Box 14301
    Cincinnati, OH 45250
PHONE: (606) 441-7300
FAX: (606) 442-2088
URL: http://www.dav.org
E-MAIL: ahdav@one.net
NATIONAL COMMANDER: Andrew A. Kistler

WHAT IS ITS MISSION?

According to the organization, the Disabled American Veterans (DAV) is "made up exclusively of men and women disabled in our nation's defense." Further, the DAV "is dedicated to one, single purpose: building better lives for all our nation's disabled veterans and their families." Soldiers who return from war often bear its scars for the rest of their lives. For example, many DAV members lost an arm or a leg while serving in the Korean War, some suffer the lingering effects of exposure to the herbicide Agent Orange used in Vietnam, and some were deafened by explosions in World War II.

"Treaties are signed and the battles of nations end," says the DAV Web site, "but the personal battles of those disabled in war only begin when the guns fall silent. These men and women must struggle to regain health, reshape lives shattered by disability, learn new trades or professions, and rejoin the civilian world. At each step, they need help to help themselves. For three quarters of a century now, that aid has come from the Disabled American Veterans, a nonprofit organization of more than one million veterans disabled during time of war or armed conflict." The DAV assists veterans with benefits claims, represents veteran concerns to the government, and strives for equal employment opportunities for its members.

HOW IS IT STRUCTURED?

DAV is led by its National Executive Committee (NEC), composed of a national commander, the immediate past national commander, national senior vice commander, four national junior vice commanders, and a representative from each of 21 geographical districts. The national commander is assisted by a national judge advocate and a national chaplain, both of whom are elected annually, and a national adjutant who is appointed and acts as the chief executive officer of the DAV. Together these supporting officers form a small advisory board for the national commander, who oversees the day-to-day operations of the DAV.

DAV membership is open to any honorably discharged veteran who was injured in the line of duty, either during war, or conditions similar to war. In 1998 just over one million such veterans, from every major U.S. military conflict from World War I on, were DAV members. This membership is divided into 21 geographical districts across the United States. Each district elects a representative to serve a two-year term on the NEC.

PRIMARY FUNCTIONS

The DAV works on both a national and local level to meet the needs of its members. On the national level, the DAV strives to protect and expand the laws and programs that have been enacted over the years to help disabled veterans. At the local level, the DAV helps its members make sense of these benefits, and provides other services to improve their quality of life.

The DAV's legislative staff, made up of combat-disabled vets, monitors national policy initiatives as they relate to disabled veterans. They lobby for increased government funds dedicated to veterans' medical and disability compensation. They also seek to protect present laws and benefits, a necessity according to the organization's Web site because "the understanding of the American public and their elected representatives for the problems of disabled veterans fades as the memory of war grows weaker. . . . The pressure to cut federal spending is intense, and the temptation to economize at the expense of needed veterans' programs is more than many politicians can resist. Under such circumstances, a man or woman injured in wartime hostility can be injured again by peacetime apathy." The DAV's legislative staff also works closely with the Department of Veterans Affairs (VA), in efforts to improve claims processes and delivery of care to low-income veterans.

The DAV's National Service Officers (NSOs), themselves disabled vets, advise and counsel veterans in regard to the benefits and options available to them. They counsel current members of the armed forces on potential benefits, often visiting patients at military hospitals; help secure medical or disability benefits for injured veterans; and seek out homeless vets to assure they receive the benefits owed them. They also help veterans obtain medical treatment at VA hospitals, occasionally coming to a veteran's aid when the VA requires a formal

hearing to determine if the vet truly deserves benefits. In such cases the NSOs organize medical evidence, draft statements, and sometimes deliver testimony on behalf of the veteran. The DAV also retains national appeals officers who represent veterans appealing their judgments. In 1996 the NSOs helped 239,487 veterans receive $1.8 billion worth of benefits. The services of the NSOs are available through 69 offices and open to all disabled veterans, not only DAV members.

Employment

National unemployment figures for veterans and for the disabled are higher than the national average, therefore disabled veterans have a high rate of unemployment, well above the national average. The DAV works with the president's Committee on Employment of Persons with Disabilities, the Department of Labor, and the Office of Personnel Management to provide employment opportunities for disabled veterans. The NSOs help veterans with federal government placement assistance and they assist disabled veterans, who feel they have been discriminated against, file claims.

PROGRAMS

Through its programs, the DAV meets the many special needs of its members and of veterans of the U.S. Armed Forces in general. A variety of DAV activities are carried out through its National Voluntary Service Program. DAV members and volunteers in the Transportation Network operate at VA hospitals around the country, transporting disabled veterans to and from medical appointments. Volunteers also help care for disabled veterans within VA hospitals, clinics, and treatment centers.

The DAV helps soldiers who are not members through its Transition Assistance Program (TAP). As part of this program, the NSOs visit military bases around the country, talking to men and women who will be leaving military service and helping prepare them for life outside of the armed forces. The DAV opened offices specifically for this purpose in the areas around Norfolk, Virginia, and San Diego, California, where there are numerous military installations.

BUDGET INFORMATION

The DAV had total revenues of $125 million in 1996. Of these revenues, $105 million came from contributions and donations. The remaining $20 million included $8 million in membership dues, and $12 million from DAV financial investments.

The DAV spent $108 million in 1996. The DAV's greatest expenses were the National Service program and

BUDGET:

1996 DAV Revenue

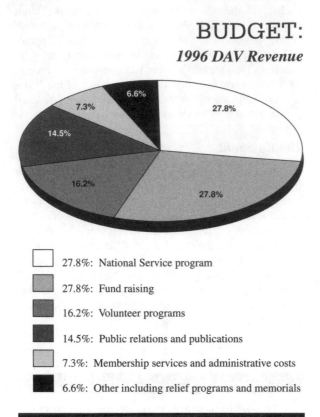

- [ ] 27.8%: National Service program
- [ ] 27.8%: Fund raising
- [ ] 16.2%: Volunteer programs
- [ ] 14.5%: Public relations and publications
- [ ] 7.3%: Membership services and administrative costs
- [ ] 6.6%: Other including relief programs and memorials

the organization's fund-raising efforts, costing the DAV approximately $30 million each. The organization spent $17.5 million on its volunteer programs. The DAV spent $13 million to public relations efforts meant to raise public consciousness of the DAV and the problems of disabled veterans. Membership services cost the DAV $4.4 million and administrative costs were another $4 million. Appropriations for DAV relief programs and memorials amounted to $4 million. DAV publications and other communications cost $2.5 million. The DAV spent $580,000 on legislative efforts. The DAV allocated $200,000 to its National Employment Program in 1996.

HISTORY

When the 4.7 million U.S. soldiers who served in World War I (1914–18) returned home, many of them formed small, local organizations to share the process of civilian life readjustment. These organizations provided a way for veterans to help other veterans overcome the emotional and physical scars of the war. These groups also provided more tangible assistance, such as understanding the government's system of benefits. As the groups grew in size, the veterans became aware that government agencies were more responsive to the requests of veteran groups than to the requests of individual veterans.

On September 25, 1920, a coalition of local groups, made up of some 300,000 Americans wounded in World War I, united as the Disabled Veterans of the World War (DAVWW). They named Robert Marx their first national commander and immediately organized into a national body with the structure the organization retains today. Shortly after the DAVWW's formation, 1920 Democratic presidential nominee James Cox invited National Commander Marx to join him in a whistle-stop campaign across the country. Marx seized the opportunity to recruit more disabled veterans groups for his coalition. Due to Marx's efforts, the DAVWW quickly gained national attention. It held its first national meeting in Detroit, Michigan, on June 27, 1921.

The DAVWW's initial goal was to force the government to create one agency for all veteran services. At the time, veterans had to file separate claims with different organizations and branches of the government to receive the benefits that were available to them. It was a confusing, frustrating, and overly bureaucratic process for veterans seeking benefits. The DAVWW and other veteran service organizations (VSOs), such as the American Legion, pressed the federal government for action. The government responded by creating the Veterans Bureau, the forerunner of today's VA. In its first full year of operation, the DAVWW assisted 7,000 claims with different government agencies.

The DAVWW Women's Auxiliary was created at the DAVWW's second national convention in San Francisco, California in 1922. The Women's Auxiliary was open to the female relatives of disabled veterans, as these family members also carried much of the disabled veterans burden.

The Great Depression of the late 1920s and 1930s had an incredible effect on the DAVWW. Disabled veterans faced with economic hardships joined the DAVWW in great numbers. They felt the DAVWW could obtain economic relief for them more effectively than they could on their own. In 1928, before the Great Depression began, the DAVWW's membership was 23,700, but by 1932 it had almost doubled to 41,000.

The DAVWW began a highly successful Idento-tag fund-raising campaign in 1941. Idento-tags were small replicas of license plates sold by DAVWW chapters. In the first year of the program, Idento-tags raised $800,000 for the DAVWW. Sale of these tags continued for more than 30 years.

The DAVWW changed its name to Disabled American Veterans (DAV) in January 1941. Less than a year later, the United States entered World War II (1939–45). The DAV reacted quickly to U.S. involvement in World War II, calling for updates to government policies on the now increasing number of veterans. The DAV also trained 354 new NSOs to meet the demands of newly discharged veterans. Over 670,000 U.S. soldiers were wounded in World War II, and the membership of the DAV swelled to 105,000. During and after the war, the DAV lobbied Congress for legislation and funds for disabled veterans. Between 1943 and the start of the Korean War (1950–53), Congress enacted 500 laws that affected veterans benefits and services. Among the most famous of these was the GI Bill, which provided soldiers returning home after the end of World War II with college educations and low-interest homes loans.

In 1960 DAV member John F. Kennedy was elected president. President Kennedy, wounded in World War II, was a champion of the disabled. He formed the Committee on the Employment of the Handicapped, a national program designed to eliminate employment barriers imposed on the disabled. President Kennedy's successor, Lyndon B. Johnson, was also vigilant in support of the disabled and veterans. In 1966 President Johnson signed the Veterans Readjustment Act. The act extended federal medical and service benefits for veterans to include those who served in the Vietnam War (1959–75). This was significant because the United States never officially declared war with Vietnam. However, soldiers who returned from the fighting in Vietnam needed and demanded the same financial and medical benefits accorded veterans of other U.S. conflicts. The Veterans Readjustment Act granted Vietnam veterans those benefits.

In the late 1960s and early 1970s, the DAV once again saw its membership rise, as large numbers of disabled veterans returned from Vietnam, with membership reaching 300,000 in 1973. It is believed that 15 percent of Vietnam veterans suffered from post traumatic stress disorder (PTSD), but this disorder was little understood in the 1970s. The DAV initiated one of the first research projects that examined the effects of this condition, one of extreme emotional distress brought about by exposure to intense situations, such as war or kidnapping.

The1970s and 1980s saw the DAV struggling to defend cuts to veterans benefits, as the economy performed poorly, and the Vietnam War dropped out of the nation's immediate memory. The DAV did not forgot, however, and on Memorial Day, 1983, the DAV opened its DAV Vietnam Veterans National Memorial in New Mexico. In 1985 the DAV's membership passed 1 million for the first time. The membership of the DAV rose again in the early 1990s to approximately 1.1 million, as soldiers returned home from the Persian Gulf War (1991). In the late 1990s, DAV coordinated with the efforts of other veterans groups in attempting to have a portion of the federal budget surplus devoted to the VA.

CURRENT POLITICAL ISSUES

The DAV's political activities are very limited in their focus, as the organization does not wish to become overly involved in partisan issues. In fact, the DAV insists it is not a political organization, stating in its

FAST FACTS

The U.S federal government paid $13 billion in compensation to disabled veterans in 1997.

(Source: The United States Department of Commerce, 1998.)

membership literature that "[i]ts members reflect all shades of American political opinion. They count on the DAV to advocate their needs as disabled veterans, and the DAV concentrates its attention and resources on this single, nonpartisan concern. Unlike some other veterans' groups, the DAV has no political action committee and does not endorse candidates for political office." However, the DAV does work with government on issues that affect disabled veterans.

Generally, the DAV seeks to protect and increase medical and disability-related benefits. To this end it opposes attempts to eliminate, tax, use means-testing for, or otherwise reduce VA-disability compensation. The DAV also opposes any efforts to include VA hospitals in a national health insurance plan. Likewise DAV supports cost-of-living increases for disability benefits and the extension of disability compensation to all soldiers who have radiogenic diseases. Additionally the DAV wants to expand the VA's responsibility to include residential care for home-bound veterans.

The DAV's education- and employment-related goals include retention of affirmative action practices in federal hiring, financial support for VA job training, and placement programs. The DAV has also pushed for legislation that would require the government to provide headstones for deceased veterans, and for the establishment of national military cemeteries in every state.

Case Study: The Persian Gulf War Syndrome

In the years that followed the Persian Gulf War, many veterans who had served there complained of health problems. Symptoms varied widely from one veteran to another, but included fatigue, skin rashes, depression, muscle and joint pain, headaches, loss of memory, and respiratory problems. By August of 1997, over 100,000 veterans had registered health complaints with the VA for what was being termed the Gulf War Syndrome, and the number of complaints continued to rise.

Despite the large number of complaints, throughout the early 1990s the Department of Defense (DoD) denied the existence of a Gulf War Syndrome. The DAV and other veterans organizations called for a thorough investigation of the veterans' claims. The DAV feared that exposure to toxic substances during the war, including chemical weapons, might be to blame. The DoD maintained that U.S. soldiers had never been exposed to chemical weapons during the conflict. In 1996, however, it was revealed that the demolition of an Iraqi weapons facility after the conclusion of the war might have released deadly chemical weapons and nerve gases.

The revelations about possible exposure to chemical weapons angered the DAV, and other veterans organizations. The DAV demanded that further investigations be made, outside of DoD control. The DAV claimed that the military had a poor record of informing veterans of the health risks they may have faced, and a history of covering up information that would reveal the military had unnecessarily risked the health of its soldiers.

The DAV was successful in persuading the Clinton administration to create a Gulf-illness review committee independent of the DoD in 1998. The Presidential Advisory Committee on Gulf Veterans' Illnesses was created to oversee military investigations into the Gulf War Syndrome and included representatives of the veteran community. The committee found that the DoD's investigation of the illness up to that point had been superficial and unlikely to answer any questions, and pushed for more thorough investigations. Meanwhile, the National Institute of Environmental Health Sciences began funding studies into the origins and possible treatments for the syndrome.

FUTURE DIRECTIONS

More than 40 percent of DAV members are World War II veterans, all of whom are in their 70s or older. As these members move into old age, the DAV will face the difficulties of providing for their increasing needs, and ensuring that funding for the VA also keeps up with demand. This is complicated by the fact that, as the WW II soldiers begin to leave the organization, its membership and influence will decrease. DAV National Adjutant Arthur Wilson specifically addressed how these demographic trends might affect veterans. Wilson said in 1998, "Reduced numbers of veterans can only make it harder to defend veterans to make sure government gives them the justice and dignity they have earned and deserve." In response, the DAV has created the DAV Endowment Fund. The fund is meant to secure the

DAV's services for future veterans who may lose money and political power as their numbers dwindle.

GROUP RESOURCES

The DAV maintains a Web site at http://www.dav.org with information on the DAV's activities and concerns, as well as contact information. On-line copies of DAV's press releases and speeches are also available. The DAV makes its annual report available to all inquiries; it contains comprehensive financial information and reports on the organization's yearly activities. Questions about the DAV may be directed to: Disabled American Veterans, 3725 Alexandria Pike, Cold Spring, Kentucky 41706; or contact DAV by phone at (606) 441-7300.

GROUP PUBLICATIONS

The DAV publishes *DAV Magazine* bi-monthly. *DAV Magazine* is mailed free to DAV members, but nonmembers may subscribe to the magazine for $15 per year. For information, write to DAV Magazine, PO Box 14301, Cincinnati, OH 45250-0301; or call the DAV at (606) 441-7300, or (202) 554-3501 for TDD.

BIBLIOGRAPHY

Amador, Ronald. "Disabled Vets." *Los Angeles Times*, 26 May 1997.

Autry, Dave. "White House Heeds DAV Call for Gulf Illness Probe." *DAV Magazine*, January/February 1998.

Crispell, Diane. "Mustering Out." *American Demographics*, November 1993.

Cuhane, Charles. "Veterans Groups Urge Expanded Eligibility for VA Care." *American Medical News*, 10 August 1992.

Dethlefsen, Merle and James Canfield. *Transition from Military to Civilian Life*, Harrisburg, Penn.: Stackpole Books, 1984

Fisher, Ernest. *Guardians of the Republic: A History of the Noncommissioned Officers Corps of the United States Army*, New York: Ballantine, 1994.

Hart, Max. "Chalk One Up for the DAV." *Fund Raising Management*, May 1990.

Snyder, Keith and Richard O'Dell. *Veterans Benefits*, New York: Harper Collins, 1994.

Waldrop, Judith. "27 Million Heroes." *American Demographics*, November 1993.

Eagle Forum

WHAT IS ITS MISSION?

A lobbying and political education group, the Eagle Forum states it has been "leading the profamily movement since 1972." Through its efforts, the Eagle Forum seeks to advance its conservative agenda of a less intrusive national government, free enterprise, traditional morality, and other issues. According to the organization's mission statement, the Eagle Forum's mission is "to enable conservative and profamily men and women participate in the process of self-government and public policymaking so that America will continue to be a land of individual liberty, respect for family integrity, public and private virtue, and private enterprise."

HOW IS IT STRUCTURED?

Phyllis Schlafly is the founder and president of the Eagle Forum, and plays a major role in determining the group's agenda. Schlafly and the organization's national administration communicate with the 80,000 members of the Eagle Forum through the organization's publications, and its state affiliates. While members can communicate their concerns to the national organization through these and other channels, there is no formal method for setting policy, which is primarily determined by the president and other executives.

The Eagle Forum's Operations Center is located in Alton, Illinois. To better conduct the organization's work with Congress and the federal government, the Eagle Forum also has an office in Washington, D.C. The Eagle Forum's Education Center, located in St. Louis, Mis-

ESTABLISHED: 1972
EMPLOYEES: 15
MEMBERS: 80,000
PAC: Eagle Forum PAC

Contact Information:
ADDRESS: PO Box 618
    Alton, IL 62002
PHONE: (618) 462-5415
FAX: (618) 462-8909
E-MAIL: eagle@eagleforum.org
URL: http://www.eagleforum.org
PRESIDENT: Phyllis Schlafly

souri, manages the organization's educational efforts and publishes the *Education Reporter*, a monthly journal of national reports on education-related issues. The Eagle Forum has a staff of approximately 13 employees at these three offices.

PRIMARY FUNCTIONS

The Eagle Forum's primary activity is persuading lawmakers to enact legislation that addresses the concerns of the organization. Through the Eagle Forum PAC, the organization provides campaign funding to candidates who support the organization's views. Representatives of the Eagle Forum, most notably President Schlafly, speak before Congress to present the concerns of the organization and its members, and otherwise lobby Congress on behalf of conservative issues. Through the organization's Web site and periodicals, the Eagle Forum encourages its members to petition and write congressional members in support of particularly important or urgent conservative issues.

The Eagle Forum also engages in a number of educational activities designed to raise public awareness of conservative issues and alert conservatives to issues of concern. Activities in this arena are also led by Schlafly. Her weekly radio commentary is carried on 270 stations across the United States and her newspaper column is syndicated to more than 100 newspapers. She is also the author of sixteen books on issues ranging from national defense to child care.

PROGRAMS

Most of the Eagle Forum's programs are designed to assist its lobbying efforts, by informing the public and gaining support for conservative issues. One such program is the Eagle Forum's Score Board, which rates how U.S. senators and representatives voted on issues of importance to the organization. Through Score Board, the Eagle Forum can keep its supporters informed of who in Congress is working for, and against, their agenda, information which supporters can then use when it comes time to vote for their congressional representatives.

The Eagle Forum Court Watch project was initiated to counter what the Eagle Forum sees as disturbing trends in the federal judiciary. The Eagle Forum believes that liberal federal judges are abusing their power by issuing rulings that force their views on the public, without any legal or constitutional justification. To stop these judges, the Eagle Forum Court Watch works to publicize judicial rulings and opinions that it considers unconstitutional in their scope. The project also gathers information on potential court appointees, and lobbies Congress to oppose the appointment of liberal activist judges.

BUDGET INFORMATION

Not made available.

HISTORY

Phyllis Schlafly was already a prominent conservative author and lawyer when she founded the Eagle Forum in 1972. Schlafly believed "progressive" political and social developments of the 1960's had contributed to an antifamily atmosphere in the United States. Schlafly founded the Eagle Forum as a way of advocating conservative, traditional profamily values. One of the first objectives of the Eagle Forum was the defeat of the Equal Rights Amendment (ERA).

The ERA was designed to add an amendment to the United States Constitution that would assure women the same political, legal, and economic rights as men. First introduced in 1923, it finally passed Congress in 1972. However, for a constitutional amendment to become law, the amendment must be ratified, or approved by 38 states. After the ERA was passed in Congress, it went to the states, where it struggled to win approval.

Phyllis Schlafly viewed the ERA as "the principal legislative goal of the radical feminists." She believed the ERA, along with *Roe v. Wade,* the Supreme Court decision that made abortion legal, were two direct assaults on the U.S. family. The Eagle Forum spent 10 years fighting the ERA. Because of its work opposing the amendement, the Eagle Forum could take partial credit for the ERA's defeat. The proposed amendment effectively died when the time limit designated for the its approval expired in 1982 without the approval of the 38 states necessary for ratification.

In the 1970s, the Eagle Forum was part of a coalition of conservative political organizations that became known as the "New Right." Members of the New Right each had their own cause: some wanted lower taxes; others struggled to overturn *Roe vs. Wade*; and some worked for increased defense spending. During this decade, the Eagle Forum worked for all of these issues, thus establishing itself as a general advocate for the New Right. The election of Republican Ronald Reagan to the presidency in 1980 brought even greater voice and visibility to the Eagle Forum. Many of the Eagle Forum's policies were enacted by the Reagan administration. The Eagle Forum supported President Reagan's national defense budget, tax cuts, and conservative social positions, and the organization became closely aligned in the public's mind with the administration.

With the election of Democrat Bill Clinton to the presidency in 1992, the Eagle Forum was once again opposed to the policies of the administration in charge. However, the congressional elections of 1994 gave Republicans a majority in Congress after years of being the minority party. While this meant that the Eagle Forum enjoyed greater influence in Congress than it had previously, it did not affect the Eagle Forum's intense campaign against the Clinton administration. The Eagle Forum was vocal in its opposition to President Clinton's early efforts to reform the U.S. health care system and opposed his administration's proposals on issues from taxes to health care. As Clinton appointed new federal judges that the Eagle Forum considered dangerous liberals, the organization became increasingly concerned about the effects that rulings by these judges could have on the nation. In response, the group formed the Eagle Forum Court Watch project. The Eagle Forum was disappointed by Clinton's reelection in 1996, and called for his impeachment based on allegations of illegal fundraising during his campaign. They supported the 1998 impeachment of Clinton for perjury and obstruction of justice, and were disappointed when the Senate failed to convict the president and remove him from office. In 1999 the Eagle Forum called for an end to U.S. involvement in Kosovo, only to see the United States engage in a major military operation there.

CURRENT POLITICAL ISSUES

In the 1990s the Eagle Forum lobbied vocally on a wide variety of policy issues. In the arena of domestic policy, the Eagle Forum has rejected tax increases and lobbied instead for tax cuts. The organization believes that the federal government is too large and too intrusive in the lives of U.S. citizens, and should drastically reduce its size and cut its spending. In line with these views, the Eagle Forum was among the opposition that defeated President Clinton's health care reform measures in 1994.

In matters of foreign policy, the Eagle Forum believes that the United States should be much less involved in the affairs of other countries. The organization does not believe that the U.S. should act as a "police force for the world" by sending U.S. troops to restore order in the world's trouble spots. Accordingly, the Eagle Forum disagreed with decisions to send U.S. soldiers to intervene in conflicts in Bosnia, Somalia, and Kosovo. The Eagle Forum also opposes the signing of United Nations (UN) and other international treaties, which it believes endanger the sovereignty and independence of the United States by forcing it to comply with global laws.

Case Study: Global Warming

In 1992 nations around the world began to develop what became known as the UN Framework Convention on Climate Change (UNFCCC). The purpose of the UNFCCC was to combat the greenhouse effect, an atmospheric phenomenon that traps heat in the earth's atmosphere. The greenhouse effect occurs when solar radiation, which has entered the earth's atmosphere,

becomes trapped by gases such as carbon dioxide to create a heating effect. Many scientists believe that in the past hundred years, the release of large amounts of carbon dioxide and other chemicals into the atmosphere by automobiles and industrial manufacturing has increased the greenhouse effect. These scientists are concerned that if this unnatural increase continues, it will cause global warming, or a permanent rise in temperatures around the world. This would have serious effects on global weather patterns and sea levels.

When diplomats convened in Kyoto, Japan, in 1997, they agreed that global warming was a serious problem that required immediate attention. Accordingly they drafted what became known as the Kyoto Protocol. The authors of the Kyoto Protocol felt that global warming can be averted by reducing worldwide emissions of carbon dioxide and other greenhouse gases. The protocol set limits on greenhouse gas emissions by the nations that would sign it. It also called for its signatories to take other steps to reduce the amount of greenhouse gases in the atmosphere, such as planting more trees, which absorb carbon dioxide. The Kyoto Protocol was the first agreement produced by the UNFCCC that established legally binding emissions limits on its participants.

The Eagle Forum strongly opposed the UNFCCC and stated that there were a number of reasons that the United States should not ratify the Kyoto Protocol. First and foremost, the Eagle Forum pointed out that the greenhouse effect and global warming are only theories of what is happening, and what might happen, to the earth. While there is scientific evidence to support these theories, there is also scientific evidence that disputes them. The Eagle Forum, citing studies that claim the greenhouse effect does not exist, argued that the UNFCCC is unnecessary.

The Eagle Forum also opposed the UNFCCC and the Kyoto Protocol because the organization feels they are harmful to the U.S. economy. In order to control greenhouse gas emissions in the United States, supporters of the Kyoto Protocol proposed a system of economic controls, starting with the government increasing taxes on fuels and energy sources that produce emissions. The tax increase would raise consumer prices, thus lowering product demand. In turn, manufacturers would decrease production, which would lead to less emissions. The Eagle Forum argued that these higher prices would also force many U.S. industries that rely on cheap fuels to close or relocate to countries whose emissions laws were not as strict.

For these reasons, the Eagle Forum has fought the UNFCCC since it began in 1992. The Eagle Forum sees the Senate as its best chances for defeating the Kyoto Protocol. Before the Kyoto conference had even begun, the Senate passed a resolution stating that it did not intend to sign any agreement that bound the United States to emissions limitations, unless it also restricted the emissions of developing nations. The Kyoto Protocol did not include such restrictions and many senators urged President Clinton not to sign it. The Eagle Forum considered the placing of restriction on developed countries such as the United States, without similar limitation on developing nations of Asia or Africa, to be unfair. The organization went so far as to question the true motives for the treaty, claiming that it was really intended to redistribute wealth from richer nations to poorer ones.

Despite the protests of the Eagle Forum and the Senate, President Clinton signed the Kyoto Protocol on November 12, 1998. However, the treaty could not be binding until it was ratified by a Senate vote. In light of the strong opposition to the treaty in that body, Clinton decided not to submit the treaty to the Senate for a vote until additional restrictions for developing nations would be included. While the president had hoped these restrictions would be added in 1999, Senate support for the treaty is doubtful. It is certain, however, that the Eagle Forum will exert its full influence to block any ratification efforts.

FUTURE DIRECTIONS

Global governance will remain a major issue for the Eagle Forum in the future. In addition to continued opposition to the Kyoto Protocol, the Eagle Forum hopes to see U.S. troops pulled out of volatile regions such as the former Yugoslavia. To this end, the Eagle Forum will also push for stronger limitations on the use of executive orders by the president. The organization feels that these orders are being used to unconstitutionally take over a variety of rights and privileges that are reserved for Congress, such as the ability to legislate and form international treaties.

GROUP RESOURCES

The Eagle Forum can be contacted by mail at Eagle Forum, PO Box 618, Alton, IL, 62002; and by phone at (618) 462-5415. The Eagle Forum also maintains a Web site at http://www.eagleforum.org. The Web site contains information about the organization, its policies, and founder Phyllis Schlafly. Through the Web site, one can also join the Eagle Forum mailing list, and receive E-mail updates.

Radio Live with Phyllis Schlafly is the Eagle Forum's daily radio broadcast. On the radio show, Schlafly discusses major issues in the news, and topics of concern to the Eagle Forum. Visit http://www.eagleforum.org/radio for a list of radio stations that carry Radio Live, as well as recordings of recent shows.

GROUP PUBLICATIONS

The Phyllis Schlafly Report is the main publication of the Eagle Forum. It is a monthly issues-oriented newsletter sent to Eagle Forum members. It contains Eagle Forum articles on issues of the day, such as tax cuts and U.S. involvement in Bosnia. The Eagle Forum also publishes a monthly journal called the *Education Reporter*. This journal provides updates on federal, state, local and judicial actions and rulings that affect education, and articulates the Eagle Forum's opinions on education policy. Both of these periodicals are available by subscription to the general public.

The Eagle Forum offers for sale a number of books by Phyllis Schlafly. Available titles include *Pornography's Victims* and *Child Abuse in the Classroom*. Also available is *The Sweetheart of the Silent Majority*, a biography of Phyllis Schlafly. All Eagle Forum publications can be ordered on-line at http://www.eagleforum.org/order; by mail at Eagle Forum, PO Box 618, Alton, IL 62002; by phone at (618) 462-5415; or by fax at (618) 462-8909.

BIBLIOGRAPHY

Beinart, Peter. "Degree of Separation." *New Republic*, 3 November 1997.

"Green Blues." *National Review*, 4 May 1998.

Gingrich, Newt. "Conservatism Now!" *National Review*, 22 December 1997

Jacobson, Louis. "The Eagle Has Landed." *National Journal*, 25 October 1997.

Jacoby, Henry D., Ronald G. Prinn, and Richard Schmalensee. "Kyoto's Unfinished Business: Kyoto Protocol on Climate Change Incomplete." *Foreign Affairs* July-August 1998.

McGinnis, John. "The Origin of Conservatism." *National Review*, 22 December 1997.

Electronic Frontier Foundation (EFF)

WHAT IS ITS MISSION?

The mission of the Electronic Frontier Foundation (EFF) is to ensure "that the civil liberties guaranteed in the United States Constitution and the Bill of Rights are applied to new communications technologies."

HOW IS IT STRUCTURED?

The Electronic Frontier Foundation (EFF) is a non-profit, civil liberties organization based in San Francisco, California. It is headed by a 17-member board of directors made up of some of the most illustrious names in the high-tech industry, as well as prominent writers and social critics. In 1997 the board included Esther Dyson, an MIT professor and writer; John Perry Barlow, one-time Grateful Dead lyricist and Internet expert; Mitchell Kapor, president of the Lotus Corporation; Stewart Brand, author of *The Whole Earth Catalog*; and Steve Wozniak, co-founder of Apple Computers.

Board decisions and policy are supported and implemented by eight full-time staff members, as well as several consultants and volunteers. Staff members are responsible for areas such as programs, membership, legal issues, and administration.

PRIMARY FUNCTIONS

The Electronic Frontier Foundation's primary function is to protect and promote the civil liberties of people

ESTABLISHED: July 1990
EMPLOYEES: 8
MEMBERS: 3,000
PAC: None

Contact Information:
ADDRESS: 1550 Bryant St., Ste. 725
    San Francisco, CA 94103-4832
PHONE: (415) 436-9333
FAX: (415) 436-9993
E-MAIL: ask@eff.org
URL: http://www.eff.org
EXECUTIVE DIRECTOR; PRESIDENT: Tara Lemmey
CHAIRMAN: Lori Fena
VICE-CHAIR: John Perry Barlow

FAST FACTS

Between 1992 and 1998, the number of host computers connected to the Internet rose from 1 million to nearly 30 million. Nearly 20 million of those hosts came on-line between July 1996 and January 1998.

(Source: Robert H. Zakon. "Hobbes' Internet Timeline." April 12, 1998.)

who use on-line technology. In effect, the EFF is dedicated to defending free speech on the Internet by educating policymakers, law enforcement officials, and the general public about issues that affect current and future communications technologies.

The EFF uses a variety of techniques to get its message across. It has participated as a friend of the court in several major legal cases where it believes users' on-line civil liberties have been violated and has challenged proposed legislation aimed at curbing free speech on the Internet such as the Communications Decency Act (CDA). It monitors legislation and agency actions that may affect the on-line community and works at the federal, state, and local levels to change legislation. Members participate in these activities primarily through electronic mail campaigns and on-line political organizing.

In addition to political and legal action, leading EFF board members and staffers write articles for newspapers and magazines expressing the organization's viewpoint, and speak to law enforcement organizations, state attorney bar associations, conferences and summits, and university classes about the technical, social, and political issues and implications of the rapidly expanding on-line world. The EFF also produces official reports about the civil liberties implications of actions by telephone companies, public utility commissions, and network service providers.

PROGRAMS

As a relatively small organization, the EFF has yet to establish long-term programs aimed at supporting its membership. It does, however, actively sponsor and participate in a number of national and international coalitions and campaigns aimed at promoting on-line freedom of expression. These include the Blue Ribbon Online Free Speech Campaign, which encourages Web masters

worldwide to place a blue ribbon logo on their Web sites in support of free speech on the Internet, as well as the Global Internet Liberty Campaign—a broader-based campaign aimed at preventing individual countries from imposing restrictions on Internet activity.

The EFF established the Pioneer Awards in 1991 to recognize individuals who, according to the group, significantly contributed "to the development of computer-mediated communications or to the empowerment of individuals in using computers and the Internet." Awards are presented annually at the Conference on Computers, Freedom, and Privacy, which is attended by Internet policy makers and members of the Internet industry.

The organization is also a member of the Internet Free Expression Alliance and the Digital Future Coalition. These groups of like-minded organizations work together to convince government policy makers and industry leaders of the importance of permitting the Internet to remain a center of free expression.

BUDGET INFORMATION

The EFF operates with a relatively small annual budget of approximately $1 to $2 million. Like many other public interest advocacy groups, the EFF sustains its activities through membership dues, individual donations and gifts, and foundation and corporate grants. Major individual donations and foundation and corporate grants range from $10,000 to over $250,000. The EFF also receives many smaller donations from individuals who support its work. Membership dues range from $10 to $500 annually (average membership dues are $40 per year). Special projects and programs such as the EFF/Aerosmith Virtual World Tour of Cyberspace also generate funding. The money is used to cover staff and administrative costs, and to fund legal actions and publications.

HISTORY

According to John Perry Barlow, co-founder of the organization, the Electronic Frontier Foundation began with a visit from the Federal Bureau of Investigation (FBI). "In late April of 1990," writes Barlow in his *A Not Terribly Brief History of the Electronic Frontier Foundation,* "I got a call from Special Agent Richard Baxter of the Federal Bureau of Investigation. He had been sent to find out if I might be a member of the NuPrometheus League, a dread band of info-terrorists who had stolen and wantonly distributed source code normally used in the Macintosh ROMs."

Barlow neither knew of nor was a member of the NuPrometheus League, but he was concerned that government agents were monitoring his on-line activity. Barlow subsequently posted an account of his experience on the WELL, an electronic bulletin board system (BBS) in Sausalito, California, which at the time was the digital home of some of the nation's most "technically hip folks," including Mitch Kapor, the inventor of Lotus 1-2-3, one of the world's most popular spreadsheet programs.

Kapor had had a similar experience with the FBI and after reading Barlow's account he contacted Barlow and suggested they meet. Together they conceived the Electronic Frontier Foundation to help support legal actions on behalf of computer software publishers and BBS operators whose First Amendment rights may have been challenged. The new organization also stepped in when searches and seizures appeared to have exceeded the authority of the Fourth Amendment, where the government seemed to have violated the Electronic Communications Privacy Act, and where warrants had been issued with insufficient cause.

An early case involved a role-playing games publisher named Steve Jackson whose office equipment was seized by the Secret Service. His equipment was confiscated in an effort to prevent publication of a game called *Cyberpunk* which agents believed, incorrectly, to be "a handbook for computer crime." Another case involved Craig Neifdorf, who had published an internal BellSouth document in his electronic magazine *Phrack*. Although Neidorf's action was completely legal, he was charged with interstate transport of stolen property with a possible sentence of 60 years in jail and $122,000 in fines.

These cases and others highlighted what Barlow described as the "symptoms of a growing social crisis: Future Shock." "America," wrote Barlow, "was entering the Information Age with neither laws nor metaphors for the appropriate protection and conveyance of information itself."

In the early 1990s, confusion and misunderstanding about the Internet and other computer networks was rampant. Sourches such as the *Washington Post*, the *Wall Street Journal*, and *Time* published stories about hackers, crackers, and Internet pornography which had little basis in fact and only served to inflame policy makers and ordinary citizens. The *Wall Street Journal*, for example, published a piece alleging that the document Niedorf had published was a computer virus capable of bringing down the emergency telephone system for the entire country.

The EFF filed an *amicus brief* (friend of the court) in support of Neidorf and introduced his lawyer to an expert witness whose testimony helped force the government to abandon the case after only four days. As it turned out, the document Niedorf had reproduced in his electronic magazine dealt only with the bureacratic procedures of 911 administration in the BellSouth region and contained nothing that could not easily be obtained through legal means.

The formation of the Electronic Frontier Foundation was officially announced at the National Press Club in Washington, D.C., on July 10, 1990. One of its first official acts was to grant an organization called Computer Professionals for Social Responsibility (CPSR) $275,000 for a project on computing and civil liberties. EFF leaders met with congressional staffers, civil libertarians, and officials from the Library of Congress and the White House to discuss issues such as intellectual property, telecommunications policy, and law enforcement techniques in cyberspace.

In addition to organizing legal actions and lobbying for "rational" computer security legislation, the EFF set up two Usenet newsgroups, established an electronic mailing list, and launched EFF forums on the Well and CompuServe to help raise public awareness of the new civil liberties issues being generated by the computer revolution. In 1991, the organization began publishing a newsletter called *The EFFector* to spread its message to people who might be interested in their work but were not on-line.

During its first year, the EFF also helped organize a major international conference on Communications, Privacy, and Freedom that was to be held in San Francisco in March of 1991. It also helped convince Governor Dukakis of Massachusetts not to sign a computer crime bill which the EFF called "misguided" and organized an effort to rewrite the bill for re-submission to the Massachusetts legislature. The rewritten EFF legislation made a clear distinction between computer trespass and actual malice, proposing appropriate penalties for each.

By 1994 the EFF had grown into a full-fledged nonprofit organization with a full-time staff, paid membership, and tax-exempt status. That same year it finally won the case in which Steve Jackson was involved. Among other things, the federal court's final decision stated that electronic mail could not be read by law enforcement officers without a court-authorized wiretap warrant.

1994 also saw the EFF face its greatest challenge yet—the "Clipper Chip" key escrow encryption proposal. The Clipper Chip was a cryptographic device intended to protect private communications while at the same time permitting government agents to access encrypted private communications using "keys" held by two government "escrow agents." These "keys" could be obtained upon presentation of "legal authorization."

The EFF coordinated a massive grassroots and private industry campaign to prevent the proposal from being signed into law, arguing that "privacy protection will be diminished, innovation will be slowed, government accountability will be lessened, and the openness necessary to ensure the successful development of the nation's communications infrastructure will be threatened."

The Clipper Chip proposal was eventually abandoned, but the EFF soon found itself facing an even greater challenge—the Communications Decency Act (CDA) of 1995. Developed in response to reports in the media about the prevalence of pornography on the Internet, the CDA was intended to prohibit the "the [computer] equivalent of obscene telephone calls and the distribution to children of materials with sexual content." According to the EFF, however, the legislation would restrict content on the Internet, effectively limiting freedom of speech on the Internet that would far exceed restrictions applied to any other communications media.

When the bill was signed into law by President Clinton in February 1996, thousands of Web pages went black for 48 hours in protest. The EFF immediately announced its intent to challenge the new legislation in court and together with the American Civil Liberties Union (ACLU) and other like-minded groups requested an injunction against the CDA. On June 12, 1996, a panel of three federal judges in Philadelphia granted a preliminary injunction against the Communications Decency Act, and just over a year later, on June 26, 1997, the Supreme Court ruled unanimously that the Communications Decency Act violated the First Amendment and that all provisions of the CDA were unconstitutional.

The death of the CDA may have been an important victory, but on-line civil libertarians still faced many challenges. By the late 1990s the Internet had gone mainstream and was dominated by commercial interests and "surfed" by millions of ordinary citizens around the world. Like any start-up organization, the EFF now had to adopt a more institutional approach if it intended to keep up. It did this by bringing in Barry Steinhardt, the former associate director of the ACLU, to serve as EFF's president and CEO. Appointed in 1998, Steinhardt immediately set about formulating an overall strategy and working to overcome the organization's financial problems. And, according to Steinhardt, "Since the CDA decision there has been a headlong rush to embrace tools that may well create a regime of private-sector censorship that's every bit as troubling as the CDA." Battling these new forms of censorship would be EFF's next task.

CURRENT POLITICAL ISSUES

The Internet has been in existence since the 1970s, but until the 1990s it was used primarily by scientists and researchers to exchange information with colleagues. However, with the development of the World Wide Web and new graphics-based "browsers," interest in the Internet grew exponentially as businesses and individuals began to see the enormous potential of this new medium. But the same things that made the Internet so attractive to so many people also made it the subject of significant debate concerning governance and jurisdiction. The new digital media did not easily fit into existing frameworks and many established legal principles and cultural norms could not easily be applied to a medium that was "nowhere and everywhere at the same time."

The EFF arose in response to this confusion, determined to protect the freedom that existed on the Internet, while helping to establish fair and appropriate principles to govern its content and use. The EFF's main goal is to ensure that "common carriage principles" are maintained in the information age. Common carriage principles require that network providers carry all speech, regardless of its content. The EFF is also working to convince Congress that laws should be enacted enabling broader public access to information.

Aside from freedom of speech issues, one of the EFF's primary concerns is privacy in communications. The organization advocates measures that ensure the public's right to use the most effective encryption technologies available, and opposes any efforts by government to implement measures that would allow government agencies to "eavesdrop" on those communications.

Case Study: The Clipper Chip

On April 16, 1993, the White House officially announced a new encryption technology called the Clipper Chip. Developed by the National Security Agency (NSA), and implemented by the National Institute for Standards and Technology (NIST), the Clipper proposal was designed to provide the private sector with a secure system for encrypting data, primarily telephone communications, while at the same time allowing law enforcement agencies to tap into these encrypted communications with approval from the Attorney General.

The concept behind the Clipper Chip was simple: Clipper Chip installation would provide encryption of telephone calls or fax transmissions between two phones or fax machines. To prevent monitoring by unauthorized parties, the signal would be scrambled, making it unintelligible to all but the intended recipients. The only catch was that, in order to allow surveillance by law enforcement agencies, the scrambled signal could be decoded by using two data 'keys,' each held by a different government agency and released only when the Attorney General approved a request for them.

The proposal immediately sparked a furious debate. On-line activists and private industry were virtually unanimous in their opposition, claiming that Clipper threatened the future of personal privacy in the United States. Questions were raised about whether the government could be trusted to hold the keys to this system and whether it would actually be effective in fighting violent crime, terrorism, and drugs.

Another fear was that by making Clipper a standard and demanding its incorporation in products made for export, the initiative would cripple U.S. companies and allow overseas competitors to dominate the international markets for encrytion software. After all, as many pointed out, why would anyone want to purchase encryption software or equipment that would allow surveillance by the U.S. government? Despite widespread opposition, President Clinton persisted with the proposal, announcing on February 4, 1994, that Clipper would be a Federal Data Processing Standard, and he backed that statement up by placing an immediate government order for 50,000 Clipper devices.

THe EFF and other anti-Clipper groups such as Computer Professionals for Social Responsibility (CPSR) responded by organizing an anti-Clipper petition that eventually collected more than 40,000 signatures. They submitted testimony before congressional committees and lobbied for relaxed export controls on encryation devices. Above all, they brought the issue to the attention of the mainstream media.

Soon Clipper was the talk of the nation. Few Americans really understood the technology or the issues involved. All they knew was that Clipper would allow the government to listen in on private communications. That alone was enough to turn public opinion against the proposal: a CNN/Time Magazine poll found that 80 percent of the American public was opposed to Clipper.

By the end of 1994, the Clipper Chip was, for all intents and purposes, dead. However the government refused to give up. Later proposals from the administration included Clipper II and Clipper III, software-only versions that would require users to give a copy of their encryption keys to a government-certified agent who would hold them "in trust." Opposition has remained stiff and none of these proposals has yet to win acceptance.

SUCCESSES AND FAILURES

Over the years, the EFF has racked up an impressive number of victories at the federal level. It won the Steve Jackson Games case in which a federal court affirmed that electronic mail could not be read by law enforcement officers without a court-authorized wiretap warrant), helped kill the initial Clipper Chip proposal, and took part in a broad and successful coalition to oppose the Communications Decency Act.

None of these victories have been decisive, however. Even as late as 1998, the federal administration was still pushing to impose variations of the original Clipper proposal and despite the Supreme Court's declaration that the Communications Act was unconstitutional, 11 states passed online censorship laws in 1995 and 1996. New attempts to censor Internet content through the use of "anti-porn filters" also proved difficult to halt and in 1998 the Senate Commerce Committee approved the Coats and McCain bills, which among other things would force libraries and schools to use software to filter "indecent speech."

FUTURE DIRECTIONS

According to a 1998 survey conducted by the Federal Trade Commission (Privacy Online: A Report to Congress), privacy continues to be the number one concern for users of the Internet. This is especially true when it comes to conducting on-line business transactions. To that end, the EFF has been working with Microsoft Corp. on a proposition called the Privacy Preferences Project (P3P). If adopted, P3P will allow Web sites to quickly and easily post privacy policies and help safeguard e-commerce transactions.

GROUP RESOURCES

The EFF publishes an electronic bulletin, EFFector Online, as well as a hard copy newsletter, *EFFector*. It also maintains extensive electronic archives on the Internet at ftp.eff.org, gopher.eff.org, and http://www.eff.org/, and hosts Internet and Usenet conferences, including comp.org.eff.talk. The EFF also maintains active conferences on the Whole Earth 'Lectronic Link (WELL), CompuServe (CIS), and elsewhere. The organization also provides a free telephone hot line for members of the on-line community who have questions regarding their legal rights.

To access the EFF's archives, refer to the general EFF brochure (http://www.eff.org/pub/EFF/about.eff) or send queries to ask@eff.org. Other resources include: the Online Activism Organizations List, a listing of regional, national and international groups sharing goals similar or complementary to EFF's; the Online Activism Resources List which lists on-line and offline resources for computer-assisted advocacy and grassroots political action; and the FOIA Toolkit, which includes introductory materials and required forms for requesting government information under the Freedom of Information Act. For more information about the organization, write to the Electronic Frontier Foundation, 1550 Bryant St., Ste. 725, San Francisco, CA 94103-4832, call (415) 436-9333 or E-mail mech@eff.org.

GROUP PUBLICATIONS

EFF publishes an electronic bulletin, "EFFector Online," as well as a hard copy newsletter, "EFFector." For more information on EFF publications, write to the Electronic Frontier Foundation, 1550 Bryant St., Ste. 725, San Francisco, CA 94103-4832, call (415) 436-9333 or send E-mail to pubs@eff.org.

BIBLIOGRAPHY

Barlow, John Perry. *A Not Terribly Brief History of the Electronic Frontier Foundation.* San Francisco: Electronic Frontier Foundation, 1990.

———. "Jackboots on the Infobahn: Clipping the Wings of Freedom?" *Wired,* April 1994.

Bottoms, David. "Cyber-cowboy . . . or Prophet?" *Industry Week,* 4 December 1995.

Bruning, Fred. "Stay In Center Lane; Maintain Speed; Caution, Advanced Culture Ahead." *Newsday,* 31 January 1994.

"Communications Decency Act 96: First Wave Of Lashbacks." *Online Libraries and Microcomputers,* 1 March 1996.

Diamond, Edwin, and Stephen Bates. "Law and Order Comes to Cyberspace." *Technology Review,* 1 October 1995.

Dyson, Esther, and George Gilder, Jay Keyworth, and Alvin Toffler. "A Magna Carta for the Knowledge Age." *New Perspectives Quarterly,* 22 September 1994.

Hirschkop, Ken. "Democracy and the New Technologies." *Monthly Review,* 17 July 1996.

Levy, Stephen. "Clipper Chick." *Wired,* September 1996.

Sussman, Vic. "Policing Cyberspace." *U.S. News and World Report,* 23 January 1995.

Trumball, Mark. "Futurist Sees Laissez-Faire Internet." *Christian Science Monitor,* 14 November 1995.

EMILY's List

ESTABLISHED: 1985
EMPLOYEES: 50
MEMBERS: 45,000
PAC: EMILY's List

WHAT IS ITS MISSION?

According to its 1998 statement of purpose, "EMILY's List identifies viable pro-choice Democratic women candidates for key federal and state political offices and supports them in three ways; raising campaign contributions, building strong campaigns, and mobilizing women voters." EMILY is an acronym for "Early Money is Like Yeast"—yeast being the ingredient that makes dough rise. Concerned by the small number of women in the U.S. Congress, and discouraged by the growing political power of the pro-life movement, political activist Ellen Malcolm founded this political action committee (PAC) to provide campaign money to pro-choice Democratic female candidates. Group initiatives have brought EMILY's List into the forefront as a political force behind the Democratic Party.

Contact Information:

ADDRESS: 805 Fifteenth St. NW, Ste. 400
    Washington, DC 20005
PHONE: (202) 326-1400
FAX: (202) 326-1415
E-MAIL: emilyslist@emilyslist.org
URL: http://www.emilyslist.org
PRESIDENT: Ellen R. Malcolm

HOW IS IT STRUCTURED?

EMILY's List is a political action committee based in Washington, D.C. It was founded by Ellen Malcolm, who still serves as president. Malcolm helps recruit and select EMILY's List candidates, assists in development efforts, and remains the public face of the organization. Although EMILY's List has been called an autocracy and Malcolm has been accused of running EMILY's List too rigidly, under her guidance EMILY's List has grown from a tiny coalition of concerned individuals to a political network with more than 45,000 members.

Perhaps because of this growth, Malcolm has delegated some of her administrative duties. Executive Direc-

tor Mary Beth Cahill directs EMILY's List' political strategies and programs, manages day-to-day operations, and conducts long-term strategic planning. An advisory board composed of a small number of pro-choice activists contributes time and resources to the management of EMILY's List. The advisory board assists in development efforts as well as the recruitment and selection of the organization's candidates.

Together, Malcolm, Cahill, and the advisory board design group policies, programs, and strategies. This highly centralized organization has no local chapters or delegates. Regional offices of EMILY's List are essentially local fund-raising centers. "Members" are donors who meet EMILY's List contribution requirements by donating at least $100 annually to the organization and $100 to two of its candidates during a two-year election cycle. Members of the Majority Council are individuals whose contributions to EMILY's List political programs exceed $1,000 per year. Members of the Majority Council and EMILY's List rank-and-file have the opportunity to effect change or steer policy at the organization's annual national convention in Washington, D.C.

PRIMARY FUNCTIONS

EMILY's List strives to help pro-choice Democratic women win state and federal elections primarily through three methods: raising campaign contributions, building effective campaigns, and mobilizing female voters.

The members of EMILY's List firmly believe that it takes money to win elections, therefore the group's main function is to raise money for its candidates. Campaign finance laws, however, prohibit groups or individuals from donating more than $5,000 to any candidate in any campaign. To circumvent the restrictions of this law, EMILY's List uses a technique called "bundling." When a person becomes a member of EMILY's List, he or she is required to make donations of $100 or more—although not exceeding $5000—to two or more candidates sponsored by EMILY's List. The donations are then "bundled" together and sent to the candidates. Bundling is a common practice for PACs and grassroots networks. Using this method 50,000 individuals raised more than $7.5 million for EMILY's List candidates in 1998. EMILY's List is so successful at providing funds for its office seekers it has become one of the largest sources of contributions for federal candidates.

The second priority of EMILY's List is to provide support resources for its candidates. It conducts training workshops for campaign managers, press secretaries, and fund-raisers. Through *The Women's Monitor*, it provides candidates with insight into voters' opinions on current issues. With a staff of political campaign veterans, the organization gives candidates practical support in the field, including refocusing candidates' messages, counteracting negative attacks by opponents, and designing

media strategies. EMILY's List also helps to staff campaigns through its job bank program.

EMILY's List focuses on mobilizing female voters because, according to President Emily Malcolm, "when women vote, women win." With the assistance of local Democratic organizations, EMILY's List coordinated a massive 34-state voter-encouragement campaign directed at 3.4 million women prior to the 1998 general election.

PROGRAMS

EMILY's List seeks to increase campaign effectiveness through its training department and job bank. Between 1995 and 1996, the training program educated more than 450 campaign workers. Participants are selected based on political experience and willingness to relocate.

Four seminars form the core of the training program. The Campaign Management Seminar educates participants in all aspects of a political campaign from budget to media and field skills. The Fundraising Seminar familiarizes participants with the tools of fund-raising such as direct mail and telemarketing, as well as the methods of financing a major campaign. The Press Seminar teaches students how to write press releases, how to generate press coverage, and how to prepare a candidate for debate and interview. Research Seminar participants learn the value of proper compilation and analysis of research.

The job bank is a service that places capable campaign workers into the campaigns of EMILY's List candidates in need of qualified staff. It maintains a database of 800 campaign professionals.

In 1994, EMILY's List launched WOMEN VOTE!, a get-out-the-vote project meant to target, contact, and mobilize female voters through phone calls and direct mail. Aside from getting women to go to the polls, WOMEN VOTE! assists state parties in upgrading and building their voter files. In 1996 WOMEN VOTE! reached 3 million voters in 31 states. WOMEN VOTE! is an ongoing initiative that is expected to spend $10 million before 2000.

BUDGET INFORMATION

EMILY's List began fiscal year 1995-96 with a budget surplus of $500,000. It raised an additional $21,498,168 to increase its total by 37.8 percent from 1994-95. Contributions came entirely from EMILY's List members.

Of that $22 million, 30 percent ($6,717,970) went directly into the campaigns of EMILY's List candidates; 26.3 percent ($5,794,105) was spent on development efforts, the bulk of that figure going toward fund-raising for candidates and EMILY's List; and 13 percent ($2,896,993) went toward the WOMEN VOTE! initiative. Another 9.4 percent ($2,077,759) of the budget went toward the group's "Building Effective Campaigns" division, which included research and training seminars. Administrative costs, including an 11-person payroll, consumed 10 percent ($2,219,925) of the EMILY's List budget, and 4.6 percent ($1,000,000) was spent in soliciting new members. Communications, including the publishing of *The Women's Monitor* and the creation of a new Web site, consumed 4 percent (876,869) of the budget.

HISTORY

EMILY's List was founded in 1985 by Ellen Malcolm and 25 friends as a grassroots coalition of pro-choice activists. Discouraged by a lack of women congressional representatives and the growing political power of the pro-life movement, the group formed a political action committee to provide campaign money for pro-choice Democratic women candidates. At the time of EMILY's List's establishment, there were no women U.S. senators; EMILY's List began donating funds to this cause immediately.

Within a year of its founding, the EMILY's List membership rolls topped 1,100 and the group celebrated its first success as a contributor to a successful campaign. In 1986 Barbara Mikulski of Maryland became the first Democratic woman senator elected in her own right. By 1988 EMILY's List had become the nation's largest financial resource for Democratic women, and in 1990 donations to EMILY's List exceeded $1 million for the first time. In the same year EMILY's List contributed to the successful gubernatorial races of Ann Richards of Texas and Barbara Roberts of Oregon.

In the early 1990s, one of the most important events in the history of EMILY's List occurred—Supreme Court Justice Clarence Thomas's confirmation hearings. During the hearings, lawyer Anita Hill accused the Supreme Court nominee of having sexually harassed her while she worked under him at the Equal Employment Opportunity Commission. Despite Hill's charges, Thomas was confirmed by Congress, and many angry women joined EMILY's List in order to express their dismay politically. These voters believed they could send a message to Congress through the polls. To understand the effect of the Hill-Thomas hearings on EMILY's List, one needs only to look at the organization's membership rolls, which grew 600 percent from 3,500 members before the hearings in 1991, to 24,000 members in 1992, after the hearings.

These freshly mobilized female voters, combined with EMILY's List contributions, helped 1992 become "The Year Of The Woman." A record four Democratic women were elected to the U.S. Senate and 21 to the U.S. House of Representatives. It was the biggest one-time

BUDGET:
1996 EMILY Expenses

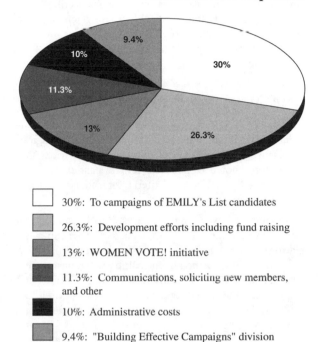

☐	30%: To campaigns of EMILY's List candidates
▢	26.3%: Development efforts including fund raising
▢	13%: WOMEN VOTE! initiative
▢	11.3%: Communications, soliciting new members, and other
▢	10%: Administrative costs
▢	9.4%: "Building Effective Campaigns" division

electoral gain for women in U.S. history. In 1996 the 45,000 EMILY's List members donated more than $6.7 million to candidates, making EMILY's List the largest source of contributions to Democratic female federal candidates.

CURRENT POLITICAL ISSUES

Although EMILY's List is primarily concerned with one political issue, reproductive rights, the group has invariably found itself in the midst of others. Most notably, EMILY's List has been at the center of a battle over the practice of bundling, an effective method of avoiding campaign contribution restrictions. Although no measures have yet been passed regarding this type of campaign funding, Congress has considered legislation prohibiting bundling three times since 1992. EMILY's List believes it should be exempt from any such legislation because it is a non-lobbying PAC, meaning it theoretically expects nothing in exchange for contributions. To combat restrictive legislation, EMILY's List hired lobbyists to oppose bundling reform initiatives.

As a decidedly pro-choice organization, EMILY's List is under constant criticism by conservative pro-life writers and politicians. The group's liberal endorsement policy also sometimes brings EMILY's List into affiliation with candidates whose views are not always mainstream. This further attracts attention from critics who label EMILY's List a "radical" group. Such negative attention has, at times, colored the way the organization is viewed by the public and may harm its political effectiveness.

Case Study: Garamendi vs. Pombo

In 1992 EMILY's List donors gave Democratic candidate Patti Garamendi $60,000 toward her campaign to represent California's 11th Congressional District. As a viable, pro-choice Democratic female candidate, Garamendi met EMILY's List criteria for endorsement and campaign support.

Garamendi was running against Republican Richard Pombo in a conservative district. As part of her campaign platform, however, she actively supported rap musician Ice-T in his First Amendment battles with conservative commentators and politicians over his song "Cop Killer." Garamendi attacked her opponent for not supporting Ice-T's First Amendment rights. She ran advertisements that showed burning crosses and accused Pombo of racism. This support of Ice-T's First Amendment rights, although not radical in theory, was poorly executed during Garamendi's campaign. The attacks and advertising did more to stigmatize Garamendi than her opponent, and Garamendi ultimately lost the election.

This type of situation has the potential to harm EMILY's List in its mission. If the group is branded too radical because of associations with candidates, prospective donors may be reluctant to give money to the organization. Candidates might also believe involvement with EMILY's List may hurt their candidacy. And potential workers may be reluctant to work for an organization whose beliefs are inconsistent with their own.

SUCCESSES AND FAILURES

When EMILY's List was founded in 1985, no Democratic woman had ever been elected to the U.S. Senate in her own right. In the U.S. House of Representatives, the number of elected women had been declining for 11 years. But by 1988, those trends were reversed when EMILY's List supported campaigns of pro-choice Democratic women candidates. By 1998 EMILY's List had contributed to the successful campaigns of 42 pro-choice female U.S. Representatives, 6 U.S. Senators, and three state governors.

Perhaps a better measure of the success of EMILY's List is the phenomenal reaction by other interest groups.

Several have since copied the fund-raising methods and unique organizational structure of EMILY's List. There has also been an explosion of similar PACs. PAM's List (an acronym for Power and Money) and W.I.N. (Women in the Nineties) are two state-level imitators. In 1992 the Labor Party in England formed EMILY's List, United Kingdom, with ambitions similar to those of the U.S. organization. Most strikingly, a group of moderate Republican women have started WISH List (Women in the Senate and House)—an organization designed to provide financial and tactical support to the candidacies of pro-choice Republican women.

FUTURE DIRECTIONS

EMILY's List seeks to do more than build campaign war chests. Through its training programs and its WOMEN VOTE! initiative, EMILY's List wants to become a full service political organization that provides candidates with interpretations of voter trends, demographic analysis, and funding patterns. In the words of Ellen Malcolm, "We expect to be one of the major political centers. Our slogan could be, 'if you want to understand women as political force, come to EMILY's List.'" A current goal is to nurture more candidates at the local and school board level by dedicating more money to those races. This will help ensure candidate loyalty as a candidate moves up the political ladder.

GROUP RESOURCES

EMILY's List maintains an extensive Web site at http://www.emilyslist.org. The Web site, which is open to non-members, offers campaign updates, budget information, and *The Women's Monitor*, the organization's poll of female voters. Parties interested in EMILY's List's annual convention (The Majority Council Conference), EMILY's List Training Department programs, or EMILY's List may telephone (202) 326-1400 or write to Early Money is Like Yeast's List, 805 Fifteenth St., Ste. 500, Washington, DC 20005 for more information.

GROUP PUBLICATIONS

EMILY's List distributes *The Women's Monitor*, the organization's poll of female voters, to its candidates. In 1996 EMILY's List research staff published nine issue-briefing books for its candidates and two issue-briefing books for Democratic nominees and progressive organizations. These briefing books were information updates on legislation concerning abortion, agriculture, the federal budget, civil rights, congressional reform, crime, defense, education, the environment, foreign affairs, health care, labor, and welfare reform

EMILY's List keeps its members updated on its candidates with *News from EMILY*, an E-mail newsletter. *Notes from EMILY* is also available via the World Wide Web at http://www.emilyslist.org/el-join/notes.html.

BIBLIOGRAPHY

Brotman, Barbara. "GOP Version of EMILY's List." *Chicago Tribune*, 16 June 1992.

Corn, David. "EMILY's Pissed: EMILY's List Versus Campaign Finance Reform." *The Nation*, 3 May 1993.

Ferguson, Andrew. "The Year of the Female Impersonator." *Washingtonian*, November 1994.

Freidman, Jon. "The Founding Mother." *New York Times Magazine*, 2 May 1993.

Hirschmann, Susan. "EMILY's List: Chicks with Checks: The Year of the Woman Produces the PAC of the Year." *American Spectator*, April 1993.

Kemper, Vicki. "The Year of the Woman's Wallet: Election Fundraising in 1992." *Common Cause Magazine*, Winter 1992.

Kretchmar, Laurie. "IBM Heir: Cash for Democratic Women." *Fortune*, 6 April 1992.

McCarthy, Abigail. "Women and Money and Politics." *Commonweal*, 15 August 1997.

Madigan, Charles. "Angry Women Voters Turning to Dems." *Chicago Tribune*, 12 May 1996.

Pilger, John. "EMILY Wouldn't Like It: EMILY's List OK on the Labor Party's Social Justice Agenda." *New Statesman*, 7 July 1995.

Rudy, Kathy. *Beyond Pro-Life and Pro Choice: Moral Diversity in the Abortion Debate*. Boston: Beacon Press, 1996.

Staggenborg, Susan. *The Pro-Choice Movement Organization and Activism in the Abortion Conflict*. New York: Oxford University Press, 1991.

Families and Work Institute (FWI)

ESTABLISHED: 1989
EMPLOYEES: 18
MEMBERS: None
PAC: None

Contact Information:

ADDRESS: 330 7th Ave., 14th Fl.
New York, NY 10001
PHONE: (212) 465-2044
FAX: (212) 465-8637
E-MAIL: afarber@familiesandwork.org
URL: http://www.familiesandworkinst.org
PRESIDENT: Ellen Galinsky

WHAT IS ITS MISSION?

According to the organization, "The Families and Work Institute is a nonprofit organization that addresses the changing nature of work and family life. We are committed to finding research-based strategies that foster mutually supportive connections among workplaces, families, and communities. We: identify emerging work-life issues, considering the entire life cycle, from prenatal and child care to elder care, and all levels of employees, from managers to assembly-line workers at all types of organizations; benchmark solutions to work-life problems across all sectors of society—business, education, community, and government—and serve as a broker to build connections among these sectors; and evaluate the impact of solutions on employees, their families, their communities, and on the productivity of employers."

As American women have entered the workforce in increasing numbers, families have sought new ways to deal with issues such as child care and career mobility. Single-parent families, too, are increasingly faced with the challenges of managing work and family. Employers have started to consider issues such as child care leave, flexible time, and alternative working conditions such as telecommuting. Through its research, consulting, and information sharing activities, the Families and Work Institute (FWI) tracks the implications of family and work trends in the United States and offers strategies for dealing with these trends.

HOW IS IT STRUCTURED?

The FWI headquarters are located in New York City. A 12-member board of directors works with FWI staff to advise, create recommendations, and set policy. Board members serve three-year renewable terms; a smaller nominating committee selects individuals for board or executive positions, including the president of the organization. The president serves for an indefinite term at the discretion of the board.

Because FWI staff numbers are small, employees rotate among administrative and program coordination responsibilities. Staff members have backgrounds in consulting and research, in areas including business, public policy, early childhood development, and psychology. The organization has no affiliates or members, but FWI staff frequently hire or collaborate with outside resources, such as polling firms and universities, to carry out large-scale research.

PRIMARY FUNCTIONS

FWI is primarily a research organization that is concerned with work and family issues like early childhood development and the family-friendly employer. It makes its research reports available to the general public, corporations, and government in order to provide tangible facts that will shape debates around family and work issues.

FWI also works to educate the public on how to improve the family and workplace through conferences, workshops, and other projects. An annual FWI conference is open to all and draws attendees from all over the United States. The organization also holds workshops aimed at helping employers and employees deal with work and family issues. Workshops have addressed general topics like evaluating and developing family policy, but FWI also works directly with companies to address their particular concerns.

PROGRAMS

In keeping with the organization's mission, FWI programs seek to improve the understanding of the relationship between families and workplaces. FWI research targets a variety of issues, and through its educational programs informs the public of the results and their significance.

One of FWI's main research and education programs is the Fatherhood Project, which was founded by Dr. James Levine in 1981 and became part of FWI in 1989. This project is an ongoing effort to study and strengthen the role of the father in the family—particularly a father's contribution to raising children. The Fatherhood Project

carries out its goals through training, workshops, consultation, and media presentation. For example, the project aired a PBS program in 1998 called *Fatherhood USA*, which examined the stereotypes and issues around fatherhood and suggested ways to strengthen a father's role. As part of the federal government's Head Start program to improve the lives of underprivileged children, the Fatherhood Project trains professionals to get fathers more involved in the lives of their children.

The Community Mobilization Forum is an FWI program created to gather the input of working citizens. The forum is a process designed to help communities discuss issues and improve circumstances that relate to families and community life. The Community Mobilization Forum provides process tools such as assessing the problem being addressed, getting appropriate people involved, maintaining momentum, measuring results, and financing the process. An FWI Web site bulletin board facilitates additional discussion about the forum among a wide audience.

BUDGET INFORMATION

FWI is a national nonprofit organization. Funding for FWI research comes from U.S. foundations and corporations. For fiscal year 1997, FWI had a total of $4,108,828 in revenue; this included grant supported research ($3,526,209), client supported research ($223,502), publications and information services ($200,899), contributions ($169,500), interest income ($40,176), and other income ($16,954). Expenses for fiscal year 1997 totaled $4,020,175 and included: Program Services including Community Life ($2,231,416), Families ($408,591), and Work Life ($712,591); Information Services ($96,800); and Support Services including administration ($493,732) and fund raising ($77,045). In a separate expense breakout, largest expenses went toward salaries ($1,090,154) and consultants ($1,834,224).

HISTORY

FWI was founded in 1989, when two researchers in the fields of families and work issues—Dana Friedman and Ellen Galinsky—saw a need for more information on related issues. Combining diverse backgrounds from both academia and the business world, the women created what started out as both a consulting and research organization. Friedman served as president until 1996, when Galinsky took over.

While FWI provided corporate consulting at first, it gradually moved away from this service to concentrate on independent research. By 1996 FWI had completely left the consulting arena. FWI first gained national recognition in 1991 with the release of their first study, a cor-

BUDGET:

1997 FWI Revenue

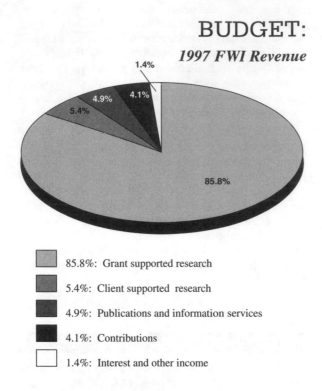

- 85.8%: Grant supported research
- 5.4%: Client supported research
- 4.9%: Publications and information services
- 4.1%: Contributions
- 1.4%: Interest and other income

1997 FWI Expenses

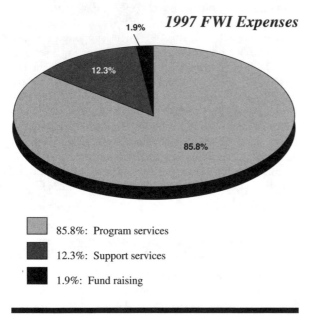

- 85.8%: Program services
- 12.3%: Support services
- 1.9%: Fund raising

porate guide to work and families. The study, which was unlike anything previously published, rated corporations on what they offered families and employees. Not only did it provide recognition for the organization, but it's ratings and information about various U.S. corporations laid out benchmark data for future studies. The organi-

zation went on to study issues that connected work and family life, such as child care, elder care, fatherhood, and community programs. By the late 1990s FWI had published 40 such studies.

FWI played a part in the early 1990s in gaining legal rights for working families. Data from a 1992 FWI study was used in congressional debates to shape the Family and Medical Leave Act—a piece of legislation that was later passed and which required employers to offer 12 weeks of unpaid leave to qualified employees to care for family members in situations such as the birth of a child or the illness of an elder relative. The study assessed programs in several states that were already offering mandatory leave to employees.

During the late 1990s the organization continued to monitor social issues that affected work and families, including the changing aspects of the workforce. In 1997 the organization published *The 1997 National Study of the Changing Workforce,* which compiled the results of interviews with almost 3,000 employees. Among the findings of the study was that work benefits which facilitate better family life have not improved substantially. Also, people are spending more time working, men are taking on more of traditional women's roles at home, and workers have more opportunities for autonomy and less for advancement.

CURRENT POLITICAL ISSUES

While FWI is strictly a research organization and does not advocate for particular issues, the organization's research does affect political change. Many areas of interest to FWI are also a source of great social concern and political debate. For example, FWI has carried out research that looks at a father's role in the family and how that role is affected by work. The need for single parents, male and female, to work and therefore spend less time with their children has been linked to a number of social ills including drug abuse and dropping out of school.

Another area of interest to FWI is women in the workplace who also have families. As more women enter the workforce, Americans have had to reevaluate traditional family roles. According to data cited in a *Knight-Ridder/Tribune News Service* article (May 16, 1995), 57.5 million women were working in 1995. More than half of these women provided at least half of their total household income. Studies done in the late 1980s and 1990s indicated that women also have a psychological attachment to their careers—a 1989 survey of 745 Detroit women who worked, found that these women, when they stopped working to care for their children, were 30 percent more distressed than their counterparts who returned to work. Overall, FWI research showed that work, for women and men, goes beyond income considerations and that psychological and other value considerations do come into play.

Case Study: Family Medical Leave—Working Parents Dilemma

Prior to 1993 no policy existed in the United States that required employers to grant time off after the birth of a child or for other family medical events. An employer could legally punish parents who did not return to work immediately after having a baby, regardless of the impact on the family or on newborn care. While maternity leave might be provided, no provisions were legally available for the father in a household.

FWI was interested in this issue because it affected both work and family life. The organization studied the effect of leave on employee productivity in the 1992 study *Parental Leave and Productivity: Current Research*, which looked at the cost of replacing the employee versus granting the leave and summarized manager experiences with leaves. Earlier FWI studies— *The Family-Friendly Employer: Examples from Europe* (1992) and *The Implementation of Flexible Time and Leave Policies: Observations from Employers* (1990)— provided an overview of innovative leave and flexible work policies in European countries, and possible applications in the United States of America.

Studies like these were cited and used heavily by Congress in an attempt to pass Family Medical Leave legislation that would allow employees to take time off for family medical situations. These initiatives were twice vetoed by President Bush. As the next U.S. president, Bill Clinton signed into law the Family Medical Leave Act (H.R. 1 ENR) which requires companies over a certain size to provide 12 weeks of unpaid leave to employees with a new baby in the family. The law gives employees the ability to take time off from work to deal with a myriad of details such as care of a newborn and other family adjustments.

Public Impact

The passage of the Family and Medical Leave Act gave families new legal rights in dealing with medical issues. Eligible employees (usually those who had worked for an employer for at least 12 months) were now entitled to 12 weeks of unpaid leave for situations that could include the birth of a baby or the adoption of a child. Qualified employees were now also eligible for unpaid leave to deal with any personal and serious medical situations or illnesses that prevented them from carrying out their jobs. Upon returning from the leave, employees were entitled to be reinstated in their previous job or given an equivalent position.

SUCCESSES AND FAILURES

While FWI has provided research that has influenced government policy, the fact that their research has

FAST FACTS

By 1998 almost half of the people in the United States felt that society incorrectly emphasizes work over leisure. Only 28 percent of Americans felt that way in 1986.

(Source: U.S. News and World Report and Bozell Worldwide 1997 poll data cited in: Stephanie Armour. "Working Less, Stressing More: Blame it on Downsizing, E-Mail, Laptops and Dual–Career Families." *USA TODAY,* March 13, 1998.)

not been received or used in college business curricula is a disappointment to the organization. FWI feels that their work is particularly relevant in a business education setting, where future business leaders learn how to run an effective company. According to the organization, FWI lacks the resources to forge and maintain an effective relationship with business educators.

FUTURE DIRECTIONS

Telecommuting, a trend that gathered momentum in the late 1990s, has the potential to redefine the relationship between families and work. According to an article in the *Jerusalem Post* (December 25, 1996), telecommuting grew at a rate of 10 to 15 percent per year between 1992 and 1996. The same article cited research from the New York market research firm Link Resources, which indicated that more than a third of American households had a least one person who worked from home. Many of these telecommuters are self-employed (45 percent, according to a survey by Find/SVP) and telecommuters who work for a company often foot much of the bill to set up an office at home. Telecommuting will impact many areas that FWI studies, including family relations, child care, and employer policy.

GROUP RESOURCES

The FWI Web site at http://www.familiesandworkinst.org. includes press releases, announcements of new publications, a place to order all publications, and a discussion forum at http://www.familicsandworkinst.org/forums/index.html. For more information on FWI programs or research, call (212) 465-2044 or write to 330 7th Ave., New York, NY, 10001.

GROUP PUBLICATIONS

FWI offers about two dozen reports of research findings that address family and work issues. Publications include *College and University Reference Guide to Work-Family Programs, Working Fathers: New Strategies for Combining Work and Family, Women: The New Providers: Whirlpool Foundation Study, Part One*, and *The Role of Child Care Centers in the Lives of Parents. Child Care Aware: A Guide to Promoting Professional Development in Family Child Care*, (Amy Laura Dombro, 1995) is a guidebook for communities in implementing effective childcare and is based on interviews and experiences of Child Care Aware staff in the United States. Another FWI publication, *The Study of Children in Family Child Care and Relative Care: Highlights of Findings* (Ellen Galinsky, Caroline Howes, Susan Kontos, and Marybeth Shinn, 1994) looks at what elements in child care programs are important, and how the addition of these elements affect children. The 1996 publication *Rethinking the Brain: New Insights into Early Development* summarizes the results of a FWI Brain Research Convention and the implications of current early development research. Publications may be ordered at the FWI web site http://www.familiesandworkinst.org, by faxing (212) 465-8637, or by mailing requests and payment to 330 7th Ave., New York, NY 10001.

BIBLIOGRAPHY

Boyd, Leslie. "Family: Giving Children a Good Start." *Gannett News Service*, 28 August 1996.

Chen, Edwin. "Parties Vying to Be a Woman's Best Friend." *Los Angeles Times,* 2 March 1998.

Dillner, Becky. "Single-Parenting Success." *Gannett News Service,* 27 January 1995.

Donahue, Tim. "Men Can Be Devoted Dads, Have Successful Careers, Too." *Gannett News Service,* 18 June 1995.

Frandsen, Jon. "Conservatives Say Emphasis on Day-Care Punishes Parents Who Stay at Home." *Gannett News Service,* 11 February 1998.

Franke-Folstad, Kim. "When Praising Families Don't Forget Single Parents." *Rocky Mountain News,* 24 February 1997.

Fyock, Catherine D. "Unretirement: A Golden Opportunity." *Human Resources Forum,* 1 February 1998.

Hochman, Nancy K. S. "Dr. James Kevine: Developing Child Care as a Man's Issue." *New York Times,* 28 December 1997.

Lewin,Tamar. "For Centers, Balancing Quality and Cost of Care." *New York Times,* 27 April 1998.

———. "Men Assuming Bigger Share at Home, New Survey Shows." *New York Times,* 15 April 1998.

Lynch, Michael, and Katherine Post. "What Glass Ceiling?" *The Public Interest,* 1 June 1996.

Rubenstein, Carin. "Superdad Needs a Reality Check." *New York Times,* 16 April 1998.

Simons, Janet. "Kid-Friendly Advocate For Child-Care Reform Out To Make It Everyone's Cause." *Rocky Mountain News,* 2 February 1998.

"The Workplace Turns to Telecommuting to Drive Productivity; Survey Reveals a Gap in Employer Responsibility, Leaving Opportunity for Corporate Leadership." *Business Wire,* 5 April 1998.

Whitmire, Richard. "Fatherless America: What Can Be Done?" *Gannett News Service,* 25 January 1995.

Family Research Council (FRC)

WHAT IS ITS MISSION?

In the words of the organization, "the Family Research Council (FRC) exists to reaffirm and promote, nationally, the traditional family unit and the Judeo-Christian value system upon which it is built. To accomplish this task, the Council will: promote and defend traditional family values in print, broadcast, and other media outlets; develop and advocate legislative and public policy initiatives which strengthen and fortify the family and promote traditional values; establish and maintain an accurate source of statistical and research information which reaffirms the importance of the family in our civilization; and inform and educate citizens on how they can promote Biblical principles in our culture."

Since its inception in 1983, the FRC has become one of the foremost groups to advocate for family values. The group, under the aggressive leadership of President Gary Bauer—a former White House policy adviser during the Reagan administration—has worked to ensure that the right-wing Christian perspective plays a role in U.S. policy development. FRC, in some ways, is more outspoken and radical than other Christian right-wing groups, according to an article in *Fortune* (September 8, 1997). For example, the FRC has advocated strongly against gay rights and trade with China—issues that some other Christian groups have taken a softer stance on. The FRC deals with a wide variety of issues that include AIDS funding, adoption and child care, publicly funded arts, drug abuse, pornography, the military, and welfare reform.

ESTABLISHED: 1983
EMPLOYEES: 100
MEMBERS: 450,000 constituents
PAC: Campaign for Working Families

Contact Information:

ADDRESS: 801 G St. NW
    Washington, DC 20001
PHONE: (202) 393-2100
TOLL FREE: (800) 225-4008
FAX: (202) 393-2134
E-MAIL: corrdept@frc.org
URL: http://www.frc.org
PRESIDENT: Gary L. Bauer

HOW IS IT STRUCTURED?

The FRC's main office is located in Washington, D.C. Heading the office is the president. The office includes a vice president for program planning, a director of communications, an assistant press secretary, policy analyst positions, and a vice president for resource development. Also housed in the Washington, D.C., office are the director of the Military Readiness Project, the chairman of the Cultural Renewal Initiative, a director of Cultural Studies, and a senior education adviser. FRC also supports and directs its political action committee (PAC), the Campaign for Working Families, which lobbies for legislation and candidates that support the organizational agenda.

The FRC has no affiliated state organizations, but does work closely with independent state Family Policy Councils (FPCs). FRC assists the FPCs with advocacy work by providing literature and resources when needed and sending representatives when on-site assistance is needed.

As a nonprofit organization, FRC has no dues-paying members but as many as 450,000 constituents receive FRC material and the organization's action alerts. As a nonprofit organization, FRC relies on grassroots mobilizing strategies that include calling on constituents to contact congressional members on particular issues. However, FRC works closely with a similar organization (American Renewal Association) and constituents can tap into that group if they want to take more action on a particular issue.

PRIMARY FUNCTIONS

The FRC works to advance its agenda in a number of ways. As part of its mission, the organization lobbies for legislation that supports its views of family values. FRC staff watch the legislative process closely, testify at hearings, coordinate the activities of the group's PAC, and meet with key policymakers. For example, in 1997, the organization unsuccessfully worked to influence Congress to override President Bill Clinton's veto of the Partial Birth Abortion Ban (H.R. 1122). This legislation would have penalized doctors who performed this controversial, late-term abortion procedure. A more favorable outcome occurred when the FRC and other similar groups successfully lobbied for and achieved the passage of the Taxpayer Relief Act of 1997 (H.R. 2014), which introduced tax credits of $500 per child for families.

Although the FRC does not have an organizational structure that extends to the grassroots level, it is aggressive in getting its message to people across the country. In 1997 members of the organization visited almost every state to make people aware of what they call the "pro-family" message. FRC representatives appeared at church functions and schools as well as other civic loca-

tions. The FRC sponsors seminars and organizes pro-family events. It also lends support for research projects. The FRC works closely with 35 state FPCs, which operate independently, but work to advance an agenda similar to the FRC's.

The organization makes aggressive use of media outlets and written informational material. President Gary Bauer hosts a daily radio commentary *Washington Watch*, which was broadcast on over 400 radio stations across the country in 1997. The FRC also produces a variety of publications, including the *Gary Bauer Monthly Newsletter* and *Washington Watch*, a publication that comes out 10 times a year and was circulated to 313,000 families in 1997. FRC staff members field media inquiries and make appearances on television shows such as *Good Morning America*. The organization also sponsors what it considers to be pro-family advertising. In a California 1997 legislative campaign, for example, Bauer and the FRC contributed $100,000 to an ad campaign that gave negative publicity to moderate Republican house candidate Brooks Firestone, who had refused to support the Partial Birth Abortion Ban.

Many of the issues that the FRC is concerned with deal with the choices that children and young adults in United States face. The FRC wants to influence the decision young people make regarding teen pregnancy, becoming sexually active, and having a sexual relationship and living with someone without being married. The FRC attempts to reach the young segment of the population by devoting a staff position in Washington to deal with these issues. HRC launched a newsletter in early 1998 called *i.e.* which is aimed at young adults and addresses pro-family issues. The premier issue covered topics such as abstinence and cohabitation.

PROGRAMS

FRC carries out a number of programs that advance its agenda. The Military Readiness Project is an informational initiative to get information out on military issues that concern FRC. FRC's positions on military-related issues include: banning gays in the military, prohibiting sale of pornography in military commissaries, and opposing women in combat. The project publishes the *One Minute Briefing*, a bimonthly newsletter mailed to military personnel and families, as well as others interested in these issues.

FRC's Cultural Renewal Initiative is directed by a chairperson; that person is responsible for speaking publicly and writing about certain family issues. Some of the issues that the project focuses on include childrearing in families, marriage and divorce, family work trends, and human sexuality.

In May 1997 FRC initiated the Witherspoon Fellowship Program, an internship program for college-age juniors and seniors. The program offers work experience and leadership development for up to 14 U.S. students annually. The FRC hopes, through the program, to create future leaders who will carry on the organization's mission and defend Christian and family values. Students serve an apprenticeship at FRC and contribute to research, articles, and other written material.

BUDGET INFORMATION

The FRC's growth in influence and effectiveness is reflected in its budget growth. According to a January 19, 1998, article in *Time*, FRC President Bauer transformed the organization when he took over in 1988, resulting in a growth in membership (from a 3,000-member mailing list to 455,000 members) and a budget that grew from $200,000 to $14 million.

In 1995 the organization had total revenue of $11,096,336, including $10,479,712 in contributions, $127,888 in program service revenue, $341,945 in interest, $92,860 in rental income, and $53,931 in other revenue. Expenses in 1995 totaled $10,296,719 and included: $8,159,821 in program services, $1,535,442 in management, and $601,456 in fund-raising. Of total expenses, some of the largest expenditure areas included salaries ($2,916,624 plus director's salary of $150,404) and printing and publications ($1,881,811).

HISTORY

The FRC was originally founded in 1983 as a conservative organization that advocated for issues affecting U.S. families. Key to the creation of the organization was James Dobson, a televangelist. In 1988 the FRC merged with Focus on the Family, another pro-family advocate group. In 1992 the HRC reorganized to become a distinct 501(c)(3)(h) nonprofit organization that allowed tax deductibility for contributors. The FRC is supported by grants and donations with the majority of donations coming from individuals.

In 1988 Gary Bauer took over as president of FRC, giving the organization an increasingly credible and aggressive demeanor. Bauer had previously served in the Reagan administration, first as a top education department official and then as director of the White House Office of Policy Development. Bauer came into FRC with a belief that Republican policies should be built on religious conservatism. Under his leadership, the FRC was involved in an increasingly broad range of family issues, some of which didn't necessarily match the moderate Republican party line. For example, Bauer and the FRC opposed certain initiatives that favored big business—initiatives that Republicans typically support—such as trade with China and the privatization of social

BUDGET:

1995 FRC Revenue

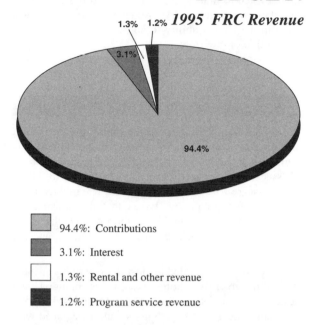

1.3% 1.2%

3.1%

94.4%

- ▨ 94.4%: Contributions
- ▨ 3.1%: Interest
- ☐ 1.3%: Rental and other revenue
- ▧ 1.2%: Program service revenue

1995 FRC Expenses

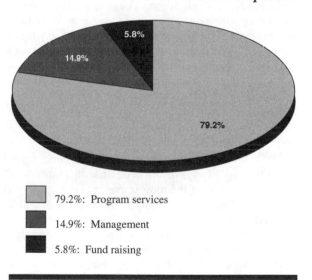

5.8%

14.9%

79.2%

- ▨ 79.2%: Program services
- ▨ 14.9%: Management
- ▧ 5.8%: Fund raising

security. The growth and broadening of the FRC agenda reflected the savvy that other groups of the religious right were acquiring. Once the butt of TV talk-show jokes, conservative religious groups such as FRC were developing the political savvy necessary to effectively shape public policy and make their message known.

The FRC continued to increase its effectiveness in 1996 when Bauer formed the organization's political action committee (PAC)—the Campaign for Working Families. It quickly grew into one of the largest PACs, raising $1.4 million (with 25,000 donors) in the next two years. A December 22, 1997, article in *National Review* called this an astonishing achievement for an organization devoted to family issues, but PAC officials claimed that the growth in the PAC reflected donor disappointment in the GOP's ability to address social issues such as abortion or gay rights.

CURRENT POLITICAL ISSUES

Given that the FRC exists to promote the family unit and the Judeo-Christian value system upon which it is built, the organization deals with a tremendous variety of issues. These issues range from gay rights to AIDS, from daycare to homeschooling, and from government reform to foreign policy. Issues that the organization dealt with in the 1990s included: abortion and other sanctity of life issues, social security privatization, and tax relief for families.

FRC has long battled against the gay rights agenda. According to FRC, homosexuality is immoral and destructive to society, individuals, and families. The FRC does not believe that gay rights should be equated with civil rights, and thus opposes gay initiatives such as same-sex marriage, benefits for partners, and adoption and custody privileges for gay couples. The organization takes the position that a gay lifestyle is a choice and can be unlearned. To advance their agenda in the gay rights arena, FRC produces issue statements and publications that explain their viewpoint. The organization is also active in supporting legislation that would slow the gay rights movement. For example, the FRC lobbied successfully for the Defense of Marriage Act (S.B. 1740), which was created to prevent the definition of marriage from expanding beyond the traditional union of man and woman. The legislation passed in late 1996.

FRC has always maintained that the sanctity of human life is one of the most important issues that they defend. To this end, the organization opposes abortion, assisted suicide, euthanasia, experimentation on unborn children, and cloning. These actions, FRC maintains, cheapen the value put on human life and contribute to societal decay. The FRC encourages legislation that would restrict doctors' ability to provide assisted suicide or euthanasia measures. The organization spoke out against cloning, calling it a procedure that transformed procreation into the customized production of humans or other species. FRC works to encourage the president of the United States to appoint pro-life Supreme Court judges, since many precedents around abortion issues have been set in court. FRC also took an active role in monitoring legislation that would imposed penalties on doctors for performing certain late term abortion procedures (the Partial Birth Abortion Ban, H.R. 1122); the legislation was passed by the House and the Senate in 1997 but later vetoed by President Clinton.

Although abortion and gay rights initiatives are probably some of the most controversial issues that FRC was involved with in the late 1990s, family tax reform is also an issue that the organization advocated successfully for in 1997.

Case Study: Taxpayer Credit for Families with Children

Taxpayer relief for families is a cause that pro-family groups such as FRC have long advocated for. One of the provisions that these groups have lobbied for includes a $500 per child tax credit for families. Once proposed as part of the "Contract With America" that Republicans backed in 1994, the legislation resurfaced in 1997 as the Taxpayer Relief Act (H.R. 2014). Specifically, HRC believed that passage of such legislation would strengthen U.S. families and finances, encourage family savings, and ensure that the best investment for children is made by parents who know what is best for their children.

Opponents of tax relief argued that such legislation would increase the federal deficit and spur inflation. But FRC maintained that the cost to the deficit would be more than made up by the strength to families that such legislation would provide. FRC felt that the cost of not providing such family relief would result in weaker family systems, and lead to increased divorce and crime.

In 1997 President Clinton signed into law the Taxpayer Relief Act, which included a provision for family tax credits of $500 per child. FRC played a large part in pushing for this legislation, using the usual lobbying strategies and producing media material on the subject. FRC President Bauer called the passage a win for U.S. families.

Public Impact

Opponents of the $500 credit for families with children point out that the policy benefits the middle class and upper middle class. This benefit phases out for households with combined income over $110,000. The benefit does not extend to individuals who do not make enough money to pay taxes, or who cannot afford to have children. The tax credit, opponents argue, also discriminates against those who may have children but are not recognized for tax purposes as families, such as same-sex couples. But such a bill supports everything that the FRC advocates for; the affirmation of the traditional family unit.

SUCCESSES AND FAILURES

While the passage of the 1997 Taxpayer Relief Act was FRC's biggest win during that year, the organization's greatest defeat was the failure to pass the Partial-

Birth Abortion Ban (H.R. 1122). Although FRC and other conservative religious and pro-life groups mounted an involved campaign against the late-term abortion procedure, President Clinton (traditionally a supporter of abortion rights) vetoed the proposed ban on the grounds that the procedure is necessary in cases where the mother's life may need to be saved. FRC and other antiabortion groups will continue to fight to eliminate abortion in the United States, or at least restrict certain types of procedures. FRC maintains that the sanctity of human life must continue to be protected, and that abortion rights have not contributed to stronger families or the well-being of women.

FUTURE DIRECTIONS

Although FRC and the religious right have come a long way toward becoming a serious force in politics, FRC may play an even bigger role in politics if its president, Gary Bauer, as has been rumored, runs as a GOP presidential candidate in 2000. The Republican Party perceives FRC and Bauer as being to the right of the moderate Republican stances, and fear that if he ran in the Republican primaries, the vote could split the party and weaken GOP effectiveness for the presidential bid. Nevertheless, Bauer and the FRC will continue to aim efforts at continuing to refocus the Republican Party and its agenda. The organization maintains that the GOP needs to focus its efforts to affirm the traditional family system. By doing so, the FRC says that the party will speak for a strong constituency that is looking for representation.

GROUP RESOURCES

FRC maintains a Web site at http://www.frc.org. The Web page offers detailed information on FRC positions, ways of providing support, and research and information related to issues on the FRC agenda. Such materials include newspaper editorials, transcripts of FRC speeches, a monthly fax of "Drug Facts," news releases, and policy papers. FRC makes publications, videos, and other merchandise available either by calling the organi-

zation directly, or ordering on the Web at http://www.townhall.com/cgi-bin/laforg. The FRC also maintains a Legislative Hotline. By dialing (202) 783-4663, you can access current information on pending family issues in Washington, D.C.

GROUP PUBLICATIONS

FRC publishes the *Washington Watch* 10 times per year, the *Gary Bauer Monthly Newsletter*, *Ed Facts* (weekly and available for a fee), *Family Policy* (six issues annually) and numerous press releases. Publications may be ordered by calling the organization directly or accessing their Web site at http://www.frc.org.

BIBLIOGRAPHY

"Abortion and the Republicans: Idealists v Realists." *The Economist,* 24 January 1998.

Borjas, George. "How Not to Save American Jobs." *National Review,* 22 December 1997.

Brogan, Pamela. "Industry Proposes Ways to Keep Kids From Gaining Access to Internet Smut." *Gannett News Service,* 1 December 1997.

Elsner, Alan. "Conservatives Score Upset in California Vote." *Reuters,* 14 January 1998.

Henderson, Rick. "MFNemies: Beijing's Atrocities Put Free-traders on the Defensive," *Reason,* 1 July 1997.

Innerst, Carol. "Some Kindergartners Are Taught About Homosexuality." *Washington Times,* 7 December 1997.

Swomley, John M. "New Strategies, New Groups (Activities of Right-wing Organizations)." *The Humanist,* 13 March 1997.

Wetzstein, Cheryl. "Anti-Porn Groups Say Clinton Let Them Down." *Washington Times,* 9 November 1997.

Whitwill, Stuart C. A. "Christian Conservatives Organize to Criticize ALA." *American Libraries,* November 1995.

Willis, Ellen. "Sunday Focus/Moralism and the Body Politic." *Newsday,* 1 February 1998.

Zabarenko, Deborah. "Gay Marriage Latest Family Values' Campaign Issue." *Reuters,* 14 June 1996.

Fraternal Order of Police (FOP)

ESTABLISHED: 1915
EMPLOYEES: 18 (1997)
MEMBERS: 277,000

Contact Information:

ADDRESS: 1410 Donelson Pike, A-17
    Nashville, TN 37217
PHONE: (615) 399-0900
TOLL FREE: (800) 451-2711
FAX: (615) 399-0400
E-MAIL: glfop@grandlodgefop.org
URL: http://www.grandlodgefop.org
NATIONAL PRESIDENT: Gilbert Gallegos

WHAT IS ITS MISSION?

The Fraternal Order of Police (FOP) is a labor union that bills itself as "the world's largest organization of sworn law enforcement officers." According to the organization's Web site, it is "committed to improving the working conditions of law enforcement officers and the safety of those who serve through education, legislation, information, community involvement and employee representation."

HOW IS IT STRUCTURED?

The FOP's day-to-day affairs are administered by a 15-person staff at the organization's national headquarters in Nashville, Tennessee. Daily operations are supervised by the national secretary, who is one of a seven-member executive board that oversees all FOP operations. The executive board is elected by FOP membership at the group's biennial conference. Overall FOP policy is set by its board of directors. The board of directors, which consists of the Executive Board, past presidents of the FOP, and a trustee from each state lodge, meets twice yearly.

Members of the FOP belong to local lodges, which cover cities or regions. The more than 2,000 FOP local lodges are organized into 42 state lodges, each of which has a voice on the FOP's board of directors. The FOP also has two affiliated organizations. The Auxiliary Group is a support organization for the wives and adult family of FOP members. The Fraternal Order of Police Associates is open to membership by anyone in the general public who wishes to support the FOP and law enforcement officers.

PRIMARY FUNCTIONS

As a labor union, the primary function of the FOP is to win the best possible wages and benefits for its members from their employers. For the most part, FOP negotiations take place at the local level. The FOP also works to organize new collective bargaining units, thereby increasing its membership and overall effectiveness. For instance, in 1997 the FOP successfully organized the 720-member Capitol Hill police force.

The FOP also seeks to influence legislation and public opinion about issues of concern for its members, and police in general. Through its Washington D.C., office, the FOP lobbies Congress for legislation that supports issues such as firearms laws. On occasion, the FOP challenges laws in court that it considers unjust. Through public education efforts, the FOP encourages the general public to support their local law enforcement.

PROGRAMS

FOP programs are designed primarily to provide special services and benefits to members of the union. For example, the FOP Legal Defense Plan makes special liability insurance coverage available to FOP members at an affordable price. The plan includes coverage that will assist an officer in paying legal fees if he or she is the subject of a lawsuit or administrative action. Liability insurance for special events such as concerts, dances, conventions, or other large gatherings where police officers might be hired to handle security in their off duty hours, is also available. The FOP also maintains educational and professional development seminars for its members, which help them stay at the top of their profession.

On May 15th of each year is National Peace Officers' Memorial Day. On this day, people around the country join in remembering police officers who have died in the line of duty. The FOP and FOP Auxiliary sponsor an Annual Memorial Service every May 15th, when the family and comrades of officers who lost their lives gather on the steps of the U.S. Capitol.

BUDGET INFORMATION

Not made available.

HISTORY

The FOP was created in 1915, during a time when "the life of a policeman was bleak," according to FOP literature. Officers were called on to work extremely long hours, and had few official outlets for complaint. In Pittsburgh, Pennsylvania, two patrol officers, Martin Toole and Delbert Nagle, decided to organize their fellow officers. They and 21 other officers seeking better working conditions met on May 14, 1915 to form an organization. William H. Larkin was the first president. Initially known as the United States Association of Police, within a year the group had adopted as its name the Fraternal Order of Police.

Bowing to the anti-union sentiment of the time, the FOP's constitution declared that it was not a labor union, and denounced the use of strikes by police officers. They called the units lodges rather than locals, the first was named Fort Pitt Lodge No. 1. The group's union-like aims were quickly apparent, however. Members went to Pittsburgh Mayor Joe Armstrong and announced their intention to bring their concerns over hours and pay before the city council.

By 1917 the FOP had grown to approximately 1,800 members. Under the leadership of Delbert Nagel, the FOP began to expand into a national organization. Its first national convention was held in Pittsburgh, Pennsylvania, in 1917, and in 1918 it began to publish the *FOP Journal*. The FOP began to quickly expand across the country, and police officers agitated, but did not strike, for higher pay and better working conditions. The organization was popular in the many areas where formal labor unions for police were illegal. The FOP's denunciation of the 1919 Boston police strike, and support of Governor Calvin Coolidge's use of state militia and firing of the officers who had gone on strike, gained the FOP national attention and the approval of the general public.

The 1920s saw significant gains for police officers in pay and benefits, including the enactment of an eight-hour workday law in Pennsylvania. The FOP supported efforts to arrest and deport seditious aliens during the so-called Red Scare, and pushed for federal handgun control laws. In the 1930s the main concern of the FOP, as it was for everyone, was the Great Depression. The FOP's efforts to maintain police officer's wages were largely unsuccessful, as were their protests against the extension of federal income taxes to include state and municipal employees by the Revenue Act of 1936.

Another concern of the FOP that developed during this period and continues to this day is the portrayal of police in the media. The FOP routinely protested against movies that glorified criminals while depicting police officers as brutal and inept. In the 1950s, its protests against NBC's teleplay *A Long Way Home* led the program's sponsor to withdraw its support. On the other hand, the organization approved of the television program *Dragnet,* and awarded its producer a special plaque for positively portraying police officers.

The late 1950s and 1960s saw police routinely involved in breaking up civil rights and anti-war demonstrations. Increasingly, such activities led to negative publicity for police officers, and the FOP defended officers against many charges of police brutality. The FOP also worked to defend its members from investigations by internal review boards, which were becoming increasingly common across the United States. The FOP maintained then and now that review boards are often unfair and unjustly deprive officers of the right to a fair hearing. The FOP protested against the U.S. Supreme Court's 1966 Miranda decision. This was the ruling which held that police officers must inform a suspect of their rights when they are arrested. The FOP felt that the Miranda decision placed undue restrictions on police officers and would only serve to hinder efforts to catch criminals.

In 1965 the FOP was an important supporter of federal legislation which led to the enactment of a federal survivorship benefit for the family of officers killed enforcing a federal law. Continued lobbying by the FOP led to the enactment of the 1976 Public Safety Officers Benefit Act, which paid $50,000 to the survivors of an officer who died while enforcing any law.

In 1982 the FOP Auxiliary and the FOP began to observe National Peace Officers' Memorial Day with a service at the U.S. Capitol in Washington, D.C. Although May 15th was designed as National Peace Officers' Memorial Day by President Kennedy in 1962, this was the first major service dedicated to fallen law enforcement officers.

In the 1980s and 1990s, enactment of a "Law Enforcement Officers' Bill of Rights" was a priority for the FOP. The rights that the FOP seeks are mostly protection for law enforcement officers under review by their own agencies, and include such concerns as the right to be informed of any investigations into their past activities, and the right to legal counsel at administrative hearings. The FOP's efforts have so far been unsuccessful. The FOP has also pushed for the enactment of laws that would allow public safety employees (police officers and firefighters) to join formal unions and bargain collectively for wages and benefits.

CURRENT POLITICAL ISSUES

The FOP supports legislation that helps law enforcement and labor unions including proposals to increase gun control measures and to protect and expand collective bargaining and organizing rights. Conversely, the organization fights legislation that it perceives would hurt the mission of police or organized labor.

For example, in the 1990s the FOP was among the groups that successfully opposed the various bills, usually referred to as the National Right to Work Act, that would have weakened labor unions by making it illegal to require members to pay dues. In 1998 the FOP succeeded in winning passage of a federal law that exempted law enforcement offices from following state and local laws that prohibited the carrying of a concealed weapons. The FOP's efforts to organize law enforcement officers can also lead to political controversy. In the late 1990s the FOP was critical of the Clinton administration for not allowing their union to organize the Secret Service.

Case Study: The Lautenberg Law

In the closing days of the 104th Congress in 1996, a bill called the Domestic Violence Offender Gun Ban was passed, over the protests of the FOP. This bill, often called the Lautenberg law, after its author, Senator Frank Lautenberg (D-N.J.), prohibited anyone who had ever been convicted of or pled guilty to a domestic violence charge, including a misdemeanor, from owning or carrying a gun.

The FOP began campaigning for changes to the Lautenberg law as soon as it was passed. The reason for the FOP's urgency was that, in a departure from other federal gun ban laws, the Lautenberg did not exclude law officers from the ban. Even worse, in the FOP's eyes, was the fact that the law applied to any domestic violence convictions, even those decades in the past. These two facts combined to mean that police officers with years of distinguished service but also with a domestic violence offense in their past, could lose their jobs because the Lautenberg law prevents them from carrying a weapon.

The FOP believes that such firings are unnecessary and unjust, but many supporters believe that the law should apply to everyone, including law officers, and regardless of when the crime was committed. Supporters of the law feel that domestic violence is a serious problem, and that preventing offenders from carrying a gun is a preventive measure. The FOP agrees that domestic violence is a serious problem that needs to be addressed. The organization points out that police officers are frequently called in to deal with domestic violence, and thus they are well aware of the potential danger. The FOP claims that officers are much more likely to be attacked during a domestic violence call than, for example, during an arrest.

The main objection the FOP has to the Lautenberg law is not that it applies to police officers, but that it covers crimes committed long before the law was ever passed. As a representative of the people who must enforce this law, the FOP feels that it places an impossible burden on the police. Because there was no national effort to track domestic violence offenses before the Lautenberg law, it is nearly impossible to identify past offenders. Therefore, few industries actually enforce the background check. Indeed, the FOP asserts that the only place where the backgrounds of potential gun carriers are being checked are law enforcement agencies.

The FOP has pursued changes to the Lautenberg law on several fronts. They have supported bills introduced by Representative Bob Barr (R-Georg.) that would make the Lautenberg law apply only to domestic violence crimes committed after the law was enacted. There has been opposition, however, from those who feel that no one who as committed an act of domestic violence should be employed by a police agency anyway. The FOP agrees that no police department would ever knowingly employ a domestic abuser. Another obstacle to passage of Representative Barr's bill has been the presence of other proposals, including some that would repeal the Lautenberg law outright, or cause it to no longer apply to law enforcement officers. The FOP does not endorse these bills, as they feel that the ban for domestic abusers is a good idea in principle, even when applied to law enforcement officers.

To address the urgent concern of police officers being fired from their jobs, the FOP also challenged the Lautenberg law in court. This effort has met with mixed results. While their initial case was thrown out of court, an appeal led to a verdict that sections of the Lautenberg law that could cost law officers their jobs were unconstitutional. The government then appealed the case, and in April of 1999 the verdict was reversed again, with the Lautenberg law being found fully constitutional. The FOP has vowed to appeal this verdict to the U.S. Supreme Court.

FUTURE DIRECTIONS

While the late 1990s saw a nationwide drop in crime, there are many trends which the FOP finds troubling. The FOP is disturbed by the trend toward more violent acts by younger and younger teens and even children, as well as the spread of lethal technology such as armor-piercing bullets and guns that can evade X-ray devices. The FOP plans to push for new legislation that addresses these issues. Some of the ideas that FOP hopes to see implemented include a ban on ammunition capable of piercing body armor, higher penalties for criminals who use firearms equipped with laser sights, and tougher penalties for juvenile criminals.

GROUP RESOURCES

The FOP maintains a Web site at http://www.grandlodgefop.org, with information for the public about the organization and its concerns. Available information includes details on the group's officers and major activities, links to lodges and affiliated groups, and updates on laws, lawsuits, and legislation that are important to the FOP.

GROUP PUBLICATIONS

The FOP has a periodical publication, *National F.O.P. Journal*, that discusses the organization's activities, and issues of concern to the law enforcement field. The magazine is free for members and $10 per year for nonmembers. For information, contact the FOP by mail at FOP Grand Lodge, 1410 Donelson Pike, A-17, Nashville, TN 37217, or call (615) 399-0900.

BIBLIOGRAPHY

Bridger, Chet. "Police Want Arrest Rights." *Federal Times*, 31 March 1997.

Church, George J. "The Ad Wars Turn Nasty." *Time*, 30 September 1996.

Clinton, Bill. "Teleconference Remarks to the Fraternal Order of Police." *Weekly Compilation of President Documents*, 7 August 1995.

Daniel, Lisa. "Capitol Hill Police Elect First Union." *Federal Times*, 30 June 1997.

"Fight for the Light." *The Nation*, 26 June 1995.

"Fond Memorial." *Billboard*, 7 June 1997.

Howard, Theresa. "Calling All Cops: Let LJ's Campaign Drive Full Speed Ahead." *Nation's Restaurant News*, 13 October 1997.

Rivenbark, Leigh. "Police Balk at Gun Law." *Federal Times*, 10 February 1997.

Rivenbark, Leigh. "Secret Service: Cops or Not?" *Federal Times*, 27 May 1996.

Winters, Paul. *Policing the Police*. San Diego, Calif.: Greenhaven Press, 1995.

Gray Panthers

ESTABLISHED: August 1970
EMPLOYEES: 5 (1997)
MEMBERS: 35,000 (1997)
PAC: None

Contact Information:

ADDRESS: 733 15th St. NW #437
     Washington, DC 20006
PHONE: (202) 466-3132
TOLL FREE: (800) 280-5362
FAX: (202) 466-3133
E-MAIL: info@graypanthers.org
URL: http://www.graypanthers.org
EXECUTIVE DIRECTOR: Dixie Horning

WHAT IS ITS MISSION?

The Gray Panthers is an advocacy organization whose members politicize for social change in many areas including health care, social security, housing, environment, education, and peace. The name of this organization can be deceiving because membership in the Gray Panthers is not restricted to senior citizens. The Gray Panthers' motto, in fact, declares, "Age and Youth in Action." This underlying theme of Gray Panthers is unique because it, ". . . distinguishes [itself] from conventional groups for older people [by refusing] to pit the interests of the old against those of the young. [T]he Panthers fight for everyone's place at the table," as reported in *Nation*.

HOW IS IT STRUCTURED?

The Gray Panthers maintains a national headquarters in Washington, D.C. A board of directors oversees the group at the national level. The board hires an executive director, deputy director, director of public policy and media, and a grass roots organizer. Local chapters are convened into 17 regional networks; a "convenor" directs each network.

The national organization holds biennial conferences where the delegates define agendas and assign the members to assorted task forces. Each task force addresses a specific arena of concern, such as foreign policy, sustainable environment, national health care, and affordable housing.

Local chapters of the organization are self-governing. Meeting attendance is generally free, and official membership is available through local chapters. The general membership comprises people of all ages, as the organization reiterates in its published description, "[J]ustice is sought for all age groups."

PRIMARY FUNCTIONS

The Gray Panthers engage in a wide and varied array of activities. Members testify before legislators and other civic bodies. They also participate in political demonstrations and seek media attention in order to focus public attention on the organization's key issues.

Information Dissemination and Community Activism

The Gray Panthers upholds specific political principles and priorities as defined by the organization at the national level. These principles include the need for an equitable and universal health care system, the need to reduce military spending, the need for affordable housing, the need to preserve the environment, and the need to end discrimination. Local chapters of the Gray Panthers organize groups who work to resolve and address the political agenda as defined by the national Gray Panthers organization. For instance, a local Gray Panthers chapter might collaborate with a county-sponsored health insurance counseling program to educate seniors on new changes in Medicare. The Gray Panthers take advantage of, and participate in, public statewide conferences on environmental topics such as the protection of public resources. Regional meetings of the Gray Panthers are held periodically to discuss topics such as the future of Medicare. Seminars are likely to focus on any Gray Panthers agenda, in association with other advocacy groups such as the Older Women's League (OWL).

Legal and Legislative Activities

The Gray Panthers confronts various issues that are important to its members. In 1996, for example, the National Gray Panthers Project Fund filed *amicus curiae* (friend of the court) briefs in collaboration with other social justice groups in support of the right of every person to receive assisted suicide as a medical treatment. The amicus curiae briefs were filed in a case before the Supreme Court of the state of Washington.

Aside from legal advocacy, the Gray Panthers respond to emergency situations worldwide with whatever resources it can muster. After Hurricane Mitch in 1998, the Gray Panthers collected money and medicines to send to the afflicted areas. Gray Panther representatives further contacted political officials in Washington, D.C. to encourage the U.S. government to forgive all debts to the afflicted countries and to convince the members of the International Monetary Fund (IMF) to do the same.

PROGRAMS

The Gray Panthers' programs revolve primarily around public education. By utilizing its resources, the organization hopes to further its vision of a social structure in which the young and old can live in relative harmony; educating the public through its programs is an effective way of accomplishing this goal.

National Committee for Responsive Philanthropy (NCRP)

NCRP, founded in 1976, by a group of prominent nonprofit organizations—including the Gray Panthers, the National Congress of American Indians, and the NOW Legal Defense and Education Fund—calls attention to unfair practices involving charity fundraising. NCRP reports on philanthropic organizations, especially with respect to "alternative" funding sources, for non-traditional groups including women, aged, gays, and other advocacy charities. NCRP, for example, protests the policies of the United Way campaign which ignores the concerns and needs of non-traditional charities. In essence, the NCRP is a radical group that exists in contention with traditional charities that fail to share resources with non-traditional and advocacy organizations.

The NCRP continually conducts research and issues reports. The NCRP has released approximately one dozen reports about charities, especially those promoted in the workplace. The NCRP reports discussed the inequities of some charities. A report on "Women's Funds" was published in 1986, and in 1990 a report on "Right wing Attacks on Corporate Giving" was issued. "United Way's Donor Choice: Who Benefits?" appeared in 1992. The NCRP's flagship report, "Moving a Public Policy Agenda: the Strategic Philanthropy of Conservative Foundations" appeared in July of 1997. That report studied the impact of conservative foundations and institutions on politics and on public opinion. Additionally NCRP publishes periodic reports on corporate grant-making policies, and offers technical assistance to start-up alternative funds.

Age and Youth in Action Summit

The first National Age and Youth in Action Summit held on May of 1997 in Washington, D.C. was hosted by the Gray Panthers, the United States Student Association (USSA), the Students Environmental Action Council (SEAC), the Older Women's League (OWL), and other groups. It concentrated its efforts upon creating a forum for common dialogue between young and old and identifying solutions to common problems.

BUDGET INFORMATION

The National Gray Panthers Project Fund (NGPPF), with reported assets of $684,275 in 1995, operates on a budget of approximately $200,000 per year. In 1997 the Gray Panthers Project Fund budget of $260,000 went to support efforts toward the establishment of a national health care system. In the process of accomplishing its ends the project fund supports a staff of five employees, including one executive director, one fund-raiser, two office mangers, and one writer. All of the funding for the Gray Panthers is the result of direct mail campaigns.

HISTORY

The Gray Panthers was the brainchild of social activist Margaret Kuhn of Buffalo, New York. Kuhn, along with a handful of her friends, founded the organization in 1970 in reaction to a forced retirement imposed upon her at age 65 by the United Presbyterian Church of New York, her employer of 25 years. The group initially called themselves Consultation of Older and Younger Adults for Social Change. Their purpose was to redefine the role of senior citizens in U.S. society and to unite older and younger Americans behind social change.

Almost immediately the small group of seniors joined with a band of college students to protest the U.S. war effort in Vietnam. One year later the fledgling organization had multiplied, from Kuhn and her original five organizers to 100 members. The group gained increasing visibility and established an office in the basement of an old church in Philadelphia, Pennsylvania. Around the same time the Consultation of Older and Younger Adults for Social Change was attracting media attention and the name Gray Panthers was coined by a TV reporter in 1972. Eventually the name was officially adopted by the organization. It called attention to the parallels between the militant Black Panthers of the Civil Rights movement and the radical ideas of the Consultation of Older and Younger Adults for Social Change.

In 1973 the Gray Panthers merged with a group called the Retired Professional Action Group, an organization directed by consumer activist and attorney, Ralph Nader. Nader personally donated a generous sum of $25,000 to the organization. The combined group studied the conditions and quality of U.S. nursing homes in 1977 and issued a publication called "Nursing Homes: A Citizens' Action Guide." Additionally, the newly merged group established a "Media Watch" program to revise the media image associated with the aged. The Gray Panthers also presented papers to the American Medical Association (AMA) protesting the profit motive that overshadows health care in the U.S. health care industry.

During the 1980s the Gray Panthers were involved in organized protests in support of a federally supported national health care system. The group continued to support reductions in military spending and environmental interests. It was during that time, in the early 1980s, that the Gray Panthers earned recognition as a non-government organization (NGO) by the United Nations.

In 1985 the group expanded its operations and opened an office in Washington, D.C. The Gray Panthers' national operations were centralized there in 1990. Founder Maggie Kuhn died in 1995 at the age of 89 years, just weeks after she attended the 10th biennial convention of the Gray Panthers. The Gray Panthers membership was declining in the 1990s and their numbers had dwindled to 40,000 by the time of Kuhn's death. In an effort to regroup from the loss of Kuhn, the Gray Panthers held its first annual National Age and Youth in Action Summit and selected a new board of directors in 1997.

CURRENT POLITICAL ISSUES

Political issues espoused by the Gray Panthers typically focus on the importance of life, and the need to protect and preserve it. Anti-war demonstrations, improvements in nursing home facilities, and better access to health care are among the humanitarian causes espoused by Gray Panthers over the years. With regard to the issue of euthanasia, the Gray Panthers nonetheless uphold the right of the individual to choose to die.

Case Study: Assisted Suicide

Assisted suicide is a procedure whereby a person who is experiencing exceptional suffering from a terminal illness may be permitted to employ the services of a doctor, in order to further hasten imminent death. Assisted suicide is a highly emotional issue. Results of various opinion polls in this matter indicate that the general population is divided almost equally over assisted suicide.

During the 1994 elections in the state of Oregon, a ballot initiative called Measure 16 or "Death with Dignity" won approval by the voters by a two percent margin. Under Oregon's Measure 16, a doctor was allowed to prescribe a lethal prescription to a patient under certain conditions: at least two doctors needed to concur that the patient was terminally ill and could not possibly live longer than six months and the patient made persistent requests for assistance in suicide. Some believed that Measure 16 won voter approval because few voters were aware that the measure would support physician-assisted suicide through the Oregon Health Plan. Efforts made by groups such as the National Right-to-Life Committee to overturn the measure were unsuccessful through mid-1999. The measure continues to be challenged, however, at the state and federal level.

Shortly before Measure 16 appeared on the Oregon ballot, Attorney General Dennis Vacco of New York brought suit in his state to challenge the legality of assisted-suicide legislation. In his arguments Vacco suggested the scenario that cost-conscious managed care facilities might find it lucrative to encourage patients to request assisted suicide rather than to become involved in expensive medical treatment. This point was clearly demonstrated by the case of one health maintenance organization (HMO) in the State of Oregon that agreed to pay the cost for physician-assisted suicide, but denied reimbursement to AIDS patients for costly HIV medications. In New York, as well as Oregon, the court banned the assisted suicide procedures as unconstitutional.

A group of doctors in New York contested the ban on assisted suicide and were joined in their argument by the late Rita Barrett, a cancer patient with only slim hope for survival. As her legacy, she collaborated with the doctors who contested the ban on assisted suicide. Barrett died a natural death before the matter went to trial, but in December 1994 Judge Thomas Griesa of the U.S. District Court reinforced the ban. The case was appealed at the same time as an appeal of a similar ban in Washington state, brought about in an action by Attorney General Christine O. Gregiore.

Gray Panthers was cited in the press as the only seniors group to come forward publicly and take a stand on the issue of assisted suicide. Bobi Gary, then co-president of the Portland Gray Panthers chapter, agreed that there are drawbacks and risks associated with the administration of doctor-assisted suicide. She acknowledged the valid concern that persons at the lowest income levels might become easy prey for managed care organizations which might encourage the procedure because it is less costly than expensive life-saving therapies. Gary supported the measure nonetheless because it affords the patient a "choice in your own death," as quoted in Portland Skinner in 1997.

When the appeal was heard in 1996 by the Supreme Court, the International Anti-Euthanasia Task Force filed a friend-of-the-court document in support of the state's arguments. Documents defending assisted suicide were filed by the Gray Panthers Project Fund and the Gray Panthers of Washington, along with activist groups including the American Civil Liberties Union, Japanese American Citizens League, Hemlock Society USA, Coalition of Medical Professionals, and National Women's Path Network. The pro-euthanasia arguments by the Gray Panthers and affiliated groups maintained the rights of terminally ill patients to obtain due process and equal protection under the Fourteenth Amendment of the Constitution. It was argued in the court briefs that patients suffered discrimination, who were not provided with appropriate medical assistance in ending their own suffering by ending their own lives. Much to the chagrin of the Gray Panthers and the other concerned parties, the Supreme Court ruled unanimously in June 1997 to uphold the decision of the court of appeals, thus stating that New York's ban on assisted suicide did not violate the Fourteenth Amendment. The Gray Panthers continues to support initiatives that favor the legalization of assisted suicide.

SUCCESSES AND FAILURES

The Gray Panthers was successful in establishing the National Media Task Force. In 1975 that group was instrumental in bringing about a revision to the National Association of Broadcasters' Code of Ethics, which discouraged age stereotyping in television broadcasting. Persistent efforts of the Gray Panthers also contributed to the passage of the Discrimination in Employment Act in 1978—legislation that raised the mandatory retirement age from 65 to 70.

FUTURE DIRECTIONS

Although Gray Panther membership suffered a decline over recent years—most notably since the death of founder Margaret Kuhn—the organization will take measures it hopes will revitalize its ranks. The organization hopes to accomplish this through the establishment of new Gray Panther networks, including scheduled start-ups in New Mexico and in Pennsylvania. Additionally there are other groups in other communities that are investigating the feasibility of establishing local chapters.

GROUP RESOURCES

The Gray Panthers National Office maintains a library on aging. The Gray Panthers has created a Web site at http://www.graypanthers.org; while not fully functional, the site contains some information about what the organization does as well as how to contact the various regional offices throughout the United States. For more information on the organization, write to the Gray Panthers, 733 15th St. NW #437, Washington, DC 20006 or call (202) 466-3132. Information regarding the local chapter in a specific area is also available through the Gray Panthers' toll-free number at 1-800-280-5362.

GROUP PUBLICATIONS

Network is the biannual national newspaper of the Gray Panthers. Subscriptions are available at a rate of $20 per year. Points for Prowling, published bimonthly, offers "how-to" information and tips for problem resolution and fundraising. Other publications from the Gray Panthers Project Fund include "Bridging Generations for a New Social Contract" and "Age and Youth in Action Summit Final Report."

Information on obtaining the organization's publications may be requested by writing to the Gray Panther

National Headquarters, 733 15th St. NW #437, Washington, DC 20006 or by calling 1-800-280-5362. Many regional Gray Panthers organizations publish local newsletters as well. These are available from the respective chapter offices.

BIBLIOGRAPHY

Brown, Dave. "Senior Power." *Social Policy,* Spring 1998.

"Gray Power." *Nation,* 28 May 1990.

Hessel, Dieter, ed. *Maggie Kuhn on Aging: A Dialogue.* Philadelphia: Westminster Press, 1977.

Kuhn, Margaret E. *Get Out There and Do Something about Injustice.* New York: Friendship Press, 1972.

Kuhn, Margaret E., with Christina Long and Laura Quinn. *No Stone Unturned: The Life and Times of Maggie Kuhn.* New York: Ballantine Books, 1991.

Nichols, John. "Gray Panthers Still Nipping at Congress." *Capital Times,* 2 November 1995.

Quirk, Barbara. "Panthers Founder a True Leader." *Capital Times,* 2 May 1995.

Greenpeace USA

ESTABLISHED: 1971
EMPLOYEES: Not made available
MEMBERS: 1.6 million
PAC: None

WHAT IS ITS MISSION?

A nonprofit, nonviolent organization, Greenpeace USA's mission is to protect the global environment. It believes that determined individuals can alter the actions and purposes of even the most powerful by 'bearing witness' and drawing attention to an abuse of the environment through their unwavering presence at the scene, whatever the risk. Greenpeace USA focuses its efforts on four major areas of environmental protection: global warming, ancient forests, toxic substances, and the Earth's oceans.

Contact Information:
ADDRESS: 1436 U St. NW
         Washington, DC 20009
PHONE: (202) 462-1177
TOLL FREE: (800) 326-0959
FAX: (202) 462-4507
E-MAIL: info@wdc.greenpeace.org
URL: http://www.greenpeaceusa.org
EXECUTIVE DIRECTOR: Kristen Engberg

HOW IS IT STRUCTURED?

Greenpeace USA is the U.S. branch of the Greenpeace International organization. Greenpeace International is headquartered in Amsterdam, the Netherlands, and has branches in more than 25 countries around the world. Greenpeace USA is headquartered in Washington DC, with four regional offices for the northwest, northeast, Great Lakes and southwest areas. The Greenpeace USA board is responsible for coordinating the organization's activities in the United States. Board decisions and policy are overseen, reviewed and in some cases directed by the seven-member board of directors of Greenpeace International to which Greenpeace USA sends a trustee.

Greenpeace USA employs a wide variety of staff, including scientists, environmental activists, and media specialists. Greenpeace USA also has access to the

Greenpeace activists protest the French government's plans for nuclear testing on the South Pacific island of Mururoa in 1995. (Photograph by Joerg Sarbach, AP/Wide World Photo)

research facilities of the international organization's two laboratories in the United Kingdom and Ukraine as well as Greenpeace Marine Services, an experienced seaborne group specializing in the identification of marine pollution, destruction and over-fishing, as well as peaceful, but obstructive demonstration.

Greenpeace USA welcomes anyone interested in supporting its interests to become a member. Members donate a minimum of $30 annually and receive such benefits as access to restricted portions of the organization's Web site as well as *Greenpeace* magazine.

PRIMARY FUNCTIONS

Greenpeace USA has two primary methods by which it works to achieve its goals: activism and information dissemination. Subscribing to no political agenda, Greenpeace USA endorses a broad environmental mandate. The organization stages protests and gives speeches in order to combat such environmental problems as global warming, nuclear weapons testing, and the destruction of old-growth forests. For instance, Greenpeace USA's defining moment was its sailing of a boat into a U.S. nuclear testing area in Alaska in 1971, causing the testing to be postponed. In addition to the staff's mobilization in environmental crisis situations, the group also encourages its members to act by sending letters and faxes to their local lawmakers in the hope that their voices will enable legal change.

Greenpeace USA also does a great deal of research which it furnishes to both the public and legislators. It attempts to expose various offenses to the environment by issuing reports on topics such as "Salmon and Climate Change," "Can Genetic Engineering Feed the World," and "The Chlorine Crisis: Time for a Global Phase-out." The organization employs multimedia experts that catalog various environmental situations through the medium of video and photography. Using press releases and its Press Alert Network, Greenpeace USA keeps all those interested up-to-date on the most recent events in environmental issues.

PROGRAMS

Greenpeace USA plays an active role in developing and supporting programs for both the United States and the international arena. These programs focus on both public education and activism. One such program is its Green Room, a Web site devoted to making learning about the problems of environmental waste more interactive. Visitors to the site, accessible at http://www.greenpeaceusa.org/green, are able to take an on-line quiz to test their knowledge about environmental toxins, send a virtual postcard, or visit the Kid's Clubhouse, a special portion of the site dedicated to children.

In addition to its standard membership program that requires the donation of at least $30 annually, Greenpeace USA has also introduced a new kind of membership program: FRONTLINE. A member of Greenpeace USA participating in the FRONTLINE program is responsible for donating at least $10 per month and in return gets the assurance that these donations are sustaining the organization's activities. In addition to the normal membership benefits such as a subscription to *Greenpeace* magazine, members of the FRONTLINE program also receive invitations to the group's special events and boat tours.

BUDGET INFORMATION

Greenpeace USA is a registered 501(c)4 nonprofit, tax-exempt organization funded almost entirely by the individual contributions of its members and supporters as well as by sales of merchandise. In 1995 membership contributions, grants and donations to Greenpeace USA, amounted to $15.9 million, while merchandising and interest receipts contributed a further $220,000, to bring

FAST FACTS

Since 1945 there have been 2,050 tests of nuclear devices, about one every nine days for the last 51 years

(Source: Greenpeace. "Nuclear Test Ban Treaty," 1998.)

the total to $16.14 million. Disbursements, which ran to a total of $17.16 million, were made for a variety of programs including biodiversity ($125,000), Toxics ($220,000) and Nuclear Disarmament ($194,000), as well as program-support financing of $8.9 million for media & communications and public information & outreach. Fundraising itself represented a charge of more than $5.1 million, while administrative costs totaled $2.45 million.

Grants, donations and accrued interest to Greenpeace USA's charitable foundation amounted to $7.28 million, while disbursements for programs, program support, and administration totaled $5.62 million.

The Greenpeace charitable foundation was also responsible for a grant of $3 million to Greenpeace International, where the funds are used to finance smaller Greenpeace offices unable to fully fund their own operations. Funds from the international body also help Greenpeace obtain the highest quality scientific information; operate a fleet of ships worldwide; and use the latest communications technology to get its message to the concerned public as quickly as possible.

HISTORY

Greenpeace was conceived in 1971 when members of the Don't Make A Wave Committee in Vancouver, Canada, renamed their organization Greenpeace the better to express their purpose of creating a green and peaceful world. The newly formed organization was brought into the international spotlight when 12 of its members sailed a small boat, *Phyllis Cormack*, into the U.S. atomic test zone off Amchitka in Alaska in 1971. Their plan was to "bear witness" to environmentally harmful activities and draw the attention of the global community.

Initially Greenpeace was primarily concerned with the dangers of nuclear weapons and the testing of these items. After the actions of the crew of the *Phyllis Cormack* in Alaska, the United States announced that it would end its nuclear tests in the Aleutian Islands "for

FAST FACTS

Over 80 percent of the world's ancient forest has already been destroyed or degraded by human activity.

(Source: Greenpeace. "Greenpeace Celebrates Landmark Victory In Forest Debate," 1998.)

political and other reasons." On the heels of that success, the Greenpeace sailed its ship, *Vega*, to the Polynesian Islands, a long-standing French nuclear testing site. While staging a protest, French paramilitary officers boarded *Vega* and attacked the crew. Greenpeace subsequently won in a trial over the incident; in 1974 the French government agreed to limit their underground nuclear testing.

Based on its successes with nuclear testing, Greenpeace opened its first offices in the United States in San Francisco, California and Portland, Oregon in 1975 and expanded their activities. The organization began working in earnest to stop the exploitation of various endangered animal species. Greenpeace activists went to great lengths to protect marine mammals from being hunted for their valuable pelts or oils, even going so far as to step in the way of the guns and harpoons of hunters. These actions paid off; seal hunting had bans placed on it worldwide and the International Whaling Committee (IWC) banned the hunting of sperm whales in 1981. An even greater victory occurred a year later when the IWC voted to end all commercial whaling by 1985.

However, 1985 was also a year of terrible tragedy for Greenpeace. Its ship, the *Rainbow Warrior*, was heading to a French nuclear test site when a bomb exploded, allegedly planted by French secret service agents. Noted Greenpeace photographer Fernando Pereira was killed. Four years later the organization christened the *Rainbow Warrior II* in memory of Pereira.

The 1990s was a period of great activity for Greenpeace as it focused its activism on a number of different areas. After almost a decade of attempts to protect the continent of Antarctica, it is turned into a world park in 1991 with the signing of the Madrid Protocol. Another success came three years later when 65 nations agreed to end the practice of exporting hazardous waste to developing nations at the Basel Convention in Switzerland. In 1996 one of Greenpeace's most long sought after objectives was achieved when the five nuclear powers, the United States, United Kingdom, Russia, China, and France, signed the Comprehensive Nuclear Test Ban

Treaty. The following year marked another huge success: the Kyoto Convention results in most of the industrialized countries of the world agreeing to reduce the emission of greenhouse gases.

CURRENT POLITICAL ISSUES

As both a national organization and a member of Greenpeace's International Coordinating Committee, Greenpeace USA plays a role in both domestic and international issues. One important campaigning issue has been the urgent need for reductions in the accumulation of toxic wastes. Countering what it refers to as one of the major myths of the industrial era, Greenpeace has insisted that there are no safe or acceptable levels of toxic pollution. Its advocacy of this cause has been given greater urgency by the realization that those who bear the burden of toxic poisoning—ethnic, poor, and rural communities, and children—are the least able to influence decisions about the use of toxic materials and pollution.

Greenpeace has also championed the cause of the silent with its crusades against deforestation and overfishing. Port blockades and other forms of peaceful civil disobedience, including two activists suspending themselves from a Seattle bridge to focus attention on the environmental damage caused by factory trawling, have helped turn the attention of the media, the people, and finally governments to the critical issues affecting the environment.

One of the most prominent examples of Greenpeace's coordinated, worldwide efforts has been its opposition to nuclear testing.

Case Study: Nuclear Testing

Since its inception in Canada in 1971, Greenpeace has opposed nuclear testing. Its first act of 'bearing witness' that year involved members chartering a boat to sail into the US nuclear testing grounds on Amchitka Island in Alaska. Such actions have continued, often risking member's lives in an effort to draw the world's attention to the risks inherent in nuclear bombs, the inevitable pollution following their testing, and the sensitivity with which governments regarded the issue.

Changes on the world political front, such as the collapse of the United Soviet Socialist Republic, combined with the vociferous anti-testing opposition of Greenpeace and similar organizations, seemed to encourage steady progress during the late 1980s and early 1990s. However in 1995 rumors that Israel, India, and Pakistan were developing nuclear weapons began to alter that perception. Then, in May of 1995, China held a nuclear test with France following suit in both September and October. Greenpeace joined the voices of many nations in protest against these actions that had reversed so much of the feelings of global good will. Against this backdrop of Greenpeace's activism and the worldwide outrage generated by the tests, Australia, one of the many non-nuclear countries affected by nuclear testing, presented a draft test-ban treaty to the United Nations. The Australian draft, known as the Comprehensive Nuclear Test Ban Treaty, received the support of 158 countries with just three, India, Pakistan and North Korea, voting against.

The vote for the treaty was a triumphant success for Greenpeace USA activists but only a temporary respite. Many countries, including the United States, stalled in ratifying the new treaty. President Bill Clinton attempted to introduce the treaty to the Senate in September of 1997 but hearings were not held on whether or not it should be ratified. Another severe blow to any mood of optimism that may have developed following the introduction of the Comprehensive Nuclear Test Ban Treaty came in May of 1998 when both India and Pakistan conducted a series of tests. Nations worldwide once again condemned the actions of India and Pakistan. Despite the ratification of the treaty by France and the United Kingdom, the United States has yet to do the same. Greenpeace USA continues to advocate the logic and necessity of all nations to sign the treaty, especially the United States.

FUTURE DIRECTIONS

The work of Greenpeace has only just begun. Many of its most prominent and successful campaigns have started to make a mark on the public and political consciousness: increased public awareness of issues like toxic pollution, global warming, factory fishing and the dangers of nuclear testing and nuclear energy are a testament to the dedication of the more than 5 million Greenpeace activists worldwide, but the exploitation of the earth continues almost unabated.

With this in mind, Greenpeace will continue to champion the rights of the 200 million people around the world who depend on forests for their livelihood, food and medicine. It will defend the rights of the earth's children for whom global warming and the effects of fossil fuels are a forbidding inheritance. It will again press the US government and NASA to end their use of plutonium-based energy sources in spacecraft, and it will extend its advocacy of alternative energy sources like wind and solar power to replace the diminishing and polluting stocks of fossil fuels. It will also continue to extend and strengthen its representation in the East, where economic development and environmental pollution continue to go hand-in-hand and run apace. And with recent nuclear tests in India and Pakistan in mind, Greenpeace will put further pressure on the world's governments to make nuclear disarmament a top international priority.

GROUP RESOURCES

For current campaign issues and developments as well as membership details, access the Greenpeace USA Web site at http://www.greenpeaceusa.org. The site also includes press releases and background analysis on various issues of interest to Greenpeace. For international information and access to the Greenpeace Archive, check the Greenpeace International Web site at http://www.greenpeace.org. For more information on Greenpeace USA write Greenpeace USA, 1436 U St. NW, Washington, DC 20009 or call (202) 462-1177.

GROUP PUBLICATIONS

Greenpeace produces a magazine, *Greenpeace*, available to supporters making an annual donation of $30 or more. Its Web site also contains numerous research reports on such topics as toxins, oceans, forestry, energy, nuclear and Greenpeace fleet activities. On-line publications can be accessed at http://www.greenpeaceusa.org/media/publications.htm. For more information on how to obtain the organization's publications, write Greenpeace USA, 1436 U St. NW, Washington, DC 20009 or call (202) 462-1177.

BIBLIOGRAPHY

Corder, Mike. "Greenpeace Works to Rebuild Interest: Environmental Group has Fallen victim to Its Success, Some Say." *Dallas Morning News*, 16 November 1997.

"French Commandos Seize Greenpeace Ship." *Star Tribune*, 10 July 1995.

Johnson, Rebecca. "The In-Comprehensive Test Ban." *Bulletin of the Atomic Scientists*, 21 November 1996.

Lemonick, Michael D. "Special Report: The Ragtag International Band Of Ecowarriors Known As Greenpeace." *Time International*, 7 November 1994.

Lewis, Paul. "World Forestry Talks in Split on Curbing Logging." *New York Times*, 22 February 1997.

Manning, Robert A. "Cold War Has Ended, Why Is Nuclear Arms Race Still Here?" *Los Angeles Times*, 7 July 1996.

Nicoll, Ruaridh. "Fight for the Final Frontier." *Guardian*, 19 November 1997.

North, Richard D. "Greenpeace, Please Grow Up!" *Independent*, 26 September 1996.

"Nuclear Test Ban Treaty." *Earth Explorer*, 1 February 1995.

Poole, Teresa. "Peking Survives Its Trial by Greenpeace." *Independent*, 13 June 1996.

Segal, David. "Greenpeace Says Toys Contain Toxic Substance." *Washington Post*, 14 November 1998.

Handgun Control, Inc. (HCI)

ESTABLISHED: 1974
EMPLOYEES: 70
MEMBERS: 400,000
PAC: Voter Education Fund

Contact Information:
ADDRESS: 1225 Eye St. NW, Ste. 1100
      Washington, DC 20005-3991
PHONE: (202) 898-0792
FAX: (202) 371-9615
URL: http://www.handguncontrol.org
PRESIDENT: Robert J. Walker
CHAIRMAN: Sarah Brady

WHAT IS ITS MISSION?

According to the Web site maintained by Handgun Control, Inc. (HCI), the organization tries to "prevent gun-related violence injuries and deaths so people can live in a safer America." The HCI works to convince Congress to pass responsible federal, state, and local gun control laws centered on this ideal. However the organization notes that it "does not seek to ban legitimate handguns, rifles or shotguns."

HOW IS IT STRUCTURED?

HCI headquarters are located in Washington, D.C.; satellite offices are located in San Francisco, California; Los Angeles, California; Chicago, Illinois; and Cleveland, Ohio. The HCI is led by a 15-member board of trustees that designates a president; the president and board chairman work with the board to compose the direction and policy of the HCI. Other positions, such as treasurer and general counsel, are appointed by the board.

The Center for the Prevention of Handgun Violence (CPHV) is the education, research, legal action, and entertainment outreach arm of the HCI. CPHV's national initiatives include prevention programs for parents and youth on the risks associated with guns; legal representation for gun violence victims, and outreach to the entertainment community to encourage the industry not to make guns seem sexy or wonderful.

The HCI invites anyone who shares the organization's interest in controlling handguns to make a monetary contribution and join. HCI's 400,000 members come from a wide variety of backgrounds but are united in their effort to lobby Congress and educate the general public about handguns. Occasionally the HCI coordinates some activities with several state organizations that have similar interests and concerns. They are not directly linked but they do come together to work on projects. These groups include Virginians Against Handgun Violence, Texans Against Violence and the Massachusetts-based Stop Gun Violence.

PRIMARY FUNCTIONS

Through lobbying, litigation, education, and research, the HCI seeks to control the use and sale of handguns in the United States. The HCI, while not advocating a complete ban on guns, lobbies members of Congress on a variety of gun-related issues. Assault weapons bans, increased child protection, and mandatory waiting periods before the purchase of a firearm are all topics on which the HCI believes that congressional action could make a significant difference.

Through the CPHV the HCI provides legal services in gun-related court cases. The HCI also files *amicus* (friend of the court) briefs on behalf of individuals suing gun manufacturers or dealers and city, county, and state governments that enact gun control laws.

In an effort to educate the public and legislators, the HCI forms coalitions with doctors, researchers, law enforcement officials, community leaders, and even some pro-gun groups that share similar views on particular issues. The organization prints pamphlets and brochures that discuss the impact of gun violence, how young people are affected, and ways to try to prevent gun deaths and injuries. The HCI keeps statistics on gun usage, the number of people killed by guns, and the number of guns sold annually in the United States. The organization compiles information and statistics on gun control laws and crime in various communities. The CPHV also conducts polls on various aspects of the public's gun-related habits.

PROGRAMS

The CPHV is the branch of the HCI that is centrally responsible for public programs. These programs educate the public about handgun risks and pursue a legal agenda for those harmed by handguns or handgun manufacturers.

Straight Talks About Risks (STAR)

Over the last several years the CPHV has brought "Straight Talk About Risks" (STAR) to more than 70 municipalities across the country. Some of the larger school districts that use the program include schools in

James Brady looks on as his wife Sarah Brady, chairman of HCI, testifies at a congressional hearing on handgun control. James Brady, former press secretary to President Reagan, was severely wounded during the 1981 assassination attempt on the president. (The Bettmann Archive)

New York, New York; Los Angeles, California; Chicago, Illinois; and Dade County, Florida. The gun-violence prevention program is geared to children in pre-kindergarten through grade 12. STAR focuses on messages about the dangers of guns and activities to help young people develop the motivation and skills to stay safe. Children role-play situations involving guns and learn how to tell the difference between real and toy guns.

STAR materials include classroom activities, posters, handouts and videos and are available in both English and Spanish. Program organizers have contacted researchers, educators and students in developing the program. Organizations that helped review and guide the program include the American Academy of Child and Adolescent Psychiatry, National Association for the Education of Young Children, National Urban League, National PTA and National Crime Prevention Council. More than 2,000 educators have been learned how to teach the STAR program, and more than 150,000 students have taken STAR instruction.

Steps to Prevent (STOP) Firearm Injury

According to CPHV literature, "One in five pediatricians nationwide has treated a child for a gunshot

BIOGRAPHY:

Sarah and James Brady

Gun Control Activists (S. Brady: b. 1942) (J. Brady: b. 1940) While on vacation in 1985, Sarah and James Brady's then five-year-old son, Scott, picked up a loaded gun from the seat of a friend's pick-up truck and pointed it at his mother. Ironically, the gun their son had picked up was the same type used four years earlier to seriously wound and permanently disable his father. James Brady, White House press secretary, had been shot in the head during an attempt on President Ronald Reagan's life in 1981. The image of her son with a handgun, and its potential for disaster, prompted Sarah Brady to action: "I called Handgun Control, Inc., and said, 'Can I do anything to help?' " It was a question that would change the lives of both Sarah and James. As Washington insiders and victims of a high-profile tragedy, the Brady's decision to get involved was a boon for gun-control advocates. Sarah Brady proved a powerful and prolific speaker across the United States and both Bradys testified repeatedly before federal legislators. In 1987, as vice chair of Handgun Control, Inc., Sarah Brady met with lawmakers who were piecing together a tougher gun-control bill. In the course of the six-year campaign to win passage of the legislation, it became popularly known as the Brady Bill. In *USA Weekend* Sarah revealed, "I really do enjoy the politics of it. I love the fight in a campaign. I want to *win*." Jim added, "You should see her chasing a congressman down the hall. She's yelling, 'Congressman!' and he's running as fast as he can go. 'Here comes that woman from gun control. We know what you want.' "

---

injury. Recent research has shown unequivocally that a firearm in the home increases risks for domestic homicides, suicides and unintentional shootings. Yet, many parents keep loaded, unlocked firearms easily accessible in their homes." With the American Academy of Pediatrics, the Center created STOP, a program that gets children's doctors and medical workers to talk to parents and youths about the risks of having guns in the home. Program materials include a cassette and brochures that are dedicated to presenting the facts about in-home handgun accidents. CPHV estimates that more than one million families have received STOP messages since its inception. In June of 1998 STOP2, a rededication of the STOP program, was initiated.

Legal Action Project

This program has started several activities since it was established in 1989. It represents victims of gun violence in court cases and lawsuits, files court briefs, and helps attorneys in cases against gun manufacturers and dealers. Cases have included suits against gun manufacturers such as Beretta USA and dealers such as K-Mart.

BUDGET INFORMATION

For 1996 the HCI reported approximately $6.6 million in total revenues and $7 million in total expenses. That lowered the agency's total assets to $1.2 million by the end of 1996, compared with $1.6 million at the end of 1995, according to information that the HCI released.

Among the major revenues the organization listed were $3.8 million in membership dues and $2.6 million in general contributions. Among expenses, the organization spent $2.6 million on legislation and legal activities, $1.2 million on fund-raising, $936,000 on member services, $903,000 on membership development, $873,000 on public education and $109,211 on political action. The HCI's political action committee, the Voter Education Fund, spent $310,000 in 1996 and raised $268,000 in revenues.

HISTORY

The HCI was founded in 1974 by Dr. Mark Borinsky, who was a victim of gun violence. The organization called itself a citizens' gun control lobbying organization. Borinsky was later joined by N. T. "Pete" Shields, whose son Nick was killed because of random handgun violence during the "Zebra" killings in San Francisco in 1973–74. In 1975 Shields became executive director of the HCI and was later elected its chair.

Looking to increase the HCI's legal and educational faculties, Shields founded the CPHV in 1983. Sarah Brady, wife of James Brady, Ronald Reagan's former press secretary shot in 1981, joined the HCI in 1985 and later became chair of both the HCI and the CPHV. James Brady also became a CPHV board member. In 1986 the HCI began a nationwide campaign to pass the Brady Bill, which would require a background check on the intended handgun purchaser and a five-day waiting period before buying a handgun.

In 1993 President Bill Clinton signed the Brady Bill into law; it went into effect on February 28, 1994. The HCI reported that in the first two years after its enactment, more than 100,000 potential criminals were not allowed to purchase a handgun. However in 1997, the HCI's efforts were dealt a blow when the Supreme Court ruled that background checks of would-be handgun buyers violated their constitutional rights and thus should not be enforced.

CURRENT POLITICAL ISSUES

The HCI has been involved in some very high profile political issues in the 1990s. In part, due to research and testimony provided by the HCI, the Brady Bill was pushed through in 1993. A year later, the HCI once again lobbied Congress and set about a public education campaign to ensure the passage of the Violent Crime Control and Law Enforcement Act, which banned the manufacture of certain types of assault weapons. One of the less well-publicized issues, but one of the group's most important, involves mandatory handgun locks.

Case Study: Gun Safety Locks

Although HCI has a long history of supporting safety equipment for handguns, its endorsement of trigger locks is best understood in the context of its likely policy alternatives. While HCI wants to see a law enacted that requires mandatory trigger locks, the group believes that locks are only a first step toward greater gun safety. In fact HCI was critical of an October 1997 agreement between the Clinton administration and the gun manufacturing industry in which eight of the largest gun manufacturers in the United States agreed to sell 80 percent of their guns with a safety lock. HCI spokesperson Robin Terry suggested that there was much more that the gun industry and the government could do to enhance gun safety.

HCI pushed for mandatory indicator mechanisms that signal when a gun is loaded and the installation of transmitter chip technology that renders handguns unusable for anyone other than the gun owner. This transmitter chip technology—an example of which is Colt Manufacturing's "Smart Gun"—requires a transmission from a chip worn by the gun owner in order for the gun to fire. More than simply hoping for better and safer technologies, HCI also objected to the agreement because of its reliance on voluntary compliance by the gun industry, the limitation of the agreement to only eight manufacturers, and its application to only 80 percent of participating manufacturers' weapons. In all, HCI objected because they saw the voluntary agreement as a means by which the gun industry could forestall mandatory and more far-reaching federal legislation.

Thus, despite the voluntary agreement HCI and other gun control advocates continued to push for federal legislation. After a series of school shootings in Pearl, Mississippi; West Paducah, Kentucky; Jonesboro, Arkansas; Springfield, Oregon; and Edinboro, Pennsylvania, during the 10 months between October 1997 and July 1998, Representative Carolyn McCarthy (D-N.Y.) introduced the Children's Gun Violence Prevention Act. According to

BUDGET:
1996 HCI Expenses

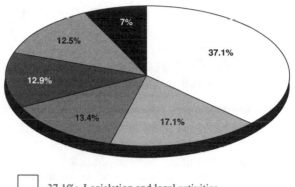

☐	37.1%: Legislation and legal activities
▨	17.1%: Fund raising
▨	13.4%: Member services
▨	12.9%: Membership development
▨	12.5%: Public education
■	7%: Political action and other

an HCI press release, the act would impose safety standards on the gun manufacturing industry including child trigger resistance and child safety locks; authorize the Consumer Product Safety Commission to test various technologies related to "making guns more child-resistant;" prohibit the sale of assault weapons—those not covered by the 1994 assault weapons ban—to individuals under 18; increase criminal penalties for those convicted of selling guns to juveniles; and require gun owners to "store loaded guns in a place that is reasonably inaccessible to children, or use a device to lock the gun." Despite the fact that Representative McCarthy introduced the legislation in June of 1998, Congress adjourned in October of 1998 without considering it. Republican leaders, many of whom are opposed to various forms of gun control, did not schedule it prior to adjournment, effectively killing the legislation for the 105th Congress.

In their continuing effort to quell public outrage at the series of schoolyard shootings in 1997 and 1998, Handgun Control, Inc. head Sarah Brady joined Senator Ted Kennedy (D-Mass.) and Representative McCarthy on March 24, 1999—the one year anniversary of the school shootings in Jonesboro, Arkansas—to announce the reintroduction of comprehensive legislation designed to protect children from guns. In a Handgun Control, Inc. press release Brady was quoted saying "Everyday, 14

FAST FACTS

Every day in the United States 14 children, ages 19 and under, are killed with guns.

(Source: Handgun Control Inc., 1999.)

children are killed in gun homicides, suicides, and unintentional shootings—that's an entire classroom of children every two days." The gun control debate was further fueled in April 1999 when two seniors at Columbine High School in Littleton, Colorado, waged a one-day rampage that resulted in the death of at least 12 students and one teacher. Thus, despite its earlier legislative defeats and its desire for more far-reaching and technologically advanced means of improving gun safety, the HCI, along with its allies in Congress, will continue in its support of gun safety lock technology.

FUTURE DIRECTIONS

The portion of the Brady Bill that mandated a five-day waiting period before the purchase of a handgun expired in November of 1998. The HCI will dedicate itself to a reinstitution of this mandate in some form, believing that it is an essential component of gun control. While last-ditch efforts by several members of Congress were unsuccessful in reinstating a waiting period, Sarah Brady, chair of the HCI and the CPHV vowed in a press release that "the fight over the waiting period is far from over."

GROUP RESOURCES

The HCI maintains a Web site at http://www.handguncontrol.org, which contains information on HCI programs, recent activities, and handgun statistics. For more information on the HCI, write to Handgun Control Inc., 1225 Eye St. NW, Ste. 1100, Washington, DC 20005, or call (202) 898-0792.

GROUP PUBLICATIONS

The HCI publishes a newsletter, *The Progress Report,* which is delivered to members three times a year. The legal department prints the *Legal Action Report* four times a year, which details the various lawsuits HCI has filed against the gun industry. Project Lifeline publishes the *Project Lifeline News*. It comes out four times a year and urges doctors and other health care workers to discuss gun violence issues. Information on the availability of these publications can be obtained by writing to Handgun Control Inc., 1225 Eye St. NW, Ste. 1100, Washington, DC 20005, or by calling (202) 898-0792.

BIBLIOGRAPHY

Cottrol, Robert J., ed. *Gun Control and the Constitution: Sources and Explorations on the Second Amendment.* New York: Garland Publishing, 1994.

Eby, Lloyd. "Brady Act Attacked in Supreme Court." *World and I,* February 1997.

Edel, Wilbur. *Gun Control: Threat to Liberty or Defense Against Anarchy?* Westport, Conn.: Praeger Publishers, 1995.

"Getting Organized: American Firearms Organization." *Field and Stream,* August 1995.

Gibbs, Nancy. "The Littleton Massacre." *Time,* 3 May 1999.

Greenhouse, Linda. "Justices Limit Brady Gun Law as Intrusion on States' Rights." *New York Times,* 28 June 1997.

Kruschke, Earl R. *Gun Control: A Reference Handbook.* Santa Barbara, Calif.: ABC-CLIO, 1995.

LaPierre, Wayne R. *Guns, Crime and Freedom.* Washington, D.C.: Regnery Publishing, 1994.

Larson, Erik. *Lethal Passage: How the Travels of a Single Handgun Expose the Roots of America's Gun Crisis.* New York: Crown Publishers, 1994.

Malcolm, Joyce Lee. *To Keep and Bear Arms: The Origins of an Anglo-American Right.* Cambridge, Mass.: Harvard University Press, 1994.

Rosenberg, Merri. "Up in Arms." *Scholastic Update,* 2 November 1998.

"The Sheriff's Revenge." *Economist,* 7 December 1996.

Spitzer, Robert J. *The Politics of Gun Control.* Chatham, N.J.: Chatham House, 1995.

Witkin, Gordon. "Handgun Stealing Made Easy." *U.S. News and World Report,* 9 June 1997.

Zeskind, Leonard. "Armed and Dangerous." *Rolling Stone,* 2 November 1995.

Health Insurance Association of America (HIAA)

WHAT IS ITS MISSION?

According to the HIAA its mission "is to be the most influential advocate for the private, free enterprise health care system." It supports a vision of health care in the United States in which government, health insurance companies, and health care providers "will build upon our employer-based system to create a consumer-responsive, prevention-focused, affordable and cost-effective health care system which fosters individual responsibility, human dignity, improved human status, and enhanced quality of life for all."

HOW IS IT STRUCTURED?

The HIAA is a Washington, D.C.-based trade association and is governed by a board of directors. The board's chairman is elected by the membership. The work of the HIAA is managed by key staff members including a president, a chief of staff, and a range of vice presidents who develop policy through consultation with leaders from member companies and HIAA policy committees.

The HIAA offers services to its members through various departments and divisions. The Federal Affairs and State Affairs offices monitor and lobby on legislation and regulation that affect the health insurance industry. The Policy Development department conducts research, analyzes legislation and regulations, and develops policy proposals. The Legal department files lawsuits and provides information to the courts on legal issues from the perspective of the insurance industry. The

ESTABLISHED: 1956
EMPLOYEES: 100
MEMBERS: 250
PAC: Health Insurance Political Action Committee (HIPAC)

Contact Information:

ADDRESS: 555 13th St. NW, Ste. 600
    Washington, DC 20004
PHONE: (202) 824-1600
FAX: (202) 824-1722
URL: http://www.hiaa.org
PRESIDENT: Charles N. Kahn
CHAIRMAN: Leonard Schaeffer

public affairs office handles relations with the media and the public and organizes campaigns on public policy proposals. Other departments distribute information on and to the insurance industry, produce publications, and provide education for insurance professionals.

Most members are companies that offer or manage a combination of medical, disability, and long-term care insurance plans. Member companies include commercial insurers, health maintenance organizations (HMOs), preferred provider organizations (PPOs), and Blue Cross/Blue Shield plans. In 1996 the HIAA membership was opened to include companies that offer products or services to the health insurance industry such as benefit-consulting firms and medical care providers.

PRIMARY FUNCTIONS

The primary function of the HIAA is to monitor and shape public policy proposals that affect the health insurance industry. The organization provides members with regular updates and bulletins on the status of important regulations and legislation at the national and state levels and gives an analysis of the likely effects such proposals could have on the insurance industry. HIAA members have access to an on-line service that offers instant legislative updates. HIAA staff and leaders from member companies lobby legislators and regulatory agencies and appear before congressional hearings. They are also frequently appointed to public policy committees to represent the insurance industry. For example, HIAA President Bill Gradison served on the Federal Medicare Reform Commission charged with developing solutions to problems in the federal government-run program that covers medical care for all senior citizens.

In order to influence legislation the HIAA also coordinates major efforts to shape public and policymaker opinion. It does this by traditional lobbying, such as letter-writing campaigns and meetings with representatives, as well as advertising in newspapers and on television. Although the HIAA focuses more on lobbying than on elections, it does operate a political action committee, Health Insurance Political Action Committee (HIPAC), which contributed $112,862 in the 1997–98 federal election cycle, of which 76 percent went to Republican candidates.

Another major function of the HIAA is to conduct research and collect information and data on the health insurance industry for use by its members, policymakers, and consumers. The organization also serves as a forum for debate among members on health care issues and public policy through committees, task forces, and working groups. The HIAA attempts to identify and address emerging issues in health care and to build consensus in the insurance industry on issues of public policy. Additionally, the HIAA offers teleconferences, seminars, and workshops on particular issues.

PROGRAMS

In addition to its lobbying and research efforts the HIAA administers a number of programs. The HIAA runs the Prevailing Healthcare Charges System (PHCS), which collects insurance claims information used to determine how much health care providers and companies that sell drugs, medical equipment , and supplies typically charge for services or products. The program, which was started in 1973, is the nation's largest database of health care charges. Health care insurers use the data to evaluate and set rates for reimbursement for health services provided to their customers. In addition to insurance companies, HMOs, PPOs, consultants, government agencies, and a range of other health services organizations rely on the data. HIAA members receive discounted subscriptions to PHCS.

HIAA members receive discounted access to the HIAA's Insurance Education Program. This program offers coursework by mail on all aspects of the health insurance industry to over 30,000 insurance professionals and other students a year.

The HIAA also holds an annual conference, the Insurance Forum, that is open to both members and non-members. The forum includes an exhibit hall and special sessions on new products, insurance markets, and public policy issues.

BUDGET INFORMATION

Not made available.

HISTORY

The HIAA was formed in 1956 by the merger of the Bureau of Accident and Health Underwriters and the Health and Accident Underwriters Conference. For most of its history the HIAA has been the voice of traditional fee-for-service health insurers. Health maintenance organizations (HMOs) and preferred provider organizations (PPOs) offer access to a limited number of doctors and often charge patients and their insurers a set rate regardless of how much care patients use. Fee-for-service insurers generally pay a percentage of a patient's health care bills and the patient has free choice of doctors and service providers. From its founding the HIAA has opposed most legislative efforts to expand the regulation of the private insurance market and to establish national health insurance that would make the government the provider of universal health coverage to all citizens, a system in place in Canada and most Western European countries.

The HIAA became active in Washington, D.C., in the 1970s. Battles over ways to control rising medical care costs often pitted the insurance industry against health care providers such as doctors and particularly hospitals. The establishment in the 1960s of Medicare, a government program providing health care coverage for all elderly citizens, and Medicaid, a government program providing coverage for the poor, and the programs' expansion in the early 1970s meant that the federal government played an increasingly greater role in the health care industry. The HIAA pushed for a federal health-planning bill that eventually passed in 1974 despite the opposition of doctors and hospitals. Most HIAA members also supported the efforts of Democratic President Jimmy Carter, elected in 1976, to impose cost controls on hospitals.

The HIAA opposed a proposal by Republican President Ronald Reagan, elected in 1980, to control health care costs by increasing competition in the already competitive health insurance industry rather than regulating hospitals. Reagan administration cuts in Medicare and Medicaid payments to health care providers resulted in many providers making up the difference by charging more to privately insured patients. Facing an uphill battle in Congress to increase Medicare and Medicaid payments, the HIAA launched a national advertising campaign to make the public and policymakers aware of this cost shifting, often called the hidden tax.

Issues in the 1980s

An economic recession and increasing health care costs increased the number of uninsured people in the 1980s. The number of Americans without health insurance coverage increased by 6 million between 1979 and 1984. Millions more had inadequate coverage. The insurance industry was criticized for failing to address the problem. In the late 1980s the HIAA recommended a program to increase access to medical care in the hopes of convincing policymakers that the industry was committed to solving the growing health care crisis. Proposals included the expansion of Medicaid to cover a greater number of the disadvantaged, changes in regulations to make it easier for insurers to offer low-cost plans to small businesses, and tax incentives for individuals who purchase their own insurance. The HIAA also proposed regulations to help insurance companies share the risks for insuring people they might ordinarily deny coverage to, such as those with medical conditions requiring costly treatments. The HIAA made several other public efforts to encourage companies to provide preventive medical care for their employees and to encourage individuals to purchase long-term care insurance that covers expenses such as extended nursing home care for the elderly or disabled.

A Change in Position

The future of the HIAA seemed uncertain in the early 1990s as health care reform became a hot issue. Recognizing that reforms that could benefit large insurers in turn could harm small insurers, the HIAA

supported partial reforms that would satisfy all its members. But it became increasingly difficult for the HIAA to hold its members together after the 1992 election of Democratic President Bill Clinton, who promised a major overhaul of the nation's health care system. By early 1993 the country's five largest health insurers had ended their HIAA membership. Several small insurers founded a splinter group, the Council on Affordable Health Insurance.

Facing the building political momentum for comprehensive health care reform, the HIAA's board of directors reversed its past positions and endorsed a proposal calling for universal coverage, in which all citizens have health insurance supported by a government mandate that employers provide coverage for their employees. Employers providing benefits greater than a standard, national package would be taxed. The board also supported unspecified government controls on rapidly escalating health care costs.

In the midst of the turmoil, the HIAA's president of five years, Carl J. Schramm, announced he was leaving at the end of 1992. Congressman Willis D. Gradison, a Republican from Ohio and the ranking member on the House Ways and Means Health Subcommittee, was chosen to replace Schramm. Although the HIAA did not stop voicing its support for health care reform and universal coverage, as Clinton's doomed health care plan unfolded, the HIAA became one of its most vocal opponents.

Moving Forward

In 1998 Charles Kahn was chosen to replace Gradison as president. He had been the HIAA's key staff member in the fight against Clinton's health care plan but had left HIAA to become a high-level congressional staff member after his long-time friend and political ally Republican Newt Gingrich became Speaker of the House of Representatives following the 1994 elections. In Congress Kahn helped engineer the passage of a 1997 Medicare reform plan endorsed by the HIAA that encouraged seniors to pursue private-sector insurance. As HIAA president, Kahn tried to bring back the members who left in the early 1990s and to attract members from the managed health care industry away from the American Association of Health Plans (AAHP), the leading trade association in managed care. The HIAA has been very active on managed-care issues, joining the Coalition for Affordable Quality Healthcare, which launched a major effort in 1998 to improve the industry's public image and to fight congressional efforts to increase the regulation of managed-care plans.

CURRENT POLITICAL ISSUES

The HIAA is active in public policy proposals that have the potential to affect the health insurance industry.

In the area of health care reform the HIAA opposes any efforts to make the government the provider of health care or health insurance except for the most needy members of the population. Instead it supports the expansion of the private health insurance market with reforms based on a number of principles. According to the HIAA, government policy should encourage employers to provide or contribute to their employees' health insurance; if individuals are not insured by their employers they should take personal responsibility for getting their own coverage. Also individuals should receive tax advantages for purchasing health insurance just as companies do. Government regulations should not increase insurance costs and it should allow insurance markets to operate with minimal interference to meet consumer demand. Government regulations should not restrict the ability of insurance companies to deny coverage to individuals or to set a price for insurance coverage adequate to cover the individual's health risks.

Case Study: The HIAA v. Clinton Administration Health Care Reform

When President Clinton took office in 1993, most health insurers and health care providers, who had resisted comprehensive changes in the health care system, felt that major reform was inevitable due to increasing public outrage at the cost of health care. As the president's task force on health care reform, led by his wife, Hillary Rodham Clinton, swung into action, groups such as the HIAA started lobbying to make sure that their interests were taken into account in the formulation of any new plan. Advised by political consultants that the public distrusted the insurance industry, the HIAA set up a front group, the Coalition for Health Insurance Choices, which began to run television ads in the spring of 1993 endorsing the HIAA's vision of reform. At the time, the HIAA's membership was composed of small and medium sized companies that felt they might be forced out of business or absorbed by larger companies under the reform plan that was emerging in the fall of 1993.

The Initial Campaign

Early efforts by HIAA leaders to negotiate with the task force were undermined by the administration's attacks on the insurance industry for price gouging and profiteering. Although still hoping there would be room for compromise, the HIAA decided to run a more aggressive series of television advertisements that depicted a middle-aged, middle-class couple, named Harry and Louise, discussing Clinton's health care proposal at their kitchen table. The ads capitalized on public distrust of government bureaucracy by emphasizing that a complex Clinton plan would mandate that the government make decisions about health care rather than individuals and their doctors. The announcer in one of the ads observed, "The government may force us to pick from a few health care plans designed by government bureaucrats." Louise

then asserts, "Having choices we don't like is no choice at all." Harry responds, "They choose," Louise completes the thought, "We lose."

While a Gallup poll taken in the month the ads began running showed 56 percent of the public approving of Clinton's health care proposal and only 24 percent disapproving, four months later, most polls found that those who disapproved outnumbered those who approved. The HIAA spent an estimated $14 to $15 million on advertising. It targeted a limited number of media markets such as New York and Washington, D.C., where national opinion leaders such as journalists, policymakers, and corporate executives live as well as other states in which members of Congress were considered vulnerable to influence. The ads were so effective in undercutting support for Clinton's plan that Dan Rostenkowski (D-Ill.), a key congressional committee leader, brokered a deal with HIAA leaders to pull the Harry and Louise ads off the air while his committee considered the proposal. Rostenkowski assured the HIAA that its cooperation would result in a final version of the plan more favorable to its members' interests. The ads returned to the air when Rostenkowski, facing unrelated charges of ethics violations, had to turn over his chairmanship to Sam Gibbons (D-Fla.), who refused to honor the deal. When the Clinton administration attacked the ads as deceptive and alarmist, their attacks only increased the media attention given the Harry and Louise campaign. The HIAA also received free publicity when television news programs ran the ads as part of stories on health care reform lobbying efforts and the sour relationship between the federal government and reform opponents.

Reform supporters, including the American Association of Retired Persons and the League of Women Voters, tried to counter the Harry and Louise campaign with ads of their own but these failed to resonate with the public or policymakers. In addition, the reform supporters had much smaller advertising budgets and their ads were not nearly as well-targeted or effective as those of the HIAA.

Other Tactics and Supporters

In addition to its media efforts, the HIAA also launched a grassroots campaign that resulted in hundreds of thousands of phone calls, letters, and visits to congressional members. Employees of HIAA member companies and insurance agents across the country who felt their economic well being was threatened by the Clinton plan participated in the lobbying effort. The HIAA employed organizers in a number of states where congressional support was considered crucial. Field organizers then asked individuals, who had personal or professional ties to congressional members, to present the organization's case to targeted representatives.

Members of small business organizations, such as the HIAA and the National Federation of Independent Business, were early opponents to the president's plan because its universal coverage might have required small businesses, which do not offer employee insurance, to do so. Some businesses, however, might have benefited from the proposed reforms. Hospitals, which care for uninsured patients who can't pay for medical care, recoup some of these costs by charging higher fees to insured patients. These fees are in turn passed on in the form of higher insurance premiums to those businesses that insure their workers. Thus if more businesses were required to insure employees, the hospital charges would be spread out among more insurers and might therefore lower premiums for some companies. For this reason, organizations such as the United States Chamber of Commerce, the National Association of Manufacturers (NAM), and the Business Roundtable were initially supportive of the administration's efforts. The Harry and Louise ads and other lobbying, however, began to reverse the momentum in favor of health reform. As opponents stood firm in their opposition, business supporters of reform backed down. The Chamber, the Roundtable, and NAM all came out against the plan in the winter of 1994. By the late summer of 1995 it was clear that Clinton's plan of comprehensive health reform was not going to garner enough congressional or public support to pass.

Public Impact

The proposed health reform plan was intended to stem the rapid growth in health care costs and make health care accessible and affordable for everyone without destroying the U.S. system of private health insurance. Many critics of the plan argued that it would not achieve these goals and it might create new problems, such as the rationing of health care in which patients would not have access to some services or would have to wait to receive them. However, the failure of the Clinton administration, Congress, and groups such as the HIAA to reach a consensus on comprehensive reform leaves problems unsolved. Health care costs continue to grow and increasing numbers of people do not have health insurance or access to medical care.

FUTURE DIRECTIONS

Although congressional efforts to increase the regulation of managed health care plans such as HMOs failed in 1998, proponents are determined to push for such legislation in the future. The HIAA's legislative efforts will be focused on fighting these measures. Because the public's negative opinion of health insurance companies has encouraged politicians to further regulate the industry, the Coalition for Affordable Quality Healthcare, of which the HIAA is a key member, launched a major advertising campaign to improve the industry's image at the end of 1998. This campaign will be expanded in the future.

FAST FACTS

It is estimated that every one percent increase in health insurance premiums results in roughly 200,000 people losing or failing to get health coverage.

(Source: Health Insurance Association of America. "Press Release." November 19, 1998.)

GROUP RESOURCES

The HIAA maintains a Web site at http://www.hiaa. org that contains information about the association's goals, activities, and membership. The site also contains press releases, congressional testimony, and position statements as well as many of the reports prepared by the HIAA. For more information about the HIAA, contact the Health Insurance Association of America, 555 13th St. NW, Ste. 600, Washington, DC 20004 or call (202) 824-1600.

GROUP PUBLICATIONS

In addition to the *HIAA Reporter,* a bimonthly newsletter that updates members on HIAA activities and insurance industry issues, the HIAA produces the *Source Book of Health Insurance Data,* which details various statistics that relate to health insurance as well as the industry's history. The HIAA also offers a wide range of publications relevant to the insurance industry and health care provision including brief white papers on particular topics such as managed care, insurance buying guides, compilations of data from the health insurance industry, and public opinion research. A listing of current titles is available on the HIAA's Web site at http://www.hiaa.org/ hiaapubs/index.html. Publications can be ordered by writing to the HIAA Distribution Center, 9050 Junction Dr. Annapolis, MD 20701, by calling (800) 828-0111 or by faxing (301) 206-9789.

BIBLIOGRAPHY

Demkovich, Linda E. "Health Insurers Favor Budget Cutting—But Not If It Means They Must Pay More." *National Journal,* 21 November 1981.

Goldreich, Samuel. "Chip Kahn—Should Hill Enact Managed-Care Reform?" *Washington Times,* 10 August 1998.

Johnson, Haynes, and David S. Broder. *The System: The American Way of Politics at the Breaking Point.* Boston: Little, Brown, and Co., 1996.

Judis, John B. "Abandoned Surgery: Business and the Failure of Health Care Reform." *The American Prospect,* Spring 1995.

Kosterlitz, Julie. "Harry, Louise and Doublespeak." *National Journal,* 25 June 1994.

———. "Shaky Times for Insurers." *National Journal,* 21 November 1992.

Scarlett, Thomas. "Killing Health Care Reform: How Clinton's Opponents Used a Political Media Campaign to Lobby Congress and Sway Public Opinion." *Campaigns and Elections,* October 1994.

Serafini, Marilyn Werber. "The Toughest Sell in Town." *National Journal,* 19 September 1998.

———. "A New Growth Chart for Health Insurers," *National Journal,* 25 April 1998.

Spragins, Ellyn E. "Making HMOs Play Fair," *Newsweek,* 4 May 1998.

Human Rights Campaign (HRC)

WHAT IS ITS MISSION?

The Human Rights Campaign (HRC), is a national lesbian and gay political organization that "envisions an America where homosexuals are ensured of their basic equal rights—and can be open, honest, and safe at home, work and in the community." The HRC has approximately 200,000 members, both gay and nongay, all committed to making this vision a reality.

HOW IS IT STRUCTURED?

The HRC includes the Human Rights Campaign (a 501(c)4 organization to which contributions are not tax deductible) and the Human Rights Campaign Foundation (a 501(c)4 organization where donations are tax deductible). The Human Rights Campaign is governed by a 21-member board of directors; the board heads the organization and has the ultimate authority for making budget decisions and policy decisions regarding the operations of the HRC. The board of directors is cochaired by three members, two of whom also cochair the HRC Board of Governors. The board of governors—a large body with over 90 nationwide members—is responsible for the nationwide coordination of HRC volunteers, as well as fund-raising activities.

The HRC Foundation is headed by a five-member HRC Foundation board, including a president, vice president, and treasurer/secretary. This board oversees all foundation activity, which includes work that is not legislative or political, such as the Coming Out Project, educational outreach, and funding for these efforts.

ESTABLISHED: 1980
EMPLOYEES: 60
MEMBERS: 200,000 (1997)
PAC: Human Rights Campaign Political Action
    Committee

Contact Information:

ADDRESS: 919 18th St. NW
        Washington, DC 20006
PHONE: (202) 628-4160
TOLL FREE: (800) 777-4723
FAX: (202) 347-5323
E-MAIL: hrc@hrc.org
URL: http:\\www.hrc.org
EXECUTIVE DIRECTOR: Elizabeth Birch

The HRC office is located in Washington, D.C., and is headed by an executive director. This position is appointed by the board and has no set term. The HRC departments at the Washington office include: the Executive Offices (which house the executive director and staff); the Political Department (responsible for work with the PAC, lobbying, field organizing, and monitoring federal legislation); the Communications Department (which interacts with the media and commissions public opinion polls as needed by independent polling firms); the Education Department (which develops the Web site, the magazine, and does research); the Membership/Development Department (responsible for outreach and fund-raising); and the Finance/Administration Department (which manages the finances of the organization).

The field-organizing function of the Political Department is the means through which the HRC mobilizes support at the grassroots level. This program establishes district coordinators that serve two-year terms. The HRC works with the coordinators to conduct activist training and to conduct activist weeks (week-long training on how to lobby, how to run town meetings, and other aspects of grassroots work). These district coordinators make up the HRC Action Network.

The HRC has more than 200,000 members nationwide, both gay and heterosexual, who support the organization's vision. Members not only support the HRC's efforts through membership fees (ranging from $20 to over $1,200) but are given options for other ways to contribute such as committing to donating a certain amount per month or sponsoring another person's membership.

PRIMARY FUNCTIONS

The HRC works to influence and shape federal policy that will impact gays, lesbians, and bisexuals. The HRC continuously lobbies for federal legislation that will support its agenda. According to the HRC, the organization has the largest full-time lobbying team in the United States. The HRC works at every stage of the legislative process, including monitoring legislation, testifying at hearings, and mobilizing supporters to contact their congressional representatives. The HRC also works to defeat bills that would violate the basic human rights of gays, lesbians, and bisexuals. Through effective lobbying, the HRC was responsible (with the collaboration of other gay-rights groups such as AIDS Action Council and the American Foundation for AIDS Research) for passing such legislation as the 1990 Ryan White Care Act and the Americans with Disabilities Act (July 1990), as well as creating programs for research and for screening of breast and cervical cancer. The HRC's lobbying efforts also helped to defeat antigay legislation at the state level in Oregon and Idaho (1994) and Maine (1995).

The HRC uses its political action committee (PAC) to support HRC-endorsed federal legislative candidates from all parties. In 1996 the HRC contributed more than $1 million to assist HRC-endorsed candidates for federal office. The HRC funded candidates in more than 170 races in 1996—out of these races, 83 percent of HRC-endorsed candidates were winners; an increase from 67 percent in 1994. Besides funding, the HRC provides material to candidates it has endorsed to assist the candidate in understanding and speaking about gay, lesbian, and bisexual issues.

The organization supports and sponsors public poll research on the subjects of gay and lesbian equal rights, as well as AIDS policy. The HRC commissions independent polling firms to carry out the polls. The HRC uses this research to try to gain public support—and ultimately, to provide support for shaping policy—on issues of AIDS and human rights. For example, in 1996, the HRC conducted a survey to gauge the impact of gay issues in that year's political campaign. Five percent of respondents who voted (up 3 percent from 1992 and 1994 surveys) identified themselves as gay, lesbian, or bisexual. The 1996 poll found that 70 percent of respondents believed that gays and lesbians should be protected from workplace discrimination. Regarding other issues on the HRC's agenda, 80 percent of respondents stated that increasing funding for AIDS research and prevention was "very important" or "one of the most important issues." A law that would increase the penalties for hate crimes aimed at gay people was favored by 75 percent of the respondents. The findings from these public opinion polls are consolidated for HRC-endorsed candidates to provide them with background and to help them speak clearly about the issues.

The HRC works at the grassroots level to advance its agenda. To mobilize grassroots support, the HRC coordinates a 10,000-member Action Network. The Action Network is headed by the field division (under the Political Department) of the HRC. Action Network members receive mailings (Action Alerts), which encourage them to respond to specific legislative initiatives that promote the HRC agenda. The HRC also has an Action Center on its Web site, a feature that ranks a congressional representative's voting record on HRC issues and allows HRC supporters to send instant messages to legislators.

PROGRAMS

HRC programs support the organization's agenda to advance the human rights of gays, lesbians, and bisexuals. Most of its largest programs are educational. For example the organization sponsors the National Coming Out Project. This program uses local events, public service announcements, and celebrity speaking engagements to encourage gays, lesbians, and bisexuals to be open about their sexuality. According to the organization, this type of honesty is the best route for a gay person to follow because it may open up a dialogue between gays and heterosexuals.

The National Coming Out Project encompasses many events. National Coming Out Day is held annually on October 11, and honors the 1987 march for gay rights in Washington, D.C., on that date. On this day, speeches and rallies are held in colleges, businesses, churches, and community centers across the country. On National Coming Out Day, the HRC also conducts a media campaign using radio, television, and magazines.

The National Coming Out Project works year round with lesbian and gay groups on college campuses, providing them with materials to plan for the annual Coming Out Day and to encourage these organizations to register young gay voters. The HRC also produces the *Resource Guide to Coming Out*, which gives readers resources and helps them through the coming out process. In 1997 the HRC coordinated hundreds of events on Coming Out Day and distributed 25,000 copies of the *Resource Guide to Coming Out*.

The HRC also coordinates an Academic Internship Program. College students may apply for part-time or full-time internships. Interns may work in several areas, including: communications, electronic media, field organizing, merchandise, PAC department, administrative, membership, legislative, development, or the National Coming Out Day Project.

The HRC held a Youth College for Campaign Training in 1996. This program trained 25 young activists and placed them in congressional campaigns that were key to the HRC's agenda. In 1996 the HRC also carried out The California Project, in which HRC worked with local activists in an attempt to defeat extremist campaigns for positions in the California Assembly.

BUDGET INFORMATION

In fiscal year 1996–97, the HRC and the HRC Foundation had combined revenues of $11,153,350 —a record number since the organization's inception. Revenue came from the following sources: Federal Club members and other major donors ($4,105,084); regular membership ($3,587,069); events ($2,666,319); earned income and other revenue ($512,085); and bequests and foundation grants ($282,793). Programs made up the largest expense in the HRC's budget—federal and field advocacy ($4,155,166); communications ($1,195,199); and membership ($1,560,678). Other expenses included administration ($1,576,533) and fund-raising ($2,353,969). The HRC's and the Foundation's combined net assets at the end of the year were $1,221,641.

The HRC's PAC contributed more than $1.1 million to the campaigns of HRC-endorsed candidates in 1996. Of these 170 political races, 83 percent of the HRC-endorsed candidates were successful in winning their races.

BUDGET:

1996 HRC Revenue

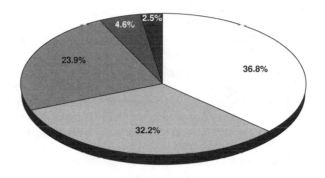

☐ 36.8%: Federal Club members and other major donors

▨ 32.2%: Regular membership

▨ 23.9%: Events

▨ 4.6%: Earned income and other

■ 2.5%: Bequests and foundation grants

1996 HRC Expenses

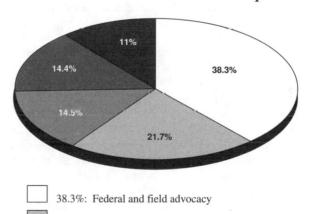

☐ 38.3%: Federal and field advocacy

▨ 21.7%: Fund raising

▨ 14.5%: Administration

▨ 14.4%: Membership

■ 11%: Communications

HISTORY

The HRC was founded in 1980 with the name of the Human Rights Campaign Fund. At the time that the HRC was founded, the gay rights movement was over a decade old. Gays were taking steps to be accepted by the rest of society. The focus of gay rights groups such as the HRC, as well as more radical gay rights groups (like Act Up), was on equal rights issues such as employee discrimination, hate crimes, adoption, and custody rights. The AIDS epidemic also directed the efforts of these groups toward fighting HIV-related discrimination, advocating for confidentiality in treatments, and promoting research to lead to more effective treatments.

Gay rights groups faced hostile opposition from the Christian right wing, a well-organized coalition of groups, politicians, and supporters that had unified in the 1970s and opposed gay rights on the basis that homosexuality violated biblical tenets. The Christian Coalition became a viable opponent to gay rights groups and remained so throughout the 1980s and 1990s.

In February 1993 the HRC merged with what was then known as National Coming Out Day (NCOD). NCOD had begun in October 11, 1988, to commemorate a 1987 march on that day in Washington, D.C., for gay rights. Under the HRC, the program evolved into the National Coming Out Program, a year-round effort to encourage people to live openly as gays and lesbians, and to be honest about their sexuality.

Since President Bill Clinton was elected in 1992, and reelected in 1996, the HRC has had generally good relations with the White House and worked with a presidential administration that claims to be supportive of gay and lesbian issues. The Clinton administration, for example, supported 1995 legislation that would bar discrimination based on sexuality from the workplace. In 1997 President Clinton made historic gay rights news by being the first president to speak at a gay rights function, which was sponsored by the HRC.

However, the Clinton administration angered the gay community and gay rights groups when he signed the Defense of Marriage Act (1996), a law that makes it possible for states to refuse to recognize same-sex marriage performed in another state. The president also lost points with gay activists when he compromised by endorsing the "Don't Ask, Don't Tell" policy for gays in the military. This policy called for the military not to question recruits about their sexual orientation, but only protected gay and lesbian military personnel so long as they kept their homosexual lifestyle a secret.

The organization faced changes in 1995 when the board of directors appointed Elizabeth Birch as executive director of the HRC. In 1996 Birch changed the organization's name to "Human Rights Campaign," dropping the word "Fund" from the title. The purpose of the name change was to show that the HRC did more than raise money for political candidates.

In 1996 the HRC coordinated OutVote '96, the first national lesbian and gay political convention. The convention took place in Chicago and was held between the Democratic and Republican Conventions. In 1997 HRC expanded its field programs by appointing many new district coordinators, and beginning such new programs as activist training and action weeks at the local level.

CURRENT POLITICAL ISSUES

The HRC is involved in a number of issues that affect gay and lesbian civil rights, such as hate crimes against gays. According to the organization, gays are increasingly targets of these crimes, but the federal government has difficulty prosecuting the crimes under laws designed primarily to stop hate crimes based on religious or ethnic differences. Thus the HRC has pushed for revisions and expansions of hate crime laws, at both a national and state level.

The HRC is also concerned with the treatment of gays in the workplace. No federal law currently exists to protect gays from job discrimination. At the state level, protection exists only in 11 states. In the other 39 states, an employer may fire a person based solely on that person's sexual orientation. The HRC has been a strong supporter of the Employment Non-Discrimination Act (ENDA), first proposed in 1994, which would outlaw discrimination based on sexual orientation. Attempts to pass the bill in the House of Representatives have failed.

Another major issue that gays and lesbians face both in and out of the workplace is partner benefits. Currently, gays and lesbians are not able to legally marry, and therefore do not enjoy the same rights and privileges that heterosexuals can gain through marriage. Partner benefits such as health insurance, adoption of children, and joint tax status are not generally available to the gay community. The HRC has sought these rights for gay and lesbian couples on many fronts. Attempts to legalize marriage in states such as Hawaii have been unsuccessful, but the HRC has enjoyed some smaller successes.

In the workplace, the HRC has pursued changes that would allow same-sex couples to enjoy some of the financial and social benefits of marriage. These benefits can often be quite substantial, including health, dental, and life insurance. The HRC maintains that same-sex partners are entitled to these benefits, and has played an active role in advocating for them in particular cases. Many companies have voluntarily expanded the benefits programs to cover gay and lesbian couples, allowing these partners, while not married, to enjoy better insurance coverage. In some cases, however, these moves have led to controversy.

Case Study: Can Ross Perot Make Room for Gay Benefits?

In early 1998, the HRC learned that the Perot Systems Corp., an information technology company owned by billionaire and one-time presidential candidate Ross Perot, might be retracting its policy of offering same-sex benefits to homosexual employees. The policy had been put in place during Perot's absence from the company. Upon his return, he commented that he might end the benefits.

After hearing of the possible withdrawal, the HRC monitored the situation at Perot Systems to see what direction the company would take. The HRC also took direct action by contacting Perot personally and requesting him not to rescind domestic benefits for same-sex partners of employees. The organization issued press releases with contact information for the company, and urged members and supporters to write or call Ross Perot and urge him not to withdraw the policy.

Shortly after HRC launched its action, Perot modified his position and said that he would consider the situation further before withdrawing the policy. However, in April 1998, after Perot had returned, the company withdrew the policy and began excluding gay and lesbian employees from receiving partner benefits.

Public Impact

The setback for same-sex partner domestic benefits at Perot Systems was a disappointment for the HRC. Ever since Lotus Notes became the first public company to offer such benefits in 1991, information technology companies, such as Perot Systems, have been among the leaders in extending benefits to same-sex partners. The benefits have tremendous positive financial impact for recipients and, according to HRC studies, cost the granting companies very little. Gay right groups believe that granting same-sex partner benefits would be the first step for improving the situation of homosexuals in the workplace and beyond. Same-sex partner benefits, the HRC feels, foster a better acceptance of gay and lesbian relationships in the workplace, and help broaden society's definition of a domestic partner.

FUTURE DIRECTIONS

As the HRC looks toward the future, elections and polls seem to indicate that voters are favoring moderate approaches that bring people together. The HRC will continue to make an effort to educate "fair-minded" people about its work, and present opportunities to bring these people into the policy-shaping process at the grassroots level. For example, the HRC will be expanding its cadre of district coordinators, with a goal of one coordinator for each legislative district. The HRC will continue to encourage gay and nongay support for coming out, believing that honesty and courage will foster progress and necessary dialogue.

Additionally, the HRC will continue to fight AIDS—until a cure is found—by lobbying for necessary funding and research. The HRC will continue to advocate that the federal ban on needle-exchange programs

FAST FACTS

Hate crimes against lesbians, gays and bisexuals increased nationally by 6 percent in 1996.

(Source: The New York City Gay & Lesbian Anti-Violence Project, "National Coalition of Anti-Violence Programs 1996 Annual Report.")

be lifted and that the Medicare system go through the appropriate reforms so that those who are covered can receive the AIDS treatments that they need.

GROUP RESOURCES

The HRC maintains a comprehensive Web site at http://www.hrc.org; the site includes: news releases; information about the organization's issues, missions, and programs; information on getting involved; and a feature that allows users to send messages directly to their legislator. Through the Web page, users may access voting records on gay rights-related issues. The organization sells merchandise that features the HRC logo—available through the Web site or by contacting the organization directly.

As part of the National Coming Out Project, the HRC produces the "HRC Resource Guide To Coming Out." This pamphlet is designed to help people deal with the difficult issues surrounding coming out. It can be accessed on-line at http://www.hrc.org/ncop/guide.html. For more information, contact the Project directly at 1-800-866- 6263.

GROUP PUBLICATIONS

The HRC produces the *HRC Quarterly*, a publication that members receive four times a year. The *HRC News*, which can be accessed at the organization's Web site at http://www.hrc.org, contains current and past press releases and information from the HRC. The organization also publishes a legislative report card, summing up voting records for the most recent legislative session. For information on these and other HRC publications, call the organization at (202) 628-4160, or write to The Human Rights Campaign, 919 18th St. NW, Washington, DC 20006.

BIBLIOGRAPHY

Baker, Daniel, Sean O'Brien Strub and Bill Henning. *Cracking the Corporate Closet: The 200 Best (and Worst) Companies to Work for, Buy from, and Invest in if You're Gay or Lesbian—and Even if You Aren't*, New York: HarperBusiness, 1995.

Black. Chris. "Senate Begins Gay-Rights Debate." *The Boston Globe*, 7 September 1996.

Burr, Chandler. "The AIDS Exception: Privacy vs. Public Health." *The Atlantic Monthly*, June 1997.

Isikoff, Michael. "Gingrich: Newt's Gay Sister Gets Out Front." *Newsweek*, 13 March 1995.

Lurie, Peter and Ernest Drucker. "An Opportunity Lost: HIV Infections Associated with Lack of National Needle Exchange Programme." *The Lancet*, 1 March 1997.

Montgomery, Lori. "Gay Group Protests Congressional Inquiry into Teaching of Homosexuality in Public Schools." *Knight-Ridder Tribune News Service*, 4 September 1995.

Simons, Todd. "The End: Has the Gay Movement Met Its Match?" *The Advocate*, 24 January 1995.

Thurman, Skip. "Clinton to Openly Advocate Gay Rights." *The Christian Science Monitor*, 7 November 1997.

Walker, Paulette. "Law Makers Push NIH to Spend More on the Most Prevalent Diseases." *Chronicle of Higher Education*, 18 April 1997.

Winfeld, Liz and Susan Spielman. *Straight Talk about Gays in the Workplace*, New York: Amacom, 1995.

Humane Society of the United States (HSUS)

WHAT IS ITS MISSION?

Promoting the humane treatment of animals is the chief mission of the aptly named Humane Society of the United States (HSUS). The organization was founded on that philosophy more than 40 years ago and has since grown into the largest animal protection organization in the United States. Originally, the HSUS was primarily concerned with the treatment of domestic and farm animals, but today organizers are also involved in protecting exotic species around the globe, from African elephants to whale populations off the coast of Norway.

The HSUS has also initiated numerous campaigns that indirectly impact the welfare of animals. One arm of the HSUS, for example, preserves wildlands, while another focuses on education, informing everyone from grade school children to animal shelter professionals. Despite its varied list of campaigns, the first and foremost concern of the HSUS, according to HSUS President and Chief Financial Officer Paul Irwin, is the "continuing effort to eliminate the tragic surplus of homeless dogs and cats and the suffering these animals experience."

ESTABLISHED: November 22, 1954
EMPLOYEES: 300
MEMBERS: 5.4 million
PAC: None

Contact Information:
ADDRESS: 2100 L St. NW
    Washington, DC 20037
PHONE: (202) 778-6132
FAX: (202) 452-1100
E-MAIL: webmaster@hsus.org
URL: http://www.hsus.org
PRESIDENT; CEO: Paul G. Irwin

HOW IS IT STRUCTURED?

The HSUS is a private, nonprofit, charitable organization funded exclusively by membership dues, contributions, grants, and bequests; in other words, the HSUS receives no state or federal money. The HSUS maintains its headquarters in Washington, D.C., and at the national level is governed by a board of seven officers and 25 directors. Among the prominent directors is

Jane Goodall, the famous primate researcher. While HSUS staff are charged with carrying out daily operations, the president is responsible for running the administration on behalf of the board of directors. The treasurer prepares the annual operations budget for approval by the board and oversees HSUS assets, making disbursements for expenses and maintaining the financial records required to meet federal and state reporting requirements.

The HSUS maintains nine regional offices, which oversee operations in 46 states. Each regional office serves different needs. Officers in Alabama, for example, uncovered horse cruelty during the equestrian event at the 1996 Summer Olympic. Videotapes of the mistreatment, captured by undercover HSUS investigators, "garnered international media attention," according to the *HSUS News,* "and focused public outrage on this little-known event." In Minnesota, local investigators exposed the ill treatment of dogs in a Dalmatian breeding mill.

The HSUS also has an international arm, the Humane Society International (HSI). With offices in Australia, Columbia, and Europe, HSI provides the HSUS with global influence.

PRIMARY FUNCTIONS

The HSUS attempts to make the world a safer place for animals by working through three major channels: legal, legislative, and educational. To many Americans the HSUS is synonymous with Humane Society animal shelters around the country. In fact the HSUS does not offer the shelters financial assistance—it merely provides them with guidelines for shelter policies and operations, conducts training for staff, sponsors a trade show for animal care and control workers, and publishes *Animal Shelter* magazine. The shelters, in turn, give the HSUS a highly visible community presence. It is here that many people learn about the main mission of the HSUS, which is to end pet overpopulation through sterilization programs and adoption, and how to prevent animal cruelty.

The HSUS has three organizations dedicated to promoting its educational message. To address issues in higher education the Center for Respect of Life and Environment (CRLE) was founded in 1986. Its goal is to foster compassion toward "all sentient beings and respect for the integrity of nature." According to information posted on the HSUS Web site, "CRLE focuses on higher education, religion, the professions, and the arts in promoting a humane and sustainable future." In addition to hosting annual seminars, the organization supports six theological institutions committed to teaching students about the ethics of maintaining a "humane" environment. In the early 1990s CRLE was also credited with helping to create a greater public respect for animals through its publication of *Earth Ethics: Evolving Values for an Earth Community.* The journal was widely distributed and used in college classrooms.

Primary and secondary school level education is provided by the National Association for Humane and Environmental Education (NAHEE). Based in East Haddam, Connecticut, NAHEE serves as a resource for youths and educators and reaches its audience primarily through the publication *KIND News* (Kids In Nature's Defense). Finally the HSUS operates the International Center for Earth Concerns (ICEC). From its headquarters in Ojai, California, ICEC "works internationally in collaboration with other organizations and individuals to support effective animal-protection and nature-conservation projects," according to the HSUS Web site.

The HSUS also seeks to preserve wildlands through its Wildlife Land Trust and to improve the environment through EarthKind. In 1996, according to that year's HSUS annual report, the Wildlife Land Trust accepted "permanent protection responsibility" for 1,739 acres located in Arkansas, Maine, New Hampshire, and New York. Meanwhile, EarthKind, the environmental arm of the HSUS, aims to improve energy efficiency and biodiversity around the world.

A leader in efforts to strengthen anticruelty laws and promote the enforcement of those laws, the society maintains a government affairs office in Washington, D.C. This office monitors legislation involving wild captive domestic animals and works to influence policy at the federal and state level. The HSUS was successful, for example, in gaining congressional support to drop a $2 million annual subsidy for the mink industry. Moreover since 1982 the HSUS has successfully lobbied to end cruel hunting and trapping methods—such as body-gripping traps and bear baiting—in Massachusetts, Washington, Oregon, Arizona, and Colorado.

To help back up some of its initiatives in Washington, the HSUS has proved itself skilled in the business of undercover investigations. HSUS professional investigators routinely conduct research on animal abuse in circuses, factory farms, rodeos, and zoos. Among its many victories, HSUS investigations have helped to shut down a major California dogfighting operation and to convict an animal-sacrificing practitioner in Florida.

In its attempt to foster "compassion for all creatures," the HSUS often finds itself playing hardball in the political arena. As President Irwin admitted in the fall 1997 issue of the *HSUS News,* the society "has never had trouble identifying our political adversaries. From the beginning in 1954, their ranks have included puppy mill operators, furriers, cockfighters, whalers, and an array of others who needlessly exploit animals." Subsequently, the list of HSUS opponents has also included major government agencies, including the U.S. Department of Agriculture—which the HSUS has charged with failing to enforce laws intended to protect animals—and the U. S. Fish and Wildlife Service—which the HSUS criticizes for allowing hunting on federal land designated as wildlife refuges.

Within the range of animal-protection organizations, the HSUS is not as militant as the Animal Liberation Front or People for Ethical Treatment of Animals (PETA) but it is more staunchly protective of individual animal rights than the World Wildlife Fund.

PROGRAMS

The HSUS sponsors a number of campaigns and programs to bring about its mission, such as celebrating Animal Shelter Appreciation Week in November, funding television broadcasts on the My Pet Television Network, and promoting educational travel through the HSUS Journey of Awareness program. In 1997, the HSUS launched the First Strike Campaign to address the rise of violence against animals and people. "This campaign," wrote Randall Lockwood, HSUS vice president of training initiatives, in the summer 1997 issue of *HSUS News*, "is a long-term effort with two goals: to increase awareness of the well-documented connection between violence against animals and violence against people and to encourage all those involved in antiviolence efforts to work together." As part of the campaign, the HSUS produced brochures, a handbook, and other educational literature for professionals and the general public. The HSUS also established a toll-free number (1-888-213-0956) for individuals and groups hoping to organize local anti-violence coalitions.

Hoping to sensitize children to unnecessary cruelty to animals, the HSUS also coordinated an anti-dissection campaign in 1997. The program was designed to provide students with an early awareness of harmful animal classroom exercises, namely the biology class frog dissection project. The campaign provides teachers with alternative teaching tools, such as CD-ROMs, charts, diskettes, models, and videos.

One of the most visible HSUS programs is its anti-fur campaign, thanks to a succession of Hollywood stars that have promoted the cause, including actresses Candice Bergen and Betty White, and supermodel Cindy Crawford. Started in 1988, the campaign urges consumers to avoid fur products through ads in the print and broadcast media, as well as on kiosks, buses, and billboards. "Your fur coat is a luxury our family can't afford," declared the bold message on one billboard depicting three furry pups; another well-publicized campaign featured Cindy Crawford and several other supermodels promoting the slogan "I'd Rather Go Naked Than Wear Fur."

BUDGET INFORMATION

The HSUS is supported primarily by membership dues, contributions, grants, and bequests. In 1996 con-

A young girl embraces the dog her grandmother adopted for her during the 1998 "Meet Your Best Friend at the Zoo" day in Royal Oak, Michigan. The Michigan Humane Society says the annual event is the largest off-site animal adoption program in the nation. (Photograph by Richard Sheinwald, AP/Wide World Photo)

tributions and grants totaled $31,372,968, by far the largest chunk of its income. Bequests amounted to $7,701,753, while investment income provided $7,838,583. Total income in 1996 was $48,002,654 and total expenses amounted to $41,654,779. The HSUS spends a large portion of its budget on fundraising ($12,070,900) and producing public education and mem-

BUDGET:

1996 HSUS Revenue

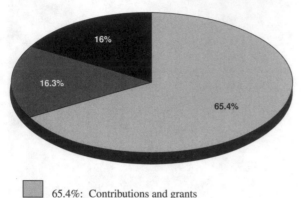

- [ ] 65.4%: Contributions and grants
- [ ] 16.3%: Investment income
- [ ] 16%: Bequests

1996 HSUS Expenses

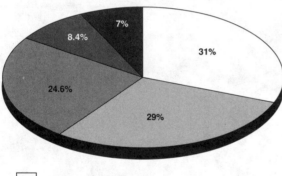

- [ ] 31%: Administration
- [ ] 29%: Fund raising
- [ ] 24.6%: Producing public education and membership literature
- [ ] 8.4%: Wildlife, animal habitat, and sheltering programs
- [ ] 7%: Cruelty investigations

bership literature ($10,259,383). Wildlife, animal habitat, and sheltering programs cost the HSUS $3,477,450, while cruelty investigations amounted to $2,899,918. The HSUS budget supports about 300 employees, including its administrative staff in Washington, D.C.

The HSUS was born out of a movement that swept the nation following the establishment of the first Society for Prevention of Cruelty to Animals in New York in the late 1800s. On November 22, 1954, in Washington, D.C., a small group of activists, determined to eliminate animal abuse and neglect, formed the HSUS. In the early days the organization reflected its founders' vision, primarily promoting humane treatment of farm and domestic animals. Today the HSUS is the largest animal protection organization in the United States with a staff of more than 300 nationwide and a constituency of more than five million.

Over the years the HSUS's focus on farm animals, in particular, has intensified with the growth of "factory farms." Farming used to be an industry of small, family-owned farms; today large factory-like operations prevail. Partly as a result of the booming agri-business industry, Americans are more aware of the food they buy and increasingly they are demanding organic products. Given this heightened consumer awareness, the HSUS lobbies for organic labeling that includes the humane treatment of animals.

The rise of industry—including the housing boom in the United States—has also prompted the HSUS to increase its effort to protect wildlife and animal habitat. Like the treatment of farm animals, the plight of wildlife in urban areas has captured the public's attention in recent years because many people have personally come face to face with the conflicts. The HSUS is developing solutions, for example, to reduce the number of deer hit by motorists, such as installing roadside reflectors to inhibit deer from crossing the road or building bridges that the animals can use to bypass busy roads.

In part technology has helped the HSUS pursue its mission. "The computer has had an enormous impact on our ability to influence," Patricia Forkan Looks, HSUS senior vice president, told the *HSUS News* in 1990. "When I first became involved in the animal-protection movement, we had no computers and were doing all the mailings by hand. If someone suggested that we get the mailings out quickly, it was nearly impossible. Computers have made a huge difference in our ability to talk to our members quickly and, in turn, we know they are doing excellent work out in the trenches."

Not surprisingly advances in the modern world have also increased the HSUS's burden. In response to the increasingly industrialized world, the HSUS has expanded its mission, from cruelty investigations to enacting legislation dealing with trapping, captive wildlife, wildlife refuges, endangered species, predator control, and marine mammals. As the organization's promotional literature asserts: "With programs in animal research issues, companion animals, farm animals and bioethics, humane education and wildlife and habitat protection, the HSUS touches on every issue affecting animals."

CURRENT POLITICAL ISSUES

In recent years the fight for animal rights has become more politicized. On one end of the political spectrum is PETA, far smaller than the HSUS with only 600,000 members and an annual budget of $13 million. Unlike the HSUS, PETA has advocated for complete vegetarianism among humans and the abolition of zoos. The HSUS assumes a more moderate position on these issues, as well as on the controversial practice of using animals for medical testing. "Our view is that much more needs to be done to reduce the suffering of animals in laboratories, but we stop short of calling for the complete abolition of animal testing," Martin Stephens, HSUS vice president for animal research issues, told *Insight on the News* in 1997. "We've forged alliances with several federal agencies and companies involved in testing animals. We may not agree with them 100 percent across the board, but it's better to work together on reform than shout insults across the divide." In fact forming partnerships with other animal rights organizations, state and federal governments, and large corporations has helped the HSUS maintain a formidable presence in the global debate on animal rights.

Case Study: Saving the Dolphins

The plight of the dolphins caught and killed in tuna nets in the Pacific made international news in the 1980s. Tuna fishers, trying to haul in the largest catches possible, ensnared hundreds of dolphins in their nets. The tuna fishers, of course, weren't interested in the dolphins but rather the schools of tuna that swam underneath the dolphins, and so they used whatever means necessary—sometimes helicopters and speed boats—to chase the dolphins and capture the tuna below. One report put the dolphin death toll at 100,000 per year during the 1970s and 1980s. A public outcry in the late 1980s led major U.S. tuna canners, including Starkist, Bumblebee, and Chicken of the Sea, to agree not to purchase any tuna caught by dolphin chasing. Shortly after that Congress enacted laws that produced standards for companies to market their goods with a "dolphin-safe" label. Several countries, however, continued to import tuna caught by outlawed, dolphin-chasing practices. The HSUS called for tighter policing but faced considerable resistance from the Clinton administration, largely due to pressure from Mexico and other Latin American nations.

Working with other organizations, including the Sierra Club, the HSUS lobbied long and hard to ensure tough enforcement of the dolphin-safe standards on products sold in U.S. markets. In the end, they won a battle, but not the war. Although companies could import tuna caught by chasing dolphins, those companies could not market their products with the dolphin-safe label. "Amendments to the original dolphin-deadly legislation were secured," noted one report in the fall

FAST FACTS

It is estimated that shelters in the United States take in 8 to 12 million animals each year. Approximately four percent of cats and 14 percent of dogs are returned to their owners; 25 to 35 percent of all animals are adopted by new owners, and depending on the geographic region, about 30 to 60 percent are euthanatized.

(Source: Humane Society of the United States. "Pet Population Fact Sheet," 1998.)

1997 issue of *HSUS News*, "but the legislation remains unacceptable." The dolphin-tuna case illustrates the HSUS's role in monitoring and changing laws that protect animals. And like many of HSUS's campaigns, the fight wages on.

FUTURE DIRECTIONS

In the twenty-first century, the HSUS and other animal-rights protection groups will only face bigger battles as industry continues to swallow up wildlife habitat. As HSUS President Paul Irwin wrote in the foreword to *Wild Neighbors: The Humane Approach to Living with Wildlife*, "Eight out of every ten Americans now live in municipalities of fifty thousand residents or more. Every other American lives in one of our thirty-nine largest cities. More than 70 million acres of land have been taken to build cities and suburbs, while an urban "shadow"—an area reflecting the effects of urbanization—spreads over the countryside." While the HSUS will continue its effort to make sure wildlife living in our midst, and in our homes, is treated humanely, the organization intends to continue acquiring wildlife land through its Land Trust."

GROUP RESOURCES

The HSUS maintains a Web site at http://www.hsus.org which provides information on specific HSUS campaigns, events, and actions. The HSUS produces frequent press releases on political issues which are also available on the Web site. For more information about the various HSUS educational organizations contact the HSUS Wildlife Land Trust by E-mail at hsuswlt@ix.netcom.

com or call 1-800-729-SAVE; contact NAHEE at PO Box 362, East Haddam, CT 06423-0362; phone (860) 434-8666 or E-mail at nahee@snet.net; contact CRLE via email at crle@aol.com or access its Web site at http://www.center1.com/crle.html.

GROUP PUBLICATIONS

The HSUS has many publications including *Animal Activist Alert,* a quarterly newsletter covering animal legislation; *HSUS Close-Up Reports,* a quarterly magazine covering society activities; *Wild Tracks,* a quarterly newsletter sent to wildlife- and habitat-protection activists; *KIND News* and *KIND Teacher,* educational program information and activities for teachers and students, which is printed throughout the year; *Shelter Sense,* a newsletter designed for shelter staff or animal control professionals; *Earth Ethics,* a quarterly journal with articles concerning issues connected with the HSUS Center for Respect of Life and Environment division. The HSUS also publishes many brochures, such as *Working for Animals: A Handbook for Lobbyists* and *Make It a Safe Trip for Your Dog,* as well as books, including *Wild Neighbors: The Humane Approach to Living with Wildlife.* These and other publications can be obtained by contacting the HSUS at (202) 452-1100.

BIBLIOGRAPHY

Dorsey, Chris. "License Fees Fund the Antics." *Sports Afield,* February 1993.

Hadidian, John, Guy R. Hodge, and John W. Grandy. *Wild Neighbors: The Humane Approach to Living with Wildlife.* Golden, Colo.: Fulcrum Publishing, 1997.

Hanson, Gayle M. B. "AID Trophy-hunt Funding Jogs Use vs. Abuse Issue." *Insight on the News,* 9 December 1996.

Hepner, L. H. *Animals in Education: The Facts, Issues and Implications.* Albuquerque: Richmond Publishers, 1994.

Horvitz, Leslie Ann. "Are Animal Advocates Biting the Hand of Dedicated Docs?" *Insight on the News,* 19 May 1997.

Magner, Denise K. and Paulette Walker Campbell. "Activists Push to Expand U.S. Rules On Animal Research to Cover Birds, Rats, and Mice." *The Chronicle of Higher Education,* 12 February 1999.

Nieves, Evelyn. "A Campaign For a No-Kill Policy for the Nation's Animal Shelters." *New York Times (Late New York Edition),* 11 February 1999.

Reiger, George. "Wishful Wildlife Management." *Field & Stream,* October 1994.

Schmiedeskamp, Mia. "Crimes Against Nature." *Scientific American,* March 1999.

Stanglin, Douglas. "Animal Antics." *U.S. News & World Report,* 17 June 1996.

Independent Insurance Agents of America (IIAA)

WHAT IS ITS MISSION?

According to the organization, the mission of the Independent Insurance Agents of America (IIAA), "is to be the unrelenting advocate for independent insurance agents and to fulfill the educational, political, and business needs of its members." The IIAA is a professional association of independent insurance agents—agents who sell policies written by several different insurance companies, as opposed to company or captive agents, who work exclusively for a single large insurer. It has consistently advanced the perpetuation of the independent agency system, and the overall well-being of the insurance industry itself. Among the IIAA's declared Fundamental Values is a pledge to "commit the resources necessary to achieve a legislative, regulatory, and legal environment most favorable to independent agents and consumers."

ESTABLISHED: September 29, 1896
EMPLOYEES: 70
MEMBERS: 300,000
PAC: InsurPAC

Contact Information:

ADDRESS: 127 S. Payton
    Alexandria, VA 22314
PHONE: (703) 683-4422
TOLL FREE: (800) 221-7917
FAX: (703) 683-7556
E-MAIL: info@iiaa.org
URL: http//www.independentagent.com
PRESIDENT: William B. Greenwood
EXECUTIVE VICE PRESIDENT: Jeffrey M. Yates

HOW IS IT STRUCTURED?

The IIAA is a federation of local chapters operating in all 50 states; delegates from the chapters elect national officers at an annual convention. The president, vice president, and president-elect each serve one-year terms. A permanent administrator, the senior executive vice president and general counsel, are appointed positions and oversee the day-to-day operation of the organization. At its national headquarters in Alexandria, Virginia, and a branch office on Capitol Hill, the IIAA maintains a combined staff of 70 full-time employees.

IIAA programs are run by specialized committees within the organization. For instance, political activities

are the primary responsibility of the Government Affairs committee, through its three subcommittees: one for organizing grassroots action among the membership, one devoted to state government, and the IIAA's political action committee, InsurPAC. In addition, the group organizes an annual Legislative Conference in Washington, in which members from the state and local associations coordinate IIAA strategy and meet with their congressional representatives.

PRIMARY FUNCTIONS

Through a wide range of ambitious programs, the IIAA serves its members in three distinct arenas: within the insurance industry itself, between the industry and the general public, and between the industry and government.

The IIAA provides training and educational programs for its members, and has helped set the professional standards used in the regulation and accreditation of insurance agents. It is the advocate for independent agents, when their interests conflict with those of other insurance professionals. Although the IIAA is not a union, it has been involved in the negotiation of contracts between agencies and large companies, and works to maintain the competitive viability of independent agents.

At other times—particularly on political and regulatory issues—the IIAA has joined forces with insurance companies and other agent associations, cooperatively forming a unified voice for the insurance industry in government and consumer affairs. It sponsors an innovative program called Future One, an agent/company coalition focusing on industry research and state government affairs. In February 1998 the IIAA formed a strategic alliance in the areas of legislation and education with two of the largest agent groups, the National Association of Life Underwriters (NALU) and the Life Underwriter Training Council (LUTC). The alliance represents a combined membership of 500,000 agents and agency employees.

IIAA public relations programs promote a positive image of member-agents, and of the insurance business in general. Independent agents are represented as business professionals who work in their customers' best interests. On its own behalf, the IIAA presents itself as a consumer advocacy organization, rather than a vehicle for the professional self-interest of its members. IIAA media outreach programs ensure that the group's positions receive coverage in local and national news reports.

In both state and federal government, the IIAA conducts extensive political lobbying on issues affecting the conduct and regulation of the insurance business. In the words of an IIAA publicity release, it is "renowned for its effectiveness on Capitol Hill and in state houses around the country, and has been recognized as one of the top Washington lobbying groups by *Fortune* and *Roll Call*, among others." The same document notes that the group takes a proactive approach, "working behind the scenes to influence legislation before it becomes law." IIAA research programs provide industry data to legislators, and staff members are sometimes involved in drafting the texts of bills affecting the industry. In addition, the IIAA is a major campaign contributor, and operates a grassroots organization of 5,000 member-agents who directly lobby their local legislators through visits, phone calls, letters, faxes, and E-mails.

PROGRAMS

The IIAA's most visible programs are its public relations efforts, particularly its long-running media advertising campaign on behalf of independent agents. Since 1956 IIAA advertising has promoted an image of its member-agents as trusted business advisers whose primary loyalty is to their customers, not their companies. The ads imply that only agents displaying the "Big I" logo have the flexibility and independence to offer consumers the best coverage at the right price. In addition, the IIAA produces educational consumer guides and brochures on various insurance products, distributing some 300,000 such publications a year.

Since 1969 the IIAA has sponsored the nation's largest junior golf tournament, the Independent Insurance Agent Junior Classic. Attracting 10,000 participants a year, the competition includes local and state qualifying tournaments, which are run by member volunteers.

Within the insurance industry, the IIAA is known for its Best Practices Program, providing research and training on sales techniques, business strategies, and ethics. In 1970 the association launched the InVEST Program (Insurance Vocational Education Student Training), offering training classes at the high school and junior/community college level. As an outreach project, InVEST recruits young people for careers in insurance, with particular emphasis on increasing the numbers of women, ethnic minorities, and urban residents in the field.

IIAA legislative programs are relatively unpublicized, despite their impressive scale. Between 1979 and 1992, InsurPAC contributed a total of $4.2 million to U.S. congressional campaigns. Beyond its efforts on Capitol Hill, IIAA programs direct considerable resources to state and local government, where much of insurance regulation takes place. Future One's Insurance Campaign Institute trains insurance professionals to run for political office, and its state grant program encourages local initiatives to "significantly improve the insurance climate in a particular state."

BUDGET INFORMATION

Not made available.

HISTORY

The IIAA traces its beginnings to a meeting of 16 independent agents at Chicago's Great Northern Hotel on September 29, 1896, organized by Robert S. Brannen of Denver, Colorado. Established as the National Association of Local Fire Insurance Agents (NALFIA), its membership expanded to include 5,216 agents, in 36 state organizations, by 1913. In that year, the NALFIA voted to include casualty and surety agents, taking the name "National Association of Insurance Agents" (NAIA). The current name, Independent Insurance Agents of America, was adopted in 1975.

The association opened its first Washington, D.C., office in 1934. The first federal legislative committee was formed in 1945; among its priorities was the passage of the McCarran-Ferguson Act, which gave primary responsibility for insurance regulation to the states. The "Big I" logo and national advertising campaign were introduced in 1956, and the Insurance Youth Golf Classic (now the IIA Junior Classic) was established in 1969. The current Alexandria, Virginia, headquarters, owned by IIAA, was opened in 1989. The Capitol Hill office began operations in 1992.

NAIA membership grew to include over 30,000 independent agencies by 1952, and nearly 36,000 by 1965. Because of company mergers and market changes, the number of member-agencies dropped to 28,000 by the mid-1990s. However, the IIAA's 300,000 individual members represent a significant part of the industry workforce, and a majority of U.S. independent agents.

CURRENT POLITICAL ISSUES

The IIAA involves itself in law and policy issues that affect the insurance industry, on both the state and the federal level. Since most Americans are consumers of insurance, the regulations governing the industry have a clear public impact. However, quite often these issues receive little attention outside the insurance field, although they may have a tremendous impact on the operations of insurance companies. The focus of IIAA lobbying in the late 1990s included: pension regulation, corporate-owned life insurance, natural-disaster protection, banking policy, and crop insurance. Because many insurance-related issues involve technical details whose significance is unclear to nonspecialists—including many lawmakers-industry groups such as the IIAA often function as expert advisers to legislators. In addition, the associations serve as advocates for the professional interests of their membership.

While it joins a united front on many issues affecting the industry as a whole, IIAA positions on regulatory issues often differ from those of other agent associations and the large insurance companies. As the chief representative of independent agents, the IIAA breaks from the other industry associations to promote competition among companies and informed comparison-shopping by consumers. The IIAA believes it is in the public good to offer buyers a wide variety of insurance products. Addressing the 1997 IIAA Legislative Conference, House Banking Committee Chairman Jim Leach noted that within the insurance field, "every group pursues its own vested interest," but expressed his opinion that "the vested interest of IIAA members is fairly close to the national interest" on most issues.

Case Study: Banking and Insurance

Insurance is marketed not only as protection against possible catastrophe but as an investment toward financial security. Because of their dual nature—as instruments for risk-management, and as money-making investments—many insurance products (such as pensions, annuities, and life policies) can be seen to occupy a gray area between the domains of banking and insurance. Beginning in the 1980s, bankers and other financial professionals sought permission to market certain kinds of coverage that had traditionally been available only through insurance agents. Ever since, the two industries have battled over the issue of competition. The progress of that struggle highlights the many resources and strategies the IIAA employs, and the evolution of its agenda in response to changed conditions.

The IIAA's original position, joined by most other industry organizations, was definitive: banking and insurance should remain separate and noncompetitive, each marketing its own, exclusive, range of products and services. The banking industry countered by appealing to popular sentiment for deregulation and the consumer benefits of increased competition. Even as banks achieved limited access to particular markets, insurance lobbies fought for the principle of separation, winning several showdowns on the issue. For example, in 1991 the IIAA led efforts in the House of Representatives to defeat a proposed omnibus banking bill, which would have expanded the role of the banks. Reporting on the fierce lobbying battle, the industry publication *American Banker* concluded that "insurance agents routed the administration and banking interests whenever it came down to issues pitting one industry against another. Faced with a strong push to give banks more authority to sell and underwrite insurance, the insurance lobby successfully watered down the proposal. Indeed, the resulting amendments would have ended up rolling back the limited insurance powers banks already have" (American Banker, October 6, 1991). Through the early 1990s, the IIAA and its allies worked to stalemate any expansion of banking into the field of insurance.

FAST FACTS

According to 1996 Census Bureau statistics, the insurance industry employs a total of 2.4 million people in the United States.

(Source: *Life Insurance Fact Book*, 1997.)

Changing Focus

Two Supreme Court decisions in the mid-1990s changed the legislative playing field. *NationsBank of North Carolina, N.A. v. Variable Annuity Life Insurance Co. (1995)* ruled that national banks could sell fixed and variable annuities from their small-town branches. One year later, in *Barnett Bank of Marion County, N.A. v. Nelson*, the court held that state laws prohibiting such sales were preempted by federal law. In the wake of these rulings, the position of strict separation was no longer tenable. The IIAA's focus shifted to two major concerns: influencing the state regulations that would govern bank insurance sales, and defending the primacy of the states (not the federal government) in regulating insurance.

The IIAA drafted model laws regulating bank sales, and lobbied for their adoption in state houses. In some cases, the IIAA models were believed to impose such severe restrictions that it was possible most banks would not want to sell insurance. Agent groups supported placing restrictions on the banking industry's ability to sell insurance because they felt that banks had an unfair competitive advantage. The agents argued that the banks could use the confidential customer information they had to create an environment where customers would feel they had to buy insurance from the bank if they wanted to get credit (*Best's Review*, September 1996). In the name of consumer protection, insurance interests managed to achieve restrictions in many states that regulated which banks could participate in selling insurance and which sales techniques they could use.

Equally important, agent groups like the IIAA have been negotiating strategic relationships between banks and insurers. As a result, insurance agents are now allowed to sell certain financial products in competition with banks. While the marketing turf battles have continued, the insurers have also sought common ground and cooperation with banks, acknowledging that both industries are experiencing rapid reorganization. This new approach was underscored in January, 1997, when the IIAA "endorsed legislation to let banks and insurance companies own each other." In a dramatic reversal for a group that had "opposed bank entry into the insurance field for over 100 years," IIAA President Ronald A. Smith addressed his former adversaries: "To the banks we say: Come talk to us. If you want to sell insurance, come talk to the insurance experts. Additionally, many IIAA member agencies want to explore offering your products to our customers." Given the changes in government policy, IIAA Public Affairs Vice President Paul Equale observed, "It was our responsibility to adapt" (*American Banker*, January 17, 1997). Although it applied considerable lobbying muscle, the IIAA's preferred position on banking and insurance did not prevail; but through its willingness to compromise, and its long-term relationships with legislators, it continues to promote the competitive interests of its members in a changing marketplace.

SUCCESSES AND FAILURES

The IIAA can claim many legislative victories in its long history; and, as the battle over bank insurance sales illustrates, its flexibility and constant lobbying presence have allowed it to minimize many apparent defeats. A primary concern, underlying the IIAA's position on a number of issues for over 50 years, has been to establish and defend the principle of individual state's rights on insurance regulation.

Like most industry groups, the IIAA supported the passage of the 1945 McCarran-Ferguson Act, the statutory foundation for state regulation. McCarran-Ferguson placed the insurance business under state control on all matters not specifically covered by federal legislation, and granted the industry a limited exemption from federal antitrust laws. Since its passage, the IIAA has opposed several attempts to repeal or amend McCarran-Ferguson. It has also resisted most efforts to expand federal oversight of insurance, either through national legislation or the initiative of federal administrators. (In the banking battle, for example, it has been particularly outspoken against expanding the powers of the comptroller of the currency to regulate bank sales.)

McCarran-Ferguson faced a serious challenge in 1994, when a popular health care reform bill included provisions to eliminate the federal antitrust exemptions. Fearing the bill would pass, the IIAA negotiated a compromise that would have upheld most state powers. The bill was eventually defeated, along with the threat to repeal McCarran-Ferguson, but in the aftermath, IIAA leaders were widely criticized by some members and other industry groups for having accepted even a mild compromise on the issue.

The IIAA's long-standing support of state regulation indicates that, for all its effectiveness on Capitol Hill, it is even more confident of its ability to achieve its goals at the state level. While many observers feel that some increased federal presence is inevitable, the IIAA's contribution to maintaining state regulation for over a half-century must be counted among its lasting achievements.

FUTURE DIRECTIONS

The IIAA sees itself as one of the top lobbying organizations in Washington and is committed to remaining so by being vigilant in a fast-changing market and regulatory environment. Recent initiatives include mentoring programs to promote greater diversity in the field, a drive for increased participation by IIAA members, and a program to help members better utilize the Internet and related business technologies.

GROUP RESOURCES

The IIAA operates separate Web sites for membership and consumer affairs. The site at http://www. independentagent.com offers consumer access to IIAA educational and public-relations material, as well as an automated agent-referral system and links to the home pages of individual insurance companies. Research requests should be directed to Public Relations at the Alexandria headquarters.

GROUP PUBLICATIONS

IIAA's monthly magazine, *Independent Agent*, provides members with industry news, reports on IIAA activities, and business advice, particularly sales techniques. Another monthly, *Management Services*, focuses on agency management issues; the bimonthly *Action-*

gram provides updates on government and regulatory affairs. In addition, the IIAA produces many brochures and handbooks on insurance, intended both for consumers and the media, and available through the IIAA Consumer Communications/Press Relations office.

BIBLIOGRAPHY

Atkinson, Bill, and Robert M. Garsson. "Agents Outlobbied Bankers." *American Banker*, 6 November 1991.

Brooks, Jack. "Deception, Overreaction, Inertia Mar McCarran Reform Debate." *National Underwriter Property & Casualty*, 17 October 1994.

Brostoff, Steven. "IIAA Looks to Put Together Broad Coalition on Bank Bill." *National Underwriter Property & Casualty*, 17 July 1995.

de Senerpont Domis, Olaf. "A Friend of Newt Helps Insurance Agents Write Banking Policy." *American Banker*, 25 August 1995.

Fisher, Mary Jane. "Agent Groups Are Hefty Campaign Contributors." *National Underwriter Life & Health*, 5 April 1993.

Gardner, Jonathan. "Pols PAC It In: Campaigns Draw $42 Million from Healthcare Interests." *Modern Healthcare*, 20 January 1997.

Hofmann, Mark A. "McCarran Reform Fears: AIA Compromise Comes Under Fire." *Business Insurance*, 7 March 1994.

McConnell, Bill. "Agents Endorse Measure That Would Let Banks Own Insurers." *American Banker*, 17 January 1997.

McDaniel, Dave. "Banks Face Sales Barriers as Agents Lobby States." *Best's Review Life & Health*, September 1996.

Mulcahy, Colleen. "IIAA Draws Fire on McCarran Reform." *National Underwriter Property & Casualty*, 22 August 1994.

Pasher, Victoria Sonshine. "The IIAA Celebrates 100th Anniversary, Looks Ahead." *National Underwriter Property & Casualty*, 18 September 1995.

International Association of Machinists and Aerospace Workers (IAM)

ESTABLISHED: May 5, 1888
EMPLOYEES: 170
MEMBERS: 700,000
PAC: Machinists' Non-Partisan Political League (MNPL)

Contact Information:

ADDRESS: 9000 Machinists Pl.
   Upper Marlboro, MD 20772
PHONE: (301) 967-4500
FAX: (301) 967-4586
URL: http://www.iamaw.org
PRESIDENT: R. Thomas Buffenbarger

WHAT IS ITS MISSION?

The primary goal of the International Association of Machinists and Aerospace Workers (IAM) has always been to improve the wages, benefits, and working conditions of its members. The IAM's mission includes cooperating with management in the training and apprenticing of workers. Over its history, the union has developed a commitment to ensuring a safe and healthy workplace that is free from discrimination on the basis of sex, race, or national origin. The IAM has become increasingly concerned with ensuring job security for its members in a global economy marked by intense competition.

HOW IS IT STRUCTURED?

The IAM is governed by an executive council composed of the international president, a secretary-treasurer, a headquarters vice president, and six other vice presidents who are representatives of regions or major industries. Every five years conventions of delegates sent by the roughly 1,300 local lodges are held to elect these officers, set policy priorities, and amend the organization's constitution. The locals, which elect their own officers, are affiliated with roughly 100 district lodges that coordinate their activities and serve as intermediaries with the headquarters located in Washington, D.C.

The headquarters is composed of numerous departments. The Aerospace, Transportation, and Woodworkers departments handle issues specific to these industries. There are departments for collective bargaining, organizing, and political and legislative action that assist and coordinate the activities of the locals and districts in these areas. The Communications Department manages the IAM Web site, organizes the conventions, and puts out the IAM's publications, videos, and press releases. The Human Rights Department works primarily on civil rights issues, including discrimination and affirmative action, within the organization and in public policy.

The International Department works with international organizations and foreign unions on issues of interest to IAM members and to promote international labor rights. The IAM has a Women's Department to handle special issues such as workplace sexual harassment. There are also departments for research and legal affairs that assist the other departments in performing their functions. The IAM's political action committee, the Machinists Non-Partisan Political League (MNPL) is based at the organization headquarters.

The IAM has members in the United States, Canada, the Panama Canal Zone, Puerto Rico, and Guam. Significant segments of its membership are employed in the aerospace industry and in transportation, including the airline, railroad, automotive, and trucking industries. Others work in the defense, tool and die, wood and paper, electronics, construction, mining, and product manufacturing industries.

The IAM is affiliated with the American Federation of Labor and Congress of Industrial Organizations (AFL-CIO), the Canadian Labor Congress (CLC), the Railway Labor Executives' Association, the International Labor Organization, the International Metalworkers Federation, and the International Transport Workers' Federation.

PRIMARY FUNCTIONS

The IAM's main function is to enter into collective bargaining with employers to form contracts outlining such things as wages, benefits, and work rules. The IAM oversees roughly 7,000 contracts. During these negotiations the union members may authorize a strike to force employers to address their concerns or they may use such tactics as "slowdowns" where workers refuse to perform their duties at the normal pace. This practice was used against Northwest Airlines in 1998 negotiations and resulted in delayed or canceled flights for more than 100,000 passengers. The IAM also organized a rally attended by politicians and labor dignitaries to support the workers' demands in these negotiations.

In the political sphere the IAM seeks to protect its members' interests through lobbying and mobilization of its members at elections and on legislative issues. As IAM President Buffenbarger observed of the union's political foes, such as big business, "We can't match them dollar-for-dollar in the political derby. But we sure out-work them, out-organize them and out-vote them on election day." The IAM conducts voter registration and get-

out-the-vote drives as well as member education on political candidates and election issues. The union also alerts its members to key political issues and encourages them to contact their representatives, which can be done through the IAM Web site. The headquarters periodically hosts legislative conferences where activist members learn about upcoming issues and develop political strategies.

Besides lobbying, the IAM works with the government in a number of ways. Leaders give testimony before congressional hearings and inform legislators of the impact of bills on IAM members, affected industries, and the public. The IAM participates on various government advisory boards such as the Aviation Rulemaking Advisory Committee. It also works with the Federal Aviation Administration, the National Transportation Safety Board, the Occupational Safety and Health Administration, and other such agencies to help them set and enforce safety standards and work practices. The IAM also runs a number of federally funded worker training programs.

PROGRAMS

The IAM runs a variety programs, with some devoted to political action and others to expanding services and benefits for its members. In addition to the activities of the Political and Legislative Affairs Department, the IAM was an active participant in "Labor '98," the latest version of a coalition of unions organized by the AFL-CIO to strengthen organized labor's impact on the elections. The effort included major drives to register voters and get them to the polls, distribution of voter education guides, and political rallies and other events mobilizing members around important workers' issues such as pensions, wages, health care, and workplace health and safety. Although labor leaders will sometimes argue the effort is nonpartisan, the ultimate goal is to return control of the U.S. Congress to the Democrats.

The IAM operates a program that provides assistance to members and their families who are experiencing crisis, ranging from damage to a home by natural disaster, to personal problems. Locals and districts operate Community Services committees which are assisted by a national department.

As part of its efforts to serve the community, the IAM operates the IAM Center for Administering Rehabilitation and Employment Services (IAM CARES). This nonprofit organization works in collaboration with community based organizations to help individuals with disabilities to prepare for and secure employment. It also promotes the hiring of individuals with disabilities by labor, business, and industry.

The IAM runs the William W. Winpisinger Education and Technology Center in Maryland, which was founded to develop union members' leadership skills.

Through an emphasis on labor history and labor's role in society, students are taught that they "are part of a larger movement toward economic and social justice with dignity on the job." The school offers general leadership training and classes in areas such as organizing, collective bargaining, and strategic planning.

In 1994 the IAM launched a program to assist members and their employers in building High Performance Work Organization partnerships, a program of labor-management cooperation designed to improve productivity and industrial competitiveness—with the goal of protecting good jobs for union members. The program includes training for labor and management representatives and field visits to work sites. The program involves examining and restructuring company processes such as work procedures and the pricing of materials.

BUDGET INFORMATION

Not made available.

HISTORY

The Knights of Labor, an activist labor movement formed after the close of the Civil War, began to fall apart in the mid-1860s. Several railroad machinists who desired to break away from the Knights gathered on May 5, 1888, in Atlanta, Georgia, to found the Order of United Machinists and Mechanical Engineers, which subsequently became the International Association of Machinists when it admitted Canadian members. The organization, led by Thomas W. Talbot, sought to strengthen solidarity and skills within the trade and to provide its members with insurance for accidents, illness, and unemployment. Although the union grew quickly in the South and Midwest, by the mid-1890s the organization was dominated by Northeastern members.

In 1893 James O'Connell was elected to lead the union. He sought affiliation with the American Federation of Labor (AFL), which was reluctant to accept the IAM because of its policy of admitting only white, practicing machinists. O'Connell pushed the union to remove the whites-only provision from its constitution and gained a charter from the AFL in 1895, although the union continued to discriminate on the basis of race. O'Connell took an active role in helping the IAM's local unions with organizing and collective bargaining contract negotiations. In 1900 he helped negotiate a short-lived agreement with the National Metal Trades Association, an employer group, that set up collective bargaining, overtime pay, a nine-hour day, and guidelines for apprentice training and dispute arbitration.

Dissatisfaction with O'Connell's leadership led to the election of a socialist, W. H. Johnston, in a close race in 1911. Under Johnston the union was opened to women and to unskilled as well as skilled workers in the machine industry. After a series of unsuccessful strikes, the IAM's fortunes improved with the onset of World War I (1914–18), which increased demand for machinists' labor. By 1918 membership reached over 330,000 and many locals had negotiated an eight-hour day. Most of the membership gains were lost in the early 1920s, however, and Johnston resigned in 1926.

The union became more politically active in the 1920s. In 1924 the IAM ventured into presidential politics by supporting the unsuccessful Progressive Party candidacy of Robert La Follette. The IAM encouraged the passage of the Railway Labor Act in 1926 that required railroad companies to bargain with unions and forbid discrimination against union members. The following year the IAM pushed for ratification of amendments to the U.S. Constitution that would forbid child labor.

The IAM's membership was severely reduced by the Great Depression of the 1930s, when almost 30 percent of union members were unemployed. The IAM backed the economic recovery policies of democratic President Franklin Roosevelt, who was elected in 1932. The IAM took advantage of the provisions of the Wagner Act of 1935, which committed the federal government to protecting the right of workers to unionize and to bargain collectively with their employers, and launched an organizing effort in the aircraft assembly industry. The union endorsed Roosevelt in the 1936 presidential election.

World War II (1939–45) brought unprecedented membership gains to the IAM. Union growth in new industries led to jurisdictional conflicts with other unions that resulted in temporary disaffiliation from the AFL. The IAM pledged full support to the war effort and adopted the "no-strike" pledge encouraged by the Roosevelt administration. Membership soared to over 700,000 by 1944. In 1948 the IAM expanded its commitment to including members of all races. Despite widespread layoffs after the war, IAM contracts reflected gains in wages, hours, paid vacations and, by the mid-fifties, health and welfare benefits.

Labor's gains led to a political backlash culminating in the passage of the Taft-Hartley Act in 1947 over President Truman's veto, which restricted labor's ability to organize and participate in politics. Recognizing the need to defend its political interests, the IAM responded by forming its own political action committee (PAC), the Machinists' Non-Partisan Political Action League. But the activities of the PAC were rarely nonpartisan and the IAM almost always endorsed Democrats.

The 1960s were a time of greater prosperity for the IAM. In 1960 the union established the Labor-Management Pension Fund. Wages continued to rise and in 1966 the union led a strike at five major airlines that ended a cap on annual wage increases. By 1968 membership in what was now called the International Association of Machinists and Aerospace Workers passed the million mark. Programs on the union's political agenda, such as social security increases, Medicare, and Medicaid, passed under the leadership of IAM-endorsed president Lyndon Johnson in the mid 1960s. The IAM led an effort to push occupational health and safety legislation and the first bill passed Congress in 1970.

The Vietnam War (1959–75) hurt the relationship between labor and the Democratic Party, but in 1972, the IAM was one of a handful of AFL affiliates to endorse George McGovern, the Democratic nominee for president. Economic recession and defense cutbacks reduced IAM membership. Republican President Nixon appointed IAM President Floyd Smith to a labor-management board set up to control wages and prices during the massive inflation of this period, but in 1972 he resigned along with other labor members in protest of the board's pro-employer bias. To address the organization's changing needs, the 1976 IAM convention set up departments for organizing and civil rights.

In 1977 William W. Winpisinger, a charismatic new leader who described himself as "a seat-of-the-pants socialist," was elected IAM president. He was a staunch advocate of labor organizing and called for government ownership of airlines, banks, the oil industry, railroads, and utilities. During the 1970s energy crisis, he formed a coalition with environmentalists, civic groups, and others to work for lower energy costs and publicized oil companies' high profits. Within the labor movement, he pushed for a more active political and organizing role for the AFL-CIO and called for its elderly President George Meany to retire. Within the Democratic Party, Winpisinger tried to get then-president Jimmy Carter—who he described as the best Republican president since Herbert Hoover—off the 1980 Democratic ticket. The election brought Republican Ronald Reagan to power, whom Winpisinger criticized for advancing economic policies that were destroying the nation's industrial base and benefiting the wealthy at the expense of working people.

The 1990s brought mixed fortunes for the IAM. The IAM, like most of the labor movement, contributed to the successful election of Democratic president Bill Clinton in 1992 after twelve years of Republican control. The Clinton administration proved hospitable to labor but its support of the North American Free Trade Agreement (NAFTA), that opened up trade with Mexico and Canada and has contributed to the movement abroad of some unionized jobs, caused some bitterness. The election of a Republican Congress in 1994, produced a wave of anti-labor proposals, but few made it into law due in large part to the efforts of organizations like the IAM.

The decline of labor success in organizing, collective bargaining, and politics led IAM President George Kourpias to commit to an alliance with two other unions, the United Steel Workers of America (USWA) and the United Auto Workers (UAW) in the summer of 1995. The merger would create the largest industrial union in North America. President Tom Buffenbarger, elected in 1996, supervised the merger while also working to turn

around a decline in membership that began in the 1970s. In response to the growth of a global economy dominated by multi-national corporations, the new president emphasized building ties to unions in other countries.

CURRENT POLITICAL ISSUES

The IAM supports traditional labor issues endorsed by the AFL-CIO, such as occupational health and safety regulations, increases in the minimum wage, and opposition to free trade agreements such as NAFTA. The union supports social welfare programs such as Social Security, Medicare, and Medicaid and social policies such as affirmative action.

The IAM works on issues that are of particular relevance to the aerospace industry, where significant numbers of the union's members are employed. It has lobbied President Clinton to support its efforts to restrict the aerospace industry's use of "offsets" to sell its products abroad. In this practice, foreign countries will condition their purchase of significant numbers of airplanes on the aircraft manufacturer's agreement to build a certain amount of its products in the foreign country rather than in the United States. This results in the export of technology and high-wage manufacturing jobs. An issue of importance in the airline industry is the servicing and repair of U.S.-based airlines' planes abroad.

Case Study: The Aircraft Repair Station Safety Act

Changes in federal aviation regulations in 1988 resulted in the Federal Aviation Administration (FAA) no longer being required to ensure that foreign repair stations certified for domestic airline use meet the same maintenance standards as those located in the United States. Some major airline companies and legislators plan to further loosen the regulatory standards to allow the foreign countries rather than the FAA to certify the stations. Because aircraft maintenance is a major part of an air carrier's budget, the IAM argues that low fare start-up airlines may attempt to cut costs by sending their aircraft (including second-hand, aging planes that are often purchased by such airlines) to repair shops in nearby areas such as Central America. The intense competition among airlines means that the larger, older airlines, who have typically done their own maintenance, will be pressured to go abroad as well. The IAM points out that this practice not only exports jobs abroad, it undercuts the FAA's strict safety standards and endangers the flying public.

Thus the IAM has been a major supporter of the Aircraft Repair Station Safety Act, a bipartisan bill introduced in the Congress in 1997. This bill addressed some of the concerns of Vice President Gore's Commission on Aviation Safety and Security. It was drafted to make it

FAST FACTS

The United States is considered to have the best airline safety record in the world. The accident rate is one-third that of European countries and one-tenth that of developing countries.

(Source: R. Thomas Buffenbarger. "Testimony before the Subcommittee on Aviation of the Committee on Public Works and Transportation," October 9, 1997.)

more difficult for airlines to repair domestic aircraft abroad and would also crack down on the use of uncertified parts—which may be defective or worn out—in repairing planes. Delegates to the IAM Legislative Conference held in Washington, D.C., took their cause to Capitol Hill and convinced twenty House members to sign on as co-sponsors of the bill. Some of the major airlines, who have significant investments in in-house, domestic repair facilities, have joined the IAM in supporting the proposal.

The bill was sponsored in the House of Representatives by Robert Borski (D-Pa.) and Christopher Shays (R-Conn.), and by Arlen Spector (R-Pa.) in the Senate. In both chambers of Congress, the bill made it to committee where it was deliberated upon but not passed. The IAM continued to lobby on the issue and IAM President Buffenbarger testified in support of the bill before congressional hearings. The IAM urged all its members to let their representatives in Congress know that they favor the bill and provided them with the means to E-mail members of Congress through the IAM Web site. The IAM continues to pursue the issue with Congress.

FUTURE DIRECTIONS

Hammering out the details of the proposed merger with the USWA and the UAW will be occupying much of the IAM's attention. Some labor analysts argue that the merger may never go through because of the different organizational cultures and the difficulties faced in eliminating duplicate positions at all levels. But the unification committee composed of representatives from all three unions is actively developing a strategic merger plan and cooperative arrangements have been set up in legislative affairs, communications, and organizing.

GROUP RESOURCES

The IAM maintains an extensive Web site at http://www.iamaw.org. It includes information from the officers and the various departments, press releases and back issues of the *IAM Journal*, and information on political issues and upcoming events. For more information, contact the IAM by writing the International Association of Machinists and Aerospace Workers, 900 Machinists Pl., Upper Marlboro, MD 20772 or by calling (301) 967-4500.

GROUP PUBLICATIONS

The IAM distributes the quarterly *IAM Journal* to all members. There is also a fax newsletter, published at least weekly, to keep local union leaders current on important matters. Both are available on the IAM Web site, http://www.iamaw.org. IAM publications may also be obtained by writing the International Association of Machinists and Aerospace Workers, 900 Machinists Pl., Upper Marlboro, MD 20772 or by calling (301) 967-4500.

BIBLIOGRAPHY

Bernstein, Aaron. "Look Who's Pushing Productivity." *Business Week*, 7 April 1997.

———. "Now Departing for China: Boeing Jobs." *Business Week*, 27 November 1995.

Bernstein, Aaron, and David Leonhardt. "Divided at United." *Business Week*, 10 August 1998.

Dine, Philip. "Union Chief Mixes Insight and Instinct; Machinists Leader is Building Ties." *St. Louis Post-Dispatch*, 15 June 1998.

Edsall, Thomas B., and Frank Swoboda. "Clinton Celebrates Labor Day With Union Leaders in Maine; Shipyard Pact Cited as Model of Defense Conversion." *Washington Post*, 6 September 1994.

Garland, Susan B., Kevin Kelly, Dave Sedgwick, and Stephen Baker. "Breath of Fire or Last Gasp?" *Business Week*, 14 August 1995.

Holmes, Stanley. "Machinists, Boeing Working to Forge New Cooperative Spirit." *Seattle Times*, 17 December 1995.

Smith, Joel. "Problems at Northwest Airlines: Airline Breaks Silence in Dispute: It Blames Machinists for Slowdowns, Cancellations." *Detroit News*, 1 May 1998.

Verespej, Michael A. "Mega-Unions, Mega-Headaches?" *Industry Week*, 4 September 1995.

International Brotherhood of Electrical Workers (IBEW)

WHAT IS ITS MISSION?

According to its constitution, the goals of the International Brotherhood of Electrical Workers (IBEW) are to organize all electrical industry workers in the United States and Canada into local unions and to pursue for these workers employment, adequate pay and benefits, and safe working conditions. Another of its objectives is to settle disputes between employers and employees through arbitration if possible and to "cultivate feelings of friendship" among members in the industry. The IBEW wants, through "legal and proper means, to elevate the moral, intellectual and social conditions of [its] members, their families and dependents, in the interest of a higher standard of citizenship."

HOW IS IT STRUCTURED?

The international office, located in Washington, D.C., has six major departments based on employment jurisdictions: Construction and Maintenance, Manufacturing, Government Employees, Broadcasting and Recording, Telecommunications, and Utilities. These departments handle issues of interest to members in the different industries and coordinate activities within their branches. Other important departments include: Safety and Health, which provides information on worker health and safety regulations and potential hazards associated with members' jobs; the Research and Technical Services Department, which collects economic and industry information, analyzes collective bargaining contracts, and prepares special reports for use in areas such as contract negotiations, organizing, and government hearings; and

ESTABLISHED: November 28, 1891
EMPLOYEES: 200
MEMBERS: 700,000
PAC: IBEW Committee on Political Education (COPE)

Contact Information:
ADDRESS: 1125 15th St. NW
    Washington, DC 20005
PHONE: (202) 833-7000
FAX: (202) 728-6056
E-MAIL: IBEWnet@compuserve.com
URL: http://www.ibew.org
INTERNATIONAL PRESIDENT: John J. Barry
INTERNATIONAL SECRETARY-TREASURER: Edwin
    Hill

the Journal and Media Relations Department, which handles public relations, media affairs, and publications. IBEW's political action committee (PAC), IBEW Committee on Political Education (COPE), is also located in the Washington office.

The IBEW holds a convention every five years in which governing officers are elected and policy proposals are considered. Delegates from local unions vote for union leadership, which includes a president, secretary-treasurer, and the eight-member International Executive Committee, which members are elected by district although its chairman is elected at large. There are also 12 vice presidents, elected from 11 regional districts plus an additional "district" representing the railroad industry. The international office provides assistance to the staff and officers of the 12 districts that oversee and service the approximately 1,100 local unions. Members elect local union officers.

The IBEW has members in the United States, Canada, and Puerto Rico. The vast majority of IBEW members are located in the construction, electrical utility, electrical manufacturing, and railroad and telecommunications industries, as well as in government. Membership by industry includes such diverse fields as jukebox and X-ray equipment repair. The IBEW is affiliated with the American Federation of Labor and Congress of Industrial Organizations (AFL-CIO) and the Canadian Federation of Labour.

PRIMARY FUNCTIONS

The IBEW lobbies Congress and the executive branch to promote the interests of its members. Union leadership appears at congressional hearings and has regular contact with legislators and officials within the executive branch. The IBEW's political action committee endorses candidates, raises and distributes campaign contributions, coordinates the union's political activities on behalf of candidates, and monitors legislation. Its directors have been credited with marshaling the support of other labor lobbyists for favored candidates. At the state and local level many larger IBEW locals are influential in races because of their ability to recruit members as campaign volunteers and to turn out voters.

The union engages in collective bargaining with employers to protect members' jobs and ensure high wages and benefits. Sometimes these negotiations are cooperative but the union has also resorted to staging strikes or a "day of action," a short-lived protest at company plants or annual stockholders' meetings to protest planned job, wage, or benefit cuts. The IBEW has built alliances with other unions representing workers in the same industries, such as the Communications Workers of America (CWA), in order to coordinate bargaining or organizing. Because of the growth in the number of multinational companies, these unions have also built ties

with unions in other countries to strengthen members' positions. The IBEW also attempts to convince workers in non-unionized businesses to join the IBEW. During these organizing campaigns, the IBEW has often been forced to file charges with the National Labor Relations Board and stage protests against companies engaging in unfair labor practices.

The IBEW also works with employers to ensure safe working conditions and provide adequate worker training. Representatives from the union and management have also worked with federal agencies such as the Occupational Safety and Health Administration (OSHA) to establish standard work practices.

PROGRAMS

Apprenticeship and training has been one of the IBEW's central programming activities since the time of its founding. After years of collaborative effort, the National Joint Apprenticeship and Training Committee was established by the IBEW and the National Electrical Contractors Association (NECA) in 1947. This committee promotes a highly skilled and productive work force in the electrical industry by encouraging apprenticeship and training. It develops standard working procedures, prepares training materials, and offers classes to IBEW members and contractors.

Organizing

To address a decline in membership in the latter half of the twentieth century, the IBEW has developed a number of innovative organizing techniques. The Construction Organizing Member Education Training (COMET) program, which has been endorsed by the AFL-CIO, encourages rank-and-file support and participation in organizing new members. Local union leaders are trained and given a highly structured but interactive lesson plan that is used in seminars with union members. Unionists in the skilled trades have historically viewed unions as a way of restricting access to a limited number of jobs, making them reluctant to bring in large numbers of new members that might hurt the job prospects of the existing membership. The COMET program is largely geared to overcoming this resistance. It also teaches members about labor law and organizing techniques such as "salting," in which union members obtain jobs with non-unionized contractors and then "work from the inside" to convince workers to unionize. The IBEW is credited with developing the controversial practice of salting and has successfully defended it before the U.S. Supreme Court.

Member Services

The IBEW helps oversee pension funds as well as health and welfare funds in some areas. The National

Employees' Benefit Board includes representatives of the union, NECA, and the public and oversees the operation of the Pension Benefit Trust Fund and the Employees' Benefit Agreement that offers pensions to participating members. The union also offers a low-interest credit card, insurance program, reduced cost legal services, and a scholarship program for members and their families.

BUDGET INFORMATION

Not made available.

HISTORY

The emergence of a large-scale light and power industry during the last decades of the nineteenth century significantly increased the number of electrical workers. Most of these workers were involved in stringing outdoor power lines and wiring existing buildings. At this time the work was long, difficult, low-paying, and extremely dangerous. There was only limited worker training and there were virtually no safety standards. According to the IBEW, the national death rate for electrical workers was double the rate for all other industries.

Linemen and wiremen who had gathered at a year-long exposition on the wonders of electricity in St. Louis, Missouri, in 1890 came together a year later to form a union to address the deplorable conditions in the industry and immediately sought assistance from the American Federation of Labor (AFL). The union was chartered by the AFL as the National Brotherhood of Electrical Workers, but changed its name in 1899 to the International Brotherhood of Electrical Workers when its jurisdiction was extended to Canada. The first president of this small union, Henry Miller, and his supporters hoped to form a national organization of all electrical workers, including those in the telephone, telegraph, electric power, electrical contracting, and electrical equipment manufacturing industries that would be able to effectively confront the large corporations developing in these areas. One of the first actions of the union was to establish an apprenticeship system designed to improve training and safety in the industry. Early growth was limited in the face of hostile employers, anti-union sentiment, and a poor economy. The union almost went bankrupt offering a funeral benefit to members and their spouses.

The union grew stronger in the first two decades of the twentieth century. Because unauthorized strikes by local unions hurt the authority of the international union leadership in its relationship with employers, attendees of the 1903 convention elected F. J. McNulty the first full-time, paid president, hoping to bring discipline and stability to the operation of the union. In subsequent years the high rates of membership turnover decreased. Despite a temporary split of the organization into competing factions, the union grew to almost 150,000 members in 1919, in large part due to the economic effects of World War I (1914–18). Control of the union became more centralized and a strike fund was established. In 1920 the IBEW and what would become the National Electrical Contractors Association (NECA) formed the Council on Industrial Relations, a joint venture to settle disputes through labor-management cooperation that through its success earned the electrical construction industry the nickname "the strikeless industry." Many employers tolerated unions because they needed their skilled members during the labor shortage produced by the war. However, these employers went on the offensive during the postwar economic downturn that weakened the position of unions by creating a surplus of workers. Moreover, employers and politicians who felt labor unions had gained too much power during the war succeeded in getting restrictive labor laws passed. By 1925 the IBEW's membership had declined to 56,349.

The onset of the Great Depression of the 1930s decimated many unions. The IBEW's membership losses were not as great, in part because members did not want to lose eligibility for a pension plan adopted in 1927 that required members to stay in good standing for 20 consecutive years. During the Depression more than 50 percent of the membership was often unemployed at any given time. Because of financial difficulties there was no international convention between 1929 and 1941. Despite the union's financial weaknesses, its political fortunes improved. The IBEW supported many of the successful initiatives of President Franklin Roosevelt's administration designed to revamp the economy and create a social safety net. The IBEW's president for much of the 1930s left in 1940 to become an assistant secretary for labor in Roosevelt's administration. Largely as a result of passage of the National Labor Relations Act of 1935, which gave legal protections to labor unions and their members, the IBEW experienced new organizing successes at utility companies, manufacturing plants, and in the railroad and radio broadcasting industries, and could boast almost 200,000 members by 1941.

The demand for electrical workers during World War II (1939–45) brought even more members into the IBEW. The union worked with the government to ensure that defense jobs were adequately staffed and placed greater emphasis on training new members. In 1946 the IBEW negotiated an agreement with the NECA establishing a benefit fund based on employer payroll contributions and in 1947 they agreed on a cooperative program to train electrical workers. In the political arena the IBEW, along with other unions, confronted a backlash against organized labor stemming from its stunning growth and economic gains in the postwar period. It fought, unsuccessfully, two major pieces of legislation aimed at regulating the labor movement, the Taft-Hartley Act of 1947 and the Landrum-Griffin Act of 1959. Traditional skilled craft unions such as the IBEW had not been very active in politics compared to the industrial unions, but these defeats, coupled with the increased role of the government in industrial affairs in the wake of the New Deal and the war, spurred new efforts by the entire labor movement to involve its members in politics. Joseph Keenan, International Secretary from 1955 to 1976 and director of the AFL-CIO's Committee on Political Education (COPE), placed increased emphasis on educating IBEW members on political issues and getting them to register and vote.

The IBEW reached its peak with roughly a million members in the early 1970s. In this same decade, economic stagnation, foreign competition, and technological change began to erode the basis of the IBEW's membership. The conservative turn in national politics symbolized by Ronald Reagan's election to the presidency in 1980 and again in 1984 made new organization more difficult. Deregulation, particularly in the telecommunications industry, further cut into IBEW unionized jobs. Outdated union organizing techniques were in part responsible for the decline in membership and in the late 1980s the leadership of the union responded by launching aggressive organizing programs, particularly in the construction industry, with limited success. The IBEW has supported Democratic presidential candidates including the successful candidacy of Bill Clinton. In an effort to establish what unions term a "pro-worker" majority the IBEW has also been very active in congressional elections, particularly since the Republicans took control of Congress in 1994 and pursued a legislative agenda strongly opposed by organized labor.

The 1996 IBEW International Convention was the scene of a battle in the elections for the presidency and other offices within the union. The constitutional structure of the IBEW has long been criticized by advocates for union democracy as restricting the ability of insurgents to challenge the incumbent leadership. Michael Lucas, the challenger in the presidential election and a former executive assistant to John Barry, the incumbent up for reelection, was unsuccessful in a push to have a secret ballot in the elections so that officers would be unable to reward or punish delegates for their votes. The election was framed as a battle over the future direction of the union. Lucas, 55, who developed several confrontational organizing techniques at the IBEW and portrayed himself as the advocate of aggressive organizing and bargaining, criticized his opponent for being out of touch, timid, and too cozy with management. Barry, who had worked closely with management to preserve union jobs, portrayed himself as the voice of reason, dedicated to organizing but willing to cooperate with employers to achieve gains for union members. While Barry held onto his office, a committee was appointed to study the IBEW's structure and constitution.

CURRENT POLITICAL ISSUES

In general the IBEW endorses the broader political agenda and activities of the AFL-CIO, including support for social welfare programs, greater worker protections, an increased minimum wage, and opposition to international free trade initiatives such as the North American Free Trade Agreement (NAFTA). The union also spearheads legislative efforts on issues of particular relevance to its own members at the national and state levels. In the defense area, the IBEW lobbied Congress to cut spending on an Israeli missile in favor of purchasing Patriot missiles produced by unionized workers in U.S. plants. It encouraged states to require the licensing of all installers of telecommunications cabling, thereby privileging workers in unions such as the IBEW who run training and licensing programs.

The IBEW opposes efforts to deregulate unionized industries and open them up to the competition that usually results in a loss of unionized jobs and downward pressure on wages and benefits. It has joined the Communications Workers Union in opposing further deregulation in the telecommunications industry. These two unions have requested federal and state agencies to halt mergers in this area, such as the union of Bell Atlantic and NYNEX, although despite their efforts that merger was ultimately approved. The IBEW has also tried to block mergers of electrical suppliers through lobbying and lawsuits. It has been particularly active in fighting the move toward deregulation and competition in the provision of electricity.

Case Study: Deregulation and Retail Competition in the Electric Industry

Following a general trend towards deregulation and heightened competition in utility industries, states and the federal government began considering bills to open up the provision of electricity. Electrical customers, whether homeowners or businesses, would be able to choose among competing suppliers of electricity much like they choose among competing providers of long-distance telephone service. The logic is that consumers would benefit from free market competition to provide better service and lower rates, rather than being protected by government regulation of prices and service as has historically been the case.

Unions such as the IBEW fear that the increased competition will lead to job cuts, reduced worker training, and lower worker safety standards. The IBEW also argues that retail electrical competition will hurt consumers because only large users of electricity, such as industrial manufacturing plants, will have the market power to be able to bargain for lower prices. Suppliers will be encouraged to make up the money lost in such bargains by charging higher rates to small businesses and homeowners. Moreover, the IBEW argues that many power providers might find it too costly to service the diffuse residential market, or that a few mega-companies might emerge to monopolize the industry, and thus real choice for consumers may never materialize. They also argue that competition will lead providers to cut corners in maintenance and repair, potentially resulting in poor and unreliable service such as frequent blackouts and extended downtime during weather emergencies.

Some electric companies, large consumers of electrical power, middlemen who market electricity, and public-interest groups like Citizens for a Sound Economy (CSE) that are dedicated to encouraging free-market principles endorse unregulated retail competition. A CSE report highly criticized by the IBEW argued that although residential consumer prices would not decline as much as those paid by industrial and commercial users, they would still fall under competition. Proponents also argued that lower costs would stimulate productivity growth in industries using large amounts of electricity and that this would further increase U.S. competitiveness and job growth in a world economy. Moreover, competition would reduce unreasonable regional differences in power rates.

Although the IBEW claims it is not opposed to competition in general, it has lobbied against numerous proposals it believes do not provide adequate protections for workers and consumers. When House Commerce Energy and Power Subcommittee Chairman Dan Schaefer conducted several hearings around the country to drum up grass roots support for his deregulation bill, members of IBEW locals garnered press attention by staging protests outside the meeting rooms and placing members in the audience. The president of the International also testified in congressional hearings on proposed federal legislation. The IBEW lobbied the Clinton administration to reshape its proposal, which included consumer protection provisions endorsed by the IBEW but inadequate worker protections according to union members. The union leadership vowed to continue to fight to include such provisions in any federal legislation.

In states such as Ohio, where deregulation has been actively pursued, the IBEW has joined opposition coalitions. Some environmental groups, such as the National Resources Defense Council, fear that competition will hurt efforts to both lower the demand for electricity and explore alternative ways to generate power, thus making it harder to reduce pollution. Those companies and associations that explore and offer renewable sources of power and those that help large electrical users reduce their demand are also concerned. Some consumer and low-income advocacy groups have also joined various coalitions in opposing retail electrical competition.

In other states, such as California, where deregulation has already begun implementation, the IBEW and other utility unions such as the Utility Workers of American (UWUA) obtained provisions to soften the blow of the transition to competition. State regulators approved a plan to cover retraining, early retirement,

FAST FACTS

Although proponents of deregulation in the electrical industry argue it will reduce prices and improve U.S. competitiveness worldwide, industrial electric prices in North America are the lowest among the world's leading industrial countries.

(Source: International Brotherhood of Electrical Workers. "Will Deregulation Short-Circuit North America's Power Supply?")

and severance pay costs for utility workers displaced by deregulation. As cities such as Los Angeles respond to the state legislation, IBEW locals planned to work to ensure their interests will be protected through favorable contracts requiring unionized public utilities.

Ultimately, the effect of competition on jobs and prices is unclear. Although more than a dozen states have pursued deregulation, none had completed the process of deregulation by the late 1990s. Even where legislation had yet to pass, however, many existing energy providers began to downsize and restrict wages in anticipation of competition. While there has existed a clear momentum behind deregulation at the federal level, the activities of groups such as the IBEW successfully prevented a consensus from forming behind any one bill. Despite the introduction of numerous bills between 1997 and 1999, none passed the committee review level.

FUTURE DIRECTIONS

A major goal for the IBEW is to reverse the decline in membership and bargaining clout by organizing non-union sectors of the industry. It has set a goal of organizing 15 percent of underrepresented workers in each of its employment jurisdictions. Each district vice president will be required to set up a strategic organizing plan of action that will be entered into a computer program and made available nationwide to the locals. The union has also pledged to identify promising new growth areas, such as computer technology, teledata, and solar energy, and to develop training programs in these new areas to give its members advantages in the labor market.

GROUP RESOURCES

The IBEW's Web site at http://www.ibew.org includes an extensive history of the organization, recent publications and press releases, and information on current political issues, as well as health and safety information for members. There are also links to IBEW district and local Web sites. More information about the IBEW can be obtained by writing to the International Brotherhood of Electrical Workers, 1125 15 St. NW, Washington, DC 20005 or by calling (202) 833-7000.

GROUP PUBLICATIONS

The *IBEW Journal*, distributed to all members, is published ten times a year and recent issues are available through the IBEW's Web site at http://www.ibew.org/reference.htm. Other publications outlining issue positions such as the pamphlet "Will Deregulation Short-Circuit North America's Power Supply?" are available from the Journal and Media Relations Department which can be contacted by writing to the International Brotherhood of Electrical Workers, Journal and Media Relations Department, 1125 15 St. NW, Washington, DC 20005; or by calling (202) 833-7000.

BIBLIOGRAPHY

Antolovich, Gabrielle. "Electrical Union Looks to Recruit More Women." *Business Journal,* 17 February 1997.

Bass, Holly. "Union Opposition Emerges as a Threat to Revision of Telecommunications Bill." *Wall Street Journal,* 11 August 1994.

"ESCOs, Environmentalists, and Unions Join to Form Anti-Wheeling Coalition." *Electric Utility Week's Demand-side Report,* 17 March 1994.

Grabelsky, Jeffrey. "Lighting the Spark: COMET Program Mobilizes the Ranks for Construction Organization." *Labor Studies Journal,* 22 June 1995.

"IBEW Shadowing Schaefer Hearings to Protest National Competition Bill." *Electric Utility Week,* 21 April 1997.

Irwin, Patricia. "Threatened: Unions Warn of Deregulation's Downsides." *Electrical World,* January 1997.

Kass, John. "Those in the Know Seek out the Power of Electricians' Local." *Chicago Tribune,* 14 May 1998.

Knell, Michael E. "Raytheon Union Targets Missile Dollars." *Boston Herald,* 4 January 1994.

Korman, Richard. "Vote to Signal IBEW's Direction." *Engineering News-Record,* 9 September 1996.

Moore, Michael T. "Achilles' Heel of the DWP Deregulation Plan: Union Clout." *Los Angeles Times,* 21 December 1997.

"Retail Competition Would Save Consumers Over $100 Billion Annually, Study Finds." *Foster Electric Report,* 12 June 1996.

"Union Pickets Electricity Hearing." *National Journal's Congress Daily,* 16 April 1997.

International Brotherhood
of Teamsters
(IBT; Teamsters)

WHAT IS ITS MISSION?

The International Brotherhood of Teamsters (IBT or Teamsters) is one of the largest unions in the United States, representing workers of highly diverse occupations, including truckers, food-processing workers, entertainers, and flight attendants. Traditionally, the IBT has fought for higher salaries, better benefits, and more job security, in particular for truckers. The IBT Web page elaborates on Teamster priorities as being "strength for working families, working for better communities, winning rights on the job, [and] building a strong, democratic union."

ESTABLISHED: 1903
EMPLOYEES: 300 at the national level
MEMBERS: 1,400,000
PAC: D.R.I.V.E.

Contact Information:
ADDRESS: 25 Louisiana Ave. NW
    Washington, DC 20001
PHONE: (202) 624-6800
FAX: (202) 624-6918
URL: http://www.teamster.org
PRESIDENT: James Hoffa, Jr.

HOW IS IT STRUCTURED?

National leadership of the union is headed by an executive board, which is made up of one president, 22 vice presidents, and a secretary/treasurer. Three international trustees are also part of the centralized leadership. Officials serve five-year terms.

Members are organized into local chapters, or locals, by profession. Members vote for their local officials at the roughly 600 local chapters, and since the 1991 restructuring of voting procedures, individual members have also been able to vote for top officers. Members were also given the right to vote for representatives who determine policies and finances, as well as the opportunity to vote alongside employers on actual union contracts. Thus the organization has evolved into a structure in which each faction monitors the other. The changes in voting procedures have attempted to correct long-

standing power imbalances favoring the national union at the expense of local chapters.

Since the 1950s, the practice of "business unionism" or running the union like a large business, has made a stronger, more centralized national organization of the IBT. At the same time, the national leadership has expressed an interest in augmenting the strength and numbers of the local chapters.

PRIMARY FUNCTIONS

The IBT spends a significant amount of time negotiating contracts with employers in order to secure better working conditions and more competitive wages and benefits for its members. In the case of a failed contract negotiation, the union bears the responsibility of organizing a strike and helping its workers weather the strike in numerous ways, often by providing strike pay. The IBT may also call for consumer boycotts as a means of leverage. Because the IBT is affiliated with the American Federation of Labor-Congress Industrial Organization (AFL-CIO) and the Canadian Labor Commission (CLC)—national federations that coordinate individual unions in the U.S. and Canada, respectively—it may also provide various kinds of support for other unions through coalitions and alliances.

Another top priority is organizing new members and creating new locals. If enough workers at a nonunionized business express their desire to organize, elections are held that determine what union will represent the workers at the business. The IBT is always trying to convince workers at nonunionized workplaces to call for elections, and to vote for the IBT as their representatives.

The IBT is also active on the community level. The roughly 600 IBT locals do grassroots organizing in areas such as registering voters and working with community groups that address environmental, religious, and women's issues. The IBT is also frequently active in the community as volunteers, particularly in disaster mobilization. During Operation Desert Storm, 1,000 IBT flight attendants volunteered to serve flights transporting troops, supplies, and mail.

The IBT monitors and frequently testifies to Congress on behalf of or against proposed legislation that could affect its members, particularly regarding tax and trade legislation. These lobbying activities have become increasingly important as labor's striking power has decreased. For instance, on March 5, 1997, IBT President Ron Carey explained the possible negative effects that the North American Free Trade Agreement (NAFTA) might have on the working family when he testified before the House International Relations Subcommittee on International Economic Policy and Trade.

PROGRAMS

The IBT has a number of programs to educate and mobilize its members and supporters. These programs focus on the organization's overall goal of securing good wages and working conditions. With the decline in the power of organized labor's traditional tool, the strike, lobbying the government and educating the public are of increasing importance to the IBT.

The Eyes on Congress E-Mail Network is an educational program that works to increase the organization's political influence. Once members join the network, they are kept informed about legislation in Congress that will impact their lives. Through the network, the IBT also provides suggestions on how to most effectively support or fight legislation.

Fighting discrimination is also a top priority for IBT. To accomplish this, the IBT implemented the Human Rights Commission in 1992 as a reform instrument. The IBT has held conferences on human rights (1997), civil rights (1995), and women's rights (1993) in the past, and will continue to do so in the future. In particular, the union is concerned with producing publications for Spanish-speaking workers.

BUDGET INFORMATION

Not made available.

HISTORY

The modern day IBT evolved from the Team Drivers International Union (TDIU), which was founded in 1899, in Detroit, Michigan, to address the poor working conditions and salaries of drivers of horse-drawn vehicles. By 1902 the TDIU had grown from 1,200 to 30,000 members and was involved in several strikes and pickets to improve driver wages. That same year, a splinter group, the Teamsters National Union, emerged and the two groups joined together in 1903 at a Niagara Falls convention to found the IBT. Cornelius Stein was elected as the first president of the new union. The IBT organization consisted of small, local groups that operated fairly independently. Locals joined together to form joint councils that oversaw mostly ceremonial activities. The national office had little influence over the small powerful locals, particularly those in Chicago, New York City, Boston, and St. Louis.

In 1907 Stein was forced out of the IBT after being charged with extortion, and Daniel Tobin was elected president. Tobin would hold the office until 1952 and see membership grow from 40,000 in 1907, to 125,000 in 1933, to 1,100,000 in 1952. Throughout his term, Tobin primarily devoted himself to national labor issues and legislation, and paid little attention to the activities of

There were many violent encounters between the Teamsters, hired strikebreakers, and the police during the 1934 strike. As a result of the strike, the Teamsters received seniority rights and higher wages. The successful strike served as a catalyst for expansion of the union. (National Archives and Records Administration)

locals. For the first 20 years of Tobin's term, the locals in major cities expanded gradually, organizing drivers of the new motorized vehicles, as well as warehouse workers. In the 1920s, and 1930s, there were frequent local strikes aimed at raising hourly wages. These strikes, which were against the law at the time, led to frequent and violent confrontations with the police and with strikebreakers hired by employers.

Strengthening of the National Union

In 1934 a successful strike in Minneapolis, Minnesota, led by Farrell Dobbs, won seniority rights and

higher wages for local Teamsters. Dobbs wanted to expand these benefits to other locals, and felt that a strong national union was the best way to do so. His plan was to recruit long-distance drivers into the IBT and therefore create an industry-wide membership, rather than one limited to local commerce. Meanwhile, new laws were passed that greatly expanded the rights and power of organized labor. Despite Tobin's resistance to the plan, Dobbs began a successful campaign under these new laws to recruit long-distance drivers and membership grew by leaps and bounds. Although Dobbs left the IBT in 1940, several other organizers including Dave Beck and Jimmy Hoffa continued to aggressively recruit new

BIOGRAPHY:

James R. Hoffa

Union leader (1913–1975?)   On July 30, 1975, James R. Hoffa disappeared. The de facto leader of the International Brotherhood of Teamsters had accepted a lunch invitation from two organized crime figures at a Southfield, Michigan, restaurant and was never seen again. Hoffa's life journey to that fateful day is the stuff of Hollywood movies. As a teenager working for a grocery store and charged with unloading a truck of perishable strawberries, Hoffa organized his first strike that resulted in a contract within an hour. His union, the "Strawberry Boys," merged with another local union. By the end of the decade, Hoffa had grown the 40-member union group into a 5,000-member union group with $50,000 in the bank. As president of a Detroit local, Hoffa called upon gangsters to muscle his competition. His ties to the mob were firmly established, a fact Hoffa never made a secret

of. In 1957 Hoffa succeeded Dave Beck as president of the Teamsters. Charges of corruption plagued Hoffa throughout his career, and in the late-1960s he served five years of a 13-year sentence that was commuted by President Richard Nixon. In one interview with the *Detroit News* Hoffa reminisced, "When you went out on strike in those days, you got your head broken. The cops would beat your brains out if you even got caught talking about unions." Although his body was never found, Hoffa was declared "legally dead" in 1982.

members. They also began to organize IBT locals under powerful regional councils. During the 1940s, locals were put under trusteeships by these regional councils, meaning that their finances were controlled by the regional councils and that national officers were elected by regional council delegates, rather than individual members.

In 1952 Dave Beck, an IBT official from California became president of the union when Tobin retired. Beck formally organized the joint councils into five regional conferences, which took over the political and organizing functions for the locals. Each local continued to negotiate and administer their own contracts. In the 1940s and 1950s, IBT contracts were among the first to give workers health care benefits and provide generous pension benefits. In 1957 a U.S. Senate committee began a two-year investigation into allegations of union corruption. Beck resigned after the committee accused him of misappropriating hundreds of thousands of dollars of union funds for his own use and accepting payoffs from employers. Beck was convicted in 1959 and went to prison. Due to the continuing investigations into IBT corruption, the AFL-CIO expelled the Teamster's from the national labor organization.

Jimmy Hoffa succeeded Beck as IBT president. He had risen to prominence and power in the Detroit local, and had a reputation for using ruthless and violent strategies to solidify his control over the union. Under Hoffa's leadership, the IBT's membership grew to include sanitation and garage workers, and workers in the food and soft drink processing fields. He negotiated contracts that provided Teamster's with the most comprehensive health

care package in the country and substantial wage increases.

However, Hoffa became the target of continued investigations into his corrupt practices and ties to organized crime. He was ultimately convicted of mail fraud in 1964, but appeals kept him out of prison until 1967. Hoffa's hold on the Teamster's was so strong that he continued to serve as president from prison. In 1971 Hoffa agreed to resign as president as a condition of his sentence being commuted by President Richard Nixon. Hoffa handpicked his successor, Frank Fitzsimmons, and continued to run the union from behind the scenes. In 1975 Hoffa was preparing his plans to regain the IBT presidency when he disappeared. Although he is presumed dead, Hoffa's body has never been found and what happened to him remains a mystery.

The Post-Hoffa Years

In 1977 the federal government forced the IBT to give control of its giant Central States pension fund to independent managers because the union officials had mismanaged it repeatedly. And in 1978, Fitzsimmons and other officials were indicted for misappropriating pension funds and taking bribes from employers to stop strikes. In 1981 Fitzsimmons died and Roy Williams became president of the IBT. He resigned in 1984 after being convicted of offering to bribe a senator to influence his vote on antiunion legislation. The next IBT president, Jackie Presser, was a strong supporter of President Ronald Reagan and had been considered for the post of undersecretary of labor. Presser was indicted on charges of embezzlement and racketeering in 1986, and died in 1988 while awaiting trial.

In addition to corrupt officials, IBT members also had to cope with economic problems in the 1980s. The reduction of federal regulation in the transportation and trucking industries had allowed small companies to compete with large firms. As several large companies closed due to increased competition and high labor costs, many Teamsters lost their jobs. Workers took jobs with nonunion companies and IBT was forced to make concessions when contracts were negotiated. In addition, Teamster membership began to fall from its record high of 2,000,000 members in the late 1970s.

In 1987 the U.S. Justice Department filed a lawsuit against the IBT under the Racketeer Influenced and Corrupt Organizations (RICO) Act. The IBT was accused of allowing known crime figures to control the union and its funds. To protest the government using the RICO Act against unions, the AFL-CIO readmitted the IBT. Ultimately, the IBT and the government reached a compromise in 1989. The federal government agreed to drop the charges in exchange for the resignation of several top officials and the guarantee of fair and direct election of officials. A three-person Independent Review Board (IRB) was also established to oversee Teamster activities. The IRB consists of one member appointed by the U.S. Attorney General, one member appointed by the IBT, and one mutually agreed upon member.

The first direct election of a Teamster president took place in 1991 and saw reform-minded Ron Carey win. Many of the rank-and-file members were angry over the way officials had abused their funds and their union, and were determined to take back control. Many Teamsters supported Carey and his efforts to clean up the union by expelling hundreds of shady officials and reducing perks for officials.

In 1996 Carey's traditionalist opponents chose Chicago lawyer James Hoffa, son of the notorious Jimmy, to run against Carey, and the battle between the two men was fierce and expensive. Carey narrowly won the election, but eventually had to return questionable campaign funds and was forbidden by federal monitors to run for reelection. Fueled by Carey's scandal and his father's legacy, James Hoffa won the Teamster presidency in 1999. The future of the IBT under Hoffa and into the twenty-first century is uncertain. Membership has stalled at about 1,400,000 members and potential recruits are reluctant to join the scandal-ridden union. Reformers are discouraged by the failures of Carey, and only one out of every four Teamsters voted in the 1999 elections.

CURRENT POLITICAL ISSUES

The U.S. Labor Department's Bureau of Labor statistics show that as much as 18.3 percent of the work force is composed of part-time workers, a major point of concern for IBT officials. For example, the hiring of part-time, nonunion labor instead of full-time union employees with benefits was one of the major issues in the 1997 United Parcel Service (UPS) strike. The union eventually forced UPS to reduce the number of part-time workers it employs and increase the number of full-time hires.

Another method of bypassing union labor is subcontracting, or "outsourcing," which is the practice of contracting with nonunion companies for cheaper goods and services. For instance, an automobile company with a unionized workforce will buy parts from nonunion companies for a lower cost than if the auto producer was to pay its union employees to make the same parts. The degree to which employers depend on this practice to cut costs was evident in the IBT's marginal victory in the 1997 warehouse driver's strike against Giant Foods. While the union won the job security guarantees that it sought, the IBT failed to convince Giant to offer exclusive union delivery contracts outside of the Washington-Baltimore area, a primary objective of the strike. As a result, the company continues to subcontract many of its delivery contracts outside of its immediate area to nonunion truckers.

Case Study: The Teamsters and the North American Free Trade Agreement (NAFTA)

The effects of NAFTA on the IBT's trucking constituents, and on working families in the United States and Mexico, are of great concern to the Teamsters. NAFTA is a major trade agreement between Canada, Mexico, and the United States. Signed in 1994, its purpose is to eliminate most trade barriers and tariffs between the three nations. Specifically, the IBT is concerned with the NAFTA provision that allows Mexican trucks to cross into the United States. Fearing that the provision could shift contracts away from union workers to Mexican truckers, the IBT mobilized against the measure, generating press releases and testifying in front of elected officials, as well as launching a public relations campaign pointing out the risks that NAFTA poses.

The IBT argued that the foreign trucks are not properly insured, don't conform to U.S. environmental standards, are older and heavier than U.S. trucks, and often not in good repair. The General Accounting Office (GAO) confirmed these allegations. A GAO study found that fewer than one percent of the 3.3 million trucks crossing into the United States each year are inspected, and that nearly half of those inspected provide reason for safety concerns. The IBT also pointed out that Mexican drivers don't have the same training in the handling of hazardous materials that U.S. truck drivers do, and computerized data is not available on Mexican truckers' driving records and violations involving drugs and alcohol. The IBT further argued that the NAFTA provision would cost thousands of U.S. jobs, and exploit Mexican truck drivers, who, according to IBT sources, earn as little as $7 a day.

As a result of IBT efforts, implementation of the trucking provision, scheduled for 1995, was delayed several times. Mexican trucks were banned from delivering merchandise beyond a narrow strip of U.S. territory bordering Mexico. A significant number of political and environmental institutions and organizations stood with the IBT in opposition to the trucking provision, including the majority of the U.S. House of Representatives. However other well-known political figures, such as Governor Pete Wilson of California, and Governor George W. Bush of Texas, encouraged President Bill Clinton to lift the ban. The Mexican government also pressured the Clinton administration to fully implement the NAFTA agreement. In September 1998, after the ban had been extended several times, Mexico filed a formal complaint against the United States, demanding that the trucking provision be implemented, or else pay compensation to Mexico. In response, the United States agreed to implement the provision in 2000.

SUCCESSES AND FAILURES

The potential of Teamster power was evident in the 1997 strike against shipping giant UPS. According to the union, 60 percent of the 200,000 employed by UPS at the time of the strike were working part time, earning about half the wages of full-timers. UPS management had refused to budge on the issue in protracted negotiations. In a June 26, 1997, IBT news release, Teamster President Ron Carey, who was a former UPS delivery driver, explained that "UPS used to be a place where you could come on as a part-timer and work your way up to a good, full-time job. But today's UPS management has slammed the door of opportunity in the faces of its part-time workers."

On August 1, 1997, when the contract between the company and the union expired, 301,000 UPS employees went on strike. Settlement seemed in the best interest of both sides, as the strike burdened the union's resources, and UPS saw over half of its business going to competitors, such as Federal Express, resulting in a significant loss of revenue. On August 19, 1997, the strike came to an end, with the union garnering such significant gains as 10,000 new full-time jobs over the following five years, pension increases, limits on outsourcing (subcontracting), wage increases, and increased safety protections.

However, the Detroit newspapers strike, which lasted from 1995 to 1997, illustrates a less successful use of strike power to influence negotiations. Teamster Local 372, representing more than 1,000 circulation, distribution, and transportation workers, was one of six unions that struck against the *Detroit News* and the *Detroit Free Press*, which are published separately but conduct business under a joint-operating agreement. The major negotiation issues were job security and pay. During the strike, the newspapers continued to publish, using management and replacement workers to pick up the slack. Despite significant loss of revenue (the parent company of the *Free Press*, Knight-Ridder, admitted in November 1995 that the papers suffered a 20 percent loss in daily circulation, and that advertisers were being offered a 25 percent discount) and despite persistent national pressure on behalf of the union (including a campaign to boycott K-Mart stores, which advertise in the papers) the company held a firm line. As a result, many striking workers crossed the picket line and returned to work within the first six months of the strike.

In April 1996, the union dropped key demands for increased pensions, more jobs, and higher commissions for single-copy distributors (items that newspaper management claimed would cost $71 million over the following three years), but to no avail. Eventually, in 1997, all strikers made an unconditional offer to return to work. Not all strikers were asked to return to work, however, and the National Labor Relations Board (NLRB) is in the process of judging whether the companies are guilty of unfair labor practices.

FUTURE DIRECTIONS

The IBT will continue to fight for better wages, benefits, and working conditions for its members, perhaps more vigorously in the wake of the success of the 1997 UPS strike. However, the IBT also identifies several other areas it will focus on in the future.

While the image of IBT President Ron Carey as the Teamster reformer was tainted by accusations of improper campaign contributions in the 1996 election, the union has continued to move forward (with the help of the federal government) in terms of keeping reform at the forefront of the union's agenda. An additional concern is the declining membership of organized labor in general, and in particular the drop from 2 million IBT members in 1974 to 1.4 million in 1997, a decline which has encouraged the union to successfully seek out new members in more diverse fields of employment.

The IBT's main challenge may be dealing with the changing face of its organization, including the diversification of union members. Eight to 10 percent are Hispanic, and this number increases yearly. Additionally, one-third of all Teamsters are women. While the union as a whole voted to reject President Carey's proposal to adopt a nongendered organizational name, IBT officials are becoming aware of the needs of Spanish-speaking members and issues such as sexual harassment in the workplace.

GROUP RESOURCES

The IBT Web page at http://www.teamster.org provides background information on the organization, recent press releases, references to relevant news articles, as well as a weekly updated congressional report. The IBT also has a members-only reference library with 30,000 holdings.

GROUP PUBLICATIONS

The *Teamster Magazine* is published eight times per year for members. Recent issues can be accessed on-line on the Web site at http://www.teamster.org. Other Teamster materials, including leaflets on issues currently concerning the union, and Teamster videos such as *Freight '98: Fighting for Our Future*, and *Teamsters: Stronger Than Ever* can be ordered through the Web site, or by writing to Teamsters Education Department, 25 Louisiana Ave. NW, Washington, DC 200001. You can also contact the department by phone at (202) 624-8117 or by fax at (202) 624-6851.

BIBLIOGRAPHY

Blackmon, Douglas A. "Mediator Suspends UPS Labor Talks with Pilots Union." *Wall Street Journal*, 3 June 1997.

Brill, Stephen. *The Teamsters*. New York: Simon & Schuster, 1978.

Cohen, Warren. "Big Labor's Big Challenge." *U.S. News and World Report*, October 1996.

Dine, Philip. "Vote Count for Hard-Fought Teamsters Election a Study in Contrasts." *St. Louis Post Dispatch*, 20 December 1996.

Lichtenstein, Nelson. "Teamsters Fight Vital to Reviving Unions." *Detroit News*, 16 January 1997.

Press, Margaret Webb. "Giant Looking Beyond Strike to Regain Stride." *Washington Post*, 2 January 1997.

Scherer, Ron. "The New Teamster: Rig No Longer Required." *Christian Science Monitor*, 11 December 1996.

————. "Teamster Tattoo Politics: As Genteel as a Tire Iron." *Christian Science Monitor*, 17 July 1996.

Swoboda, Frank. "Talks Between Teamsters, Giant Food are Halted." *Washington Post*, 4 January 1997.

Japanese American Citizens League (JACL)

ESTABLISHED: April 6, 1929
EMPLOYEES: 24
MEMBERS: 24,500
PAC: None

Contact Information:

ADDRESS: 1765 Sutter St.
　　San Francisco, CA 94115
PHONE: (415) 921-5225
FAX: (415) 931-4671
E-MAIL: jacl@jacl.org
URL: http://www.jacl.org
NATIONAL PRESIDENT: Helen Kawagoe
NATIONAL DIRECTOR: Herbert Yamanishi

WHAT IS ITS MISSION?

The stated mission of the Japanese American Citizens League (JACL) is to preserve the rights, culture, and heritage of U.S. citizens of Japanese ancestry. It is further committed to the development of an understanding among people of all cultural backgrounds. As stated by Senator Joseph Scott at the organization's 1932 national convention, JACL exists to remind its members "to be proud Americans, but to never forget their heritage."

HOW IS IT STRUCTURED?

JACL is a nonprofit organization with federal 501(c)3 filing status. National leadership is divided between the national president and the national director. The president is the chief volunteer officer (CVO) of JACL and is elected to a two-year term at each national convention. The director is the chief executive officer (CEO), a full-time, paid position. The director controls JACL's day-to-day business and is hired by a national board of directors headed by the president. The organization has a full-time national staff of approximately 20 employees, with roughly half employed at the main office in San Francisco, California. The remaining staff members coordinate the efforts of the 112 chapters of JACL at the local level. Local headquarters are maintained in such cities as Chicago, Illinois; Seattle, Washington; and Washington, D.C.

JACL's chapters belong to one of eight districts. District councils meet several times annually to discuss issues of local concern. At the national convention, held every two years, the national council of chapter delegates assembles to discuss plans of action, national dues, and other issues that affect the entire organization.

PRIMARY FUNCTIONS

JACL was founded to secure and maintain the rights of Japanese Americans and to promote and preserve Japanese-American heritage. The organization serves as a link between Japanese American communities scattered across the United States. In its early years JACL devoted much of its efforts to securing basic rights for Japanese citizens and resident aliens in the United States, and this remains an important part of the organization's purpose. Over the years, however, as the Japanese American community has grown and became more accepted, other activities have become prominent as well. These include supporting qualified Asian American candidates for political office, and educating the public about Japanese American history and culture. In general the organization seeks to increase the visibility and acceptance of Japanese Americans.

PROGRAMS

JACL sponsors a number of programs for its members as well as a few programs for non-members. Members receive a subscription to *Pacific Citizen*, a bimonthly magazine which has acted as JACL's official newsletter since 1932. The JACL Credit Union serves members nationwide but one of the group's biggest perks is only available to California residents. When early members expressed concern over the health of their aging parents, the organization established the JACL Health Trust. Underwritten by Blue Shield of California, this program provides basic long-term, major medical and catastrophic health care coverage. Smaller benefits, such as rental car discounts, warehouse shopping discounts, and a JACL credit card round out the membership package.

JACL also maintains a number of scholarships and grant programs, some of which are open to non-members. The JACL National Scholarship and Awards Program distributes over $75,000 annually for aid at all educational levels. Through its Mike M. Masaoka Congressional Fellow Program, JACL enables upper-level college students and graduate students to serve in the office of a U.S. congressperson.

BUDGET INFORMATION

The 1998 operating budget of JACL was $1.56 million, the vast majority of which was obtained through membership dues and donations. JACL is a nonprofit organization and accepts charitable contributions.

HISTORY

JACL was founded at a time in U.S. history when the nation was less than receptive to its growing Asian population. California's Anti-Alien Act of 1913 stated that no person of Japanese ancestry could own land, while the Immigration Act of 1924 barred the entry of any new Japanese into the United States. The Cable Act revoked the citizenship of any female U.S. citizen who married a Japanese national. Such groups as the Japanese Exclusion League, formed in 1920, were dedicated to the preservation of such laws and the sponsorship of new ones. It was clear that there was a need for leadership in the Japanese-American community.

Traditionally, the eldest members of a Japanese community would assume leadership roles. However, in the West coast "Little Tokyo" communities of the 1920s and 1930s, the older an individual was, the less likely it was that he or she spoke English or was even, in fact, a U.S. citizen. This meant that leadership would have to come from the younger, U.S.-educated *Nisei*. *Nisei* is Japanese for "second generation." The first generation, or *Issei*, bristled at the thought of young men and women, some of whom were viewed as radicals, guiding the community. Only through an unswerving dedication by JACL founders was the organization able to bridge the generation gap.

When JACL was founded in 1929, it was conceived as a group that would serve the needs of the Japanese-American population of Los Angeles. However, contact was soon made with the Progressive Citizens' League, a Seattle group with similar interests, and the organization began to look outside regional boundaries. Other chapters soon filled in the span of miles between the two cities and JACL became a league in function as well as name. However, the state of communication and transportation in the early 1930s meant that chapters had little actual contact with each other. JACL was incorporated under California law in 1937.

Two early issues facing the organization were the Cable Act of 1922, and a promise made to World War I veterans. Japanese resident aliens—non-citizens residing legally in the United States—were told that they could receive citizenship if they served in the army in World War I (1914–18). Fifteen years after the end of the war, none of those who served had been granted citizenship based on these grounds. This issue found popular support with such veterans' groups as the American Legion (which was, in fact, a member of the Japanese Exclusion League). In 1935 a law was passed granting citizenship to all resident aliens who served in World War I. The repeal of the Cable Act was another issue that found JACL working with other special-interest groups. With the assistance of prominent women's groups such as the League of Women Voters in lobbying on behalf of JACL, the Cable Act was amended in 1931.

Executive Order 9066, signed by President Roosevelt after the Japanese bombing of Pearl Harbor, forced the evacuation of 120,000 Japanese Americans, most of them U.S. citizens by birth. Families were instructed to bring only what they could carry to the detention camps. (National Archives and Records Administration)

World War II (1939–45)

As a response to the Japanese attack on Pearl Harbor on December 9, 1941, swift action was taken against Japanese Americans and Japanese resident aliens. By December 11 over 2,000 *Issei* had been detained and classified as "enemy aliens." Respected newspaper columnists Damon Runyon and Walter Lippmann called for the deportation of all people of Japanese ancestry. By the end of 1941 the U.S. Army and the Department of Justice had settled on a plan to "evacuate" all persons of Japanese descent from the West Coast of the United States. On

February 19, 1942, a little more than two months after the events at Pearl Harbor, President Franklin Roosevelt signed Executive Order 9066, which essentially declared martial law in the western United States. The "evacuation" had begun.

JACL found itself in an extremely difficult situation. Its protests were ignored in Washington, D.C., and the general population feared and distrusted Japanese Americans. It appeared that nothing could be done to stop the evacuations or the internment camps set up in the central United States. Faced with this situation, the organization made the highly controversial decision to assist the government and do everything it could to ensure that the evacuation and internment went as smoothly as possible.

While critics in later years would accuse JACL of "selling out," it may have been the most prudent course of action at the time. By cooperating, the organization hoped to demonstrate to the government and the public that Japanese Americans were good citizens who supported the United States and its government and would not betray the country to Japan. Also, by maintaining a good relationship with the federal government JACL could still hope to influence how the prisoners were treated.

Throughout the rest of the war, JACL fought for better conditions in the relocation camps and the right of Japanese-American men to serve in the armed forces. They successfully opposed several state initiatives designed to strip anyone of Japanese ancestry of their U.S. citizenship. JACL also served as a de facto government in many relocation camps, acting as a liaison between the camps and the federal government. While some accused the organization of collaborating with the federal government, the organization continues to maintain that it protected the interests of its members in the most effective way possible.

Postwar

In the years following World War II JACL continued to face the challenge of discrimination against and misunderstanding of Japanese Americans. Throughout the 1950s the organization worked to eliminate the many barriers to full and equal participation by Japanese Americans within U.S. society. With the 1952 Immigration and Naturalization Act JACL won a major victory: immigration quotas that discriminated against people from Asia and the Pacific Rim were lifted and *Issei* were granted the right to become citizens of the United States. Amendments to this Act in 1965 completely eliminated race as a barrier to immigration.

JACL played a significant role in the civil rights movement of the 1960s. It was one of the founding members of the Leadership Conference on Civil Rights in 1948. JACL members joined in Dr. Martin Luther King Jr.'s famous March on Washington in 1963. In 1964 JACL launched its successful campaign against anti-miscegenation laws. Many states at that time had laws against miscegenation (literally, "the mixing of races," the marriage of a white to a non-white).

Throughout the post-war period, JACL pushed the U.S. government to acknowledge its mistake in holding Japanese Americans in relocation camps during the war. As U.S. society gradually became more accepting of minorities after the civil rights efforts of the 1960s, JACL's efforts began to bear fruit. In 1978 a Commission on Wartime Internment and Relocation of Civilians was established by the U.S. Congress. Its findings further highlighted the injustice underlying the government's actions. Based on the recommendations of this commission, and under heavy pressure from JACL, Congress passed the Civil Liberties Act of 1988, which provided an apology and $20,000 in compensation to all then-living individuals who had been interned or had their rights abridged during World War II. The Civil Liberties Act also provided $4 million in grants to be used in educational efforts about the internment.

With the elimination of anti-miscegenation laws in the 1950s and 1960s, marriages between Japanese Americans and U.S. citizens of other backgrounds greatly increased. A 1993 study found that more than half of all Japanese-American marriages were to someone of a different racial or ethnic group, the highest such percentage for any minority group. Thus, in the 1990s it became a priority for JACL that the children resulting from such marriages be counted properly by the U.S. Census and not be forced to represent themselves as being a part of only one ethnic heritage.

CURRENT POLITICAL ISSUES

Over the course of six decades JACL has fought to establish and defend the rights of Japanese and other Asian Americans. Since the civil rights movement of the 1960s, the barriers facing Japanese Americans have changed for the better in many ways, but JACL continues to ensure that a unified voice representing Japanese Americans is still heard in politics and society.

Case Study: The 2000 Census

The accuracy of the U.S. census is of great concern to JACL. The national census, conducted every 10 years, is the constitutionally required count of all people in the United States. Data from the census is used to determine the number of U.S. Representatives from each state, draw the boundaries of congressional districts, and allocate hundreds of billions of dollars in federal grant money. Historically, the census has tended to undercount minorities, meaning that the regions in which they live receive less representation in government and less federal funding.

JACL is particularly concerned about how the census tracks a respondent's race. The organization is opposed to adding a new "multiracial" category to the census, as are many other groups that represent minorities. These groups feel that adding a general multiracial category will only lead to misrepresentation. For example, an individual of African and white background would be counted the same as someone who is Asian and Native American. Lumping people of such different backgrounds together, JACL argues, would not provide any useful information. Furthermore, opponents of the category argue, because the official counts for distinct minority populations would drop, the groups that represent them would lose some of their power and effectiveness. JACL feels that Asian Americans, who have relatively high intermarriage rates and thus more mixed-race children, would be particularly hard hit by the adoption of a multiracial category.

JACL has suggested several ways to improve the accuracy and reporting power of the census without harming how it measures membership in its established racial categories. In order to improve the census's counting of minority group populations, JACL has called for the use of statistical sampling, rather than the traditional head-count method of census-taking. Through the use of statistical sampling, only part of the population would be directly measured, and this information would be used to estimate the rest. JACL also proposes that the census bureau allow respondents to signify their multiracial status, not through the use of a new category, but by selecting all of the existing categories they feel apply to them.

JACL saw a number of initial victories on census issues. A Clinton administration task force agreed that the multiracial category did not serve a well-defined purpose and would only generate more confusion and racial tensions if adopted. JACL was also pleased when the Census Bureau proposed a 2000 census that would combine traditional head-counting methods with statistical sampling. However, there were many opponents to this plan.

Most Republicans disliked the idea of using statistical sampling. They questioned whether it would really be more accurate than the head-count measure, or if it would simply be inaccurate in different ways. Since the minorities and poor that the traditional method supposedly undercounts tend to live in Democratic congressional districts and often vote for Democrats, many Republicans felt that this was an attempt by the Democratic administration of President Bill Clinton to increase the power of the Democratic party. Opponents of the plan challenged it in court, claiming that it violated the constitutional requirement that the census actually count each person in the United States. In January of 1999, the case reached the U.S. Supreme Court.

JACL authored an *amicus curiae* ("friend of the court") brief supporting the sampling method. They claimed the constitutional requirement held by opponents of sampling to require an actual count of each person was incorrect. Furthermore, JACL attorneys argued that the Constitution did not permit the traditional method to be used if another method believed to be more accurate, the sampling method, was available.

In its decision, the Supreme Court determined that sampling was not legal if it was being used to determine either the number of U.S. Representatives that a state received or its votes in a presidential election. However, the Court allowed sampling to be used to determine the population count for such purposes as drawing congressional districts and assigning federal funds. This was a bittersweet victory for JACL. While it did not gain everything it wanted, the limited use of sampling would translate into more government funding for areas with minority populations, and more equitable congressional districts, which could lead to better representation in state and national legislatures.

FUTURE DIRECTIONS

The campaign to create a truly representative multiracial category for the census remains one of JACL's highest priorities. The organization continues to support Asian American political candidates at the state and federal level. Two of the most important issues for JACL have remained unchanged since its foundation: family and education. The scholarship program and group insurance plan are just two examples of the organization's continued commitment to these key areas.

GROUP RESOURCES

JACL's national Web site can be found at http://www.jacl.org. From this site, various chapter sites, as well as individual members of JACL leadership, may be contacted. The national office in San Francisco may be contacted in writing at Japananese American Citizens League, 1765 Sutter St., San Francisco, CA 94115 or by phone at (415) 921-5225. The Washington, D.C., Public Affairs Office is responsible for press releases and can be contacted at (202) 223-1240.

GROUP PUBLICATIONS

A subscription to *Pacific Citizen,* the newsletter of JACL, is included with the price of JACL membership. Published bi-monthly, *Pacific Citizen* has served as the voice of the organization since 1932. Subscription information is available at (800) 966-6157 or by E-mail at PacCit@aol.com. There are also books on the history of Japanese Americans available through JACL, such as *Planted in Good Soil* and a JACL study guide on the Japanese-American experience. For more information, visit JACL's Web site at http://www.jacl.org, or write to Japanese American Citizens League, 1765 Sutter St., San Francisco, CA 94115, or call (415) 921-5225.

BIBLIOGRAPHY

"The Census: Count 'em, Every One." *Economist,* 30 January 1999.

"Counting Race." *Fortune,* 16 October 1995.

Golden, Tim. "Group Seeks Reparations as Detainees." *New York Times*, 29 August 1996.

Hosokawa, Bill. *JACL: In Quest of Justice* . New York: Morrow, 1982.

"Interned Justice." *New Republic*, 28 September 1987.

"A Time of Agony for Japanese Americans." *Time*, 2 December 1991.

Matsumoto, Gary. "Lost Years, Lost Peace." *New York Times*, 19 August 1995.

O'Hare, William. "Managing Multiple-Race Data." *American Demographics*, April 1998.

John Birch Society (JBS)

ESTABLISHED: December 9, 1958
EMPLOYEES: 95 (1997)
MEMBERS: 50,000 (1997)
PAC: None

Contact Information:

ADDRESS: PO Box 8040
     Appleton, WI 54913-8040
PHONE: (920) 749-3780
FAX: (920) 749-5062
URL: http://www.jbs.org
PRESIDENT: John F. McManus

WHAT IS ITS MISSION?

According to the organization, the purpose of the John Birch Society (JBS) is to "promote less government, more responsibility, and a better world."

The John Birch Society was founded to expose and thwart the internal and international Communist conspiracy that its founder, Robert Welch, believed is working to destroy U.S. independence and create a world government. In his view, as expounded in the November 1966 issue of *American Opinion,* a conspiracy of strategically placed "insiders" whose origins date back to 1776, seeks to gain control of the world. The group sees many of the innovations in U.S. government over the past hundred years, such as the Federal Reserve System and the direct election of U.S. senators, as undermining U.S. society and the Constitution, and part of the insiders' plans. The society has fought back throughout its 40-year history by promoting militant Americanism in defense of individual freedom and national independence.

The JBS's political activities support traditional Judeo-Christian moral values and honor the family unit. They endorse the free-market system, competitive capitalism and private enterprise, and see the proper role of government as limited to protecting the rights to life, liberty, and property. The JBS welcomes participation in its ranks by individuals from all ethnic, racial, and religious backgrounds.

HOW IS IT STRUCTURED?

National headquarters have been located in Appleton, Wisconsin, since 1989. The JBS is incorporated under the laws of Massachusetts as a nonprofit corporation, and operates as a nonprofit, despite not having applied for federal tax-exempt status. It is run along corporate lines. The governing body is a council with 28 to 30 members serving as a board of advisers, from which 8 to 10 are selected for an executive committee. The committee in turn functions as a board of directors, appointing the CEO, and usually, the president and vice president. The CEO is in charge of daily operations, while the president oversees publications and public relations. The vice president is responsible for home-office operations, with the director of field activities directly under him who is in charge of coordinators and other field staff. There are 30 to 35 staff coordinators and some 40 to 45 field staff on the payroll.

The JBS has more than 1,000 local chapters, run by volunteer leaders, appointed by either a volunteer section leader or staff coordinators. There is at least one chapter in each of the 50 states. In 1997 the field staff was reorganized to place new emphasis on building membership and recruiting married couples. Annual dues are $60 for husband and wife, $48 for individuals and $24 for youth up to age 21. Application forms stipulate that membership may be revoked at any time by an officer of the JBS with no reason given and with a pro-rated refund of dues paid.

PRIMARY FUNCTIONS

The JBS is a nonpartisan political action organization. Its educational objective is to build a base of understanding concerning the proper role of government and the need for citizens to be vigilant in order to protect their freedoms. The JBS organizes members to support measures that will reduce the size and scope of government. Limited governmental authority is in line with the organization's ideal of a federal government that serves only to protect its citizen's lives, liberty, and property rights.

The council develops a program for action, upon which local chapters base their activities. The council's program is outlined in the monthly JBS *Bulletin,* which is mailed to all members. The paid professional field staff coordinates member activity. A comprehensive program of education, publishing, and communication includes the Internet, production and distribution of video and audio programs, and issue-oriented fliers. Speakers tour the country, region by region, throughout the year, addressing public audiences and appearing on radio and television shows. In the 1990s, speaking topics included "Crises in our Schools" and "Eco-Fraud."

The JBS also seeks to educate the public and influence the course of government through the media. JBS representatives take positions on governmental appointments and develop and distribute investigative reports in an effort to bring issues that the group is concerned about to the public's attention. The resulting surge of public support, or opposition, to an issue often influences policy. For example, in 1996 the JBS was opposed to President Bill Clinton's attempt to appoint his National Security Adviser, Anthony Lake, to be director of the Central Intelligence Agency. An article highly critical of Lake's politics ran in the JBS's *New American* magazine, and was widely distributed on the Internet. The article cited policy recommendations made by Lake in the 1970s as evidence of his weak stand against Communism. When Lake withdrew his nomination in March 1997, the JBS hailed it as a major victory.

PROGRAMS

Most JBS programs are designed to inform members, and the general public, about important issues, and motivate them to take action in defense of the organization's principles. One example is the Tax Reform Immediately (TRIM) program. TRIM is a nationwide network of committees and individuals working to rein in federal spending by pressuring the U.S. House of Representatives—which controls the federal budget—through voter education. Three times a year, TRIM issues report cards on each of the 435 House members' votes on major spending bills. In the 1996 elections, the JBS credited its TRIM reports with a role in defeating big spenders in Congress, as well as helping incumbent fiscal conservatives win against well-financed challengers.

Another major JBS initiative is its Conservative Index. The Index scores every U.S. Representative and Senator based on how they voted on 20 recent proposals. These proposals are selected by the JBS to cover a wide range of issues that the organization considers particularly important or particularly symbolic of a congressperson's views. Selected proposals might address such topics as the United Nations, abortion, term limitations, and federal spending. Congressional members' scores represent how closely their votes match those that the JBS prefers. The index is published in JBS's *New American* magazine twice a year (or four times every congressional session); once every summer and again in fall or winter. Distribution of the last edition in each session usually takes place shortly before federal elections, and are intended to guide organizational supporters on whether or not to support an incumbent candidate.

BUDGET INFORMATION

The JBS reports revenues of approximately $6 million annually. The society, not required to disclose budget information, reveals only that its largest sources of revenue are contributions (not counting dues) from members, and advertising in the *New American* magazine.

HISTORY

The John Birch Society began with a group of 11 business friends brought together by Robert Henry Winborne Welch, Jr. to mobilize against the Communist conspiracy, which Welch believed threatened the nation and the world. Welch never met the man for whom he named his society, U.S. Army Air Force Captain John Birch, the missionary-turned-soldier who was murdered in China by the Communists in 1945 at the of World War II. Welch honored Birch as the first U.S. casualty of the Cold War, that era of ideological competition between the Western democracies and Communism that began at the end of World War II and lasted for almost five decades.

The end of World War II was followed by the spread of Communist-led governments across Central and Eastern Europe, backed by Soviet troops. Winston Churchill, England's wartime prime minister, spoke of an "iron curtain" descending across the European continent. The United States, Great Britain, and other western nations undertook a strategy of "containment" to counter the expansion of Communism. The Soviet Union and the United States settled into the uneasy standoff of the Cold War. In Asia, China came under Communist control in 1949. The Cold War flared briefly into a military conflict during the Korean War (1950–53). After the fighting ended, Korea was split into two separate Communist and non-Communist nations. In Southeast Asia, the United States was being drawn into a futile effort to prevent Communist encroachment in Vietnam. It was against this backdrop of ideological struggle that Welch, a retired Boston candy manufacturer, proposed the creation of a nonpartisan organization to promote an aggressive agenda of anti-Communist education and action under his leadership.

The society emerged into public view in 1960 when Welch charged that President Dwight D. Eisenhower was "a dedicated, conscious agent of the Communist conspiracy". The charge against the popular ex-war hero, a moderate Republican, created a firestorm, and although Welch softened it in subsequent versions of *The Politician,* the publication in which it originally appeared, the Birchers thereafter found themselves considered extremists.

Despite controversy, the JBS was mobilizing, in part benefiting from an increasing conservative frustration over the United States government's inability to counter Communist advances around the world. In 1960 U.S. Senator Barry Goldwater of Arizona, a conservative and early opponent of U.S. involvement in Vietnam, made a bid for the Republican presidential nomination. He had the backing of Welch and the JBS, but lost to Richard Nixon, Eisenhower's vice president.

The 1960s: A Traumatic Decade

The JBS's membership continued to grow, reaching nearly 100,000 by 1964, fueled by a series of traumatic events that seemed to confirm Welch's darkest fears. In 1961 the United States was humiliated in its disastrous failed attempt to trigger a revolution against Fidel Castro, Cuba's Communist president. Later that year, the East Germans built a wall that physically divided Communist East Germany from non-Communist West Germany. The following year, the United States and the Soviet Union went to the brink of war over the installation of Soviet nuclear missiles in Cuba. In Southeast Asia, the United States was being drawn into a war between pro-and anti-Communist forces in Vietnam. At home, the civil rights movement, which Welch saw as a cover for Communist activity, was gaining momentum.

In 1964 the JBS again supported Goldwater for the Republican nomination. At that year's Republican convention there were bitter fights over platform planks proposed by moderates to disavow the John Birch Society and other so-called extremists, and to take a stronger stand in favor of civil rights. Goldwater refused to repudiate the JBS and went on to say in his acceptance speech that "extremism in defense of liberty is no vice." His campaign attracted strong conservative support, including Birchers, but incumbent President Lyndon Johnson defeated Goldwater in a landslide.

After Goldwater's crushing defeat, Republican leaders wanted the Birchers out of their party. A prominent conservative, Senator John Tower (R-Tex.), denounced the JBS for its interference. William F. Buckley Jr., editor of the conservative *National Review* magazine, agreed with Tower's statements. While continuing to be active after 1964, the JBS no longer played a prominent role in Republican politics. The society faded into relative obscurity, marginalized by its conspiratorial world view and crusading anti-Communism. The JBS was further eclipsed in the 1970s, as new coalitions formed and gathered strength within the Republican party, bringing together conservative and Christian elements that would help elect Ronald Reagan to the presidency in 1980.

After the death of founder Welch in 1985, the organization regrouped, closed its offices in Belmont, Massachusetts, and San Marino, California, and moved its headquarters to Appleton, Wisconsin.

CURRENT POLITICAL ISSUES

The JBS takes an active position on many different issues, most of them controversial. In the 1990s the JBS has spoken out against increased trade and improved diplomatic relations with the Communist People's Republic of China. Unsatisfied with federal and media investigations of the bombing of the Alfred P. Murrah Federal Office building in Oklahoma City, Oklahoma, in 1995 the JBS supported the convening of an Oklahoma grand jury to further investigate that tragedy. The JBS was also an early leader in the drive to remove President Clinton from office in the late 1990s, beginning its Impeach Clinton A.C.T.I.O.N. (Activate Congress to

Improve Our Nation) campaign in November 1997. One of the most prominent and long-standing concerns of JBS, however, is U.S. involvement in the United Nations.

Case Study: Get US Out!

Since its founding, the JBS has been a major source of opposition to the United Nations (UN), an organization that Welch said was conceived, created, and controlled by Communists, and constantly furthering Communist objectives. Starting in 1962, the drive against the UN was made a regular item on the agenda of the monthly *Bulletin* mailed to members. Almost four decades later, the JBS remains frustrated in its major aim: getting the United States out of the UN. Its original slogan "Get the US out of the UN and the UN out of the US" has been shortened to "Get US Out!" But objective and tactics remain unchanged. In 1966 Welch urged the formation of local committees "To Restore American Independence Now" (TRAIN). The JBS headquarters produced a full array of materials, including a film on the world organization, postcards, bumper stickers, and a special $2 packet of information with an anti-UN book and an exposé of the World Health Organization, a specialized agency of the UN. The campaign also included massive letter-writing efforts.

In observance of the UN's fiftieth anniversary in 1995, the Birchers mobilized an all-out educational campaign with pressure tactics similar to the ones that had been used by the organization's founder almost 30 years earlier. The JBS distributed 1.1 million anti-UN pamphlets and "Get US Out" bumper stickers and billboards, scheduled speaking tours and media appearances, and peppered local newspapers with letters to the editor.

The society took a strong position in 1996 against deployment of U.S. troops to Bosnia as part of UN and North Atlantic Treaty Organization (NATO) peacekeeping operations in the former Yugoslav republics. The JBS objections to U.S. involvement in UN operations rest on fears of "insider" plans to empower the UN with its own military, and make the U.S. military into an arm of a New World army. Birchers see the transfer of U.S. troops to UN command as confirmation of that belief. The JBS declared itself to be the only significant voice explaining how NATO was actually an adjunct of the UN, adding that the resulting decline in popularity of the world body contributed to the "charade" of sending U.S. troops to Bosnia as a NATO rather than UN operation. Members distributed over 100,000 copies of the "A Dozen Good Reasons to Bring Our Troops Home from Bosnia Now!" pamphlets and placed ads in numerous local newspapers.

As additional proof that U.S. military power is being undermined by the UN, the JBS cites the case of Army Specialist Michael New. Stationed in Germany in 1995, New learned that members of his U.S. Army 3rd Infantry Division were to be deployed in Macedonia. As a UN peacekeeping force, they would serve under the command of a Finnish general, and they would be required

to remove the U.S. flags from their uniforms and replace them with UN flags. New was the only one of the 550 soldiers in his battalion that refused his orders on the grounds that his oath to uphold the U.S. Constitution did not allow him to wear a UN uniform. On January 24, 1996, he was court-martialed and sentenced to a bad conduct discharge.

A special report entitled "Beasts in Blue Berets" in the September 29, 1997, issue of the *New American* provides another example of why the JBS considers participation in the UN to be bad for the United States. The report details atrocities, such as a photograph of UN soldiers torturing a Somali child over a fire. It also reports numerous incidents of drunkenness, looting, use of child prostitutes and criminal abuse of diplomatic immunity during a number of UN operations. The report concludes that the escalating scandal of unpunished atrocities committed by UN peacekeepers illustrates that the "planetary police" are beyond accountability.

Public Impact

While the JBS has thus far failed in its goal of having the United States withdraw from the UN, it points to action in the U.S. Congress as proof that its message is having an impact. The society's annual report for 1996 cited the close defeat (210 to 218) in the U.S. House of Representatives of a measure, sponsored by Robert Dornan (R-Calif.), to cut off all funding for deployment of U.S. troops to Bosnia. Perhaps even more significantly, in 1997 Representative Ron Paul (R-Tex.) succeeded in obtaining the first vote ever in Congress on a measure to get the U.S. out of the UN. While the measure failed, 54 representatives were in favor, and the JBS sees it as an important first step in accomplishing its goal.

FUTURE DIRECTIONS

The JBS has acquired and dedicated a building in Appleton to serve as the future Robert Welch University (RWU). In time, the JBS hopes to build the university into a four-year, degree-granting, institution. The university serves as a research center for the organization, and there is an internship program, although not yet on a regular schedule and only occasionally for college credit.

GROUP RESOURCES

JBS maintains a Web page at http://www.jbs.org offering a wide variety of information. There are FAQs and special reports on many topics important to the JBS, such as abortion, war and peace, and China. The Web site also features the latest editions of TRIM and the Conservative Index. The JBS E-mail Alert Network offers updates on fast-breaking legislation and major events.

The JBS assigns top priority to equipping members, and a wider public audience, with information on government and public policy. A well-stocked research library is currently housed in the building near the Appleton headquarters, which will be the home of the future Robert Welch University. It is open to the public by appointment, with for-fee research services available to JBS members.

GROUP PUBLICATIONS

The John Birch Society maintains an active publishing and distribution network, making information available in a wide variety of formats. Foremost among them is the *Bulletin,* a 32-page periodical, the society's official voice. It contains the action agenda recommended to members and has been published continuously since 1959. The biweekly *New American* magazine, published by an affiliated corporation, is available by subscription, on newsstands and on the Web site. Reprints of special issues are available for $2.50 a copy and $75 for 100 copies. Special issue themes include Immigration, Educating for Global Control, Communism, Toward a Police State, and Conspiracy. Regular paid circulation is about 55,000.

Through its American Opinion Book Services (AOBS), the society publishes and distributes titles through a chain of 20 bookstores run by volunteer members. In addition, field staff maintain wholesale accounts with AOBS; titles are also distributed to another 25 to 30 wholesale and direct-mail company accounts. About 300 titles are available at any given time, a third of which are published by the JBS or one of its affiliates (RWU, American Opinion Publishing, A.C.T.I.O.N., Western Island Publishing, Youth Needs Truth Foundation, and Americanism Foundation). Topics include history, economics, education, biography, political science, health, the writings of Robert Welch, and the McGuffey Readers. The book division sells several hundred other items, including *New American* reprints, flags, bumper stickers, yard signs, and computer software. Videos are also available, including "Welcome to Membership," "The Vital Weapon of Truth," "The John Birch Society Speaks," and "Leadership in the John Birch Society." All of the JBS's publications can be ordered on-line at the AOBS Web site at http://www.jbs.org/aobs, or by mail at JBS, PO Box 8040, Appleton, WI.

BIBLIOGRAPHY

Barrett, Todd. "Once a Red, Always a Red." *Newsweek,* 17 September 1990.

Buckley, William, James Burnham and Frank S. Meyer. "John Birch Society. (Special six-part section on the JBS threat to the conservative movement)." *National Review,* 19 October 1965.

Epstein, Benjamin and Arnold Forster. *The Radical Right.* New York, N.Y.: Random House, 1966.

Feldman, Paul. "Conspiracy Talk a U.S. Tradition." *Los Angeles Times,* 29 May 1995.

Kreyche, Gerald F. "Resentment of Government Hits New Heights." *USA Today Magazine,* March, 1996.

Reed, Mack. "Birch Society Is Not Dead—and Even Now Is Anti-Red." *Los Angeles Times,* 27 September 1993.

Rivenburg, Roy. "Camp Conspiracy: Canoeing, Archery—and Lessons about 'Insiders' and Worldwide Plots." *Los Angeles Times,* 25 July 1996.

Sahagun, Louis. "A Wave of Distrust in the West." *Los Angeles Times,* 3 February 1995.

Sargent, Lyman Tower. *Extremism in America: A Reader.* New York: New York University Press, 1995.

Shogan, Robert. "Voice Regained." *Los Angeles Times,* 26 June 1990.

Smith, Doug. "Birch Society Is Alive, Well and to the Right of Newt Gingrich." *Los Angeles Times,* 23 February 1995.

Udall, Stewart L. and W. Kent Olson. "Me First, God and Nature Second." *Los Angeles Times,* 27 July 1992.

Knights of Columbus (K of C)

WHAT IS ITS MISSION?

The Knights of Columbus (K of C) bills itself as the "world's largest Catholic family fraternal service organization." It helps Catholics materially through insurance benefits and spiritually through fraternization with other devout Catholics. The group also places a strong emphasis on works of charity, which follows in the Catholic tradition of helping others. The four principles of the Knights of Columbus, which correspond to the four degrees of membership, are charity, unity, fraternity and patriotism. The knights' motto is "protecting families for generations," a goal they strive for not only through charitable programs that help individual families but also by pushing for conservative policies the group believes help families in an overall sense.

HOW IS IT STRUCTURED?

The Knights of Columbus is a fraternal organization with headquarters located in New Haven, Connecticut. It also has an office in Washington, D.C. The chief executive officer is the Supreme Knight who, along with the organization's other executive officers, runs the group's operations with the oversight of a board of directors.

The organization is open to men, 18-years-of-age and older who are "practical" Catholics. Members belong to councils, which are generally organized along the lines of a church parish. There are 11,000 councils across the United States, Canada, Mexico, the Phillippines, Puerto Rico, Cuba, the Dominican Republic, Panama, the Bahamas, the Virgin Islands, Guatemala, Guam, and

ESTABLISHED: 1882
EMPLOYEES: 600
MEMBERS: 1.6 million
PAC: None

Contact Information:

ADDRESS: One Columbus Plaza
New Haven, CN 06510
PHONE: (203) 772-2130
FAX: (203) 773-3000
URL: http://www.kofc-supreme-council.org
SUPREME KNIGHT: Virgil C. Dechant

Saipan. Members attend an annual Supreme Council meeting, during which they vote on resolutions that guide the organization's activities.

PRIMARY FUNCTIONS

As a fraternal organization, offering quality member services is important to the Knights of Columbus. Member activities include family awards programs, athletic programs for youth, scholarship funds, and initiatives that in general promote the well-being of families. The insurance benefits, in particular, are generous. According to the *Boston Globe,* which wrote a series of articles on the Knights of Columbus in 1995, the organization's insurance program, which is run out of the New Haven office, had $4.6 billion in assets and ranked in the top one percent of 1,700 life insurance companies in the United States.

The group is especially dedicated to its wide-ranging charity initiatives. According to the K of C, in the 1990s members volunteered more than 397 million hours of service to various causes and donated $945 million to charity. Examples of those activities include running religion programs for youths, participating in blood drives, volunteering at veterans' hospitals, delivering communion to the homebound, and sponsoring the Special Olympics World Games for mentally challenged athletes. Since 1976, the knights have also underwritten the cost of telecasting the Christmas papal mass at midnight from St. Peter's Basilica in Rome. Although the K of C is not formally affiliated with the Catholic Church, the group is linked through members, activities, and common goals.

The group is tax-exempt and does not actively support political candidates, but members can make individual contributions. In 1997, for example, Supreme Knight Virgil Dechant donated $500 to the Republican National Committee. While it is not a partisan organization, the knights do actively push conservative causes. It has committed millions to anti-abortion crusades and is a principal sponsor of March for Life, an annual anti-abortion rally in the nation's capital. In 1996 the knights organized a grassroots campaign asking its U.S. members to send postcards urging members of Congress to overturn President Clinton's veto of the partial-birth abortion ban act. The K of C estimates that approximately 2.5 million cards were sent. The Knights of Columbus also files *amicus curiae* (friend-of-the-court) briefs in cases which involve issues the group considers important.

PROGRAMS

Programs sponsored by regional K of C groups are geared toward the needs of individual communities. All funds raised at the local level remain in the community and focus on one of the following areas delineated in the national "Surge . . . with Service" program: church, community, council, family, or youth.

The Knights of Columbus support the Special Olympics and many other programs that benefit individuals who are mentally challenged. Members serve as coaches, officials, and trainers at state and local Special Olympics games and the national organization sponsors the Special Olympics World Games, held in New Haven, Connecticut. At the 1995 games, the Knights of Columbus contributed $1 million and provided more than 7,000 volunteers.

Programs that support the "family initiative" include Knights of Columbus Family Week, which is held every August. Regional councils hold family Masses, picnics, prayer services, dinners and other activities to, according to K of C fact sheets, "promote and highlight both family interaction and the family focus of the Knights." New members are also initiated during the Family Week celebrations. These initiations, called exemplifications, correspond with the birth and death dates of Father Michael J. McGivney, the order's founder.

Among the many youth-oriented K of C offerings is the leadership training program called Columbian Squires; local branches are called circles. The program is geared toward young men between the ages of 12 and 18 who, under the guidance of member-Knights, perform service programs to benefit their communities. There are more than 25,000 Squires in approximately 1,100 circles in the United States, Canada, the Philippines, Mexico, Puerto Rico and Guam.

BUDGET INFORMATION

Not made available.

HISTORY

The circumstances under which the Knights of Columbus was born are detailed in Christopher Kauffman's comprehensive history of the group called *Faith and Fraternalism: The History of the Knights of Columbus.* In Kauffman's analysis, a number of economic and social factors gave rise to fraternal groups in general and the knights in particular. One reason Kauffman cites were the conditions in Ireland that drove a large number of Catholic immigrants to the United States in the mid-nineteenth century; the immigration wave fueled anti-Catholic sentiment among many Americans, creating the need for Catholics to band together in order to form a unified voice.

There were already a number of Catholic organizations in existence in 1882, when the knights began, most of which provided basic insurance benefits for sickness and death. In fact, the nucleus for the K of C came from another Catholic organization, the Red Knights. The Knights of Columbus founder, a 29-year-old priest named Father Michael J. McGivney, approached several groups for help in forming an association and received the most welcome reception from former Red Knights. The cleric envisioned only a small organization when he called a meeting in the basement of St. Mary's Church in New Haven. The name of the new group derived from Irish immigrants' pride in the fact that America had been discovered by a Catholic, Christopher Columbus. The term "knights" symbolized the perceived need for a militant struggle against anti-Catholicism.

The group's original mission statement called for unity and charity, adding: "secondly, our object is to unite men of faith . . . to aid each other in time of sickness, to provide for a decent burial, and to render pecuniary assistance to the families of deceased members." The group did not succeed in its efforts immediately. In some cases, church hierarchy resisted welcoming them into parishes, thinking the group would usurp control over parishioners. But by the end of 1884, the K of C had extended to 12 councils in Connecticut.

By 1891 the knights had extended to New York, and by 1892 to Massachusetts. John J. Phelan, who was Supreme Knight from 1886 to 1897, pushed the group toward nationwide expansion. Phelan was a successful lawyer and politician with big ambitions. In 1897, a council was established in Quebec, Canada marking the knights' international expansion. Mexico City, Mexico and Manila, Philippines followed in 1905. In 1904 the first women's auxiliary was formed, the Daughters of Isabella.

By 1906 the knights had councils in every state, most of the provinces in Canada, and were in or about to enter four other countries. It was also in 1906 that the group moved its headquarters into a four-story building in New Haven. An indication of the group's growing prominence and influence was its persuasion of Congress to appropriate $100,000 for a Columbus Memorial in Washington, which was unveiled in 1912. Another indication was that also by 1912, the group's advocacy of a holiday to honor Columbus had helped bring about such a celebration in 30 states.

World War I (1914-18) worked to further increase the organization's prominence. During that period, the U.S. War Department approved the knights as providers of official recreation centers for soldiers, along with the Young Men's Christian Association and the Young Men's Hebrew Association. Such centers were opened stateside and overseas. The official role helped increase Knights of Columbus membership from 389,000 in 1917 to 782,400 in 1922.

But events that would escalate into controversy had already begun in 1917. In that year, Mexico adopted a constitution that placed severe restrictions on the practice of Catholicism, which leftists considered a threat to their revolutionary goals. While U.S. government and political leaders struggled to condemn such religious persecution without a full-scale diplomatic break with its neighbor to the south, the knights pushed for stronger measures and stronger rhetoric.

The Mexican Knights of Columbus, meanwhile, became involved with the *Cristeros,* a group of armed rebels fighting the persecution. The church-state troubles continued into the 1930s, and the Knights of Columbus campaign for strong resistance to the Mexican government caused division among U.S. Catholics and anger among some government officials.

In some ways the knights' modern era began in 1964 when John McDevitt became the Supreme Knight. McDevitt was the first Supreme Knight born in the twentieth century and that was reflected in his attitudes. One of the first things he did was push through a mandatory retirement age of 70 for Supreme Officers, a change designed to modernize the organization's outlook. It was certainly a necessary change in the 1960s, when the Second Vatican Council had prescribed modernization of Catholicism and patriotic groups were under attack by anti-war protesters.

McDevitt took the group's reins at a time when conservative ideals were under attack. He reaffirmed the group's stance on such matters as the role of women, divorce, birth control, abortion and pornography. McDevitt also worked to modernize the knights' internal workings, including the initiation rituals and, in perhaps the most symbolic action, he presided over the move to a new glass-faced 23-story headquarters in New Haven. He also strongly and successfully urged the elimination of the system under which applicants for membership could be blackballed, a system widely perceived to be responsible for the low number of African American members.

Under Supreme Knight Virgil Dechant, who took over from McDevitt in 1977, the K of C insurance program experienced a period of extraordinary growth. Dechant, a self-made millionaire who owned large agricultural operations in Kansas, first began to modernize the insurance program in 1969 when he served as the group's Supreme Secretary. As Supreme Knight, Dechant expanded, improved and computerized the operation. By 1976, the group's insurance in force grew to $3.6 billion, and to $6.4 billion in 1981. During the same period, the group's assets grew from $656 million to more than $1 billion.

By 1995, the question was not whether the business side of the knights' operations was healthy enough, the question was whether it was too healthy. That was the question posed in an investigative series that appeared in the *Boston Globe* in 1995. The newspaper reported that Dechant was paid a salary of at least $524,000 per year, not including use of a $95,000 Mercedes Benz, and membership in the New Haven Country Club.

Dechant defended his position, claiming that other insurance companies compensated their top executives at similar levels. Detractors, however, complained that the knights enjoyed an unfair advantage—their tax-exempt status. The *Globe* quoted Robert McIntyre of Citizens for Tax Justice as saying: "Their activities are by no stretch of the imagination something that should be called non-profit and they ought to be taxable like other business."

CURRENT POLITICAL ISSUES

Although, as a tax-exempt organization, the Knights of Columbus is restricted in its ability to support or oppose political candidates, the group does not hesitate to become involved in the political process—especially when its economic interests are at stake.

Case Study: Fight Over Tax-Exempt Status

In the mid-1980s Reagan administration officials proposed taxing fraternal benefit societies as part of a controversial plan to eliminate loopholes in the tax code. Fraternal organizations won their tax exemption "when large parts of the United States were rural and agricul-tural and when many individuals were unable to obtain insurance from commercial companies," Treasury Department officials argued.

In 1984 the Treasury estimated that by ending tax breaks for fraternal organizations that provide insurance, $275 million would be raised by 1990. Fueled by such statistics, then Secretary Donald Regan formally pro-posed the plan and attached it to federal budget legisla-tion. Fraternal organizations mounted a grassroots cam-paign coordinated by the National Fraternal Congress, which represented about 100 groups, including the Knights of Columbus. According to the *Boston Globe*, Virgil Dechant was one of the prime movers when it came to contacts on Capitol Hill and in the White House.

The knights were well-positioned, being in synch with the Reagan administration on many social issues. Also, Dechant had made $2,000 in personal donations to the Republican National Committee. The knights supple-mented the combined drive with the group's own attor-neys and lobbyists. In the two months after the proposal surfaced, the knights spent $209,000 to preserve their tax-exempt status, much of that on mailings urging members to oppose the tax. According to the *Globe*, more than 88,000 letters poured into the White House and White House phones rang off the hook. When the Reagan admin-istration's final tax-reform plan was unveiled in May 1985, the proposed tax on fraternal organizations was not included.

FUTURE DIRECTIONS

Possibly the biggest, and most elusive, goal of the Knights of Columbus is to recapture the soul and spirit of the organization. While the 1995 *Boston Globe* series was vehemently disputed by the knights, as well as by church hierarchy, criticism still came from members. Many knights were concerned that the measures taken to attain financial success had overshadowed the group's dedication to spiritual ideals.

Among the dissidents quoted in the *Globe* series was Dean Robertson, a former grand knight from California, who complained: "I realized that these shining knights, whose compass of virtue always pointed to charity, as we learned in the first degree, were really . . . bottom-line businessmen."

GROUP RESOURCES

The K of C maintains a museum and library, which is open to the public and contains volumes on history of the organization and the Catholic church. The group also has a Web site (www.kofc-supreme-council.org), which contains detailed information about the group's activities.

GROUP PUBLICATIONS

The knights publish the monthly flagship magazine *Columbia,* as well as two monthly newsletters, *Knight-line* and *Squires.* For subscription rates and information, call (203) 772-2130.

BIBLIOGRAPHY

Franklin, James L., Meg Vaillancourt, and Patricia Wen. "Doing Good and Doing Well." *Boston Globe,* 2 April 1995.

Franklin, James L., Meg Vaillancourt, and Patricia Wen. "Fra-ternal Group Uses Clout to Safeguard its Interests." *Boston Globe,* 3 April 1995.

Kauffman, Christopher J. *Faith and Fraternalism: The History of the Knights of Columbus, 1882-1982.* New York, N.Y.: Harper & Row, 1982.

"Knights Charity Said to Begin at Home." *National Catholic Reporter,* 14 April 1995.

"Law Urges Knights to be Consistent." *National Catholic Reporter,* 11 August 1995.

Schmitt, Frederick. "Knights of Columbus Sued Over Sales Prac-tices." *National Underwriter,* 2 September 1996.

Spalding, Matthew. "Knight Vision." *Policy Review,* May/June 1996.

Slawson, Douglas. "The National Catholic Welfare Conference and the Mexican Church-State Conflict of the mid-1930s: A Case of Deja Vu." *Catholic Historical Review,* January 1994.

Unsworth, Tim. "Knights of Peter Claver in the Shadows." *National Catholic Reporter,* 25 August 1995.

Wen, Patricia. "Top Knight Known for Acumen, Emphasis on Control." *Boston Globe,* 3 April 1995.

Knights of the Ku Klux Klan (KKKK)

WHAT IS ITS MISSION?

The term Ku Klux Klan is a general one used to affiliate a group with the original Ku Klux Klan formed in 1865. The phrase is deemed part of the public domain and no single group can claim it as referring only to itself. There are some 200 Klan organizations throughout the United States whose views and agendas vary, with some articulating a definitively racist agenda and others a more moderate stance. All, however, promote white Christian American culture and seek to protect white Christians from political and social movements perceived as detrimental to them. "We believe as shown by the writings of our forefathers that America was founded by white Christians *for* white Christians," says KKKK literature.

HOW IS IT STRUCTURED?

The Knights of the Ku Klux Klan (KKKK), headed by Pastor Thomas Robb, considers itself a quasi-political party and is the preeminent Klan organization in the United States with a political agenda. The KKKK adopted its modern structure in the 1970s under the directorship of David Duke. They phased out titles like "Grand Wizard," "Grand Klaliff," and "Grand Kludd" in favor of titles used by other social action groups. However, many Klans not affiliated with Robb's group still use the traditional classifications set forth in the 1920 Klan constitution.

The KKKK is located in Harrison, Arkansas, and is headed by a national director who is responsible for the organization and direction of individual KKKK units.

ESTABLISHED: 1956
EMPLOYEES: Not made available
MEMBERS: Not made available
PAC: None

Contact Information:

ADDRESS: PO Box 2222
    Harrison, AR 72601
PHONE: (870) 427-3414
E-MAIL: knights@kukluxklan.org
FAX: (870) 427-3414
URL: http://www.kukluxklan.org
NATIONAL DIRECTOR: Pastor Thomas Robb
NATIONAL TREASURER: Rachel Pendergraft

The national director serves as chief director and president of a board of directors, which provides oversight and guidance at a national level. The Grand Council also advises the national director. Although the KKKK often refers to itself as a political party, the Knights Party, it is registered with the federal government as a nonprofit organization.

Below national leadership are ten regional districts, which are composed of state "Realms." For example, District 3 encompasses the Realm of Pennsylvania, the Realm of New Jersey, and the Realm of Delaware. Below Realms are units (previously Klaverns or Dens), the local groups in which citizens participate in the KKKK. Within each unit there is a unit coordinator who is responsible for local organizing. The coordinator appoints additional unit officials: an assistant unit coordinator, a secretary, a treasurer, an ombudsperson, and an expediter. A unit recruiter organizes and recruits members at the local level.

KKKK members begin as Klansmen and Klanswomen. All members are Christians who certify that they are white, not of racially-mixed descent, are not married to or do not date nonwhites, and have no nonwhite dependents. Klansmen and Klanswomen may achieve the rank of Page, then Squire, through activities and study. They may become Knights if they have a high school diploma or GED certification and pass a written test administered by the KKKK. Unit coordinators must have earned the rank of Knight, and unit recruiters must have earned at least the rank of Squire, have a high school diploma or GED certification, and have been approved by the national office. The assistant unit coordinator also must have obtained the rank of Squire. All members of a unit must have earned the minimum rank of Page.

PRIMARY FUNCTIONS

The KKKK, a self-described "grass-roots movement to take back America," carries out an array of activities aimed at bringing the group into recognition as the voice of the white rights movement. The group seeks to win this recognition in society and politics through its integrated efforts to get publicity and votes for the KKKK, its causes, and the candidates it supports.

The KKKK disperses its message through several avenues. Local units and members distribute literature in their communities; sponsor newspaper, radio, and television ads; work on petition drives to get Klansmen and Klanswomen on campaign ballots; and organize voter drives for candidates and referendums. The KKKK also employs professional media representatives to answer queries from the media and the public and to speak at schools, churches, or other institutions. Robb and other top leaders have been heard and seen on radio and television programs and in newspapers and books. They have also taken part in debates. The organization produces literature and videos designed for broadcast on public access cable television and for distribution to the public. These types of activities are aimed at getting positive publicity and recruiting new members. Much of the work of the KKKK is also geared toward separating Robb's group from other Klans and dispelling popular negative beliefs about the KKK.

The KKKK is perhaps best known for its public rallies and demonstrations. For example, since 1986 the KKKK has held annual protests in opposition to recognition of Martin Luther King, Jr. Day, a national holiday. Since its first protest in Pulaski, Tennessee, the KKKK has expanded this effort. Now, each January, KKKK members and supporters distribute literature and deliver speeches explaining their belief that King was a Communist and did not live by Christian values and, therefore, should not be honored. Such rallies have been held in Springfield, Illinois; Topeka, Kansas; and Austin, Texas. KKKK members wear plain street clothes at such events, as opposed to other Klan members who wear robes and hats. Rallies are organized by the national headquarters in Arkansas and members do not rally with other Klan groups.

PROGRAMS

The KKKK leads programs largely centered around education. For example, the steps toward becoming a full-fledged Knight involve social and religious study about white Christian culture and history. Earning the rank of Knight means being able to articulate the beliefs of the KKKK and back them up with knowledge of the U.S. Constitution and the writings of prominent early Americans like James Madison, Noah Webster, and John Jay. The Re-educate the Educators program is concerned with educating teachers about the ideals of the KKKK. The group's national headquarters prepares materials for students and teachers, including a workbook for teachers and aspiring teachers which deals with opposition to social trends faced by youth, such as homosexuality, interracial dating, and drug use. Also Pastor Robb teaches a week-long Christian leadership seminar at the Soldiers of the Cross Bible Camp, and KKKK members are invited to attend the annual National Klan Congress in Arkansas.

The Sleeper Program

The KKKK sponsors a unique program designed for those who support the KKKK but want to keep KKKK affiliation confidential because of political involvement. As part of the Sleeper Program, an anonymous member may participate in politics as part of the Democratic or Republican parties. The politician then works with the intent to win seats in government and create easier access to elections for Knights who wish to run for political office.

BUDGET INFORMATION

Not made available

HISTORY

The history of the Ku Klux Klan is a confusing and controversial one. Many groups of the KKK have broken off from the parent organization, some to be reabsorbed in later years. The current Klan is as fractured now as it ever has been. Its history is further obscured not only by codes of secrecy but also by its past disbandings, resurgences, bankruptcies, and trial cases. The Klan has a self-endorsed history, which it delineates by eras.

During Civil War Reconstruction the dissention in the South was widespread. With the emancipation of slaves and the new civil liberties they were entitled to by Unionist/Republican decree, the white South boiled with discontent and the Ku Klux Klan emerged. By most historical accounts the Ku Klux Klan began in Pulaski, Tennessee, in 1865 (although some claim it was formed in 1864) when it was established as a social fraternity devoted to white supremacy. In 1867 Confederate General Nathan Bedford Forrest solidified the group and the Ku Klux Klan was considered formally organized, with Forrest as its first Imperial Wizard. This period is referred to as the First Era of the Order by the Klan.

The First Era of the Order

The Ku Klux Klan appealed to disenfranchised Southerners and the group flourished. The initial activity of the Ku Klux Klan was restricted primarily to the southern states. The early deeds of the Ku Klux Klan were often crimes of terror and hate against blacks or anyone thought to be positively affiliated with blacks. Murders, burnings, and rapes were often attributed to the Klan. Many local governments in the South allowed the Klan to be above the law, either by ignoring racially-motivated crimes or, in many cases, by actively supporting and belonging to the ranks of Klansmen.

Due to the increasing violence of the group, Forrest ordered the Ku Klux Klan disbanded in 1869. Regardless, KKK membership was estimated at 550,000 in the South in 1870. The crimes of the KKK continued to run unchecked until 1871, when the U.S. Congress enacted the KKK Act, which outlawed the then not-so-secret fraternity as a conspiracy to deprive people of their civil liberties. President Ulysses Grant dispatched federal troops to put down the still active dens. By the mid 1870s, membership severely dropped off and the Klan was considered dead by most.

The Second Era

The first two decades of the twentieth century saw a resurgence of participation in the Ku Klux Klan. This second revival was led by William Joseph Simmons beginning in 1915 at Stone Mountain, Georgia. This date marks the beginning of what the Klan calls the Second Era of the Order. High levels of immigration to the United States had created new social tension and KKK activity was no longer confined to the South nor was its hostility limited to blacks. Jews, Catholics, and all nonwhites were now targets of the Ku Klux Klan, and the group took hold in states traditionally untouched by sentiments of the KKK, like Oregon, Oklahoma, and particularly Indiana. The Klan boasted members in every level of government. By 1920 membership had risen to 4 million.

D. C. Stephenson emerged as a powerful member of the Klan, as Grand Dragon of Indiana and as head of the operation of an additional 22 states. However, the fall of the Second Era of Order was credited to Stephenson after he was convicted in 1925 of the brutal rape and murder of Matilda Oberholtzer. This high profile incident discredited the Klan among the public, and many Klan members abandoned the group in its wake. After Stephenson's conviction, many Klan secrets were discovered, leading to a round of trials of state and federal officials for bribery and misappropriation of funds.

Third and Fourth Eras

From 1950 through the end of the 1960s comprised the Third and Fourth Eras of the Order, as named by the Klan. During the 1950s the Klan was investigated by the House Committee on Un-American Activities. The simmering, and later raging, disputes over civil liberties and desegregation was a national concern and brought tension to southern states in particular. The KKK again made a stronghold for itself in the South, where racism was more tolerated.

Three major organized Klan groups emerged during this time: the United Klans of America, The US Klans, and the Knights of the Ku Klux Klan. The Knights of the Ku Klux Klan (KKKK) was founded in 1956 in Louisiana. The unification of the US Klans and the United Klans of America occurred in 1961 under Robert Shelton. The combined estimated membership of various Klan organizations in the 1960s was approximately 50,000.

The civil rights movement of the 1960s brought considerable media coverage of the injustices suffered by blacks and civil rights supporters in the South. High profile murders and hate crimes were often spotlighted, but while Klansmen were tried for these misdeeds, they were rarely convicted, even when pursued at the federal level by the Federal Bureau of Investigation.

The 1963 bombing of the 16th Street Baptist Church in Birmingham, Alabama, killed four young girls and brought national media coverage to Klan involvement in crimes of terrorism. In 1964 the burning of the Mount Zion Baptist Church in Mississippi brought further negative attention to the Klan, which was widely suspected of being responsible. The high profile Alabama murder of Viola Liuzzo, a white civil rights advocate, led President Lyndon Johnson to make a public address denouncing the Klan.

Fifth Era of the Order

Due to negative media coverage, splintering of the KKK, and association of the group with violence, membership dwindled to only about 1,500 in the early 1970s. The leadership of Shelton ran unchallenged until David Duke started changing the face of the KKKK during the beginning of the Fifth Era of the Order. In 1975 Duke emerged as the national director of the KKKK. Shortly thereafter he ran for election in Baton Rouge's sixth senatorial district, running a strong but unsuccessful campaign. Duke was considered responsible for the rise in KKKK membership in the 1970s. While he was often closemouthed about KKKK membership numbers, combined Klan membership was then estimated at 12,000 members.

Duke was ousted as national director after a recording of a phone conversation was discovered in which he discussed selling the KKKK membership list for $35,000. Media coverage of this incident reduced Duke's acceptance among the KKKK and the group's membership was compromised. In 1989, no longer affiliated with the KKKK, Duke was elected to the U.S. House of Representatives. He went on to make unsuccessful bids for the governorship of Louisiana and also U.S. president.

The 1980s saw the rise of many different Klan groups. A 1987 wrongful death civil suit, brought against the United Klans of America by Morris Dees of Klanwatch, resulted in the award of $7 million to the victim's mother. The United Klans of America was forced into bankruptcy. The KKKK, in the late 1980s and the 1990s, was represented by Pastor Thomas Robb of the Church of Jesus Christ in Bergman, Arkansas. Robb had previously served as national chaplain and national organizer in association with Duke. His leadership marks the sixth Era of the Order.

CURRENT POLITICAL ISSUES

In keeping with the belief that the United States was formed as a Christian nation, the KKKK opposes the separation of church and state and favors legislation that promotes traditional Christian behavior. Accordingly, the KKKK believes interracial marriage and homosexuality should be illegal, as should abortion except in cases of rape, incest, or in situations where the mother's life is at risk. The group advocates the rights for home schooling and private schooling options. The KKKK supports legislation requiring welfare recipients to pass drug tests to be eligible for aid and for caps on welfare benefits.

The KKKK favors foreign policy that puts the United States, white Christians particularly, first in all matters. The group opposes free trade agreements, like the North American Free Trade Agreement (NAFTA), on grounds that free trade takes jobs away from Americans, and the KKKK opposes the purchase of U.S. property and industry by foreign corporations and investors. Similarly the group advocates for an immediate end to foreign monetary and military aid and for much stricter border controls to stop illegal immigration. However, the KKKK believes immigration of white Christians into the United States should be unrestricted. To that end the KKKK also supports the voluntary repatriation or relocation of those who do not wish to live under white Christian rule and the abolition of minority-advancement programs like affirmative action. Likewise the group supports the right to racially discriminate when hiring, selling, renting, socializing, or conducting business.

The KKKK takes an equally conservative approach to economics, believing that American money should remain in American hands. The group advocates for conservative economic policies like the repeal of the Federal Reserve Act, which provides for the foundation of the nation's economy as it currently operates; as well as a balanced budget and a flat income tax. The KKKK is also concerned with the environment and advocates that the United States should make nations that want to trade with the United States adhere to strict environmental protections. The KKKK supports efforts to search for and implement energy-conserving measures like the use of solar energy.

Yet such moderate, mainstream-conservative views tend to be overshadowed by the more radical positions for which the Klan has been criticized by civil rights groups. For example, HIV/AIDS advocacy groups strongly oppose the KKKK proposition that all HIV-positive people be quarantined in national hospitals in order to stop the spread of the disease. Such proposals, and particularly those in defense of racial discrimination, often alienate even the most conservative-minded, leaving the KKKK open to attack from minority organizations, gay and lesbian rights groups, and others, many of whom are white Christians, who believe the KKKK goes too far.

A major battle of the KKKK is to protect the First Amendment right to freedom of speech and, thereby, the group's right to advocate even its most unpopular views. On this issue the KKKK has the support of the most influential liberal-minded organization in the country, the American Civil Liberties Union (ACLU).

Case Study: KKKK v. KWMU-FM

In search of new members and a new outlet for its message, the KKKK Realm of Missouri sent a check to KWMU-FM to underwrite a National Public Radio program that the radio station airs. Underwriting works much like advertising in that the money funds the radio station and in return the underwriter is recognized on-air as a program sponsor. Specifically, the Missouri Klan wanted to air the slogan "a White Christian organization, standing up for the rights and values of White Christian America since 1865," according to the *St. Louis Post-Dispatch.*

But KWMU and the University of Missouri at St. Louis, which holds the station's operating license, refused to accept the underwriting from the Klan. "We believe that the [Federal Communications Commission] and federal law requires broadcasters to serve the public interest and permits broadcasters to exercise editorial discretion in selecting the messages that they broadcast," said university spokesman Bob Samples in *Law Journal EXTRA!.* Furthermore, the university argued for the station's right to choose all material it broadcasts.

Seeing this as an infringement on free speech, a right given by the First Amendment of the U.S. Constitution, the KKKK Realm of Missouri unit coordinator Robert Cuffley sued the university and the KWMU station manager. The KKKK based its argument on the premise that, as a public radio station, KWMU is a public forum that may not discriminate against or reject any particular viewpoint. The suit was filed in federal court. In September of 1998 the court ruled against the Klan, which had asked for a court order forcing KWMU to accept and publicly identify it as an underwriter. The Klan lost again on first appeal to federal district court, and the Realm of Missouri has appealed to the 8th U.S. Circuit Court of Appeals.

The KKKK's legal battle over its right to participate fully in public radio underwriting programs will have implications for a very important First Amendment rights issue. For this reason the ACLU, which is generally opposed to Klan beliefs on grounds that they violate minority rights, has spoken in defense of the KKKK in relation to this case. "This is a publicly owned radio station," said Deborah Jacobs, executive director of the ACLU of Eastern Missouri, according to *Law Journal EXTRA!* "Once they have established the forum of opening underwriting spots to anyone who wishes to purchase one, they cannot turn around and deny one particular group the right to purchase the spot."

If the 8th Circuit Court of Appeals and the U.S. Supreme Court rule in favor of KWMU, public radio stations nationwide will be allowed to refuse underwriting to any group on the basis of a disagreement with the message to be underwritten. If the KKKK ultimately wins, public radio stations will be forced to accept underwriting from any group, no matter its message, perhaps challenging the open-mindedness of their audiences.

FUTURE DIRECTIONS

The future plans of the KKKK are comprehensive and ambitious. As the KKKK enters it sixth era, it intends to increase membership and organize programs that

FAST FACTS

The fiery symbolic cross adopted by the Klan is derived from the Scottish tradition of lighting a cross to symbolize obedience to God and the opposition of tyranny.

(Source: "Ku Klux Klan." http://www.kukluxklan, 1999.)

---

increase their name recognition and voter base. The KKKK is already trying to achieve equal ballot access to local, state, and federal offices. Long-term goals include the repeal of NAFTA and GATT trade treaties and the cessation of foreign aid, with the allotted monies reallocated to programs such as Social Security and Medicare. The KKKK will also urge the creation of programs that prohibit trade with countries that fail to establish strict environmental laws and the search for nonpolluting energy sources in the United States. Drug testing for welfare recipients, abolition of antigun laws, and prohibition of illegal, nonwhite, and non-Christian immigration are just a few of the issues the KKKK will pursue in the future.

GROUP RESOURCES

The Knights of the Ku Klux Klan maintain an Internet Web site at http://www.kukluxklan.org which offers general information about the group and its beliefs, how to join, a gift shop, and weekly commentaries. The organization also provides speakers for functions or gatherings upon request. Further information is available by calling or faxing (870) 427-3414 or by writing to PO Box 2222, Harrison, AR 72601.

GROUP PUBLICATIONS

The KKKK offers several publications through its national office. An on-line bookstore at http://www. kukluxklan.org/book.htm offers all individuals pamphlets dealing with Klan issues. It also provides the *Knights' Party Handbook,* the *Knights Party Unit Handbook,* and the *Handbook for Knights* to members of the appropriate rank. Members also receive *Robb's Victory Report.* The KKKK publishes the *White Patriot News*

Report, which can be subscribed to for $15. In addition, the introductory video *This is the Klan* is available through the national office, as is a general newsletter. Both can be obtained for a modest donation. Several videos are available for the purpose of sponsoring public access cable programming. Publications may be obtained by writing to Patriot Supplies, PO Box 2222, Harrison, AR 72601.

BIBLIOGRAPHY

Alexander, Charles C. *The Ku Klux Klan in the Southwest.* Norman, Okla.: University of Oklahoma Press, 1995.

Bryant, Tim. "Judge Favors UMSL in Dispute with Klan KKK Wants to Underwrite Program on Public Radio." *St. Louis Post-Dispatch,* 30 September 1998.

———. "Klan Loses Bid to Underwrite Public-Radio Programming at UMSL University Station Does Not Have to Accept, Broadcast KKK Messages, Judge Rules." *St. Louis Post-Dispatch,* 11 December 1998.

Chalmers, David Mark. *Hooded Americanism: The History of the Ku Klux Klan.* Durham, N.C.: Duke University Press, 1987.

The Emergence of David Duke and the Politics of Race. Chapel Hill, N.C.: University of North Carolina Press, 1992.

"Five Injured at Klan Protest." *New York Times,* 10 May 1998.

"Klan Must Pay $37 Million for Inciting Church Fire." *New York Times,* 25 July 1998.

Lutholtz, M. William. *Grand Dragon: D.C. Stephenson and the Ku Klux Klan in Indiana.* West Lafayette, Ind.: Purdue University Press, 1994.

Newton, Michael. *The Ku Klux Klan: An Encyclopedia.* New York: Garland, 1991.

Oshinsky, David. "Should the Mississippi Files Have Been Reopened?" *New York Times,* 30 August 1998.

Ruiz, Jim. *The Black Hood of the Ku Klux Klan.* San Francisco: Austin and Winfield Publishing, 1998.

Sims, Patsy. *The Klan.* Lexington, Ky.: University Press of Kentucky, 1996.

Wade, Wyn Craig. *The Fiery Cross: The Ku Klux Klan in America.* New York: Oxford University Press, September 1998.

Laborer's International Union of North America (LIUNA)

WHAT IS ITS MISSION?

The Laborers' International Union of North America (LIUNA) strives to improve the condition of skilled and unskilled laborers in the workplace and increase laborer competitiveness in the marketplace. According to the organization's president Arthur A. Coia, "LIUNA's mission has remained the same since its founding: to empower working men and women, especially those starting out on the lowest rungs of the economic ladder. To raise laborers' living standards. . . . To give them a strong voice in the workplace. . . . To provide skills so that members can achieve their full potential. . . . To protect members' health and safety. . . . And most of all to ensure dignity, respect, and security."

HOW IS IT STRUCTURED?

There are three tiers to the Laborers' Union: the international union, district councils, and local unions. The general executive board, LIUNA's national leadership officers, consists of the general president, general secretary-treasurer, and 14 vice presidents. Since 1996 all general executive board members have been elected by rank and file members. The union's officers are elected every five years. The international union in Washington, D.C., governs the smaller divisions of the union and defines the powers and jurisdictions of local unions and district councils. The international union also provides guidance for the local unions and district councils in matters such as bargaining, research, public affairs, legal issues, and political action. There are nine regional international union offices in the United States, one in

ESTABLISHED: April 13, 1903
EMPLOYEES: Not made available
MEMBERS: 750,000
PAC: The Laborers' Political League (LPL)

Contact Information:
ADDRESS: 905 16th St. NW
    Washington, DC 20006
PHONE: (202) 737-8320
FAX: (202) 737-2754
URL: http://www.liuna.org
GENERAL PRESIDENT: Arthur A. Coia

Canada, and two sub-regional offices in Canada. These offices administer the executive affairs of the union.

There are 60 district councils throughout North America, which are grouped by state and occupation. The primary function of the district councils is to conduct bargaining for the local unions and help them collaborate to meet common objectives. There are over 650 local unions in the United States and Canada, each of which are affiliated with the district councils and international union. Members of the local unions elect their own officers. The officers are not considered direct employees of the international union.

The Laborers' Union represents a wide range of laborers across North America covering over 50 different industries. The scope of its membership encompasses laborers in diverse occupations including: construction; environmental remediation (hazardous waste removal); maintenance; food service; health care; clerical; local, state, and federal government service; custodial services; and shipbuilding. Among its members are Alaskan pipeline workers; nurses in the United States and Canada; airplane machinists and mechanics at Dulles International Airport in Virginia; and maintenance and display workers at Disneyland.

LIUNA is affiliated with the American Federation of Labor-Congress of Industrial Organizations (AFL-CIO), a voluntary federation of American trade unions. The Laborers' Union is also affiliated with the Canadian Labour Congress (CLC). Since its inception in 1903 LIUNA has diversified and expanded its trade jurisdiction by aligning with several trade unions. These trade unions include: the Compressed Air and Foundation Workers International Union; the Tunnel and Subway Constructors International Union; the International Union of Pavers, Rammermen, Flag Layers, Bridge and Stone Curb Setters and Sheet Asphalt Pavers; the Journeymen Stone Cutters Association of North America; the National Postal Mail Handlers Union; and the National Federation of Independent Unions.

PRIMARY FUNCTIONS

LIUNA strives to improve the welfare of laborers in a variety of occupations. Consequently, many of its functions revolve around the political arena. LIUNA tracks congressional voting patterns to determine which candidates strongly support labor views; tracks legislation and makes public stands on positions to influence representatives; and promotes voter registration among union members to increase the chances of union-sympathetic candidates winning office. In 1996 the Laborers' Union nearly doubled the amount of voters participating in the congressional elections within its organization from the 1994 turnout. The campaign helped 12 labor-friendly candidates win seats in Congress. LIUNA uses its political action committee (PAC), Laborers' Political League

(LPL), to fund candidates for federal office and promote legislative programs.

Another of the primary activities of the Laborers' Union has been extending financial support to congressional and presidential candidates. It is not uncommon for labor unions to support Democratic candidates and the LPL has been particularly active in its support. The LPL grew from being the sixteenth largest labor PAC in the 1993 to 1994 election cycle to the fourth largest in the 1995 to 1996 election cycle. The LPL ranked twelfth on a list of the fifty top PAC contributors to candidates from 1995 to 1996 donating over $1.9 million.

The Laborers' Union also provides a number of benefits and services to its members. The Laborers' Union offers hundreds of pension, health and welfare, and training funds to its members. LIUNA members also have access to Union Privilege, an AFL-CIO-sponsored program designed to provide financial support to laborers. Some of the Union Privilege benefits include a no annual-fee credit card, mortgage assistance, legal assistance, credit counseling, consumer advice, and assistance for laid off or disabled workers. LIUNA also offers courses on important labor issues such as union leadership, public-sector bargaining, and industrial bargaining through the George Meany Center for Labor Studies.

PROGRAMS

LIUNA's membership base has been what historically was considered unskilled laborers, such as construction workers and hazardous waste removal workers. One of the initiatives LIUNA has taken to increase the security of its members in the marketplace is to provide education and training programs. At one time construction work could be performed by any unskilled general laborer; because of technological advances in construction work, however, the job has become more demanding. LIUNA's answer to the increase in skill level required for construction work is to equip its members with background training.

In 1967 LIUNA took the initiative to develop a training program to cater to an increasingly competitive market. LIUNA managed to secure several federal grants to fund its training projects. In 1969 LIUNA joined with the Associated General Contractors to form the Laborers-Associated General Contractors Education and Training Fund (L-AGC). The group is independently funded and coordinates training projects in 73 sites across North America. The L-AGC provides training for skills required in the construction and environmental fields as well as workplace literacy and career path guidance.

In addition to training construction workers, the L-AGC fund also provides hazardous waste removal training. Members are offered an 80-hour certification program in which they learn how to clean up everything from toxic chemicals to radiation. Trainees are introduced to current methods in hazardous waste removal through simulated hazardous waste sites designed by a U.S. environmental firm. LIUNA currently has 69 state-of-the-art training facilities in North America. Because of the increasing demand for hazardous waste laborers, the L-AGC training program has been extremely successful in placing its trainees and anticipates future success as well.

Apart from committing to improving working conditions and job security for its members through job training programs, LIUNA also offers consumer benefits and services such as pension and health care benefits. LIUNA offers financial consulting for its members to plan for the future, low-rate mortgages, research services to help find the right health care package, and special interest rates for loans and credit cards. The Laborers' Union also provides assistance for members who have been laid off or are disabled. These incentives are offered through the Union Privilege program, part of a larger program offered to AFL-CIO affiliates.

BUDGET INFORMATION

LIUNA has three primary funding units called Labor-Management Cooperatives in their Tri-Fund network. These units consist of management and laborers who work together to fund various projects. The three Labor-Management Cooperatives are: Laborers-Employers Cooperation and Education Trust (LECET); the Laborers-Associated General Contractors Education and Training Fund (L-AGC); and the Laborers' Health and Safety Fund of North America (LHSFNA).

In 1998 LIUNA had net assets of roughly $129.7 million. That year it disbursed approximately $100.3 million. The largest amount, 39 percent, was spent on the purchase of investments and fixed assets. The next-largest expenditures were salaries for its employees and officers (14 percent), direct and withholding taxes (12 percent), and benefits (11 percent). Other expenditures included professional fees (8 percent) and office and administrative expenses (7 percent). The final 9 percent of LIUNA's budget was spent on miscellaneous costs such as organizing expenses, convention expenses, and educational and publicity expenses.

HISTORY

During the period between 1877 and 1914, the United States became one of the world's most powerful industrial nations. Much of the economic success of the United States during the Industrial Revolution occurred at the expense of laborers. Businesses often used child labor, forced unlimited workdays, provided poor and

BUDGET:
1998 LIUNA Expenses

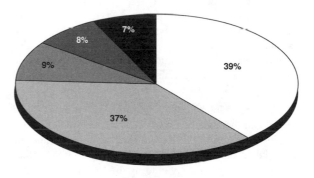

☐ 39%: Purchase of investments and fixed assets

▢ 37%: Salaries and benefits

▨ 9%: Miscellaneous, including organizing expenses, convention expenses, and educational and publicity expenses

▨ 8%: Professional fees

■ 7%: Administrative expenses

even hazardous working conditions, and offered disgracefully low wages for cumbersome work. Labor unions formed to protect workers against these conditions. Originally there were two general types of labor unions that emerged in response to the Industrial Revolution: craft, or horizontal unions which organized by skill; and industrial, or vertical, which organized by industry. The Laborers' Union was an industrial union originally designed to serve construction workers.

Early craft unions organized by the Knights of Labor (1869–1917) eventually gave way to larger, more inclusive, craft unions such as the American Federation of Labor, which was founded in 1886. In the early 1900s, poor working conditions and low wages brought on a series of protests and strikes from the International Workers of the World. After a strike by the International Ladies' Garments in 1910 a small number of collective bargaining agreements (peaceful protest of working conditions considered to be unfair) emerged.

The first really successful unions were trade unions for specialized crafts such as the Cigarmaker's and Seamen's unions. When the United States began to industrialize, larger unions designed to represent laborers in a particular industry began to develop. Unions for steelworkers and autoworkers represented both skilled and unskilled laborers.

During the early 1900s, the United States experienced a sharp increase in building construction. With so much new business the number of jobs in construction grew immensely. Samuel Gompers, the president of the American Federation of Labor, hoped to see these new workers unified in such a way that their strength in numbers could work to their advantage. After communicating this to the country's labor leaders, a collection of representatives met in Washington, D.C., and this conference led to the formation of the International Hod Carriers' and Building Laborers' Union of America on April 13, 1903.

The new International Union was extremely successful and membership swelled to 100,000 in the 1920s. It enjoyed a growing influence over labor issues and the other labor unions in the United States. Other trades began to join the union, including the International Compressed Air and Foundation Workers Union, the Tunnel and Subway Constructors International Union, and the International Union of Pavers, Rammermen, Flag Layers, Bridge and Curb Setters and Asphalt Pavers.

Membership in the International Union lagged during the Great Depression in response to poor economic conditions. Part of the New Deal legislation, introduced by President Franklin D. Roosevelt to combat the effects of the Great Depression, included the Wagner Act or National Labor Relations Act (1935). The Wagner Act guaranteed organizing and collective bargaining rights allowing unions to peacefully protest working conditions they considered unfair. During the World War II industrial efforts, membership increased dramatically to 430,000 in 1942. However, later legislation such as the Taft-Hartley Act or Labor-Management Relations Act (1947) and the Landrum-Griffin Act (1959) put labor unions at a disadvantage in their efforts to win concessions from big business. Although the Taft-Hartley Act defined "unfair labor practices," it banned boycotts, sympathy strikes, and strikes in inter-union disputes. The Taft-Hartley Act also permitted the president to issue an injunction to stop a strike in the case of a "national emergency." The Landrum-Griffin Act was designed to curb labor corruption.

The International Union became affiliated with the newly combined AFL-CIO's Union Department in 1955 and to this point catered exclusively to construction workers. The post-World War II (1939–45) industrial boom in the United States ushered in a demand for labor representation. In response the Laborers' Union began to diversify its membership to include nonconstruction workers. In 1965 the union officially changed its name to the Laborers' International Union of North America to correspond to the expanding and diversifying enrollment trend of the union. In 1968 LIUNA accepted the Mail Handlers Union into its fold and during the 1970s Canadian membership in LIUNA topped 50,000.

The 1980s and 1990s were a time of transition for LIUNA. Accusations of links to organized crime and mis-

guided contributions to presidential campaigns forced LIUNA to try to alter its image. It attempted to increase its focus on membership and, in so doing, decrease the focus on its alleged illegal activities. For example, in 1994 LIUNA celebrated the news that the Department of Labor considered construction work (or "Construction Craft Laborer") as an apprenticeship occupation. Other initiatives by LIUNA included a pledge to eradicate any links that the organization might have had to organized crime.

CURRENT POLITICAL ISSUES

Recent political issues of importance for LIUNA have had to do with the targeting of specific legislative initiatives to support or defeat in the political arena. For example, LIUNA collaborated with the AFL-CIO, the National Education Association, and other large labor unions to defeat California's Proposition 226 (the Paycheck Protection Act). The legislation would have required unions to seek annual permission from its members to use funds for political or legislative activities. Labor unions outspent proponents of the legislation $30 million to $4.5 million on advertising, canvassing, and lobbying against the Paycheck Protection Act.

LIUNA's General President Arthur A. Coia argued that Proposition 226 unfairly targeted labor unions in the use of membership funds for political activity when big business already outspends labor unions in the political arena by a margin of 11 to one. The Paycheck Protection Act would have placed restrictions on labor unions' funding of political initiatives while leaving corporations and other special-interest groups free to support their own initiatives. In March of 1998, the House voted down a similar bill (H.R. 2608), a national Paycheck Protection Act, which LIUNA was also instrumental in defeating. In June of 1998, LIUNA celebrated the signing of Transportation Equity Act for the 21st Century (TEA-21), which is another example of labor unions' use of micro-campaigning to support or defeat legislation. The Transportation Construction Coalition (TCC), of which LIUNA is a key participant, has worked to secure legislation committed to improving the nation's transportation infrastructure.

Case Study: Cleaning Up Its Act

Perhaps the most important political concern of the Laborers' Union in recent years has been the reconstruction of a public image that has been tainted by certain union officials' association with members of organized crime. In 1986 the President's Commission identified LIUNA, along with the Teamsters, the Longshoremen, and the Hotel Employees and Restaurant Workers, as having "clear ties" to organized crime.

The Department of Justice (DOJ) drafted a complaint against LIUNA in February of 1995. In a Racketeer Influenced Corrupt Organization (RICO) complaint which was not filed, the DOJ accused LIUNA President Arthur Coia of looting union health and welfare benefit funds. The report also accused Coia of stealing union funds from upstate New York. He was alleged to have shared the stolen money with an East Coast Mafia member. The DOJ insisted that Coia and other members of the Laborers' Union suspected of having ties to organized crime be removed from the organization and that the union must initiate broad reforms.

Three months after the racketeering charges were drafted in the RICO investigation, the DOJ unexpectedly dropped the complaint. The DOJ then handed over the duties of cleaning up the union to Coia himself under an oversight agreement. Under the agreement, if the union failed to disassociate itself from organized crime, the DOJ would take over a substantial portion of the union as it had with the Teamsters in 1989. Some contend that the mysterious dismissal of the RICO action was influenced by Coia's close political and personal relationship with President Bill and Mrs. Hillary Clinton. The Laborers' Union has been a generous contributor to the Democratic Party in recent years and this may have afforded them special treatment by the White House. For instance, in 1998 the House Judiciary subcommittee documented 120 social interactions between Coia and the Clintons, including breakfasts at the White House and trips on Air Force One.

In July of 1996 House Republicans held hearings to determine whether the DOJ was persuaded by the Clinton administration to drop the RICO complaint. The hearings did not turn up any convincing evidence that the White House influenced the investigation. In November of 1997 Robert D. Luskin, a LIUNA attorney who was designated chief prosecutor of corruption for the reforms, indicated he intended to charge Coia with corruption. However, nothing ever came of the charges.

The Laborers' Union has instituted reforms and terminated much of its connections to organized crime. Some of the Union's reform efforts have included adopting an ethics and disciplinary code, initiating investigations in major regions throughout the country, and overhauling its contract procedures. In addition, in 1996 the Union held its first rank election for LIUNA officers. The election was supervised by an independent election official, Stephen Goldberg, a law professor at Northwestern University. Incumbent Arthur A. Coia defeated challenger Bruno Caruso by a comfortable margin. In a press release issued by the DOJ, Scott Lassar, U.S. attorney for the Northern District of Illinois and member of the DOJ oversight team said, "[p]rogress has been made, but the work of reforming the Laborers' Union has not been completed." Coia began rooting out corrupt union officials prior to the DOJ's 1995 intervention. He welcomed the opportunity to "once and for all" rid the union of corruption.

In January of 1999 the DOJ extended their oversight agreement with LIUNA to January 31, 2000. Apparently

FAST FACTS

The Laborer's Union was the largest union contributor of "soft money" to the Democratic Party in 1996. "Soft money" refers to the unlimited amount of money interest groups are entitled to give for the purpose of strengthening state party organizations.

(Source: Kenneth R. Weinstein. "LIUNA, Organized Crime, and the Clinton Administration." *The Heritage Foundation*, October 20, 1996.)

satisfied with the reform efforts LIUNA has initiated, the DOJ has softened the conditions under which it would impose the consent decree that would allow it to take over the reform efforts itself. Since the Laborers' Union began its reform efforts, 450 investigations have been opened, 132 charges filed, and 189 members have been forced out of the union.

FUTURE DIRECTIONS

The Laborers' Union has been expanding and diversifying its membership base by recruiting new and different types of members. In November of 1998 LIUNA reported that over six hundred health care workers in New England joined the union. LIUNA won allegiance from nursing home employees in Greenwich, Connecticut, Pawtuxet Village and Warwick, Rhode Island, and Somerville, Massachusetts. LIUNA grew from 425,000 members in 1996 to 750,000 in 1998. It represents a diverse range of occupations, including construction, environmental remediation, maintenance, food service, health care, and clerical workers. The Laborers' Union plans to take advantage of its numerical strength and focus on expansion of its broad membership base in the upcoming decade.

GROUP RESOURCES

For more information about LIUNA, contact its national headquarters by writing to 905 16th St. NW, Washington, DC 20006 or by phoning (202) 737-8320. For public affairs information, including current news releases, consult their public affairs link at http://www. liuna.org/pages/public-affairs/liunanews.html. To learn the perspective of LIUNA members on LIUNA's affairs, access the Web site of the Laborers' at http://www. laborers.org. This site has many links to articles published on LIUNA as well as links to sites of interest for laborers. LIUNA also provides information about current political issues of concern to the union, such as election news and legislative proposals, at a Laborers' Political League newsletter posted on-line at http://www.liuna.org /pages/legislative/legislative.html.

GROUP PUBLICATIONS

The Laborer magazine is LIUNA's primary publication. While a print version via subscription is only available to LIUNA members, recent issues of *The Laborer* can be viewed on-line at http://www.LIUNA. org/pages/public-affairs/liunanews.html. Current news releases are also available from LIUNA's public affairs office on-line at http://www.liuna.org/Pages/Public-affairs/ newsreleases/newsrelease.html.

BIBLIOGRAPHY

Bradford, Hazel. "Laborers to Clean Up Corruption." *Engineering News Record*, 27 February 1995.

Church, George W. "Fruits of Their Labor." *Time*, 24 June 1996.

Goodman, John F. "A Union Trains for the Future." *Training and Development*, October 1992.

Greenhouse, Steven. "Union Monitor Seeking to Oust Laborers' Chief." *New York Times*, 23 October 1997.

Isikoff, Michael, and Daniel Klaidman. "The Mob, the Clintons and the Union Boss." *Newsweek*, 20 May 1996.

Johnson, Dirk. "At Prosecutors' Prodding, Laborers' Union Opens Up Elections." *New York Times*, 2 February 1996.

Levine, Bruce, et al. *Who built America?: Working People and the Nation's Economy, Politics, Culture, and Society.* New York: Pantheon Books, 1992.

Mulligan, John E., and Dean Starkman. "An F.O.B. and the Mob." *Washington Monthly*, May 1996.

Weinstein, Kenneth R. "LIUNA, Organized Crime, and the Clinton Administration." *Heritage Foundation*, 20 October 1996.

Winston, Sherie. "Laborers Have Election Contest." *Engineering News Record*, 7 October 1996.

York, Byron. "Mob Rules." *The American Spectator*, April 1997.

Lambda Legal Defense and Education Fund (LLDEF)

WHAT IS ITS MISSION?

According to the organization, the Lambda Legal Defense and Education Fund (LLDEF) is a "national organization committed to achieving full recognition of the civil rights of lesbians, gay men and people with HIV through impact litigation, education and public policy work." The organization's mission is "to provide legal assistance and education to lesbians and gay men and to promote the availability of legal services to homosexuals by encouraging and attracting homosexuals into the legal profession."

More simply, LLDEF mainly works toward its goals in the courtroom by taking on cases with the hopes of setting legal precedents that advance the civil rights of gays and lesbians. To this end, LLDEF has focused its efforts in the following areas: employment and housing discrimination, gay military personnel issues, Autoimmune Deficiency Syndrome (AIDS) and Human Immunodeficiency Virus (HIV) policy and reform, marriage and parenting issues, and immigration.

ESTABLISHED: 1973
EMPLOYEES: 43
MEMBERS: 14,000

Contact Information:
ADDRESS: 120 Wall St., Ste. 1500
    New York, NY 10005
PHONE: (212) 809-8585
FAX: (212) 809-0055
E-MAIL: general@lambdalegal.org
URL: http://www.lambdalegal.org
EXECUTIVE DIRECTOR: Kevin Cathcart

HOW IS IT STRUCTURED?

LLDEF is a nonprofit organization that maintains a national headquarters in New York, New York. It is staffed by an executive director, a deputy director, legal director, managing director, and several project directors. LLDEF is governed by a board of directors with two co-chairs, a secretary, a treasurer, and a 25-member group representing states all over the nation. The board of directors and the executive director are responsible for the

overall direction of LLDEF, but it is the legal department of the organization, with input from other branches, that decides which cases and strategies to pursue. As members are not part of the organization's policy-making structure, membership in LLDEF is strictly a sign of support, although members are kept informed of all LLDEF activities.

LLDEF has three regional offices: the Western Regional Office located in Los Angeles; Midwest Regional Office in Chicago; and the Southern Regional Office in Atlanta. Each regional office is responsible for cases specific to their area, as well as for local media relations and publicity.

PRIMARY FUNCTIONS

LLDEF's main function is to pursue litigation to achieve improved civil rights for lesbians, gays, and people infected with HIV/AIDS. To this end, LLDEF selects and advocates court cases that advance the civil rights of their members, or that will set precedents that will hopefully prompt legislation if a favorable verdict is returned. At any time LLDEF has an active docket of about 60 court cases, encompassing such areas as equal employment rights and benefits; discrimination in housing; public benefits; tax and insurance; access to HIV/AIDS-related treatments and healthcare; child custody and visitation; and sodomy laws. LLDEF also plays a key role in challenges that involve gays and lesbians in military service and the organization is attempting to litigate marriage rights for gays and lesbians through its Marriage Project.

LLDEF fights proposed legislation and ballot initiatives that it believes would restrict or discriminate against lesbians, gays, and HIV/AIDS carriers. The organization campaigns against such initiatives and, if they do become law, challenges them in court.

A majority of LLDEF's cases are brought to them through its referral/intake service, which receives about one hundred calls per week from individuals or their attorneys seeking assistance. About one-third of these calls fall outside the organization's mission and are referred to an appropriate agency if possible. The remainder of the callers are given some form of assistance by LLDEF, usually in the form of investigation services, litigation services, or written resources. Most incoming calls concern employee discrimination.

To garner public support for its causes, LLDEF maintains an active coalition-building process. The organization briefs and meets with such related groups as: the Human Rights Campaign, the National Gay and Lesbian Task Force, the Gay and Lesbian Alliance against Defamation, Gay and Lesbian Advocates and Defenders, the Black Gay and Lesbian Leadership Forum, and many others. These groups, as well as other activists at both community and state levels, use LLDEF-prepared resources such as brochures, training manuals, and archives of media coverage in organizing their particular activities.

LLDEF also disseminates information and education about the fight for improved civil rights for lesbians and gays through conferences and seminars at which member-attorneys speak on current issues and court cases. The organization works to keep the media informed on the issues, and LLDEF attorneys can be found on television and radio and in print, serving as an authority not only on LLDEF cases, but also on gay and lesbian civil rights issues in general. To build support within government for upcoming cases, LLDEF provides issue-related briefing material to legislators and members of the judiciary.

PROGRAMS

LLDEF programs target a number of different issues, including employment, military, and reproductive rights. Four specific initiatives—the AIDS Project, the Anti-Gay Initiatives Project, the Family Relationships Project, and the Marriage Project—serve as good examples of LLDEF's efforts.

The AIDS Project uses litigation, education, and policy analysis to secure access to adequate health care for those with HIV/AIDS. This program also fights discrimination on the part of health insurers such as AIDS-specific payment "caps" and coverage exclusions of life-prolonging treatments. The AIDS Project also works to ensure that HIV/AIDS carriers are protected against other forms of discrimination by federal law.

Under the Anti-Gay Initiatives Project, the LLDEF works to prevent anti-gay legislation from becoming law, and challenges any such laws that are enacted. LLDEF and other gay and lesbian civil rights groups celebrated a major victory in this area in May, 1996, when the U.S. Supreme Court ruled Colorado's Amendment Two unconstitutional. In *Evans v. Romer*, the court struck down the amendment that made illegal the enactment of laws protecting gays and lesbians from discrimination.

The Family Relationships Project seeks to attain the same rights for lesbian and gay couples that non-gay couples enjoy—including the right to adopt, child custody and guardianship rights, and inheritance rights. This project also works in a broader sense to expand the definition of "family" to reflect America's increasing diversity.

LLDEF's Marriage Project was initiated in 1994 to lay the legal groundwork to provide same-sex couples the right to marry. According to LLDEF, many lesbian and gay couples share in the same responsibilities as married couples but are denied the legal and social support that comes with being married. LLDEF's Marriage Project works toward ending what it calls "second-class status" accorded same-sex couples.

BUDGET INFORMATION

When LLDEF formed in 1973, it had virtually no budget and was run by volunteer lawyers and staff. By the mid-1980s, however, AIDS became a larger part of the news and donations to LLDEF increased phenomenally. By 1993 LLDEF's budget reached $2 million.

With members joining at rates between $40 and $1,500 or more, 1995 brought in more than $4 million in total public support (contributions, gifts, and grants). An additional $34,768 was earned from program services such as the speakers bureaus and attorneys' fees; interest on investments provided $94,946.

Total LLDEF expenses for 1995 were $2,822,186. Expense categories included $1,857,435 in program services, $505,133 in management/general expenses, and $459,558 in fundraising expenses. In each of these categories salaries and compensations for organization officials accounted for almost half of the category totals.

HISTORY

LLDEF, the largest and oldest U.S. organization to deal with attaining equal rights for gays and lesbians, was founded in 1973 after its founder, William Thom, won his legal battles focusing on the proposed organization's right to non-profit status. In 1972 a New York court had turned down Thom's application for nonprofit status. The court found that the proposed gay legal defense group's "stated purposes are on their face neither benevolent nor charitable, nor, in any event, is there a demonstrated need for this corporation." According to the court, "it does not appear that discrimination against homosexuals, which undoubtedly exists, operates to deprive them of legal representation." The ruling was overturned in 1973 by the New York Supreme Court, but the state of New York still refused to grant incorporation to a group that used the word "gay" in its title. The fledgling organization substituted the word "lambda"—a Greek letter that also is a pictograph of the scales of justice.

During its first several years, LLDEF operated on a very small budget, depending on the help of volunteer lawyers and staff. One of its first staffers was Copy Berg, who had been ousted from the Navy in 1976 for being gay. Berg was one of the first to challenge the military ban on gays and, as a volunteer staffer, he typed his own briefs for the organization that agreed to represent him. Despite the efforts of Berg and others, challenges to the military's ban on gays would be unsuccessful until the 1990s.

BUDGET:
1995 LLDEF Expenses

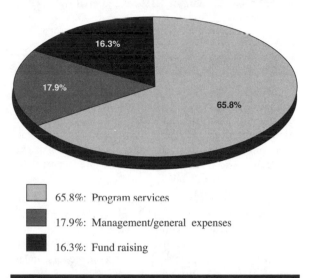

- 65.8%: Program services
- 17.9%: Management/general expenses
- 16.3%: Fund raising

In the 1980s the gay community reportedly became increasingly aware that they faced discrimination on several fronts. LLDEF fought discrimination in many arenas, including a landmark 1980 court case that was the first challenge to AIDS discrimination. The case involved a physician who treated AIDS patients and who was denied renewal of his office lease because nearby tenants feared they would catch the disease. The case was settled with the provision that the lease be renewed and that neighboring tenants not discriminate against either the physician or his patients in the future, a victory for AIDS activists and LLDEF. The organization also served as legal counsel in the 1986 Supreme Court Case *Bowers v. Hardwick*, which upheld the power of the states to enforce sodomy laws. LLDEF believes that sodomy laws, which prohibit "unnatural" sexual intercourse, stigmatize lesbians and gays (although they do also apply to heterosexuals). In the 19 states in which sodomy laws remain in effect, gay sexual union could still be illegal and punishable by law. After this decision, LLDEF continued to pursue litigation nationwide with the goal of eradicating these laws on a state level.

Throughout the 1990s LLDEF saw success in its challenges of the U.S. military's restrictive policies on gays. When Bill Clinton became president in 1993, he promised to end the ban on gays in the military, and a federal court ruled the ban unconstitutional in January of that year. The ban was replaced by a "don't ask, don't tell" policy, that allowed gays to join the military so long as they kept silent about their sexuality. LLDEF challenged this policy as well, and in 1997 it too was ruled unconstitutional by the courts.

As a result of its increasing involvement in high-profile cases, LLDEF's membership and budget grew throughout the 1980s and 1990s, and with it the scope of its activities. In 1996 the organization was involved in 50 cases across the United States that dealt with some aspect of gay, lesbian, or HIV-related civil rights.

CURRENT POLITICAL ISSUES

Many of the battles LLDEF faces result from public objections to gay and lesbian lifestyles. Others involve fear and misunderstanding about the causes and the contagiousness of the AIDS/HIV epidemic. The combined effect of these two areas has led to the restriction of gays and lesbians from enjoying the same life opportunities afforded to heterosexuals.

One major issue LLDEF deals with is employee discrimination against gays and lesbians. Legal protection from gender-based discrimination exists in only 11 states; in other states it is possible for lesbians and gays to be fired for being gay, and they have no legal recourse unless they work in a locality with its own anti-discrimination ordinance. LLDEF takes the position that lesbians and gay men should not be fired, harassed, held back, or given unequal benefits because of their sexual orientation. It mainly battles this issue, as well as others involving health care for AIDS and patients, by pursuing "test cases" with the potential to advance workplace protections and promote equal employment benefits for lesbian and gay workers.

In addition to discrimination in the workplace, LLDEF battles discrimination in society at large. Although many same-sex couples share the same responsibilities as married couples, gay and lesbians receive none of the same benefits and rights currently held by married couples. Such rights include joint insurance (including health) and equitable division of property. LLDEF has established the Marriage Project and has created a national coalition aimed at winning lesbians and gays the freedom to marry nationwide.

Case Study: Same-Sex Marriage in Hawaii

LLDEF's Marriage Project was initiated in 1994 after an important preliminary ruling in a Hawaii Supreme Court case. *Baehr v. Lewin* originated when three gay couples sought, through the court system, the right to obtain a same-sex marriage in the state of Hawaii. In 1993 a judge ruled in *Baehr v. Lewin* that refusing to grant marriage licenses to the gay plaintiffs was sex discrimination and violated the constitutional guarantee of equal protection.

After the ruling, LLDEF became involved in the initiative to secure same-sex marriage rights. The organization founded the Marriage Project, which assumed the role of coordinating the legal and activist work needed

to forge ahead on the marriage issue. LLDEF formed the National Freedom to Marry Coalition with other like-minded organizations to coordinate national and local efforts directed at public education and political organizing. The latter function was planned in a state-by-state basis, since LLDEF and other organizers predicted a backlash from several states. LLDEF staff also stepped in to provide legal counsel after the *Baehr v. Lewin* case was remanded to a lower state court. The lower court ruled, in December 1996, that the state had not shown compelling reasons why only heterosexual couples should be allowed to marry.

Hawaii's battle over same-sex marriage rights was far from over, however. The December 1996 ruling was appealed, and had yet to be decided by 1999. In 1996 the U.S. Congress passed a "Defense of Marriage" act granting states the right to refuse to recognize same-sex marriages from other states. A number of state legislatures have enacted similar laws.

The most serious response to LLDEF's actions came from conservatives and religious leaders in Hawaii. Opposed to same-sex marriages on moral or religious grounds, they proposed a 1998 ballot initiative that would amend the Hawaiian constitution to allow the legislature to determine if same-sex marriages should be legal. LLDEF and its partners campaigned vigorously against this ballot initiative, but it was passed in a 1998 election. Another measure, passed in Alaska on the same day, defined "marriage" as a union between one man and one woman.

Public Impact

While the passage of the Hawaiian and Alaskan ballot initiatives are a serious setback for same-sex marriages, LLDEF has not given up, noting that the struggle in Hawaii received national attention and that some gains were made. LLDEF's "Marriage Project Director's Update: October 1997," states that "Newsweek's latest poll reported that opposition to [gay and lesbian] marriage among the general public had dropped to only 56% nationwide." LLDEF plans to continue the fight for same-sex marriages through legal action. If and when same-sex marriage is legalized in some or all states, it will have an enormous impact on the lives of gay and lesbian couples. Custody and adoption, insurance coverage, divorce issues, estate planning, and employment benefits are only a few of the areas in which same-sex couples hope to benefit.

SUCCESSES AND FAILURES

LLDEF has been an effective participant in the movement to ensure and improve domestic partner benefits. According to LLDEF, employers such as big business, universities, and the public sector are increasingly offering domestic partner benefits. In 1994 estimates of the number of entities providing such coverage hovered around 200; by the spring of 1997 the *New York Times* reported that "[a]n estimated 500 companies, including IBM, Apple Computer, Walt Disney and Levi Strauss, as well as many colleges, universities, states, and municipalities, now offer health and other benefits to domestic partners." Of companies with more than 5,000 employees, one in four now offers coverage for the spousal equivalents of unmarried employees.

LLDEF continues to push for domestic partner benefits by taking on relevant court cases. In October 1997 it helped defend the City of San Francisco's policy of contracting only with businesses that extend employee spousal benefits to unmarried as well as married workers. The city was one of the first to provide domestic partner benefits to its own employees and enacted the Equal Benefits Ordinance in June 1997. San Francisco's pro-domestic benefits policy has actually spurred private-sector companies like the San Francisco 49ers, Pacific Bell, and Chevron Oil Corporation to offer these benefits to their employees.

FUTURE DIRECTIONS

Though LLDEF has been widely successful in securing medical benefits for domestic partners, many employers still refuse to provide them. But while LLDEF will continue to fight on that front, the issue stands a chance of resolving itself if LLDEF is successful in its most ambitious endeavor—making gay marriages legal. LLDEF calls on its constituency to realize that the same-sex marriage issue is not only about getting the right to marry, but about laying the groundwork now to keep the rights to same-sex marriage, and to achieve recognition of same-sex marriage in all states.

GROUP RESOURCES

LLDEF maintains a Web site at http://www.lambdalegal.org that provides a synopsis of the issues the organization deals with, as well as summaries of related court cases, news events, and reports. LLDEF's current docket can obtained by calling the organization. On television, LLDEF produces "Update," which is broadcast as part of *Gay USA*, a program on the Gay USA Network. On the show, which airs in an increasing number of cities nationwide, LLDEF provides updates about current cases and issues. For more information on the organization, write to the Lambda Legal Defense and Education Fund, 120 Wall St., Ste. 1500, New York, NY 10005, call (212) 809-8585, or fax (212) 809-0055.

GROUP PUBLICATIONS

LLDEF publishes a tri-annual newsletter, *The Lambda Update*, which contains information about current concerns of the organization and reports on the status of court cases that LLDEF is involved in. LLDEF produces 14 publications that are available for purchase, as well as various legal papers and memos that are distributed free of charge. Examples of publications include "Civil Marriage for Lesbians and Gay Men: Organizing in Communities of Faith" and "OUT on the Job, OUT of a Job: A Lawyer's Overview of the Employment Rights of Lesbians and Gay Men." LLDEF also makes legal briefs available for a nominal copying cost. For more information on the organization's publications, write to the Lambda Legal Defense and Education Fund, 120 Wall St., Ste. 1500, New York, NY 10005, call (212) 809-8585, or fax (212) 809-0055. Information on publications can also be found at the organization's Web site at http://www.lambdalegal.org.

BIBLIOGRAPHY

"The Thorn in His Side. Clinton and the Military Ban on Gays." *Advocate*, 2 April 1996.

Curiel, Jonathan. "The Little City that Could. San Francisco, CA, Forcing Big Business to Offer Domestic Partner Benefits." *Advocate*, 18 March 1997.

Goldenberg, Carey. "Gain for Same-Sex Parents, At Least; Finding in Hawaii Case May have Impact on Custody Disputes." *New York Times*, 6 December 1996.

Moss, J. Jennings. "Lesbian Baiting in the Barracks." *Advocate*, 4 February 1997.

————. "Losing The War. Harassment of Gays and Lesbians in the Military." *Advocate*, 15 April 1997.

Neff, Joseph. "Dad's Fight for Custody Heads for High Court; Gay Man's Fitness as Parent at Issue." *News and Observer*, 12 May 1997.

Scott, Janny. "Judge Broadens Rejection of Military Gay Policy." *New York Times*, 3 July 1997.

Rothman, Clifford. "A Stand for Human Worth School Officials Should've Stopped the Anti-Gay Abuse, Says Jamie Nabozny. A Jury Agreed." *Los Angeles Times*, 26 February 1997.

Sullivan, Andrew. "Telltale: Recommiting to the 'Don't Ask, Don't Tell' Gays in the military policy. An Agenda For A Second Term." *New Republic*, 11 November 1996.

League of Women Voters of the United States (LWV)

ESTABLISHED: February 14, 1920
EMPLOYEES: 49
MEMBERS: 132,212

Contact Information:

ADDRESS: 1730 M St. NW
　　　Washington, DC 20036-4508
PHONE: (202) 429-1965
TOLL FREE: (800) 249-8683
FAX: (202) 429-0854
E-MAIL: lwv@lwv.org
URL: http://www.lwv.org
PRESIDENT: Carolyn Jefferson-Jenkins

WHAT IS ITS MISSION?

According to organization literature, the League of Women Voters of the United States (LWV) is a nonpartisan political organization that "encourages the informed and active participation of citizens in government and influences public policy through education and advocacy." While the achievement of women's suffrage in the early 1900s was an impetus for founding the organization, the vision of the LWV has moved beyond women's voting rights to address political involvement for all citizens. The organization is involved in a wide variety of issues ranging from environmental concerns to international relations to public health; the crucial theme that links all issues for the LWV is facilitating effective public involvement, whether through voting, community dialog, or grassroots mobilization.

HOW IS IT STRUCTURED?

Based in Washington, D.C., the LWV is a political organization with 501(c)4 nonprofit status, meaning it is allowed to lobby and influence legislation. Its partner organization is the League of Women Voters Education Fund (LWVEF), a 501(c)3 nonprofit organization that functions in a complementary fashion, pursuing research and outreach efforts. The LWV is headed by a 15-member, geographically representative board of directors, each member of which serves a two-year term.

The LWV has affiliate chapters at the state level in all 50 states, the District of Columbia, and the Virgin Islands; local chapters exist in over 1,000 communities.

At each level, local and state chapters set their own initiatives based on the national policy agenda. Members join the LWV at a rate of $45 for individuals or $60 per household (1999 figures), and can then join state and local chapters. In line with the organization's diversity policy, both men and women can join the organization, provided they are U.S. citizens and are at least 18 years of age. Members have the opportunity to become involved in grassroots lobbying tactics, including letter writing, phoning legislators, and participating in local chapter initiatives.

PRIMARY FUNCTIONS

The LWV has the ultimate goal of promoting citizen involvement in government processes. Specifically, the group facilitates grassroots involvement in policy formation by encouraging members and citizens to vote and educating all potential voters. According to an LWV survey taken in 1996, lack of information rather than disinterest or apathy prevents citizens from voting. According to another LWV survey, more than 76 percent of Americans felt that they lacked adequate information to make informed decisions at the polls. In response, the LWV launched a "Get out the Vote" campaign incorporating information hot lines, magazine articles, and town meetings to inform the public about upcoming elections.

The LWVEF serves as the outreach and research arm of the organization, and its work is driven by the overriding belief that informed and empowered citizens are better able to influence public policy. The Fund studies and generates information, intended to be unbiased, that will give the public a better understanding of timely policy issues. For example, the LWVEF produced a report called *Charting the Health of American Democracy* in June 1997 that proposed that democracy in the late twentieth century was seriously being challenged. The causes cited included low voter turnout, decreasing citizen confidence in government, and lack of responsiveness on the part of government institutions. The LWVEF also educates citizens about how to register to vote and how to encourage participation in local community government.

The LWV attempts to influence public policy. Although it is nonpartisan and does not support political candidates, the organization does take positions on relevant political issues. Positions for the organization are debated and decided at the membership level; in this way members help shape the overall national agenda. Members at the local level interface with the community through the use of media, surveys, and community meetings. Once the league's agenda is formulated, organization staff and board members work with policy makers to lobby for particular issues, testify before congressional and government committees, form coalitions with other supportive groups, track pending legislation, contact policy makers, and create media campaigns.

PROGRAMS

LWV programs share one similarity: they serve to educate members and the general public about public policy and they encourage civic involvement. The organization's programs include the "Making Democracy Work" campaign finance reform program, the Drinking Water Protection Project, and the Wetlands Citizen Education Program.

"Making Democracy Work" is an ongoing initiative designed to facilitate citizen involvement in public policy at all levels. While local and state LWV chapters design their own approach in carrying out the initiative, "Making Democracy Work" generally focuses on areas that the organization feels are indicative of healthy civic involvement: increasing voter turnout, advocating for campaign finance reform, expanding citizen education and participation, and increasing the diversity of elected officials. LWV chapters carry out the program using such means as public surveys, media campaigns, or coalition building with other supportive civic groups.

LWV's Wetlands Citizen Education Program began in 1996 as an effort to facilitate discussion and create community-based initiatives related to wetlands health. The organization trained members to lead community projects and open the lines of dialog. By mid-1998 the group's local chapters instigated a variety of wetland-related projects, including producing videos, creating educational kits, and organizing workshops with the community.

The LWV does not limit its initiatives to the United States. Since its inception, one of its mandates has been to assist groups in countries with emerging democracies. That vision is encompassed in the organization's Global Community Dialogue Program, which was established in 1992 with the primary goal of training civic leaders and organizations in other countries. Training may include U.S. internships for civic leaders, workshops, teleconferences, and partnering projects. Recent target areas have included Central Europe, Latin America, the former Soviet Union, and Africa.

BUDGET INFORMATION

In fiscal year 1996, which ended in June of 1997, the LWV had revenue totaling $2,518,837, which included direct public support ($578,766), program service revenue ($87,959), membership dues ($1,503,779), interest on savings ($2,607), dividends ($32,612), sales of assets ($217,889), and sales of inventory ($95,225). Expenses totaled $2,871,096 and included program services ($1,519,087), management and general ($649,859), and fundraising ($702,150).

The LWVEF had revenues in fiscal year 1996 that totaled $5,171,454 and included direct public support

BUDGET:

1996 LWVUS Revenue

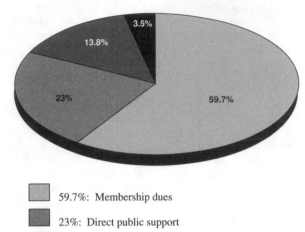

- [ ] 59.7%: Membership dues
- [ ] 23%: Direct public support
- [ ] 13.8%: Interest, dividends, and sales of assets and inventory
- [ ] 3.5%: Program service revenue

1996 LWVUS Expenses

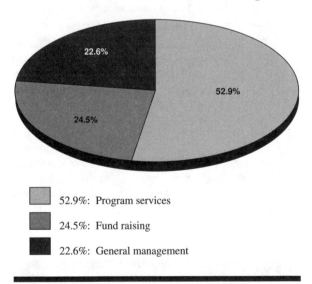

- [ ] 52.9%: Program services
- [ ] 24.5%: Fund raising
- [ ] 22.6%: General management

($369,899), indirect public support ($2,853,731), government contributions ($1,814,572), program service revenue ($47,677), interest on savings ($5,705), dividends ($24,942), sale of assets ($55,440), and loss on sales of inventory (-$512). Expenses for 1996 totaled $4,236,614 and included: program services ($3,105,015), management and general ($485,667), and fundraising ($645,932).

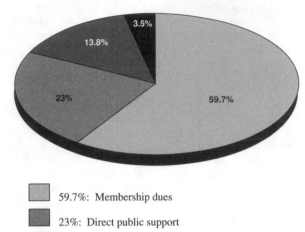

HISTORY

Suffrage groups, including the National Woman Suffrage Association and American Woman Suffrage Association, existed in the United States as early as 1860. These groups, although not always sharing the same philosophy, laid the groundwork for women to achieve the right to vote. During a meeting of the National American Woman Suffrage Association, the National League of Women Voters was founded in 1920, in part due to the vision of women's rights advocate and peace activist, Carrie Chapman Catt. The founding occurred just six months before the passage of the 19th Amendment which gave women the right to vote. Maud Wood Park served as the League's first president.

Once women won the right to vote, they began to use their new power to influence and shape public policy. Women formed legislative councils, monitored policy initiatives, and formed targeted groups to deal with specific issues. LWV members quickly got involved with shaping legislation and advocated successfully for the passage of the 1921 Sheppard-Tower Act, which provided government funding for maternal and children's programs.

Women's activism and membership in groups like LWV dropped sharply during the Great Depression of the 1930s because the economic downturn was the universal concern of the day. During this period the LWV did, however, focus on reforming local election processes, and began researching the status of election procedures. After World War II (1939–45) women redoubled their advocacy efforts, pushing as early as the late 1940s for adoption of an equal rights amendment to the U.S. Constitution. The LWV had opposed an earlier version of such an amendment in 1921 on the grounds that it would compromise labor rights for women in nonunionized jobs.

The LWV continued to extend its interest into a variety of civic issues. In the 1930s the organization advocated for natural resource measures that would reclaim areas damaged by floods during the Depression. In the 1950s members took a strong stand against the congressional investigations being launched by Senator Joseph McCarthy, and advocated for what they called the necessary freedom to disagree within a democracy. Later in the decade the organization established the LWVEF to strengthen public outreach and research.

The resurrection of a strong women's movement in the 1960s affected the agenda of groups like the LWV, which began to advocate for such feminist issues as equal rights and the demise of sexism. In 1974, for example, the LWV formed a coalition with other feminist groups such as the National Organization for Women (NOW) and Girls in Education to pursue federal monies that would address sexism in school materials. Against little resistance, legislation passed providing the financial means to create curricula addressing issues of sexism.

BIOGRAPHY:
Maud Wood Park

Activist (1871–1955) After fifteen years of speaking and lobbying for woman's suffrage, Maud Wood Park was chosen to serve as the first president of the League of Women Voters (LWV). The nonpartisan group was formed from the National American Woman Suffrage Association (NAWSA) in 1920 after passage and ratification of the Nineteenth Amendment to the U.S. Constitution, guaranteeing women the right to vote. Park had worked to pay her own way through school and graduated with top honors from Radcliffe College in 1898. After graduation, she became active in civic work to improve the lives of the disadvantaged around her and at the same time promoted woman's suffrage. She chaired the Massachusetts Woman Suffrage Association in 1900 and helped found the College Equal Suffrage League in 1904. Traveling extensively to promote the cause of suffrage to college women across the country, her popular lectures drew large audiences. In 1916 her friend, Carrie Chapman Catt,

head of the NAWSA, convinced the charismatic speaker to go to Washington, D.C., and lobby legislators for a woman's suffrage amendment. Passage of the amendment was a testament to Park's skills as a lobbyist. Under Park, the LWV adopted a thirty-eight point program of legislative measures. Recognizing strength in numbers, she collectivized nine other women's groups under one banner, the Women's Joint Congressional Committee (WJCC). Leading the WJCC, Park successfully leveraged the political muscle of all nine groups. Despite illness that forced her retirement in 1924, Park continued to lecture and support women's rights and causes.

The LWV also joined with other feminist groups in the unsuccessful attempt to ratify the Equal Rights Amendment (ERA) in the early 1970s. At the same time, the organization changed its bylaws in 1974 to allow men to join. Several men since then have served as president.

In the 1980s many of the initiatives crucial to the organization's mission involved making the U.S. government, specifically the idea of a democratic system, more accessible to the individual citizen. The League targeted two initiatives in particular: voter participation and campaign finance reform. The organization sponsored and televised presidential debates to provide citizens with information on the issues and the candidates. Acting in the legislative arena, the LWV played a part in passing the Federal Election Campaign Act of 1974—legislation that installed campaign reform and set up public financing of campaigns. Later, in the 1990s, the organization worked to streamline the voter registration process and helped enact the National Voter Registration Act, which conveniently tied in voter registration with motor vehicle registration.

Toward the end of the 1990s the LWV continued to stay involved in issues such as campaign finance reform, a hotly debated issue with much at stake for all political parties. The organization claimed the situation had become so unbalanced that politicians were most influenced by special interest money, giving the average citizen little say in what was supposed to be a democratic process.

CURRENT POLITICAL ISSUES

The LWV advocates for a variety of issues, both domestic and international, that relate to preserving democracy and facilitating civic involvement. On the international level, the group supported the United Nations request for prompt payment in early 1997 when the United States was late in paying its UN dues of over one billion dollars. In September, 1998 the LWV put in place an absentee voting process that allowed Bosnians living in the United States to participate in their country's elections that month. This involved setting up a multilingual hotline to dispense voting information to refugees and working with refugee agencies.

On the domestic front, the LWV has tackled a wide range of issues. Concerned over the state of the environment, it advocates for policies designed to protect the integrity of natural resources. For example, the LWV pushed for the demise of the Nuclear Waste Policy Act of 1997 on the grounds that the suggested storage site in Nevada was not geographically safe and had not been adequately studied. In a defeat for the LWV, the bill passed the Senate. The LWV also advocates for social policies such as a citizen's right to basic health care. According to the organization, even though increasing numbers of Americans are participating in managed health care plans (73 percent in 1995 as opposed to 27 percent in 1988), many are being denied the care and services that they need. The organization advocated for passage of the proposed Patients' Bill of Rights Act of 1998 that would streamline access to necessary and emergency care, facilitate a grievance process, and guarantee confidentiality of medical records.

Campaign finance reform has been a goal of the LWV since 1973. In August of 1998 the organization made significant headway toward realizing their agenda when an amendment for campaign reform passed the House.

Case Study: Bipartisan Campaign Reform Act

According to the LWV, the issue of campaign finance reform is critical to the essence of democracy. The existence and evolution of campaign finance laws have given special interest groups tremendous power to sway candidates—power that overrides the influence of the voting public. The LWV believes the ability of the U.S. citizen to influence public policy is a right inherent in democracies that should not be lost. Opposition to their position on the part of powerful, key policy makers has made the fight for campaign finance reform an uphill battle.

During the 1998 congressional session, Representatives Christopher Shays (R-Conn.) and M. Meehan (D-Mass.) sponsored a campaign finance reform amendment to the Bipartisan Campaign Reform Act of 1998 (H.R. 2183). The act was originally introduced as a bill to amend the Federal Election Campaign Act of 1971 in order to reform the campaign financing for federal elections. Shays' amendment proposed to ban "soft money" contributions—money from corporations, special interests, and the very wealthy—and what LWV terms "sham issue ads": ads that, due to a legal loophole, allow special interests to advertise for a particular candidate and avoid contribution limits and disclosure rules that would otherwise apply. In a unique congressional phenomenon called "Queen of the Hill," the amendment had to get more votes than all other amendments to the House bill before it could be considered for a second and final vote.

To both ensure that the amendment outcompeted other amendments and that it passed the House, LWV leadership and other coalition groups met with sponsors, held press conferences, and targeted "swing" voters, policy makers that might vote either way on the issue. To influence swing voters, their constituents were approached by the LWV and asked to contact their congressional representative. The organization also provided a sample "Letter to the Editor" for constituents. Lobbyists further urged policy makers to vote against the other H.R. 2183 amendments so that the campaign reform amendment would have a better chance at passage.

In August of 1998, due in part to the efforts of the LWV and other coalition groups, the campaign finance reform amendment beat out 57 other amendments and passed the House. By mid-1999, the bill was pending in the Senate.

FUTURE DIRECTIONS

LWV staff, board members, and organization members collaborated to create *Vision 2000,* a plan identifying the League's direction at the beginning of the twenty-first century. Initiatives include increasing diversity among members and programs, advocating for increased representation of women and minorities among policy makers, maintaining voter turnout at or above 85 percent, and increasing community involvement through the formation of Citizen Education Centers. The organization also expects to step up global involvement through its Global Community Dialogue/ Grassroots Internship Program.

GROUP RESOURCES

The LWV Web site at http://www.lwv.org includes a catalog of publications, up-to-date information on organization policy initiatives, and timely action alerts. Included is information on becoming involved in civic policy and on joining the organization. The League Action Line targets how to effectively communicate to policymakers and includes government access information. Contact the organization directly by writing to 1730 M Street NW, Washington, DC 20036-4508; by phone at 1-800-249-VOTE; or by E-mailing lwv@lwv. org for information on registering to vote or becoming a member.

GROUP PUBLICATIONS

The LWV produces a number of pamphlets, brochures, books, and information kits that educate citizens and promote grassroots community involvement. A bimonthly journal called *National Voter* is available to members. Among the titles available to the public is *Tell It to Washington: A Guide for Citizen Action,* which details why individuals should interact with policy makers and how to effectively make one's views heard. It also includes a directory of addresses and contacts. Other publications cover such topics as political effectiveness, international affairs, natural resources, and social policy. All materials can be ordered by contacting the organization's publishing clearinghouse at (301) 362-8184; fax (301) 206-9789; or E-mail: lwv@pmds.com. A list of LWV publications can be found on the Web site at http://www.lwv.org.

BIBLIOGRAPHY

Baker, Nancy Kassebaum, and Walter F. Mondale. "Campaign Finance System Must Be Repaired Soon." *Star Tribune,* 25 July 1997.

Baldauf, Scott. "GOP Builds Party in Texas via Grass Roots, Not Glitz." *Christian Science Monitor,* 8 January 1998.

Cain, Becky. "Learning from the Suffragists." *Social Education,* September 1995.

"High Profile Pair Push Senate on Campaign Funds." *Rocky Mountain News,* 1 October 1997.

Genis, Sandra. "Here's One Vote for Checking ID at Registration; It Shouldn't Be Easier to Get a Ballot Than a Library Card." *Los Angeles Times,* 27 April 1997.

Kessler, Glenn. "Bitter Medicine Reform Is Coming; and This Could Be Painful." *Newsday,* 11 April 1993.

Kimmel, Michael S. "In the Public Interest: The League of Women Voters, 1920–1970 by Louise M. Young." *Journal of American History,* March 1991.

Morality in Media (MIM)

ESTABLISHED: 1967
EMPLOYEES: 13
MEMBERS: 14,000
PAC: None

Contact Information:

ADDRESS: 475 Riverside Dr., Ste. 239
New York, NY 10115
PHONE: (212) 870-3222
FAX: (212) 870-2765
E-MAIL: mimnyc@ix.netcom.com
URL: http://pw2.netcom.com/mimnyc/index.html
PRESIDENT: Robert Peters

WHAT IS ITS MISSION?

The stated mission of Morality in Media (MIM) is to use "its knowledge of the law and the vigorous involvement of informed citizens to address . . . the exploitation of obscenity in the marketplace, and the erosion of decency standards in the media." Arguing that pornography "degrades men and women, violates children, destroys marriages, serves as a training manual for sexual psychopaths in our midst, threatens public health and causes deterioration of entire neighborhoods," MIM uses its legal and publicity resources to promote stronger anti-pornography legislation, to provide information to the public about media and "decency issues," and "to intervene as a friend of the court in cases involving challenges to anti-pornography laws." Although MIM claims that it "does not believe in censorship," it "does believe that those who traffic in obscenity are responsible before the law."

HOW IS IT STRUCTURED?

The nonprofit MIM is governed by a board of directors, which averages 19 members and meets about four times a year. Day-to-day operations are directed by a president and executive staff. The president is also a voting member of the board. MIM has affiliates in Louisiana, Massachusetts, Puerto Rico, South Dakota, and Wisconsin; and chapters in Michigan, Missouri, and Buffalo, New York. These chapters and affiliates operate independently of the national organization and are not supported financially through it or monitored by it. The national organization often does provide local chapters with publications and legal materials; experts to speak at local public meetings; analysis of legislation; and advice. In addition to its regional structure, MIM established its National Obscenity Law Center to act as its research arm.

PRIMARY FUNCTIONS

While MIM's staunch opposition to pornography and obscenity frequently involves it in efforts to shape and promote tougher legislation to curb "indecency" in the media, the organization's primary focus is to use its legal resources to support existing anti-pornography laws in the face of court challenges. In 1996, for instance, the organization played a key role in a Supreme Court decision which ruled that cable TV operators can prohibit indecent material on channels leased to independent programmers—a key provision of the Cable TV Act of 1992—and has been a major contestant in the battle to control obscenity on the Internet. Morality in Media also provides information about pornography and media decency issues to the general public through its membership newsletter and other publications, its public inquiry services, public speaking activities, and interviews with print and broadcast journalists.

Perhaps the most important resource in Morality in Media's anti-pornography information campaign is its National Obscenity Law Center (NOLC). Based in New York, the National Obscenity Law Center compiles information on obscenity and indecency laws and makes it available to individuals, civic groups, attorneys, legislators, law enforcement agencies, and prosecutors at all levels of government. The NOLC maintains the most comprehensive collection of materials related to obscenity law in the United States and its bimonthly newsletter is subscribed to by federal and state prosecutors, police and other public officials, law libraries, and other groups and individuals.

PROGRAMS

MIM runs a number of different programs, most centering around educating the public about its agenda. In support of its legal and legislative activities, MIM sponsors several programs aimed at increasing public awareness of pornography in media. Chief among these is the annual White Ribbon Against Pornography Campaign (WRAP), which is run in conjunction with a related program called Pornography Awareness Week (PAW). To show their opposition to pornography, citizens are encouraged to display white ribbons as a symbol of "community standards of decency" and to demand that obscenity laws be enforced. The 1997 WRAP campaign collected thousands of signatures on a petition to President Clinton calling for more vigorous enforcement of federal

obscenity laws. In ironic testimony to the efficacy of the WRAP campaign, free speech supporters on the Internet launched their own Blue Ribbon Campaign to show their opposition to MIM-supported legislation aimed at curbing on-line pornography.

One of the most pressing items on Morality in Media's anti-obscenity agenda has always been sex on television. To protest the "growing assaults on standards of decency and civility that have become all too common TV fare," MIM annually sponsors a national Turn Off TV Day. In 1997, MIM permanently fixed its Turn Off TV Day on Valentine's Day, February 14. In addition to turning their televisions off for one day, participants are also urged to express their concerns about television programming to advertisers and network heads.

BUDGET INFORMATION

MIM's 1996 budget was $610,602. Most of this (more than $580,000) came from contributions, with the remainder derived from legacies and bequests, newsletter income, and investment income. MIM spent more than 70 percent of this money on its various programs, with about $120,000 going to the National Law Obscenity Center, $175,000 going to public education, and another $120,000 split between the newsletter and research and publication. Fund-raising accounted for about 20 percent of expenses.

HISTORY

The idea for Morality in Media began in Manhattan in 1962 with a Catholic priest, an Orthodox Jewish rabbi, a Lutheran pastor, and a Greek Orthodox priest. Led by Father Morton A. Hill, S.J. (Society of Jesus), the group initially came together in response to the complaints of a mother who had discovered that pornographic magazines were circulating among sixth grade boys at the local school.

Working out of a small office in St. Ignatius Loyola parish rectory in Manhattan, the group set about researching the problem of pornography and the law, sharing what they learned with local church groups and organizations, appearing on radio and television whenever possible, and distributing a mimeographed newsletter. By 1966, at about the same time as the United States Supreme Court handed down its Fanny Hill decision which stated that a work must be "utterly without redeeming social value" to be declared obscene, the organization's activities had expanded to the point where it was forced to relocate to larger commercial quarters. There, in 1967 with the assistance of three volunteer lawyers, a newly established board of directors, and a professional writer, the fledgling organization, now called Morality in

Media, incorporated as a not-for-profit corporation in the state of New York.

Word of MIM soon spread throughout the United States and in 1968 Father Hill was appointed by President Lyndon B. Johnson to a Commission on Obscenity and Pornography. As it turned out, the commission's 1970 majority report recommended that all "adult" obscenity laws be repealed. Condemning the report as "flawed" and calling it a "Magna Carta" for the pornographers, Father Hill co-authored a minority report recommending enforcement of obscenity laws and the establishment of a national research and reference library on the Law of Obscenity. MIM followed this recommendation when it established the National Obscenity Law Center in 1976. Thanks in no small part to the efforts of Father Hill and MIM, the majority report was eventually rejected by President Nixon and the Senate. Hill's minority report on the other hand was cited no less than four times by the Supreme Court in 1973 in upholding obscenity laws.

MIM's efforts to clean up the media paid off again in the landmark 1978 *FCC v. Pacifica* case. The case originated in 1973 when MIM member John H. Douglas made a complaint to the Federal Communications Commission (FCC) in 1973 regarding the afternoon broadcast of George Carlin's "Seven Dirty Words" monologue, arguing that Carlin's broadcast violated the Federal Broadcast Indecency Law. In 1978 the U.S. Supreme Court upheld the decision made by the FCC that the Carlin monologue was "indecent" and should be prohibited.

In 1983 Father Hill met with President Reagan to discuss what MIM regarded as the failure to enforce the Federal Obscenity Laws. The meeting eventually led to the formation of the Attorney General's Commission on Pornography which issued a final report in 1986. MIM lobbying also prompted the establishment of a permanent Child Exploitation and Obscenity Enforcement Section in the Department of Justice in 1987 and led to the extension of the Federal Racketeer Influenced Corrupt Organizations (RICO) Act to include obscenity offenses. This law allows the government to confiscate the assets of convicted pornographers. Morality in Media submitted briefs in support of the law in two court challenges brought before the Supreme Court. The group also figured prominently in the drafting of the 1984 Child Pornography Act and later supported it before the Supreme Court.

With the explosion of new media in the 1990s, Morality in Media became more vocal than ever, leading the battle to force broadcasters to rate television programs, pushing for a tougher and more explicit ratings code for movies, and calling for federal legislation to control obscenity and pornography on the Internet and online services. In 1996 MIM helped defeat a court challenge to a key provision of the Cable TV Act of 1992 which allowed cable TV system operators to ban indecent programming on leased access channels. In upholding the provision, the Supreme Court also effectively ruled for the first time that government can regulate indecent programming on cable TV. The same year also saw the culmination of a long struggle to extend the ban on broadcast indecency by two prime-time hours, to 10 P.M. instead of 8 P.M.

CURRENT POLITICAL ISSUES

MIM faces a number of political issues in an effort to accomplish its objectives. In 1999, for example, the organization issued statements regarding new Calvin Klein children's underwear advertisements that some critics thought were inappropriate and possibly pornographic. In addition, MIM maintains a position on the amount of violence that should be allowed on television and advocates legislation to control such material. One of the most controversial cases that MIM has been involved in was the battle over restrictions to free speech on the World Wide Web.

Case Study: The Communications Decency Act

In the early to mid 1990s a new front was emerging in MIM's ongoing battle against pornography—the Internet. Once an academic backwater used primarily by scientists and researchers to communicate with colleagues, the Internet's popularity exploded when new hypertext software made it easier to explore the Internet's vast resources. With graphics and multimedia capabilities added, the Internet began growing at an exponential rate.

By 1994 the Internet was host to millions of companies, organizations, and individuals. Users reveled in the new medium's anarchic spirit and pornographers were able to take advantage of it to publish and distribute material. Corporations jumped aboard to push their products. The mainstream media began to issue reports about the Internet's dark side, of a cyberspace inhabited by pedophiles and stalkers. The perception that the Internet was dangerous and unsafe for children grew even stronger when *Time* magazine published a cover story on "Cyberporn" featuring a study that supposedly proved the existence of a massive pornography industry on the Internet. Although the study was later shown to be grossly inaccurate, it spurred an onslaught of demands from organizations such as MIM that the federal government legislate pornography off the Internet.

In early 1995, in a move that infuriated the Internet community (and especially Internet providers), Senator Jim Exon (D-Neb.) introduced Senate Bill 314—the Communications Decency Act (CDA). Expanding current FCC regulations on "obscene" and "indecent" telephony and telegraphy to cover any content carried by all forms of electronic communications networks, the CDA made telecommunications and network providers criminally liable if their network was used in the transmission of any material deemed to be "obscene, lewd, lascivious, filthy, or indecent," as provided under the Communications Act of 1934. In order to comply with this bill, Internet providers would either have to restrict the activities of their users or monitor every private communication, file transmission, E-mail message, and Web site to ensure that no activity for which they could be held liable was taking place.

Not surprisingly, MIM supported this effort to regulate the Internet, although the organization was critical of the bill as it was written, fearing that it was too vague and all-inclusive and would be vulnerable to a court challenge. These fears were well founded. Congress never held hearings on Senator Exon's bill and the legislative process took place mostly "behind closed doors." Rushed to completion so that it could be included as part of the Telecommunications Act of 1996, the CDA was signed into law by President Clinton on February 8, 1996. In the single largest demonstration from the Internet community in history, thousands of world wide Web pages went black for 48 hours to protest the new law. Newly formed Internet advocacy groups such as the Citizens Internet Empowerment Coalition (CIEC), the Electronic Frontier Foundation (EFF), and the Center for Democracy and Technology (CDT), together with the American Civil Liberties Union (ACLU) immediately launched a court challenge on the basis that the CDA violated the First Amendment.

Notwithstanding its concern that the CDA's proponents had not done their homework, MIM, along with other conservative anti-pornography groups such as the National Law Center for Children and Families, the Family Research Council, Enough is Enough!, and the National Coalition for the Protection of Children and Families, filed an *amicus curiae* (friend of the court) brief supporting the act. MIM's position was made clear in the brief's introduction, which stated that "In their zeal for unfettered freedom to distribute all material, however pornographic, without any consideration for the larger audience of children on-line, Plaintiffs urge this Court, in effect, to surrender the legislature's compelling interests in protecting children in favor of the economic interests and ideological wishes of computer indecency providers."

In the end, the court, unmoved by the arguments of MIM and its allies, came down firmly on the side of the plaintiffs. On June 12, 1996, a panel of three federal judges in Philadelphia granted the Citizens Internet Empowerment Coalition's request for a preliminary injunction against the Communications Decency Act, unanimously ruling that "in the absence of evidence to the contrary, we presume that governmental regulation of the content of speech is more likely to interfere with the free exchange of ideas than to encourage it." Just over a year later, on June 26, 1997, the Supreme Court ruled unanimously that the Communications Decency Act vio-

FAST FACTS

Gross revenues for the pornography industry in 1996 were larger than the domestic box office receipts for mainstream Hollywood movies.

(Source: "The Business of Porn." *U.S. News and World Report,* February 1997.)

lated the First Amendment, finding that all provisions of the CDA were unconstitutional as they applied to "indecent" or "patently offensive" speech.

Although not surprised by the decision, MIM was nevertheless disappointed, stating in a press release that the decision meant that "children now have no protection under the law from indecent explicit sexual depictions on their home computers." MIM also criticized the Supreme Court justices for failing "to provide guidance on how the Communications Decency Act could be amended to constitutionally protect the children of our nation from this vile material." In view of this, the organization announced that it would request Congress to appoint a Blue-Ribbon Commission "to come up with a practical, effective, and constitutional solution".

FUTURE DIRECTIONS

While MIM has gained some headway against the amount of indecent media, there are several problems on which it will focus special attention in the coming years. These problems include inadequate or non-existent state law in ten states, failure of prosecutors to enforce obscenity laws, and inadequate enforcement of indecency laws by the Federal Communications Commission. To counter these problems, MIM is working on proposals for new laws that would control indecency on cable TV and the Internet to be introduced in Congress by the end of 1999. It also plans to increase its efforts to provide the public with "how-to" information, resource materials, and leadership.

GROUP RESOURCES

Providing information resources is central to MIM's activities. The organization's extensive NOLC library includes copies of all reported obscenity cases since

1800, copies of all federal and state obscenity laws, copies of many anti-pornography ordinances and model laws, a Brief Bank Index, and monographs for recurring inquiries. The center also publishes a digest of obscenity cases, a handbook on the prosecution of obscenity cases, and a bi-monthly newsletter. Other resources include Morality in Media's Web site at http://pw2.netcom.com/mimnyc/MAINPAGE.HTM which includes an order form for MIM publications as well as press releases, briefs, a history of the organization, news about its campaigns and other information. The NOLC also maintains an extensive Web site http://pw1.netcom.com/nolc/index.html featuring articles from the center's current news bulletin, a subscription form, and a detailed description of the *Obscenity Law Reporter,* the NOLC's leading publication. For more information on either MIM or the NOLC, write to Morality in Media, 475 Riverside Dr., Ste. 239, New York, NY 10115 or call (212) 870-3222.

GROUP PUBLICATIONS

Among MIM's regular publications are the bi-monthly *Morality in Media* newsletter for all members. The organization also publishes booklets, pamphlets, and study reports on a variety of subjects related to obscenity and indecency. These include: *How to Win the War in Your Community: The People vs. Pornography, Pornography's Effects on Adults and Children,* and *Cliches: Debunking Misinformation about Pornography and Obscenity Law.* NOLC publications include: *The Obscenity Law Reporter,* a 3-volume ring-binder digest of obscenity cases decided since 1800; *Handbook on the Prosecution of Obscenity Cases,* a comprehensive guide for prosecutors, from investigation through trial to final appeal; and *The Obscenity Law Bulletin.* For more information on any of these publications, contact Morality in Media's Publications Department by calling (212) 870-3222, write to MIM at 475 Riverside Dr., Ste. 239, New York, NY 10115, or send E-mail to mimnyc@ix.netcom.com or nolc@ix.netcom.com.

BIBLIOGRAPHY

Abernathy, J. "Net Censorship: Alternatives Gain Momentum." *PC World,* September 1995.

"The Business of Porn." *U.S. News and World Report,* February 1997.

Cleaver, Cathleen A. "Cyberspace Cleanup or Censorship." *Washington Times,* 11 February 1996.

Dworkin, A., and C. A. MacKinnon. *Pornography and Civil Rights.* Minneapolis, Minn.: Organizing Against Pornography, 1988.

Dyson, E. "If You Don't Love it, Leave it," *New York Times Magazine,* 16 July 1995.

El Nasser, H. "Challenges to Cyberporn Bill Could Clog Courts." *USA Today,* 19 July 1995.

Elmer-DeWitt, P. "On a Screen Near You: Cyberporn." *Time,* 3 July 1995.

Family Research Council. "Smut: Out-of-Line Online." *Washington Watch,* 26 February 1996.

Goss, N., and G. Ricks. "Pulling Plug on Cyberporn." *Santa Barbara News-Press,* 8 October 1995.

Healey, J. "Clashing over Obscenity in Cyberspace." *Congressional Quarterly Weekly Report,* 8 July 1995.

"How Time Fed the Internet Porn Panic." *Harper's Magazine,* September 1995.

Huffington, Arianna. "Internet Evils Beyond the Indecency Limits." *Washington Times,* 16 March 1996.

Levy, S. "A Bad Day in Cyberspace: The Senate Takes a Sledgehammer to Our Communications Future." *Newsweek,* 26 June 1995.

Lynch, Stephen. "The Rating Game." *Orange County Register,* 31 March 1996.

Meeks, B. N. "The Obscenity of Decency: With Senator James Exon's Communications Decency Act, the Barbarians Really are at the Gate." *Wired,* June 1995.

Wallace, Jonathan, and Mark Mangan. *Sex, Laws and Cyber-Space: Freedom and Censorship on the Frontiers of the Online Revolution.* New York: Henry Holt and Co.,1996.

Weingarten, Fred W. "Debate over Indecency on the Net Reveals Deep Divisions." *Computer Magazine,* February 1996.

Zillmann, D., and J. Bryant. "Effects of Prolonged Consumption of Pornography on Family Values." *Journal of Family Issues,* 1988.

Zipperer, J. "The Naked City: 'Cyberporn' Invades the American Home." *Christianity Today,* 12 September 1988.

Mothers Against Drunk Driving (MADD)

WHAT IS ITS MISSION?

Mothers Against Drunk Driving (MADD) provides support and assistance to the victims of accidents that involve drunk driving. Additionally MADD embraces the goal of discouraging everyone from driving after drinking. MADD is not a temperance association and it is not concerned with restricting the availability of alcohol for consumption by adults, under appropriate circumstances.

Contact Information:
ADDRESS: P.O. Box 541688
    Dallas, TX 75354–1688
PHONE: (214) 744-6233
TOLL FREE: (800) 438-6233
FAX: (214) 869-2206
E-MAIL: info@madd.org
URL: http://www.madd.org
NATIONAL EXECUTIVE DIRECTOR: H. Dean
    Wilkerson, J.D.

HOW IS IT STRUCTURED?

MADD is a nonprofit organization based in Irving, Texas, that operates with a limited staff and relies heavily on volunteer participation at the national, state, and local chapter levels. At the national level, MADD is headed by a national executive director who also functions as the chief executive officer. The organization is also governed by an elected national president who presides over the entire organization for a set term of office. A board of directors, including 24 members plus a chairman of the board, operates at the national level. Representatives from local MADD chapters comprise two-thirds of the board; the remaining one-third is composed of private sector members-at-large. Other national officers include a secretary, a treasurer, and three vice presidents who address field issues, victim issues, and public policy. Officer elections are held at an annual conference of the MADD board of directors.

In 1997 MADD reported operations in 37 states, with 339 local chapters, and 225 community "action" groups.

These numbers include affiliates in Great Britain, Canada, and Australia. Local chapters often operate exclusively through volunteer efforts. Mirroring the national office, most local chapters elect a president and board of directors to oversee the day-to-day activities and to communicate with the state and national offices. MADD chapters work closely with local law enforcement agencies and other nonprofit organizations to prosecute drinking-and-driving offenders and to educate young people about the dangers and risks of underage drinking.

Public service and philanthropic organizations including the Community Tool Box and the American Public Health Association work with MADD to disseminate information and services. The Alcohol Policies Project of the Center for Science in the Public Interest backs political issues in cooperation with MADD, in an effort to eradicate the socially destructive effects of alcohol abuse. Campus and fraternal organizations such as Sigma Phi Epsilon sponsor alcohol awareness programs in conjunction with the MADD agenda. MADD also collaborates with manufacturers of alcoholic beverages to discourage underage drinking.

Despite its name MADD is not an organization composed exclusively of mothers. Membership includes mothers, fathers, family members, young people, law enforcement representatives, and other individuals who have been affected by, and hope to prevent, drunk driving.

PRIMARY FUNCTIONS

To achieve its mission MADD works in four areas: victim assistance, public awareness, strengthening of public policies with regard to drunk driving, and discouraging and preventing illegal drinking by minors through public education.

Victim Assistance

MADD, to a large degree, is a human services organization. The organization's advocacy training helps chapters provide a full range of victim support services. Chapters offer group support and counseling for families of victims and survivors of drunk driving accidents. Victim services include referrals to counselors and support groups and assistance to victims' outreach facilities including Internet support groups. MADD sponsors and organizes candlelight vigils and it participates in the construction and dedication of monuments to the memory of drunk driving victims. The organization also coordinates victim impact panels in conjunction with civil probation offices to provide confrontation between victims and drunk driving offenders. Victims can also turn to MADD for assistance with legal procedures, including applications for Crime Victims Compensation funds.

Public Policy Department

On the political front MADD has impacted state and national laws that involve drinking and driving through its lobbying efforts. The national president of MADD works to keep the organization involved in a wide array of political activities through participation in national and international conferences. MADD also trains public policy liaisons through its national office in order to better coordinate political activity. The public policy department tracks legislation as well as statistical information, at both the state and national levels, and makes the information available to the public. Trained liaisons also prepare testimony for presentation before state and national legislatures. Additionally MADD volunteers track and observe drunk driving cases in the courts and report the outcome to the public media. In this way MADD uses media pressure as a tool to ensure that justice is served and that victims are diligently represented by prosecutors. MADD workers also solicit policy funding through grants.

Educational Programs

MADD activists work to discourage and prevent illegal drinking by minors through public education. MADD conveys this message through symposiums such as the MADD National Youth Summit to Prevent Underage Drinking, an assemblage of high school students from around the United States; as well as through Safe & Sober Workshops.

PROGRAMS

The hundreds of MADD chapters across the United States continually initiate new programs to further the MADD agenda. Among MADD's most popular programs is a holiday promotion called the red-ribbon campaign, inspired by the motto "Tie One on for Safety." Program participants wear a red ribbon to remind others of the dangers of drinking and driving. Additionally MADD promotes practical action programs. The Designate a Driver Program encourages party-goers to travel in groups which include a designated driver. The designated driver abstains from drinking alcohol in order to ensure the availability of a sober driver for the return trip home. In the metropolitan Detroit area, a St. Patrick's Day Program to provide free public transportation to revelers met with success. Party-related businesses have supported MADD policies with helpful programs such as one conceived by tuxedo rental parlors, in which rented apparel is accompanied by a written reminder to not drink and drive. MADD's Safe Party Guide gives tips for ways to entertain without encouraging others to drink

Among MADD's more emotionally-charged efforts is the memorial marker program initiated by a MADD chapter in Boulder, Colorado. Signs depicting criss-

Candy Lightner founded MADD in 1980 after her 13-year-old daughter was killed in a hit-and-run accident. After the man responsible received only a two-year sentence, the group worked to obtain harsher penalties for drunk drivers. (AP/Wide World Photos)

crossed red ribbons inside a white diamond-shaped caution symbol are erected at the site of fatal drunk driving accidents. MADD supports outreach programs for youth, including the release of a 1998 parenting project on CD-ROM. The CD, called *The Key,* is an interactive learning tool for families to enjoy together. Integral to the MADD mission is the MADD impact panel program, whereby victims and survivors of drunk driving accidents confront convicted DWI offenders.

In keeping with a MADD campaign to encourage corporate sponsorship, telecommunications giant AT&T initiated a funding program in conjunction with MADD. Under the provisions of the agreement instituted in 1997, AT&T offers customers the option of designating a portion of their long distance telephone bill payments to MADD. In some areas local call charges are also eligible under the program provisions. Funds acquired through AT&T are earmarked to support victim assistance programs and legislative initiatives. Through such cause-related marketing promotions MADD is able to appeal to a vast number of consumers; the AT&T program alone reached 90 million contacts across a customer base including business, government, and private individuals.

A similar arrangement with Traveler's Group stipulates that the corporation will pay to MADD a $10 donation for each new Travelers' Group credit card issued. A percentage of each credit card purchase also goes to MADD. In an agreement between MADD and software publisher Sierra Online Dynamix, that company promised to donate a portion of the profit from every sale of the company's *Driver's Education '98* CD-ROM, a driver's simulation software which includes alcohol impairment experiences.

BUDGET INFORMATION

As a nonprofit organization under U.S. tax code 501(c)3, MADD is required to spend at least 60 percent of its funds on programs in keeping with the purpose of the organization. MADD reported in 1992 that 70.1 percent of its total income went toward community programs. By 1994, however, the organization was operating with a cash flow totaling $45.5 million, of which amount an estimated $18.3 million (40 percent of total income) went to salaries, commissions, and expenses. Since that time MADD reported its administrative expenses at 13 percent, and fund raising overhead at 19 percent of total funds raised, or 17 percent of total income. Of funds secured at the national level, 80 percent was distributed to local chapters and 20 percent was retained at the national level. Overall 70 percent of total funds went directly to program expenses. Program funds are disbursed by the national office to the state offices and local chapters of the organization. All monies raised locally remain in the hands of the local organization.

In 1996 MADD took in $40 million in funds through telemarketing and direct mail campaigns. Corporate contributions totaled 5 percent of MADD funding sources in 1996, with sponsors including AT&T, KMart, and Alamo Rent A Car. Individual contributions, at 79 percent, remained the mainstay of the organization. Government grants made up 4 percent of MADD's funding resources. Twelve percent of MADD's funds came from miscellaneous sources, including interest, membership fees, and special events.

HISTORY

MADD was founded in May 1980, in the home of Candy Lightner in Fair Oaks, California. Lightner, a real estate agent, was motivated after the death of her 13-year-old daughter, Cari, who was killed in a hit-and-run accident. The man responsible for the girl's death was Clarence Busch, a drunk driver with two prior convictions who had been previously incarcerated for a total of

less than two days. Despite a two-year sentence imposed from the hit-and-run incident involving Lightner's daughter, Busch served his time in minimum security institutions and a halfway house. The original MADD organizers joined together to find ways to enforce stricter penalties for drunk driving, in order to prevent the thousands of deaths and injuries associated with drunk driving each year.

By 1997 MADD had grown to over 300 chapters and included three million members. Many chapters were founded by parents and relatives of accident victims under circumstances similar to Lightner's. For example the Long Island Chapter was founded in 1982 by Celia and Marvin Strow in memory of their 22-year-old daughter, Janice. That chapter worked to pass "zero tolerance" laws for convicted drunk drivers under the age of 21 in Long Island.

In 1983 Lightner relocated the MADD national headquarters from its roots in California to Hurst, Texas. Lightner resigned from MADD in 1985 in opposition to a restructuring by the MADD board of directors which would have removed her from the role of CEO and executive director.

Political and Legislative Milestones

In the years since the inception of MADD in 1980, the group has been successful in affecting public policy and legislation. Due to MADD's persistent efforts, a presidential commission was formed in December 1983 to encourage all states to raise the legal drinking age to 21. The first incentive measure that passed the legislature in response to that presidential commission was in June 1984, when the House of Representatives passed a measure to reduce federal highway funding for states that did not make 21-years-old the minimum legal drinking age. Under the resulting legislation, a state would lose five percent of its federal highway funds. Consequently judges and prosecutors became more alert and sensitive to the need for adequate and appropriate punishment in drunk driving cases. For instance, in the criminal sentencing of one drunk driver following a fatal automobile accident in 1982, a judge in North Carolina revoked the convicted driver's license for five years. The judge further sentenced the motorist to donate blood to help accident victims on a bimonthly basis, for the duration of the five-year "no-driving" period.

Over time, and in part through the vigilance of MADD, the death toll on U.S. highways declined. During the New Year's Eve weekend of 1984, highway casualties reached a 35-year low. In June of the same year, a landmark ruling by the New Jersey Supreme Court allowed that the host of a party may be held liable should a guest suffer injuries in a car crash after leaving the party in a drunken state. Similarly the Texas Supreme Court set a precedent that year, that employers could be held liable for allowing intoxicated workers to drive themselves home if a crash ensued as a result.

In 1990 the MADD board of directors voted to institute Rating the States (RTS), an assessment of highway safety in the individual states, in conjunction with the National Highway Traffic Safety Association (NHTSA). MADD released RTS reports in 1991, 1993, and 1995. By this time MADD's public reputation and visibility was so strong that the results of the RTS served as sufficient incentive for a number of state governments to reevaluate and improve their drunk driving policies and regulations. In one instance the governor of Alabama assigned MADD representatives to a special task force on drunk driving in April 1994. The governor of Missouri made similar appointments in reaction to RTS results. Also in response to an RTS rating, the governor of Virginia signed into law a .08 blood alcohol content (BAC) ceiling as the legal limit for drivers. Other states including Idaho, Michigan, California, Missouri, and Pennsylvania reacted to RTS results with positive action against drunk driving.

Legal Challenges

In 1992 the organization ceased its practice of preparing a financial report for publication, which solicited questions and accusations regarding MADD's spending standards. The National Charities Information Bureau further suggested that MADD failed to meet the requirement that a minimum of 60 percent of organizational expenditures go toward beneficial programs. In 1993, and again in 1995, MADD was saddled with additional legal resistance regarding the attempted seizure of local MADD assets by the national organization. The national office further demanded power of attorney to tap into local funds at will. In Michigan the state chapter obtained an injunction against the seizure of funds early in 1995. Other MADD chapters withdrew from the national organization over similar grievances.

CURRENT POLITICAL ISSUES

MADD has ignited political controversy over personal freedom issues and often sparked the ire of corporate concerns in its attempts to eliminate drunk driving. During the 1980s MADD focused attention on a need to return the national legal drinking age to 21-years-of-age, a move which conflicted with the corporate interests of the alcoholic beverages industry. This enormous lobby, combined with the restaurant and entertainment industries and other corporations—such as commercial airlines, which serve alcoholic beverages—created political friction against the MADD proposal. Ultimately MADD accomplished its goal of raising the drinking age nationwide, and alcohol-related fatalities were reduced dramatically. In Minnesota, for example, alcohol-related fatalities dropped from 43 percent of all motor vehicle accidents in 1985 to 35 percent of such accidents in 1994.

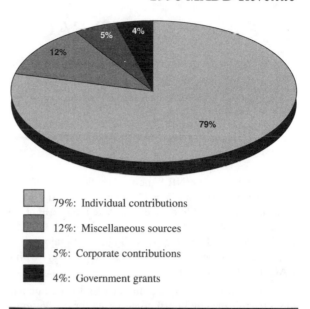

BUDGET:
1996 MADD Revenue

79%: Individual contributions

12%: Miscellaneous sources

5%: Corporate contributions

4%: Government grants

In 1996 MADD enlisted support from the U.S. Department of Transportation and other groups, to further reduce alcohol-related traffic fatalities. The group formed an alliance called Partners in Progress, which set a goal for the year 2005, to reduce highway deaths from drunk driving to below 11,000 fatalities.

Case Study: A .08 BAC Limit Nationwide

Seeking the support of the media and the medical community, Partners in Progress set out to revise the legal definition of drunk driving from .10 percent blood alcohol content (BAC) to .08 percent. The issue triggered considerable hostility, and although certain states passed legislation conforming with MADD's proposal, the issue generated extensive controversy. By August 1998 less than one-half of the United States was in compliance with the MADD recommended .08 percent BAC.

The American Beverage Institute, a liquor lobby group, came forward in emphatic opposition to .08 BAC. The institute presented arguments to the legislature as well as to the press that virtually any drinking of alcohol would cause drunkenness under such terms. The NHTSA countered with statistics to show that states enforcing .08 BAC experienced a significant drop in alcohol-related fatalities.

The National Restaurant Association (NRA), also in opposition to .08 BAC, rebutted NHTSA with arguments in support of the states' rights to determine appropriate

FAST FACTS

Approximately two people are injured in an alcohol-related car crash every minute.

(Source: "MADD Statistics: 1998 Summary of Statistics," 1999.)

BAC levels. In an NRA newswire the association's Senior Vice-president Elaine Graham was quoted, "It will punish the responsible drinker and take the spotlight off the real problem—chronic alcohol abusers." Graham noted unspecified statistics that, "[T]he vast majority . . . of all alcohol related deaths are caused by drivers with a BAC of 0.14 or higher."

Nationally syndicated columnist Eric Peters upheld the NRA posture in an article he wrote for the *National Review*. He accused MADD and the NHTSA of presenting intentionally inaccurate or misleading driving statistics. Peters maintained that alcohol-related incidents as defined by the NHTSA could refer to any accident in which alcohol at any level might be detected in any person, including passengers, in any car involved in a particular accident. According to the NHTSA definition such statistics are irrelevant to substantiate arguments favoring the reduction of the legal BAC level for drivers. Peters challenged other statistics touted by MADD as biased and, in some cases, completely inaccurate.

Undaunted, MADD asserted that .08 BAC would ultimately serve to reduce fatalities at least by virtue of the heightened public awareness of blood alcohol levels. MADD also contended that any amount of alcohol impairs driving ability and therefore any reduction of the BAC limit is a valid deterrent to drunk driving accidents. MADD's rebuttal to opposing statistics maintained that the likelihood of a crash increased noticeably at .05 percent BAC and then increased sharply at .08 percent. MADD emphasized that too many drivers are able to plea bargain a DWI indictment down to reckless driving when they are caught with a BAC that measures only slightly above the legal limit of .10 percent and suggested that a .08 percent would reduce the number of plea bargains.

MADD meanwhile voiced support for all states to pass the .08 BAC legislation in the form of an amendment to the Intermodal Surface Transportation Act of 1997 (S. 1173). The amendment tied federal highway funding to a stipulation that each respective state would reduce its legal DWI limit to .08. The act was not passed, however, and the amendment was then attached to

another bill, the Federal Highway Bill, which was postponed by unanimous consent by the Senate in April 1998. MADD vowed to keep pressing for legislative progress on the issue with the Congress elected for 1998–2000.

FUTURE DIRECTIONS

One of MADD's most pressing initiatives is its 20 by 2000 program. Since 1995 MADD has sought to decrease by 20 percent the proportion of alcohol-related fatalities on U.S. roads by 2000. MADD is focusing on five areas to achieve its goal: youth issues, such as fake I.D. confiscation measures; enforcement, such as highway sobriety checkpoints; sanctions, such as plate or vehicle confiscation; self-sufficiency, such as funding programs through fines; and responsibility marketing and service, such as promoting the idea of the designated driver.

MADD will also press for amendments to all state constitutions to authorize comparable restitution for victims of drunk driving accidents as for victims of other crimes. The amendments include "deep pockets" protection that would hold liable those persons who knowingly serve alcohol to already intoxicated individuals or to minors. Child endangerment laws would also be expanded to apply to convicted drivers of DWI incidents in which children were transported in the car.

GROUP RESOURCES

The MADD National Office Victim Services at 1-800-438-6233 provides victim advocate services, victims tributes, congressional contacts to encourage support of victims rights, and access to the National Victims' Constitutional Amendment Network. Victim support groups are available through many local chapters of MADD.

MADD provides an Internet-based legislative tracking service for legislative bills concerned with alcohol, underage drinking, and drunk driving. It also provides congressional schedules and a congressional directory. The legislative tracking service is available through Internet links to the Health Policy Tracking Service (HPTS) at the National Conference of State Legislatures. Search the databases at http://www.madd.org/pub_pol/default. shtml, or E-mail specific queries to assist@hpts.org.

GROUP PUBLICATIONS

MADD publishes and supplies a wide collection of pamphlets, posters, and instructional brochures. MADD literature is available through the MADD Bookstore; by mail at the Fulfillment Center, 8220 Ambassador Row,

Dallas, TX 75247; by fax via (214) 638- 7833; and on-line at http://www.madd.org/store.

Examples of MADD publications include how-to guides such as, *A How-to Guide for Victim Support Groups* and *A How-to Guide for Candlelight Vigils.* Brochure-length publications are priced from 15 cents to 55 cents, and included titles such as *Your Grief: You're Not Going Crazy* and *Drunk Driving: An Unacknowledged Form of Child Endangerment.* Some brochures are available in Spanish. MADD also offers an assortment of posters with messages such as "If you're going to drink and drive tonight, don't forget to kiss your mother good-bye," and "You can't replace your face."

MADD publishes an informative newsletter, *Driven: A Publication of Mothers Against Drunk Driving*, which is available on-line at http://www.madd.org/driven/default.shtml. *Driven* publishes articles of general interest regarding public policy, grass roots movements, victim remembrance and victim support, and public awareness. Additionally a number of MADD chapters publish newsletters at their own local level. Contact the National MADD headquarters at (214) 744-6233.

BIBLIOGRAPHY

Grollman, Earl. *Straight Talk About Death for Teenagers.* Boston: Beacon Press, 1993.

Kennedy, Joey. "Drunk Driving Makes a Comeback." *Redbook,* May 1997.

Lightner, Candy, and Nancy Hathaway. *Giving Sorrow Words.* New York: Warner Books, 1990.

Lord, Janice Harris. *Beyond Sympathy.* Ventura, Calif.: Pathfinder Publishing, 1990.

———. *No Time for Goodbyes.* Ventura, Calif.: Pathfinder Publishing, 1991.

McGowan, Richard. *Government Regulation of the Alcohol Industry: The Search for Revenue and the Common Good.* Westport, Conn.: Quorum Books, 1997.

Nikkel, Cathy. "Lowering the Boom on Drunk Driving." *Motor Trend,* June 1998.

"Road Warrior." *People,* 4 May 1998.

Russell, Anne, Robert B. Voas, William DeJong, and Marla Chaloupka. "MADD Rates the States: A Media Advocacy Event to Advance the Agenda Against Alcohol-Impaired Driving." *Public Health Reports,* May-June 1995.

Sellinger, Margie Bonnett, "Already the Conscience of a Nation, Candy Lightner Prods Congress into Action against Drunk Drivers." *People,* 9 July 1984.

Stanglin, Douglas. "Last Call?" *U.S. News & World Report,* 19 May 1997.

Travisano, Jim. "For Safety's Sake . . . Join the Club." *Current Health 2,* December 1997.

Motion Picture Association of America (MPAA)

ESTABLISHED: 1922
EMPLOYEES: 120
MEMBERS: 7
PAC: Motion Picture Association of America, Inc.
    Political Action Committee

Contact Information:

ADDRESS: 1600 Eye St. NW
    Washington, DC 20006
PHONE: (202) 293-1966
FAX: (202) 296-7410
URL: http://www.mpaa.org
PRESIDENT; CEO: Jack J. Valenti

WHAT IS ITS MISSION?

According to Motion Picture Association of America (MPAA) President Jack Valenti, the association's goal is "nothing more than a free, open and fair marketplace where our stories on film and videotape can compete honestly with all others. That is our goal and to that objective we direct all our energies and our skills." The MPAA works to protect the interests of its member companies through legal, legislative, and public educational means.

HOW IS IT STRUCTURED?

The MPAA is a trade association for seven major Hollywood studios: Walt Disney Co., Sony Pictures Entertainment, Inc., Metro-Goldwyn-Mayer, Inc., Paramount Pictures Corp., Twentieth Century Fox Film Corp., Universal Studios, Inc., and Warner Brothers. The chairmen and presidents of these studios comprise the MPAA board of directors.

The MPAA works and serves its members out of offices in Washington, D.C., and Los Angeles, California. The office in Washington, D.C., provides its member companies with regular updates on legislation and proposed regulatory changes that may affect the motion picture industry. MPAA operates the Title Registration Bureau that registers the titles of motion pictures to be released in U.S. theaters. The MPAA is affiliated with the Alliance of Motion Picture and Television Producers (AMPTP), the National Association of Broadcasters (NAB), and the National Cable Television Association (NCTA).

PRIMARY FUNCTIONS

MPAA serves as the voice and advocate for its member companies before Congress, the executive branch, the Federal Communications Commission (FCC), the Office of the United States Trade Representative, and other relevant federal and state regulatory agencies and commissions. The MPAA addresses federal and state legislation as well as regulatory proposals that would impact the production and distribution of motion pictures, television programs, and home video. For example it fights to ensure First Amendment rights for motion picture and television producers. The association also assists its member studios with the international distribution of their products, advises them on taxation, and conducts a nationwide public relations program for the film industry.

The chief executive officer of the MPAA and the president of the National Association of Theatre Owners administer the policy review committee that monitors the Classification and Rating Administration (CARA), which is the motion picture rating system. MPAA companies do not participate in the film rating system. Once CARA rates a film, all advertising and promotional material must be given to the Advertising Administration of the MPAA for review and approval.

The MPAA also attempts to protect the rights of copyright owners and prevents illegal copying of motion pictures through its anti-piracy program. The organization collaborates with police to identify and track-down those who pirate films and works to ensure the conviction of criminals.

PROGRAMS

The MPAA anti-piracy program was started in 1975 to prevent the illegal copying of videos and other copyrighted material and to prevent Internet piracy, which includes the copying of computer games, video games, and recorded music. According to the MPAA Web site, "the program has several objectives: to strengthen industry security measures, to strengthen existing copyright protection through legislation activity, to assist local governments in the investigation and prosecution of piracy cases and to provide technical support in the criminal and civil litigation generated by such investigations." The biggest piracy issue involves the copying of videos, which causes motion picture companies to lose about $250 million in revenues every year.

The MPAA offers a $15,000 reward for information that leads to a piracy-related arrest, and a $2,500 reward is offered to those who reveal the location of video piracy labs that are equipped with at least 30 VCRs used to illegally copy motion pictures. The number to call to inform the MPAA is 1-800-662-6797.

BUDGET INFORMATION

Not made available.

HISTORY

The Motion Picture Producers and Distributors of America (MPPDA), a coalition of 15 movie production companies, was founded in 1922. The organization was formed to unify the interests, opinions, and voices of the industry. The first order of business was to improve public perception about the motion picture industry. In the 1920s the American public was concerned with the pervasive portrayal of violence, sex, and lawlessness on movie screens. Thus, the MPPDA looked for a way to regulate what was depicted in film. Its first president, Will H. Hays, invented the Hays Production Code in 1934 to establish benchmarks for moral standards in motion pictures.

The new code defined the degree of "objectionable" material that could be shown on screen. For example, the Hays Code prevented film makers from showing a criminal profiting from a crime. Films were also required to positively portray family, marriage, U.S. government, and religion. While many felt the Hays Code stifled creativity, it did serve its purpose to mollify the public.

In 1945 the organization's name was changed to the Motion Picture Association of America and Eric Johnston became its second president. These changes were a precursor to several larger ones that would substantially change the motion picture industry. In its landmark 1952 case *Joseph Burstyn, Inc. v. Wilson, Commissioner of Education of New York, et al.*, the Supreme Court ruled that the state of New York could not censor a film it considered sacrilegious. Often referred to by the name of the film involved, *The Miracle,* the court decided that motion pictures could be classified as "press" and were therefore protected under the First Amendment. While the Hays Code was challenged by this verdict, it remained virtually unchanged for another decade.

The 1960s marked a shift in the social structure of the United States; racial, sexual, and moral revolutions were unfolding as women and African Americans demanded equal rights. Other protests erupted over the U.S. involvement in the Vietnam War (1959–75). This upheaval had a serious affect on the MPAA and the motion picture industry as a whole.

Jack Valenti became the MPAA's third president in 1966. Recognizing that a new form of American cinema was emerging in response to this radical movement, Valenti decided to replace the Hays Code with a new set of guidelines. In November 1968, the MPAA created the Classification and Ratings Administration (CARA), which designated films with one of four ratings: G for general audiences, M for mature audiences, R for movies

FAST FACTS

Movie industry exports contribute more to the U.S. economy than automotive, aircraft, apparel, or chemicals.

(Source: Dyan Machan. "Mr. Valenti goes to Washington." *Forbes,* December 1, 1997.)

---

in which children under 16–years-old should not be admitted without a parent or guardian, and X for movies in which children under 17 should not be admitted. The M rating was soon changed to PG-13 for movies, which meant that parental guidance was suggested. The motion picture industry was not forced to follow these guidelines but nearly all did so.

Along with the 1970s came a rise in new motion picture technology. The VHS (video home system) format for VCRs (videocassette recorders) was introduced and was greeted as a mixed blessing by the MPAA. On the one hand, the motion picture industry had a new market, on the other hand movie piracy became cheaper, faster, and was less-easy to detect. By 1975 the MPAA began their anti-piracy program to quell the emerging black market of film prints.

In 1990, in response to complaints from film makers, the MPAA changed its X rating designation to NC-17 for no children under 17 admitted. This was done in response to critics, who claimed that artistic movies that contained adult themes were being unfairly classified with more graphic and hard-core pornography films.

The companies that are associated with MPAA are now diversified entertainment organizations with interests that include cable TV, the Internet, pay-per-view, home video, and satellite distribution.

CURRENT POLITICAL ISSUES

Because of the international nature of the film industry's consumer base and the difficulty of enforcing copyright laws overseas, MPAA has taken public policy stances on numerous international trade issues. Like many industries with a large international consumer base, the MPAA supports free trade and Fast Track authority for the president and the continued strength of the World Trade Organization (WTO).

The MPAA is also concerned with movie piracy, which takes the form of videotaping films and selling

them without paying royalties to studios and artists who are protected by intellectual property laws. Although MPAA offers rewards for information leading to arrests for such behavior, its ability to ensure enforcement overseas is limited. According to the MPAA's Web site, more than $2 billion dollars a year is stolen in intellectual property. The problem is becoming increasingly difficult to counter given recent advances in pirating technology and a growing industry reliance on foreign markets. According to *Billboard*'s Eileen Fitzpatrick, such concerns have led MPAA to sign both "a 'memorandum of understanding' with Beijing designed to improve enforcement of anti-piracy and copyright laws" and "a similar memorandum with the World Customs Organization." In recent years MPAA's concerns over intellectual property issues has put the organization in the forefront of a struggle attempting to get the United States to ratify the World Intellectual Property Treaty.

Of course, MPAA has domestic political concerns as well. Where art, film, and culture meet broader societal concerns, MPAA is an organizer and advocate of both industry standards and free expression. Since its early years under the leadership of Will H. Hays, MPAA has been concerned with the maintenance of moral standards in the film industry. In recent years, MPAA has expanded its efforts to regulate the content of print, television, and radio advertisements of studios and studio productions and to meet growing parental concern regarding Internet decency, MPAA announced in March of 1998 that beginning in June of that year it would impose its standards on Internet Web sites maintained by its member studios.

The MPAA is steadfastly opposed to government regulation of the film industry. By establishing self-imposed rating standards it attempts to uphold the First Amendment rights of film makers and hopes to keep government censorship at bay. This logic also dictated MPAA's involvement in a television rating system that would utilize program blocking technology known as the "V-chip."

Case Study: The MPAA and the V-Chip

The Telecommunications Act of 1996 required that all new television sets with screens larger than 13 inches be equipped with a V-chip device, which would allow parents to block out television shows based on industry-imposed ratings. The Federal Communications Commission determined that the broadcast industry would "voluntarily" provide such ratings. When V-chip technology first became a hot topic, MPAA was highly critical of the technology and the politicians pushing the industry toward compliance. Cynthia Littleton of *Broadcasting and Cable* magazine quotes Valenti: "The V-chip is a charade . . . [program] labeling is a charade. . . . The V-chip is a quick-fix political remedy. Politicians have learned that their numbers go up if they trash TV."

In its opposition, MPAA first voiced practical concerns. Where the movie rating system monitors 1,200 hours of film per year, such an effort to rate television would require an estimated 611,520 hours. Moreover, some have questioned the effectiveness of the V-chip considering both news and sports programs, which in many cases are chief sources of television violence, are exempt from ratings. In addition, industry leaders predicted that few, if any, television programs would receive anything other than a PG-13 rating. Indeed, some opponents suggested that the ratings system would actually give license to television programs to increase the level of sex, violence, and language. In an effort to forestall the push for a ratings system, the industry established a $2 million fund to investigate an alternative blocking device that would not require ratings; the technology did not materialize, however.

The MPAA eventually became a leader in the advancement of V-chip technology. In MPAA's tradition of seeking to self-regulate rather than open itself to government regulation, Valenti led a charge in which the industry would voluntarily impose ratings compatible with V-chip technology. Moreover, Valenti warned members of Congress as well as FCC officials that efforts by the government to impose such a system on the industry would result in legal challenges. As long as the effort was voluntary, however, the industry would direct the process. Along with Decker Anstrom of the National Cable Television Association (NCTA), Eddie Fritts of the National Association of Broadcasters (NAB), and Martin Franks of CBS, Valenti worked closely with Clinton administration officials as well as members of Congress to establish the industry's ratings system. Despite efforts from such critics as the Center for Media Education to impose ratings that would specify the content of programming with S, L, and V ratings (for Sex, Language, and Violence), the MPAA and its allies were only committed to an age-based ratings system.

Valenti revealed the industry's ratings system before the National Press Club on December 19, 1996. On January 17, 1997, Valenti, Anstrom, and Fritts wrote a letter to the FCC outlining the industry's six rating categories, which ranged from TV-Y (suitable for all children) to TV-M (for mature audiences only). By July 10, 1997, the industry once again compromised a previous stance by adding content-based ratings in addition to the age categories it had preferred. Under continued pressure from parents' advocacy groups, MPAA and its allies adopted the content ratings that included S, L, and V; they also adopted FV (for fantasy violence) in children's programming.

FUTURE DIRECTIONS

The MPAA is constantly looking for ways to expand its relationship with the global film community. To that end, in March of 1999 the MPAA announced that it would be staging a Chinese film festival later that year

or in 2000. The festival will likely take place in Los Angeles or New York, and will feature some of China's finest film makers. While bringing the richness of foreign film to the United States is the MPAA's main objective in holding the festival, it also hopes to promote goodwill between China and American film. Presently China greatly restricts what U.S. films enter its marketplace; the MPAA would like to see those restrictions decreased.

GROUP RESOURCES

The MPAA maintains a Web site at http://www.mpaa.org that gives information about the association, their movie rating system, their TV parental guidelines, and includes press releases from President Valenti. Information about the MPAA may also be obtained by writing the MPAA at Motion Picture Association of America, 1600 Eye St. NW, Washington, DC 20006, or by phoning (202) 293-1966.

GROUP PUBLICATIONS

The MPAA publishes a pamphlet about the association that provides extensive information on its history, functions, accomplishments, and its future goals. Another publication is the *U.S. Economic Review,* which is published annually. This item gives non-confidential statistics on the motion picture industry such as information on theatrical data, VCR Cable (basic, addressable, pay) data, television data, and computer/Internet statistics. This is available on the MPAA Web site at http://www.mpaa.org/useconomicreview. Both publications are also available by contacting the MPAA at Motion Picture Association of America, 1600 Eye St. NW, Washington, DC 20006 or by phoning (202) 293-1966.

BIBLIOGRAPHY

Albiniak, Paige. "Who Makes What in Washington?" *Broadcasting & Cabling,* 8 January 1998.

Carney, Dan. "Industry Agrees to TV Ratings." *Congressional Quarterly Weekly Report* 2 March 1996.

Fink, Mitchell. "Bells Went Off at the Motion Picture Association of America." *People Weekly,* 27 October 1997.

Fitzpatrick, Eileen. "MPAA Cracks Down on Piracy." *Billboard,* 3 January 1998.

Fleming, Heather. "No Ratings Change Without Parents Say So." *Broadcasting & Cable,* 14 April 1997.

Karon, Paul. "MPAA 75th Year Under Fire." *Variety,* 28 September 1997.

Littleton, Cynthia. "Valenti Calls V-chip 'Quick Fix'." *Broadcasting & Cable,* 8 July 1996.

Machan, Dyan. "Mr. Valenti Goes to Washington." *Forbes,* 1 December 1997.

McClellan, Steve. "It's Markey v. Industry on V-chip: IRTS Panel Debates Program-Blocking Technology." *Broadcasting & Cable,* 30 October 1995.

Mifflin, Lawrie. "F.C.C. Approves Rating System for TV: Sets With Blockers Will Be on Market Within a Year." *New York Times,* 13 March 1998.

"TV Ratings Brought About by Unprecedented Cooperation." *Communications Daily,* 1 March 1996.

Valenti, Jack. "TV Parental Guidelines: Keeping Faith with Parents Who Truly Care About the TV Watching of Their Young Children." Speech Before the Annual Convention of the National Association of Broadcasters, 7 April 1997.

Weinraub, Bernard. "Hispanic Film Audience Grows Fastest." *New York Times* 11 March 1998.

National Abortion and Reproductive Action League (NARAL)

WHAT IS ITS MISSION?

According to the organization, the mission of the National Abortion and Reproductive Action League (NARAL) is "to secure and protect safe, legal abortion; and to make abortion less necessary—not more difficult or dangerous."

NARAL, founded in 1969, deals with abortion issues and issues of contraception, childbirth, sexuality, and pregnancy. NARAL fights ongoing legislative efforts to ban abortion, and combats efforts from pro-life factions that make access to the abortion process difficult. Facing an increasingly conservative political climate since its inception, the organization has been forced to operate on the defensive as legislatures at the state and federal level whittle away at abortion rights. Though the landmark *Roe v. Wade* 1973 court decision may never be overturned, states have made great strides in increasing restrictions that impact reproductive rights.

ESTABLISHED: 1969
EMPLOYEES: 40
MEMBERS: 500,000
PAC: NARAL-PAC

Contact Information:

ADDRESS: 1156 15th Street NW, Ste. 700
      Washington, DC 20005
PHONE: (202) 973-3000
FAX: (202) 973-3096
E-MAIL: naral@newmedium.com
URL: http://www.naral.org
PRESIDENT: Kate Michelman

HOW IS IT STRUCTURED?

NARAL consists of three organizational entities. NARAL, Inc., is a 501(c)(4) nonprofit organization that carries out lobbying initiatives (including testifying at hearings and monitoring the entire legislative process), mobilizes grassroots support, and plans strategy for the legislative policy-making process, both at the federal and state level. NARAL, Inc., is governed by a 24-member board of directors, each of whom serve three-year terms and are selected by a nominating committee. Members of the nominating committee serve one-year terms and are elected by the membership.

Before the Freedom of Access to Clinic Entrances Bill of 1994, patients seeking reproductive services were harassed by crowds of anti-abortion protestors. (UPI/Corbis-Bettmann)

NARAL-PAC, the organization's political action committee, works to put pro-choice candidates into office. The PAC provides campaign support for these candidates through funding, advertising, and other forms of coaching.

The NARAL Foundation is a 501(c)(3) charitable organization that was founded in 1977 and is governed by a 12-member board. The board meets four times a year and manages a budget for the foundation, which in 1997, was approximately $1.6 million. Through the funds that it raises, the foundation sponsors research on abortion and reproductive topics, funds NARAL's educational efforts, and provides training for pro-choice grassroots activists.

NARAL's office is based in Washington, D.C. Departments include: Executive, Development, Government Relations, Political, Communications, Legal, and Finance and Administration. The central NARAL office networks with 35 state affiliates that launch grassroots initiatives impacting both state and federal issues.

Members join NARAL by paying dues ranging from $20 to $250. Additionally, members can choose to pledge a monthly amount to the organization. NARAL members have the opportunity to vote for board members, who cannot be elected unless at least 100 members vote.

PRIMARY FUNCTIONS

As a pro-choice organization, NARAL carries out its mission of ensuring reproductive rights and choice by working in two areas. NARAL seeks to shape and influence related federal and state public policy. The organization also pushes to advance these rights by educating the public and policymakers, and by providing outreach services to those who need them.

NARAL uses a variety of strategies to influence and shape relevant public policy. The organization advocates for pro-choice policies including: the continued right for a woman to have an abortion (even in late term), funding for abortion and reproductive services, safe access to clinics, and support for physicians that do the procedure. NARAL also advocates for policies such as pregnancy prevention programs and programs that provide contraception or sex education. NARAL carries out public policy research on topics including abortion and politics, late-term abortion, religion and abortion, and abortion as an issue in voting.

Based in Washington, D.C., the national office—with resources from its Political, Legal, and Government Relations departments—monitors reproduction-related legislation. NARAL staff testify at hearings, meet with legislators, and brief congressional members. NARAL-

PAC raises funds to support the campaigns of pro-choice candidates. NARAL-PAC provides these candidates, as well as pro-choice policymakers who are already in office, with background information about relevant issues.

NARAL is also active at the state level; ensuring that the pro-choice agenda advances at the grassroots stage. Thirty-five states have NARAL affiliate offices, which lobby for supportive state legislation and fight anti-choice policy and legislation. State NARAL affiliates hold fund-raising events, support pro-choice campaigns, identify voters, support pro-choice candidates, send action alerts to members, distribute voting records, produce newsletters, and speak out in the media. State affiliates also make use of NARAL STAR, a computerized database that tracks the current status of state abortion-related laws and legislation.

NARAL also gets information out to the public and the media about the pro-choice agenda. The organization creates advertising that supports pro-choice causes and is used in a variety of media outlets. The NARAL Foundation funds research on reproductive and abortion issues, and circulates the findings. For example, in the annual publication *Who Decides? A State-by-State Review of Abortion Rights,* the NARAL Foundation summarizes current abortion information from each state, including voting records and recent legislative activity.

NARAL organizes events that advance or commemorate the pro-choice cause. On January 22, 1998, NARAL and other allied organizations including Planned Parenthood Federation of America (PPFA) and National Organization for Women (NOW) organized "Speak Out." The gathering was a forum for women to share their stories and experiences about abortion. The event commemorated the twenty-fifth anniversary of the *Roe v. Wade* court decision that legalized abortion. NARAL also holds national and state conferences.

The organization carries out public education efforts on the topics of pregnancy prevention, family-planning services, contraception, and sex education. For example, NARAL publishes fact sheets on emergency contraception and maintains a hot line for information on these types of contraception. The hot line received 100,000 calls in the two years following its inception. The organization also publishes fact sheets on mandatory waiting periods regarding reproductive decisions and on the controversial RU486 birth control drug. The organization makes available research on the status of sex education across the United States.

PROGRAMS

NARAL programs serve to educate the public about reproductive choices and to empower the public to make these choices. Programs provide services, call for activist assistance, and provide information about reproductive

choice issues. For example, supporters can target the government and policymakers by participating in Choice Watch, a NARAL program that publishes action items and asks supporters to write letters or call policymakers on a particular issue. The NARAL campus-organizing program brings public education of reproductive issues onto college campuses and seeks to involve students in shaping advocacy efforts. NARAL assists with clinic protection efforts in various states. The organization sponsors an annual conference, which in 1997, met in Washington D.C. After the conference, participants visited Capitol Hill, where they lobbied for reproductive choice initiatives.

The NARAL "Who Decides?" program is an ongoing campaign created to make the public aware of the barriers that prevent a woman from having the freedom to choose to have an abortion. As part of this program, a report is produced regularly that outlines the status of reproductive rights in every state. Details include the status of abortion legislation, whether sex education is required, whether insurance companies cover contraception, and what percentage of women in each state are at risk of unintended pregnancy. In 1998 the program produced a special edition of the report to honor the twenty-fifth anniversary of the *Roe v. Wade* court decision.

Among the key findings in the report was a trend on the part of states to restrict access to abortion, decreased access to abortion providers (due in part to fear among medical professionals of harassment), a need for organized, quality sex education, and private insurance coverage for contraception. The report also listed anti-abortion initiatives and gains in that year's Congress, as well as the status (by state) of such related laws as mandatory waiting periods, public funding for abortion, restriction on minors' access to abortion, and bans on the partial birth abortion and other procedures.

BUDGET INFORMATION

NARAL, Inc., had revenue totaling $5,012,971 in the year ending March 31, 1997. Revenue included: direct public support ($4,858,570), program service revenue ($166,557), interest on savings ($35,528), and other revenue ($4,939). There also was a net loss from special events (−$52,623) for that year. Expenses for 1996 totaled $4,703,737 and included: program services ($3,050,341), management and general ($458,343), and fund-raising ($1,195,053). In a separate breakdown of NARAL, Inc., expenses, the highest expenses included salaries ($814,548) and telephone charges ($717,261).

NARAL Foundation revenue for the same period totaled $2,957,058 and included: direct public support ($2,931,270), dividends and interest from securities ($16,652), and net income from special events ($9,136). Foundation expenses totaled $1,711,071 and included:

program services ($1,148,240), management and general ($195,930), and fund-raising ($366,901).

HISTORY

NARAL's history has been shaped and influenced by the ongoing abortion debate in the United States. NARAL was formed in 1969. The organization and other pro-choice allies celebrated an enormous victory on January 2, 1973, when the U.S. Supreme Court handed down the court decision *Roe v. Wade*, which effectively legalized abortion in the United States. However, NARAL had little time to relish the victory. Anti-abortion forces mobilized quickly and, over time, attempted to control or limit aspects of the abortion process.

In the late 1970s, NARAL continued to face well-organized and powerful opposition to the pro-choice agenda. The conservative presidential candidate, Ronald Reagan, added an anti-abortion plank to the GOP campaign in 1976. Members of the Republican party were also successful in creating alliances to their conservative cause with segments of the religious community, such as Catholics, who disagreed with abortion on religious and moral grounds. To carry out the organization mission more effectively, NARAL founded its partner organization, the NARAL Foundation, in 1977 to provide further financial support for public education campaigns, policy and legal research, and leadership training for NARAL affiliate leaders.

In 1985 Kate Michelman, former executive director for Planned Parenthood Federation of American (PPFA), became NARAL's executive director. She brought a background in education to the organization, and real-life experience in having to deal with difficult choices about reproductive issues. Michelman made the choice to have an abortion when her husband left her abruptly and she was faced with the prospect of having to support four children on her own. Her abortion occurred three years before the *Roe v. Wade* decision. Several years after making her difficult decision, Michelman decided to devote her life to fighting for reproductive rights.

Conservative politics continued to grow as a powerful anti-abortion force in the 1980s and 1990s. Republican-dominated federal legislatures were common and legislation passed and proposed during this period reflected the conservative movement in the Congress. For example, the federal government's Medicaid program was repeatedly prohibited from paying for abortions. As this program pays for much of the health care bills of the poor, NARAL denounced these bans as eliminating the choice of abortion for the poor of the United States. Pro-choice advocates also suffered a setback in 1992, with the outcome of a Pennsylvania court decision *Planned Parenthood of Southeastern PA v. Casey*. The decision gave states the power to regulate abortions unless the plaintiff (the woman or the abortion providers) could prove that regulation would cause undue burden.

Another area of great concern to NARAL has been violence directed at those who seek or provide abortions. Hundreds of violent acts were commited at abortion clinics in the 1980s and 1990s, including bombings that killed dozens of people. One victory against clinic violence was the Freedom of Access to Clinic Entrances Bill of 1994 (S.636), which NARAL lobbied extensively for and which penalizes those who conduct violence or harm against patients seeking reproductive services from facilities. Also in the 1990s, NARAL lobbied consistently to get President Bill Clinton to sign several executive orders that reversed years of anti-choice policy. These advances included removal of bans for importing the RU486 birth control drug and allowing the use of fetal tissue in medical research.

NARAL publications reflected the increased role of the state abortion related policy and in 1995, NARAL's annual report *Who Decides?* was expanded to include the status of state statutes in areas of sex education, access to family planning programs, welfare policies that limited reproductive choices, and minors' access to abortion providers and contraception. Though it may have appeared that pro-choice groups were losing ground as states made advances to limit reproductive freedom, NARAL was still noted for its effectiveness in pursuing its agenda. In 1993 an O'Leary/Kamber Report titled the "Best of New Washington, D.C.," ranked NARAL as one of the top three special interest groups that lobbied at the Capitol. Michelman was ranked as the most effective spokesperson for a political action committee.

NARAL and other pro-choice groups continue to face challenges from the pro-life movement. Since *Roe v. Wade* abortion opponents have not focused on overturning that decision but have directed efforts at outlawing certain abortion procedures and creating barriers for access to abortion (such as the Hyde Amendment). Pro-life groups were, in 1996 and 1997, instrumental in bringing the partial-birth abortion issue to the public. The partial-birth procedure is used after 20 weeks of pregnancy. Pro–choice supporters maintain that such a procedure should be allowed if it saves the life of the mother. Anti-abortion activists, on the other hand, claim that the procedure is brutal and close to infanticide. Anti-abortion advocates were successful in lobbying for legislation to ban the partial-birth abortion (H.R. 1122), but the bill was vetoed by President Clinton in late 1997. NARAL and other pro-choice groups continue to face strategic and well-planned opposition from pro-life supporters.

CURRENT POLITICAL ISSUES

Because of the contentious nature surrounding the issue of abortion and reproductive rights, every NARAL initiative is extremely political. Issues that the organization is involved with include: fighting for the right to have an abortion, providing safe access to abortion clinics, ensuring availability of abortion providers, and working to make sure that parental consent issues and waiting periods do not erode reproductive rights. Beyond protecting the ability of women to have abortions, NARAL works to expand the birth control options available to women, and thereby reduce the need for abortions. Efforts in this area include lobbying for increased funding for contraception research and for public family-planning clinics, and also for approval of the French-developed drug RU486, the so-called abortion pill.

Abortion that occurs at more advanced stages of pregnancy such as the second and third trimester became a major legislative concern in the 1990s. NARAL has been particularly involved in fighting to retain the right to receive late-term abortion; sometimes referred to as partial-birth abortion. The procedure is controversial and fiercely opposed by anti-abortion activists who claim that it is brutal and unnecessary.

Case Study: The Partial-Birth Abortion Legislative Ban Vetoed

The partial-birth abortion procedure is typically performed between the twentieth and the twenty-fourth week of pregnancy. It is characterized by a partial live delivery of the fetus, after which several medical procedures are performed that culminate in the fetus being born dead. NARAL maintains that late-term abortion procedures such as this should be available to women, particularly in cases where the mother is in danger. Pro-life advocates claim that the procedure is brutal. The National Right to Life Committee (NRLC), one of the leading pro-life groups in the United States, says the procedure is "close to infanticide." Pro–life advocates claim that partial-birth abortion is performed much more often than official figures indicate, and that the procedure is often performed as an elective procedure rather than a necessary one.

In 1995 pro-life advocates, conservatives, and members of Congress launched a powerful initiative to ban partial-birth abortions. The Partial Birth Abortion Ban Act (H.R. 1122) proposed criminal penalties for doctors who performed the procedure. To gain support for the bill, anti-abortion activists used publicity and testimony that graphically described the procedure. According to an article in *USA Today* (November 17, 1997), the depiction and publicity surrounding the procedure has disturbed many citizens, including some pro-choice policymakers. The same article cites evidence from a USA Today/CNN/Gallup Poll that shows that since the partial-birth abortion became an issue, the number of people that believe that any type of abortion should be allowed dropped by one-third. The bill passed in Congress in mid-1997, but was vetoed by President Clinton.

Public Impact

While attempts to pass the Partial Birth Abortion Ban over Clinton's veto were unsuccessful, the issue is

FAST FACTS

Nearly one-half of all women in the United States have an abortion during their lifetime.

(Source: Bob Dart. "Roe v. Wade: 25 Years Later." *The Atlanta Journal and Constitution,* January 18, 1998.)

far from over. Pro-life forces continue to rally support, using strategies such as distributing mass amounts of postcards to church communities and supporters. Despite failure to pass the bill, the debate surrounding the partial-birth abortion issue benefited opponents of abortion, such as the National Right to Life Committee (NRLC). Contributions to NRLC jumped 30 percent in 1995, and between 1995 and mid-1998, 28 states enacted partial-birth abortion bans of their own, bans which NARAL plans to challenge in court.

FUTURE DIRECTIONS

Pro-choice organizations claim that their opponents are only whittling away at pieces of the abortion issues. However, many pro-lifers have a goal of completely reversing the 1973 *Roe v. Wade* court decision. NARAL recognizes that a strategy that focuses only on certain aspects of abortion (such as the partial-birth abortion procedure) allows abortion opponents to change public opinion incrementally. Directions that NARAL takes in the future will be affected not only by their ability to deal with opponents' strategies, but by the political tenor of future legislatures and support or opposition of future presidential administrations. Recognizing the need to continue building support at the state level, NARAL will concentrate its efforts in strengthening grassroots activities by providing training and support. NARAL will also work with its PAC to target efforts in candidate races where reproductive rights issues can make or break the election.

GROUP RESOURCES

NARAL maintains a Web site at http://www.naral.org, which includes press releases, current issues, historic court cases, links to state affiliate offices, and links to other Web sites with contraceptive or reproductive rights information. NARAL maintains a toll-free hot line (1-888-NOT-2-LATE) that provides information on emergency contraceptives and referrals to health care professionals. NARAL produces fact sheets on relevant issues that can be accessed through the Web site or by calling the NARAL Washington, D.C., office at (202) 937-3000. Results from public opinion polls are also accessible on the Web site.

GROUP PUBLICATIONS

NARAL produces the *NARAL News*, a quarterly publication available to members and also accessible on the Web site. Other reports include *Sexuality Education in America* and *State by State Review of Abortion and Reproductive Rights: Who Decides?. Choices: Women Speak Out About Abortion* features 12 women's stories concerning reproductive rights—including NARAL President Kate Michelman, actress Polly Bergen, and has a preface by Anna Quindlen, Pulitzer Prize-winning columnist and novelist. The NARAL Web site features links to other allied organizations' publications. Contact the organization for information on ordering at 1156 15th St. NW, Ste. 700, Washington, D.C., 20005; or by phone: (202) 973-3000; or fax: (202) 973-3096.

BIBLIOGRAPHY

Ackerman, Elise et al. "Who Gets Abortions and Why." *U.S. News & World Report,* 19 January 1998.

Dart, Bob. "Roe v. Wade: 25 Years Later." *The Atlanta Journal and Constitution,* 18 January 1998.

Dowling, Katherine. "Adult Support System Knows Best? A California Law Requiring Parental Notification of an Adolescent's Abortion Is Being Challenged." *Los Angeles Times,* 14 May 1997.

Kerr, Kathleen. "Abortion Pill Still Just a Trial." *Newsday,* 21 January 1998.

Lewis, Shawn D. "Catholic Church's Postcard Campaign Against Partial Birth Abortion Criticized." *Gannett News Service,* 28 June 1996.

Mathis, Deborah, and Carl Weiser. "Jane Roe Pleases Ashcroft with Her Abhorrence of Abortion." *Gannett News Service,* 21 January 1998.

"On the Hill; Federal Spending Bills Move Forward with Some Reproductive Health Limits." *Reproductive Freedom News,* 8 August 1997.

Rosin, Hanna. "Walking the Plank. Republican Party Platform Chair Henry Hyde's View Against Abortion." *The New Republic,* 19 August 1996.

Singer, Jeremy, and Carl Weiser. "Protesters Condemn Violence Against Abortion Clinics While Condemning Abortion." *Gannett News Service,* 22 January 1997.

"What's Ahead in Battle over Abortion." *Gannett News Service,* 9 January 1998.

National Academy of Sciences (NAS)

WHAT IS ITS MISSION?

According to National Academy of Sciences President Bruce Alberts, the organization was created to "validate scientific excellence; maintain the vitality of the scientific enterprise; apply the judgments of science to public policy; and to communicate the nature, values, and judgments of science to governments and to the public." The National Academy of Sciences (NAS) is an advisory board created in 1863 by the United States government to help it process and evaluate the scientific and technological innovations made during the American Civil War.

HOW IS IT STRUCTURED?

The 2,100 members of the NAS are accomplished scientists from across the country. These scientists are elected by active members of the NAS and serve unrestricted terms. They are divided into their fields of expertise, representing all of the sciences including anthropology, psychology, genetics, and mathematics.

NAS management is done by committee. The NAS has 17 active committees, each with different responsibilities. For instance the Committee on International Security and Arms Control gathers analysis and monitors developments related to nuclear weapons proliferation. The NAS Finance Committee manages the financial concerns of the organization.

The Council of the National Academy of Sciences is the governing body of the NAS. It is comprised of 17 members, each elected by the NAS general membership. Five of the 17 are officers acting as treasurer, foreign

ESTABLISHED: March 3, 1863
EMPLOYEES: Not made available
MEMBERS: 2,100
PAC: None

Contact Information:

ADDRESS: 2101 Constitution Ave. NW
    Washington, DC 20418
PHONE: (202) 334-2000
E-MAIL: wwwfdbk@nas.edu
URL: http://www.nas.edu
PRESIDENT: Bruce Alberts

Wreckage from the Challenger *explosion on January 28, 1986, was recovered from the Atlantic Ocean and examined by the National Academy of Sciences as part of their investigation of the disaster.* *(Corbis/Bettmann)*

secretary, home secretary, vice president, and president. The Council is further divided into five subcommittees—Executive Committee, Budget and Internal Affairs, International Affairs, Membership Affairs, Scientific Programs—which supervise the operation of the institution.

The National Research Council (NRC) is the arm of the NAS that researches, prepares, and delivers reports to the U.S. Congress on different scientific and technical issues. It has a committee system, with divisions such as the NAS. NRC committees include non-scientist members. For example, the behavioral sciences committees are made up of professors, police chiefs, mayors, social workers and welfare officers. The subjects of NRC work is determined by the NAS.

The NAS created two organizations, the National Academy of Engineering and the Institute of Medicine to help it meet growing scientific, technological, and medical demands. These organizations are independent research groups that function in the same manner as the NAS.

PRIMARY FUNCTIONS

The future of the sciences in the United States has always been a major concern of the NAS. It prepares reports on the state of science education in terms of its

effectiveness and well being. The NAS believes the future of the United States is linked to the quality of its science education. Therefore it has presented reports and testimony to Congress calling for increases in public funding for science education. It also assists Congress in determining the proper allocation of federal funds. For instance, the NAS published *Allocating Federal Funds for Science and Technology* in 1995, as requested by the Senate Appropriations Committee. The report was designed to establish a set of rules for the Appropriations Committee to follow when it distributed federal funds. It tried to reveal where federal dollars should go and how much funding was recommended.

The NRC is actively involved in providing the federal government with advice on funding and legislation that affects the sciences or that may be affected by science or technology. While NRC researches and composes the reports, NAS determines the direction of the projects, committee appointments, and approves the final drafts of the reports. These reports are diverse reference materials for all of the federal government. The reports cover a wide variety of subjects. *Use of Reclaimed Water and Sludge in Food Crop Production* (1996) and *Information Technology for Manufacturing* (1995) are two NRC reports.

NAS also acts as an advocacy group for science. It attempts to persuade Congress to spend more money on research and development grants by emphasizing the critical necessity of technology and science. The NAS also attempts to raise public consciousness of the importance of science. NAS has established an Office of News and Public Information, which acts as a press agent for the organization. It has created the Public Welfare Medal to scientists who further science's public relations effort.

The NAS also acknowledges and rewards accomplished scientists. Election to membership in NAS is a widely recognized honor for scientists. Members often receive funding dollars before other scientists because of their association with the NAS. The NAS also recognizes excellence with approximately fifteen prizes and cash awards for scientists who distinguish themselves in their disciplines. The awards vary in amount and frequency of presentation.

PROGRAMS

Diminished federal spending in the 1990s forced changes in many government organizations. Fiscally conservative congressional budget committees felt many programs, or "entitlements," should be eliminated and searched for reasons to cut these programs. While NAS funding was never in peril, the group has recognized the necessity of good public support. The NAS has created several programs, most notably the Regional Symposia, that are designed to educate the public and raise awareness of the importance of science.

The NAS sponsors forums or "symposia" at which the public may learn about scientific developments. Presented nationwide throughout the year, they are open to the public and feature eminent scientists who deliver papers and present findings on subjects from black holes to genetics.

The Frontiers of Science program is a similar initiative. The Frontiers of Science is an annual symposium held in November for young scientists from academic, industrial, and federal laboratories. Some 100 scientists under age 45 discuss approximately 25 different scientific issues.

The NAS created the Colloquia series in 1991. The Colloquia are not open to the public. The Colloquia retreats, which are generally two days long, bring scientists together to concentrate discussion on one topic. Such immersion on one project by many experts helps stimulate diverse, high quality work. The results of the Colloquia are published in the journal *Proceedings of the National Academy of Sciences* or *PNAS*. A colloquy is held four to five times a year.

Beyond Discovery was also designed to increase public understanding of how science works. Beyond Discovery is an educational program that brings the confusing process of scientific innovation into clearer focus. It tries to describe the research that occurs between a scientific discovery and its eventual effect on the public.

Beyond Discovery publishes accounts of scientists work from first hand notes and reports. These reports help to explain the importance and necessity of basic science. A typical Beyond Discovery report might be an examination into the role of genetic coding in people who develop cancer. A science writer accumulates and examines scientists' notes and accounts and adapts them into a final report. The Beyond Discovery program starts new projects every four months. The reports are made available through the NAS Web site and *PNAS*.

BUDGET INFORMATION

Eighty-five percent of the NAS' revenue is derived from its work with the federal government. The NAS took in approximately $170 million in the fiscal year ending 1996. Federal government contracts made up $146 million of that income. Those contracts were split among different government departments. For instance the NAS billed the Environmental Protection Agency (EPA) $6 million for research projects. The NAS' biggest federal government client was the Department of Transportation, which did $38 million in business with NAS in 1996. Department of Transportation studies included *Use of Shoulders and Narrow Lanes to Increase Freeway Capacity* and *Airport and Air Transportation Issues*. The NAS derives $22 million (15 percent) of its revenue from private contracts and private contributors.

The organization divides its expenditures between "direct" and "indirect" costs. Direct costs are expenses incurred in the production of NAS studies. These costs include the preparation and reproduction of reports, the salaries of staff, and expenses such as travel and meals that may be incurred in the preparation of a NAS project. Indirect management costs include services such as personnel, communications, administration, and building maintenance.

HISTORY

During the Civil War the United States government and the Federal Army were overwhelmed with proposals for new weaponry and new inventions to help the war effort. Contractors, seeking lucrative government deals to manufacture goods, drafted proposals and brought them to the War Department. The War Department lacked the resources to thoroughly evaluate the proposals and it did not have the knowledge to investigate the technological innovations of inventors.

Scientists who favored the creation of a national science organization seized the opportunity and lobbied the War Department. Their goal was to create a private, autonomous organization that would objectively evaluate inventors and contractors claims. The government could use the advice of this science organization to determine the worthiness of a proposal.

The War Department approved of the concept and recommended it to Congress. Congress and President Abraham Lincoln signed the organization into existence on March 3, 1863. The NAS began its work investigating ways of preventing corrosion on the Navy's new iron-hulled ships. Near the conclusion of the Civil War the NAS researched the longevity of metal headstones made for soldier's graves. Subsequently the organization became largely inactive after the Civil War.

By 1914 the NAS had become so ineffectual that a group of members, led by astrophysicist George Ellery Hale, pushed for the creation of a new research group within the NAS. These members wanted to reinvigorate the NAS and believed the United States would likely be drawn into World War I and would thereby need an active and effective NAS. The President of NAS William Welch agreed and on September 20, 1916, the National Research Council was created. The NRC and NAS missions were nearly identical, except that the members of NRC were not exclusively scientists. The NRC grew to assume control of NAS' research activity. Part of the NRC's growth was due to the creation of the National Research Council Fellowships in 1919. The fellowships were an important resource for American scientists for forty years, training research support staff for the scientific community.

In 1929 an Academy Committee delivered an important report that led to the formation of the prestigious Woods Hole Oceanographic Institution. The institution, located in Woods Hole, Massachusetts, is now a world-famous meteorological, oceanographic, geologic, and biological research center.

In 1941 the organization published *Recommended Daily Allowances* (RDA), a dietary reference guide for Americans created by NAS' Committee on Food and Nutrition. The *Recommended Daily Allowances* was simply a list of foods and their proper quantity which the organization believed Americans should consume in the course of a day to remain healthy.

The NAS made many significant contributions to the medical sciences during World War II (1939–1945). Beginning in 1940 the organization conducted research in aviation medicine, emergency treatment on the battlefield and new drugs and medicines, including the synthesis of penicillin. Immediately after the war the NAS began tracking the physical effects of the atomic bomb on the 100,000 survivors of Hiroshima and Nagasaki; these efforts would continue for more than half a century.

The effects of radiation in general were a preoccupation of the NAS during 1956–59. The organization's Committee on Biological Effects of Atomic Radiation helped form public policy on the debate over nuclear power and the nuclear industry. In 1959 the organization signed an exchange program with the Soviet Union to create joint research projects and conduct panel discussions.

Since the creation of the NRC the NAS formed two organizations to keep up with the rigorous medical and technological developments of the twentieth century. In 1964 the NAS formed The National Academy of Engineering (NAE) to research and advise on engineering issues. In 1970 the NAS created the Institute of Medicine (IOM) to research and advise on contemporary medical concerns.

During the 1980s and 1990s the NAS researched a number of high profile issues. In 1986 the space shuttle Challenger exploded shortly after liftoff, killing all seven people on board. The NAS conducted an investigation and prepared a report on the disaster. In the early to mid 1990s the NAS investigated and help confirm existence of Gulf War syndrome. Some soldiers returning from service in the Persian Gulf War (1991) suffered mysterious symptoms of an unknown illness. The soldiers publicly demanded an investigation into the causes of their sickness. The federal government used the NAS' investigations to form its Gulf War syndrome policy.

During the mid 1990s the NAS responded to a perceived crisis in the American school system. Educators feared that U.S. students were falling behind their international classmates in many areas. The NAS believed it was necessary to develop national science standards that would be guidelines for forming classes and writing lesson plans. The NAS first drafted a comprehensive list of standards in 1995–96. They separated students into three levels: kindergarten through fourth grade, fifth grade through eighth grade, and ninth through twelfth. The standards recommend what subjects students should be taught at these levels. The standards are voluntary and serve as recommendations for school boards.

CURRENT POLITICAL ISSUES

The NAS has attempted to avoid political controversy for the most part. It has, however, investigated and delivered reports on many controversial issues including *Preventing HIV Transmission: The Role of Sterile Needles and Bleach* and *Continued Review of the Tax Systems Modernization of the Internal Revenue Service.*

One area in which the NAS has become engaged in controversy is regarding the degree to which the NAS was independent of public and federal monitoring. The issue came to a head in the mid to late 1990s.

Case Study: The NAS and the Federal Advisory Committee Act

The Animal Legal Defense Fund and two other groups filed a lawsuit against the NAS in 1994. They were seeking access to an NAS committee that was composing a manual for the care of animals used in scientific testing. The animal rights groups were denied access and consequently sued the NAS. The groups believed that the NAS was subject to the Federal Advisory Committee Act (FACA), a 1972 law that requires all agencies and committees that advise the federal government to open their meetings and proceedings to the public. FACA also requires the presence of a government official at those meetings. Therefore, the Animal Legal Defense Fund argued, the NAS must allow the public to attend its meetings. A Federal District court initially ruled in the NAS' favor but a subsequent U.S. Court of Appeals rulings in January of 1997 agreed with the animal rights groups.

These rulings caused an institutional crisis at the NAS. The NAS was concerned that scientists attending committees would be fearful of speaking freely. Scientists that received Federal funding might be reluctant to criticize the government or government policy. This would be especially true with the presence of a representative from Congress at NAS meetings.

The NAS also believed it must remain independent from government or public interference. The NAS maintained that to keep its scientific objectivity it must not be affected by social or political pressures. Too much outside influence could negatively affect the NAS committees' rulings. The NAS asserted that FACA would make the NAS a useless organization by taking away its independence. The NAS argued that the American people would no longer be able to assume the NAS' recommendations and rulings were credible.

The NAS then attempted to take the matter to the Supreme Court. In early November of 1997, however, the Supreme Court decided not to hear the case because it did not believe that the NAS had enough evidence for an appeal. Thus despite the NAS' best efforts the ruling of the U.S. Court of Appeals stood. The NAS would have to open its meetings to the public and allow representatives from Congress to attend their proceedings.

The NAS presented its case to Representative Steve Horn (R-Calif.) immediately following the Supreme Court rejection in the hopes of affecting a legislative change that would allow the organization a special exemption. Representative Horn brought the case before the House of Representatives. Just days after the Supreme Court refused its appeal, the NAS was elated when the House passed a bill that allowed the NAS to be exempted from the restrictions of FACA. While the new bill did ask for several concessions from the NAS, including that it make the summary of closed meetings available to the public, the NAS felt that the bill would allow the organization to maintain its independence and credibility. The bill was passed by the Senate on November 10, 1997 and signed into law by President Bill Clinton on December 17, 1997.

FAST FACTS

The NAS's membership includes more than 160 Nobel Prize winners.

(Source: National Academy of Sciences, 1999.)

FUTURE DIRECTIONS

In early 1999, the NAS introduced a new initiative, the Campaign for the National Academies, that it hopes will guide U.S. scientific endeavor for the years to come. The campaign is broken down by seven strategic areas on which the NAS will focus. These areas are science, medicine, and engineering advances; making scientific knowledge more accessible and understandable; increasing the education of youth; preserving environmental resources; enhancing the quality of health care; stimulating U.S. involvement in the global economy; and ensuring a safe and peaceful world. The NAS will be investing a large amount of its resources in the pursuit of the goals of the campaign; it will host conferences and seminars as well as research and publish reports to further the campaign's objectives.

GROUP RESOURCES

The National Academy of Sciences maintains a Web site at http://www.nas.edu. The Web site contains brief historical information, NAS awards updates, lists of NAS committees and members, and NAS reports on a number of topics. Those interested in further information may contact the organization by calling (202) 334-2000 or writing to the National Academy of Sciences, 2101 Constitution Ave. NW, Washington, DC 20418.

GROUP PUBLICATIONS

The NAS publishes the *Proceedings of the National Academy of Sciences* (*PNAS*), a journal that reports the findings of NAS committees, scientific discoveries, and issues. *PNAS* is available to the public by writing to the Proceedings of the National Academy of Sciences, PO Box 5030, Brentwood, TN 37024, calling (877) 314-2253, faxing (615) 377-3322, or E-mailing subspnas@nas.edu. An on-line version is available via the World Wide Web at http://www.pnas.org.

The NAS also distributes *Reports and Events. Reports and Events* is a guide for the news media that provides a monthly digest of NAS meetings. It is available on-line at http://www2.nas.edu/whatsnew/events.html.

The National Academy Press is the publisher for the NAS. The National Academy Press publishes notable NAS reports in book form. These reports are available at many public and university libraries across the country.

BIBLIOGRAPHY

Culotta, Elizabeth. "Science Standards Near Finish Line." *Science*, 16 September 1994.

Cushman, John. "Scientists Reject Criteria for Wetlands Bill." *New York Times*, 10 May 1995.

Danir, Mubarak. "Integrating the Science Curriculum." *Technology Review*, May/June 1995.

Goodwin, Irwin. "Federal Court Rules NAS Must Open Advisory Panels, Threatening Its Independence." *Physics Today*, June 1997.

Greenwood, M.R.C. "Raiders of the Last Bastion." *Science*, 11 July 1997.

Holden, Constance. "National Standards." *Science*, 9 December 1994.

National Issues in Science and Technology, 1993. Washington, D.C.: National Academy Press, 1993.

"New Members of NAS." *Science*, 16 May 1997.

Ozone Depletion, Greenhouse Gases and Climate Change. Washington, D.C.: National Academy Press, 1989.

Wade, Nicholas. "Academy of Sciences, Fighting to Keep its Panels Closed is Rebuffed by Supreme Court." *New York Times* , 4 November 1997.

National Association for the Advancement of Colored People (NAACP)

WHAT IS ITS MISSION?

According to the organization, the mission of the National Association for the Advancement of Colored People (NAACP) is "to ensure the political, educational, social and economic equality of minority group citizens of the United States. . . . The NAACP is committed to achievement through non-violence and relies upon the press, the petition, the ballot and the courts, and is persistent in the use of legal and moral persuasion even in the face of overt and violent racial hostility." The NAACP is primarily concerned with civil rights issues as they pertain to African Americans and has remained one of the cornerstone operations in the fight for civil liberties.

ESTABLISHED: 1911
EMPLOYEES: 104
MEMBERS: 500,000
PAC: None

Contact Information:
ADDRESS: 4805 Mt. Hope Dr.
   Baltimore, MD 21215
PHONE: (410) 358-8900
FAX: (410) 486-9257
URL: http://www.naacp.org
PRESIDENT; CEO: Kweisi Mfume
CHAIRMAN: Julian Bond

HOW IS IT STRUCTURED?

The NAACP is a national, nonprofit, social action group headquartered in Baltimore, Maryland. A president and a board of directors leads the NAACP by providing general oversight and directing policy in terms of prioritizing issues and initiatives. The NAACP president also serves as spokesperson for the organization, particularly in media coverage of issues of great importance to the NAACP. Board officers include a chairman, a vice chairman, an assistant secretary, a treasurer, and an assistant treasurer. These national officers are elected by the board and serve for an undetermined length of time.

The full board numbers about 60 members elected by NAACP members to serve staggered, three-year terms. The board and a nominating committee select the

pool of candidates up for election. The board, and particularly its officers, is composed of civil rights activists with extensive experience in politics—board members are attorneys, former state and national legislators, task force leaders, university board members and professors, and political analysts and advisors, among a myriad of other political players.

Below national leadership are seven regional offices that serve as links to the 2,200 chapters and branches that can be found in the United States, Japan, and Germany. Regional divisions exist so that each branch or chapter has a larger pool of members to work with when mobilizing. Chapters and branches are essentially the same; groups with college ties are considered chapters, such as the Princeton University chapter. The 500,000 individual NAACP members generally get politically involved through these branches and chapters rather than through the national organization. Membership fees range from $3 to $2,500 because of the wide variety of membership options, such as corporate membership. But the organization stresses that it invites all Americans to join regardless of race, gender, ethnicity, religion, or any other factor.

The NAACP also maintains a bureau in Washington, D.C., enabling it to work directly with the U.S. government. Although closely affiliated with the NAACP, the NAACP Legal Defense and Education Fund (LDEF) has been an independent entity since 1957. Founded by the NAACP, this group provides legal representation and advice for minorities whose civil liberties may have been violated. However, the NAACP sometimes teams up with otherwise-unaffiliated special interest groups too, as when it worked with People for the American Way in a campaign for the protection and improvement of public education.

PRIMARY FUNCTIONS

The NAACP operates at all levels in its efforts to influence elections, policy and legislation, and social norms. Its membership of more than 500,000 illustrates the group's emphasis on grassroots involvement. The group maintains an active membership through educational initiatives, such as issue alerts made available on the NAACP Web site, and conferences and leadership programs. The focus of educational initiatives range from health and labor issues to guidance on voter registration. Voter drives for candidates and referendums, marches, and demonstrations are one of the mainstay techniques used at the grassroots level to affect change. Often, the NAACP seeks media attention for its initiatives. For example, its protest of the inclusion and definition of the word *Nigger* in publisher Merriam Webster's dictionary was covered by media powerhouses National Public Radio and the *New York Times*.

Perhaps the NAACP's strongest weapon is its legal team. The group's earliest legal work focused on chang-

ing the many raced-based laws that restricted minorities, such as voting requirements that hampered African Americans' right to vote. Now that U.S. laws generally prescribe a more egalitarian nation, NAACP attorneys seek to set case precedents and gain reparations for minorities for the decades of bias they were subjected to and, according to the NAACP, still feel the effects of. The LDEF provides legal representation and advice for minorities whose civil liberties may have been violated. Working in concert with attorneys are NAACP lobbyists who fight for or against legislation pending in Congress. The NAACP asserts that it lobbies the government for what it deems to be in the best interest of all Americans, not just NAACP members.

PROGRAMS

Members of the NAACP have access to a full spectrum of civil rights activities, leadership development opportunities, and educational programs. Through its programs the organization seeks to raise the level of education and achievement of minorities so they will have access to life-enriching opportunities. For example, the Back-to-School/Stay-in-School program focuses on lowering the high school dropout rate and the illiteracy rate among minorities and increasing the number of minorities attending college. NAACP adult branches, college chapters, youth councils, churches, schools, community organizations, and businesses provide advising and tutoring services for those in the program.

Similarly, the Afro-Academic, Cultural, Technological, and Scientific Olympics, known as ACT-SO, is a year-long program designed to encourage those African American high school students evidencing academic or other talent through 24 categories of competition that include the sciences, humanities, and performing or visual arts. African American high school students may compete in up to three categories for scholarships, prizes, and medals.

Community Development Resource Centers

The NAACP started installing Community Development Resource Centers in selected minority-populated areas in 1992, and the multifaceted educational program has been expanding ever since because of its high success rate. The program is designed to increase the economic vitality of minority areas. Specifically, it pairs businesses and families with experienced professionals so that the rates of home ownership and development of businesses and economic opportunities in a given area will increase.

Each center maintains a staff of professionals with experience in economic issues pertaining to the community in which it is located. The center develops community needs assessments and advises consumers, businesses, and real estate buyers in areas such as starting and operating a business, buying property, credit issues, technology, and general money management. In addition to one-on-one counseling, centers provide workshops.

BUDGET INFORMATION

The NAACP's estimated budget for 1999 was $17 million.

HISTORY

The idea for the NAACP was born in 1908, when William English Walling published an editorial in the *Independent* asking, "who realizes the seriousness of the situation? What large and powerful body of citizens is ready to come to the Negro's aid?" Walling's article led to a meeting in January 1909 in New York City, where he met with Mary White Ovington and Henry Moskowitz to discuss the formation of a multiracial organization to address the racial inequities of the United States. They first set out to recruit prominent African Americans and whites, among them Bishop Alexander Walters, Reverend William Henry Brooks, and Oswald Garrison Villard, grandson of abolitionist William Lloyd Garrison and publisher of the *New York Evening Post.* A total of 60 such personalities signed the document written by Villard titled *The Call,* which announced the newly formed alliance and invited the public to its upcoming public meeting.

The group produced a set of resolutions demanding that Congress and the president enforce constitutional amendments guaranteeing civil and voting rights for African Americans and that African Americans receive the same educational opportunities as whites. The organization behind these resolutions adopted its name in 1910 and in 1911 the NAACP was incorporated in New York with Villard as its first chairman and white attorney Morefield Storey as president.

Early Victories

The first initiatives of the NAACP were to get the word out, increase membership and donations, and heighten awareness and esteem among African Americans. It started publishing *Crisis* magazine, edited by W. E. B. Du Bois, which had 10,000 subscribers by the end of its first year. The organization started to grow as branches budded across the country, with New York City, New York, Boston, Massachusetts, Chicago, Illinois, Philadelphia, Pennsylvania, and Washington, D.C., in the lead. These branches fought local battles; for instance in 1915 several branches went to work protesting showings of silent film director D.W. Griffith's *Birth of a Nation,*

which characterizes African American males as having a lust for white women. By 1920 membership exceeded 50,000. More than 350 branches had formed, one third of them in the South where attempts by African Americans to form any sort of organization were often met with violence on the part of whites.

When communities would not voluntarily change, NAACP attorneys stepped in and the organization began the process of chipping away at laws restricting African American's civil rights. Early successes included the 1917 Supreme Court decision that a Louisville, Kentucky, ordinance requiring African Americans to live in certain sections of the city was unconstitutional, paving the way for further residential segregation litigation.

With its strength and prominence growing, the NAACP began the fight in earnest for the African American franchise. It started a sequence of legal challenges to state laws that, although not banning African Americans from voting per se, had the effect of doing so. For example some states required literacy in order to vote even though literacy among Southern African Americans was low. Its first success came with the final ruling on *Guinn v. United States,* in which the U.S. Supreme Court struck down the literacy requirement enacted by the Oklahoma legislature. NAACP attorneys celebrated a similar Supreme Court success in 1944. In *Nixon v. Herndon* the high Court ruled against a Texas law that specifically banned African Americans from voting in primary elections.

African Americans seemed to find a genuine advocate with the 1945 election of President Harry S Truman, whose Commission on Civil Rights produced the report *To Secure These Rights,* which sparked formation of the NAACP National Civil Rights Emergency Mobilization. This committee lobbied for implementation of the measures spelled out in the report, leading to passage of the Civil Rights Act of 1957 that established the U.S. Commission on Civil Rights as a permanent entity, and made it a federal crime to interfere with voting rights.

In 1954 the NAACP celebrated the now-famous U.S. Supreme Court decision that ended the legal segregation of public schools. Although no single legal team can take credit for the *Brown v. Board of Education* ruling, NAACP attorneys were heavily involved in several of the cases that merged into the one decided by the high Court. The NAACP's 1954 annual report, titled "The Year of the Great Decision," noted that the decision "put the law of the land unequivocally on the side of human rights."

Yet the true desegregation of schools was still years away as the white-dominated society refused to make changes mandated by the federal government. Many African Americans, particularly those in the South, feared retaliation for exercising the voting rights they had won. This fear was perpetuated by a Southern environment where white supremacy groups like the Ku Klux Klan were becoming more active in response to the fed-

BIOGRAPHY:

W(illiam) E(dward) B(urghardt) Du Bois

Educator; Activist; Author (1868–1963) W. E. B. Du Bois was a tireless, lifetime proponent of unconditional equal and civil rights for all African Americans. Prior to earning his Ph.D. from Harvard, Du Bois was awarded a grant to complete his thesis at the University of Berlin. It was Du Bois's travel and studies overseas at the age of 25 that opened his eyes to the racially based social structure of the United States. For more than 10 years following his return, Du Bois worked as a professor and wrote prolifically to educate the public about the effects of racism on the African American community and his social science solutions. Feeling that his proposals for change were virtually ignored by the white power structure, Du Bois grew convinced that only through an organized campaign of African American protest would social change occur. In 1910 Du Bois was the leading founder of the National Association for the Advancement of Colored People (NAACP). For 25 years, Du Bois was

charged with editing *Crisis*, the NAACP's official publication. Over time, his views expressed in *Crisis* became more radical and separatist, opposing those of NAACP board members and other African American leaders and eventually resulting in his resignation in 1934. From the mid-1940s until his death in 1963, Du Bois became increasingly tied to his support of socialist politics and communism. Of capitalism, Du Bois said, "No universal selfishness can bring social good to all." Upon his death at the age of 95, *Crisis* eulogized him as, "the Prime Minister, philosopher, and father of the Negro protest movement."

eral civil rights legislation. To counter this, the NAACP sought strength in numbers by initiating voter drives in the South. NAACP members served as advisors and escorts, eventually adding 700,000 African American voters to the rolls by the mid-1960s.

Dramatic Change

Still, civil rights victories in the years just after World War II (1939–45) were scarce and were generally not enforced. For example, some schools remained segregated despite the Supreme Court decision. Dissatisfaction among African Americans was growing, leading to the rise of new, more visible groups like the Nation of Islam, led by Elijah Muhammad and Malcolm X; the Congress of Racial Equality; the Southern Christian Leadership Conference, led by Martin Luther King Jr.; and Stokely Carmichael's Student Non-Violent Coordinating Committee.

The NAACP recognized that the organization was not receiving the level of public exposure that other groups were commanding. But while its legal battles played out in the background, the organization soon became involved in the sit-ins and demonstrations staged by activists in attempts to desegregate restaurants, theaters, and just about every place imaginable. In fact, the famous bus boycott in Montgomery, Alabama, was sparked by NAACP Montgomery Branch secretary, Rosa Parks. Also, much of the NAACP's work during this time was defending individuals who were arrested or injured

for taking part in such activism. By the late 1960s the civil rights movement had come of age as activists realized their efforts would be met with violence in the form of riots, police brutality, and assassinations. It was no longer a question of whether or not African Americans would gain equal citizenship, but how and when.

The NAACP continued to promote voting as the way to bring about change. The Civil Rights Act of 1960 had already strengthened voting rights by providing federal supervision of voter registration, but the NAACP pushed for even stronger federal legislation that would abolish the poll tax. The Civil Rights Act of 1964 did this, and the Civil Rights Act of 1965 outlawed the oral and written exams required of potential voters in some states, character references, and other voting barriers. Armed with this new legislation, the NAACP helped another 84,000 African Americans register to vote, and an additional 350,000 registered when federal examiners arrived to ensure African Americans were not intimidated or otherwise kept from registering.

Increasing their representation at the polls brought new political power to African Americans, allowing them to have a dramatic effect on elections. Carl Stokes became the first African American mayor of a major U.S. city when he was elected in Cleveland, Ohio, in 1967, and by 1970 more than 1,000 African Americans had been elected to public office throughout the country. The NAACP continued its focus on multiracial participation and solutions throughout the 1960s and 1970s. NAACP lobbyist Clarence Mitchell was instrumental in the passage of the Fair Housing Act (1968) that outlawed restrictive covenants in sale and lease contracts, as well as other devices used to try to keep African Americans out of white neighborhoods. Also, the NAACP won the court battle that desegregated the University of Mississippi via the court-ordered enrollment of James Meredith and his subsequent federally escorted entrance into the school, despite protests by then-Mississippi Governor Ross Barnett. Former NAACP attorney Thurgood Marshall was appointed to the U.S. Supreme Court, and presidents John F. Kennedy and Lyndon B. Johnson worked directly with the NAACP and reinforced the organization's message with their radio and television announcements urging peaceful resolution to the civil rights war that had erupted in the form of riots in many major cities.

However, while the NAACP's multiracial emphasis caused some to gravitate toward the NAACP, it caused others to move away, like Fred Hampton, a youth activities organizer. Hampton left the NAACP for the Black Panther Party and was later killed in a Federal Bureau of Investigations (FBI) raid of his apartment sparked by his Black Panther connections. The highly publicized incident led to the discovery that the U.S. government, through an FBI counterintelligence operation, was monitoring all civil rights groups, including the NAACP. Although the NAACP had built strong ties with the government, it had also taken on the cases of several activists who were being tried because of their civil rights activism.

Despite its advocacy of nonviolence, the NAACP may have helped to bring about riots and militancy. In 1974 NAACP attorneys won a federal class-action suit brought by African American parents against the Boston School Committee. The committee was found guilty of consciously maintaining two separate school systems, one for whites and one for African Americans, and was ordered to remedy the situation immediately. When bussing of students began the following fall, starting the process of integration, both predominantly African American and white schools experienced race-based boycotts, demonstrations, and violence. NAACP surveys of African Americans bussed to South Boston High School found that racially based tension had increased throughout Boston as a result of the NAACP-achieved court ordered bussing.

Even after the beating of a African American man by whites led to widespread violence, a public statement by President Gerald Ford in opposition to bussing in Boston, a near-hostage situation at South Boston High, and the refusal of the Boston School Committee to further comply with the court order, the decision of Judge W. Arthur Garrity Jr. stood. "Time will bring about an understanding on the part of most people that there's no alternative but compliance with the principles set out by the Supreme Court of the United States," Garrity wrote. It later became clear that NAACP attorneys had only paved the way for the organization's branches to begin their work in Boston. In 1977, for the first time in the

FAST FACTS

In 1996 13.6 percent of African Americans aged 25 or over had completed four years of college, compared to 24.3 percent of whites.

(Source: U.S. Bureau of the Census. *Current Population Survey: Educational Attainment in the United States, March, 1996,* 1997.)

twentieth century, an African American was elected to the Boston School Committee. The events that transpired in Boston exemplify the way in which the NAACP brought changes in education, housing, and employment across the country well into the 1980s.

Affirmative Action

Soon the NAACP became the premier defender of affirmative action, the federal government's attempt to compensate minorities for decades of prejudice and exclusion. In general terms, the policy provided for African American's increased inclusion by requiring public institutions, like governments and universities, to admit and hire more minorities. While the NAACP was successful as a watchdog force in ensuring that affirmative action policies were followed, it did not fare as well in the precedent-setting U.S. Supreme Court case that challenged the legality of affirmative action. The case of *Bakke v. Regents* would decide if the University of California's affirmative action policy, and affirmative action in general, illegally damaged non-minorities by shrinking their opportunities in admissions and hiring decisions.

The Supreme Court's decision was close, with a five to four decision that affirmative action policies are permissible, but not mandatory. This decision left it up to the states and public institutions to decide if and how they want to include more minorities. The decision also allowed for further challenges to the program. In the 1996 general elections, California voters passed a referendum outlawing affirmative action policies in their state, initiating the most significant challenge to affirmative action since its inception. The law was prevented from taking effect due to the efforts of NAACP attorneys, members, and other civil rights organizations, which questioned its constitutionality. Ultimately, however, the Supreme Court will have to rule again on a challenge to affirmative action, with the NAACP again in the vanguard of the policy's defense. In the meantime, the NAACP's defense of affirmative action spread as additional states,

FAST FACTS

In 1995 about 29 percent of African Americans were in a household earning an income below the poverty line, as compared to about 30 percent of Hispanics and 11 percent of whites.

(Source: U.S. Bureau of the Census. Current Population Reports, 1998.)

including Michigan and Texas, initiated anti-affirmative action legislation similar to California's.

CURRENT POLITICAL ISSUES

The U.S. Constitution protects racial prejudice as a matter of free speech, but when prejudice is put into practice it becomes discrimination, a federal offense. The NAACP involves itself in such discrimination cases when it believes a minority person's rights have been infringed upon. Many suits involve equal employment issues and affirmative action. For example, in 1998 the City of Baltimore was brought under investigation for its disciplinary actions against African Americans, and the termination of employees after discrimination charges were aired. In regard to equal employment, the NAACP argues African Americans remain disadvantaged by current wage and hiring practices. The privatization of social security—putting control of the program into the private sector—is another political issue the NAACP is concerned with as it claims privatization would affect minorities most harshly due to their greater dependence on those benefits. Another example of an issue that on the surface might not seem to affect minorities differently than non-minorities is the way the U.S. Bureau of the Census collects data about the people of the United States.

Case Study: Census 2000

Every ten years the Bureau of the Census compiles and analyzes population information in order for the government to understand how the country's population is fluctuating, so that it can make policy and legislation decisions accordingly, including the redrawing of political boundaries. Perhaps more importantly, census data is used to determine how many federal dollars will be disbursed to a given area for public programs like health care, education, and recreation. Collection of data for the 2000 census was a concern for the NAACP because past censuses tended to inaccurately reported the numbers of minorities for a variety of reasons. Data for minority groups can be difficult to obtain as minorities tend to have a poor rate-of-return when submitting mail-in census questionnaires. They are also sometimes missed on the Bureau of the Census's second flush of obtaining data due to inaccurate and inconsistent address information. According to the Cable News Network (CNN), in 1990 approximately 11,000 children went uncounted in Baltimore, Maryland, a city with a African American majority. "In terms of hard cash, it was $640 per child through the course of a year," said NAACP President Kweisi Mfume.

For the 2000 census, the NAACP pledged to aid the Bureau of the Census in taking the most accurate census yet, its reason being to help obtain accurate data pertaining to minority populations so that policy decisions and legislation based on census figures can be more effective. While the bureau is responsible for the accuracy and completion of the census, it asked various groups to assist in its efforts since community-based groups such as the NAACP have established trust in the communities in which they exist.

The organization issued numerous bulletins to its local organizations in the hopes of utilizing grassroots support in achieving the NAACP's goal. The NAACP suggested that by mid-April of 2000, groups kick off the census drive by organizing educational events that explain the census process and what the information is used for. After April 15, the NAACP hoped that local groups would obtain the cooperation of local media in an effort to get the public to open its doors to the census takers.

The national NAACP coordinated local and national programs that included education about census-taking methods and purposes. The NAACP stressed the point that it is illegal, through a law of confidentiality, for census data to be used for any purpose other than to provide the government with summary information about the population, in order to reassure those who for some reason wished to remain anonymous and uncounted. The NAACP's hope is that someone uninterested in being involved in the census will be less resistant to including themselves. The NAACP further aided the Bureau of the Census by organizing members to aid in the distribution of questionnaires in places housing those with no permanent addresses, such as soup kitchens and homeless shelters. Local programs also distributed surveys to those who for some other reason might be missed in typical census sweeps.

FUTURE DIRECTIONS

With the futures of affirmative action, Social Security, and Medicare uncertain as the United States crosses the threshold into the twenty-first century, the NAACP will be busy rallying support for maintenance of these programs. The organization will continue its efforts to forestall any attempts to pass anti-affirmative action policies at the state level, while it argues its way up to the U.S. Supreme Court. In terms of Social Security and Medicare, the NAACP planned to scrutinize the proposals that legislators, including President Bill Clinton, promised will come in efforts to stabilize these entitlements. The organization, being generally opposed to any cuts to the programs, considered coordinating efforts with other like-minded groups such as the American Association of Retired Persons (AARP).

The NAACP also planned to evaluate major U.S. industries in regard to their return on consumer dollars. As part of the Economic Reciprocity Initiative the NAACP will rate industries based on the amount of income they generate from minorities, primarily African Americans, and ranking them according to their reciprocity in terms of advertising and marketing, vendor relationships, and employment for minorities. By 1998 the NAACP had released a comprehensive analysis of the telephone industry's reciprocity, and it urged members to boycott companies that showed low ratings. If such boycotts prove successful, the NAACP could have a great impact on changing the practices of industries that have historically excluded minorities.

GROUP RESOURCES

The NAACP maintains a Web site at http://www.naacp.org. Included at this site are issue alerts, links to local branches, an on-line membership and donation application, and other general information about the group and current issues. The national hot line at (410) 521-4939 provides a recorded message about issues relevant to the NAACP. For additional information, call national headquarters at (410) 358-8900. The national headquarters also maintains the Henry Lee Moon Library and the National Civil Rights Archives; these resources are located at 4805 Mt. Hope Dr., Baltimore, MD 21215.

GROUP PUBLICATIONS

The NAACP publishes the *Crisis* 10 times per year. The magazine discusses current issues, major legal cases, and news stories affecting minorities. It comes with most membership options or may be subscribed to by writing: The Crisis, 4805 Mt. Hope Dr., Baltimore, MD 21215. Some NAACP branches and chapters publish their own newsletters covering local issues.

BIBLIOGRAPHY

Arenson, Karen W. "Civil Liberties Groups Sue City University over Remedial Program." *New York Times,* 9 December 1998.

Bivins, Larry. "Scandals Plague NAACP Board." *Detroit News,* 30 October 1997.

Bronner, Ethan. "Black and Hispanic Admissions off Sharply at U. of California." *New York Times,* 1 April 1998.

————. "Rights Groups Are Suing Florida for Failure to Educate Pupils." *New York Times,* 9 January 1999.

Finch, Minnie. *The NAACP: Its Fight for Justice.* Metuchen, N.J.: Scarecrow Press, 1981.

Greenberg, Jack. *Crusaders in the Courts.* New York: Basic Books, 1994.

Harris, Jacqueline L. *History and Achievement of the NAACP.* New York: African-American Experience, 1992.

Holmes, Steven A. "N.A.A.C.P. Post Gives Julian Bond New Start." *New York Times,* 28 February 1998.

Johnston, David Cay. "Pensions Battle: Modern-Day Separate but Equal." *New York Times,* 11 October 1998.

Moreno, Sylvia. "A Blessing for Bayview." *Washington Post,* 25 December 1998.

Ovington, Mary White. *Black and White Sat down Together: The Reminiscences of an NAACP Founder.* New York: Feminist Press, 1995.

"Racial Profiling Protested in Connecticut." *New York Times,* 7 July 1998.

Sack, Kevin. "In the Rural White South, Seeds of a Biracial Politics." *New York Times,* 30 December 1998.

"Tampa Schools Fail to End Desegregation Order." *New York Times,* 29 October 1998.

Wendin, Carolyn, and David Levering Lewis. *Inheritors of the Spirit: Mary White Ovington and the Founders of the NAACP.* New York, N.Y.: John Wiley, February 1999.

Williams, Julian. "The Strangest of Bedfellows." *Newsweek,* 14 September 1998.

National Association of Broadcasters (NAB)

ESTABLISHED: April 26, 1923
EMPLOYEES: 165
MEMBERS: 7,500
PAC: TARPAC

Contact Information:
ADDRESS: 1771 N St. NW
    Washington, DC 20036
PHONE: (202) 429-5300
FAX: (202) 429-3931
URL: http://www.nab.org
PRESIDENT AND CEO: Edward Fritts

WHAT IS ITS MISSION?

According to the organization's Web site, the mission of the National Association of Broadcasters (NAB) is to "maintain a favorable governmental, legal and technological climate for the constantly evolving and dynamic business of free over-the-air broadcasting." NAB is a leading private, nonprofit organization representing the broadcast community and promoting the benefits of commercial radio and television broadcasting.

HOW IS IT STRUCTURED?

The Washington, D.C.-based NAB represents radio and television stations as well as networks and has associate members who supply programming and equipment to the industry. International memberships are available for individual stations and broadcast corporations operating outside the United States. NAB maintains committees on children's television, the future of radio broadcasting, the future of television broadcasting, and on-air initiatives. It also houses a reference library with some 10,000 holdings, employs a staff of 165, and is associated with the Television and Radio Political Action Committee (TARPAC). NAB divisions include Television, Radio, a Career Center, Research and Information, Science and Technology, and Legal and Regulatory. The organization also operates the NAB Education Foundation (NABEF) which conducts research, education, and other activities related to broadcasting.

PRIMARY FUNCTIONS

The overriding goal of NAB is to encourage the development, promotion, and implementation of new broadcasting technologies, develop effective management techniques, and formulate and implement appropriate broadcasting policies and regulations. These concerns require NAB to function in the areas of advocacy, litigation, education, public and industry information, technological research, and networking.

NAB serves as both a direct resource for its members and as a network for national and international exchange. The organization maintains information services and a career center and customizes seminars for different member needs and interests. NAB's Legal and Regulatory Department provides legal guidance to members through Counsel Memos, NAB HelpFax documents, departmental publications, and phone or fax consultations. Similarly the Science and Technology Department offers information on current technological topics such as "Y2K": the concern over computer programming failure triggered by the turn of the century. The organization holds annual trade shows and conventions, including the vast international NAB convention held each April in Las Vegas.

NAB often represents broadcasters before the Federal Communications Commission (FCC) and other federal agencies, courts at all levels, and other legal and regulatory bodies. The organization files statements of opinion with regulatory bodies and offers testimony during the development and modification of relevant legislation and regulations. The group also files lawsuits asserting the rights of broadcasters according to these rules. Furthermore NAB monitors government activities and mobilizes members to act on a local level to influence elected officials.

PROGRAMS

NAB runs a number of programs, many focusing upon educating either its members or the general public. Providing opportunities for face-to-face industry meetings, as well as hands-on experience of the latest technologies, is the role of NAB conventions. Held in both the spring and fall, with international participation representing 20 percent of total attendance, the conventions help broadcasters familiarize themselves with regulatory, technical, and service developments by introducing, explaining, and discussing the latest changes in the industry, both in the United States and overseas. NAB also organizes an annual European conference for radio managers.

Through the NAB Education Foundation (NABEF), the organization offers the NABEF Summer Fellowship Program and the NABEF Professional Fellowship Program. The Summer Fellowship Program is open to students and provides a stipend of $3,000 to pursue educational opportunities by working with NAB staffers and broadcast industry volunteers as well as through contacts with national policy makers. In addition, NABEF provides opportunities for practical experience at radio and/or television stations. The Professional Fellowship Program provides management training for radio and television broadcasters of demonstrated ability who show promise for future advancement in the industry.

In addition to these programs, NAB provides members with numerous benefit programs. These include providing information and analysis of important issues of relevance to the broadcasting industry as well as discounts on its conventions and publications.

BUDGET INFORMATION

Not made available.

HISTORY

Like many professional organizations, NAB was born of controversy, in this case a reaction to the 1923 decision by the American Society for Copyright and Artist Protection (ASCAP) to revoke all radio station licenses for broadcasting popular music. ASCAP threatened violators with prosecution and linked future licenses to music fees of up to $5,000. NAB founding members attended an informal meeting in Chicago; they included such personalities as Thorne Donnelley and Elliot Jenkins of WDAP and William Hedges, former radio editor for the *Chicago Daily News* and manager of Chicago station WMAQ.

The founders quickly agreed on a name, the National Association of Broadcasters, and hired retired piano roll businessman Paul Klug as managing director because of his experience with composers and lyricists. Their initial plan was to create their own music license bureau and library of music to compete with ASCAP.

By January of 1924 NAB had organized itself into four bureaus: music release, legislative and legal, radio programs, and copyright revision. Almost immediately NAB set about lobbying for a revision of the copyright laws by proposing an amendment to Section 1 of the 1909 Copyright Act, to the effect that: "Copyright control shall not extend to public performances, whether for profit or without profit, of musical compositions where such performance is made from printed or written sheets or by reproducing devices issued under the authority of the owner of the copyright, or by use of radio or telephone or both." It was a popular and successful cause which provoked more telegraphs to the senator introducing the amendment than any other single event except the response to the U.S. declaration of war in 1917.

In 1926 the National Broadcasting Company (NBC) made the first official national radio broadcast from the Waldorf-Astoria with an audience of more than 11 million listening in. Two other networks were soon on the air: the Blue Network from WJZ and the Red Network from WEAF. A year later the Radio Act of 1927 became law, establishing a station licensing system for distributing the radio spectrum. The act also established the Federal Radio Commission, predecessor to the Federal Communications Commission (FCC). NAB was incorporated that same year.

In 1928 William Paley bought a chain of stations, creating the Columbia Broadcasting System (CBS) as a major competitor in radio broadcasting. The stock market crash the following year reinforced the importance of radio as a free source of information and family entertainment. Behind the scenes, NAB continued to disseminate information, encourage new developments, and promote the industry as a whole. At the 1931 NAB convention Radio Manufacturers Association vice president Ben Geddes announced that several of the largest motor manufacturers would equip their automobiles with radio sets. In 1933 NAB helped boost President Franklin D. Roosevelt's National Recovery Act by rallying broadcasters to the cause while radio listeners were treated to the first of his famous "fireside chats" broadcast from WEAF New York. In the following year the FCC was established by the Communications Act of 1934, an event that coincided with the invention of FM radio.

By 1938, the year actor Orson Wells terrified listeners with his *War of the Worlds* radio broadcast realistically describing an attack by aliens, there were 847 on-the-air radio stations. NAB, now with 461 members, established a full-time president with the selection of former mayor of Louisville, Kentucky, Neville Miller. Miller soon had the membership approval necessary to set up a new musical publishing company, BMI, which would become America's largest musical publishing company within ten months of opening. The war years made tremendous demands on the country as a whole but the technological developments in broadcasting were undiminished, with both the NTSC television broadcast standard and commercial television broadcasting being approved by the FCC during this time.

While NAB's relationship with the FCC was sometimes strained during this period due to a difference in views over the best way to operate the industry, its relations with the government as a whole were not. NAB members lead the industry in complying with regulations during World War II (1939–45) and by providing important information to the public. These efforts were later recognized in a letter from President Harry S Truman thanking broadcasters for the part they played in winning the war.

The first postwar NAB industry convention attracted 3,000 attendees. At this time radio was the main business concern, although developments in television were also a subject of interest. The industry was just two years away from the debut of commercial television broadcasts. While television and radio would soon be competing for advertising revenues, the technologies, philosophies, and appeals of the two broadcasting mediums were almost identical, so much so that in 1951 the Television Broadcasters Association merged with NAB to become the National Association of Radio and Television Broadcasters. This appellation lasted for seven years until the organization reverted to NAB with the announcement by organization chairman Merrill Lindsay that, "The membership has arrived at a place of mutual understanding; where both radio and television broadcasters can stand side by side and proclaim that each is a part of the great American electronics communications medium."

However, all was not completely well with NAB. In 1959 it was alleged that certain television quiz shows were rigged; in what were dubbed the Payola Hearings it was discovered that this was indeed the case. NAB's television board immediately denounced such practices and its Standards of Good Practices Committee recommended strengthening the voluntary code of conduct for the nation's radio broadcasters.

The 1960s was a time of amazing technological advancements within broadcasting. In 1962 the first broadcasting satellite was launched and the following year marked the first time that a television program had ever been beamed to the earth. Americans had unprecedented coverage of violent conflict as broadcasters helped bring the Vietnam War into television sets across the country. In 1969 the Apollo 11 lunar landing was broadcast to nearly a billion people around the world.

The 1980s were an era of great change for NAB. In 1982 a federal court struck down the NAB code, claiming that its guidelines for television and radio violated anti-trust laws. In the same year NAB contributed to the formation of the ATSC standard for digital television, marking the start of a long debate about digital and high-definition television (HDTV). In 1984 NAB began to provide stations with Public Service Announcements and community-oriented campaign materials. It also received FCC approval of its request to give stations the authority to sponsor candidate debates. In 1986 the National Radio Broadcasters Association became a part of NAB, and radio station membership approached the 5,000 mark.

In the 1980s NAB also began a significant image overhaul. It began the decade without a reputation as an effective lobbying group, but that would all change when former radio broadcaster Eddie Fritts became president and CEO in 1982. Fritts began hiring Washington, D.C., insiders and focusing on issues that would benefit NAB members' financial welfare. Under Fritts, NAB increased its influence through the Television and Radio Political Action Committee (TARPAC), and non-PAC fund-raisers for individual broadcasters. During this era NAB effectively stopped a Mothers against Drunk Driving

(MADD) effort to take beer ads off television by offering to finance public service announcements (PSAs) about alcohol abuse.

In the early to mid-1990s NAB achieved several major legislative goals with the signing of the Cable Act in 1992 and the Telecommunications Act in 1996. The Cable Act, made law despite the veto of President George Bush, ensured that cable providers carried local stations and allowed local authorities to regulate cable rates. The Telecommunications Act deregulated much of the communications industry, making it easier for small companies to do business.

By the late 1990s NAB had become one of the nation's most influential lobbying organizations. In 1998 *Fortune* magazine named it the 18th top lobbying group in Washington, D.C. Banking on its strength, the group was now preparing to address the issues of equal employment opportunities and minority ownership, as well as government influence on programming content. NAB was also active in advancing the interests of radio broadcasters impacted by the issues of subscription radio via digital satellite transmission, low power "pirate" radio stations, and fledgling on-line radio services.

CURRENT POLITICAL ISSUES

Many of NAB's interests involve government oversight and place the group's representatives in the midst of FCC and congressional debate, as well as in the courts. Technological issues are often central to these activities, as are issues of competition between different elements in the television industry.

For example NAB has filed suits seeking protection for local television stations against digital broadcast satellite (DBS) providers who are supplying customers with illegal distant network signals. In early 1999 some 2 million viewers in Florida risked losing network programming when NAB asked for a federal court order stopping PrimeTime 24 from offering CBS and Fox programs. NAB wants Congress to create legislation requiring DBS companies to give customers only local network affiliates and to provide all such local stations.

Other regulatory issues affecting NAB's television constituency are the creation of content ratings and the v-chip—a device used to block programming deemed unacceptable for children; a proposed end to local marketing agreements (LMAs); and a proposed easing of station ownership caps. An unusual regulatory battle involving radio interests escalated in 1999 between NAB and community radio operators, or "pirates" operating low-powered radio stations without FCC licenses; such operations are also known as "microradio." NAB worried that FCC approval of low-power stations would create interference for conventional broadcasters' new digital signals.

FAST FACTS

The first TV broadcast in the United States was in 1927, from New York City to Washington, D.C. It was transmitted by wire and the picture was composed of just fifty lines.

(Source: National Association of Broadcasters, 1999.)

NAB's biggest challenge, however, has been influencing the transition from analog to digital transmission of television broadcasts. The organization has sought to shape FCC policy regarding technological standards, spectrum distribution, and a plan for serving analog and digital viewers until the transition is complete.

Case Study: Digital Television Implementation

The FCC has mandated that television broadcasters must convert their operations to replace analog signal transmission with digital signal transmission. Digital signals can accommodate more information and provide viewers with greatly improved picture and sound quality. New services will include HDTV programming and datacasting—the transmission of information supplementing television programming. The FCC has the authority to determine when the transition should begin and end, what technologies will be used, how the digital spectrum will apportioned and paid for, and whether must-carry rules for cable television providers will cover both types of transmission.

The first major debate regarding digital transmission occurred over technological standards. During the 1990s two digital systems emerged as the best options, one known as 1080 interlace technology and the other as 720 progressive technology. However broadcasters, cable operators, and others did not agree on which of these systems was best and each claimed that using one particular technology was vital to their interests. NAB and television manufacturers favored the interlace technology because it provided the best picture quality; the cable, satellite, and computer industries wanted the progressive system because it took up less space in the transmission process and was more compatible with computer technologies. It was expected that one format would be selected by the FCC, causing heated debate on the subject. However regulators decided to avoid setting a standard prematurely, and have allowed broadcasters to choose their own formats during the first stage of digital transmission.

Broadcasters in major markets were given a date by which they were required to begin broadcasting digitally, and in November of 1998 some 42 stations began transmitting two signals. However there was not much evidence of change for the general public. Most broadcasters began by simply converting their programs to the digital format without any increase in resolution, and high-definition programming was scarce. At the time a Mitsubishi HDTV receiver cost about $7,000 and, not surprisingly, few viewers had made this kind of investment in the new technology.

Other major issues remained to be resolved. A bitter fight over the expansion of "must carry" rules to include digital signals was in full swing in early 1999, when the FCC began a proceeding considering the issue. FCC rules require cable operators to carry most local broadcast programming. Expanding "must carry" rules to include digital signals would eventually double the space occupied by local broadcasters. The cable industry insists that most cable systems do not have the room to accommodate this doubling of local channels, and would be forced to dump cable channels in order to comply. NAB responded that broadcasters will not be able to finance the government-mandated switch to digital technology if there is no guarantee that cable viewers will get the improved service.

The FCC loaned broadcasters space on the digital spectrum during the transition from analog to digital. Well before the first mandated digital broadcasts began, however, elected officials were debating new fees and the possibility of auctioning off the digital spectrum, which had an estimated value of up to $70 billion in 1995. President Bill Clinton suggested broadcasters trade air time for candidates for federal elective offices for their space on the digital spectrum. In 1997 he established the Advisory Committee on Public Interest Obligations of Digital Television Broadcasters, more commonly known as the Gore Commission, to make recommendations to the FCC.

Many analysts expect the analog-to-digital transition to be a lengthy process, longer than the 10-year span named by the FCC. As Joel Brinkley noted in the *New York Times,* it is a transition unlike any seen before: "Nobody was forced to trade a horse for an automobile, a Victrola for a radio, a typewriter for a computer."

FUTURE DIRECTIONS

In an effort to further public education about the ways in which broadcasters attempt to benefit their communities, NAB hosted its first annual Service to America program in June of 1999. The program recognizes and rewards broadcasters who have attempted to further political debate, performed a public service, or brought about closer ties between the broadcast industry and the communities in which they reside. Colin Powell, former chairman of the Joint Chiefs of Staff, was the first keynote speaker of the program.

In the case of program content labeling, NAB wants to ensure that parents are the judge of their effectiveness and that any related legislation be prohibited for several years. The organization hopes to show its support of minority ownership by participation in an investment fund created by the television industry. In February of 1999 NAB became the first group to make a pledge to the fund. NAB was expected to give some $10 million to the fund, which organizers hoped would total $200 million. The money would be made available to help minorities buy television and radio stations.

GROUP RESOURCES

The NAB Information Resource Center (IRC) is designed to serve NAB staff and members. Located at NAB headquarters in Washington, D.C., the IRC houses approximately 6,500 books and reports on the broadcasting industry, as well as 100 magazines, journals, and newsletters. NAB-generated publications and reports, including member newsletters, news releases, convention programs, and engineering conference papers are also available at the IRC. Some material from the IAC is also available at http://www.nab.org/nac.

NAB also maintains a Web site at http://www.nab.org that contains a good deal of information about NAB programs, policies, issues, and member benefits. For more information write to NAB Services-Department 955, 1771 N St. NW, Washington, DC 20036, or call 1-800-368-5644.

GROUP PUBLICATIONS

NAB publishes a variety of newsletters and information sources for its members, including *NAB World,* a monthly International Member newsletter. An on-line catalog is available at the NAB Web site at http://www.nab.org and on-line ordering is possible. For more information about NAB publications write to NAB Services-Department 955, 1771 N St. NW, Washington, DC 20036; call 1-800-368-5644; or E-mail nabpubs@nab.org.

BIBLIOGRAPHY

Albiniak, Paige. "Gore Commission Seeks New Delay." *Broadcasting and Cable*, 24 August 1998.

Brinkley, Joel. "The Dawn of HDTV, Ready or Not." *New York Times*, 26 October 1998.

Halonen, Doug. "NAB Now Rides a Wave of Capitol Clout." *Electronic Media*, 14 December 1998.

Jaquet, Janine. "Taking Back the People's Air." *Nation*, 8 June 1998.

McConnell, Bill. "NAB Offers $10M for Minority Plan." *Broadcasting and Cable*, 22 February 1999.

"Steady as She Goes." *Broadcasting and Cable*, 16 November 1998.

Zoglin, Richard. "Chips Ahoy: As a New Study Warns that Violence Saturates the Airwaves, a Technological Quick Fix Promises to Help. But Will the V-Chip Really Protect Our Children?" *Time*, 19 February 1996.

National Association of Home Builders (NAHB)

ESTABLISHED: 1942
EMPLOYEES: 340
MEMBERS: 195,000
PAC: Build-PAC

Contact Information:

ADDRESS: 1201 15th. St. NW
    Washington, DC 20005
PHONE: (202) 822-0200
TOLL FREE: (800) 368-5242
FAX: (202) 822-0559
E-MAIL: info@nahb.com
URL: http://www.nahb.com
PRESIDENT: Donald D. Martin
EXECUTIVE VICE PRESIDENT; CEO: Thomas M.
    Downs

WHAT IS ITS MISSION?

Dubbing itself the "Voice of America's Housing Industry," the National Association of Home Builders (NAHB) is a not-for-profit trade association based in Washington, D.C. The NAHB represents the interests not only of builders, but of remodelers, subcontractors, material manufacturers, equipment suppliers, and architects. The organization's primary goal is to keep the housing industry as one of the nation's top national priorities.

Among the NAHB's other goals is providing consumers with safe, decent, and affordable housing. To this end, the organization promotes the expansion of opportunities for home construction, financing, and remodeling; easing of regulatory burdens faced by professionals in the industry, and the development and monitoring of the various professions involved in delivering housing to consumers.

HOW IS IT STRUCTURED?

The NAHB is a federation of more than 850 state and local home builders' associations throughout the United States. About one-third of the association's 195,000 members are either home builders or remodelers, or both; the remainder are associates who work in closely related fields in the housing industry, such as building products and services, mortgage finance, or equipment rental. Membership in the NAHB occurs automatically when an individual joins his or her local builders association.

The NAHB is staffed by a core group of over 300 employees based in Washington, D.C., that is led by an executive vice president/chief executive officer. This executive also functions as primary spokesperson for the organization. The Washington staff is divided into more than 50 divisions and committees, the most significant of which are councils that offer advice and information to professionals in specific fields or demographic areas. For example, the National Council of the Housing Industry (NCHI) is a special standing committee whose purpose is to provide building suppliers with access to NAHB's builder members and to make sure that suppliers are represented during policy-development activities. Represented on this council are corporations that manufacture lumber, pipes, fixtures, windows, carpet, paint, and other materials. Other well-known councils are the Multifamily Council, for professionals involved in the construction and finance of multifamily dwellings such as apartment buildings; the Commercial Building Council; the National Sales and Marketing Council; the Remodelers Council; and the Women's Council.

Other divisions within the organization serve primarily to perform research, analyze policy issues, and present statistics and findings on different aspects of the housing industry. The most important division involved in information-gathering is the Economics Department. The Public Affairs Division publishes press releases and produces a regular report titled *Housing Facts, Figures, and Trends*.

The NAHB also participates in the operation of two important subsidiary organizations that focus on specialized aspects of the housing industry. The Home Builders' Institute (HBI), the educational arm of the NAHB, operates training and apprenticeship programs for workers in residential construction. The NAHB Research Center, located in Maryland, keeps builders up-to-date with the latest technology and changes in the industry. The center's staff includes scientists, engineers, architects, and economists who perform testing and certification programs on a variety of new building products.

PRIMARY FUNCTIONS

One of the most significant functions of the NAHB is its role as a political lobbying organization. NAHB divisions analyze policy issues and closely monitor proposed legislation and regulations put before Congress. Because of the complexity of the home-buying process many issues affect the home construction industry, among them mortgage financing and lending rates, mortgage interest tax deductions, building codes, labor policies, and environmental concerns.

The NAHB works closely with legislators and federal agencies, making its position known—in press releases, press conferences, or formal reports—as laws are drafted and discussed. The organization tries to make housing a national priority whenever laws are made and policies are established. To that end, the NAHB realizes

that its greatest political strength comes from highly organized, well-trained, and knowledgeable members. Its councils and its affiliates, the NAHB Research Center and the Home Builders' Institute, all work to this end. When new materials, methods, standards, or equipment are introduced to the industry, the Research Center develops, tests, and evaluates them in order to improve on any new technology and make it more affordable. The HBI helps its members professional development, providing them with continuing education programs, training in specific construction trades, apprenticeships, and job placement services.

The NAHB hosts the International Builders' Show, an annual convention and exposition where more than 1,000 manufacturers introduce building products and services to industry professionals from around the world. A similar convention, the Remodelers' Show, is held each year to provide remodeling contractors with information about computers, business management, sales techniques, personnel training, and other aspects of the trade.

PROGRAMS

Most of the NAHB's programs are carried out by its affiliate organizations, the NAHB Research Center, and the Home Builders' Institute. Among recent Research Center initiatives is the National Housing Quality Program, established in 1993 with funding from both the NAHB and the Department of Energy Advanced Housing Technology Program. The primary purpose of the program is to promote quality management principles and practices in the home building and remodeling industries. Each year the program presents a National Housing Quality (NHQ) Award, recognizing a U.S. home builder for "customer-focused business excellence and quality achievement."

Another important Research Center program is the International Housing University, a joint venture with GMA/International Ltd. Builders. The university provides builders from around the world with the opportunity to learn and apply certain principles or techniques—such as land development, marketing, and management—that are integral to the U.S. building industry.

The NAHB's Home Builders' Institute conducts a variety of education and training programs, including certification programs for members who want to earn titles such as Certified Graduate Remodeler or Graduate Master Builder. The Institute also heads a remarkable number of community outreach programs. One such program, CRAFT (Community, Restitution, Apprenticeship-Focused Training), is a national training program for at-risk and "adjudicated" youth—that is, teens who have appeared before the juvenile justice system. CRAFT provides participants (who must be 17 or older) with 21 weeks of training in the home-building field, including hands-on work opportunities on community-service pro-

FAST FACTS

In the 1990s development fees and charges faced by builders and land developers added more than $12,000 to the cost of a typical new home.

(Source: National Association of Home Builders. "How Regulation Affects the Cost of Housing." Government Regulations and Fees Survey, 1995.)

jects. Participants learn skills such as basic carpentry or building maintenance, or focus on one of a variety of trades. After a participant leaves the program, an HBI project coordinator assists the graduate with his or her transition back into the community and provides supportive services for six months.

BUDGET INFORMATION

According to the NAHB, its political action committee, Build-PAC, is the third-largest trade association PAC in the United States, raising more than $2 million every election cycle. To avoid conflicts with the political wishes of NAHB members, Build-PAC's contributions are not funded through membership dues but solicited directly from members as contributions.

HISTORY

The origins of the NAHB are in its former parent organization, the National Association of Real Estate Boards (NAREB). NAREB formed a builder division in 1923 but problems arose in the early months of World War II (1939–45). Because of the war effort the housing industry was faced with two special problems: overall housing shortages and a question about whether or not the government should construct housing for workers in war-related industries. In 1942 NAREB's directors decided to make their builder division independent, thereby allowing it the independence it needed to focus on ways to tackle shortages and keep construction in the private sector.

The newly independent organization changed its name to the National Association of Home Builders and in 1944 established its headquarters in Washington, D.C. Later that year the organization's first annual convention

was held in Chicago. With fewer than 1,000 members, the group began with a focus that was necessarily narrow: wartime needs.

In the postwar years, however, the NAHB began to expand its focus, adopting a long-term view as a way of protecting the industry's interests. This often involved incorporating into its ranks men and women representing other aspects of the housing industry, such as the 1964 creation of the National Council of the Housing Industry to represent the building products sector. After a dramatic expansion of the number of members specializing in remodeling occurred in the 1980s, the NAHB added organizations and services devoted to the particular interests of remodelers.

Over the years the NAHB has also adapted to the changing social and economic demands of the nation's home buyers. For example, when the Arab oil embargo of 1973 forced the United States to deal with shortages of oil and natural gas, home builders were called upon to make homes more energy efficient. The NAHB played a significant role in this effort, and today maintains a focus on environmentally conscious construction. In 1988 the organization turned its attention to the problem of homelessness, hosting a national symposium that resulted in several important publications on the issue.

The NAHB expanded its capabilities significantly in 1983 with the establishment of the Home Builders Institute (HBI), its educational arm. The HBI was created to offer a range of educational and job training programs that would contribute to the professional development of members.

CURRENT POLITICAL ISSUES

During the last two decades of the twentieth century, the NAHB benefited from a boom in its most favored demographic segment—suburban new-home buyers. Since 1975 the percentage of U.S. residents living in the suburbs climbed from 37 percent to 47 percent, signaling a large-scale shift in the way we live. This has generally been good news for home builders, of course, as they have increased production to meet the rising demand. Other groups, most notably environmentalists, take a different stance.

Case Study: Controversy over Suburban Sprawl

In the late 1990s questions began to be raised regarding the suburban population shifts begun in the 1950s, the potential drawbacks of the rush to develop vast suburban communities, and the manner in which such development had been accomplished by private enterprise. Often, some argued, development planning was flawed, resulting in a phenomenon that has become known as suburban sprawl. The suburban rings around cities were growing faster than their infrastructures—roads, sewer and water systems, waste disposal, and the like—could support.

In 1998 the Sierra Club, a national group promoting environmental consciousness, published a report titled *The Dark Side of the American Dream: The Costs and Consequences of Suburban Sprawl.* The report defined sprawl as "low-density, automobile-dependent development beyond the edge of service and employment areas." Increasingly, the report claimed, the results of such development were harmful: "The consequences of decades of unplanned, rapid growth and development are evident all across America: increased traffic congestion, longer commutes, increased dependence on fossil fuels, crowded schools, worsening air and water pollution, lost open space and wetlands, increased flooding, destroyed wildlife habitat, higher taxes and dying city centers." The report listed several prominent examples of sprawl, including the city of Las Vegas, Nevada, whose population had increased an incredible 238 percent from 1990 to 1996.

Voters in cities and towns across the United States expressed their own concerns about urban sprawl, approving more than 200 local ballot initiatives in 1998 that set strict growth boundaries for their communities and levied taxes for the purchase of land that would be permanently set aside as open space. Vice President Al Gore praised the new anti-sprawl movement, calling it "a brand new path that makes quality of life the goal of all our urban, suburban and farmland policies."

The NAHB voiced strong opposition to the Sierra Club's report. For one thing, they countered, there was no such thing as "unplanned" growth in these areas; most urban localities had comprehensive growth plans, and any change from these plans requires government approval from a wide range of agencies. Home building was further restricted through public hearings, reviews, and approvals. In highly regulated markets, the NAHB claimed, it could take two or three years to receive all the approvals necessary before breaking ground. The NAHB also took issue with the Sierra Club's definition of cities as employment areas, citing statistics indicating that employment in the suburbs was increasing nearly five times as rapidly as in the cities.

The NAHB's most strenuous objection, however, was the report's failure to even mention the main force behind today's urban growth. The U.S. population is projected to increase from 268 million to 300 million by 2010, the NAHB pointed out, with new households forming at a rate of 1.3 million per year. Though the Sierra Club has advocated higher-density housing in already-developed markets, an NAHB poll showed 82 percent of Americans "preferred purchasing a single family home in an outlying area as opposed to a smaller home or townhouse at the same price located closer to the central city." As long as consumers demanded suburban housing, stated the NAHB, ballot measures limiting suburban growth were meaningless.

FAST FACTS

About 6,790,000 new homes will have been sold in the United States between 1990 and 1999.

(Source: National Association of Home Builders. "Housing Facts, Figures, and Trends," 1998.)

SUCCESSES AND FAILURES

While the NAHB can list many accomplishments, it sometimes fails to fulfill its promise to members to make housing a top priority. For many builders some of the most frustrating obstacles to housing development are posed by environmental regulations. In particular, the Endangered Species Act has kept builders away from land considered ripe for development. One such dispute erupted in Southern California's San Bernardino County. A rare native species of fly, the Delhi Sands flower-loving fly, had been granted endangered status in 1993 because 97 percent of its habitat, the sandy inland dunes of Southern California, had already been destroyed by development. It now occupied only a small area within the county.

Land developers saw this area as important to the economic development of the area's communities, in particular the nearby city of Colton. The California State Assembly and the NAHB came to the aid of these developers, arguing that the fly's endangered status should be lifted by the U.S. Fish and Wildlife Service—it was already so threatened, they argued, that it was not expected to survive past 2000. The NAHB went so far as to challenge the validity of the fly's protected status on the grounds that the fly lived only in California, and the act applied only to interstate commerce. This argument was a particularly crucial one for the future of endangered species legislation—about half of all endangered species live in only one state. The NAHB pushed its appeal of the fly's listing through the courts before it was dismissed by the Supreme Court in 1998; the area remains undeveloped.

Despite such legal setbacks, NAHB councils work diligently on behalf of members. In the 1990s, with the assistance of the NAHB's Women's Council, many women successfully broke into the executive ranks of the home building industry. Builders—mostly small, family-run operations—have traditionally been male-dominated businesses, with women often relegated to marketing or interior design positions. Of the 133,000 women estimated to be working in the home building industry in 1996, very few held executive positions. But the gender gap has gradually narrowed, thanks, many believe, to the women who first broke through gender barriers several years earlier. The NAHB Women's Council works to ensure that it is never again as difficult for qualified women to earn positions of authority in the industry.

FUTURE DIRECTIONS

Much of the NAHB's future depends on the impact of national developments on the housing industry. If the country undergoes an economic recession, for example, with a corresponding adjustment in interest rates, or if regulatory legislation comes before Congress, the NAHB will respond to defend and promote the interests of its members. In addition to reacting to current market variables, the organization also identifies long-term trends in the housing industry and works to keep its members informed and prepared. One recently spotted trend is the boom in home buyers over the age of 55. Older Americans, the fastest-growing market segment with a growth rate of twice the overall population, are generally wealthier and more informed than other potential home buyers. The NAHB plans to assist members in capitalizing on this emerging market segment.

Another growing trend in the housing industry is "green" building: building homes with sustainable materials that employ energy-efficient features such as built-in kitchen recycling centers and composting toilets. Until the late 1990s the movement consisted of a series of local programs driven by consumer demand that were sparked in 1991 after the city of Austin, Texas, created the first city-funded green building program. The NAHB, with help from the Environmental Protection Agency (EPA), has given the movement national attention by sponsoring the first annual National Green Building Conference, held in Denver in April of 1999. Billed as "the first conference on resource-efficient construction for the mainstream home builder," the event presented builders with information about how to make homes more environmentally sensitive.

GROUP RESOURCES

The NAHB's Web site, http://www.nahb.com, is one of the most comprehensive sources of information about the organization's activities and interests. The site contains links to both the Research Center and the Home Builders' Institute, as well as links to government agencies whose decisions affect the housing industry. Some of the information on the NAHB Web site, however, is accessible only to NAHB members. For further information about the NAHB, contact the Public Affairs Division at (202) 368-5242, ext. 253.

GROUP PUBLICATIONS

The NAHB releases a vast number of publications. Of particular interest to the public is its semimonthly newsletter, *Nation's Building News*, which provides the latest information on issues in the housing industry. Other periodical publications include *Builder Magazine* and *Housing Economics*. Most of the councils within the NAHB also publish periodicals that focus on certain aspects of the industry—the Multifamily Council, for example, publishes *Hotline*, providing the latest news on markets, sources of financing for multifamily projects, legislative issues, and management.

The Economics Department of the NAHB is a source of many different reports on the state of the industry, including the *Housing Opportunity Index*; *Existing Home Prices*; and *Housing Affordability and Interest Rates*. Most publications of broad public interest, however—such as press releases and *Housing Facts, Figures, and Trends*—are published by the Public Affairs Division. A few NAHB publications are written in conjunction with federal agencies, such as the *NAHB/OSHA Jobsite Safety Handbook*.

Many NAHB publications can be viewed or downloaded from the organization's Web site. For further information about NAHB publications, contact Public Affairs at (202) 822-0406.

BIBLIOGRAPHY

Building Better Communities through Regulatory Reform: A Guide to Regulatory Change. U.S. Department of Housing and Urban Development, 1987.

Burkitt, Janet. "'Green Guides' Encourage Earth-Friendly Building." *Seattle Times*, 13 June 1998.

Egan, Timothy. "Dreams of Fields: The New Politics of Urban Sprawl." *New York Times*, 14 November 1998.

Freedman, Allan. "Property Rights Advocates Climb the Hill to Success." *Congressional Quarterly Weekly Report*, 25 October 1997.

Harris, Sandra Ann. "Building Women: More and More Run the Show for Major Building Firms but Some Sexism Remains." *San Francisco Examiner*, 22 March 1998.

Hays, R. Allen, ed. *Ownership, Control, and the Future of Housing Policy*. Westport, Conn.: Greenwood Press, 1993.

Iovine, Julie V. "When 'What You See Is All You Get,' What Does $620,000 Buy?" *New York Times*, 23 January 1997.

Miniter, Richard. "We are Suburbanites, Hear Us Roar!" *Seattle Times*, 25 December 1997.

Morcombe, Keith N. *The Residential Development Process: Housing Policy and Theory*. Brookfield, Vt.: Gower Publishing, 1984.

Petit, Jack. *Building Greener Neighborhoods: Trees as Part of the Plan*. Washington, D.C.: Home Builder Press, 1995.

Robinson, Susan G. *Building Together: Investing in Community Infrastructure*. Washington, D.C.: National Association of Counties, 1990.

National Association of Letter Carriers (NALC)

WHAT IS ITS MISSION?

The primary mission of the National Association of Letter Carriers, according to its Public Relations Department, is "to represent the city delivery letter carriers in collective bargaining with the U.S. Postal Service." The NALC represents the interests of its members through contract negotiations, grievance procedures, improvement of working conditions, and lobbying of Congress about bills that directly affect the Postal Service.

HOW IS IT STRUCTURED?

The NALC is a labor union that had approximately 315,000 members in 1999. About 223,000 members are active city-delivery letter carriers; the remainder are retired letter carriers. The NALC consists of 2,909 branches in 50 states, DC, Puerto Rico, Virgin Islands, and Guam. NALC's branches are the equivalent of locals in other unions. Most rank-and-file contact with the union is made through its branches; the election of local and national union officers, the filing of grievances, and votes on proposed union contracts are done on a by-branch basis.

The union is administered by ten resident officers who are elected to four-year terms by the national rank and file. The NALC is headed by a president who oversees the day-to-day operations of the union and who, together with the executive vice president and vice president, formulates union strategy for NALC's contract negotiations with the United States Postal Service (USPS). The NALC secretary-treasurer and assistant secretary-treasurer are responsible for the union's finances.

ESTABLISHED: August 30, 1889
EMPLOYEES: 60
MEMBERS: 315,000

Contact Information:

ADDRESS: 100 Indiana Ave. NW
Washington, DC 20001
PHONE: (202) 393–4695
FAX: (202) 737-1540
E-MAIL: nalcinf@access.digex.net
URL: http://www.nalc.org
PRESIDENT: Vincent R. Sombrotto

When the first convention of the National Association of Letter Carriers was held in August 1890 there were 4,600 members throughout the United States. In 1999 the union had grown to 315,000, including a reported 223,000 active city delivery letter carriers. (United States Postal Service)

The director of City Delivery works on issues directly affecting the delivery of mail by letter carriers. The director of Safety and Health, the director of Retired Members, the director of Life Insurance, and the Health Benefit Plan director are the four other resident officers.

NALC has 15 regions in the United States, each headed by a national business agent. The regional membership elect business agents, who then work in the NALC Washington, D.C., headquarters. The fifteen business agents and ten resident officers make up the NALC national executive council. There are 50 NALC state asso-

ciations as well, which conduct regular state conventions and work on legislative issues important to letter carriers.

The NALC is affiliated with the AFL-CIO. It is also part of the Communications International, an international association of communications unions.

PRIMARY FUNCTIONS

The most important function of the NALC is to bargain with the United States Postal Service (USPS) for the wages, benefits and working conditions of its members. Collective bargaining agreements have typically been negotiated for four year periods. Because letter carriers are considered federal employees, they are not allowed to strike. If a collective bargaining agreement cannot be reached with the USPS, it goes to binding arbitration.

The NALC handles grievances against the USPS made by letter carriers. A grievance is normally filed when one or more employees at a particular post office branch or group of branches believe that the Postal Service has violated their rights as described in the current collective bargaining agreement. Local leadership then attempts to resolve grievances at the branch level. If it is unable to do so, the issue is passed on to the regional business agent at national headquarters.

On the public front, NALC promotes the USPS as a financially sound entity. This is important work because NALC is a single-employer union, meaning that all its members work for the USPS. Congress regularly threatens to privatize the Postal Service or handicap it through legislation that would strengthen competition from companies like the United Parcel Service (UPS). Because such legislation would pose a potential threat to NALC members as well, the union concentrates a good part of its lobbying efforts on keeping the USPS strong.

PROGRAMS

The NALC is responsible for a number of programs that benefit its members and reach out to local communities. A major union program is the annual NALC National Food Drive, the largest of its kind in the nation, if not the entire world. During the months of April and May, letter carriers throughout the United States collect canned food from postal patrons along their routes. The food remains in the communities in which it is collected, going directly into local food banks. In 1998 the program marked its sixth consecutive year, and letter carriers collected a record 62.5 million pounds of canned goods. That figure included a 10 million-pound donation from Campbell Soup Co. The city of Milwaukee, Wisconsin, brought in the most food, with more than 1.3 millions pounds; Nashville, Tennessee, was number two, collecting 1.14 million pounds.

Every fall the NALC holds its annual Hero of the Year awards ceremony to honor letter carriers who have performed courageous deeds far above the call of their jobs. Letter carriers assist many individuals in the areas they serve: they have put out fires, saved children from drowning, and assisted the elderly with serious medical problems that would have otherwise gone unnoticed. The 1998 winner was a letter carrier in East Syracuse, New York, who noticed smoke coming from a retirement home on his mail route. After instructing passers-by to call the fire department, the letter carrier entered the building, warning residents to leave. He kicked in the door of the apartment where the fire started and found the tenant asleep. Because of the postal employee's prompt action, no lives were lost.

NALC national conventions are held every two years. In 2000 the 62nd convention was scheduled to be held in Chicago, Illinois. Elected delegates from every branch attend these conventions to consider constitutional amendments, deliberate key issues in standing committees, and establish national policy for the NALC. In addition, delegates at every alternate convention nominate national officers for election.

BUDGET INFORMATION

The union does not publish an annual report detailing its yearly budget. However, according to the NALC Public Relations Department, virtually all of the union's budget comes from dues collected from its members.

HISTORY

The National Association of Letter Carriers resulted from the struggle of letter carriers for an eight-hour work day that was waged through much of 1888 and 1889. Finally Some 60 mailmen from 18 states met in Milwaukee, Wisconsin, and on August 30, 1889, passed the resolution that formed the NALC. William Wood of Detroit, Michigan, was the organization's first president. Unfortunately letter carriers from many large cities, like New York and Philadelphia, were not represented at that first meeting, but were brought into the union the following summer. When the first national convention was held in August 1890, the NALC had 52 branches and 4,600 members throughout the United States.

Despite retaliation by the USPS—for example, the postmaster in St. Louis fired all local NALC leaders—the union continued to grow and by 1892 had 335 branches. The first major issue attacked by the union was the eight-hour work day. Although the right to work no longer than eight hours had been granted by the Post Office Department (the precursor to the USPS), it was being systematically ignored at branch post offices throughout the nation. The NALC fought the problem fiercely and won a Supreme Court decision in 1893 that awarded letter carriers $3.5 million in overtime.

In 1895 the U.S. government began restricting the rights of postal workers with the first of a series of executive orders. It forbade postal employees to travel to Washington, D.C., to lobby Congress. In 1902 President Theodore Roosevelt issued his so-called "gag order" which banned all federal employees, mail carriers included, from soliciting Congress individually or through associations, for pay raises or other legislation. The ban lasted until 1912 when the Lloyd-LaFollette Act was passed. The gag order also forbade federal workers from affiliating with any organization that might require workers to strike against the federal government. The measure was aimed specifically at the AFL, which was then considered a dangerous radical group. The NALC finally joined the AFL on September 20, 1917.

The Post Office Department's stance toward the NALC became less adversarial when President Warren Harding appointed William Hays Postmaster General. Hays instituted what he called an "open-door policy toward unions," meeting often with union officials. Relations were so cordial that when Hays resigned, he was made a full-fledged member of the NALC, and he continued as a dues-paying member until his death in 1954.

The onset of the Great Depression brought hard times to union ranks. One of the first actions of President Franklin D. Roosevelt after taking office in 1932 was to cut the wages of letter carriers by 15 percent. Only hard and constant lobbying on the part of the NALC restored the lost earnings in 1935. Mail carrier wages suffered so much during the 1930s that in 1941 Edward Gainor, president of the NALC for 27 years, was ousted from office by disgruntled employees, and replaced by William Doherty. Unfortunately for Doherty, the United States entered World War II that same year. Not only were letter carrier's wages frozen, they were expected to perform additional work as well, such as the delivery of ration books.

Letter carriers finally got their long-awaited pay increases after the war ended. In 1949 the NALC got pay rates for letter carriers equalized throughout the United States. From that point on, all city letter carriers received the same pay, regardless of the size of the community in which they worked.

The administration of President Dwight Eisenhower was a difficult time for the NALC. Eisenhower vetoed a series of pay increases passed by Congress and gave the Post Office Department free reign in its treatment of postal workers. In response, in 1960 the NALC launched a "Crusade for Economic Equality" aimed at educating congressmen and persuading them to pass a pay increase for mailmen. The effort was successful, and Congress managed to override Eisenhower's veto, one of only two presidential vetoes overridden during Eisenhower's eight years in office.

Despite the pay increase, the rate of inflation in the 1960s quickly ate into the wages of mail carriers, particularly in big cities where their incomes approached the poverty level. When President Richard Nixon offered a meager 4.1 percent raise in 1969 protest erupted in the NALC. As the Christmas mail rush neared, Nixon met with NALC president James Rademacher in the White House to look for a compromise. The union had fiercely opposed Nixon's proposed reform of the Post Office Department. The president's plan called for the creation of an independent United States Postal Service that would have dealt directly with postal unions. Congress would

no longer be responsible for providing wages or benefits for postal workers. Rademacher and Nixon agreed that in exchange for a pay raise the NALC would drop its opposition to Post Office reform.

NALC rank-and-file members opposed the compromise and calls for strikes were heard throughout the country. On March 17, 1970, the New York City branch voted to strike; within days employees at other branches had walked out as well. Eventually Nixon had to call out 25,000 soldiers to deliver the mail. The strike finally ended when the government agreed that, as part of postal reform, postal workers would have rights to collective bargaining as defined by the National Labor Relations Board. The 1970 strikes led to the growth of a grassroots movement within the NALC. Direct election of officers was introduced to replace the old proxy system that had kept many rank-and-file members from being able to break into the union's power structure. In 1978 Vincent Sombrotto, the man who had led the New York strike, was elected national president.

In the 1990s the NALC twice went to binding arbitration in its negotiations with the USPS. At the same time, the union developed its own privately owned and administered medical and life insurance plans, which are considered among the best available for federal and postal employees. It also opened its own retirement community in Florida called Nalcrest.

CURRENT POLITICAL ISSUES

Like all labor unions, the NALC is concerned with a number of issues that affect its membership. In fall 1998 the union began negotiating a new contract with the USPS and an increase in letter carrier wages took priority. Previously the union had fought to control automation of the Postal Service, a process that would inevitably have led to layoffs for some workers and changed or increased responsibilities for others. A battle the NALC has waged for some time, and continues to wage, is to prevent the privatization of the USPS.

Case Study: Blocking USPS Privatization

Privatization of USPS has meant two things through the years: a change in USPS structure and a liberalization of federal laws. The USPS is a public governmental body whose guiding principle has been to provide a necessary service for the American public; privatization would transform it into a private business whose guiding principle is operational profitability. Privatization would also mean the liberalization of laws governing the mail so that private companies would be allowed to offer services previously limited to the post office. The NALC has opposed both aspects of postal privatization.

The issue of privatization is as old as the Post Office itself. It arose for the first time in the 1800s when private firms were allowed to transport all types of mail in direct competition with the government-run Post Office Department. These private companies serviced only the most profitable routes, those within and between large cities. The most expensive routes to operate were left for the Post Office, which was required by law to provide the whole nation with uniform service at a uniform price. The problem eventually led to the private express statutes which prohibited private firms from delivering certain types of mail.

By the 1990s the USPS had a monopoly on the delivery of normal first-class mail; the so-called "private express statutes" state that private companies such as FedEx, UPS, and Airborne can only offer to deliver special types of first-class, for example overnight delivery. Furthermore, when private companies deliver first-class mail, they are bound by the "double postage rule" which states they must charge twice as much as the USPS does for the same service. So, for example, UPS is required to charge at least $20 for overnight delivery because the USPS charges at least $10 for the same service. In addition, only the USPS has been allowed to put mail in mailboxes; private firms are required to deliver mail to a person or leave it in the door.

The Postal Reorganization Act of 1970 semi-privatized postal service in the United States. But the USPS, which was formed by the act kept its monopolies on first-class mail and mail box access and postal employees, like the Letter Carriers, continued to be treated more like federal employees than private employees. For example, they were not allowed to strike the USPS. Privatization of the Postal Service was advocated, unsuccessfully, by the administration of President Ronald Reagan who saw it as a way of limiting government presence in the private sector.

The latter half of the 1990s saw the introduction of a new flurry of bills designed to privatize the U.S. mails. Some of the new bills, such as House Resolution 1717, would have eliminated the private express statutes and opened up first-class mail delivery and access to mail boxes to private delivery companies like UPS or Federal Express. It would have transformed the USPS into a completely private corporation as well. Senate Bill 1107 would have eliminated the double postage rule, allowing private companies to offer express services at a lower cost than the USPS. Conversely, House Resolution 198 would have prohibited post offices from offering any but "core" postal services. If passed, post offices could no longer maintain public copy machines or offer packaging services.

The Northrup Amendment to the 1997 House Treasury Appropriations Bill would have limited USPS's international mail service, which was seen as unfairly competing with UPS. In Summer 1998 the most critical proposal was House Resolution 22, known as the Postal Reform Act of 1997, which would have eliminated the double postage rule and opened private mail boxes to pri-

FAST FACTS

On average, 24 pieces of mail are delivered to each U.S. household every week. This amounts to approximately 3.4 billion pieces of mail delivered across the United States each week.

(Source: United States Postal Service. "Postal Facts," May 1998.)

vate delivery firms. Newly instated Postmaster General Bill Henderson even commented publicly that he believed it was only a matter of time until the USPS lost its historic monopoly on first-class mail.

Public Impact

NALC has worked against Congress's efforts to privatize the delivery of first-class mail through its lobbying arm as well as by mobilizing its members to write to members of Congress. Union opposition has been aimed at protecting the USPS, its members, and the American public. NALC has pointed out that opening segments of mail delivery to private companies would lead to a situation similar to that in the nineteenth century. Private companies would "cherry pick" the choicest, most profitable routes, leaving the USPS to make do with the rest. For letter carriers higher USPS expenses would mean layoffs and wage cuts. For the public at large, this new postal market competition would result in higher USPS rates across the board as the Postal Service struggled to provide uniform service as required by law. Inevitably those individuals most hurt would be Americans in lightly populated, rural areas and poor Americans in neighborhood and communities the private companies chose not to service.

SUCCESSES AND FAILURES

The NALC considers its role in reforming the Hatch Act one of its most important successes. The original act, passed in 1937, put tight restrictions on the political activities of federal employees and their families. They were not allowed to participate in election campaigns, serve as a delegate to a party convention, raise money for a candidate or issue on a ballot, or run for partisan political office. Hatch Act reforms were passed in the late 1980s only to be vetoed by President George Bush.

Another bill, passed and signed into law by Bill Clinton in 1993, while not removing all restrictions from political activity by federal employees, did relax the restrictions considerably. USPS employees still cannot run for partisan office or raise campaign funds for a partisan candidate from non-union sources. However, they can now work in partisan campaigns, can hold office in a political party, and can serve as delegates to a party convention. In addition, there are no restrictions on activity in nonpartisan elections.

FUTURE DIRECTIONS

As the twentieth century was drawing to an end, the NALC was concerned about building a solid relationship with the new Postmaster General, Bill Henderson. In the view of the NALC, relations with previous postmasters general had been characterized by suspicion, a lack of forthrightness, and an unwillingness to bargain in good faith. Those qualities led to an inability to reach agreements on NALC contracts without going to binding arbitration. The union remained hopeful that the new postmaster general will be more receptive to the wealth of knowledge the NALC believes it can offer to the USPS in helping the government agency remain competitive in both the national and international market.

GROUP RESOURCES

The NALC maintains an informative Web site where union news is posted regularly. Back issues of the *NALC Bulletin*, the internal union newsletter, *The Postal Record*, the union's monthly magazine, and union press releases are also available. The NALC Web site can be accessed at http://www.nalc.org. Many NALC branches maintain Web pages as well.

GROUP PUBLICATIONS

The two main publications of the NALC are *The Postal Record*, the union's monthly magazine, and the *NALC Bulletin*, an internal newsletter that appears approximately every two weeks. Annual subscriptions to *The Postal Record* are available for $16 by writing: Membership Dept., National Association of Letter Carriers, 100 Indiana Ave. NW, Washington DC 20001-2144. Selected articles from *The Postal Record* are posted on the NALC Web site. Subscriptions are not available for the *NALC Bulletin,* however it is available at the NALC Web site.

BIBLIOGRAPHY

Adie, Douglas K. *Monopoly Mail: Privatizing the United States Postal Service.* New Brunswick, N.J.: Transaction Publishers, 1989.

"Carriers Work a Food Miracle on Streets of America." *The Postal Record,* July 1998.

Coleman, Rufus. "Local Mail Carriers Join in U.S. Protest." *Dallas Morning News*, 20 June 1996.

Conkey, Kathleen. *The Postal Precipice: Can the U.S. Postal Service Be Saved?* Washington, D.C.: Center for the Study of Responsive Law, 1983.

Cullinan, Gerald. *The Post Office Department.* New York: Frederick A. Praeger, 1968.

Fuller, Wayne E. *The American Mail: Enlarger of the Common Life.* Chicago: University of Chicago Press, 1972.

"Postmaster General Sends the Wrong Signal on Privatization." *NALC Bulletin,* 1 September 1998.

"Proud to Serve." *The Postal Record,* July 1998.

Sorkin, Alan L. *The Economics of the Postal System.* Lexington, Mass.: Lexington Books, 1980.

Vincent, Stuart. "Posting a Food Drive Record." *Newsday,* 15 May 1996.

National Association of Life Underwriters (NALU)

WHAT IS ITS MISSION?

According to the official mission statement of the National Association of Life Underwriters (NALU), the organization's mission is "to improve the business environment, enhance the professional skills, and promote the ethical conduct of agents and others engaged in insurance and related financial services who assist the public in achieving financial security and independence."

An association of professional insurance agents, the NALU concentrates on the areas of "legislation, education and reputation." For over a century, NALU programs have sought to influence state and federal regulation of insurance; to provide its members with training in product lines, business skills, and ethical practices; and to promote a positive public image of agents and the insurance industry.

ESTABLISHED: June 18, 1890
EMPLOYEES: 100
MEMBERS: 108,000
PAC: Life Underwriter's Political Action Committee (LUPAC)

Contact Information:

ADDRESS: 1922 F St. NW
    Washington, DC 20006-4387
PHONE: (202) 331-6000
TOLL FREE: (888) 515-6258
FAX: (202) 835-9601
E-MAIL: bhollis@nalu.org
URL: http://www.nalu.org
PRESIDENT: Larry M. Lambert
EXECUTIVE VICE PRESIDENT; CEO: Arthur D. Kraus

HOW IS IT STRUCTURED?

The NALU is a federation of local associations, the "umbrella" organization for some 950 state and local agent groups, ranging from 25 to 2,500 members each. Local associations operate in all 50 states, as well as Puerto Rico, the Virgin Islands, Guam, and the District of Columbia. There is also a European association that is primarily for agents who serve Americans living abroad. While NALU membership and interests were originally restricted to the specialty of life insurance, its bylaws have been amended to include professionals dealing in other kinds of insurance, and to address all aspects of the business.

National officers are elected at an annual convention, by delegates representing the members through their local associations. A 12-member board of trustees serves for a term of two years, while the president, secretary, and treasurer each serve one-year terms. The immediate past president, and the president-elect for the coming year, also serve as voting officers. Day-to-day management of the association is directed by a permanent executive vice president and CEO appointed by the board.

The national organization is divided into 16 specialized committees and conferences. Their general areas of responsibility are: public relations (the Community Service and Public Relations Committees); member services (the Membership, Associations, Convention, Professional Development, and Recognition of Quality and Achievement Committees, along with the Association Executives Advisory Council); political activity (the State Law and Legislation, Political Involvement, and Federal Law and Legislation Committees, as well as the organization's political action committee); and industry affairs (the Field Practices Committee, Association for Advanced Life Underwriting, Association of Health Insurance Agents, and a conference of field managers known as GAMA International). In 1996, the group formed a subsidiary, the NALU Service Corporation (NALUSC), to centralize all for-profit activities and separate them from other NALU programs.

PRIMARY FUNCTIONS

The NALU serves its member agents in many ways. On an individual level, it provides training programs to help agents improve and update their professional skills, as well as forums, where agents can share experiences and ideas with their colleagues. More important, the NALU represents their common, collective interests in several crucial arenas: within the industry itself, before the general public, and between the industry and government. Like any professional association, it seeks to maintain the profitability and competitive strength of its membership. The NALU has also been instrumental in developing and enforcing ethical standards within the field, and generates publicity promoting a positive image of the insurance business as a whole, to consumers and lawmakers alike.

In state and national government, the NALU has been an influential, well-funded, and well-organized lobbying force on laws affecting insurance. It is a major contributor to congressional campaigns, and maintains a grassroots network of member-contacts with legislators, as well as a full-time staff of lobbyists. Because NALU has first-hand knowledge of industry issues, it often serves as an unofficial expert advisor to lawmakers and government agencies. NALU uses industry data, produced by its research programs, to support legislation that serves the interest of its members. In addition

to maintaining a substantial presence on Capitol Hill, the national association also devotes considerable resources to strengthening state and local NALU chapters, and coordinating political efforts at the local level. Under the 1945 McCarran-Ferguson Act, the regulation of insurance is primarily a state function. The act gave the industry a limited exemption from federal antitrust statutes, and established that state regulations would prevail in any case not specifically covered by federal law. As a result, state legislatures and regulatory commissions tend to be far more significant to insurance agents than to those in other professions, and are a major focus of NALU lobbying.

NALU's campaign-funding arm, LUPAC, is the largest political action committee (PAC) in the insurance industry. Out of 4,079 federally registered PACs, it ranked twenty-sixth in receipts and twenty-eighth in disbursements in 1996, placing it in the top one-half percent of all PACs in the country. In the 1995–96 election cycle, LUPAC contributed over $1.3 million to a total of 407 U.S. House and Senate candidates, 329 of whom were elected. At least 22 percent of NALU members contributed to the organization's two-year fund-raising goal of $2.2 million.

Through its State and Federal Law and Legislation committees, and its full-time legal staff, the NALU monitors developments in government, advances its positions on insurance-related legislation, and organizes grassroots action by its members. In addition, a Political Involvement Committee (LUPIC) organizes a network of members to serve as personal liaisons with lawmakers. LUPIC established legislative contacts for 98 percent of the 105th Congress, which was elected in 1996, and included 90 freshman lawmakers.

Other NALU projects help advance its political goals. For example, NALU research programs serve not only to educate members, but also to inform legislators on industry conditions. NALU staff members routinely draft model laws that express the association's policies; these are submitted to lawmakers, and portions of them are often reproduced in the bills presented for legislative debate. NALU public relations programs also reinforce the lobbying effort, by promoting goodwill and ensuring that the association's viewpoint is well-represented in the media.

PROGRAMS

Through its committees, the NALU sponsors a wide range of projects to advance its stated mission. It provides its members with extensive training programs on product lines, sales techniques, and business strategies, and conducts conferences on such specialties as life underwriting, health insurance, and field management. Through the Field Practices Committee, it promotes a professional code of ethics, and involves itself in disciplinary proceedings when an agent's ethics are questioned.

Public relations programs include the Media Outreach Network, in which members volunteer as contact-people for local media outlets whenever news stories involve the insurance business. As part of the network, the volunteers represent the NALU and help explain the organization's policies. As of 1997, 647 such media managers were in place, from 415 local associations. The national organization also encourages local chapters to develop volunteer and service projects in their own communities.

BUDGET INFORMATION

The NALU reported a total income of $15,286,286 for the fiscal year ending August 1997. Fifty-two percent of that total came from member dues, and another 31 percent from the sale of advertising in the NALU publication *Life Association News*; the rest is listed as derived from "product sales" (primarily training materials sold to members), "convention," and "other [sources]." The breakdown of expenditures includes: 28 percent for publications, 24 percent on legislative and regulatory activities, and 11 percent for public relations programs. NALU administrative costs accounted for nine percent of spending, while another 14 percent went to maintain state and local associations. The final 14 percent was divided between educational programs and the national convention.

HISTORY

The NALU was organized on June 18, 1890, at a meeting of 70 life insurance agents at the Parker House Hotel in Boston, Massachusetts. In its first 15 years, the NALU concentrated on expanding its membership base and by 1905, it had 2,302 members, in 45 state and local chapters. During this time, the organization also promoted higher standards of conduct.

The association faced a crisis in 1905, when allegations that many of the largest insurance agencies were guilty of unethical business practices and wasteful mismanagement, prompted government investigations. The NALU, already an advocate for reform, moved to the forefront as credible voice for the embattled industry. Its leaders noted the rapid decline of public confidence and trust, as well as its members' fears that the clamor for reform would go too far, leading to intrusive over-regulation. To address these needs, the NALU crafted a four-point response: 1) to "seize every opportunity to influence all proposed legislation affecting the business," assuring that it is "timely, well-thought-out and highly coordinated;" 2) to strengthen and enlarge the NALU

BUDGET:
1997 NALU Revenue

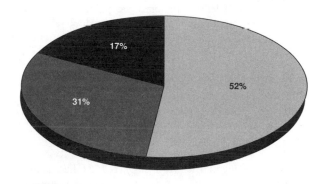

■ 52%: Member dues

■ 31%: Sale of advertising in NALU newsletter

■ 17%: Product sales, convention, and other sources

1997 NALU Expenses

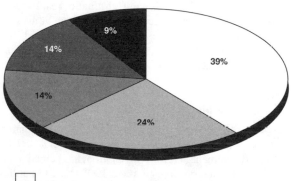

□ 39%: Publications and public relations programs

■ 24%: Legislative and regulatory activities

■ 14%: Educational programs and the national convention

■ 14%: State and local associations

■ 9%: Administrative costs

itself, and extend its operations; 3) to "seek the cooperation of the [insurance] companies in launching publicity campaigns to restore the tarnished image of the business and educate the public in an appreciation of the value of life insurance;" and 4) to "raise the occupation of agent to that of a profession," by establishing qualifying credentials, offering training in ethical sales practices, and disciplining dishonest or incompetent agents (Norris, 72). This four-point program helped restore the industry's public image and provided the framework for NALU activities ever since.

The NALU soon assumed a leading role in agent education. In 1916 it sponsored the publication of the first standard textbook in the field, S. S. Huebner's *Life Insurance: A Textbook*, and established the American College of Life Underwriters for professional training in 1927. The NALU worked to promoted self-regulation and ethical conduct, and through its state associations contributed to the development of regulatory and licensing standards for the industry.

Legislative Action

On the legislative front, the NALU had grown strong enough by 1913 to achieve a major victory in the legislation that created the federal income tax. The original bill had considered dividends from insurance policies to be taxable income, but the NALU lobbied to make them tax exempt. Two NALU officers met with President Woodrow Wilson at the White House to argue their case, the only representatives of the industry to receive such an audience. Later that week, NALU scored a victory when the bill's language was changed to include the exemption (Norris, 95–6). While few of its efforts have yielded such dramatic results, the NALU has maintained access and influence at all levels of government. The association supported the McCarren-Ferguson Act, and has opposed efforts to repeal it. The act's importance has caused the NALU to give almost as much priority to lobbying efforts in state houses and regulatory commissions as to its efforts in Washington, D.C.

In terms of public relations, the NALU's campaign to expose and punish wrongdoers in the field, and its active involvement in reform legislation, has helped rehabilitate the industry's image since 1905. NALU publicity has consistently promoted an image of agents as responsible business people, active in their communities and concerned with the public's best interest. The association's positions on regulatory issues, for example, are often presented as efforts to protect consumer rights and privileges, rather than to advance the interests of the membership.

The NALU itself has seldom been the target of media or government scrutiny, except in late 1940s. At that time, Nola Patterson was an outspoken NALU member who believed the rank-and-file force of field-agents was not adequately represented in the organization, and charged that it was dominated by agency executives and managers whose primary loyalty was to their companies. Denied the opportunity to address the 1948 convention, she filed charges against 183 insurance companies with the National Labor Relations Board (NLRB), alleging that the NALU was a "labor organization" under the Wagner and Taft-Hartley Acts, and that the companies'

managers were engaged in unfair labor practices by exerting control in an association of workers.

The NALU countered that it was a "professional association," not a union, and had never engaged in collective bargaining on behalf of members. Before the NLRB ruled on the case, a settlement was reached in which the NALU admitted none of the charges and maintained its nonunion status, but agreed to eliminate programs (notably the Agency Practices Agreement) in which NALU conferences addressed management issues and agent compensation. (Norris, 210–13).

NALU established its current Washington headquarters in 1960, and founded LUPAC in 1966. Membership has declined in recent years (down to 108,000 from a high of 140,000 at the time of its 1990 centennial), reflecting an industry-wide trend of reorganization in response to a fast-changing marketplace. While it is a concern, the drop in numbers does not necessarily indicate a decline in the NALU's position in the industry, or its effectiveness as a lobbying force.

CURRENT POLITICAL ISSUES

On both the state and federal level, the NALU is involved in legislative and policy issues that affect the insurance industry. In recent years, its primary concerns have included: banking policy, tort reform, long-term care insurance, accelerated death benefits, corporate-owned life insurance, pension regulations, natural disaster protection, and the taxation of income from various insurance products. These types of issues have a great impact on the insurance community, where even small changes in insurance regulations can affect a company's long-term planning and profitability. But these issues also affect the American public, who purchase and rely on insurance in times of need. Even so, it is rare to have an insurance topic be the subject of heated public controversy.

Case Study: Health-Care Reform

One high-profile exception to this rule is the long-running national debate over healthcare—and even in this case, the role played by the NALU and its allies has been far less visible than those of other concerned parties, such as the American Medical Association, the large health-insurance providers, and reform-minded activists.

In its first term, the Clinton administration made healthcare reform a high priority. Amid wide concern about spiraling medical costs, and with at least 15 percent of the population either ineligible for health care insurance or unable to afford it, President Clinton pledged to reinvent the health care system, guaranteeing universal coverage and more-efficient operation. In a major defeat, the president was unable to get any comprehensive reform plan through Congress; but the issue became the subject of vigorous—and continuing—debate.

Even before the administration released its proposal in September of 1993, the NALU and other agent associations responded to leaked and rumored "indications that the Clinton plan will have little or no role for [insurance] agents," and would "severely limit or eliminate" their place in the health care system (NU, 9/13/93). A grassroots NALU campaign developed around one feature of the plan, the creation of regional health alliances to regulate health coverage. As proposed, the alliances would study local needs, then certify a small number of companies to offer medical insurance in each region, requiring them to offer a standard benefit package and to accept all applicants, regardless of medical status or history. The NALU objected to these alliances on the grounds that they would: eliminate competition in health insurance; deprive consumers of the savings and choices that competition encouraged; create significant unemployment in the insurance business (particularly in underwriting departments, which would be unnecessary under universal coverage); and become another level of government bureaucracy, leading to waste and higher costs for all.

In April of 1994, NALU Vice President and CEO William Regan III reported that while the lobbying efforts were going as the organization had hoped, the issue was still in transition. He noted that by November—two months after the proposal was released—NALU member-agents had held more than 250 meetings with members of Congress on the issue in their home states and districts. On November 16, 1993, more than 200 agents visited Washington, D.C., to meet with 325 congressional members. And back in the congressional districts, there were over 120 meetings between agents and congressional representatives from the time Congress adjourned in late November and reconvened in January.

The level of this grassroots response reflects the scope and effectiveness of NALU political activity. While it supported neither the Clinton plan nor any of the alternatives offered by Congress, NALU's lobbying presence gave it a voice in each proposal, just as each proposal included elements that the NALU had advocated. In the continuing debate, the NALU is committed to "the goal of assuring universal, affordable health insurance coverage for all Americans," and to reforming healthcare; but it tends to prescribe careful adjustments to the present system, rather than radical changes. It opposes any nationalized, government-run health care system, arguing that the private-sector insurance market, augmented by programs like Medicare and Medicaid, can best meet consumers' needs (*L&R Issues*).

SUCCESSES AND FAILURES

As in the health care debate, the NALU's political effectiveness is measured not only in clear-cut successes but also in its ability to maintain a constant, influential

FAST FACTS

When the NALU was founded in 1890, the total annual income of U.S. life insurance companies was slightly less than $1 billion a year. In 1986 U.S. life insurance companies took in $286 billion and ten years later in 1996, the figure was $546 billion.

(Source: *Life Insurance Factbook,* 1997.)

voice on industry-related issues. By taking a proactive, bipartisan approach, forming long-term relationships with legislators, and being flexible in its positions, the NALU is often able to affect the law. But, this process can be a long one, with setbacks along the way. For example, NALU and other agent associations, particularly the Independent Insurance Agents of America, spent years working against bills that would allow banks to compete with insurers in the sale of certain insurance products. Then, two Supreme Court decisions (*Nations-Bank of North Carolina, N.A. v. Variable Annuity Life Insurance Co.,* 1995, and *Barnett Bank of Marion County, N.A. v. Nelson,* 1996) ruled that national banks could sell fixed and variable annuities, and that state laws prohibiting such sales were preempted by federal law. Despite the ruling, agent groups have continued lobbying, working on the regulations that govern these transactions, in order to strengthen the competitive position of agents. Along the way, they have achieved restrictions on which banks may participate and what sales techniques they may use, as well as provisions allowing agents to sell certain financial products in competition with banks. Adjusting to changed conditions, the agent associations have been able to diminish some of the threat to their members' interests.

FUTURE DIRECTIONS

Aside from continuing its current programs and maintaining its vigilance on legislative and regulatory issues, the NALU has begun drives to increase both its total membership, and the level of participation by existing members. Industry changes in the 1990s, especially reductions in the recruitment of new agents, have forced agent associations to eliminate some programs that were no longer considered critical, and to find more effective ways of financing their activities. In February 1998 the NALU formed a strategic alliance with two of its fellow

FAST FACTS

Approximately 22 percent of Americans have no life insurance coverage.

(Source: *Life Association News,* November 1998.)

agent associations, the Independent Insurance Agents of America (IIAA) and the Life Underwriter Training Council (LUTC). Representing a total membership of 500,000, the alliance will coordinate programs for education and legislation, combining the resources of the three groups.

GROUP RESOURCES

NALU's Web site at http://www.agents-online.com/nalu, is primarily a resource for its member-agents, allowing them to access industry data, professional news, and legislative and regulatory reports. Research inquiries and publication requests should be directed to Public Relations at the national office in Washington, D.C.

GROUP PUBLICATIONS

Introduced in 1906, the monthly magazine *Life Association News (LAN)* provides NALU members with industry news, instructional articles on sales and management techniques, and legislative updates. While it remains the primary house organ of NALU, *LAN* has

recently been supplemented by a video newsmagazine, *NALU Video Journal.* The association also distributes several newsletters, including *NALU Outlook, LUPIC Washington Update,* and *LUPIC LifeLines,* and periodically issues legislative Action Alerts to rally grassroots action by members. A book-length history of the organization, *Voices From the Field* , by George Norris, was published in 1989 to celebrate NALU's centennial. In addition, the NALU prints several booklets and pamphlets, both for members and consumers, on insurance products and issues. For information on the group's political activities, two annual publications, the *Digest of Committee and Conference Activities* and the handbook of current *Legislative and Regulatory Issues,* are particularly useful. Requests for NALU publications should be directed to the Public Relations staff at 1922 F St. NW, Washington, DC, 20006-4387, or by phone at (202) 331-6000.

BIBLIOGRAPHY

Arndt, Sheril. "NALU Boasts Impressive Lobbying Record." *National Underwriter Life & Health,* 18 September 1989.

Atkinson, Bill, and Robert M. Garson. "Insurers Outlobbied Bankers." *American Banker,* 6 November 1991.

Brostoff, Steven. "Battle Lines Drawn in Health Reform." *National Underwriter Property & Casualty,* 13 September 1993.

———. "Regan Satisfied with Agents Reform Battle So Far." *National Underwriter Life & Health,* April 11, 1994.

Fisher, Mary Jane. "Agent Groups Are Hefty Campaign Contributors." *National Underwriter Life & Health,* 5 April 1993.

King, Carole. "NALU Undertakes Strategic Plan to Broaden Membership." *National Underwriter Life & Health,* 16 September 1996.

Norris, George W. *Voices from the Field: A History of the National Association of Life Underwriters.* Washington, D.C.: NALU, 1989.

Zinkewicz, Phil, Robert E. Vagley, et al. "Insurance . . . at the Crossroads." *Forbes,* 17 October 1988.

National Association of Manufacturers (NAM)

WHAT IS ITS MISSION?

According to the Web site of the National Association of Manufacturers (NAM), its mission is "enhance the competitiveness of manufacturers and improve living standards for working Americans by shaping a legislative and regulatory environment conducive to U.S. economic growth, and to increase understanding among policymakers, the media and the general public about the importance of manufacturing to America's economic strength." Primarily NAM seeks to promote the growth of the manufacturing industry through public education and the petitioning of legislators.

HOW IS IT STRUCTURED?

NAM is led by a 220-member, annually elected board of directors and a president. Directors' terms generally run from three years to a maximum of seven years. The board of directors invites member input through surveys and meetings and works with the president to establish NAM policies. The president is then responsible for the organization's day-to-day operations and decision-making.

With much of its lobbying efforts focused at the federal level, NAM maintains its main office in Washington, D.C., with 10 regional offices spread throughout the United States. NAM works together with a network of affiliated groups such as manufacturing trade associations and state manufacturing and employer associations. Rather than individuals, the NAM's membership is made up of more than 14,000 companies and subsidiaries

ESTABLISHED: January 1895
EMPLOYEES: 180
MEMBERS: 14,000
PAC: None

Contact Information:
ADDRESS: 1331 Pennsylvania Ave. NW
     Washington, DC 20004
PHONE: (202) 637-3000
TOLL FREE: (800) 736-6627
FAX: (202) 637-3182
E-MAIL: manufacturing@nam.org
URL: http://www.nam.org
PRESIDENT: Jerry Jasinowski

FAST FACTS

Federal regulations and legal costs impose an estimated $750 billion—about $7,500 per employee—on business.

(Source: The Manufacturing Institute. "America Needs a Raise—and How To Get It." Washington, D.C.: National Association of Manufacturers, 1997.)

across the nation, including about 10,000 small manufacturers. The companies that NAM represents run the gamut of the manufacturing industry and may have as few as 10 employee to several thousand. According to NAM, its membership accounts for about 85 percent of the goods manufactured in the United States and employs more than 18 million workers.

The Manufacturer's Institute is the educational and research arm of NAM. The institute employs scientists and other researchers whose work is aimed at ensuring that policymakers and the media gain a better understanding of NAM's positions. Supplementing the work of NAM are a number of more specialized organizations that function more or less as subsidiaries of the parent organization. These subsidiaries are engaged in various activities such as research, public relations and education, and legislative reform. The most important of these groups is the Associations Council. Made up of more than 215 different manufacturing trade associations, the Associations Council provides a mechanism for industry or product specific manufacturing trade associations to join with NAM to develop legislative, regulatory, economic, and educational policies. With its own board of directors and three representatives on NAM's board, the Associations Council is an essential component of NAM's strategy, enabling it to marshal the immense resources of about 60,000 manufacturers across the United States.

PRIMARY FUNCTIONS

As NAM's primary focus is to promote a pro-growth, pro-manufacturing policy agenda virtually all of its activities center around government legislation. It lobbies Congress to support new legislation that is beneficial to its members or stirs up opposition to bills it believes will have an adverse effect on industry.

NAM's efforts to influence policy range from the grassroots level—members are encouraged to write to Congress expressing their views—to national media campaigns. In addition to national advertising campaigns, NAM uses its influence to have its positions reported in newspapers and magazines across the country, as well as on influential television programs such as ABC's *Nightline* and PBS's *Nightly Business Report*. Through press conferences, interviews, and opinion editorials, NAM promotes the manufacturing industry and works to discredit charges against it.

Through its *Briefing* newsletter and other publications, NAM keeps its membership informed about all of the issues affecting manufacturers and outlines the steps it is taking to promote their interests. In many cases, this involves a considerable educational effort as many members rely on NAM to analyze how complex legislation might affect them.

PROGRAMS

To further its goals, NAM sponsors a variety of programs and campaigns. Most are centered around providing additional opportunities for growth to its members. A key component of NAM's strategy to promote support and understanding of manufacturing is the annual National Manufacturing Week expo and program in Chicago, Illinois, which the NAM has been co-sponsoring since 1991. Attended by about 65,000 manufacturing engineers and executives, the National Manufacturing Week exposition typically features up to 1,800 exhibitors and is considered to be the most comprehensive industrial trade show in North America. Among the shows that are part of National Manufacturing Week are the National Design Engineering Show and Conference, the National Plant Engineering and Management Show and Conference, the National Industrial Automation, Integration and Control Show and Conference, and the Manufacturing Enterprise IT Solutions Center. The exposition also features talks by technical experts from the world's leading manufacturers, major universities, industry publications and consulting firms. With the extension of the North American Free Trade Agreement (NAFTA) to Mexico, NAM is also sponsoring a Mexican Manufacturing Week aimed at promoting U.S. technology to management and technical staff from major industries in Mexico.

One of NAM's newest efforts is the Center for Workforce Success. Dedicated to helping U.S. companies educate and train their employees, the center includes an industry center, a school-to-work program designed and driven by manufacturers, a national skill standards project, and special publications. In addition the organization sponsors the NAM Awards for Excellence that rewards the most effective manufacturing team in the United States each year.

With the globalization of U. S. trade, NAM facilitates forums for international conferences such as the one held at the Hong Kong convention center, July 3, 1998. President Clinton spoke to Hong Kong community and business leaders about the city's potential as an international port. (Photograph by Anat Givon, AP/Wide World Photo)

BUDGET INFORMATION

NAM has an annual budget of approximately $16 million. This is used to cover employee salaries, public relations, and day-to-day operations. Membership dues account for 86 percent of the budget; meetings, investments, and publications account for the remaining 14 percent. Additional funds for specific projects are raised as needed.

HISTORY

Founded in Cincinnati, Ohio, in 1895 while the United States was in the midst of a deep recession, NAM was originally conceived as a vehicle for helping U.S. manufacturers locate new markets for their products in other countries. The first meeting was held January 22–25, 1895, and was attended by a total of 583 association and manufacturing executives from across the nation. Among the objectives adopted by the organizing convention were to maintain and supply the domestic market with U.S. products, extend foreign trade, and develop reciprocal trade relations between the United States and foreign governments.

The name National Association of Manufacturers of the United States of America was formally adopted at the

next annual convention in January of 1896. The fledgling association moved quickly to exert its influence, successfully pushing for higher tariffs and bilateral reciprocity (known as "two-way trade") during the McKinley administration (1897–1901). It also called for the creation of the Department of Commerce, which was established in 1903. NAM's determination to keep a lid on labor unrest also manifested itself early on with the establishment of an internal department to advocate open shop labor policies.

During the first two decades of its existence, NAM focused on such issues as education, safety, and fiscal responsibility. Its call for vocational education programs in 1910 and 1911 led to the adoption of such programs in schools throughout the country, and in 1916 it cooperated with three other associations to establish a program to standardize safety devices. NAM also called for workmen's compensation laws two years before they were advocated by the American Federation of Labor.

The Great Depression

In October of 1929 the New York stock market crashed, plunging the United States into the Great Depression. Although many factors contributed to the Depression, industrial overproduction and the lack of a social safety net are generally considered to have played key roles both in provoking the Depression and causing it to drag on throughout the 1930s. The fact was that U.S. manufacturers were producing more goods than people could afford to buy.

In 1934, alarmed by the threat of government interference posed by President Franklin Roosevelt's New Deal proposals, NAM launched a major public relations campaign "for the dissemination of sound American doctrines to the public." Over the next 13 years, NAM spent more than $15 million on leaflets, movie shorts, radio speeches, educational films, and other public relations efforts including a daily NAM column which appeared in 260 newspapers.

During World War II (1939–45), much of NAM's activity revolved around boosting production and raising worker morale. Its efforts included a plant-level employee morale program entitled "Soldiers of Production," community relations activities, and programs to help companies deal with such wartime problems as priorities, allocations, and labor relations. After the war, in 1947, NAM helped push through the Taft-Hartley Act, overriding President Harry Truman's veto. The act placed new restrictions on the rights of workers and gave manufacturers more flexibility in labor relations.

The Postwar Boom

With the end of World War II, the United States emerged as the world's predominant industrial power, accounting for half the world's gross domestic product (GDP). As many economists point out, the American "decline" in the latter part of the century had more to do with other countries rebuilding themselves and resuming their positions on the world stage than with any loss of U.S. economic prowess. Nevertheless, NAM continued to wage war on the perceived inefficiencies, calling for an end to excessive government spending, tax reductions, reevaluation of U.S. labor policies, and steps to increase international trade. On this last point, NAM scored a victory in 1962 with the enactment of the Trade Expansion Act, which resulted in lower tariffs.

On other fronts NAM was more proactive; it supported the Civil Rights Act of 1964, and conducted seminars around the country to help employers understand their responsibilities under Title VII of the new law. NAM also cosponsored Equal Employment Opportunity-Affirmative Action conferences in 1968.

Revitalizing American Industry

As the boom years of the 1950s and 1960s subsided into the financial decline of the 1970s and 1980s, NAM redoubled its efforts to promote its pro-business agenda. To increase its presence in the nation's capital, the association moved its headquarters from New York to Washington, D.C., in 1974, and in 1978 it successfully derailed union-backed labor law reform legislation that was killed in a Senate filibuster. The legislation would have provided unions with what NAM called unfair legal powers

in organizing activities, and would, so NAM claimed, have had adverse effects on the economy.

In October of 1979 NAM launched its "Program to Revitalize American Industry," releasing a six-point "Revitalization Agenda" aimed at reducing inflation and reinvigorating manufacturing and the economy. Three of the agenda's six points were enacted by Congress in 1981. NAM also led the way in urging the Treasury Department to reverse its exchange rate policy and conduct a major international effort to lower the value of the dollar—its excessive value being seen as a major contributor to the massive U.S. trade deficit. In the late 1980s NAM began working closely with the Canadian Manufacturers Association to promote free trade, playing a major role in the ratification of the historic U.S.-Canada free trade accord.

By the end of the Reagan and Bush presidencies in 1992, NAM had been so successful in pushing its agenda that many of its opinions were seemingly accepted without question by politicians, the media, and the general public. Its massive and well-orchestrated public relations efforts helped to propel NAM into the forefront of the pro-business lobby. NAM lobbyists helped defeat President Bill Clinton's 1993 BTU tax scheme, prevented the enactment of striker replacement legislation, and helped override a presidential veto of securities litigation reform legislation in 1995. In 1997 NAM pushed for and achieved a tax break and established the Center for Workforce Success.

CURRENT POLITICAL ISSUES

NAM's agenda is simple: to promote economic growth and protect the interests of American manufacturers. Anything that impinges on the ability of manufacturers to produce goods at low cost becomes a target for NAM lobbyists. In general this means that NAM opposes legislation that would raise the costs of doing business—whether it is granting more powers to labor, raising the minimum wage, or imposing stricter environmental legislation. At the same time NAM supports legislation that would give businesses more freedom and reduce its regulatory burdens. Free trade, tax reductions, and less government-imposed paperwork are among the issues that NAM supports. Probably one of the most controversial issues tackled by the NAM is that of the manufacturing industries' relationship with the environment.

Case Study: Clean Air Standards

In February of 1997, when the Senate Environment and Public Works Clean Air Subcommittee began holding hearings on an Environmental Protection Agency (EPA) proposal for new clean air standards, NAM launched a massive lobbying and public relations campaign to prevent the new rules from going into effect.

According to the EPA, the new standards, which mandated a one-third reduction in ozone levels nationwide and would also regulate smog and soot from smokestacks, trucks and buses, would result in 20,000 fewer premature deaths per year from respiratory problems.

Claiming that air quality is already greatly improved from past levels and that the new rule would impose an intolerable burden on manufacturers, NAM launched a massive counterattack, rallying a 500-member coalition, the Air Quality Standards Coalition, to try and stop the implementation of these regulations. With an estimated budget of $2 million, NAM blitzed the media, the government, and its own memberships with ads attacking the EPA and debunking its evaluation of hundreds of independent studies as "junk science." Arguing that the costs of compliance were simply too high, NAM and its allies disputed the health benefits of the new standards and warned consumers that passage of the new rule would drive up the cost of cars, and prevent people from using household goods like barbecues and lawnmowers.

Not surprisingly, the coalition's assertions drew an angry response from environmental organizations. Claiming that NAM was grossly overstating the costs of compliance and pointing out that childhood asthma deaths have more than doubled since 1980, environmental groups organized their own grassroots effort to promote the new standards. The Sierra Club, for example, spent $50,000 on an ad series supporting the clean air rules and Internet sites invited visitors to fax NAM and the Senate expressing their views. The supporters of the new environmental legislation accused NAM of setting up organizations to fight control of pollution with names that suggested just the opposite.

Ultimately NAM was unsuccessful in its bid to defeat the EPA's efforts. In spite of NAM's best efforts and that of many other business advocacy groups, the new rules were approved in the summer of 1997. At the very least, NAM looks to prevent further increases in environmental standards and for methods of helping its members minimize the financial affects of the newly approved laws.

GROUP RESOURCES

NAM offers a variety of information resources. It maintains a Web site at http://www.nam.org that outlines the organization's policies, history, and goals, as well as provides access to NAM's *Briefing* newsletter, news updates, and upcoming events. The site also includes a members-only area where NAM members can access detailed reports and a variety of business resources.

NAM also provides a variety of services aimed at supporting U.S. manufacturers such as the Export Hotline that gives information on trade regulations, key contacts, business etiquette and protocol, transportation, shipping, foreign trade zones, documentation, and legislation. The service covers more than 80 countries and is available 24 hours a day on fax or on the World Wide Web at http://www.exporthotline.com.

Another NAM resource is Manufacturing Pulse-Mark, an industry database that allows manufacturers to measure their performance and compare it to other companies in their industry. NAM members can also take advantage of NAMnet, an on-line legislative and regulatory information service available via the World Wide Web, and NAM PolicyFAX which provides access to issue papers, newsletters, and analyses.

GROUP PUBLICATIONS

Publications available from the National Association of Manufacturers include *The Facts About Manufacturing,* which shows "manufacturing's strength and positive effect on the American economy," *Eye on Manufacturing,* a quarterly update from the Manufacturing Institute, and the *Briefing* newsletter. President Jerry Jasinowski has also co-authored a book called *Making it in America,* which features 50 case studies of American firms that have climbed to success. Most of these publications are available by E-mailing mfg.inst@nam.org, by calling the NAM's Publication Center at 1-800-637-3005, or by writing to the National Association of Manufacturers, 1331 Pennsylvania Ave. NW, Washington, DC 20004.

BIBLIOGRAPHY

Eisen, Phyllis. "Back to Basics," *The Journal of Commerce,* 17 July 1997.

Finlayson, Ann. *Naming Rumplestiltskin: Who Will Profit and Who Will Lose in the Workplace of the 21st Century.* Toronto: Key Porter Books, 1996.

Jasinowski, Jerry. "Environmental Extremism at the E.P.A." *Washington Times,* 9 June 1997.

————. *Making It In America: Proven Paths to Success from 50 Top Companies.* New York: Simon and Schuster, 1995.

Lemonick , Michael D. "The Queen Of Clean Air." *Time,* 7 July 1997.

Miller, William H. "The New Congress." *Industry Week,* 4 January 1999.

Pope, Carl. "A Good, Clean Fight." *Sierra.* March-April 1997.

Rifkin, Jeremy. *The End of Work.* New York: G.P. Putnam, 1995.

Watzman, Nancy, and James Youngclaus. "Environmental Give and Take." *Capital Eye,* 1 November 1995.

Workman, Andrew A. "Manufacturing Power: The Organizational Revival of the National Association of Manufacturers, 1941–1945." *Business History Review,* Summer 1998.

National Association of Realtors (NAR)

ESTABLISHED: May 12, 1908
EMPLOYEES: 350
MEMBERS: 710,000
PAC: REALTORS Political Action Committee (RPAC)

Contact Information:

ADDRESS: 430 N. Michigan Ave.
    Chicago, IL 60611-4087
PHONE: (312) 329-8200
FAX: (312) 329-8576
URL: http://nar.realtor.com
PRESIDENT: Sharon A. Millett

WHAT IS ITS MISSION?

The mission of the National Association of Realtors (NAR), since its inception in 1908, has been to work for the benefit of property owners in the United States. To accomplish this mission, the NAR exerts pressure on the government for affordable housing, better housing standards, improved home financing, and the prevention of real estate fraud. Other matters of concern to the association are community revitalization, protecting private property rights, encouraging beautification of land, and ensuring fair real estate taxation.

HOW IS IT STRUCTURED?

The NAR consists of two main offices. Its headquarters, where the business of running the association and building membership takes place, is in Chicago, Illinois. Representatives of the organization are also located in Washington, D.C., where they regularly meet with legislators and keep tabs on issues affecting members. The organization's press office is also located in Washington.

A staff of 350 runs the daily operations of the association. Officers include a president, a president-elect, a first vice president, a treasurer, a vice president and liaison to committees, and a vice president who is liaison to members. The officers are elected annually during the association's convention. The association also elects 13 vice presidents from 13 designated regions around the United States who serve as members of the board.

Membership is composed of residential and commercial Realtors—brokers, salespeople, property managers, appraisers, counselors, and others engaged in all aspects of the real estate industry. Members belong to one or more of some 1,700 local associations or boards and 54 state and territory associations affiliated with NAR. The state and territory boards represent a particular region, and members attempt to educate the public and influence governmental policy at the state or regional level. These boards are headed by elected officials who create policy at the local level and represent local interests to the state boards and the national NAR membership.

There are thousands of state and local real estate associations around the United States. In some cases, they are affiliated with the NAR and follow its guidelines and policies; in other cases, they are not members and act according to their own guidelines. Individual real estate agents—although they may be associated with a particular agency—are, in fact, self-employed. Although they may have an office in an agency, they are responsible for generating their own sales and creating their own advertising. They pay part of their commission to the agency in exchange for the office space and affiliation. Most real estate agents do not receive benefits packages because, technically, they are not considered employees. Because of this professional independence, some agents may choose to join NAR; others in the same office may not. Only members of NAR may call themselves "Realtors." Others call themselves real estate agents.

Someone who is a "Realtor" must follow the standards set by the NAR and, if consumers have complaints, they can take them to the association. If the association determines that a "Realtor" has not acted according to its ethical guidelines, membership may be revoked.

In addition to the state and local boards, the NAR is affiliated with the Commercial Investment Real Estate Institute, Counselors of Real Estate, and the Institute of Real Estate Management.

PRIMARY FUNCTIONS

According to the NAR, it "provides a facility for professional development, research and exchange of information among its members, to the public, and government, for the purpose of preserving the free enterprise system and the right to own real property." In its first role as an association of professionals, the NAR emphasizes training and education of its members to enhance the skills and uphold the reputation of all Realtors. It also actively recruits new members as a way of increasing its influence.

The NAR has nine affiliated institutes, societies, and councils that provide a wide range of programs and services to members. The Commercial Real Estate Institute, through publications and an extensive education curriculum, enhances professional development for those working in commercial-investment real estate. The Counselors

of Real Estate provide NAR members with advice on money management, reducing debt, the best use of land studies, and economic and market analyses. The Institute of Real Estate Management helps Realtors become Certified Property Managers (CPM) through its training program; the CPM designation demonstrates proven experience and ethical conduct in managing properties.

The Real Estate Brokerage Managers Council provides members with information, networking opportunities, and professional recognition for brokerage owners and managers. The Realtors Land Institute brings together real estate professionals interested in improving their skills in activities related to the land, including land brokerage, agri-business, land management, planning and developing, appraising, and acquiring. Through two specialized councils (Residential Sales Council and the Real Estate Buyer's Agent Council) and extensive education and training programs, the Realtors National Marketing Institute promotes professional competence in real estate sales and brokerage, and real estate brokerage management. The Society of Industrial and Office Realtors is an international organization whose 1,700 members specialize in a variety of commercial real estate activities, including the marketing of industrial and office properties. The Women's Council of Realtors provides an extensive referral network and education programs for personal and career growth, as well as increasing opportunities to be more productive and earn more.

The NAR, through its well-mobilized membership and powerful REALTORS Political Action Committee (PAC), influences federal legislation affecting Realtors and property owners. It does this by maintaining an active core of lobbyists; working with agencies such as the Department of Housing and Urban Development (HUD); and preparing informational and educational materials for its members, as well as the public and the media. The NAR has succeeded in helping the public by lobbying hard for a reduction in the amount of taxes a homeowner must pay on the profits from the sales of a home. In part because of the association's efforts, Congress reduced the tax rate from 28 percent to 20 percent, saving property owners an estimated $3 billion in tax payments over five years. In addition, the NAR has worked with HUD to create a Fair Housing Partnership Agreement, which commits Realtors to promoting equal housing opportunities for low-income individuals

PROGRAMS

The NAR hosts a multitude of programs and initiatives geared toward servicing its members, influencing public policy, and educating the public. In 1998 it launched a three-year national media campaign designed to educate the public about the "vital roles our members play in the real estate transaction." The tag line of the campaign was "We're REALTORS. Real Estate is our

FAST FACTS

The median price for a home in the Western United States in 1998 was $160,800; in the South, $111,300; in the Northeast, $145,600; and in the Midwest, $108,200.

(Source: National Association of Realtors. "PR News Wire," 1999.)

Life." The national campaign appeared on network television programs, including *Good Morning America, ABC World News Tonight,* the *CBS Evening News,* and the *NBC Nightly News.* Spots were also broadcast on national cable networks such as CNN, A&E, Discovery, and Lifetime.

A major initiative launched in 1998 was the "At Home with Diversity: One America Certificate" program. Created in conjunction with HUD, the goal of the program is to help real estate agents meet the needs of a widely diverse real estate market. Courses are offered in 30 states and agents are awarded certificates upon completion of training.

BUDGET INFORMATION

The NAR's gross revenues for 1997 were $65 million, most of which was generated by member dues; its expenses amounted to $61 million. Twenty-four percent of the NAR's budget is spent on informational materials to keep its members and the media updated; 21 percent goes toward strategic planning, the annual convention, and governing the organization; 19 percent is spent on political activities; and 10 percent is spent on maintaining its property. The remainder of the budget goes toward installing new technological developments, building membership, and educational and legal matters.

HISTORY

The NAR was founded in 1908 as the National Association of Real Estate Exchanges. Three earlier attempts to form a national real estate group had met with failure. The first effort, in 1891, resulted in the creation of the National Real Estate Association, which survived only 19 months, two other efforts also died quickly.

On May 12, 1908, 120 men representing 19 real estate boards from 13 states met in Chicago, Illinois, to try again. Their objective was to "unite the real estate men of America for the purpose of effectively exerting a combined influence upon matters affecting real estate interests." The group authorized employment of an executive secretary and general counsel and discussed areas of interest including taxation, state and municipal legislation, the organization of local information exchanges and the development of a code of ethics.

In 1913 the organization established an official ethics code for its members. Three years later, Charles N. Chadbourne, a Minneapolis real estate broker, devised the term Realtor to identify real estate agents who are members of the association and follow its standards.

The early years of the association were spent battling what members believed to be excess taxes on property and mortgages. After World War II (1939–45), Realtors formed their PAC. During the same period, Realtors worked successfully to oppose the imposition of a ceiling on the price of real estate. As a consequence, the cost to buy a home has steadily risen over the years to hundreds of thousands of dollars, and even millions, and thus makes purchasing a home unaffordable to many.

In the 1950s, the organization was successful in urging the government to allow people to defer paying taxes on capital gains, or profits, from the sale of their home if they purchased another home of equal or greater value within two years. This helped home buyers afford the down payment on a new home, which kept sales, and the economy, strong.

In the 1960s the association helped convince the government to give tax relief to people age 65 and older by allowing them to exclude paying taxes on the first $30,000 of profit they made from the sale of their home; by 1982, the government had raised that limit to $125,000.

One of the organization's ongoing battles, which began in 1976, has been to help defeat the government's efforts to limit tax deductions for mortgage interest payments as a way to raise additional tax revenues. The fight continues today as legislation periodically is introduced that would limit the amount of homeowners' mortgage deductions, causing them to pay higher federal income taxes.

In the 1990s the NAR looked inward and initiated campaigns to "clean up" the perceived image of realtors. Over the years, the real estate profession had gathered a reputation as a group of salespeople who disregarded the needs of the consumer and focused on a sale at all costs. An official, revised ethics policy, adopted in 1996, is part of that image renovation. In particular, the NAR will attempt to counter accusations of racial steering—showing properties to selected individuals on the basis of race.

CURRENT POLITICAL ISSUES

The "Voice for Real Estate" is the NAR's operation for government affairs in Washington, D.C. Through this operation, the NAR lobbies Congress and government offices for public policies that encourage home ownership and support a free-enterprise system for the buying and selling of property. The NAR has worked for tax incentives for real estate investors and home owners and advocates for private property rights. Issues including natural disaster insurance, fair-housing practices, protections for on-line property listings, and modernizing financial services, have been the focus of many of the NAR's political activities.

Case Study: FHA Loan Limits

During the 1990s the NAR worked hard to convince Congress to raise the Federal Housing Administration's (FHA) mortgage insurance limits. The FHA is a division of HUD, which provides loans. These loans are officially called mortgage insurance and are offered at low interest rates, with low down payments, to citizens who want to purchase homes but who do not qualify for non-government, or private, financing. Although the amount that people could borrow from FHA had risen over the years, the NAR felt that loan limits had not kept up with actual housing prices.

Critics of the proposed budget claimed that raising the FHA loan limits would not really help lower income borrowers, but would simply allow higher income borrowers to obtain cheap home loans through the FHA. The NAR argued that such claims were not realistic by pointing out that in 1996, 34 percent of people with FHA loans, had incomes that were less than 80 percent of the national average income. The NAR also argued that passage of the FHA increase would not only help buyers whose income was not enough to make loan payments, but also those buyers who did not have large amounts of money to make the big down payments required by many private-lending sources. Nontraditional borrowers, such as single parents, minorities, and unmarried couples, who had difficulty obtaining mortgage insurance from private sources, would also benefit from increased FHA loan limits.

The NAR pointed out that increasing loan limits so that more people could buy homes, would not only benefit the buyers, but their communities and the federal government as well. Home ownership provides stability in neighborhoods and draws businesses into these areas. The NAR estimated that over five years the loan limit increase would allow 175,000 additional households to purchase homes and generate over $715 million in additional government revenue.

The NAR's efforts paid off in early 1998 when members in both houses of Congress introduced legislation to increase the FHA budget, so that loan limits could be increased. The NAR supported this legislation through public statements, press releases, informational materials,

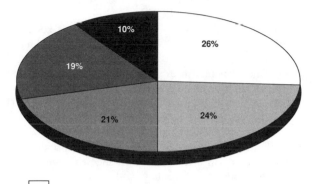

BUDGET:
1997 NAR Expenses

- 26%: Technological developments, building membership, education and legal expenses
- 24%: Information materials
- 21%: Strategic planning, the annual convention, and governance
- 19%: Political activities
- 10%: Property maintenance

and members' testimony to Congress. In October 1998 President Bill Clinton signed into law a bill that raised the FHA's mortgage insurance limits. The new limits were between $109,032 and $197,620 (different limits apply to different parts of the country depending on average home prices for that area.) The new law also provided for simpler calculation systems for FHA loans and a more uniform way to determine loan limits for a given region.

The NAR honored four U.S. Senators and eight members of the U.S. House of Representatives at their first Realtors Legislative Awards in November 1998, for their work in passing the legislation increasing FHA loan limits. In turn, the NAR also received an award in November 1998 from HUD for leading the drive to make FHA loans more accessible to citizens.

In January 1999 the loan limits were increased again to $208,800 in high-cost areas, and $115,200 in lower-cost areas.

FUTURE DIRECTIONS

With a new long-term strategic plan as its touchstone, NAR officials say they will focus on five areas that most directly impact the success and profits of its members: creating broader relationships with other organizations and businesses; building public awareness of the value of Realtors; increasing professionalism in the industry; providing aggressive leadership in the association; and increasing the value of the organization to its members by offering more services.

In the future, the organization plans to become involved with legislative policy that reaches beyond narrowly focused real estate issues, as a way to build coalitions with other industries. It also will enforce its Code of Ethics through a national system of trained hearing panels. In the future, members will have more ability to exchange information globally through the Internet. In addition, the NAR will work to raise consumer awareness about Realtors and will offer a benefits package to members that will offer health insurance and other coverage regardless of where they work.

GROUP RESOURCES

The NAR is a member and consumer-oriented organization and, as such, makes a wide variety of resources available. "One Realtor Place" is an extensive on-line resource for NAR members that provides up-to-date real estate information and offers networking opportunities through on-line discussions. The REALTORS Information Center is home to a vast amount of information available for loan to members.

The NAR hosts an extensive Web site at http://www.realtor.com, geared toward both realtor members and home buyers. Of particular interest to consumers is the Finance Center site that offers tools and resources to help sort through the process of buying a home. Tools and resources include electronic personal planners, worksheets to help compare mortgages and detail income and debt, calculator tools, and a glossary of terms.

For general information about NAR resources, contact the National Association of Realtors at 430 N. Michigan Ave., Chicago, IL 60611. For information on legislation or for press inquiries, contact NAR at 700 Eleventh St., Washington, D.C. 20001-4507; phone (202) 383-1188

GROUP PUBLICATIONS

Today's REALTOR™ is the NAR's official magazine and provides members with the latest news surrounding the real estate industry. The NAR also publishes a monthly magazine, *Real Estate Outlook,* which predicts trends in the market. Nine times each year it publishes *Real Estate Today,* a magazine which provides information and ideas for those in residential, brokerage, management, and commercial investment real estate. *Realtor News* is a biweekly publication providing timely articles on industry developments.

BIBLIOGRAPHY

"Buying a Home: Part 1." *Consumer Reports,* May 1996.

Caggiano, Christopher. "Low Rent." *Inc.,* July 1997.

"Democracy Campaign Reports Realtors Give Cash to Get Action." *Capital Times,* 13 April 1998.

"Plan to Raise FHA Limits Could Boost Buying." *USA Today,* 13 April 1998.

"Putting the Realtor on the Buyer's Side." *Consumer Reports,* July 1997.

"Real Estate Now a Better Investment." *USA Today,* 15 April 1998.

Somerville, Glenn. "U.S. Home Sales Soar: Durable Goods Fall." *Reuters News Service,* 25 March 1998.

National Audubon Society (NAS)

WHAT IS ITS MISSION?

According to its mission statement, the National Audubon Society (NAS) works to conserve and restore natural ecosystems, focusing on birds and other wildlife for the benefit of humanity and the Earth's biological diversity. The scope of NAS's efforts is wide-ranging and its reach is boundless: from repelling oil-drilling efforts in the Arctic National Wildlife Refuge to preserving the beauty of California's Mono Lake to educating children and adults about rare wetlands fowl through its magazines and field guides. The national organization and its various chapters have, in effect, staked claim to all of planet Earth in a desire to maintain its natural integrity.

ESTABLISHED: January 5, 1905
EMPLOYEES: 300
MEMBERS: 550,000
PAC: None

Contact Information:

ADDRESS: 700 Broadway
    New York, NY 10003
PHONE: (212) 979-3000
FAX: (212) 353-0377
URL: http://www.audubon.org
PRESIDENT: John Flicker
VICE CHAIRMAN: John B. Beinecke
VICE CHAIRMAN: Ruth O. Russell

HOW IS IT STRUCTURED?

The National Audubon Society is a nonprofit advocacy group located in New York City. NAS activities and overall operations are charted by an elected president and board of directors consisting of approximately 32 members. Most directors are nominated by regional chapters and subsequently elected by the membership. Directors come from a broad range of backgrounds including industry, science, and policy. Donald C. O'Brien, for example, who is chairman of the board until 2000, is a senior partner in a law firm and a former Commissioner of Connecticut State Board of Fisheries and Game.

The National Audubon Society is a three-tiered organization. At the national level, it maintains a Washington staff of 25 government affairs specialists who

serve as the society's main lobbying arm. The work of this office includes writing policy recommendations, organizing grassroots members and activities, and influencing and educating key decision makers. At the regional level, the society's field staff, which includes ecologists, biologists, and environmental scientists, provides that same voice in the various state Houses and conducts independent field studies and conservation projects. Also, at both the national and regional levels, the members of the society's 510 chapters provide support in the form of letter-writing campaigns, phone calls, and personal visits to decision makers. In addition to regional and state offices, the National Audubon Society operates 14 Education Centers across the United States and 27 Sanctuary Departments to administer the 102 wildlife sanctuaries sponsored by the NAS.

PRIMARY FUNCTIONS

In order to carry out its conservation efforts, the NAS is involved in a wide variety of initiatives. At the Washington level, the NAS is one of the most established and respected special interest groups and has consistently exerted a significant influence on legislation. Members testify before Congress and provide research surrounding all aspects of environmental protection. Collections of biological and botanical findings by NAS field workers have been used by local, state, and national governments to determine the fate of millions of acres of natural lands. At the community-based "chapter" level, NAS mobilizes an effective grassroots effort. Members are encouraged to write letters in support of or in opposition to legislative agenda, make phone calls and personal visits to state legislators and members of congress, and participate in clean-up efforts.

The NAS is also keenly aware of the importance of the so-called "fourth branch of government," the media. Through its own *Audubon* magazine and various field guides, and via aggressive lobbying of national magazines and journals to promote "green" causes, the NAS maintains a consistently high profile in the public eye.

Education has always been a primary tool of the Audubon societies in their work. Early in the society's history, a focus on children was established as a means of shaping the way future adults (potential hunters) viewed the natural world. Mabel Osgood Wright, president of the Connecticut Audubon Society at the turn of the twentieth century, compiled a booklet for Connecticut schoolteachers, *A Year with Birds,* which served as a guide to the one hundred birds most commonly seen in the state, and whose hope was that children who came to recognize the uniqueness of a given species would be less likely to indiscriminately kill a feathered creature.

The NAS not only advocates for and educates the public about the environment, it also takes a very active role in environmental protection. One direct method is to acquire lands on which birds and mammals exist in high concentration or in precious uniqueness. One such acquisition by the NAS took place in 1924, when its president, Gilbert Pearson, saw an opportunity to acquire a remarkable sanctuary in Louisiana. This land, 40-square-miles of marsh, had been owned by Paul J. Rainey, who used it as a shooting grounds. At Pearson's suggestion, Rainey's sister gave the land (and an endowment of $156,786) to the National Audubon Society, to be maintained as the Paul J. Rainey Wildlife Sanctuary.

PROGRAMS

The NAS sponsors many campaigns and programs that focus both on direct preservation and conservation, as well as public education. Living Oceans is a marine conservation program that uses science-based policy analysis, education, and grassroots advocacy to promote protection of marine fish and ocean ecosystems. The Endangered Species Campaign calls for stringent enforcement of the Endangered Species Act (ESA) as well as changes to the ESA to improve protection of endangered and threatened species. The Agriculture Policy Program focuses on conservation of prairies and wetlands and protection of marginal lands from being brought into intensive row crop production. The Everglades Ecosystem Restoration Campaign is the largest-scale ecosystem restoration project ever attempted anywhere in the world. The Forest Habitat Campaign seeks to sustain and restore forest ecosystems in the United States and the habitat they provide to birds and wildlife and the Wetlands Campaign, has the goal to preserve and restore the nation's wetland ecosystems.

Current educational and field programs of the National Audubon Society include Audubon Adventures, a curriculum-based program used primarily in grades four through six. Adventures attempts to teach children about science, environmental topics, and respect for nature while at the same time, help them practice language and communication skills. The materials are written and developed by professional educators and present basic scientific facts about birds, wildlife, and their habitats and needs. The program develops student skills in multiple disciplines and supports the teaching standards recommended by the National Academy of Science and the National Research Council.

For its adult members, Audubon Expedition Institute (AEI) prepares hundreds of college and graduate students for environmental careers. Through the use of mobile classrooms traveling the country, AEI, fully accredited through Lesley College in Boston, brings students in direct contact with invaluable learning experiences. By combining academic studies with hiking in canyons and mountains to explore geology, visiting industry to learn about business concerns, speaking with authors and scientists to hear current perspectives, and attending congressional briefings, students learn first-hand about the issues facing our environment.

BUDGET INFORMATION

The budget of the NAS comes primarily from member dues, contributions, and from sales of *Audubon* magazine and the various field guides. In 1997 the society's budget totaled $52,582,869. The largest single source of income came from contributions and bequests, which accounted for almost $22 million, or about 42 percent of the total. Membership dues of $9,426,741 accounted for another 18 percent. A substantial portion of the budget, close to $9 million, resulted from earned income and royalties, while the remainder came from investment income and profits from sales of investments.

By far the bulk of expenses—65 percent, or more than $35 million—was spent on program services including environmental education and information, publishing, wildlife preservation, and research. Fund-raising activities accounted for another 23 percent and management for about 12 percent.

HISTORY

The NAS has its roots in one hunter's love for wildlife, and his desire to see winged creatures proliferate and not perish. In 1886 *Forest and Stream* editor George Bird Grinnell was appalled by the negligent mass slaughter of birds that he saw taking place. As a boy, Grinnell had avidly read *Ornithological Biography,* a seminal work by the great bird painter John James Audubon; he also attended a school for boys conducted by Lucy Audubon. So when Grinnell decided to create an organization devoted to the protection of wild birds and their eggs, he did not have to go far for its namesake.

The public response to Grinnell's call for the protection of fowl was said to be instant and impressive: within a year of its foundation, the early Audubon Society claimed 39,000 members, each of whom signed a pledge to "not molest birds." Prominent members included jurist Oliver Wendell Holmes, abolitionist minister Henry Ward Beecher, and poet John Greenleaf Whittier. Such an organization was not wholly new.

Devastation and Dangers in the Plume Trade

Before Grinnell's Audubon Society, the American Ornithologists' Union, founded in 1883, was already aware of the dangers facing so many birds in the United States. The pressure on migratory and nonmigratory fowl was two-fold. Pressure from shooting enthusiasts was

BUDGET:

1997 NAS Revenue

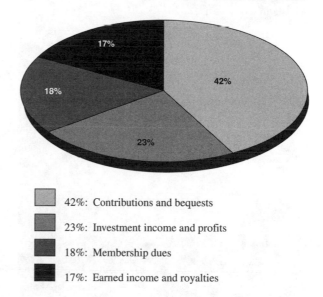

- 42%: Contributions and bequests
- 23%: Investment income and profits
- 18%: Membership dues
- 17%: Earned income and royalties

1997 NAS Expenses

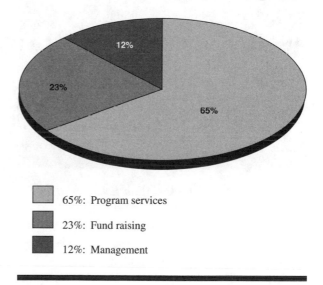

- 65%: Program services
- 23%: Fund raising
- 12%: Management

intense: great auks, for example, whose habit of crowding together on rocks and beaches made them especially easy to hunt, had been driven to extinction early in the century. During one week in the spring of 1897, nature author Florence Merriam claimed to have seen 2,600 robins for sale in one market stall in Washington alone. By the turn of the century, the sale of bird flesh was never greater.

A snowy egret (Egretta thula) *on Estero Island, Florida. This species, once hunted to near extinction by the millinery trade, became a symbol for the early conservationist movement in the United States and is the National Audubon Society's emblem. (Photograph by Robert J. Huffman, Field Mark Publications)*

The second equally greatest threat to the bird population, was the desire for their plumage. In the late 1890s the American Ornithologists' Union estimated that five million birds were killed annually for the fashion market. In the final quarter of the nineteenth century, plumes, and even whole birds, decorated the hair, hats, and dresses of women.

But public opinion soon turned on the fashion industry. Bolstered by the support of hunter/naturalist President Theodore Roosevelt, who was an avowed Audubon Society sympathizer, and a widespread letter-writing campaign driven by church associations, many of whom distributed the Audubon message in their various newsletters, the plume trade was ultimately eradicated by such laws as the New York State Audubon Plumage Law (1910), which banned the sales of plumes of all native birds in the state.

In 1918 the NAS actively lobbied for the Federal Migratory Bird Treaty Act. In the 1920s, the organization also played a vital role in convincing the U.S. government to protect vital wildlife areas by including them in a National Wildlife Refuge system. The association also purchased critical areas itself and to this day continues to maintain an extensive sanctuary system, of which the largest is the 26,000-acre Paul J. Rainey Sanctuary in Louisiana, acquired in 1924. After nearly three-quarters of a century, the National Wildlife Refuge Campaign remains a key component of overall NAS policy.

Prosperity through Publication

In 1934, with membership at a low of 3,500, and with the nation in the throes of the Great Depression, John H. Baker became the NAS president. Baker, a World War I aviator and ardent bird lover, was also a businessman, and he set about to invigorate the society and bolster its budget. Baker's innovation was to begin publishing book-length descriptive and illustrated field guides on major forms of bird and mammal life. Soon, in association with New York publisher Alfred A. Knopf, the Audubon *Field Guides* became a staple of every artist's and environmentalist's library.

Modern Issues: DDT and the Prairie Dog

During the post-World War II period, the NAS was consumed by the battle over the pesticide DDT. As early as 1960, the society circulated draft legislation to establish pesticide control agencies at the state level. In 1962 the publication of *Silent Spring* by long-time Audubon member Rachel Carson gave the campaign against "persistent pesticides" a huge national forum. Following her death in 1964, the NAS established a fund devoted strictly to the various legal fights in the war against DDT.

The poison was aimed chiefly at coyotes and prairie dogs, both considered pests by the politically influential local stockmen of the western United States. This provoked the ringing question, "What constitutes a 'good' versus a 'bad' animal?" In addition to the prairie dog, DDT was responsible for the near-complete extinction of the black-footed ferret. In the five years leading up to 1972, nearly 40,000 acres of Dakota prairie dog towns were saturated with DDT. Backed by scientific findings on DDTs long lasting and carcinogenic qualities, the NAS campaigned successfully to convincing governments worldwide to ban the chemical for use or production.

Through the 1960s and 1970s, the society began to use its influence to focus attention on a wider range of environmental issues and became involved in developing major new environmental protection policies and laws. Audubon staff and members helped legislators pass the Clean Air, Clean Water, Wild and Scenic Rivers, and Endangered Species acts. In 1969 the society opened an office in Washington, D.C., in an effort to keep legislators informed of Audubon's priorities.

By the 1970s the NAS had also extended to global interests. One area that NAS became actively involved with was whaling. Between 1973 and 1974 alone, the poorly regulated whaling industry had succeeded in eliminating 30,000 whales. But by 1985, following the 37th annual meeting of the International Whaling Commission in Bournemouth, England, which was attended by officials from the National Audubon Society and other U.S.-based environmental organizations, a worldwide moratorium on whale "harvesting" was approved. So successful has this moratorium been in restoring populations of many whales, that "non-consumptive uses of whales" may once again be permitted in some areas.

In 1995 the NAS elected as its president John Flicker, attorney and the former head of The Nature Conservancy. In his leadership of The Nature Conservancy, Flicker raised funds for purchasing key Everglades and unique wilderness lands in the state of Florida. As a seasoned lobbyist, Flicker has set about increasing NAS presence in the halls of Congress. High atop his list of goals for the NAS in the late twentieth century was the preservation of the Arctic National Wildlife Refuge from oil drilling interests, and the uniting with rainforest activists to protect tropical hardwood areas from excessive deforestation.

CURRENT POLITICAL ISSUES

Ever since its inception as an organization devoted to the protection of birdlife, the NAS has sought to maintain an aggressive lobbying presence in Congress and the various state houses. Early in NAS history, the organization was fortunate to have within its ranks several high-profile personalities whose vigor and often scathing wit succeeded in affecting and overturning legislation that the NAS deemed critical to bird life survival.

Since those early victories, the NAS has broadened its concerns to cover virtually the entire gamut of environmental issues. Major efforts for the 1990s included protecting ancient forests in the Pacific Northwest, preserving wetlands, and re-authorizing the Endangered Species Act.

FAST FACTS

One-half of the original Everglades marshes have been drained and lost forever to urban and agricultural development.

(Source: National Audubon Society. "Everglades Ecosystem Restoration Campaign," 1996.)

Case Study: Oil Drilling in Alaska Wildlife Refuges

One of the National Audubon Society's greatest challenges in recent years came in the wake of the 1994 election of a Congress that appeared determined to weaken or eliminate environmental protection laws in order to foster short-term economic growth. From logging in national parks to development of Everglades wetlands, this new Republican-dominated Congress challenged environmental organizations such as the NAS on every front.

One of the biggest skirmishes was fought over the Arctic National Wildlife Refuge, originally created in 1980 as part of the Alaska National Lands Act. Home to "an unparalled diversity of wildlife," this vast region of tundra "represents one of the largest intact ecosystems in the world." Yet from the outset, the new refuge was besieged by oil and mining interests determined to exploit its natural resources.

In 1990, a nationwide survey of the Refuge System conducted by the Fish and Wildlife Service (FWS) found 57 different secondary uses occurring on Alaska's wildlife refuges. Twenty of these uses were identified as harmful and another 23 as inappropriate by Alaskan wildlife refuge managers. The FWS's ability to control these harmful and illegal activities was severely hindered by funding limitations, staff shortages, and the size and remoteness of Alaskan wildlife refuges. It also faced a powerful Alaska congressional delegation, which attempted to push through legislation that would give away land to Native corporations and that would open the Arctic Refuge to oil drilling.

In its 1996 Annual Report the NAS pointed out that even by the most optimistic industry predictions, oil from the Refuge would add a mere 0.4 percent to the world's oil reserves. Nevertheless, the Alaskan delegation was determined to have its way and succeeded in inserting an Arctic oil drilling provision into the 1995 federal budget bill. In response, the Audubon Society rallied its grassroots membership, deluging Senators with more than 4,000 letters and calls supporting an amendment to remove the provision from the bill.

These efforts helped sway key swing votes in the Senate, but ultimately the amendment to remove the provision was narrowly defeated by a margin of 48 to 51. The society and its allies continued to lobby against the provision and convinced President Clinton to veto any bill that contained provisions to develop the Arctic Refuge. Finally, after numerous government shutdowns and acrimonious budget negotiations, the Arctic oil drilling provision was killed.

FUTURE DIRECTIONS

In 1996 the Audubon Society decided it was time "to prepare ourselves to lead the environmental movement boldly forward into the new millennium." A long-term 25-year strategic plan dubbed "Audubon 2000" was prepared that calls for the society to sharpen the focus on the conservation of birds, other wildlife and their habitats, to expand its educational programs, and to increase investment in its grassroots network "as the primary instrument of our environmental advocacy."

GROUP RESOURCES

The NAS maintains one of the largest and most extensive Web sites of any of the environmentalist associations. It includes news about legislation and campaigns, education efforts, a search mechanism for locating local chapters, and news of the NAS in national and local media. Other information sources include various chapter-run bookshops. Since 1984 Audubon Productions has maintained its original commitment to providing quality entertainment that educates and informs people about the environment. Audubon Productions has produced over 40 "World of Audubon" Specials for Turner Broadcasting System (TBS), a series of natural

history programs entitled "Audubon's Animal Adventures" for the Disney Channel, as well as various other videos and interactive products.

GROUP PUBLICATIONS

Publications available from the National Audubon Society include: *Audubon,* a bimonthly magazine featuring articles on wildlife topics (free to members; $20/yearly to nonmembers); *Audubon Activist,* published bimonthly; *Audubon Adventures,* a bimonthly children's newspaper; and *Field Notes,* a bimonthly journal.

The National Audubon Society also publishes, in association with Alfred A. Knopf, a wealth of field guides, including *The Audubon Society Field Guide to North American Birds, The Audubon Society Field Guide to Wild Animals,* and *The Audubon Society Field Guide to North American Mammals.*

BIBLIOGRAPHY

Backman, Marjorie. "Changing of the Guard." *Audubon,* July/August 1995.

Cockburn, Alexander. "The Green Betrayers." *Nation,* 6 February 1995.

Conservation Foundation. *State of the Environment: An Assessment at mid-Decade,* Washington, D.C.: Conservation Foundation, 1984.

Flicker, John. "Local Voices in a National Debate." *Audubon,* January/February 1996.

Jasinowski, Jerry. "Environmental Extremism at the E.P.A." *Washington Times,* 9 June 1997.

McGowan, Kathleen. "Audubon On-Line." *Audubon,* May–June 1997.

Pope, Carl. "A Good, Clean Fight." *Sierra,* March–April 1997.

Salisbury, David F. "Beyond Environmental Extremism; Finding the Middle Ground Between Business and Conservation." *Christian Science Monitor,* 3 August 1982.

National Automobile Dealers Association (NADA)

WHAT IS ITS MISSION?

The National Automobile Dealers Association (NADA) represents new car and truck dealers, dealership managers, and other dealership employees in the United States, whether they are dealers of domestic or imported vehicles. One of the association's main goals is "to preserve the value of the franchise system. NADA policies and actions forcefully communicate dealer views and concerns to the executive, legislative, and judicial branches of the federal government, to manufacturers, distributors and industry, and to the public." NADA keeps a close eye on Congress and regulatory agencies, making sure proposed legislation is beneficial, or at least not detrimental, to auto dealers' interests. According to the organization, "Every year, NADA analyzes hundreds of legislative proposals and evaluates their effects on dealers. . . . Positions on specific legislative and regulatory issues are developed by NADA's officers and Government Relations Committee in cooperation with its members. These positions are presented as the collective view of dealers to Congress, the courts, federal agencies and the public."

ESTABLISHED: 1917
EMPLOYEES: 400 (1997)
MEMBERS: 19,500 franchise owners (1997)
PAC: Dealers Election Action Committee

Contact Information:

ADDRESS: 8400 Westpark Dr.
    McLean, VA 22102
PHONE: (703) 821-7000
TOLL FREE: (800) 252-6232
FAX: (703) 821-7075
E-MAIL: nada@nada.org
URL: http://www.nada.org
CHAIRMAN: Paul J. Holloway

HOW IS IT STRUCTURED?

NADA headquarters are located in McLean, Virginia, a suburb of Washington, D.C. Another smaller suite of offices, where legislative activities are handled, is maintained on Capitol Hill. The majority of NADA's 400 employees work in McLean. The president represents the organization in public settings, serving as an authority for the media in interviews, and for Congress

FAST FACTS

Over 198 million vehicles are in operation in the United States today.

(Source: *National Automobile Dealers Association Data,* 1998.)

through testimony. NADA's day-to-day operations are run by an executive vice president. Frank McCarthy, who had been serving as vice president since in 1968, was named Association Executive of 1997 by *Association Trends.* NADA staff closely monitors laws and regulations that affect auto and truck dealers. Its officers and government relations committee work to develop positions on various issues, and are overseen by both an executive committee and NADA's board of directors.

NADA officers—president, first vice president, secretary, and treasurer—serve one-year terms and are elected at annual meetings in October. These officers, plus eight vice chairmen, comprise the executive committee, which meets three times a year. The vice chairmen come from different regions of the country, thereby ensuring input from a geographically diverse group of members.

The board of directors consists of up to 63 members, also from around the country, with at least one member representing each state. Board members, who are selected by nominating ballots sent out in the mail, serve staggered three-year terms, and the board meets annually.

NADA members must hold an auto or truck sales and service franchise. A yearly membership ranges from $65 to $400, depending on the sales volume of the member dealership. In return NADA provides advocacy, information, and discounts on products and services. Franchised medium- and heavy-duty truck dealers generally join the American Truck Dealers (ATD) division. ATD dues range from $125 to $300 per year, and members receive the same benefits as do NADA members, although publications and services are customized to meet truck dealers' specific needs.

NADA and NADA-ATD members are directly affiliated with the national organization; there are no NADA chapters. However statewide auto dealer associations cooperate and often work closely with the national group. These state associations are bound to NADA by common interest only; they have their own boards, funding, and operations and are completely independent of NADA.

Additionally, NADA's for-profit entity, NADA Services Corp., publishes NADA's popular used-car guide, known as the "Blue Book," and a monthly magazine.

PRIMARY FUNCTIONS

From its legal defense fund for members in judicial and regulatory proceedings to financial aid for auto dealership employees hit by natural disasters, NADA performs a wide variety of services for its members. Professional training, trade information, and financial consulting services are also provided. The association's Industry Relations department acts as a go-between for dealers and auto manufacturers, helping dealers win better franchise agreements and solve problems, while the staff of the Industry Relations department conducts a biannual dealer attitude survey used to help communicate dealer concerns to manufacturers and distributors.

NADA primarily acts as a watchdog, protecting the interests of dealers in both legislative and regulatory processes. When necessary, NADA mobilizes masses of auto dealers to lobby for their interests, and NADA officers often testify before Congress on legislation that affects dealers. For example NADA filed comments with the National Highway Traffic Safety Administration (NHTSA) when it was drawing up rules for installation of on/off switches for airbags. The issue is of particular interest to NADA since the switches have to be installed by dealers. NADA closely scrutinized the rules and the language of them to ensure not only that maximum safety standards were maintained, but also to make certain that liabilities would not fall on dealers for any injuries resulting from use of the switches.

Dealers Election Action Committee

The Dealers Election Action Committee ranks among the biggest-spending political action committees (PACs) in the nation. According to Elections Commission records, it spent more in candidate contributions than all but four other PACs in 1995 and 1996, giving more than such high-profile groups as the National Education Association (NEA), American Medical Association (AMA), and National Rifle Association (NRA). Indeed, the Center for Responsive Politics (CRP), which monitors campaign finances and the connection between money and politics, suggests NADA has ample influence over legislation. An October 1996 CRP report listed NADA as second in campaign contributions for the 1996 elections, after the Association of Trial Lawyers of America.

CRP's report credited NADA with having had a significant influence on the fall of the auto luxury tax, reporting that it doled out $119,500 to members of the House and Senate tax-writing committees who had jurisdiction over the bill. CRP's report also claimed lobbying efforts by NADA and auto manufacturers had resulted in Congress's denial of funds for the development of new Corporate Average Fuel Economy standards that would have specified how far a car must go on a gallon of gasoline. NADA's PAC donated $7,000 to Rep. Tom DeLay (R-Texas), who authored the measure denying the funds, the CRP report stated.

PROGRAMS

NADA provides a number of programs designed to improve dealers' operations and make them more profitable. The Management Education department publishes management guides, conducts training programs, and produces instructional videos, and the Dealer Academy prepares people to take over dealerships and trains dealership managers. NADA also hosts annual conventions and expositions featuring displays of equipment, educational workshops, and prominent speakers, such as then-President George Bush, who was a speaker in 1986. The group also offers pension, profit-sharing, and insurance plans for members.

NADA events sometimes involve the public as well. Among its public education efforts, in 1995 the association launched a nationwide campaign to get motorists to use anti-lock brakes properly. And in 1996 it pledged to help the government with a public education campaign on how to minimize air bag dangers.

BUDGET INFORMATION

NADA is a nonprofit agency funded partly by membership dues based on gross dealer sales. Dues revenue is subsidized by income from NADA's for-profit entity, NADA Services Corp., which publishes NADA's used-car guide and monthly magazine. This also keeps dues down. "Because of this structure," the group's literature says, "NADA has not raised its dues in more than 10 years and does not plan to raise them in the foreseeable future."

As for revenue to fund its PAC, the Dealers Election Action Committee, NADA encourages members to make voluntary donations, and they do. Reports on file with the Federal Elections Commission (FEC) show a number of donations—large and small—from dealers around the country. NADA's PAC raises over $1 million annually from car and truck dealers.

HISTORY

Thirty dealers went to Washington, D.C., in 1917 to change Congress's perception of the automobile. According to NADA's Web site, "By convincing Congress that

FAST FACTS

Three percent of the total revenue of all states is the result of sales tax generated by the sales of new cars and trucks.

(Source: *National Automobile Dealers Association Data,* 1998.)

cars weren't luxuries, as they had been classified, but were vital to the economy, the group prevented total factory conversion to wartime work and succeeded in reducing a proposed 5 percent luxury tax to 3 percent." Realizing a continuous presence was needed, the dealers organized the National Automobile Dealers Association, with headquarters eventually founded in St. Louis, Missouri.

To develop its membership roster NADA had an effective solution—annual conventions held at the same time and location as auto shows. By 1924, 2,000 of the country's 20,000 car and truck dealers attended the NADA's annual convention. The group's budget was also growing, reaching more than $50,000 per year.

The growth of the fledgling auto industry in the 1920s fueled NADA growth. The organization quickly expanded its member services to include insurance, credit, and such important information resources as used-car values, increasingly valuable because of the fact that used cars were beginning to outsell new cars by more and more each year. The car values determined by NADA ultimately evolved into the U.S. government-endorsed *Official Used Car Guide.*

The Great Depression of the 1930s was tough on auto dealers and NADA barely survived it. Customerless dealers could not pay their dues and dropped out, leaving NADA with such limited funds that it was forced to fire workers and seek cheaper office accommodations. Finally the New Deal policies of President Franklin D. Roosevelt helped boost the economy and NADA. Particularly, the proposed Code of Fair Competition for the Motor Vehicle Retailing Trade renewed interest in advocacy as it sought to implement mandatory standards for all auto dealers. NADA regained its momentum as the voice of dealers nationwide by acting as a center of discussion and input. Also at this time, dealers began to realize that policies not directly related to the auto industry could still affect them. For example, Prohibition resulted in dealer losses when cars not fully paid for were being confiscated by the Revenue Department after their owners violated the alcohol ban. The need for NADA was clearly growing and by the time its headquarters moved to the "Motor City" (Detroit, Michigan) in 1936, the group had bounced back and formed new programs and departments.

World War II (1939–45) brought new difficulties, however. A 1942 Census Bureau report showed the auto industry hardest hit of any business surveyed. Wartime rationing of cars had the biggest impact, as sales and delivery of new vehicles were frozen, used-car sales dropped due to fears that similar restrictions would be placed on them, and gas rationing rendered any car purchase futile.

After the war there was still a shortage of vehicles, and NADA's challenge became changing the perception that dealers were somehow getting rich off the shortage. Rumors of this nature had become increasingly prolific as disgruntled customers signed onto long waiting lists in order to buy their cars, eager to answer the call of the nation's newly built highways and interstates. Before the industry had a chance to recover its reputation, operations were again disrupted by war, this time the Korean War. Now not only was steel for building autos under tight rations, but a seven percent excise tax was levied on automobiles to help pay for the war effort. NADA's fight against this tax was unsuccessful, despite the fact that its headquarters had moved to Washington, D.C., to facilitate closer work with government agencies and legislative activities.

New challenges arose for auto dealers in the 1970s when the energy crisis, the Clean Air Act, and other emissions standards shifted sales to smaller vehicles. Japan's share of the auto market was increasing due to their marketing of smaller, more fuel-efficient cars, while U.S. manufacturers like Studebaker were going under. NADA fought several pieces of legislation proposed by Congress in response to the tightened oil supply that it determined would negatively impact dealers—against mandatory conservation, it favored voluntary conservation instead—but to no avail. The government raised gasoline taxes and imposed fuel economy standards. Fluctuating consumer tastes because of the government's conservation policies also hurt dealer sales, as not only smaller cars, but also public transportation, grew in popularity. By the late 1970s much of NADA's efforts went toward resisting such restrictions on auto use and rebuilding the public's image of auto dealers.

The 1980s and 1990s brought relative stability for auto dealers and, perhaps, re-validation of the notion that American's love affair with the automobile will never die. The nation's success in the Persian Gulf War in the 1990s helped ensure a long-term supply of relatively inexpensive fuel that would likely keep that love affair alive for a very long time. But by the end of the 1900s, as more global focus caused attention to turn toward controlling environmental pollution, NADA saw new challenges in its efforts to fight initiatives it believes to be unfair or burdensome to dealers. For instance, it continues to lobby against strict Corporate Average Fuel Economy (CAFE) standards, as well as provisions of the Superfund law that level penalties against dealers retroactively for improper disposal of hazardous wastes.

CURRENT POLITICAL ISSUES

NADA staff members scour legislative and regulatory proposals for measures that could affect auto and truck dealers. Often, in seeking to protect the interests of its members, NADA takes positions contrary to those taken by consumer groups. And these clashes ultimately affect car and truck buyers. But, NADA argues, its efforts can benefit consumers by preventing what seem to be overly broad federal regulations that limit consumer choice.

Sometimes policy can impact dealers indirectly, like Superfund pollution clean-up measures that have, according to NADA, punished "persons who were not themselves negligent and who made sincere efforts to act in an environmentally responsible manner." In other instances, the policy in question is directly aimed at changing or controlling certain particulars within the auto industry, such as fuel economy and emissions standards, and plenty of activity is devoted to safety standards issues. According to NADA's Web site, "dealers support realistic measures that prevent injuries and save lives. NADA supports safety belt use as the most effective, economical and practical means of occupant protection. NADA works with ... other safety groups to educate the public regarding seat belts, child safety seats, rear-seat shoulder-belt retrofitting, and other occupant protection systems."

Case Study: "Off" Switches for Air Bags

The controversy over on/off switches for airbags is one that clearly illustrates NADA's influence. In January of 1997 the National Highway Traffic Safety Administration (NHTSA), in response to a number of cases where children and sometimes adults were injured or killed by air bags, proposed a rule allowing vehicle owners to request that dealers deactivate air bags.

NADA and other auto industry interests immediately challenged the proposal, favoring instead, cut-off switches to deactivate the air bags in certain situations. Allowing permanent deactivation "would send the wrong message to the motoring public regarding the safety efficacy of air bags and would likely decrease motor vehicle safety," a NADA press release stated. Dealers also feared that they could be held liable for injuries or deaths resulting from dealer deactivation of air bags. Air bag benefits outweigh risks in all but a few situations, NADA argued, making cut-off switches a better solution than permanent deactivation. Its efforts to kill the deactivation rule included testimony before Congress by former NADA president Ramsay Gillman.

In March of 1997 the Clinton administration postponed the deactivation rule due to pressure from automobile and insurance concern. The NHTSA eventually adopted a rule that allows some vehicle owners to have dealers install cut-off switches. The regulation went into effect in January of 1998. Gillman stated, in his column in the association's magazine, *Automotive Executive,* that the cut-off switch rule "was a direct result of NADA action."

SUCCESSES AND FAILURES

Although NADA has often found itself on the losing end when it has tried to prevent public policies seen as serving some greater good, such as its efforts to prevent energy conservation measures in the 1970s, the group has had substantial success in its efforts to defend or promote the relatively narrow interests of auto dealers. In the fall of 1997 after three years of negotiation with the Internal Revenue Service over some new-car dealers' use of the "last in, first out" or LIFO accounting method as a way of reducing their taxes, NADA reached an agreement under which 4,000 dealers paid an average of $47,000 in fines. This agreement was a win for NADA, which said it saved dealers millions of dollars and won assurances from the IRS that no dealers would be forced out of business because of this tax dispute.

Killing a Tax

The automobile luxury tax enacted in 1990 had been repealed for all items except luxury cars by 1993. It was, perhaps, fitting that NADA led the fight against this tax; the organization had originally come together in 1917 in an effort to, among other things, persuade Congress to lower a five percent luxury tax on autos. Now NADA initiated an industry-wide coalition against the tax that included auto manufacturers Ford and General Motors as well as other dealer associations. The coalition met frequently at NADA's legislative office in Washington, D.C., to iron out a politically acceptable compromise to the tax. In August of 1996 President Bill Clinton signed a law that would phase out the tax, eliminating it altogether by 2002. John Peterson, then NADA's president, was invited to the bill-signing—a privilege generally accorded those influential in a law's enactment.

With growing concerns among government officials about such environmental issues as global warming and ozone depletion, there will likely be a steady stream of new initiatives from Washington affecting the auto industry, notably, standards for vehicle emissions and fuel economy. NADA will monitor such changes to ensure that they are not too burdensome to the automobile and truck industries or harmful to sales.

NADA must also help its members cope with changes coming not from Washington, but from auto

This woman had an on-off airbag switch installed after recovering from serious facial injuries resulting from being struck by the driver's side airbag after deployment. The National Automobile Dealers Association tries to ensure that maximum safety standards are maintained when new switches are installed. (Photograph by Greg Nelson)

manufacturers who have been trying to buy out dealerships, and from new forms of competition like the CarMax used-car superstore chain and sales via the Internet. In helping its members, however, NADA must be careful not to be too aggressive. In 1995 the organization reached a settlement with the Justice Department over alleged antitrust violations after a department probe into recommendations the association had made to members concerning pricing, inventory, and other business practices. *Automotive News* called the probe "puzzling." Although NADA denied fault and paid no fines in the end, the group agreed to 10 years of Justice Department scrutiny.

GROUP RESOURCES

NADA has a Web site at http://www.nada.org that offers basic information about the group, including details about its programs, its legislative and regulatory concerns, and its history. Various documents the group has available can be obtained through the Fax-on-Demand service at

(800) 778-7209. Also, the group has a convention hot line number: (703) 821-7188; and a Retirement Plan Information Center that can be reached at 1-800-4-NADART.

GROUP PUBLICATIONS

Members receive several bulletins, guides, and a faxletter. *Automotive Executive* is the association's monthly magazine with news about the association, the auto industry, and happenings in Washington; call (703) 821-7150 or (800) 252-NADA, ext. 8, to subscribe. The *N.A.D.A. Official Used Car Guide,* also published monthly, is a guide to vehicle retail, loan and trade-in values. The public may subscribe to this guide by calling 1-800-544-NADA.

BIBLIOGRAPHY

Ball, Jeffrey "GM Jumps Into the Safer Air-Bag Fray With a New Child-Detecting System." *Wall Street Journal (Eastern Edition),* 11 February 1999.

Carney, Dan. "High-Tech Airbags On the Horizon." *Popular Science,* January 1999.

Freedman, Eric. "LIFO in Limbo: Dealers and IRS Are Trying to Resolve Dispute over How Adjustment Is Reported." *Automotive News,* 27 January 1997.

Harris, Donna Lawrence. "Dealers Favor On-Off Air Bags." *Automotive News,* 10 February 1997.

Kim, Dong-Young. *Campaign Finance Decision-Making and Strategies of Trade Association PACS: Two Case Studies.* Washington, D.C.: Georgetown University, 1992.

"NADA Launches ABS Campaign." *Automotive News,* 7 August 1995.

"NADA Reaches Agreement with IRS to Untangle LIFO Dispute." *Automotive News,* 29 September 1997.

"NADA Tripped on Three Issues." *Automotive News,* 2 October 1995.

Nomani, Asra Q., and Gabriella Stern. "Clinton's Air-Bag Proposal Faces Delay by Regulators after Industry Pressure." *Wall Street Journal,* 11 March 1997.

Sawyers, Arlena. "Relax the Tax: Phase-out of Charge on Luxury Vehicles Was Highlight of '96, Outgoing Chief Says." *Automotive News,* 27 January 1997.

"U.S. Ends Puzzling Price Quiz at NADA." *Automotive News,* 25 September 1995.

Watzman, Nancy, Jay Youngclaus, and Jennifer Shecter. *Political Pacanalia.* Washington, D.C.: Center for Responsive Politics, 1996.

National Cable Television Association (NCTA)

ESTABLISHED: 1952
EMPLOYEES: 85
MEMBERS: 100
PAC: None

WHAT IS ITS MISSION?

According to the Web site of the National Cable Television Association (NCTA), the organization's mission is to "advance the public policies of the cable television industry before Congress, the executive branch, the courts and the American public . . . [and] present the industry's interests to organizations representing state and local policy makers." Primarily the NCTA provides its members with a strong national presence by providing a single, unified voice on issues affecting the cable industry.

Contact Information:
ADDRESS: 1724 Massachusetts Ave. NW
        Washington, DC 20036
PHONE: (202) 775-3629
FAX: (202) 775-1055
URL: http://www.ncta.com
PRESIDENT: Decker Anstrom
CHAIRMAN: Leo Hindery, Jr.

HOW IS IT STRUCTURED?

The NCTA's leadership is composed of a board of directors selected from the CEOs of NCTA member companies. Working committees, such as the Satellite Network Committee and the Public Affairs Committee, help keep the board up-to-date on the latest issues facing the cable industry. NCTA activities are broken down into the following departments and offices: administration, association affairs, Office of Cable Signal Theft, Office of Small System Operators, government relations, industry affairs, National Academy of Cable Programming, legal, program network policy, public affairs, and science and technology. The NCTA's membership is composed of cable program networks and the organization represents hardware suppliers and other services to the industry and approximately 50 million cable subscribers.

PRIMARY FUNCTIONS

NCTA's primary goal is to promote legislation favoring cable television and to reduce governmental regulation of the industry. To this end, the organization represents its members before federal, state, and local governing bodies. The NCTA also presents industry opinions and programs to the media and the public in addition to serving as a conduit for information to its members.

The NCTA promotes policies favoring cable television by addressing Congress, the courts, and the executive branch of the federal government—namely, the Federal Communications Commission (FCC). Federal regulations have affected the industry by controlling such things as cable system ownership, subscription rates, and access to programming. Technological advances have greatly complicated regulation of the larger television industry, which has grown beyond broadcast and cable providers to involve the satellite, telephone, and computer industries. At the same time, cable operators have been given the opportunity to provide telecommunications services including local and long distance telephone services and high speed computer data transmission. Serving as both a monitor and advocate, the NCTA seeks to derail regulation that would unequally benefit competing industries or otherwise hurt the cable industry.

Through its alliance with state cable associations, NCTA works to advance cable interests with state and local policy makers. Such representation is important because municipalities contract with cable operators on an individual basis and have their own power to regulate some aspects of cable company operation.

Filling a public relations capacity, the NCTA works to present a positive image of its members by advancing public service programs as well as promotional campaigns. The organization has focused on supporting the interests of children, most notably in its commitment to gain free Internet access for all schools. In the face of criticism on such issues as rate increases and poor customer service, the NCTA has sought to improve the image of cable providers with their customers.

NCTA also serves as an important communications tool within the industry. The organization helps its members respond to issues in an organized way and keeps them educated about technological developments. The use of fiber-optic cables, digital transmission, interactive programming, and cable modems can revolutionize cable services, but implementing these technologies is expensive and complicated. NCTA assists members by organizing the industry's trade show and by providing relevant information through its science and technology department.

PROGRAMS

As the representative organization of an industry that is undergoing significant technological and regulatory rev-

olutions, NCTA is involved in a number of important ongoing programs. NCTA hosts the industry's annual trade show, which typically features more than 300 exhibiting companies and attracts more than 30,000 attendees.

One of its most popular and successful initiatives has been the development of the cable industry's On-Time Service Guarantee (OTG). Responding to public perception that the success of the cable industry in extending its customer base had resulted in a preoccupation with numbers and fees at the expense of service, the OTG required participating cable companies to pledge on-time installation appointments or, failing that, free installation and on-time service appointments or a $20 refund. Launched on March 1, 1995, the campaign's immediate success has led to continuing extensions and nationwide participation by almost all of the country's 8,000 cable companies. NCTA has supported these developments by organizing OTG advertising campaigns, news letters, nationwide teleconferences, cable company awards, employee recognition awards, and company visits by CEOs, members of Congress and state policymakers.

Another industry program in which NCTA has played an important role is in the initiation, financing, and follow-up to the National Television Violence Study. Commissioned by the cable industry in 1994, this three-year, $3.5 million study delivered its final report in April of 1998. The findings are now under industry review, and additional research has also been commissioned to follow up on consumer experience with a new TV-rating system and the V-chip. NCTA has also pledged to create and distribute a pair of free videos to help parents develop the critical viewing skills needed to protect their children from excessive violence.

BUDGET INFORMATION

Not made available.

HISTORY

A precursor to the NCTA, the National Community Television Association, was founded in 1952 by a very different cable industry than the one that exists today. Originally cable technology was introduced solely as a conduit for local broadcast TV. It served households that were unable to receive direct transmissions from local broadcast antennas because of the surrounding terrain. To solve the problem, antennas were erected at geographic high points and homes were hard wired to these towers. In 1950 there were 70 cable systems serving just 14,000 subscribers nationwide.

Late in the 1950s and early 1960s, cable systems realized the business potential of retransmitting signals from distant broadcasters. This extension of service and program choice quickly developed into a major attraction for television viewers and, almost as quickly, as a major bone of contention between NCTA members and conventional terrestrial TV broadcast companies. The business benefits to the cable operators were obvious, as cable companies totaled 800 and subscribers numbered 850,000 by 1962. However this growth also brought the industry under the scrutiny of the FCC, following broadcasters' objections. The FCC froze further development in major markets, making the industry an unwilling subject to the regulating body.

In 1969 the National Community Television Association was renamed the National Cable Television Association. The decade that followed saw constant NCTA lobbying at federal, state, and local levels for a lifting of restrictions. At first cable operators were not allowed to import distant signals and could only offer movies, syndicated programs, and sporting events. A trend toward deregulation by the FCC coupled with cable's pioneering of satellite communications technology, eventually resulted in improved services to consumers and a corresponding increase in cable subscribers. By the end of the decade, almost 15 million households across the United States were cable subscribers.

The 1980s began with NCTA pressing for further deregulation, arguing that it would be good for the consumer, good for the technologies which were already gobbling up hundreds of millions of development dollars, and of course, good for the industry it represented. The turning point for NCTA deregulation efforts came with the 1984 Cable Act, which virtually deregulated the industry. The act spurred investment in the industry into the 1990s, which NCTA describes as a $15 billion rewiring of America and the biggest private construction project since World War II.

In the 1990s key issues for NCTA were digital signal transmission, competition by direct satellite providers, content ratings, interactive services, Internet access, and as always, the specter of regulation or re-regulation. New competition from emerging technologies and converging industries often involved regulatory changes, with groups representing satellite providers, broadcast television, telephone companies, and the computer industry all attempting to influence legislation and regulations. Passage of the Telecommunications Act of 1996, which allowed cable operators to enter the telecommunications industry and telephone companies to deliver television programming via phone lines, was expected to result in dramatic changes, including broadcast, cable, and telephone company mergers.

NCTA also sought to shape developments outside of government jurisdiction. In 1998 NCTA worked with the Consumer Electronics Manufacturers Association to form an agreement regarding technical standards for digital television sets that would ensure product compatibility with cable services.

FAST FACTS

In 1998 more than six out of ten U.S. households subscribed to cable TV.

(Source: National Cable Television Association, 1999.)

CURRENT POLITICAL ISSUES

The often antagonistic relationship between NCTA and the FCC stems from the highly political nature of many cable industry issues. While NCTA has seen dramatic advances in the area of deregulation, technological issues have kept the organization focused on developing FCC policies. The transition from analog to digital signal transmission has NCTA warning policymakers that a proposed expansion of the "must carry" rule to require cable operators to carry most local stations' analog and digital signals would put broadcasters' interests ahead of those of cable operators. The group is also battling efforts by Internet access providers including America Online to convince the FCC to give them access to cable's broadband link to cable customers; such "open access" or "unbundling" of cable services is vehemently discouraged by NCTA.

Perhaps the greatest political gain for NCTA is the passage of the Telecommunications Act of 1996, which was designed to stimulate new telecommunications services and providers by allowing cable and telephone companies into each others' fields.

Case Study: The Telecommunications Act of 1996

The Telecommunications Act of 1996 opened up the telecommunications market to cable companies, and the cable market to telecommunications companies. With cable companies putting down expensive new, high-volume fiber-optic cables, the added revenue from telephone and data traffic was vital to continuing service upgrade and development, according to NCTA. The act also ended price regulation, a long-standing obstacle for NCTA.

The cable industry, however, was not always interested in entering the telecommunications market. Just a few years prior, the NCTA members were firmly against any such change. In 1993, however, cable operators considered the legislative, judicial, and regulatory pressure they faced, and quietly reassessed their position. In early 1994 the industry began to publicize its new willingness to let phone companies into cable if reciprocal privileges were granted. Subsequently NCTA identified a few basic goals for the new telecommunications legislation and pressed for these policies in a relatively low-key manner.

Implementation of the resulting telecommunications act has not moved rapidly. The Bell telephone companies decided to contest the constitutionality of three of the provisions of the bill. The provision deregulating fees for large cable systems did not go into effect until March 1999. Moreover the considerable expenditures required to enter the new markets were being made more slowly than anticipated.

FUTURE DIRECTIONS

With the FCC mandate to transition from analog to digital signal transmission by 2006, NCTA is faced with a major battle in the familiar arena of cable versus broadcast interests. Already discontent about the "must carry" rule requiring cable operators to carry the analog signals of most local stations, NCTA has balked at proposals expanding the policy to include both digital and analog formats, saying that some two-thirds of cable operators do not have the capacity to comply. NCTA warns that under such rules cable programming will be dropped to accommodate broadcast signals. At the same time, broadcasters assert that they need the promise of "must carry" to convince investors to finance their switch to digital equipment.

In early 1999 both NCTA and broadcast representatives maintained no-compromise stances on the digital "must carry" issue, as the FCC began proceedings to determine future policy. In 1997 NCTA had challenged existing "must carry" rules in the Supreme Court, but was disappointed by a 5 to 4 decision affirming the constitutionality of FCC "must carry" rules.

The first digital transmissions in the United States began in late 1998, including the presentation of the first high definition television (HDTV) programs, which have superior picture and sound quality. At the time, however, few broadcasters had HDTV programming to offer and few stores offered the digital-HDTV receivers required by HDTV programs. The 2006 deadline, when broadcasters would give up rights to the analog spectrum, is likely to be extended if a sufficient number of viewers have not purchased digital TV sets. NCTA would like to see such market forces control the transition from analog to digital, rather than the FCC.

GROUP RESOURCES

For details about current issues and technological developments as well as membership information, access the NCTA Web site at http://www.ncta.com. For more information about the NCTA write to the National Cable Television Association, 1724 Massachusetts Ave. NW, Washington, DC 20036 or call (202) 775-3669.

GROUP PUBLICATIONS

The NCTA's primary form of publication is its press releases, covering the latest cable industry issues. Occasionally the organization also releases research reports as well. For more information on any of the NCTA's publications, write to the National Cable Television Association, 1724 Massachusetts Ave. NW, Washington, DC 20036 or call (202) 775-3669.

BIBLIOGRAPHY

Aversa, Jeannine. "Bill Would Extend Power of FCC Over Cable Rates." *Rocky Mountain News*, 26 February 1998.

Beltz, Cynthia. "Talk is Cheap." *Reason*, 18 August 1996.

Blake, Kevin. "Cable vs. Satellite TV: The Battle Heats Up." *Consumers' Research Magazine*, 1 March 1997.

Eisenberg, Daniel, and Brian Roberts. "Q&A: Brian Roberts Thinks Cable Will Deliver." *Time*, 1 December 1997.

Haddad, Charles. "AT&T Bids For TCI: Effect On The Cable Industry." *Atlanta Journal and Constitution* , 26 June 1998.

Halonen, Doug. "NCTA, CEMA Set Digital Standards." *Electronic Media*, 8 November 1998.

———. "NCTA Vows to Fight Digital Must-Carry." *Electronic Media*, 19 October 1998.

Hearn, Ted. "Anstrom Ponders Telecom Act Fallout." *Multichannel News*, 26 February 1996.

Lieberman, David. "Cable Industry Polishes Image." *USA Today*, 2 December 1997.

———. "C-SPAN Chief: Digital TV May Hog Cable Space." *USA Today*, 2 June 1998.

"NCTA Says Mandatory Unbundling Will Reduce Infrastructure Investment." *Communications Today*, 11 December 1998.

Sanger, Elizabeth. "TV's Money Box." 1 March 1998.

National Cattlemen's Beef Association (NCBA)

WHAT IS ITS MISSION?

The National Cattlemen's Beef Association (NCBA) identifies itself as "the marketing organization and trade association for America's one million cattle farmers and ranchers." With offices in Denver, Chicago, and Washington, D.C., the NCBA is a consumer-focused, producer-directed organization representing the largest segment of the nation's food and fiber industry. The NCBA works to achieve the vision set forth in its Web site: "A dynamic and profitable beef industry, which concentrates resources around a unified plan, consistently meets consumer needs, and increases demand."

HOW IS IT STRUCTURED?

NCBA headquarters are located in Denver, Colorado, and house the organization's communications, association, and administrative functions. The CEO presides over all staff functions and serves until he or she resigns. A Chicago branch office carries out marketing, advertising, market and nutrition research, and new product development. The Washington, D.C., office—known as the NCBA Center for Public Policy—coordinates policy development and government-related affairs. Functions at the center include monitoring legislation, lobbying, and otherwise encouraging congressmen to support the organization's agenda. The NCBA political action committee (PAC), which raises campaign money for political candidates supportive of the organization's mission, operates primarily through the Washington, D.C., office.

ESTABLISHED: 1898
EMPLOYEES: 165
MEMBERS: 40,000
PAC: National Cattlemen's Beef Association PAC

Contact Information:
ADDRESS: 5420 South Quebec St.
    Greenwood Village, CO 80111-1904
PHONE: (303) 694-2851
FAX: (303) 694-0305
E-MAIL: cows@beef.org
URL: http://www.beef.org/ncba.htm
PRESIDENT: Clark Willingham

The organization is governed by four officers who each serve one-year terms (including president, vice president, president-elect, and chief executive officer or CEO). Immediately beneath the officers are two boards; the Dues Division Board and the Checkoff Division Board. The boards preside over a number of policy-setting committees focusing on the following industry areas: consumer marketing, communications, quality, public policy, and association services and administration. Additional committees are responsible for such administrative areas as audit, budget, evaluation, planning, nominating, and the formulation of resolutions addressing NCBA administrative issues. Each committee is headed by a chairperson and vice chairman who work with NCBA staff support.

The NCBA has two divisions: the Checkoff Division and the Dues Division. The Checkoff Division of the NCBA is responsible for beef product promotion and research and is financed by the "beef checkoff," a beef industry self-help program that collects $1 per head of cattle sold, including imports. Checkoff funds are administered by the Cattlemen's Beef Research and Promotion Board, a 111-member group appointed by the U.S. Department of Agriculture that is separate from the NCBA but that shares a budget as part of a joint operating agreement with the NCBA. The NCBA's Checkoff Division also oversees 45 State Beef Councils, which receive 50 cents for every dollar collected in checkoff funds for use in local programs that will promote and increase the demand for beef in the United States. The NCBA's Dues Division, which is financed by organization members, works to influence government policies through both lobbying for the development of pro-NCBA policies and government monitoring.

The NCBA forms alliances with related industry groups. For example, American National CattleWomen is a 5,600-member group that has a working arrangement with the NCBA. The NCBA also works closely with the Cattlemen's Beef Research and Promotion Board, which represents U.S. and overseas beef producers, as well as the U.S. Meat Export Federation, a group devoted identifying and expanding foreign markets for U.S.-reared beef.

Cattlemen join the NCBA at a dues rate based on an initial figure and adjusted according to how many head of cattle they own. Members receive organization publications and have one vote each in policy formulation, regardless of the size of their herd. Any beef producer, regardless of the size of his or her operation, may join the organization. The NCBA's policies are developed by members within the organization's committee structure. Policies and programs are approved or modified at an annual NCBA Stakeholder Congress, where each member is allowed to cast his or her vote on the proposals under consideration.

PRIMARY FUNCTIONS

The activities of the NCBA are guided by one overriding goal: to ensure the health and growth of the beef industry. Consequently, the organization's constant focus is to initiate and support the passage of legislation that supports its member's interests. This is sometimes accomplished in concert with other groups. For example, in April of 1998 the NCBA, along with the American Farm Bureau Federation and the National Farmers Union, requested that the U.S. Senate conduct a hearing to study the reason behind the consistently low to-market prices in the livestock industry. The NCBA has also lobbied for the expansion of international trade through international trade agreements like the North American Free Trade Agreement (NAFTA).

The NCBA carries out educational programs, seminars, and conferences that benefit those in the beef industry. Regional meetings are sponsored by the organization throughout the year, one of several ways the NCBA alerts its members to beef marketing and production trends. In May of 1998, for example, the organization's *National Cattlemen* magazine reported that demand for prepared beef products (such as ready-to-eat pot roast, as well as more typical beef deli selections) was on the rise because U.S. consumers have exhibited a trend of spending less and less time cooking meat for their eat-at-home meals. In response to this trend, the NCBA formed a Prepared Beef Task Force to monitor the changing consumer market and report to its members so operations can be made more profitable.

The NCBA also plays a role in shaping the direction of industry research. At the organization's 1998 Centennial Convention members established priorities for research focusing on the pathogen *E.coli* 0157:H7, which had sparked media attention due to its presence in infected meat in the 1990s. *E.coli* is a bacterium that is toxic if ingested, and its growth is promoted in undercooked meat such as the ground beef used in hamburgers.

Finally, the NCBA promotes beef consumption among consumers. For example, the Idaho NCBA council hosted a Celebrity Beef Challenge in which celebrities judged various beef dishes. The Florida Council created a brochure which pointed out how beef can be part of a healthy diet for women. When local promotions like these prove successful, the councils share their strategies so other states can use them.

PROGRAMS

NCBA programs all work toward the organization's goal: to promote beef consumption, expand awareness of the product, and create new markets. To this end the organization encourages its members to promote beef through the sharing of information or through advocacy efforts. One example of such a networking and information-gathering opportunity for members is the NCBA's annual Cattle Industry Conference; the 1998 conference included seminars on such topics as irradiated beef, product demand, the future retail beef market, and new products.

Programs like the NCBA's *Carcass Data Service,* which allows members who pay a fee to receive information—including marbling and fat content—about their cattle after they are slaughtered, promote education and awareness among members. Information and research regarding quality issues are shared through the NCBA's Beef Quality Assurance (BQA) program, an ongoing effort to monitor quality and to bring industry stakeholders together.

The program that has one of the greatest impacts on the NCBA's mission is the Checkoff Division's beef checkoff program. Founded in 1985 and administered by the government-run Cattlemen's Beef Research and Promotion Board, the program collects $1 for each head of cattle sold in the United States, including cattle imported into the country. Fifty percent of this money is returned to the NCBA for use in beef marketing and awareness programs at the state council level. Between 1987 and 1997 the checkoff, which is assessed to all sellers of cattle regardless of their membership in the NCBA, generated $890 million in revenue.

According to NCBA reports, the checkoff program has been an effective way to create beef marketing opportunities. The program funded a TV ad campaign titled *Beef: It's What You Want* that aired almost 3,000 television commercials promoting beef between 1997 and 1998. Checkoff funds are also used to develop and distribute recipes in advertising supplements to give consumers new ideas for preparing beef. Checkoff funds also finance nutrition campaigns about beef—one such program circulated information showing beef to be superior in nutritional quality to chicken or fish.

The funds from the checkoff program also drive research that works to eliminate contaminants in beef, and to assure consumers that beef is safe to eat. Checkoff funding also allows the NCBA to develop and promote new beef products, such as the rotisserie beef roast the organization created as an alternative to similar chicken products. Programs may also include educating beef sellers and consumers on the value of underutilized cuts of meat.

BUDGET:
1996 NCBA Revenue

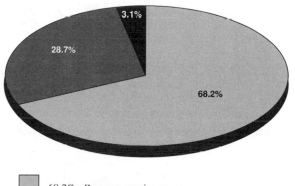

■ 68.2%: Program service revenue

■ 28.7%: Member dues

■ 3.1%: Sales from inventory, rental income, and other sources

1996 NCBA Expenses

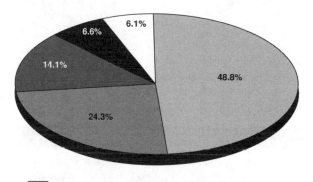

■ 48.8%: Consumer marketing

■ 24.3%: Communications, general service and administration

■ 14.1%: Compensation of officers, employee salaries and benefits

■ 6.6%: Quality initiatives

□ 6.1%: Association services and public policy

BUDGET INFORMATION

The NCBA developed a joint 1998 budget with the Cattlemen's Beef Board of $74.3 million. This budget included $55.8 million from state funding and checkoff-program monies that were earmarked for promotion (including export promotion), research, and consumer information programs. An additional $18.4 million in

income anticipated from member dues and other non-checkoff sources was earmarked for policy and governmental affairs initiatives, as well as foreign market development. NCBA member dues provide much-needed support for the organization's lobbying efforts, since checkoff money cannot legally be used to support political initiatives.

FAST FACTS

A single hamburger can contain meat from 100 cattle raised in four different countries.

(Source: Attributed to Nicols Fox, author of a book on food poisoning in: "As Hamburgers Go, So Goes America?" *Economist*, August 23, 1997.)

1996 tax records showed the NCBA with total revenue of $48,681,874 (including $234,031 in contributions from General Motors, Bayer, Walco, and other corporations with shared interests). The total revenue consisted of $33,179,080 in program service income; $13,907,588 from member dues; $188,081 in rental income; $681,870 in sales from inventory; and $351,303 from other sources. Expenses for 1996 totaled $48,649,596: $1,371,950 for compensation of NCBA officers, $5,140,713 for other salaries, $356,707 for employee benefits, $23,744,438 for consumer marketing, $3,215,356 for quality initiatives, $7,571,977 for communications, $1,870,469 for association services, $1,104,154 for public policy, and $4,273,832 for general service and administration.

HISTORY

The NCBA was founded in Denver, Colorado, in 1898 as the National Live Stock Growers Association. Three previous attempts had been made to create such a national organization. The cattlemen who created the organization that would later become the NCBA wished to create an organization that would be free from the influence of political promoters. They anticipated meeting once a year to discuss issues that affected them collectively. While the first annual organization convention was spent structuring the new association and voting in its first officers, the 1899 convention focused on identifying issues important to the organization's growing membership: rapid and more humane rail transportation, high bred stock, the modernization of meat packing houses, national and state quarantines, and thorough live stock inspection by states.

Prior to the turn of the twentieth century it was legal to sell food containing small amounts of chemicals harmful to human health. In 1901 the founder of the Food & Drug Administration assembled a "poison squad" to identify poisons in food that were toxic to humans. The

findings resulted in the Pure Food and Drug Act of 1906 and the Meat Inspection Act of 1906. These two acts reshaped the beef industry, as they created the first nationwide regulations concerning the quality and safety of meat. Exactly what regulations are applied to beef has remained one of the NCBA's greatest concerns since this time. Concerns about the risk of contaminated beef increased throughout the century, as researchers identified harmful bacteria such as *E.coli* that thrived in organic environments like undercooked beef.

Establishing Revenue-Producing Checkoffs

In 1922 the first voluntary checkoff initiative was established by the National Live Stock and Meat Board, at 5 cent per carload of animals. This checkoff would serve as the predecessor of the NCBA checkoff, and brought in $70,000 during its first year. Checkoff initiatives were largely supported by beef producers; when California founded the first state Beef Council in 1954, the state enacted a voluntary 10 cents per head assessment for cattle sold that was strongly supported by California Cattlemen.

While beef was a staple of the U.S. diet throughout the first half of the 20th century, the demand in beef began to drop in the 1960 and 1970s as health-conscious Americans began favoring poultry and fish, or experimenting with vegetarianism. This consumer trend may have contributed to a decline in the number of producers. According to an article in *USA Today*, the number of cattle growers had plummeted from 2.7 million in 1959 to 900,000 by 1996. The decline in consumer demand for beef products forced the NCBA to develop new ways to increase the demand and marketability of beef.

1985 Legislation Changes Industry

The 111-member Cattlemen's Beef Research and Promotion Board was established as part of the 1985 Federal Farm Bill as a vehicle for administering a national beef checkoff program. Checkoff funds continued to be largely supported by the industry; in a referendum in 1988, 79 percent of beef producers favored continuing the checkoff. In 1996 the National Cattlemen's Association merged with the National Live Stock and Meat Board to form the NCBA. Part of the purpose of the merger was to simplify operations, and bring both membership income and checkoff funds together under one plan and one budget. The Beef Board remained a separate entity from the NCBA, although the two have continued to operate under a joint agreement.

The passage of the 1996 Farm Bill was also significant for the agricultural community as a whole since it initiated the phase-out of government subsidy of agricultural crops that had been in place since the Great Depression of the 1930s. The NCBA supported the phase out, which was scheduled for implementation over the next seven years, claiming that government subsidies created unrealistic economic situations, raised the cost of producing beef, and made it hard for beef producers to be flexible in marketing their product.

In 1997 the NCBA also had a hand in lobbying for and achieving tax relief that indirectly benefited beef producers. Some of the favorable tax legislation included fully deductible health insurance for self-employed people by the year 2007 and an increase in the exemption that family businesses can take on their taxes—up from $600,000 to $1.3 million per business.

CURRENT POLITICAL ISSUES

The NCBA keeps a close watch on a number of issues that have the potential to impact the beef industry. For example, the organization is interested in promoting export markets for beef. When demand for beef began sagging in the United States in the 1980s, the beef industry was forced to look for other accessible markets. According to the organization, rapidly growing countries with young populations and disposable income had the potential to create overseas markets for U.S. beef. To ensure that federal policy facilitated such international agricultural trade, the NCBA lobbied Congress to continue funding the International Monetary Fund and the Market Access Program, programs that support such trade. The NCBA has also pushed for policy that would extend credit to financially troubled countries that wanted to import U.S. beef.

One long-standing barrier to exports faced by the NCBA is the European Union's ban on U.S. beef, begun in 1989 in objection to the growth hormones fed to U.S. cattle. According to the NCBA, growth hormones—used in 90 percent of U.S. cattle—have been proven safe in many studies. Several European countries, however, have feared the health impacts of the hormone on consumers. According to a *Time* article, the ban resulted in $140 million dollars lost to the U.S. beef industry during its first year, and at least an equivalent loss in potential sales every year since. The World Trade Organization ultimately ruled that the European Union's ban was unfair and in violation of free trade agreements, giving the European Union until May 13, 1999 to lift the ban or suffer U.S. retaliation.

Another great concern to the beef industry has been the decline in demand for beef by U.S. consumers. While some data suggest that Americans still eat plenty of convenience beef foods like hamburgers, many are switching to poultry or fish. Consumers cite inconsistency in quality as part of the problem. In an article in *USA Today*, consumers were dissatisfied with the quality of 20 percent of the beef they ordered or purchased.

Addressing consumer concerns both domestically and abroad, the NCBA is working hard to improve beef's

FAST FACTS

Per capita beef consumption went from 85 pounds a year per person in 1970 to 67 pounds in 1996. Per capita poultry consumption, meanwhile, jumped from 40.6 pounds in 1970 to nearly 72 pounds in 1996.

(Source: Rae Tyson. "Beef Industry Hits Hard Times," *USA Today,* March 5, 1996.)

image with the public, and is attempting to convince U.S. consumers that beef is both safe and healthy to eat. Many steps have been taken, including multi-million dollar advertising campaigns and the passage of special libel and defamation laws in several states. These laws have made it easier for businesses to sue individuals who criticize an industry's products and discourage others from buying them. When, in early 1996, television personality Oprah Winfrey seriously questioned the safety of beef on her popular talk show, these libel laws were put into action.

Case Study: Oprah Winfrey and Mad Cow Disease

In April of 1996 Winfrey interviewed former rancher-turned-vegetarian Howard Lyman on her show. Lyman suggested that "mad cow disease," a disease of unknown origin that had swept through the cattle population of Great Britain and killed several people, was quite possibly a threat in U.S. beef. The disease, which has been linked to cows eating the by-products of dead cows, causes brain disease and death in cattle and is also harmful and potentially fatal to humans who eat the infected beef. After hearing Lyman's story, Winfrey claimed: "It has just stopped me cold from eating another burger!"

Immediately after the popular show aired on national television, the beef industry claimed beef commodities plummeted. Citing Winfrey's comment as the cause for the industry setback, Pal Engler, an NCBA official, and other associated Texas cattlemen sued Winfrey, stating the show had caused beef prices to hit a 10-year low and seeking compensatory damages of $11 million. One plaintiff claimed he lost $6.7 million as a result of the show.

During the trial, which began in early 1998 and lasted six weeks, the NCBA took advantage of the publicity and media attention to tell everyone that beef produced in the United States was not infected with mad cow disease. On February 26, 1998, a jury held that

Winfrey's statements were protected as free speech by the First Amendment. NCBA officials issued a statement saying that it was extremely disappointed in the outcome and concluded that its case may have been weakened by the jury's determination that Winfrey's comments did not apply specifically to cattle owned by the suing party and a bench ruling that certain provisions of the product libel law did not apply to the case. But the organization concluded that, along with increased awareness of mad cow disease, the trial had also generated an increased awareness that no health threat was posed by American beef. "We made a point emphatically that U.S. beef is safe," said Engler after the conclusion of the trial.

FUTURE DIRECTIONS

The NCBA will continue to concentrate on making U.S. beef desirable to a changing U.S. consumer, and to opening foreign markets. While customers in the 1940s wanted a tasty, juicy steak, the consumers of the 1990s were clamoring for leaner products that are convenient to prepare. Such changing trends will continue to affect how industry members breed cattle, as well as prompt them in areas of new product development, such as the successful prepared pot roast. The NCBA will also work toward stabilizing the demand for beef, which will involve focusing on product safety, product quality, and consumer marketing.

The organization will also continue to promote beef products that are convenient to prepare. According to the organization, U.S. households—particularly those containing working women—are increasingly pressed for time. NCBA research indicates that these consumers are looking for ways to eliminate time pressure in their lives and often resort to compressing such family activities as "the dinner hour." The organization recognizes that convenience of food preparation—resulting in less time in the kitchen—is a benefit that customers will pay a premium for.

In its long-range plan, the NCBA has deemed it imperative to stabilize the demand for beef by 2001. Strategies to attain this goal include: targeting information campaigns that promote both the safety and the nutritional value of beef; adding value at all stages of the beef production and marketing processes; and clearly identifying and prioritizing issues so that the organization and the industry it serves can best orchestrate efforts to influence beef-related policy.

GROUP RESOURCES

The NCBA Web site at http://www.beef.org features a number of resources, including recipes (http://www.beef.org/fh_recip/recipes.htm), cooking tips, NCBA merchandise (http://www.beef.org/organzns/ncba/ncba_

merchandise.htm; which feature a centennial line of gifts, clothing, and jewelry), and diaries from actual family cattle ranch operations (http://www.beef.org.inddiary/diarists.htm). The organization offers a link to a Web site dealing with safety and food-borne illness (*Fight BAC* at http://www.fightbac.org). *Ask a Dietitian* (http://www.beef.org/saf_libr/ask_an_expert.htm) is a Web site link designed to answer questions about beef nutritional issues. Also included at the NCBA Web site are current press releases and policy initiatives covering the following categories: conservation, farm policy, federal lands, food/nutrition, foreign trade, property rights, science/regulatory, and tax/credit.

GROUP PUBLICATIONS

The NCBA publishes the monthly magazine *National Cattlemen* and the weekly newsletter *Beef Business Bulletin* for members. A Web site library at http://www.beef.org/library.htm includes several publications, among them *Industry Statistics, The Beef Brief,* the monthly *NCBA Policy Report,* and "Wow That Cow." For more information, contact the NCBA by mail at 5420 South Quebec St., Greenwood Village, CO 80111; by phone at (303) 694-0305; or by fax at (303) 694-2851.

BIBLIOGRAPHY

"As Hamburgers Go, So Goes America?" *Economist,* 23 August 1997.

"Beef—It's Still a Winner." *Food Service Distributor,* 1 July 1996.

Birnbaum, Jeffrey H. "The Power 25: Washington's Power 25. Which Pressure Groups Are Best at Manipulating the Laws We Live By?" *Fortune,* 8 December 1997.

Frazier, Deborah. "Safe Meat Sells, Agriculture Chief Glickman Tells Cattlemen." *Rocky Mountain News,* 6 February 1998.

Groves, Martha. "Raising the Steaks." *Los Angeles Times,* 9 February 1997.

Lameiras, Maria M. "Make Theirs Meatless: Health, Ethics Prompt Many to Go Vegetarian." *Atlanta Journal & Constitution,* 16 January 1998.

Ochs, Ridgely, Jamie Talan, Bob Cooke, Tom Maier, and Dana B. Silverstein. "What's Good to Eat?" *Newsday,* 7 July 1996.

"Oprah: Broadcast Offered Both Sides." *Star Tribune,* 5 February 1998.

Tyson, Rae. "Beef Industry Hits Hard Times." *USA Today,* 5 March 1996.

Strickland, Debbie. "Family Pride at Steak: For Georgia's Cattlewoman of the Year, Beef Is More than Just What's for Dinner." *Atlanta Journal and Constitution,* 11 April 1996.

"Will *E.coli* Scare Make Mincemeat of the Burger?" *Rocky Mountain News,* 24 August 1997.

National Coalition Against Domestic Violence (NCADV)

WHAT IS ITS MISSION?

According to the organization's 1997 annual report, the National Coalition Against Domestic Violence (NCADV) was founded in 1978 in order to "empower battered women and their children, and to eliminate personal and societal violence in the lives of women and their children." It is the only national organization representing state and local organizations and individuals working to help battered women and their children. Specifically, the NCADV works to facilitate or coordinate the efforts of domestic violence programs at the community and state levels to raise money and develop services.

ESTABLISHED: 1978
EMPLOYEES: 10
MEMBERS: 1,700
PAC: None

Contact Information:

ADDRESS: PO Box 18749
    Denver, CO 80218
PHONE: (303) 839-1852
FAX: (303) 831-9251
URL: http://www.webmerchants.com/ncadv
EXECUTIVE DIRECTOR: Rita Smith

HOW IS IT STRUCTURED?

The NCADV is a nonprofit, feminist organization based in Denver, Colorado. The NCADV is governed by a board of directors that consists of women from around the country who work on behalf of domestic violence programs within their own communities. The board also consists of representatives from the various task forces within the coalition. These task forces, which include battered and formerly battered women; women of color; jewish women; and lesbians of color, were created soon after the NCADV was formed in 1978 in order to address the problems many feminist organizations found themselves facing on the local level, namely that the factionalization of many feminist organizations along lines of race, class, and sexual orientation sometimes caused communication problems. The task forces research and address issues affecting the groups they represent, ensur-

FAST FACTS

Women are 10 times as likely as men to be abused by their partners.

(Source: U.S. Department of Justice, 1994.)

ing that no members are left without representation at the national level.

The NCADV operates two offices. The office in Washington, D.C., includes a membership specialist, and a public policy specialist. The public policy specialist tracks and analyzes all legislation affecting the concerns of the organization and its members as well as the women they serve. She also testifies at congressional hearings and works with others to develop and lobby for legislation beneficial to victims of domestic abuse and their children. The NCADV office in Denver is larger, and serves as the headquarters for the organization. This location has offices for executive, membership, finance, and resource development directors, as well as for information specialists and conference coordinators.

In 1997 the NCADV boasted a membership base of approximately 1,700 coalitions, organizations, and individuals organized into several categories. Active organizational members are the only members who enjoy voting privileges and who are allowed to participate in NCADV policy decisions. Active organizational memberships are primarily made up of programs and institutions that work directly on behalf of battered women and their children. Organizations are carefully screened by the NCADV before being granted membership at this level. In order to become an active organizational member, organizations must reflect feminist principles and cultural diversity. For example, each organization must include women from a variety of ethnic, cultural, and socio-economic backgrounds.

Other levels of membership are not screened because such levels do not confer policy and voting rights. These other membership levels include small donors, youths, supportive organizations, supportive individuals, and major donors.

PRIMARY FUNCTIONS

Since its inception, the NCADV has worked to create a national network of state and local agencies dedi-

cated to helping victims of domestic abuse. The NCADV provides these local programs and agencies with information about funding as well as technical assistance. It has also helped to create model treatment programs, such as the Small Business Project, which helps women achieve economic independence, allowing victims to break the patterns of dependence that contribute to their inability to escape from abusive situations.

The NCADV also works to educate the public about domestic violence. It sponsors a bi-yearly conference on the subject and also sponsors Domestic Violence Awareness Month each October, where communities throughout the country hold special events designed to draw attention to the seriousness and magnitude, of domestic violence. Finally, through its Washington, D.C., office, the NCADV monitors, drafts, and lobbies for legislation that affects battered women and their children. The NCADV has also gathered and presented testimony before congressional task forces investigating family violence and has worked with Congress to develop funding for domestic abuse programs.

PROGRAMS

The NCADV sponsors several programs supporting local and community organizations dedicated to helping battered women and their children. Most of these programs are designed either to aid women who are the victims of domestic violence, or to publicize the issue of domestic violence and educate the public.

The NCADV publishes the *National Directory of Domestic Violence Programs,* which contains information on over 2,000 domestic violence programs across the country. The organization also works through its Public Policy Program, not only to identify concerns about pending legislation concerning domestic abuse, but to generate and publish updates and alerts that are distributed to local and community domestic abuse programs as a means of organizing public and political response. Through its Information and Referral Services, the NCADV responds to requests from individuals and agencies concerning domestic abuse programs and public awareness. It responds to lawyers, doctors and clinics, police officers, the media, shelters, and the battered women themselves, as well as concerned friends and family members. In addition, the NCADV has established the Face to Face Program, which helps women find plastic surgeons who will remove the physical scars left from domestic violence injuries at no charge.

The NCADV attempts to generate national and international awareness about domestic violence. Its Remember My Name Project consists of a national registry listing the names of women who were killed by their husbands or boyfriends. Working with *Ms.* magazine on an annual basis, the organization collects names and produces a poster for Domestic Violence Awareness

Month that lists the preceding year's victims. Through its International Project, the NCADV also works to create a connection between the battered women's movement in the United States and international efforts to address issues of violence against women.

BUDGET INFORMATION

In 1995 the NCADV reported an income of $270,427, and assets of $98,939. The NCADV receives approximately 23 percent of its funding from membership dues; 17 percent from product sales; 15 percent from combined federal campaigns; 30 percent from corporate grants; 11 percent from foundation grants; three percent from individual contributions and one percent of its revenue from other sources.

HISTORY

The NCADV was created in Washington, D.C., in 1978, during hearings being conducted by the U.S. Commission on Civil Rights on battered women. Although the battered women's political movement had been active since the early 1970s, there was no organized national coalition to address the issues of battering and domestic violence. The major concern of feminists discussing the formation of a national coalition was the struggle for financial resources. They feared that the creation of a national organization would drain donations from local agencies and shelters that were already struggling to keep themselves financially solvent. However, the Civil Rights Commission's hearings helped convince activists that a national coalition would be a valuable asset for local agencies dedicated to helping battered women and their children, not only helping to create and maintain lines of communication between these separate agencies, but also helping them to locate and take advantage of new sources of funding. By the end of the Civil Rights Commission's hearings, the NCADV had formed a steering committee whose purpose was to research and suggest an organizational structure, and plan a national conference.

During the first years of its existence, the organization devoted most of its resources to planning a national conference and finding the financial resources which would allow it to continue its operations. In addition, the coalition also began monitoring national legislation affecting victims of domestic abuse and their children. Its first national conference took place in 1980.

In 1981 the NCADV established its first annual Day of Unity, which is observed on October 1. The purpose of the Day of Unity was to raise the public consciousness about the presence and prevalence of domestic violence in their communities and to connect agencies and individuals working on behalf of battered women. The

BUDGET:
1995 NCADV Revenue

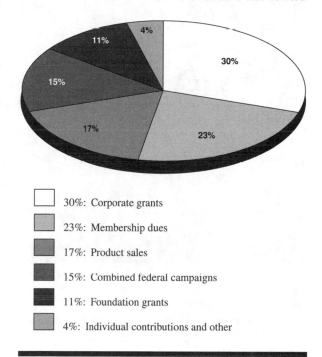

- ☐ 30%: Corporate grants
- ☐ 23%: Membership dues
- ☐ 17%: Product sales
- ☐ 15%: Combined federal campaigns
- ☐ 11%: Foundation grants
- ☐ 4%: Individual contributions and other

Day of Unity is still observed, and activities include purple ribbon campaigns and library displays. Community activists distribute purple ribbons to clergy members, police chiefs, judges, librarians, and other public figures as a means of remembering victims of domestic abuse and raising public awareness about the issue. Library displays serve the same purpose, often exhibiting posters and flyers published by the NCADV.

By 1987 the Day of Unity had evolved into the Domestic Violence Awareness Month (October), during which local shelters distributed information and resources about domestic violence to the public. During this month, activists from the NCADV also appear on national television and radio programs in their efforts to raise funds for shelters and to raise awareness about domestic abuse. In 1989 the NCADV opened its first national toll-free hotline, providing information services to battered women as well as to those agencies and individuals dedicated to helping them, including police officers, judges, shelter personnel, and emergency-room doctors and nurses. Also that year Congress passed the first Domestic Violence Awareness Month legislation, officially reserving the month of October for this purpose; the NCADV has worked to ensure that similar legislation is passed every year.

Demonstrations outside the residence of O. J. Simpson. Simpson had a documented history of spousal abuse against his ex-wife. The National Coalition Against Domestic Violence works to protect battered women and their children. (Photograph by Paul Sakuma, AP/Wide World Photo)

During the 1990s the NCADV initiated several innovative projects and programs designed to raise money for shelters and to raise public awareness about the issue. In 1992 the NCADV created a legislative committee based in Washington, D.C., the purpose of which was to support legislation affecting battered women and their children, increase public awareness of issues related to violence against women, and serve as a communications bridge between state legislatures. In 1994 it established the Teen Dating Violence Video Resource Project with the video *Rough Love,* describing the symptoms and effects of violent relationships among teenagers. This video project was a response to the growing research which suggested that many victims of domestic abuse had become involved with their batterers while they were still teenagers, entering into a pattern of abuse that was difficult to break later on.

Also in 1994 the organization supported a Colorado bill that declared menacing and harassing a woman to be against the law. When the "stalker bill" was passed, the media relations specialist for the NCADV was present, bearing a poster the NCADV had created with a picture of a coffin with flowers on it and the message: "He Beat Her 150 Times. She Only Got Flowers Once." The poster quickly became one of the NCADV's best-selling products.

The NCADV's legislative committee also lobbied for the passage of 1994's Violence against Women Act, which set aside special funds for the building and support of battered women's shelters. At the 1997 White House Conference on Hate Crimes, the organization's legislative committee lobbied for inclusion of crimes against women as a hate crime under the new laws.

CURRENT POLITICAL ISSUES

The NCADV has addressed many challenges since its creation. Some of the most serious of these involve the coalition's ongoing efforts to define its beliefs and principles and then operate according to them. In its efforts to connect activists and shelters across the country and to act on behalf of all battered women, the NCADV has been forced into confrontations with other lobbying groups, government agencies, and even members of its own organization.

As a result of its feminist philosophy, the NCADV is dedicated to diversity among its members and staff. Since domestic abuse affects women from all social and economic classes, as well as all races and ethnicities, the NCADV wants to ensure that its membership reflects this diversity. However, this diversity sometimes contributes to conflicts between members. Activists working against domestic violence have often criticized the fact that the feminist movement seems to focus on issues affecting middle- to upper-middle-class white women at the exclusion of women of color, poor women, and lesbians. Sensitive to such criticism, the NCADV formed several task forces immediately after its creation to ensure inclusiveness and diversity at the national level.

Although the NCADV immediately addressed concerns about divisiveness based on differences in race, social class, and sexual orientation, some of its other feminist principles have been more painful to honor. In 1987 it was awarded a substantial grant from the Johnson & Johnson Company that allowed the coalition to create and maintain a national domestic violence hot line. The hot line was in service 24 hours a day and operators took calls from battered women from around the country, providing information about local shelters and domestic abuse centers in their areas.

In 1989, however, the NCADV learned that Johnson & Johnson had financial holdings in South Africa. At this time, the South African government was operating under a system of apartheid, or forced segregation. The apartheid system did not allow black South Africans to hold political office or hold any public service job that would allow them any authority over white South Africans. By accepting a grant from a corporation who was still financially supporting this system of government, critics argued that the NCADV was itself implicitly supporting, or at least profiting from, the system of apartheid. The coalition returned the money in 1989.

The NCADV's work on behalf of the 1990 Immigration Fraud Act also illustrates the organization's belief that the protection of battered women knows neither borders nor class distinctions. The NCADV worked diligently to ensure that the act contained a provision allowing battered immigrant women to seek waivers to deportation laws. In order to stay in the United States, an immigrant must be married for two years to a U.S. citizen. Immigrant women who were abused were often threatened with deportation by their spouses if they tried to seek counseling or help from the police. Because of the NCADV's influence, the law included provisions allowing battered immigrant women to escape from their abusive spouses without being shipped out of the country.

In 1997 the legislative committee of the NCADV was also heavily involved in the White House Conference on Hate Crimes, lobbying to make sure gender was included as a hate-crime designation during the drafting of hate-crime laws. Hate-crime laws are designed to add special penalties to violent crimes committed against someone because of their race and/or religious persuasion. The NCADV legislative committee lobbied successfully to ensure that violence against women, in the form of domestic abuse and rape, was included among these definitions.

FUTURE DIRECTIONS

The NCADV has expanded its base to begin addressing issues of child custody, working to ensure that women who are abused do not lose custody of their children to their abusers, and preventing organizations from passing any legislation that might erode the rights or safety of battered women and their children. For example, the NCADV continues to effectively lobby against the National Rifle Association's efforts to overturn the Domestic Violence Offender Gun Ban Law, which prohibits men convicted of domestic abuse from owning a gun.

GROUP RESOURCES

The NCADV maintains a Web site at http://www.webmerchants.com/ncadv which provides information on the history and background of the coalition. The NCADV also provides information and referral services through its office, which can be reached by calling (303) 831-9251 or by writing to the National Coalition Against Domestic Violence, PO Box 18749, Denver, CO 80218. The NCADV also publishes an information packet about domestic abuse and a yearly edition of its *National Directory of Domestic Violence Programs,* both of which can be obtained by contacting the coalition at any of the addresses listed above.

GROUP PUBLICATIONS

The NCADV publishes several informational brochures and directories for individuals and agencies working with battered women and their children. These include the *National Directory of Domestic Violence Programs;* a Rural Resource Task Force information packet; the *Domestic Violence Awareness Month Manual,* a guide for agencies and individuals who want to participate in NCADV activities; and its *Open Minds, Open Doors: Working with Women with Disabilities Resource Manual.* In addition, the NCADV publishes and distributes the *Teen Dating Violence Resource Manual* and the *Rough Love Video and Teaching Guide* focusing on violence against teenage women. The coalition also offers a broad variety of other publications, posters, T-shirts, pins, and bumper stickers that can be used for training and awareness activities. The NCADV prints a full publication and product catalog that can be obtained by calling the NCADV at (303) 831-9251, by writing to the National Coalition against Domestic Violence, PO Box 18749, Denver, CO 80218, or by visiting the NCADV Web site at http://www.webmerchants.com/ncadv.

BIBLIOGRAPHY

Berry, Dawn Bradley. *Domestic Violence Sourcebook*. Los Angeles: RGA Publishing Group Inc., 1995.

Blair, Anita K. "Against the Violence against Women Act." *New York Times*, 25 July 1995.

Brott, Armin A. "Is Domestic Violence Really That Prevalent?" *Washington Post*, 31 July 1994.

"The Case for Nicole." *New York Times*, 19 June 1994.

Forster, Jeff. "OJ Simpson and Domestic Abuse." *Patient Care*, 30 September 1994.

"Healing the Scars of Abuse." *Austin American Statesman*, 24 April 1995.

Jones, Ann. *Next Time She'll Be Dead*. Boston: Beacon Press, 1994.

"National Coalition Against Domestic Violence." *CQ Press*, 1995.

Russell, Diana E. *Rape in Marriage*. New York: Macmillan, 1982.

Schecter, Susan. *Women and Male Violence*. Boston: South End Press, 1983.

National Coalition for the Homeless (NCH)

ESTABLISHED: 1982
EMPLOYEES: 7
MEMBERS: 1,500
PAC: None

WHAT IS ITS MISSION?

According to the organization, "the mission of the National Coalition for the Homeless (NCH) is to end homelessness. Toward this end, the NCH engages in public education, policy advocacy, and grassroots organizing." Homelessness is a problem that has grown in the United States during the late twentieth century. Many factors contribute to the phenomenon, including lack of affordable housing, inadequate transitional facilities or support services for the mentally ill, and a minimum wage that makes it hard to afford decent living conditions. Homelessness is a problem that, according to advocate organizations like the NCH, can be solved by directly addressing such issues.

Contact Information:
ADDRESS: 1012 Fourteenth St. NW, #600
　　　　Washington, DC 20005-3406
PHONE: (202) 737-6444
FAX: (202) 737-6445
E-MAIL: nch@ari.net
URL: http://nch.ari.net
EXECUTIVE DIRECTOR: Mary Ann Gleason

HOW IS IT STRUCTURED?

NCH is an advocacy organization based in Washington, D.C. It is headed by an executive director who is assisted by a small staff including a health care policy analyst; a field organizer who liaisons with state and local groups working on homeless issues and also handles civil rights issues; and a public education coordinator who develops policy and education for homeless children and monitors welfare reform in conjunction with other groups such as the Children's Defense Fund.

The NCH is governed by a geographically and ethnically diverse 40-member board of directors. Individuals who were formerly homeless comprise 31 percent of the board. The board meets twice annually and, along with the executive director and NCH staff, sets policy

and direction. Board members develop organization vision along four workgroup areas: housing, health care, income, and civil rights. Board members serve indeterminate terms and are nominated and elected by a small board-nominating committee. A smaller executive committee deals with board administration; each member serves a two-year term.

Although NCH has a relatively small membership base, it has a much larger network, which includes independent Housing and Homeless Coalitions in all states except Kansas. The NCH liaisons and builds grassroots support with its network and members by keeping them informed of issues and legislative initiatives through monthly mailings of newsletters, fact sheets, and legislative alerts. Individuals and organizations pay membership dues ranging from $12.00 to $500.00 (1999). Members receive the NCH newsletter and a discount on publications.

PRIMARY FUNCTIONS

NCH takes a three-pronged approach to carrying out its mission of permanently ending homelessness. First, the organization carries out public education efforts. It maintains an on-line research library that, according to NCH, is the only one of its kind. The on-line resource offers information on all aspects of homelessness and contains research not normally found in other libraries. NCH staff frequently speak at workshops and conferences and address community groups, researchers, legislative staff, and the media on homeless issues. The organization publishes a bimonthly newsletter called *Safety Network* and fact sheets on homeless topics such as domestic violence and AIDS. NCH also carries out a number of ongoing public education programs.

Second, the NCH plays a major role in influencing and promoting legislative policy that affect the homeless. NCH staff monitor pending legislation, such as amendments to the McKinney Homeless Assistance Act of 1987 and proposed policy that would improve access to affordable housing, health care, or jobs. The organization provides Legislative Alerts (accessed on-line and through the mail) that summarize the policy in question and specifically recommend action.

In addition to harnessing grassroots efforts through Legislative Alerts and the publication of policy information, NCH mobilizes support by connecting with Housing and Homeless Coalition groups at the state and local level. NCH provides support and advocating skills to these groups by sharing written publications and visiting on site when needed. NCH also coordinates ongoing programs at the grassroots level, such as the National Homeless Civil Rights Organizing Project.

PROGRAMS

In accordance with its mission, NCH carries out a number of programs that deal with homeless issues. These programs are aimed both at educating the public about the state of homelessness in the United States and assisting homeless people to attain basic human rights such as decent housing, food, and education.

Several NCH programs serve as public education efforts. The Art and Literature Project aims to make the voices of the homeless heard through their art and writing. The project was established with the immediate, tangible goal of publishing a book featuring poetry and prose written by homeless individuals, illustrations by homeless artists, and a listing of organizations that feature visual art created by the homeless. The long term goal of the project is to create a better understanding of the struggles faced by individuals who are homeless.

The Homeless Voices Project brings a local understanding of homelessness to the general public by profiling homeless people throughout the United States. The project began by profiling the story of two homeless men in Seattle, Washington, and can be accessed on the NCH Web site.

NCH co-sponsors National Hunger and Homelessness Awareness Week with the National Student Campaign Against Hunger and Homelessness. The annual event takes place one week before Thanksgiving and the NCH offers tips available for planning local events. Examples include: fund-raising for a local homeless shelter or the Grate American Sleep Out. The Sleep Out is an awareness-raising activity where college students spend a night outside to "discuss, think, and learn about homelessness."

National Homeless Person's Memorial Day takes place every year on December 21 and honors homeless people who have died across the United States. NCH has sponsored the event since 1990 in Washington, D.C., but also encourages other cities and regions to hold events of their own. Events include candlelight vigils, religious services, and theatrical plays about homelessness. In addition to providing planning tools to communities that want to participate, NCH has released reports in conjunction with the event that summarize the status of homelessness and that recommend actions.

The NCH serves as a coordinator of street newspapers that are created by homeless populations in different locations. The Street Newspaper Project maintains a directory of these papers, sponsors conferences for networking among newspaper creators, maintains a press service for the papers, and helps new organizers get their paper off the ground. These papers not only serve a public education purpose, but provide meaningful work and financial assistance to the individuals that create them.

Other NCH programs offer direct assistance to the homeless population by improving their access to education or organizing advocacy for basic civil rights. For example, the Educational Rights Project was established to inform homeless families of their right to obtain public education for their children. According to NCH, homeless children are often denied access to educational facilities even though these restrictions are illegal. A 1996 study (Shinn and Weitzman) found that children made up 40 percent of the homeless in the United States and were the fastest growing segment of the homeless population. Another study (National Association of State Coordinators for the Education of Homeless Children and Youth, 1997) found that budget cuts in the 1990s had worsened the educational opportunities for homeless children. NCH claims that homeless children face barriers to education including transportation difficulties, immunization requirements, lack of clothing, and poor health. NCH has developed an informational packet that summarizes educational rights for children and is distributed to shelters and directly to homeless families.

The National Homeless Civil Rights Organizing Project is an ongoing program to document and fight civil rights abuse. Field offices in several urban locations across the United States are staffed with homeless or formerly homeless advocates who work with all local homeless groups to advance their efforts. The program documents instances of abuse to the homeless on videotape and uses the footage in advocacy and education efforts.

NCH's "You Don't Need A Home to Vote" program was established in 1992 with the goal of registering homeless people to vote. While initial attempts were successful and registered over 200,000 homeless voters, subsequent drives produced less registration activity. Part of the reason, suggests author and professor Joel Blau in a *Newsday* article (October 8, 1995), is that "They're too busy meeting their daily needs. It's hard to be politically active if you don't know where you're going to sleep tonight."

BUDGET INFORMATION

NCH is funded through member contributions, telemarketing efforts, assistance from foundations, and special event fund-raising. The Combined Federal Campaign, which allows federal employees to contribute part of their wages to a selected charitable cause, has historicaly provided over one-quarter of NCH's budget.

In 1997 NCH had support and revenue totaling $564,545, The largest source of revenue came from telemarketing ($221,627), followed by fees and honoraria ($54,929); dues and contributions ($50,542); grants ($22,084); publications ($15,648); appeals ($15,188); Combined Federal Campaign ($4,262); interest ($2,318); and other ($163,004).

NCH expenses in 1997 totaled $534,717 including public education ($155,371); policy advocacy ($113,056);

BUDGET:
1997 NCH Revenue

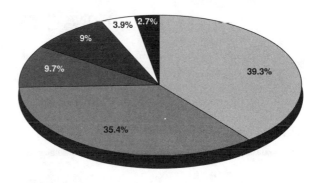

▣	39.3%: Telemarketing
▣	35.4%: Other including combined federal campaign
▣	9.7%: Fees and honoraria
▣	9%: Dues and contributions
□	3.9%: Grants
▣	2.7%: Appeals

1997 NCH Expenses

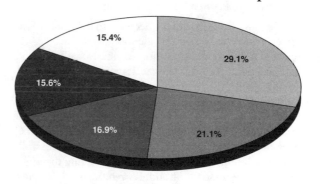

▣	29.1%: Public education
▣	21.1%: Policy advocacy
▣	16.9%: Fund raising and administration
▣	15.6%: Technical assistance
□	15.4%: Grassroots organizing

grassroots organizing ($82,292); technical assistance ($83,459); fund-raising ($90,629); and administration ($9,910).

FAST FACTS

One-third of all homeless men are combat veterans from the Korean, Vietnam, or Persian Gulf conflicts; 42 percent of these are Vietnam veterans.

(Source: Veterans Day Survey by International Union of Gospel Missions cited in: *Rocky Mountain News,* November 9, 1997.)

HISTORY

The NCH was founded by Robert Hayes, a New York city attorney whose interest in the homeless was sparked in the late 1970s. This interest grew as he began to talk to the many homeless individuals he passed on his way to and from work. He became actively involved when he worked on a case for his firm of Sullivan and Cromwell to secure shelter for more than 2,000 homeless New York men. Hayes soon became well known all over the city for his public interest efforts and over the years, expanded his talents to include a mastery of the legislative process and of public relations.

In 1982 Hayes made the decision to forsake his Wall Street career to work for the homeless. In 1984 he founded the National Coalition for the Homeless with a $10,000 grant from his previous law firm, as well as government and private sources of funding. The coalition started out with a $75,000 annual budget. The coalition, under Hayes, originally linked advocates from New York to Seattle. The organization added Washington D.C. operations in 1985. The Washington offices successfully achieved a number of policy initiatives during the 1980s including the removal of address requirements in qualifying for veteran's benefits.

While the NCH counted its various victories, concern was also on the rise about the Reagan administration's seeming unwillingness to address the growing problems surrounding the homeless. The administration did establish the first homeless task force in 1983, but it failed to implement any lasting policy or programs. Homeless advocates continued to push for the problems to be noticed and succeeded in proposing the Homeless Persons' Survival Act of 1986 (S. 2608, H.R. 5140,). Although the proposed policy contained what advocates such as NCH saw as far-reaching solutions to homelessness, only small parts of the original proposal were adopted. These included the Homeless Eligibility Clarification Act of 1986 (H.R. 5139), which facilitated ease in obtaining certain federal benefits like social security or food stamps, and the Homeless Housing Act (H.R. 5134), which earmarked funds for shelters and transitional housing.

In 1987 NCH achieved a hard-won milestone after lobbying for and passing the McKinney Homelessness Assistance Act (H.R. 558, Public Law 100-77), which, according to NCH, was only reluctantly signed by President Reagan. The act was the first, and as of 1999, the only federal legislative response to homelessness. Its provisions provided funding for shelter and food for the homeless, created opportunities for acquiring buildings for shelters, and made available programs to the homeless such as mental illness support services and drug abuse treatment. The NCH followed up by suing the federal government to enforce the McKinney Act and working with the New York law firm of Kaye, Scholer, Fierman, Hays & Handler, on a lawsuit to force the government to comply with a section of the act. In December 1988 NCH won a victory when the suit resulted in a permanent injunction requiring the government to comply with the act. NCH continued to lobby for amendments to the act in successive years; some of the new amendments addressed the needs of homeless children and individuals with AIDS.

Over the years, because of Hayes's high profile and his knack for public relations, the NCH's budget grew. By the late 1980s it was not uncommon for NCH to receive unsolicited donations, including $50,000 from First Boston Corporation. By 1989 the NCH budget had grown to $2.5 million and a staff of 20 people. But Hayes also had a reputation for not being a team player, which angered potential allies involved in homeless issues. An example is when he refused help of co-counsel from groups like the American Civil Liberties Union on a case involving housing rights for HIV positive homeless people.

Seven years after he founded the NCH, Hayes left to work for another New York law firm, under the condition that he spend one-third of his time in homeless advocacy efforts. But in 1992, Hayes surprised the New York law community and homeless advocates by relocating to Maine. He cited reasons such as wanting to devote more time to family and community causes, such as homeless advocacy.

The NCH continued to lobby on behalf of the McKinney Act throughout the 1990s when funding for the act went up and down. Allocations reached a record high of $1.4 billion in Fiscal Year 1995, however, programs were cut by 27% in FY 1996. NCH maintained that the act was a landmark first step, but only an emergency response to the problem of homelessness. According to NCH, homelessness in the United States will continue to increase if the causes are not effectively addressed by local, state, and federal government.

CURRENT POLITICAL ISSUES

The NCH advocates for issues that will improve conditions for homeless people in the United States and that would ultimately eradicate the instance of homelessness altogether. One issue that the organization addresses is the lack of affordable housing in the United States. According to a Housing and Urban Development report (April 28, 1998), the supply of affordable housing has continued to decrease and 5.3 billion households are living in a worst case scenario, meaning that these households pay more than half their income for rent or they live in substandard housing. These households are at risk of facing homelessness.

NCH advocated for policy that supports affordable housing opportunities for the potentially or already homeless, and fights legislation that would deny such opportunities. For example, NCH called on its supporters to urge congressional members to vote down the Fair Housing Amendments Act of 1998 (H.R. 3206). The proposed legislation would allow communities to deny the construction of group homes for people with disabilities. NCH and other advocates for the homeless also fought the signing into law of the Supplemental Spending Bill (H.R. 3579), which would cut funding for housing reserves ($2.3 million) and redirect it toward disaster relief and military spending. The NCH was unsuccessful in this campaign, and the bill became law in May 1998.

NCH is also concerned with the amount of the minimum wage. According to the organization, an hourly wage of $10.73 is required to afford a two-bedroom apartment that amounts to 30 percent of income. The minimum wage in 1999 was $5.15 per hour, or half that ideal. According to NCH, many homeless people are working part- or full-time jobs at substandard wages and are still unable to afford a permanent home. A 1997 survey conducted by the Conference of Mayors found that in 29 U.S. cities, 20 percent of homeless people worked part-time or full-time jobs. The NCH believes that minimum wage should be set at and related to housing costs; in May 1998, they urged supporters to push their legislators to pass proposed policy (S. 1805 and H.R. 3510) that would increase the minimum wage to $6.15 by 2000.

Homeless children, in particular, face unique obstacles and barriers. One right that is perennially denied to them is the right to an education. In 1997 using successful grassroots strategy, NCH helped restore funding to education programs for homeless youth that had suffered funding cuts in 1996.

Case Study: Funding for Homeless Youth Education

When federal programs that impacted education for homeless youth were slashed by 23 percent in 1996, many states had to shut down programs that allowed homeless children to access educational opportunities. NCH took immediate action to get funding restored in

FAST FACTS

It is estimated that over 760,000 people are homeless on any given night in the United States.

(Source: National Coalition for the Homeless. Fact Sheet, 1999.)

the following fiscal year. Staff monitored appropriations funding, paid many visits to Washington, and presented key decision makers with statistics from their constituencies. Most effectively, NCH enlisted the advocacy of two teachers from Pennsylvania.

In a meeting with staff of a key committee member, NCH let the teachers do the talking. NCH had hoped to restore funding to its previous level, but the teachers' testimony proved even more successful. With the passage of the appropriations bill for Fiscal Year 1998 (H.R. 2264), funding was restored to the original $4 million. In addition, the bill delivered another $2 million in program funding. This additional funding meant that school districts had the increased ability to offer homeless children and youth services that included transportation, school supplies, and after school programs.

FUTURE DIRECTIONS

In the future, NCH will focus on monitoring the impact of welfare reform on the homeless. According to the organization, although the federal government claims that the first two years of welfare reform (1996–1998) have proven successful, families and the homeless still need assistance and viable alternatives. Specifically, NCH will identify actions that can be taken by policy makers to create options to welfare and to low-wage employment.

GROUP RESOURCES

The NCH library is an on-line resource that compiles a number of reports and information on the homeless. It can be accessed on the NCH Web site at http://nch.ari.net/database.html. Publications in the library can be ordered by contacting the organization directly at 1012 Fourteenth St. NW #600, Washington, DC 20005-3406;

A homeless family has their Thanksgiving dinner on the grounds of the U.S. Capitol. The National Coalition for the Homeless engages in public education and grassroots organization to raise public awareness of the plight of the homeless.

(Reuters/Corbis Bettmann)

phone (202) 737-6444; fax (202) 737-6445. The NCH Web site also includes resources for monitoring legislation, including summarization of congressional testimony, reports, and a listing of congressional committees that deal with homeless issues. The Web site also includes tips for grassroots advocates to communicate with legislators.

GROUP PUBLICATIONS

Safety Network is the bimonthly newsletter of the NCH and is available by contacting the organization. NCH publishes fact sheets on homeless issues and reference sources such as *The Essential Reference on Homelessness: An Annotated Bibliography* and *A Directory of Statewide and National Homeless/Housing Advocacy Organizations.* The organization publishes dozens of reports on homeless issues that range in cost from $3.00 to $5.00. Publications can be obtained by contacting NCH at 1012 Fourteenth St. NW #600, Washington, DC 20005-3406; phone (202) 737-6444; fax (202) 737-6445.

BIBLIOGRAPHY

Campbell, Colin. "Media's Portrayal of Homeless Issue May Make it Worse." *Atlanta Journal and Constitution,* 14 December 1997.

Chawkins, Steve. "Building for the Future: In Complex Transaction, Social Agency Obtains Housing for Homeless and Couple Gain a Big Tax Break." *Los Angeles Times,* 23 February 1998.

Franklin, Marcus. "Homeless Vets Advocate Leads Conference."*Atlanta Journal and Constitution,* 2 May 1997.

"Taking Homeless Agencies To Task." *Newsday,* 2 February 1994.

Taylor, Kimberly Hayes. "Empty Promise Land: Poor Families Find the Downside to State's Booming Economy." *Star Tribune,* 22 February 1998.

Wilentz, Amy. "Cold Comfort for the Homeless Seeking Shelter and Compassion." *Time,* 19 January 1988.

National Committee for an Effective Congress (NCEC)

WHAT IS ITS MISSION?

The National Committee for an Effective Congress (NCEC) is dedicated to electing progressive individuals to the Senate and House of Representatives by contributing money, work, and campaigning expertise to candidates who support its principles. The NCEC advocates the traditional principles of American political liberalism: supporting women, minorities, the environment, civil rights, healthcare, housing, and the welfare safety net. It opposes what it considers extremism and the radical right.

HOW IS IT STRUCTURED?

The National Committee for an Effective Congress is a small organization with offices in Washington, D.C., and New York City. It is headed by a board of directors. The size of the board varies, but it may have as many as 50 members at any particular time. The board is appointed by the national director and its primary responsibility is to evaluate candidates for seats in Congress and to give them the NCEC's endorsement.

The Washington office is headed by the NCEC director. The director, who is selected by the national director and approved by the board of directors, is responsible for maintaining the NCEC's comprehensive databases of congressional and electoral information. The director also serves as a liaison between the organization and Congress.

Most of the NCEC's staff are based in Washington, however there is a staff located in New York City. The

ESTABLISHED: 1948
EMPLOYEES: 14
MEMBERS: 60,000
PAC: None

Contact Information:

ADDRESS: 122 C St. NW
    Washington, DC 20001
PHONE: (212) 686-4905
TOLL FREE: (800) 547-5911
E-MAIL: info@ncec.org
URL: http://www.ncec.org
NATIONAL DIRECTOR: Russell Hemenway

FAST FACTS

Only one-half of one percent of all Americans donate money to political candidates. Of those who do contribute, 85 percent are white males who earn $100,000 a year or more.

(Source: National Committee for an Effective Congress, 1998.)

group's national director oversees the New York office and is responsible for coordinating much of the NCEC's fundraising efforts. The national director is also the primary contact between the NCEC and its members.

NCEC members are its contributors. Membership confers no special privileges or benefits other than the opportunity to support the NCEC's work. NCEC members are located throughout the United States, but are concentrated in the Northeast and in California.

PRIMARY FUNCTIONS

The primary function of the NCEC is to support the election of progressive candidates to Congress. When making candidate endorsements, the NCEC considers a variety of criteria. Candidates must support programs and policies traditionally associated with political liberalism: civil rights; government aid to those in desperate need; open and ethical government; the environment; gun control; and freedom of choice. Candidates must be involved in races the organization judges to be "marginal," meaning key races where NCEC support could be the deciding factor.

An NCEC candidate must genuinely need the resources the group offers; the NCEC does not support candidates whose election is felt to be a sure thing. However candidates must have a real chance of being elected; the NCEC does not squander its resources on long shots. Besides endorsing candidates already running, the NCEC evaluates which incumbents might be easily beaten in an election. When such a seat has been found, the group goes to work recruiting an appropriate progressive challenger.

Candidates endorsed by the NCEC qualify for various kinds of assistance. The NCEC provides money for campaigns; however, direct financial contributions to campaigns are limited to $5,000 per candidate. However, private liberal contributors often rely on information pro-

vided by the NCEC to select candidates to support financially. On occasion the NCEC will introduce its members to candidates whose campaigns are in financial need.

The various information services the NCEC can provide to a candidate are often more important than financial aid. Staff members visit a candidate's headquarters and examine the budget, fundraising, and campaign strategies. The NCEC advises campaign teams how to make the best use of limited campaign resources, how to use the media effectively, and how to plan a candidate's schedule. Key aides are debriefed for information on their candidate, and his or her relations with the media and other politicians in the state.

Candidates endorsed by the NCEC gain access to its comprehensive databases of electoral and demographic information. The databases, considered among the very best and most comprehensive in the nation, contain detailed information on voting and voters for every precinct in the country. The Democratic National Committee provides the NCEC with its own polling data. Data also comes from members of Congress, their staffs, trade unions, and other sources. All NCEC information resources are provided at no charge to its candidates. NCEC technical information services include electoral and demographic precinct targeting, voter profile analysis, get-out-the-vote plans, candidate scheduling plans, media market analyses, and polling sample selections. One important advantage of NCEC data is that it enables candidates to efficiently allocate campaign resources by focusing on reaching important "swing votes"—votes that could go to either candidate—which frequently decide the outcome of an election.

The NCEC uses its databases in determining marginality ratings. These ratings assess and quantify—on a scale of 1 to 10—a candidate's real chances of winning an election. The NCEC's marginality ratings are used to determine which candidates the group will endorse. They are also used by a wide spectrum of other political groups to decide which candidates to support. These groups include the Democratic National Committee, EMILY's List, the AFL-CIO and other labor, women's, and environmental groups.

PROGRAMS

The NCEC is essentially a single-issue organization: to elect as many progressive candidates to Congress as possible. The organization's small staff devotes most of its time and energy to the information gathering, analysis, and fundraising that is essential to this work.

The NCEC has been greatly involved in the congressional redistricting. Every 10 years, following the U.S. census, Congress redraws district lines to account for growth, decline, and shifts in the population. This task can have dramatic implications for political parties and

BIOGRAPHY:
Eleanor Roosevelt

U.S. First Lady; Humanitarian (1884–1962) Eleanor Roosevelt is widely regarded as the most effective woman in the history of U.S. politics. As first lady, Roosevelt broke the "social hostess" mold her predecessors had cast. She held weekly press conferences that were limited to women reporters, wrote newspaper and magazine columns that addressed personal and political issues, had a highly successful radio program, and commanded exorbitant fees for lecture tours. For Depression-era work-relief programs, Roosevelt fought for equal access by African American citizens to available jobs. Said Roosevelt, "It is a question of the right to work and the right to work should know no color lines." She found government posts for many qualified women and never failed to use her unique access to the president to lobby his attention to the causes of the oppressed. Following the death of Franklin Roosevelt, President Harry Truman appointed her one of five U.S. delegates to the first United Nations General Assembly. Within six months,

she began work as chairman of the UN Human Rights Commission. Roosevelt was the driving force behind the Universal Declaration of Human Rights, which was ratified by the General Assembly on December 10, 1948. She refused in 1947 to support the newly formed Progressive Party, but formed with others the following year, the National Committee for an Effective Congress. For

the last dozen years of her life, Eleanor Roosevelt maintained an active and high-profile role in both national and world political arenas. At her funeral in 1962, former presidential candidate Adlai Stevenson said of Roosevelt, "She would rather light candles than curse the darkness."

voters alike. If lines are drawn so that a minority population is concentrated in a single district, they will often be more likely to elect a minority representative to Congress. On the other hand, if minority populations are split up between different districts where they are outnumbered by other voting groups, their distinct voice as a section of the population will be neutralized.

Politicians, officials, and party organizations ask for the NCEC's advice on redistricting because of its extraordinary database of voter information. These databases show the demographic makeup of each precinct on a street-by-street basis. NCEC experts work closely with the congressmen responsible for redistricting: they interpret data, point out voting blocs, and the like, to ensure that no group is excluded from the political process and that no group receives disproportionate influence from the new district lines.

BUDGET INFORMATION

The NCEC's budget in 1998 was approximately $1.2 million. Virtually all of the group's money came from member contributions. Some additional funds were earned by selling information to the DCCC. As a political organization, the NCEC is not eligible for foundation endowments or other grants.

HISTORY

The National Committee for an Effective Congress was founded in 1948 by Eleanor Roosevelt and a group of friends. They formed a nonpartisan group in response to the increasingly isolationist mood in the United States following World War II. The strategy they developed was to pool contributions from a committed group of donors and use the money to help elect candidates to the Senate and House of Representatives who recognized the responsibility of the United States as the leader of the free world. In its first year, the group endorsed and raised money for six candidates for Congress. They included mayor of Minneapolis Hubert Humphrey, Chicago alderman Paul Douglas, and Tennessee congressman Estes Kefauver. All six were elected.

During the late 1940s and early 1950s, the NCEC was an important part of a bipartisan coalition to fight Senator Joseph McCarthy and the anti-communist hysteria he unleashed in the United States. When the Senate finally voted to censure McCarthy for misconduct in 1954, both McCarthy and the press said NCEC was responsible for the vote. Its work exposing Senator McCarthy solidified the group's reputation as an opponent of the radical right in American politics. In later years, it would combat other right wing groups, such as the Ku Klux Klan, the John Birch Society, and the Moral Majority.

In 1958 the NCEC was responsible for the formation of the Democratic Study Group, a group of liberal

Congressmen who were opposed to Judge Smith, who, as chairman of the House Rules committee, had prevented civil rights legislation from reaching the floor of the House of Representatives. The Democratic Study Group was on the leading edge of liberal thinking in the House during 1959–60. The NCEC also supported the Wednesday Group and Republicans for Progress, two liberal Republican organizations. The NCEC recognized that important legislation, particularly that dealing with civil rights, could not be passed without bipartisan support. It continued to assist progressive Republicans as well as Democrats until the 1980s, when the religious right began to dominate the Republican Party. As a result, by 1998, the group was supporting Democratic candidates exclusively.

In 1965 Russ Hemenway was asked to take over the NCEC. Hemenway, who had been actively involved in reform politics in New York State, accepted the offer because he thought the NCEC could be transformed into an anti-war organization. When he joined the NCEC, the United States anti-war movement was still in its infancy. There was very little organized opposition to the country's involvement in Vietnam. The NCEC began supporting anti-war candidates and helping create anti-war coalitions on Capitol Hill. The group worked closely with Senator William Fulbright, who became one of Washington's most outspoken critics of the government's Vietnam policy, and supported Senator Eugene McCarthy's anti-war candidacy, which helped bring down the presidency of Lyndon Johnson. Hemenway's work made such an impact in Washington that his name was included in Richard Nixon's first Enemies List, an acknowledgment Hemenway calls the high point of his career.

In 1970–71 the NCEC wrote and saw passage of the 1971 Campaign Finance Act. That act was initiated when the NCEC realized that television stations were charging NCEC candidates the highest advertising rates possible. The act required that candidates be charged no more for TV advertising than the rates stations charged their best customers. It also contained provisions requiring that candidates disclose the sources of their funding. Most activist groups in Washington did not believe the bill had a chance and refused to support the project. When the bill passed after more than a year's work, the *New York Times* gave NCEC full credit for the bill and editorialized "When Richard Nixon signs the bill, he should give a pen to Russ Hemenway."

The NCEC was active in the fight to impeach Richard Nixon for his involvement in the Watergate scandal. It financed the first national poll on impeachment done by the Gallup organization. The poll showed overwhelmingly that Americans belived Nixon's personal involvement in the Watergate crimes should be investigated.

Campaign reform legislation that was passed in 1974 changed the way NCEC operated in congressional races. Suddenly the contributions it could make to a candidate were limited to $5,000. Barred from the $50,000 to $60,000 contributions it had been making, the organization had to find ways to translate that $5,000 into the greatest amount of political leverage possible. It began to develop the campaign services and electoral databases that later became the hallmarks of its work.

The NCEC worked hard in 1997–98 to win passage of a new campaign reform act. A slim majority of senators was scraped together in support of the bill, but a filibuster kept it from going to a vote in the Senate. The senators leading the filibuster offered compromises but others involved in the fight, who disagreed with the NCEC's policy of approaching issues one small step at a time, kept the compromise plans from going through. After the fight the NCEC believed that the only way a campaign reform bill could pass the senate was for the Democrats to win back majority status.

CURRENT POLITICAL ISSUES

The NCEC began its support of liberal candidates around the middle of the 1900s. By the 1990s the religious right within the Republican Party had gained unprecedented influence by refining its campaign organization and techniques. In 1994, largely as a result of this influence, the Republicans won a majority in both houses of Congress for the first time since 1955. Political observers in the media said a massive shift of political loyalties was underway in the United States. Newt Gingrich, the leader of the new Republican majority in the House, proclaimed his conservative program, "Contract with America." At the same he announced the end of the liberal movement that had begun with Franklin Roosevelt's New Deal in the 1930s. The NCEC looked like the last remains of a dying progressive movement.

Case Study: The 1998 Election

The Republicans had another strong showing in the 1996 congressional elections, gaining seats in the Senate and retaining control of the House. They continued to look strong going into the 1998 races. For the Democrats the election year got off to a particularly bad start. Early in the year, Independent Prosecutor Kenneth Starr charged President Clinton with carrying out an illicit love affair with White House intern Monica Lewinsky, allegedly instructing Lewinsky to lie about it if asked, and then lying about it himself while under oath. The scandal peaked in late summer when Lewinsky's grand jury testimony, which detailed her sexual history with the president, was released to the media.

Clinton was accused of perjury and obstruction; Republicans in Congress called for impeachment hearings. Democrats were in an uncomfortable position: all members of the House of Representatives were up for reelection at the end of the year. They had to defend the president while trying to distance themselves from him and the scandal at the same time. As a result, most observers believed that the affair could only lead to the loss of more democratic congressional seats.

Throughout, the NCEC worked as usual on behalf of its endorsed candidates. Most analysts continued to predict defeats in the 1998 elections, estimating a loss of between four and six seats. Predictions were based partly on Clinton's political problems and partly because the president's political party historically loses seats in an off-year election during a second term. The NCEC predicted a year-and-a-half before the election that this conventional wisdom probably would not hold in 1998. Unlike most reelectd presidents, Clinton had not carried many Democrats into the House on his coattails. Consequently, NCEC reasoned, there would not be a voter backlash against those House members. In fall 1998, NCEC intelligence indicated that the party might at worst lose two seats and at best gain two seats. The group endorsed 109 congressional candidates, 21 running for Senate seats and 88 running for House seats.

Public Impact

In the 1998 elections, contrary to all conventional wisdom, the Democrats picked up five seats in the House and lost no seats in the Senate. While it is impossible to quantify the effect any single group has on the outcome of an election, the candidates supported by the NCEC did very well. Sixty-one of its House candidates and 16 of its Senate candidates were elected—more than 66 percent and 75 percent, respectively. The gain in the House left Democrats confident that they could regain a majority in the 2000 election.

Such numbers are particularly important in the eyes of the NCEC. The increased effectiveness of right-wing campaign organizations, such as the Moral Majority, has made modern elections, in the words of NCEC National Director Russ Hemenway, "a game of numbers." Every single vote is significant, and the party best able to identify and reach voters likely to vote for them, will win. The narrow margin between electoral success and failure was illustrated by data gathered by the NCEC which showed that a shift of only 9,600 votes in six congressional districts would have given the Democrats a majority in the House of Representatives.

FUTURE DIRECTIONS

The NCEC will be overhauling its Web site completely in the first half of 1999. The revised resource will include expanded election information in the form of graphs, maps, and statistics. A more critical concern for the future of the NCEC, and for American liberal politics in general, is the age of most NCEC contributors—who are in their sixties or older. The group is developing outreach programs to find committed young contributors to carry on the progressive fight in the twenty-first century.

GROUP RESOURCES

The NCEC Web site at http://www.ncec.org contains information about congressional candidates, congressional races, as well as the voting record of incumbent members of Congress. Following elections, the organization posts the results of all congressional races and, in particular, how NCEC-supported candidates fared. The NCEC DataLine provides information on current members of Congress, including voting records, campaign finance information, and analysis by the NCEC of how members voted on liberal issues. Individual members of Congress can be called up by name, district, state, or zip code. The database also includes addresses, phone numbers, and E-mail and Web addresses for congressmen. The NCEC Web site posts news daily about progressive politics. It plans to initiate news groups, where people can discuss political issues with others on-line. The organization also posts its newsletter on-line.

GROUP PUBLICATIONS

The NCEC's *Comprehensive Congressional Vote Analysis* reviews where representatives and senators stand ideologically based on nearly 200 House votes, and over 100 Senate votes in which liberals opposed conservatives. This sourcebook of progressive politicians in Congress can be ordered free of charge at the NCEC Web site or by calling 1-800-547-5911.

BIBLIOGRAPHY

Curran, Tim, and John Mercurio. "The Democrats Strike Back: Republicans Lose Five Seats In House, Members Blast Leaders." *Roll Call.* 6 November 1998.

Mercurio, John. "As Voting Looms: Looking Back Down the Road To a Status Quo Election." *Roll Call,* 2 November 1998.

National Committee for an Effective Congress. "1998 Rematches Hold Key to Control of the House." *Election Update,* October/November 1997.

Ornstein, Norman J. "Elections Lack Big Picture, But There Are Some Issues to Watch." *Roll Call,* 2 November 1998.

Rothenberg, Stuart. "Democrats' Win Not Really That Big, But GOP Still in Trouble." *Roll Call,* 9 November 1998.

Scoble, Harry M. *Ideology and Electoral Action: A Comparative Case Study of the National Committee for an Effective Congress.* San Francisco: Chandler Pub. Co., 1967.

Wilson, James Q. *Political Organizations.* Princeton, N.J.: Princeton University Press, 1995.

Wright, John R. *Interest Groups and Congress.* Boston: Allyn and Bacon, 1996.

National Committee to Preserve Social Security and Medicare (NCPSSM)

ESTABLISHED: 1982
EMPLOYEES: 70
MEMBERS: 5.5 million
PAC: National Committee to Preserve Social Security
   and Medicare Political Action Committee

Contact Information:
ADDRESS: 10 G St. NE, Ste. 600
   Washington, DC 20002
PHONE: (202) 216-0420
TOLL FREE: (800) 966-1935
URL: http://www.ncpssm.org
PRESIDENT: Martha A. McSteen

WHAT IS ITS MISSION?

As its name suggests, the mission of the National Committee to Protect Social Security and Medicare is to ensure the preservation of the federal programs of Social Security and Medicare. Through its educational efforts, the national committee keeps its members informed of changes in Social Security, Medicare, and other legislative issues that affect senior Americans. The national committee encourages its members to influence legislation through grassroots efforts such as petitions, telephone calls, and postcards. Also, the national committee staff directly lobbies members of Congress on issues related to seniors. Through these efforts, the national committee seeks to safeguard the federal government programs earmarked for millions of older Americans.

HOW IS IT STRUCTURED?

The national committee maintains its headquarters in Washington, D.C.; its president oversees daily operations. It is governed by a 14-member board and its headquarters is staffed by 70 people.

Along with the staff that works out of the national headquarters, the national committee also has employees across the United States. These regional coordinators work at the local level with officials, community groups, and individuals. Membership in the national committee is open to anyone who shares an interest in the issues of Social Security and Medicare and who desires to advocate for these programs. Membership information can be obtained by calling the toll-free number 1-800-966-1935.

The national committee's Political Action Committee (PAC) is nonpartisan. It supports both Republican and Democratic candidates—incumbents and challengers alike—who have shown strong commitment to issues important to senior Americans and support the views of the national committee.

PRIMARY FUNCTIONS

Through education, grassroots organizing, and its lobbying efforts, the national committee attempts to influence legislation that impacts Social Security and Medicare, along with other programs and issues that affect senior Americans. With over 5.5 million members, the national committee has the ability to carry a strong message of support for its views to congressional leaders. The organization's various branches, such as the Minority Affairs Department and the Grassroots Outreach Services Department, address specific areas of concern to the national committee.

The national committee keeps its members educated about issues relevant to seniors and informed of pending legislation. The group conveys this information through letters to members, *Secure Retirement*, a bi-monthly member magazine, a toll-free information hotline, a legislative alert service, and periodic newsletters to community groups that advocate on behalf of seniors. The national committee also makes available numerous educational brochures, including "Social Security Disability Benefits," "Supplemental Security Income," and "What You Need to Know about Entitlements." The brochures are available to members and groups that support senior adults.

The Minority Affairs Department works to increase awareness and sensitivity to the special concerns of minority, low-income, and disadvantaged seniors. Specifically, the department conducts workshops and seminars dealing with minority issues and concerns, reviews and analyzes legislation affecting minorities, provides consultation and training on minority issues, and provides educational and resource materials.

Volunteer Advisors is a group of 16 retired Social Security Administration (SSA) and Health Care Financing Administration (HCFA) executives who meet periodically with the national committee staff to exchange ideas, reflect on current issues, and offer advice. The Volunteer Advisors also attend informational forums with members of Congress and provide expertise as speakers and participants at workshops and conferences.

Grassroots Organizing

The theme for the national committee's Grassroots Outreach Services Department is "Empowering Seniors, Strengthening Ties." The mission of the Grassroots Outreach Services is to coordinate and implement the political and legislative agenda for the national committee at local, regional, and state levels. The Grassroots Outreach Services also maintains a network of informed members and activists, supports efforts and activities that promote the issues of retirement and aging and increase awareness of these issues.

The Grassroots Outreach Services fulfills its mission to organize, inform, and assist its members in two ways. First, regional coordinators work in the field around the country. They communicate with elected officials, educate and update members on legislation of concern, and work with aging agencies and community groups to coordinate informational forums, seminars and other events that increase awareness of issues of concern to seniors. Second, the national committee's member-services representatives operate from the organization's Washington headquarters. The member-services representatives answer letters and telephone calls that ask about the national committee and pending legislation. They also deliver petitions to members of Congress, assist in coordinating legislative alert phone campaigns, and maintain up-to-date member information in the organization's database.

The legislative staff of the national committee directly lobbies Congress on issues it considers important to seniors, including Social Security and Medicare. Policy analysts study proposed legislation to determine its effect on seniors. They track the progress of legislation through the process, and they advise lobbyists and grassroots workers on the meaning and implications of pending legislative actions. The national committee legislative staff informs congressional members of legislation that the organization both supports and opposes and explains the impact that the legislation might have on senior Americans. To make its message heard, the national committee uses television and radio commercials, visits to congressional offices, and letter and petition campaigns.

PROGRAMS

The national committee's programs are primarily educational in nature. The organization's "Ask Mary Jane" program is designed to answer some of the most commonly asked questions regarding Social Security and Medicare. Appearing both in the magazine, *Secure Retirement*, and on the organization's Web site (http://www.ncpssm.org), the column "Ask Mary Jane" is written by Mary Jane Yarrington, a senior policy analyst for the national committee. Common questions fielded by Yarrington include who is eligible for benefits and how to obtain benefits. Anyone can submit questions either in writing or by E-mail at the "Ask Mary Jane" Web site.

In addition to educational programs for members, the national committee sponsors special events to increase public awareness of the issues surrounding

FAST FACTS

Since 1936, over 390 million Social Security numbers have been assigned.

(Source: Social Security Administration, http://www.ssa.gov.)

Medicare and Social Security. For example, in 1998, the national committee aired a teleconference, live via satellite across the United States, called "Social Security: A New School of Thought." The national committee also sponsors national and regional events, such as the Annual Southwest Society on Aging Conference, held in Austin, Texas, in 1998.

BUDGET INFORMATION

The national committee is a tax-exempt organization under section 501(c)(4) of the Internal Revenue Code. Under this status, contributions and membership dues to the national committee are not considered charitable donations for federal income-tax purposes.

For the fiscal year ending March 31, 1997, the national committee reported an income of $38,814,180. Membership dues and contributions accounted for 89 percent of that total. Six percent came from advertising income, four percent came from list rental income, and one percent came from investment income.

Expenses, which totaled $35,421,956, were divided into administrative, fund-raising, and program. Administrative expenses were $6,362,361; fund-raising costs for direct mail, membership appeals, grant proposals, and television and radio time totaled $3,698,968; and program expenses accounted for $25,360,627. Program expenditures were broken down into five line items: legislation, $10,388,571; education, $8,413,570; member services and development, $5,531,282; political and other contributions, $678,204; and grant expenditures, $349,000.

CURRENT POLITICAL ISSUES

The national committee was founded in 1982 to protect funding for Social Security and Medicare at a time when the economy was weak and the federal government was looking to cut costs. Throughout its history, the organization's priority has been protection of these benefits. The national committee has also pushed for legislation which would make the Social Security and Medicare systems more efficient and easier to use.

In the late 1990s the main focus of the national committee was the future solvency of Social Security. In 1955, 8.6 workers supported every Social Security recipient; by 1995, that number had dropped to 3.3 workers per recipient. In 2040, there will only be two workers or less for every person receiving Social Security benefits. As the population grows older and the work force grows smaller in comparison, the federal government has a growing demand for benefits, but fewer tax dollars with which to pay for them. According to a report issued by the Social Security Board of Trustees in April 1998, Social Security in its current form will deplete its trust funds in the year 2032. All parties agree that something must be done to salvage Social Security. The debate grows loud, however, when the discussion turns to exactly what should be done. Two common solutions—with many variations of each—have been put forth: maintaining benefits and partial privatization.

Case Study: The Debate over Social Security Reform

In July 1998 bills were introduced in the House of Representatives (H.R. 4256) and Senate (S. 2313) that would have dramatic effects on how Social Security operates. These bills were in large part created by the National Commission on Retirement Policy (NCRP) of the Center for Strategic and International Studies (CSIS), a public policy research organization.

The Social Security reform bills, introduced by congressional members who belong to the NCRP, recommended that two percent of the current payroll tax that supports Social Security be directed into Individual Savings Accounts (ISAs) with additional voluntary contributions up to $2,000. These accounts would allow individuals to invest some of the money that had been going to Social Security into the stock market, or other ventures, that generally have had a higher rate of return than the Social Security program's investments generate. Other aspects of the reform plan include a gradual increase of the eligibility age for full retirement benefits, provisions for different investment alternatives, and the creation of additional poverty protections by guaranteeing minimum benefits.

According to the NCRP, as stated in the information provided at its Web site at http://www.csis.org/retire, this proposal would modernize Social Security, making it viable for the next 70 years without tax increases. The proposed system would allow more personal choice and greater financial growth potential. It would eliminate penalties for earnings after age 65, thus encouraging those who want to continue working to do so even after they are eligible for benefits. Older workers staying in their jobs would increase the U.S. workforce—which funds Social Security—without taking benefits away from those who need them. According to NCRP figures, a single person retiring at the age 65 in the year 2030 would benefit from a 9.4 percent increase in retirement income compared to the current system. An individual retiring at age 67 in 2060 would earn a 38.4 percent increase.

The national committee reacted quickly to the NCRP's report and the subsequent bills H.R. 4256 and S. 2313. In a press release issued on April 28, 1998, national committee president Martha McSteen said, "For all the good intentions which may have gone into this bill, the privatization plan it proposes will shred the six-decade-old Social Security safety net and leave millions of retirees in future decades on the edge of poverty."

The national committee cited figures from the Congressional Research Service, which reported that based on the NCRP's plan, the average wage earners retiring in 2025 would experience a 33 percent reduction in guaranteed benefits paid by the government. By 2070, that number could swell up to 48 percent. These large reductions in guaranteed benefits are supposed to be made up by the profits individuals earn from their ISAs. Profits from the ISAs are not guaranteed, however. It is possible, argued the national committee, that the ISA would not generate sufficient profits to make up the losses in guaranteed benefits, thus leaving Social Security recipients without enough money. While the NCRP views the ISAs as an opportunity for increased growth, the national committee sees potential for disaster. The organization also opposed a provision in the bills that would require 40 years of work to qualify for full social security benefits. It considers this prejudicial against low-income workers and women because, for example, many women take years off of work in order to raise children.

The national committee is a strong supporter of maintaining Social Security as a fully funded federal program and strongly objects to any efforts to privatize. Although the national committee acknowledges the need for reform, it rejects the notion that Social Security is in need of drastic, and risky, change. The national committee notes that the projections for Social Security funding improved from 1997 to 1998. Projections in 1997 indicated that trust funds would be depleted in 2029; in 1998, those projections changed to 2032. Furthermore, according to the Social Security Board of Trustees, income from taxes devoted to Social Security would still be able to support approximately 75 percent of the program cost in 2032. Thus while the reserve funds of Social Security would be exhausted in 2032, the majority of the necessary funding would still be available.

Citing the Social Security Board of Trustees' report, McSteen announced a Web site "Newflash" that the "report confirms that the constant predictions of bankruptcy by privatization enthusiasts are wildly exagger-

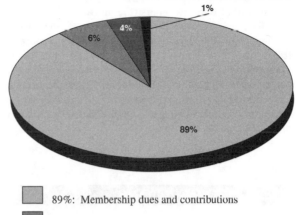

BUDGET:

1997 NCPSSM Revenue

- 89%: Membership dues and contributions
- 6%: Advertising income
- 4%: Rental income
- 1%: Investment income

1997 NCPSSM Expenses

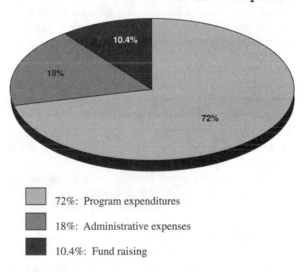

- 72%: Program expenditures
- 18%: Administrative expenses
- 10.4%: Fund raising

ated. The report should assure today's workers and retirees that the Social Security system is sound in the near term, and there is ample time to carefully and thoughtfully address and correct the long-term solvency imbalance." With the current system still capable of fullfiling most of Social Security's funding needs, the national committee believes that reform, rather than radical changes, is the best approach to the problems with Social Security.

Public Impact

Bowing to the pressure of the national committee and other groups, neither the House nor the Senate passed the NCRP proposal. This does not mean that the debate over how to fix Social Security is over, however. The so-called Baby Boomers (the unusually large number of Americans born between 1946 and 1964) began turning 50 in the mid-1990s, with 78 million more to follow in the coming years. Between 2010 and 2030, the number of people between the ages of 65 and 84 is projected to increase by 80 percent. Given these numbers, the strain on Social Security will not subside for years to come, and changes of some sort will probably have to be made.

FUTURE DIRECTIONS

The national committee is interested in any issue which affects the welfare of the elderly. In addition to its involvement in the long-running debates over Medicare and Social Security, the organization is pushing for minimum staffing requirements in nursing homes. The organization is also seeking legislation which would reform the health care system. The national committee wants health care providers and insurers to provide more information and choices to patients. A constant concern of the organization is to ensure that Social Security does not suffer funding cuts in federal budget calculations.

GROUP RESOURCES

The national committee maintains a Web site, which can be accessed at http://www.ncpssm.org. The Web site offers a variety of information concerning Social Security, Medicare, and senior issues. For example, the site provides a link to current and past press releases, a listing of legislation endorsed by the national committee, and almost 30 articles under the heading *Viewpoints,* which include "Social Security and Money's Worth Considerations," "Medicare Improvements," and "Social Security and the Budget." The national committee's Legislative Action Center link provides current information on legislative activities and information on how to contact lawmakers. The Web site also provides an on-line version of *Update on Congress,* and *Ask Mary Jane.* Other information provided include a "news flash," which deals with an up-to-date important issue; a bulletin board; a listing of current activities; and a link to the Minority Affairs Department. The site also provides links to other sites of interest such as the SSA, HCFA, the Administration on Aging, and House of Representatives and Senate, and the National Council on Aging.

The national committee also offers "Senior Flash," a toll-free telephone hotline. A caller can listen to a weekly synopsis of legislative actions, upcoming votes, and scheduled hearings. The hot-line telephone number is 1-800-998-0180. The national committee puts on *Secure Retirement,* a radio show. It airs weekly around the nation on various radio stations. For more information about the organization, write to the National Committee to Preserve Social Security and Medicare, 10 G St. NE, Ste. 600, Washington, DC 20002 or call (202) 216-0420.

GROUP PUBLICATIONS

The national committee produces *Secure Retirement,* a bi-monthly magazine that includes articles on Social Security, Medicare, and health care. It periodically carries special features, such as a biennial Congressional Scorecard that breaks down each lawmaker's voting record on issues important to seniors. *Secure Retirement* is distributed to national committee members and others including lawmakers, senior centers, the media, and public libraries.

Update on Congress is published monthly during times when Congress is in session. The report focuses on current happenings and issues in the legislative arena. It is distributed to activists, senior organizations, and the media, and can be accessed on-line at http://www.ncpssm.org.

The national committee also produces informational brochures that are available to its members and other senior support groups. Titles include "What You Need to Know about Entitlements," "Supplemental Security Income," "Questions and Answers," "Social Security Disability Benefits," and "Buying Your Medigap Policy." For more information on the organization's publications, call 1-800-966-1935 or write to the National Committee to Preserve Social Security and Medicare, 10 G St. NE, Ste. 600, Washington, DC 20002.

BIBLIOGRAPHY

Downing, Neil. "Go Figure When It Comes to Social Security. Because They're Calculated in Different Ways, Taxes Will Increase Nearly Six Times as Much as Benefits in 1999." *Chicago Tribune,* 11 November 1998.

Spragins, Ellyn. "Surviving the Medicare Mess." *Newsweek,* 16 November 1998.

Stevenson, Richard W. "Social Security Is Issue, But Solution Is Elusive." *New York Times,* 11 November 1998.

Updegrave, Walter. "Breaking the Rules of Retirement." *Money,* December 1998.

National Conference of Catholic Bishops (NCCB)

WHAT IS ITS MISSION?

The National Conference of Catholic Bishops (NCCB) was established by the Second Vatican Council, which was called by Pope John XXIII from 1962 through 1965 to modernize the Roman Catholic Church. Through the NCCB, Catholic bishops attend to the Church's affairs in the United States. According to *The Official Catholic Directory, 1998*, "Its purpose is to foster the Church's mission by providing the Bishops of the United States of America with an opportunity to exchange views and insights of prudence and experience and to exercise in a joint manner their pastoral office." Under certain conditions, as specified in the documents of the council, the NCCB can initiate actions that are binding on all the bishops of the United States, but it is primarily a vehicle for study and an arena where bishops can coordinate solutions to common problems and develop cooperative initiatives.

ESTABLISHED: 1966
EMPLOYEES: 400 (1997)
MEMBERS: 392 (1996)
PAC: None

Contact Information:

ADDRESS: 3211 4th St. NE
       Washington, DC 20017
PHONE: (202) 541-3000
FAX: (202) 541-3322
E-MAIL: webmaster@nccbuscc.org
URL: http://www.nccbuscc.org
PRESIDENT: Bishop Joseph A. Fiorenza
GENERAL SECRETARY: Rev. Msgr. Dennis M. Schnurr

HOW IS IT STRUCTURED?

The NCCB is composed of all the Catholic bishops in the United States, who meet twice a year (in June and November). The conference elects its own president; other officers include a vice president, secretary, and treasurer. The president, with the concurrence of an administrative board, nominates a general secretary who must then be elected by the whole body. The general secretary, elected for a five-year term, directs the day-to-day operations of NCCB staff. He can be re-elected for additional one-year terms.

The conference operates through 29 standing committees, some of which have full-time staff. It is within these committees that policy initiatives begin and where bishops study issues and present proposals for action to the NCCB body for deliberation and decision. Representatives to these committees come from the 13 regions that the Church in the United States is divided into. Some committees have representation from each region. The NCCB also has ad hoc (temporary) committees that are organized as the need arises. For example, in 1997 ad hoc committees dealt with such issues as health care and sexual abuse.

Together, NCCB officers, the chairs of each of the standing committees, a representative from each of the 13 regions and, for one year, the immediate past president of the conference, comprise the Administrative Committee. This committee decides what issues are presented to the main body, although it rarely refuses the recommendations of a committee chair. It also speaks for the conference between meetings of the whole body, and can give approval for a standing committee to issue official statements.

One last member of the Administrative Committee is the elected representative from the United States Catholic Council (USCC). NCCB sponsors the USCC, an organization that assists the bishops in their service of the Church. NCCB and USCC are so closely related that NCCB's Administrative Committee is identical to USCC's Administrative Board, and the NCCB General Secretary is also the General Secretary of USCC. Given the fact that the USCC takes its direction from the NCCB and is staffed by the same people, it is difficult to maintain a clear distinction. As such, NCCB concerns itself with the internal affairs of the Church, while the USCC is the public outreach that directly interacts with the government and society at large.

PRIMARY FUNCTIONS

The NCCB's efforts fall primarily into two categories: educating Catholics and the general public about the moral aspects of policy issues, and influencing government action on these issues. The NCCB studies issues and develops positions representing Catholic teaching, which are then expressed in major pastoral documents such as "A Catholic Framework for Economic Life," a summary of ten key principles of Catholic teaching in regard to economic justice. On occasion the conference also issues statements directed at issues of the moment. An example was a statement issued in November 1997. Concerned that funding for Food Stamps for many legal immigrants had been abolished by federal welfare reform, the bishops urged the federal government to "remember the plight of hungry legal immigrants" when formulating the 1999 Federal Budget.

Since 1976 the NCCB Administrative Committee has issued a statement on "Political Responsibility" prior to each presidential election. The statement urges Catholics to vote but does not recommend specific candidates. It lists issues of concern to the bishops and reflects in summary form positions already taken by the conference.

The NCCB also develops a legislative agenda and through the USCC lobbies for this agenda. The committees of the conference concerned about public policy issues determine their legislative priorities and present them to the Administrative Committee for review, changes, and approval. The USCC Office of Government Liaison coordinates the actual lobbying efforts. The conference provides testimony before congressional committees and more frequently writes letters to the president of the United States and other federal officials urging the passage or defeat of legislation. The conference is considered by many observers to be very effective, especially compared to other religious lobbies. One reason is because it is clear who it represents, the Catholic Church in the United States. Another reason is that the Catholic Church is a major provider of services, Catholic Charities USA being the largest charity in the United States according to the *Non-Profit Times*.

The USCC's Department of Social Development and World Peace is involved in many areas of public policy. It is concerned with issues such as abortion, euthanasia, health care, poverty at home and abroad, and international disarmament. At the direction of the USCC, the department studies such issues and makes proposals on policy to the NCCB. Working through the USCC's Office of Government Liaison, department members provide testimony before Congress. They also sponsor an annual conference on social ministry in the Church and training workshops for Church workers at the local level. Most of the statements and publications of the USCC that have attracted public attention have resulted from this department or its related offices.

In addition to lobbying Congress, the General Counsel of the USCC will occasionally file *amicus curiae* (friend of the court) briefs in federal court cases. Notable 1990's involvement included Supreme Court cases on physician-assisted suicide.

PROGRAMS

According to the NCCB Web site, "The programs of NCCB/USCC range over the spectrum of Catholic concerns—from prayers and worship to the state of the economy, from revitalizing parishes to averting nuclear war, from promoting vocations to protecting life at all stages."

Of the more than 30 NCCB committees, all but a few are dedicated to internal conference administration or narrowly Catholic matters. Others, by the nature of their focus, are more heavily involved in studying issues and developing policy positions, and ultimately trying to influence the government and society as a whole. The Pro-Life Activities Committee addresses issues like abortion and euthanasia. Its ultimate goal is the passage of a constitutional amendment that would reverse the effect of *Roe v. Wade,* the 1973 Supreme Court decision that secured the legality of abortion in the United States. To this end it created the Committee for a Human Life Amendment, a separate organization that promotes grassroots activities against abortion.

The Ad Hoc Committee on Health Care Issues and the Church lobbies against legislation and regulation that would force Catholic hospitals and health care professionals to perform abortions or other procedures that violate Catholic moral teaching. It also works to ensure adequate health care for the poor.

The Committees on the Laity, on Marriage and Family Life, and on Women in Society and in the Church are all concerned with matters of public policy. Among their goals are legislation and regulation that promotes traditional family life, that allows mothers to stay at home with their children, and that strengthens job security for all workers.

Other committees and departments are means through which the Church reaches out to particular groups. The NCCB funds projects through grants and also provides advocacy services. The Campaign for Human Development, for example, has distributed over $250 million in its 27-year history. The Migration and Refugee Services resettled nearly 16,000 refugees in the United States in 1997.

BUDGET INFORMATION

As a church entity, the NCCB is not required to disclose its finances in detail, although some information is readily available on its Web site. The NCCB derives most of its operating income from an assessment from each diocese, the church unit that is headed by a bishop, based on the number of Catholics in a community. The USCC budget is also provided primarily from this income, although some specific projects operated through the USCC receive funding from the federal government and private foundations.

According to *Associations Unlimited* (Gale Research, 1997), the NCCB budget for 1996 was $42,000,000. Several committees oversee special collections each year in Catholic churches throughout the country. For example, in 1997 the USCC Campaign for Human Development awarded $8 million in grants to local self-help projects combating poverty. This money came from an annual collection made in most parishes in November. USCC Migration and Refugee Services receives money from a collection called the American Bishops Overseas Appeal, but also receives funds from government grants that are used for direct assistance to

refugees, administration of diocesan resettlement programs, and program management at the national level. The USCC also generates some income for the NCCB from the publication and sale of the major statements of the NCCB, as well as books, pamphlets and videos.

HISTORY

The NCCB was created in 1966, after the Second Vatican Council mandated national episcopal conferences. The United States, however, was one of several countries that already had an established national Catholic bishops' conference and a related civil entity. During World War I U.S. bishops formed the National Catholic War Council to facilitate support by Catholics of the spiritual and recreational needs of servicemen. In 1919, with the encouragement of Pope Benedict XV, U.S. bishops began to meet annually to continue their collaboration, and formed the National Catholic Welfare Council. Soon the word "council" was replaced by "conference," and a second organization, the NCWC, Inc. was established to allow bishops to work through their staffs in areas of education, immigration and social action. In 1966 the NCWC and the NCWC, Inc., were replaced by the NCCB and the USCC, its public policy arm.

The new organizations were quite different from their predecessors in both structure and focus. The new statutes established a more democratic structure in which cardinals (the highest position in the Roman Catholic Church next to the pope) and archbishops (chief bishops who lead the largest dioceses in the country) had no different authority or position than an ordinary bishop. The NCCB was also more focused on internal church matters than the NCWC, which was created to provide an effective means for the Church to relate to the federal government.

In public policy areas, the NCCB did continue the tradition of the NCWC in speaking out on issues of concern to the Church. Part of the agenda has always been issues that impact the financial and legal well-being of the institutional Church: aid to Catholic schools, funding of Catholic social services and so on, but the Church's concern for social justice and morality has also led the conference to address policy issues of the moment. At its first meeting in 1966, the NCCB spoke in cautiously approving tones about the U.S. involvement in Vietnam. In 1968 the NCCB issued "Human Life in Our Day," a statement primarily about birth-control, that also raised questions about the war. By 1971 in a "Resolution on Southeast Asia," the bishops judged that the war was immoral because the destruction it caused was so much greater than the good that it could achieve. In 1976 and again in 1982 the NCCB issued major documents that condemned the use of nuclear weapons and called for deep negotiated cuts in nuclear arsenals.

Although the conference has a very definite policy against endorsing or opposing political candidates,

BIOGRAPHY:

Joseph Louis Bernardin

Cardinal; Activist (1928–1996)   Late in his life, Cardinal Joseph Louis Bernardin was widely regarded as the most respected official of the Roman Catholic Church in the United States. Bernardin was an active leader who worked hard to address contemporary issues while reinforcing what he saw as the Church's primary obligation: to minister and bring social services to the poor. Appointed archbishop of Cincinnati in 1972, Bernardin immediately did away with the lavish trappings traditionally associated with the office and instead worked long hours to address both local and national issues. Bernardin personally visited prisons and migrant worker camps. From 1974 to 1977, Bernardin served as president of the National Conference of Catholic Bishops. In the early 1980s, Bernardin succeeded the late Cardinal Cody as archbishop of Chicago and was named cardinal himself one year later. While he was known for his social liberalism, Bernardin remained steadfast in traditional Church positions on issues such as abortion and homo-

sexuality. In the mid-1990s, a terminal cancer diagnosis prompted him to write, with desperate intensity, a book on his condition titled, *The Gift of Peace.* In Bernardin's final months, President Clinton awarded him the Presidential Medal of Freedom, the nation's highest civilian honor for an individual's contribution to his or her community. Said the cardinal of his pending death, "When

one comes face to face with the reality of death as a cancer patient, one's perspective on life is altered dramatically. What seemed so important before, now is seen as trivial, and what is truly important invites new commitment and a realignment of priorities."

the nature of the Catholic Church in the United States led it to be sympathetic with the Democratic Party and its policies up until the 1970s, when issues like abortion, gay rights, and feminism changed the political landscape. Since then the conference has found itself aligned with Democrats on some issues and Republicans on others.

CURRENT POLITICAL ISSUES

The NCCB regularly issues statements on many areas of public policy, but the NCCB, and the Catholic Church in general, has long been seen as focusing almost exclusively on the issue of abortion. In the mid-1970s Joseph Bernardin, then president of the conference, led the NCCB in shifting attention to other public policy issues. A conscious effort was made to ground all public policy activities in what Bishop Bernardin called "a consistent ethic of life."

The NCCB has spoken against the death penalty, arguing that executing criminals diminishes society's respect for life and that the modern prison system can adequately protect society against even violent criminals while offering the possibility of rehabilitation. In the area of welfare reform, the conference has cautioned against reforms that would in effect abandon elements

of society that are already marginalized, such as immigrants and the elderly.

This is not to say that abortion has not remained a central concern of the NCCB. Catholic teaching insists that it is immoral to take any action that directly takes the life of an innocent person, including an unborn child from the moment of conception. For some of the bishops, abortion is the decisive issue, and it is the issue on which the conference has been able to generate the most grassroots activity.

Case Study: Partial-Birth Abortion Ban

During the first session of the 104th Congress a bill was introduced that would ban the procedure that is widely known as the partial-birth abortion, a late-term abortion in which the fetus is partially delivered, the skull punctured and the brain removed, and then the skull collapsed for easier delivery. The Committee for Pro-Life Activities of the NCCB lobbied vigorously for passage of the ban, and in November of 1995 it passed handily in the House, 288 to 139. In December it passed with amendment in the Senate, by a much closer margin, 54 to 44. The House accepted the Senate's amendments in March of 1996, 286 to 129. As he had earlier indicated, President Clinton vetoed the bill on April 10, because although it did allow the procedure in cases where the woman's life was threatened, it did not allow its use in cases where there was just a "serious health risk," but not danger of death.

The NCCB continued to lobby Congress, as actions to override the presidential veto were already underway. Millions of Catholics were urged to send postcards to Congress. In July, an official of the House of Representatives said that more than 2.4 million cards had been delivered to members of that House, with an unknown number waiting to be processed. In September 1996 the House overrode the President's veto, 285 to 137, but the Senate failed to override,.

When the 105th Congress convened in 1997, another bill was introduced, virtually identical to the previous. Action was taken more quickly this time, and the bill passed the House on March 20, 295 to 136. It passed the Senate with amendment on May 20, 64 to 36, only three votes short of the two-thirds majority needed to override the expected presidential veto. The House accepted the Senate amendments on October 8. Bishop Anthony M. Pilla, the President of the NCCB, immediately wrote a letter to President Clinton urging him to sign the bill, but on October 10, Clinton vetoed it. The NCCB sponsored another postcard campaign that began the weekend after January 22, 1998, the 25th anniversary of the Supreme Court's *Roe v. Wade* decision which secured the legality of abortion in the United States.

Public Impact

During the 104th and 105th Congresses the NCCB's goal of a ban on one particular form of abortion moved closer to achievement. How much the change in the votes between 1995 and 1997 is the result of their efforts is difficult to determine. Some commentators argue that in general the Catholic position on abortion is closer to the opinion of the country at large than the pro-choice position. In January 1996 the Secretariat for Pro-Life Activities sponsored a poll of 1,000 registered voters nationwide which found that 71 percent favored the ban on partial-birth abortions. In May 1997 the American Medical Association decided to support the Partial-Birth Abortion Ban Act.

How often this form of abortion is used is a matter of some controversy. Abortion rights activists say only 500 to 600 times a year, while doctors interviewed in such newspapers as the *American Medical News* and the *Washington Post* acknowledge performing thousands each year. Eighteen states have enacted bans on the procedure, most modeled on the federal legislation, although several state laws have been blocked by the courts. It may be that the procedure itself is so controversial that a ban is inevitable, but it is probably safe to say that the postcard campaign of the NCCB has ensured that Congress is aware of the strength of the pro-life forces on this issue at least.

FUTURE DIRECTIONS

In the 1990s the NCCB paid relatively more attention to internal Church affairs and less to public policy matters. Nevertheless, given its history and what it sees as its mission, both to protect the vital interests of the institutional Church and to share and apply Catholic social teaching, the conference will continue to be a strong voice on a number of issues. The growing movement for physician-assisted suicide will elicit further efforts in the courts and in the Congress to prevent the establishment of a "right to die" that would require Catholic hospitals and health care workers to support this practice. And the conference will continue to work to reverse the effects of *Roe v. Wade*, hoping ultimately to pass a Human Life Amendment.

GROUP RESOURCES

The NCCB/USCC maintains an extensive Web site at http://www.nccbuscc.org with pages dedicated to its departments, offices, and activities including action alerts and lobbying efforts. Press releases are also available at the site.

GROUP PUBLICATIONS

The USCC Publishing and Promotions Services publishes the bishops' major statements and other Church documents, which are available at http://www.nccbuscc.org. Several departments publish monthly newsletters or quarterly reports. Cassette tapes and videocassettes are also produced by NCCB. J. P. Kenedy and Sons each year publishes *The Official Catholic Directory,* which lists all the committees of the USCC and their members, along with other official information about the conference and the Catholic Church in the United States.

BIBLIOGRAPHY

"Bishops Blast GOP Budget." *The Christian Century,* November–December 1995.

"Bishops Warn Against Anti-immigrant Views." *The Christian Century,* 8 December 1993.

Byers, David M. "Religion and Science: The Emerging Dialogue." *America,* 20 April 1996.

"A Community of Conscience." *America,* 9 December 1995.

Gonzalez, David. "Bishops Assail Rule Hostile to Immigrants." *New York Times,* 18 November 1994.

———. "Bishops Vote to Expand Women's Roles in Church." *New York Times,* 17 November 1994.

Greenhouse, Linda. "Justices Uphold Laws Banning Assisted Suicide." *New York Times,* 27 June 1997.

The Official Catholic Directory, 1998. New York: P. J. Kenedy and Sons, 1997.

"Starving the Poor: Views of Catholic Bishops." *New York Times,* 24 November 1994.

Steinfels, Peter. "Bishops Steer Middle Course on Politics." *New York Times,* 5 November 1995.

———. "U.S. Catholic Bishops Open Drive against Doctor-Assisted Suicide." *New York Times,* 21 March 1996.

Steinfels, Peter, and Gustav Niebuhr. "Shift to Right Looms at Top for U.S. Catholics." *New York Times,* 3 November 1996.

National Congress of American Indians (NCAI)

WHAT IS ITS MISSION?

The National Congress of American Indians (NCAI) is a national organization dedicated to improving the general status and welfare of American Indians and Alaskan Natives through broad-based representation of Indian people and tribes across the United States. The preamble to the organization's constitution states that the NCAI seeks "to secure to ourselves and our descendants the rights and benefits to which we are entitled under the laws of the United States . . . to enlighten the public towards a better understanding of the Indian race; to preserve Indian cultural values; to seek an equitable adjustment of tribal affairs; to secure and preserve rights under Indian treaties with the United States; and otherwise to promote the common welfare of the American Indians." The organization also promotes American Indian participation in, and influence over, the decision-making processes that affect them.

ESTABLISHED: November 1944
EMPLOYEES: 15
MEMBERS: 2,685 (1997)
PAC: None

Contact Information:

ADDRESS: 1301 Connecticut Avenue NW, Ste. 200
    Washington, DC 20036
PHONE: (202) 466-7767
FAX: (202) 466-7797
URL: http://www.ncai.org
EXECUTIVE DIRECTOR: JoAnn K. Chase

HOW IS IT STRUCTURED?

The NCAI claims to be the largest, as well as the oldest, national American Indian organization. The executive council, which acts as the NCAI's governing body, has a complex structure involving several levels of representation. The administrative board consists of five positions. The president, vice president, and recording secretary are all elected to two-year terms by delegates at national conventions. The council then elects a treasurer and hires an executive director who serves as head of the Washington, D.C. headquarters and oversees a small staff of secretaries and associates. Unlike the exec-

FAST FACTS

According to the Bureau of Indian Affairs, unemployment on Indian reservations nationwide stood at 49 percent in 1997.

(Source: Tony Pugh. "Because of Government Treaties and Promises, Welfare Reform Involves Deeper Issues for American Indians." *Knight-Ridder/Tribune News Service*, September 23, 1997.)

utive director, other board members operate mainly from their home communities.

The executive council also includes 12 area vice presidents from geographic regions across the country. Finally, in addition to the administrative board and the area vice presidents, the council includes a voting delegate from each member tribe.

Within the NCAI, individual committees oversee a number of priority issues. These committees deal with economic development, education, health and housing, human resources, Indian elders, Indian veterans, jobs, training and Indian preference, legislation and litigation, national Indian nuclear waste policy, natural resources, political resources, and treaty and land rights. Committee members include both NCAI staff and tribal members.

NCAI's membership includes both tribes and individuals; in 1997 185 tribes representing 800,000 American Indians as well as 2,500 individuals comprised the Congress. Non-Indians can also participate in the NCAI as non-voting associates.

The NCAI frequently allies itself with other Indian-oriented organizations that support one or more of its goals. On a national and international level, it has worked with the National Tribal Chairmen's Association, the National Indian Gaming Association, and the World Council of Indigenous Peoples. It also often allies itself with individual tribal governments or other local tribal organizations.

PRIMARY FUNCTIONS

The NCAI functions primarily as a political lobbying group for American Indian interests. In fulfilling this function it acts as a liaison between the federal government and individual tribes or other Indian communities and local groups. It also works to bring a variety of Indian perspectives together and achieve some sort of consensus that can then translate into positions and proposals.

In its role as political liaison and lobbyist, the NCAI carries out a number of activities. At its Washington headquarters, members monitor specific legislation that affects American Indians as well as the general trend of Indian policies over time. When a piece of legislation seems particularly alarming or relevant to Indian interests, the NCAI alerts tribes and communities and receives feedback. Armed with this grassroots input, it uses its national meetings and conferences to formulate positions it then presents to the federal government, either by testifying before Congress or by providing information to committees and individuals on a more informal level. The NCAI routinely puts pressure on Congress, the Department of the Interior, the Bureau of Indian Affairs (BIA), and the Indian Health Service (IHS) to change policies it deems harmful to the well-being of American Indians. The organization also keeps track of ongoing concerns among tribes and other communities and strives to make federal officials aware of them.

Beyond these lobbying efforts, the NCAI performs other functions as well. It serves as a central point of communication and contact for tribes that go to Washington to conduct business with the federal government. Occasionally it provides legal support to tribes in court. The organization conducts surveys, compiles research, and makes the results available both to Indian groups and to the government. It also works to educate the public through conferences, media campaigns, and publications. The NCAI sometimes joins with other Indian organizations—such as the National Indian Gaming Association and the National Tribal Chairmen's Association—to push for certain issues, and it employs a New York law firm in an advisory capacity.

PROGRAMS

Most of the NCAI's organizing efforts go toward bringing its members together at various gatherings to share information and formulate policy stances. Each fall it holds its annual national convention, and it also sponsors an annual meeting every summer. These mid-year meetings include speakers, panels, workshops, and sessions wherein delegates draft committee reports. Executive council meetings also convene throughout the year.

The NCAI's 50th annual national convention, held in November of 1994, demonstrated both the range of issues the organization tends to address and the level of importance it wants American Indian issues to attain with federal policymakers. At the week-long convention, entitled "Fifty Years of Enduring Spirit: Visions for the Future," attendees expressed concern over nuclear waste storage, the status of Indian gaming operations, the state of BIA-run prisons, and health services for American Indian communities. Participants also voiced dissatisfaction with what they saw as the federal government's lack of commitment to acting on the NCAI's concerns and improving the lives of American Indians. The NCAI's president at the time, Wisconsin Chippewa leader Gaiashkibos, criticized Transportation Secretary Federico Pena and Housing Secretary Henry Cisneros for failing to speak at the convention as expected. He also faulted Vice President Al Gore for not scheduling an appearance at the congress while in Denver for a meeting of the Council of Jewish Federations.

In addition to its regular conferences, the NCAI also reaches out to the public, hoping to increase public awareness of American Indian issues. Occasionally the organization launches educational media campaigns in conjunction with other Indian organizations; it also created a high school textbook to teach students about tribal government.

BUDGET INFORMATION

In 1997 the NCAI had an operating budget of approximately $1,400,000. Funding sources include contracts with the federal government, private donations, and membership dues. For tribes, the amount of dues depends on tribal population. The organization regularly administers a charitable and educational fund called the NCAI Fund.

HISTORY

The NCAI emerged in 1944, at a time of great change for American Indian generally, as well as for federal Indian policy. Prior to the 1940s the most influential national organization concerned with American Indians was the Society of Americans Indians (SAI); this group, conceived and dominated by non-Indians with a Christian reformist bent, passed into obscurity in the 1920s. By 1944, however, several factors combined to allow the birth of an organization of Indian leaders. Many American Indians who had left their reservations for the first time to serve in the armed forces or work in war industries during World War II (1939–45) felt the government owed their people better treatment for their patriotic service; they also learned how to function within white society and, through contact with other tribes, gained a sense of pan-Indian identity.

Within the federal government, Commissioner of Indian Affairs John Collier pushed an Indian policy that also set the stage for the development of the NCAI. Collier opposed the government's previous policy of assimilation through which it sought to eradicate local tribal identities and fully "Americanize" American Indians politically, socially, and culturally. Collier's philoso-

phy—eventually christened the "Indian New Deal"—supported the survival of tribes as distinct political and cultural entities. One of his policies, the Indian Reorganization Act (IRA), encouraged tribes to create official tribal governments patterned on Euroamerican institutions, to interact with Washington, administer federal funds, and provide services for their reservations. When some of Collier's initiatives met with opposition from white politicians and American Indians alike, he decided that an Indian-led organization might find better success at pushing for change. In the spring of 1944 a Collier aide gathered a group of Indian leaders together to discuss the creation of such an organization. These men, many of whom had gained experience in the U.S. political system through the IRA or the BIA, convened a national conference on Indian affairs in November of 1944, setting the groundwork for the NCAI. In its structure, methods, goals, and personnel the organization owed much to the Indian New Deal.

From its beginning, the NCAI operated under a very different philosophy than that of its predecessor, the SAI. The differences, however, sometimes went unnoticed by non-Indian policymakers until they became too obvious to ignore. While the SAI had encouraged Indians to assimilate into mainstream U.S. culture, the NCAI firmly supported tribal survival and the preservation of Indian culture and spirituality. At the same time, however, NCAI leaders insisted that American Indians deserved the same civil rights as U.S. citizens. They therefore pushed for such measures as veterans' benefits, voting rights, the repeal of restrictive liquor laws on reservations, and the establishment of an Indian Claims Commission to settle outstanding Indian grievances over treaty violations and loss of lands.

To white politicians and their Indian supporters who, despite Collier's efforts, still supported assimilation as federal policy, the NCAI's support of such measures fit neatly with their desire to eradicate American Indian cultural and political uniqueness. Yet as Alison Bernstein noted in her 1991 study *American Indians and World War II*, the NCAI firmly believed that "individuals could be both Native Americans and Indian Americans, and that they should not be forced to give up their cultural identity to enjoy the rights and responsibilities of citizenship."

The latent conflict between NCAI and assimilationist philosophies, which had remained hidden throughout the 1940s, clearly emerged in the early 1950s during the debate over termination. In 1953 the bipartisan resistance to Collier's programs that had developed since the war emerged as the official federal Indian policy of termination. This policy again fully embraced assimilation as the best way to deal with American Indians. Its major component included provisions to terminate the federally recognized—and financially supported—status of those Indian tribes and reservations that seemed most ready for such a move. Termination legislation also included a relocation program that sought to move Indian people from reservation communities into major cities as a means of acculturating them more quickly into mainstream society.

The NCAI firmly opposed termination and eventually had a hand in derailing it. Termination contradicted one of the NCAI's top priorities, the survival of American Indian tribal and cultural identities. The NCAI used all of its lobbying skills and contacts developed over the previous decade to lead the fight against termination. By insisting that, under the democratic principle of needing the consent of the governed, Washington could not terminate tribes without their consent, the NCAI helped to stall and deflect these efforts. By 1958 it was official government policy that tribes must consent to their own disbandment, and termination came to an end. Though only about three percent of existing tribes actually suffered termination during the 1950s, the policy signalled to many Indian leaders that they could not trust the federal government; even when it seemed to support them it could turn on them unexpectedly.

The 1950s and early 1960s proved to be the heyday of the NCAI's status and influence as the single representative of national Indian concerns. In later decades other organizations emerged whose differing tactics, agendas, and resources led them to challenge NCAI authority. In 1961 the NCAI endorsed and attended a conference organized by anthropologist Sol Tax and the University of Chicago, where Indian leaders gathered to discuss the past and future of federal Indian policies. Out of this conference emerged the National Indian Youth Council (NIYC), a group composed mainly of American Indian college students heavily influenced by the African American civil rights movement.

From the mid-1960s into the early 1970s the NIYC and the American Indian Movement (AIM)—which was established in Minneapolis, Minnesota in 1968—criticized the NCAI for its moderate stance and its position within the mainstream political system. These younger groups opted instead for confrontational protest and militant rhetoric to transform American Indian's inferior political and social position. In the later 1970s and 1980s, as the federal courts became a more effective site of activism than traditional lobbying efforts, the NCAI again lost some of its prominence. Though the NCAI now shares the national stage with a number of other spokespeople for American Indian interests, it remains an influential component of Indian efforts to inject their perspectives into national policy.

CURRENT POLITICAL ISSUES

As an advocate for American Indian concerns, the NCAI continues to make its voice heard on a variety of political issues. For legislators and reporters seeking an American Indian perspective, the NCAI provides tribal feedback on everything from treaty disputes over land and resources, to the protection of American Indian religious freedom and sacred sites, to social conditions on reservations. In the mid-1990s the organization became increasingly concerned with proposed funding cuts for federal Indian programs. The NCAI opposed these proposals as threats to tribal governments' ability to provide their people with basic services, and as violations of the tribes' treaty-established, government-to-government relationship with the United States.

Case Study: American Indians and Nuclear Waste

The NCAI has concerned itself with the impact nuclear testing and nuclear waste have on American Indian communities. Many facilities that produce and/or store nuclear waste are located near reservations, so the possibility of radioactive waste leaking into the environment is a major concern for the inhabitants. In 1983 the organization forged a cooperative agreement with the U.S. Department of Energy (DOE) through the DOE's Office of Civilian Radioactive Waste. Under this agreement the NCAI provides information to tribal governments, delivers tribal feedback to the DOE, trains Indian communities in proper radiological emergency response, and generally works to make the tribal-federal relationship a more cooperative one regarding nuclear waste issues. In addition to these ongoing efforts, the NCAI pays close attention to potential transportation routes for nuclear waste. It also supports Indian communities struggling with nuclear-related environmental contamination and health problems.

The federally owned Hanford Nuclear Facility opened in south-central Washington State in 1943 as a center for nuclear weapons research, plutonium production, and uranium and plutonium reprocessing. The largest nuclear weapons manufacturing facility in the United States, its production facilities were closed in 1989, but millions of gallons of nuclear waste is stored there.

In April of 1997 members of five tribes living near the Hanford site filed suit for damages resulting from the release of radioactive substances. Over 150 plaintiffs from the Colville, Nez Perce, Umatilla, Warm Springs, and Yakama reservations, claiming that radioactive materials released at Hanford constitute wrongful human radiation experimentation, targeted several federal government agencies and contractors for compensation. According to the plaintiffs, toxic substances released at Hanford have taken multi-level environmental and human tolls. They cited declassified DOE documents tracking the release of radioactive iodine, phosphorous, plutonium, and zinc into the air, groundwater, and surface water for hundreds of miles surrounding the site. The toxic substances have contaminated fish, game, and vegetation ingested by people in the area, resulting in an array of human health problems, including high instances of arthritis, diabetes, and cancer, as well as blood, reproductive, and autoimmune disorders. The pollutants have also disrupted traditional native cultural patterns, which rely heavily on the consumption of local plants and wildlife. Stored nuclear waste at the site compounds threats to area groundwater and the Columbia River.

Situations like Hanford make the NCAI concerned with proposals to centralize all the nuclear waste from across the country into one central storage site. The Nuclear Waste Policy Act of 1997 represented an attempt to do exactly that. Many in Congress supported the bill because it would allow the federal government to fulfill its legal obligation to take possession of nuclear waste produced at private facilities. The NCAI, and others, feared the risks involved in moving such a large amount of waste and questioned if it would be stored safely. All of the proposed sites for storing the nuclear waste were on or near reservations. Even more crucially, plans to move the nuclear waste to its final destination involved transporting tens of thousands of truckloads along major interstates through 43 states. With government estimates of over 300 expected accidents, the potential threat to the U.S. public as a whole seems clear. Procedural motions by members of Congress from Nevada, where the waste was to be temporarily stored, eventually defeated the act.

Public Impact

The issue of nuclear waste storage is important, not just to the NCAI and American Indians, but to all U.S. citizens. Many people living near the Hanford facility are not American Indians, and the NCAI lawsuit was one of several brought against the facility. On this, and many other issues, the NCAI has acted in the interest of all Americans.

FUTURE DIRECTIONS

In coming years the NCAI will most likely continue to view federal funding for Indian programs as a priority. It also remains strongly committed to protecting religious freedom and securing reclamation and protection of geographic sites that hold spiritual significance for Indian communities. In the future, as it has throughout its history, the NCAI will take up any issue it perceives as central to its goal of promoting tribal self-determination and cultural survival among Indian people.

The NCAI faces a number of challenges as it works to achieve a broadly representative consensus among the nation's diverse Indian population. Some politicians regard the NCAI as "the" Indian voice in Washington. Though this was the case in the 1940s and 1950s, it no longer remains true. Multiple Indian perspectives exist on every issue, emanating from localities across the country and represented by a number of national Indian organizations. In order to remain a significant voice, the organization needs to find a way to work with, rather than against, other Indian groups whenever possible.

NCAI leaders also must strive to remain connected to grassroots experiences and opinions while also maintaining their organization's unique niche as a political lobbyist with a well-established reputation in Washington.

GROUP RESOURCES

In its role as lobbyist and liaison, the NCAI compiles statistics and other research on a great variety of American Indian issues. It maintains a database and mailing lists, and has a library that includes volumes on Indian history, art, and contemporary issues; the library is open to the public and is located at the organization's Washington office at 2010 Massachusetts Ave. NW, 2nd Fl., Washington, DC 20036. To find out more about NCAI resources, call the Washington office at (202) 466-7767, or visit its Web site at http://www.ncai.org.

GROUP PUBLICATIONS

The NCAI publishes a newsletter, the *Sentinel*, for its member tribes that provides updates on the federal budget, proposed legislation, and legal decisions of interest to American Indians. It also publishes results of NCAI surveys and includes information on upcoming conferences, as well as a calendar of other events. Former publications have included the *Information Letter*, published from 1955 to 1958, and the *Sentinel Bulletin*, published from 1947 to 1973.

For information about accessing NCAI publications, write the Washington office at: 2010 Massachusetts Ave. NW, 2nd Floor, Washington, D.C. 20036 or call (202) 466-7767.

BIBLIOGRAPHY

Bee, Robert. *The Politics of American Indian Policy*. Cambridge, MA: Schenkman Publishing, 1982.

Chase, JoAnn K. "Sen. Gorton and the Indian Treaties." *Washington Post*, 20 September 1995.

Denver Post staff and wire services. "Indians Can't Count on Continued Subsidies, Espy Warns." *Denver Post*, 15 November 1994.

Edwards, Robin T. "Advocacy Group Fighting for Native Rights." *National Catholic Reporter*, 2 February 1996.

Hilliard, Carl. "Absence of Two Cabinet Members Irks Indians." *Denver Post*, 17 November 1994.

MacPherson, Karen. "Ad Campaign Says Indians Are Taxpayers Too." *Scripps Howard News Service*, 15 April 1997.

———. "Indian Tribes Launch Education Campaign to Keep Federal Funds." *Scripps Howard News Service*, 13 March 1996.

Michel, Karen Lincoln. "Shaped by the Hand of God." *Dallas Morning News*, 1 June 1996.

Miniclier, Kit. "Tribes Converge on Denver for National Congress." *Denver Post*, 11 November 1994.

Overton, Penelope. "Mashantuckets Pledge to Join Appeal of Ruling." *Day*, 8 February 1996.

Reeves, Tracey A. "Indians Blast Idea That U.S. Funding to Tribes Be Cut because of Casino Profits." *Knight-Ridder/Tribune News Service*, 16 June 1995.

Sabbatini, Mark. "Native Conference Opens." *Juneau Empire*, 9 June 1997.

National Congress of Parents and Teachers (PTA)

WHAT IS ITS MISSION?

The National Congress of Parents and Teachers—known popularly as the National Parents and Teachers Association, or PTA—was started more than 100 years ago to relieve the suffering and improve the lives of children. As part of that mission, the group has a strong (although by no means exclusive) focus on public schools. The PTA calls itself "the largest volunteer child advocacy group in the United States. An organization of parents, educators, students and other citizens active in their schools and communities, the PTA is a leader in reminding our nation of its obligations to children." The group cites a threefold mission: to support and speak on behalf of children and youth in the schools, in the community, and before governmental bodies and other organizations that make decisions affecting children; to assist parents in developing the skills they need to raise and protect their children; and to encourage parent and public involvement in U.S. public schools.

ESTABLISHED: February 17, 1897
EMPLOYEES: 80
MEMBERS: 6.5 million
PAC: None

Contact Information:

ADDRESS: 330 N. Wabash Ave., Ste. 2100
    Chicago, IL 60611
PHONE: (312) 670-6782
TOLL FREE: (800) 307-4782
FAX: (312) 670-6783
E-MAIL: info@pta.org
URL: http://www.pta.org
PRESIDENT: Lois Jean White

HOW IS IT STRUCTURED?

The PTA is headquartered in Chicago, Illinois, and directed by a volunteer, 87-member board of directors made up of state PTA leaders, officers, and additional members appointed by the PTA president. The board is led by an executive board consisting of eight officers, who are elected every two years. Both the board of directors and the executive board meet four times a year. Day-to-day operations and PTA administration are handled at the Chicago office. The PTA also maintains an Office of

Governmental Relations in Washington, D.C., that coordinates its legislative activities.

Despite the group's name, membership is not limited to parents and teachers; rather, it is open to "anyone who believes in the National PTA Mission," according to PTA literature. Members help guide the group by voting on policy statements, resolutions, and position statements, which are further refined into legislative directives that guide the Washington staff. Members are organized into more than 26,000 local units and branches in all 50 states as well as overseas Department of Defense branches.

PRIMARY FUNCTIONS

The PTA works to improve the lives of children in a variety of ways. One way is through special observances that raise awareness about problems that affect children, or generate support for education. For instance, in April 1998, the PTA celebrated Earth Week, during which members focused on environmental issues relevant to youth. In May, the PTA holds Teacher Appreciation Week, during which members conduct activities to strengthen respect and support for teachers. Ideas for such activities are posted on the PTA's Web site. And every year, the PTA sponsors American Education Week, during which members around the country conduct appreciation activities for teachers and administrators.

The PTA has several programs aimed at children's health, welfare and safety. Among these are "Be Cool. Follow the Rules," a program designed by PTA and Navistar International to help communities improve school bus safety through TV public service announcements, a guide for bus drivers, safety tip cards for parents and children, and a video on school bus safety. Another example is the Family and Community Critical Viewing Project, which provides workshops on controlling the impact of violence and commercialism on television as well as a video narrated by TV talk show host Rosie O'Donnell aimed at giving parents and teachers skills to help children become smarter TV viewers.

Awards are another means the PTA uses to achieve its goals. The PTA encourages excellence in education through the Hearst Outstanding Educator Award, given annually to an educator whose commitment inspires student excellence. Two other awards—the Outstanding Unit Award and the Together Everyone Achieves Membership (TEAM) Award—motivate PTA involvement by recognizing the outstanding work of state and local units.

The PTA offers training to members through workshops on such topics as advocating for children before government agencies, managing finances, and working with the media. The national office also conducts training sessions that prepare state-level leaders to train local leaders. The national convention offers all members the

opportunity to participate in the PTA. Convention delegates vote on policy statements, which are broad statements on children's issues that form the basis for resolutions and position statements. After approval by convention delegates (or by the board of directors) policy statements must then be approved by 60 percent of state PTA units.

The group's legislative directives are based on resolutions and position statements and are set by the PTA's executive board, after review by the full board of directors. The directives are set every two years, just before the start of a new Congress, and lay out the PTA's priorities for legislation for that session. The legislative directives govern the activities of the Office of Governmental Relations in Washington, D.C., which lobbies legislators and federal agencies in an attempt to achieve the PTA's objectives. The PTA does not endorse candidates however, since it is a tax-exempt, nonprofit, and nonpartisan organization.

The Washington office also analyzes the activities of Congress, regulatory agencies, and the courts and informs members and local PTA units of developments of interest to them through a newsletter ("What's Happening in Washington"), through a legislative hot line (888-4ALLKDS), and through other means. The PTA also has an annual national legislative conference, although that is a smaller, invitation-only gathering. At the conference, state legislative chairs and others receive updates on and learn about various legislative issues of concern to the organization.

PROGRAMS

The PTA has a number of programs designed to train teachers, to help parents get involved with their children's education, and to protect children and help them succeed. These programs include: Reflections, an arts recognition and achievement program for students in preschool through grade 12 in literature, musical composition, photography, and visual arts. More than 600,000 students participate each year in the program, which began in 1969. The Teacher Education in Parent/Family Involvement Training program, begun in 1995, is a partnership program with the American Association of Colleges for Teacher Education. The program trains teachers on how to bring about parent and family involvement in education.

The Ebony/National PTA Guide to Student Excellence is produced in partnership with Johnson Publications. The program is designed to motivate young people and to help them develop academic readiness, self-esteem and ethnic pride. The Technology/Internet Safety program, which began in 1996, was developed in collaboration with the Children's Partnership and National Urban League. The program aims to safeguard children from harmful materials on the Internet through distribution of information to parents. The Family Nest is a Spanish-language program aimed at fostering parental involvement. Begun in 1994, the program includes a video and parent's tip sheet developed in collaboration with the ASPIRA Association and the Mexican-American Legal Defense and Education Fund.

BUDGET INFORMATION

Not made available.

HISTORY

The national PTA was born in the late nineteenth century, in an era before many of the current child protection laws were enacted. Alice McLellan Birney, a businesswoman and mother of three daughters, wrote: "Oppressed with a sense of needless suffering, I asked myself for the thousandth time, 'How can it be prevented?' How can the mothers be educated and the nation made to recognize the supreme importance of the child?' Congress was in session at the time, and I knew how its doings were telegraphed to all parts of the earth . . . and then like a flash came the thought: Why not have a National Congress of Mothers, whose growth would quickly become international?"

Together with Phoebe Apperson Hearst, mother of newspaper publisher William Randolph Hearst, Birney began planning the congress. The theme of the first meeting in February 1897 was "All Children Are Our Children." The group was a success from the outset, when 2,000 women showed up for the first meeting at the First Baptist Church in Washington, D.C. Birney was elected the first president, and Hearst was elected the first vice president. A constitution and bylaws were adopted in 1898, and in 1900 the charter was signed and the National Congress was incorporated under the laws of the District of Columbia. In 1897 the New York Assembly of Mothers became the first state branch, and in 1899 the first local association formed in Kansas City. In 1908 the National Congress changed its name to the National Congress of Mothers and Parent-Teacher Associations.

From the outset, the group lobbied for legislation to protect children. In 1899 a convention resolution urged Congress to create a national health bureau; 14 years later the U.S. Public Health Service was formed. In 1906 the PTA succeeded in getting the Pure Food Bill enacted into law, and in 1912 the PTA successfully led a fight for the U.S. Children's Bureau. That same year PTAs sponsored hot lunch programs in a number of schools. In 1918, the group purchased a headquarters building in Washington, D.C. By 1920, it had grown to 189,282 members in 37 state branches. In 1924 the group adopted the name National Congress of Parents and Teachers.

Another turning point came in 1926, when Selena Sloan Butler formed the National Congress of Colored Parents and Teachers (NCCPT) to carry on PTA goals in the South's segregated schools. The National Congress of Parents and Teachers cooperated closely with the NCCPT, and in 1970, after the end of legally segregated schools, the two groups merged. In 1933 the Great Depression forced the bankruptcy of some school districts and suspended some PTA activities. But by 1935 the group had grown to 1.7 million members and 49 state branches. In 1939 the group's headquarters was moved from Washington, D.C., to Chicago, Illinois.

In 1941 the National Congress initiated a nationwide school lunch program. The group's wartime activities included promoting programs to save the nation's resources. The group participated in a conference that led to the formation of the United Nations in 1944. By 1945, state branches extended to all 50 states and membership had increased to 3.5 million.

In 1954 the PTA helped field test the Salk polio vaccine and campaigned for acceptance of its use and by 1956 membership topped 10 million. The European Congress of American Parents and Teachers was organized in 1958. In 1965 the PTA sponsored the Books for Appalachia program, which brought one million books to mountain schools. In 1966 the group launched a national project on smoking and health with support from the U.S. Public Health Service. However the 1960s also began a 20-year decline in membership.

In 1974, the PTA set up five pilot projects on school absenteeism. In 1976 the group began a federally funded program to combat alcoholism. In 1977 a project aimed at television violence involved hearings in eight cities. That same year, the PTA opened its Office of Government Relations in Washington, D.C. Among the congressional battles the group fought in the late 1970s was legislation allowing parents tax credits for tuition paid to private schools, a measure the PTA successfully argued would hurt public schools.

In the early 1980s the PTA fought against cuts in federal aid to school lunch and child nutrition programs. In 1984 the group saw an increase in membership for the second year in a row, but even then membership was only 5.4 million, less than half of what it had been in 1960. In the late 1980s the PTA began efforts to raise awareness about AIDS, then a relatively unknown disease.

In 1990, the PTA launched the Common Sense drug prevention program, and the national PTA president was named to President George Bush's Education Policy Advisory Council. The group also launched many of the programs that continue today, such as "Safeguarding Your Chilren" and "Be Cool. Follow the Rules." In 1996, in time to celebrate the group's 100th anniversary, the PTA launched its World Wide Web site. In 1997, as the group celebrated its centennial, Lois Jean White was elected the first African American national president.

CURRENT POLITICAL ISSUES

Over the years, the PTA has successfully pushed for the passage of hundreds of laws affecting children at the national, state, and local level. It has promoted the teaching profession through a number of donations to scholarship programs. It has also used its prominence as the premiere child advocacy group to raise awareness about a number of issues that affect children and schools.

The National PTA is credited with, among other achievements, establishing juvenile courts for minors, pioneering hot lunch programs, establishing childcare centers for children of working mothers, improving public school curricula, increasing teachers' salaries, arranging for physical examinations of millions of preschool children, and sponsoring hundreds of recreation centers for teenagers.

Public Impact Case Study: TV Ratings

In 1996 the television industry, in response to widespread criticism that too many programs were unsuitable for children, was in the process of developing a voluntary rating system. The system was to be used with the V-chip, new technology that would allow parents to block out programs with ratings unsuitable for children. The PTA, which had been a leading advocate of improving the quality of children's television programming for more than 25 years, had worked hard to secure passage of the V-chip legislation, and the group took an active interest in shaping the ratings system.

On November 21, 1996, the PTA released the results of a survey of 679 randomly selected parents. The survey showed that 80 percent of parents preferred a ratings system that went beyond simply showing what age group a show was appropriate for. Parents wanted a system that gives information about why a program is unsuitable for children, such as whether it contained sex or violence, so they could judge for themselves whether programs were appropriate for their children. "Parents have spoken loud and clear," then-PTA president Joan Dykstra said in a statement after the survey results were released. "They want objective information about television content so they can make informed choices about what their children watch."

The following month, however, television industry executives introduced a ratings system based only on age-appropriateness and not on program content. The PTA launched an effort to revise the ratings system. "The television industry had an opportunity to show itself as responsive and responsible to American consumers, and today it has failed to do so," Dykstra said in December 1996 when the ratings system was introduced. The PTA put out a call for members and parents around the country to contact the Federal Communications Commission (FCC), which was threatening to step in if the television industry did not effect changes in the rating system.

The industry responded to the pressure. In June 1997 the PTA played a key role in negotiating a new system with the television industry. A revised ratings system was announced in July. The new system, which went into effect October 1, 1997, added the letters S, V, L and D to the age-based ratings—for Sexual situations, Violence, Language, and Dialogue. The ratings also have an FV rating for "fantasy violence," a descriptor used for animated programs. In December 1997, the PTA's role in creating the ratings was recognized when PTA national president Ginny Markell was appointed as one of the five non-TV industry members of the 24-member board set up to monitor the application of the ratings. In February 1998, the PTA, together with the cable industry and other child advocacy groups, launched a program to help parents understand and utilize the ratings. The program is called "Tools You Can Use to Help You Choose: A Family Guide to the TV Ratings System."

FUTURE DIRECTIONS

PTA literature hints at reasons why the group's membership declined from its peak of about 12 million in the 1960s: "Today, the PTA is shedding the old, mistaken image of a cookie-baking, fund-raising women's group." The group began a number of programs in the mid-1990s aimed at the environment, violence, Internet pornography, parental involvement in schools and other pressing issues, and the group launched its own Web site in 1996. But although PTA membership inched up from 5.3 million in 1983 to 7 million in 1991, reversing a 20-year decline, membership has since ebbed to 6.5 million. It is uncertain that the PTA will ever be able to push membership up to levels it has achieved in the past.

It is unclear how widespread the viewpoint is, but in 1995 Charlene Haar wrote in an editorial in *Insight on the News* magazine that PTAs were ineffective as a parent advocacy organization because they had become captive of teacher unions. Domination by such unions, especially the National Education Association, often forced the PTA to push the union agenda even when that was not in the best interests of parents, Haar wrote. The PTA responded in the same edition that teachers were indeed a large part of the organization, but that the group's sources of financial support and interests were broad enough that it could be considered independent and unbiased. "The National PTA cooperates with many partners but is subservient to none," a group representative argued.

GROUP RESOURCES

The PTA has an extensive Web site at http://www.pta.org, that offers information about the group's history, programs, activities and positions. The group also publishes a number of resources for parents, teachers, and child advocates. Among these are "The Parents Guide to the Information Superhighway," and "Teacher's Guide to Parent and Family Involvement." For more information on activities, materials, and publications, call 1–800–USA-LEARN.

GROUP PUBLICATIONS

The group offers a wealth of material and publications to members to help them in their efforts to improve education and child safety. For instance, the *National Standards for Parent/Family Involvement* handbook offers educators information about successful programs for increasing parental involvement in education. The PTA's *Our Children* magazine is published nine times a year. The magazine explores education issues, has information about PTA activities, and includes other articles of concern to parents and educators. A subscription is $25 a year ($15 for PTA members). For more information, call (312) 670-6783. The *What's Happening in Washington* newsletter is published 10 times a year. A one-year subscription is $6. For more information, call (202) 289-6790. Recorded information about legislative

activities is available at (888) 4ALLKDS. The group publishes *The PTA Story: A Century of Commitment to Children,* which details the group's history. The book costs $34.95 and is available through the group's Web site or by calling 1-800-369-2646, ext. 3339.

BIBLIOGRAPHY

Cantor, Joanne, Suzanne Stutman, and Victoria Duran. "What Parents Want in a Television Rating System: Results of a National Survey." National PTA, 1996.

"Don't Be a Trigger to Violence: Keep Handguns Out of the House." *Our Children,* October 1997.

Goll, David. "PTA Leaders to Gather to Celebrate Organization's 100th Anniversary." *Contra Costa Times,* 14 February 1997.

Haar, Charlene. "PTA Serves Teacher Unions, Not Parents." *Insight in the News,* 27 March 1995.

"Looking to Our Roots: A History of the PTA." Chicago, Ill.: The National PTA, 1997.

Rubenstein, Carin. "Parent Power." *Good Housekeeping,* October 1994.

Whitfill, Kathryn. "Don't Fault the 'T' in the Nation's PTAs." *Insight in the News,* 27 March 27.

National Cotton Council of America (NCC)

ESTABLISHED: November 1938
EMPLOYEES: 100
MEMBERS: 21,794
PAC: Cotton Action Committee

Contact Information:
ADDRESS: 1918 N. Parkway
     Memphis, TN 38112
PHONE: (901) 274-9030
FAX: (901) 725-0510
E-MAIL: info@cotton.org
URL: http://www.cotton.org
PRESIDENT: Jack Hamilton

WHAT IS ITS MISSION?

The National Cotton Council (NCC) describes itself as "the unifying force of the U.S. raw cotton industry's seven segments: producers (those who grow cotton), ginners (those who separate fiber from seed), warehousemen (those who store baled cotton), merchants (those who market the fiber), cottonseed crushers (those who process the seed), cooperatives (those who process, handle or market cotton or cottonseed for their producer), and textile manufacturers (those who spin the fiber into yarn)." The organization's purpose, as outlined in its mission statement, is "to ensure the ability of all industry segments to compete effectively and profitably in the raw cotton, oilseed, and value-added product markets at home and abroad." The NCC is the only U.S. organization representing all seven cotton industry segments.

The United States is the largest cotton exporter in the world. One-fourth of all cotton exports come from the United States and cotton makes up $60 billion of the nation's economy. Cotton has multiple uses; a familiar textile, its seed also provides feed for animals as well as serving as the basis for cotton seed oil. The NCC advocates for a viable and profitable U.S. cotton industry and deals with challenges that include tax policy, environmental regulation, increasing international competition, and natural pests that attack the plant. The organization's prime strategic focus is profitability for all segments of the cotton industry.

HOW IS IT STRUCTURED?

The NCC structure reflects the organization's wide-ranging focus, encompassing markets both nationally and internationally. The main office is located in Memphis, Tennessee, with a branch office located in Washington, D.C. The NCC also has offices in London; Seoul, South Korea; and Hong Kong. NCC policies are developed through a group of delegates representing each cotton industry segment who vote on all measures submitted to them. Each year these delegates appoint a 35-member board of directors that directs NCC business and offices. The board, in turn, elects the organization's officer positions of president, vice presidents, and treasurer.

The NCC has several committees that develop recommendations during the year and submit these recommendations to a vote at the annual delegate meeting. These committees include: Farm Program and Economic Policy; International Trade Policy; Public Relations and International Market Development; Research and Education; Packaging and Distribution; and Health, Safety and Environmental Quality. Recommendations adopted by the delegates become part of the NCC's plan of action for the year and are implemented by NCC staff.

NCC staff positions include managers of Washington operations, economic services, technical services, and field services. Most staff work is performed out of the Tennessee office, with 12 staff members working as field staff and based in the Washington office and an additional 12 staff members working collectively in the London, Seoul, and Hong Kong offices.

The NCC also oversees the Cotton Council International (CCI), an organizational arm that promotes U.S. cotton export and receives directions from the Public Relations and International Market Development committees. The CCI fosters relationships with international markets by holding tours and advertising campaigns. The NCC is also affiliated with the Cotton Foundation, a separate, 501(c)3 organization supported by more than 70 corporations and donors who are not members of the NCC but who support the NCC's mission. The Cotton Foundation supports research and education relevant to the cotton industry.

NCC membership is available to any industry firm or individual who is employed in one of the industry segments. Dues vary according to segment. Members receive publications and other informational resources from the NCC, as well as preferred status when participating in Cotton Foundation educational programs. Members are also issued Action Requests (by mail, Web site, or fax) and encouraged to contact their representatives regarding particular issues or legislation relevant to the cotton industry.

PRIMARY FUNCTIONS

The NCC performs various functions in its effort to maintain a healthy U.S. cotton industry. The organization works to ensure the profitability of the industry through its own research and by encouraging legislative and regulatory reforms. Through its research arm, the Cotton Foundation, the NCC studies ways to reduce costs and improve yields in the cotton industry. One of its 1997 studies looked at increasing the Vitamin E content of cottonseed oil to enhance its nutritional content and its use as a cooking staple. Another 1997 foundation initiative brought producers, ginners, and textile representatives together to identify the most pressing research priorities to focus on in order to keep the cotton industry on the cutting edge. These priorities, when identified, were shared with agencies such as the U.S. Department of Agriculture (USDA) and with key policymakers.

The NCC carries out activities designed to improve the global competitiveness of U.S. cotton. For example, members of the NCC worked together to address competitiveness provisions for cotton that were outlined in the Federal Agriculture Improvement and Reform Act of 1996 (FAIR). NCC representatives crafted changes to the act that they considered to be necessary to the cotton industry; these changes were later adopted in agriculture appropriations legislation passed in 1998. The NCC opposes what it considers to be unfair trade policies or practices that might impede cotton exports. For example, the organization opposed a Brazilian policy restricting the use of private credit to purchase imported products. The organization wrote letters to both the U.S. trade representative and the Foreign Agricultural Service protesting the policy.

As the NCC's foreign market arm, the CCI works to establish and promote exports of cotton products to markets around the world. This involves both encouraging foreign markets to purchase U.S. cotton and assisting U.S. producers in selling their products overseas. In 1997 CCI members visited potential market sites in China and Latin America to promote the U.S. cotton industry. The CCI also carried out studies of potential markets in China, Germany, Japan and three other countries in order to make market information available to U.S. cotton manufacturers.

PROGRAMS

In addition to its research activities, the NCC carries out a number of programs designed to promote cotton and cotton products and educate individuals about the cotton industry. The NCC promotes education in the industry by hosting annual Beltwide Cotton Conferences. These educational seminars are held at various locations in the cotton-growing region of the southern United States, and provide information designed to assist NCC members improve their profitability and keep them informed of new developments in the industry. The 1997 conferences, for example, included information on contamination prevention. The NCC also produces a number of trade and educational publications that cover a multitude of industry-related topics such as crop monitoring or the most recent research findings.

The program *Cotton Cares* is coordinated by NCC's Health, Safety, and Environmental Quality Committee. Focusing on environmental considerations as they relate to cotton production, the program is carried out by member producers who volunteer their time speaking to the Environmental Protection Agency (EPA), businesses, and student groups.

The *Cotton USA* program, managed by the CCI, encourages consumers to be on the lookout for products made with U.S.-grown cotton. A special *Cotton USA* trademark logo is key to the program. Companies whose products use U.S. cotton are allowed to use the logo on these products. *Cotton USA* has its own Web site (http://www.cottonusa.org), which includes a database of worldwide manufacturing companies eligible to use the *Cotton USA* logo on their products.

BUDGET INFORMATION

The NCC is funded with dues from its members and reports an average annual operating budget of $8 million. NCC supports the CCI and contributed $850,000 to that subsidiary organization in 1997. As part of its 1997 contributions the CCI also received $2 million from Cotton Incorporated, $9.2 million from the United States Department of Agriculture that was earmarked for *Cotton USA* activities, $100,000 from the American Textile Manufacturers Institute, and another $100,000 from the New York Cotton Exchange.

The Cotton Foundation, the not-for-profit research affiliate of the NCC, had a 1997 budget of $1.6 million. Included in those revenues was $351,000 from supporting member firms—up 30 percent from 1996. Additional revenues from 18 other member firms further enhanced the budget for the Foundation's research and education projects.

HISTORY

The NCC was founded in 1938 in Memphis, Tennessee, in response to a sluggish cotton economy. During the Great Depression of the 1930s, cotton supply exceeded demand and exports of cotton began declining, causing a drop in cotton prices. Additionally, rayon and synthetic fibers were being developed, creating a new and competitive textile market. Concerned industry members saw the need to unite and formulate strategies that would

keep the cotton market healthy without relying totally on the government for support. The NCC was formed to represent the needs of all segments of the industry.

Cotton continued to compete with other synthetic fibers into the 1960s and 1970s. In 1966 Congress passed the Cotton Research and Promotion Act which established Cotton Incorporated, an organization designed to carry out the research and marketing necessary to maintain cotton's competitive edge. Cotton Incorporated's work helped cotton reestablish a viable market position.

The world economy became increasingly interconnected in the 1970s, and more and more foreign companies became viable competitors in many industries. As a result the cotton industry was forced to rethink the way it did business. Technological advances contributed to the globalization of the economy—methods of communication and transportation had become faster, making it possible for manufacturers to locate industry segments in a variety of foreign locations where costs—usually labor costs—might be cheaper than in the United States. Another arrangement, known as the Caribbean Basin Initiative (CBI), allowed finished textile production to take place abroad using base fabrics manufactured in the United States. Due in part to these changes, domestic jobs in the textile and apparel industries decreased 40 percent between 1973 and 1996.

The 1990s saw substantial changes in the international textiles market. In 1994, after a seven-year-long debate among the participating countries, Congress agreed to phase in the General Agreement on Tariffs and Trade (GATT) over a 10-year period and phase out the Multifiber Arrangement, which had governed textile trade since 1973. The NCC supported the GATT phase-in, as well as the signing of the North American Free Trade Agreement (NAFTA). The NCC believed that these treaties would create a more open trading environment in the textile industry and would open up more export markets to the U.S. cotton industry. The first impacts to the textile and apparel industries included cuts in import tariffs and an expanded export market as the cooperating nations agreed to open their markets to more imports.

With these trade changes in place the NCC changed its focus from protecting domestic manufacturers by limiting the import of competing products into the United States, to exploring opportunities for U.S. exports. In an effort to remain competitive, the cotton industry now works to cut costs in production and experiments with research and technology to achieve lower production costs.

CURRENT POLITICAL ISSUES

The NCC is involved in a number of issues impacting the profitability of the cotton industry. For example, the organization must maintain a viable share in the global cotton market. The entrance of foreign competitors into the market, made possible by the increasing globalization of the economy in the 1980s and 1990s, has forced the cotton industry to adopt new marketing strategies and to advocate for trade policy that will be advantageous to the U.S. cotton industry. In addition to monitoring and influencing legislation, the international marketing arm of the NCC, Cotton Council International, carries out activities to expand cotton's international markets. The CCI meets with foreign representatives from the industry, conducts tours of U.S. and foreign operations, and launches promotions to increase the awareness of cotton worldwide.

Cotton pricing has been and will continue to be an issue faced by the industry on a daily basis. In late 1997, and early 1998, the price of cotton dropped, partly as a result of the Asian financial crisis and a resultant decrease in demand for U.S. cotton from Asian countries. The price drop manifested itself in yet another way—the total acreage of cotton decreased as farmers and producers, discouraged by the price drop, planted available land with other crops. In a February 1998 issue of the NCC newsletter, the organization president stated that cotton acreage and production were at their lowest since 1989. In response, the NCC worked to increase awareness of the implications of low cotton price to the media, the public, and to key policymakers by providing press releases to numerous publications. The NCC also went public with its support for providing U.S. assistance during the Asian financial crisis.

In addition to marketing cotton, the agricultural aspects of cotton production are also of concern to the NCC. Producers often resort to the use of pesticides to enhance and protect their valuable crops. The NCC assists in the development of relatively safe pest control methods, and lobbies to gain the necessary government approval for their use, even in the face of opposition from environmental groups.

Case Study: Crop Management

The cotton crop is subject to a number of natural pests, including the boll weevil—a pest that originated in Central America in the late 1890s, made its way into North America, and costs the cotton industry $300 million annually. The organization supports the use of Integrated Pest Management, or IPM, in managing cotton crops. IPM is a technique whereby all available pest control techniques—natural, genetic, cultural, and chemical—are evaluated and then combined, based on each particular situation, into a pest management program. According to the NCC, IPM programs avoid economic damage and minimize environmental disturbances. Proponents of organic farming, however, oppose any use of chemicals for crop production.

The NCC has been a strong supporter of boll weevil eradication programs, which use the IPM technique.

FAST FACTS

In 1996 the textile industry employed 624,000 workers, with the majority working in three states: Georgia, North Carolina, and South Carolina. Nearly half of the textile workers employed in 1996 were women.

(Source: Mark Mittelhauser. "Employment Trends in Textiles and Apparel, 1973-2005," *Monthly Labor Review*, August 1, 1997.)

The organization claims that this method reduces the pesticides that would normally be needed to eradicate the boll weevil by at least 70 percent. Organic farming of cotton is not feasible, according to the NCC, because of the increased time and energy needed to raise cotton organically. Additionally, the NCC claims that enough acres are not available to offset reduced yields if a significant amount of cotton was grown organically.

To ensure that the cotton industry received support for pest eradication, the NCC lobbied Congress to make money available in 1998 for the National Boll Weevil Eradication Program. Due in part to NCC's advocacy, the USDA made loans to several state eradication programs. The NCC achieved a victory in the pest management arena when the EPA approved a request from Texas cotton producers in 1998 to use the insecticide Furadan to control aphids on cotton plants.

The NCC has voiced objections to the EPA's regulatory role in crop management, stating that the EPA shows inconsistency in making decisions about which pesticides are or are not safe to use. The EPA is making decisions about pesticides as part of the implementation of the Food Quality Protection Act; applicable here since cotton produces a food by-product. Though the NCC complains that the EPA needs to have a regulatory policy based on sound science, it is possible that the effects of insecticides on humans are not entirely understood.

FUTURE DIRECTIONS

As the NCC looks to the future, trends such as an increase in international trading, advancing technology, and an environmentally astute public have the potential to affect the demand for U.S. cotton. In response, the NCC will continue to pursue international markets for cotton products, while also staying at the technological forefront—even though technological advances may be quickly overrun by competitors—and will continue to invest in research aimed at technological procedures.

GROUP RESOURCES

The NCC provides a great deal of information through its Web site. In its Economic Information section, accessible at http://www.cotton.org/ncc/econinfo. htm, one can visit the WeatherCenter to find out about weather conditions across the United States. Prices and other economic information about cotton are also available. The CCI maintains its own Web site, with information on the international cotton market, at http://www. cottonusa.org/cci.htm. For more information, contact the CCI at 1521 New Hampshire Ave. NW, Washington, DC 20036, or call (202) 745-7805.

GROUP PUBLICATIONS

The NCC provides educational resources that tell the story of cotton; these include teaching kits, booklets, and other classroom resources and can be ordered through the Web page at http://www.cotton.org/ncc/public/ncc/ stycottn.htm, or by mail at National Cotton Council, ATTN: Communications Services Dept., Box 12285, Memphis, TN 38132. The NCC also publishes a variety of material for members, including *Cotton's Week*

newsletter, *Cotton Economic Review*, and the *Cotton Physiology Today* newsletter.

BIBLIOGRAPHY

"Economic Research Service: Cotton and Wool Outlook." *M2 PressWIRE*, 15 April 1997.

Groves, Martha. "True Colors; Biotech Company Calgene Patents Gene to Control Cotton Pigment." *Los Angeles Times*, 24 July 1996.

Iritana, Evelyn. "Southeast Asia's Economic Survival Depends on Exports." *Los Angeles Times*, 21 November 1997.

McCurry, John W. "Exports: The New Gospel of Textiles: Foreign Sale of U.S. Products Continue Breaking Records as More Manufacturers See Global Market as a Key to Survival." *Textile World*, 1 August 1994.

Rostler, Suzanne. "Texas Crop Shrinks, Farmers Soft on Grains." *Reuters*, 7 June 1996.

Sharma, Mukul. "India-Labor: Liberalization Kills Textile Workers." *Inter Press Service English News Wire*, 27 September 1995.

"The Week in Georgia." *Atlanta Journal & Constitution*, 15 March 1998.

Walker, Tom. "How Georgia Stocks Fared: Economy, Markets Being Good to Most Textile Companies." *Atlanta Journal & Constitution*, 3 April 1998.

White, Fred C., and Michael E Wetzstein. "Market Effects of Cotton Integrated Pest Management." *American Journal of Agricultural Economics*, 1 August 1995.

National Council of La Raza (NCLR)

WHAT IS ITS MISSION?

According to the organization's Web site, "the National Council of La Raza (NCLR) is a private, non-profit, nonpartisan, tax-exempt organization established in 1968 to reduce poverty and discrimination, and improve life opportunities for Hispanic Americans." NCLR seeks to advance its mission in the United States by employing a wide spectrum of activities ranging from political advocacy work to media outreach. The organization also carries out an extensive community and organizational development program.

By working with Hispanic communities in the United States and by serving as an advocate for these communities, NCLR seeks to help an often disadvantaged and misunderstood segment of the population. One basic goal of the organization is to teach Americans that the term Hispanic refers to a broad ethnic group which includes many nationalities and to dispel the common stereotype of Hispanics as immigrants who are poor, uneducated, and probably illegal. The group seeks to counter the discrimination that is fed by such misconceptions and to thereby improve economic, health, educational, and civil rights conditions for Hispanics.

ESTABLISHED: 1968
EMPLOYEES: Not made available
MEMBERS: Not made available
PAC: None

Contact Information:
ADDRESS: 1111 19th St. NW, Ste. 1000
Washington, DC 20036
PHONE: (202) 785-1670
FAX: (202) 776–1792
URL: http://www.nclr.org
PRESIDENT: Raul Yzaguirre

HOW IS IT STRUCTURED?

The NCLR is governed and directed by a 30-member board of directors, which is diverse geographically and represents a variety of nationalities. The board is required to have at least half of its members represent regional affiliates or constituencies, and to be made up of

half female and half male members. The NCLR has a main office in Washington, D.C., which includes the organization's Policy Analysis Center, and regional offices in: Los Angeles, California; Phoenix, Arizona; Chicago, Illinois; and San Antonio, Texas. Field offices provide support (including organizational development, management assistance, and resource development) to the NCLR's 200 affiliates (which represent 37 U.S. states, Puerto Rico, and Washington, D.C.) and to at least 20,000 independent Hispanic groups and individuals needing services.

NCLR members pay annual dues of $35 and have the option of becoming an NCLR associate. Associates receive a discount on publications, the quarterly newsletter, and notification of pending legislative or policy issues. Members are asked through Action Alerts to contact policymakers on pending initiatives that affect the Hispanic community.

PRIMARY FUNCTIONS

To carry out its mission, the NCLR functions in a number of ways. The organization is an advocate for issues that affect the Hispanic community. Advocacy efforts include lobbying, testifying at congressional hearings, and commenting on policy. The range of issues that the NCLR is involved with is wide, including education, health, foreign trade, farmworkers rights, civil rights, economic mobility, and poverty.

The NCLR also engages in research and policy analysis that complements and supports the organization's advocacy efforts. For example, the NCLR researches citizenship proceedings in order to make sure that they are fair and efficient for Hispanic applicants. Other areas that the NCLR monitors are U.S. census practices, and conditions for migrant Hispanic farmworkers in the United States.

The NCLR offers organizational development support to Hispanic communities in rural and urban settings. These efforts are designed to strengthen and assist Hispanic organizations and include consulting in the areas of management, operations, leadership development, and resource development. Goals of such programs may include the construction and planning of housing, schools, community centers, or business centers.

The council uses media outreach to complement its initiatives and to advance its mission. The NCLR forms coalitions with like-minded organizations (such as the National Coalition on Health Care) and provides an organizational model for other evolving initiatives or organizations in the Hispanic community. The organization has an interest in collaboration, and staff is involved with other private-sector or nonprofit organizations whose missions overlap with that of the NCLR.

The NCLR partners with the private sector to enhance its outreach programs. For example, since 1991 the organization has partnered with Prudential Life Insurance, which helped sponsor the annual NCLR conference and other NCLR programs such as the College Leadership Forum, the NCLR Congressional Awards, and the ALMA Awards.

PROGRAMS

NCLR programs are created to carry out the organization's mission and as such, directly serve Hispanic communities. For example, NCLR education programs include EXCEL and EXCEL-MAS, programs that develop supplementary curricula for Hispanic children in school and for after-school programs. The Proyecto Educar: Community Service Leadership in Action program enlists the help of volunteers to assist Hispanics with literacy, English language fluency, and preparation for General Equivalency Diploma (GED) exams. Project LEER (Literacy Education Employment Readiness) develops job-training programs for Hispanics in communities across the United States.

To address human rights issues in Hispanic communities, the NCLR's Hispanic Poverty and Employment Project uses data the organization has collected to assess the effect of these issues on the Hispanic population. For example, the project monitored the effect of tax policy on Latino workers.

The organization is also involved in addressing the housing needs of the Hispanic community. According to the NCLR, many Hispanics live either in economically declining rural or inner-city areas. Hispanics may be living in substandard, deteriorating housing. The organization works to put programs in place that will ensure quality, affordable housing for Hispanic communities. The NCLR's Southwest Initiative program worked with 25 different organizations to provide remodeled or new housing for Hispanics. The program also carried out community development initiatives in Hispanic communities, including the planning and building of schools, business areas, and community centers.

The NCLR also operates the Home-To-Own program, active primarily in Denver, Colorado, and Phoenix, Arizona. The program is operated from the organization's southwest regional office, and assists low-income Hispanics with purchasing their first home. The program incorporates flexible mortgage qualifications and counseling to facilitate the home-buying process for program clients.

BUDGET INFORMATION

Not made available.

HISTORY

The term "Hispanic" or "Latino" refers to ethnicity rather than race and includes a variety of nationalities. Hispanics occupied the geographic United States long before Anglo-Saxon settlement and had established cultural traditions and societies on the continent. Public perception of the Hispanic community in the United States, however, has been shaped more recently by this ethnic community's large population increase in the United States and its interaction with other U.S. majority and minority ethnic groups. When immigration rules in the United States were modified and relaxed in 1964, the number of Latinos immigrating to the United States increased substantially.

By 1995 there were 22.4 million Latino students in K-12 schools across the United States. Many of the Hispanic immigrants were eager to take advantage of work and educational opportunities that were unavailable in the countries where they had came from, such as Mexico or Cuba. As the numbers of Hispanics in the United States grew Hispanics faced increased discrimination and a mounting resistance to affirmative action. Many Hispanics who were legal residents were mistakenly assumed to be illegal aliens. That, coupled with a poor understanding of the cultures that the term "Hispanic" encompasses, often put barriers of many types in front of Hispanics looking to achieve success in the United States.

According to Dr. Rebozo de la Garza, the director of a Hispanic organization in Texas (*Hispanic Outlook in Higher Education,* February 21, 1997), increasing numbers of Latino immigrants competed for dwindling resources in educational and financial support—leading to financial stagnation and a general barrier to upward mobility. Because many Hispanics were recent immigrants they could not speak English well and faced language barriers. In 1968 an organization was founded in Arizona named the Southwest Council of La Raza, to address the issues that U.S. Hispanics were facing and to advocate for this growing community. According to the organization, the term La Raza was not meant to be read as "The Race," a common misinterpretation of the phrase that implies exclusivity. Rather, La Raza was chosen as part of the organization's name because it means "The People," or "The Hispanic people of the New World." This is meant to symbolize the mixture inherent in the Hispanic community, which has roots in Native American, European, Arab, and African culture.

In 1970 the council, which had thus far focused its efforts on improving conditions in the Southwest United States, opened an office in Washington, D.C., to provide both greater visibility, and to be near the nation's capitol in order to affect policy decisions. This was the beginning of the organization's focus on community-building efforts as well as research and advocacy. In 1972 the Southwest Council of La Raza changed its name to the National Council of La Raza, reflecting its increasingly national focus.

The next 10 years were a time of growth for the NCLR, as it expanded into a major national Hispanic advocacy group, and continued its community-building efforts. The NCLR developed more than 150 affiliations with local and regional groups, and established regional offices in: Chicago; Phoenix; Los Angeles; and McAllen, Texas. In 1980 the NCLR established its Policy Analysis Center. This think tank greatly increased the NCLR's researching and policy-recommending capabilities. Soon, the organization had established itself as one of the United States' most important Hispanic advocacy groups, and the organization's opinions on issues affecting Hispanics were frequently solicited by the federal government.

During the late 1990s the NCLR actively sought to improve the Hispanic community's portrayal in the media. According to NCLR, portrayal of Hispanics is often unrealistic and not representative of the Hispanic population. According to an article in the *Los Angeles Times* (December 13, 1997), a 1997 NCLR study found that portrayals of Hispanics in prime-time television had improved only slightly but were still quite stereotypical. To combat the problem, NCLR established a partnership with the Disney-owned ABC network to air the 1998 American Latino Media Arts Awards. The NCLR purchased a block of advertising time during the show and kept the advertising revenue it was able to raise. The organization claimed that airing the awards on ABC was a big step for Disney and the Hispanic community. The National Hispanic Media Coalition, however, criticized the NCLR for partnering with Disney, claiming that in so doing the council was indirectly endorsing Disney's discriminatory hiring practices.

According to the NCLR, Hispanics in the late 1990s were the most undereducated ethnic group in the United States. Hispanics drop out of high school at a statistically noticeable rate, and may face barriers to education due to poverty or English language difficulties. The NCLR and other Hispanic advocacy groups achieved a victory in 1998 when President Bill Clinton allocated $600 million for an action plan that would address Hispanic education issues. The program included improved college outreach to high schools and increased teaching resources for education in the English language.

CURRENT POLITICAL ISSUES

Many of the issues that the NCLR advocates for on behalf of Hispanics relate to basic civil and human rights. As a community subject to misunderstanding, stereotyping, and racism in the United States, Hispanics have had to work hard to obtain access to decent wages and other opportunities such as quality housing. Hispanics are often assumed to be immigrants (legal or otherwise), when in fact most Hispanics are native born U.S. citizens, a fact that the NCLR strives to make the public more aware of.

FAST FACTS

In 1998 Latino children and young adults made up 14 percent of the school-age population, and are projected to grow to 22 percent by 2020.

(Source: "Gore Announces $600 Million Hispanic Education Action Plan," *US Newswire,* February 2, 1998.)

However, there are many Hispanics who still have close relatives living in South or Latin America, and immigration laws are therefore a major concern. For example, in 1998, when some in Congress proposed to limit immigration based on level of education (forcing immigrants with less education than others to wait as long as five to 20 years to enter the United States), NCLR spoke out strongly in a public statement and claimed that the restrictions would make it very difficult for Hispanic families to reunite in the United States.

Case Study: Arizona's "English-Only" Law

In 1988, a ballot initiative in Arizona was passed, with a 50.5 percent majority, that amended the state constitution to require "the state and all political subdivisions to act in English and in no other language." This was one of many so-called English-only laws passed in states across the country in the 1980s and 1990s. Many considered the state English-only laws to be essentially symbolic in nature, along the same line as naming a particular plant to be the official state flower. Others, however, including the NCLR, viewed Arizona's law as potentially very restrictive and unjust.

While supporters of the law claimed that it would only affect legally binding documents, such as court documents, its opponents challenged it as an unconstitutional restriction on the First Amendment right to free speech. A lawsuit was soon filed on behalf of Maria-Kelley Yniguez, a state employee who sometimes used Spanish in her reports, and when communicating with Spanish-speaking customers. She was later joined by Arizona State Senator Jaime Gutierrez, who claimed that the law prevented him from communicating with his constituents in Spanish. The NCLR feared that the law would be applied to groups that received funds from the state, including the NCLR itself. This would then prevent the NCLR, the group claimed, from such common-sense

activities as posting fliers in Spanish that advertise classes in English as a second language.

The law found little support from within the government of Arizona. The state government declined to enforce the measure, and when a federal district court found the law unconstitutional, the state declined to appeal. At this point, the supporters of the ballot initiative stepped in and appealed the case to the circuit court. Once again, it was ruled unconstitutional. In 1995 the case was presented to the U.S. Supreme Court. The NCLR filed an *amicus curiae* (Friend of the Court) brief with the Court, outlining why it felt the law was unconstitutional. In a surprising move, the Supreme Court threw out the case, declaring that it was not a matter for federal jurisdiction.

Continuing their challenge in the state courts, the NCLR and the law's other opponents, secured a unanimous decision from the Arizona Supreme Court in 1998. The court found the law to violate the First Amendment right to freedom of speech, because it blocked the "free discussion of governmental affairs." The court also found the law in violation of the right to equal protection under the law, because it placed an undue burden on non-English speakers.

FUTURE DIRECTIONS

In the 1998 elections Hispanic voters turned out in record numbers and had a noticeable influence on the vote in heavily Hispanic-populated states such as California. According to an article in the *Dallas Morning News* (September 20, 1998), Hispanics represent the largest growing segment of the Democratic Party. The NCLR will work to ensure that the Hispanic vote remains a force in developing policy that will advance the civil and human rights of U.S. Hispanics.

GROUP RESOURCES

The NCLR offers a Web site at http://www.nclr.org, as well as publications and resources for communities on topics such as leadership training and economic development assistance. Contact the organization directly by mailing 1111 19th St. NW, Ste 1000, Washington, DC, 20036, or by the telephone at (202) 785-1670 for information about resources, programs, and publications.

GROUP PUBLICATIONS

NCLR publications include *Agenda,* a quarterly newsletter, and other newsletters that focus on issues of importance to the organization such as education, poverty, and HIV/AIDS. The organization's Publications Guide or specific publications may be obtained by contacting the NCLR distribution center at: The National Council of La Raza (NCLR) Distribution Center, P.O. Box 291, Annapolis Junction, MD 20701-0291. Examples of NCLR reports include: *Hispanic Health Status: A Disturbing Diagnosis* and *Burden or Relief? The Impact of Taxes on Hispanic Working Families.*

BIBLIOGRAPHY

"Census 2000; Hispanic Issues and Answers." *Hispanic Outlook in Higher Education,* 27 June 1997.

DePass, Dee. "Bienvenidos Business; Hispanic-Owned Companies Fighting for Market Share." *Star Tribune,* 15 June 1997.

Domhoff, G. William, and Richard L. Zweigenhaft. "The New Power Elite: Women, Jews, African Americans, Asian Americans, Latinos, Gays and Lesbians." *Mother Jones,* 13 March 1998

Garvin, Glenn. "Bringing the Border War Home." *Reason,* 1 October 1995.

Hernandez, Carol. "Cultural Divide; Latin Couples from Different Countries Often Find Out They Don't Know a Hill of Beans (Black or Pink) About Each Other's Customs." *Newsday,* 30 December 1997.

Hispanic Yearbook, TIYM Publishing Co. Inc.: McLean, Va.

McConnell, Scott, "Americans No More?" *National Review,* 31 December 1997.

"Misconceptions Surround the Ethnicity of Hispanics." *La Prensa de San Antonio,* 13 July 1997.

Romano, Michael. "U.S. West Chief Blasts Media on Race; Industry Aids in Keeping Hispanics the Target of Prejudice, Stereotypes." *Rocky Mountain News,* 14 October 1997.

Torres, Mark Anthony. "Oppressors' Roots Shouldn't Be Recognized." *University Wire,* 6 July 1998.

National Council on Crime and Delinquency (NCCD)

ESTABLISHED: June 14, 1907
EMPLOYEES: 50
MEMBERS: 500
PAC: None

Contact Information:

ADDRESS: 685 Market St., Ste. 620
    San Francisco, CA 94105
PHONE: (415) 896-6223
FAX: (415) 896-5109
URL: http://www.nccd.com
PRESIDENT: Barry Krisberg

WHAT IS ITS MISSION?

The National Council on Crime and Delinquency (NCCD) is a nonprofit organization with the broad mission of reducing crime and making sure the U.S. criminal justice system is effective, humane, fair, progressive, and cost-effective. Unlike many groups in Washington that have arms-length relationships with government because they have partisan goals or narrow ideological concerns, the NCCD conducts research and provides consulting work for federal, state, and local government agencies.

HOW IS IT STRUCTURED?

The NCCD is headquartered in San Francisco, California, and has offices in three other cities—Washington, D.C., New York City, New York, and Madison, Wisconsin. The group's day-to-day affairs are run by officers spread out among the various locations. The president is based in San Francisco, the executive vice president is located in Washington, D.C., and the vice president is in Madison. Each office has a specific focus: in San Francisco, juvenile justice; in Madison, child protection; and in Washington and New York, adult crimes. There are no regional or local chapters.

The NCCD's 18-member board of directors provides broad oversight for the group's activities, including the review of the annual budget and direction of the overall mission. The board meets once a year and is made up of judges, attorneys, and others with experience in the criminal justice field. Members can attend the annual meeting and vote for the board members. They may also vote by proxy.

In more than 20 states, the NCCD has citizen action committees—groups of citizens interested in the probation, parole, and juvenile justice systems. The NCCD, with a grant from the Ford Foundation, helped establish the committees, which are composed of business, labor, and civic leaders throughout the United States. The purpose of forming the committees was to build support among public opinion leaders for the type of juvenile and criminal justice reforms advocated by the NCCD. The committees are independent and self-sustaining but are affiliated with the NCCD; for instance, information about the committees can be obtained through NCCD offices or through its Web site.

PRIMARY FUNCTIONS

The NCCD is an assembly of individuals who are experts on criminal and delinquency matters, and who pride themselves on their international reputation for sponsoring quality research, training, and professional programs. The NCCD offers its expertise to public policymakers in a variety of ways. The council supplies reports directly to legislators and their staff that are used to help draft legislation. It produces policy papers, ranging from treatises on preventing hate crimes to evaluations of jail-based drug treatment programs. As of 1998 the NCCD had 40 such policy papers available to the public, ranging in price from $3.50 to $10.40. Examples include an essay on solving prison overcrowding problems, which is a document useful for state corrections officials; and a resource guide for preventing hate crimes, which is a manual intended not only for lawmakers but for advocacy groups concerned about hate crimes.

The council conducts research and provides consulting for the U.S. Department of Justice and other federal agencies. The NCCD is a primary consultant to the Justice Department in the areas of violence prevention and juvenile justice reform. The NCCD also acts as a resource for the House and Senate Judiciary committees and for other lawmakers on criminal justice matters through live testimony. The group regularly holds educational forums on Capitol Hill for Members of Congress and their staffs. The council also works with government agencies in almost every state. It provides consulting work that involves projecting prison populations, developing and evaluating new programs for correctional systems, and assisting in development of plans for compliance with court-ordered mandates for prison systems.

PROGRAMS

The NCCD has a variety of contracts with government agencies, including the Children's Research Cen-

A boot camp in Bushnell, Florida. These juvenile criminals did not successfully complete the boot camp program and were sent to prison to complete their sentences. (Photograph by Pete Cosgrove, UPI/Corbis-Bettmann)

ter. Begun in 1991, the center works with state and local agencies to bring about decision-making systems for child protection. These systems have a dual goal: to provide workers with simple, objective and reliable methods for making decisions in child protection cases; and to provide managers with case information for improved planning and resource allocation.

The Comprehensive Strategy for Serious, Violent, and Chronic Juvenile Offenders helps communities to develop a comprehensive system for preventing juvenile crime, intervening in early criminal behavior, and responding to "serious, violent, and chronic offending." The NCCD offers regional training workshops, community needs and risk assessments, and technical assistance. Workshops and training are currently being offered in California, Florida, Iowa, Maryland, Rhode Island, and Texas.

BUDGET INFORMATION

The NCCD's annual budget is approximately $4 million, most of which comes from government contracts. Other sources of revenue include dues and foundation grants.

FAST FACTS

The annual cost of jailing a drug addict is $25,900; the annual cost of drug treatment programs ranges from $1,800 for outpatient treatment to $6,800 for long-term hospitalization.

(Source: Raja Mishra. "Doctors: Drug Treatment Beats Jail." *News & Observer,* March 18, 1998.)

HISTORY

According to the NCCD's journal, *Crime & Delinquency,* the council began on June 14, 1907, when 14 probation officers met in Plymouth Church, Minneapolis. Their goal was to form a professional association, where they could share information and advocate for reform of the criminal justice system. The officers were responding to a perceived need for reform. At the time, many of the standards and processes of the modern criminal justice system, such as nationwide probation, parole, and a juvenile court system, had not yet been created.

That early group became known as the National Probation Association (NPA). Among its achievements were assisting Virginia in drafting its first probation law, persuading Congress to create the U.S. Probation and Parole Service, helping the U.S. Childrens Bureau publish the nation's first standards for juvenile court and writing several model legislative codes that were enacted across the United States.

An early concern of the NPA was the number of children being held in jails and the inadequacy of juvenile detention centers. The group launched a nationwide program of studies and recommendations designed to improve these practices and, soon, the group was being called upon to conduct surveys of juvenile courts in virtually every major urban area. Following these studies, the NPA helped local groups enact laws, promote resources for juvenile courts, and establish state standards.

In 1954 the council launched an effort to involve citizens in the criminal justice reform effort, figuring that such involvement would focus the nation's attention on the need to improve the system. By 1960 the NPA had expanded its scope well beyond the focus of the probation officers who had founded the group. To reflect the group's broader membership and concerns, the NPA changed its name to the National Council on Crime and Delinquency.

In the late 1960s President Lyndon Johnson formed the National Commission on Law Enforcement and asked the NCCD to conduct a national survey on the status of the juvenile corrections systems. The resulting report helped set a national agenda for corrections reform efforts. As the federal government expanded its role in criminal justice matters, the NCCD emerged as a major consultant to the federal Justice Department. In the 1970s the group expanded its research, training and technical assistance resources.

In the 1980s the NCCD went through a period of financial hardship that almost destroyed it. The primary reason was that Reagan administration budget cuts dried up federal grants that had previously sustained it. The council was able to rally from those hard times by turning increasingly to private funding through foundations, corporations, and philanthropists. The NCCD was able to win grants from, among other sources, the Edna McConnell Clark Foundation, Bristol-Meyers, the Pfizer Corp., and AT&T.

By the late 1990s the NCCD was back on firm footing. "Today," NCCD President Barry Krisberg wrote in 1998 "the council enjoys unparalleled national prestige and is actively helping almost all 50 states and the District of Columbia to analyze and solve their criminal justice problems."

CURRENT POLITICAL ISSUES

Over time, the NCCD has attempted to steer public policy on crime in a wise direction by providing comprehensive and objective studies so that policies are not based solely on assumptions and rhetoric. One area in which the group has been particularly influential is juvenile justice.

Case Study: Juvenile Justice

In 1967 the NCCD issued a report that documented "the indiscriminate mixing of all types of prisoners—the sick and the well, the old and the young, hardened criminals and petty offenders . . ." in correctional facilities. The study helped bring about the Juvenile Justice and Delinquency Prevention Act of 1974, which led to substantial changes in the way juvenile offenders are handled in the justice system. For instance, every state and five U.S. territories comply with the act's mandate that juveniles and adults in confinement be separated.

By the early 1990s, however, there was a backlash of public opinion about the need to crack down on youthful offenders. Particularly, there was wide public perception that the criminal justice system was not dealing with young criminal offenders, especially repeat offenders, harshly enough. Media reports indicated that violent trends were increasing among America's young, thus driving crime rates to record levels. Conservative members of Congress and other public officials called for get-tough alternatives like orphanages and boot camps, along with laws to abolish the special legal status that protected young criminals from being fully prosecuted.

The NCCD helped to shed light, rather than heat, on the discussion. They released a report in 1995, which revealed that arrests of youths for violent crimes had risen only one-half of one percent between 1982 and 1992. The report also indicated that twice as many children were killed by their parents or guardians than by other children. The findings "go far to refute misconceptions," the magazine *Education Digest* reported.

Some get-tough legislative measures have been enacted, including the Juvenile Crime Bill (S.10) sponsored by Senator Orrin Hatch (R-Ut.) in 1997. One of the bill's provisions allows for children 14 years and older to be tried as adults if they commit federal felonies. Other juvenile crime-deterrants that were suggested in the early 1990s, such as orphanages, have not been widely adopted. Boot camps, once so popular that they were in operation in every state, have fallen out of favor; a number of the camps have closed. While it is difficult to say how much the NCCD influenced the juvenile crime debate in the 1990s, it is apparent their research bears consideration.

FUTURE DIRECTIONS

In 1993 the NCCD advocated for a change in the war on drugs, claiming that too much money was spent on enforcement of anti-drug laws and not enough on treatment. But that approach has not become the predominant public policy in the United States. In fact, with tougher drug-related sentences, the number of federal prisoners sentenced for drug violations had reached 60 percent by 1997.

In March 1998 there was a significant boost for the NCCD's approach when a panel of medical experts reported that drug treatment programs are, in fact, effective. The panel urged that more emphasis be placed on treating drug addicts and less on incarcerating them. While the Clinton administration acknowledged the validity of the findings, as of 1999 there was still little change in federal funding. To that end, the NCCD will continue to push for federal monies to be spent on drug treatment programs.

Another goal the NCCD continues to pursue is an end to capital punishment. Capital punishment is a decision adopted at the state level. As local groups push for initiatives to abolish capital punishment the NCCD helps those efforts by providing studies that show, for example, that the death penalty is unevenly applied to offenders of various races.

GROUP RESOURCES

The council's Research and Information Center, which it touts as the world's largest private library collection of criminal justice materials, is located at the James Cotton Library of Rutgers University in Newark, New Jersey. For more information about the center, call (973) 353-5522. The NCCD has a Web site at http://www.nccd.com that offers background on the group's mission, programs and staff, announcements on upcoming events, and a listing of the group's policy papers, along with an on-line order form.

GROUP PUBLICATIONS

The NCCD's quarterly journal, *Crime & Delinquency,* examines criminal justice issues. A subscription costs $66 per year, and is available from Sage Publications, (805) 499-0721. The council also publishes research briefs, and policy papers which can be ordered on-line at http://www.nccd.com. NCCD "Charter" members (those who contribute $50 or more) get research briefs quarterly; "Advocate Members" (individuals who contribute at least $130) also get a discount subscription to the journal. "Institution" and "Organization" members ($200 contribution or more) get, in addition to the briefs and discount journal subscription, copies of each NCCD publication.

BIBLIOGRAPHY

Butterfield, Fox. "Three Strikes' Rarely Invoked In Courtrooms." *New York Times,* 10 September 1996.

Dohrn, Bernadine. "Undemonizing Our Children." *Education Digest,* December 1995.

Howell, James C. "NCCD's Survey of Juvenile Detention and Correctional Facilities." *Crime & Delinquency,* January 1998.

"The Jailhouse Door." *Economist,* 18 September 1993.

Krisberg, Barry. "The Evolution of an American Institution." *Crime & Delinquency,* January 1998.

Mishra, Raja. "Doctors: Drug Treatment Beats Jail." *News & Observer,* 18 March 1998.

"Now the Hard Part of the Crime Fight: Money." *U.S. News and World Report,* 14 March 1994.

Rector, Milton G. "Tribute to Don Gottfredson, Former Director of Research of the National Council on Crime and Delinquency." *Crime & Delinquency,* February 1996.

National Education Association (NEA)

ESTABLISHED: 1857
EMPLOYEES: 519
MEMBERS: 2,400,000
PAC: National Education Association Political Action
   Committee

Contact Information:

ADDRESS: 1201 16th St. NW
   Washington, DC 20036
PHONE: (202) 833-4000
URL: http://www.nea.org
PRESIDENT: Robert F. Chase
VICE PRESIDENT: Reginald Weaver

WHAT IS ITS MISSION?

The National Education Association (NEA) was founded to "advance the interest of the profession of teaching and to promote the cause of education in the United States." Today the organization's stated purpose is to seek "a quality education for each child in safe schools where children can learn the basics, practice values such as responsibility and teamwork, and prepare for jobs of the future." The NEA's leadership has made the issue of quality education the top priority of the organization's advocacy efforts in lobbying, public relations, and collective bargaining with employers.

HOW IS IT STRUCTURED?

The NEA has a headquarters office in Washington, D.C., and six regional offices. It is governed by a Representative Assembly (RA) which meets once a year and is attended by roughly 10,000 delegates elected at the state and local level. The RA debates and sets NEA policy and elects national officers. Between annual meetings, policies are made and implemented by the 159-member board of directors and an executive committee that includes the NEA's president, vice president, secretary-treasurer, and six other members.

The headquarters office assumes a number of responsibilities such as lobbying at the federal government level, providing public relations with the national media, and coordinating activities among the state associations and local affiliates. The regional offices serve as links to the state and local associations. The 52 state asso-

ciations sponsor activities that include lobbying state governments, advocating higher professional standards for educators, and filing legal actions to protect academic freedom and members' interests. Organized beneath the state associations are 13,000 local affiliates that: negotiate collective-bargaining contracts covering pay, benefits, and working conditions with employers where allowed by law; offer professional development workshops on educational issues; and represent members before school administrators and the local community.

NEA members include elementary and secondary public school teachers, educational support staff, school administrators, college and university faculty, retired educators, and college students who intend to teach.

PRIMARY FUNCTIONS

The NEA functions as both a professional association and a union. In states that do not allow public employees, including public school teachers, to unionize or bargain collectively over pay and working conditions, NEA affiliates serve as an informal voice for the interest of its members. In other states, the NEA acts as a union, negotiating contracts with employers and handling members' work-related grievances.

As part of its goal to improve public education, the NEA analyzes and conducts research and shares information on educational issues with policymakers, the public, and its members through press releases, reports, journals, and books. Since 1983 the NEA has spent over $70 million on education improvements. An example is a program launched by the NEA in 1996 to spend $1.5 million to set up five charter schools. Charter schools are alternative public schools in which the standing bureaucratic rules are scrapped and school district authorities have a limited role in the schools' operation. Another NEA program provides small grants to grassroots education initiatives in urban areas. The NEA offers materials and workshops to members to improve their teaching skills and encourages affiliates to experiment with and develop new techniques. It also works to build public support for the public school system. A public relations campaign started in 1997 publicizes the everyday successes of public education through a series of paid television spots.

The NEA is considered by national, state, and local policymakers to be one of the most politically powerful interest groups. In the 1995–96 election cycle the NEA's Political Action Committee (PAC) gave $2,356,006 to candidates for federal office. Although roughly a third of NEA members favor the Republican Party, over 98 percent of NEA contributions went to Democrats. The NEA rates the voting records of candidates, makes valuable endorsements, distributes campaign literature, and organizes drives to turn out voters. NEA members are also a reliable source of volunteers for political campaigns.

Because so many decisions are made at the local level in the United States' decentralized education system, NEA affiliates are also active in local school board elections where NEA members often run for office. In addition to its election efforts, the NEA maintains an extensive lobbying operation, spending nearly a million dollars to lobby the federal government in 1996. The NEA monitors federal and state legislation and alerts members to issues affecting their interests. Members are encouraged to contact their representatives and can do so through E-mail from the NEA Web site.

PROGRAMS

The NEA institutes a variety of programs to promote education. These programs primarily focus on improving either teaching methods or students' abilities.

As part of its public relations efforts and its goal to improve children's education, in 1998 the NEA sponsored "Read Across America," an event to encourage early childhood literacy and a love of reading. The Senate passed a resolution declaring March 2, the birthday of children's author Dr. Seuss, as Read Across America Day. The NEA announced a national read-in in which adults across the country were encouraged to read with children through thousands of local events sponsored by NEA affiliates. Keeping with the Dr. Seuss theme, legislators donned the famous striped stovepipe hat worn by the Cat in the Hat and school cafeterias served green eggs and ham. Sports stars, movie actors, First Lady Hillary Clinton, Vice President Al Gore, Speaker of the House Newt Gingrich, governors, and mayors read with children in public events. Over one million adults and ten million children were estimated to have participated and the event resulted in 3,000 newspaper articles and 500 radio and television news stories.

In conjunction with The Learning Channel and Discovery Communications, Inc., the NEA has developed TeacherTV, a series of TV shows that film teachers and students involved in the use of innovative education methods in their classrooms. Episodes cover topics including the incorporation of technology in the educational process, dealing with violence in school, and encouraging diversity. Copies of TeacherTV can be ordered through the NEA.

BUDGET INFORMATION

Not made available.

HISTORY

The National Teachers' Association, which later became the National Education Association, was formed

Striking teachers rally in front of city hall in Daly City, California. The NEA vigorously lobbies federal and state legislatures, as well as local governments, in an effort to improve the quality of education and teacher compensation. (AP/Wide World Photos)

by a group of educators meeting in Philadelphia in 1857 on behalf of ten state teachers' groups that wanted a national organization. While the NEA began as little more than a debating society, by the turn of the century it was an influential force in U.S. education. Its leaders created a public educational system that had professional educational bureaucrats controlling educational decisions rather than politicians or people outside the education field. In this system, public schools were organized like businesses with a hierarchical decision-making process led by school administrators. This model became the basis of early twentieth-century educational reform.

For roughly half a century the leadership and policy making of the NEA were dominated by male school administrators and college professors rather than the mostly female public school teachers that formed the majority of the membership. The NEA thought that teachers should be selfless public servants who should not demand better pay and working conditions but instead focus on improving their status as professionals. But schoolteachers revolted against this notion and in 1910 elected Ella Flag Young, the first woman president.

Young, and a series of presidents that came after her, paid attention to issues such as improved salaries, a voice for teachers in school decisions, and larger political issues like women's suffrage. However, the old guard managed to pass a number of structural reforms at the 1920 convention that destroyed the rebellious teachers' influence. Dissatisfaction with the NEA led to the founding in 1916 of the rival American Federation of Teachers (AFT) as a labor union dedicated to improving teachers' pay and benefits. The NEA, however, criticized the AFT as being unprofessional. At the NEA's urging, employers encouraged or even coerced teachers to join the NEA over the AFT, which led to substantial membership growth for the NEA.

As the NEA grew it hired more staff and developed a greater capacity for policy making. The Research Division, formed in 1922, became a major source of educational data used by federal, state, and local governments. The NEA's Educational Policies Commission, formed in 1935, had a tremendous impact on U.S. educational policy. It produced a set of statements outlining the relationship between education and democracy that were adopted as goals by numerous school districts. Throughout the 1950s, the NEA attempted to persuade policymakers through research and information rather than through the issue advocacy and lobbying done by most interest groups.

The NEA changed considerably during the 1960s. Most U.S. presidents had recognized the NEA's influence and appointed an NEA leader or staff person to advise on educational policy. However, President John F. Kennedy, elected in 1960, brought in a maverick who challenged the NEA's monopoly on educational policy and as a result, the NEA increased its lobbying activity. The organization pushed for increased federal funding of education, which was almost completely funded at the state and local level, and in 1966 Congress passed the landmark Elementary and Secondary Education Act, which significantly increased federal involvement in public education. Subsequent legislative battles over the amount of federal funding to be distributed under the act led to the creation of the Committee for Full Funding of Education, a coalition that included the NEA, the AFT, the National School Boards Association, and the American Association of School Administrators.

By the end of the 1960s the NEA had transformed itself from a conservative professional association to a more militant advocate of improvements in teachers' working conditions. In the 1970s the NEA became increasingly active politically. Although the NEA did not make an official endorsement, it backed the Educators for McGovern-Shriver, a group favoring the Democratic presidential nominee in the 1972 campaign. In 1976 the NEA made its first presidential endorsement in backing Democrat Jimmy Carter who advocated the NEA's proposal of establishing a cabinet-level department of education. The work of the Liberal-Labor Coalition led by the NEA and the United Auto Workers (UAW) on behalf of Carter in the 1976 primary season helped ensure his nomination and eventual successful presidential bid.

In 1980 Republican President Ronald Reagan proposed eliminating the newly created Department of Education and thereby reducing the already limited federal role in public education. President Reagan appointed a commission to evaluate the state of U.S. public schools, which released an influential report, "A Nation at Risk: The Imperative for Educational Reform," that was critical of teachers and teachers' unions. In contrast to AFT leaders who agreed that educational reform was needed, the NEA forcefully attacked most of the commission's recommendations. The report marked the rise of an adversarial relationship between teachers' unions and conservative politicians and political organizations that attacked the unions as barriers to educational reform and promoters of policies such as sex education and tolerance of homosexuality.

The NEA provided early and crucial support for Democratic presidential candidate Bill Clinton helping him gain his party's nomination and win the 1992 election. Although not in complete agreement with the NEA on educational reform, President Clinton supported increased aid to education. He has also successfully fought proposals by the Republican-controlled Congress that the NEA viewed as undermining public education. Examples of Republican-backed proposals include tax credits for private school expenses and a voucher program in the District of Columbia that would allow public school students to use government certificates to attend private schools. In an effort to build a better relationship with the Republican Party, the NEA supported a few moderate Republicans in the 1998 elections.

Under the leadership of President Robert Chase, elected in 1996, the NEA accepted a range of public school reforms it previously opposed in an effort to build support for the public school system. To that aim, the NEA now endorses standardized tests of student performance, national educational standards, experiments with charter schools in which union contract provisions are relaxed, and a peer review process where experienced teachers evaluate other teachers.

Chase's other major focus has been on merging the NEA and the smaller, traditionally more militant AFT. Many of the differences between the NEA and the AFT have shrunk over time and leaders hope a unified organization will strengthen membership clout in schools and the political arena. A merger requires the support of two-thirds of the NEA's RA. However a plan presented in 1998 was supported by only 42 percent of the delegates and thus dealt a blow to the NEA's leadership. While some delegates felt the merger plan was too vague, many delegates opposed it in part because the unified organization would adopt the AFT's affiliation with the AFL-CIO, the 13 million-member federation of organized labor.

CURRENT POLITICAL ISSUES

At all levels of government, the NEA supports increased funding for public education and actively opposes efforts to introduce market-based educational reforms such as vouchers and privatization, where private-sector businesses take over some or all of the management responsibilities of public schools. The NEA also lobbies for legislation to benefit children. In 1997 it joined the American Medical Association and the National Parent and Teachers Association to push for an agreement between Congress and television networks to label programs for violence, sexual content, and strong language so parents could make informed decisions about what their children watch.

The NEA has also been active in protecting the organization's political clout. In 1998 the NEA joined other unions such as the American Federation of State, County, and Municipal Employees to successfully wage a battle against California's Proposition 226 that would have required unions to get members' written permission to use any portion of their dues for political activity. In 1998 the NEA was also active in lobbying to protect federal policies that would connect schools and libraries to the Internet at reduced costs.

Case Study: E-Rate

In the late 1990s, there were concerns that technological advances such as computers and the Internet could widen social and economic inequalities between those who have access to technology and those who can't afford it. In response to these concerns educators and the Clinton administration, particularly Vice President Al Gore, pushed for a provision in the 1996 Telecommunications Reform Act that ordered the Federal Communications Commission (FCC), the agency responsible for regulating telephone companies, to find a way to give public and nonprofit schools and libraries access to information technology and to require telephone companies to provide them with discounted services.

The FCC responded by developing the e-rate, short for education rate, program. The FCC reached an agreement with long-distance providers such as AT&T, MCI, and Sprint in which these companies would get regulations that lowered their operational costs in exchange for supporting the e-rate program through contributions to a government-administered fund. The fund would be used to help schools and libraries pay for wiring and Internet services. President Clinton promised that "the e-rate will ensure for the first time in our nation's history, a child in the most isolated inner city or rural town will have access to the same universe of knowledge as a child in the most affluent suburb."

The long-distance companies responded, however, by adding a surcharge to their customers' bills to pay for the program and, according to critics, pocketed the savings offered by the FCC as profits. The surcharges—as much as 4.9 percent of the total phone bill—led to an outcry among customers who complained to the FCC and to their congressional representatives. Conservatives began to call the surcharge the Gore tax because of the vice president's role in pushing for e-rate. In 1998 Congress pressured the FCC to cut the funds for e-rate, reducing the program from $2.25 billion to $1.275 billion. However, the uproar led several congress members to demand the FCC stop collecting funds for the e-rate altogether unless Congress passed a law specifically setting up an e-rate program.

The political fight over Internet access then moved on to the Internet. The NEA led a coalition of groups, including the National Association of School Administrators, the National Association of Independent Schools, and the National Catholic Educational Association in an effort to preserve the e-rate program. The coalition set up a World Wide Web site explaining e-rate and its benefits. The site provided information on lobbying techniques and urged visitors to send E-mail messages from the site to Congress, the FCC, and the phone companies. The site even offered sample wording for messages. In the site's first three weeks more than 10,000 messages were sent to lawmakers. The National Taxpayers Union, a 300,000-member conservative organization that often fights government spending programs, launched its own site to fight the e-rate-related surcharge.

Vice President Gore attacked Congress for pressuring the FCC to cut back e-rate funding in a speech at the NEA's 1998 convention. Schools and libraries applied for over $2 billion dollars in aid but with the FCC cuts, many requests had to be denied. The NEA's efforts were successful in fending off further congressional attacks on the program and the NEA continues to lobby for increased funding. The political wrangling, however, delayed the distribution of e-rate funds and students gaining access to the Internet through their schools.

SUCCESSES AND FAILURES

Education is a hot issue among voters and the NEA's primary goal of increased educational funding was achieved in the 1999 federal budget, which raised education spending by 12 percent, despite tension between the NEA and the Republican-controlled Congress. While Congress voted to partially fund President Clinton's NEA-endorsed proposal to reduce class sizes by hiring 100,000 new teachers, it failed to pass a major funding initiative that would have paid for school construction and modernization.

FUTURE DIRECTIONS

In 1997 NEA President Bob Chase launched a major campaign endorsing a "new unionism." In announcing the campaign he declared the "challenge is clear: Instead of relegating teachers to the role of production workers— with no say in organizing their schools for excellence— we need to enlist teachers as full partners, indeed, as comanagers in their schools. Instead of contracts that reduce flexibility and restrict change, we—and our schools—need contracts that empower and enable. . . ." The major focus of the new unionism campaign is to improve education while protecting employee rights by emphasizing three points: collaboration and cooperation with administrators, parents and business leaders; the personal responsibility of teachers for student achievement; and risk taking by using new and experimental educational methods. Local unions are encouraged to keep these goals in mind when they negotiate their contracts. The national office is publicizing the successes of local affiliates so that others may imitate them.

GROUP RESOURCES

The NEA has an extensive Web site at http://www. nea.org that includes information on the organization, legislation and issues in public education and teaching, and NEA projects and programs. MediaLine, a weekly E-mail update on NEA news, can be subscribed to by E-mailing a request to lyris@list.nea.org. For further information write the National Education Association, 1201 16th St. NW, Washington, DC 20036 or contact the NEA Communications office at (202) 833-4000.

GROUP PUBLICATIONS

NEA Today is the organization's major journal published nine times a year. An on-line version is available at the NEA's Web site at http://www.nea.org/neatoday. The *NEA Higher Education Advocate* is a newsletter available to members on issues in higher education published eight times a year. The NEA also produces a range of reports, manuals, and books on a variety of education issues. A current listing of publications is available on-line at http://www.nea.org/publications. Publications available to the public can be obtained from the NEA Professional Library at 1-800-229-4200 or by writing to the National Education Association, 1201 16th St. NW, Washington, DC 20036.

BIBLIOGRAPHY

Baker, Peter. "President Vetoes School Tax Breaks." *The Washington Post,* 22 July 1998.

Chaddock, Gail Russell. "Teachers Unions Jump on Bandwagon of School Reform." *Christian Science Monitor,* 14 October 1997.

Gergen, David. "Chasing Better Schools." *U.S. News and World Report,* 8 December 1997.

Gleick, Elizabeth. "Mad and Mobilized." *Time,* 9 September 1996.

Ratnesar, Romesh. "The Bite On Teachers." *Time,* 20 July 1998.

Roman, Nancy E. "How Much Clout Does E-mail Have in Congress?" *The Washington Times,* 8 June 1998.

Sanchez, Rene. "Teachers Union on Defensive in School Reform Struggle." *The Washington Post,* 3 June 1996.

———. "Teachers Union Merger Rejected." *The Washington Post,* 6 July 1998.

Schneider, William. "Voluntary or Not, Is It Censorship?" *The National Journal,* 19 July 1997.

Stanfield, Rochelle L. "Remedial Lessons." *The National Journal,* 11 November 1997.

Toch, Thomas. "Will Teachers Save Public Schools." *U.S. News and World Report,* 20 July 1998.

"Unions Consider Charter Schools of Their Own." *New York Times,* 22 September 1996.

Worth, Robert. "Reforming the Teachers' Unions: What the Good Guys have Accomplished—and What Remains to be Done." *Washington Monthly,* May 1998.

National Federation of Independent Business (NFIB)

ESTABLISHED: May 20, 1943
EMPLOYEES: 600–700
MEMBERS: 600,000
PAC: NFIB SAFE Trust (National) and State SAFE Trust
    (36 states)

Contact Information:

ADDRESS: 53 Century Blvd., Ste. 300
    Nashville, TN 37214
PHONE: (615) 872-5300
TOLL FREE: (800) 634-8663
E-MAIL: comments@nfibonline.com
URL: http://www.nfibonline.com
PRESIDENT: Jack Faris

WHAT IS ITS MISSION?

The stated mission of the National Federation of Independent Business (NFIB) is "to influence public policy at the state and federal level for the benefit of small and independent business in America." The NFIB hopes that, through the efforts of both the organization's leadership and members, it can ensure a marketplace in which a small business can survive and prosper.

HOW IS IT STRUCTURED?

The NFIB is led by a president and a 12–member board of directors, elected every three years, that plan and prioritize NFIB's national programs. Information and other resources provided to NFIB members clearly reflect the leadership's position on issues. With a headquarters in Nashville, Tennessee, federal legislative offices in Washington, D.C., and legislative offices in all 50 state capitals, the NFIB voices the concerns of small business to key lawmakers throughout the country.

While led by its president and board, NFIB policies are determined by the overall membership. NFIB members vote five times a year to determine the organization's position on federal legislative issues and at least once a year on state issues. Once the ballots are tallied, NFIB lobbyists work to convince Congress and state legislatures of the merits of the organization's views. The NFIB's membership is composed of small and independent business owners from a diverse range of industries. In order to maintain its democratic structure, a cap is placed on membership dues in order to prevent any member or group of members from exercising undue influence over the organization. Minimum dues are $100 and the maximum contribution is $1,000.

At the state level NFIB leadership councils, consisting of representative small business owners, provide advice and counsel on state ballot issues, assist with political action activities, prioritize legislative activities, provide testimony to legislative committees, and serve on state boards and task forces. The NFIB Education Fund, established in 1980, is an affiliate of the national organization. The NFIB Education Fund conducts research of small business issues for NFIB, and publishes *Small Business Economic Trends*.

PRIMARY FUNCTIONS

The central function of the NFIB is to lobby the federal and state governments of the United States on issues that are crucial to small and independent businesses. NFIB members and staff testify before U.S. and state legislatures on a regular basis, to ensure that the small business point of view on a wide range of bills and issues is clearly heard and understood. By letting legislators know how small business owners feel about particular issues, the NFIB hopes to convince lawmakers that voting in accordance with the organization's views will help ensure them reelection. To this end the NFIB also conducts voting analyses and reports regularly to its members on the voting records of all legislators with regard to small business issues. Organization at the grassroots level is also a key component of NFIB's lobbying strategy. Members are encouraged to contact lawmakers directly by letter, E-mail, or fax, provide testimonials, and serve on advisory committees.

The NFIB also works to disseminate vital information to its members and the public-at-large regarding issues that affect small and independent business owners. This occurs through its publications, newsletters, E-mail, and Web site services. For instance, realizing that many business owners were having difficulty preparing for the Y2K bug, the NFIB set up a Web-based resource center so that its members might be better able to anticipate and solve problems that might arise.

PROGRAMS

The NFIB runs a variety of programs, most focusing either upon membership privileges or grassroots legislative lobbying. In the way of incentives for its membership, the NFIB offers a wide range of services. They include benefits such as medical savings accounts through Wells Fargo Bank, a "Small Business Works for America" credit card, a workman's compensation program in 21 states, as well as numerous programs run by

individual state-level efforts. Additionally the NFIB keeps its members abreast of current issues through membership subscriptions to several of its publications.

The NFIB's Guardian Program gives members who have an interest in grassroots campaigning an opportunity to work in the organization's recruiting and education efforts. NFIB guardians receive special material about issues that the organization is working on so that they can disseminate it to the general membership population. These guardians are also asked to present their findings to federal task forces.

Another program designed to support NFIB's lobbying efforts is the Key Contact program. The NFIB invites those members who are personally familiar with federal legislators to become "key contacts," willing to talk or write to these lawmakers in an effort to make NFIB views known to them. These contacts can then act to establish a working dialogue between the general membership and the legislators who serve them.

BUDGET INFORMATION

The NFIB's 1997 budget totaled $71 million, all of it derived from membership dues. The money is used to support the NFIB's lobbying activities, cover administrative, publishing, and membership costs, and fund research and other activities of the NFIB Education Foundation. A limited amount of money is occasionally disbursed in the form of grants and fellowships.

HISTORY

The NFIB was founded in San Mateo, California, in 1943 by C. Wilson Harder. Employed by the National Chamber of Commerce at the time, Harder felt that the Chamber showed little concern for the needs of the small business owner and worried that the development of big business monopolies would further stifle the growth of small business. In January of 1943 he quit the Chamber of Commerce to form a nonprofit organization dedicated to championing small business interests in Congress. On May 20 the National Federation of Small Business (NFSB) was incorporated and Harder signed up his first seven members.

Taking the advice of members of Congress with whom he had spoken while working for the Chamber of Commerce, Harder was determined to ensure that his new organization would truly represent the interests of its membership and not simply the views of a committee claiming to speak for members. To find out what members wanted, Harder implemented a survey called *Mandate* which included no more than 10 questions on each economic or political issue Harder felt was important for small businesses. The ballots were collected and

FAST FACTS

Small businesses make up 98 percent of all businesses in the United States and employ almost 60 percent of the workforce.

(Source: National Federation of Independent Business. "Editor's Guide to Small Business." Washington, D.C., 1995.)

---

tabulated by the organization's district chairmen and then forwarded directly to Congress, along with the original questionnaire.

Thanks largely to a dedicated sales force and a policy of face-to-face membership renewals, the NFSB grew much faster than its rival, the National Small Business Association (NSBA; later National Small Business United), even though the NSBA had started several years earlier. In 1949 the National Federation of Small Business changed its name to the National Federation of Independent Business to better distinguish itself from the NSBA. By 1958 the NFIB had grown enough to initiate state surveys in conjunction with the federal *Mandate*. By the time of Harder's death in 1968 the NFIB was well established as one of the preeminent small business organizations in the country.

Leadership of the NFIB was taken over in 1969 by Wilson S. Johnson, who immediately set about restructuring the organization, establishing a mission statement, and implementing overall policy guidelines. Johnson also increased the size of the membership sales force, added more staff to the Washington, D.C., office, developed new selling tools, and upgraded the accounting, data processing, purchasing, and public relations departments. The result was a tremendous surge in membership. Between 1969 and 1977 membership nearly doubled, from approximately 266,000 to more than half a million.

In 1971 Johnson began to meet quarterly with White House staff to discuss small business problems. In conjunction with this effort, the organization began producing the *Quarterly Economic Report*, a publication whose timely studies and detailed statistics boosted the NFIB's visibility and credibility on Capitol Hill and led to the formation of a full-fledged research department.

By 1977 the NFIB was beginning to change its role from that of an information provider to a major player in policy debates. A political action committee (PAC), now called the NFIB Save America's Free Enterprise Trust

(SAFE Trust), was established and action councils were formed to support NFIB's legislative staff by writing, calling, and visiting their legislators. Later renamed NFIB Guardians, action council members headed grassroots mobilization efforts on legislative issues, testified at state and federal levels, and helped raise funds for political action committees.

In 1983 Johnson handed over presidency of the NFIB to John Sloan Jr., a former member of the U.S. Chamber of Commerce's Small Business Council who had served three terms as chairman of the Small Business Administration National Advisory Council. Sloan further streamlined the NFIB's management and administrative structure and made more concerted efforts to elect members of Congress sympathetic to NFIB aims by upgrading the SAFE Trust PAC. A full-time PAC director was hired and fund-raising was intensified.

Sloan died unexpectedly in 1992 and was replaced by Jack Faris, who furthered efforts to strengthen the NFIB's political muscle. A vocal opponent of President Bill Clinton's 1993 health care initiative, the NFIB was active in killing the legislation. In the late 1990s the organization began to focus on revising the U.S. Tax Code, which the NFIB viewed as an impediment to small business ventures. It hoped to convince members of Congress to back legislation that would ensure substantial tax reform.

CURRENT POLITICAL ISSUES

The NFIB tends to be fiscally conservative and is dedicated to minimizing, to the greatest extent possible, government interference in the economic arena. Tax cuts, a balanced budget, and an end to government mandates have been and continue to be leading issues on which the NFIB focuses its legislative efforts. Its top priority, however, has been to slim down the amount of involvement government has in the affairs of small businesses, ranging from taxation levels to health care reform.

Case Study: The NFIB versus the Clinton Health Care Proposal

When Bill Clinton was elected president in 1992 he promised to make health care reform a top priority and established a task force to investigate the issues and make recommendations for government action. In 1993 the task force's report, with its suggestions for improving health care, was returned to the Clinton administration. The administration then proposed the Clinton Health Security Plan to Congress. One of the many proposals in the plan required that all employers provide health care insurance to employees that was partially paid for by the employer.

As early as 1991 many small business and business organizations, including the NFIB, the National Restaurant Association, and the National Wholesale Grocers

Association, had declared their support for health care reform in general. However they also made it clear that they would oppose any attempt to require employers to pay for employee health insurance. When the Clinton plan was presented to the public and Congress, the NFIB led the fight to ensure that the plan would not be adopted.

NFIB objected to the plan for two major reasons. Members were concerned about their ability to pay the ever escalating cost of insurance for their employees. Many member businesses employed under eight people, and with limited resources it would be difficult to obtain lower group insurance rates. Business owners were concerned that their already small profits would be eaten up by health care costs. Even more than the cost itself, however, NFIB members questioned the government's right to require them to pay health care costs. The NFIB stood opposed to an expanded government bureaucracy that would impose more rules on independent businesses.

Supporters of the Clinton plan, including the Small Business Coalition for Health Care Reform, the Ford Motor Company, and the American Association of Retired Persons, tried to counter the objections of the NFIB and other business organizations, stressing that medical costs were already enormous because of the number of Americans without medical insurance and would only increase without the intercession of Clinton's plan. People without insurance often used expensive emergency room services for basic care and often required more expensive care for illnesses that had grown worse from lack of treatment. The cost of treating uninsured patients was passed on to other patients through higher insurance premiums and higher costs for health care services. Supporters of the plan argued that universal health insurance coverage would lower health care costs for everyone by eliminating the need for the insured to pay the cost of treating the uninsured.

President Clinton and others in favor of the plan also pointed out that small business employers would only be required to pay a portion of employee health insurance costs. Employees would contribute toward insurance costs, as would the government. Plans were also discussed that would create insurance pools whereby small businesses could join together to purchase group health insurance at lower rates.

Despite the president's arguments and proposed revisions favoring small businesses, the NFIB continued its opposition to the plan. The organization sent action alerts to all its members urging them to contact legislators and voice their opposition to the plan. In the spring of 1994 the House Energy and Commerce Committee worked out a compromise health care bill that addressed some of the NFIB's concerns but still required some employer contributions. In response the NFIB arranged meetings between its members and legislators and conducted a public relations campaign against any compromise plans requiring employers to provide insurance benefits and pay part of the cost. It also worked to influence physicians to oppose health care reform plans. Physicians were warned that if employers were forced to pay for health care insurance, they would pressure the government to regulate and limit medical fees.

Ultimately, the NFIB and other business organizations were successful in preventing any health care reform legislation from coming to a vote in Congress. The original Clinton Health Security Plan had been revised several times, including the compromise plan of the Energy and Commerce Committee, but none of the plans were acceptable to the independent business community. By late 1994 sweeping health care reform was clearly impossible to enact as legislators and the public could not agree over what needed to be done. Public attention turned to other issues and the NFIB emerged victorious from the political battle over health care reform.

FUTURE DIRECTIONS

One of the most important goals that the NFIB hopes to achieve is the complete reformation of the U.S. Tax Code by December of 2000, thereby reducing the regulations the organization believes discourage investment and stifle economic activity. On March 16, 1999 the NFIB began a 30-day campaign to educate the public about what it feels is an outdated and over-complicated system that does not tax fairly. The NFIB will continue organizing similar grassroots efforts in order to enable legislative action to eliminate the code.

GROUP RESOURCES

The NFIB provides an extensive Web site at http://www.nfibonline.com that includes updates and background on many small business-related policy issues. The NFIB provides a variety of information resources, including newsletters highlighting current legislative measures the organization is supporting or opposing and regular reports on Congressional voting records. For more information on the NFIB, write to the National Federation of Independent Business, 53 Century Blvd., Ste. 300, Nashville, TN 37214 or call (615) 872-5300.

GROUP PUBLICATIONS

The NFIB publishes several magazines and newsletters, including *Independent Business*, a national magazine published six times a year that focuses both on the day-to-day aspects of running a small business as well as reporting on political issues. News on NFIB activities and legislative issues is covered in the monthly newsletter *Capitol Coverage*. Other publications include *Small*

Business Economic Trends and *How Congress Voted.* For more information on these publications, write to the National Federation of Independent Business, 53 Century Blvd. Ste. 300, Nashville, TN 37214; or call (615) 872-5300.

BIBLIOGRAPHY

"Big Brother May Be Watching." *Industry Week*, 16 February 1998.

Clausing, Jeri. "Legislation Limiting Year 2000 Liability Is Introduced." *New York Times*, 24 February 1999.

"Face to Face with the IRS." *Business Week*, 18 March 1996.

Love, Alice A. "The 104th's Lobbyist 'In Crowd': A New Pecking Order in Special-Interest Washington." *Roll Call*, 1995.

"Mandate Ballot the Source of Small Business Voice." *Independent Business*, September/October 1997.

Skocpol, Theda. *Boomerang: Health Care Reform and the Turn against Government.* New York, N.Y.: W.W. Norton, 1997.

Skrzychi, Cindy W. "Dome Alone II: How Small Business Won Congress's Heart." *Washington Post*, 6 January 1995.

Stevenson, Richard W. "The Long Arm of Small Business: Delivering a Big Blow to the Death Tax." *New York Times*, 12 June 1997.

Wagner, Lynn. "Business Keeps Heat on Clinton Plan." *Modern Healthcare*, 28 February 1994.

Weisskopf, Michael. "Small Business Lobby Becomes a Big Player in Campaigns." *Washington Post*, 9 August 1996.

National Federation of the Blind (NFB)

WHAT IS ITS MISSION?

The National Federation of the Blind (NFB) is a national organization dedicated to serving the needs and protecting the rights of the United States's blind citizens. The NFB is one of the largest service organization dedicated to the blind. According to the NFB's 1998 Statement of Purpose, "the ultimate purpose of The National Federation of the Blind is the complete integration of the blind into society on a basis of equality. This objective involves the removal of legal, economic, and social discriminations; the education of the public to new concepts concerning the blind; the achievement by all blind people of the right to exercise to the fullest their individual talents and capacities. It means the right of the blind to work along with their sighted neighbors in the professions, common callings, skilled trades, and regular occupations."

ESTABLISHED: 1940
EMPLOYEES: Not made available
MEMBERS: 50,000
PAC: None

Contact Information:

ADDRESS: 1800 Johnson St.
   Baltimore, MD 21230
PHONE: (410) 659-9314
FAX: (410) 685–5653
E-MAIL: epc@roudley.com
URL: http://www.nfb.org
PRESIDENT: Marc Maurer

HOW IS IT STRUCTURED?

The governing body of the NFB consists of a president and a 17-member board of directors. This governing body is entirely composed of blind NFB members. Below the board of directors are 700 chapters that service the individual NFB members. In locations where there are no chapters, members-at-large serve as representatives of the organization. Local chapters are responsible to send delegates to the NFB's annual national convention, where they elect the board of directors. Membership in the NFB is free and open to any blind person who wishes to join. People with sight may also

Protestors at a 1978 rally in Washington, D.C., express opposition to Federal Aviation Administration policies that are perceived to be discriminatory to disabled travelers, including the blind. (AP/Wide World Photos)

become "associate" members of the NFB, which requires a minimum donation of $10.

There are several organizations affiliated with the NFB that pursue similar goals. The American Action Fund for Blind Children and Adults provides services to blind people who cannot obtain the same services from the government. The National Organization of Parents of Blind Children is a support and services network for parents of visually impaired children. These organizations share The National Center for the Blind (formed in 1978) with the NFB. The National Center for the Blind is a medical center where different medical disciplines come together to make care more efficient.

PRIMARY FUNCTIONS

The NFB works to lessen the difficulties that its members face living in a society of sighted people. This involves both assisting its members in dealing with the problems they face, while also working to eliminate the economic and social barriers against the blind in U.S. society. NFB chapters offer members a support system that allows them to discuss concerns, problems, and ideas. This support network is a critical facet of service organizations like the NFB, by not only assisting with

finding pragmatic solutions to problems, but also providing emotional support. The organization also helps its members to understand how federal and state policies concerning the blind affect their lives.

The NFB maintains a civil rights organization that provides legal assistance to its membership. The NFB represents blind individuals in legal actions involving such things as job discrimination, housing discrimination and child custody matters. The NFB also provides legal counsel designed to help blind people obtain Medicare and Social Security Disability Insurance benefits, information regarding blind students' rights, and information on guide dog discrimination.

Another civil rights activity of the NFB is to raise public awareness of issues that affect blind people. Efforts are generally directed at educating the public through publications and media to be more aware, responsive, and sensitive to the particular needs of the blind. For instance, the NFB has composed *The Courtesy Rules of Blindness;* a list of points that teaches sighted people how to treat blind people with more sensitivity. But the NFB's educational efforts also attempt to bring respect to the blind community. In the NFB's literature the organization states, ". . . members of the NFB strive to educate the general public to the fact that the blind are normal individuals who can compete on terms of equality with others."

There are many tools and devices designed to assist the blind. These "adaptive" products range from white canes to guide dogs to clocks that tell time audibly. The NFB purchases these devices, which can be expensive, and offers them to blind persons at substantial discounts through its Materials Center. The Materials Center makes these adaptive goods accessible to individuals with limited financial resources. The Materials Center also offers publications with information on every aspect of blindness. These publications are available on cassette tape and in the Braille language.

Technology designed to assist the blind often changes. To assure blind individuals access to these technologies, the NFB maintains the International Braille and Technology Center (IBTC). The IBTC is an evaluation and demonstration center that houses over a million dollars worth of adaptive technology. The ascent of computer technologies and their effect on adaptive tools have made the IBTC a helpful place for blind people and their families. The IBTC introduces and instructs individuals to new adaptive goods.

PROGRAMS

The NFB has developed several programs, all designed as self-help initiatives for its members. In cooperation with the United States Department of Labor, the NFB created Job Opportunities for the Blind (JOB). JOB is a free recruitment, referral, and assistance program created to place blind people in gainful employment. JOB publishes bulletins that advise blind people on insurance matters, hiring practices, and employment trends. More than thirteen hundred blind individuals are registered with JOB and six thousand employers receive information about the program.

The NFB maintains a number of scholarships for blind students, ranging in value from $3,000 to $10,000. The student must be legally blind, pursuing a full-time, post-secondary education, demonstrate academic excellence and financial need, and meet any special criteria associated with a particular scholarship. For example, the $3,000 Hermione Grant-Calhoun Scholarship is specifically designated for blind women. Although the NFB's scholarship program is administered by the NFB's Scholarship Committee, applicants need not be members of the NFB to obtain a scholarship.

The NFB also believes an important element of its function is to keep blind people adequately informed of news events. To address this problem, the NFB developed a program called *Newsline for the Blind. Newsline for the Blind* is a "talking newspaper" which is a spoken text version of *USA Today,* the *New York Times,* and the *Chicago Tribune.* This service is made possible through a computer program that translates the appropriate text into spoken word. Users access *Newsline for the Blind* through their touch-tone telephones. *Newsline for the*

Blind enables the blind to get a regular stream of information on a number of different issues. Although the service is expanding, *Newsline for the Blind* is not yet available in all areas.

BUDGET INFORMATION

The NFB is a nonprofit institution. Public support is the main source of the organization's revenue. It raised $14,533,380 in 1996, approximately $12,600,000 from donations and contributions, $1,800,000 from donated services, and $375,000 from government grants. The NFB raised $277,812 from sale of aids, appliances, materials and publications. It garnered $260,000 from investments and $54,000 in royalties.

The NFB spent $13,407,760 in 1996, with $5,700,000 spent on education, and $1,600,000 on legal advocacy and assistance. The NFB spent $3,700,000 on specialized programs such as the IBTC, publications, and *Newsline for the Blind.* The NFB spent $2,295,040 on support services. Approximately $2,000,000 was spent on fund-raising for the organization, and $280,000 was spent on management and administrative costs.

HISTORY

The NFB was founded in 1940 when representatives from seven blind assistance organizations from different states met in Wilkes-Barre, Pennsylvania. These groups consolidated to form the NFB and used a California organization, the California Council of the Blind as their model. The founder of the California Council of the Blind, Jacobus tenBroek, is widely recognized as the founder of the NFB and was its first president

In 1964 the NFB persuaded U.S. president Lyndon B. Johnson to sign a bill that designated a White Cane Safety Day because blind people use a long white cane to identify and avoid physical impediments or obstructions they are unable to see as they walk down the street or move about a room. The White Cane Safety Day was established to raise public awareness of the problems blind people face as they travel in and move about communities. In 1968 tenBroek died and was succeeded as president of the NFB by Kenneth Jernigan.

In 1978 the NFB opened the National Center for the Blind (NCB). The NCB was meant as a one-stop resource location for the blind. It housed the American Action Fund for Blind Children and Adults and the National Organization of Parents of Blind Children, as well as the NFB and eventually the International Braille and Technology Center (IBTC). In 1979 the NFB formed Job Opportunities for the Blind (JOB), the job referral and employment network dedicated exclusively to the blind. The NFB presidency again changed hands in 1985 when

Kenneth Jernigan retired and Marc Maurer was elected president in 1986. In 1990 the NFB opened the International Braille and Technology Center at the NCB. The IBTC was designed to give the blind and families of the blind access to adaptive technologies.

CURRENT POLITICAL ISSUES

The NFB is a civil rights organization, yet it is relatively apolitical; it does not lobby the U.S. Congress on behalf of its members. However, it does counsel Congress on the issues the blind face. The NFB also pursues legal action when necessary to preserve the civil rights and benefits due blind individuals. These cases are generally lawsuits over job discrimination or Social Security benefits.

Part of the NFB's political agenda is to nurture a positive public perception of blind people. The organization fights negative stereotypes (such as the ones that portray the blind as incapable) in all aspects of society. A notable conflict over stereotypes was the NFB's high profile battle with the Walt Disney company over its film *Mr. Magoo.*

Case Study: NFB vs. Mr. Magoo

Mr. Magoo was a cartoon character created in 1949 as a parody of Joseph McCarthy, the Republican senator who conducted controversial investigations in his quest to eradicate communism in the Department of State and in the film industry. The creators poked fun at McCarthy by making Mr. Magoo see only what he wanted to see. In the 1950s the cartoon Mr. Magoo evolved into a crabby blind man who stumbled into ridiculous situations and misunderstood the people and things around him. Mr. Magoo movies and cartoon serials appeared on television for many years but the character's popularity waned in the 1970s. The Walt Disney company, however, saw potential in the comedic aspect of the character and acquired the rights to him, planning to produce a live action film to be released in December 1997.

The NFB, for its part, had been a long-standing critic of Mr. Magoo. Former NFB President Kenneth Jernigan related stories of comparisons between the blind and Mr. Magoo in the NFB's annual convention speech in 1975. When the organization learned that Disney was planning to resurrect Mr. Magoo, it immediately sprang into action. The NFB was not alone in its dislike for Magoo; major media forces such as the *Los Angeles Times*, *New York Times*, and *Wall Street Journal* questioned the wisdom of doing a Magoo film at the time Disney acquired the rights to the character in 1995.

In an effort to change Disney's mind the NFB made direct appeals to the corporation. At the organization's July 1997 convention, the NFB passed a series of resolutions condemning Disney for *Mr. Magoo* and recommended a boycott of Disney products. NFB President Marc Maurer composed a personal appeal to Disney's Chief Executive Officer Michael Eisner requesting him to abandon the Magoo project. Additionally the organization publicized their objections at press conferences, in speeches and by soliciting television news programs to carry the organization's objections to the film.

Disney was then forced to respond to the NFB. The film company said that Magoo was not blind but rather simply "visually limited" and that no offense was meant to the blind. Leslie Nielsen, the actor who portrayed Mr. Magoo said that he felt the character was an admirable, heroic person. Finally, in the hopes that it could pacify the NFB and other critics, Disney allegedly altered harsher aspects of the Magoo character's limitations to appear less offensive. Despite this, however, the NFB maintained its opposition. Disney went ahead with its altered version of the film which opened as scheduled. Though the NFB was unable to prevent its release, the organization took some satisfaction in the fact that the film was recognized as a commercial and critical failure.

FUTURE DIRECTIONS

A significant challenge facing the NFB is how to make the latest technology available to the blind. Computer innovation made information more accessible to the blind and the NFB used it to create *Newsline for the Blind*. Developments in medical technology such as corneal transplant (the procedure by which a donor's cornea may restore sight for some blind people) has the capacity to quickly and radically change what it means to be blind. The International Braille and Technology Center (IBTC) will become a more visible part of the NFB's activities in its efforts to ensure that its membership is kept informed and has access to useful technology.

GROUP RESOURCES

An excellent overview of what blindness is and what the NFB does is the organization's *If Blindness Comes.* Written by former NFB president Kenneth Jernigan, *If Blindness Comes,* is a comprehensive collection of information about the NFB. Individuals interested in purchasing *If Blindness Comes* or other information about the NFB may write the organization at the National Federation of the Blind, 1800 Johnson St., Baltimore, MD 21230 or may telephone the NFB at (410) 659-9314. In addition the NFB maintains a Web site at http://www. nfg.org. It contains a great deal of information on the NFB, including an overview of some of the programs and services it offers to its members.

GROUP PUBLICATIONS

The NFB publishes a broad range of manuals, magazines, and information books. These publications are available in Braille, large type, or as audiocassettes. The NFB's Kernel Books is a series of books by blind writers. These books are autobiographical accounts of the authors' personal experiences. The books are meant as inspirational stories for blind as well as sighted people.

The NFB publishes two magazines aimed at special audiences. *Future Directions* is a quarterly magazine for parents and educators of blind children. It is available in print and audiocassette. *Voice of the Diabetic*, another quarterly publication covers issues, problems and concerns of those blind because of diabetes.

The main publication of the NFB is the *Braille Monitor,* a monthly publication dedicated to keeping the blind informed of state and federal legislation, legal actions affecting the blind, and technological updates. The *Braille Monitor* also contains recipes, advice, obituaries, and classifieds. It is available in Braille, print, and audiocassettes. It can be accessed via the World Wide Web at http://www.nfb.org/bralmons.htm.

Information on how to obtain all of the NFB's publications may be obtained by writing the National Federation of the Blind, 1800 Johnson St., Baltimore, MD 21230 or by telephoning the NFB at (410) 659-9314.

BIBLIOGRAPHY

Bannon, Lisa. "The Vision Thing." *Wall Street Journal,* 31 July 1997.

Brandt, John. "Magic Kingdom is Under Attack." *Industry Week,* 15 September 1997.

Gashel, James. "Social Security, SSI, and Medicare Facts for 1998." *Braille Monitor,* January 1998.

Grann, David. "Eyes of the World." *New Republic,* 24 March 1997.

Grover, Ronald. "Duck, Goofy: Why so Many Groups are Taking Potshots at Disney." *Business Week,* 1 September 1997.

Jernigan, Kenneth. "The Day After Civil Rights." *Vital Speeches of the Day,* 15 August 1997.

————. *If Blindness Comes.* Baltimore, MD: The National Federation of the Blind, 1994.

————. "Language and the Future of the Blind." *Vital Speeches of the Day,* 15 October 1989.

The National Federation of the Blind. *Julie and Brandon: Our Blind Friends.* Boise, ID: The National Federation of the Blind, 1995.

Nussbaum, Debra. "Bringing the Visual World of the Web to the Blind." *New York Times,* 26 March 1998.

Trapp, Greg. "Understanding Your Rights During the Job Interview." *Braille Monitor,* January 1998.

National Gay and Lesbian Task Force (NGLTF)

ESTABLISHED: 1973
EMPLOYEES: 16
MEMBERS: 18,000
PAC: None

Contact Information:

ADDRESS: 2320 17th St. NW
    Washington, DC 20009
PHONE: (202) 332-6483
TDD (HEARING IMPAIRED): (202) 332-6219
FAX: (202) 332-0207
E-MAIL: ngltf@ngltf.org
URL: http://www.ngltf.org
EXECUTIVE DIRECTOR: Kerry Lobel

WHAT IS ITS MISSION?

According to the organization, "The National Gay and Lesbian Task Force (NGLTF) works to eliminate prejudice, violence and injustice against gay, lesbian, bisexual and transgender people at the local, state and national level. As part of a broader social justice movement for freedom, justice and equality; NGLTF is creating a world that respects and celebrates the diversity of human expression and identity where all people may fully participate in society."

NGLTF advocates for gay rights on issues such as the right to marry, housing and job discrimination, sodomy laws, hate crimes, and gay service in the military. The movement has been opposed by right wing religious and conservative groups that hold the opinion that the homosexual lifestyle is not only morally wrong, but a choice that can be changed. Against this backdrop, the NGLTF and other gay rights groups (such as the Human Rights Campaign and LAMBDA Legal Defense and Education Fund) continue the fight to advance gay civil rights in the United States.

HOW IS IT STRUCTURED?

For tax purposes, the NGLTF is actually two entities. The National Gay and Lesbian Task Force, Inc. is the group's lobbying division. The Policy Institute is the nonprofit portion of NGLTF that members may make tax-deductible contributions to. The Institute carries out research initiatives, acts as a liaison with the media, and conducts educational outreach. Both parts of the NGLTF receive guidance from a board of directors.

NGLTF is headed by an executive director, who is selected through a search process coordinated by the board of directors. Beneath the executive director is a political director who oversees: field organizing, public advocacy, media relations, and the Policy Institute work. Under the executive director, a development director works toward increasing support for NGLTF, including membership funding.

NGLTF does not have state or regional affiliate groups. Instead the organization, through its field-organizing function, provides contacts and information resources for state and local gay and lesbian groups that are working on legislative issues. Members do not have voting privileges, but receive a quarterly newsletter. Monthly sustainers (members who give on an ongoing monthly basis) receive a monthly newsletter.

PRIMARY FUNCTIONS

The fight for gay, lesbian, bisexual, and transgender (GLBT) rights is carried out by NGLTF in a variety of ways. The organization is different from other advocacy groups in that it does not create state or regional affiliates. Instead, NGLTF serves as a coalition builder by tracking relevant legislation at the state and local level, and by making the information available to other gay rights advocate groups. The organization has, since 1995, produced a yearly report (*Capital Gains and Losses: A State by State Review of Gay, Lesbian, Bisexual, Transgender, and HIV/AIDS Related Legislation*) that tracks the status of state GLBT legislation. In early 1998 the organization was actively tracking 24 legislative initiatives.

NGLTF employs a field organizer who shares current legislative information with like-minded advocate groups. The organization also provides guidelines on lobbying for the layperson, and these are available on the NGLTF Web site. In another attempt to harness grassroots support, the organization provides Web site visitors the opportunity to register for E-mail updates that provide information on current legislative initiatives and gay rights issues. The organization also offers training and consultation for local activists in areas such as media relations.

In addition to acting as a coalition builder, the NGLTF also functions as a lobbying organization and attempts to influence public policy at the state and federal level on gay rights issues. NGLTF also acts as a research clearinghouse—both in the initiation of new research on relevant issues and as a translator of academic information into tools that activists can use. The organization convenes roundtables and conferences to share ideas among analysts, academics, and thinkers that have an interest or involvement in gay rights issues.

As part of its effort to educate the public about its

Police and demonstrators clash in New York City's Times Square following a candlelight vigil held in October 1998 in memory of Matthew Shepard. Shepard was a gay college student who was found tied to a fence post and beaten to death. Hate crimes have been a major concern of the National Gay and Lesbian Task Force since its founding.

(Photograph by Suzanne Plunkket, AP/Wide World Photo)

mission, the organization works closely with the media to get its message out. NGLTF works with both mainstream and gay media to field information requests, to ensure that GLBT issues are covered fairly, and to combat prejudice in society.

PROGRAMS

NGLTF programs work toward goals that will accomplish the organization's mission—to secure civil and humans rights for the GLBT community. Programs accomplish this through public education, as well as information and networking opportunities within the GLBT community. For example NGLTF hosts the annual Creating Change Conference, which presents new research findings and gives participants the chance to strategize and launch new initiatives. In November 1997 the conference drew 1,500 gay rights activists.

In line with the collaborative role of NGLTF, many groups including the Federation of Statewide Lesbian,

Gay, Bisexual and Transgender Political Organizations attended and participated in electing new task force officials. A new group was formed at the conference—The National Consortium of Directors of Lesbian, Gay, Bisexual and Transgender Resources in Higher Education. Sixty activists of various faiths also met to develop political strategies with a spiritual focus.

NGLTF programs also educate the gay community and the public on barriers and opposition that the movement faces. Some of the most formidable opposition to the gay rights movement in the United States has originated from right-wing religious or political groups. NGLTF, through its Fight the Right Program, attempts to give supporters concrete ways of dealing with these impediments. The program produces publications, media materials, and resources including: *Countering Right Wing Rhetoric*, a *Fight The Right Video List*, an update on state right-wing attacks and conservative referenda that impede the gay rights movement, *Organizations Fighting the Right*, and a *Fight The Right Action Kit*.

To educate members or supporters who have on-line access, NGLTF coordinates an Activist/Organizer Mailing List. Those on the list receive E-mail updates and press releases on relevant issues in the gay community and actions that need to be taken.

BUDGET INFORMATION

The NGLTF has an annual budget of over $2 million. The two branches of the NGLTF are similar in that they both rely on public donations for support, but the nonprofit branch, the Policy Institute, is far ahead in both revenues and expenses. Most of the money given to the NGLTF is in the form of membership fees, which range from $35 to $1,200 a year.

In 1996 the National Gay and Lesbian Task Force, Inc. (the group's lobbying division) had total revenue of $140,118 from public support. Expenses included program services ($74,869), management and general ($52,519), and fundraising ($31,118). The 1996 revenue for the NGLTF Policy Institute (the nonprofit branch) totaled $2,324,816; the bulk of revenue came from public support ($2,103,930) followed by program service revenue ($201,967), interest on investments ($11,738), and other revenue ($7,181). The 1996 expenses for the Policy Institute totaled $2,234,037 and included program services ($1,838,658), management and general expenses ($342,594), and fundraising ($52,785).

HISTORY

Advocacy for gay rights is a relatively young movement. Its beginnings can be traced to 1969 after a clash erupted between police and clientele at a New York City gay bar, the Stonewall Inn. Although police often raided gay bars, clientele seldom fought back. However, that night, the bar's patrons rioted against the police. That incident launched a social revolution that, according to an article in *Time* (June 27, 1994) "is still changing the way Americans see many of their most basic institutions including family, church, schools, the military, media and culture." Against the backdrop of these social changes, gay rights advocate organizations formed and NGLTF was founded in 1973.

As the gay rights movement gained momentum in the 1970s and early 1980s, the issues for gays went beyond acknowledging their existence and moved into the realm of acknowledging their equality. Issues involving equal rights for gays (who have compared their movement to the 1960s civil rights movement) began to shape the agendas of organizations like NGLTF. In the meantime, increased numbers of gays and lesbians were making their presence known by coming out, that is acknowledging publicly that they were homosexual. Gay activism during the late 1970s also changed toward less radical, aggressive measures of protest. Groups such as Act Up (a radical gay and lesbian advocate group) found constituents more interested in pursuing activism by writing letters to Congress or aligning with more centrist (and less radical) groups like NGLTF or the Human Rights Campaign.

In the early 1980s the rising AIDS epidemic became a prevalent social issue that occupied a high place on the agendas of gay rights groups such as NGLTF. These groups fought for AIDS-related civil rights, such as housing and job discrimination, insurance coverage, and the privacy of medical records. In 1992 after years of conservative Republican presidents, Democratic President Bill Clinton was elected and proved to be more sympathetic to gay rights causes. However, the president disappointed NGLTF and other gay groups by his failure to abolish the military ban on gays. Instead, he endorsed a "don't ask, don't tell" policy that most gays and lesbians viewed as an unwelcome compromise—they could serve in the military as long as they didn't talk about their sexuality. The outcome of the military ban issue caused NGLTF and other gay groups to look at the way they were mobilizing their support and to begin to concentrate their efforts outside of Washington, D.C.

The gay rights movement encountered opposition from the religious right in the late 1970s and the religious right has remained an opponent over the years. The right-wing faction has done an effective job of organizing and gathering resources. This conservative sector argues that not only are gay and lesbian lifestyles immoral, but they are choices that gays and lesbians could opt out of if they chose. Further, opponents feel that gays and lesbians do not have the justification to ask for special treatment. To counter these attacks, the focus of the NGLTF changed slightly when Kerry Lobel took over as executive director in 1996. Lobel wanted to forge partnerships with other similarly aligned groups. Lobel stepped to the forefront of the group after executive directors Torie Osborn resigned in 1993 and Peri Jude Radecic resigned in 1994 during a period of financial struggle within the organization.

In the 1990s, many gay rights issues have originated at the state level, and have become part of the agenda of NGLTF and other groups. Some of these include state antigay referenda, the fight for same-sex marriage that began with a court case in Hawaii, and state legislation that deals with issues such as sodomy laws, domestic benefits, and adoption.

CURRENT POLITICAL ISSUES

NGLTF advocates to advance the rights of the GLBT community. The organization has been involved in issues such as hate crimes against the gay community, housing and job discrimination, and advocating for improved legal rights. A national resource center for gay, lesbian, bisexual, and transgender grassroots organizations, NGLTF often plays a coordinating role; directly linking activists and information where needed. But NGLTF also participates in the political process at the national level by meeting with the president, participating in summits, and speaking out about relevant issues.

Hate crimes against the GLBT community have always been a concern of NGLTF. According to the organization, 1996 FBI statistics showed that among 8,759 total reported hate crimes in 1996, over one thousand were based on the victim's sexual orientation. However, NGLTF claims that many hate crimes aimed at the gay community go unreported because of fear that police will discriminate or show a lack of interest in pursing the case. During 1997 NGLTF executive director Lobel traveled across the United States and listened to testimony about hate crimes aimed at the gay community. NGLTF collected signatures on a petition during the tour and presented them to President Clinton at a hate-crime summit held in November, 1997—a summit which NGLTF and the American Civil Liberties Union had advocated for. The summit was part of efforts to get hate crimes acknowledged and recognized at the national level.

NGLTF is also involved in the fight to end discrimination against gays and lesbians in the workplace. In a 1991 example, Robin Shahar, a lesbian and attorney who had been offered a position with the Georgia Attorney General's Office, had the offer rescinded when then-Attorney General Michael Bowers discovered that Shahar was planning a commitment ceremony with her same-sex partner. Bowers claimed that Shahar's lesbian relationship violated Georgia's sodomy law. In this instance, the gay community suffered a setback when in January 1998, the Supreme Court declined to hear Shahar's case.

In a victory for gays regarding workplace discrimi-

nation, President Clinton signed an executive order in May of 1998 banning discrimination based on sexual orientation in the federal workplace. Although gay rights opponents mobilized quickly to resurrect an amendment to block the executive order, the amendment was voted down in the House by 252 to 176, thus killing the measure.

NGLTF also maintains that state sodomy laws, while rarely enforced, are used as the basis for other discrimination against the gay community as in the Shahar case. In mid-1997, twenty states still had sodomy laws on the books. However, NGLTF and other advocate groups achieved a victory in July 1997 when Montana's Supreme Court struck down that state's sodomy law in the case of *Grayczan v. Montana*. According to NGLTF Executive Director Lobel, this outcome was the result of 25 years of work by organizations like NGLTF.

Some of the most visible gay rights issues concern amendments that would limit civil rights for the gay community. NGLTF and gay advocate groups worked hard for, and achieved defeat of, an antigay rights referendum in Colorado. In May 1996 the Supreme Court struck down Colorado's Amendment 2 which voters passed in 1992, and would have eliminated protection against discrimination based on sexual orientation. However, NGLTF and gay rights groups were unsuccessful in upholding an antidiscrimination law in Maine in early 1998.

Case Study: Maine Repeals Civil Rights Law

The Maine Human Rights Act was passed by that state's legislature and became law in May 1997. This act banned discrimination based on sexual orientation in Maine. However, right-wing forces in the state (including the Christian Coalition's Maine chapter and the conservative Christian Civic League) were able to put the amendment to public vote, using a Maine "people's veto" provision. These conservative groups argued that the gay and lesbian community should not be entitled to special rights.

NGLTF assisted the Maine grassroots group, "Maine Won't Discriminate," in an effort to overturn a possible voter's veto. The NGLTF field organizer spent a number of weeks in the state working with the grassroots group to organize volunteers and help with efforts. Hundreds of volunteers made over ten thousand phone calls in an attempt to mobilize support and educate the Maine voters on the upcoming vote. Nonetheless, voters repealed the amendment. This repeal reduced the number of states with legal protection against discrimination based on sexual orientation to ten.

The repeal of this law means that in Maine (and other states that don't ban such discrimination) members of the GLBT community may possibly face legal discrimination when applying for jobs, housing, and credit. The opposition continues to argue that the gay community should not be afforded special rights and that a homosexual lifestyle is a choice that is immoral.

FUTURE DIRECTIONS

As NGLTF looks toward the future it will focus on coordinating and assisting grassroots efforts in issues of importance to the GLBT community. The organization will continue to collaborate and build coalitions with other supportive groups—a focus that was brought to NGLTF when Kerry Lobel took office in 1996. After the brutal murder of Matthew Shepard in October of 1998 drew national attention to the issue of hate crimes against gays and lesbians, the NGLTF teamed with other organizations to renew the push for hate crime laws. The organization is also working to ban sexual-orientation discrimination and sodomy laws in all states. NGLTF will continue to fight for gay civil rights, such as adoption, tax status, and other family rights. And in perhaps the biggest issue revolving around civil rights, NGLTF will play a role in organizing grassroots efforts in support of same-sex marriage.

GROUP RESOURCES

NGLTF maintains a Web site at http://www.ngltf. org. The Web site includes press releases, a list of publications and resources, legislative updates, and status of laws that affect the GLBT community. For information about NGLTF resources, publications, or organizational initiatives, write to National Gay and Lesbian Task Force, 2320 17th St. NW, Washington, DC 20009; call (202) 332-6483; or fax (202) 332-0207.

GROUP PUBLICATIONS

NGLTF issues reports and larger publications, some of which are available in full text on-line. The list of publications includes: *Income Inflation: The Myth of Affluence Among Gay, Lesbian, and Bisexual Americans, Out & Voting: The GLB Vote in Congressional House Elections, GLBT Campus Organizing: A Comprehensive Manual*, and *To Have & To Hold Organizing for Our Right to Marry*. NGLTF also produces a yearly report, *Capital Gains and Losses*, which summarizes yearly legislation affecting the GLBT community. Costs for materials range from $10 to $25. The organization also compiles maps (available on-line) that show the status of hate crimes, sodomy laws, marriage laws, and civil rights across the United States. Publications may be ordered by mailing 2320 17th St. NW, Washington, DC, 20009; over the phone at (202) 332-6483; or by fax at (202) 332-0207.

BIBLIOGRAPHY

Cusac, Anne-Marie. "Urvashi Vaid. (Gay-lesbian Activist/ Author) (Interview)." *The Progressive,* 1 March 1996.

Holland, Beth. "Raising Money, Hopes and Consciousness. Fighting Anti-Gay Violence." *Newsday,* 1 August 1996.

Kompas, Kate. "Traveling Exhibit Shows Gay, Lesbian Families." *University Wire,* 4 February 1998.

McAllester, Matthew. "What A Difference A Modem Makes; In Cyberspace, Long Island's Gay Teenagers are Finding the Freedom to be Open Without Fear. They're also Finding There are Risks." *Newsday,* 28 January 1997.

Murphy, Kim. "No Place to Rest." *Los Angeles Times*, 20 December 1995.

Nichols, Bill. "Gay Gathering Takes Gauge of President Clinton Lauded, Warily, as Would-be Heirs are Warned." *USA Today,* 7 November 1997.

Rios, Delia M. "Disappointment Overshadows Gays' Support for Clinton." *The Atlanta Journal and Constitution,* 8 October 1995.

Scanlon, Bill. "Hate Crimes on Campus Against Gays, Lesbians Up." *Rocky Mountain News,* 12 November 1997.

Steyn, Mark. "Culture Vultures; Everybody Out! Ellen DeGeneres Ignites Lesbian Fever." *The American Spectator,* 1 June 1997.

Wright, Elizabeth. "In the Name of 'Civil Rights'." *Issues & Views,* 15 May 1996.

National Governors' Association (NGA)

WHAT IS ITS MISSION?

The National Governors' Association (NGA) is the only bipartisan national organization "of, by and for the nations' Governors." According to the organization's Web site, the NGA's mission is "to provide a forum for Governors to exchange views and experiences among themselves; assist in solving state focused problems; inform one another on state innovations and practices; and provide a bipartisan forum for Governors to establish, influence and implement policy on national issues." Through the association, governors collaborate on public policy issues and work collectively on matters of governance at both the state and federal levels. Issues of importance range from education and emerging environmental challenges to welfare reform and maternal and child health initiatives.

ESTABLISHED: 1908
EMPLOYEES: 90
MEMBERS: 55

Contact Information:
ADDRESS: 444 North Capitol St. NW
     Washington, DC 20001–1512
PHONE: (202) 624-5300
FAX: (202) 624-5313
URL: http://www.nga.org
CHAIRMAN: Thomas R. Carper
VICE CHAIRMAN: Michael O. Leavitt
EXECUTIVE DIRECTOR: Raymond C. Scheppach

HOW IS IT STRUCTURED?

The NGA is a nonprofit organization headquartered in Washington, D.C. It is led by a nine-member executive committee with a chairman and vice chairman at its head. To ensure that the NGA remains bipartisan, its statutes require that the chairman and vice chairman be of opposing political parties, and that the vice chairman replaces the chairman each new year. The executive committee is always made up of four members of the chairman's political party, and five members of the opposing party. The executive committee oversees a finance committee, which manages the association's finances, and a legal affairs committee, which reviews cases of impor-

tance to the states and files briefs to reflect the governors' views.

The NGA has three standing committees: Economic Development and Commerce, Human Resources, and Natural Resources. These committees not only help governors develop policy, but may splinter into special task forces to focus on issues that are particularly timely, usually in conjunction with the NGA Center for Best Practices.

The NGA Center for Best Practices is a 501(c)3 corporation that works with the NGA. It is governed by a board of four state governors, which reports to the NGA executive committee. The Center for Best Practices is the primary research division for the NGA, and helps to develop policy for the NGA as well. The center also develops methods through which the NGA's policies can be put into practice. As part of this mission, the center identifies ideas that have worked well in particular states, and then helps other states to implement these so-called best practices. Along with helping to facilitate the sharing of ideas among the states, the center assists governors by identifying emerging public policy issues, developing strategies to improve current state programs, seeking ways to transfer responsibility from the federal government to the states, and establishing both public and private partnerships among federal, state, and local governments. The five divisions of the Center for Best Practices are: Employment and Social Services; Economic Development and Commerce; Education; Health; and Natural Resources.

The NGA membership is composed of governors from the 50 U.S. states, from the U.S. commonwealths of Puerto Rico and the Northern Mariana Islands, as well as governors from the U.S. territories of American Samoa, Guam, and the Virgin Islands. The NGA often works closely with other state and regional organizations, particularly the National Conference of State Legislatures, and the National Association of State Budget Officers. The NGA and the National Conference of State Legislatures co-sponsor the Federal Funds Information for States.

PRIMARY FUNCTIONS

The NGA is designed to help the governors of each state communicate with each other, so that they can share ideas and develop positions as a unified group. Governors discuss public policy issues through conferences and brainstorming sessions. Through these meetings, governors can decide how best to apply national policy to their states, and how to ensure that the concerns of the states are addressed at the national level.

Beyond fostering communication among U.S. governors, the NGA and in particular the Center for Best Practices develops concrete policies and ideas on how to improve government at a local, national, and especially, state level. The center and the committees of the NGA also study how the various levels of government can best serve their citizens. Based on these findings, the NGA can promote reforms and shape legislation to better serve the states and territories of the United States.

PROGRAMS

The programs of the NGA are designed to meet the needs of its members, the governors of the United States, and are almost entirely research oriented. The exact nature of the organization's research programs varies, depending on what issues are of particular concern. Most research is carried out through the Center for Best Practices, and through NGA's standing committees. One exception is the Federal Funds Information for States. This subscription service, co-sponsored by NGA and the National Conference of State Legislatures, is devoted to monitoring federal spending decisions. This information is of crucial importance to all branches of state government. Subscribers are provided with regular reports on the federal budget and federal grant programs; they also receive special reports on major spending issues.

BUDGET INFORMATION

In the 1997-98 fiscal year the NGA operated from an $11 million budget. State dues funded NGA's lobbying, general administration, public information, and management services activities. In addition, dues fund three federally-oriented groups that provide lobbying and policy support for priorities implemented by the NGA standing committees. The Center for Best Practices, composed of five policy studies divisions, receives funding from a variety of grants, contracts, fee-for-service programs and corporate contributions.

HISTORY

When Theodore Roosevelt became president of the United States, he realized that his programs to manage and preserve the nation's natural resources would need cooperation from the states to be successful. Roosevelt decided that the best way to ensure this cooperation would be to bring state governors together in an organization to discuss national issues that affected states. On May 13, 1908, Roosevelt convened the first meeting of the new Governors' Conference at the White House. Roosevelt remained in charge of the conference throughout his term and used the governors to lobby for his legislative initiatives.

In 1910 Roosevelt's successor, William Howard Taft, encouraged the governors to meet without the president in attendance and the Governors' Conference became independent of the White House. Without the president to guide their activities, the conference became unfocused. Governors of larger states argued that they should determine the conference's agenda because their states had more voters and a greater stake in national issues. Governors of smaller states were reluctant to give up their power. Endless discussions were held to try to clarify the conference's purpose and structure.

By the 1930s, the Governors' Conference had become primarily a social organization with no political agenda or power. Less than half the members regularly attended meetings, and those that did come did so mainly to meet other governors and to try to gain media attention. The Great Depression of the 1930s crippled the nation, and saw people increasingly turning to the federal government, rather than the states, for help. Against this backdrop, the Governors' Conference had little role to play.

During World War II (1939-45), the Governors' Conference did enjoy some resurgence. Members came together to discuss civil defense, the management of increased industrial production, and ways to support the war effort. After the war ended and into the 1950s, the conference tried to become an effective, unified body, but failed. Discussions on issues such as states' rights, Social Security, the budget, and social programs went on and on, but there was seldom any consensus reached on resolutions and very little action. The few resolutions that were passed and sent to the president and Congress had little impact on national policy or legislation.

In the 1960s a new breed of governors began to be elected. They were activist governors, elected to deal with the tremendous social and economic changes of the late 1950s and 1960s. The Governors' Conference developed into a more influential and effective body, as the governors developed clear and unified agendas for coping with state and national problems. The Governors' Conference became an advocate for stronger state governments that would take back many of the responsibilities that had shifted to the federal government.

The recommendations from a 1965 reorganization study were implemented fast and furiously. The word "national" was added to the organization's name to symbolize its new unity. The conference also established its Office for Federal-State Relations in Washington, D.C., to serve as a full-time lobbying organization. Standing committees on important subjects such as transportation, education, and labor were established, and charged with developing policy resolutions.

By the 1970s the National Governors' Conference had been revitalized and was an important voice in national politics. In 1974 the conference created the Center for Policy Research and Analysis to provide research on issues such as energy, economics, and health care. Such research would be used to develop conference resolutions and to lobby Congress. In 1975

the conference oversaw the building of the Hall of States, which would house the various state lobby groups that had previously been scattered throughout Washington, D.C. In 1977 the conference changed its name to the National Governors' Association. The organization felt that "association" reflected their commitment to full-time, continuous work.

Throughout the 1980s, the NGA supported the Reagan administration's efforts to sort out federal functions and determine which functions should be taken over by states. Reagan proposed that states should assume responsibility for many social and transportation programs that were currently being administered by the federal government. The NGA provided research, proposed service models, and made legislative recommendations to facilitate these changes. Bill Clinton, then governor of Arkansas, guided the NGA through the complicated process of reforming the federal welfare system into alternative state programs.

In the 1990s, the NGA continued to work on the issues of welfare reform, education, excise taxes, and fiscal problems. The NGA has become a leading voice on issues that involve federal and state governments and represents a unified membership.

CURRENT POLITICAL ISSUES

Almost every event or issue of significance anywhere within the United States is also important to the NGA. The organization develops policy and makes recommendations on issues ranging from the environment to technology to health care. Certain issues are of particular concern to the states and the NGA, because they fall under the constitutional or traditional authority of the states, while others are of special concern because they are so widespread.

For example, the NGA is very active in education, an area for which the states are constitutionally responsible. NGA policy forums and regional conferences have enabled state policymakers to promote standards-based education and develop school-to-work transition skills and to discuss education curricula, instruction assessment, and credentialing. With technology playing an increasing role in the education system, the NGA actively has promoted the use of educational technology (computers and other multimedia systems) so students can compete effectively in the global marketplace of the twenty-first century.

In the late 1990s most states faced problems with so-called brownfields. The term brownfields refers to over 450,000 former industrial and commercial sites across the U.S. that are contaminated by industrial waste, and lie unused and abandoned. Often found in the middle of major cities, they discourage local growth and stifle economic expansion. The NGA and its Center for Best

Practices have aggressively pursued methods of cleaning up and rebuilding brownfields.

One of the oldest and most difficult issues facing state governors is that of states' rights. Ever since the founding of the United States, there has been controversy over which branch of government—state or federal—should have authority over various aspects of society and government. While the Civil War established that the national government was the final authority, the states have continued to assert the right to govern their citizens in the manner they see fit.

Case Study: States' Rights and the 1998 Tobacco Settlement

The NGA has consistently worked to defend and, on occasion, expand the power and authority of state government. The organization believes that the states, and their governors, have a better understanding of the needs of their state's citizens than the federal government, which is responsible for all U.S. citizens. Others feel that the federal government can do a better job of serving the needs of U.S. citizens. They argue that states can more easily be dominated by particular political parties or interest groups, and that state governments may neglect important national concerns in favor of regional ones. In these and other cases, opponents of states' rights feel the federal government must step in and ensure fair treatment for all.

States' rights can be found at the core of many of the issues that concern the NGA. One example is the organization's position on the tobacco industry settlement of 1998. In November of 1998, the states and the largest tobacco and cigarette producers in the United States reached a historic legal settlement. The states had been pursuing lawsuits against the tobacco industry for knowingly damaging the public health, and costing the state governments billions of dollars in health care costs. In exchange for dropping these lawsuits, the tobacco industry agreed to give the states more than $200 billion over 25 years, as well as make a number of changes in their advertising methods.

Almost immediately, controversy arose over who was entitled to the money from the tobacco settlement, and what it should be spent on. The states maintained that they should get all of the money, and that it was entirely their decision as to what it should be spent on, but others disagreed. By law, the federal government was entitled to a share of any money awarded to repay Medicaid costs, for which the federal government provides 57 percent of its funding. Also, many people felt that some of the money from the settlement should be devoted to programs designed to prevent smoking, and help those who smoke quit. They were dismayed by proposals, such as one made in Florida, that the funds be spent in other areas such as road improvement, and pushed the federal government to place restrictions on how the states used their settlement money.

In 1999 the NGA and other groups representing the states lobbied Congress heavily to leave the tobacco settlement money under their control. On March 15, 1999, Governor Paul E. Patton of Kentucky presented the opinion of the nation's governors to the U.S. Senate. Patton argued that the states were entitled to all of the money from the tobacco settlement. He pointed out that Medicaid costs were only one of many complaints filed by the states, which included charges of racketeering, endangering the public health, and violations of various state laws. He further pointed out that the federal government had declined invitations to join the states in their legal action, leaving all the risks inherent in a lawsuit to the states. For these and other similar reasons, the NGA believed that the states had sole claim on the tobacco settlement.

Patton also took a strong states' rights stand on the issue of what the settlement funds should be spent on. He argued that it was up to each state to decide exactly how much money to spend on smoking prevention programs; "Although states will spend significant amounts of money on programs that improve the health, education, and welfare of their citizens, states do not need to be told how to spend any portion of their money."

The NGA's lobbying efforts in the House paid off in March of 1999, when a bill was passed that would allow the states to keep all of the settlement money. As of April 1999, however, the NGA was still trying to convince the U.S. Senate to pass similar legislation. It also remains to be seen if the states will be allowed complete control over the funds, as strong efforts continue in Congress to regulate how the states can use their tobacco settlement money. Despite these obstacles, the NGA remains committed to protecting the tobacco settlement, which the organization calls its top priority for 1999.

FUTURE DIRECTIONS

In the coming years, NGA will devote much of its attention to issues in education, such as accountability in education, harnessing the potential of technology, and expanding opportunities for learning. The NGA believes that schools should be judged not by the number of books in their libraries, but by their ability to improve student achievement and produce graduates who can excel in college and the workplace. The Center for Best Practices held two regional forums in 1998 to address the accountability issues facing state policymakers, and plans on future discussion sessions. Since advances in technology are expected to transform the economy and workplace at the beginning of the twenty-first century, the NGA will continue to examine methods in which states and local school districts can use computers, multimedia presentations, and other advanced technology to support instruction.

GROUP RESOURCES

The NGA's extensive Web site can be accessed at http://www.nga.org. The site includes information on NGA's policy stances on education and welfare reform, environmental protection, economic development, and other public policy issues of statewide and national importance. The NGA Center for Best Practices also maintains a Web site at http://www.nga.org/cbp.

For further information about the NGA write to the National Governors' Association, 444 North Capitol St., Washington, DC 20001-1512 or phone (202) 624-5300. The most recent edition of *NGA Chairman's Agenda,* issued annually at each year's winter meeting, can be obtained free of charge by calling (202) 624-5301.

GROUP PUBLICATIONS

The NGA has an extensive list of publications, including a newsletter, statistical reports, and many research and policy reports. Annual publications include the *Directory of Governors of the American States, Commonwealths and Territories* (published in January), the *Governors' Staff Directory* (published in March and September), *The Fiscal Survey of States* (published in April and October) and *Policy Positions.* The *Governors' Bulletin: An Insider's Perspective* is a biweekly publication that is available by subscription. The NGA also publishes hundreds of books and pamphlets, and issue briefs dealing with subjects such as: agricultural and rural development, state budgeting, social services, brownfields, transportation, and education. Virtually all NGA publications may be purchased on-line via the NGA Book Store, at http://st7.yahoo.net/governors. For more information on NGA publications, write to National Governors' Association, 444 North Capitol St., Ste. 267, Washington, DC 20001-1512; or call (301) 498-3738.

BIBLIOGRAPHY

Brown, Patricia, and Paul D. Goren. *Ability Grouping and Tracking: Current Issues and Concerns.* Washington, D.C.: National Governors' Association, 1993.

Donlan, Thomas G. "Listen to the Governors; A Compromise on Welfare Reform Is Worth Adopting." *Barron's,* 19 February 1996.

Donohue, John W. "Of Many Things." *America,* 23 March 1996.

"Gerstner: Education Is Slipping." *Industry Week,* 21 August 1995.

Gruenwald, Juliana, "Governors Offer Alternative to Hill's Internet Tax Bills." *Congressional Quarterly's Weekly Report,* 28 February 1998.

Lawrence, Jill. "Gubernatorial Reapproachment: Partisan Rivalry Almost Destroyed the National Governors' Association. Now Things are Under Control Again." *Governing,* April 1996.

Nelson, Matthew. "Internet Tax Resolution Creates Stir." *InfoWorld,* 2 March 1998.

Pavetti, LaDonna. "How Much More Can they Work?: Setting Realistic Expectations for Welfare Mothers." Washington, D.C.: The Urban Institute, 1997.

Shafroth, Frank. "Governors Agree to Overhaul of Deferral Poverty Programs." *Nation's Cities Weekly,* 12 February 1996.

Thompson, Gov. Tommy G., and Gov. Thomas R. Carper. "State Innovations Prepare Today's Students for the Workplace of Tomorrow." *Voice of the Governors,* Washington, D.C.: National Governors' Association, 1998.

Walters, Jonathan. "The Disappearing Policy Advisers." *Governing,* July 1997.

The National Grange

ESTABLISHED: December 4, 1867
EMPLOYEES: 20
MEMBERS: 290,000
PAC: None

Contact Information:

ADDRESS: 1616 H St. NW
      Washington, DC 20006-4999
PHONE: (202) 628-3507
TOLL FREE: (888) 447-2649
FAX: (202) 347-1091
URL: http://www.nationalgrange.org
NATIONAL MASTER: Kermit W. Richardson

WHAT IS ITS MISSION?

The National Grange was founded in 1867 and is the oldest farm organization in the United States. According to the organization, "the National Grange is the country's foremost family-oriented, community service organization with a special interest in agriculture related issues."

The National Grange serves as a unifying voice for the agricultural community as well as rural non-farm interests at the national, community, and state levels. The National Grange philosophy encompasses rural and agricultural health, and promotes strong community and family values in rural areas. Although not strictly a lobbying organization, the National Grange's ability to unify many agricultural constituents has made its lobbying efforts some of the most successful among agricultural organizations. The National Grange's programs cover a wide variety of functions, including lobbying developed from grassroots, non-partisan input, and promoting community development in rural communities. Since its inception, the organization has broadened its focus from agricultural politics and has taken on the additional role of promoting the health of rural communities.

HOW IS IT STRUCTURED?

The National Grange is a fraternal farm organization with headquarters located in Washington, D.C. The organization is headed by a National Master, a position which is synonymous with executive director or president. The National Master and the Overseer (the organization vice president) serve on a six-member executive committee which provides overall guidance to the organization and whose members are elected by delegates for staggered three-year terms. The Washington office houses the Legislative Affairs office and oversees programs that are carried out by the Grange departments. Organization departments are headed by representative members across the nation and include: Membership Development, Women's Activities, Deaf Activities, Junior Grange Activities, Youth/Young Adult Activities, Community Service, and the Lecturers' Department. The latter is headed by the National Grange Program Director, who is responsible for coordinating the organization's national convention, where organizational directives and policy initiatives are formed.

National Grange policy initiatives are debated once a year during a week-long convention. Proposals are first suggested either at the national level or at the local level, within local (or Subordinate) Grange groups or county (Pomona) Grange groups. Local proposals are debated and adopted at state Grange conventions. At the national convention, all proposed policy from the states and from the national level is debated and adopted by delegates; delegates consist largely of Masters and their spouses from the county and local Grange groups for each state. The conference culminates with decisions on policy and direction that address issues relevant to agriculture and rural communities. Results of the conference are published annually in the *National Grange Journal of Proceedings*, and initiatives are forwarded to government policymakers.

State chapters of the National Grange operate in the District of Columbia and 37 states. Each state group is structured like the national organization, is headed by a Master, and carries out the same programs. There are some 5,200 local Grange groups located across the nation.

Grange members typically join local (Subordinate) groups. Members are 14 years or older, and pay dues to support activities at the local, state, and national level. Women have equal membership in the National Grange and all members have the ability to help develop policy directives. Members receive benefits such as discounts on merchandise, phone service, and insurance.

PRIMARY FUNCTIONS

The National Grange serves agricultural and rural communities in a number of ways. The organization has always been known for its ability to influence policy making. The National Grange's legislative agenda is guided by the organization's policy-making process, in which all members participate. From the local to the national level, all Grange members have a chance to propose policy and direction for the organization. Resulting initiatives are distributed annually to congressional members as well as to the media and other organizations. For

example, a 1998 policy directive was the *Blueprint for Rural America* which pinpointed ten actions that the organization supports, including. stabilizing the price of milk, making funding available to restore rural schools, and improving rural road systems. Legislative directors in the organization use policy directives as a guide in lobbying for or against related government legislation and policies. Members are kept informed of Grange initiatives through Action Alerts on the organization Web site.

PROGRAMS

The National Grange carries out a number of programs that improve the quality of life in rural or agricultural communities. These programs address a variety of rural issues, such as geographic isolation, emergency response time, farm safety, homelessness, and community economic development.

The National Grange's Community Service Program encourages local Grange groups to carry out community service work as a way to promote healthy and effective rural communities. Community service work includes creating community response teams to deal with natural or medical emergencies, helping with community economic development, and carrying out programs that support farm safety. In 1998 this program launched the National Grange Community Service Recognition Program, which was created to recognize outstanding firefighters and law enforcement officers in rural communities.

The Grange Deaf Project provides resources and funding that promote an understanding of deafness among Grange and non-Grange members. The organization distributes educational materials about deafness, such as posters and publications. The National Grange offers forms of financial support to those who are affected by deafness. The Mandy Project awards funds annually to one Grange family to assist with their deaf child's hearing care expenses. The organization has established an endowment to make it possible for deaf students to attend Gallaudet University. The National Grange also sponsors hearing testing in communities.

The Junior Grange Program is geared toward children ages five to 14 and sponsors a variety of projects for this age group, such as community cleanup efforts and work with housebound residents. The program also coordinates a number of projects such as Stop the Violence, which teaches Junior Grange members how to deal with conflict constructively; Farm Safety Just for Kids; and the Family Outreach Program, which sponsors activities for Grange families to do together.

The Grange Youth Program focuses on members ages 14 to 35 and offers regional conferences as well as leadership development activities and public speaking contests. The Grange Women's Activities Department carries out programs such as the Community Awareness Project, which gives assistance to homeless people in rural communities; and the Health Initiative, which works with hearing-impaired people and promotes community activities such as hearing testing. The National Grange also sponsors an annual program addressing health. In 1997 the Let's Beef it Up campaign educated Grange members about the value of eating beef and how to incorporate it into a family diet.

BUDGET INFORMATION

In fiscal year 1997 the National Grange had total revenues of $1,030,231 (up from $953,343 in 1996) and expenses of $1,318,902 (up from $1,203,604 in 1996). Major revenues included dues from Subordinate Grange groups ($857,937) and sales income ($109,616). Other revenue categories included dues from other types of Grange groups, newsletter income, tape sales, and interest income.

Grange expenses in 1997 included (but were not limited to): general and administrative ($291,805), legislation ($185,287), national convention ($178,781), and sales ($161,743). Salaries for fiscal year 1997 totaled $502,579. The organization projected total revenue for 1998 at $1,384,619 and total 1998 expenses at $1,336,320.

HISTORY

The history of the National Grange is significant because it spawned the Granger movement, a phenomenon which enabled farmers to think about their vocation in economic terms and to take political action. The National Grange was founded in 1867 by Minnesota farmer and activist Oliver Hudson Kelley and six other like-minded peers. Kelley had served as a clerk for the Commissioner of Agriculture in Washington, D.C. and was sent on a tour of the country in 1866—during the aftermath of the Civil War (1860–65). Disheartened by the destruction to farmland that had occurred during the war, Kelly and his peers felt that farmers needed a union-like organization to represent them and their concerns. Farmers felt they needed to address issues such as establishing fair market value for their products and dealing with exorbitantly high railroad shipping rates. Often separated from each other by great distances, farmers faced difficulty organizing.

Initially the National Grange hoped to ally with one of the two major U.S. political parties, the Republican Party or the Democratic Party, in order to address farmers' issues. Not finding what they wanted in either party, the group developed its own political party which had strong Midwestern support and was known alternately as the Independents, Reformers, Anti-Monopolists, or Farmers' Party. Some of the National Grange's accomplishments during this time included establishing cooperative arrangements that benefited farmers, such as stores, grain elevators, and mills. Cooperative arrangements put farmers in more direct contact with consumers and eliminated middlemen in agricultural transactions, thereby achieving one of the National Grange's goals.

In 1876, a year after membership climbed to a peak level of over 850,000, it became clear that much of the National Grange's constituency didn't favor any political party alliance, and the Grange became more of an advocacy organization than a political party in its own right. The movement continued to serve to unify the farm vote and advance the ideals of farmers, which were expressed under the umbrella of Populism and the Greenback Movement. During this period, pressure from the organization was felt in the outcome of the Supreme Court case *Munn v. Illinois* (1876) which upheld the legality of state regulation of railroad shipping and grain elevators.

The National Grange did not entirely remove itself from politics. In 1919 the organization opened its lobbying office in Washington, D.C. The group worked, at times in coalition with other farm groups, to promote and lobby for policies which would advance the agenda of farmers in the United States. Lobbying successes included the establishment of the U.S. Extension Service, a program which conducts agriculturally related research and offers services and outreach for farmers, and passage of the Capper-Volstead Act (1922), which legalized farmers' cooperatives.

Farming in the United States has always been particularly affected by economic hard times, and this was never more true than during the Great Depression of the 1930s. Farm prices were extremely low during this period, and many farmers, especially small farmers, struggled to make ends meet. Terrible droughts turned much of the central United States into a so-called Dust Bowl and drove farmers off the land. The National Grange supported President Franklin Roosevelt's efforts under his New Deal program to raise farm prices, most notably the Agricultural Adjustment Act. In the years after World War II (1939–45), the Grange continued to back federal subsidies and support for farmers. However, other farming groups, such as the American Farm Bureau Federation (AFBF) and the National Farmers Union (NFU) grew in strength during the 1950s and 1960s and began to replace the National Grange in the public eye.

The 1970s were a good time for farmers, with prices and sales high. Many small operations expanded and borrowed money to purchase equipment—assuming that the economy would remain healthy. The U.S. recession of the 1980s devastated many small farms, and owners were often forced to give away or auction off property that they could no longer afford to maintain. More than 20,000 such auctions occurred in 1981. The farmers' plight was intensified by the strength of the dollar, which made U.S. agricultural products too expensive to buy abroad. During this time the National Grange played a role in lobbying for legislation that would help small farmers through the recession, such as the Tax Reform Act of 1986 which lowered tax rates, and amendments to the Farm Credit Act which helped keep farmers from going bankrupt.

In 1995 the Grange joined other organizations to protest pork pricing, which they claimed was too low and was controlled by a small monopoly of packing and processing plants. Farming organizations lobbied the U.S. Department of Agriculture, requesting that the Department ensure that its market price reporting system accurately reflected prices the market would bear.

In 1998 the National Grange expressed their approval when Congress presented what the Grange considered a unified suggestion for policy that would, according to the Grange, strengthen U.S. agricultural commodity markets. Highlights of the suggested initiative included reintroducing fast track legislation (whereby trade legislation could become effective without congressional approval), renewing China's status as a Most Favored Nation (thereby removing barriers to trade with China), lifting export restrictions in India and Pakistan, and supporting increased funding for the International Monetary Fund (IMF). The Grange will be monitoring strides in these areas and lobbying for their success.

CURRENT POLITICAL ISSUES

The National Grange is involved with political issues that impact the U.S. agricultural community or other rural constituents. For example, the National Grange opposed the Global Climate Treaty, which was proposed in 1997 by a number of countries around the world. The organization took the position that all nations (including Mexico, China, and India) should have to comply with the treaty; otherwise participating nations would suffer competitively since they would be bound by emission control regulations imposed by the treaty. The National Grange claimed that the Global Climate Treaty could also impact the price of fertilizer, and could take productive agricultural land out of use. National Grange leaders spoke at White House Conferences in conjunction with other interest groups and called for further research on global warming to address the impact to the U.S. agricultural sector.

The National Grange supports international trade policy which expedites international trading and opens up new markets. In 1997 the group advocated for the installation of fast track legislative policy, which would expedite trade agreements around the world.

BUDGET:

1997 GRANGE Revenue

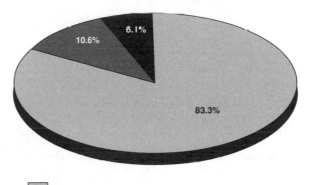

- 83.3%: Dues from subordinate grange groups
- 10.6%: Sales income
- 6.1%: Other

1997 GRANGE Expenses

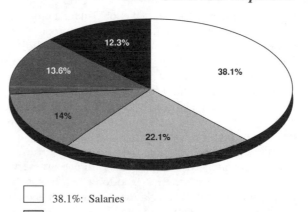

- 38.1%: Salaries
- 22.1%: General and administrative
- 14%: Legislation
- 13.6%: National convention
- 12.3%: Sales

Case Study: Increasing Agricultural Exports

The Grange and other agricultural groups have supported the North American Free Trade Agreement (NAFTA), which will be fully implemented by cooperating countries in 2005 and which facilitates U.S. exports. According to the Grange, trade policies like NAFTA

FAST FACTS

According to the National Grange, the average farmer counts on exports for about one-third of his or her income.

(Source: Ellyn Ferguson, "Administration Support Pledged for Small Farmers." *Gannett News Service*, January 22, 1998.)

have achieved healthy trade surpluses for the agriculture industry, including a $28.5 billion surplus in 1997. Additionally the National Grange claims that each dollar in trade surplus contributed an additional $1.39 to the U.S. economy. The organization feels that demand for agricultural exports is growing and that policy that expedites international trade should be implemented.

In 1997 the National Grange lobbied for a proposal called "fast track" trade legislation; the proposal, if passed, would have prohibited Congress from modifying any proposed trade legislation. The proposal was attractive to supporters of international trade because, as pointed out in a *USA Today* article (April 16, 1998), "countries are much less likely to go through the tedious negotiations that trade pacts require if they know that a deal can be rewritten by Congress." What was the point of having the president negotiate treaties, argued fast track's supporters, if Congress could throw out everything that had been agreed to, and force negotiations to begin all over again? The National Grange lobbied for the proposal in coalition with other like-minded groups. Additionally, they created information for members and legislators to better understand why fast track legislation would benefit international trade. The proposal, facing opposition from both parties in Congress, was withdrawn by the president and the House Speaker in late 1997.

Public Impact

While it seemed unlikely that Congress would freely give up their power to modify legislation, opponents of fast track trading policies had other issues with the idea. Workers' unions opposed it on the same grounds that they had opposed NAFTA, claiming that U.S. jobs would be lost to workers in foreign countries because U.S. companies would be encouraged to relocate outside of the United States. In *Reuters Business Report* (September 25, 1997), a spokesperson for the

International Union of Electronics Workers claimed that the union had lost 5,000 to 6,000 jobs to Mexico, after the NAFTA installation began in 1993. Other unions estimate that trade agreements like NAFTA have resulted in the loss of more than 420,000 U.S. jobs. The AFL-CIO spent $1 million on an advertising campaign to defeat the fast track proposal, claiming that they supported international trade policy as long as countries traded on equal terms and were held to the same environmental and workers rights conditions as the United States.

FUTURE DIRECTIONS

The National Grange will be focusing on initiatives that benefit agricultural and rural communities. This includes pressuring the Department of Agriculture to make good on a promise to make more loan money available to small farmers, including changing language in the 1996 Farm Bill which denied credit to farmers who had been delinquent or had defaulted on a U.S. Department of Agriculture (USDA) loan. Grange lobbyists will also push for rural highway money when Congress debates how road money will be allocated. The organization will continue to advocate for technological improvements in rural schools, including the use of computers and interactive video technology which make it possible for education resources to be offered via satellite in the schools.

GROUP RESOURCES

The National Grange makes educational resources available to members including classroom materials on the subject of hearing loss, camps for children, regional conferences, and farm safety programs. Information can be obtained by contacting the National Grange office by phone at (202) 628-3507 or by writing to 1616 H St. NW, Washington, DC 20006-4999. The organization's Web site is located at http://www.nationalgrange.org.

GROUP PUBLICATIONS

National Grange publications include: *Blueprint for Rural America* (a ten-point program of initiatives for the future), *National Grange Journal of Proceedings* (from the annual Grange conference), *People, Pride and Progress: 125 Years of the Grange in America*, by David H. Howard (Washington, D.C.: National Grange, 1992, cost $12), and *The Grange—Friend of the Farmer*, by Charles M. Gardner (Washington, D.C.: National Grange, 1949). To order publications, contact the National Grange by phone at (202) 628-3507; write to 1616 H St. NW, Washington, DC 20006-4999; or access the organization Web site at http://www. nationalgrange.org.

BIBLIOGRAPHY

Arcellana, Nancy Pearson. "Making a Lot Out of a Little." *Women in Action,* 3 January 1997.

"Bank of America Makes Biggest Bank Commitment Ever For Rural Community Development Lending." *Business Wire,* 1 October 1997.

Ehrbar, Aloysius, and John Steinbreder. "Facts vs. the Furor over Farm Policy." *Fortune,* 11 November 1985.

Eisenberg, Richard. "How City Slickers Can Live Off the Land." *Money,* 1 January 1988.

Knight, Danielle. "Food: Quit Hogging the Environment." *Inter Press Service English News Wire,* 7 April 1998.

Marti, Donald B. *Women of the Grange: Mutuality and Sisterhood in Rural America, 1866-1920,* New York: Greenwood Press, 1991.

Mason-Draffen, Carrie. "Bankrupting A Tradition, Mounting Bills, Higher Costs Threaten State's Dairy Farms." *Newsday,* 8 February 1998.

White, Kristine. "Making a Life and a Livelihood Down on the Farm." *The Columbian,* 8 February 1998.

Woods, Thomas A. *Knights of the Plow: Oliver H. Kelley and the Origins of the Grange in Republican Ideology,* Ames, Iowa: Iowa State University Press, 1991.

Zepeda, Lydia, and Marco Castillo. "The Role of Husbands and Wives in Farm Technology Choice." *American Journal of Agricultural Economics,* 1 May 1997.

National Organization for the Reform of Marijuana Laws (NORML)

ESTABLISHED: 1970
EMPLOYEES: 6
MEMBERS: 7,000

Contact Information:

ADDRESS: 1001 Connecticut Ave. NW, Ste. 700
    Washington, DC 20036
PHONE: (202) 483-5500
FAX: (202) 483-0057
E-MAIL: norml@norml.org
URL: http://www.norml.org
EXECUTIVE DIRECTOR: R. Keith Stroup

WHAT IS ITS MISSION?

Believing marijuana is a drug far less dangerous than other legal drugs such as alcohol, the National Organization for the Reform of Marijuana Laws (NORML) concentrates its efforts on bringing about the legalization of marijuana for industrial (hemp-related), medicinal, and recreational use. Through legislative and educational efforts, NORML aims to rid the U.S. public and government of the stigma attached to marijuana use.

Unlike other pro-marijuana organizations, NORML is willing to compromise and supports legislative changes that bring marijuana closer to legalization, such as reduced fines and sentencing, or legalization of the drug for medicinal use. Even so, according to NORML Director R. Keith Stroup, "the ultimate goal of NORML is to end prohibition. We believe it should be legal for adults to smoke marijuana privately. The federal anti-marijuana laws would be removed and states should be encouraged to experiment with different models of legalization. We will continue to pursue efforts to remove the marijuana smoker from the criminal justice system altogether."

HOW IS IT STRUCTURED?

Originally founded in 1970 by R. Keith Stroup, NORML split in the summer of 1997 into two complementary but separate organizations: NORML, which is primarily a lobbying organization, and the NORML Foundation, which carries out the organization's educational and advocacy functions. Both groups work toward the same goals and operate out of the same address in

Washington, D.C. This arrangement enables the organization to carry out lobbying activities and still offer tax-exemption to donors who wish to support NORML's cause. Donations to NORML Foundation became tax-deductible in 1997 when the Internal Revenue Service granted the organization nonprofit status.

The NORML Foundation functions as an umbrella organization for a national network of citizen activists who are affiliated through 70 local chapters located in nearly every state in the United States, as well as Puerto Rico, Australia, Canada, New Zealand, Norway, and the United Kingdom. While the local chapters tend to function fairly autonomously, they may seek legal advice from the national staff or educational materials from the national clearinghouse to assist them with local efforts and activities. Supporters may choose to join the national chapter, a local chapter, or both.

Stroup presides over NORML Foundation in the same capacity that he did NORML before the division, acting indefinitely as executive director. Stroup's responsibilities include not only overseeing the organization itself, and occasionally defending citizens being prosecuted for marijuana-related offenses, but networking with people who work in a legislative, governmental, research or celebrity capacity who may be sympathetic to NORML's cause.

A legal committee, the NORML Amicus Curiae Committee, monitors marijuana-related legal actions. When such initiatives are pending, Stroup's NORML Foundation notifies the public about the situation and attempts to gain support for the organization's stance. Meanwhile, NORML lobbies and testifies in Congress for policy favored by NORML. This half of the organization is headed by Allen St. Pierre, the previous deputy director, who serves as executive director of NORML for an unspecified period.

A 17-member board of directors serves both organizations. The board is composed of attorneys, doctors, scientists, and researchers, including Nobel Laureate chemist Kary Mullis. Board members are often called upon to testify on NORML's behalf in front of various government bodies.

PRIMARY FUNCTIONS

NORML's efforts include influencing public opinion, organizing and activating people who advocate the use of marijuana, and lobbying the government to make marijuana laws less restrictive. The historical purpose of NORML has been primarily to influence legislation. The organization believes, however, that legislative and judicial changes, whether in favor of or against the decriminalization of marijuana, are often the result of the evolution of public opinion, and public opinion on marijuana has tended to shift radically over the past 30 years. There-

fore, NORML has consistently attempted to balance its legal assaults on marijuana laws with educational materials aimed at convincing the U.S. public that marijuana has been unfairly demonized in a way that alcohol and legal pharmaceutical substances (schedule II drugs) have not.

Government and Legislative Advocacy

NORML's primary activity is to monitor marijuana-related legislation at the national and state levels, lobbying legislators and providing expert testimony to support efforts to decriminalize or legalize marijuana and hemp, and to gain approval for the use of marijuana for medicinal purposes. The NORML Amicus Curiae Committee files briefs in a capacity as a friend of the court on important or new marijuana-related legal action at the appellate court level. NORML persistently tries to engage federal government representatives in public debate. In February of 1996, NORML's then Deputy Director Allen St. Pierre debated Lee Brown, former head of the Office of National Drug Control Policy, on an America On-line forum.

NORML also constantly monitors the activities of the federal government, particularly in light of the much-publicized "war on drugs." Mandatory minimum drug sentences, the civil rights of suspected drug dealers, and the invasive use of drug testing are all concerns of NORML. National and local chapters have been active in defending citizens arrested or incarcerated for marijuana use, particularly those who have grown or used marijuana to treat illnesses. Local chapters may also hold or attend rallies or conferences to raise money to assist someone arrested for a marijuana-related offense, to support local legislation, or to educate and mobilize marijuana users.

NORML relies on its extensive network of 70 local chapters to organize and apply pressure at the grassroots level. Chapters attend and sponsor conferences and events that bring media and public attention to marijuana issues and encourage those sympathetic to become members and active in the movement. In addition, NORML has worked closely and maintained alliances with organizations such as the American Civil Liberties Union (ACLU), the Cannabis Action Network, Partnership for Responsible Drug Information, and the Campaign for the Restoration and Regulation of Hemp, as well as numerous international groups, particularly those located in the Netherlands where marijuana is legal and regulated by the government. Director Stroup has been successful in associating a variety of marijuana-sympathetic celebrities, scientists, and government officials with the organization, including former Attorney General Ramsey Clark, cartoonist Gary Trudeau, Hugh Hefner of the Playboy empire, author Hunter S. Thompson, and performers such as Willie Nelson and more recently, the rock band the Black Crowes and rap group Cypress Hill.

NORML acts as an information resource for the media on marijuana-related issues, as well as a national

FAST FACTS

In 1996 there were over 641,000 marijuana-related arrests in the United States.

(Source: *FBI Report*, October 4, 1997.)

clearinghouse for information useful to marijuana law reform efforts.

PROGRAMS

While national NORML does not conduct ongoing programs, local NORML chapters can be counted on as regular supporters and participants in several annual events dedicated to marijuana legalization and culture. For instance, the Massachusetts chapter holds a yearly "Mass/Cann Freedom Rally," which, according to NORML records, has drawn as many as 50,000 supporters. And NORML chapters in Michigan are an organizing force for the yearly "Hash Bash" held on the campus of the University of Michigan every April. NORML concedes that a primary goal of these local rallies is to have fun, but also clearly states on their Web page that: "For a rally to be truly successful, organizers and participants have the responsibility to ensure that more is achieved than mass euphoria." NORML encourages organizers to think strategically, targeting upcoming legislation as a focal point for the rallies, pushing for the best media coverage possible, and setting a tone that shows spectators that marijuana legal reformers are "rational, intelligent, clean, nice, moral, 'norml' citizens."

BUDGET INFORMATION

NORML began 1995 with $45,485 in net assets and fund balances and $13,856 in assets ($7,256 in noninterest-bearing cash and $6,600 in inventories for sale or use). In the same year the group took in $397,693. Of that, $149,628 arrived in the form of contributions, gifts, and grants, and $248,064 was generated from other income-producing activities. This includes $72,862 from program services ($69,047 from a 1-900 information hotline and $3,815 from a seminar); $108,875 from membership dues and assessments; $5,011 from sales of

inventory; and $61,315 from record sales and special grants.

Meanwhile, the group spent $345,233 on program services (the bulk of which went toward public education efforts); $196,949 on management and general expenses; and $71,049 on fund-raising activities. This brought NORML's total expenditures in 1995 to $613,231.

Once the nonprofit NORML Foundation was initiated in 1997, budgets for the two components of the full organization were separated to comply with tax laws that prohibit nonprofit organizations from conducting lobbying activities. In 1997 both groups together brought in about $900,000 of which almost equal portions went to NORML and NORML Foundation.

HISTORY

NORML was founded in 1970 by attorney Keith Stroup, primarily to function as a national lobby for legal reform on marijuana-related issues. One of NORML's first major activities was to serve as a public watchdog for the Nixon administration's Commission on Marijuana and Drug Abuse. NORML was instrumental in convincing the bipartisan commission to let several reform advocates testify. The culminating report, *Marijuana: A Signal of Misunderstanding*, recommended decriminalization of marijuana.

NORML was most influential and productive between the years of 1973 and 1978, when public opinion was more favorable to decriminalization efforts and the federal government, in general, was less concerned with drug use in the country. In fact, President Jimmy Carter endorsed decriminalization early in his 1976 presidential campaign bid. During this period, NORML was instrumental in bringing about decriminalization laws in 11 states: Alaska, California, Colorado, Maine, Minnesota, Mississippi, Nebraska, New York, North Carolina, Ohio, and Oregon. In all of these states, except Alaska, marijuana use has remained decriminalized (punishable by a small fine, instead of a prison sentence and/or a criminal record).

After 1978 NORML's push for legalization focused on medicinal marijuana. From 1978 to 1992 NORML assisted in efforts that encouraged numerous states to pass statutes or resolutions that endorse the medicinal use of marijuana. The federal government, however, has remained unconvinced, and maintains a strict anti-marijuana stance with respect to the treatment of illnesses. In 1988 NORML won a 16-year lawsuit to compel the federal government to make marijuana available as medicine. However, the Drug Enforcement Agency (DEA) has subsequently rejected this ruling.

In 1994 NORML sponsored "National Medical Marijuana Day," to focus national attention on the perceived need for legalization of medicinal marijuana. In 1995

NORML encouraged and assisted Rep. Barney Frank (D-Mass.) in putting together a federal medical marijuana bill (H.R. 2618), which was introduced into the house, and a similar bill (H.R. 1782) in 1997. These bills would have removed federal restrictions that prevent physicians from legally prescribing marijuana. NORML testified on behalf of H.R. 2618 in 1996, and a NORML board member, Dr. Lester Grinspoon, testified on behalf of H.R. 1782 in 1997. While neither of these federal bills were passed, NORML had a success at the state level. NORML members in California and Arizona were active in getting medicinal marijuana issues placed on the ballot, and both passed in the November 1996 elections. The law was circumvented in Arizona by the governor and legislature, but was put into practice in California, in direct opposition to the federal government.

CURRENT POLITICAL ISSUES

While the public sometimes tends to think of marijuana reformers as radical and anarchistic, NORML persistently tries to present its cause in moderate and reasonable terms. On its Web page NORML delineates the "Principles of Responsible Cannabis Use," which include limiting marijuana use to adults only, making it illegal to drive and operate dangerous machinery while under the drug's influence, stopping drug abuse, and showing sensitivity to others who choose to use marijuana.

Starting in the early 1980s, the federal government adopted a "war on drugs" stance, which was carried on in the 1990s by President Bill Clinton. This antidrug position has played a crucial role in NORML history, keeping the organization busy challenging new and restrictive drug policies. NORML has been especially critical of involuntary drug testing, and the organization's staff uses a 900 hot line number to answer questions on the legality of drug testing in various situations.

NORML is also concerned with the numerous efforts at the state level to implement stiffer criminal penalties on those who use or sell drugs, such as California's crime-related "Three Strikes" law. NORML claims such efforts have disproportionately affected drug-related offenders over other criminals. So while the group is concerned with the drug war and the manner in which it affects the civil rights of all drug users, NORML's official efforts are generally focused on marijuana, and on convincing the U.S public that marijuana has been unfairly targeted and grouped with more dangerous drugs such as cocaine and heroine.

The issue of medicinal uses of marijuana, however, has captured public sympathy. NORML has been busy rallying and testifying on behalf of state laws and initiatives that promote legalization for those who have medical conditions with symptoms that are alleviated by marijuana, including AIDS, multiple sclerosis, glaucoma, and cancer.

BUDGET:
1995 NORML Revenue

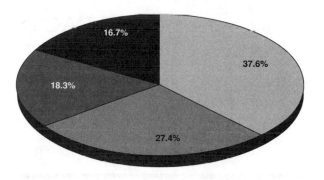

- 37.6%: Contributions, gifts, and grants
- 27.4%: Membership dues and assessments
- 18.3%: Program services
- 16.7%: Other

1995 NORML Expenses

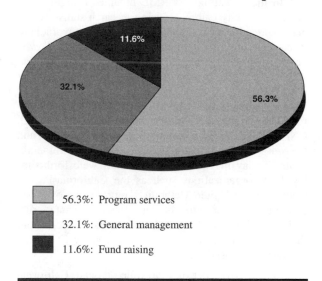

- 56.3%: Program services
- 32.1%: General management
- 11.6%: Fund raising

Case Study: California State Proposition 215

California's Proposition 215 not only instigated public debate regarding marijuana, but also called into question the extent the federal government can legitimately interfere with or override laws made at the state and local level, and the right of the federal government to interfere in the doctor-patient relationship.

FAST FACTS

According to an an ACLU study, 47 percent of Americans believe that it is a "very good" idea "to legalize marijuana for medical use if prescribed by a doctor"; 32 percent believe it is a "somewhat good" idea; and 16 percent called it a "somewhat bad" or "very bad" idea.

(Source: *ACLU Study* by Belden & Russonello (B&R) Research and Polling Firm, January 1995.)

In 1995 the California state legislature legalized marijuana use for anyone holding a doctor's prescription. California governor Pete Wilson, however, vetoed the legislation. California NORML and other marijuana activists responded by gathering 750,000 signatures, well over the amount required to place the initiative on the ballot for public referendum in November of 1996.

In the meantime, NORML mounted a highly successful publicity campaign using research statistics and personal testimony that resulted in editorials favorable to its cause in mainstream publications such as *USA Today*, prestigious health publications such as *The New England Journal of Medicine*, and conservative ones such as *The Orange County Register*. Even conservative William F. Buckley came out in support of, not only the medicinal marijuana issue, but of decriminalization in general. CNN, CNBC and PBS featured specials on the topic, and the *New York Times* featured the controversy prominently in its Sunday magazine. Endorsements were forthcoming from organizations such as the California-Pacific Conference of United Methodists, representing over 400 churches from the cities of San Francisco, Santa Cruz, and West Hollywood; the California Nurses Association; the Los Angeles AIDS Commission; and the California Multiple Sclerosis Society.

When November of 1996 rolled around, California voters approved the initiative as did Arizona voters, who passed a similar state law, Proposition 200. While Arizona legislators circumvented Proposition 200 by passing legislation that mandates that doctors cannot prescribe marijuana until it is approved by the Food and Drug Administration, California's law has raised numerous legal issues, as well as the disapproval of the federal government, which maintains a strict antidrug stance toward marijuana.

On December 30, 1996, the Clinton administration threatened to use federal laws to prosecute doctors who prescribe marijuana to their patients. Barry McCaffrey, director of the Office of National Drug Control Policy, stated in a press release that: "The recent passage of propositions which make dangerous drugs more available in California and Arizona poses a threat to the National Drug Control Strategy goal of reducing drug abuse in the United States." Attorney General Janet Reno echoed the statements of McCaffrey when she threatened to use the power of the Justice Department to criminally prosecute doctors who prescribe marijuana to patients.

On April 11, 1997, U.S. District Judge Fern Smith made a temporary injunction prohibiting the federal government from interfering with California doctors who prescribe marijuana. This came as the result of a lawsuit filed by California physicians. On May 1, 1997, the same judge finally ruled against the federal government saying, ". . . this case is about the ability of doctors, on an individualized basis, to give advice and recommendations to bona fide patients suffering from serious, debilitating illnesses regarding the possible benefits of personal, medical use of small quantities of marijuana."

Despite the injunction, on April 21, 1997, federal agents raided and confiscated 331 marijuana plants and associated growing equipment at a San Francisco buyer's club, one of 15 in the city that sells marijuana to clients holding prescriptions with the cooperation of local law enforcement and health officials. The move angered local officials, including District Attorney Terence Hallinan, who questioned the federal government's right to enforce local laws through federal courts and stated at a press conference the following Tuesday that the raid "shouldn't have happened."

California NORML Coordinator Dale Gieringer immediately denounced the act as "federal piracy," and, in conjunction with Americans for Medical Rights, a California health organization, mobilized a public relations campaign against federal interference. Three days after the raid, the nearby city of San Jose voted to regulate cannabis buyers' clubs, further underscoring the potential for the federal government to clash not only with state government, but with local governments as well. The Office of National Drug Control Policy, however, has stood firm. Action will be taken against those who grow and sell marijuana for as long as federal law forbids these activities, says the office.

FUTURE DIRECTIONS

Hoping that the recent publicity over California's Proposition 215 will help them push legislation through, NORML will be testifying and lobbying on behalf of bills that attempt to legalize medical use of marijuana at the state and federal levels. In 1997 10 states introduced legislation related to medicinal marijuana, and NORML testified on behalf of most of them. The organization expects more initiatives in the future, and plans to testify on behalf of as many as possible. In addition, the organization intends to monitor the federal government's level of compliance with state and local mandates that have legalized medicinal use.

GROUP RESOURCES

NORML has a Web site (http://www.norml.org) that offers information on how to become a member and on current issues and research, as well as a guide to marijuana laws and an on-line shopping catalog. The site also provides links to other advocacy Web sites and local NORML chapters. The public can E-mail NORML at norml@aol.com, write to 1001 Connecticut Ave., NW, Suite 1010-C, Washington, DC 20036, or call (202) 483-5500. NORML also provides a 900 toll number that costs callers $2.95 a minute and offers legal advice on drug testing and marijuana laws: 1-900-97-NORML. NORML maintains an extensive library with publications on marijuana issues that is open to the public at the NORML headquarters.

GROUP PUBLICATIONS

To order any of the following publications, write 1001 Connecticut Ave. NW, Ste. 1010-C, Washington, DC 20036, or call (202) 483-5500. NORML Foundation publishes a bimonthly newsletter, *Freedom@NORML*, monthly newsletters, *Ongoing Briefing* and *Pot Pourri*, and a bimonthly update, *Legislative Bulletin*. A weekly

media advisory is sent to 2,000 media outlets, and NORML also periodically publishes special research reports. NORML also produces the brochures *About Normal* and *Industrial Hemp*.

BIBLIOGRAPHY

Anderson, Patrick. *High in America: The True Story Behind NORML and the Politics of Marijuana*. New York: Viking Press, 1981.

Associated Press. "Anti-Marijuana Efforts Failing, Group Charges." *Las Vegas Review-Journal*, 2 August 1997.

Associated Press. "Bids to Curb Pot Failing Despite Funds, Group Says." *Arizona Republic*, 2 August 1997.

"Bait and Switch of Pot Legalizers." *Washington Times*, 5 January 1997.

Owen, Rob. "NORML Continues to Fight to Legalize Marijuana." *Richmond Times-Dispatch*, 7 June 1996.

"Pro-Marijuana Group Optimistic." *Washington Times*, 11 September 1989.

Rehg, Rob. "Campaign to Legalize Pot Resembles a Pipe Dream." *San Francisco Chronicle*, 20 August 1989.

Rosin, Hanna. "The Return of Pot." *New Republic*, 17 February 1997.

Stroup, R. K. "The Pot Lobby." *New York Times*, 21 January 1973.

Tannenbaum, Rob. "The Disciples of Pot." *Rolling Stone*, 28 May 1992.

National Organization for Women (NOW)

ESTABLISHED: June 30, 1966
EMPLOYEES: 34
MEMBERS: 250,0000
PAC: NOW/PAC; NOW Equality PAC

Contact Information:

ADDRESS: 1000 16th St. NW
     Washington, DC 20036
PHONE: (202) 331-0066
TDD (HEARING IMPAIRED): (202) 331-9002
FAX: (202) 785-8576
E-MAIL: now@now.org
URL: http://www.now.org
PRESIDENT: Patricia Ireland

WHAT IS ITS MISSION?

According to the National Organization for Women's (NOW) 1966 Statement of Purpose, "The purpose of NOW is to take action to bring women into full participation in the mainstream of American society, exercising all the privileges and responsibilities thereof in truly equal partnership with men." By the 1990s that mission had expanded. In 1996, according to NOW president Patricia Ireland, "Feminism is not just about women's rights. NOW's purpose must offer a clear understanding of what it means to be a feminist organization concerned with ending race, class, and other issues of oppression that come from a patriarchal structure."

NOW has always maintained that its focus was to better the position of women in society, working toward equality in every arena. Over its 30-plus year history, NOW has defined and redefined its own goals in response to changing times and a changing membership. In 1966 NOW was concerned with economic and social issues in the United States. Today the organization concerns itself with women's issues worldwide.

HOW IS IT STRUCTURED?

NOW has national headquarters based in Washington, D.C. It is headed by four national officers, who are elected to four-year terms by a delegate assembly. Officers must be members of NOW for at least four years and have served as a state or chapter leader for one year prior to election. They may serve for only two consecutive terms in any one office. The president acts as the

main spokesperson for NOW as well as its chief executive and financial officer. The officers also sit on the National Board and conduct all national meetings.

A National Convention is held each year in June or July. Delegates to the convention vote on all aspects of NOW policy, and it is through the convention that the main architect of organization is formalized. If a local chapter initiates a national action, it must first be proposed, then approved at the National Convention by a majority of the delegates. Only then does it become binding on the entire membership.

NOW's national board meets every two months and votes on any policy matters that arise between national conferences, as well as on any disciplinary actions toward members, chapters, or officers deemed to have violated NOW policy.

The state organizations largely mirror the national structure, with bylaws and officers and a governing board all drawn from local chapters. Each state coordinator either serves as a lobbyist to the state legislature on behalf of the state organization in matters of policy or hires one to act in her place. There are also nine regional chapters. Each region elects a representative to the 42-member national board.

NOW has over 550 local chapters. The chapters elect officers, who are usually unpaid except in large urban chapters. In addition, the chapters elect delegates to the national convention. The parent organization depends on its chapters to generate interest in its work, and frequently it is at the local level that timely issues first arise and come to national notice. Los Angeles NOW, for example, was very active during the O.J. Simpson case, highlighting the issue of violence against women. A Rochester, New York, chapter fought a sustained campaign against alleged pornography on a cable-access channel. Each chapter tailors task forces to meet the particular needs of their community.

PRIMARY FUNCTIONS

NOW remains focused on its original goals of supporting sexual, racial, economic, and constitutional equality for all people. NOW leaders are highly visible, lobbying for social issues such as gay/lesbian rights and organizing public actions to capture the attention of the public and the media. Special events such as demonstrations and marches are an important part of NOW's public awareness strategy. A favorite method is the "Zap action," which is a protest action designed to attract public and press attention to an issue. An example occurred in 1992 when a young pregnant woman protested the FDA ban on the drug RU486, which induces abortion. Having had a U.S. physician prescribe the pill, she obtained it in Europe where it is legal. When she arrived at Kennedy Airport in New York, the woman was greeted by NOW President Patricia Ireland and Feminist Majority President Eleanor Smeal. Customs confiscated her prescription, resulting in a controversial media event.

NOW's president serves as the group's chief lobbyist, attempting to gain support for legislation NOW supports as well as expressing the organization's opposition to new or existing legislation. NOW has consistently supported the 1973 Supreme Court decision *Roe v. Wade,* which struck down existing state laws prohibiting abortion, and has worked to repeal legislation that restricts reproductive freedom. NOW frequently issues press releases defining the organization's stance on pending legislation or socially significant cases pending in the court system and announcing new initiatives by the organization.

NOW also provides advocacy for individual cases that have feminist repercussions and often enters debates as a means of exposing an issue to closer scrutiny. Through its education and litigation arm, the NOW Foundation, Inc., the organization enters court actions as amicus curiae, or "friend of the court." NOW was instrumental in freeing Dr. Elizabeth Morgan, a mother imprisoned for civil contempt in a child custody case in 1987 and finally released in 1989. The "Morgan Bill" signed that year limited the time a person could be incarcerated for contempt to 18 months.

PROGRAMS

Because NOW is an organization that actively rallies for change, it sponsors a number of programs and initiatives directed toward securing basic human rights. Programs are educational, thought provoking, and always action-centered.

NOW launched the Women-Friendly Workplace Campaign on March 8, 1997, International Women's Day. The program aims to address the ongoing problem of sexual harassment, unequal compensation, and workplace hazards. A letter from the officers of NOW to NOW activists suggested a plan of action at the chapter level, specifically targeting one company for scrutiny. The letter offered a pledge for employers and another for consumers that asked employers to "provide a workplace free of discrimination based on sex, race, sexual orientation, age, marital or family status, pregnancy, parenthood, disability, or size." Local politicians were also urged to sign the pledge. National NOW targeted Mitsubishi Motor Manufacturing, citing a lawsuit by the Equal Employment Opportunity Commission alleging that "300 to 500 women had been verbally harassed and physically assaulted by co-workers and supervisors." NOW termed Mitsubishi a "Merchant of Shame" in 1996 along with brokerage firm Smith Barney.

NOW president and abortion rights supporter Patricia Ireland stuffs a court order in the pocket of Keith Tucci, executive director of Operation Rescue outside an abortion clinic. The order was a temporary injunction prohibiting anti-abortion activists from coming within 100 feet of a clinic that provides abortion services. (AP/Wide World Photos)

BUDGET INFORMATION

In 1997 NOW's total income was $5,585,500 against total expenses amounting to $5,854,920. NOW depends on membership dues ($4,007,500) and contributions ($1,170,000) for most of its income. The national organization funds state and local chapters primarily through renewal dues; approximately 37 percent of the dues paid each month goes directly to the chapters. Chapters also fund raise themselves for any other needed income. Political projects and communication initiatives receive a significant portion of NOW's budget, as do education and actions (rallies and marches), fund raising, and membership development. NOW's Washington staff is paid out of its administrative budget.

HISTORY

NOW was established on June 30, 1966, in Washington, D.C., by women attending the Third National Conference of the Commission on the Status of Women. First held in 1961, the commission reported "that despite having won the right to vote, women in the United States still were discriminated against in virtually every aspect of life." NOW began with 28 core activists. Among the first leaders were Betty Friedan, author of the best-selling *The Feminine Mystique* (1963), considered the first manifesto of the modern women's movement; and the Rev. Pauli Murray, an Episcopal priest and African American author and activist.

As a leader in the Women's Liberation movement, NOW quickly gained national attention through demonstrations, grassroots activism, and often sensationalist media coverage. Such attention drew celebrity followers; activist and actress Marlo Thomas and her spouse, popular talk show host Phil Donahue were among the early well-known members of NOW.

"Consciousness raising" in the 1960s took form for feminists with the "Click!," the experience of gaining sudden insight into the innate sexism in everyday life. The "Click!" was a concept popularized by journalist Gloria Steinem, founder and editor of *Ms.* magazine, established in 1972. NOW greatly benefited by the popularity of *Ms.,* which while not officially affiliated with NOW directed attention to the group's political and social agendas. *Ms.* became an outlet for feminist writing and squarely targeted the industry of advertising that feminists considered "sexist." Certainly the magazine encouraged active participation in feminist politics, and editor Steinem continued to work closely with the organization, while not participating in NOW's political structure.

As NOW grew rapidly in size and political effectiveness, factions within the organization became more vocal and diverse. Specifically division centered around membership inclusion. While the stated aim of feminism was to represent all women, the early appeal of NOW was primarily to educated, middle-class white women. Member friction forced NOW to significantly evolve in order to better represent the needs of all women, notably women of color and lesbians.

Over the years diversity became an important thread running through the organization. In 1973 it formed its first task force on women of color. In 1980 NOW launched an internal affirmative action program, and by 1999 women of racial and ethnic diversity comprised one-third of the organization's national board and 19 percent of its staff. In February of 1998 NOW organized a Women of Color and Allies Summit called "Linking Arms in Dangerous Times." Approximately 600 activists attended the summit to investigate strategies to eliminate racism, classism, and sexism.

By 1975 the support of lesbian rights became one of NOW's priority issues. National conferences were held in 1984 and 1988. NOW activists were key players in the 1979 *Belmont v. Belmont* case that expanded the definition of family to include lesbian partners and awarded a lesbian mother custody of her children.

The Reagan-Bush era of the 1980s was generally regarded as a period of lost ground for feminists in general. The Conservative Far Right was overtly hostile to NOW, declaring feminism responsible for the erosion of the family. Patrick Buchanan, Republican columnist and one-time political candidate, declared feminism "out of touch with the times and the country." In particular, the defeat of the Equal Rights Amendment (ERA) in 1983 was a significant blow to NOW. When the amendment failed NOW scrambled to regroup and energize its followers.

The organization experienced a resurgence in the 1980s when NOW activist Ellie Smeal returned to office in 1985. Smeal's presence marked the return to a more aggressive grassroots effort harkening back to NOW's earliest days. Her dynamic style helped make NOW seem less "mainstream" and more assertive during a time when the organization needed an image boost. This push to the fore was in response to the cultural conservatism exemplified by the prominence of Phyllis Schlafly, a long-time conservative activist who had created the STOP ERA organization. Claiming that women would be forced into combat duty and compelled to share unisex toilets, Schlafly helped successfully foil NOW's all-out effort to pass the ERA. Her group Eagle Forum campaigned to defeat feminist and gay/lesbian political initiatives and achieved significant influence in the Republican Party.

In the 1992 presidential campaign, NOW and other feminist groups who repudiated the social policies of the Reagan-Bush era threw their support behind Democratic candidate Bill Clinton. Women's issues were discussed extensively during the campaign, and NOW/PAC and EMILY's List, a political action group that supported Democratic women running for office, were instrumental in electing senators, notably the first African American woman senator, Carol Mosely Braun of Illinois. With the election of Bill Clinton in 1992, women's groups expected a significant reward for their support.

The media dubbed 1992 the "Year of the Woman" as women were elected in record numbers to offices across the country. During the 1990s NOW continued to be heavily involved in electoral politics, viewing women in politics as essential to fundamental societal change. But the organization also often opposed the policies of the Clinton administration, claiming that many campaign promises were broken. In particular, they disparaged Clinton's welfare reform proposals as harmful to women and children

CURRENT POLITICAL ISSUES

NOW has become immediately identified with social issues that have concerned women for decades and has proven to be a major force in effecting change for women. NOW's official priorities include "winning economic equality and securing it with an amendment to the U.S. Constitution that will guarantee equal rights for women; championing abortion rights, reproductive freedom and other women's health issues; opposing racism and fighting bigotry against lesbians and gays; and ending violence against women."

In the 1990s NOW activists lobbied for the Family Leave Act signed into law by President Clinton in 1993, and turned its attention to marriage and family law, children's rights, and preserving social programs that benefit families. Defining the new families (gays and lesbians raising children, as well as single parent families) continued to be a controversial issue. And reproductive rights, a rallying point for NOW from its inception and always bitterly contested in U.S. politics, reached crisis proportions.

Case Study: Abortion Clinic Violence

Since the late 1960s NOW has "supported access to safe and legal abortion, to effective birth control, and to reproductive health and education. We oppose attempts to restrict these rights through legislation, regulation, or constitutional amendment." It was a strong proponent of the groundbreaking 1973 *Roe v. Wade* decision that recognized a women's right to abortion and it continues to protect this decision even though the high court ruling has been challenged time and again by individual states.

Equally strong in their beliefs are individuals and organizations who support the anti-abortion, Right-to-Life movement. Staging marches and demonstrations, the Right-to-Life movement gained strength throughout the

BIOGRAPHY:
Betty Friedan

Author; Activist (b. 1921)   Betty Friedan is one of the world's foremost spokespersons on women's rights issues. Her radical viewpoints emerged in her first book published in 1963. Said Cornell University President Hunter Rawlings in 1998, "Betty Friedan redefined the place of American women in society with the publication, thirty-five years ago, of *The Feminine Mystique*." Friedan was not born the feminist activist. Following World War II (1939–45), the former university honors student accepted society's expectations that she give up her career as a reporter to make room for the men returning from the war. She quit her job, married, had three kids, and accepted her role as a suburban housewife. She slowly came to see herself mirrored in women's magazines of the day, but found herself at odds with the reflection. She turned to writing. After the success of *The Feminine Mystique*, Friedan spearheaded efforts to organize delegates representing women's groups nationwide, founding the National Organization for

Women (NOW). In her 1981 book, *The Second Stage*, Friedan tackled an issue she'd pondered for ten years–the problem of a divisive, growing polarization of the sexes. Heavily criticized for betraying the women's movement, Friedan's book favors male-female equality and contrasts it with the myth that grew out of the feminist movement of the superwoman who

juggles career, marriage, and family. Friedan's ability to cut her own path, and the requisite tolerance for controversy, have made her a popular lecturer well into her seventies. Her most recent work, *The Fountain of Age* (1993), challenges conventional perceptions surrounding the process of aging.

1980s and early 1990s, peaking with a speech by President George Bush at the March for Life in 1992. He told the assembled crowd of 70,000, "I'm with you in spirit." Peaceful marches were not enough for some fringe groups, who took their beliefs to the extreme.

Doctors and clinics performing abortions were targeted by Operation Rescue, a radical group dedicated to shutting down clinics by blocking entrances with their bodies. Over 2,000 people were arrested in Wichita, Kansas, in 1991. After Wichita, Operation Rescue targeted Buffalo, New York, in 1992. NOW drew volunteers from across the country to Buffalo to form a human barricade around the clinics, barring Operation Rescue protesters. President Patricia Ireland moved NOW's national board meeting to Buffalo, public support for Operation Rescue did not materialize, and the protest ended two weeks later. Called "Operation Fizzle" by the press, Operation Rescue steadily lost support, only to be replaced by a more radical and violent group called the Lambs of Christ, who first came to prominence at the Republican National Convention in Houston, Texas.

Once again, NOW effectively foiled the protest, but the Lambs went underground and began to target doctors, picketing their homes and threatening their lives. When clinic workers and doctors were murdered in Florida, NOW stepped up the pressure on the Justice Department to investigate clinic violence. In 1994 NOW successfully petitioned the Supreme Court in *National Organization for Women, Inc. v. Scheidler* to apply the

RICO Act (a federal anti-racketeering act which had been used against criminal organizations) to clinic violence. In 1998 a federal jury supported the 1994 findings and declared that Joel Scheidler, executive director of the Pro-Life Action League, and members of Operation Rescue were guilty of racketeering, essentially using intimidation tactics to bar women from their right to abortion.

This legal victory significantly slowed the incidence of violent protests, but did not deter incidents altogether. In January of 1998 a bombing occurred at a Birmingham, Alabama, clinic, killing a security guard and seriously injuring a nurse. In October of 1998 Dr. Barnett Slepian was shot and killed in his home outside Buffalo, New York. NOW, along with other feminist and abortion rights groups as well as the American Medical Association, appealed for a federal investigation. The Justice Department announced that it would form a task force to investigate a possible network linking episodes of clinic violence, take measures to prevent such violent incidents, and prosecute individuals and organizations.

SUCCESSES AND FAILURES

NOW's most significant disappointment has been the failure to enact the ERA, which has been NOW's major legislative objective since its inception. A 1978

"Declaration of a State of Emergency" stated: "The ERA is the foundation on which all our gains rest. If the ERA is defeated, it will be perceived as a vote against equality for women. The gains women have made in the past 15 years will be eroded and erased. Worse yet, every future effort we make will be dismissed with the excuse that when the ERA failed, it proved that the women of this country didn't want equality."

The ERA was first written in 1921 by suffragist Alice Paul and has been introduced in every session of Congress since 1923. It passed Congress in 1972, but was only ratified in 35 out of a necessary 38 states by the July 1982 deadline. Section 1 of the amendment declares, "Equality of Rights under the law shall not be denied or abridged by the United States or any state on account of sex."

Despite unprecedented effort, the ERA was eventually defeated because of a perception on the part of the public that society would be adversely affected by the amendment. The Religious Right gained tremendous momentum by depicting the amendment (and feminism) as destructive to family life, promoting homosexuality, and blurring gender roles. However, the failure of the amendment galvanized NOW to reassess and refine its goals. The "failure" has helped NOW rally support for a variety of causes and to become a powerful political network that focuses two political action committees, NOW/PAC and NOW Equality PAC, on electing pro-ERA candidates.

FUTURE DIRECTIONS

NOW has made a concerted effort to attract young women into its membership. In April of 1997 high school- and college-age women met at a "Young Feminists Summit." Sexual harassment, acquaintance rape, reproductive rights, body image, and eating disorders were among the workshop topics. Amy De Bower, a member of NOW's national young feminist committee, stated "We're going to have an effective third wave of feminism because we're addressing the needs of the people who are going to fuel it." NOW continues working hard to combat that the idea that feminism is irrelevant to today's women, an assertion made among others by Christina Hoff-Sommers, an academic who claimed the

feminist "elite" has alienated women in her widely reviewed book *Who Stole Feminism?*

GROUP RESOURCES

NOW maintains a Web site at http://www.now.org that incorporates many key documents relating to its history, issues, and legislative activities. It produces frequent press releases on political issues, available on the Web site, and informational videos on NOW history. The organization's "Action Alert List" E-mails updates on issues and appeals to its membership to ask for letter-writing and phone campaigns targeting legislators or corporations, soliciting funds, and other purposes.

GROUP PUBLICATIONS

NOW publishes *National NOW Times*, a bimonthly newsletter, and informational brochures, such as *Together We Can Change the World* and *Valuing Diversity*. These and other publications can be obtained by contacting NOW at (202) 331-0066 or via E-mail at now@now.org.

BIBLIOGRAPHY

Carabillo, Toni, Judith Meuli, and June Bundy Csida. *The Feminist Chronicles 1953–1993*. Los Angeles: Women's Chronicles, 1993.

Forman, Gayle. "The Nuts 'n' Bolts of NOW." *Ms.*, July/August 1996.

Goldberg, Carey. "Thousands March to Battle New Right." *New York Times*, 15 April 1996.

Gornick, Vivian. "Who Says We Haven't Made a Revolution? A Feminist Takes Stock." *New York Times Magazine*, 15 April 1990.

Idelson, Holly. "Abortion Clinics Can Use RICO to Fight Violence. (National Organization for Women, Inc. v. Scheidler)." *Congressional Quarterly Weekly Report*, 29 January 1994.

Schneir, Miriam. *Feminism in Our Time: The Essential Writings: World War II to the Present.* New York, N.Y.: Vintage, 1994.

Sommers, Christina Hoff. *Who Stole Feminism? How Women Have Betrayed Women.* New York, N.Y.: Simon & Schuster, 1994.

National Organization on Disability (NOD)

ESTABLISHED: 1982
EMPLOYEES: 13
MEMBERS: None
PAC: None

Contact Information:

ADDRESS: 910 16th St., Ste. 600
    Washington, DC 20006
PHONE: (202) 293-5960
TDD (HEARING IMPAIRED): (202) 293-5968
FAX: (202) 293-7999
E-MAIL: ability@nod.org
URL: http://www.nod.org
PRESIDENT: Alan A. Reich
CHAIRMAN: Michael R. Deland

WHAT IS ITS MISSION?

According to the organization, the National Organization on Disability (NOD) "promotes the full and equal participation of America's 54 million men, women, and children with disabilities in all aspects of life. NOD was founded in 1982 at the conclusion of the United Nations International Year of Disabled Persons. NOD is the only national disability network organization concerned with all disabilities, all age groups, and all disability issues." NOD is an action group that seeks the economic and social advancement of all disabled persons, unlike groups organized around a specific disability.

HOW IS IT STRUCTURED?

The decision-making council of NOD is composed of a board of directors and an executive director. NOD is managed by a staff of approximately 13, five of whom administer NOD programs. Other personnel include a development officer, a community affairs director, and executive assistants. State representatives of NOD help execute NOD programs, but they also hold positions in and have responsibilities with other organizations. NOD is a nonprofit organization, and it has no political action committee (PAC) that lobbies Congress on its behalf. While NOD does not have a membership in the traditional sense, it works on behalf of the 54 million disabled Americans who participate in or affected by NOD's work.

PRIMARY FUNCTIONS

NOD is an advocacy and action organization created to eliminate the barriers disabled people face. These may be the social barriers of discrimination and prejudice, the physical challenges of using public transportation, or economic barriers like the high unemployment rate among the disabled. Although there are exceptions, such as NOD's Start on Success (SOS) Internship Program, NOD generally does not work directly with individuals. Instead NOD takes a top-down, institutional approach to helping the disabled. It works with local governments, churches, and communities. For instance NOD's Community Partnership Program provides cash awards to communities whose efforts for the disabled are extraordinary. NOD's Religion and Disability program "That All May Worship" is designed to make places of worship more accessible and accommodating to those with disabilities.

NOD also encourages existing institutions to be more responsive to the needs of the disabled. For example NOD attacks the high unemployment rate that plagues its constituency through its CEO Council Program that recognizes and rewards chief executive officers (CEOs) of corporations who work to employ more disabled people. It also advises businesses on disability-related issues. It is NOD's hope that changing social institutions changes our society. Sometimes NOD's work is meant to change the public's perception of the disabled and their contributions to society. For instance NOD worked to have a wheelchair added to the President Franklin Delano Roosevelt (FDR) Memorial in Washington, D.C. to illustrate the capability of disabled persons. The absence of the wheelchair reflected the fact that it was not widely known that Roosevelt used a wheelchair during his presidency.

The Franklin D. Roosevelt Memorial in Washington, D.C., opened in 1997. Roosevelt spent most of his adult life in a wheelchair as a result of polio. The National Organization of Disability protested the fact that the memorial did not depict Roosevelt in a wheelchair. (Photograph by Brian K. Diggs. AP/Wide World Photo)

PROGRAMS

NOD has developed several major initiatives that apply a societal approach to helping the disabled. They represent distinct efforts designed to address the unique problems of the disabled in a variety of arenas. Many focus on educating people about those with disabilities, while others focus on helping the disabled to enjoy fulfilling lives.

Community Partnership Program (CPP)

The CPP is an educational program for towns, cities, and counties. Used by 4,500 communities, the CPP's goal is to train and assist communities to be more responsive to disabled citizens. NOD offers instruction in the form of advice and manuals.

Communities apply NOD instructions customized for their needs. For example, communities might use NOD resources to help educate its citizens to be more aware of the needs of the disabled. A town may need NOD to help local business implement reforms that are part of the Americans with Disabilities Act (ADA). NOD offers cash awards to communities that are exceptionally successful at implementing a CPP program. These awards, for excellence in training, education, or awareness, are sponsored by United Parcel Service (UPS) and are meant to help initiate community participation in the CPP.

World Committee on Disability

The World Committee on Disability is an international NOD program that seeks to enforce the United Nations (UN) World Programme of Action Concerning Disabled Persons, a global version of the kinds of activities NOD carries out locally. This UN program resulted from a resolution to bring economic and social reforms to countries whose policies toward the disabled may be less advanced or progressive than those of other nations.

Start on Success (SOS)

SOS is a unique program for NOD because of its direct contact with individuals with disabilities. SOS works to counteract the chronic unemployment that many disabled people face by offering disabled high school students paid internships in partnership with businesses nationwide. These jobs range from dough maker at a pizza parlor to clerk at a law office, and help to illustrate the idea that the interns can be as successful as anyone else in the business world.

BUDGET INFORMATION

NOD is a 501(c)(3) tax-exempt, nonprofit organization. NOD receives no government funds and is supported entirely by private donations from individuals, corporations, and foundations. Information detailing NOD funding and spending was not made available.

HISTORY

Established in 1982 at the conclusion of the UN International Year of Disabled Persons, NOD was created as an all-purpose advocacy group for the disabled. Before the creation of NOD, a general disability advocacy group did not exist. Organizations tended to be specialized, working specifically for a group such as the blind (the National Federation of the Blind) or for individuals whose disability was incurred during military service (Disabled American Veterans). At the time many individuals were concerned about threatened cuts in social spending by President Ronald Reagan. These cuts meant reduced government spending on Medicaid, education, and other social welfare programs which often direct some of their funding toward assisting the disabled.

In 1985 NOD created the World Committee on Disability to help implement the UN's World Programme of Action. The newly-formed committee conducted conferences and events and worked with leaders of disability organizations in other nations. In the late 1980s, and in keeping with the belief of the UN that all people were entitled to a set of basic human rights, NOD began to push for legislation that would guarantee such rights to the disabled.

NOD reached this goal in 1990 with the signing of the Americans with Disabilities Act (ADA). Prior to this legislation if a disabled individual felt discriminated against, the person had virtually no legal recourse. Lawsuits could be based on the rights guaranteed by the 1964 Civil Rights Act, but that legislation made no specific provisions for the disabled. If the physical characteristics of an office building, such as a lack of elevators, prevented a disabled person from working there, the disabled person simply would not be able to work there. The ADA established new rights meant solely for the disabled including the requirement that public transportation and buildings be wheelchair accessible.

Although passage of the ADA could not be attributed solely to NOD, the organization was a member of the coalition that worked for adoption of the legislation. The ADA helped change the structure of NOD. NOD discovered that businesses and communities needed help in understanding and implementing the ADA and the organization experienced associated growth throughout the 1990s.

While the ADA was a step in the right direction, the organization realized that there were still major obstacles to overcome for those with disabilities. In the early 1990s NOD focused on attacking the unemployment problem. In 1991 it created the CEO Council Program, encouraging a large number of businesses to rethink their stance on hiring the disabled. Several years later the SOS program was established and NOD was able to provide internships with businesses.

The end of the decade marked a period of success for NOD. In 1997 it was able to persuade a congressional committee to construct an FDR memorial to include a wheelchair, as a way of celebrating the former president's ability to accomplish so much in the face of his disability. Also that year Christopher Reeve, an actor who became paralyzed after being thrown from a horse, joined NOD as its vice chairman.

CURRENT POLITICAL ISSUES

Generally NOD does not directly engage in policy making or attempt to affect legislation. However NOD, on occasion, does become involved with political issues. For instance NOD was part of the coalition that supported passage of the ADA. One of the biggest and most visible of NOD battles and victories was its campaign to force the federal government to add a wheelchair to the FDR Memorial.

Case Study: A Wheelchair-less Memorial for a Wheelchair President

The FDR Memorial in Washington, D.C. is intended to honor the accomplishments of President Franklin Delano Roosevelt, who used a wheelchair for many years. NOD discovered in 1995 that the proposed memorial, however, contained no reference to the fact FDR relied on a wheelchair after contracting polio, an omission NOD felt was an oversight at best and an insult at worst. The exclusion of a wheelchair could be construed as an endorsement of the perception that his illness was a weakness. NOD saw it as a prominent and unacceptable symbol of society's prejudice toward the disabled.

NOD chairman Michael R. Deland met with the FDR Memorial Commission, a group established in 1955 to decide upon an appropriate memorial to the former president. He petitioned the commission to add a wheelchair and initially it refused. In the face of this,

NOD started its "FDR in a Wheelchair Campaign." Fifty-three disability groups endorsed NOD's campaign. It was largely a media campaign, with articles and editorials reminding Americans about Roosevelt's disability and the symbolic importance of including a wheelchair in the Memorial. It included a letter-writing campaign that brought thousands of letters into the offices of the FDR Memorial Commission. In addition the organization staged protests; a member of NOD's board of directors promised to chain himself to the White House fence if the government refused to add the wheelchair. Throughout 1996 and 1997 support for the addition came from President Bill Clinton, former Presidents George Bush, Jimmy Carter, Gerald Ford, and sixteen FDR grandchildren.

Eventually the commission came to agree with NOD. Just days before the memorial's dedication in May 1997, the Senate unanimously approved the resolution adding a depiction of a disabled Roosevelt in the Memorial. However, the Senate put a private funding stipulation onto the resolution to pay for the proposed $1.5 million addition. Subsequently the FDR in a Wheelchair Campaign became the FDR Wheelchair Fund, a capital campaign to pay for the addition to the FDR Memorial. The organization is in the process of soliciting contributions through its partnerships including the CPP, its Web site and through direct mail.

Public Impact

While Roosevelt was president, many people did not know that he needed a wheelchair. During his lifetime, the media was complicit in keeping the fact he was in a wheelchair a secret from the public. It was considered a courtesy not to mention it and his disability was seen as a possible sign of vulnerability. The public's belated discovery of Roosevelt's use of a wheelchair has help change the public's view of disability. Roosevelt's tenacity in the face of his disability can be seen as a symbol of the man's strength of character.

FUTURE DIRECTIONS

The challenges of disability may be eased by society's growing interest in being more responsive, but many obstacles remain. Even with the changes brought about by the ADA, the unemployment rate among the disabled remains disproportionate, at approximately 67 percent annually. To combat this, the organization plans to expand its CEO Council Program and SOS program. NOD hopes that this, along with the continuing shift in the public's perception of the disabled, will help its constituency become more self-supporting and fulfilled.

FAST FACTS

The percentage of companies that have employed people with disabilities rose two percent (62 percent to 64 percent) from 1986 to 1995.

(Source: The National Organization on Disability, 1997.)

GROUP RESOURCES

NOD maintains a Web site at http://www.nod.org that contains a condensed version of rights guaranteed by the ADA, a list of NOD publications, detailed information on NOD programs such as CPP, and a list of NOD State Representatives. Those interested in contacting NOD with further questions may write to the National Organization on Disability, 910 16th St. NW, Ste. 600, Washington, DC 20006, call (202) 293-5960, or E-mail the organization at ability@nod.org. NOD also offers a fact sheet about the organization, a brochure describing its programs, and the organization's annual report. These resources are free and available to the public by contacting the organization.

GROUP PUBLICATIONS

One of NOD's central publications is the *Disability Agenda* newsletter, containing information on the most recent efforts of NOD. It is available on-line at http://www.nod.org/attitudes.html. NOD also makes a variety of other publications available, including four NOD-cosponsored surveys of Americans with disabilities. Additional publications include fact sheets, annual reports, brochures and other publications about NOD. Instructions on establishing CPP, NOPP, and Religion and Disability programs are available in the form of guides like the *Guide to Organizing a Community Partnership Program* and *That All May Worship,* which provides instructions for religious organizations that want to make services and facilities more accessible to individuals with disabilities. A list of NOD's publications is available via the World Wide Web at http://www.nod.org/info.html#publications. Persons interested in obtaining more information about NOD's publications may write the organization at National Organization on Disability, 910 16th St. NW, Ste. 600, Washington, DC 20006 or call (202) 293-5960.

BIBLIOGRAPHY

DeMasters, Karen. "Hiring of Disabled is Strong." *New York Times*, 28 October 1998.

Gest, Ted. "Diplomacy on Wheels." *U.S. News and World Report*, 29 July 1996.

Karr, Albert. "A Court Ruling Would Expand Firms' Duty to Find New Jobs for Disabled Workers." *Wall Street Journal*, 17 November 1998.

Koretz, Gene. "A Law That Put People to Work." *Business Week*, 10 February 1997.

Leo, John. "Let's Lower the Bar." *U.S. News and World Report*, 5 October 1998.

Morris, Jenny. *Pride Against Prejudice*. Philadelphia: New Society, 1991.

Noah, Timothy. "Get Me Harry Hopkins." *U.S. News and World Report*, 13 July 1998.

Pear, Robert. "Clinton Proposes Aid for Disabled Returning to Jobs: No Penalty for Working; Health Benefits Would Be Paid by Expanding Budgets for Medicaid and Medicare." *New York Times*, 30 November 1998.

Thomas, Evan. "Remembering FDR: Disability Activists Win a Round in a Fight Over Presidential Public Image and Memorial Politics." *Newsweek*, 5 May 1997.

York, Thomas. "IT Offers Opportunities for Workers with Disabilities." *InfoWorld*, 21 September 1998.

National Restaurant Association (NRA)

WHAT IS ITS MISSION?

The objectives of the National Restaurant Association (NRA) are to represent, educate, and promote the food service industry. The food service industry includes owners and employees of full-service restaurants, cafeterias, quick service restaurants, and providers of food at institutions. The association's membership also extends to businesses that supply products and services to the food service industry, such as food suppliers or manufacturers of cooking equipment.

HOW IS IT STRUCTURED?

The NRA is a membership organization with national offices located in Washington, D.C. It is composed of six primary offices and divisions including the Executive Office, the Administrative Division, the Communications Division, the Convention Office, and the Government Affairs and Membership Division.

The Executive Office includes the president and vice presidents of the organization and their staffs. The president is selected following a national search and is hired by the board of directors. Members of the Executive Office oversee broad issues affecting the membership, such as new legislation. This office helps to create policy and programs for the NRA and works closely with the board of directors, which includes restaurant owners who are elected from the general membership.

The Administrative Division oversees activity within the organization, and it contains four departments: administration, finance, human resources, and legal. The

ESTABLISHED: 1919
EMPLOYEES: 276
MEMBERS: 32,000 members representing more than 170,000 restaurant outlets
PAC: National Restaurant Association PAC

Contact Information:

ADDRESS: 1200 Seventeenth St. NW
Washington, DC 20036
PHONE: (202) 331-5900
TOLL FREE: (800) 424-5156
FAX: (202) 331-2429
E-MAIL: info@dineout.org
URL: http://www.restaurant.org
CEO: Herman Cain

administration department oversees the daily operations of the organization, while the finance department deals with all financial matters. The human resources department attends to issues concerning employees, and the legal department represents the organization in legal matters and monitors its actions to make sure it complies with all federal regulations.

The Communications Division offers a wide variety of services to members. It includes the research department, the technical services department, the information response department, the public health and safety department, and the information services and technology department. This division responds to inquiries from members about issues or crises that might prompt attention from the media; it also responds directly to calls from the press and feeds information pertinent to the restaurant industry to news organizations. It also creates and distributes a wide variety of publications and sponsors the Great Menu Contest, a competition open to all restaurateurs that looks for excellence in the design and marketing of their menus.

The Convention Office prepares for the yearly exhibition of products, technology, and services, as well as educational programs, at NRA's trade show, held each May in Chicago. The event, which is free to members, draws about 100,000 visitors.

Staff in the NRA's Government Affairs Division liaison with national political leaders and, through its political action committee, contribute funds to legislators sympathetic to NRA's cause. It also organizes grassroots programs which are active in speaking out for or against legislation, and it organizes a yearly conference between restaurateurs and political leaders. The Membership Division offers a variety of benefits to members, including insurance coverage, car rental and hotel discounts, and a credit card program.

PRIMARY FUNCTIONS

Through the various initiatives of its divisions and departments, the NRA functions primarily to serve the needs of its members and to promote issues key to the food service industry. Through its political action committee and its grassroots efforts, it actively represents the views of its membership to legislators. It provides an extensive number of programs to educate members about all areas of the food service industry, that are ever broadening to meet changing industry trends. It also focuses on promoting the food service industry to the public and can be credited with improving the overall quality of eateries in the United States by constantly surveying patrons about their dining-out habits and passing that information along to NRA members, who strive to meet consumer demands.

The Information Services Department and the Technology Department respond to general questions about restaurant operation from restaurant owners, while the Information Response Department answers specific inquiries about restaurant facilities and equipment. The Public Health and Safety Department helps restaurateurs follow standards that ensure clean and safe food and surroundings for consumers.

The Research Department performs surveys on topics relating to restaurant trends, ranging from wages and benefits to consumer demands. It publishes its survey results in the NRA's monthly magazine, "Restaurants USA." The department also publishes a variety of how-to manuals on topics critical to running a restaurant, such as hiring, marketing, and accounting, and maintains computerized listings of consultants and software vendors that serve the restaurant industry.

PROGRAMS

The NRA offers a variety of programs for members. In the area of government affairs, members can become involved in the Grassroots Program, which organizes and coordinates a network of local representatives who communicate regularly with federal legislators and government officials in order to gain mutual understanding. The Congressional Leadership Forum is a political education program that promotes contact between food service operators, suppliers, and federal government officials at a variety of events.

Educational Foundation

NRA is affiliated with the Educational Foundation, which offers training and testing programs for restaurant servers, managers, and security personnel. It also produces materials, including books, manuals and videotapes, for training managers and employees.

The Educational Foundation offers a Foodservice Management Professional (FMP) Certification Program which recognizes successful professionals who meet education requirements, have specified experience in the industry, and pass a comprehensive examination. The Management Skills Program provides training for managers in key areas such as administration, finance, human resources, marketing, and operations.

The SERVESAFE Program teaches people how to train restaurant staff in areas such as food safety, responsible alcohol service, and employee and customer safety. The Customer Service and Serve Skills Program are dedicated to helping staff give quality service and increase customer satisfaction. The Foodservice Security Program offers comprehensive training focusing on maintaining a security staff and keeping the restaurant safe for employees and customers.

BUDGET INFORMATION

In 1997, the NRA received more than $25 million of its $40.5 million in annual revenues from the sale of books and other educational materials, and admissions and purchases at its annual convention. It earned more than $6 million from membership fees and its investments. Donations accounted for another $3 million, and the remainder was earned from rental income, auxiliary services, and other miscellaneous sources. Because it is a nonprofit organization, the funds it receives are used to pay staff salaries and to continue its overall operation.

HISTORY

On October 16, 1916, a group of seven Kansas City restauranteurs met to discuss their mutual goals and concerns. One of the leaders of the group, Myron Green, reportedly declared, "If you have an idea and I have an idea and we trade them, then we each have two ideas." With this founding principle, the group began working for the interests of the restaurant industry.

The first meeting of the national organization was held on March 13, 1919, and the first convention took place in Kansas City that December. Sixty-eight restauranteurs from 16 states attended the original convention—an event that now draws more than 100,000 people from around the world to Chicago each May. The first president elected was John Welch, a restauranteur from Omaha, Nebraska.

Early Challenges

No sooner was the organization in place than Congress passed the Volstead Act ushering in Prohibition. Up to that time, many restaurants made most of their profits from the sale of alcohol, with food serving a secondary role. Leaders of the fledgling organization helped members adapt to the liquor-free environment by adding soft drinks and new food items to their menu. They also helped to find new outlets to sell food. And so was born the Howard Johnson franchises and White Castle, one of the country's first hamburger chains.

The Depression presented another crisis for the food service industry. Although Prohibition had ended by this time, fewer consumers had the money to pay for the luxury of dining out. The association offered its members moral support as well as practical suggestions on cutting food costs, managing labor problems, increasing business volume, and responding effectively to government action.

World War II and the Post-War Era

As the country plunged into World War II, restaurants faced food, equipment, and labor shortages. NRA

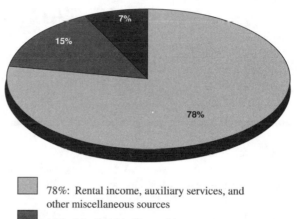

BUDGET:
1997 NRA Expenses

- 78%: Rental income, auxiliary services, and other miscellaneous sources
- 15%: Membership fees and investments
- 7%: Donations

conventions were canceled in 1941 and 1945 because of gasoline rationing and restrictions on travel. Nevertheless, the number of meals served in restaurants tripled from a prewar level of 20 million meals per day to 60 million per day.

In the decade after World War II, every aspect of the food service industry expanded to meet the demands of a thriving economy. During the 1950s, the association launched an industry lobbying effort to influence proposed federal minimum wage legislation, and it endorsed the use of credit cards.

The 1960s and 1970s

During the 1960s, the NRA continued to grow and encourage its members to adapt to the changing times. Lifestyles changed as young people rejected traditional values and turned to experimentation—an attitude that would leave a lasting impression on the food service industry. In the 1960s, for example, American restauranteurs escaped from the traditional French mode of cooking and began trying new ethnic foods and locally grown produce, a trend which continued throughout the next decade.

In 1979, the organization moved its headquarters from Kansas City, Kansas, to Washington D.C., occupying a building two blocks from the Capitol. The move signaled NRA's intention to become more active in politics. During that same period, it formed its Political Action Committee and began grappling with issues such

FAST FACTS

Approximately 50 billion meals are eaten at restaurants and school or work cafeterias each year.

(Source: "National Restaurant Association Industry Fact Book," 1999.)

as reporting tips, business meal deductions, labor laws, and the minimum wage—issues which are still relevant today.

The 1980s and Beyond

The association began taking an active stance on far-reaching social issues. It worked to increase the awareness of alcohol abuse, and it produced materials to help restaurant operators handle issues such as employees with HIV and AIDS, food allergies among consumers and staff, and proper nutritional labeling of food. NRA leaders also became more highly visible and outspoken, appearing on national news programs and helping to generate more than 8,000 newspaper articles a year on dining out.

The recession of the early 1990s brought economic difficulties to the restaurant industry. The industry also faced other hurdles in the form of more government regulations, such as the Family Leave and Medical Act, which required employers to allow staff members to take leaves of absence for designated reasons; the Americans With Disabilities Act, which required restaurants to spend money on making their facilities accessible to the disabled; and the business meal deduction, which reduced the tax deductible spending of business people who were dining out. "The government has become our greatest competitor," said Boston restaurant owner Stephen Elliott, adding that regulations steadily reduce a restaurant's profits. "There is a true need for us to bond as an industry in order to survive."

CURRENT POLITICAL ISSUES

The NRA has lent its voice to many issues facing the food service industry. Its lobbying and grassroots efforts have tackled legislation involving tax issues, labor issues, tourism, food and health safety, and licensing. Specifically, the NRA opposes any increase of the min-

imum wage from $5.15 an hour, which was instituted in September 1997, to $7.25 an hour. Their view is that restaurants are usually small businesses with extremely narrow profit margins. Restaurant owners object to even more profits being taken from their bottom line for wages. They also contend that minimum wage hikes would reduce the number of entry level jobs available, causing special difficulty for the scores of young people who work in these positions. It would also take away potential employment for the millions of people who are just off welfare and are entering the labor market.

The issues that are most controversial for the NRA involve perceived government interference into the food service industry.

Case Study: Tip Reporting

Frustrated by widespread underreporting of tips, the Internal Revenue Service (IRS) attempted to adopt a tracking process called the Tip Reporting Alternative Commitment (TRAC), which is an agreement between individual restauranteurs and the IRS. Under the agreement, restaurant owners would be mandated to educate employees about tip reporting and to ensure that employees honestly report their charge-card tips. The TRAC also threatened that the IRS would audit a restaurant's financial records back to 1988; normally, audits only target one to four years in the past. Such an audit would show how much the restaurant earned and give the IRS a better picture of how much servers and bartenders earned in tips and how much should have been reported. The NRA sees this type of aggressive auditing as an attempt to intimidate the industry.

In 1998 Congress passed a law to prevent the IRS from coercing restauranteurs into signing the Tip Reporting Alternative Commitment (TRAC). This victory was short-lived, however, when in October 1998 the U.S. Court of Appeals overturned a lower-court decision made in *Bubble Room, Inc., v. U.S.* The National Restaurant Association originally filed the case in 1996 on behalf of a member restaurant located in Florida. The IRS charged the restaurant for nearly $32,000 in back taxes after informing restaurant owners that employees had not reported all their tips. NRA's contention was that employees should be responsible for reporting their own income accurately, and the IRS should not make the employers responsible.

According to a news release issued October 21, 1998, by NRA CEO and President Herman Cain, the decision essentially will "force restaurant owners to become the 'tip police.'" At issue is whether the IRS has the right to charge a restaurant employer for tip income that employees earned but failed to report. The courts remain split on whether or not to uphold the latest decision. The NRA remains clear in its contention that it is the responsibility of the employee to declare tips and the responsibility of the restaurant employer to report the tips to the IRS.

FUTURE DIRECTIONS

The NRA will continue to be actively involved in monitoring legislation that affects the industry and speaking out on issues such as unionization, a requirement to provide employee health insurance, and efforts on the part of some musicians to collect fees from restaurants for playing the recorded music of their clients.

One area that is raising keen debate among members is a proposal that would prohibit smoking in all U.S. restaurants, not including bars. NRA membership is mixed in its reaction. Some believe the law would drive away business, while others, who already have voluntarily banned smoking in their establishments, say they have seen their business increase by as much as 15 percent. So far, the NRA has not adopted a position on the proposal because of the variety of views expressed by members.

GROUP RESOURCES

The NRA maintains an extensive Web site at http://www.restaurant.org, geared toward addressing the needs of its members. It includes a virtual Reading Room sponsored by the NRA's Educational Foundation that highlights industry statistics and regulations. The site also features press releases, consumer study reports, industry forecasts, and suggestions for grassroots involvement in food industry key issues.

GROUP PUBLICATIONS

The NRA makes numerous publications available to its members. *Food Service Information Abstracts* is a biweekly publication that compiles blurbs from a variety of trade magazines in the food service industry. "National Restaurant Association: Washington Weekly" is a newsletter that reports on legislation and regulatory issues affecting the food service industry. *Restaurant Industry Operations Report* offers an annual update on the condition of the industry across the United States, while *Restaurants USA* is a monthly magazine that keeps food service managers and operators abreast of trends and developments in the industry. In addition, the association publishes a variety of books, catalogs, pamphlets, and films on issues of interest to members.

The NRA publishes *Fork in the Road*, which is available twice per year, in March and September. This publication is aimed at high school students and offers a look at the restaurant industry and restaurant careers. The NRA offers one copy of *Fork in the Road* free of charge to the career counseling office of every public high school in the United States. Additional copies are available by calling 1-800-424-5156, ext. 5989. All other publications can be obtained by contacting the NRA's Communication Division at 1200 Seventeenth St. NW, Washington, DC; phone (202) 331-5900; fax (202) 331-2429.

BIBLIOGRAPHY

Ballon, Marc. "The Cheapest CEO in America." *Inc. Magazine Online,* October 1997.

Bianchi, Alessandra. "No Experience Required." *Inc. Magazine,* September 1997.

Parch, Lorie. "Beyond Alice's Restaurant." *Working Woman,* May 1998.

Scheidel, Carmen. "Where There's Smoke. . . There's Ire: Michigan Operators Sue Over Ban." *Restaurant Business,* 1 January 1999.

National Rifle Association of America (NRA)

ESTABLISHED: 1871
EMPLOYEES: 400
MEMBERS: 2.8 million
PAC: NRA Political Victory Fund

Contact Information:

ADDRESS: 11250 Waples Mill Rd.
    Fairfax, VA 22030
PHONE: (703) 267-1000
TOLL FREE: (800) 672-3888
FAX: (703) 267-3989
E-MAIL: nra-contact@nra.org
URL: http://www.nra.org
PRESIDENT: Charlton Heston
EXECUTIVE VICE PRESIDENT: Wayne R. LaPierre, Jr.

WHAT IS ITS MISSION?

According to the history of the National Rifle Association (NRA), it was originally established in 1871 "to provide firearms training and encourage interest in the shooting sports." Over 100 years later, the NRA continues that mission: "What members share with every other member is an appreciation of the shooting sports and . . . most of all, a commitment to safety, responsibility and freedom." Also integral to the NRA mission is the belief in the constitutional right to keep and bear arms. Specifically, the NRA maintains there should be no limits placed on the Second Amendment to the U.S. Constitution, which states: "A well-regulated militia, being necessary to the security of a free State, the right of the people to keep and bear Arms, shall not be infringed."

HOW IS IT STRUCTURED?

The NRA is a membership and lobbying organization based in Fairfax, Virginia. At the national level it is headed by a president, first vice president, second vice president, and executive vice president. Other officers include secretary, treasurer, and executive director of the NRA Institute for Legislative Action (ILA). The NRA's 76-member board of directors selects all posts except the executive director of the Institute, who is appointed by the executive vice president. All officers serve one-year terms; the only paid positions are executive vice president and executive director of the NRA-ILA. The executive vice president handles day-to-day operations of the organization. The president, vice presidents, and NRA board oversee the duties of both paid positions. The board meets about once a month.

On the board of directors, 25 members are elected annually to three-year terms. According to published reports, only life and five-year members may vote for these board members. A 76th member serves as director, a position created in 1994. The director is elected for a one-year term at the annual convention and, unlike the other 75 board positions, all NRA members may participate in the vote. The association has 36 standing and special committees.

The NRA has three regional divisions: eastern, central and western. The regions are further divided into 37 areas, or districts. Each area usually includes one or two states, and has its own representative.

In 1997, the NRA-Institute for Legislative Action and representatives of 21 firearms owners and industry groups around the world, met in Belgium "to formally establish an international organization dedicated to preserving the shooting sports worldwide." According to a NRA press release, "The World Forum on the Future of Sportshooting Activities will serve as an information-sharing round table, designed to keep the world's national and international firearms groups informed on threats to sportshooting." Other forum members included the British Shooting Sports Council, the Sporting Shooters' Association of Australia and the International Practical Shooting Confederation.

PRIMARY FUNCTIONS

As a membership organization the NRA is committed to providing service to its over 2 million members all of whom are sporting enthusiasts. To that end, the NRA has a number of divisions and departments devoted to all aspects of the shooting sports. Divisions include: firearm safety efforts, firearms training, law enforcement programs, junior shooting activities, women's issues, hunter/hunting services, recreational shooting, competitions, and gun collecting. Especially valued are the various gun safety and education initiatives because, according to the NRA, it is the responsibility of all gun owners to fully understand the laws regarding gun purchase and how to properly store, transport, and use all firearms.

Key to the NRA's mission is the defense of the Second Amendment. According to NRA released statements, if the Second Amendment is not upheld their other initiatives would not be possible. To that end the NRA wields a tremendous amount of clout politically, both in lobbying congressional members and giving campaign money to candidates who support the NRA's views and goals. The organization's Institute for Legislative Action follows and lobbies Congress to enact laws favorable to gun owners. Through the ILA's Grassroots Division, the NRA is particularly effective in mobilizing members to

action. In addition to promoting the passage of NRA-favored legislation, the organization also monitors proposed legislation, staunchly fighting any perceived attacks on the Second Amendment. The NRA has been extremely critical of the Clinton administration's anti-firearms position, especially its support of the Brady Act and the ban on assault weapons.

When legislation that challenges gun-owner's rights is enacted, the NRA continues to fight. For example, the NRA helped pay for appeals to the U.S. Supreme Court that overturned part of the Brady Act. In an effort to garner public support when these legislative battles arise, the NRA takes its case to the media. The NRA-ILA frequently issues press releases, criticizing any attempt to limit the Second Amendment. The organization also has considerable print press exposure featuring celebrity NRA members such as Tom Selleck, and air time on television and radio, including a radio talk show hosted by executive vice president Wayne LaPierre.

PROGRAMS

The NRA sponsors a variety of programs that focus on issues such as gun safety, firearms education, competitive shooting, hunting, personal protection, and gun collecting. The organization has 34,000 certified instructors nationwide who participate in the NRA's Basic Firearm Training Program. Courses offer hands-on training on how to safely and properly use weapons such as pistols, rifles, and shotguns. Other courses focus on areas such as home firearm safety.

The NRA is especially proud of its Eddie Eagle program, a gun safety program that serves nine million children in pre-school through sixth grade. For teenagers, the NRA sponsors a Youth Sports Fest Program that, according to its literature, "introduces young people to the NRA and to the fun and rewards of the shooting sports. Young people learn gun safety and participate in a variety of shooting sports activities in a well-supervised, positive environment."

"Project Exile" is an example of a program where the NRA works in collaboration with federal, state, or local government efforts to uphold existing gun laws. It is a program led by the United States Attorney's Office in Richmond, Virginia, to "banish armed criminals from city streets." Essentially the initiative mandates that when law enforcement officers apprehend a felon who is in possession of a gun, he or she will be swiftly prosecuted and "exiled" to a federal prison to serve a minimum five-year sentence. The NRA endorses and supports the program through its CrimeStrike Division. When the program began in 1998, Richmond had the second highest per-capita homicide rate in the United States. After the first six months of the program, city reports indicated that the homicide rate was cut in half.

National Rifle Association executive vice president Wayne LaPierre introduced Eddie Eagle at a 1997 press conference. The NRA hopes the mascot will be utilized to teach young children the importance of gun safety. (Photograph by Dennis Cook, AP/Wide World Photo)

BUDGET INFORMATION

NRA 1996 figures reported $140,580,668 in revenues. Members' dues accounted for $70,722,184; contributions were $38,425,937; program fees were $22,575,920; and investment income was $4,986,074. Expenses included $109,079,872 in program services; $16,733,522 in administrative costs; and $7,705,673 in fund-raising. Over a recent 8-year period, the NRA estimated that it spent more than $100 million on firearms safety and training.

The agency's political action committee is a key contributor to pro-gun and Republican candidates. A 1996 *Mother Jones* article noted the wealth of the NRA's Political Victory Fund, which the magazine says is the nation's largest political action committee: "In 1994, this PAC outspent all other groups with $5.3 million in direct campaign contributions, 'independent expenditures' on behalf of pro-gun candidates, and money for phone banks and mailings to NRA members telling them how to vote."

HISTORY

According to NRA literature, Col. William C. Church and Gen. George W. Wingate, who both served

in the Army of the Potomac during the Civil War, helped found the NRA a few years after the war ended in 1865. Both men felt that militia units at the time lacked marksmanship skills, that the New York area did not have enough shooting ranges, and that an organization could help develop shooting facilities in New York. Wingate's *Manual of Rifle Practice,* that appeared in six installments in the *Army and Navy Journal,* also helped spawn the push to establish the NRA. The organization gained a certificate of incorporation in New York state in 1871. The early NRA established gun training programs and competitions both within and outside the military and helped train future soldiers for World War I (1914–18). Prominent civilians who joined the NRA included inventor Thomas Edison.

Over the years, the NRA increasingly became concerned over anti-gun legislation, beginning with passage of the Sullivan Act in New York in 1911, all the way through the Brady Act of 1993. The NRA's Institute for Legislative Action, founded in 1975, "has since been the fighting force . . . for American firearm owners" to battle any attempt to enact gun control legislation. Such an escalation in political involvement has led some observers to strongly criticize the NRA. A July 1996 article in *Mother Jones* magazine asserts the NRA took a radical shift at its 1977 convention that moved the organization "from the hands of traditional sportsmen to those of militant political hard-liners." The story points to Neal

Knox, the politically influential former first vice president who has been on the NRA's board of directors, as the strong force pushing the NRA to a more hard-line stance.

The NRA's reputation was further tarnished when some NRA board member were accused of ties to militia groups. This was especially true following the 1995 bombing of the Murrah federal building in Oklahoma City. According to a 1997 article in *U.S. News and World Report* "Timothy McVeigh didn't help matters when, soon after being arrested for the Oklahoma City bombing, he proudly declared that he is an NRA member."

To combat such criticism and to bolster their image, the NRA launched a media blitz in the late 1990s, that called on a number of celebrity supporters. The most outspoken of these supporters was actor Charlton Heston, longtime NRA member and advocate. Heston's participation in the NRA escalated when he was elected president of the organization at the 127th national meeting in 1998. Said NRA's executive vice president, ". . . Moses is on our side."

BUDGET:
1996 NRA Revenue

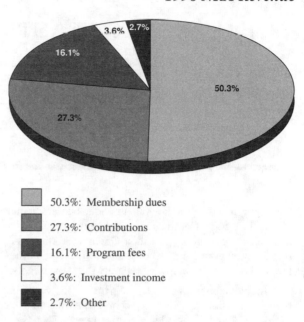

- 50.3%: Membership dues
- 27.3%: Contributions
- 16.1%: Program fees
- 3.6%: Investment income
- 2.7%: Other

CURRENT POLITICAL ISSUES

A strong lobbying presence on Capitol Hill and an influential financial supporter of congressmen, the NRA finds itself involved in a number of political issues. In particular the NRA works to influence or enact legislation to weaken or eliminate gun control laws. In the late 1990s, for instance, it was a harsh critic of proposals that would allow gun rationing, restrict licensing, transnational gun control, and legislation to force citizens to use gun trigger-locks.

A particular piece of legislation that was targeted by the NRA in the 1990s was the Brady Act of 1993. The Brady Act was named after James S. Brady, the former presidential press secretary who in 1981 was severely wounded in an assassination attempt on President Ronald Reagan. The NRA had said publicly the Brady law is flawed and does not work.

Case Study: The Brady Act

On November 30, 1993, President Bill Clinton signed the Brady Bill into law. This legislation required a five-day waiting period for individuals who were purchasing a handgun. The waiting period was intended to give local law enforcement officers time to check the background of potential gun buyers, and block the sale of a weapon if the buyer should not legally own a gun. The Brady Bill had first been introduced in the House of Representatives in 1987. The length of the battle over the generally popular legislation was attributed by many to the strength of the NRA's lobbying and public mobilization efforts. The *1993 CQ Almanac* described the Brady Bill as "the first major gun control legislation to

pass Congress since 1968." Although most advocates of the legislation conceded that it would have little effect on deterring crime, they touted the legislation as a good first step to reducing gun violence, as well as a chance to demonstrate that the powerful NRA could be dealt a legislative loss.

Despite its overall loss, the NRA was able to win a significant battle in the legislative war. Although the Brady Bill passed the House of Representatives by a vote of 238 to 189 and the Senate by a vote of 63 to 36, pro-Second Amendment legislators were able to enact a "sunset" provision as part of the bill. This provision, called the Gekas Amendment after Pennsylvania Republican Representative George Gekas, limited the period of time that the bill's five-day waiting period would be in effect. This meant that the five-day waiting period would expire on November 30, 1998, five years after passage of the legislation.

For years the NRA argued that the Brady Bill was not only an infringement upon Second Amendment freedoms, but that it also brought into question the balance of power between the national government and the states. In the June 1997 *Printz v. United States* case, the U.S. Supreme Court ruled in a five to four decision that the Brady law's provisions requiring state and local officials to conduct background checks during the five-day waiting period was unconstitutional. The case was brought by sheriffs from Montana and Arizona who claimed that

FAST FACTS

According to the Bureau of Alcohol, Tobacco, and Firearms, of the nearly 70 million individuals who own firearms in the United States, 11% have used them for defense.

(Source: Bureau of Alcohol, Tobacco, and Firearms, 1999.)

---

the requirements of the law put an undue burden on their offices in terms of both time and money. According to *New York Times* reporter Linda Greenhouse, the Court ruled that by giving directives to state officers, the Brady law violated the "principle of separate state sovereignty."

In November of 1998, the Brady Bill's waiting period provisions expired in accordance with the time limit imposed by the Gekas Amendment. They were replaced by a program known as the National Instant Criminal Background Check System (NICS). NICS had originally been proposed as an alternative to the Brady Bill in 1993, but had failed to pass. The NRA had advocated for an instant check system as a more effective crime prevention policy, and as a fully constitutional alternative to the five-day waiting period. According to the NRA Web site, the FBI—which administers the background check system—describes NICS as a "national database containing records of persons who are disqualified from receiving firearms." The NRA claims that the NICS computer system is able to check and clear gun purchases in less than two minutes and will be available from 9:00 A.M. to 2:00 A.M. Eastern Standard Time, seven days a week, closed only on Thanksgiving and Christmas. Such a system, the NRA contends, will provide a much more effective answer to gun control.

FUTURE DIRECTIONS

In the twenty-first century the NRA will, of course, continue to monitor and lobby against anti-gun legislation. It will also continue efforts to find more places and ranges to shoot safely and to improve the attitude of the public toward the legal, legitimate use of firearms. NRA administration also hopes to see a resurgence in membership: there were 2.8 million members in 1997, down from 3.5 million in 1995. Upon taking over the presidency, Charlton Heston made it a goal to not only increase membership, but to diversify membership to include more women and minorities. According to 1998 NRA estimations, only ten to fifteen percent of its membership were women.

GROUP RESOURCES

The NRA opened a National Firearms Museum in 1998 to showcase the history of firearms. Considered one of the most extensive collections of firearms in the United States, the museum is located at NRA national headquarters in Fairfax, Virginia. Admission is free and the museum is open to the public daily from 10 A.M. to 4 P.M. For more information, call (703) 267-1600.

The NRA maintains an extensive Web site at http://www.nra.org that provides members and the public insight into NRA's legislative activity. There are pages dedicated to children's education and safety information, as well as press releases and action alerts on timely issues.

The NRA Grassroots Division may be reached by calling 1-800-392-8683.

GROUP PUBLICATIONS

The NRA publishes several magazines available to members only including the *American Rifleman, American Guardian,* and *American Hunter.* Each magazine is published monthly, except for a combined November-December issue for each magazine. *InSights* is a magazine geared toward younger shooters and *NRA Shooting Education Update*, is published for members who are gun instructors and coaches. The organization produces a variety of educational and informational publications for all ages including brochures such as *A Parent's Guide to Gun Safety,* and videos including *Fundamentals of Gun Safety.*

Through its Research and Information Division, the NRA researches and analyzes election results, opinion polls, and legislation. It then produces brochures, pamphlets, and fact sheets that are distributed, upon request, to the press, legislators, and the public. Brochures include *The False Promise of Gun Control,* fact sheets include *NRA Firearms Glossary.* Full text of most are available on-line at http://www.nra.org. For more information, contact the NRA by mail at 11250 Waples Mill Rd., Fairfax, VA 22030; or by phone at 1-800-672-3888.

BIBLIOGRAPHY

"After the Fall." *New Republic,* 26 May 1997.

Anderson, Jack. *Inside the NRA: Armed and Dangerous.* Beverly Hills, Calif.: Dove, 1996.

CQ Almanac. "President Signs 'Brady' Gun Control Law." *1993 CQ Almanac,*.

Dreyfuss, Robert. "Good Morning Gun Lobby!" *Mother Jones,* July/August 1996.

Getlin, Josh. "Heston Chosen to Lead NRA Back to Mainstream." *Los Angeles Times,* 9 June 1998.

"Massachusetts Takes Aim at Gun Safety." *Nation's Health,* 1 December 1996.

Metaksa, Tanya. "Freedom, Guns and Women." *Economist,* 14 June 1997.

"Moses Fights for Gun Rights." *U.S. News and World Report,* 19 May 1997.

"NRA Challenge Ended." *New York Times,* 6 February 1997.

Seelye, Katherine Q. "The NRA Woos the World." *New York Times,* 6 April 1997.

———. "Gun Lobby in Bitter Power Struggle." *New York Times,* 30 January 1997.

"Thou Shalt Not Take the NRA's Name in Vain." *Time,* 19 May 1997.

National Right to Work Committee (NRWC)

ESTABLISHED: 1955
EMPLOYEES: 40
MEMBERS: Nearly 2 million
PAC: Right to Work Political Action Committee

Contact Information:

ADDRESS: 8001 Braddock Rd.
   Springfield, VA 22160
PHONE: (703) 321-9820
TOLL FREE: (800) 325-7892
FAX: (703) 321-7143
E-MAIL: info@nrtw.org
URL: http://www.nrtw.org
PRESIDENT: Reed Larson

WHAT IS ITS MISSION?

The National Right to Work Committee (NRWC) describes itself as "the only national organization that exclusively and solely promotes the right of an individual to work without being forced to join a labor union or pay union dues." The committee calls a system of forced dues "compulsory unionism," and its chief goal is to persuade Congress to pass a law making it illegal, nationwide. The group also fights what it perceives to be the abuses of unions. For instance, the committee wants to strengthen penalties for acts of violence committed by members of labor organizations during labor disputes.

HOW IS IT STRUCTURED?

The NRWC is an advocacy group with national headquarters located in Springfield, Virginia. It is staffed by approximately 40 employees, who are overseen by the group's officers, including a president, vice president for legislation, vice president for communication, and director of news and information. The National Right to Work Legal Defense Foundation is also housed at Virginia headquarters and functions as the NRWC's tax-exempt sister organization. The foundation takes on legal battles for individuals or groups of employees seeking to fight compulsory unionism and other perceived union abuses. So, while the Legal Defense Foundation works in the courts to win favorable interpretations of existing laws, the committee works in Congress and state legislatures for new laws. Both groups try to use the media and other public forums to sway public opinion.

The NRWC maintains an Institute for Labor Relations Research, which supplies studies and reports on issues related to compulsory unionism. It also has a political action committee (PAC), the Right to Work Political Action Committee, which was started by NRWC president Reed Larson, but is technically and legally a separate entity.

More than 30 state groups pursue the same cause as the National Right to Work Committee, but are not directly affiliated with nor have any legal ties to it. The national committee may, however, provide in-kind assistance and advice to these groups, but no funds or formal supervision. Some state groups take the advice and follow the lead of the committee to a greater extent than others. The majority of the local groups—and all of the most active ones—are located in states that do not have laws prohibiting unions from forcing employees to pay dues.

PRIMARY FUNCTIONS

One of the main functions of the NRWC is its effort to mobilize the public to contact Congress and state legislatures in support of laws that would prohibit compulsory unionism. The committee boasts of its ability to generate thousands of letters, telegrams, and telephone calls from its members when such laws are up for consideration. Around election time, the committee sends out hundreds of thousands of issue advocacy mailings—documents that inform the public of the voting records and positions of candidates on right-to-work issues, but do not endorse or oppose any particular candidate, since that would violate tax laws.

Committee officers also actively lobby elected officials and testify in hearings on alleged union abuses. The committee's Institute for Labor Relations Research provides studies backing its positions to legislators and state right-to-work groups across the United States. For instance, the committee offers data showing the relative economic performance of right-to-work states versus non-right-to-work states.

Through the National Right to Work Legal Defense Foundation, the organization provides free legal aid to employees or groups of employees. It does not accept cases from businesses. The foundation takes on cases with two objectives in mind: to enforce employee's existing rights against union abuse and to break new legal ground in expanding these rights. In addition to litigation, foundation attorneys and academic consultants work to develop new legal theories, economic data, and social science findings.

PROGRAMS

The NRWC has no dues requirements and maintains a loose criteria for membership; one has to simply donate

money or actively support the group's work to be considered a member. To that end, it provides no structured, formal member services. Member participation is limited to donating money and writing letters to politicians in support or opposition of legislation.

BUDGET INFORMATION

The NRWC gets no government funding and has no endowment. According to the committee's 1997 financial report, it received $8.5 of its $8.7 million in revenue from dues and contributions. The rest came from investment returns and miscellaneous income. The committee spent $6.9 million on its activities, including communication and other services for members, legislative activities, and activities to spread message to the public. The remainder of the group's $8.5 million in expenditures went for administrative and support services, including fund-raising activities.

HISTORY

In most states labor unions can deduct union dues from workers' paychecks whether they agree or not, and a union can establish itself as the representative for all employees in its bargaining unit in negotiations over pay and working conditions, whether or not a particular employee wants the union to represent them. Before 1958, this was the case in all states, which, according to some, represented a violation of workers' rights.

The National Right to Work Committee was founded in 1955 by conservatives who felt that unions had too much power. Longtime president Reed Larson explained the motivation for starting the group in a speech in 1996, "I've been working at this problem for more than 40 years, having decided many years ago that, unless we curtail the excessive political power of organized labor, the free enterprise system as we know it is destined for extinction in our country."

Since its formation the committee has fought tooth-and-nail against organized labor to establish right-to-work laws—laws that prohibit unions from requiring employees to pay dues. The first law of this type was passed in Kansas in 1958, where Reed Larson—a conservative World War II veteran and then-president of the Kansas Jaycees—directed the campaign. However attempts by national right-to-work committee members and their supporters to win such laws in five other states that year failed. Getting right-to-work laws through state legislatures has sometimes taken years, but the committee's successes are adding up. By 1998, 21 of the 50 states had enacted right-to-work laws. Those states, predominantly in the South and West, predictably had less unionized work forces in comparison to states that have not passed right-to-work laws.

FAST FACTS

In 1997 the median weekly earnings for unionized workers was $640; nonunion workers earned an average of $478 per week.

(Source: U.S. Department of Labor, 1998.)

National Right to Work Committee Legal Defense Foundation

Larson said it became clear to him in the latter half of the 1960s "that employees rights could be adequately defended only through a broad-based litigation program. I asked my board of directors to give me permission to organize a separate litigating organization," and in 1968 the National Right to Work Committee Legal Defense Foundation was born. When the foundation is successful, it often sets landmark precedents. For example, it was involved in the 1988 U.S. Supreme Court ruling in *Beck v. Communication Workers of America,* which established that the only activities for which private sector unions can force payment of dues, are activities related to collective bargaining. This means that if a worker objects to the way his or her dues are being used, they can request that a portion of their dues be refunded.

This was an important legal precedent for the foundation because it established the principle that unions cannot use dues to lobby, to help political candidates, or for any cause the worker does not support. The victory was seen by the committee as an important right for workers, although labor advocates argue that it is unfair to impose such rules on unions when corporations are not required to get shareholder approval for political activities.

Attempts to Pass a National Law

As well as triumph, the committee has also met with defeat, particularly in its efforts to establish a national right-to-work law. Larson claims the committee's efforts have been unsuccessful because the committee is outgunned. "Over the years," Larson said in a letter he sends to those seeking information about the group, "union bosses have proven themselves masters at controlling key federal positions (regardless of who's in charge), thereby dictating our country's labor policy. And they have billions of dollars, all accrued through forced union dues, at their disposal to try to block or reverse Right to Work's progress."

In attempts to wield similar power in Congress in the name of the right-to-work movement, the Right to Work Political Action Committee (PAC) has donated more than $800,000 to political candidates between 1987 and 1996. In the 1995–96 reporting year, the Right to Work PAC gave $142,080 in political contributions to Republicans, including North Carolina senator Jesse Helms and Congressmen Ernest Istook of Oklahoma.

CURRENT POLITICAL ISSUES

The committee involves itself in a number of issues relating to unions. Generally, it takes the position that workers should be empowered as individuals—the opposite from unions which emphasize strength in numbers. For example, the committee supports the right of employees to represent themselves rather than having a union represent them in negotiations over wages and benefits. Additionally, the committee has aided the defeat of bills that would have relaxed laws prohibiting the right to picket or strike. For instance in 1992 and 1994, Massachusetts Senator Edward Kennedy tried to pass a bill making it easier for unions to call strikes. The committee successfully worked against the bill, which it asserted "would have given big labor unprecedented power to call and win massive, job-crippling strikes."

But the committee's primary concern is gaining the right for employees to refuse to have union dues withheld from their paychecks. Employees have long exercised the right to have their dues used only for specific purposes, and to get a dues refund if their dollars are used for political purposes. But allowing workers to withhold dues altogether would take worker freedom to a new level—a level that labor organizations say could hurt unions' very existence.

Laws that bar such practices have become known as right-to-work laws, and 21 states have them. The National Right to Work Committee continues to work on further implementation of such laws, state by state. But their ultimate goal remains to have a national law passed.

Case Study: National Right-To-Work Act of 1996

In 1994 Republicans won control of both houses of Congress for the first time in decades, with some nine out of ten new Republican members pledging support for some type of right-to-work law. By 1996, with the presidential elections upcoming and a chance to put a national spotlight on the issue, the time seemed ripe to make an all-out effort to pass a national right-to-work law.

Senator Lauch Faircloth (R-N.C.), had introduced just such an act in 1995, which failed to pass. He reintroduced it as the National Right-to-Work Act of 1996. The bill would prohibit unions from requiring workers at unionized companies to pay dues or other union fees.

Essentially, paying dues would be voluntary. "We now have the makeup of Congress to make a real fight for it," said the committee's Martin Fox, according to a January 24, 1996, article in *The Detroit News*. "The president would veto it. But we think it's time to find out who's for freedom and who's for coercion." To show support the NRWC flooded the Senate with postcards, letters, petitions and phone calls urging passage of the act. They also had the backing of Majority Leader Trent Lott, a Mississippi Republican. But organized labor, which had spent millions of dollars on congressional campaigns in 1996, also had plenty of allies in Congress, not to mention nation-wide grassroots opposition from those who felt the act would weaken unions and lower wages.

In July, not long before the national conventions of the two political parties, the issue came to a head. Democrats threatened to filibuster a vote; Republican backers moved to "invoke cloture," or limit debate, a maneuver that would have the effect of forcing a vote. A cloture motion needs three-fifths of the Senate, or 60 senators, to pass. The act fell far short of passage with 31 votes for and 68 votes against; all 47 Democratic senators voted to kill the bill. However Larson still called it a "tremendous victory" because Senators were at least put on record as being for or against the bill, and he pledged to renew the quest for a right-to-work act with increased vigor.

The bill was re-introduced in 1998. Larson says the bill is in its "strongest legislative position ever," but unions have vehemently fought the legislation in the past and are continuing to do so. Legislators, particularly in states where organized labor is strong, continue to endorse right-to-work legislation at their peril. For instance, when Rep. Dan Burton (R-Ind.) came out in support of the National Right-to-Work Act of 1998, Labor News, a Web site in Indianapolis, Indiana, maintained by labor unions, put out a notice on its site that Burton was supporting the legislation. "In November," the notice said, "working Hoosiers will once again have the opportunity to use their votes to repeal Congressman Burton's right to work." Burton successfully ran for and was elected to a ninth term.

FUTURE DIRECTIONS

The committee continues to push new right-to-work laws at the state and national levels, but it will also have to work to prevent erosion of already-won gains as labor unions are actively pushing repeal of right-to-work laws. Additionally, unions threaten to dilute right-to-work laws with initiatives such as a bill banning companies from replacing striking workers. Organized labor may be able to pass such measures if the pendulum of political support swings in the direction of Democrats.

GROUP RESOURCES

The National Right to Work Legal Defense Foundation maintains a Web site at http://www.nrtw.org, that contains updates on issues key to compulsory unionism. The site includes court opinions, speeches, press releases, and a history of the foundation. Publications and answers to union questions are available through the NRTW Public Affairs Office; call 1-800-325-7892.

GROUP PUBLICATIONS

The committee publishes a monthly newsletter for members, the *NRTW Newsletter*. Any donor who gives more than $10 becomes a member and gets a six-month subscription. For $15, a donor gets a one-year subscription. The newsletter informs members on the committee's activities and provides updates on union issues. Copies of the newsletter may be obtained by writing: 8001 Braddock Rd., Springfield, VA 22160; or calling 1-800-325-7892.

BIBLIOGRAPHY

Broder, David. "Making an Issue of Labor's Contributions Could Backfire." *News & Observer,* 6 October 1997.

Burkins, Glenn. "Unions Are Set Back on Dues Disclosure." *Wall Street Journal,* 17 January 1997.

Lewis, Bill. "Will Dole and Gingrich Let Congress Vote?" *Human Events,* 23 June 1995.

Pepper, Jon. "Workers Forced to Pay Union Dues May Get Their Just Due Under Legislation." *Detroit News,* 24 January 1996.

"Right to Work Bill Killed in Senate." *Congressional Quarterly Weekly Report,* 13 July 1996.

Rose, Robert L., and Glenn Burkins. "Unions Win Partial Victory in Case on Dues." *Wall Street Journal,* 30 January 1996.

Simpson, Glenn R. "Democrats to Swivel Spotlight to 'Mush Money' Threat." *Wall Street Journal,* 19 September 1997.

Turow, Scott. "Money=Speech=Trouble." *News & Observer,* 14 October 1997.

Weiberg, Neil. "Extortion's Extinction?" *Forbes,* 8 May 1995.

National Right-to-Life Committee (NRLC)

ESTABLISHED: 1973
EMPLOYEES: 46
MEMBERS: 1 million
PAC: National Right to Life Political Action Committee

Contact Information:

ADDRESS: 419 7th St. NW, Ste. 500
    Washington, DC 20004-2293
PHONE: (202) 626-8800
FAX: (202) 737-9189
E-MAIL: nrlc@nrlc.org
URL: http://www.nrlc.org
PRESIDENT: Wanda Franz, Ph.D.

WHAT IS ITS MISSION?

According to the organization, the National Right to Life Committee (NRLC) "employs educational, charitable, scientific, and political activities to promote respect for the worth and dignity of all human life, particularly the life of the unborn child from the moment of conception." NRLC works to preserve human life and opposes procedures that they believe unnecessarily or immorally end life, including abortion, infanticide, euthanasia, and assisted suicide.

HOW IS IT STRUCTURED?

NRLC has a central office located in Washington, D.C. The organization is governed by a 53-member board of directors, which includes each NRLC state director and three members at large. The board sets policy for the NRLC and many members work actively in their state offices to keep abreast of pro-life issues at the state and local levels. An appointed president manages the day-to-day operations at the national office. Other officers include: vice president, chairman of the board, treasurer, and secretary.

NRLC's office also houses the NRL Educational Trust Fund, an entity that contributes to NRLC's pro-life agenda by raising funds through participation in the Combined Federal Campaign. This campaign makes it possible for federal and military workers who support pro-life work to contribute through payroll deduction. The trust fund has used proceeds to create educational advertisements on issues such as partial-birth abortion and health care rationing. The trust fund also funds the Association of Interdisciplinary Research in Values and Social Change, a group of scholars and professionals that is interested in advancing pro-life research.

The central NRLC office oversees 50 state affiliates, whose directors serve on the NRLC board. Affiliate offices oversee regional chapters in each state and monitor and influence relevant policy at the state level.

PRIMARY FUNCTIONS

NRLC functions with one main directive—to advance pro-life causes—but pursues this cause through many different avenues. At the NRLC Annual Convention, members gather to network and to discuss current right-to-life issues. For example, at the 1999 conference, participants discussed what NRLC could do to carry out its initiatives in the new millennium. The 1999 conference also incorporated a special focus on chapter needs. Through the annual conference, right-to-life supporters from across the nation learn about the latest NRLC activities and strategies and find out about new ways to advance the right-to-life agenda in their own area.

Legislation is an important part of NRLC. The organization lobbies for pro-life policies through its federal and state legislation departments. The staff of these two departments monitor pro-life policies throughout the entire legislative process. Staff members testify on legislation, meet directly with key legislators, and prepare written materials for policymakers and others in the pro-life movement. The NRLC Political Action Committee (NRLC PAC) is the largest pro-life PAC in the country and it funds and otherwise supports pro-life candidates at the federal level. In the 1996 election campaign, the NRLC PAC raised more than $2 million to support over 100 pro-life congressional candidates. The NRLC PAC also works with political candidates to educate them on pro-life issues.

Because the organization works at both the federal and the local level, NRLC is able to generate grassroots support from members. The *NRL News* informs subscribers about current right-to-life legislation and lets readers know, through Action Alerts, specific actions that they can take, such as contacting congressional members about an upcoming bill, in support of the pro-life movement.

NRLC promotes scientific activity to advance its mission. The organization sponsors and coordinates the Association for Interdisciplinary Research in Values and Social Change. This group is a collaboration of medical professionals, academics, researchers and lawyers who meet to share information and to present research findings on right-to-life issues in conjunction with the NRLC annual convention. The association publishes a newsletter six times a year in which members publish new

research and analyze and review the existing research on abortion, assisted suicide, and euthanasia.

PROGRAMS

NRLC's programs generally serve the purpose of conducting outreach and education for the pro-life cause. For instance, the organization's American Victims of Abortion (AVA) program provides information and speakers on post-abortion syndrome. Post-abortion syndrome is the psychological aftereffect a woman may experience after she has had an abortion. According to NRLC, research shows that women who have post-abortion syndrome may abuse drugs and alcohol, suffer in relationships and have difficulty communicating, suffer from decreased self-esteem, and may be more likely to attempt suicide. The AVA program also focuses on issues such as informed consent (for those who are deciding whether or not to have an abortion), fathers's rights, and parental notification. The American Victims of Abortion Program also collaborates with other pro-life groups that are concerned with post-abortion problems.

NRLC sponsors three outreach programs that are aimed at specific segments of the U.S. population. National Teens for Life was formed by pro-life teens in 1985. In 1997 the program included thousands of teen members from all 50 states. The program attempts to educate teens on the abortion issue. Members have lobbied at the state level and have volunteered in political work for pro-life candidates. National Teens for Life hosts two annual events—a congressional reception every January 22 (after the annual March for Life in Washington, D.C.) and an annual convention held in conjunction with the NRLC convention.

The Black Americans for Life (BAL) program conducts outreach activities to pro-life supporters in the black community. According to BAL, for every 10 African American babies born, another five are aborted. Since 1973, when abortion was legalized, it is estimated that nearly 11 million African American babies have been aborted, according to data from The Alan Guttmacher Institute and the National Abortion and Reproductive Rights Action League (*The Christian Science Monitor*, April 30, 1997). In order to educate the black community about abortion and other pro-life issues, BAL sponsors a 60-second radio announcement for use on local and religious radio stations. BAL also publishes its own newsletter and works with NRLC state affiliate groups to form BAL groups on the state and local level.

The National College Students for Life (NCSL) program was established in 1995, by college students that supported the pro-life movement. These students saw a need for a pro-life organization for college students because, as the program believes, college campuses often house strong support for the pro-choice movement. NCSL educates college peers about abortion and pro-life

The National Right to Life Committee uses demonstrations to promote respect for the worth and dignity of all human life particularly the lives of unborn children. The main thrust of their campaigns has been to have abortion declared illegal. (AP/Wide World Photos)

issues, registers college voters, produces several publications, and holds an annual convention in concert with the NRLC annual convention. NCSL also works with the NRLC state affiliate groups to distribute printed material in the community.

BUDGET INFORMATION

Contributions to the NRLC increased throughout the 1990s, due in part to the widespread media coverage of the partial-birth abortion issue. For example the NRLC's 1997 annual report showed total 1997 contributions at $2,819,518 and 1996 contributions at $2,102,954. Organization tax records for 1996 showed total revenue at $2,978,348 (including $2,476,141 in direct public support, $343,457 in indirect public support, $37,461 in program service revenue, $59,100 in interest, and $62,189 in other revenue). Expenses in 1996 totaled $2,041,265 (including $1,598,519 in program services, $148,088 in management, and $294, 658 in fund-raising).

HISTORY

On January 22, 1973, the U.S. Supreme Court made history with its ruling in the cases *Roe v. Wade* and *Doe v. Bolton*. These court decisions struck down restrictive abortion laws in all 50 states and replaced them with a national policy that allowed abortion for any woman requesting the procedure. The federal court thus legalized abortion in all 50 states.

Following these landmark court decisions, leaders of the movement against legalized abortion saw the need to create an organization that would speak for the pro-life cause. In June of 1973, supporters met in Detroit, Michigan, and formed the National Right to Life Committee (NRLC). NRLC was created as a nonprofit, nonsectarian organization to coordinate the pro-life efforts across the United States and to influence federal policy regarding pro-life issues. The first president was Edward Golden of New York who served a one-year term. The presidents that followed Golden served terms of one to seven years. Four of the organization's presidents have been medical doctors.

The pro-life movement gained a victory with the election of Henry Hyde (R-Ill.) to the House of Representatives in 1974. Hyde went on to become an outspoken supporter of pro-life policy. In 1976 Hyde successfully proposed an amendment to federal spending bills for that year which stopped almost all federal funding for abortions. This amendment continued to be adopted in the years that followed, and is often called the Hyde Amendment. In 1978 five pro-choice senators were replaced with pro-life senators as the NRLC and other pro-life groups continued to gain allies.

A crucial milestone in the history of the NRLC was the formation of its PAC in 1980. Due in part to the PAC's efforts, many new pro-life senators were elected that year and a few pro-choice senators were defeated, including George McGovern. In total, 11 Senate seats changed from pro-choice supporters to pro-life supporters. 1980 also saw the election of pro-life President Ronald Reagan. For the first time since 1952, Republicans had a majority in the Senate.

By the time George Bush became president in 1988, 33 percent of polled voters claimed that a candidate's abortion stand was a very important issue in deciding for whom they should vote. In 1992, pro-choice candidate, Bill Clinton, was elected president. His election, however, did not stop the pro-life movement, which still had many congressional members on its side. In fact, by 1994, 80 percent of Republicans and 20 percent of Democrats in Congress were pro-life supporters. These strong pro-life numbers were a result of elections held that year when Republicans gained control of the Senate as well as the House (the latter had not had a Republican majority since 1954). The new membership was to have an impact on the kinds of legislation that Congress voted on. For example, during the Reagan and Bush administrations, when Democrats had control of Congress, the House and Senate averaged nine votes per year that dealt with abortion. In 1995 and 1996, with Republicans in control, Congress had 53 votes that touched on abortion.

CURRENT POLITICAL ISSUES

NRLC's stated mission is to advance the cause of the pro-life movement, and to restore and maintain legal protection for the lives of all defenseless human beings. The organization carries out such work by advocating and becoming involved in issues including: infanticide, abortion, assisted suicide, and euthanasia. NRLC is also involved with issues concerning free speech and campaign reform in an attempt to preserve special-interest group access to congressional voting records.

To oppose euthanasia and assisted suicide, NRLC publishes scientific research on topics such as mental illness, pain control (and how it can be improved), and depression. On the political level, the organization lobbies for policies that will make euthanasia and assisted suicide illegal. NRLC played a major role in lobbying for the passage of the Federal Assisted Suicide Funding Restriction Act of 1997, which denies federal funding for assisted suicide. NRLC has been instrumental in helping develop laws in several states that ban assisted suicide. This strategy was given a major boost when the U.S. Supreme Court decided in 1997, that the decision by many terminally ill people to end their lives, often called the right to die, was not protected by the Constitution.

The major issue for NRLC, however, is abortion. NRLC was formed in 1973 as a direct response to the *Roe v. Wade* court decision that legalized abortion. NRLC opposes abortion on all fronts. Some of NRLC's specific anti-abortion efforts include lobbying against allowing the French-made RU486 abortion pill to be sold in the United States, and teaching women about alternatives to abortion through publicity campaigns and crisis pregnancy centers (volunteer organizations that provide assistance with adoption, financial assistance, education, and other assistance for pregnant mothers). But perhaps the largest and most controversial abortion issue that NRLC has lobbied against is the partial-birth abortion procedure.

Case Study: NRLC Fights for Ban on Partial-birth Abortion Procedure

NRLC and other pro-life groups have always maintained that human life begins at conception, thus making abortion an act of killing. Such groups find the partial-birth abortion procedure particularly brutal. This procedure, usually performed between 20 and 24 weeks of pregnancy, partially delivers the baby from the womb, at which time several medical procedures are performed that result in the fetus being born dead.

The partial-birth abortion debate began to draw national attention in the early 1990s, and quickly ignited controversy, within both the pro-life and pro-choice movements. Judie Brown, president of the pro-life American Life League felt the focus on partial-birth abortions would hurt the pro-life movement. "We've shot ourselves in the foot. What we've done here is said, 'Here's a really bad kind of abortion,' and the implicit message is that all other kinds of abortion aren't as bad. That undermines what this movement is trying to do, which is ban all abortions, period" (*USA Today* November 17, 1997).

On the other hand, NRLC maintained that the partial-birth abortion debate forced people to consider abortion as a choice about a baby, rather than a more removed, ideological construct about a woman's choice. Pro-choice advocates defended the procedure, claiming that it is performed only when medically necessary. They also claimed that the procedure would actually be less common if it was easier for women to get an abortion early in their pregnancy. Pro-choice groups further argued that NRLC and other pro-life groups, by cutting federal aid to the poor for abortions, lobbying against access to the RU486 abortion pill, and other measures, have made it necessary for some women to have partial-birth abortions. While some pro-choice leaders, such as U.S. Representative Barbara Kennelly (D-Conn.), admitted that they find the procedure to be brutal, they maintained that the decision should still rest between the woman and her doctor.

With media coverage turning public opinion against partial-birth abortions, NRLC pushed hard for laws banning the procedure. An attempt to pass a federal ban was vetoed by President Bill Clinton in 1996, but NRLC and other pro-life organizations kept the pressure on. Many states, beginning with Ohio in 1995, enacted some form of partial-birth abortion ban. By mid-1998, 28 states had partial-birth abortion bans. It is unclear, however, if these bans will stand up to court challenges. The Ohio law was found to be unconstitutional in 1998, but this decision did not extend to other, more carefully worded, state laws.

In 1997 another attempt was made to pass a national partial-birth abortion ban. NRLC members testified before Congress on their support for such a ban. They pointed out that earlier claims of the procedure's necessity and low frequency were in dispute. Ron Fitzsimmons, a pro-choice activist and director of the National Coalition of Abortion Providers, admitted in early 1997 that previous remarks he had made about the low frequency of the procedure were untrue. He stated in a *New York Times* article (February 26, 1997) that the partial-birth abortion was performed much more often than his colleagues have admitted and on healthy women bearing healthy babies. NRLC also argued against accepting a compromise proposed by President Clinton, which the organization claimed was a phony ban that, through confusing language, would sound like it was preventing partial-birth abortions without actually restricting the procedures at all. The Partial-Birth Abortion Ban Act was passed by the House and the Senate in 1997, but once again President Clinton vetoed the ban. Attempts to overturn Clinton's veto, and enact the law anyway, failed. The House mustered the necessary two-thirds majority but the Senate fell two votes short.

FUTURE DIRECTIONS

NRLC will continue to strategically focus on fighting for legislation that bans partial-birth abortions. Although unsuccessful, the publicity surrounding the issue has actually helped the organization's mission. More people have become aware of the procedure and, according to the organization, are against it, even though they might otherwise support abortion. Additionally, NRLC will attempt to limit minors' access to abortion services by pushing for the reenaction of the Child Custody Protection Act, which would make it illegal for a nonparent to assist a minor in getting abortion services in another state. In other initiatives involving health care reform, NRLC will attempt to stop any measures to legalize assisted suicide.

GROUP RESOURCES

NRLC communicates with the public through many mediums. The organization maintains a Web site at http://www.nrlc.com that includes current press releases, Action Alerts, information about outreach programs, and information about pro-life issues. The National Right To Life Center toll-free hot line—a referral line offering information about crisis-pregnancy centers—can be reached at 1-800-848-LOVE. NRLC compiles and makes public, congressional voting records on pro-life issues, that can be accessed by phone at (202) 393-LIFE. The organization also produces a daily radio commentary, "Pro-life Perspective." The show is broadcast primarily on Christian radio stations and includes information on current legislative initiatives as well as abortion, crisis pregnancy, assisted suicide, and euthanasia.

GROUP PUBLICATIONS

NRLC publishes *NRL News*, a newspaper that comes out 18 times a year. The organization also provides free, upon request, a partial-birth abortion packet that includes a bumper sticker, brochure, petition, and church bulletin. The packet can be ordered on-line using the order sheet located at http://www.nrlc.org/abortion/pba/free.html. These and other publications are also available by phone at (202) 626-8800, or by mail at 419 7th St. N.W., Ste. 500, Washington, DC 20004-2293.

BIBLIOGRAPHY

Abrams, Jim. "N.J. Congressman Makes Anti-Abortion Fight His Life's Work." *The Columbian*, 3 November 1997.

Dawnay, Ivo. "Focus Roe vs. McCorvey: This is the Woman Who Stands Accused of Starting the Slaughter of More than 35 Million Babies." *The Sunday Telegraph*, 11 January 1998.

Goldman, Jane. "Should Doctors Help Us Die?" *Newsday*, 13 July 1997.

Hunt, Liz. "U.S. Scientists Link Abortion to Breast Cancer." *Independent*, 12 October 1996.

Maier, Thomas. "Targeting Right-to-Die Battles: Supporters Shift Focus to State Level." *Newsday*, 29 June 1997.

Sisson, Bob. "Doctor-Assisted Suicide For Oregon Residents Only." *The Columbian* 6 November 1997.

Skorneck, Carolyn. "Opponents Say Campaign Bill Is Dead." *The Columbian*, 8 October 1997.

Thomas, Cal. "Medical Ethicists Take a Long Slide Down Slippery Slope to Infanticide." *Newsday*, 25 November 1997.

National Small Business United (NSBU)

ESTABLISHED: 1937
EMPLOYEES: 24
MEMBERS: 65,000
PAC: NSBU Small Business Victory Fund

Contact Information:
ADDRESS: 1156 15th St. NW, Ste. 1100
      Washington, DC 20005-1711
PHONE: (202) 872-8543
FAX: (202) 293-8830
E-MAIL: nsbu@nsbu.org
URL: http://www.nsbu.org
PRESIDENT: Todd O. McCracken
CHAIRMAN: Thomas Farrell

WHAT IS ITS MISSION?

The nation's second largest small business advocacy group, National Small Business United's (NSBU) stated mission is "to keep the concerns of small business owners before Congress and the Administration and to promote national policies that are supportive of small business." NSBU works closely with members in the House of Representatives and the Senate to promote or oppose legislative and regulatory initiatives that affect the small business community. It also encourages its own members to take action to protect their interests. NSBU sees itself as a nonpartisan organization working "for the common interest of all small businesses."

HOW IS IT STRUCTURED?

The NSBU's day-to-day operations are handled by a small staff of professionals, but its priorities and positions are formulated by a 32-member board of trustees (all volunteer small-business owners) nominated and elected by the general membership. Board members serve three-year terms, while board officers are elected every year. Meeting several times throughout the year, members of the board of trustees are also heavily involved in local, state, and regional organizations. Some also serve on regional Small Business Administration committees.

NSBU membership is composed of a diverse group of small business owners, including carpenters, consultants, manufacturers, retailers, grocers, designers, contractors, and many other businessmen. Representing more than 65,000 small businesses in all 50 states, NSBU

includes affiliated state and regional small-business groups as well as NSBU chapters. Many states are in the process of building chapters. Nonetheless, NSBU remains a distant second to the National Federation of Independent Business, the largest small business advocacy group with over 600,000 members.

PRIMARY FUNCTIONS

NSBU works to influence public policy at both the national and regional levels. Once the organization's priorities have been set by its 32-member board of trustees, NSBU's Washington-based lobbyists set out to persuade policymakers to support their positions. At the same time, the membership is kept informed of evolving policy issues and the stance taken by the board of trustees through publications, policy forums, conferences, and action alerts. Members are encouraged to support NSBU actions through such grassroots initiatives as letter-writing campaigns. Through its political action committee, the NSBU Small Business Victory Fund, NSBU provides financial support to the campaigns of politicians that it endorses.

NSBU members testify regularly before congressional committees like the Occupational Safety and Health Administration (OSHA) and Environmental Protection Agency (EPA) on issues such as taxes, federal bureaucracy, health care, and product liability. When not working to support the national organization, NSBU chapters and affiliates concentrate on influencing state policies that may help or hinder small business growth. In Texas, for example, Small Business United of Texas is working to improve access to reduce regulations on small businesses and to improve health benefits and workers compensation.

PROGRAMS

As NSBU's activities are focused on lobbying Congress and other legislative bodies to promote the interests of small businesses, it has relatively few programs. NSBU does provide its membership with a range of benefits including low-cost insurance protection, a long distance telephone program in cooperation with AT&T and various partners, foreign currency exchange discounts, overnight delivery discounts, and fax, copier, and printer supplies.

NSBU also sponsors an Energy and Enterprise program. Through this program, NSBU provides its members with information on how to improve the efficiency of their business and reduce energy costs. In one example, NSBU used the occasion of its own move into new office space to point out to members the benefits of new light fixtures.

BUDGET INFORMATION

The NSBU's annual budget varies from year to year, ranging from $1 million to $2 million. The money is raised from members' dues of $150 annually. The organization's 1996 budget was $1.2 million.

HISTORY

NSBU's origins date back to November, 1937, a time when the United States was still suffering in the Great Depression. For small business owners, it was an especially difficult time. DeWitt Emery, a small business owner from the Midwest, felt that President Franklin Roosevelt's New Deal laws were not equally benefiting small businessmen, and in some ways were proving to be harmful. Emery decided to take action.

Convinced of the importance of the role of small business in the nation's economy and the necessity for its voice in national affairs, Emery drafted a letter calling for small business owners to form an association to represent their interests in Washington. He sent out the letter to 200 firms across the United State and received support from 160 of them. Emery called the new organization the National Small Business Men's Association.

The fundamental objectives of the National Small Business Men's Association were formulated at the organization's first national convention in Pittsburgh in September of 1938 and continue to shape NSBU policy to this day. The fledgling organization demanded that the government stay out of private business affairs, that laws under which congressional powers were delegated to others be repealed, and that Social Security and other tax forms be simplified. Other objectives included reducing government expenses, balancing the federal budget, freedom of speech, and equal rights for employers and employees. Finally, the National Small Business Men's Association insisted that government should encourage small business growth by restructuring the tax system to be lighter on small businesses, and to cease attempts at reforming the economy at the expense of recovery. In 1962, the National Small Business Men's Association changed its name to the National Small Business Association (NSBA) to include the numerous women who own small businesses.

One of NSBA's biggest successes was the formation of the Small Business Administration's (SBA) Office of Advocacy. Created in 1974 as a result of NSBU lobbying, the Office of Advocacy conducts research on issues of concern to small business and represents the small business sector before Congress. The SBA itself is an independent agency of the federal government whose mission is to aid, counsel, assist and protect the interests of small business concerns. In existence since 1953, the SBA came very close to being abolished in the 1980s by the Reagan administration. NSBU played a leading role in preventing this from happening and helped initiate the White House Conference on Small Business in 1980, 1986, and 1995.

In 1981, another organization was formed, called Small Business United (SBU). SBU fought for many of the same issues as NSBA, and in 1986, the two decided to combine their efforts to become a more powerful organization. Thus, in 1986 SBU and NSBA merged to form one association—National Small Business United (NSBU).

Over the years, NSBU has been instrumental in pushing through a number of laws aimed directly at promoting small business interests such as 1979's "Rule of Two," which requires all federal contracting officers to set aside certain government contracts exclusively for small business if offers can be obtained from at least two. Other pieces of legislation promoted by NSBU included 1982's Small Business Innovative Research Act, which mandates federal agencies with substantial research and development budgets to direct a fixed percentage of those funds to qualified small businesses, and 1980's Regulatory Flexibility Act, which mandates that the federal government review all regulations to make sure they do not adversely affect small businesses.

The 1980s and early 1990s were good years for National Small Business United. Under the guidance of John Galles—president from 1987 until the end of 1996—the organization not only scored numerous legislative triumphs, but also quadrupled its revenues and increased its funds balance eightfold.

CURRENT POLITICAL ISSUES

NSBU is dedicated to promoting and protecting the interests of American small business. Consequently, its political agenda often echoes that of other corporate and industry groups, although, in some cases, NSBU's concern is not always shared by its corporate brethren. Indeed, on occasion, NSBU's stance is more likely to resemble that of the average consumer than big business. In other areas such as credit reform, where state and federal governments tend toward a pro-consumer approach, NSBU comes out squarely on the side of business. Generally speaking, anything that increases operating costs or paperwork for small businesses is staunchly opposed by NSBU lobbyists, while anything that lightens the burden is aggressively promoted. A simplified tax structure, the extension of tax benefits enjoyed by big business to smaller businesses, and less government-imposed bureaucracy are all among the policy initiatives supported by NSBU.

Case Study: 1997 Taxpayer's Relief Act

In 1997, NSBU's top priority was gaining some measure of tax relief for its members. For years, the orga-

FAST FACTS

Between 1992 and 1995, the SBA doubled its loan volume to small businesses—from 27,000 loans in 1992 to 57,000 loans—in spite of the fact that its budget shrank by nearly one-third.

(Source: Jerry Useem. "It's the New Economy, Stupid" *Inc. Online*. August 27, 1996.)

nization had been pushing for tax reforms that would directly benefit small businesses, pointing out that smaller companies seldom were able to take advantage of the tax write-offs available to larger firms, yet they still had to comply with costly and time-consuming tax filing procedures. According to NSBU, small businesses were at a competitive disadvantage with larger firms because of the tax system, and that they only wanted changes to level the playing field.

To call attention to the plight of small business, NSBU drafted a letter to Congress containing an itemized list of recommendations that included a $1 million estate tax exemption for family businesses, a graduated capital gains tax to encourage long-term investments in small businesses, clarification of independent contractor status, a 100 percent health care deduction for the self-employed, expansion of the home office deduction, and a halt to the expansion of payroll taxes. While their proposals were being debated in Congress and the Senate, NSBU released a steady stream of news releases re-emphasizing their demands and criticizing any proposals that in their view did not go far enough. Members were encouraged to write to Congress expressing their views and regular news conferences were held to keep the issue in the public eye.

When the Taxpayer's Relief Act, as it was called, was finally agreed on in July 1997, NSBU was elated. Although the agreement failed to address some of the items on the small business wish list, it went a long way toward "leveling the playing field." Among the measures included in the act were an increase in the estate tax exemption, a phased-in increase in the allowable health insurance deduction to 100 percent by 2007, a reduction in capital gains tax rates, and expansion of the home office deduction. Although the phase-in periods for some of the new exemptions and deductions were slower than NSBU would have liked and the demand for clarification of independent contractor status was ignored, the advocacy group declared victory, calling the 1997 Taxpayer's Relief Act "the largest small business tax cut in history."

SUCCESSES AND FAILURES

One of NSBU's biggest victories occurred in 1994, when it helped defeat an employer health care mandate that would have required all employers to provide their employees with a specified set of health care benefits. NSBU felt that this law would have placed a massive new burden on small businesses. NSBU was also a leading proponent of the Paperwork Reduction Act—which is meant to reduce the amount of paperwork associated with compliance with government regulations. One of six associations in the Paperwork Reduction Coalition, NSBU worked closely with members of Congress for over six years until the act was signed into law in 1996.

In 1997, NSBU was also handed one of its biggest defeats when a series of strict new anti-pollution measures proposed by the Environmental Protection Agency (EPA) were approved by the White House. Along with the National Association of Manufacturers (NAM), the National Federation of Independent Business (NFIB) and other business advocacy groups, NSBU had waged a bitter campaign to prevent implementation of the new standards, claiming that they were based on unscientific data and would cripple the nation's small businesses. With the enactment of the new standards, NSBU, together with many other business groups, vowed to challenge the EPA in court on the grounds that the new Clean Air Standards were unconstitutional.

FUTURE DIRECTIONS

One of NSBU's biggest goals is to increase its membership. But achieving that goal could be difficult. Hamstrung by its lack of size and money, NSBU is unable to generate the kind of clout in Washington that would draw new members to the organization. Even worse, NSBU is facing competition from dozens of "small business organizations" formed in the 1990s, all of whom are fighting to increase their membership. For the future, NSBU's primary concerns are likely to continue to revolve around

many of the same issues that have dominated its recent history. Tax reform remains an important issue to NSBU, as does regulatory reform, health care reform, utility deregulation, and federal deficit reduction.

GROUP RESOURCES

National Small Business United offers a variety of information resources. It maintains a Web site at http://www.nsbu.org, which outlines the organization's policies, history, and goals, and provides access to NSBU news releases, white papers, and legislative issues briefs. NSBU members can also take advantage of services like SBU NET, a weekly news and views fax service, and the Small Business Tool Kit, which offers instruction on how to write your member of Congress and how to write a letter-to-the-editor.

GROUP PUBLICATIONS

National Small Business United publishes *Small Business* USA six times a year. Subscriptions are automatically included with membership. The organization's weekly newsletter is available via E-mail, fax, or on-line at http://www.nsbu.org. Other publications include *Capitol Focus* and *Annual Survey of Small and Mid-Size Businesses*. For more information, E-mail nsbu@nsbu.org, or call (202) 293-8830.

BIBLIOGRAPHY

Arthur Andersen's Enterprise Group. "Small and Mid-Sized Businesses Gearing Up for Growth." *News Release*, 27 June 1996.

Mukherjee, Sougata." Business Group Looks Within for Chief." *Triangle Business Journal*, 30 December 1996.

———. "Congress Takes Notice of Small Biz." *Denver Business Journal.* 30 September 1996.

Murphy, Shelby L. "Apathy into Action." *Austin Business Journal*, 13 January 1997.

Useem, Jerry. "It's the New Economy, Stupid" *Inc., Online*. 27 August 1996.

National Taxpayers Union (NTU)

WHAT IS ITS MISSION?

According to the Web site of the National Taxpayers Union (NTU), "The NTU works for Constitutional amendments to curtail deficit spending and restrict tax increases, lower taxes for all people, taxpayer rights, eliminating wasteful and inefficient government spending, reducing spending, bureaucracy and regulation at all levels of government, and accountability from our elected officials."

HOW IS IT STRUCTURED?

The nonprofit, nonpartisan NTU is led by a president and chairman who help to oversee the day-to-day operations of the organization. Policy and direction are provided by its board of directors, led by the chairman. The NTU has 300,000 members nationally. While members do not direct NTU policy, their opinions about various issues are surveyed. These surveys help the organization direct its lobbying efforts. Membership requires payment of at least $15 annually.

The NTU also runs the National Taxpayers' Union Foundation as its educational and research arm. It is the foundation that analyzes the supposed cost of congressional voting patterns through the VoteTally and Bill-Tally programs.

Contact Information:
ADDRESS: 108 N. Alfred St.
  Alexandria, VA 22314
PHONE: (703) 683-5700
FAX: (703) 683-5722
E-MAIL: ntu@ntu.org
URL: http://www.ntu.org
CHAIRMAN: David Stanley
PRESIDENT AND CEO: John Berthoud

PRIMARY FUNCTIONS

The NTU believes it best represents taxpayer interests through congressional action, which includes lobbying, giving testimony to congressional committees, and educating politicians. The organization also pursues this agenda in state legislatures.

The NTU works to convince members of Congress to add a balanced budget amendment (BBA) to the Constitution. This would affect many government policies and programs but its main purpose would be to eliminate deficit spending. Other issues that the NTU addresses through its lobbying efforts include an extensive revision of the current income tax system, endorsement of a flat tax, and the elimination of what it considers wasteful government spending.

Besides lobbying, the NTU offers congressional testimony. In 1997, for example, the NTU gave important testimony on behalf of the line-item veto, a mechanism by which the president of the United States may remove individual spending measures from congressional budgets. The NTU has proposed Internal Revenue Service (IRS) reforms and protested the political influence of the American Association of Retired Persons (AARP).

A significant portion of the NTU's activities involves research. The NTU created the National Taxpayers Union Foundation (NTUF) expressly for this purpose. This research arm investigates patterns and effectiveness of congressional spending and tracks congressional votes on key tax issues. The NTU uses this research in congressional testimony and to shape public opinion about tax issues. An example of NTUF research is a published report that showed how congressional term limits would have helped pass the Balanced Budget Amendment (BBA).

PROGRAMS

The majority of NTU programs are directly connected to research done by the NTUF. Besides researching ways that the federal government could reduce its expenditures, the NTUF also conducts audits of congressional activities in two categories. Through these programs, the NTUF hopes to make every member of Congress accountable.

The NTUF's Bill Tally is an inventory of bills, legislation, and spending appropriations initiated by each member of Congress. Bill Tally assesses how much those actions cost taxpayers and identifies the representative or senator who introduced them. The goal is to make known to the public who spends taxpayers' money and how. Vote Tally also assesses the cost of congressional actions. However, instead of looking at bills various legislators have initiated, Vote Tally looks at the estimated cost of the floor votes that are cast by each member of Congress.

BUDGET INFORMATION

NTU brought in $3,075,622 of revenue in 1997. The vast majority ($2,960,135) came from contributions from members and other organizations interested in supporting NTU activities. For example, Iowans for Tax Relief donated $200,000 for NTU's efforts to pass a Balanced Budget Amendment (BBA). Approximately $115,000 came from other sources such as investments.

NTU spent a total of $2,836,792 in 1997: $1,637,571 was spent on program services, with $908,792 going for research and public education. NTU spent $377,484 lobbying legislatures, $213,000 on field services, or special projects, and $138,295 on publications. Support services amounted to $1,199,221, including $845,606 on management and $353,615 on fund-raising. Management costs were dedicated mostly to mailings ($384,495), printing ($227,917), salaries ($236,256), and professional fees ($101,506).

HISTORY

The NTU was founded by James Davidson and a small group of his friends in 1969, because no other group existed to defend taxpayers in the way that he envisioned. Davidson believed that exorbitant high taxes were unjust impositions on American taxpayers and that the situation could only get worse. Further, he felt the Vietnam War and "Great Society" social programs created by President Lyndon Johnson would create a great burden on the federal government's financial resources.

One of the first things the NTU tackled was the formation of a balanced budget amendment (BBA) to the Constitution. The NTU began working on a BBA in 1975, many years before the U.S. public at large became interested. According to the NTU, federal spending on all but essential programs would have to be eliminated. Soon after, the explosion of the national debt in the 1980s made many people believe a BBA might be necessary.

The election of President Ronald Reagan in 1980 helped the NTU achieve many of its goals. President Reagan lowered taxes and enacted taxpayer friendly legislation such as the NTU-backed Tax Reform Act of 1986, which substantially lowered taxes for many Americans. Ironically, while President Reagan eased tax burdens, government spending rose and the combination of the two factors caused an explosive increase in the national debt.

Another significant victory for the NTU was passage of the Taxpayer Bill of Rights in 1988. This new bill gave taxpayers more legal and financial recourse when dealing with the Internal Revenue Service (IRS). Among the many concessions it allowed to taxpayers was the ability to recover damages from the IRS due to improper seizures or unjustified actions.

The 1990s were a mixture of successes and failures for the NTU. Despite the fact that the Republican party controlled Congress for much of the decade, the organization was unable to obtain passage of a BBA it proposed in 1995. Two years later, however, the NTU endorsed another Taxpayer Bill of Rights and it passed, offering taxpayers even more rights when confronted by the IRS. Random audits could no longer be performed by the IRS and the IRS must establish a mediation division to better deal with taxpayer complaints.

CURRENT POLITICAL ISSUES

The NTU supports legislation that promotes less government taxation and opposes any that challenges its goals. For instance, the NTU fought a 1998 Transportation Bill that the organization felt was "pork-barrel" legislation, which means it was laden with unnecessary funding targeted for particular congressional districts. Through such legislation, representatives attempt to "bring home the bacon" to their districts and constituents. Despite the organization's objections, the Transportation Bill was passed in Congress because it created jobs, improved districts, and would win votes for those members of Congress that voted for it.

The NTU also works as a watchdog of various organizations that it believes may have undue influence over governmental policy. Such is the NTU's relationship with the American Association of Retired Persons (AARP).

Case Study: NTU vs. AARP

The NTU has been an outspoken critic of the AARP, a prominent national political organization consisting of older Americans. Its 30 million members make it a significantly powerful political force; it contributes extensively to congressional campaigns and lobbies Congress aggressively. Its publications *Modern Maturity* and *AARP Bulletin* enjoy enormous popularity. Among the AARP's goals are increases in Social Security and Medicare benefits.

These interests lie in direct conflict with the NTU's purpose of reducing what it considers to be extensive government spending. In 1995 the NTU and the NTUF conducted a study of the AARP, its agenda, and practices. After the completion of several studies, NTU executive director Paul Hewitt gave congressional testimony that criticized the AARP's goals and tactics, warning that its agenda would ultimately raise the average annual tax on American households by $13,000. According to Hewitt, the AARP recommended tax increases of $1.3 trillion a year to pay for its proposals.

To limit the power of nonprofit special interests such as the AARP, the NTU advocates three special interest reforms. It proposes elimination of government grants to organizations that spend 5 percent or more of

BUDGET:
1997 NTU Expenses

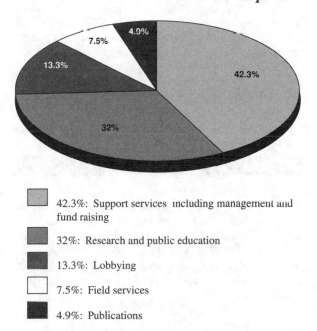

- ■ 42.3%: Support services including management and fund raising
- ■ 32%: Research and public education
- ■ 13.3%: Lobbying
- □ 7.5%: Field services
- ■ 4.9%: Publications

their budgets lobbying Congress. This ensures grants will be given based on merit rather than as a return on an investment. Additionally the NTU hopes to have a cap placed on postage subsidies that charitable organizations receive for their mailings. Finally, NTU believes for organizations to maintain their nonprofit status, they must not receive more than 20 percent of their revenue from untaxed commerce. Despite the NTU's ardent advocacy of these principles, legislators have been slow to respond to its requests. None of the organization's revisions of special interest group law have been enacted.

SUCCESSES AND FAILURES

The BBA is likely the NTU's greatest success and its greatest failure. The NTU has been working on and advocating a BBA since 1975. For many years it warned of the consequences of the national debt to Congress and to the public, stating that government spending was out of control. The NTU essentially sparked the contemporary public debate over irresponsible federal financial policy. The *Wall Street Journal* commented in 1995, "Since 1975, the NTU has been working quietly, rallying support for an amendment requiring a balanced federal budget. Now the drive is grabbing headlines from coast to coast and Congressional powers who long ignored the idea are taking it seriously."

However, its efforts to have Congress enact a BBA have failed consistently. In 1995 one version passed the House of Representatives but was defeated in the Senate. Soon after, the measure lost some of its immediacy with Congress due to the explosive growth of the U.S. economy. Because of the excellent economy, the federal government enjoyed a federal budget surplus in 1998. The national debt actually began decreasing from an estimated high in 1995 and with it, NTU's chances of having a BBA added to the Constitution.

FUTURE DIRECTIONS

With the federal budget surpluses anticipated until at least 2008, and with plans for a BBA committed to the background for the present, the NTU will research and publish studies on how to use the surplus funds. By early 1999, the NTU had already issued several statements regarding various strategies for the excess funds, rejecting one plan by members of Congress to raise their salaries.

GROUP RESOURCES

The NTU maintains a Web site at http://www.ntu.org that contains information on the NTU's policies and programs, and hyperlinks to other organizations that share similar views. For more information about the organization, write to the National Taxpayers Union, 108 N. Alfred St., Alexandria, VA 22314, or call (703) 683-5700.

GROUP PUBLICATIONS

The NTU publishes two newsletters, "Dollars and Sense" and "Capital Issues." Both contain articles on the most recent happenings at the NTU as well as current issues that the organization is working on. They are available via the World Wide Web at http://www.ntu.org/pubs/newsltrs.htm. The NTU also publishes numerous issue briefs and policy papers such as "Opposing Tax Relief: The Big-Government Agenda" and "Federal Campaign Contribution Habits of Forbes 400." These are available at http://www.ntu.org/pubs/pubs.htm. For more information on the NTU's publications, write to the National Taxpayers Union, 108 N. Alfred St., Alexandria, VA 22314 or call (703) 683-5700.

BIBLIOGRAPHY

Chadd, Edward A. "Manifest Subsidy." *Common Cause*, fall 1995.

Davidson, James Dale. "Should the Senate Pass a Balanced Budget Amendment to the U.S. Constitution." *Congressional Digest*, March 1997.

De Senerpont Domis, Olaf. "Taxpayer Group Joins Effort to Block Fed's Bid for Tax Payment System." *American Banker*, 7 July 1994.

McNamee, Mike. "A Kindler Gentler IRS?" *Business Week*, 1 February 1999.

Tauzin, W. J. "Act Now to Put IRS in the Dustbin of History." *Insight on the News*, 24 August 1998.

"USA's Money Pits Keep Growing." *USA Today*, 14 February 1996.

Wagner, Elizabeth, et al. "Panel on IRS Restructuring." *National Tax Journal*, September 1998.

Worsham, James. "Can the IRS be Fixed?" *Nation's Business*, May 1998.

National Trust for Historic Preservation (National Trust)

WHAT IS ITS MISSION?

According to the mission statement of the National Trust for Historic Preservation, the organization "is a private, nonprofit organization dedicated to protecting the irreplaceable. It fights to save historic buildings and the neighborhoods and landscapes they anchor. Through education and advocacy, the National Trust is revitalizing communities across the country and challenges citizens to create sensible plans for the future."

HOW IS IT STRUCTURED?

The National Trust is essentially organized into a two-tier structure with a national headquarters in Washington, D. C. responsible for developing a coordinated national policy, and a network of seven regional and two branch offices responsible for implementing policy locally, developing grassroots support, and identifying local conservation issues, which could possibly be incorporated into national plans. The headquarters office as a whole is responsible for overseeing administration of the National Trust's award schemes and coordinating the organization's local campaigns. The office supports the regional and field offices with a variety of publications, newsletters, financial disbursements, fund-raising activities, legal services, and policy guidance.

The National Trust's board of trustees is responsible for setting national conservation goals and priorities. It is supported in these efforts by a staff of professional lawyers and lobbyists who represent the interests of the National Trust and its members before government and

ESTABLISHED: 1949
EMPLOYEES: Not made available
MEMBERS: 275,000
PAC: None

Contact Information:
ADDRESS: 1785 Massachusetts Ave. NW
    Washington, DC 20036
PHONE: (202) 588-6000
TOLL FREE: (800) 944-6847
FAX: (202) 588–6223
E-MAIL: resource@nthp.org
URL: http://www.nthp.org.
PRESIDENT: Richard Moe
CHAIRMAN: Nancy Campbell

the courts. Additionally the National Trust set up the National Trust Legal Defense Fund to initiate litigation if a historic site is threatened. A communications department provides informational and public relations support through regular press releases, newsletters, and a World-wide Web site.

At the grassroots level, the National Trust's branch network communicates the organization's aims and encourages support among local communities for the local and national conservation issues identified by the National Trust. The regional and branch offices are located in Chicago, Illinois; Denver, Colorado; Boston, Massachusetts; Philadelphia, Pennsylvania; Charleston, South Carolina; Washington, D. C. ; Fort Worth, Texas; San Francisco, California; and South Pasadena, California.

The National Trust membership, organized under its branch network, consists of people from many different backgrounds but united by their common interest in preserving U.S. historical sites. Members pay annual dues of $20 and receive National Trust publications and discounts on entrance fees to National Trust sites and museums.

PRIMARY FUNCTIONS

The National Trust operates in many different capacities to achieve its goals. Identification of sites, communities, and even historical events play an important role in the National Trust's activities. Each year the organization prepares a list of 11 of the most endangered historic places in the United States. The National Trust draws public and legislative attention to sites it deems highly significant symbols of U.S. heritage that are threatened by neglect, deterioration, lack of maintenance, insufficient funds, inappropriate development, or insensitive public policy. The National Trust has also joined forces with groups such as the National Parks and Conservation Association to identify more complex historical phenomena like the National Underground Railway Network, a patchwork of more than 400 historic sites commemorating the people, places, and events that formed a part of the United States's opposition to slavery.

The National Trust also educates the public about ways in which it can assist in the preservation effort of the sites it identifies. The National Trust is active both as an owner of such sites and as a facilitator that encourages others to restore or preserve buildings they own or for which they are responsible. The National Trust provides matching funds or low-interest loans for the restoration of historic sites and communities, or for urban renewal initiatives.

Finally the National Trust maintains a lobby and its National Trust Legal Defense Fund. It lobbies Congress for legislation to support its preservation efforts. National Trust board members testify before members of Congress on such issues as urban sprawl and national landmarks. The legal defense fund becomes involved in litigation if a site is threatened.

PROGRAMS

Identification and preservation of historic sites, education, funding and advocacy in support of the preservation of those sites, and recognition of the people and institutions who have made significant contributions to the preservation of the historic heritage of the United States are all aims of programs developed and administered by the National Trust.

The National Main Street Center was created in 1980 as a human resource and technical reference center for towns and small cities to access when they undertake economic development within the context of historic preservation. Training courses, technical assistance to states and towns, and help in building business and government partnerships are available through the center. From this initiative the Main Street Membership Network evolved through which communities receive current information on revitalization techniques and activities nationwide, as well as technical advice and referrals on issues of local concern.

The Gifts of Heritage program offers individuals an opportunity to preserve their homes and properties, give a lasting gift to their community, and participate personally in the preservation of America's cultural heritage. To ensure that donated properties receive the protection they require, the National Trust conducts a complete preservation survey of the property and places protective easements on historically and architecturally significant aspects of the house and landscape. These easements become part of the deed, defining the standards by which all subsequent owners must maintain the property.

The National Trust's Rural Heritage program has worked on rural historic preservation issues since 1979. The program focuses on building a rural constituency for historic preservation, creating forums for education, publishing information on rural historic preservation, providing technical assistance to rural communities, and influencing public policy to conserve America's rural heritage. In the urban forum, the National Trust supports sensitive urban renewal with its Community Partners program, a neighborhood initiative that seeks to promote the use of historic preservation as a tool for revitalizing America's historic urban neighborhoods by creating partnerships between community development and historic preservation groups at the national, state, and local levels to demonstrate the effectiveness of preservation-based community development.

BUDGET INFORMATION

The National Trust's 1996 operation budget totaled $37,096,265 with revenues of $32,301,713. Nearly 32 percent ($9,277,983) of the National Trust's revenues were derived from contributions, while membership dues accounted for 10.5 percent ($4,213,455). Investment income and capital gains accounted for almost 21 percent of total revenues, while federal appropriations and other grants accounted for another 15 percent. The remainder was derived from a variety of sources including property admissions and special events, investment income, contract services, article sales, advertising, and rentals. Well over half of the 1996 budget (over $20 million) was devoted to historic sites and preservation services. Membership services and fund-raising accounted for just over 20 percent, (about $7.8 million). Another $7.2 million was spent on education and publications. Nearly $3 million, or 7.4 percent, was allocated for general and administrative costs.

HISTORY

The early decades of the twentieth century witnessed a number of events that had a profound effect on the development of the conservation movement. Most notable among these were the passing of the 1906 Antiquities Act, the first major federal preservation legislation passed to preserve archeological sites; the 1909 opening of America's first outdoor museum of historic buildings in Salem, Massachusetts; the 1910 incorporation of the Society for the Preservation of New England Antiquities, America's first regional preservation organization; and the creation in 1916 of the National Park Service to care for the nine existing National Monuments.

The focus on preserving the past continued during the 1920s and 1930s. Greenfield Village, Henry Ford's collection of historic buildings and artifacts was opened in Dearborn, Michigan, and Williamsburg, Virginia, was restored under a plan formulated by W. A. R. Goodwin with funding from John D. Rockefeller, Jr. In 1935 the National Historic Site Act authorizing the Department of the Interior to survey historic sites under a National Historic Landmarks Program and to acquire historic properties for public use was passed.

While efforts by particular state and city governments and private individuals were obviously making a difference, preservationists recognized the need for a nationwide organization that could cover a broader range of challenges. Interest remained high despite World War II (1939-45), and in 1947 the National Council for Historic Sites and Buildings was established as the first nationwide private preservation organization. Two years later, the National Trust for Historic Preservation was established.

BUDGET:
1996 NTHP Revenue

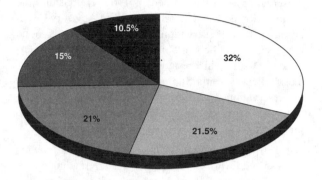

- ☐ 32%: Contributions
- ▨ 21.5%: Other
- ▨ 21%: Investment income and capital gains
- ▨ 15%: Federal appropriations and other grants
- ■ 10.5%: Membership dues

1996 NTHP Expenses

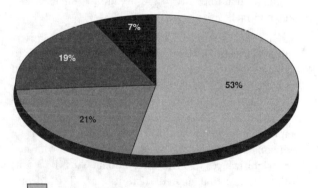

- ▨ 53%: Historic sites and preservation services
- ▨ 21%: Membership services and fund raising
- ▨ 19%: Education and publications
- ■ 7%: General administrative

In 1951 the National Trust acquired Woodlawn Plantation in Virginia and restored the mansion that overlooks Mount Vernon. The following year the first issue of *Historic Preservation* magazine appeared. In 1954 the National Council for Historic Sites and Buildings merged with the National Trust to strengthen its efforts.

The following decade was a mixture of success and failure for the National Trust. In 1960 the National Trust issued its first Crowninshield Award to the Mount Vernon Ladies' Association of the Union, and published the first issue of *Preservation News*. The National Historic Preservation Act was passed in 1966, establishing the National Register of Historic Places, an Advisory Council on Historic Preservation, and matching grants-in-aid to the states and the National Trust to be used for preservation. Despite this progress, the demolition of New York's Pennsylvania Station in 1963 was a major blow to preservationist efforts. The beautiful but aged structure was destroyed despite widespread public outrage and picketing.

In 1971 the National Trust responded to a growing interest in its work by opening a western regional office in San Francisco, California, its first regional office. Two years later National Historic Preservation Week was declared, and momentum continued to mount as the national bicentennial approached. In 1976 the Tax Reform Act provided tax incentives for the rehabilitation of income-producing properties that have been certified historical, while the Public Buildings Cooperative Use Act encouraged restoration and adaptive use of historic buildings for federal use. More progress followed in 1978 when the U.S. Supreme Court ruled in its first major preservation case, involving New York's Grand Central Terminal, that the city's preservation ordinance was constitutional.

In 1980 amendments to the National Historic Preservation Act were passed that directed federal agencies to nominate and protect historic federal properties and broadened participation in the National Register listing. A year later the Economic Recovery Tax Act provided significant new investment tax credits for rehabilitation, helping the National Trust to give businesses and private individuals good reasons to restore properties with historic significance. In 1988 the National Trust issued its first "11 Most Endangered Historic Places" list, detailing the plight of 11 historic locations that were most in danger of being destroyed.

The 1990s began well for the National Trust as President George Bush reinstated substantial funding for preservation in his proposed budget. A significant achievement and symbol of this new attitude was the December 12, 1997, reopening of the landmark St. James Hotel in Selma, Alabama. Part of an ongoing redevelopment of Selma's historic downtown area, the plan was partially financed and guided by the National Trust. There was more success a year later when, in February 1998, it was announced that the organization would be a key partner with the White House on the Save America's Treasures Millennium Program, a new initiative to keep the rich heritage of the United States alive.

CURRENT POLITICAL ISSUES

During the 1990s there has been significant legislative support for the National Trust's programs, and a look at the condition of the sites it protects confirms its success in achieving many of its most cherished ambitions. But challenges remain when private, government, or individual interests come into conflict over sites. The issue of Route 710 is illustrative.

Case Study: Long Beach Freeway Extension

In 1949 the California Highway Department (now known as CalTrans) proposed to construct an extension of Route 710, the Long Beach Freeway. This addition would connect the San Bernadino and Foothill Freeways. After much study, in 1964 the California Highway Commission chose a route that would pass through the city of South Pasadena. The proposal was immediately rejected by local residents, the National Trust, and other conservationist groups, as well as by mayors, city officials, and a variety of government departments. After a decade of legal wrangling, a successful lawsuit by the city of South Pasadena in 1973 forced the project to be evaluated for an Environmental Impact Statement. When this became finalized in the early 1990s, CalTrans proposed to proceed with a new plan that would incorporate several compromises that were worked out with a community group. However, the freeway would still pass through the cities of El Soreno and South Pasadena. Again, residents and local government rejected the new proposal as shortsighted. It was estimated that as many as one thousand homes of a historic nature and thousands of mature trees in the affected area would be destroyed or suffer adverse effects through their proximity to the freeway. The National Trust was monitoring this issue and added its voice to those that opposed the extension.

"In an era when Americans are rediscovering the importance of nurturing strong communities, the Route 710 Freeway Extension should never be built," said Richard Moe, president of the National Trust. "This freeway project would destroy some of the most stable, historic communities in the Los Angeles Basin, cost more than a billion dollars for 4.5 miles of pavement, and move traffic less than one mile an hour faster than a low-build alternative. Bulldozing stable neighborhoods for freeway construction is a crude, outmoded approach to transportation and a waste of taxpayers money."

CalTrans, the proposed contractors, and local representative Matthew G. Martinez (D-CA) lobbied hard for continuation of the project; on the other hand, a low-build alternative was supported by a broad coalition of environmentalists, city officials, and government departments, and it appeared as though this alternative would be the one used. In a March 20, 1998, letter to President Bill Clinton calling for him to strongly consider a low-build alternative, the Advisory Council on Historic

Preservation, an independent federal agency, cited the 710 project as " . . . one of the most important historic preservation cases ever to come before the Council." The Environmental Protection Agency (EPA) and the Department of the Interior also opposed the 710 Freeway Project and voiced their own concerns about the project's impact on the environment and its effects on stable, historic communities.

The case against the freeway looked solid, yet on April 21, Rodney Slater, secretary of the U.S. Department of Transportation, signed a record of decision that essentially allowed for CalTrans to extend the Long Beach Freeway through the historic communities. The National Trust and its president were stunned: "In approving the 710 Freeway, Secretary Slater missed an opportunity to require the Federal Highway Administration to conduct a fair and objective study of a Low Build Alternative," said Moe. "This study, required by law, would address transportation needs and provide jobs now, without destroying neighborhoods and likely saving billions of taxpayer dollars."

Issuing a protest was not enough for the National Trust. Along with the Sierra Club, the Los Angeles Conservancy, and the South Pasadena Unified School District, the National Trust joined in a lawsuit that the City of South Pasadena filed against the U.S. Department of Transportation. The lawsuit asked for an invalidation of the record of decision which had been signed over the objections of the City of South Pasadena and other parties. The suit claimed that the Federal Highway Administration's decision to approve the project violated several federal laws and failed to comply with clean air requirements, as well as failing to adequately address several alternatives that had been presented, including South Pasadena's own "multi-modal, low build" alternative presented earlier that decade.

The Department of Transportation stated that they had fully complied with all legal requirements and considered and implemented strict conditions to lessen the impact of the extension on the neighborhoods. Yet the EPA mandated that the newest plans, which call for a new trench-and-tunnel route through El Sereno and South Pasadena, must also undergo the same rigorous environmental impact study that the previous plan underwent before work could begin. It remains unclear as to whether the revised plans could even be brought to fruition, as there are as yet no funds allocated for the project. The cash-strapped agency responsible for coming up with the funds—the local Metropolitan Transportation Authority—may be unable to do so. Costs that were estimated at $1.4 billion are now thought to be wildly inaccurate since the price was based on surface-level extension plans made years before, and have failed to take into account the trench-and-tunnel route.

By mid-1999 there was still no resolution to the lawsuit brought about by the National Trust and others. CalTrans continued to publicize the advantages of the addi-

FAST FACTS

Independence Hall in Philadelphia and the Old South Meeting House in Boston were both intended for demolition before authorities stepped in to save them.

(Source: National Trust for Historic Preservation, 1999.)

tion and seemed confident that it would eventually be allowed to go ahead with its plan. However, the National Trust also continued to voice its side of the issue with updates to its Web site and notices in its publications.

FUTURE DIRECTIONS

One of the most exciting new opportunities for the National Trust is its role in the White House Millennium Council, a multi-year initiative to mark the end of the twentieth century and the beginning of the new millennium. As part of the council, the National Trust will sponsor the "Save America's Treasures Millennium Program." President Bill Clinton's budget for fiscal 1999 allocated $50 million for historic preservation. The National Trust also hopes to add private contributions to that money.

While the plans are still under development, the National Trust actively seeks grassroots input to help identify significant sites that are threatened. The program does not limit its work only to the most famous landmarks and documents, but also seeks to preserve the streets and older neighborhoods that are part of everyday communities as well. According to National Trust President Richard Moe, the "program has the potential to be the most significant public/private effort to preserve our heritage in the nation's history."

GROUP RESOURCES

The National Trust Library is located at the University of Maryland's College Park campus and is maintained as a separate collection in the Architecture Library. For more information about the library, call (301) 405-6320. The National Trust also provides a Legislative Hot Line number (1-800-765-6847) to inform the public regarding the Law and Public Policy Department's advo-

FAST FACTS

The nation's first historical site renovation was the 1828 restoration of Touro Synagogue, Newport, Rhode Island.

(Source: National Trust for Historic Preservation, 1999.)

cacy efforts and late-breaking developments in Congress. In addition to these efforts, the public policy department of the National Trust maintains the Sprawlwatch Clearinghouse Web Site at http://www.sprawlwatch.org, which has information on urban sprawl and planning growth.

For information on current concerns and developments as well as membership details, the National Trust Web site at http://www.nthp.org is an excellent source of information. The site also includes press releases, publications details, and background analysis on various issues. For more information about the organization, write to the National Trust for Historic Preservation, 1785 Massachusetts Ave. NW, Washington, DC 20036, call (202) 588-6000, or E-mail resource@nthp.org.

GROUP PUBLICATIONS

The National Trust publishes a number of fact sheets and newsletters. Legal developments are covered by the organization's *Preservation Law Reporter*, and heritage tourism in *Getting Started: How to Succeed in Heritage Tourism* and *Touring Historic Places: A Manual for Group Tour Operators and Managers of Historic and Cultural Attractions*. Members of the Preservation Faxboard Network receive *Preservation Advocate News*, a monthly fax newsletter. *Preservation News*, the National Trust's magazine, is available to all members. For further information relating to legal department publications or the faxboard network, contact the Law and Public Policy Department at (202) 588-6254. For information on other publications write to the National Trust for Historic Preservation, 1785 Massachusetts Ave. NW, Washington, DC 20036, call (202) 588-6000, or E-mail resource@nthp.org

BIBLIOGRAPHY

Baer, William C. "When Old Buildings Ripen for Historic Preservation: A Predictive Approach to Planning." *Journal of the American Planning Association*, 1 January 1995.

Baum, Geraldine. "National Perspective; Culture; Benefactors Are Now Paying the Price for Historic Preservation . . . " *Los Angeles Times*, 20 July 1998.

Dickinson, Rachel. "Heritage Tourism is Hot." *American Demographics*, 1 September 1996.

Ewing, Reid. "Is Los Angeles-Style Sprawl Desirable?" *Journal of the American Planning Association*, 1 January 1997.

Laskar, Devi Sen. "Keepers of the Past: Roswell Groups Working to Keep History-Minded City from Losing its Appeal." *Atlanta Journal and Constitution*, 13 August 1998.

Prost, Charlene. "Historic Preservation Trust Seeks to Gain Backers." *St. Louis Post-Dispatch*, 5 October 1993.

Rochell, Anne. "History at Risk: Preservationists Sounding Alarms as Southern Treasures Fall by the Way." *Atlanta Journal and Constitution*, 25 May 1997.

Stokes, Samuel N., Elizabeth Watson, and Shelley S. Mastran. *Saving America's Countryside*, 2d ed. Baltimore: Johns Hopkins University, 1997.

National Urban League (NUL)

WHAT IS ITS MISSION?

According to the National Urban League (NUL) its mission is "to assist African Americans in the achievement of social and economic equality. The Board of Trustees of the National Urban League and all of its affiliates reflect a diverse body of community, government, and corporate leaders. The League implements its mission through advocacy, bridge building, program services and research." A community-based organization that serves more than 2 million people per year, the NUL works to fight discrimination and ensure equal opportunity for African Americans and other minorities in education, employment, housing, health, and welfare.

HOW IS IT STRUCTURED?

The NUL is a federation of 115 local affiliates in 34 states and the District of Columbia. The national headquarters is located in New York, New York, and, while the national organization offers assistance and makes policy recommendations to these affiliates, it does not oversee their daily operations. The NUL is led by a president and chief executive officer. The president is in charge of the national organization's daily operations and acts as the principal representative of the NUL to the media.

The NUL is staffed by more than 3,000 professionals, with the assistance of more than 25,000 volunteers serving on local boards, advisory committees, and auxiliaries. The national office is home to three important departments: Development and Communications, Operations, and Finance and Administration. In Washington,

ESTABLISHED: 1910
EMPLOYEES: 3,000
MEMBERS: 50,000
PAC: None

Contact Information:
ADDRESS: 120 Wall St.
　　　New York, NY 10005
PHONE: (212) 558-5300
FAX: (212) 558-5332
E-MAIL: info@nul.org
URL: http://www.nul.org
PRESIDENT; CEO: Hugh B. Price

BIOGRAPHY:
Whitney Moore Young, Jr.

Author; Activist; Professor (1922–1971) A recruiter for the head position of the Omaha, Nebraska, chapter of the National Urban League, described Whitney Moore Young, Jr., as poised, self-confident, articulate, dynamic—"the kind of guy that I think would impress whites." This 1950s characterization of Young was accurate. He was an effective intermediary between African Americans and whites of that era and persuaded wealthy white men to support the African American cause. After serving in the U.S. Army during World War II (1939–45), Young earned his master's degree from the University of Minnesota's School of Social Work and became Director of Industrial Relations for the St. Paul, Minnesota, chapter of the Urban League. Young was successful in facilitating the league's mission to broaden employment opportunities for African Americans with his visits to St. Paul employers. This success was duplicated in his work for the Omaha chapter. In 1961 Young was chosen president of the National Urban League.

Young instituted a host of new programs aimed at training African American workers and saw the league's number of affiliates grow from 63 to 98 and its budget increase tenfold. Young's diplomatic skills were constantly tested as he balanced the favor of liberal whites who funded his organization against that of militant African Americans who courted his African American audience. At the time of his death, only 10 years after assuming leadership, the *New York Times* hailed the National Urban League under Young as, "one of the nation's primary non-government forces working towards the self-sufficiency of the Black American poor."

D.C., the NUL operates two additional departments: a Public Policy/Government Relations Office and a Research Department.

The policies of the organization are formulated once a year by the board of trustees at the annual convention. The board is a large, interracial group composed of business, professional, religious, and local governmental leaders and is typically chaired by a person, usually a business executive, with a public profile equal in stature to the president. At the annual convention, NUL affiliates send delegates to make their positions on policy known to the board. The NUL does not have a membership base in the traditional sense; community leaders volunteer to lead and operate programs primarily at the affiliate level.

PRIMARY FUNCTIONS

The NUL works on several levels to improve social and economic conditions for African Americans and other minorities in U.S. cities. The organization offers a number of direct services, such as technical assistance, employment training, and business management training, in order to help develop a greater degree of self-sufficiency in urban minority communities. In recent years, the group's focus on youth has led it to establish a number of educational, internship, and awareness pro-

grams, often accompanied by awards programs that recognize individual and group achievement. In specific cases—for example, helping a small business owner to win an important contract or fighting a particular instance of discrimination—the NUL helps arrange advocacy for people in need of legal or promotional help. The organization also provides referral services that direct people, especially business owners or career seekers, to professionals who can best help with particular issues.

As the central body of a national federation, the NUL also serves the important function of gathering and disseminating information. Its Washington, D.C., office conducts research on the social and economic aspects of African American life and publishes its findings. It monitors legislation that might affect urban minorities, and publicizes proposed bills on its Web site. The organization makes a point of distributing this information not only to its members and clients, but to journalists, researchers, and legislators, in order to promote dialogue and awareness.

PROGRAMS

Although most NUL programs are designed and implemented by affiliates to address specific community issues, the national organization conducts a number of programs in areas such as education, employment, health, social welfare, and the administration of justice. In some cases, such as the organization's on-line Career Center, programs are forums that will help people connect, network, and solve problems. NUL programs are often designed and executed in collaboration with other minority advocacy groups.

One of the most significant and far-reaching activities started in the late 1990s was the Campaign for African American Achievement, launched in 1997 by the NUL and 20 other national black organizations. The aims of the program are to improve the academic standing of young African American students by encouraging and rewarding excellence in the classroom, as well as improving the education delivered in public schools. The program operates at the national level through the establishment of a National Achiever's Society, and it operates locally during September, designated as Achievement Month. During Achievement Month, NUL affiliates and local organizations conduct high-profile events celebrating the efforts of academically successful students.

One of the most important components of the NUL since 1969 has been the Black Executive Exchange Program (BEEP), a program that addresses the need to provide high-quality education for African American students who are interested in high-level industry and government careers. The program links university students to African American role models employed in high-ranking positions, in order to provide practical, real-world business experience and aid the professional advancement of young African American professionals.

BUDGET INFORMATION

Not made available.

HISTORY

The period of Reconstruction following the Civil War in the United States was a time of change for former slaves in the South. The federally mandated reforms of Reconstruction came to an end, however, in 1877, and many southern whites immediately set out to erode or even eliminate the new political and economic freedoms that African Americans had gained in the last decade. As a result of this backlash, African Americans, primarily rural slaves in the antebellum South, undertook a large-scale migration to Northern cities such as Chicago, Detroit, and New York. The industrialized cities offered steady work in the factories and an escape from the harsh and often dangerous life in the rural South.

It soon became clear, however, that a U.S. city was not a place where an already economically disadvantaged person could easily adapt. In the spirit of Booker T. Washington, who had been a tireless advocate of education and self-reliance among black Americans until his

FAST FACTS

According to a survey conducted in the mid-1990s, the household income of African Americans is about 62 percent of that earned by white households.

(Source: William Raspberry. "Inheriting Wealth." *Washington Post,* August 10, 1998.)

death in 1915, a group of black and white professionals founded the National Urban League in 1910. The organization began as a collaboration between several existing social welfare groups, with a primary goal of training African American social workers at Fisk University to work among black immigrants in New York City.

Early Leadership

In its early years, the NUL directed its efforts toward employment and social integration, stressing self-reliance rather than pressuring the government to pass laws that would ensure equality. It also urged southern blacks to exercise caution, migrating north only after provisions for employment and housing had already been arranged. This pragmatic stance, fairly conservative when compared to the more militant black activist groups of the time, earned the NUL a reputation among many black leaders for being too moderate and stodgy—a reputation which persists in some circles today.

Under the leadership of Edwin Kinkle Jones and T. Arnold Hill, the NUL's early years were spent largely in attempts to penetrate northern labor markets. In 1925 Jones created a Department of Industrial Relations within the NUL to administer vocational guidance and education, while Hill attempted to ease rising tensions between the growing number of black workers and the existing white labor unions. Together, the two tended to downplay the inflammatory issue of race, instead concentrating on finding common ground.

World War II and Beyond

Lester B. Granger took charge of the NUL in 1941, the year the United States entered World War II (1939–45). Under Granger's aggressive leadership, blacks made substantial progress in the military and were able to participate in the economic boom that followed the war. However, the NUL was less successful with its efforts to eliminate the rampant discrimination in the housing industry. Led by Granger, the NUL had limited success in the battles for public housing waged throughout the 1940s and 1950s. Once again the NUL was criticized as too cautious by more activist groups such as the National Association for the Advancement of Colored People (NAACP) and the Southern Christian Leadership Conference (SCLC).

When Whitney Young Jr. was installed as the new executive director of the NUL after Granger's exit, the organization believed it was acquiring more militant leadership. Young, however, was much more than a skillful negotiator and diplomat, he was able to greatly expand economic opportunities for blacks through his dealings with powerful U.S. business leaders. It was Young, more than any other NUL leader, who transformed the organization from a seemingly marginal movement into a powerful and independent link between the civil rights community and the government in Washington, DC.

Young's successor, Vernon Jordan, carried on in this tradition, assuming leadership of the NUL after he had already become a significant Washington power broker. Jordan added to Young's legacy by strengthening the relationship between the NUL and corporate America. The NUL also tragically garnered unanticipated attention when Jordan was non-fatally shot in 1981 in Indiana. Though the NUL lost ground during the conservative government administrations of the 1980s, the leadership of President Hugh Price, begun in 1994, injected the organization with renewed power and hope. Under Price, the NUL restored its financial power and enlarged its public endowment; restructured the board and staff; redesigned a new strategic purpose for the coming millennium; and launched its flagship program, the Campaign for African American Achievement.

CURRENT POLITICAL ISSUES

The 1990s were characterized by both a rapidly expanding technological economy and shifting demographics in the United States. The NUL struggled not only to keep up with these dramatic changes in society, but to maintain its hold on the gains made by African Americans in the past. For example, in the technological boom of the Information Age, the NUL sees a potential threat to poorer urban families, who may become even further marginalized by their lack of access to sophisticated computers or electronic equipment. At the same time, as U.S. society becomes more pluralistic, ethnic and racial minorities are forced to deal with a changing mindset about programs enacted during the civil rights era—programs that were designed to combat discrimination and unequal opportunities.

Case Study: The Erosion of Affirmative Action

The affirmative action laws enacted throughout the 1960s and 1970s were intended to remedy past discrimination and provide minorities and women a level playing field in workplace hiring and promotion, the awarding of government contracts and housing, and admission to institutions such as colleges and universities. While most Americans agreed with the idea of helping minorities expand their opportunities for success, the quota system that awarded jobs, contracts, and other assignments to minority candidates was controversial. The quota system required that a certain percentage of government contracts or university admissions be set aside for minorities or women. Critics of the quota system argued these set asides sometimes meant that more qualified white males were denied contract awards or entrance to university programs.

The anti-affirmative action movement did not gain real political power until the 1990s. In California, one of the first states to seriously debate a retraction of affirmative action laws, Governor Pete Wilson began to voice his opposition. Though the NUL had long advocated self-reliance for blacks, it believed affirmative action to be an important safeguard against discrimination, and came out strongly against the governor's public statements, going so far as to move its scheduled 1996 annual convention out of Los Angeles. The urban league's high-profile protest, however, failed to stop the passage of Proposition 209 in November 1996. Proposition 209 was a state ballot initiative that effectively ended affirmative action programs in state and local government employment, contracting, and college admissions.

For a time, the NUL and other defenders of affirmative action feared that Proposition 209 would be the beginning of a domino effect—that affirmative action programs across the country would continue to fall in the wake of this changing political climate. This proved not to be the case. A similar measure failed in Houston, Texas; organizers in Florida failed to gather enough signatures to place a statewide initiative on the ballot, and Republicans in Congress proved unwilling to do away with affirmative action in contracting and hiring by federal agencies.

A 1998 initiative to end affirmative action in the state of Washington, however, had the NUL and other black activist groups concerned. Washington was not traditionally a state with a particularly powerful or mobilized minority voting bloc, and the ballot measure, known as Initiative 200, was almost certain to pass. Still, the NUL did what it could, spending $10,000 of its own money, and an additional $40,000 donated by local affiliates, in an attempt to defeat the measure. Ultimately the measure passed easily, by a margin of 58 to 42 percent.

Though ideologically opposed to the measure, the NUL seemed less concerned than other groups about the passage of Initiative 200. Most major corporations and universities, the NUL reasoned, were still committed to diversity, and would work to achieve it even without affirmative action legislation. President Hugh Price summed up the NUL's reaction to the California and

Washington repeals with these words in the *San Francisco Chronicle*: "I know of no corporation or university that wants to go backwards on this issue. The tools for accomplishing diversity and inclusion may change, but the fundamental objective is as sound as ever."

FUTURE DIRECTIONS

The trend toward the erosion of state affirmative action laws and practices has led black leaders to reevaluate the ways in which African Americans work to secure economic opportunity and success, and the NUL is leading the way by developing new strategies. In its report *The State of Black America 1998*, the NUL acknowledges the weakening of affirmative action laws and practices established during the civil rights era, and recommends new strategies for gaining black economic power and independence. The best long-term answer, according to the report, is the gradual accumulation of assets and wealth, even by poor families. With this as a goal, the NUL is already developing programs that will help urban minority families learn the basics of open-market investments such as stocks, bonds, and securities in order to build wealth and ease the financial burden on coming generations.

GROUP RESOURCES

The best source of information about the NUL is the organization's Web site, accessible at http://www.nul.org. The site includes information about many NUL programs, links to each of the 115 local affiliates, and the organization's Virtual Library, a searchable archive for viewing and downloading archived speeches, news, and other publications. The organization can also be reached by E-mail at info@nul.org. For further information about programs or administration, contact the national headquarters at (212) 558-5300. For information about legislation, policy, or research, write the Washington Office, National Urban League, Inc., 1111 14th St. NW, 6th Fl., Washington, DC 20005, phone (202) 898-1604 or fax (202) 682- 0782.

GROUP PUBLICATIONS

The premier publication of the NUL is its annual study, *The State of Black America*, a highly respected and widely quoted examination of current social and economic challenges facing African Americans. The organization also publishes various periodicals, such as the *BEEP Newlsetter*, *The National Urban League Equal Opportunity Journal*, the *Urban League News*, and the *Urban League Review*. The NUL also releases occasional reports on its research into particular issues, for example the recent special report *Losing Ground Bit by Bit: Low-Income Communities in the Information Age*.

Each week Hugh B. Price, president of the National Urban League, writes a weekly column, "To Be Equal," on important issues facing minorities in the United States. This column as well as the entire text of *The State of Black America*, selected reports, and other publications archived in the Virtual Library can be viewed at the NUL Web site at http://www.nul.org. For further information about NUL publications, send a request in writing to the National Urban League, Inc., 1111 14th St. NW, 6th Fl., Washington, DC 20005 or phone (202) 898-1604.

BIBLIOGRAPHY

Bivins, Larry. "Race Initiative Fails to Produce National Dialogue." *The Detroit News*, 16 June 1998.

Black Americans and Public Policy. New York: National Urban League Staff, 1988.

Dickerson, Dennis C. *Militant Mediator: Whitney M. Young, Jr.* Lexington, Ky.: University Press of Kentucky, 1998.

Freedberg, Louis. "Initiative Wins in Washington State." *San Francisco Chronicle*, 5 November 1998.

Gilliam, Dorothy. "Seeking Power Through the Purse." *Washington Post*, 9 August 1997.

Hamilton, Dona Cooper and Charles V. Hamilton. *The Dual Agenda: The African American Struggle for Civil and Economic Equality*. New York: Columbia University Press, 1997.

Herbert, Bob. "The Success Taboo." *New York Times*, 14 December 1997.

Johnson, Roy S. "There Is Opportunity and There Is Action: A Conversation with Hugh Price of the National Urban League." *Fortune*, 4 August 1997.

Moore, Jesse Thomas. *A Search for Equality: The National Urban League, 1910- 1961*. University Park, Pa.: Pennsylvania University Press, 1981.

Parris, Guichard and Lester Brooks. *Blacks in the City: A History of the National Urban League*. Boston: Little, Brown and Company, 1971.

Raspberry, William. "Inheriting Wealth." *Washington Post*, 10 August 1998.

National Wildlife Federation (NWF)

ESTABLISHED: 1938
EMPLOYEES: 600
MEMBERS: 4.4 million
PAC: None

Contact Information:
ADDRESS: 8925 Leesburg Pike
    Vienna, VA 22184
PHONE: (703) 790-4000
TOLL FREE: (800) 822-9919
FAX: (703) 790-4488
E-MAIL: info@nwf.org
URL: http://www.nwf.org
PRESIDENT; CEO: Mark Van Putten

WHAT IS ITS MISSION?

The National Wildlife Federation (NWF) states that its mission is "to educate, inspire, and assist individuals and organizations of diverse cultures to conserve wildlife and other natural resources and to protect the earth's environment in order to achieve a peaceful, equitable, and sustainable future."

HOW IS IT STRUCTURED?

The nonprofit NWF is led by a president and chief executive officer, who guides the organization's day-to-day operations. A 28-member volunteer board of directors includes 13 regional directors from across the United States who work with regional organizers to implement the organization's conservation programs and policies at a grassroots level. Beneath the board is a national network of 10 field offices and 46 affiliated organizations throughout the United States and its territories. The conservation programs and policies pursued by NWF's field offices are set each year by elected delegates from its state affiliates. NWF's regional organizers promote ongoing collaborative efforts between its field offices and affiliate organizations.

The 10 regional field offices assist individuals and grassroots groups nationwide, (including NWF state affiliates and like-minded organizations) on specific conservation issues. NWF's nationwide network of 46 state organizations elects key members of NWF's leadership through an annual resolution process. These affiliates are independent statewide organizations that support the purposes and objectives of NWF at the grassroots level by working to educate, encourage and facilitate the conservation efforts of their distinct base of members and supporters.

The NWF oversees a number of subsidiary organizations. The National Wildlife Federation Endowment was established in 1957 as a separate corporation to manage gifts and bequests that support the activities of the parent organization. The National Wildlife Productions, Inc., was formed in October 1994 to produce television and mass media projects; these include films, television programs, IMAX movies, and other media products. DeSoto Greeting, a wholly owned taxable subsidiary of the NWF, produces educational materials for the study of nature. Finally Wildlife Productions, Inc., established in 1996, focuses solely on producing the educational film *Whales*.

PRIMARY FUNCTIONS

The NWF performs its work primarily through two forums, education and activism. In the area of education the organization runs many programs designed to inform the public and the media. The NWF acts in cooperation with schools, community groups, and churches to increase knowledge about problems facing the environment and wildlife. The organization hopes that by increasing awareness about these issues, the public will be convinced to do its part in helping to preserve these resources.

The NWF promotes grassroots campaigning as the most effective way to achieve its goals. The organization organizes regional and local groups through its field offices to get them to advocate the cause of preservation. The NWF also advocates its position before both local lawmakers and Congress and supports legislation that furthers its causes.

PROGRAMS

The majority of NWF projects fall into community- and classroom-based categories. One of the most successful community-based projects has been the Backyard Wildlife Habitat program, which aids and encourages landscaping with the needs of wildlife and the health of the environment in mind. Through this program, NWF has certified over 20,000 properties worldwide. Building on the program's success, NWF's Schoolyard Habitats and Workplace Habitats programs create wildlife habitat learning places at educational institutions and corporate locations nationwide.

Classroom education activities focus on the hugely popular Animal Tracks program, which offers both online and printed conservation materials geared toward

elementary and middle schools to assist teachers in instructing children about the environment and how to care for it. In addition the NWF has also established a National Wildlife Week program, which reaches more than 20 million students by distributing free conservation curriculum materials to more than 620,000 teachers nationwide.

The National Conservation Achievement Awards program, created in 1965, recognizes individuals and organizations who have provided leadership in disseminating the conservation message and made great strides in helping protect the natural world.

BUDGET INFORMATION

NWF's 1996 revenues totaled $84,079,000, while total expenses were $83,284,000. Well over half ($52,051,000) of NPCA's revenues were derived from sales of publications, films, and educational materials. Membership dues accounted for about $11 million while donations and bequests accounted for another $10 million. The bulk of the remaining revenues came from royalties and investment income. A substantial portion of NPCA's budget ($9,974,402) was spent on conservation advocacy programs, education outreach, publications, films, and educational material. All told, program expenses accounted for about 50 percent of the total budget. Over $8 million was spent on management and general expenses and nearly $12 million on program development.

HISTORY

In February 1936, the new chief of the U.S. Biological Survey, Jay "Ding" Darling, convinced President Franklin Roosevelt to invite 1,500 conservationists to Washington, D.C., for a conference. The gathering allowed Darling to make his dream of melding conservationist groups into a national grassroots organization that would protect U.S. resources and wildlife into a reality. The General Wildlife Foundation was formally organized at the Washington meeting.

The fledgling group plunged into activism and was instrumental in the passage of the Federal Aid in Wildlife Restoration Act of 1937. The act provided federal funds for many wildlife programs for the first time. In 1938, the organization changed its name to the National Wildlife Federation. Darling also painted 16 different animals for the stamps that would become the group's trademark and primary fund-raiser. Each successive year the stamps featured different wildlife and became valuable collectibles.

During the 1940s, the NWF struggled to survive. World War II (1939–45) diverted funds, members, and

BUDGET:

1996 NWF Revenue

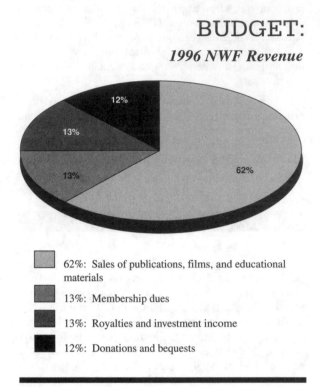

- 62%: Sales of publications, films, and educational materials
- 13%: Membership dues
- 13%: Royalties and investment income
- 12%: Donations and bequests

public interest from the conservation agenda. Yet, the federation managed to implement several new initiatives, which included broadcasting radio programs on conservation topics, providing educational pamphlets on conservation to schools, and publishing the "Conservation News" newsletter in 1945.

In the 1950s the NWF set up a scholarship fund for undergraduates and sponsored its first annual conservation conference. In 1953, through the efforts of the NWF and the Boone and Crockett Club, the Key Deer National Wildlife Refuge was established. Ranger Rick, a character created by NWF to educate children about conservation, made his first appearance in 1958 in a book titled, *The Adventures of Rick Raccoon.* And in 1959, the NWF broke ground for a new headquarters building in Washington, D.C.

NWF made quantum leaps forward on several fronts in the 1960s. *National Wildlife* magazine was launched in 1962 and increased membership and revenues. The first wildlife magazine for children *Ranger Rick* began publication in 1967. Congress passed the Clean Air Act and President Johnson signed the Wilderness Act into law. NWF had strongly supported and vigorously lobbied on behalf of both major pieces of conservation legislation. The first Endangered Species Act, also pushed by NWF, became law in 1966.

The 1970s saw a great expansion of activity by the NWF in many areas including education, research, lobbying, legal, publishing, and working with affiliates at

the grassroots level. Since conservation had become a global concern, NFW started a new magazine, *International Wildlife,* in 1970. The Clean Water Act was passed in 1972. In 1973 the NWF opened the Laurel Ridge Conservation Education Center in Virginia. That same year, the Endangered Species Act was passed, establishing a system by which plants and animals on the edge of extinction could be systematically protected. The following year, the NWF launched its Backyard Wildlife Habitat Program in 1974. Regional legal clinics were established in four sections of the United States, staffed by NWF attorneys, to work with affiliates and other local organizations on conservation problems.

In 1982 the NWF made a breakthrough in environmental protection by forming the Corporate Conservation council to encourage private enterprises to cooperate with conservation groups. Throughout the 1980s, NWF representatives testified at hundreds of congressional hearings on issues such as the Environmental Protection Agency's Superfund for toxic pollution cleanups, acid rain, and grazing reforms. The fight to preserve coastal wetlands became a top priority for the NWF in the late 1980s.

In 1994 the NWF heralded a victory in the fight begun in 1972, to restore the endangered bald eagle population when the bird was downgraded to the less-dire "threatened" status. The NWF had set up a data bank on bald eagles to help researchers and helped establish a refuge for the birds. As part of a plan to restore Yellowstone National Park's ecosystem to its natural state, the NWF successfully campaigned to return timber wolves to the park in 1995. In the late 1990s, many NWF programs began a comprehensive examination of how solutions to conservation problems involve entire ecosystems. This holistic environmental health approach to conservation issues will be a priority for the NWF through the twenty-first century.

CURRENT POLITICAL ISSUES

The NWF is concerned with almost every political issue that arises in an environmental context. Such issues include the effect of explosive population growth on the environment, the endangerment of fish by the construction of dams and reservoirs, and the poisoning of the environment because of industrial waste dumping. However, one issue of central importance to the NWF is the best method of balancing environmental and economic concerns. The organization realizes that the more profitable it can make the preservation of the environment, the more likely individuals and businesses will be to support its efforts.

Case Study: The NWF and Habitat Conservation Plans

The Endangered Species Act of 1973 was a landmark in habitat conservation efforts. It established a sys-

BIOGRAPHY:
Jay Norwood Darling

Environmentalist; Political Cartoonist (1876–1962)
At the beginning of the twentieth century, successful newspaper sketch artist Jay Norwood Darling drew a piece supporting President Theodore Roosevelt's proposal for a national forestry service. It was the first of many conservation-oriented sketches the artist would eventually publish. By 1917, Darling (known by his pen name "Ding") saw his work nationally syndicated in over 130 newspapers and was both a millionaire and the foremost political cartoonist in the United States. Using his drawings to reach what he perceived as a disinterested populace, Darling was ahead of his time in depicting issues like soil erosion and pollution. His sharp satire and detailed and distinctive drawings earned him the Pulitzer Prize for cartooning in 1923 and 1942. In 1934 United States Secretary of Agriculture Henry A. Wallace asked him to be chief of the U.S. Bureau of Biological Survey, forerunner of the U.S. Fish and Wildlife Service.

Although it represented a $92,000 per year salary decrease compared to his non-government work, Darling ran with the opportunity and worked to conserve the nation's wildlife with a zeal that had not been seen before. During his 20-month term, he secured $17 million for wildlife habitat restoration and established the Migratory Bird Conservation Commission. When he left his post, Darling led a successful effort to collectivize the myriad small environmental groups around the United States, and ultimately helped organize and lead the National Wildlife Federation. Before succumbing to illness in 1962, Darling received the Audubon Medal in 1960.

---

tem by which endangered species could be identified and protected. One of the act's greatest attributes was its ability to balance ecological needs with the economic needs of landowners. Through the development of habitat conservation plans (HCPs), non-federal landowners are allowed to knowingly harm an endangered species or its habitat in the pursuit of lawful economic pursuit. HCPs establish guidelines for how a landowner can go about doing this. The plan the landowner submits must contain methods of restoring and preserving the habitat and any species affected and must be approved by either the secretary of the interior or commerce.

However, the NWF and other like-minded groups claim that during the Clinton administrations, too many HCPs have been approved. In 1997 the NWF noted that prior to 1993, the year that the Clinton administration took office, merely a dozen HCPs were in effect and covered barely 1,000 square miles of land. Four years later, however, more than 200 had been approved and the land area affected was nearly 9 million square miles. According to the NWF, this was far too great a number; the organization questioned whether or not sustainable levels of endangered species were being maintained with so many sites for the government to keep track of. Especially distressing were the HCPs approved for logging companies that offered huge amounts of land and a period of more than 25 years to use it.

The NWF set about uncovering methods to enact a change in the legislation, specifically to make the requirements for obtaining an HCP more stringent. It

organized public education drives to get the word out about the possible abuses of HCPs that were taking place. It also petitioned the U.S. Fish and Wildlife Service and National Marine Fisheries Service, two federal agencies in part responsible for creation of HCP guidelines, to consider the ramifications of an abused HCP system. The organizations stated that they would assess the situation and decide if the guidelines needed to be changed. More than a year later, in March of 1999 the Fish and Wildlife Service released a five-point improvement plan for the HCP process. Much to the dismay of the NWF, these new guidelines fell short of the organization's expectations. It planned on using a hearing process offered by the Fish and Wildlife Service to communicate ways that the guidelines should be revised by the end of 1999.

FUTURE DIRECTIONS

In its constant pursuit to find new ways to get its message to the public, the NWF plans to take advantage of partnerships with other nonprofits and corporations to utilize the Internet. While the NWF has had a fairly extensive Web site since the mid 1990s, the organization is looking to use its World Wide Web presence to further the range of its advocacy. Already in early 1999 the NWF had created a virtual bookstore that, in conjunction with

FAST FACTS

Scientists have estimated that the current accelerated loss of species in some parts of the world is 1,000 to 10,000 times the natural rate.

(Source: National Wildlife Federation, 1999.)

barnesandnoble.com, offered a visitor the chance to purchase NWF publications.

GROUP RESOURCES

The NWF Web site at http://www.nwf.org contains information on current campaign issues and developments, press releases, and membership details. For more information about the organization, write to the National Wildlife Federation, 8925 Leesburg Pike, Vienna, VA 22184.

GROUP PUBLICATIONS

The NWF has many publications that it offers to promote environmental conservation. Both *National Wildlife* and *International Wildlife* magazines educate readers about sustainability and the conservation issues impacting wildlife and people around the globe. *Ranger Rick* magazine is directed toward children and uses photographs and exciting stories to get them interested in conservation and preservation issues. In addition, the NWF publishes various reports on environmental issues such as "International Trade and the Environment."

Many of the NWF publications are available via the World Wide Web at http://www.nwf.org. For more information on obtaining the organization's publications, write to the National Wildlife Federation, 8925 Leesburg Pike, Vienna, VA 22184.

BIBLIOGRAPHY

Brick, Phil. "Determined Opposition: The Wise Use Movement Challenges Environmentalism." *Environment*, 1 October 1995.

DiSilvestro, Roger. "What's Killing the Key Deer?" *National Wildlife*, 12 February, 1997.

"NWF Celebrates Conservation Win in 1996 Farm Bill." *International Wildlife*, 17 July 1996.

Turbak, Gary. "Seeking the Missing Lynx; Researchers Use a Novel Technique to Pin Down the Exact Status of the Declining Lynx."*National Wildlife*, 10 December 1997.

Wiley, Karen B., and Steven L. Rhodes. "From Weapons to Wildlife: The Transformation of the Rocky Mountain Arsenal." *Environment*, 1 June 1998.

National Women's Political Caucus (NWPC)

WHAT IS ITS MISSION?

The mission of the National Women's Political Caucus (NWPC) "is to identify, recruit, train and support women seeking elected and appointed office." Toward that end, the organization organizes women throughout the United States at the grassroots level, seeks out and trains potential candidates for office at all levels of government, and evaluates candidates' support for a wide range of feminist issues. The NWPC is completely nonpartisan; its political activity is based on the liberal feminist principles of equal rights for women, government support of child care, and abortion rights.

HOW IS IT STRUCTURED?

The NWPC is a nonprofit group that organizes women throughout the United States through its national office and its network of state and local chapters. The national office is based in Washington, D.C., and is responsible for developing the organization's programs and determining the candidates it will endorse for national office. The local chapters are responsible for endorsing and supporting women running for local public office, finding viable women candidates for local, state and federal office, organizing women at the grassroots level, and hosting NWPC training seminars. The national office often bases its endorsements of candidates for national office—for example, seats in the House of Representatives—on recommendations made by the state caucuses. The national office will formally endorse a candidate for local office—any office below the gubernato-

ESTABLISHED: July 11, 1971
EMPLOYEES: 8
MEMBERS: 10,000
PAC: Campaign Support Committee (CSC); Victory Fund

Contact Information:

ADDRESS: 1211 Connecticut Ave. NW
    Ste. 425
    Washington, DC 20036
PHONE: (202) 785-1100
TOLL FREE: (800) 729-6972
FAX: (202) 785-3605
E-MAIL: WinNWPC@aol.com
URL: http://www.nwpc.org
PRESIDENT: Anita Perez Ferguson

rial level—if the state chapter believes the endorsement may be critical to the candidate's success.

Every two years, the state chapters send delegates to the national convention where the NWPC president and national governing board are elected. The president, the NWPC's official head, is responsible for the day-to-day management of the organization. She oversees the Washington office, its staff, and NWPC finances, is the organization's official public spokesperson, and serves as a member of the board. The NWPC presidency is a paid, full-time position. The national governing board is composed of approximately 48 NWPC vice presidents and committee leaders. The board sets policy for the group and organizes its various organizational interests and priorities at its quarterly meetings. In addition to the elected president and board, the NWPC hires an executive director who runs its Washington headquarters and coordinates the group's fund-raising efforts. The executive director is responsible to the national governing board.

The NWPC has two task forces, one for Republican women and one for Democrats. The task forces search out viable candidates in their respective parties and develop strategies to attract more women into politics. The Republican women's task force also fights the growing radicalization of the party by the religious right. Task force leaders attend the quarterly board meetings.

PRIMARY FUNCTIONS

The NWPC uses many means to aid women in winning political office. These include training seminars in campaign techniques, financial and expert support of candidates, promoting women candidates for appointed positions, acting as a clearinghouse for information about female candidates and women in politics in general, and sponsoring special events where women can network and learn about the activities of the NWPC.

The National Women's Political Caucus provides high-quality training for women in important campaign and political skills. Its leadership seminars are offered regularly across the nation through NWPC state and local chapters. The seminars cover every element of a political campaign, including development of a campaign plan, motivating volunteers, using the media, and raising money. Every election cycle, the NWPC trains more than 2,000 women candidates and campaign workers.

The NWPC endorses and gives financial support to candidates for political office at the local, state, and national levels. The national organization supports candidates in federal and gubernatorial races. The state chapters support lower state positions and local offices. The national office plans to become more involved in mayoral elections in the future. NWPC support takes different forms. It campaigns for candidates; it mounts fund-

raising drives; it provides campaign funds to some candidates; its volunteers go door-to-door to get voters to the polls. The NWPC also gives public endorsements to candidates. Candidates are first considered by the NWPC political planning committee who then recommends names to the National Steering Committee. The political planning committee considers a candidate's political record, her position on issues like abortion rights, child care, and the Equal Rights Amendment, and evaluates her ability to win the election, before recommending an endorsement to the board.

The caucus uses its influence to support the appointment of women to important posts in government. The NWPC worked with the Coalition for Women's Appointments to evaluate the credentials of hundreds of women. They compiled a list of 200 women and presented it to the Clinton administration during the 1996 election campaign. Secretary of State Madeline Albright, Secretary of Labor Alexis Herman, and Small Business Administrator Aida Alvarez were among the women recommended by the coalition.

The NWPC publishes and distributes information about women involved in politics. It compiles candidate lists and reports about women running for high office. Its *Directory of Women Elected Officials* is a source book of women serving in federal, state, and many local elective offices. The NWPC has documented the progress women have made in the political sphere in its "Fact Sheet on Women's Political Progress." The caucus sponsors research about women and their role in the political process.

The caucus sponsors a variety of events throughout the United States intended to raise the awareness of women's issues and women candidates, to mobilize women at the grassroots level, and to create opportunities for women to meet and network. Events include the caucus's three yearly steering meetings and its two award ceremonies. The Good Guys Awards recognize men who have made an outstanding contribution on behalf of women. The Exceptional Merit Awards (EMMAs) honor exceptional coverage of women's issues by members of the media. Every two years the group holds its national convention.

PROGRAMS

A critical element of the NWPC's work is its political and leadership skills programs for women of almost all ages. It introduced its Girls' Leadership Training Program in 1997. Aimed at girls 12 to 14 years of age, the training focuses on three areas: civic participation, organizing a group to take action, and public speaking and presentations. Each seminar, which is open to no more than 25 girls, lasts a full day; a second follow-up session occurs six months after the first.

The caucus offers its Young Women's Campaign Skills Training every two years. Recognized experts teach the basics of campaigning skills in a day-long session. More than 350 women between the ages of 18 and 35 attended the 1996 sessions in Washington, D.C., and Los Angeles. An information and job fair staffed with representatives from various political organizations is held along with the training, providing an opportunity for attendees to meet and network.

The caucus has been offering its Basic and Advanced Campaigning Skills Training—the core of its training programs—since 1991. The courses are intended to give women a solid grounding in the art of successful political campaigns. They are taught throughout the United States by experts in the field, using books written by NWPC representatives. Since it was initiated, more than 5,000 women have completed the seminars. Prices depend on the chapter that is sponsoring the event. Corporate training is held for female executives, to improve their management skills and encourage their involvement in the political process. The NWPC started its International Orientation Program in 1995. It is designed to teach women from abroad and their women's organizations about the activities of the NWPC.

BUDGET INFORMATION

The national office of the NWPC has an annual budget of approximately $750,000. About one-third of that sum comes from dues paid by members. Each state chapter sets its own membership dues. Approximately $20 of each member's dues go to the national office. Another third of the budget comes from outside contributions, and the final third comes from corporate and government grants. Most of the corporate money is used to finance the various leadership training programs run by the organization. Money used in candidate campaigns is not part of the NWPC budget. It comes exclusively from the two NWPC PACs: the Campaign Support Committee and the Victory Fund. The former accepts donations only from NWPC members. The latter was established to enable nonmembers to make donations that would support candidates endorsed by the caucus.

HISTORY

The NWPC was founded at the height of the mid-1900's American women's movement when 320 women from 26 states met under the leadership of feminists such as Shirley Chisholm, Bella Abzug, Gloria Steinem, and Betty Friedan to form the caucus on July 10 and 11, 1971. It's first statement of purpose pledged to fight sexism, racism, institutional violence, and poverty. The means they chose for the fight were the reform of the major

political parties, the election of women to public office, the advocacy of women's issues, and the support of feminist candidates regardless of party. It was, according to Sue Thomas and Clyde Wilcox, the first time the strategy of electing women to act for women's interests had been explicitly followed.

In the first three years of its existence, female state officeholders increased by 36 percent, partly the result of NWPC recruitment and leadership programs. The passage of the Equal Rights Amendment was a major priority of the NWPC and in 1975 the organization established the election of pro-ERA candidates as its top priority. By 1976 the organization was on secure enough financial footing to form a political action committee and began contributing financially to selected races. In 1977 it adopted explicit guidelines for candidate endorsements: candidates had to be feminists; they had to have shown support for caucus positions in the past, and to openly express support for them. Specifically, they had to advocate passage of the ERA, women's freedom to get an abortion, and publicly-funded child care.

In 1977–78, during the 95th congressional session, the caucus began to compile a chart of how congressmen and senators voted on women's issues. Decisive issues that session included equal representation on the National Commission of Neighborhoods, tax deductions for home day-care services, flextime for federal workers, the extension of the food stamp program, federal funding for abortion, the Humphrey-Hawkins full employment bill, and raising the minimum wage. By the 101st Congress in 1989–90, the most important issues were federal funding for child care programs, family and medical leave, the Civil Rights Act of 1990, and the availability of abortion.

The late 1980s and early 1990s were difficult years for feminists. Ten years of conservative Republican administrations had dismantled gains made over the previous decades in abortion, and federal funding of programs important to women. In 1991 when the Senate Judiciary Committee reacted with hostility to Anita Hill's claims that she had been sexually harassed by Supreme Court nominee Clarence Thomas, it seemed just one more sign of the new low to which women's issues had sunk in Washington. In reply, the caucus took out a full-page ad in the *New York Times* that asked "What if 14 women instead of 14 men, had sat on the Senate Judiciary Committee during the confirmation hearings of Clarence Thomas?" The following year contributions to the NWPC were twice as high as they had been two years earlier.

In 1993 and 1994, the NWPC instituted a drive at its national office to find new women candidates. Gains were small, however, and the group shifted the focus of the efforts onto its state organizations. Nonetheless during the 1993–94 election cycle, the caucus trained 2,500 women candidates and campaign workers in its seminars, a record number. The national Steering Committee put

BIOGRAPHY:

Shirley Chisholm

Legislator; Activist (b. 1924) "I ran because someone had to do it first," said Shirley Chisholm of her symbolic bid for the Democratic presidential nomination in 1972. This groundbreaking move was only one milestone in a long, distinguished political career. Beginning as a district representative in her own state's assembly, in 1968 Chisholm parlayed her success and popularity into a seat in the United States House of Representatives. Even before her landslide victory, Chisholm envisioned her role in the House as an advocate for disadvantaged groups. In her book, *The Good Fight,* written after her 1972 campaign, Chisholm asks rhetorically, "Could it be that the persistence of poverty, hunger, racism, war, semiliteracy, and unemployment is partly due to the fact that we have excluded so many persons from the processes that make and carry out social policies?" In addition to sponsoring bills to help the poor and disadvantaged, during her 14-year tenure, the staunch Democrat served on the Veterans'

Affairs Committee, the Education and Labor Committee, and the influential House Rules Committee. After leaving office in 1982, Chisholm became the Purington Professor of Political Science at Mt. Holyoke College in Massachusetts. In 1984 she cofounded the National Political Congress of Black Women, a group that sent a 100-woman delegation to the 1988 Democratic

National Convention. A strong supporter, Chisholm joined both of activist Jesse Jackson's presidential campaigns. "Jackson is the voice of the poor, the disenchanted, the disillusioned," she was quoted as saying in *Newsweek*, "and that is exactly what I was."

together seminars in which state leaders could examine and learn from past campaigns. In the congressional elections of 1998, the NWPC saw women make great strides in winning office. They held 67 seats in the 106th Congress—58 in the House and nine in the Senate. As recently as the 102nd Congress, women had held only 30 seats in both houses.

CURRENT POLITICAL ISSUES

The NWPC has been involved in most women's issues in U.S. political life. It is a special interest group in the classic sense, serving the political interests of a well-defined segment of the population. Its fundamental principle is that women are best able to advocate issues important to other women. In 1994, however, it released a report that addressed the "gender gap" in American politics, and reached the surprising conclusion that women—the NWPC's constituency—were not a separate predictable political bloc.

Case Study: The Political Gender Gap

According to conventional political wisdom, women are much more likely than men to vote for Democratic candidates. That assumption, however, did not play out in the 1994 elections, during which large numbers of women switched unexpectedly to Republican candidates. In 1994 the NWPC issued a report just after the Repub-

licans won a majority in the House of Representatives for the first time in decades. The NWPC suggested that the difference between the way men and women vote— the so-called gender gap—was not a particularly important factor in American partisan politics. It was a conclusion that contradicted an assumption many analysts and groups held almost without question. The NWPC wrote "women voters are not monolithic and do not constitute a voting bloc in the same sense as blacks or Jews."

Statistics did show an 11–percentage-point difference between how men and women voted in 1994, which reflected a much greater split than in previous elections. But, as the NWPC pointed out, there was a wider gap between other voter categories including: how married and single individuals voted, which resulted in a 12–point difference, or the 30-point gap between someone who lived in an urban area versus the country. Essentially, the NWPC implied, other factors like race, income, and where one lives, are much more important in predicting how a woman will vote than the simple fact that she is a woman. For example, there was a 50-point difference between black and white party preference, and a 35-point difference between Jewish and non-Jewish voters. The NWPC concluded "it makes no sense to talk about 'the women's vote' as though all women vote the same."

Public Impact

Other feminist and liberal groups disputed the findings. Emily's List, a group that supports women candidates with money and advice, called the findings "utterly mistaken" in the *Washington Times,* adding the gender gap was indeed "a political fact . . . the candidates had better heed." Mark Gersh of the National Committee for an Effective Congress told the *Washington Post* that there was "a huge cleavage in the electorate" between white men and women. Katherine Deans, the communications director of the Democratic Party in Florida called the 11-point gap between male and female voters "the Grand Canyon of gaps." Deans further contended that there are issues that affect women disproportionately, such as health and child care, the minimum wage, and Medicare. Candidates could attract significant numbers of women voters by addressing those issues, Deans said.

The fact that the report was released by a group that for more than 20 years had worked to further the special interests of women in the electorate and to find candidates that addressed those particular interests made the findings all the more surprising. It seemed to contradict the very basis of NWPC activism. According to the NWPC, however, the report was very much in line with the group's nonpartisan politics. One position paper advocating reaching out to Republican women stated, "Concerns of special interest to women are not the ones we want as partisan issues! We in NWPC are fighting so that issues especially pertinent to women become accepted by both parties." According to the NWPC, women's issues transcend any gender gap or party preferences. Because of that, the NWPC suggested, the Democrats could not simply take the women's vote for granted.

SUCCESSES AND FAILURES

NWPC claims at least partial responsibility for the success women candidates had at the polls in November 1998. The reelection of Senators Patty Murray in Washington State and Barbara Boxer in California, after very hard-fought, close races, were significant victories for the women's groups who supported them. In 1998 the NWPC reported an increase in qualified candidates—candidates who had already held office—for federal office. Those numbers increased because of the activities of local NWPC caucuses and the group's leadership seminars for candidates and campaign workers.

FUTURE DIRECTIONS

The focus of the organization through the first decade of the twenty-first century, according to its president Anita Perez Ferguson, is to vigorously pursue its primary organizational goal of increasing the number of women in elective office from the federal level down to the local levels. State chapters will integrate structures and programs developed by the national office. For example, the California NWPC is organizing an appointments project to recruit women candidates for appointive office and encourage state officials to select women for those offices. State chapters will be examining the open mayoral elections and looking for viable candidates to run for the seats in 2000, with assistance from the national office in selecting cities of 100,000 or more population. A critical element of both long- and short-term plans is the NWPC leadership seminars to train women candidates, which will be held regularly in different parts of the country.

GROUP RESOURCES

The NWPC Web site at http://www.nwpc.org contains a wealth of information about the group, women in politics, and political issues that affect women. News about caucus events, the candidates for state and national office that the caucus has endorsed, and statements by caucus leaders on current affairs are posted. Information about job openings at NWPC is available at 1-800-729-NWPC. A schedule of caucus leadership seminars together with price, location, and registration information, is available on the Web site. It can also be obtained by writing the NWPC, 1211 Connecticut Ave. NW, Ste. 425, Washington, DC 20036 or by calling (202) 785-1100.

GROUP PUBLICATIONS

The NWPC publishes a quarterly newsletter, *Women's Political Times,* about women in politics. A sample copy may be requested by writing the NWPC, 1211 Connecticut Ave. NW, Suite 425, Washington, DC 20036 or by calling (202) 785-1100. The *Directory of Women Elected Officials* lists contact information for women federal and state officials as well as many local officials. The "Fact Sheet on Elected Women Officials" tracks women officeholders from the 1970s to the present. Both are available free of charge by writing or phoning the NWPC. The "Fact Sheet on Women's Political Progress" documents the progress women have made in political life since the 1970s. A complete list of caucus publications can be obtained by calling (202) 785-1100.

BIBLIOGRAPHY

Barta, Carolyn. "Women's Caucus Work is Never Done." *Dallas Morning News,* 20 August 1997.

Burrell, Barbara C. *A Woman's Place Is in the House.* Ann Arbor, Mich.: University of Michigan Press, 1994.

Conway, M. Margaret, Gertrude A. Steuernagel, and David W. Ahern. *Women and Political Participation.* Washington, D.C.: Congressional Quarterly Press, 1997.

Evans, Sara. *Born for Liberty: A History of Women in America.* New York: Free Press. 1989.

"Historic Efforts." *Dallas Morning News,* 20 August 1997.

O'Donnell, Norah M. "Gender Gap?: Lincoln, Six New House Members Set Record for Women." *Roll Call,* 5 November 1998.

Raasch, Chuck. "Gender Gap Overplayed, Study by National Women's Political Caucus Shows." *Gannett News Service,* 24 August 1995.

Thomas, Sue, and Clyde Wilcox. *Women and Elective Office.* New York: Oxford University Press, 1998.

Zepatos, Thalia, and Elizabeth Kaufman. *Women for a Change: A Grassroots Guide to Activism and Politics.* New York: Facts On File, 1995.

Operation Rescue National (ORN)

WHAT IS ITS MISSION?

The mission of Operation Rescue National (ORN) is to stop abortion and to enlist the support of Christians in opposing its practice. While other pro-life organizations attempt to halt the practice of abortion through legislation, ORN chooses directly confrontational methods. ORN is most known for organizing nonviolent, yet controversial protests at abortion clinics. ORN feels strongly that abortion is not a political issue but a moral issue dictated through Christian gospel.

HOW IS IT STRUCTURED?

Operation Rescue National is a coalition of Christians with national headquarters located in Dallas, Texas. Separate Operation Rescue organizations exist at the state and local levels and are called upon to assist the national organization when help is needed with protests or other initiatives. ORN is a nonprofit group that receives funding solely from supporters. Contributions are not tax deductible.

The group is headed by an executive director, who serves an undetermined length of time. The executive director is the spokesperson for ORN and holds a particularly visible leadership position. As the face and voice of ORN, directors have repeatedly been put in jail for civil disobedience. ORN is also headed by a board of directors, which oversees organization administration and policy. The ORN national office has no paid staff and no membership system, instead the group relies on volunteer supporters across the country to carry out initiatives.

ESTABLISHED: 1987
EMPLOYEES: Not made available
MEMBERS: Not made available
PAC: None

Contact Information:

ADDRESS: PO Box 740066
    Dallas, TX 75374
PHONE: (972) 494-5316
FAX: (972) 276-9361
E-MAIL: orn@airmail.net
URL: http://www.orn.org
DIRECTOR: Rev. Philip L. Benham

PRIMARY FUNCTIONS

Although it protests against other issues, ORN's main mission is to prevent abortions from occurring and to spread information about what the organization calls the brutality of abortion. Most notably, the organization conducts acts of civil disobedience by protesting at or near abortion clinic facilities. Since ORN is committed to upholding biblical principles in its endeavors, the organization's methods are usually nonviolent but are often controversial. Many of the protests have resulted in arrests of ORN supporters. At the protests, ORN supporters use methods such as chanting, rushing clinic clientele, and displaying graphic posters of aborted fetuses. In some cases, protesters do dissuade individuals from entering the clinics and having an abortion; the group considers these instances to be successful "rescues." ORN most often succeeds in closing the clinics down for several hours during the protests.

ORN also places emphasis on educational protests meant to be proactive. Specifically, the group targets high school students by organizing anti-abortion protests on or near public high school grounds. Reasoning that a high school student needs to be informed about abortion before becoming pregnant, ORN supporters gather in front of schools, giving students information about abortion and displaying large posters that depict abortion. Use of the posters has been controversial because they are often quite graphic. One mother, quoted in an article from the *Dallas Morning News* (October 5, 1996), claimed that her 2-year-old daughter was traumatized by the explicit images. ORN also uses graphic posters in protests aimed at the general public and has, on occasion, not hesitated to target young school children.

ORN also attempts to dissuade people from supporting or receiving abortions by publishing materials including books, posters, videos, and bumper stickers. The organization provides supporters and protesters with material to hand out in confrontational situations and a list of questions and answers so that protesters are prepared when challenged.

ORN's activities are not limited to protesting against abortion. The organization creates campaigns to fight trends and events that they believe oppose the values of the Christian belief system. For example, ORN worked in coalition with the American Family Association (AFA) to protest at the entrance of Disney World in Orlando, Florida. The organization and other Christian groups opposed Disney World's stand on homosexuality: Disney World has long endorsed gay-friendly policies in its organization and a Disney-owned TV network aired the April 1997 episode of the program *Ellen*, in which a gay character "came out" on television. ORN has also organized protests at Barnes and Noble bookstores in the United States, claiming the stores carry books that contain child pornography.

PROGRAMS

ORN programs are short term efforts to deal with a current issue or concern of the organization. In 1993, for example, the organization launched the Cities of Refuge Campaign. This effort organized clinic protests, rallies, and picketing in many U.S. cities including Minneapolis-St. Paul, Minnesota; Cleveland, Ohio; Philadelphia, Pennsylvania; Dallas-Fort Worth, Texas; San Jose, California; Jackson, Mississippi; and the area around Melbourne, Florida. The goal of the campaign was to ensure that any individual would be within a day's drive of rescue from abortion. In a Knight-Ridder/Tribune News Service article dated July 17, 1993, ORN claimed to have rescued and prevented 39 abortions during the campaign.

In an effort to address what ORN considers the "godlessness" of public schools in the United States, the organization launched the God is Going Back to School Campaign in early 1997. According to ORN, Christian influence has been steadily declining in public schools. The organization cites evidence of this by pointing to increased school violence, drug use, and decreasing test scores. The program was created to expose students to Christian ideals and to educate high school students about abortion and get them thinking about the issues before decisions about pregnancy became a factor in their lives. To carry out the campaign, ORN supporters hand out literature at or near high school grounds and engage students in discussion about abortion and Christian principles. During the campaign, ORN claims to have prevented abortions, converted students to Christianity, and convinced students to postpone becoming pregnant.

BUDGET INFORMATION

Not made available.

HISTORY

The anti-abortion movement began to gather momentum in 1973, when the landmark Supreme Court case *Roe v. Wade* legalized abortion in all 50 states. In the years following the court decision, anti-abortion groups mobilized their forces and began to build power. Operation Rescue was founded in 1987 by Randall Terry, a lay Christian Minister. Terry proved to be an adversarial and uninhibited leader of the organization. According to his own accounts, he spent seven months in jail and had been arrested 35 times for protesting abortions. In 1993 Terry—still an anti-abortion activist but no longer leader of ORN—was sentenced to five months in prison when he aided another activist in presenting a human fetus to President Bill Clinton at the Democratic convention in New York City. Throughout the 1990s

Terry remained in the news; an article in *The Nation* (August 22, 1994) claimed that Terry was organizing a training camp at his New York estate that would produce militant and fierce followers. In 1998 Terry entered politics in a bid for a seat in the United States Congress.

Kevin Tucci replaced Terry as executive director in 1990. At this point, Operation Rescue became Operation Rescue National (ORN). A former Assemblies of God minister, Tucci had a lower-key style of leadership but was no less afraid of being arrested for the anti-abortion cause. He was first arrested in 1988 at an anti-abortion rally that Terry had invited him to and which he spoke at. During Tucci's leadership, ORN continued to add to its arsenal of protest tactics. New methods included picketing abortion providers at their homes. And, in instances where ORN supporters were unwilling to be arrested, adopted more passive methods of protest like prayer vigils.

In 1991 ORN made national news when the organization held a 46-day blockade of a clinic in Wichita, Kansas. The blockade ground city operations to a halt and resulted in 2,600 arrests. The organization continued to intensify its tactics, and offered supporters a training camp in Melbourne, Florida—complete with subjects ranging from sidewalk counseling to surveillance.

By 1993 more mainstream pro-life factions (including politicians and the Minnesota Catholic Archbishop) deplored the tactics used by ORN, which had escalated to include displaying "wanted posters" of abortion providers and harassing providers' families. ORN had also developed and mailed letters to patients of gynecologists—the letters were intended to dissuade the recipients from considering abortion.

One abortion protester, who was allegedly associated with ORN, went too far in 1993 and broke the organization's code of nonviolence. Rachelle Shannon entered an abortion clinic in August and shot abortion provider and physician George Tiller. Shannon was perceived among abortion activists that knew her as a generally peaceful woman, and had often appeared on videotapes of Operation Rescue protests. While ORN leaders claimed they didn't know Shannon, her act caused a rift between anti-abortion groups as they struggled to decide which tactics were and were not appropriate.

In February 1994 repercussions from the Shannon incident led to division among ORN leadership as the group continued to struggle with the role of violence in anti-abortion protests. Tucci wanted ORN leaders to sign an agreement that they would not discuss violence of any kind at all. Several of the leaders disagreed and Tucci resigned shortly thereafter. He was replaced by Reverend Philip Benham, a pastor and founder of the Dallas contingent of Operation Rescue, and ORN headquarters moved from Melbourne to Dallas.

ORN celebrated a huge public relations victory in 1995 when Norma McCorvey (also known as Roe in the famous 1973 *Roe v. Wade* decision that legalized abor-

Operation Rescue National uses confrontational methods, like this 1992 sit-in in Buffalo, New York, to achieve its goal of stopping abortion. (AP/Wide World Photos)

tion) became a Christian and announced her opposition to abortion except in cases of fetal deformity or when necessary to save the mother's life. McCorvey originally met ORN Director Benham when she worked for the Choice for Women Abortion Clinic in Dallas. Benham befriended McCorvey and invited her to a church service where she was baptized as a Christian.

Benham's extreme tactics, however, have lost the organization some supporters. Among them is conservative televangelist Rev. Jerry Falwell who supported ORN until Benham took over. As a countermeasure Benham targeted Falwell's Liberty University bookstore with a protest in 1998, claiming it sold controversial material that was pornographic in nature.

CURRENT POLITICAL ISSUES

ORN's involvement with current issues takes a religious rather than a political focus. As such, the group does not attempt to influence the political system using methods like lobbying for bills or directly challenging abortion policy. Instead, the group seeks to bring their message to the public and to change public opinion specifically about abortion. ORN uses similar strategies

FAST FACTS

If current rates are sustained, approximately 43 percent of women in the United States will have an abortion in their lifetime.

(Source: Data from Alan Guttmacher Institute cited in: "Abortions in America." *U.S. News & World Report,* January 19, 1998.)

when combating other issues such as homosexuality and pornography. At times, organization supporters and leadership have committed acts of civil disobedience in carrying out protest activities in an attempt to bring their message to the public. By the late 1990s such activities were being seriously challenged.

Case Study: ORN Tactics Challenged in Court

In November 1997, ORN launched an abortion protest at the E. C. Glass High School in Lynchburg, Virginia. The protest was part of ORN's God is Going Back to School Campaign, which targets high schools for abortion protest. ORN enlisted the help of a nearby Christian college, Liberty University, for assistance with the protest. On the day of the demonstration, 300 Liberty students and the executive director of ORN, Reverend Philip Benham, gathered outside the school to advocate against abortion and engage high school students in discussion.

Although ORN claims that they were not trespassing and that protesters moved off private property when told by local police, Benham and the leader of another anti-abortion organization were arrested and later convicted of trespassing in February 1998. Because the judge refused to let Benham leave the state of Virginia, Benham chose to begin serving his six month jail sentence immediately. Both leaders filed appeals. The organization was outraged by the sentence, claiming that in this case, peaceful Christian activists had been given harsher jail terms than "true criminals."

Public reaction to ORN's high school demonstrations have been mixed. The organization plans to continue with the God is Going Back to School Campaign, but Benham's arrest in Virginia may set a precedent for whether the demonstrations continue, or how ORN plans to carry them out in the future. What may also affect ORN's future tactics is the outcome of an April 1998 Supreme Court ruling. In a case that began with the

National Organization of Woman (NOW), Inc. v. Scheidler (January 1994), the court ultimately ruled that ORN was subject to the Racketeer Influence and Corrupt Organization (RICO) statute because of its threatening and confrontational tactics at abortion clinics. This meant that illegal actions at protests could be prosecuted under federal racketeering laws and that organizations such as NOW or Planned Parenthood could sue ORN for damages.

While a 1997 court ruling (*Scenic vs. Pro-Choice Network*) had affirmed that groups like ORN could protest in front of abortion clinics because it constituted the right to free speech, the 1998 interpretation of RICO proposed that organizations like ORN could be held accountable for anything construed to be "part of a pattern of criminal activity." As a result of the 1998 court case, ORN was liable for almost $86,000 in damages to two clinics, and faced the possibility of a nationwide injunction that would ban all ORN protest activities involving clinics. In the case of ORN's high school demonstrations, an interpretation of RICO could hold the entire organization responsible for any act of civil disobedience perpetrated by any ORN supporter.

FUTURE DIRECTIONS

According to the organization, ORN will direct its future efforts wherever God calls. Although protesting against abortion remains a focus of ORN, the organization will continue to organize demonstrations at businesses such as Disney World or Barnes and Noble where there is a perceived anti-family element. The organization will also broaden its focus beyond abortion in order to address other issues of concern to Christians such as pornography or homosexuality. The organization also plans to continue its goal of returning Christian values to public schools.

GROUP RESOURCES

ORN maintains a Web page at http://www.orn.org; the site includes press releases, articles, text of newsletters, information on the organization's latest initiatives, and links to other pro-life and Christian-related sites.

GROUP PUBLICATIONS

ORN sells books, videos, posters, and bumper stickers that deal with the issue of abortion—publications can be ordered by contacting the organization (address: PO Box 740066, Dallas, TX., 75374; phone: 972-494-5316; fax: 972-276-9361). Book titles include *Grand Illusions: The Legacy of Planned Parenthood* and *Accessory to*

Murder. Publications may be ordered by contacting the National ORN office. ORN also produces the *Operation Rescue National Newsletter*, available monthly and on the Web site. Call ORN for hard copy subscriptions to the newsletter.

BIBLIOGRAPHY

Cunningham, Amy. "Who are the Women Who are Pro-Life?" *Glamour,* February 1994.

Demchak, Patricia. "Former Clinic Owner Crusades Against Her Own Past." *University Wire,* 22 January 1998.

"Falwell Stung by Protestors Claims of Porn at LU Bookstore." *Church & State,* May 1998.

Gold, Jeffrey. "Harassment Ban at NJ Clinics Used To Defend Abortion Foe." *Rocky Mountain News,* 28 March 1998.

Means, Marianne. "Abortion Still Irreconcilable Issue." *Rocky Mountain News,* 17 November 1997.

Snyder, Jodie, and Susie Steckner. "Nightmare at Abortion Clinic: Police Report Details Medical Chaos Death." *Arizona Republic,* 15 December 1998.

Waldman, Steven, Elise Ackerman, and Rita Rubin. "Abortions in America." *U.S. News & World Report,* 19 January 1998.

"Where Have All The Babies Gone?" *Life,* 1 January 1998.

Williams, Dick. "Roe v. Wade at 25: Tide May be Turning on Abortion." *Atlanta Journal,* 20 January 1998.

Ybarra, Michael J. "Tracing the Evolution of the Abortion War." *Los Angeles Times,* 22 January 1998.

Organization of Chinese Americans (OCA)

ESTABLISHED: 1973
EMPLOYEES: 4
MEMBERS: 4,000
PAC: None

Contact Information:

ADDRESS: 1001 Connecticut Avenue NW, Ste. 707
    Washington, DC 20036
PHONE: (202) 223-5500
FAX: (202) 296-0540
E-MAIL: oca@ocanatl.org
URL: http://www.ocanatl.org
NATIONAL PRESIDENT: George Ong
EXECUTIVE DIRECTOR: Daphne Kwok

WHAT IS ITS MISSION?

According to the organization's Web site, the Organization of Chinese Americans (OCA) is a "national non-profit, non-partisan advocacy organization of concerned Chinese Americans. OCA is dedicated to securing the rights of Chinese Americans and Asian American citizens and permanent residents through legislative and policy initiatives at all levels of the government. OCA aims to embrace the hopes and aspirations of the 1.6 million citizens and residents of Chinese Ancestry in the United States as well as to better the lives of the 7.6 million Asian Americans across the country. OCA's primary objectives include promoting active participation of Asian Americans in both civic and national matters; securing social justice, equal opportunity, and equal treatment of Asian Americans; eliminating prejudices, stereotypes and ignorance of Asian Americans; and promoting the cultural heritage of Chinese and other Asian Americans."

As Asian Americans have established a growing presence in the United States, the need has grown for advocacy organizations to defend their interests. OCA is such an organization—one of six national Asian American advocacy organizations in the United States and the first advocacy organization for Chinese Americans. Of all Asian American groups in the country, Chinese Americans represent the largest segment, making up seven percent of the U.S. population. The organization focuses mainly on civil rights advocacy and education and plays an active role in policy making that includes affirmative action, welfare reform, immigration, and campaign finance reform.

HOW IS IT STRUCTURED?

OCA's main office is located in Washington, D.C. The organization is headed by a national board chaired by a national president and including members from an executive council, presidents of each chapter of OCA, and other membership representatives. The national board sets policy and direction for the organization. OCA's executive council receives guidance from the board and is responsible for implementing organizational policy initiatives. The 14 members of the council serve two-year terms and are elected by OCA membership. A small staff assits the council.

The organization has 41 state chapters throughout the United States, a chapter in Hong Kong, and 32 college affiliates representing an estimated 10,000 people in 1998, including 4,000 paid members. The national office provides some financial assistance to state chapters, including help with administrative costs and assistance so that young OCA members can attend the organization's annual convention.

Members join OCA at rates varying from $10 (student) to $250; privileges include being able to vote for the executive director and receive benefits such as the OCA publication *Image*, access to a job bank, credit card discounts, and long-distance phone service discounts

Student affiliates are not considered state chapters. Instead they link directly to the national organization. These groups pay no membership dues their first year, and $20 annually thereafter. While student groups may be independent entities, they must subscribe to the same values as the national organization. Student affiliates may participate in all OCA activities and receive member benefits such as updates on issues, notification of internships, and publications.

PRIMARY FUNCTIONS

OCA primarily functions as an advocacy organization for the civil rights of Chinese Americans and Asian Pacific Americans (APAs). To this end, OCA—both at the federal and state level—monitors relevant policy and fights for legislation that will advance the quality of life for APAs. The organization, for example, has lobbied against laws that would recognize only the English language at the state level. Other issues that the organization is involved with include hate crimes, immigration, and voter rights. In addition to legislative work at the national level, the organization assists chapters with grassroots work by providing them with materials such as sample press releases, fundraising tactics, examples of testimony, and other technical assistance. OCA also counsels members who may travel to Washington, D.C., to meet with legislators on relevant issues, prepping and briefing members on the issue in question. When needed, the organization identifies and networks with other coalition groups or assists chapters in pursuing coalition opportunities.

In addition to advocacy, OCA carries out a number of public education efforts at the national and state level, such as hosting an annual convention for its members. Convention topics in 1998 included policy updates; tours and meetings with key policymakers; discussion of relevant issues like hate crimes, racism, and interracial marriage; and leadership training for APA youth. The organization assists chapters with ad campaigns, such as campaigns not to drink and drive, or information on job discrimination, by providing materials or financial assistance.

OCA attempts to bring an understanding of the issues faced by the Asian American community to children as well as adults. The organization speaks at colleges and administers a number of programs aimed at youth, such as an internship program, leadership training, Youth Day, and College Day. The organization also receives grants for outreach and information gathering work, such as grants from the U.S. Department of Justice to get the word out to the APA community regarding the Immigration Control and Reform Act.

PROGRAMS

OCA programs provide opportunities for the Chinese American community, such as networking, job placement, personal development, and the pursuit of higher education. For example, the organization carries out several educational programs geared toward Chinese American youth, including those in college. It administers the Presidential Classroom Scholarship and holds an annual essay contest for students in grades 9 through 12. The contest features a theme relative to the Asian American community, and winners receive cash prizes and have their essays presented at the annual OCA convention. The OCA Avon College Scholarship provides financial assistance for APA women entering their first year of college.

For Chinese American youth in general, the Young Organization of Chinese Americans is a subset of the larger organization and an opportunity for younger Chinese Americans to form their own chapters. Local OCA chapters provide assistance with setting up youth chapters. Youth chapter members take part in OCA programs including: Youth Day (held at the OCA National Convention), OCA summer internships, and eligibility for scholarships.

The OCA Alcohol and Traffic Safety Awareness Project has been funded by the U.S. Department of Transportation since 1993 and is an outreach program of OCA. Outreach initiatives are undertaken at the local level through OCA chapters, and include activities like workshops, illustrative skits, and publications.

The organization is also interested in promoting personal development within the Chinese American community, and administers several leadership development programs, an internship program, and a number of awards. In a similar vein, OCA offers an annual journalism award that features the best essay or article published that addresses issues of interest to the Asian Pacific community.

BUDGET INFORMATION

Not made available.

HISTORY

The late 1800s saw tremendous advances in transportation, technology, and industry worldwide. The rapidly expanding U.S. economy led to a wave of immigration to the United States from European and Asian countries. During this period many Chinese immigrated to the western United States. These Chinese immigrants were often willing to do difficult jobs for little money, resulting in widespread fear among other workers that the Chinese would take their jobs. Objections became so vocal that in 1882 the U.S. Congress passed the Chinese Exclusion Act, which banned further immigration from China. This act remained in effect until 1943. Throughout this period Chinese Americans were subject to racism and stereotyping.

During World War II (1939–45), when China fought alongside the United States against Japan, the Exclusion Act was lifted, and many more Chinese began to immigrate to the United States. The Chinese who were part of this new wave of immigrants were by and large better educated than previous immigrants had been, particularly in the years after the war ended as many intellectuals fled the communist takeover of China. According to some sources, China lost 300,000 holders of advanced educational degrees during this period.

As more and more Chinese began to immigrate to the United States, community leaders saw a need for an organization that would advocate for the civil rights of the Chinese American community. Particularly in the 1960s and 1970s Chinese Americans realized that their community needed a unified voice that had the ability to push for and monitor legislation related to their needs. Chinese Americans were particularly concerned about instances of anti-Chinese discrimination. In response to such concerns OCA was founded in 1973.

In the 1990s APA communities continued to combat discrimination and stereotyping when several incidents involving Asian or Asian American communities were spotlighted in the media. Charges of illegal campaign donations from Asian countries to the Clinton/Gore campaign were uncovered; central to the scandal was an Indonesian (adopted and raised by Chinese parents) named Ted Sioeng who donated money to the Democratic National Convention that was suspected of having been illegally funneled from Beijing, China. The illegal donation scandal was a major concern to OCA and to the APA community in general for two reasons: it again underscored the tendency of non-Asians to clump all Asian nationalities together; and it perpetuated the stereotype that APAs are not trustworthy.

In another move that thrust APAs reluctantly into the news, Republicans in Congress blocked President Bill Clinton's nomination of Bill Lan Lee, an Asian American, to a top administration civil rights post as assistant attorney general for civil rights. OCA and the APA community were upset by the blocking of Lee's confirmation, since he would have been the first Asian American to hold this important position. The organization pointed out that even Republicans recognized that Lee was qualified for the job and that denying him the position was a direct attack from Republicans who opposed Clinton's policy on affirmative action.

CURRENT POLITICAL ISSUES

As an advocacy group, OCA works in a number of areas in order to advance the civil rights of Chinese Americans and APAs. For example the organization supports immigration policies that will remain open for Asians wishing to live in the United States. OCA advocates for the removal of barriers to legal immigration and for policies which discourage discrimination toward legal or illegal immigrants. The organization feels that many U.S. lawmakers who wish to limit the number of people who can immigrate to the United States to join family members fail to understand the importance to many Chinese Americans of the traditional Chinese family, which can be broader than that of the typical nuclear American family.

OCA also works to provide APAs with as great an opportunity to learn English and improve their education as possible. According to OCA, APAs realize that although it is crucial to learn English in order to succeed in the United States but policy makers cut English programs under the assumption that APAs don't want to learn the language. OCA also advocates bilingual educational programs, which they feel are necessary for APAs to make the transition to a new life.

While OCA supports the concept of welfare as a safety measure rather than a way of life, the organization opposes the perception by some that APAs came to the United States to take advantage of welfare benefits. Similarly, the organization opposes policies that limit APA eligibility for public services such as education benefits, housing programs, and job services. The organization feels that APAs pay taxes for these programs and should have equal access to them. In mid-1998 the organization lobbied to restore cuts in food stamps that, in the organization's opinion, would have seriously impacted tax-paying legal residents of the Asian American community.

Case Study: OCA Helps to Restore Food Stamp Benefits

In 1996 a number of reforms were implemented within the federal government's welfare system. Among those reforms were cuts in the amount of food stamp benefits the government provided, and new restrictions on who was eligible for them. Legal permanent residents of the United States—people from other countries who have the right to live in the United States but are not U.S. citizens—were no longer eligible for benefits under the reformed system. This change was made for many reasons, but one that particularly troubled OCA was the perception of lawmakers that foreigners were coming to the United States to abuse the welfare system.

According to OCA the food stamp cuts seriously impacted legal permanent residents of the United States. In the Asian American community the changes particularly impacted immigrants who were disabled, very young, or elderly, and Hmong and Laotian residents who had been uprooted from their native land as a result of the Vietnam War. According to the organization, some Asian permanent residents even committed suicide when their benefits ran out.

Many permanent residents of the United States are recent immigrant in the process of attaining full U.S. citizenship, which, in many cases, takes several years. According to OCA, Asian Pacific Americans are one of the largest groups of immigrants into the United States, and thus make up one of the largest groups of legal resident aliens. OCA takes the position that legal permanent residents are paying taxes for programs such as food stamp benefits, and therefore should be able to access these benefits.

OCA lobbied against the new food stamp system from the beginning, and pushed for a restoration of benefits to permanent residents. In 1998 it rallied behind legislation in Congress that was a first step towards achieving this goal. The organization tracked the initiative in Congress and urged members to write their legislators and express their support for the measure. Members were advised to secure press opportunities for impacted Asian Americans to tell their story, particularly some of the most vulnerable sufferers, such as the elderly and the disabled.

As a result of the work of OCA and other APA groups, Congress voted in the fall of 1998 to restore food stamp benefits to legal permanent residents, designating $818 million for this purpose. OCA applauded the legislation as an important first step, but believed that there was much still to be done. The restoration provides ben-

FAST FACTS

The Asian Pacific American population increased nine times between 1965 to 1995, though the proportion of those originally born in their native countries dropped from 60 percent to 30 percent.

(Source: Xiao-huang Yin Yin. "Immigration and the Asian-American Experience." *The World and I*, February 1, 1998.)

efits to only 250,000 legal immigrants out of 935,000. This number includes many of the most vulnerable immigrants, such as refugees, the elderly, and children, but still excludes most healthy, adult, immigrants, regardless of their need. OCA continues to fight to regain eligibility for benefits for all legal permanent residents.

FUTURE DIRECTIONS

As 2000 approaches, OCA intends to focus on the census as a way to better describe the APA community. It plans to work not only to advocate for a fair count, but to educate the APA community on the importance of participating in the census counts. The national census has a major impact on how electoral districts are drawn up, and on how federal funding is handed out, so OCA wants to ensure that no one in the APA community is left uncounted. Beyond the census, OCA remains committed to winning back food stamp and other welfare benefits for the taxpaying legal permanent residents who lost them under the 1996 welfare reforms.

GROUP RESOURCES

OCA offers a number of resources to its members and to members of the Asian Pacific American community. Some of these include: job bank information, internships and scholarships, and networking opportunities such as conventions or workshops. Resources can be accessed by visiting the OCA Web site at http://www. ocanatl.org. For more information about the organization, write to the Organization of Chinese Americans, 1001 Connecticut Ave. NW Ste. 707, Washington, DC 20036, E-mail oca@ocanatl.org, or call (202) 223-5500.

GROUP PUBLICATIONS

OCA publishes the magazine *Image*, which covers issues in the Asian American community and outlines the work of the national organization and state chapters. The organization also publishes a directory of Asian Pacific American businesses that includes profiles of key APA policymakers and census data on the APA population, as well as an annual *APA Issues Paper* summarizing current issues and concerns of interest to the APA community. Publications can be ordered by contacting the organization directly at 1001 Connecticut Ave., Suite 707, Washington, DC 20036; phone: (202) 223-5500; fax (202) 296-0540; or E-mail oca@ocanatl.org.

BIBLIOGRAPHY

Elias, Thomas D. "Prop 209 Helps Asian Students." *Newsday*, 23 February 1998.

Epstein, Warren. "Nothing to Be Sorry For." *Knight-Ridder/Tribune News Service*, 25 May 1994.

Jackson, Robert. "Chinese American Sociologist Broke New Ground with '60 Report." *Rocky Mountain News*, 24 May 1997.

Jacobs, Paul, and Alan C. Miller. "State Treasurer Linked to Asian Funds, Records Show." *Los Angeles Times*, 25 February 1998.

Kang, K. Connie. "Americans Bristle at Democrats' 'Interrogation'." *Los Angeles Times*, 27 February 1997.

Miller, Alan C. "A Partisan Tangle over China-Linked Donors." *Los Angeles Times*, 23 February 1998.

Page, Clarence. "Labeling Americans by Race Adds to Census Confusion." *St. Louis Post-Dispatch*, 16 July 1997.

———. "'Model Minority' Still on the Fringe." *St. Louis Post-Dispatch*, 26 May 1995.

Streisand, Betsy. "Real-World Troubles." *U.S. News and World Report*, 18 September 1995.

Tang, Bonnie, Julie Su, and Stewart Kwoh. "Asian Americans Will Not Become a Wedge Group." *Los Angeles Times*, 31 May 1996.

Wax, Emily. "Mother's Fray/Culture Clash Puts Special Strain on Immigrant Moms and Daughters." *Newsday*, 10 May 1998.

Peace Action

ESTABLISHED: 1957
EMPLOYEES: 12
MEMBERS: 55,000
PAC: Peace Action Political Action Committee

Contact Information:
ADDRESS: 1819 H St. NW, Ste. 425
    Washington, DC 20006
PHONE: (202) 862-9740
FAX: (202) 862-9762
E-MAIL: peaceaction@igc.apc.org
URL: http://www.peace-action.org
EXECUTIVE DIRECTOR: Gordon S. Clark

WHAT IS ITS MISSION?

Peace Action began in 1957 to prevent nuclear war, which at that time seemed a very real possibility. The group's focus broadened and evolved over the years as it reacted to changing threats and as it attempted to reach out and bring in a greater number of members. In general, Peace Action aims to abolish nuclear weapons, end international arms trade, and refocus economic spending from weapons to economic development. The group's agenda also includes broader issues such as human rights and environmental protection because its leaders believe peace and justice are inexorably linked.

The group's goals are best summed up in its vision statement: "We share a vision of world peace: where the menace of nuclear weapons has forever been erased from our planet, where war has been abolished as a method of solving conflicts, where all human beings are assured the wherewithal to live in health and dignity, where no one is denied the opportunity to participate in making decisions that affect the common good."

HOW IS IT STRUCTURED?

Peace Action is a nonprofit organization, but it does engage in lobbying and is therefore not tax-exempt. The national offices are located in Washington, D.C., and are headed by an executive director, an executive committee, a national congress, and a board of directors. The executive committee oversees the general day-to-day activities of the group. The national congress, which meets once per year, is responsible for the "big picture"

strategy and setting broad political directions. The board meets at least three times per year and is responsible for administrative matters such as the budget and specific strategy decisions. The group has 27 state affiliates and more than 100 local chapters. The local chapters as well as the state affiliates are autonomous, however the state affiliates do help set policy for the national group by sending at least one member to the national group's 45-member board of directors.

Peace Action's sister organization is the Peace Action Education Fund (PAEF), which is located in New York City. The fund is a 501(c)3, tax-exempt organization, which has the goal of educating and mobilizing the public around various issues related to peace, disarmament, and justice. PAEF includes an International Office, also based in New York City, that monitors peace and disarmament work in the United Nations and promotes Peace Action's message globally.

Peace Action is one of more than 160 organizations in the United States that is part of the Fifty Years Is Enough Network, a coalition trying to change the lending policies of the World Bank and the International Monetary Fund—policies that the coalition believes promote "inequitable and unsustainable development overseas that create poverty while destroying the environment."

Peace Action also has a Political Action Committee (PAC). While it is not considered a major player in the political process financially—the PAC made only a little more than $1,000 in disbursements in 1997, according to Federal Election Commission reports—it does help candidates with grassroots organizing, personnel, and in-kind contributions, according to Peace Action staff.

PRIMARY FUNCTIONS

According to Peace Action, its mission since inception has been to abolish nuclear and conventional war and "to help lead the world away from war and toward peace and justice." To accomplish its goals the group places particular emphasis on education. Peace Action targets its members by offering instruction on how to be effective organizers. It also attempts to educate the public and policymakers on armament issues that affect individuals around the globe. Peace Action is known for its strong grassroots efforts, its ability to mobilize rallies and demonstrations, and its lobbying presence.

Peace Action conducts regional meetings and holds an annual congress to train and organize activists and decide on future policy. During "Congressional Education Days," held in Washington, D.C., activists are briefed on the issues and meet with elected representatives. Both Peace Action and PAEF produce resources for peace activists around the country including fact sheets, briefing papers, press releases, videotapes, and radio commercials. Peace Action also publishes an

annual voting record for every member of Congress and puts out an annual report documenting contributions to members from military-oriented PACs. Peace Action does this because effective organizers who are educated on the issues have historically led successful campaigns for change.

Although Peace Action's PAC does not make notably substantial political donations, Peace Action is active in the political process. Its members are known to be particularly vocal on Capitol Hill in their attempt to effect legislative change. Its annual Peace Voter campaign reaches millions of voters in congressional districts across the nation. During the 1996 elections, under its Peace Voter '96 initiative, the group distributed more than one million Peace Voter guides and made efforts to mobilize voters in 60 congressional races. In 1998 the Peace Voter campaign targeted 50 pivotal House and Senate races and distributed four million voter guides.

Peace Action aligns with like-minded groups to further strengthen its causes. The group forms coalitions with labor unions, antiviolence groups, environmental groups, and civil rights proponents. Peace Action also maintains a strong international presence. Members serve as representatives to the United Nations and participate in forums on a multitude of issues, advocating for peace and justice around the world.

PROGRAMS

Peace Action sponsors a number of programs and initiatives designed to influence public policymakers and members of Congress, to educate and assist grassroots activists, and to galvanize and mobilize the public.

A Student Peace Action Network (SPAN) is designed to bring students into the peace movement and to link student groups across the nation dedicated to peace and social justice. The network, run by a full-time campus organizer based in Washington,, D.C., arranges speaking tours, distributes mass communication through the Internet and mailings, and organizes student activist summits. As of 1999, SPAN was operating on more than 80 campuses around the United States.

BUDGET INFORMATION

In 1996 Peace Action raised $849,122 in revenues: $449,901 from contributions, $115,566 from grants, $108,249 from membership dues, $47,220 from corporate support, $35,792 from conferences, $22,000 from bequests, and $70,394 from other sources. That year, the group spent $757,005: $528,708 for programs, $148,287 for fund-raising, and $90,010 for administration costs.

HISTORY

The genesis for Peace Action came in aftermath of the United States dropping atom bombs on the Japanese cities of Hiroshima and Nagasaki in 1945, at the end of World War II (1939–45). Countries banded together to ensure that such devastation would never happen again and individuals around the world formed peace groups to "ban the bomb." Public sentiment was particularly roused in 1957 when philosopher and humanitarian Dr. Albert Schweitzer published "Call to Conscience," where he revealed the dangers of nuclear radiation. Its publication in *The Saturday Review,* sparked Saturday Review editor Norman Cousins to call a meeting of activists willing to confront nuclear testing. Peace Action's roots were formed when this group of intellectuals, pacifists, and various prominent citizens gathered in the New York apartment of a poet named Lenore Marshall in 1957.

At the time the group met, the Cold War (the sustained political and sometimes military conflict between the world's Communist and capitalist superpowers) was at its height and nuclear war seemed a real threat. That first meeting gave rise to Peace Action's forerunner—the National Committee for a Sane Nuclear Policy (SANE). SANE's message struck a responsive chord, and it grew in support and influence to the point where, in 1960, it called upon distinguished speakers such as Eleanor Roosevelt, widow of former President Franklin Roosevelt, and Republican presidential nominee Alfred Landon for a rally in New York City.

Communist Infiltration

The ups and downs that have characterized the group's history began early on. As documented in Milton Katz's comprehensive history of SANE, the group struggled almost from the beginning with Communist participation. Communists were attracted to SANE because its pacifist ideology coincided with the goals of the Communist activity in the United States at that time. Consequently some politicians accused SANE of having a serious Communist infiltration problem. These accusations were especially troublesome because this period in the United States was marked by widespread fear of Communist control of U.S. organizations and institutions.

SANE's attempts to protect its credibility by ridding itself of Communists offended many within the group and caused resignations and the breaking away of some chapters. Meanwhile, tensions between the United States and the Soviet Union were heating up. By 1962 the two nations had resumed atmospheric testing of nuclear weapons. SANE responded with protests and an antinuclear advertising campaign featuring Dr. Benjamin Spock, a pediatrician and author of best-selling books on child care. This was to be the beginning of Dr. Spock's long and high-profile involvement with SANE.

BUDGET:

1996 Peace Action Revenue

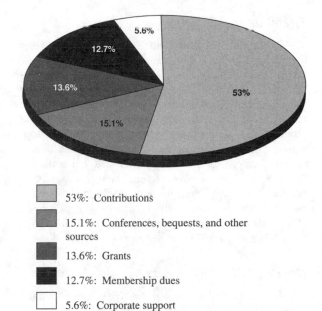

■ 53%: Contributions

■ 15.1%: Conferences, bequests, and other sources

■ 13.6%: Grants

■ 12.7%: Membership dues

□ 5.6%: Corporate support

1996 Peace Action Expenses

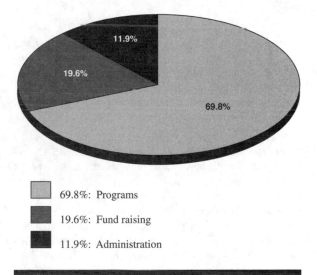

■ 69.8%: Programs

■ 19.6%: Fund raising

■ 11.9%: Administration

In 1963 SANE co-chairperson Norman Cousins met with U.S. President John Kennedy and Soviet Premier Nikita Kruschev and helped bring about a partial nuclear test ban treaty between the two nations, limiting nuclear testing to underground testing. It was one of the group's biggest successes. Kennedy sent his personal thanks and an original, signed copy of the treaty to Cousins in appreciation for Cousin's role. Into the 1960s, however, interest among the general public in the nuclear threat—and in SANE—waned. By 1964 SANE was in debt and some members of its board of directors argued that the group should cease to exist. But the group prevailed and broadened its interests as the decade progressed.

The War in Vietnam

Public antiwar sentiment began to heat up when President Lyndon Johnson began escalating U.S. involvement in the Vietnam War (1959–75). In November of 1965, SANE organized an antiwar march in Washington, D.C., that drew 35,000 people. As the war raged on, internal divisions once again plagued the group. Some members argued that SANE should adopt a more militant stance rather than the mainstream, middle-class approach that the group had been taking. While SANE's early efforts to end the war were unsuccessful, it is likely that pressure from antiwar groups such as SANE did eventually contribute to the decision of President Richard Nixon to withdraw U.S. troops from Vietnam in 1973.

Renewed Nuclear Fears

Before the end of the war, SANE, in 1969, took the word nuclear out of its title, changing its name to SANE: A Citizen's Organization for a Sane World. Among the issues SANE advanced in the 1970s were disarmament and the conversion of military resources to economic resources.

The 1980s saw a renewal of interest in the nuclear threat especially during the Reagan administration when anti-Soviet rhetoric flared and there was a massive build-up of the Pentagon budget. SANE's opposition efforts to President Ronald Reagan's military budgets included booklets, slide shows, radio broadcasts, fact sheets, fliers, Capitol Hill briefings, and press conferences.

There was another development, perhaps motivated by the renewal of the Cold War, that benefited SANE— the rise of the nuclear-freeze movement. Starting at the grassroots level, the movement worked for a mutual freeze on all testing, production, and deployment of nuclear weapons and gained support across the nation. The strength of the public's views on peace were shown in 1982, when one million people took part in an antiwar march in New York City, the largest antiwar demonstration in U.S. history.

With growing public support, SANE prospered and began to flex its muscle. It moved into a permanent headquarters in Washington, D.C., and began a political action committee to help elect people to Congress who shared its goals. The organization continued to grow as the nuclear freeze movement gained popularity. By 1984, SANE's PAC had raised more than $250,000 for political candidates—part of more than $5.4 million raised by peace-oriented PACs around the country. By December 1984 SANE had more than 100,000 members.

Merger with the Freeze Campaign

The cooperation between SANE and another group on the freeze movement, the Nuclear Weapons Freeze Campaign, led to a merger of the two groups in 1987. The new combined group became SANE/Freeze, and the name was changed to Peace Action in 1993. The group's evolution to its modern focus can be seen in the report of the commission formed to define a mission for the combined group: "True peace is more than the absence of war. It requires an unceasing effort to eliminate the causes of war and violent solutions to conflict—especially militarism, racism and social and economic injustice."

CURRENT POLITICAL ISSUES

Throughout its history Peace Action has been actively involved in issues surrounding nuclear and conventional war worldwide. Peace Action members have worked toward the ratification of the Comprehensive Test Ban Treaty (CTBT), the Nuclear Non-Proliferation Treaty, and the World Court ruling against nuclear weapons. They continue to monitor legislation involving a weapons trade Code of Conduct, military budget cuts, and land mine legislation. And while Soviet-U.S. tensions have eased, other conflict areas have shifted to the foreground including the incidents of nuclear testing by Pakistan, India, and North Korea in 1998 and the production of biological weapons and frequent threat of war with Iraqi leader Saddam Hussein.

Case Study: Land Mines

Peace Action joined with other peace groups in the 1990s to protest against the production and use of land mines, devices concealed under the ground that explode by pressure. Peace Action urged countries worldwide to ban further use of land mines, destroy their stockpiles, and work to demine areas where land mines exist. An estimated 100 million land mines in 68 countries, kill or maim over 26,000 people per year. Although most mines were placed during wars, and intended for use against enemies, most areas with land mines are now relatively at peace, and the mines are killing civilians. Land mines also prevent farmers from tilling the soil, people and animals from reaching water sources, relief shipments from being delivered, and refugees from returning home.

Efforts by the United Nations to address the land mine issue were producing few results, and so representatives from several countries and peace groups met to discuss alternatives. These talks led to an announcement by Canada in October 1996, that it would host a conference with the purpose of enacting a treaty banning land mines to be signed by December 1997. Initially, the

BIOGRAPHY:
Dr. Benjamin Spock

Pediatrician; Author; Peace Activist (1903–1998)
Dr. Benjamin Spock acquired worldwide fame and popularity with the enormous, enduring success of his parenting handbooks. Beginning in 1962, Dr. Spock's focus on child rearing shifted to a deep concern for the hazards associated with nuclear testing. That same year he became co-chairman of the National Committee for a Sane Nuclear Policy (SANE). When critics of his politics asked about this shift, Dr. Spock replied, "I'm ashamed to say that it took me so long to realize that politics is a crucial part of pediatrics. How else are we going to get better schools, health care for our children, and housing for their families, if not by political activity?" His celebrity status and early, outspoken involvement with the group helped SANE to become an effective national voice for nuclear disarmament. In the late 1960s, Dr. Spock retired from practicing medicine to devote full attention toward protesting the highly politi-

cized war in Vietnam. He helped organize and lead the 35,000 person March on Washington in November of 1965; three days later he was joined by two other SANE leaders to meet with Vice President Hubert Humphrey to discuss proposals to end the war in Vietnam. In 1972 Dr. Spock ran for president of the United States as a can-

didate for the People's Party, a group "committed to issues of social justice." Dr. Spock spent the last two decades of his life as an influential member of the advisory council of Americans for Humanitarian Trade with Cuba, a coalition to end the U.S. embargo on food and medical sales to Cuba.

United States refused to participate in what became known as the Ottawa Process, called that because representatives met in Ottawa, Canada. President Bill Clinton felt that the Ottawa Process would move too quickly and preferred to support the long-term approach of the United Nations. Although President Clinton had publicly committed to working to ban land mines, he and the Department of Defense felt that alternative technology must be developed to replace the strategic uses of land mines during wartime. President Clinton advocated for the use of "safe" land mines, mines that would self-neutralize or self-destruct within a fixed amount of time, as well as other replacement weapons.

In the summer of 1997, legislation to ban the sale and use of land mines by the United States was introduced in both houses of Congress. Peace Action began a campaign asking citizens to call President Clinton and voice their support of the legislation against land mines and of U.S. participation in the Ottawa Process. With the death of Princess Diana, who had been a global spokesperson for the need to ban land mines and had publicized the destruction caused by land mines, the public grew even more aware of the issue, and the call-in campaign was extended.

The outpouring of support for the Ottawa Process resulted in the United States relenting and agreeing to participate. The final Ottawa Treaty established a commitment to ban the use, production, stockpiling, and transfer of anti personnel mines (commonly known as land mines), and sets time frames for the removal of existing land mines. In December 1997, 122 countries signed

the treaty. It was agreed that the Ottawa Treaty would go into effect six months after 40 countries had ratified the treaty by having their governments vote for formal approval. The United States did not sign because the treaty did not include two exceptions that the United States insisted upon: the retention of land mines laid along the demilitarized zone in Korea, and an exemption for the "safe" mines.

As of March 1999, 67 countries had ratified the Ottawa Treaty, and it had gone into effect months before. Although there is often a lapse in a country's commitment to the provisions of a treaty, and acting on those commitments, many countries that ratified the Ottawa Treaty are honoring their commitment. Canada, for example, destroyed its stockpile of land mines and made it a crime for any citizen to make, use, or transfer land mines.

Land mine legislation in the United States stalled for lack of support and the issue received less public attention after the brief interest created by Princess Diana. Despite the lack of change in U.S. land mine policy, Peace Action continues to work to educate legislators and citizens on the horrors of land mines and the need for a truly global ban.

FUTURE DIRECTIONS

Peace Action will continue to work toward its long-range goals of abolishing nuclear weapons, reducing worldwide military spending and, in general, creating

---

FAST FACTS

Peace Action estimates that 45,000 nuclear warheads exist on the planet. Combined, they represent the explosive equivalent of 200,000 Hiroshima bombs.

(Source: Peace Action Fact Sheet, 1998.)

more just societies with a greater respect for human rights. Among its specific initiatives is its fight to close the School of the Americas, a training institution in Georgia for Latin American soldiers run by the U.S. military. The school's graduates have long been associated with atrocities in Latin America, but legislation offered by members of Congress to close it have been avidly opposed by the Defense Department, which insists the school does not teach torture or other abuses. Despite public pleas that have included hunger strikes on the steps of the Capitol building, legislation banning the school has failed year after year.

Another initiative is the Global Network for the Abolition of Nuclear Weapons Peace Action International, a network of over 1,000 organizations calling for a convention abolishing nuclear weapons.

GROUP RESOURCES

In keeping with Peace Action's proactive stance, the group maintains an extensive Web site at http://www. webcom.com/peaceact. The site provides information about all Peace Action programs, policies, and state affiliates. It also includes interactive fact sheets and invites concerned individuals to respond to the issues by signing on-line petitions.

The Peace Voter program issues voters guides of all kinds and offers training packets for activists in how to influence the media and how to conduct grassroots campaigns. For more information, call (202) 862-9740, ext. 3002 or ext. 3006. The Student Peace Action Network has developed materials Peace Action affiliates can use to reach out to college campuses. Call (202) 862-9740, ext. 3051.

The Peace Action Peace Empowerment Program is a resource geared toward mobilizing thousands of Peace Action members across the United States. Peace Empowerment Program members receive monthly action alerts on key policy issues. In turn, program members generate thousands of letters and calls to policy makers and provide monthly donations of as little as five dollars.

GROUP PUBLICATIONS

The quarterly newsletter, *Peace Action,* is free to members. It includes updates on the group's activities, information on how to become more active in the peace movement, descriptions and order forms for the group's T-shirts and other products, and various other information. Nonmembers may order the newsletter by calling (202) 862-9740.

The group also publishes a variety of books, pamphlets, brochures, and information packets. Titles such as *The Big Book for Peace,* a peace book for children, can be viewed on the Peace Action Web site at http://www.peace-action.org and ordered by writing to the general mailing address.

BIBLIOGRAPHY

Cortright, David. *Peace Works.* United States: Westview Press, 1994.

Houk, Lyn Adele Martin. *The American Peace Movement, 1954-1963.* Houston, Texas: University of Houston, 1990.

Katz, Milton. *Ban the Bomb: A History of SANE, the Committee for a Sane Nuclear Policy, 1957-1985.* New York: Praeger, 1987.

"Land Mines: Another Pro-Life Issue." *America,* 27 February 1999.

Lerman, David. "Lawmakers Push Ban of Land Mines." *The Chicago Tribune,* June 13, 1997.

Mann, David Leon. *The Historical Origins of the American Peace Test.* Las Vegas, Nev.: University of Nevada-Las Vegas, 1991.

Polsby, Nelson W. *Political Innovation in America: the Politics of Policy Initiation.* New Haven, Conn.: Yale University Press, 1984.

Thiede, Barbara. *Anti-Nuclear Liberals and the Bomb: A Comparative History of Kampf Dem Atomtod and the Committee for a Sane Nuclear Policy, 1957-1963.* Columbia, Missouri: University of Missouri-Columbia, 1992.

Thompson, Kurt Alan. *Social Theory and the Origin of the Modern Peace Movement in the United States.* Berkeley, Calif.: University of California-Berkeley, 1991.

People for the American Way (PFAW)

ESTABLISHED: 1980
EMPLOYEES: 65
MEMBERS: 300,000
PAC: People for the American Way Voters Alliance

Contact Information:
ADDRESS: 2000 M St. NW, Ste. 400
    Washington, DC 20036
PHONE: (202) 467-4999
TOLL FREE: (800) 326-7329
FAX: (202) 293-1672
E-MAIL: pfaw@pfaw.org
URL: http://www.pfaw.org
PRESIDENT: Carol Shields

WHAT IS ITS MISSION?

People for the American Way (PFAW) was created in 1980 to "monitor and counter the divisive agenda of the Religious Right political movement" (PFAW Web site). The "religious right" is a broad term which refers to organizations that advocate socially conservative political policies based on christian principles, such as overturning *Roe v. Wade,* the Supreme Court decision which made abortion legal in the United States; reinstituting prayer in public schools; and opposing sex education in public schools.

People for the American Way promotes ideals of "pluralism, community, and tolerance" (PFAW Web site). The organization works through grassroots organizing, lobbying, and the legal system to engage citizens in political action, and to defend and protect institutions such as public education and public broadcasting, as well as individual and religious civil rights. PFAW works on behalf of important legal cases, supports liberal candidates for political office, and actively monitors the funding activities and funding sources of various religious right organizations.

HOW IS IT STRUCTURED?

People for the American Way is a nonprofit, nonpartisan organization with 501(c)3 status. It represents more than 300,000 members and activists, and has its headquarters in Washington, D.C. The organization is governed by a board of 51 directors. PFAW employs approximately 65 staff members who are charged with

carrying out the organization's daily operations. The president of the organization is responsible for running the necessary administration on behalf of the board of directors. Along with managing the staff, the president's duties also include issuing press releases and organizing and attending news conferences.

PFAW maintains six regional offices in California, Colorado, Georgia, Florida, New York and Texas. These regional offices oversee activity in all 50 states. Each regional office serves local constituents by providing assistance with political organizing and training; obtaining information on federal and state legislation; locating speakers for meetings, programs, and panels; obtaining research materials about the religious right; and coordinating activities among progressive groups.

People for the American Way Foundation is an affiliate organization to PFAW. While PFAW primarily focuses on lobbying for progressive legislation and building communities of activists, the PFAW Foundation conducts research, provides legal assistance, promotes educational programs, and monitors the religious right. The PFAW Foundation provides information to policymakers, scholars, and activists nationwide. In addition to the foundation, PFAW has established the People for the American Way Voters Alliance. The Alliance was formed in 1998 as a political action committee whose focus is on lobbying government officials and organizing voters.

PRIMARY FUNCTIONS

PFAW protects progressive ideals through three major channels: public education and activism, legislative lobbying, and legal advocacy. The organization has identified six issues of primary political importance: education, free expression, religious liberty, equal rights, building democracy, and monitoring conservative religious organizations such as the Christian Coalition.

The organization's primary function is to educate the general public about threats to its basic freedoms, and then to organize them against these threats. PFAW uses its field offices to organize members at the grassroots level and to encourage members to operate as its "eyes and ears" in monitoring the activities of conservative religious organizations. PFAW relies on members to supply information from local newspapers and media related to important political issues at the state and local levels. The group's Activist Network uses this information, along with information from direct mailings, Internet sites, and television and radio broadcasts of conservative religious groups to chronicle and publish the activities of the religious right in the PFAW newsletter and on its Web site. This information is updated every four to eight weeks.

PFAW also provides political toolkits and organizing assistance to local constituencies. When local political issues become linked to one of the six national issue areas, PFAW arms local activists with the latest information and rapid organizing resources. It also links local political constituencies with each other, thereby increasing their resources and influence.

In addition to its local organizing and information efforts, PFAW lobbies government officials in an effort to pass progressive legislation. PFAW Foundation researches government policies and legislation, as well as their impact upon the liberties and ideals PFAW is dedicated to defending. PFAW notifies and mobilizes its members, as well as the general public, to conduct calling and letter–writing campaigns. PFAW also funds national and local advertising campaigns aimed at passing or defeating relevant legislation.

Finally, PFAW uses litigation to focus public attention and educate the public on issues, and to counter the effects of right-wing activities. PFAW provides legal assistance to individuals and organizations on issues concerning constitutional freedoms. In other instances, the PFAW joins cases being presented by other progressive political organizations, such as the American Civil Liberties Union (ACLU).

PROGRAMS

People for the American Way sponsors numerous campaigns and programs to achieve its political goals. As part of its equal rights program, PFAW sponsors Students Talk About Race (STAR), a program which promotes dialogue among young people with different racial backgrounds. Each year PFAW also publishes *Hostile Climate*, a report of anti-gay activities. As part of its efforts to monitor conservative religious organizations, PFAW established the Religious Right Monitoring Network which publishes and reports on the activities of conservative religious organizations such as the Christian Coalition.

PFAW has established a Lawyers Network which works with lawyers in private law firms who provide their services on a pro bono (free) basis. Lawyers working for PFAW focus on cases where constitutional rights are at stake. In 1998, for example, PFAW lawyers, working with the ACLU, took on a case involving freedom of expression. The Loudoun County library system in Loudoun County, Virginia, had decided to use filtering software on all of its computer terminals in order to block library patrons' access to sexually graphic material on the Internet. Lawyers representing the Loudoun County library system argued that allowing patrons access to such material via the library's computer system could create a hostile working environment for library employees who might also be subject to these images while performing their daily duties. PFAW and ACLU lawyers argued that the blocking software violated the guarantee of free speech in the First Amendment and was, therefore, unconstitutional. In November 1998, PFAW and the ACLU won their case.

In 1998 PFAW established the Voters Alliance, a political action committee formed to get voters to the polls and to assist activists in setting up and managing political campaigns. In one of its most visible programs, PFAW Voters Alliance spent nearly $2 million on an advertising campaign with the message, "Let's Move On." Television, radio, and print ads were designed to tap into voters' discomfort with the continuing Republican focus on the President Clinton-Monica Lewinsky political scandal.

BUDGET INFORMATION

In 1996 the budget for PFAW was approximately $10 million. PFAW is a nonprofit organization funded by donations, dues, contributions, grants, and bequests. In 1996 membership contributions made up 31 percent of its income; special donations also made up 31 percent of its income. Income from special events constituted 20 percent of PFAW income, and foundation grants constituted 12 percent. Interest income, in-kind contributions, state operations, and the sale of books and materials each accounted for 1 percent of its annual income. PFAW's budget supports approximately 100 staff members, including professional and administrative staff, as well as paid interns.

HISTORY

People for the American Way was formed in 1980 in response to a broad conservative social movement. The most prominent member of this movement was Ronald Reagan, who was elected president in 1980. Reagan's election gave political power to the most conservative wing of the Republican Party, citizens who condemned *Roe v. Wade* (the Supreme Court decision which legalized abortion), supported prayer in schools, and fought for taxes and other political aid to support traditional families, among other things.

In reaction to this broad-sweeping political and social agenda, television producer Norman Lear joined forces with religious, business, and media figures in an effort to counterbalance the effects of Ronald Reagan's "conservative revolution." Soon after the elections of 1980, Lear broadcast a series of television commercials stating that conservative leader Reverend Jerry Falwell's "message of Christian superiority was not the 'American Way'." These television ads were so well-received that Lear, with help from others, planned and established People for the American Way. The founders wanted an organization which could combat the religious right, and which would be committed to the values of diversity, and freedom of religion and expression.

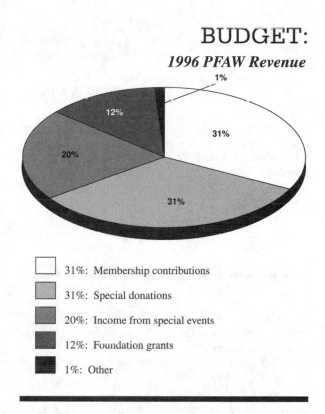

BUDGET:
1996 PFAW Revenue

- ☐ 31%: Membership contributions
- ☐ 31%: Special donations
- ☐ 20%: Income from special events
- ☐ 12%: Foundation grants
- ■ 1%: Other

Since its formation, the major focus of PFAW has been a public education campaign conducted via the mass media to make citizens aware of threats to their constitutional rights as well as misconceptions about important issues. PFAW has also compiled statistics on successful challenges to artistic expression, the banning of books, and various other activities which the organization views as threatening to civil liberties.

PFAW has established many special programs to monitor the activities of the religious right and to lobby goverment officials. For example, in 1995, conservatives attacked court decisions and laws which they claimed made it illegal for children to pray while in school. PFAW joined forces with a diverse coalition of religious and civil liberties groups to oppose these conservative attacks. PFAW conducted a campaign informing Americans that while teacher-led prayer and instruction was illegal, children were not prevented from praying in public schools.

Over the years, PFAW has enjoyed a close relationship with other civil liberties groups, particularly the ACLU. In fact, Lear founded PFAW while he was on the board of directors for the ACLU. Between 40 and 45 percent of PFAW members are also ACLU members. This has raised concerns over the years, since both groups compete for the same foundation funding. Although the activities of PFAW focus primarily on public education and outreach, since the late 1980s the organization has

FAST FACTS

Library filters installed to restrict sexually explicit material from library computers often block legitimate (or non-sexually explicit) material as well. In one case, a frequently used filter blocked Web sites put up by the Quakers and the American Association of University Women.

(Source: Pamela Mendels. "Judge Rules Against Filters at Library." *New York Times,* November 23, 1998.)

begun to take a more active role in litigation. In 1986, and 1987, PFAW and the ACLU shared funding responsibilities in an important court case in which conservative Christian parents challenged the curriculum of the local public school.

PFAW expanded its activities again in 1998, with the formation of PFAW Voters' Alliance, which serves as a political action committee for the organization. Ironically the Voter's Alliance is roughly modeled after conservative organizations which have been highly successful in organizing grassroots campaigns on local issues and getting members elected to local political offices, such as school boards. PFAW Voters' Alliance distributes information on organizing and conducting effective political campaigns, as well as publishing election training manuals.

CURRENT POLITICAL ISSUES

PFAW responds whenever, and wherever, the conservative Christian right gains political power. When Republicans signed the Contract with America after the 1994 elections, PFAW became even more diligent in its efforts to monitor the direct mailings, Web sites, and radio addresses of conservative religious groups. The constitutional battles that PFAW finds itself fighting often have their frontlines in small, localized issues, such as the battle over school vouchers.

Case Study: School Vouchers

Although the issue of school vouchers is part of national debate, the real political battles are taking place on a town-by-town, or district-by-district basis. Conservatives advocate the use of school vouchers as a solu-

tion for parents whose children are receiving an inadequate education in ailing public schools. The voucher system allows parents to remove their children from public schools and place them into the private school of their choice. Parents receive a "voucher" for the amount of money the government currently pays to each public school for the education and maintenance of each student. Under a voucher system, that subsidy is allowed to travel with the student. A student who chooses to attend a private school rather than a public school can then apply that subsidy toward tuition and costs at his or her private school.

PFAW, along with other progressive organizations, opposes the school voucher movement on the grounds that it will cripple an already weakened public school system, and that the goal of education reform should be to strengthen those public schools which are failing, not destroy them. PFAW also argues that parochial (religious) schools should not receive government funding in the form of voucher payments, because this would constitute governmental support for religion, in violation of the constitutional separation of church and state.

In its fight against the voucher system, PFAW has fought many battles across the country. It has supported legal challenges to the voucher system and has called on the Supreme Court to strike down voucher programs passed by voters. One example is the voucher system established in Milwaukee, Wisconsin in 1995. This system would allow a percentage of children in the Milwaukee school system to enroll in private schools, including parochial schools, using vouchers to cover the cost. This system was challenged in court by PFAW—and other organizations such as the Milwaukee Teacher's Association—soon after its enactment. PFAW also launched a media campaign against vouchers, organizing activists and speakers in Wisconsin, and in Ohio, where a similar measure had passed.

Despite early success in the form of rulings against the voucher system in the lower courts of Wisconsin, PFAW suffered a major setback when the Wisconsin Supreme Court reversed the decisions of June 1998. The court found that the voucher program, while it would lead to government money being granted to religious institutions, did not violate the First Amendment of the Constitution. They reached this decision because the voucher system had a definite purpose beyond supporting religion, and because monetary support was not provided especially to parochial schools, but rather granted to any school, regardless of its religious affiliations.

PFAW did not give up on blocking the use of vouchers. It continued to challenge the Ohio voucher program, and it appealed the Wisconsin decision to the Supreme Court. It has also published numerous articles and policy papers about the issue on its Web site. In Wisconsin, PFAW asked voters to "Stand Up For Public Schools" during a December 8, 1998, rally in Milwaukee, and the group continues to work to put people in touch with pro-public education organizations in the Milwaukee area.

FUTURE DIRECTIONS

PFAW will continue working on issues that help define the limitations and allowances of constitutional rights. The organization will continue to dedicate large amounts of resources and energy against school voucher programs. PFAW will also continue its work against censorship in school classrooms and libraries, by continuing its litigation efforts against banned books and course materials. The organization will go on publishing its analyses of the impact right-wing social programs and political stances have on populations such as gays and lesbians, and minorities. PFAW continues to broaden its litigation activities and will be active in lawsuits battling for equal rights for gay and lesbian partners, the separation of church and state as it relates to teacher-led prayer and religious instruction in public schools, and opposing Internet censorship in public institutions.

GROUP RESOURCES

PFAW offers a substantial amount of information regarding its programs and current issues. It maintains a Web site at http://www.pfaw.org, which lists specific PFAW areas of interest. Each area provides links to related news articles, scholarly papers, and editorials. The PFAW Web site also lists information on how to become a member of the Religious Right Monitoring Network. The organization can be contacted by calling (202) 467-4999 or by E-mail at RRMN@pfaw.org.

PFAW also operates a Field Department which assists activists in opposing the religious right in their own communities. The Field Department provides information on how to organize, including how to define and articulate issues, understand your opponents, develop allies, and act with authority. The Field Department operates four regional offices: Midwest, (202) 467-2364; Northeast, (202) 467-2377; West, (202) 467-2356; and South, (202) 467-2322. In addition, PFAW also provides legal help through the PFAW Lawyers' Network, which can be reached at Legal Department, People for the

American Way Foundation, 2000 M St. NW, Ste. 400, Washington, DC 20036.

GROUP PUBLICATIONS

PFAW has many publications, including the books *An Activist Guide to Protecting the Freedom to Learn*; *Artistic Freedom Under Attack*; *Hostile Climate: A State-by-State Report on Anti-Gay Activity* ; and *STAR: A New Dialogue About Diversity*. PFAW also publishes several organization reports, including *Who's Who on the Religious Right?*; *The Politics of Distortion*; and *Religious Right/Far Right Organizations on the Web*. These reports are the result of various PFAW programs which monitor the activities and effects of conservative religious organizations. PFAW Voters Alliance also publishes a free election training manual. These and other publications can be obtained by contacting PFAW on-line at http://www.pfaw.org; by phone at (202) 467-4999; or by writing People for the American Way, 2000 M St. NW, Ste. 400, Washington DC, 20036.

BIBLIOGRAPHY

Berke, Richard L. "New TV Ads Stress Issues, Not Scandal." *New York Times*, 7 October 1998.

Bork, Robert H. *Slouching Towards Gomorrah: Modern Liberalism and American Decline* New York: Regan Books, 1996.

Clausing, Jeri "In Rejecting Dismissal of Filtering Case, Judge Sets High Standard for Libraries." *New York Times*, 9 April 1998.

Garry, Patrick M. *Liberalism and American Identity*. Kent State Unversity Press, 1992.

Gates, Henry Louis, Jr. "The Debate Has Been Miscast From the Start." *Boston Sunday Globe Magazine*, October 1991.

Goodstein, Laurie. "Religious Conservatives, Stung by Vote Losses, Blame G.O.P. for Focusing on Clinton." *New York Times*, 5 November 1998.

Jackson, Kenneth T. "Too Many Have Let Enthusiasm Outrun Reason." *Boston Globe Sunday Magazine*, October 1991.

Kaplan, Carl S. "An Unusual Ally." *New York Times*, 2 October 1998.

Mendels, Pamela. "Judge Rules Against Filters at Library." *New York Times*, 23 November 1998.

Wattleton, Faye. "Which Way Black America?—Pro-Choice." *Ebony*, October 1989.

People for the Ethical Treatment of Animals (PETA)

ESTABLISHED: 1980
EMPLOYEES: 85
MEMBERS: 600,000
PAC: None

Contact Information:
ADDRESS: 501 Front St.
　　　　　Norfolk, VA 23510
PHONE: (757) 622-7382
FAX: (757) 622-0457
E-MAIL: peta@peta-online.org
URL: http://www.peta-online.org
PRESIDENT: Ingrid E. Newkirk

WHAT IS ITS MISSION?

With more than 600,000 members, People for the Ethical Treatment of Animals (PETA) claims the status as "the largest animal rights organization in the world." According to organization literature, "PETA is dedicated to establishing and protecting the rights of all animals. PETA operates under the simple principle that animals are not ours to eat, wear, experiment on, or use for entertainment." The group primarily advocates for animals who suffer on factory farms, in laboratories, in the fur trade, and in the entertainment industry. To carry out its mission, PETA works through public education, cruelty investigations, research, animal rescue, legislation, special events, celebrity involvement, and direct action.

HOW IS IT STRUCTURED?

PETA is an international, nonprofit, tax-exempt organization. Their headquarters are located in Norfolk, Virginia, but they also have administrative offices in San Francisco, the United Kingdom, Germany, and Italy. The organization is divided into five departments which approach animal rights issues in unique ways: Research, Investigations and Rescue; International Grassroots Campaign; Literature; Education; and Media. Other departments involved with the administration of PETA include Public Relations, Creative Services, and Finances.

The majority of PETA's staff of 85 work out of the organization's Norfolk headquarters. Staff at other sites

are limited; in Italy, for example, there is only one representative. PETA is governed by a three-member board and its day-to-day activities are managed by a president and a chairperson.

PETA does, at times, work with other animal rights and protection groups when they can agree on the issue. It has worked with California-based In Defense of Animals on campaigns to pressure corporate giant Proctor & Gamble into ending product tests on animals. PETA also works with state-run Humane Societies and the Society for the Prevention of Cruelty to Animals (SPCA). PETA has joined efforts with the controversial Animal Liberation Front (ALF) on a number of occasions, usually acting to publicize ALF findings.

PRIMARY FUNCTIONS

PETA approaches its goal of promoting the ethical treatment of animals from several angles. Its primary goal is to gather information on the inhumane and unethical treatment of animals, and communicate this information to the public. Through television and radio spots, newspaper and magazine articles, and billboards, PETA informs and educates millions of people on many animal rights issues and reported cases of animal abuse. Working with students in grade school through college, PETA distributes free products and information on issues ranging from dissection to vegetarianism.

Of particular concern to PETA is animal testing of cosmetics and household products. Unlike certain pharmaceuticals and chemicals, these products are not legally required to undergo animal testing prior to being sold in the United States. However, many companies still conduct such tests. PETA maintains and publishes lists of companies who do tests on animals and those that do not. By providing this information to the public, PETA hopes to alert consumers opposed to animal testing to boycott products manufactured by companies doing such testing and select similar products from manufacturers who do not.

Grassroots Efforts

PETA strongly believes in involving people at the grassroots level and encourages members to lobby public officials to enact local, state, and federal legislation that positively affects animals. Along with PETA's "Action Alert" reports on various animal rights/abuse cases around the world, PETA gives contact information about where people can write, call, or fax their opinions. In addition, they provide a guide to effective letter writing at their Web site.

The International Grassroots Campaign Department also coordinates campaigns in locations around the world where companies or organizations are involved in what PETA considers animal rights violations. Campaigns are creative and sometimes humorous, but always aim to get PETA's point across. For example, PETA members wore monkey masks and prison uniforms while demonstrating in front of Proctor & Gamble offices in several cities as a way of drawing attention to the animals caged and killed in product tests by the manufacturer.

Investigation and Rescue

PETA seeks to document cases of suspected inhumane treatment of animals in laboratories, fur farms, factory farms, slaughterhouses, puppy mills, and other industries. Undercover investigators go to these facilities to find and report violations of the Animal Welfare Act (AWA) or state anti-cruelty laws. PETA then makes their findings available to the public. As a result of some of PETA's investigations and their mobilization of public concern in the form of letter writing and demonstrations, a number of companies, organizations, and individuals have been convicted of violating these laws. Also, the U.S. Department of Agriculture (USDA) has re-examined and changed some of its regulations as a result of PETA's efforts.

PETA not only investigates incidents of animal abuse in laboratories, slaughterhouses, puppy mills, fur farms, and other endeavors where inhumane treatment has occurred, it also tries to rescue animals caught in these environments. For example, after PETA's investigation of Huntingdon Life Sciences laboratory, 40 beagles being held there were released for adoption into private homes.

PROGRAMS

PETA operates and/or participates in many programs designed to help stop animal abuse. Several programs promote a vegetarian diet. One such campaign, the Great American Meat-Out, is held every year on March 20. PETA and other organizations hold local demonstrations around the country, urging people to give vegetarianism a try for one day. Other programs have been aimed against the fur industry. PETA has held several "Rock against Fur" and "Fur Is a Drag" benefit concerts featuring such artists as the B-52's and k.d. lang.

PETA Kids is a program specifically aimed at children, although teachers and parents can also find useful information concerning animal rights issues. The program consists of a quarterly magazine called *GRRR!*, which contains articles on reported cases of animal abuse and simple ways children can help. The latest issues can be read at the Web site. "Action Alerts" for children can also be found at the site, as well as information on dissection issues in the classroom, which includes the opportunity to try the *Interactive Frog Dissection Tutorial*, part of PETA's effort to promote an alternative to dissection.

PETA members wear monkey masks and prison suits during a Washington, D.C., protest against the use of animals in laboratory research. The organization often resorts to extreme methods to advocate for its principles. (Corbis-Bettmann)

BUDGET INFORMATION

PETA is funded mainly by member donations. In 1997 contributions totaled $12,964,138. Income from gross merchandise sales was $455,073 and interest, dividends, royalties and other income totaled $457,375. Total revenue for 1997 was $13,876,586.

Total operating expense for 1997 was $10,945,052. Approximately 80 percent of its annual budget goes directly to programs that stop animal abuse. The International Grassroots Campaigns expended the most out of all the programs, using $3,112,353 in 1997. Public Outreach and Education spent $2,888,879; Research, Investigations, and Rescue used $2,409,407; and the Cruelty-Free Merchandise Program spent $498,491. Other operating expenses include Membership Development, which used $1,625,542 and Management and General, $410,380. Almost 15 percent was expended on fundraising efforts, and 3.75 percent on management and general operations.

HISTORY

PETA was established in 1980 by Ingrid Newkirk and Alex Pacheco, both of whom had backgrounds in

actively addressing animal rights issues. Believing that most people do not condone cruelty to animals, but do not know about many of them, Newkirk and Pacheco formed PETA as an information hub. Through meetings, publications, and public events they began to inform people of the treatment animals are subjected to for the "benefit" of humans or for their "entertainment." From factory farms to zoos to cosmetic tests to circuses, PETA began showing the public what was going on behind laboratory doors and backstage.

Early PETA Lab Raids

PETA came into existence at a time when animal activists were being informed and motivated to action by Peter Singer's 1975 book *Animal Liberation.* Singer wrote of inhumane actions and endeavors humans have imposed upon animals, especially in the area of scientific and medical research. Through undercover investigations and other tips and evidence gathered by animal advocates, raids began to take place at laboratories suspected of inappropriate behavior. In 1981 and 1984 PETA was involved in two historic raids on research laboratories. The first raid took place at the Institute for Behavioral Research (IBR), in Silver Spring, Maryland. While working there as a summer employee, Pacheco gathered evidence of the facility's abuse of animals involved in experiments. Acting on his testimony and that of five scientists secretly let into the lab at night by Pacheco, police conducted the first laboratory raid in the United States, on the charge that the lab violated Maryland state anti-cruelty laws. This lab was funded by the National Institutes of Health (NIH), which, within weeks of the raid, cut off funding to the lab. This kind of action by a government agency toward a research lab had never happened before. Media coverage of the case brought much attention to the cause of the animal protection movement.

The 1984 raid, although conducted by the Animal Liberation Front (ALF), was made public through the efforts of PETA. ALF members illegally entered the University of Pennsylvania's baboon head injury lab and stole 60 hours of videotapes that investigators from the NIH had made of their studies. They also sabotaged a computer and other equipment, causing damage of approximately $20,000. The ALF gave copies of the tapes to PETA members, who then acted as spokespersons and negotiators with government, media, and law enforcement officials. The videos showed gross accounts of animal abuse. A copy was submitted to the NIH, which eventually stopped its funding of these studies at the university. Excerpts appeared on NBC's *Nightly News*, *Today Show*, and the Cable News Network. Barbara Orlans, in her book *In the Name of Science*, writes that these two raids "succeeded in publicly embarrassing the animal research community and NIH and in stopping the research. Evidence from the raids played an important role in the passage of the 1985 strengthening amendments to the Animal Welfare Act (AWA)."

PETA Takes on National Companies

In addition to laboratory raids, PETA also succeeded in drawing national attention to other animal cruelty issues in the early 1980s. In 1983 it successfully campaigned against a U.S. Department of Defense plan to shoot dogs, cats, goats, and monkeys in order to produce wounds for study at a military hospital. In 1983 and 1984 PETA exposed the suffering of thousands of horses owned by the company Horses Unlimited. The company was transporting horses to ranchers all over the United States in cramped, even dangerous conditions. These ranchers were being paid to keep the horses fed until they could be slaughtered and their carcasses sold in Europe. Many of the horses were fed poorly and given no veterinary care. When Horses Unlimited stopped paying for these horses' care, thousands of the animals were allowed to starve. PETA gathered evidence of all these crimes and helped see to it that Horses Unlimited and many of the ranchers it had hired were charged with violations of anti-cruelty laws. Horses Unlimited would later go out of business.

Another major portion of PETA's time and effort has gone into efforts to stop cosmetic and household product manufacturers from conducting tests on animals. Through undercover investigations and campaigns,

BUDGET:

1997 PETA Revenue

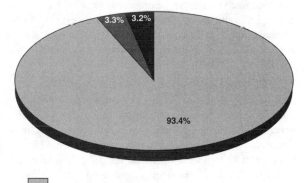

- 93.4%: Contributions
- 3.3%: Interest, dividends, royalties and other
- 3.2%: Gross merchandise sales

1997 PETA Expenses

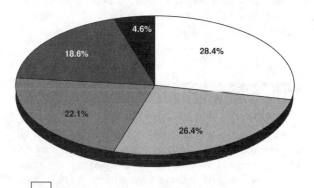

- 28.4%: International grassroots campaigns
- 26.4%: Public outreach and education
- 22.1%: Research, investigations, and rescue
- 18.6%: Membership development, management, and general
- 4.6%: Cruelty-Free Merchandise Program

PETA has been successful in stopping many large companies from performing these tests. The first major cosmetics company to stop was the Italian fashion chain Benetton, which announced in 1988 that it would no longer perform safety tests for new cosmetics and toiletries on animals. This occurred after PETA launched an international campaign against Benetton, which was triggered by PETA's undercover investigation of a lab in

Philadelphia, which Benetton had contracted with to conduct animal tests.

In 1989 other major cosmetics firms, including Revlon, Avon, Faberge, Mary Kay, Amway, Elizabeth Arden, Max Factor, Christian Dior, and Estee Lauder, also announced that they were ending, or at least suspending, all animal experimentation. A four-year international campaign organized by PETA led to the world's largest cosmetics manufacturer, L'Oreal, to also ban animal tests.

PETA has also been active in the increasing resistance to dissection traditionally performed as part of high school science curricula. Beginning in the late 1980s an increasing number of students, parents, and teachers began voicing their opposition to this practice, and PETA was there to provide information on dissection alternatives to millions of students, from elementary school through college. In 1988 a California high school student, Jennifer Graham, persisted in her right to conscientiously object to taking part in dissection without being penalized by a lower grade. Her persistence led to the passage of the California Students' Rights Bill giving students the right to refuse to take part in dissection without being penalized. Florida, New York, Pennsylvania, Rhode Island, Louisiana, and Maryland have since passed state laws that also protect a student's right to refuse to take part in dissection without penalty.

CURRENT POLITICAL ISSUES

PETA is active on a number of issues as it works toward its goal: the elimination of human mistreatment of animals. PETA campaigns against a number of different types of industries which it believes are particularly cruel in their treatment of animals. Certain types of farming, such as puppy mills, fur farms, and factory farms, concern PETA because it believes that animals in these farms are raised for economic reasons, and that they are given no care beyond that which is necessary for market purposes. Thus, PETA maintains, at fur farms animals live in small wire cages, are given no exercise, and then are killed using the cheapest, rather than most humane methods available. Fishing and hunting are other issues on PETA's list of inhumane actions against animals. According to PETA both sports cause unnecessary suffering and death to the wildlife involved.

In the area of entertainment, the animal-rights organization maintains that the inhumane treatment of animals exists in many forms, and it brings such issues to public attention as they are discovered. Horse racing, greyhound racing, circuses, rodeos, bull fighting, zoos, and marine mammal parks are just a few areas where animals risk injury in order to provide entertainment to humans.

Animal testing for medical and scientific research and for cosmetic and consumer products is perhaps the most visible issue for PETA, however. PETA believes these practices are unnecessary and cruel, and cause needless suffering and death to millions of animals.

Case Study: Huntingdon Life Sciences

Located in East Millstone, New Jersey, Huntingdon Life Sciences is an international household product and pharmaceutical testing company. In September of 1996, PETA placed Michele Rokke as an undercover investigator at the company. She was employed there as an associate technician, mainly cleaning animal cages, until May of 1997. During this time Rokke took documents from co-workers' desks, copied documents from Huntingdon's computers, and secretly videotaped employees with a tiny camera hidden in her glasses. Audiotapes were also made.

With this evidence in hand, PETA charged Huntingdon with mistreating dogs in tests it performed for Colgate-Palmolive. Colgate had hired Huntingdon to test an antibacterial agent it wanted to add to toothpaste. The organization further urged consumers to boycott Colgate products. When the news of the PETA charges reached Colgate and fearing consumer backlash, the company cancelled all its contracts with Huntingdon.

Losing more than half their clients within months of the charges, Huntingdon decided to do what most companies and research groups decline to do when investigated by PETA: fight back. Alan Staple, Huntingdon's president, sued both PETA and Rokke. The suit contended that PETA stole trade secrets and was trying to put Huntingdon out of business. Huntingdon sought unspecified damages and a court injunction to stop PETA from introducing the videotapes and documents gathered by Rokke into evidence. Huntingdon also wanted PETA to return everything it took. By issuing this multimillion dollar lawsuit, Huntingdon hoped to prevent PETA from revealing its undercover investigator's findings to the government.

Ingrid Newkirk, president of PETA, responded in the *New York Times* that the Huntingdon studies for Colgate included "the four basic tests for products: shove it in the animal's throat, poke it in the eye, shove it up the nose and rub it in abraded skin." The investigation also revealed that dogs were having their legs broken as part of a study for a Japanese company. PETA also found that monkeys were not properly anesthetized when technicians took out their organs in a study for Proctor & Gamble.

In December of 1997 PETA and Huntingdon settled the suit out of court. PETA agreed to destroy or return all documents related to the Huntingdon investigation and to relinquish the video and audio tapes as well. PETA also agreed not to do any undercover investigations of Huntingdon for the next five years. Huntingdon, in return, agreed to drop all charges against PETA.

However, as a result of the PETA investigation, the U.S. Department of Agriculture filed charges against Huntingdon citing 23 violations of the federal Animal Welfare Act (AWA). According to PETA's Web site, the USDA, "only rarely charges a registered research laboratory with violating laws protecting animals" and that the government agency "took the almost unprecedented step of charging Huntingdon Life Sciences with multiple violations of the federal Animal Welfare Act." Also included in these charges was a failure to provide adequate veterinary care for animals it poisoned in tests for major corporations. On April 8, 1998, a settlement was reached in which Huntingdon was ordered to immediately comply with all provisions of the AWA and was issued a $50,000 fine. Huntingdon was also ordered to pay $20,000 for new cages that would allow group housing for primates.

PETA's investigation of Huntingdon Life Sciences was so demanding on the organization that Newkirk decided a case this large could only be pursued every year or two. PETA's success with the Huntingdon case, however, was seen by analysts as serving notice to other testing and research sites that it is important to follow federal laws governing testing and research on animals.

FUTURE DIRECTIONS

PETA's future efforts will place more emphasis on improving conditions at factory farms, with the ultimate goal of ending this practice altogether. Along with this issue is the closely associated option of vegetarianism, which PETA will also promote with equally increased effort. Jenny Woods, a spokeswoman for PETA, stated in *Insight on the News* that "our ultimate goal is empty cages and vegetarianism."

GROUP RESOURCES

PETA maintains a Web site at http://www.peta-online.org that gives information on the organization, their activities, and recent cases. Included at their site are "Action Alerts," short reports of suspected inhumane treatment of animals, and directions on how to contact the appropriate people to voice complaints. PETA's Activist's Library is a collection of magazines, factsheets, videos, photos, and other resources that give information on how to go about holding a demonstration on a specific animal rights issue. PETA supplies those interested with fliers, videos, and media packs for their presentations. Similarly, the PETA Bookstore is a listing of dozens of books about the treatment of animals.

PETA can be contacted directly by phone at (757) 622-7382 or by E-mail at peta@norfolk.infi.net. A toll-free hot line to obtain free vegetarian recipes is sponsored by PETA at 1-888-VEG-FOOD. The Fishing Line is another telephone service sponsored by PETA. It can be accessed using the general number for PETA, then selecting the appropriate extension from the menu. The Fishing Line presents recorded information about the inhumane aspects of fishing, both commercial and "so-called" sport fishing. The Dissection Hotline is available at 1-800-922-FROG, where information and support on opposing dissection in the classroom can be obtained.

GROUP PUBLICATIONS

PETA's Animal Times is a quarterly periodical focusing on animal exploitation, rescue stories, and vegetarianism. *GRRR! The Zine That Bites Back* is a periodical geared toward children, parents, and educators dealing with animal rights issues. Also available are fact sheets and opinion pieces presenting issues in vegetarianism, animal experiments, companion animals, animals in entertainment, and wildlife.

Several publications are geared toward helping interested parties address animal rights issues in their everyday lives. *Cooking with PETA* gives favorite recipes of PETA staffers, *Shopping Guide for Caring Consumers* includes more than 500 companies and 28 product categories of "cruelty free" products, and *The PETA Catalog for Cruelty-free Living* is also available. Several videos, such as *Inside Biosearch,* are available—they document the routine treatment of animals in the product-testing industry.

All materials can be obtained by contacting PETA at their Web site http://www.peta-online.org; by telephone at (757) 622-PETA; or by writing to PETA at 501 Front St., Norfolk, VA 23510.

BIBLIOGRAPHY

Burd, Stephen. "U.S. Probes Animal-Rights Group for Link to Raids on Laboratories." *Chronicle of Higher Education,* 23 June 1993.

Carney, Eliza Newlin. "Today's Lesson: Lobbying." *National Journal,* 7 August 1993.

Gandee, Charles. "PETAphilia." *Vogue,* July 1994.

Guillermo, Kathy Snow. *Monkey Business: The Disturbing Case That Launched the Animal Rights Movement.* National Book Press, 1993.

Harnack, Andrew. *Animal Rights: Opposing Viewpoints.* San Diego, Calif.: Greenhaven Press, 1996.

Newkirk, Ingrid. *Kids Can Save Animals!: 101 Easy Things to Do.* New York, N.Y.: Warner Books, 1991.

PETA. *Shopping Guide for Caring Consumers, 1998: A Guide to Products That Are Not Tested on Animals.* Tampa, Fla.: Book Publishing Co., 1997.

Robbins, John, and Joanna R. Macy. *Diet for a New America: How Your Food Choices Affect Your Health, Happiness, and the Future of Life on Earth.* Tiburon, Calif.: H. J. Kramer, 1998.

Shiflett, Dave. "Take a Fish to Lunch: But You Better Not Eat It, Says PETA." *American Spectator,* December 1997.

Singer, Peter, and Susan Reich. *Animal Liberation,* New York, N.Y.: New York Review of Books, 1990.

Swasy, Alecia. *Soap Opera: The Dark Side of Proctor & Gamble—The Company That Brings You Crest, Ivory, Pampers, and Tide.* New York, N.Y.: Simon & Schuster, 1994.

Planned Parenthood Federation of America (PPFA)

WHAT IS ITS MISSION?

According to the organization, Planned Parenthood Federation of American (PPFA) is the world's largest and oldest voluntary family-planning organization. It is also the twelfth largest charitable organization in the United States. PPFA is "dedicated to the principles that every individual has a fundamental right to decide when or whether to have a child, and that every child should be wanted and loved."

Planned Parenthood's more than 900 health centers are spread across the United States and offer reproductive healthcare and sexual health information to men, women, and children. At a PPFA health center, clients may receive family-planning services such as counseling, abortions or abortion referral, screening for sexually transmitted diseases, contraception or voluntary sterilization, sex education, and adoption referrals. The health centers and the main organization function with one overriding goal—to provide the widest array of information possible for those who are making reproductive or sexual health choices.

ESTABLISHED: 1916
EMPLOYEES: 10,961
MEMBERS: 400,000 donors (1997); 142 affiliates
PAC: Planned Parenthood Federal PAC

Contact Information:

ADDRESS: 810 7th Ave.
New York, NY 10019-5882
PHONE: (212) 261-4302
TOLL FREE: (800) 230-7526
FAX: (212) 245-1845
E-MAIL: communications@ppfa.org
URL: http://www.plannedparenthood.org
PRESIDENT: Gloria Feldt

HOW IS IT STRUCTURED?

PPFA is overseen by a 35-member board of directors, which is geographically diverse and includes five officers. The nonprofit arm of the PPFA is headed by a 14-member board, also geographically diverse. PPFA's main office is headquartered in New York City, New York, and includes the following departments: Global Services, Family Planning International Assis-

tance (FPIA), Operations and Information Systems, Communications, Media Relations, Public Policy, Special Projects, Insurance and Claims, Quality Assurance, Field Operations, Development and Major Gifts, and Education.

PPFA has an additional office in Washington D.C., which carries out legislative and public information functions; three affiliate service centers, located in Atlanta, Chicago, and San Francisco; and 142 affiliate organizations. Affiliates oversee more than 900 health centers in 48 states and Washington, D.C. PPFA also maintains three offices through its international family-planning program—an office in Nairobi, Kenya, serves Africa; an office in Bangkok, Thailand, services Asia and the Pacific; and an office in Miami, Florida, serves Latin America and the Caribbean.

In 1997 PPFA had 142 affiliate members. Affiliate offices are located across the country and offer PPFA health and reproductive services for communities in their region. PPFA affiliates receive three memberships/votes each and board members each carry one membership/vote. Members approve long-range goals and priorities for PPFA. All attend annual meetings and vote on any special issues or elect new officers. Affiliates appoint one voting delegate for each of their three memberships. PPFA also had 400,000 donors in 1997. Donors are individuals who contribute to either the national or local PPFA programs.

PPFA provides support to the Alan Guttmacher Institute (AGI), an affiliate of PPFA which is independent and nonprofit and which carries out research and policy analysis on reproductive health issues. The PPFA Action Fund carries out political functions including lobbying, testifying, monitoring relevant legislation, and coordinating the activities of PPFA's Planned Parenthood Federal PAC.

PRIMARY FUNCTIONS

PPFA works in a number of ways to achieve its mission of providing information and services to those who are facing reproductive choices. PPFA clinics provide the following services: abortion or abortion referrals, family planning, birth control, pregnancy testing and counseling, adoption referrals, prenatal care, sex education, voluntary sterilization, HIV testing, testing for sexually transmitted diseases, and gynecological care. According to PPFA, 25 percent of women have visited a PPFA clinic at least once. Clinics provide not only health services, but counseling, educational materials, and advocacy programs. Clinics provide services to those on Medicaid insurance—people who cannot afford other insurance providers.

Occasionally PPFA clinics offer experimental treatments or services for clients who choose to participate.

For example, in 1996, 50 PPFA clinics across the United States offered a nonsurgical abortion alternative to women desiring abortions. The treatment included a combination of two drugs—methotrexate and misoprostal—that had been used for other medical purposes. Three thousand women participated in the study with the results to be used by the FDA to determine whether to approve the treatment.

In addition to the medical and educational services that take place in PPFA clinics, the organization offers sex education resources at the community level. Some of these efforts have included: sex education aimed at the family unit; presentations by PPFA staff or volunteers at community outlets such as schools, churches, or community centers; and training for medical professionals and social workers. PPFA produces an extensive collection of material that deals with reproductive and sex education topics, including brochures, reports, newsletters, and videotapes. In 1994, PPFA received a grant to carry out home parties in Detroit, Michigan. The parties were run much like Tupperware or Mary Kay gatherings, with the emphasis focused on promoting birth control and disease prevention.

Policy Shaping

PPFA not only provides resources for those concerned with reproductive choices, but the organization advocates for federal and state policy that supports the PPFA mission. To this end, the organization attempts to shape policy by working within the political process. Staff monitor legislation, meet with policymakers, conduct publicity campaigns, testify at legislative hearings, and support the campaigns of like-minded candidates for office with PAC contributions. The organization also tries to get its message to the grassroots level and creates networks at the local, state, and national level. PPFA works to create voter awareness and participation from minority populations, or from those who are young.

When necessary, PPFA has also engaged in litigation regarding reproductive choices. For example, the organization went to court in 1991 regarding the requirement for mandatory waiting periods before being able to have an abortion (*Planned Parenthood of Southeastern Pennsylvania v. Casey* No. 90-1662). In this case, the organization did not achieve their desired outcome; the court ruled that the mandatory waiting period would remain. PPFA and other abortion rights advocates have argued that a mandatory waiting period presents difficulty for poor or working women, who may be unable to make repeated trips to clinics for the procedure.

To support its programs and its work, PPFA engages in fund-raising. Funds come from individuals, patient fees, and foundations. PPFA also receives federal funding of $41 million each year from Title X of the Public Health Service Act. PPFA provides assistance to other countries that are dealing with family planning and reproductive issues. As a member of the International Planned

Parenthood Federation (IPPF), PPFA provides family planning services to 70 countries. Projects address issues such as eliminating unsafe abortions, targeting adolescents for sex education, providing contraception, and providing training and facilities for health professionals.

ing a description of each type of contraceptive, pros and cons for each, and price ranges. The Web site also offers information on other contraceptives, sexually transmitted diseases, and health issues that pregnant women need to be aware of.

PROGRAMS

PPFA programs serve to facilitate reproductive choice for the organization's constituents. Programs may include training services for professionals or initiatives that make it easier for the public to make informed reproductive choices. PPFA's Nurse Practitioner Program is a professional training resource established in 1972 to assist registered nurses to provide contraceptive medical care. Over the years, the program has evolved. In 1997, for example, the program collaborated with two graduate schools to offer nurses who had already been through the basic program an opportunity to receive academic credits toward a master's degree. The program, in 1997, began development of a curriculum that could be offered via distance-learning technologies to reach more nurse practitioners, midwives, and physician assistants.

Other PPFA training programs for health professionals offer annual seminars for nurses in women's health care, and a week-long post-graduate course for women's health professionals—the Advanced Practice Clinician Colposcopy Education Program. In the late 1990s, PPFA was also developing plans for a computer course on gynecology topics for health care professionals that could be completed from home.

PPFA also offers programs that enhance health care professionals' management skills. For example, PPFA's Leadership Institute conducts ongoing training and presentation for PPFA conventions, staff, and affiliates. In 1997 the program offered skills assessment and development workshops for PPFA CEOs, board officers, and senior managers.

PPFA may launch temporary initiatives to deal with a current issue related to reproductive rights. When abortion provider Dr. Barnett Slepian was murdered by a sniper in late 1998, PPFA launched a *Stop the Violence* campaign and collected signatures across the nation in an attempt to get Congress to take action against abortion-related violence. Other PPFA programs give members and citizens opportunities to advocate for the PPFA agenda— the Responsible Choices network allows interested citizens to add their names to an E-mail list so that they can be notified and asked to take action on current reproductive policy issues. Participants are given background on the issue and urged to contact congressional members, write letters, or take other action pertinent to the issue.

PPFA programs aim to make contraceptive services and information available to citizens. The PPFA Web site offers information on emergency contraceptives includ-

BUDGET INFORMATION

For the year ending June 1997, PPFA had a total of $530,900,000 in revenue, which included $184,300,000 in clinic income, $177,500,000 in government grants and contracts, $137,700,000 in private contributions and bequests (including corporations, foundations, individuals, federal employees through the Federal Service Campaign, and $9.5 million in bequests), $25,700,000 in other operating revenue, and $5,700,000 from the Alan Guttmacher Institute. Expenses in 1997 included: $396,100,000 in domestic programs, $401,000,000 in program services, $86,400,000 in supporting services, and $7,600,000 in other expenses.

The nonprofit arm of PPFA had total revenues in 1997 of $41,535,216 including $32,127,320 in contributions and gifts, $8,133,951 in program service revenue, $638,550 in dividends from investments, $573,036 in sales of assets, and $62,359 in other revenue. In 1997 expenses included: $30,005,216 in program services, $4,199,403 in management and general expenses, and $5,522,599 in fund-raising.

HISTORY

PPFA was founded in 1916 by Margaret Sanger. Sanger, an ardent feminist and birth control advocate, had a nursing background and was shocked when she learned that women were often forced to give abortions to themselves. She opened the first birth control clinic in the country in Brooklyn, New York, and was arrested for her efforts. She continued to advocate and help install additional clinics—collectively these became the Birth Control Federation of America.

Some historians claim that Sanger supported eugenics, or the "improvement" of the human race. In a December 16, 1996, article in *Insight in the News* Sanger is quoted as saying that "illiterates, paupers, unemployables, criminals, prostitutes, dope fiends [should be] segregated to farms where they could be reeducated regarding moral conduct." She also suggested that these people be given immediate sterilization. In 1942 public relations advisers to the Birth Control Federation suggested that its name be changed to Planned Parenthood, fearing that the original title sounded like a Nazi front and that it also suggested connotations of a conspiracy to eliminate the African American population in the United States. The name was changed, over Sanger's objections.

BUDGET:

1997 PPFA Revenue

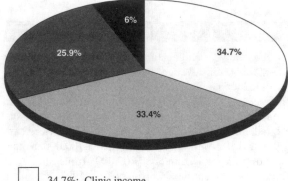

☐ 34.7%: Clinic income

☐ 33.4%: Private contributions and bequests

☐ 25.9%: Government grants and contracts

■ 6%: Other including the Alan Guttmacher Institute

1997 PPFA Expenses

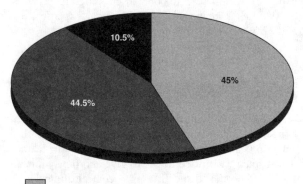

☐ 45%: Program services

☐ 44.5%: Domestic programs

■ 10.5%: Supporting services and other

Although PPFA today makes it clear that they do not support anti-Semitism or racism, the organization has continued to have its share of struggles and successes on all fronts. Several landmark events occurred in the 1960s and 1970s that affected the fight for reproductive rights. In 1965, for example, a milestone Supreme Court case (*Griswold v. Connecticut*) struck down a ban on contraceptives for married couples. In 1973 the famous Supreme Court case *Roe v. Wade* made abortion legal on

demand across the United States. And in 1974, the federal government began to provide funding annually for family-planning programs with Title X of the Health Services Act.

From 1978 to 1992, Faye Wattleton served as president of PPFA. Wattleton came from a family history of fundamentalist Christianity and had worked with PPFA at the state level. Her mother was a conservative preacher who opposed Wattleton's work with PPFA. In 1993 Pamela Maraldo replaced Wattleton, who resigned. Maraldo had previously served as director of the National League for Nursing and spent the next two years taking PPFA from reproductive health care to more of a family care focus. The PPFA board of directors disagreed with the change in focus and after two years, Maraldo resigned.

In 1996 Gloria Feldt replaced Maraldo as PPFA president. Feldt had shown considerable savvy and leadership as the director of the PPFA affiliate in Phoenix, Arizona. During her tenure there she engaged in numerous legislative battles, opened 13 new clinics, and increased fund-raising by 2,000 percent. Feldt's impetus was, and remains, to publicly challenge the conservative trend in politics and to again make PPFA a leader in the fight for reproductive health care and rights.

Throughout the 1980s and 1990s, abortion remained a contentious issue. And as the issue heated up, violence by abortion objectors, such as Rescue America and Operation Rescue, increased. More radical protesters have been responsible for serious acts of violence, killing, and injuring clinic staff or destroying facilities. In a victory for PPFA, the organization was awarded $1.01 million in damages by a Texas jury, after clinic doctors, staff and patients were harassed at a 1992 GOP convention in Houston, Texas. This ruling, however, did little to end the abortion battle.

CURRENT POLITICAL ISSUES

PPFA advocates for issues related to reproductive healthcare and rights, including the right to have an abortion. Although abortion is legal, PPFA maintains that barriers exist that can make it difficult for women to have the procedure. For instance, parental consent is often required for adolescents seeking abortion or patients experience harassment by antiabortion protesters when entering clinics. To ensure that women have access to clinics, the organization and its allies have successfully lobbied for legislation such as the Freedom of Access to Clinic Entrances Bill of 1994 (S.636), which imposed criminal penalties for those who engage in destruction of or violence aimed at abortion clinics. In 1997 PPFA and others lobbied for the demise of the Partial Birth Abortion Ban (H.R. 1122), proposed legislation that would have made this late-term abortion procedure illegal. Although the bill made it through the House and Senate,

BIOGRAPHY:
Margaret Sanger

Feminist; Activist; Nurse (1879–1966)   At the turn of the twentieth century, Margaret Sanger was one of a small minority who saw a connection between existing social ills and a lack of available birth control. Working as a nurse in the worst New York slums, Sanger repeatedly listened to the cries of poor women most already struggling to care for 10 or more children who desperately begged her to tell them some means of avoiding another pregnancy. By law, Sanger could offer no such advice. Although met by fierce opposition from almost every faction, she became consumed in her efforts to campaign for legal contraception and to establish birth control information centers nationwide. To educate the public on birth control, Sanger and volunteers published a magazine called *Woman Rebel*. Because all forms of contraception information was ruled obscene by law, Sanger was charged with nine counts of breaking obscenity laws and faced up to 45 years in prison. She fled to

London for two years before charges were finally dropped. Upon her return, Sanger abandoned the feminist stance that had characterized her movement and instead followed a more controversial path. Sanger sought the financial support of socialites and philanthropists by advocating birth control as a means of dis-

couraging reproduction by persons with undesirable genetic characteristics. Support from these individuals resulted in the establishment of what would later be the Planned Parenthood Federation of America. Before her death in 1966, Sanger helped coordinate the research that led to the eventual development of "the pill" in 1960.

---

it was vetoed by President Bill Clinton, who is generally an abortion rights supporter.

Since a large part of support for PPFA's family-planning programs comes from Title X government money, battles are waged yearly in Congress over this funding. Title X provides funding for low-income women to have access to family-planning services such as counseling, birth control, and other services. The funding does not directly sponsor abortion procedures, although opponents argue that the funding may make it easier to obtain an abortion. Congress, which had a majority of antiabortion members in both the House and the Senate in the mid-1990s tried repeatedly to limit Title X funding. PPFA, in addition to monitoring legislation and lobbying, rallied support from its grassroots Action Alert Network.

PPFA has been concerned about sex education programs in schools. Many schools are now presenting abstinence-only programs, which present abstinence as the only way to prevent getting pregnant. The Welfare Reform Act of 1997 (H.R. 1048) made $50 billion available to states for such programs. PPFA takes the position that abstinence-only education uses fear and shame tactics—the organization maintains that comprehensive sex education programs should include a balanced picture of not only abstinence, but contraceptive methods and information about disease and other health issues.

PPFA, through its membership in the IPPF, is an active force in obtaining quality family-planning services

all over the world. In 1997 PPFA lobbied successfully for reinstatement of international family-planning funds, although opponents were successful in placing conditions on abortion funding.

Case Study: PPFA's International Family Programs

PPFA believes that people all over the world should be informed of the full spectrum of family planning and reproductive alternatives. Furthermore, the organization claims that family planning is critically needed in developing countries, where overpopulation depletes scarce resources and medical facilities may be inadequate. However, aid for international family planning faced resistance from Congress during 1995 and 1996 and was completely cut at those congressional sessions.

During the following congressional cycle—the 105th Congress—PPFA lobbied hard for international family-planning funding to be put in place again and on February 13, 1997, the House voted to release funds for international family programs. Later, the Senate seconded the vote. PPFA claims that 17 international family-planning programs would have been eliminated had the funding not been reinstated. Additionally, they state, millions of women's and children's lives were saved by restoring the programs.

However, anti-abortionists in Congress have long attempted, and succeeded in some cases, in limiting how international family-planning funding can be used.

During the Reagan administration, the Mexico City Policy was in effect—policy that denied family-planning funding to overseas organizations that provided abortions or information about the procedure. In early 1998, Congress attempted once again to attach this condition to President Clinton's drive to increase funding to the International Monetary Fund (IMF).

Public Impact

According to PPFA, Congress's success in cutting international family-planning efforts had a major impact on countries where these services are needed most. PPFA claims that 350 million couples have no access to reproductive information that would help them make educated choices. Additionally, PPFA says that nearly 150 million women would stagger their pregnancies to be less frequent or avoid them completely if they had the means and information to do so. The organization states that 75 million pregnancies worldwide are unintended and that $17 billion dollars annually (more than double the expenditures in the late 1990s) would be needed to successfully address reproductive health needs in developing countries.

FUTURE DIRECTIONS

PPFA faced a number of challenges at the end of the twentieth century. Although the organization had the support of President Clinton, the Congress, during much of the 1990s, had a majority of anti-abortion members both in the Senate and the House. According to statements made by PPFA President Feldt in an article in *Cleveland Jewish News* (May 23, 1997), the organization would like to approach the future in a less defensive position. Feldt states that she would like to switch her organization's focus from responding to the agendas of other groups, such as anti-abortionists, to working on its own agenda. That agenda would include guaranteeing universal access to family planning and reproductive health, and educating the public about emergency contraceptives. PPFA has also stated as a goal that they want to double their health care clinics and maintain a presence as leader in the fight for reproductive rights.

GROUP RESOURCES

Planned Parenthood Federation of America's Katharine Dexter McCormick Library, in New York City, New York, provides information and research findings on family planning topics, population issues, and sex education. The library is located at 810 7th Ave., New York, NY, and can be reached at (212) 261-4637. The PPFA Web page includes fact sheets on family-planning topics, organization publications, Action Alerts, and ways to contact Congress members. PPFA also publishes an annual catalog, *Sexual Health Resources,* which is available by contacting the organization directly; phone (212) 261-4302; address: 810 7th Ave., New York, NY, 10019-5882; E-mail: communications@ppfa.org.

GROUP PUBLICATIONS

PPFA produces *Front Line Research,* a publication of reports on the activities of right-wing opposition to the organization's mission. PPFA makes available for sale the *Planned Parenthood Women's Health Encyclopedia* and *Talking about Sex: A Guide for Families.* A video resource, *What's Up,* is a weekly newsletter covering reproductive policy status and initiatives and is available on-line. Contact the organization for ordering information (phone: (212) 261-4302; address: 810 7th Ave., New York, NY, 10019-5882; Web site: http://www.ppfa.org; E-mail: communications@ppfa.org).

BIBLIOGRAPHY

Bethell, Tom. "Roe's Disparate Impact. (Government Stand on Abortion)." *American Spectator,* June 1996.

"Boys Have Role, Too, in Curbing Teen Pregnancy." *USA Today,* 6 January 1998.

Burns, Susan. "Sex, Lies and Politics." *Sarasota Magazine,* 1 February 1997.

Dart, Bob. "Roe v. Wade: 25 Years Later: Steadfast Right, Eroding Access: The Supreme Court Repeatedly Refuses to Overturn Roe, but Activists Have Made Abortions Harder to Obtain All Across America." *Atlanta Journal and Constitution,* 18 January 1998.

Ochs, Ridgely. "Personal Health: The Pill Works the Morning After." *Newsday,* 6 January 1998.

Smith, Evan. "Gloria Feldt. (President, Planned Parenthood Federation) (Interview)." *Mother Jones,* March-April 1997.

"Survey Shows Women Born After Roe vs. Wade Support Legalized Abortion." *US Newswire,* 20 January 1998.

Warner, Judith. "Mixed Messages: Where Is Pamela Maraldo Taking Planned Parenthood?" *Ms. Magazine,* November-December 1993.

Wattleton, Faye. "A Champion for Choice. Planned Parenthood Federation of America President Faye Wattleton." *Ms. Magazine,* September-October 1996.

Weiser, Carl. "Face of America Would Look Quite Different Without '73 Roe Ruling." *Gannett News Service,* 12 January 1998.

Project Vote Smart (PVS)

WHAT IS ITS MISSION?

Project Vote Smart (PVS) is a nonprofit organization independent of any political agenda, that researches, correlates, and distributes factual information on thousands of candidates and elected officials involved in U.S. government. PVS believes that in order to maintain the "informed electorate" that is at the basis of a functioning democracy, "abundant, accurate, [and] relevant information [must be] available free to all citizens." The organization was created to give voters an alternative to the biased information and negative advertising that often accompanies political campaigns.

HOW IS IT STRUCTURED?

PVS, which is headquartered in Corvallis, Oregon and also maintains offices in Boston, Massachusetts, is governed by a 40-member Founding Board. Members are chosen to represent an array of political viewpoints and experiences as a means of maintaining both PVS's non-partisan outlook and the objectivity of the information it makes available to the public. The Founding Board meets twice a year to vote on organization policy and direction; officers are elected annually and serve rotating terms. Board members speak on behalf of the organization, raise funds, and often participate in projects. The board also hires an executive director to manage the day-to-day operations of the organization.

PVS has no chapters or offices at state or local levels. Members may join PVS to help support the work of the organization (most members contribute at the $35

ESTABLISHED: March 1992
EMPLOYEES: 23, plus 100 interns and 154 volunteers
MEMBERS: 50,000
PAC: None

Contact Information:

ADDRESS: 129 N.W. 4th St., Ste. 204
    Corvallis, OR 97330
PHONE: (541) 754-2746
TOLL FREE: (888) 868-3762
FAX: (541) 754-2747
E-MAIL: comments@vote-smart.org
URL: http://www.vote-smart.org
BOARD PRESIDENT: Richard Kimball

FAST FACTS

According to a 1995 study by Harvard University and others, two-thirds of people interviewed could not identify their U.S. congressional representative. Forty percent of Americans could not identify the vice president.

(Source: Richard Morin. "Trust in America—Of Politics, Government: Citizen Ignorance Rampant, Costly." *Star Tribune,* February 12, 1996.)

level), but membership does not confer any special privileges. The information generated by the organization is available to anyone, regardless of whether or not they are a PVS member.

Volunteers are critical to the efforts of Project Vote Smart. Interns and volunteers comprise 90 percent of the PVS staff. These people carry out all necessary organizational tasks, including answering phones, compiling political information, categorizing issue-related speeches, pulling together descriptions of political resources on the Web, and gathering information about polling locations and hours.

PRIMARY FUNCTIONS

In order to help U.S. citizens make informed choices at the voting polls, PVS compiles and keeps current several resources that provide detailed information about political candidates. Such information includes: voting records; positions on key issues; candidate evaluations by special interest groups; campaign contribution records, including where contributions originated from; background and experience; and contact information.

Data is collected from a number of sources—for example, candidate voting records are compiled by PVS staff researchers. Campaign finance information is obtained by PVS through the Federal Election Commission, which receives its information from both candidates and political action committees (PACs). Candidate rankings are not assigned by PVS, but are collected from 83 across-the-board interest groups and compiled for the public. The candidates themselves provide background and biographical data, and are given the option of filling out PVS's National Political Awareness Test, which provides them the opportunity to state their position on rel-

evant issues. Information on candidates is available in several formats and can be accessed at the organization's Web site or by calling the toll-free voter's hot line (1-888-868-3762). PVS also makes available publications that provide information on candidates.

In addition to providing the public with information about political candidates, PVS also generates information on a number of political subjects and details, including the status of legislation; bill sponsors and co-sponsors; vetoes; public law numbers; Supreme Court decisions; polling locations and hours; election results; special interest group contact information; and issue reviews.

PROGRAMS

Many PVS programs focus on providing education and information to the voting public. Such programs include the Vote Smart Classroom, the National Political Awareness Test, and the Your Library Program. The organization's National Internship Program is another important organizational focus, as interns form a major part of the PVS workforce.

The Your Library Program encourages collaboration between libraries nationwide and PVS to create a conduit of information aimed at educating voters. Qualifying libraries receive the PVS on-line database and other resources from the organization. Sponsoring libraries also receive a computerized demonstration that allows users to download information about their elected representatives, and exhibits recounting the history of democracy and current issues in politics. Web site access is free to participating libraries.

In order to make information about candidates available to the voting public, PVS administers the National Political Awareness Test. The goal of this program is to provide a means for candidates to voice their stands on issues in a clear, unbiased way. The test, which consists of a questionnaire developed by political scientists and professionals, is sent to all presidential and gubernatorial candidates, as well as congressional candidates at the state and federal levels. PVS compiles the results and publishes them on their database. It also collects rankings for each candidate from special interest groups.

BUDGET INFORMATION

In keeping with its nonpartisan operation, PVS accepts no contributions from politically aligned organizations or corporations. The nonprofit organization receives funding from members, who may contribute $35 or more, and such nonpartisan foundations as the Carnegie Foundation and the Hearst Foundation.

In 1996 PVS had total revenues of $1,195,607, which included $1,159,360 in direct public support, $35,788 in interest on savings, and $459 in interest from securities. Expenses for the year totaled $1,465,719 and included $1,188,018 in program services, $185,493 in management and general expenses, and $92,208 in fundraising. When expenses were broken down by function, the largest categories included: salaries ($420,803), printing and publications ($259,140), and postage/shipping ($241,108).

HISTORY

The history of voter involvement in the United States is characterized by peaks and valleys. Although the first presidential election was held in 1824, only 27 percent of eligible voters chose to exercise that privilege. As the nineteenth century progressed, however, the media and campaigners learned to successfully grab and hold public interest, and by the late 1800s, 80 to 90 percent of those registered to vote were participating in elections. This trend reversed with the advent of the Progressive Movement, a social phenomenon that insisted on cleaning up government and bringing a business-like tone to government operations. With the focus on alleged government corruption, voter dissatisfaction increased and voter turnout dropped 40 percent between 1896 and 1920—a trend that would repeat itself in the 1960s.

Voter apathy and disillusionment continued to grow as campaigning styles evolved to incorporate highly paid political consultants and aggressive advertisements. Studies done in the second half of the twentieth century indicated that negative political campaigns were at least partially responsible for voters' growing lack of interest in politics. Not only were voters frustrated, but they had become so confused and overwhelmed by the proliferation of campaign rhetoric, that they refused to make an effort to fill in the gaps in their political knowledge.

PVS was founded in 1988 by political figures from both the Democratic and Republican Parties, including Barry Goldwater, George McGovern, and ex-presidents Jimmy Carter and Gerald R. Ford. PVS operations were up and running at Oregon State University by 1992, an election year. The organization announced its mission to provide a disillusioned voting public with an alternative to sensationalistic and biased political campaigns. PVS staff and volunteers were swamped with phone calls from the public requesting information on political candidates. The organization received 200,000 calls its first year of operation, 34,000 of them on election day alone.

As the demand for PVS services grew, the organization opened a second office at Boston's Northeastern University. Staff in both offices continued to assist voters over the phone and through publication mailings. PVS also launched its internship program in 1994, which allowed college students to get first-hand experience

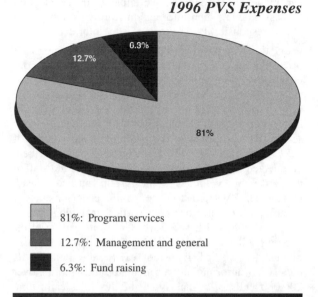

BUDGET:
1996 PVS Expenses

- 81%: Program services
- 12.7%: Management and general
- 6.3%: Fund raising

compiling information on policymakers. In an effort to broaden its reach, PVS launched its Web site in 1996. The site contains a comprehensive database of information on policymakers ranging from the president of the United States to state legislators. By 1996 the organization had distributed over one million copies of its *Voter's Self-Defense Manual* to citizens.

PVS continued to modify its National Political Awareness Test. Not surprisingly, as the organization gained recognition by voters, candidate participation rates gradually increased between 1992 and 1996, with challengers usually responding at a greater rate than incumbents. In 1996 PVS sent out 13,000 tests, including state legislators in its mailing for the first time; the mailing's total response rate reached 72 percent, the highest level in the organization's history.

CURRENT POLITICAL ISSUES

The primary issue of concern for PVS is voter participation in the United States. Many citizens are poorly informed of political proceedings and have little interest in political participation, including voting. According to PVS sources, half the country's registered voters do not cast their ballot in presidential elections and between 80 and 90 percent do not vote in local elections.

PVS maintains that this disinterest can be attributed to the inflammatory tenor of recent political campaigns.

In an attempt to counter this trend, the organization strives to provide voters with factual, nonpartisan information on candidates and issues. Such information, according to PVS, will empower voters to feel that they can make a difference by participating in the election process. Having such information readily available also places responsibility on voters to stay informed.

PVS faced its greatest difficulties while trying to get off the ground in the early 1990s. PVS originally contacted several large nonpartisan groups about doing the start-up work, but the groups backed out saying that the project was too large and would not be used by the public. Naysayers also claimed that a hot line could not be set up that could handle the predicted large volume of calls. PVS filed over 130 grant requests and saw them all rejected. Operating with minimal funding, and staffed primarily by volunteers, the group pushed ahead, undaunted. PVS enlisted the public endorsements of notable politicians from both parties, including Jimmy Carter, Gerald Ford, and Barry Goldwater, in an effort to gain publicity and establish legitimacy. To the surprise of many, it worked. PVS took off rapidly, building its database of information on candidates and handling over 200,000 calls over the course of the 1992 campaign. Soon, many of the groups which had initially turned away PVS, were eager to offer it support.

FUTURE DIRECTIONS

While the successes of the PVS Web site and hot line have been extraordinary, the organization continues to reach only a very small segment of the voting population. PVS estimates that only between five and six percent of the U.S. population uses or knows about the information PVS provides.

In mid-1998 PVS initiated a partnership with 38 newspapers and two TV stations to spread the word on services available to help the public and to facilitate candidates' efforts to provide factual information on issues affecting the public. If successful, PVS predicts that by elections in 2000 they will have created a network of thousands of news organizations able to promote and provide factual campaign data devoid of campaign rhetoric and bias.

GROUP RESOURCES

PVS provides information to educate voters via telephone at 1-888-868-3762 and on-line at http://www. vote-smart.org. This information, which is also available through many local libraries, includes PVS's candidate database and Vote Smart Classroom, a resource for teachers seeking to educate students about the importance of educated voting. PVS will also do specialized research for individuals if the organization does not have the information requested.

GROUP PUBLICATIONS

Project Vote Smart's publications include *Vote Smart Web Yellow Pages,* a compilation of PVS and other political on-line resources that is available at http://www.vote-smart.org or in print for no charge by contacting the organization. PVS also publishes the *Voter's Self-Defense Manual* and the *U.S. Government: Owner's Manual,* both of which provide detailed information on policymakers and are available on-line or by contacting PVS directly, either by mail at, 129 NW 4th St., Ste. 204, Corvallis, OR 97330; or by phone at (541) 754-2746.

BIBLIOGRAPHY

Bivins, Larry. "NAACP Gives Congress Failing Grade." *Gannett News Service,* 24 June 1998.

Boller, Gregory W. "Capitol Consumers (Research on Political Marketing)." *Business Perspectives,* 22 March 1995.

Christensen, Mike. "From Candidates to Critics, Internet Goes Political." *Atlanta Journal & Constitution,* 30 August 1995.

Cottle, Michelle. "Where Are the Good Guys When We Need Them? While the Public Interest Groups Fiddle, Campaign Finance Reform Burns." *Washington Monthly,* 1 September 1997.

Gaw, Jonathan. "Campaigns and the Internet; Voters Get Access to the Candidates with Computers." *Star Tribune,* 29 April 1996.

Gordon, Greg. "Rethinking Fund-raising; A Better Way to Finance Campaigns?" *Star Tribune,* 24 February 1997.

Milyo, Jeff. "Money Walks: Why Campaign Contributions Aren't as Corrupting as You Think." *Reason,* 1 July 1997.

"Rep. McCollum's Anti-Term Limits Move Exposed." *US Newswire,* 6 February 1997.

Shaw, David. "On the Campaign Trail, the Bad News Wins Out." *Los Angeles Times,* 18 April 1996.

Rainbow/PUSH Coalition (RPC)

WHAT IS ITS MISSION?

The Rainbow/PUSH Coalition (RPC) calls itself "a movement and a campaign of hope." Stating as its mission "to move the nation and the world toward social, racial and economic justice," it works to bring together people from different ethnic, economic, religious, and political backgrounds and to empower those who, for one reason or another, have been excluded from political and economic decision-making in the United States. The RPC strives "to make America's promise of 'liberty and justice for all' a reality."

HOW IS IT STRUCTURED?

The Rainbow/PUSH Coalition is headed by the Rev. Jesse L. Jackson Sr., its president, chief executive officer, and the founder of both Operation PUSH and the Rainbow Coalition. Its day-to-day operations are managed by a director who is assisted by a deputy director. The RPC bureau offices in Washington, D.C., and New York City each have their own directors. RPC policy is determined by a board of directors. In late 1998 the RPC board of directors consisted of 55 members and was headed by two co-chairmen.

One of the RPC's major divisions is the Ministers' Division, which is a network of ministers from various churches and denominations throughout the United States that volunteer their time. RPC's Ministers' Division is active in establishing and carrying out the organization's social activist program. It works on getting African Americans into church and mobilizing congregations

ESTABLISHED: September 1996
EMPLOYEES: 100
MEMBERS: 25,000
PAC: None

Contact Information:
ADDRESS: 930 E. 50th St.
         Chicago, IL 60615-2702
PHONE: (773) 373-3366
FAX: (773) 373-3571
E-MAIL: info@rainbowpush.org
URL: http://www.rainbowpush.org
PRESIDENT; CEO: Rev. Jesse L. Jackson, Sr.

when an important issue is at stake. The Ministers' Division also trains new ministers.

The National Field Department is the organizing arm of the RPC. It is responsible for mobilizing people across the United States to participate with Rainbow/PUSH in opposing unjust public policies and corporate practices. It also organizes new chapters. The International Trade Bureau is the economic arm of the RPC. It helps black businesses and business people gain access to corporate America through jobs and work contracts.

The M.A. Houston Prison Outpost is an outreach ministry for prisoners. It arranges visits to prisons, holds worship services, counsels inmates, and acts as an advocate for prisoners outside jails and prisons. The Political Desk oversees organizing voter participation and education. It mobilizes voters at election time to support candidates and proposals friendly to the goals of Rainbow/PUSH.

The RPC has an office in Washington, D.C., that concentrates on legislative issues, an office in Los Angeles, and a Wall Street office that handles most of its work with corporate America. RPC's state offices organize members on the local level, receive general direction from the national office, and collect annual dues. When local issues erupt that deserve national attention, they are referred to the Chicago office.

PRIMARY FUNCTIONS

The RPC is a membership organization that works very effectively as a grassroots movement. It mobilizes large numbers of local members around issues of common concern and constantly organizes new chapters throughout the United States.

An important area of activity is voter registration. The RPC uses its influence with its membership and the public at large to support candidates sympathetic to its goals. It mounts demonstrations for legislative initiatives and ballot propositions that are consistent with its program for social justice. It organizes consumer boycotts of businesses that discriminate against minorities and organizes protests against corporate and government actions that discriminate against, or outright harm, minorities, women, the disadvantaged, and the powerless.

The RPC strives to improve educational and economic opportunities for women, African Americans, and other minorities. It develops and supports progressive legislation and financial reforms that will improve educational opportunities for inner city youth. It also works directly with young people, parents, teachers, and school administrators to break the cycle of violence and lack of opportunity in which many inner-city youths are trapped. The RPC promotes legislation and directs efforts designed to increase the number of minorities in college administration, professional sports, and the entertainment indus-

tries. It actively challenges broadcast station licenses to assure employment opportunities for minorities as well as minority access to the media.

At the same time, particularly through its founder the Rev. Jackson, the organization has become actively involved in political issue negotiations. For example, Jackson and RPC representatives have attempted to influence political policy in countries such as South Africa and Haiti and to shape U.S. policy toward such nations; mediate labor disputes; and negotiate economic covenants with major corporations intended to bring work and contracts to black-owned businesses.

PROGRAMS

The RPC is an issue-oriented, program-based organization. Among the issues it believes are important are economic empowerment; employee rights and just wages; access to education, fair and decent housing; voter registration and civic education; fairness in the media and criminal justice system; trade and foreign policy; affirmative action and equal rights; gender equality; and environmental justice. A common thread running through all RPC programs is the desire to create a just society with equal opportunities for all.

Many of the organization's most important programs are administered under the umbrella of the Citizenship Education Fund (CEF). The CEF is a nationwide effort focused on education and general public policy issues. Its goal is to achieve equity in U.S. schools, thus ensuring that all students from kindergarten through university receive the best education available. The program promotes school finance reform and legislation that improves the quality of substandard schools. CEF fights legislation and judicial rulings that undermine or dismantle affirmative action statutes relating to education. Its educational mission extends beyond the schools however. CEF also educates the public-at-large about civic responsibility and the importance of participation in the political process. As part of that broader effort, the program informs the public about important public policy issues on the local, state, and national levels.

The CEF attempts to change how schools are currently funded through the School Reform Task Force. In cooperation with superintendents from 48 school districts the Task Force plans to challenge school funding in cities in federal court. The proposed lawsuits charge that current state funding practices violate the Fourteenth Amendment and the Civil Rights Act. Furthermore the Task Force continues to educate parents of children in under-financed schools on how schools are funded and what reform measures are pending. The project lobbies state legislatures on school finance reform.

The National Reclaim Our Youth Campaign, which is part of CEF, is aimed at counteracting the violence and lack of opportunity prevalent among young people, in particular among black youth in America's inner cities. The program involves the cooperation of many groups that can contribute to a solution including parents, teachers, school administrators, churches, the judicial system, community-based organizations, and members of the business community. Reclaim Our Youth has devised a "school to university plan" to put students on track to obtaining a university degree. It provides training sessions for program participants and has developed a "responsibility in media" campaign to promote positive images for young people—images that encourage academic excellence and achievement.

An important element of the Reclaim Our Youth campaign is the Juvenile Mentoring and Early Intervention Coalition Project which trains responsible, committed adults to work with abused and neglected young people and non-violent juvenile offenders. The program serves as a clearinghouse to coordinate the efforts of groups ranging from human service agencies and community organizations to churches in developing alternative ways of coping with the problems faced by urban teens.

BUDGET INFORMATION

Rainbow/PUSH has an annual budget of between $1 million and $5 million per year. Operating funds come from grants and other awards, from dues paid by the 22 state offices, and from individual, group, and business members.

HISTORY

The Rainbow/PUSH coalition has its roots in two organizations, Operation PUSH and the National Rainbow Coalition, both founded by the Rev. Jesse Jackson. Jackson joined the Southern Christian Leadership Conference (SCLC) in 1965 and became an assistant to Dr. Martin Luther King Jr. Jackson believed that African Americans, especially those living in cities, had to pursue economic emancipation. Dr. King named Jackson head of Operation Breadbasket, the SCLC economic program.

In 1971, after King's assassination and after Jackson had left SCLC, Operation Breadbasket evolved into Operation PUSH—People United to Save Humanity. The goals of PUSH were to effect increased opportunities in business, education, and employment for blacks, and to implement them the organization used tactics similar to Operation Breadbasket. Consumer boycotts were called against A&P supermarkets and Walgreens drug stores until the retailers provided more jobs to black workers, more business to black companies, and more shelf space for products produced by companies owned by African Americans. From the beginning voter registration was an important part of the PUSH program as well.

In the latter half of the 1970s, during the administration of President Jimmy Carter, PUSH for Excellence was founded with $6 million in government grants. PUSH-EXCEL, as the program was known, was a nationwide program focused on keeping young people in school and off drugs. When Ronald Reagan became president, government support for PUSH-EXCEL dried up. PUSH found itself targeted by government investigators who tried to determine if there had been any impropriety in how PUSH grants had been used. PUSH was also criticized for being essentially a one-man organization that, as Jackson moved on to new endeavors, failed to follow through on issues.

PUSH established its International Trade Bureau in 1982. At the organization's 12th annual convention in 1983 the bureau announced that it would begin to boycott companies as a way of forcing firms to share their economic power with blacks. Companies like Coca-Cola, Burger King, and Kentucky Fried Chicken agreed to sign covenants with PUSH that they would hire a specified number of African Americans and give a certain amount of business to black companies. Mark Hosenball criticized these covenants in the *New Republic,* saying Jackson used them to put together an economic patronage system. Jackson was even criticized by black business people for remarks he made that were reportedly intended to coerce brewery Anheuser-Busch, a company friendly to blacks, into signing a covenant.

In 1984, at the time of his first presidential campaign, Jackson organized the Rainbow Coalition, the political arm of his social justice movement. In 1986 its name was changed to the National Rainbow Coalition. The existence of two separate organizations, however, was seen as a financial liability. According to critics, the Rainbow Coalition was drawing money away from Operation PUSH, especially when Jackson was on the campaign trail. These charges took on special weight in the late 1980s, after PUSH said it was almost $2 million in debt. Another criticism leveled at Jackson and the Rainbow Coalition in the late 1980s was that it had squandered the publicity and support generated by his two runs for the presidency. After 1988 many of the Rainbow Coalition chapters throughout the United States simply closed.

Jackson gave up the leadership of PUSH in 1989 in order to move his legal residence to Washington, D.C. In January 1991 the organization underwent a financial crisis. Several hundreds of thousands of dollars in debt, the PUSH board of directors laid off its entire staff. Observers blamed the problems on the absence of Jackson. "I tend to think that the key to the PUSH situation is the presence or lack of presence of Rev. Jackson," National Urban League president James Compton told the *New York Times.* Following the layoff announcement, PUSH was able to raise $100,000 and had its sights set on another $1 million by spring 1992.

BIOGRAPHY:
Jesse L. Jackson, Sr.

Activist; Politician; Minister (b. 1941) With unflagging determination, Jesse Jackson combined compelling, impassioned oratory with a quick wit to emerge as the most prominent African American civil rights leader of the 1980s and 1990s. Jackson ran for the Democratic nomination for president of the United States in 1984 and 1988; his strong showing demonstrated the viability of a future African American candidate winning the presidency. Jackson grew up doubly oppressed—ostracized from the segregated community-at-large for his color, and taunted by neighborhood kids because he had no father. In Jackson, this upbringing sparked a fervent desire to both succeed and to help those who are disadvantaged or oppressed. After a successful mid- to late-1960s stint with Rev. Martin Luther King, Jr.'s, Southern Christian Leadership Conference (SCLC), in 1971 Jackson began the Chicago-based Operation PUSH (People United to Serve Humanity). In the course of the decade, Jackson rose to national prominence with his relentless appeals to end racism, militarism, and class

divisions in the United States. In a 1979 trip sanctioned by President Jimmy Carter, Jackson traveled to then segregated South Africa and delivered anti-apartheid speeches to thousands. Only the first of several such diplomatic excursions, Jackson received both criticism and applause for his meetings with leaders of troubled areas like the Middle East, Syria, Cuba, Central America, and Nigeria. In the mid-1980s Jackson resigned from

his position with Operation PUSH and established the National Rainbow Coalition, Inc. Throughout the 1990s, Jackson has worked the periphery of politics as a popular lecturer, spearheading social causes through his Rainbow Coalition, and as guest and host of numerous news-television talk shows.

PUSH and the National Rainbow Coalition merged to become the Rainbow/PUSH Coalition in September 1996, at Operation PUSH's Sterling Silver Conference. On that occasion the new organization pledged itself to the ambitious goal of founding chapters in every state as well as at colleges and high schools nationwide. The organization, still led by its founder, continued to fight for its economic and political agenda. In 1996 it led an initiative in California to vote down controversial Proposition 206, an effort to repeal affirmative action laws in the state. Jackson and the RPC traveled from San Francisco to San Diego holding rallies urging listeners to defeat the proposition. Their efforts were in vain, as it turned out, as California voters passed Proposition 206 overwhelmingly. However, the group did lead a successful fight against a Republican Party-sponsored ad that used footage of Dr. Martin Luther King's "I Have a Dream" speech to attack affirmative action. RPC efforts contributed to Bill Clinton's successful campaign for the presidency in both 1992 and 1996.

CURRENT POLITICAL ISSUES

The fight for racial and class justice has been long and arduous. The abolitionists of the nineteenth century fought slavery; civil rights activists of the 1950s and 1960s fought legal segregation of the races. The Rev.

Jesse Jackson and Rainbow/PUSH continued that fight through the 1970s. In the 1980s the organization stepped up its efforts for political enfranchisement—getting more minority candidates onto ballots and then getting minority voters to the polls to vote. In the 1990s the organization took on what it saw as the next step on the way to complete racial equality: economic empowerment.

Case Study: The Wall Street Project

The RPC's Wall Street Project was launched in 1997 on Martin Luther King Jr.'s birthday. The project's goal was to monitor diversity in hiring and leadership in companies and to guarantee that minorities received a share in decision-making and profits. Using its own funds, the RPC planned to purchase token amounts of stock—usually between $1,000 and $2,000 worth—in about 100 companies. The companies targeted would primarily be in the automobile, food, and telecommunications industries—retail sectors in which minorities traditionally bought a great deal. "We are fighting for fairness," Jackson told Cora Daniels of the Gannett News Service. "Being a shareholder gives us access to records and a basis for opening up negotiations.

By July 1997 a staff of about six working at 40 Wall Street in the heart of New York's financial district had taken on Texaco and had plans for General Motors. In mid-November 1997, in a highly publicized action, the RPC purchased stock in the largest publicly traded record companies: PolyGram, Time Warner, Sony, and EMI. The RPC was drawn into the recording industry after a senior official at PolyGram remarked during a contract dispute with an African American recording artist that virtually all black men have criminal records. Jackson used the occasion to initiate an investigation by the Wall Street Project into discrimination in the music industry.

When the RPC became involved in the issue, according to Chuck Philips of the *Los Angeles Times,* there were less than five upper-level African American executives employed at major U.S. record labels, and virtually no women or minorities. That same week, one-third of the best-selling records on the U.S. pop charts were written and recorded by women or black artists. "Corporations take the art we create and the revenues we generate but deny us access to decision-making positions of power in the industry," Jackson told Philips. "They call it show business. But the fact is we put on all the show and they get all the business."

RPC planned to evaluate each company's performance in hiring and promoting minorities and women, then use its shareholder status and its ability to mobilize 20,000 consumers in each of the nation's 50 largest cities to pressure companies to open up job opportunities for minorities. Companies that were perceived to maintain restrictive access to women, African Americans, and others risked becoming the target of a full-scale RPC consumer boycott. "We intend to open up the market," Jackson told the *Los Angeles Times,* "It is time for corporate America to open up and include people of color as more than consumers but as trading partners."

Public Impact

The impact of the RPC's Wall Street Project has been mixed. In January 1998 President Clinton publicly supported a Rainbow/PUSH conference to promote ethnic, racial, and gender diversity on Wall Street; it was attended by Federal Reserve Board Chairman Alan Greenspan and several Securities and Exchange Commission officials. Other groups, including the National Organization for Women praised the effort. As a result of the conference, the New York Stock Exchange closed in honor of Dr. King's birthday for the first time in history, although the day had been recognized as a national holiday since 1986.

The Wall Street Project has faced limitations as well. Due to the small amount of stock it owns, its vote represents only one among thousands of others at shareholder meetings. At the Texaco gathering, for example, after Jackson turned the discussion to the issue of diversity, the oil-company shareholders voted down a proposal for diversity on the Texaco board of directors. The RPC was also unable to block the merger of MCI and WorldCom, two telecommunications giants, even though it was part of an impressive alliance of consumer groups attempting to do so.

Perhaps the most disappointing setback occurred when the coalition turned its sights on the entertainment industry. The RPC called on African American actors to support its initiatives by wearing rainbow-colored ribbons to the 1997 Academy Award ceremonies. Most simply ignored the issue, while Whoppi Goldberg, the host of the event, openly made fun of Jackson at the start of the television broadcast.

SUCCESSES AND FAILURES

The Rainbow/PUSH Coalition has been involved in voter registration since its earliest days. Nonpartisan in nature, RPC's Voter Education and Registration Project reaches potential voters through radio, television, newspapers and magazines, and rallies mounted specifically to register black voters. In election years Jackson travels throughout the United States holding rallies aimed at registering new voters and encouraging voters to go to the polls. In 1984, during Jackson's first run for the presidency, the RPC registered one million new voters. In 1988, for his second campaign, they registered two million new voters. In 1998, during an off-year election, it was responsible for another 335,000 new voters.

FUTURE DIRECTIONS

The Rainbow/PUSH Coalition plans to continue its efforts to ensure that African Americans and other minorities have access to the basic opportunities that enable them to compete in corporate and economic America. In addition to its Wall Street Project, the group will be working on organizing internships and other programs for minority students that will create the contacts necessary for further advancement. For example, the organization will work on programs to get high school students part-time work in large corporations.

Jackson has set the goal of pushing RPC membership to over 100,000 in the twenty-first century, with 30 church or other organizational affiliates in every state containing at least 300 members statewide.

GROUP RESOURCES

The best source of information about the Rainbow/PUSH Coalition is its Web site which can be accessed at http://www.rainbowpush.org, http://www. rainbowpush.net or http://www.rainbowpush.com. The site includes the latest news about the RPC, speeches presented by Rev. Jackson, copies of the "Jax Fax," and press releases. The Jax Fax, written by the Rev. Jackson, spotlights important issues, new RPC programs, and new legislation introduced on Capitol Hill. Each week it is faxed to members who contribute $100 or more per year to the RPC. The Jax Fax is posted on the Web site six weeks after it has been sent to members.

GROUP PUBLICATIONS

PUSH Magazine, the RPC quarterly newsletter, is available to all Rainbow/PUSH members. Individual membership costs $35 per year. Subscribing members who contribute at least $100 per year also receive *Trading Partners*, the monthly newsletter of the International Trade Bureau, and the weekly "Jax Fax." For more information, contact the RPC by mail at The Rainbow/PUSH Coalition, 930 E. 50th St., Chicago, IL 60615-2702.

BIBLIOGRAPHY

Bailey, A. Peter. "The Reverend Jesse Jackson Moves the Rainbow Coalition into High Gear." *Essence*, September 1986.

Barrett, Todd, and Daniel Glick. "When Games Turn Nasty." *Newsweek*, 27 August 1990.

Collins, Sheila D. *The Rainbow Challenge*. New York: Monthly Review Press, 1986.

Daniels, Cora. "Jackson's Wall Street Project Targets Diversity in Corporate America." *Gannett News Service*, 7 July 1997.

Frady, Marshall. *Jesse: The Life and Pilgrimage of Jesse Jackson*. New York: Random House, 1996.

Hall, Royce T. "Jackson Leads Wall St. Push." *Newsday*, 15 January 1998.

Hosenball, Mark. "Jesse's Business." *New Republic*, 9 May 1988.

House, Ernest R. *Jesse Jackson & the Politics of Charisma: The Rise and Fall of the PUSH/Excel Program*. Boulder, Colo.: Westview Press, 1988.

McCool, Grant. "Jackson Wants Halt to MCI/WorldCom Merger." Reuters, 3 February 1998.

Nichols, John. "Over the Rainbow." *The Progressive*, December 1996.

Philips, Chuck. "Company Town: Jackson's Coalition Buys Stock in Five Record Companies." *Los Angeles Times*, 19 November 1997.

"PUSH Celebrates 25th Anniversary." *Ebony*, December 1996.

"Rainbow's Beginning." *The Nation*, 3 May 1986.

Reynolds, Barbara A. *Jesse Jackson: America's David*. Washington, D.C.: JFJ Associates, 1985.

"A Troubled Operation PUSH Struggles to Focus Its Mission." *New York Times*, 1 April 1996.

Weisberg, Jacob. "The Disorganization Man." *Newsweek*, 17 August 1987.

The Rutherford Institute (TRI)

WHAT IS ITS MISSION?

According to the organization's Web site, "the defense of civil liberties and human rights through litigation and education" lie at the core of the Rutherford Institute's purpose. Based in Charlottesville, Virginia, the Rutherford Institute (TRI) is devoted to "the defense of religious freedom, the sanctity of human life and family autonomy" in the United States and abroad. Through legal action, TRI challenges laws it believes to be unconstitutional and/or unjust, and defends clients, for free, against injustices.

HOW IS IT STRUCTURED?

TRI has 60 full-time staff members at its main office in Charlottesville, Virginia. These staff members coordinate the efforts of hundreds of attorneys throughout the world who have volunteered their time to help the organization. Branch offices are located in Bolivia, the United Kingdom, and Hungary. Representatives of TRI can also be found in Romania, the Philippines, and throughout Central America. Foreign concerns are coordinated through the European headquarters in London and the international affairs department at the main Charlottesville office. Cases are often brought to the organization by citizens who feel that their rights have been violated. The main office then finds an attorney in the appropriate location who will take the case for free or for a greatly reduced fee.

John Whitehead is the founder and president of the organization and he manages its daily activities. White-

ESTABLISHED: 1982
EMPLOYEES: 60
MEMBERS: Not made available
PAC: None

Contact Information:
ADDRESS: PO Box 7482
  Charlottesville, VA 22906
PHONE: (804) 978-3888
FAX: (804) 978-1789
E-MAIL: tristaff@rutherford.org
URL: http://www.rutherford.org
PRESIDENT: John Whitehead

FAST FACTS

In March 1998 The Rutherford Institute began publishing *Gadfly,* a magazine aimed at a younger audience. Its first issue featured articles on Jack Kerouac and the Sex Pistols.

(Source: Megan Rosenfeld. *Washington Post.* January 17, 1998.)

head is also the organization's most visible member and is heavily involved in most of the group's activities.

PRIMARY FUNCTIONS

TRI works through the court system to defend what it considers to be fundamental human and civil rights. When it considers a law to be in violation of these rights, it challenges it in court. TRI also seeks people who have had their rights violated and will act on their behalf in court. While litigation is the focus of the organization, it also devotes energy to educating the public on issues of importance to the organization, through such activities as a weekly radio program and internships for college students.

When the Rutherford Institute was founded in 1982 it was closely tied to conservative Christian groups, such as the Moral Majority. For its first 10 years, it was, according to Joshua Shenk of *Maclean's,* "the ACLU [American Civil Liberties Union] of the right." As such, it was often involved in separation of church and state issues, such as prayer in schools, and major conservative issues such as abortion. However, TRI has moderated with time. While still concerned with many of the same issues it addressed in its early days, the institute has broadened its agenda to include many other issues, including freedom of speech, defense from sexual harassment, and home schooling.

PROGRAMS

The Rutherford Institute sponsors a variety of services and programs designed to educate the public about their rights, and about issues of importance to the institute. These include books, newsletters, seminars, and a

weekly radio show. Organization president Whitehead's weekly radio address, *Freedom under Fire,* is syndicated to 1,400 stations worldwide. Listeners are invited to call the institute's Freedom Hotline at 1-800-441-FIRE and relate stories of constitutional violations. These often inspire "Action Alerts," a kind of call to arms designed to right the wrongs that have occurred. One example was a California mother who was denied child support because she taught her child at home. This triggered an avalanche of mail directed at the judge who ruled against her.

BUDGET INFORMATION

The Rutherford Institute is a 501(3) corporation. It is a nonprofit organization that relies primarily on private donations to fund its operations.

HISTORY

In 1982 author and attorney John Whitehead and film maker Frank Schaeffer saw the need for a conservative answer to the problems of the day. They were disturbed by America's divorce rate of over 50 percent, and by the fact that many children were growing up in single-parent homes. Whitehead and Schaeffer turned to a seventeenth-century Scottish minister named Samuel Rutherford for guidance. Rutherford, the author of *Lex Rex*, or "King's Law," proposed that since kings were not divine, their law should not be above God's law. Rutherford advised his followers to disobey any royal command which contradicted biblical teaching.

It was this idea that led to the formation of the Rutherford Institute. Whitehead stated in 1983 that, "courts must place themselves under the authority of God's law." The direction of the fledgling organization was outlined in Whitehead's book, *The Second American Revolution*. TRI would take a stance that advocated home schooling and prayer in public schools, while criticizing abortion and the death penalty. Influenced by the writings of minister R. J. Rushdoony and with the financial support of Jerry Falwell's Moral Majority, the institute spent its early years as a legal spearhead for the religious right.

By 1990 Schaeffer had left the organization and it appears that some of Whitehead's views had begun to change. As the 1990s progressed, TRI began to move away from a strictly Christian agenda. Whitehead even went so far as to apologize for some of the group's past activities. When confronted about a number of anti-homosexual fundraising campaigns, a penitent president told the *Washington Post:* "I should never have done those mailings. They were wrong. . . . Homophobia is wrong." While this move toward the center has alienated some of the group's early supporters, it is a circumstance

Whitehead welcomes, saying, "That leaves us free to critique everyone."

For many years the Rutherford Institute was, to the general public, a relatively unknown legal advocacy group. This situation changed dramatically when the institute agreed to represent Paula Jones in her 1994 sexual harassment suit against President Bill Clinton. Very suddenly, the institute and its founder were receiving front page news coverage. Robert Bennet, the president's lawyer, told Associated Press that the Rutherford Institute was an "extremist organization . . . trying to humiliate the president." The president's lawyers subpoenaed all of TRI's financial and membership documents, challenging its tax-exempt status. Ironically, one of the first groups to express its support for TRI was its sometime opponent, the ACLU.

The end of the twentieth century found TRI promoting a far different agenda than that first taken by Whitehead and Schaeffer in 1982. It continued to defend many of the same principles, such as home schooling, that made up its agenda in its earliest years. During the 1990s, however, the group expanded its efforts to include other, traditionally liberal, issues. For example, in 1999 TRI represented a man who claimed to have been fired because of his homosexuality and was suing for reinstatement to his job.

CURRENT POLITICAL ISSUES

Through its legal activities the Rutherford Institute inevitably becomes involved in controversy of all kinds. Throughout its history, TRI has been an important voice in debates over the First Amendment, particularly those surrounding the separation of church and state. In more recent years TRI's broader focus has involved it in many different issues, ranging from sexual harassment and sexual discrimination, to the rights of homosexuals, to its continued defense of religious freedoms.

Case Study: Asylum for Ngozi Okudoh

The Rutherford Institute has been increasingly involved in international issues, as evidenced by its representation of Ngozi Mary Ann Okudoh and her two daughters in their petition for asylum in the United States. Okudoh and her children are from Nigeria, a country where the practice of female circumcision is common. Female circumcision, where a portion of a woman's external sexual organs is removed, is a traditional practice in many African nations. Performed for a variety of traditional reasons, it is estimated that more than 50 percent of all women in Nigeria are circumcised. The procedure can have many serious effects on a woman's health, including increased chance of infection, difficulty giving birth, and debilitating pain. This, along with the fact that it is often performed on children who are unable

to understand or consent to the procedure, has outraged many from other cultures, including the United States, where it is often referred to as female genital mutilation.

Okudoh and her children had not been circumcised, but when her husband wanted to become chief of his tribe, tradition demanded that the procedure be performed. Okudoh refused to allow this, and was subjected to verbal and physical attacks from her husband, her mother-in-law, and others. In 1997 Okudoh took her children and immigrated to the United States to escape the attacks and demands that she allow herself and her children to be circumcised.

In 1999 Okudoh faced the possibility of being sent back to Nigeria, along with her children. The Rutherford Institute agreed to represent her in her effort to gain asylum in the United States. Asylum is a process whereby a person petitions the federal government to be allowed to stay in the United States, even if they would not be admitted as an immigrant under the normal rules. To be granted asylum, a person must prove that they are the victim of persecution, or have a well-founded fear of persecution, in their country of origin. "The Rutherford Institute does not believe that female circumcision is anything less than genital mutilation," said TRI legal coordinator Ron Rissler in a press release, "We will do whatever it takes to prevent such an atrocity from happening to these two girls and their mother. Although the Institute is at the forefront of protecting the free exercise of religion, we will not hesitate to assist a mother and her daughters who are being forced, under the guise of religious tradition, to adhere to a practice that is nothing less than barbaric."

TRI argued that Ngozi Okudoh and her children had been persecuted in Nigeria, and would continue to be persecuted if she returned there. Initially, it appeared that the children might be granted asylum, but that Ngozi Okudoh would be sent back to Nigeria because she did not meet all of the requirements for asylum. TRI affiliate attorney Laura Dawkins argued that Okudoh was subject to persecution in Nigeria based on her gender, and on her reproductive choice, a recent addition to the possible qualifications for asylum. As evidence of the serious negative consequences of female circumcision, Dawkins could point to a 1996 federal law outlawing the procedure on women under the age of 18, regardless of consent. After some consideration, Ngozi Okudoh and her two children were granted asylum on February 23, 1999.

FUTURE DIRECTIONS

TRI looks at the twenty-first century as a time of new challenges and concerns in the world of medicine. The legal and moral implications of such topics as cloning and genetic engineering have already sent lawmakers scrambling. TRI president Whitehead has spoken out strongly against a proposed Missouri law which would allow Death Row inmates to exchange an organ for a life sentence. He has also been a vocal opponent of the right-to-die movement. As law tries to catch up with the advances of science, the Rutherford Institute appears ready to defend its beliefs.

GROUP RESOURCES

The Rutherford Institute Web site at http://www. rutherford.org provides a wide variety of information about the institute, its publications, and current court cases. Also posted are weekly transcripts of the institute's *Freedom under Fire* radio broadcast. More information on *Freedom under Fire* can be obtained by calling 1-800-441-3473. For more information on TRI write to The Rutherford Institute, PO Box 7482, Charlottesville VA 22906. The main office can be reached by phone at (804) 978-3888 or fax at (804) 978-1789.

GROUP PUBLICATIONS

The Rutherford Institute publishes an assortment of hard- and soft-cover books, magazines, and pamphlets through its TRI Publishing wing. A complete catalog, information, and a secure order form are available online at the Rutherford Institute Web site at http://www. rutherford.com. Orders may also be placed over the phone at 1-800-225-1791. Titles available include *A*

Judeo-Christian Perspective on Law and Government, A Pro-Life Manifesto, Parent's Rights: How to Fight Back, and a pocket-sized version of the U.S. Constitution. For more information on the organization's publications write to The Rutherford Institute, PO Box 7482, Charlottesville VA 22906.

BIBLIOGRAPHY

Americans United for Separation of Church and State. *Report of Rutherford Institute's Attacks on the Clintons*, February 1998.

Burney, Melanie. "First Grader's Bible Fight Goes to Appeals Court." *Chicago Tribune*, 20 February 1998.

Cienski, Jan. "Group Backing Paula Jones Alleges Tax Intimidation by Clinton Camp." *Athens Daily News*, 4 January 1998.

Institute for First Amendment Studies, "The Rutherford Institute." *Freedom Writer*, June 1994.

"NOW Says It Won't Back Paula Jones in Her Appeal." *Chicago Tribune*, 23 April 1998.

Phillips, Andrew. "The Raucous Right." *Maclean's*, 9 February 1998.

Rosenfeld, Megan. "On the Case for Paula Jones." *Washington Post*, 17 January 1998.

"The Rutherford Institute." *Body Politic*, January 1994.

Shenk, Joshua. "Right Wing Conspiracy Facts and Fiction." *U.S. News and World Report*, 9 February 1998.

Service Employees International Union (SEIU)

WHAT IS ITS MISSION?

According to the organization, the mission of the Service Employees International Union (SEIU) is "to improve the lives of working people and their families, and lead the way to a more just and humane society." To reach these goals the SEIU is active in both the workplace and in politics. The organization serves its members by working to improve wages, benefits, job security, working conditions, and worker participation through collective bargaining contracts and the representation of workers before their employers. The union also works to improve the position of its members and other workers through the support of various legislative initiatives such as minimum wage increases, national health care reform, and family and medical leave. A union that brings together service employees of various kinds, from health care providers to zookeepers, SEIU has also been concerned with broader issues of economic and social justice such as civil rights, women's equality, and government assistance to the poor and elderly.

ESTABLISHED: April 23, 1921
EMPLOYEES: 260 (international office)
MEMBERS: 1,200,000
PAC: Service Employees International Union Committee on Political Education (SEIU COPE)

Contact Information:

ADDRESS: 1313 L St. NW
    Washington, DC 20005
PHONE: (202) 898-3200
E-MAIL: webworker@seiu.org
URL: http://www.seiu.org
INTERNATIONAL PRESIDENT: Andrew L. Stern

HOW IS IT STRUCTURED?

The SEIU is an international union with members in the United States, Canada, and Puerto Rico. It is affiliated with the American Federation of Labor, Congress of Industrial Organizations (AFL-CIO) and the Canadian Labour Congress (CLC).

The international organization is based in Washington, D.C., and is governed by an executive board of roughly 50 members. Board members and officers, which

FAST FACTS

The Service Employees International Union was the first union to organize hospital workers and by 1998 the SEIU had the largest number of unionized health care workers of any union, totaling 600,000 members.

(Source: SEIU Public Affairs Department, 1999.)

include a president, secretary-treasurer, and four executive vice presidents are elected every four years by delegates from local chapters (locals) at the union's convention. Major divisions within the international office include the Organizing Department, which oversees mobilization of new members and recruitment and training of organizing staff, and the Political Department, which directs functions such as legislative affairs and lobbying. The International Office is funded by a per capita tax paid by the locals for each union member. The International Office also maintains state councils to coordinate the political activities of the locals.

Roughly 300 autonomous locals, which have their own officers and staff, represent workers in a variety of occupations including doctors, nurses, nursing home support staff, food service workers, maintenance workers, social service workers, and even zoo keepers and Disney World workers. As of 1998 there were roughly 600,000 members in the health care industry, 585,000 members in public employment, 185,000 members in building services, 147,000 office worker members, and 80,000 amusement and industrial members.

PRIMARY FUNCTIONS

Unlike many unions in the United States that have been declining in membership, the SEIU is the fastest growing union affiliated with the AFL-CIO. The international office and the locals both participate in organizing, a priority activity on which the organization spends over 40 percent of its budget. The international office provides expertise, staff, training, and printed and audiovisual materials for organizing at the local level. Union locals dedicate a smaller percentage of their budget, but dedicate a large number of staff and volunteers to these efforts.

Local organizers try to build alliances with other unions, politicians, and community and church groups to force resistant employers to recognize or bargain with newly formed unions. Known for its aggressive organizing methods, SEIU organizers have engaged in protests, demonstrations, and civil disobedience. In 1995, as part of a campaign to organize Washington, D.C., janitors, union members blocked major thoroughfares during rush hour traffic to call attention to building owners' practices.

The union's often bitter battles to organize health care and nursing home workers have been supplemented by efforts to raise awareness about conditions at facilities and capitalize on consumers' concerns about the quality of health care. The union has commissioned studies and surveys and released reports to convince state and federal health officials and the public that certain health care facilities are understaffed or poorly run. Union staff have sent out numerous press releases, staged news conferences, run radio and newspaper ads, and scheduled interviews with local and national reporters in such efforts.

Member Services

Like most unions the primary service the SEIU offers its members is collective bargaining. Specialized staff and member representatives negotiate contracts with employers that cover areas such as wages, benefits, job security, and working conditions. The SEIU also has its own pension and medical benefit plans available to members when negotiated in collective bargaining contracts. Such provisions obtained through collective bargaining are often the major attraction drawing workers to join a union.

Political Action

The union attempts to mobilize its members in both elections and the public policy process. The national organization endorses candidates and decides if they will receive organizational and financial support based on a hierarchical decision process that involves the state councils, locals, and members. Working in coordination with the political activities of the AFL-CIO and other unions, the SEIU targets political efforts in key states and congressional districts where membership numbers are high. The union attempts to educate members on issues of relevance to campaigns by mass mailing issue papers. Union members are also encouraged to vote and volunteer in political activities.

The SEIU lobbies Congress and the executive branch on a variety of issues. International staff research issues and disseminate information to local union activists, members, and often the media and the public. The international organization also provides training materials and conferences to teach local leaders and members how to effectively lobby their representatives. Members are encouraged to contact their congressional representatives and can do so through the SEIU's Web site.

The union participates in a broad range of issues that lead it to form coalitions with other organizations. For example the SEIU has joined other unions, civil rights organizations, and women's groups at national and local levels in opposing measures scaling back or repealing affirmative action programs. On issues such as health care reform and health maintenance organization (HMO) regulation, the union has joined forces with consumer advocates.

PROGRAMS

Several major SEIU organizing campaigns are aimed at issues confronting custodial workers, nursing home workers, and health care workers. For example, "Justice for Janitors" emphasizes the need for respect for this segment of the work force, calling attention to janitors' low wages and poor working conditions and discouraging union pension funds from investing in companies linked to such practices. Similarly, the "Dignity, Rights and Respect Campaign" seeks to organize and improve the working conditions of nursing home workers. This is a multifaceted effort that includes organizing workers, lobbying state governments for greater regulation of nursing homes, negotiating patient care contracts that articulate standards for care, negotiating higher wages and benefits to discourage high levels of staff turnover, and forming coalitions with nursing home reform advocates.

In order to reinforce its efforts at organizing health care workers, the SEIU has also announced a "Choose Union Healthcare" initiative designed to encourage union-administered health plans to choose unionized firms and to encourage other unions to bargain with their employers for unionized health care providers.

Often criticized for not involving members in the international office's political decisions and stung by the Republican takeover of Congress in 1994, the national staff has launched a number of new programs to politically mobilize rank and file members. The SEIU organized a "Take the Pledge" campaign in the 1996 electoral season in which roughly 9,000 members participated in local political activities. The SEIU also organized "Decision Day" forums in electorally pivotal states; workers were brought together to call attention to issues that were important to union workers. In addition, the union sent out numerous mailings presenting information on such issues. Although the labor movement as a whole failed to reach its goal of electing a pro-labor majority to Congress, the SEIU claims to have had a significant impact on the election of pro-worker candidates in numerous districts and to have contributed to the Democratic takeover of the California state assembly.

BUDGET INFORMATION

Not made available.

HISTORY

The organization that became SEIU was originally chartered in 1921 by the American Federation of Labor (AFL) as the Building Service Employees International Union (BSEIU). This union had formed several years prior by a group of mostly immigrant janitors in Chicago who cleaned apartment buildings in exchange for low pay and unpleasant basement apartments. Like most workers who join unions, they hoped an organized membership would bring better wages and working conditions. Initially the BSEIU did not experience much growth, and prior to the Great Depression the union's strongholds were limited to Chicago and New York.

During the 1930s the union was plagued by corruption. From 1937 to 1940 union president George Scalise delivered control of the union to organized crime forces. Racketeers raided the union treasury and extorted money from employers. William McFetridge replaced Scalise as president and over the next two decades reformed the operation of the union and restored its reputation.

During the post–World War II period, the union was transformed from an organization based on private sector custodial workers to one dominated by local and state government employees. During this period the BSEIU was the first union to organize public sector employees and hospital workers. In 1968 the organization changed its name to the Service Employees International Union (SEIU) to reflect the changed composition of its membership.

During the 1980s the union experienced explosive growth. The SEIU significantly expanded its international staff and under the presidency of John Sweeney, a new generation of leadership made membership growth a top priority. Due to new organizing efforts and affiliation with other independent employee associations and unions, the SEIU nearly doubled in size from 625,000 members in 1980 to 1.2 million members in 1998. At the end of the twentieth century the union was very active in organizing segments of the work force dominated by large numbers of women and minorities such as health care and custodial workers. The composition of the SEIU, unlike many unions, thus reflects the changing face of the U.S. workforce. Fifty-eight percent of members are women and 37 percent of members are minorities.

As a result of its growth, the SEIU has gained greater influence in the labor movement as a whole. It's aggressive organizing serves as a model for other unions and President Sweeney was elected to head the AFL-CIO, the national federation with which the vast majority of American unions are affiliated. Andrew Stern, who as the assistant to the president for organizing and field services engineered the addition of 500,000 new members, was elected to replace Sweeney in 1996.

CURRENT POLITICAL ISSUES

SEIU leaders claim to be nonpartisan and to focus on issues rather than candidates, but the SEIU's political efforts, like those of most U.S. unions, tend to heavily favor the Democratic Party. During the 1995–1996 election cycle, SEIU COPE made all of its contributions to Democrats. Traditionally the SEIU has played a major role in the labor movement's efforts to pass civil rights legislation and initiatives for equal rights and pay for women. During the Clinton administration, the SEIU participated in the failed effort to reform the national health care system and the successful effort to pass the Family and Medical Leave Act, which allows employees to take time off from their jobs to care for new children or elderly parents.

Much of the SEIU's legislative efforts have been aimed at fighting changes in Medicaid and Medicare, the Occupational Safety and Health Administration (OSHA), education programs, welfare programs, and other worker protections. An increase in the minimum wage is one of the few high-priority legislative successes achieved during the Republican-dominated Congress.

The SEIU also takes an active role at the state and local levels,where it's political activities are often shaped by its constituencies. For example, SEIU has supported a number of initiatives in California, Nevada, and the District of Columbia that are tied to its efforts to organize custodial and health care workers. Shortly after taking office SEIU President Andrew Stern announced plans to increase pressure on the health care industry and asserted that the union would use "every means at [its] disposal to hold health care providers accountable to their patients and their workers." This goal was reflected in the SEIU's support for the health care reform initiative Proposition 214 in California.

Case Study: Proposition 214

As health maintenance organizations (HMOs) in California began to cut staffing levels and reassign duties in response to competitive pressures to reduce health care costs, union leaders came to the conclusion that restructuring the health care system could not be done by fighting one employer at a time. The union responded by taking the lead in developing and advocating for Proposition 214 in the 1996 California state election. In addition to requiring facilities to meet certain safe staffing levels, the initiative was designed to give patients the right to appeal health plan denials of medical services and required more disclosure of health plan policies and criteria for denying services. The SEIU was joined by the consumer advocacy group Neighbor to Neighbor, the American Federation of State, County and Municipal Employees (AFSCME), and the California Federation of Teachers in promoting the initiative. Other consumer groups and advocates for the elderly joined the effort.

The California Healthcare Association, an alliance of health care providers, and the Taxpayers Against Government Takeover, a coalition of businesses, hospital organizations, physician group practices and insurers, opposed the bill. They argued that the measure would give labor unions too much influence in staffing decisions and would raise costs for consumers. Other health policy analysts were not convinced that staffing levels had a significant impact on the quality of care or that it was possible to uniformly determine what levels were appropriate for every facility.

In supporting the initiative the SEIU hoped to build its reputation as a public defender against health care providers who lowered standards of care while fighting unions. They conducted polling and focus groups that found the proposal resonated with the public. The union pumped large sums of money into newspaper, radio, and television ads depicting managed care horror stories and highlighting HMO and insurer efforts to fight the proposition by far outspending proponents with a $5 million campaign.

Despite a narrow lead in preelection polls, the proposition failed by a margin of 58 to 42 percent. Political analysts suggested the failure was in part due to voter confusion with a similar but more radical proposition placed on the ballot by consumer advocate Ralph Nader and the California Nurses Association. But compared to the dismal failure in 1994 of an initiative that would have established universal, state-sponsored health care, the vote reflected significantly greater public commitment to change. Advocates for Proposition 214 believe the initiative furthered their cause by focusing attention on problems in the delivery of healthcare.

The failure of the initiative did not end the debate on quality-of-care issues. In early 1998 the California Assembly passed a bill to establish minimum nurse-to-patient ratios in facilities providing acute care. Similar issues have also showed up at the national level where several bills have been introduced to regulate HMOs and insurance plans.

Critics claim the SEIU pursues such reform measures merely to enrich their own members at the public's expense by raising health care costs. The SEIU, however, argues that its members, as consumers, are indeed interested in quality care as well as pride in their professions. Regardless of the the union's motives, the broad-ranging legislation endorsed by the SEIU has the potential to expand patient's rights.

FUTURE DIRECTIONS

The union intends to expand its efforts in the unionization of nursing home, health care, and home care workers. But major obstacles, like the reluctance of employers to recognize unions, will also persevere as competition and market pressure to reduce health care costs (to boost profits) reinforce this reluctance. In this age of declining unions, the SEIU will have to convince the locals to step up organization efforts so that strong collective bargaining contracts can be achieved through a larger, stronger union.

Similarly, to regain political influence the SEIU will be fervently campaigning for pro-worker political candidates to counter the conservative climate in Washington and many state houses that has impeded union legislative efforts. Having an increased role in the governors' races is one plan, and raising more money for SEIU COPE and increasing member involvement in political action are others. Additionally, the SEIU has set a goal to train and mobilize more campaign workers than any other union in the AFL-CIO.

GROUP RESOURCES

The SEIU maintains a Web site at http://www.seiu.org, which features current and back issues of the on-line publication *Bold Action News*. Information on ongoing campaigns, upcoming events, and legislative initiatives can also be found at the Web site, which is designed to allow for visitors to E-mail their congressional representatives. For more information about the SEIU, contact the Public Affairs Department at (202) 898-3200.

GROUP PUBLICATIONS

SEIU Action is published monthly and is designed to assist and inform union stewards, organizers, activists, and leaders. For information call (202) 898-3251 or E-mail action@seiu.org. Many locals also produce their own newsletters for members. The international office produces numerous materials geared toward training member activists, including *SEIU Leadership Training for the Worksite* and *Hitting Home*, a guide to lobbying, media, and other grassroots political and legislative action. To obtain SEIU publications call (202) 842-9873.

BIBLIOGRAPHY

Gustafson, Fred. "Broken Homes." *In These Times,* 14 July 1997.

Johnston, Paul. *Success While Others Fail: Social Movement Unionism and the Public Workplace.* Ithaca: ILR Press, 1994.

Kosterlitz, Julie. "Stern Measures." *National Journal,* 22 June 1996.

Moore, J. Duncan. "Looking for the Union Label: SEIU Launches Campaign to Boost Unionized Healthcare." *Modern Healthcare,* 6 October 1997.

Moore, J. Duncan. "An SEIU Victory: A Year After Union's Alert, JCAHO Downgrades Hospital." *Modern Healthcare,* 3 November 1997.

Olmos, David R. "Backers of HMO Reform Initiatives Launch Ad Blitz." *Washington Post,* 1 November 1996.

Reed, Vita. "Union Fights With Hospitals Over Staff Levels." *Las Vegas Business Press,* 2 March 1998.

Russell, Sabin. "Propositions 214, 216 Failed to Tap Outrage." *San Francisco Chronicle,* 7 November 1996.

Sweeney, John J. *America Needs A Raise.* New York: Houghton Mifflin Company, 1996.

Swoboda, Frank. "Janitors Take Fight to Wall Street: SEIU Seeks Pension Fund Help in Unionization of Downtown Workers." *Washington Post,* 17 November 1997.

The Sierra Club

ESTABLISHED: June 4, 1892
EMPLOYEES: 250 (1997)
MEMBERS: 650,000
PAC: Sierra Club Committee on Political Education
    (SCCOPE)

Contact Information:

ADDRESS: 85 Second St., Second Fl.
    San Francisco, CA 94105-3441
PHONE: (415) 977-5500
FAX: (415) 977-5799
E-MAIL: information@sierraclub.org
URL: http://www.sierraclub.org
PRESIDENT: Chuck McGrady
EXECUTIVE DIRECTOR: Carl Pope
CHAIRMAN: Michael McCloskey

WHAT IS ITS MISSION?

The Sierra Club's stated mission is "to explore, enjoy, and protect the wild places of the earth." Over the years, the Sierra Club's mission to "protect the wild places of the earth" has become the cornerstone of the organization's policy. Today, the Sierra Club is one of the best-known and most successful conservation organizations in the United States, dedicated to practicing and promoting the responsible use of the earth's ecosystems and resources, as well as to educating and enlisting "humanity to protect and restore the quality of the natural and human environment."

HOW IS IT STRUCTURED?

The Sierra Club is divided into 57 chapters, which are further subdivided into 370 groups. The Club also has 14 field offices and a lobbying office in Washington, D.C., staffed by 30 people. Chapters and groups work on regional as well as national conservation issues, publish newsletters, and sponsor local outings and activities. Chapter presidents form the Council of Club Leaders and assist the board of directors in establishing the club's national policy at an annual conference.

The board of directors, composed of 15 elected volunteers, is the governing body of the Sierra Club. The board has the responsibility and authority to oversee all staff and volunteer activities, to establish conservation priorities and internal policies, and to adopt and implement the annual budget. The board of directors elects the club's officers, including the president and executive committee. The board also annually elects an executive director, who handles day-to-day operations. Directors serve on at least one of the club's six governance committees, which focus on Communication and Education; Finance; Membership and Development; Organizational Effectiveness; Outdoor Activities; and, of course, the most important of all, Conservation. Decisions on policy, strategy, and tactics involve literally thousands of committees and more than 6,000 club members bear at least one official title.

The student arm of the Sierra Club was founded in 1991 as the Sierra Student Coalition (SSC). The coalition represents a network of thousands of young people across the United States. The aim of the SSC is to "help students become the most effective, responsible activists they can be by tailoring and amending the resources of the Sierra Club to fit their needs." The SSC is considered a Sierra Club chapter and is given an equal vote in the club's decision-making processes.

PRIMARY FUNCTIONS

The days when the Sierra Club's primary function was to help its members "explore and enjoy" the United States's wilderness have long passed. Today's politically sophisticated Sierra Club devotes far more time, energy, and money to preserving and protecting the environment than to exploring the remote backwoods of the Sierra Nevada. In fact, a Sierra Club outing in the 1990s was as likely to be a trip to clean up an oil spill as a backpacking trip through the Rocky Mountains. Yet even while its staff and management are as professional as any in Washington, grassroots activism remains one of its most effective tools of political leverage as evidenced by the Environmental Bill of Rights presented to Congress in 1995 which boasted more than one million signatures.

Much of the Sierra Club's power derives from the fact that it is generally perceived as one of the more mainstream of the environmental groups and that its members tend to vote twice as regularly as the average citizen. Members are kept informed of current issues by the club's magazine, *Sierra*, as well as by action alerts and other notices from both national and local offices. The club carefully tracks the voting records of members of the House Representatives and Senators and follows the money trails left behind by anti-environmental lobbying groups. Letter-writing campaigns are encouraged and, of course, members can use the detailed information provided them to determine their local candidate's stance on environmental issues and vote accordingly.

Newspaper advertising is also a frequently used tactic, and the club's extensive publishing wing, Sierra Club Books, not only helps promote environmental positions to the general public, but also contributes a modest surplus to the club's general fund. The club produces numerous books, calendars, and promotional materials annually. Through licensing agreements, other companies produce Sierra Club postcards, jigsaw puzzles, posters, address books, and audio and video cassettes—all of which serve to keep the organization a perpetual presence in the public eye.

In addition to its efforts to promote or oppose environmentally related legislation, the club also operates the Sierra Club Legal Defense Fund (established in 1971), which it uses to bring lawsuits against companies or governments engaged in anti-environment activities. In 1984 the club successfully brought a lawsuit against the Environment Protection Agency (EPA), compelling it to regulate the release of radioactive pollutants.

PROGRAMS

Exploring and enjoying the earth's wilderness has always been at the heart of the Sierra Club's philosophy. Even today, as environmental protection becomes an increasingly important component of the organization's mission, the club remains dedicated to providing its members with wilderness adventures around the world. Each year, the club's Worldwide Outings Program sponsors about 300 trips to 20 countries. The club offers every conceivable type of outdoor adventure—from river-running and white-water rafting to bicycle and ski tours. Members can even build trails, preserve archeological sites, and help clean up the environment on the club's service trips. Individual chapters also sponsor hundreds of outings on a regional basis.

On the environmental protection front, the Critical Ecoregions Program features multifaceted plans tailored to the particular needs of 21 different major land and water ecosystems in the United States and Canada. Each of these plans offers concrete proposals for local action to restore and protect the ecological health of the region.

Recognizing that the largest single source of greenhouse gases is the internal combustion engine, the Sierra Club has also instituted the Miles-Per-Gallon Campaign and the CAFE (Corporate Average Fuel Economy) Campaign. Arguing that making cars go further on a gallon of gas is "the biggest single step we can take to reduce oil imports, protect wilderness areas from oil drilling, decrease air pollution, and curb global warming," the club calls for accelerated efforts to improve fuel efficiency and stricter enforcement of the 1990 and 1997 Clean Air Act Amendments.

BUDGET INFORMATION

In 1996, the Sierra Club reported total revenues of $52,760,300. Almost $16 million of this came from member dues, with another $16 million in the form of grants and contributions. The remainder was drawn from

BUDGET:

1996 Sierra Revenue

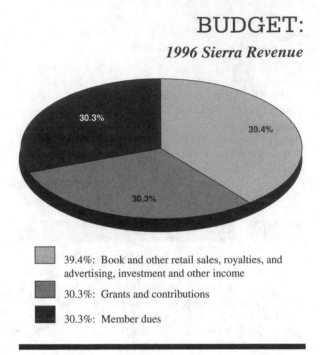

■ 39.4%: Book and other retail sales, royalties, and
advertising, investment and other income

■ 30.3%: Grants and contributions

■ 30.3%: Member dues

book sales and other retail sales, royalties, advertising,
and investment and other income. Of the $52 million, the
club spent some $34 million on program services—with
more than half of that going towards "studying and influencing public policy." Support services—including
administrative, membership services, and fund-raising
activities—accounted for close to $18 million.

HISTORY

As the Industrial Revolution steamrollered across the
vast tracts of wilderness that made up so much of the
United States in the nineteenth century, there was little
thought about what the United States would be like once
all its wild places had been tamed. Even so, as the century
drew to a close, there were men and women determined
to stop the ravaging of the country's remaining wilderness.

At the urging of one of the most renowned of these
conservationists, John Muir, the Sierra Club was incorporated on May 28, 1892, "to explore, enjoy, and render
accessible the mountain regions of the Pacific Coast; to
publish authentic information concerning them," and "to
enlist the support and cooperation of the people and government in preserving the forests and other natural features
of the Sierra Nevada." To this day, recreation, education,
and conservation have continued to define the club's mission. Over time, however, the focus of Sierra Club has
expanded to include the entire planet, rather than just the
mountains of the U.S. Pacific Coast.

National Park Expansion

Since many of the Sierra Club's original 182 charter members were scientists, the organization conducted
numerous scientific explorations of the Sierras in the
1890s. The *Sierra Club Bulletin* (first published in 1893
and continuing today as *Sierra*) included reports of excursions, guides to Sierran geography, scientific papers on
the range's natural history, and regular columns on
forestry. In its first conservation effort, the Sierra Club
led a campaign to defeat a proposed reduction in the
boundaries of Yosemite National Park and later provided
the ground work for the establishment of Mt. Rainier
National Park in 1899. The club also sponsored public
educational and scientific meetings, and in 1898 established an information center for visitors to Yosemite Valley—the first of many lodges, information centers, and
trailside shelters that the club would build and staff.

Seeking to boost the club's political influence, John
Muir supported tourism on the grounds that "if people in
general could be got into the woods, even for once, to
hear the trees speak for themselves, all difficulties in the
way of forest preservation would vanish." In 1901 the
club's board of directors decided to add an annual summer outing in an effort to encourage members and other
interested people to see firsthand the country the club
sought to preserve.

In spite of its success in attracting members and
prompting the establishment of several national and state
parks, the club's early years had ups and downs. The
Sierra Forest Reserve, once thought inviolable, was
opened to logging and sheep grazing, and in 1914 the
club conducted its last outing to Hetch Hetchy Valley,
north of Yosemite, before it was flooded by a reservoir.
That same year, automobiles first entered Yosemite Valley, inaugurating the modern era of mass tourism, and
planting the seed for future conflicts within the club.

At first, transportation seemed a boon for the Sierra
Club, as it made it easier for members to visit faraway
mountains. By the 1930s, however, the club began to
worry that its large groups and their activities could ultimately result in "loving the mountains to death."

Wilderness Conference

During this period, the club's environmentalist
stance also became more pronounced. In 1949 Club
Director and professional wilderness packer Norman
"Ike" Livermore Jr. organized a wilderness conference
attended by about 100 federal and state land managers,
outing leaders, and professional outfitters and guides.
The High Sierra Wilderness Conference was the first of
14 biennial conferences that greatly influenced subsequent conservation policy. In the same year, on the basis
of testimony by the Sierra Club, the secretaries of the
Interior and Army rejected a proposal for construction of
a dam that would have flooded 20,000 acres of Glacier
National Park.

BIOGRAPHY:

John Muir

Naturalist; Environmentalist (1838–1914) When temporarily blinded from an industrial accident, John Muir vowed that if his sight ever returned, he would leave his working life and see as much of the world as possible. When his sight returned within a month's time, he left the factory to wander. It was a few years after the Civil War when Muir settled in California's Yosemite Valley to live in a pine-log cabin he and a friend built by hand. Famous writers and botanists visited Muir and he shared his exuberance about the landscape around him. After four years, Muir left Yosemite for other travels and life experiences. He climbed Mount Shasta in northern California, and Mount Rainier in Washington, made half a dozen treks to Alaska where he climbed mountains and studied glaciers, married, and raised a family. More than 15 years passed before circumstance led Muir back to Yosemite. What he saw shocked and saddened him. During his absence, forestry and sheep herding had eroded and otherwise devastated the pristine quality of the valley and highlands. Muir's urgent campaign to increase public awareness about this tragedy paid off in 1890 when the federal government created Yosemite National Park as the first of several national preserves. In 1892, John Muir helped create the

Sierra Club and served as its first president. Impatient with the pace of the federal government in pursuing his conservationist goals, Muir spent the final years of his life traveling other continents and writing prolifically. His books are widely read today by students, naturalists, and philosophers.

The booming economy that followed the end of World War II (1939–45) saw a period of rapid development. To counter increasing recreational and commercial demands on natural lands, the Sierra Club devoted more of its time to protecting the wilderness than to exploring it. In 1951 the Club's statement of purpose was revised from "explore, enjoy and render accessible . . ." to "explore, enjoy and preserve . . ."

In 1950 the Sierra Club established its first chapter outside of California, the Atlantic Chapter, which comprised 18 eastern states and the District of Columbia. The following year, the club tested its strength by challenging a federal government proposal to build two dams in the Dinosaur National Monument. The battle continued for the next four years until 1956, when federal water developers abandoned plans to dam Dinosaur National Monument. Meanwhile, club membership had soared to 10,000.

By 1963 the Sierra Club had become the nation's leading conservationist group and opened an office in Washington, D.C., to support its increasing lobbying efforts. In 1964 Sierra Club lobbying helped push through the Wilderness Act, the first wilderness protection legislation in the world, and in 1966, the organization's outspoken opposition to proposed dams in parts of the Grand Canyon prompted the Internal Revenue Service (IRS) to take away the club's tax-deductible status. Nevertheless, the club's campaign to stop the damming of the Grand Canyon succeeded.

Electoral Politics

By the end of the 1960s the Sierra Club was a well-established political force in the United States. Its tactics and strategy served as a model for the dozens of environmental groups that arose in the environmentally conscious 1970s. Throughout the decade, the Sierra Club steadily widened the scope of its interests, establishing an International Program in 1971, and in 1973 launching a campaign to defend the Clean Air Act against opposition from the automobile industry. By 1980 the Sierra Club had decided to follow in the steps of other special-interest groups and take the plunge into electoral politics. While not actually endorsing any national candidate by name, it raised and dispensed about $100,000 to support candidates in key races. The experiment was less than successful, however, as a Reagan-led landslide wiped out many of the environmentalists in Congress whom the Club had supported.

Spurred by what it saw as a Reagan administration drive to dismantle or weaken environmental laws passed in the previous two decades, the Club endorsed some 140 candidates for the House and Senate in the 1982 election and donated approximately a quarter of a million dollars to support their campaigns. More than 75 percent of club-endorsed candidates won and the club remained active in electoral politics throughout the decade. In 1992 it raised $1 million to support favored candidates.

By 1990 the Sierra Club was a formidable political force, boasting more than half a million members. The club's new-found political activism resulted in some

FAST FACTS

According to the U.S. Forest Service, recreation, hunting, and fishing on national forests contribute over 37 times more income to the nation's economy than logging on national forests.

(Source: U.S. Forest Service. "Explanatory Notes for the 1997 Forest Service Budget," 1998.)

definitive victories. In 1987 Congress passed reauthorization and expansion of the Clean Water Act over a veto by President Ronald Reagan and, in 1990, a strengthened Clean Air Bill passed the House and Senate despite threat of veto by President George Bush. In 1995 the Club delivered over a million signatures on the Environmental Bill of Rights in opposition to the "War on the Environment" waged by Congress. Most recently, in 1997, the Sierra Club and its environmentalist allies helped pushed through strict new clean air standards proposed by the Environmental Protection Agency against a massive campaign waged by business and conservative groups.

CURRENT POLITICAL ISSUES

From its early days as an organization of conservationists, the Sierra Club has expanded its interests to cover virtually everything that impacts the environment—from a dam in California to the reduction of greenhouse emissions worldwide.

The club's concern about global warming has led it to demand more stringent controls on automobile emissions and other pollutants. It wants federal and state laws and regulations strengthened to limit pollutant emissions from internal-combustion engines to "the absolutely practicable minimum." Moreover, if emissions of a pollutant cannot be reduced to acceptable limits through existing technology, the club wants regulations to be imposed that can set limits through other means.

Other issues of concern to the Sierra Club include biotechnology, mining, nuclear power, ecotourism, and energy conservation. Among its priorities, the Sierra Club is determined to halt the destruction of forest ecosystems. Besides opposing all logging activities that it considers environmentally unsustainable, the club wants an immediate halt to all logging in remaining old-growth or roadless areas, and to ecologically destructive clearcutting.

Case Study: Salvage Rider

During the 1990s many environmental groups—including the Sierra Club—grew increasingly concerned about the government allowing the logging industry to harvest trees from national parks. While destruction of old-growth forests in British Columbia, Canada, had been a focal point for the growing antilogging movement, the Sierra Club soon found plenty to be concerned about closer to home. The 1994 Republican takeover of Congress brought issues to the forefront that had been festering for years, as the new Congress launched an immediate assault on both existing and proposed environmental legislation.

In 1995 Senators Slade Gorton (R-Wash.) and Mark Hatfield (R-Oreg.) pushed through an amendment called the "Salvage Rider" to the Federal Recissions Act (H.R. 1159; Public Law 104-19), which was an omnibus federal budget-cutting measure. The Salvage Rider was an emergency two-year salvage timber sale program, and included among other provisions that salvage could only take place on areas recommended by the Forest Service or the Bureau of Land Management. Signed into law on July 27th, 1995, the rider would, according to detractors like the Sierra Club, accelerate logging of much of the remaining old-growth forests in the United States, increase the amount of clearcut logging, and jeopardize vital habitat for endangered species. Proponents of the rider dismissed these arguments, claiming that the rider was simply an emergency measure designed to allow "salvage" logging of dead and dying trees. When a pro-environment legislator moved to eliminate the rider, his amendment failed by a 150 to 275 vote.

Environmentalists dubbed the proposed amendment the "Logging Without Laws" rider, and it soon became a leading cause of concern to conservation groups, many of which were asking for a "zero cut" policy that would not allow any logging in national forests. The Sierra Club threw its support behind the Zero Cut Campaign in the spring of 1996. Up until that time, members and chapters of the club had been prohibited from using the club's name in support of Zero Cut: most of the club's board and national leaders had been opposed to Zero Cut because it might have a negative economic impacts on rural communities, particularly in the western states. Ultimately, advocates convinced the leadership that by shifting dollars from timber subsidies into ecological restoration, both jobs and over-logged federal forests could be saved.

In spite of its efforts to emphasize the mainstream aspects of the Zero Cut policy, the Sierra Club's new stance drew howls of rage from clearcutting proponents who denounced the club for abandoning its mainstream approach and joining more radical groups. The club countered that there was nothing radical about a policy designed to prevent "the massive clearcuts, eroded hillsides, and streams filled with silt and logging debris that are the legacy of commercial logging of our public heritage." Pointing out that the logging program on national forests operated at a net loss to taxpayers of $7.3 billion between 1980 and 1991, and that national polls showed a majority of Americans were opposed to resource extraction from public lands, the club's Executive Director, Carl Pope, claimed that, in fact, the Zero Cut policy was mainstream, and that it was the clearcutters who were the radicals.

Despite repeated attempts by Sierra Club supported legislators to push through repeals of the rider, Republican control of Congress ensured that it remained in force through 1997. Nevertheless, the Club could claim a victory of sorts since its decision to support the Zero Cut policy had gained it new allies among the many environmental groups who had dismissed its previous conservative initiatives.

FUTURE DIRECTIONS

Sierra Club priorities into the twenty-first century will address environmental conservation issues such as wildlands protection and global warming. Specifically, the Campaign to End Commercial Logging on Federal Lands will emphasize public education and grassroots organizing and will continue to lobby against logging legislative attacks. The Stopping Sprawl Campaign will continue to develop strategies to help stop population sprawl at the state, regional, national, and international levels. The campaign will target initiatives that focus on land-use planning and transportation.

As the environmental wars continue, the club's mainstream approach may cause internal divisions. The controversial zero cut agenda, which the club supported following a vote by members, caused a serious split within the group. This internal split echoed what was happening in the environmental movement as a whole. As Patrick Moore, one of the original founders of Greenpeace, explained in a 1994 speech, the environmental movement in the 1990s split into two factions: those who advocated a pragmatic approach of working with business and government to promote the idea of "sustainable development," and those with more extreme positions who were in favor of taking a "zero tolerance" and "anti-development" stance at any cost. The Sierra Club has always been, and still considers itself to be, a part of the "sustainable development" camp, but its support for zero tolerance of public logging caused many to fear that it was abandoning its usual willingness to compromise.

GROUP RESOURCES

Besides an extensive Web site at http://www.sierraclub.org and numerous individual chapter Web sites, the Sierra Club provides a variety of information resources including newsletters reporting on environ-

mental news and club events and a highly successful book publishing division with more than 700 titles in print. For more information, contact the Sierra Club Information Center at 85 2nd St., Second Floor, San Francisco, CA 94105 or phone (415) 977-5653.

You can also send E-mail to information@sierraclub.org or visit the club's Web site at http://www.sierraclub.org.

GROUP PUBLICATIONS

Sierra Club publications include *Sierra*, a full-color magazine sent to members six times per year, which features environmental analysis, outdoor adventure, and tips on food, home, health, and travel. Nonmembers can subscribe for $15 a year (1999). Reprints of selected articles are available from Sierra Club Public Affairs. Call (415) 977-5653 for more information. The club also publishes *The Planet*, a newsletter that provides information to help activists fight for environmental protection at the local, state, and national level. It is available at a yearly subscription rate of $8 for members and $11 for nonmembers. For more information, contact the Sierra Club Information Center at 85 Second St., 2nd Floor, San Francisco, CA 94105 or phone (415) 977-5653. You can also send E-mail to information@sierraclub.org or visit the club's Web site at http://www.sierraclub.org.

BIBLIOGRAPHY

Bass, Rick. "The Reality of Salvage Logging Seen From Stump Level." *Sierra* July/August 1996.

Berger, John J. *Understanding Forests.* San Francisco, Calif.: Sierra Club Books, 1998.

Birnbaum, Jeffrey H. "Beating The System: This Year More Than Ever, Candidates Get Help from Special-Interest Groups That S-T-R-E-T-C-H The Rules." *Time* 21 October 1996.

Drexel, Karl. "Will the Real Sierra Club Please Stand Up?" *Christian Science Monitor* 24 May 1996.

Fox, Stephen. *The American Conservation Movement: John Muir and His Legacy.* Madison, Wisc.: University of Wisconsin Press, 1981.

Hornblower, Margot. "We Can Sit Here Bemoaning Beavis and Butt-Head or We Can Learn from Their Appeal." *Time* 9 June 1997.

Shaffer, Denny. "Why the Sierra Club Went Political." *Christian Science Monitor* 28 October 1982.

Turner, Tom. *Sierra Club: 100 Years of Protecting Nature.* New York: Henry Abrams, Inc., 1991.

Wilkinson, Todd. "New Sapling Amid Old-Growth Leaders: Internet-savvy Sierra Club President Heralds Next Generation in Environmental Leadership." *Christian Science Monitor* 9 September 1996.

Transport Workers Union of America (TWU)

ESTABLISHED: 1934
EMPLOYEES: Not made available
MEMBERS: 100,000
PAC: TWU Committee on Political Education (COPE)

Contact Information:

ADDRESS: 80 West End Ave.
New York, NY 10023
PHONE: (212) 873-6000
FAX: (212) 721-1431
E-MAIL: twu@twu.org
URL: http://www.twu.org
PRESIDENT: Sonny Hall

WHAT IS ITS MISSION?

The Transport Worker's Union of America (TWU) is a trade union representing workers from the mass transportation, airline, railroad, service, and utilities industries, as well as allied workers at universities and municipalities. Members may operate city bus, subway, or train systems; provide ground crew maintenance and baggage handling for airlines; install and repair natural gas lines; or perform railcar repair and maintenance work. The TWU describes itself as "dedicated to the promise that an organization built on trust and equality for all workers cannot be denied." To fulfill this promise, the TWU works to ensure fair pay, reasonable working conditions, a safe workplace, and job security for its members.

HOW IS IT STRUCTURED?

While the TWU is headed by an "International President" and the union is affiliated with the International Transport Workers Federation (ITF), the TWU is primarily a domestic organization. Its policy-making body is the TWU Constitutional Convention, held every four years, during which the constitution governing all TWU activities is reviewed and amended. Between conventions the president of the TWU serves as the chief executive officer and is responsible for daily decision-making and union activities. The organization also has several small administrative bureaus that report directly to the president, including the Organizing Department, which helps workers in specific areas to unionize; the Education Department, which is responsible for public relations as well as training programs for shop stewards (chief union officers at specific workplaces); and the Research Department.

Most of the internal organization of the TWU is in terms of industrial division, Transit, Air Transport, and Railroad divisions being the most important. Workers in the utilities and service industries, as well as some university and municipal workers, are organized into smaller divisions. Division councils meet regularly to discuss and formulate policies relating to their respective industries or memberships.

Despite the work that goes on in TWU divisions, the local union remains the core of the organization. Workers are organized into "locals" on the basis of interest and geographical location. Members of each local elect their own officers to handle most problems, but when a local union requires assistance, a field worker from the national is dispatched to provide professional assistance where needed—typically, legal advice, education, research, or public relations.

The TWU is affiliated with the American Federation of Labor/Congress of Industrial Organizations (AFL-CIO), the largest national federation of industrial workers' unions. All transport workers who are members of the AFL-CIO are considered members of the TWU.

PRIMARY FUNCTIONS

Although TWU objectives are typically carried out at the local level, the national organization does its part to serve and protect members. One of the most important functions of the national union is its organizing function, an ongoing process designed to bring more local members into the TWU and thereby increase the local's collective power to negotiate wage contracts, retirement plans, health and welfare benefits, and safe working conditions. Field workers from the TWU often help workers at a specific workplace to either form or join a local union.

Once a local TWU has been organized, the national union provides professional assistance in legal matters, collective bargaining, and public relations. In conjunction with the AFL-CIO, the national TWU also provides instructional programs for local union officers in all relevant areas of leadership and delivery of union services.

Through its political action committee, the Committee on Political Education (COPE), the TWU works to ensure that its members stand behind and help elect government officials who are pro-union and pro-TWU. COPE does this in two ways: by making financial contributions to political candidates who support TWU, and by making sure members are registered and voting for these candidates when an election occurs.

In the same way that it mobilizes members to vote for certain political candidates, the TWU attempts to make its members aware of items of legislation—including state or local ballot initiatives—that could affect them. Examples include regulations affecting the transport of hazardous substances, wage legislation, and regulations that set standards for occupational safety. When the TWU becomes aware of such legislation, it alerts its members, explains the potential consequences of the law, and urges them to either support or fight the measure.

PROGRAMS

Very few programs are operated from the TWU's national level. Exceptions are training programs for "shop stewards"—top union leaders who work at specific workplaces. Stewardship programs are generally carried out by field representatives from the TWU's Education Department. Shop stewards serve as primary negotiators between labor and management at particular places of employment, and their most important responsibility is presenting workers' grievances to management and representing workers at disciplinary hearings. Another national program, Member Outreach, is the TWU's organized effort to communicate with local members to encourage and influence their political involvement on key issues or local ballot initiatives. Most educational programs—on key leadership issues such as law, arbitration, workers' compensation, and organizing—that are available to TWU members are offered by the AFL-CIO through that organization's George Meany Center for Labor Studies in Maryland.

BUDGET INFORMATION

Not made available.

HISTORY

Not surprisingly, the history of the TWU began in New York City, where the nation's first extensive mass transit system was established. Previous attempts by New York's transit workers to unionize failed largely because of the power of the transit companies: strikes in 1905, 1910, 1916, and 1919 were all failures. The plight of transit workers hit rock bottom during the Great Depression of the 1930s when unemployment rates reached as high as 25 percent. New York's transit companies took full advantage of this unprecedented demand for jobs, slashing wages, imposing long hours and harsh working conditions, and hiring and firing at will.

In this environment, it would take a powerful and charismatic leader to establish a union that could succeed where others had failed. The transit workers of New York found theirs in Michael J. Quill, an Irish-born radical who worked on the IRT subway line as a change maker. Quill, a dynamic speaker, was gifted with an understanding of the power of public media to call attention to the plight of exploited workers. Although it took him and his followers a few years to solidify the TWU's influence, the union was never seriously weakened after its foundation in 1934.

Among the events that lifted the TWU to prominence, the most important was the historic Kent Avenue strike of 1937. The strike took place at a transit powerhouse where, initially, only 35 of the powerhouse's 505 workers belonged to the TWU. In order to forestall the organization of its workers, powerhouse management fired three engineers for engaging in union activity. Almost overnight 463 of the outraged workers were converted to the union cause, and together the workers staged a sit-down strike at the plant. The workers issued an ultimatum to management: either the three workers would be reinstated immediately or electric power would be shut off, affecting 2.4 million of New York's mass transit riders. A half-hour before the workers' deadline, management bowed to their demands and reinstated the fired workers. For the first time, transit workers in New York had won a major victory over management. It was a defining moment in the history of the TWU.

Expansion

In 1937 the TWU was recognized by the Congress of Industrial Organizations (CIO), the national federation of labor unions. Once it had achieved this national recognition, associated transit worker unions sprouted up across the United States throughout the 1940s and 1950s, in cities such as Akron, Ohio; Omaha, Nebraska; Philadelphia; and San Francisco.

In 1945, the TWU also began its expansion into other areas of transport labor, when employees at Pan American World Airways reached their first collective bargaining agreement with management, winning a 40-hour work week and pay for overtime. The Pan Am agreement paved the way for a similar dramatic labor victory for workers at American Airlines in 1946.

Until 1954 U.S. railroad workers were organized under the United Railroad Workers Organizing Committee, which had been formed in 1943 by the old CIO. Because the far-flung geography of railroad workers often made communication and organization difficult, the committee realized the need for association with a strong, centralized leadership organization, and voted overwhelmingly to join with the TWU in 1954. The growing union's first major achievement came a year later when workers on the Pennsylvania Railroad secured an improved maintenance plan, an end to the practice of "farming out" or subcontracting certain tasks, and providing furloughed workers with reasonable severance pay.

Since its beginnings, the TWU has maintained its status as the premier labor organization for mass transit, railroad, and airline workers by tirelessly pursuing organization at the local level and by maintaining stable leadership. Quill, the TWU's first president, served for more than 30 years. Since then the organization has been led by only five additional presidents: President Sonny Hall was elected during the 19th Constitutional Convention in 1993 and served through the end of the 1990s.

CURRENT POLITICAL ISSUES

TWU's political involvement at the national or state level is typically allied with that of other labor organizations. In California, for example, the TWU joined other organizations in the fight against Proposition 226, a 1998 ballot initiative that would have ended a traditional union practice: automatically using a portion of member dues to support political candidates and causes that are favorable to unions. Called the "Paycheck Protection Act," the legislation was sponsored by conservative groups and would have certainly eroded the financial power of U.S. unions. Despite initial polls showing that Californians favored Prop. 226 by a margin of two to one, the campaign mounted by labor unions was effective; the proposition was ultimately defeated at the polls.

Case Study: The Philadelphia Transit Strike

Typically, the TWU's most direct political involvement takes place at the local level. One such case occurred in Philadelphia in March of 1998, after the collective bargaining contract for about 5,200 workers in Transport Workers Union Local 234 expired. The workers, mostly drivers and mechanics employed by the Southeastern Pennsylvania Transit Authority's city division, could not reach agreement on issues such as work rules, wages, pensions, the hiring of part-time workers, and workers' compensation. Local 234, the city's largest transit union, operated a network of buses, trolleys, and subways that served up to 435,000 people each day. When initial negotiations failed, union leaders set a deadline of June 1 and threatened to strike if its demands were not met.

Although joined in the strike threat by suburban transit workers during the next few weeks, the drivers and mechanics of Local 234 were not able to convince Transit Authority management of the validity of their complaints. What union members found particularly offensive was a new management policy allowing liberal use of part-time workers—a policy they saw as specifically designed to weaken the union.

Management would not give in, and the workers walked out at noon on June 1. The 40-day strike paralyzed the city's trolley car and subway lines, and caused rush-hour gridlock throughout Philadelphia streets. Eventually, Local 234 and the Transit Authority reached a compromise settlement: the drivers and mechanics won a nine percent wage raise over three years and agreed to send the controversial issue of hiring part-time workers to an outside arbitrator. Although the policy on part-timers had not been abolished outright, the workers felt confident that an outsider would see the wisdom of their position. To them, the strike had produced a significant victory.

FUTURE DIRECTIONS

Among the TWU's concerns for the future has been the drainage of the federal Social Security Trust Fund, which by 2032 was estimated not to be able to pay out full benefits. Along with other labor organizations, the TWU favored a more moderate approach—such as a reduction in benefits—than many of the solutions under consideration. In particular, the TWU joined labor in its opposition to the suggested privatization of the Social Security fund through investing fund monies in the stock market. Considerable lobbying efforts were expected to be devoted to this issue in the early twenty-first century.

As it joins in finding solutions to the Social Security quandary, the TWU also continues to monitor and publicize its positions on legislation introduced in Congress, some of which has included bills that would increase the minimum wage, provide more funding to public schools, ensure equal pay for female workers, raise pension coverages, fund airport improvements, increase child care subsidies, and expand Medicare.

GROUP RESOURCES

The most comprehensive source of information about the TWU is the union's Web site at http://www.twu.org, which contains information on recent union activities, its divisions, departments, and locals. The site contains links to Web sites for TWU locals that maintain them, as well as links to relevant government agencies and political parties. For further information about TWU activities, contact the union's Education Department at (212) 873-6000, ext. 359.

GROUP PUBLICATIONS

The TWU has three major publications, all periodicals. *TWU Express*, a monthly newsletter for all TWU members, includes union news from locals around the country, as well as happenings at the national level. The *COPE Reader*, a newsletter of TWU's political action committee, provides information designed to help members become knowledgeable and influential with regard to the legislative process, and records the platforms and voting records of government officials on specific items of legislation. Another newsletter, the *Legislative Alert*, keeps members up to date on legislative issues and ballot initiatives of interest to the union. Recent editions of these newsletters can be viewed at the TWU Web site. For further information on the *COPE Reader* or *Legislative Alert*, contact COPE at (212) 873-6000.

BIBLIOGRAPHY

Chen, David W. "President of Transport Union Re-elected after Bitter Fight." *New York Times*, 22 May 1998.

Freeman, Joshua Benjamin. *In Transit: The Transport Workers Union in New York City, 1933–1966*. New York: Oxford University Press, 1989.

Greenhouse, Stephen. "Workers United? Debating Union Dues and Political Don'ts." *New York Times*, 12 October 1997.

Jennings, Kenneth M. *Labor-Management Cooperation in a Public Service Industry*. Westport, Conn.: Praeger, 1986.

Lacayo, Richard. "Will Voters Unplug Labor's Money Machine?" *Time*, 18 May 1998.

Leuck, Thomas J. "Transit Repairs Are Rushed, Unions Warn." *New York Times*, 6 October 1998.

Lieb, Robert C. *Labor in the Transportation Industries*. Westport, Conn.: Praeger, 1974.

Newman, Andy. "Direction of the Transit Union Is at Stake in Ballot Counting." *New York Times*, 16 December 1997.

Snyder, Robert W. *Transit Talk: New York's Bus and Subway Workers Tell Their Stories*. New Brunswick, N.J.: Rutgers University Press, 1997.

"Transport Workers to File Petition for Delta Vote." *Wall Street Journal*, 12 September 1997.

U.S. English

ESTABLISHED: 1983
EMPLOYEES: 15
MEMBERS: over 1.1 million
PAC: None

Contact Information:

ADDRESS: 1747 Pennsylvania Ave. NW, Ste. 1100
   Washington, DC 20006
PHONE: (202) 833-0100
TOLL FREE: (800) 873-4547
FAX: (202) 833-0108
E-MAIL: info@us-english.org
URL: http://www.us-english.org
CHAIRMAN; CEO: Mauro E. Mujica

WHAT IS ITS MISSION?

U.S. English aims to promote the use of English as the official language of the United States, either through a constitutional amendment, or through other legislative means. The organization insists that the best way to serve the varied immigrant populations in the United States is to encourage and assist them in learning English and that money spent on bilingual education should emphasize teaching students English above all else. U.S. English is perhaps most actively involved in opposing the increasing trend that not only enables, but requires non-native speakers to be able to vote, apply for driver's licenses, and perform other governmental functions in their native languages.

HOW IS IT STRUCTURED?

The organization is divided into two entities. U.S. English, Inc., concentrates on lobbying for reform on behalf of official English, with a governmental (lobbying) department, a communications department, a research department, and a development department. The 501(c)3 (tax exempt) U.S. English Foundation carries out the other functions of the organization, such as administering grants to special programs, and distributing scholarships. Both branches have three-member boards of directors chaired by the president. There are 15 employees between the two branches.

While U.S. English, Inc., may fund and participate in state and local official English campaigns and retain state council lobbyists, all efforts of both branches of the organization are centralized in its Washington, D.C., offices, which cultivate and maintain the membership of 1.3 million, whose dues augment funds solicited from other foundations.

PRIMARY FUNCTIONS

U.S. English Foundation and U.S. English, Inc., are concerned exclusively with the issue of making English the official language of the United States. Their efforts to achieve this goal, however, are diverse. The U.S. English Foundation functions primarily through grant solicitation and disbursement. The group is dedicated to funding efforts that help immigrants learn the English language, so that they can take advantage of the economic and social benefits available in the United States to the fullest extent. The foundation awards scholarships and grants designed to advance the teaching of English to immigrant groups and provides resources that explain how and where immigrants can participate in community education programs. In addition, the organization researches language policy in countries where more than one official language is present, and uses advertising and other media projects to increase public awareness of their cause.

U.S. English, Inc., the foundation's sister organization, concentrates on lobbying legislators to support federal and state legislation devised to stop the multilingual duplication of government transactions and to reallocate these funds to programs that teach English to immigrants. At times the organization is required to defend their legislative victories in court: challenges to English-only legislation in Arizona ultimately forced U.S. English to defend the law in front of the Supreme Court. They also conduct and sponsor surveys that indicate the extent of support on behalf of the American people for their cause.

PROGRAMS

The U.S. English Foundation is primarily involved in funding efforts to teach English to foreign-language speakers. For example, their funding maintains the Villa Maria Center, a school that provides free English-language training to immigrant communities in Erie, Pennsylvania. The organization also sometimes becomes directly involved in efforts to teach English. In Washington, D.C., it has adapted a literacy program to work in conjunction with tennis lessons for disadvantaged Spanish-speaking youth, modifying the program to focus on verbal skills rather than literacy. In addition the foundation sponsors two graduate scholarships through the U.S.–U.K. Fluorite Commission; recipients study methods of teaching English as a Second Language (ESL) at prestigious universities in the United Kingdom.

BUDGET INFORMATION

In 1996 the organization took in $7,438,000 in contributions, the vast majority of this sum coming from individual members. Management costs absorbed $803,000 of the total income, fund-raising $2,598,000, and programs $4,825,000. U.S. English disburses a significant amount of their revenue through grants.

HISTORY

U.S. English was founded by S. I. Hayakawa, an immigrant to the United States who received his Ph.D. in English and became a well-known semanticist and professor at San Francisco State University. In 1976 Dr. Hayakawa was elected to represent California as a Republican in the U.S. Senate. He was the first U.S. senator to introduce the English Language Amendment, a failed attempt to make sweeping official English reform through constitutional tactics. Upon leaving the Senate in 1983, he helped found U.S. English to promote an official language and presided as honorary chairman of the organization until the time of his death in 1992.

In 1986 U.S. English was active in convincing more than a million Californians to sign petitions to put Proposition 63 on the state ballot, an initiative that was to make English the official language of the state. The measure, which passed by 73 percent, has led to numerous legal disputes regarding the rights of employees to use languages other than English in the workplace. Twenty-two other states have enacted legislation that makes English their official language, although this does not always mean that government activities are limited to using English.

U.S. English has endured its share of public controversy: in 1989 former Reagan aide and senatorial candidate Linda Chavez and retired television anchorman Walter Cronkite disassociated themselves from the organization, having been president and advisory board member, respectively. Chavez and Cronkite were disturbed by the disclosure of a memo authored by the chairman of U.S. English, John Tanton. They felt the memo contained elements that were biased against immigrants. Three years later the acting director and chairman of U.S. English, Stanley Diamond, resigned after being accused of misusing the organization's funds to support political candidates in California.

Congressman Norman Shumway subsequently acted as chair for approximately six months, until the board selected Mauro E. Mujica, an architect and international businessman as well as an immigrant from Chile, to become the Chairman/CEO of U.S. English.

Since it inception, U.S. English has been active in lobbying for official English legislation, which would amend federal law to declare English the official language of the U.S. government. These efforts began to see

FAST FACTS

The 1990 U.S. Census found at least 328 languages spoken in the United States in addition to English.

(Source: U.S. English Web site, 1999.)

some success in the 1990s. In 1996 House Resolution 123 was introduced by California Representative Duke Cunningham. This bill would have established English as the official language of the federal government and required, with some exceptions, that English be used in all official government communication. The bill was passed by the House, with a vote of 259 to 169, but no action was taken by the Senate that year. The bill was subsequently reintroduced in 1997, and again in 1999. All of these bills called for the establishment of English as the official language of the federal government, one in which most (although not all) government business and communications would have to be conducted.

In 1998 U.S. English, Inc., contributed heavily to advocating and lobbying on behalf of successful legislation in California that radically reduced bilingual education in California public schools. Since this victory, the organization has been monitoring the outcome with concern, claiming that many educators have responded by defying and circumventing the law and that others were simply unprepared to accommodate the change. U.S. English, Inc., has subsequently been observing the outcomes of the lawsuits brought by parents against school districts who have allegedly not complied with the legislation.

CURRENT POLITICAL ISSUES

According to a U.S. English-sponsored poll, roughly 86 percent of Americans favor adopting English as the official national language. With such statistics as justification, the primary focus of the U.S. English Foundation has been to amend federal law to declare English the official language of the U.S. government. While Rep. Bill Emerson, who sponsored H.R. 123 for nearly a decade, was unable to push the legislation through in his lifetime, the prospects for passing official English legislation improved during the late 1990s.

The issue of official English obviously has more resonance in areas of the United States where there are large numbers of foreign speakers. Events in Arizona have illustrated the kinds of complications that have confronted U.S. English while working on behalf of state legislation. In 1988 voters in Arizona passed a referendum making English the state's official language of government, partly in response to the efforts of U.S. English. However various individuals and groups challenged the law's constitutionality and delayed its implementation. U.S. English was forced to defend the law in the Supreme Court, which upheld Arizona's official English law on March 3, 1997.

One of the most pressing issues on the organization's agenda is the possibility of statehood for the commonwealth of Puerto Rico. The possibility of a fifty-first state where less than 25 percent of the citizens speak English presents a potential conflict in implementing official English policies nationally, and is consequently a concern for U.S. English.

Case Study: Statehood for Puerto Rico

Debate over statehood has been ongoing since Puerto Rico came under U.S. authority in the nineteenth century. The succession of local governments have been granted more and more autonomy as a result of Puerto Rican nationalist movements challenging—sometimes violently—U.S. control. Today Puerto Rico is largely self-governed, while remaining under the direct authority of Congress. This is due to the fact that in 1967 a majority of its citizens voted to maintain commonwealth status rather than become a state or seek independence. However, many Puerto Ricans have become dissatisfied with the commonwealth status; many prefer statehood and some hope for complete independence.

In 1993 citizens of the island voted on whether the future of Puerto Rico's status should be commonwealth, statehood, or independence. Unlike the 1967 election, commonwealth status did not receive a majority vote, despite earning a close 48.6 percent, while the statehood option came in an extremely close second, accumulating 46.3 percent of the vote. Independence lagged behind at 4.4 percent. Because the vote was so close, and because commonwealth status did not receive a majority, there still remains much confusion over what the future status of Puerto Rico should be.

On May 21, 1997, the Resources Committee of the House of Representatives passed H.R. 856, a bill introduced by Rep. Don Young (R-Alaska), sending it to the full House for consideration. The bill would establish a referendum, to be carried out every 10 years, allowing voters in Puerto Rico to decide if the island should become a state, gain independence, or retain its commonwealth status. U.S. English has been active in the debate on whether to offer Puerto Rico statehood. Concerned with the idea of a state where (according to the 1990 U.S. Census) over 75 percent of the citizens speak only Spanish, the organization mounted a vigorous campaign to modify H.R. 856 to mandate official English regulations in the new state, should statehood become a reality.

U.S. English contracted surveys of American and Puerto Rican citizens that indicated that Puerto Ricans are too heavily invested in their own Spanish-speaking culture and identity to assimilate into an English-speaking country, and that Americans are hesitant to incorporate a state in which the vast majority of citizens don't speak English. The organization publicized this information, and emphasized the case of Quebec, a French-speaking province that has repeatedly threatened and attempted to secede from Canada, to illustrate the difficulty in incorporating a state that doesn't share a common language with the rest of the nation. Chairman Mujica's testimony before the House Committee on Resources on March 19, 1997, encouraged imposing the following conditions should Puerto Rican statehood become a reality: legislative and judicial proceedings and records must be kept in English; English fluency must be required for holding public office; public schools must teach in English; a majority of the population must speak English fluently; and a supermajority vote of 75 percent or more is needed to approve statehood.

Debate over the Puerto Rican statehood initiative continued into the late 1990s. Few legislators believed that Puerto Rico could meet the proposed requirements in the near future, particularly the requirement of an English-speaking majority in the population. When it became known that President Clinton would veto a bill which included the proposed requirements, U.S. English's proposals were abandoned by lawmakers. Nevertheless, U.S. English's arguments had an effect on lawmakers. On March 14, 1998, the House passed the bill, but by only one vote, 209 to 208. With such small support in the House, leaders in the Senate decided against considering the issue and the House bill failed to be enacted into law.

Public Impact

U.S. English believes that a non-English speaking fifty-first state would undermine their vision of official English status for the entire nation, and unravel their efforts to implement their vision at both the state and national level. Incorporating Puerto Rico into the United States without official English stipulations would create an exception that could lend support to efforts for multilingual governmental and educational structures in other parts of the country. The organization fears that this situation could create a country divided by language barriers.

FUTURE DIRECTIONS

U.S. English chairman Mauro E. Mujica has made the passage of H.R. 123 and S. 323 his top priority. "We

are beginning the next and perhaps most crucial phase of this movement," said Mujica on the foundation Web page. "For the first time, we now have a legitimate opportunity for these companion bills to be passed by the full Congress. The American people want a common-sense law recognizing English as our official language." At the same time, the organization will concentrate on continuing their successful efforts to encourage and implement state legislation.

GROUP RESOURCES

U.S. English has a Web site at http://www.us-english. org that offers extensive information on the organization and the issues that it supports, as well as how to become a member. Dues are not set at a specific amount; members contribute $10 or more. The organization maintains a database that catalogues regional resources for English classes for non-English speakers, which is also helpful for English language teachers looking for volunteer or work opportunities. Information on the database is available by calling 1-800-787-8216. Individuals can E-mail U.S. English at info@us-english.org or write to 1747 Pennsylvania Ave. NW, Ste. 1100, Washington, DC 20006. To telephone the organization, dial (202) 833-0100 or 1-800-USE-NGLI (1-800-873-6454). To fax, dial (202) 833-0108.

GROUP PUBLICATIONS

U.S. English mails a quarterly newsletter to its members, as well as monthly mailings encouraging donations, but does not publish materials for the general public. The organization's Web site (http://www.us-english.org/ foundation/reading.htm) gives a list of recommended reading, including Sen. S. I. Hayakawa's book *Language in Thought and Action.*

BIBLIOGRAPHY

Branigan, William. "Puerto Rico Winner: 'None of the Above.'" *Washington Post,* 14 December 1998.

Buckley, William F. "What is Wrong with Requiring English?" *Houston Chronicle,* 7 September 1995.

Fried, David J. "Say No to the 'English-Only' Movement." *Christian Science Monitor,* 10 May 1989.

Henry, Sarah. "Fighting Words; California's Official-Language Law Promises to Preserve and Protect English. The Question Is, Can the State Preserve and Protect its Citizens' Civil Rights at the Same Time?" *Los Angeles Times,* 10 June 1990.

Levy, Dan. "U.S. English Goes National with Campaign." *San Francisco Chronicle,* 9 July 1992.

Mujica, Mauro E. "English Unites the Nation." *USA Today,* 6 April 1995.

———. "Official Language Movement Not Same as 'English Only.'" *The Phoenix Gazette,* 29 May 1993.

Puente, Maria. "'English Only' Movement Picks Up Steam." *USA Today,* 14 March 1995.

Savage, David G. "High Courts 'English Only' Case Boils Down to Legalese." *Los Angeles Times,* 5 December 1996.

"Say, Can You See?" *Economist,* 14 March 1998.

United Automobile, Aerospace and Agricultural Implement Workers of America (UAW)

WHAT IS ITS MISSION?

The mission of the United Automobile, Aerospace and Agricultural Implement Workers of America (UAW), in the words of its constitution's preamble, is to guarantee working people "a meaningful voice in maintaining a safe and healthful workplace with decent working conditions, and . . . secured rights, together with a satisfactory standard of living and maximum job security." The UAW considers itself more than a labor union. In the words of UAW President Steve Yokich, "We in organized labor are a social movement. We're the only institution that stands up for working men and women." To achieve this aim, the UAW uses solidarity and collective action to help workers obtain decent wages, benefits, and working conditions. The organization is committed to helping its members, and other working people, stand up for their rights and live lives of dignity.

ESTABLISHED: August 26, 1935
EMPLOYEES: 500
MEMBERS: 1,275,000
PAC: Community Action Program

Contact Information:
ADDRESS: 8000 E. Jefferson
   Detroit, MI 48214
PHONE: (313) 926-5000
TOLL FREE: (800) 243-8829
FAX: (313) 331-1520
E-MAIL: uaw@uaw.org
URL: http://www.uaw.org
PRESIDENT: Stephen P. Yokich

HOW IS IT STRUCTURED?

The UAW represents workers in a broad variety of industries, in addition to auto and truck manufacturing. Other industries include aerospace, defense, farm construction, and consumer manufacturing. The organization also represents technical, office, and professional employees in state, county, and local governments, universities, and museums.

The International

The UAW International is run by an 18-member International Executive Board. It consists of six interna-

FAST FACTS

The states with the largest UAW memberships are Michigan, Ohio, Indiana, Illinois, and New York.

(Source: United Automobile, Aerospace and Agricultural Implement Workers of America, 1999.)

tional officers and 12 regional directors. Board members are elected to three-year terms at the UAW Constitutional Convention. The board oversees all UAW programs and policies, and is responsible for running the day-to-day operations of the union.

The organization's international officers are the president, secretary-treasurer, and five vice presidents. The UAW president is responsible for protecting and advancing the interests of UAW members and performing the related duties. The president is required to report to the executive committee every three months. Departments under the international president include Arbitration, Civil Rights, Community Services, UAW Retired Workers, Consumer Affairs, Education, Health and Safety, Organizing, Governmental and International Affairs, Legislative, and Women's Issues.

The secretary-treasurer is responsible for overseeing all financial operations of the UAW, including audits. The secretary-treasurer publishes an annual report on union finances in *Solidarity Magazine*. Departments under the international secretary-treasurer include Accounting, Auditing, Strike Insurance, and Veteran's Issues. The vice presidents are assigned areas of responsibilities by the president, and include collective bargaining, technical, and administrative departments. In addition to administrative personnel, the organization has staff members who are experts in collective bargaining, grievance handling, arbitration, labor law, health and safety, health care and retirement plans, unemployment insurance, workers' compensation, legislation, economics, education and training, and communications.

The collective bargaining departments are among the most important at the UAW International. There is a National Collective Bargaining Department for each of the Big Three automakers—General Motors, Ford, and Chrysler. In addition, there are departments for the aerospace industry; the agricultural implements industry; the heavy-truck industry; non-Big Three and transnational automakers; national manufacturing industries; and skilled trades and technical, office, and professional jobs.

Nationally, the UAW is divided into 12 regions, each headed by a regional director. Directors are selected at regional elections that take place during the regular UAW Constitutional Convention. Besides sitting on the International Executive Board, each regional director implements UAW programs and policies regionally, assists with contract negotiations, and oversees the enforcement of contracts at the regional level. Regional offices also administer educational, political, and other union activities in the region.

The Locals

The most important unit of the UAW is the individual bargaining unit, known as the local. The exact makeup of a local depends on the size of the company or community in which it is located. It might represent all the workers at a single factory or several; it might represent the entire workforce of a factory of a particular segment, for example the blue-collar workers, or the office and clerical staff. An amalgamated local is made up of more than one bargaining unit.

The governing body of the UAW local is the membership meeting, held regularly and open to all members in good standing. At the meeting local officials are elected by secret ballot to a term of three years. The UAW is divided into 1,086 locals throughout the United States, Canada and Puerto Rico.

Each local has a Local Union Executive Board made up of the local president, financial-secretary, and other officers. The board runs the day-to-day affairs of the local. All board actions are subject to approval of the members at the regular membership meetings.

Each local elects a bargaining committee, sometimes known as the top committee or shop committee. The shop committee, assisted by the International, negotiates contracts, deals with member grievances and, in general, acts as a liaison between the rank-and-file and the International. The locals are required to send representatives to standing union committees: Constitution and By-Laws, Union Label, Education, Conservation and Recreation, Community Services, Civil Rights, Citizenship and Legislative, Consumer Affairs, and Women's. Standing committees study problems in a specific area and make recommendations for action to the union leadership.

PRIMARY FUNCTIONS

The UAW, like most labor unions, performs a variety of functions on behalf of its members. They include organizing health and life insurance, pursuing the union's legislative agenda in Congress and state legislatures, and helping to elect candidates who support the working class. Much of the union's work involves negotiating contracts with employers, handling member grievances against employers, calling strikes, and settling health and safety problems at the workplace. Most of the UAW's operations are done at the local level.

Collective Bargaining

Perhaps the most crucial function of the UAW is the negotiation of contracts with employers, such as the Big Three automakers. This process is known as collective bargaining and the resulting contract covers workers' wages, benefits, working conditions, grievance procedures, seniority, union representation, hours of work, vacation, holidays and sick time, and deduction of union dues. All contract agreements must be ratified by the full membership, which votes by secret ballot.

Grievances

As part of each contract, the UAW negotiates the provisions for resolving problems between workers and supervision. These provisions are known as grievance procedures. UAW members can request union representation when they have a complaint that they cannot resolve themselves. A grievance might involve unfair treatment of a worker by a supervisor, or unhealthy or dangerous conditions at a workplace. The UAW representative discusses the problem with the worker and the supervisor, investigates the background of the matter, and attempts to settle it. If the problem cannot be resolved at this level, it is referred in writing to higher levels of the union and management. If the grievance still cannot be settled it will in most cases be sent to an impartial arbitrator whose decision is final.

Strikes

Sometimes the UAW calls a strike against an employer. A strike can be called for a variety of reasons, such as contract negotiations becoming deadlocked. This can happen if the union believes a company is not bargaining in good faith. A strike can also be called if a company consistently and blatantly violates the terms of a contract, or if a company refuses to correct worker health or safety issues. A call for a strike vote can be issued by either a local or the International Executive Board. First, affected members vote on the strike, then authorization to strike must be received from the International Executive Board. All members in good standing of a local or bargaining unit are entitled to vote on the strike. The strike vote is conducted by secret ballot and ballots are counted by a special committee elected by the membership for that purpose. A two-thirds majority must approve the strike before authorization can be sought from the International Executive Board. Once the board approves the strike, striking workers become eligible for benefits from the UAW Strike Insurance Fund but members must walk the picket line and participate in other strike activities to receive the benefits. Benefits include $150 per week, health care coverage, and life insurance.

Legislation

Influencing legislation is an important area of UAW activism. Most of this work is carried out through the union's PAC, the Community Action Program (CAP). CAP works in two ways: One, it actively lobbies Congress and state legislatures for the passage of progressive legislation. Two, it mobilizes the union membership to support progressive legislation and candidates, through demonstrations, vote canvassing, and letter writing campaigns. The UAW has contributed to the passage of such landmark legislation as the Medicare and Medicaid Acts, the Occupational Health and Safety Administration Act (OSHA), the Americans with Disabilities Act (ADA), and the Family and Medical Leave Act.

PROGRAMS

The UAW sponsors educational and recreational programs for members and their families. The UAW Educational Department is one of the largest in the U.S. labor movement. The department trains members in union skills as well as in specific job skills. The jewel of the union's educational efforts is the Walter and May Reuther Family Education Center on Black Lake near Onaway in northern Michigan. The 1,000-acre facility, completed in 1970, is funded by the interest from the UAW's multimillion dollar strike fund.

The center's summer scholarship program runs four one-week sessions from the end of June to the end of July and is open to all UAW members. Families learn about the principles and operations of the union, meet and interact with other union members, and take part in recreational programs. The center also provides day care activities for the younger children of visiting families.

The center holds conferences and courses for union officers on issues such as grievance handling, collective bargaining, health and safety, political action, and civil rights. The UAW regional offices use the center for their leadership courses.

Since the late 1980s, the UAW-Ford Technical Skills Program has been helping autoworkers enhance their business and technical skills. The program includes training in the skilled trades, technical business systems, new processes, and an enhanced apprenticeship program. The UAW pays for all accommodations, meals, and other program costs. It also provides transportation for members who work more than 500 miles away.

Through CAP, union members, at all levels, are encouraged to take political and social action, such as electing pro-worker candidates and working for the passage of progressive legislation. CAP works at the local, state, and national levels on issues including healthcare, public education, workplace health and safety, the environment, workers' compensation, and unemployment insurance.

BUDGET INFORMATION

In 1996 the UAW had assets worth $937.52 million. The UAW had $113.97 million in the International's General Fund that year, up slightly from 1995. The General Fund finances the union's normal costs of operation. In addition, the UAW maintains a Strike Insurance Fund, which is used to replace lost wages of striking members. In 1996 the UAW Strike Fund totaled $706.22 million.

The UAW is financed primarily by dues collected from its members. Each member pays the equivalent of two hours wages each month. Approximately 38 percent of UAW dues stay in the local unions; 32 percent goes to the International's General Fund; 30 percent goes to the Strike Insurance Fund, as long as the fund has less than $500 million. If the Strike Fund balance exceeds $500 million, the local and International get a rebate of 10 percent and five percent respectively. Public employees who are not allowed to strike do not pay into the UAW Strike Fund.

HISTORY

Henry Ford revolutionized automobile production in 1913 when he created the first assembly line and thus transformed a time-consuming and expensive job into a cheap mass industrial process. Soon, workers from across the nation swarmed to Ford's plants and others that copied his streamlined methods. Conditions in many of these factories, however, were unhealthy and dangerous. But unorganized workers could do little to force employers to make changes and often workers who tried to strike in protest were fired.

Early on, the American Federation of Labor (AFL) worked to organize autoworkers. As the size and number of locals grew, workers asked the AFL for an independent union of their own. Although the AFL agreed, autoworker delegates to the first UAW convention in Detroit, Michigan, protested when they learned that under the charter of the new union, the rank-and-file members were not allowed to elect union officials. Instead, that right was retained by the AFL leadership and AFL President William Green appointed a member of his staff, Francis Dillon, as the first UAW president.

Early on, autoworkers felt that the AFL was not serious in its efforts to organize factory workers. In response, UAW representatives and seven other unions met secretly and formed the Congress of Industrial Organizations (CIO). The AFL leadership learned of the organization and demanded that it disband. When it refused, the charters of the participating eight unions were suspended.

Sit-Down Strikes

At the second UAW convention in 1936, members demanded and were granted the right to elect their own leaders and Homer Martin was elected president. Although still affiliated with the AFL, the UAW was aligning itself more closely to the philosophy of the CIO. It adopted the CIO tactic of the "sit-down strike," in which workers occupied a factory but refused to work. That same year saw the first wave of UAW sit-down strikes across the country. The most dramatic began in December 1936 when workers occupied a General Motors plant in Flint, Michigan. The strike lasted 43 days and only ended when the governor, fearing violence against the workers, intervened and arbitrated a settlement. As a result, General Motors recognized the UAW. More strikes followed in 1937. In February, following a 15-week strike against J.I. Case, the UAW signed its first contract with an agricultural-implements manufacturer. Chrysler recognized the union in March and after that, the UAW set its sights on the Ford Motor Company.

Ford, at that time, was doing everything possible to prevent the unionization of its plants, even going so far as to intimidate its workers with threats of violence. The turning point for the UAW came in May, when Walter Reuther and other UAW organizers, who were handing out leaflets to Ford workers, were brutally attacked. Newspaper photos of the incident turned national public opinion to the union cause. Ford was not finally unionized however until April 1941, after UAW strikers organized roadblocks that effectively cut off supplies to one of Ford's plants.

In 1938 the AFL expelled the UAW after a long dispute and the union became a charter member of the CIO, which had been renamed the Congress for Industrial Organizations. In 1939 after problems connected with organizing efforts at Ford, Homer Martin was replaced by R. J. Thomas as UAW president. Martin, however, refused to go so easily and led his own renegade UAW for a short time, which eventually evolved into the Allied Industrial Workers.

The UAW Executive Board passed a motion pledging that the union would not strike for the duration of World War II (1939–45). When the war ended, there was growing anti-Communist sentiment, and union forces, led by Vice President Reuther, moved to expel communists from the ranks. When President Thomas refused to go through with the purge, he was voted out and replaced by Reuther, who went on to lead the UAW for nearly 25 years. During Reuther's time in office the UAW won pension plans, paid vacation, hospitalization and sick leave, cost-of-living increases for its members, in addition to benefits such as profit-sharing at American Motors, and an early retirement program at International Harvester. Reuther died in a plane crash in 1970, and was succeeded by Leonard Woodcock.

Troubled Times

The late 1970s were difficult for the UAW. The oil crisis of the mid-1970s and the fall of the Shah of Iran a few years later led to dramatically higher gasoline prices.

UAW workers in Flint, Michigan, staged a sit-down strike at General Motors Plant 4 in 1937. Fearing violence, the governor intervened and arbitrated a settlement between General Motors and the UAW, ending the strike after 43 days. (UPI/Corbis-Bettmann)

In response, consumers started buying energy-efficient imported autos and the U.S. auto industry entered a lengthy period of serious decline. By 1979 automakers were asking for contract concessions from the UAW. Chrysler was on the verge of bankruptcy and workers there agreed to wage concessions in order to save the company. In exchange, in 1980, the union won a seat on the Chrysler Board of Directors.

During the 1980s, the United States experienced an economic crisis and UAW members were hard hit. More than a third of all unionized auto workers lost their jobs;

half of the UAW members in the agricultural implements industry were laid off. At one point 330,640 UAW members were out of work. Even so, the UAW did manage to win two long strikes during this period; a 172-day strike against International Harvester, and a 205-day strike against Caterpillar.

Owen Bieber was elected UAW President in 1983 and under his leadership, the union intensified its political activities to prevent the loss of benefits through adverse legislation. Union attempts to get pro-worker legislation passed during the Bush administration were frequently frustrated by the president's vetoes of legislation such as the Family and Medical Leave Act and the Civil Rights Act of 1990.

As the 1990s progressed, the U.S. auto industry pulled out of the doldrums and the UAW fought to win back concessions it had made during the recession. The union also began working on new issues for organized labor, including automation and multinational companies shifting production to nonunionized Third World plants.

CURRENT POLITICAL ISSUES

The UAW involvement with political issues is consistent with the union's assertion that it is a movement for social justice. To this end, it encourages civil rights, environmental, and health care legislation. But it has never strayed far from its role as a labor union. The union's commitment to the labor issues that affect its members was made clear in the strike against General Motors in summer 1998.

Case Study: The 1998 Flint Strike

In May 1997 General Motors (GM) management reaffirmed its plans to invest $300 million in its Flint Metal Center, an engine cradle and sheet metal plant in Flint, Michigan, that employed about 4,000 members of UAW Local 659. In November of the same year it announced plans to build a $500 million engine factory in Flint. But in February 1998, in an abrupt turnabout, GM said it was suspending the investments. Although it had praised Local 659 workers just months earlier, GM maintained the reason for the action was the "uncompetitive work practices" of its workers.

The UAW felt insulted and betrayed and immediately started negotiations with GM. After four months, however, the UAW felt the talks were going nowhere. On June 5, Local 659 workers struck after they became convinced that GM had tried to remove important dies used in the production process from the plant over the Memorial Day weekend. On June 11, Local 561 struck GM's Delphi East plant in Flint, which made spark plugs, oil filters, air meters, fuel pumps, gauges, and other critical parts. In all 9,200 workers went on strike. The factories were crucial to GM's national car and truck production and the shortage of parts led to the closing of 26 of the company's 29 North American assembly plants. As a result, 175,000 GM workers were laid off.

The UAW said the strikes had nothing to do with wages or benefits—those were still covered by a 1996 contract. The critical issues, according to the union, were GM outsourcing and its compromising on health, safety and production standards. GM countered with a lawsuit in federal court, maintaining that the UAW talk of health and safety was merely a subterfuge. The real issue, GM said, was the plant investments GM had canceled. The

federal judge refused to issue a court order against the UAW and ordered the two parties to submit to binding arbitration.

The strike, the longest at GM in nearly 30 years, was finally settled on July 29, just a day before the arbitrator was to hand down a decision. Eighty percent of striking UAW members approved the settlement, over 90 percent at Flint Metal, over 60 percent at Delphi East. As part of the settlement GM agreed to make the investments at Flint Metal as it had promised. The company also agreed not to sell or close Delphi East before the year 2000. In exchange, the UAW promised not to strike either plant during the same period. The settlement also detailed a new system for UAW and GM leaders to deal with labor disputes before they reach the strike stage.

Public Impact

The strike slowed down the U.S. economy in 1998. In addition, GM and the UAW had losses from the strike. GM suffered an estimated $2 billion in lost production and UAW workers may have lost as much as $1 billion in wages. While the GM lawsuit went unsettled, the *New York Times* reported that just the threat of heavy damages that an adverse ruling could have entailed, worried the UAW. As a result, the union might refrain from authorizing strikes on similar grounds in the future.

Even more critical for the union was GM's effort to circumvent the strike by obtaining parts from outside sources, including nonunion plants in Mexico. That marked the beginning of the end of GM's vertical integration, in which everything from the smallest part to the finished automobile was produced in GM factories. The result could well mean that GM will outsource more and more production to nonunion factories in the United States and overseas. This could result in GM closing or selling its union plants, potentially leading to layoffs for thousands of UAW workers. Furthermore, it will be much more difficult for the UAW to stop GM's production nationwide by striking one or two key plants, as it did in the summer of 1998.

Immediately following the end of the strike, GM took the first step toward ending vertical integration. It announced that it intended to divest its Delphi Parts division, an action that the UAW had long opposed.

FUTURE DIRECTIONS

A critical issue that the UAW will have to deal with in the future is the increasing globalization of business. This trend hit the automobile industry in spring 1998 when two auto giants merged; Chrysler in the United States and Daimler Benz in Germany. The UAW has begun to work more closely with the German unions and it will need to cultivate ties with auto unions in other foreign countries, such as Brazil and Korea, as well. However, the union will need to address the problem of automakers outsourcing of work to countries without unions or figurehead unions.

The UAW has been negotiating a major merger with two other unions, the United Steelworkers of America and the International Association of Machinists. Once complete, the unification—known informally as "Big Steel"—will create one of the largest unions in North America. It will end overlap in areas of representation and competition for members. The UAW describes the unification as a response for the need of global unionization. The entire process will probably be completed in 2001.

GROUP RESOURCES

The UAW Web site has a wealth of informational resources, including frequently asked questions about the UAW, historical information, and news about the autoworkers and the labor movement in general. A particularly interesting and useful feature is the page on economic and labor statistics called *Jobs, Paychecks & the Economy.* Other UAW publications are also available online including *Solidarity, AMMO,* and *Washington Report.* The UAW Web page can be accessed at http://www. uaw.org. The UAW will answer E-mail inquiries sent to FAQs@www.uaw.org.

GROUP PUBLICATIONS

Solidarity, the UAW's membership magazine, presents union news, feature stories, guest columns, fiction, and readers' letters. It appears 10 times a year. An annual subscription is $5. Write Solidarity, Circulation Department, 8000 E. Jefferson, Detroit, MI 48214. It can be reached by phone at (313) 926-5373. *AMMO* is the official publication of the International UAW. It contains features on economic, social, political, and labor sub-

jects. *Washington Report* is the UAW's bi-weekly magazine on current legislative and policy news from the nation's capital. For additional information on *AMMO* and *Washington Report* write or call the UAW Publications Department, 8000 E. Jefferson, Detroit, MI 48214, (313) 926-5291.

BIBLIOGRAPHY

Asher, Robert, and Ronald Edsforth, eds. *Autowork.* Albany, N.Y.: State University of New York Press, 1995.

"Can GM and the Unions Take Each Other on Trust?" *The Economist,* 1 August 1998.

Glenn, David. "After Flint." *Nation,* 24 August 1998.

Goode, Bill. *Infighting in the UAW: The 1946 Election and the Ascendancy of Walter Reuther.* Westport, Conn.: Greenwood Press, 1994.

Groehn El-Messidi, Kathy. *The Bargain: The Story Behind the 30-year Honeymoon of GM and the UAW.* New York: Nellen Publishing, 1979.

Lichtenstein, Nelson. *The Most Dangerous Man in Detroit: Walter Reuther and the Fate of American Labor.* New York: Basic Books, 1995.

Meier, August. *Black Detroit and the Rise of the UAW.* New York: Oxford University Press, 1979.

Nauss, Donald W. "GM Plans to Spin Off Delphi Car Parts Unit." *Los Angeles Times,* 4 August 1998.

"Not Over Till It's Over." *The Economist,* 28 February 1998.

O'Dell, John. "GM Workers Begin Returning as Pact Is Ok'd." *Los Angeles Times,* 30 July 1998.

Reuther, Victor G. *The Brothers Reuther and the Story of the UAW: A Memoir.* Boston: Houghton Mifflin, 1976.

Weekley, Thomas L. and Jay C. Wilber. *United We Stand: The Unprecedented Story of the GM-UAW Quality Partnership.* New York: McGraw-Hill, 1996.

"What Price Peace?" *Business Week,* 10 August 1998.

United Farm Workers of America (UFW)

ESTABLISHED: August 22, 1966
EMPLOYEES: Not made available
MEMBERS: 26,000
PAC: None

Contact Information:

ADDRESS: La Paz PO Box 62
    Keene, CA 93531
PHONE: (805) 822-5571
FAX: (805) 822-6123
E-MAIL: UFWofamer@aol.com
URL: http://www.ufw.org
PRESIDENT: Arturo Rodriguez

WHAT IS ITS MISSION?

The largest organization of agricultural workers in the United States, the United Farm Workers of America (UFW) is a labor union devoted to improving the wages and working conditions of its members through collective bargaining and other agreements with employers. According to the organization's Web site, the UFW is fighting for "basic and simple rights" for all agricultural workers, rights which include a living wage, clean bathrooms and drinking water, job security, health insurance, and "a voice to end sexual harassment and other abuses" at the workplace.

HOW IS IT STRUCTURED?

The smallest unit of the UFW is the local chapter, which unites workers from a particular employer or a group of several employers. Local chapters elect a field committee headed by a secretary-general, and the field committees represent the various local chapters at the union's national convention, held every other Labor Day weekend. At the UFW National Convention delegates from the various chapters meet, receive updates on various local activities, and during alternate conventions elect the members of the UFW National Executive Board. The job of the executive board, which comprises a president, secretary-treasurer, and four vice presidents, is to create policy, budget the organization's resources, pass resolutions, and endorse candidates for various internal positions.

To administer the various activities of the union, the UFW is divided into several specialized departments which include the Public Action Department, Organizing Department, Communications Department, and Accounting Department. There are also 14 Public Action offices across the United States, a recruiting office in Los Angeles, and a second national office located in Washington, D.C. The Public Action offices coordinate local activities, boycotts, and publicity campaigns, as well as assist members by collecting union dues, managing retirement accounts, and finding employment for unemployed UFW members.

PRIMARY FUNCTIONS

The function of the UFW, as with all unions, is to improve the working life of its members. To a lesser extent, the UFW also works to improve working conditions for farm workers in general. The UFW's primary tool in this effort is collective bargaining.

The UFW seeks to organize farm workers into the union, so that it can represent them in negotiations with employers. Under labor laws regulating agricultural workers, if more than half of an employer's peak-level workforce signs a petition calling for a union election, by law an election must be held, with the winner obtaining the legal right to represent all the employer's workers for a minimum of one year. Having won the election, the union can assess dues and negotiate binding contracts with employers that cover issues like wages, working conditions, benefits, and grievance procedures.

Since it represents the combined influence of all of a business's employees, the UFW can usually secure higher wages and better working conditions than its members could negotiate on their own. When collective bargaining fails, the UFW may take its workers on strike until their demands are met. They may also institute a boycott. During a boycott, the union asks consumers to avoid buying certain produce or the produce of companies involved in labor disputes with the UFW.

According to the UFW, many growers actively resist efforts at unionizing their workforce through firing, threats, and other methods of intimidation. The UFW seeks to publicize anti-union activities in order to put public pressure on these businesses to allow the UFW to represent their workers. On several occasions, the UFW has organized boycotts of businesses they felt were engaging in unfair labor practices, including a boycott of non-UFW-grown California table grapes that ran from 1984 well into the 1990s. Many of these anti-union activities are prohibited by law, but the union claims such laws are poorly enforced. Accordingly, it also devotes its energies to supporting pro-union legislation and calling for stricter enforcement of the laws that protect employees and their right to unionize.

PROGRAMS

The UFW administers several programs and services for its membership. Since 1966 the union has run the National Farmworkers Service Center in Keene, California, out of which it operates a health center, a specialized housing program, and the Juan de la Cruz pension plan. These services are available for all dues-paying members of the UFW. The center also offers a comprehensive health benefits program for farm workers, the Robert F. Kennedy Medical Plan, the first such plan created in the country.

The union's Keene headquarters houses the Cesar Chávez Foundation, a nonprofit organization composed of the late labor leader's wife and family, as well as the members of the UFW's executive board. The foundation owns the rights to Chávez's name and likeness and attempts to ensure that they are used in ways consistent with UFW politics. The foundation negotiates with publishing companies, schools, and other civic groups who want to license Chávez's name or likeness for textbooks, buildings, streets, or other commemorative activities. They also review textbooks and other publications devoted to Chávez's life. In the future, the foundation plans on building a library filled with works about Chávez and the UFW.

The UFW sponsors several programs to inform the public about its efforts and encourage their support. All products grown by UFW workers are marked with the UFW symbol, a black eagle. On the UFW Web site at http://www.ufw.org, the organization provides "Action Alerts" that contain information on how to help the organization with particularly urgent issues.

BUDGET INFORMATION

The budget of the UFW is approximately $4 million, with approximately one-fifth coming from outside donations given by foundations and individual donors. Because the UFW has historically been supported mostly by donations, increasing the numbers of dues-paying members remains a top priority of the organization.

Although the AFL-CIO does not financially support the UFW, the country's largest trade union has historically contributed personnel and helped generate favorable publicity for UFW organizing campaigns, including the 1997 march through Watsonville, California, to highlight the struggle of strawberry workers.

HISTORY

The origins of the UFW can be traced back to 1951 and the passage of Public Law 78, which legalized an informal "guest worker" arrangement with Mexico. The

BIOGRAPHY:
Cesar Estrada Chávez

Labor Activist (1927–1993) In the Depression era, when Cesar Chávez was a young boy, he watched his family lose everything and join the ranks of migrant farm workers. Chávez attended more than 30 schools, suffered racism from some of his Anglo teachers, and finally dropped out after completing only the eighth grade. From these auspicious beginnings, Cesar Chávez emerged to represent those he knew, bringing dignity and strength into the lives of thousands of farm workers. As a young man living in a barrio with his new wife and family, Chávez signed up with a local parishioner to assist with a self-help social service group, the Community Service Organization (CSO). Within six years, he had worked up the ranks to be appointed general director. With Chávez at the helm, the CSO became the most powerful Mexican-American political organization in California. Nonetheless, Chávez felt that he hadn't truly brought about change for the poverty-stricken farm workers. At age 35, Chávez left his well-paying job to

start the National Farm Workers Association (NFWA). Organizing the unskilled workers proved extremely difficult even for an 'insider,' and Chávez's wife had to become a fruit picker in the fields to feed their children. Ten years later, the group Chávez gave birth to became what is now known as the United Farm Workers Union. He worked tirelessly for La Causa (as the union is called)

until his death in 1993 when more than 30,000 mourners formed a three-mile-long funeral procession to honor him. The year following Chávez's death, President Clinton awarded him the Presidential Medal of Freedom, the nation's highest civilian honor.

arrangement, called the *bracero* system, was initiated during World War II (1939–45) when agricultural growers in California and Texas faced labor shortages and wished to offer short-term labor contracts to Mexicans.

After World War II ended, growers realized that they had become dependent on seasonal Mexican laborers, who would perform the difficult, low-paying labor that most U.S. workers would not do. From 1951 to 1964 Public Law 78 encouraged the importation of thousands of migrant Mexican workers. In 1950 67,500 workers came to the United States; by 1956 that figure had increased to 445,000.

By 1965 there were thousands of Mexican laborers working and living in California alone, many of whom worked on farms as grape harvesters. By all accounts, conditions for these workers, who were non-unionized and who often spoke little English, were not good. Grape pickers in 1965 made an average of $.90 an hour, plus ten cents per basket picked. In many cases, state laws regarding working standards were simply ignored by growers. Many workers were often expected to pay for the water they drank on the job, and no ranches offered portable field toilets. The workers' temporary housing was strictly segregated by race and often lacked indoor plumbing and cooking facilities. In addition, contractors who supplied farms with laborers abused their power, playing favorites with the workers, selecting friends for the best jobs, and sometimes accepting bribes. By the

mid-1960s child labor had become rampant, as the low wages often forced entire migrant families to work in the fields.

It was largely because of these conditions that, in 1965, grape pickers in California's southern Coachella valley walked off the job. Although the bracero program had officially ended the year before, a new U.S.-Mexico agreement allowed growers to import Mexican workers as long they were paid $1.25 an hour. When Coachella growers attempted to pay the local Filipino workers less than the rate for Mexican workers, the Filipinos went on strike. Because grapes in this region of Southern California were ripening and needed to be picked and taken to market quickly, growers relented and paid all the workers $1.25, but they still refused to recognize the workers' attempt to form a union for collective bargaining purposes.

California Workers Unite

As the end of summer approached, grapes were ripening in the fields around Delano, California, and workers at nearly 30 farms, many of whom had already worked in the south and received higher wages, again went on strike for higher wages, better working conditions, and union recognition from their employers. At this point two unions—the National Farm Workers Association, founded by Cesar Chávez in 1962, and the Agriculture Workers Organizing Committee, founded by

BIOGRAPHY:

Dolores Fernandez Huerta

Labor Activist (b. 1930) In a 1976 story published in *The Progressive*, a farmer, asked about the United Farm Workers' (UFW) second-in-command, exclaimed, "Dolores Huerta is crazy. She is a violent woman, where women, especially Mexican women, are usually peaceful and calm." Huerta is not typical in any sense. The mother of 11 children dedicated most of her life towards achieving dignity for one of this country's most demeaned labor groups. Frustrated by her inability to effect change in the lives of her poorest students, Huerta abandoned her teaching career in the late 1950s and joined the Community Service Organization (CSO), a Mexican-American self-help association. In 1962 she shared migrant labor leader Cesar Chávez's concerns that the CSO was not doing enough to help rural-based farm workers and left the CSO to help Chávez establish what would become the United Farm Workers (UFW). Huerta traveled from the East to the West Coasts coordinating nationwide boycotts and

negotiating worker contracts. In the late 1970s she emerged as a strong political figure and dedicated herself to testifying before state and congressional committees on farm laborer issues like pesticide hazards and immigration policy. At a 1988 demonstration against Republican presidential candidate George Bush, Huerta was severely injured by baton-swinging police officers. Six of her ribs were broken, and she was rushed into emergency surgery to remove her damaged spleen. The current UFW president in *Hispanic* magazine said of her, ". . . she shows no sign of slowing down. [Huerta] is an enduring symbol of the farm worker movement."

Dolores Huerta in 1959—joined forces to recruit and represent both the Chicano and the Filipino workers in the area involved in the 1965 strike. Soon after the strike began, Chávez's union called upon the public to boycott grapes without a union label. On March 17, 1966, strikers marched 340 miles from Delano to Sacramento in order to publicize the use of dangerous pesticides and other mistreatment of farm laborers. They faced frustrated, embattled growers determined to break the strike by employing outside laborers and sometimes thugs to intimidate workers and strikers. In August of 1966, the unions merged and joined the AFL-CIO as the United Farm Workers Organizing Committee (UFWOC). The new union received organizing funds from the AFL-CIO, as well as strike support from other unions, including food, cash, and office equipment.

The strikes and organizing efforts continued, with the UFWOC determined to convince all grape laborers, including those employed by growers to replace the strikers, to join the union and support the strike. In 1966 the union secured contracts with two of the largest grape growers in the area, Schenley and DiGiorgio, that included an arrangement for the first benefit plan for workers; an agreement to ban the use of two dangerous pesticides deemed hazardous to workers; and a promise to provide farm workers with clean drinking water, hand washing facilities, and rest periods. This was the first collective bargaining agreement between farm workers and growers in the continental United States.

Despite that success, the UFWOC faced another obstacle to their organizing campaign when a rival union, the International Brotherhood of Teamsters, offered its services to grape growers as a more conservative representative for field workers. With controversy surrounding the question of who had the legal right to represent grape workers in union negotiations with growers, California Governor Pat Brown appointed an outside arbitrator who ordered a decisive election resulting in victory for the UFWOC in 1966. However, many growers chose instead to sign contracts with the Teamsters, who offered terms more favorable to the growers and who the UFWOC accused of intimidating workers into joining their union and breaking UFWOC-sponsored strikes.

In 1968 UFWOC leader Chávez began a 25-day fast to publicize a grape boycott and affirm the union's commitment to nonviolence on the picket lines. By 1970 televised accounts of picket-line violence, a continued boycott, and a host of bad publicity forced many grape growers to accept contracts with the UFWOC. At the end of a prolonged series of strikes and an often violent competition with the Teamsters, the UFWOC effectively organized most of the industry, claiming 50,000 dues-paying members—the most ever represented by a union in California. Contracts with growers included provisions for health clinics and health plans for workers, protective measures for the use of pesticides in the field, and extended state unemployment coverage for workers.

UFW Takes on Lettuce and Strawberry Industries

In the 1970s UFW membership peaked at about 100,000, and the union turned its attention to the lettuce industry, where lettuce growers were ignoring workplace elections for the UFWOC and negotiating contracts, or so-called "sweet heart deals" with other, less demanding unions like the Teamsters. The union called for a boycott of California lettuce even as some growers became more aggressive, threatening and firing workers involved in organizing for the UFWOC. In 1972 the UFWOC became the UFW, and after three more years of labor unrest and renewed boycotts against both the lettuce and grape industries, the UFW and California's governor persuaded the California General Assembly to pass the historic Agriculture Labor Relations Act (ALRA). The legislation created the Agriculture Labor Relations Board (ALRB) to mediate labor disputes and enforce a whole new set of labor laws designed specifically for agricultural workers. Though the 1935 Wagner Act legalized unions and collective bargaining, the law ignored agricultural laborers, many of whom are seasonal and migratory. The ALRA granted workers the right to elect unions by ballot, prohibited growers from firing workers for union activities, established minimum health and sanitation standards, and established the ALRB to investigate charges of labor law violations.

The passage of the ALRA in 1975 represented the zenith of the UFW's power and influence. By the 1980s the union's membership and political clout had declined, a 1984 boycott against grapes had yielded little progress with growers, and much of the organization's original leadership had left. By 1987 the UFW held just three contracts with major growers in California, down from 162 contracts in 1982 and 115 in 1984.

On April 23, 1993, long-time UFW president Chávez died and was replaced by his son-in-law, Arturo Rodriguez. Rodriguez, a long-time member of the union, attempted to renew the union's organizing efforts by departing from the UFW's traditional strategy of organizing workers farm by farm. Instead, the UFW targeted entire industries, and won 18 new contracts alone in 1994. With the help of the AFL-CIO, Rodriguez and the UFW targeted the $650 million-a-year strawberry industry, including growers, shippers, and grocery stores. The campaign against the strawberry growers continued into the 1990s, its success making the UFW one of the AFL-CIO's fastest growing member unions.

CURRENT POLITICAL ISSUES

Throughout its history, the UFW's greatest struggle has been to win the right to represent farm workers. Growers often maintain that their employees do not want or need a union, while the UFW claims instead that these growers are intimidating their workforce and stifling attempts to organize. One example in northern Florida is Quincy Farms, a major mushroom producer. In 1996 the company discharged 84 workers and arrested 24 for trespassing when those workers staged a lunch-hour demonstration requesting safer working conditions and higher wages. By 1998 the company still refused to recognize that the majority of its workers desired a union, even though the UFW claimed that 76 percent of the workforce expressed an interest in doing so. Workers have complained of poor pay, lack of sick leave, expensive health insurance, and high accident rates for pickers, who must climb and balance on boxes stacked five to seven feet high in order to trim and pluck mushrooms. A UFW boycott of Quincy Farm's "Prime" brand of mushrooms was organized to put pressure on the grower.

The UFW has also been involved in a long-running labor dispute with grape growers in Sonoma County, California. The organization has been boycotting all non-union California table grapes since 1984, as a means of advancing its demands of a ban on the use of certain pesticides used in growing grapes, free and fair union elections, and good-faith contract negotiations after the adoption of a union by workers. The UFW claims many growers still illegally threaten workers from joining or supporting the UFW, have delayed signing contracts with the union, or gone out of business and emerged as new corporate entities in order to avoid binding union contracts. Gallo Wine, for instance, avoided signing a union contract with the UFW for several years, although workers elected the UFW as their representative in 1994.

Case Study: Organizing the Strawberry Industry

In the late 1990s the top issue for the UFW became unionizing approximately 55,000 workers who harvest strawberries for the $584 million strawberry industry. Efforts were focused on Watsonville, California's Coastal Berry Co., the nation's largest employer of strawberry pickers. Many growers and an outspoken group of workers claim that the majority of strawberry workers in California do not want to belong to, or be represented by the UFW. Opponents of the UFW point out that though strawberry workers earned an average of $6.70 an hour in 1996, the rate at larger farms like Coastal Berry varies from $7.50 to $11.00 an hour. The workers there receive health benefits but no pension. According to industry representatives, this means that Coastal Berry's workers are among the highest-paid field workers in the nation, and see little benefit in unionization.

A UFW-led coalition of labor, civil rights, religious, and environmental groups claims that workers are being intimidated into rejecting the UFW and that despite wage increases, the workers still work 10 to 12 hour days, are often forced to use dirty drinking water and bathrooms, are still exposed to toxic pesticides, have little health insurance, and are often fired for involvement with the UFW.

The UFW has made their strawberry organizing a national issue, and has enlisted the help of labor leaders and other activists. With their "Five Cents for Fairness Campaign," the union attempts to enlist the public's support, explaining that a mere five-cent increase in the price of a pint of strawberries could result in a 50 percent increase in workers' pay. In support of this campaign, groups like the National Association for the Advancement of Colored People (NAACP), the National Organization for Women (NOW), and the Sierra Club helped form the National Strawberry Commission for Worker's Rights, an organization devoted to sending activists and volunteers to supermarkets in order to distribute pledges to consumers and ask managers to support the right of strawberry workers to hold free elections and bargain for union contracts. In 1997 over 3,000 supermarkets across the country had signed pledges supporting the workers. To create more publicity for the campaign, on June 17, 1998, activist Gloria Steinem and the UFW organized a march in New York City protesting working conditions in California's strawberry fields.

In Watsonville itself, the UFW worked to unite Coastal Berry's workforce behind them, and called for union elections. At times violence broke out between pro- and anti-UFW groups. One group of anti-UFW workers formed their own organization, called the Coastal Berry Farm Workers Committee. This group called for union elections at Coastal Berry, presenting itself as a second union, an alternative to the UFW.

From the start, the UFW claimed that the Coastal Berry Farm Workers Committee was a sham. The Committee, claimed the UFW, was developed and financially supported by the growers themselves, in violation of California law, in an attempt to take control of the unionization process. This, as well as the violence and intimidation that the UFW claimed was occurring at Coastal Berry in order to discourage employees from supporting the UFW, led the union to stay out of the July 24, 1998, election. The final tally was 523 votes in favor of representation by the Coastal Berry Farm Workers Committee, and 410 votes for no representation at all.

The UFW immediately challenged the election as illegal due to the intimidation of workers, and claimed that the Coastal Berry Farm Workers Committee and the growers had conspired to mislead the public about the nature of the committee. Meanwhile, it was discovered that 152 Coastal Berry employees had been left off the voting roll and had therefore not had a chance to vote in the election. For this reason, California's ALRB threw out the election on November 5, 1998. The Coastal Berry Farm Workers Committee appealed this decision, but doubts about that group's legitimacy continued, with the UFW producing bank records that seemed to indicate that growers were funding the Committee.

FUTURE DIRECTIONS

The UFW's future looks much the same as its present. As the strawberry industry demonstrates, the UFW's greatest struggle is to organize farm workers behind them. The union will continue to use its industry-wide organizing approach, which, while so far proving unsuccessful in the strawberry industry, has helped the organization to unionize 14 new farms and gain 6,000 new members since 1994. The UFW also hopes to develop a better relationship with California ALRB, which the UFW claims developed a pro-growers stance in the 1980s and early 1990s.

GROUP RESOURCES

Although the UFW does not offer a national publication, its various public action offices in cities around the country periodically publish newsletters and pamphlets covering the union's activities and boycotts. In addition to these publications, the National Farmworkers Service Center in Keene, California, operates several Spanish radio stations called *Radio Campesina,* one broadcasting out of Bakersfield, California, and the other operating in Phoenix, Arizona. The stations offer Spanish-speaking listeners programming and music, community service messages, and historical information about the UFW and its struggles.

On their Web site at http://www.ufw.org the union offers a list of basic grocery-store items and the brand names endorsed by the union. The lists provide the names of companies who have contracts with the UFW and who are not currently engaged in labor disputes with the union. The Web site also has information on the UFW's local branch offices.

GROUP PUBLICATIONS

The UFW puts out many publications in support of its activities. Some of them, such as *Five Cents for Fairness: The Case for Change in the Strawberry Fields,* are available free of charge on the UFW Web site, http://www.ufw.org. Others, such as the *Cesar Chávez Curriculum,* a comprehensive teaching guide and lesson plan on the life of Chávez that includes a video and worksheets, can be ordered on the Web site; by mail at UFW, P.O. Box 62, Keene, CA, 93531; or by phone at (805) 822-5571.

BIBLIOGRAPHY

Bacon, David. "Face Off in Watsonville, Strawberry Workers Pick Sides." *Progressive,* August 1997.

Barger, Walter K. *The Farm Labor Movement in the Midwest; Social Change and Adaptation among Migrant Farmworkers.* Austin: Univ. of Texas Press, 1994.

De Ruiz, Dana Catherine, and Richard Larios. *La Causa: The Migrant Farmworker Story.* Austin: Raintree Steck-Vaugh, 1993.

Ferriss, Susan, and Ricardo Sandoval. *The Fight in the Fields.* New York: Harcourt, 1997.

Henshaw, Jake. "Lawmakers, UFW Fighting Union Election." *San Jose Mercury News*, 22 July 1998.

Hornblower, Margot. "Picking a New Fight." *Time* 25 November 1996.

Meisters, Dick. *A Long Time Coming: The Struggle to Unionize America's Farm Workers.* New York: Macmillan, 1977.

Taylor, Ronald. *Chávez and the Farm Workers.* Boston: Beacon Press, 1975.

Wells, Miriam, J. *Strawberry Fields: Politics, Class, and Work in California Agriculture.* Ithaca: Cornell Univ. Press, 1996.

Zachery, G. Pascal. "United Farm Workers Discover New Life." *Wall Street Journal*, 19 December 1995.

United Food and Commercial Workers International Union (UFCW)

WHAT IS ITS MISSION?

According to the Web site of the United Food and Commercial Workers (UFCW), the organization's mission is to "improve wages, benefits, and working conditions; have a true, independent voice in the workplace;" and have workers "be treated with dignity, justice, and respect on the job." It also works to impact legislation favorable to its members, who work in many different sectors of the retail and manufacturing economy in the United States and Canada.

HOW IS IT STRUCTURED?

The UFCW is led by an international president, an international secretary-treasurer, and an international executive board, all of whom serve five-year terms and are elected at an international convention held every five years. In addition there are nine regional offices located throughout North America that are headed by regional directors. Over 1,000 local unions are organized by these regional offices in both the United States and Canada. Local unions are responsible for sending delegates to the UFCW international convention and elect the organization's officers.

The 1.4 million members of the UFCW are employed in many different trades and professions in the United States and Canada. About 900,000 members are employed in the retail and grocery industries. Another 250,000 members work in the meatpacking and food processing industries. The remaining 250,000 work as barbers and beauticians, chemical workers, garment work-

ESTABLISHED: 1979
EMPLOYEES: Not made available
MEMBERS: 1,400,000 (1997)
PAC: Active Ballot Club

Contact Information:
ADDRESS: 1775 K St. NW
 Washington, DC 20006
PHONE: (202) 223-3111
URL: http://www.ufcw.org
INTERNATIONAL PRESIDENT: Douglas H. Dority
INTERNATIONAL SECRETARY-TREASURER: Joseph T. Hansen

FAST FACTS

During a voluntary wage freeze announced by the UFCW to save jobs in meatpacking plants, the average hourly wage in U.S. meatpacking plants declined from $9.19 in January 1982 to $7.93 in January 1985.

(Source: Kim Moody. *An Injury to All: The Decline of American Unionism.* London: Verso, 1988.)

ers, textile workers, health care workers, insurance workers, bank employees, and workers in several other retail and commercial fields.

The UFCW has affiliate relations with other organized unions. Besides being a member of the American Federation of Labor-Congress of Industrial Organizations (AFL-CIO), the UFCW also works with several international unions in an attempt to address the global concerns of the workers that it represents. These include the International Federation of Commercial, Clerical, Professional, and Technical Employees; the International Union of Food, Agricultural, Hotel, Restaurant, Catering, Tobacco, and Allied Workers' Associations; the International Textile, Garment, and Leather Workers Federation; and the International Chemical, Energy, and Mining Federation.

PRIMARY FUNCTIONS

The UFCW's work is concentrated in three areas. The first provides services to current members, which includes supporting collective bargaining and enforcing contracts, working on health and safety issues, and resolving complaints. The second is to attract new members and build the strength of the union. The UFCW aggressively supports organizing drives that add new companies and new members. A third area is its efforts to influence public policy in favor of labor and unions. This includes lobbying the government to pass or fail certain types of legislation and promoting and supporting labor issues and labor-friendly candidates. The UFCW often acts in conjunction with other AFL-CIO union members. In the 1990s, some of the major issues concerning the UFCW were free trade with China, fast-track treaty authorization, and cutbacks in health benefits, all of which the UFCW opposed.

To combat the tendency of companies to compete based on who can pay the lowest wages, the UFCW concentrated on "market share" organizing programs. The goal of this campaign is to organize every non-union company and store in a particular market area. The union's aggressive organizing in the 1990s contrasted sharply with that of the 1980s, which was characterized by a shrinking membership, concessions, and a focus on job protection and cooperation with existing employers—referred to as "caretaking" uninonism.

PROGRAMS

Most of the UFCW's programs are primarily for the benefit of its membership or the union as a whole. For example, the UFCW maintains a scholarship program which awards seven $4,000 college scholarships to members or their children each year. However, the UFCW does maintain a Worker Advocacy Project which helps non-union workers establish safe and fair working conditions. The UFCW attempts to inform non-union workers about their rights in such areas as safety standards and work hours, claiming employers frequently and illegally take advantage of non-union workers. If employer abuses are found, the UFCW will assist non-union workers in obtaining help from the government. Through efforts like those associated with the Worker Advocacy Project, the UFCW demonstrates to non-union workers the value of unionization and strengthens its position.

BUDGET INFORMATION

Not made available.

HISTORY

The United Food and Commercial Workers is an amalgamated union that has grown steadily through mergers of smaller unions. The union was formed in 1979 when two large unions, the Retail Clerks Union and the Amalgamated Meat Cutters Union, merged. Prior to 1979, each of these unions already had absorbed many smaller unions. For example, the Meat Cutters had absorbed the United Packinghouse Workers in 1968, and the Barbers and Beauticians Union and the Insurance Workers had merged into the Retail Clerks Union. The newly formed UFCW became the second-largest union in North America; only the United Auto Workers (UAW) had more members.

Shortly after its creation the new union faced severe challenges, such as changes in the meatpacking industry that resulted in plant closings and downsizing. In the late

1960s and 1970s the top meatpacking companies, which up until then had maintained "pattern" or industry-wide labor agreements with their unions, were bought out by conglomerates. These huge corporate buyers often closed or sold plants and reopened others as non-union shops. The system of contract bargaining that had been established in the 1940s and 1950s broke down. In response, the UFCW began to make concessions to employers on issues like wages as an incentive to keep jeopardized plants open.

In the 1980s the UFCW also frequently consented to two-tier wage agreements, in which newly hired workers contracted for lower pay rates than workers with seniority. Between 1983 and 1985 the UFCW signed 87 two-tier agreements—more than any other union. The UFCW leadership's conciliatory approach toward employers generated friction with some rank-and-file members. The division between the union's leadership and members erupted into open warfare in the Hormel strike of the mid-1980s.

The Hormel Strike

The most publicized UFCW strike in history was one in which the union's top leadership opposed the militancy of one of its locals, P-9 in Austin, Minnesota. That local, led by its president Jim Guyette, opposed the UFCW's concession-based policies and went to war with the George A. Hormel Company, one of the nation's leading meat products manufacturers. Hormel had opened a "flagship" plant in Austin in August 1982. Guyette called for a united front in bargaining across the entire Hormel chain. But the international UFCW leadership, wanting to keep Hormel and other unionized meat companies competitive with non-union companies, were poised to agree to wage reductions, hoping to keep plants open. When the UFCW negotiated a contract with Hormel's Ottumwa, Minnesota, plant, Guyette wrote letters of protest to UFCW President William Wynn. The Ottumwa agreement included a nearly $2 drop in hourly wages. In September 1984, Local P-9 voted not to accept a wage cut proposed by the international and accepted by the other Hormel locals. Guyette said: "If concessions are going to stop, then they are going to have to stop at the most profitable company with the newest plant." The P-9 local produced T-shirts with the slogan: "If not here, where? If not now, when? If not us, who?"

When Hormel imposed the wage cut in violation of the local contract, P-9 prepared for a strike. An Austin United Support Group formed, organized mainly by Hormel workers' wives. Guyette and P-9 hired Corporate Campaign, Inc., to conduct a high-visibility anti-corporate campaign. But the UFCW leadership opposed the corporate campaign at Hormel and divorced itself from the strike. Undeterred, P-9 built up a nationwide support organization with chapters in every major city. The P-9 strike had sparked a nationwide rank-and-file campaign against concessions.

In January 1986 the UFCW's international leadership denounced the strike, just days after the Minnesota National Guard was brought in to force picketers to allow replacement workers into the Austin plant. The successful introduction of the replacement workers into the plant shifted the balance of power against the strikers. Local P-9 announced a boycott and organized pickets at other Hormel plants over the objections of union leadership. About 550 workers at other plants were fired for joining the picket lines. In June the international union put Local P-9 into trusteeship and seized its records and funds. Strikers were banned from P-9 meetings, and the replacement workers and union members who had crossed the picket line took over the local. Some of the strikers tried to reorganize under a new union, the North American Meatpackers Union.

New Strategies

The embarrassing rift between UFCW leadership and rank-and-file members during the Hormel strike was pivotal for the union. Eventually the UFCW leadership admitted that concessions did not prevent plant closings. Under the leadership of President Douglas Dority (elected in 1994), the UFCW realigned itself by adopting an aggressive, union-building strategy based on grassroots organizing and sophisticated public relations efforts. The era of concessions and cooperation between the UFCW and employers was over.

In the 1990s, the UFCW experienced rapid growth through a succession of mergers. In 1993 it absorbed the Retail, Wholesale and Department Store Union, with its approximately 100,000 members. In 1995 about 10,000 members were added with its merger with the United Garment Workers and another 10,000 members joined as the United Textile Workers became part of the UFCW. Also that year the 16,000 members of the Distillery, Wine and Allied Workers were folded into the UFCW. In 1996 the International Chemical Workers joined, adding another 40,000 members to the UFCW.

CURRENT POLITICAL ISSUES

The UFCW's primary goal of gaining the best possible wages and working conditions for its members often brings it into conflict with employers and government. There is often much more at stake when the UFCW takes a stand on an issue than UFCW jobs and benefits. For example, when the UFCW successfully lobbied against fast-track trade authority for President Clinton in 1997, it was because the union was afraid that granting the authority would lead to loss of U.S. jobs, hurting not only their own membership, but the U.S. workforce as a whole. Similarly, the UFCW's nursing home organizing efforts in 1996 and 1997 were about more than just new members for the union.

Case Study: Care for the Caregivers

The UFCW represents more than 75,000 health care workers. Many of them work in nursing homes, an industry marked by low wages, lack of benefits, rapid growth, chronic understaffing, high turnover, and a resistance to unions. In 1996 the UFCW launched a "Care for the Caregivers" campaign. Focused on nursing homes in the South, the campaign sought to connect the working conditions of nursing home employees, primarily certified nursing assistants, with the quality of care for nursing home residents. As staffing levels are cut and workloads grow, the union contends, incidents of bed sores, reports of incontinence, and the use of patient restraints skyrocket. The UFCW organized a "coalition of care" among workers, recipients, and community and religious organizations. It publicized government inspection reports at non-union nursing homes that tied poor care to low staffing levels. Focusing on Beverly Enterprises, the nation's largest nursing home operator, the UFCW made care-related issues the center of a negotiation strategy at several Beverly homes in Alabama.

Rallying community support, the UFCW also launched a "Caregivers Care-a-Van," as part of the AFL-CIO's 1996 Union Summer project, with 32 young activists joining nursing home workers in an organizing bus tour across the South. Modeled after the Freedom Rides of the 1960s Civil Rights movement, the tour began at the site of Martin Luther King, Jr.'s, assassination in Memphis, Tennessee, and retraced the landmarks of that struggle targeting the predominantly black nursing home workforce with its publicity.

In a little over a year, the UFCW's Care for the Caregivers campaign resulted in union contracts at more than a dozen nursing homes in the South. UFCW negotiations in Alabama led to new contracts for ten UFCW nursing homes in Alabama. The unprecedented contract included a $2 an hour pay raise, employer-paid health benefits, and gave the caregivers an official voice in decision-making on patient care issues.

SUCCESSES AND FAILURES

The UFCW is frequently successful in its contract negotiations with grocery chains in the United States and Canada. A contract settlement reached in August 1997 between the UFCW and the Lucky and Safeway grocery stores in northern California provides an example of the UFCW's bargaining clout. In the four-year agreement, the company pledged no takeaways on benefits or salaries, the biggest pay increases in any UFCW local nationwide, a labor-management committee, and, most significantly, the right of the UFCW to organize new or non-union supermarkets in northern California without company interference. The unionized grocery workers

also continued to receive health benefits paid for entirely by their employers. Other major retailers in the area also adopted the terms of the contract in "me too" agreements that eventually covered more than 55,000 supermarket employees.

FUTURE DIRECTIONS

The UFCW in the late 1990s took a more militant posture. Its leaders endorsed a multi-faceted approach to union-building, which included aggressive publicity efforts to expose worker and consumer health and safety issues and increasingly relied on publicity campaigns rather than unwieldy labor elections to pressure companies into accepting unions. These efforts are likely to continue, as the UFCW works to reverse its long decline in membership.

GROUP RESOURCES

The UFCW maintains a Web site at http://www.ufcw.org that contains articles, press releases, news bulletins and an archive of union-related information. Further information about the UFCW can be obtained by writing to the United Food and Commercial Workers, 1775 K St. NW, Washington, DC 20006 or by calling (202) 223-3111.

GROUP PUBLICATIONS

The UFCW produces the member publication, *UFCW Action,* six times a year. It contains the latest information on UFCW programs and activities and articles of interest to union members, including a column by the international president. It is available via the World Wide Web at http://www.ufcw.org/readaction.html. Information on subscriptions can also be obtained by writing to the United Food and Commercial Workers, 1775 K St. NW, Washington, DC 20006 or by calling (202) 223-3111.

BIBLIOGRAPHY

Buri, Sherri, "Union Drive Starts at Sony's Springfield, Oregon, Factory." *Knight-Ridder/Tribune Business News,* 5 May 1997.

Gatusso, Greg. "UFCW: Stew Leonard's Blocking Union." *Supermarket News,* 18 August 1997.

Green, Hardy. *On Strike at Hormel: The Struggle for a Democratic Labor Movement.* Philadelphia: Temple University Press, 1990.

Kinsella, Bridget, and John Moody. "Union Wins, Loses at Borders; Second NYC Store to Open." *Publishers Weekly,* 10 March 1997.

"Labor's New Organizing Tactic." *New York Times,* 26 March 1997.

Lemus, Carlos. "Unions Feel Merger Will Add Strength, Competitiveness." *Knight-Ridder/Tribune Business News,* 8 October 1995.

Moody, Kim. *An Injury to All: The Decline of American Unionism.* London: Verso, 1988.

Ramey, Joanna. "UFCW Asks Top Retailers Not to Buy from China Army." *WWD,,* 24 June 1997.

Zurales, Pete. "Union Tries to Unionize Alabama's Nursing Homes." *Knight-Ridder/Tribune Business News,* 20 June 1996.

Zwiebach, Elliott. "Food Lion Blames Union for Southwest Exit." *Supermarket News,* 29 September 1997.

United Mine Workers of America (UMWA)

ESTABLISHED: January 25, 1890
EMPLOYEES: 50
MEMBERS: 75,000
PAC: Coal Miners' Political Action Committee
(COMPAC)

Contact Information:

ADDRESS: 900 15th St. NW
Washington, DC 20005
PHONE: (202) 842-7200
FAX: (202) 842-7227
URL: http://www.umwa.org
PRESIDENT: Cecil E. Roberts

WHAT IS ITS MISSION?

The United Mine Workers of America (UMWA) was founded to improve the working conditions and pay for workers in the dangerous coal mining industry. The delegates to the organization's first convention called for miners to receive a reasonable share of the profits that was "fully compatible with the dangers of [their] calling." The union has pursued these goals through legislation and collective bargaining with employers.

HOW IS IT STRUCTURED?

The UMWA is governed by a president, vice president, and secretary treasurer elected directly by the membership every five years. These officers serve on the executive board with ten other members who are elected by region. The international union holds a convention of delegates from local unions every five years which sets policy priorities to be implemented by the executive board in between conventions. The union is divided into five districts which are primarily responsible for coordinating new organization among the local unions within their area. The international office offers assistance to the districts and locals and coordinates collective bargaining. The Washington, D.C. headquarters is divided into a number of departments including research, legislative, legal, organizing, communications, and health and safety. The Coal Miners' Political Action Committee (COMPAC) which handles the union's political operations is also located in this office.

The UMWA represents coal miners and a small number of other workers in areas ranging from health care to gun manufacturing in the United States and Canada. Anyone in these occupations is invited to join the union. It is affiliated with the American Federation of Labor and Congress of Industrial Organizations (AFL-CIO), the Canadian Labour Congress (CLC), the International Chemical, Energy, Mine and General Workers' Federation (ICEM), and the International Confederation of Free Trade Unions (ICFTU).

PRIMARY FUNCTIONS

The UMWA works to improve the wages, benefits, working conditions, and job security of its members primarily through collective bargaining with employers. The headquarters staff conduct economic, labor market, and legal research to assist the union in negotiations. Overall, the UMWA has worked to establish national wage and benefit patterns that minimize regional differences. In meeting this goal, the union maintains an ongoing contract for its members with the Bituminous Coal Operators Association (BCOA) which consists of numerous coal mine operators. When disputes with operators cannot be resolved the union organizes strikes and works to shape public opinion to put pressure on the coal companies. The union also monitors health and safety conditions and works to ensure the resolution of members' workplace grievances.

Because of technological innovation, an increase in worker productivity, and a move to cleaner forms of power generation, unemployment among coal miners is high. In a joint agreement, the UMWA and BCOA formed a training and education fund in 1988 to provide unemployed miners and their children with financial aid and other assistance so that they could be trained and find employment in other fields.

In the political sphere the UMWA mobilizes its members to vote in elections and encourages them to lobby on legislation. COMPAC, the UMWA's political action committee, raises and distributes campaign money for candidates endorsed by the union, who are generally Democrats. The union also conducts drives to register voters and get them to the polls. Most UMWA contracts specify that the leadership can call a certain number of memorial holidays, generally enacted following mining accidents. In 1996 the UMWA president declared election day a holiday giving miners more time to vote. The miners were also encouraged to spend the balance of their day driving others to the polls or making phone calls to remind friends to vote. The union also coordinates grassroots political activities, such as petition drives and protests. The international office monitors legislation, researches its potential effects on members, and alerts them when they need to take action on targeted legislation. Its leaders testify before Congress on bills of par-

ticular interest to the union and represent labor on numerous commissions such as President Clinton's Bipartisan Commission on Entitlement and Tax Reform.

PROGRAMS

Because the size of the membership determines the UMWA's clout in politics and at the bargaining table, the 1995 convention made organizing its top priority. It adopted an organizing program called Growth On All Levels, which set as its goal 15,000 person-days (the labor of one person for an average working-day) of rank-and-file member organizing every year. To finance the program, the international union contributed a million dollars annually over the regular organizing budget into a special fund which was distributed in the form of matching funds to local unions, to reimburse the lost wages of their members who participate in organizing drives. Also, as part of the Growth on All Levels program, the union provides training seminars in organizing techniques to rank-and-file members.

In the workplace, ensuring the health and safety of mine workers has always been a top priority for the UMWA. Under the direction of the vice president, the union's Department of Occupational Health and Safety works to ensure that mining operations comply with the Federal Mine Safety and Health Act and state regulations. The department oversees representatives who operate in each district. The representatives provide assistance to health and safety committees composed of full time employees elected by local union members to represent them at the mine level. Together these entities handle health and safety grievances filed by members, conduct safety inspections, investigate accidents, help prepare legal cases, and work with the various regulatory agencies.

The union also offers its members a benefits program. It includes access to such things as affordable life insurance, loans, legal services, and travel clubs.

BUDGET INFORMATION

Not made available.

HISTORY

The UMWA, once the backbone of the large scale industrial labor movement in the United States, has a long history. Efforts to unionize coal miners, who worked long hours in dangerous, unhealthy mines for low wages, began in the first half of the nineteenth century but failed in the face of factionalism, economic fluctuations, employer opposition, and anti-union violence.

BIOGRAPHY:

Mary Harris "Mother" Jones

Labor Leader (1830–1930) Mary Harris Jones, commonly known as "Mother" Jones, spent more than half her life fighting to improve conditions for workers in all fields of labor. With her working-class manner of speaking, unflagging spirit, and quarrelsome temperament, Jones was a hero to laborers, a legendary public figure for all Americans, and an antagonist to union leaders. As a paid organizer for the United Mine Workers' Union, Jones was known for her fiery speeches that rallied desperate miners. In 1893 Jones helped establish the first United Mine Workers' newspaper, *An Appeal to Reason.* Living a life that was no more luxurious than the workers she helped, Mother Jones traveled the country from one labor hotbed to another, was jailed on several occasions, and endured direct threats from company and government forces. Along the way, Jones was horrified to find young boys in the mines and young girls in textile mills working long hours

in conditions so poor that many suffered permanent injury or death. In 1903 she led a parade of 400 children from Philadelphia to New York in a bid to meet with President Theodore Roosevelt. Although Roosevelt declined to meet with the marchers, publicity generated by their efforts

compelled the Pennsylvania legislature to pass child labor restriction laws the following year. Active until the end of her life, Jones used a nationwide radio address on her 100th birthday to repeat her cry against the exploitation of labor and to urge workers to realize and use their collective power.

Two unions merged in 1890 to form the enduring United Mine Workers of America (UMWA), which was chartered by the American Federation of Labor (AFL). The union's fortunes fluctuated with the economy in the first few decades of its existence, but overall membership continued to grow reaching a quarter of a million members under the leadership of John Mitchell at the end of the century. The union called several strikes demanding higher wages, an eight-hour-work day, and official recognition by employers. One long strike that led to coal shortages in eastern cities was successfully settled after President Theodore Roosevelt intervened in 1902.

But early successes were confined to a few states—Pennsylvania, Ohio, Indiana, and Illinois. Efforts to move into areas such as Colorado and West Virginia were met with violent repression by company and local police in such incidents as the Ludlow, Colorado and Matewan, West Virginia massacres in which peacefully protesting miners or their family members were killed. Mary Harris Jones who coined the battle theme of the American labor movement—"pray for the dead, but fight like hell for the living"—earned her place in history as "Mother Jones" by offering support and advice to striking miners during this period.

The UMWA's membership increased to over 500,000 during World War I (1914–18), which brought both greater demands for coal and the need for government intervention to assure that the coal supply would remain uninterrupted. Decisions announced by President Woodrow Wilson and federal agencies that regulated

prices and wages during the war increased wages for miners significantly. A slump in demand for coal in the wake of the war coincided with the election of one of the most famous figures in labor history, John L. Lewis, as UMWA president. Lewis's refusal to make concessions to the coal companies led to a drive that almost succeeded in destroying the union. In his efforts to establish complete control over the union, Lewis destroyed all rivals and centralized authority in his office. Membership fell to under 100,000.

The UMWA's fortunes were reversed in the midst of the Great Depression by President Franklin D. Roosevelt's National Industrial Recovery Act of 1933, which granted workers the legal right to form unions and bargain collectively with employers. Lewis launched a massive campaign to unionize miners, exaggerating the truth with a flier that stated "The President wants you to join the union." Within a year over 90 percent of the coal industry was organized.

The National Industrial Recovery Act would eventually be found unconstitutional by the Supreme Court, but the Wagner Act, which passed in 1935, was upheld, and committed the government to protecting the workers' right to unionize. Lewis and others in the AFL saw this as an opportunity to organize the mass production industries, which had barely been touched by the traditional craft based unions. Faced with a conservative AFL leadership, Lewis and his allies broke away to form a rival federation, the Congress of Industrial Organizations (CIO). Lewis and the UMWA oversaw and financed the unionization of the steel industry, and within the CIO encouraged unionization in such areas as auto production against stiff, and often bloody, employer resistance.

Lewis, who had encouraged the labor movement to become more active in politics and to support Roosevelt's reelection bid in 1936, parted ways with Roosevelt over U.S. involvement in World War II (1939–45). The rest of the CIO supported Roosevelt and thus Lewis decided to withdraw the UMWA from the federation in 1940. Although most unions observed a "no-strike" pledge during the war to maintain production levels, Lewis earned public scorn by calling strikes in the coal mines. Lewis launched bitter strikes that resulted in the creation of the UMWA Welfare and Retirement Fund financed through royalties on coal production. This fund was used in part to build hospitals and clinics for the miners in the under-served region of Appalachia. Coal mine operators soon joined to form the Bituminous Coal Operators Association (BCOA) which entered into nationwide bargaining with the UMWA in 1950. Although this represented a major success for the UMWA, technological innovations in mining reduced the workforce, and thus UMWA membership declined by more than a half over the next decade to 180,000.

When Lewis resigned the UMWA's presidency in 1960 he left behind an undemocratic and centralized union structure prone to abuse. Tony Boyle, a corrupt leader who used violence to maintain his control over the union, came to office in 1962. He was challenged in the 1969 election by the Miners for Democracy movement. After a fraudulent election, Boyle is alleged to have had his opponent, Joseph Yablonski, and his family murdered. The U.S. Labor Department, under pressure from Congress, pursued a federal lawsuit that invalidated the 1969 election. In a new election held in 1972 with significant government monitoring, Arnold Miller, a member of the Miners for Democracy, established himself as UMWA president. The constitution was rewritten and the UMWA became a model of union democracy. In the midst of this confusion, UMWA members successfully lobbied for the landmark Federal Coal Mine Health and Safety Act, which regulates mining practices and provides compensation to miners with black lung disease. Another act passed in 1977 created a federal agency, the Mine Safety and Health Administration (MSHA), to oversee enforcement of regulations.

In 1982 a vigorous, young leader, Richard Trumka, was elected to head the UMWA. Under his leadership the UMWA reaffiliated with the AFL-CIO in 1989. He led several successful strikes including one against the Pittston Coal Group in Virginia in 1989. Members of labor and progressive movements, who hoped the strike would become a model for a reinvigorated union movement, rallied behind the miners. During the strike, the union used methods of civil disobedience such as blocking roads, impeding the movement of coal trucks, and occupying a coal plant. Strikers were supported by a range of visiting luminaries from Jesse Jackson of the Rainbow Coalition to a representative of Solidarity, the Polish labor move-

ment which fought for democracy and workers' rights in Poland. Trumka used the strike to bring national attention to the failure of federal labor law and the abuses of state courts. Ultimately Labor Secretary Elizabeth Dole, under pressure from President George Bush, appointed a mediator to bring labor and management to the table. Trumka was elected Secretary-Treasurer of the AFL-CIO in 1995 as part of a slate of reform candidates. UMWA vice president Cecil Roberts replaced him as president on December 22, 1995.

Between 1997 and 1998 the UMWA defeated Republican efforts in the 105th Congress to reform the regulation of mine safety, which included a proposal to abolish the Mine Safety and Health Administration, shift some of its functions to a restructured—and according to the union, a weakened—Occupational Health and Safety Administration, reduce the required number of mine safety inspections, and eliminate fines on operators for most violations of safety codes. Coal miners traveled to Washington, D.C., to attend hearings on the legislation where Trumka spoke against the bill. The union also staged protests in Congress members' districts and circulated petitions. The union did, however, reluctantly agree to the elimination of the Bureau of Mines, whose responsibilities had dwindled since its formation in 1910.

CURRENT POLITICAL ISSUES

The UMWA over its history has supported worker health and safety regulations, civil rights, and the expansion of the welfare state through federal support for such programs as social security, Medicare, and Medicaid. It has also taken a role in international affairs, fighting apartheid in South Africa and encouraging the formation of democratic unions in the former Soviet Union and developing nations.

The UMWA is often on the opposite side of the coal companies in politics but in the case of most environmental issues they unite. Because coal use produces a great deal of pollution many environmental bills aim to reduce coal consumption, hurting the industry and those who work in it. The UMWA and coal operators unsuccessfully fought a proposal made during the Bush administration to control acid rain but they have fended off efforts by the Clinton administration to raise air quality standards, which would put greater restrictions on coal mining operations. The question of U.S. participation in a global climate treaty has also pitted the UMWA against the Clinton administration, which in other policy areas, such as labor, is considered a strong ally. In 1997 the UMWA and the BCOA completed labor contract negotiations eight months in advance so they could concentrate on an attempt to defeat a treaty concerning global climate change.

FAST FACTS

To meet the terms of the global climate treaty reached in Kyoto, Japan, in December of 1997 it is projected that U.S. consumers would need to reduce their consumption of coal, natural gas, heating oil, and gasoline by one-third.

(Source: *Indianapolis Star.* December 27, 1997.)

Case Study: Global Climate Change Treaty

Delegates from the world's nations attended a meeting in December of 1997 in Kyoto, Japan to negotiate a treaty that would reduce the pollution believed to be causing global warming. A major debate was whether developing nations, those countries who are not yet fully industrialized, would be forced to reduce their emissions to levels comparable with those of the industrialized world, and possibly derail their economic growth. The UMWA and other interested parties lobbied the Clinton administration to refuse to sign any treaty evolving from the conference that did not require the participation of developing nations, arguing that to do otherwise would result in industry and jobs moving to third world countries where there are few controls on pollution. However, the treaty ultimately set binding emissions targets for only 38 industrialized countries, and called for the United States to cut its emissions of carbon dioxide, produced by burning coal, gasoline, and other fuels, to seven percent below 1990 levels by 2012. The UMWA hastened to throw its weight against the treaty.

The UMWA was joined in its criticism of the plan by the National Association of Manufacturers (NAM), the United States Chamber of Commerce (USCC), and the Business Roundtable, as well as the Global Climate Coalition, formed by oil, auto, chemical, and electric utility companies. These interests argued that reaching the emissions targets would have a devastating effect on the U.S. economy and lead to major increases in energy costs. UMWA president Cecil Roberts stated that the treaty will "throw a record-shattering number of American families out of work." Proponents of the treaty, which included environmental groups and companies that research and market technology that reduces pollution, argued that compliance with the treaty will spur innovation and economic growth. Economists gave widely varying estimates of the costs of pollution reduction and the potential impact on the economy.

The UMWA lobbied the Senate not to ratify the treaty. However, opponents feared that the Clinton administration, unlikely to get Senate support, would encourage and assist the states to voluntarily comply with plans to reduce emissions even without a formal treaty. The UMWA responded by fighting the treaty at the state level as well. The union has taken the lead in a industry-wide effort to persuade lawmakers in coal states to pass legislation preventing their states from taking action related to global warming before the Senate has acted on the proposed treaty. Legislation has been introduced in states such as Illinois, Ohio, Kentucky, West Virginia, Virginia, and Alabama where the UMWA has full time lobbyists. The UMWA has also organized rallies in coal states to publicize its criticism of the treaty's terms.

President Clinton did not submit the treaty to the Senate, perhaps anticipating defeat due to the legislative efforts of groups like the UMWA. However, bills sponsored by pro-union legislators that would have prevented federal funds from going to pay for participation in the treaty failed in both the House and the Senate. While the United States has not agreed to reforming its industrial practices, the issue of global warming and its potential consequences on the economy and the environment—good or bad—goes largely unaddressed.

FUTURE DIRECTIONS

Even if every coal miner in the United States and Canada was a member of the UMWA, the union's active membership would still be smaller than some of the other industrial unions. The UMWA hopes to expand its organizing activities into other jobs and industries in an effort to strengthen its political voice. After recruiting laborers interested in joining, the union will initiate grass-roots campaigning within the industries to swell its membership.

GROUP RESOURCES

The union maintains a Web site at http://www.umwa.org that includes information on the UMWA's history, the current activities of the various departments, press releases, and back issues of the *United Mine Workers Journal.* Some of the UMWA's historical documents are available for public research at the Historical Collections and Labor Archives at Pennsylvania University's Pattee Library, which can be reached at (814) 863-2505. For more information on the organization, write to the United Mine Workers of America, 900 15th St. NW, Washington, DC 20005 or call (202) 842-7200.

GROUP PUBLICATIONS

The *United Mine Workers Journal,* published six times a year, is distributed to all members. Issues are available on-line at http://www.umwa.org. For more information about obtaining the *United Mine Workers Journal,* write to the United Mine Workers of America, 900 15th St. NW, Washington, DC 20005 or call (202) 842-7200.

BIBLIOGRAPHY

Carey, John, and Catherine Arnst. "Greenhouse Gases: The Cost of Cutting Back." *Business Week,* 8 December 1997.

Clark, Paul F. *The Miners' Fight for Democracy: Arnold Miller and the Reform of the United Mine Workers.* New York: New York State School of Industrial and Labor Relations, Cornell University, 1981.

Dubofsky, Melvyn, and Warren Van Tine. *John L. Lewis: A Biography.* New York: Quadrangle/New York Times Book Company, 1977.

"Industry Fights Climate Change Treaty." *Coal Age,* March 1998.

Kurtz, Howard, Frank Swoboda, and Charles Babington. "Mine Workers at Work." *Washington Post,* 1 November 1996.

McKay, Jim. "UMW to Protest GOP Effort to Dismantle Safety Agency." *Pittsburgh Post-Gazette,* 28 April 1995.

———. "From Mines to Summit of Unionism." *Pittsburgh Post-Gazette,* 23 October 1995.

Victor, Kirk. "Who'll Pay the Coal Miner's Daughter?" *National Journal,* 28 October 1995.

———. "In a Deep Hole." *National Journal,* 14 August 1993.

Zieger, Robert H. *John L. Lewis: Labor Leader.* Boston: Twayne Publishers, 1988.

United Nations Association of the USA (UNA-USA)

ESTABLISHED: 1943
EMPLOYEES: 30
MEMBERS: 23,000
PAC: None

Contact Information:
ADDRESS: 801 Second Ave.
New York, NY 10017
PHONE: (212) 907-1300
FAX: (212) 682-9185
E-MAIL: unahq@unausa.org
URL: http://www.unausa.org
PRESIDENT: Alvin P. Adams, Jr.

WHAT IS ITS MISSION?

According to its 1998 statement of purpose, the United Nations Association of the United States of America (UNA-USA) is "a nonprofit, nonpartisan, national organization dedicated to enhancing U.S. participation in the United Nations system and to strengthening that system as it seeks to define and carry out its mission. UNA-USA's action agenda uniquely combines education and public research, substantive policy analysis and ongoing U.N.-U.S. dialogue." UNA-USA's ultimate goal is U.S. support for and involvement in the United Nations (UN) in the form of economic and military aid.

HOW IS IT STRUCTURED?

UNA-USA is located in New York, New York, blocks from the United Nations headquarters. An executive office conducts management of UNA-USA. Day-to-day operations are supervised by its president, chairman, and a 30-member board of directors. The UNA-USA's staff of 30 is divided into nine branches: a Washington office; policy studies; national programs; management information services and membership services; development and special events; corporate affairs; administration and finance;and the executive office.

Operating beneath the board of directors are 170 community-based chapters and divisions. They implement the organization's education and outreach programs at the local level. They also provide the means to organize the UNA-USA's 23,000 members, primarily affiliated with a particular chapter or division.

The UNA-USA invites anyone interested in furthering the United States' relationship with the United Nations to join the organization. Members pay a minimum of $25 annually and in return are sent UNA-USA publications and information. Those that join come from a variety of backgrounds but are united in their belief in the mission of the UNA-USA.

Through its Council of Organizations program, the UNA-USA is affiliated with more than 100 other groups nationwide. These groups share in the belief that the United States must expand its involvement in global affairs through participation in the United Nations. The council provides opportunities for the member organizations to participate in UNA-USA activities. In addition to its Council of Organizations, the UNA-USA has developed a special alliance with Seton Hall University in Orange, New Jersey. Seton Hall formed a School of Diplomacy and International Relations in 1997 that is dedicated to teaching students about the United Nations and international affairs.

PRIMARY FUNCTIONS

The UNA-USA is an advocate for the United Nations and U.S. internationalism, and uses policy studies and educational outreach to accomplish its goal of strengthening UN-U.S. ties.

Policy studies that research and analyze U.S. and U.N. positions in foreign affairs, represent a significant portion of UNA-USA's activities. These studies are performed by UNA-USA policy experts as well as experts outside the organization and cover subjects from human rights to nuclear proliferation. One component of UNA-USA's policy work includes surveying public opinion about U.S. involvement with the United Nations and international affairs in general. This material allows UNA-USA to alter its programs to match the needs and interests of its constituents. UNA-USA also provides the media with its studies. The media helps deliver the reports to millions more than UNA-USA is able to reach. This not only spreads UNA-USA information, but helps build public understanding of the United Nations.

The UNA-USA Washington, D.C., office occasionally provides the federal government with policy studies, results of its global policy projects, and its public opinion research. The UNA-USA hopes this information will help bolster U.S. financial support of the United Nations. UNA-USA also hopes it will help secure U.S. participation in the UN.

UNA-USA utilizes a grassroots network of community governments, institutions, and individuals to deliver its educational programs. UNA-USA also does a great deal of work at the college and university level. One notable partnership is UNA-USA's Seton Hall

Alliance. Seton Hall is a liberal arts college located in New Jersey, that maintains a School of Diplomacy and International Relations. The school's curriculum was developed with help from UNA-USA policy studies, and the association's resources and recommendations are used in Seton Hall classes.

PROGRAMS

UNA-USA has created initiatives that are extensions of the organization's educational outreach programs. Some programs attempt to bring understanding of world affairs to new audiences while others have been created to particularly build awareness of the United Nations.

UNA-USA's "Adopt-a-Minefield" program allows U.S. communities to become involved in the global effort to eliminate land mines in previous war zones. Individuals donate money that is pooled together with others in their communities. The money is used to help clear the zones of mines and aid the victims of land mine explosions.

UNA-USA's Corporate Affairs program is aimed at U.S. businesses and uses outreach specifically crafted for the corporate environment. These initiatives are sometimes coordinated with fact-finding excursions to countries aided by UN programs. The goal is to educate corporate leaders and employees about the United Nations and the benefits of multilateralism.

The Speaker's Bureau is a group of approximately 300 individuals who address audiences at UNA-USA events across the United States. The program was created as a response to demands by UNA-USA chapters and divisions who requested speakers from the national organization to address their functions. UNA-USA provides speakers as educational field officers who are generally U.S. or UN policy experts.

The Model United Nations is a student enactment of the real United Nations. Students serve as if they were ambassadors from countries throughout the world and gather to discuss issues, settle conflicts, and reach resolutions using many UN methods. Students not only learn how the United Nations works, they learn about the issues of multilateralism and how to engage in civilized, productive debate.

BUDGET INFORMATION

UNA-USA does not receive any government funding. Rather it collects all of its $4.3 million operating budget from individuals, corporations, and foundations.

HISTORY

UNA-USA's roots go back to 1923, when an organization called the League of Nations Association (LNA) was formed to encourage the United States to join the League of Nations, the forerunner of the United Nations (UN). Although the United States never joined the league, the LNA was convinced that the United States should play a greater role in international affairs.

In 1943, as the United Nations was being organized to replace the league, the LNA changed its name to the American Association for the United Nations (AAUN). When the UN was officially opened in 1946, the United States was a member nation and the AAUN, led by Eleanor Roosevelt, adjusted its purpose to focus on educating Americans about the UN and global issues. In 1947 the Department of State created the United States Committee for the United Nations (USCUN), a coalition of national organizations to organize the annual observance of United Nations Day (October 24, the day the UN was founded.) Throughout the 1950s, the two groups did very similar work, informing the public about UN activities and highlighting UN events and resolutions.

In 1964 the AAUN and the USCUN merged to form the United Nations Association of the United States of America. UNA-USA advocated that the UN should play a major role in United States' foreign policy-making processes, and pushed for public awareness of and support for UN initiatives. In addition to developing educational programs, the 1970s was a time of increasing political activity for UNA-USA.

In 1972 UNA-USA established an office in Washington, D.C. Staff in the Washington office lobbied and advised congressional representatives and executive branch staff about international affairs and UN initiatives. UNA-USA began publishing the *Washington Weekly Report* in 1974. The newsletter informed citizens and legislators on issues such as UN funding, international criminal courts, and human rights conferences and treaties.

In 1984 UNA-USA launched the Global Policy Project. To engage citizens in global issues, UNA-USA organized discussion panels in several cities across the country. The citizen panels discussed issues such as human rights, environmental campaigns, and nuclear nonproliferation. Each panel developed policy recommendations on each issue that were compiled into a national consensus report that was presented to legislators and U.N. representatives. UNA-USA also published a book titled *Successor Vision* in 1987, which detailed the organization's philosophy and discussed the increasing globalization of world affairs and economics.

The 1990s saw increased activism from UNA-USA. In 1992 the organization began the first of many fact-finding missions to inspect UN peacekeeping operations. Inspectors compiled their findings into reports that were issued to legislators, U.N. representatives, and the media. In 1995 UNA-USA published the book *How To Do Business with the UN* and began to conduct seminars for U.S. businesses explaining the UN procurement process. Better understanding of UN programs and agencies brought over $400 million in sales to U.S. companies doing business with the UN in 1997.

In 1998 UNA-USA merged with its sister organization, the Business Council for the United Nations. The two organizations joined forces to create new opportunities for members of the U.S. business and international affairs communities to come together to discuss common goals and concerns.

CURRENT POLITICAL ISSUES

The UNA-USA is involved in as broad a range of political issues as the United Nations itself. In the late 1990s, one major focus was the situation in the former Yugoslavia. With the extremity of violence proliferating the area, the issue has become a humanitarian one. The organization has worked to develop solutions that would result in a peaceful end to the conflict. Another situation with humanitarian implications involves the existence and use of land mines.

Case Study: Land Mine Ban

The land mine issue is one of the most important that the UNA-USA faced in the late 1990s. While land mines have always been dangerous weapons during wartime, they have become increasingly deadly for civilians who now occupy areas that once were battlefields. A land area that is particularly riddled with abandoned land mines is the former war-torn Cambodia. The Red Cross estimates that someone, most likely a civilian, is killed every 22 minutes by a land mine. What is more, the cost of labor and equipment used to remove just one land mine can cost as much as $1,000, and developing countries have been reluctant to commit the necessary funds.

The UNA-USA has worked for many years to encourage countries throughout the world to endorse a land mine ban. It has published reports and presented results of its research to Congress and the media about just how serious the problem is. In its effort to pursue a resolution, the UNA-USA joined with several other nongovernmental organizations to form the International and National Campaign to Ban Land Mines. This organization, together with other coalitions, was extremely pleased when its efforts resulted in a 1997 conference of UN members in Canada to discuss what could and should be done regarding this issue.

The conference was in many respects a great success; a treaty banning land mines was formulated and attendees were invited to sign on December 3, 1997, in Ottawa, Canada. The UNA-USA was active in formulating public education forums and its Adopt-a-Landmine program, and many countries agreed to a ban on the production of mines and committed to devoting resources to clearing them throughout the world. However, despite the endorsement of President Bill Clinton, the United States did not agree to sign the ban treaty. Clinton was concerned that other notable hold-outs such as China would need a less aggressive version of the treaty to sign.

To the disappointment of the UNA-USA, in May of 1998 the Clinton administration agreed to sign a comprehensive land mine banning treaty by 2006 only if the Department of Defense could come up with a viable military alternative to the weapon. While it was a blow that the United States would not commit to the treaty immediately, the UNA-USA was encouraged that at the very least, the government was willing to eventually abide by the terms of the treaty.

FUTURE DIRECTIONS

While the central goal of the UNA-USA has always been to keep the United States heavily involved in the United Nations, the United States has not always acted in accordance with that objective. This has been particularly true in the 1990s in regard to U.S. payment of dues to the United Nations. The United States has had a fairly large outstanding debt owed to the organization throught the decade; the UNA-USA has redoubled its efforts to persuade the federal government to make provisions for these payments. While in the past UNA-USA endorsed legislation has fallen flat before Congress, the organization is dedicating its efforts to ensure payment within the 106th session of Congress.

GROUP RESOURCES

The UNA-USA maintains a detailed Web site at http://www.unausa.org. It contains information about UNA-USA programs, biographies of UNA-USA executives, and select UNA-USA reports. For information about the organization write to the United Nations Association of the United States of America, 801 Second Ave., New York, NY 10017, or call (212) 907-1300.

GROUP PUBLICATIONS

UNA-USA publishes a quarterly magazine called *The InterDependent* , which is a journal of international articles and briefs. UNA-USA's Washington Office publishes *Washington Weekly Report*, which contains articles and updates about how the U.S. executive and legislative branches interact with the United Nations. The organiza-

FAST FACTS

A land mine can cost as little as $3 to manufacture.

(Source: UNA-USA's *Adopt-a-Minefield* program, 1999.)

tion also produces a number of reports on international policy and the United States. Aside from these regular publications, UNA-USA does special features. One 1998 UNA-USA special feature included a children's book about land mines called *Not Mines, but Flowers*.

Several of the UNA-USA's publications are available on-line at http://www.unausa.org/publications/index. htm. More information on the organization's publications may be obtained by writing to the United Nations Association of the United States of America, 801 Second Ave., New York, NY 10017, or calling (212) 907-1300.

BIBLIOGRAPHY

Brinkley, Douglas, and Townsend Hoopes. *FDR and the Creation of the UN*. New Haven, Conn.: Yale University Press, 1997.

Eban, Abba. "The UN Idea Revisited." *Foreign Affairs*, September-October 1995.

Halper, Stefan. "Unreformed: Kofi Annan is Subtle, Canny, and a Threat to U.S. Interests." *National Review*, 20 April 1998.

Maynes, Charles, and Richard Williamson. *United States Foreign Policy and the United Nations System*. New York: Norton, 1996.

Meisler, Stanley. *United Nations: The First 50 Years*. New York: Atlantic Monthly Press, 1995.

Negin, Elliot. "Spoiling the Party: As the UN Celebrates Its 50th Anniversary, Stinging Criticism from United States Politicians is Marring the Festivities." *Scholastic Update*, 6 October 1995.

Ostrower, Gary B. *The United Nations and the United States*. New York: Twayne Publishers, 1998.

Righter, Rosemary. *The United Nations and World Order*. Twentieth Century Fund Press, 1995.

Rubin, Amy Mangaro. "Life in a Global Society." *Chronicle of Higher Education*, 27 January 1995.

United States Department of State. "Focus on the UN: Behind-the-Scenes Benefits to Americans." *United States Department of State Dispatch*, 28 August 1995.

United States Chamber of Commerce

ESTABLISHED: 1912
EMPLOYEES: 990
MEMBERS: 180,000
PAC: None

Contact Information:

ADDRESS: 1615 H St. NW
    Washington, DC 20062-2000
PHONE: (202) 659-6000
TOLL FREE: (800) 638-6582
FAX: (202) 463-3190
E-MAIL: member@uschamber.org
URL: http://www.uschamber.org
PRESIDENT: Thomas J. Donohue

WHAT IS ITS MISSION?

The United States Chamber of Commerce's mission is to "advance human progress through an economic, political, and social system based on individual freedom, incentive, initiative, opportunity, and responsibility." In general, the chamber is dedicated to promoting the principles of free enterprise and protecting the private sector from encroachment by the federal government.

HOW IS IT STRUCTURED?

Headquartered in Washington, D.C., the chamber is administered by a full-time president and chief executive officer who reports to a volunteer board of directors. The board is composed of about 60 senior executives of corporations, chambers of commerce, and trade and professional associations. The chamber's policies on national issues are defined by membership input. Once a policy has been formulated, the chamber presents Congress with the business community's recommendations on legislative issues and government policies.

The chamber's activities are organized by departments, led by specialists in a wide range of fields including education, community development, communications, and transportation. The Office of Association Relations, and the Office of Chamber of Commerce Relations provide support and assistance to local and state chambers through advocacy, publications, and productivity tools. The chamber's communications department keeps members and the public informed of current policy issues and developments. Included within the communications department are an audio-visual department, news department, and the chamber's leading periodical, *Nation's Business*, which boasts a circulation in the hundreds of thousands.

The organization's membership is composed of individual company members in a variety of businesses as well as state and local chamber affiliates and trade and professional associations. More than 96 percent of chamber members are small businesses with 100 or fewer employees (71 percent of which have 10 or fewer employees). The remaining members include most of the United States's largest companies.

The chamber's advocacy of U.S. business is closely supported by a number of affiliated organizations including the National Chamber Foundation (NCF), a public policy research organization that analyzes economic issues and conducts training for chamber and association managers and business executives through its educational division. Other organizations include: the National Chamber Litigation Center (NCLC), a nonprofit public policy law firm that represents businesses before the courts and regulatory agencies; the Center for International Private Enterprise (CIPE), which is dedicated to promoting economic growth and democratic development in countries around the world; and the Center for Workforce Preparation (CWP), which focuses on educational reform and workforce preparation. The chamber's Small Business Center provides additional information and resources for small-business owners.

PRIMARY FUNCTIONS

The chamber's primary function is to lobby Congress and federal agencies for pro-business laws and policies. The organization forms policies on issues that affect U.S. commerce and relays these views to congressional members. For example, the chamber supports decreased taxation and increased privatization and opposes overregulation by the government and excessive environmental controls.

In addition to representing business interests before governmental bodies, the chamber also works to gain public support for business positions, such as opposition to excessive government intervention in the economy. The chamber states that "(c)ostly and far-reaching federal programs and mandates on businesses raise the costs of doing business and weaken the U.S. competitive position in the global marketplace." The chamber promotes its views through a variety of outlets, including its publication, *Nation's Business*.

The chamber also serves as a key source of information and support for U.S. businesses. To accomplish this, the chamber keeps members informed about relevant issues for U.S. businesses at home and abroad; offers a wide range of professional development and training

programs; and provides up-to-date information on trade policy, export promotion, export services and other business-related topics.

PROGRAMS

The chamber conducts a wide variety of programs including print, teleconferencing, and on-line training. GAIN—the chamber's Grassroots Action Information Network—gives members the opportunity to make their views known on Capitol Hill through broadcast video conferences and town hall meetings. Other programs include Policy Insiders, which brings business leaders together to discuss national issues and Meet-and-Greets, which allow chamber members to meet with congressional candidates for informal question-and-answer sessions.

The chamber provides members with educational opportunities. Educational programs include live video conferences via satellite—called Quality Learning Services—where experts, authors, and business consultants provide training in areas such as marketing, management, productivity, technology, and forecasting. The chamber also runs a professional development program for chambers of commerce and association executives called *Institute!*, which focuses on building leadership, management, and planning skills.

The chamber also offers a comprehensive range of services aimed at helping new and existing businesses overcome the challenges they face. Through the Small Business Institute (SBI), the chamber provides small-business professionals and their employees with self-study training programs and interactive satellite seminars. It also offers the Small Business Marketplace, an on-line catalog that features a broad selection of business-related books, audio programs, videotapes, and software. Members interested in expanding their operations to other countries can take advantage of newsletters and brochures prepared by the chamber's International Division Information Center (IDIC).

BUDGET INFORMATION

The chamber operated with a 1995 budget of approximately $72 million. While most of the money (about 75 percent) comes from membership dues and donations, the chamber does have some revenue-producing operations, such as the publishing house that produces the *Nation's Business*. Periodical and broadcast advertising income accounts for about 15 percent of the budget, while the remaining 10 percent is derived from publications sales, conferences, and other areas. The money is used to lobby the government for pro-business positions, to cover staff and operation costs, and to administer member programs.

HISTORY

By the early 1800s most U.S. cities on the Eastern seaboard had a chamber of commerce or "board of trade" and the number grew throughout the nineteenth century. Over the years, there were attempts to unite these chambers into a national federation but the first nationally based organization did not come into being until 1912.

With the active support of President William Howard Taft and his secretary of commerce and labor, a national convention was called in 1912 to examine ways in which businesses and their organizations could present a unified voice on complex national issues. The result was the formation of a government sanctioned Chamber of Commerce of the United States of America in July of 1912. Unlike its counterparts in many other countries, the new U.S. chamber was not officially sponsored by the government and to this day remains an independent voice for U.S. business.

Just two months later, on September 12, 1912, the first issue of the chamber's flagship publication, *Nation's Business* appeared. Initially printed in newspaper form, it was transformed into a magazine in 1916 and made available to readers outside the chamber's membership. The first advertisements were carried in 1917 and by 1920 the magazine had a paid circulation of 60,000 and 22,000 chamber-member subscribers. By 1937 circulation had surpassed 300,000.

The Chamber Before and After World War I

When World War I (1914–18) began, the chamber proposed an international court or council of conciliation and recommended a conference of neutral nations to formulate rules for protection from submarine attacks at sea. In 1915 President Woodrow Wilson addressed the chamber's annual meeting, publicly congratulating the chamber for its efforts. When the United States entered the war in 1917, the chamber organized more than 400 war service committees to assist the Council of National Defense, and chamber members supported a tax increase to reduce government borrowing and prevent inflation.

After the war ended, the chamber was involved in efforts to resolve postwar business problems. It called a Special Reconstruction Conference in December 1918 to consider lifting wartime restrictions on industry, and address shipping questions, labor problems, and issues arising from cancellation of war contracts. Labor unrest led to a series of postwar strikes. The chamber supported collective bargaining and the right of employees to join unions, but urged prohibition of strikes against public utilities.

Postwar Growth and the Great Depression

The 1920s marked a period of sustained growth for the chamber. Membership rose from 13,106 in 1920 to 16,257 in 1929 when agricultural organizations were invited to join for the first time. The chamber also encouraged the development of the rapidly expanding "flying industry." In 1926 the chamber launched another publication called *The Week's Work*, a newsletter for chamber members that interpreted current national issues and contained chamber plans and activities. Over the years, the newsletter went through several name changes and today is known as *The Business Advocate*.

After the stock market crashed in 1929, President Herbert Hoover asked chamber President William Butterworth to organize an executive committee of the nation's business leaders to minimize the effects of the economic disaster and help bring the country out of the depression. Nevertheless, the chamber adamantly opposed government efforts to end the depression through increased federal intervention and control. A decade later, chamber President Earl O. Shreve explained that "we saw inherent dangers of clamping ourselves into a socialized beneficent government certain to be regretted later." At its twentieth annual meeting in 1932, the chamber warned against mounting public expenditures, a warning it was to voice frequently throughout the remainder of the century.

World War II and Beyond

During World War II (1939–45), the chamber continued to resist any expansion of government powers, arguing that any new controls should be limited and strictly emergency in nature. The organization also provided advice to the government's defense and war agencies and assisted in recruiting, procurement, registering aliens, and securing local cooperation to report suspected sabotage and espionage. The chamber helped in salvaging industrial scrap, distributing information about selective service, and promoting the sale of government war bonds.

After the war the chamber's long-held interest in foreign trade was reinforced by the sudden emergence of the United States as a leading worldwide economic power. In 1947 the chamber assigned an observer to the United Nations in New York and was granted full consultative status three years later. Six years later the chamber further expanded its work in the international field by establishing an International Relations Service Department.

Rapid growth in membership led to further restructuring during the 1950s. Seventeen district managers were hired to assist the six division managers with the chamber's field work; a labor relations department and an education department were also created. Advisory committees on atomic energy and science and technology were also set up during this period.

During the 1960s the chamber laid the groundwork for more intensive political activity by establishing a program called "Action Course in Practical Politics." It also expanded its involvement in international affairs, holding regular meetings with Japanese business leaders and creating bilateral trade and investment councils with countries such as Japan, Egypt, India, and Canada. The chamber's response to President Lyndon Johnson's "Great Society" antipoverty programs mirrored its reaction to expanded government regulation during the depression, advocating that "it would be preferable to understand the nature of the poverty problem before enacting massive federal subsidy programs in a dubious effort to solve it." A task force on economic growth and opportunity consisting of the chief executive officers of 100 major corporations was created to examine the poverty issue.

In 1967 the chamber created a foundation to undertake research and to provide a "forum for private sector expertise and analysis in public policy decision making." The chamber created a council on trends and perspectives to search out new ideas and to identify and examine business, economic, and social trends that might impact U.S. business in the future.

Chamber involvement in economic, social, and political issues increased rapidly through the 1970s and 1980s. The National Chamber Litigation Center was formed to help businesses protect themselves from lawsuits and a subsidiary corporation called "Citizen's Choice" was created to act as a grassroots lobbying organization. In 1978 the chamber founded its own political action committee, the National Chamber Alliance for Politics. Endorsements were given to candidates who supported business objectives regardless of political affiliation. To help business leaders communicate more effectively, the chamber also launched the Communicator Workshop, a program that taught participants how to cope with hostile journalists, conduct news conferences, present congressional testimony, and make television and other public appearances. Similarly, the aim of the Corporate Executive Development Program was to instruct businesses in the intricacies of special-interest group politics and how to get around the complex federal government structure.

In the meantime, membership was growing rapidly, rising from 47,800 in 1973 to more than 180,000 in 1986. This strength enabled the chamber to expand its communications network to include its own satellite television network called BizNet that combined regularly scheduled programming with special videoconferencing. Chamber-produced television programs, such as "It's Your Business," "Enterprise," and "Nation's Business Today" were widely shown on cable networks across the country reaching up to 89 percent of U.S. households.

In the 1990s the chamber's position as one of the most effective business lobbies began to erode due to a combination of deteriorating economic conditions and aggressive new small business lobbies. Widely perceived as the voice of big business, the chamber's influence waned as corporate downsizing and restructuring led to a growing distrust of corporate America. Small business was increasingly seen as the "economic engine" of the United States and soon upstart business advocacy groups

such as the National Federation of Independent Business were competing directly with the chamber for political influence.

Despite its waning influence, the chamber's leadership played a decisive role in creating a pro-business environment in the mid- to late 1990s. The chamber helped push through several measures including the 1993-94 North American Free Trade Agreement (NAFTA)—an act that drastically reduced trade restrictions and tariffs among the United States, Canada, and Mexico—and the 1997 Tax Payer's Relief Act, the first tax cut in 16 years and the largest small-business tax cut in U.S. history.

CURRENT POLITICAL ISSUES

The chamber promotes business interests in domestic and foreign policy through political funds, public relations efforts, and a grassroots network of state and local chambers of commerce and their member business organizations. In the domestic policy area, the chamber opposes increases in the minimum wage and opposes efforts towards what it considers the overregulation of businesses in areas such as worker safety and the environment. It supports legal reforms in the areas of class-action lawsuits, employment law, and tort reform. For example, the chamber made efforts to limit the reach of lawsuits emanating from the Y2K (Year 2000) computer glitch.

In the area of foreign policy, the chamber is an advocate of expanding free trade and improving international trade systems. Generally, the chamber opposes the United States's use of unilateral trade sanctions. To these ends, the chamber voiced support for the extension of most favored nation trading status to China and normalization of trading relations with Vietnam. The chamber has also supported other international trade efforts such as funding of the International Monetary Fund (IMF) and the controversial NAFTA. The chamber served as a coordinator of business advocates in favor of the United States providing $18 billion for the IMF. And the chamber hailed the passing of the NAFTA as a victory for U.S. business interests. NAFTA opponents—such as organized labor and environmental groups—questioned whether the bill was beneficial to workers and the environment, but the chamber and its allies argued that the long-term benefits of the economic growth associated with expansions in free trade would eventually benefit all. The arguments used in the NAFTA debate were similar to those used in the debate over the extension of "fast-track" trade authority to the president.

Case Study: Fast-Track

Every president since Gerald Ford has enjoyed "fast-track" trading authority. Fast-track trade was established in the Trade Reform Act of 1974 and gives the president authority to negotiate trade deals upon the conditions of regular consultation with and notification of Congress and subject to an up or down vote by Congress. The act has been revised and expanded several times since 1974. The NAFTA agreement was negotiated and passed using fast-track authority. But fast-track trade authority lapsed in March of 1994 and, despite some legislative efforts to revive it, has not been renewed.

The chamber's long-standing commitment to the expansion of free trade and the belief that fast-track trading authority gave the United States a strategic advantage in negotiating trade deals, led the chamber to push for legislative renewal of fast-track authority. The chamber marshaled several arguments in support of the renewal of fast-track authority. In 1996 U.S. Chamber of Commerce Vice President Willard A. Workman told journalists that U.S. "economic interests have been hurt by not having negotiating authority." The chamber believed that both its big business and small business members were being hurt by a lack of strong and free trade. In an effort to shore up support with the small business membership, Chamber President and CEO Thomas J. Donohue wrote an editorial entitled "Fast Track: Why Workers and Small Businesses Should Care," in which he outlined, among other things, the increased reliance of small businesses on foreign markets.

The chamber also cited practical concerns regarding the negotiating processes suggesting that U.S. companies were missing opportunities in world markets. In a letter to the Senate Finance Committee, Executive Vice President for Government Affairs R. Bruce Josten wrote: "while U.S. negotiators are absent from or weakened at the negotiating table, other nations continue to negotiate trade deals which place U.S. export companies and their workers at a competitive disadvantage in some of the world's fastest growing economies." More specifically, Josten cited how a lack of such authority hurt U.S. companies trading with Chile and estimated that the United States lost half a billion dollars in potential export sales to Chile "because our exporters still pay Chile's highest duty." In September 1998 the chamber stepped up its efforts to push for fast-track authority. Citing economic crises in Asia and Latin America and a trade-deficit increase from $9.9 billion to $13.92 billion from January to September 1998, the chamber suggested fast-track authority as a potential cure for the United States's trading ills.

In support of its fast-track initiatives, the chamber and its business allies raised millions of dollars and waged a large-scale media campaign touting the benefits of free trade and the dangers of protectionism. It also made direct appeals to elected officials. In an October 1997 open letter to all Congress, the chamber emphasized its external strength and suggested that it had contacted numerous newspapers, state and local chambers of commerce, and corporations nationwide regarding the fast-track issue. The organization specified that it planned

to continue its ardent support of the reinstatement of fast-track authority.

As with NAFTA, the chamber's fast-track efforts sparked opposition from labor unions, public interest trade organizations such as the Citizens Trade Campaign and the Public Citizen's Global Trade Watch, and environmental organizations. Although not opposed to the concept of free trade, the Sierra Club, for example, raised concerns that international trade agreements needed to include provisions for greater environmental protection. Critics of fast-track charged that unregulated free trade would allow companies to avoid paying living wages to workers and to circumvent environmental regulations.

Despite the support of the administration, the Republican leadership in Congress, and powerful groups such as the U.S. Chamber of Commerce, a September 1998 House vote on fast-track authority failed. The chamber and others continue to push for executive fast-track authority. The battles over NAFTA and fast-track trading in the 1990s highlight the battles between coalitions. Opponents will continue to advocate for workers and environmental protection while businesses will highlight the beneficial financial aspects of free trade.

FUTURE DIRECTIONS

In the interest of furthering relations between the traditionally opposed business and labor organizations, the chamber has attempted to bridge the gap with the American Federation of Labor-Congress of Industrial Organizations (AFL-CIO). While chamber President and CEO Thomas Donohue acknowledged that the two organizations will not ally in regard to several issues, others, such as national defense and environmental regulations hold the potential for agreement. The leaders of both organizations spoke with the other's executive board for the first time in late 1998, and early 1999, and also issued a joint statement regarding the Federal Reserve interest rate. The chamber looks to enhance this newly formed relationship with future meetings and issue statements.

GROUP RESOURCES

The chamber offers a diverse and comprehensive range of informational resources. These include a Web site at http://www.uschamber.org, where visitors can learn about the chamber's policies, programs, history, and goals, as well as read recent press releases and find out about upcoming events. Information about the organization may also be obtained by writing to the United States Chamber of Commerce, 1615 H St. NW, Washington, DC 20062 or calling 1-800-638-6582.

Small businesses can take advantage of the Small Business Resource Catalog, which features products and training tools to fit the needs of small businesses. A free copy can be obtained by filling out an on-line form at http://www.uschamber.org/programs/sbi/marketplace-form.html.

GROUP PUBLICATIONS

The U.S. Chamber of Commerce is the publisher of *Nation's Business*, a monthly magazine widely read by owners and management of businesses. It can be accessed on the World Wide Web at http://www.nbmag.com. Also published monthly is *The Business Advocate*, which offers summaries of current administrative, legislative and legal issues. The U.S. Chamber of Commerce Policy Division publishes various materials dealing with topics such as business issues, grassroots activism, politics, employee education, and analyses of federal laws. Educational and informational books and pamphlets are also available from the Office of Chamber of Commerce Relations and the Office of Association Relations. *Small Business Financial Resource Guide*, a guide to resources and types of financing for small businesses, is published by the chamber's Small Business Center. Information about any of the organization's publications may be obtained by writing to the United States Chamber of Commerce, 1615 H St. NW, Washington, DC 20062 or calling 1-800-638-6582.

BIBLIOGRAPHY

Boroughs, Don L., et al. "What's Wrong with the American Economy." *U.S. News and World Report*, 2 November 1992.

Destler, I.M. *Renewing Fast-Track Legislation.* Washington, D.C.: Institute for International Economics, 1997.

Graham, Bob and Mike DeWine. "Fast-Track to Freer Trade Promises Bumpy Ride." *Christian Science Monitor*, 9 September 1997.

Grieder, William. "The Global Marketplace: A Closet Dictator." *The Progressive*, May 1993.

Hakim, Peter. "What the Administration Can Do to Make Up for the Loss of Fast Track." *Christian Science Monitor*, 25 September 1997.

Iritani, Evelyn. "Anti-China Mood Troubles U.S. Businesses" *Los Angeles Times*, 3 March 1997.

Kirkland, Richard I., Jr. "Today's GOP: The Party's over for Big Business in a Political Arena Now Dominated by Small-Business Populists, Anti-Government Conservatives, and the Religious Right." *Fortune*, 6 February 1995.

Magnusson, Paul. "Beyond NAFTA: Why Washington Mustn't Stop Now." *Business Week* 21 April 1997.

Schmitt, Eric. "Business Groups Press for $18 Billion for IMF." *New York Times* 5 April 1998.

Thurman, Skip. "Clinton Puts Free Trade First This Fall." *Christian Science Monitor*, 12 November 1997.

Warner, David. "Hurdles for Business in the New Congress." *Nation's Business*, February 1999.

United States Public Interest Research Group (U.S.PIRG)

ESTABLISHED: 1984
EMPLOYEES: 2 to 3
MEMBERS: None
PAC: None

Contact Information:

ADDRESS: 218 D St. SE
    Washington, DC 20003
PHONE: (202) 546-9707
FAX: (202) 546-2461
E-MAIL: uspirg@pirg.org
URL: http://www.pirg.org
EXECUTIVE DIRECTOR: Gene Karpinski

WHAT IS ITS MISSION?

According to the statement of purpose of the United States Public Interest Research Group (U.S.PIRG), the organization is a "non-profit, nonpartisan organization dedicated to serving as a watchdog for the nation's citizens and environment." U.S.PIRG works through its state organizations to lobby for pro-environment legislation and to educate the public about the importance of the environment.

HOW IS IT STRUCTURED?

U.S.PIRG is administered by an executive director and a small staff of two to three employees. Much of U.S.PIRG's legal, political, and research work is done by lawyers, lobbyists, and researchers who are contracted by the organization. There are 26 State Public Interest Research Groups (PIRGs) across the country. The State PIRGs are the primary source of finance for U.S.PIRG, supplying it with the bulk of its operating budget. These organizations are environmental protection, democracy, and consumer advocacy action groups. The U.S.PIRG Education Fund is the public education branch of U.S.PIRG.

The organization does not have a direct membership; those interested in joining are organized under the State PIRGs. Members make at least a $25 annual contribution. The State PIRG membership is composed of individuals with a diverse background but who are united by their concern in protecting the public interest

PRIMARY FUNCTIONS

There are three major forums through which U.S.PIRG conducts most of its work: the U.S. Congress, the court system, and public education. U.S.PIRG lobbies Congress and conducts congressional testimony. Through these efforts, U.S.PIRG hopes to enact or change legislation as a means of accomplishing its goals. These legislative actions may be resolutions strengthening national clean air and water standards or laws initiating campaign finance reforms. For instance, in 1996, the U.S.PIRG lobbied for passage of a congressional resolution that banned offshore oil drilling along the coasts of the United States.

If the U.S.PIRG is unsuccessful in affecting legislative change regarding a particular issue, it may resort to challenging industrial action through a lawsuit. A court order following the filing of such a lawsuit can stop industrial activities in a matter of hours. In 1996 U.S.PIRG filed a Clean Air Act lawsuit against Louisiana's Bayou Steel, which the U.S.PIRG recognized as one of the nation's worst air polluters.

U.S.PIRG also makes use of the media to further its interests. The group researches issues that impact the public and issues numerous reports about its findings. For example, as part of its consumer advocacy agenda, U.S.PIRG and State PIRGs arranged press events in 100 cities across the United States to publicize its annual *Trouble in Toyland* report. The report lists toys the organization considers unsafe. This highly visible media event reaches millions of parents helping them avoid potentially dangerous products.

PROGRAMS

U.S.PIRG does not run traditional training, education, or development programs. Rather, it sponsors projects and campaigns that are essentially divisions that uphold the organization's function. Although U.S.PIRG is also a political and consumer advocacy organization, U.S.PIRG's environmental agenda dominates the group's activities.

The Environmental Defense Campaign (EDC) is an all-purpose environmental action program that works on many different issues. In 1996 U.S.PIRG's Environmental Defense Campaign helped defend the "Superfund" law that requires industry to clean up the pollution it leaves behind. It helped protect the Endangered Species Act law and opposed changes to the Clean Water Act. With the help of other environmental groups, the EDC forced Congress to reject a proposal to open American National Parks to corporate sponsorship.

The Campaign to Cut Polluter Pork is U.S.PIRG's attempt to call attention to misguided federal subsidies paid to corporations that pollute the environment or mis-use America's natural resources. While PIRG acknowledges that corporate subsidization helps to stimulate U.S. economic growth, it objects to subsidies that go to industries that use natural resources such as timber, coal, or oil.

U.S.PIRG's Campaign for R.E.A.L. (Renewable, Efficient, Affordable, Lasting) Energy lobbies Congress to offer subsidies and increase funding for the development of new sources of energy. Many people believe the United States is too dependent on oil, coal, and nuclear power. The production of these types of energy often cause pollution. The Campaign for R.E.A.L. Energy was created to help the government promote cleaner sources of energy like solar power. One of the Campaign's successes occurred in 1994 when Congress increased funding for renewable energy programs by 14 percent.

The government agency responsible for preserving and protecting the environment, the Environmental Protection Agency (EPA), created a Community Right to Know campaign. The EPA program was designed to force industry to public disclosure of the type and amount of pollutants created by their production. U.S.PIRG created a Toxics Right to Know Campaign, which attempts to extend the EPA's program to include toxic chemical dumping.

The goal of U.S.PIRG's Consumer Watchdog Program is "to protect and expand consumers' rights to safe products; fair banking, credit card and insurance practices; truthful advertising; and the comprehensive information needed to make informed choices." This program works to protect the American consumer from unethical and unsafe corporate behavior. For instance, it is U.S.PIRG's Consumer Watchdog Program that is responsible for the organization's *Trouble in Toyland Report*.

Americans Against Political Corruption is a U.S.PIRG program that works for campaign finance reform. It advocates public financing for political campaigns, capping campaign spending, and other financing changes. The ultimate goal of the program is to reduce the influence of big money on politics.

BUDGET INFORMATION

The U.S.PIRG 1996 statement of financial activities divides the organization's assets and liabilities into two groups: the U.S.PIRG and the U.S.PIRG Education Fund. U.S.PIRG received $304,642 in total income: $293,210 came directly from State PIRG contributions; approximately $10,000 of income came from other sources including publications and interest income. U.S.PIRG spent $335,335 in 1995–96: $270,480 was spent on U.S.PIRG programs; $184,808 on research and advocacy; and $85,672 on public education. U.S.PIRG spent $64,855 on support services, which included $56,363 on general administrative costs and $8,492 on fund-raising.

Before the Superfund law of 1980 U.S. PIRG created a Toxic Right to Know Campaign to force the industry to publicly disclose the type, amount, and location of toxic chemical dumping. (Photograph by Robert Visser, Greenpeace)

The U.S.PIRG Education Fund raised $332,908 in grants and contributions. It also gathered $21,167 in interest income to bring the U.S.PIRG's Education Fund's total income to $354,075. The U.S.PIRG Education Fund spent $297,818 in 1995–96; $139,040 was spent on public education in the environmental realm; $80,007 was spent on the Toxics Right to Know program; and $21,547 was spent on U.S.PIRG's open government efforts, such as campaign finance reform. Regional environmental education programs cost the U.S.PIRG Education Fund $4,001; consumer education cost $13,782. The U.S.PIRG Education Fund spent $23,388 on general costs including administration, and $16,053 on grant development, or fund-raising.

HISTORY

The U.S.PIRG was founded in 1984, although several State PIRGs had been in existence since the 1970s. Its first significant actions involved its work in the 1986 renewals of the Safe Drinking Water Act and the Superfund law. The Safe Water Drinking Act requires local communities to maintain a safe level of contaminants in public drinking water supplies, while the Superfund law is a federal program that uses business and federal dollars to clean up areas polluted by industry. These sites, generally polluted by dangerous levels of toxic chemicals, are located across the United States.

In 1990 the U.S.PIRG was instrumental in clearing the passage of the Clean Air Act. An intense battle over the legislation took place, with environmental groups such as U.S.PIRG on one side and political action committees (PACs) representing various industries on the other. Included in the historic legislation is the prohibition of the use of such ozone depleters as chlorofluorocarbons (CFCs). CFCs were used as refrigerants in air conditioners and refrigerators and propellants in aerosol cans and are believed to erode the Earth's protective upper atmosphere ozone layer.

Three years later the U.S.PIRG contributed to passage of the Motor Voter Act that allowed US citizens to register to vote as they applied for new drivers licenses. Supporters of the Motor Voter Act believed it to be a vital tool in making the registration process more convenient, thus enabling more citizens to vote. In 1994 U.S.PIRG reports helped convince Congress to a pass a budget that included a 14 percent increase in government funding for renewable energy research and development.

In the late 1990s U.S.PIRG focused on an even more diverse range of issues than in the past, examining topics such as campaign finance reform. Additionally the

U.S.PIRG responded to the explosion in sports utility vehicle sales by conducting research in 1998 that accused makers of such vehicles with environmental negligence.

CURRENT POLITICAL ISSUES

U.S.PIRG has been a consistent supporter of campaign finance reform. Its involvement in the issue reached new proportions in 1997 after the Clinton administration was accused of inappropriate and possibly illegal fund-raising during the 1996 presidential campaign. The campaign was alleged to have received millions of dollars in illegal donations from Southeast Asian and Chinese donors. Although the Democratic Party eventually returned the money, some conservative politicians and writers called for the appointment of a special prosecutor to investigate. The Justice Department, however, found an investigation unnecessary.

These factors combined to create a sort of campaign finance reform movement. U.S.PIRG developed its own reform agenda that included the restriction of out-of-district contributions, limiting campaign contributions to $100, the institution of a spending cap, establishment of free TV and radio time and mail service to candidates, and the creation of a national referenda system. This system allows voters to directly approve policies, programs, and bills.

Case Study: Superfund

For many years U.S. industry did not dispose of its waste from production properly. Some of this waste included dangerous, toxic chemicals, which were very often dumped wherever a company wanted. The poisons from these chemicals seeped into the ground and water table. Some sites became so polluted that exposure to the air around them was considered dangerous. There are an estimated 85,000 sites like this across the United States.

Concern over these sites inspired the 1980 Comprehensive Environmental Response, Compensation, and Liability Act, known as Superfund. The Superfund was created to give the EPA the power to use legal means to clean up the worst sites. Superfund allows the EPA to bill owners and former owners of the land, tenants, and mortgage holders of the land the site is on for cleanup costs. If money from the polluters is inaccessible, a tax on petroleum and chemical companies provides the EPA with the funds to clean the polluted areas. There are 13,000 sites designated as so polluted that they require Superfund monies to be adequately recovered. U.S.PIRG has always supported the concept of the Superfund, acknowledging that without it, funding for the restoration of such sites would be difficult or impossible.

Despite the seeming benefit of this law, the tax that enabled the fund expired in December of 1995 after the 15-year period designated in the original law. Congres-

sional opponents to the tax saw this as an opportunity to prevent any efforts to reinstate it. Over the objections of the EPA, Congress did not reauthorize the bill. This had an immediate effect upon EPA efforts. After the tax expired, the EPA began losing $4 million Superfund cleanup dollars a day. U.S.PIRG lobbied hard for Congress to reinstate the tax, but were unsuccessful; the group accused Superfund opponents of illegally contributing large amounts of money for congressional support through 1995–1998. After studying the status of the fund, U.S.PIRG predicted that without congressional intervention, the money would completely dry up, which may cause many polluted U.S. land areas to remain unrecovered.

FUTURE DIRECTIONS

In the twenty-first century, U.S.PIRG will continue its campaign to inform the public about and provide legislators with research on excessive and hidden banking fees. U.S.PIRG is encouraging citizens to contact the organization with stories of their problems with bank fees and credit bureaus, which will be compiled for ongoing congressional testimony. USPIRG will advocate for changes in banking laws to ensure that banks protect the privacy of personal credit, and medical and insurance records.

U.S.PIRG will also launch a campaign to involve citizens at a younger age by researching issues of concern to college students. Through its Higher Education project, the organization will seek to educate young people about topics such as student rights, voting, environmental concerns, and consumer issues. Students will receive information and training on the participatory system and be encouraged to organize politically and make their opinions known to legislators.

In 1999 U.S.PIRG launched a long-term campaign to raise public awareness of the resurgence of toxic pollutants and the need for stricter standards. Citizens will be encouraged to voice their opinions to the Environmental Protection Agency (EPA) during a public comment period as the EPA considers restructuring toxic pollution standards. U.S.PIRG will embark on an extensive public education program to inform citizens of the types and harmful effects of toxic substances present in their work and living environments.

GROUP RESOURCES

U.S.PIRG maintains a Web site at http://www.pirg.org. It contains contact information, a list of U.S.PIRG achievements, and an inventory of available U.S.PIRG reports. For more information on the organization write the United States Public Interest Research

Group, 218 D St. SE, Washington, DC 20003, call (202) 546-9707, or E-mail uspirg@pirg.org.

GROUP PUBLICATIONS

U.S.PIRG publishes *U.S.PIRG Citizen Agenda*, a quarterly newsletter with updates of the organization's activities and environmental, consumer, and government news. U.S.PIRG publishes reports such as "Big Cars, Dirty Air" and "The Rising Cost of Global Warming." It makes many of these reports available on-line at http://www.pirg.org/reports. For more information about obtaining any of the organization's publications, write the United States Public Interest Research Group, 218 D St. SE, Washington, DC 20003, or call (202) 546- 9707.

BIBLIOGRAPHY

Berselli, Beth. "When Making Choices isn't Child's Play: Watchdog Group Says Some Toys May Cause Choking, Other Risks." *Washington Post*, 28 November 1997.

Lamiell, Patricia. "More Banks are Charging Noncustomers for ATM Use." *Denver Post*, 2 April 1998.

"Most State Advisories against Eating Mercury-Contaminated Fish are Inconsistent, PIRG Says." *Pesticide and Toxic Chemical News*, 18 February 1999.

"Study Attacks Rental Car Collision Damage Waivers." *Washington Post*, 2 September 1994.

"US Pirg Blasts Chemical Industry for Massive Discharges into Water." *Chemical Market Reporter*, 21 September 1998.

"USPIRG: 20% of Major Dischargers had Significant CWA Violations." *Air Water Pollution Report*, 17 July 1995.

United Steelworkers of America (USWA)

WHAT IS ITS MISSION?

The mission of the United Steelworkers of America (USWA) has changed little since its first convention in 1937 where delegates agreed they would unite "regardless of creed, color or nationality" all workers in the steel and iron industries "to increase the wages, and improve the conditions of employment . . . by legislation, conciliation, joint agreements or other legitimate means." More broadly, the USWA seeks to achieve economic and social justice for both its members and workers outside its membership in North America and abroad through the promotion of unionization, collective bargaining, and progressive legislation.

HOW IS IT STRUCTURED?

The USWA is governed by an executive board elected to four-year terms. The board includes a president, secretary-treasurer, two vice presidents, the directors of 12 geographic districts, and four additional representatives. Organizational policies are determined at biennial conventions attended by delegates from the organization's 2,000 local unions. Locals elect their own officers and make decisions by a democratic vote.

The USWA headquarters, which provides assistance to the districts and locals, consists of a number of departments. The Collective Bargaining and Arbitration departments work on developing and interpreting contracts with employers. The Membership Development Department provides training and educational materials in areas such as political action, organizing, collective

ESTABLISHED: June 1936
EMPLOYEES: 850
MEMBERS: 700,000
PAC: United Steelworkers of America Political Action
  Fund

Contact Information:

ADDRESS: 5 Gateway Center
  Pittsburgh, PA 15222
PHONE: (412) 562-2400
FAX: (202) 347-6735
E-MAIL: webmaster@uswa.org
URL: http://www.uswa.org
PRESIDENT: George Becker

FAST FACTS

According to the USWA, NAFTA has cost U.S. workers 500,000 jobs.

(Source: Kara Sissell. "Labor Groups Sue to Revoke NAFTA." *Chemical Week*, July 22, 1998.)

bargaining, and safety and health. The Health, Safety, and Environment Department oversees the activities of district coordinators and local union committees on occupational health and environmental issues. The Communications Department handles publications and press releases. There is also a Civil Rights Department that handles issues of particular concern to women and minorities. Various other departments service the headquarters, districts, and locals in areas such as research, legal affairs, and political mobilization. The union operates a political action committee and maintains an office in Washington, D.C. that handles legislative affairs.

The districts, organized along the same lines as political jurisdictions, coordinate and assist the activities of local unions. The locals are primarily responsible for handling grievances, contract negotiations, and labor-management cooperation. The USWA's membership is dominated by workers in the United States and Canada employed in the steel, aluminum, copper, mining, manufacturing, and chemical industries. A small percentage of members work in a range of other industries, from retail to health care. The USWA is affiliated with the American Federation of Labor and Congress of Industrial Organizations (AFL-CIO) and the Canadian Labor Congress (CLC).

PRIMARY FUNCTIONS

The primary function of the USWA is to improve the wages and working conditions of its members through collective bargaining contracts with employers and also to ensure fair treatment in the workplace. Every year a committee on wage policy meets to outline contract goals for use by districts and locals. When confronted with hostile employers the union can call strikes, but it has also developed a number of other strategies. The USWA is a pioneer in the use of "corporate campaigns" designed to hurt the targeted company's image. For example, when Japanese-owned Bridgestone, a major tire manufacturer, fired 2,000 strikers at U.S. plants, the USWA responded

by organizing demonstrations at stores that sold Bridgestone tires and at Japanese consulates. The USWA used ties to foreign unions to organize demonstrations in countries such as Brazil and Turkey. It sent some of the fired workers and their families to perform street theater in Japan to publicize their plight. The union also lobbied the Clinton administration to address the labor problem in diplomatic meetings with Japanese officials and lobbied city governments to cancel contracts with Bridgestone. In other cases the union has sent letters to investors and run ads in the financial press portraying targeted companies as bad investments. The USWA, in cooperation with other unions and the AFL-CIO, has also tried to use the clout of union financial accounts and pension funds to intimidate companies and banks into pushing hostile employers to cooperate with the union. The USWA supports these efforts with press releases, press conferences, and media ads.

The USWA also tries to improve conditions for its workers by influencing elections and legislation. The union's political action committee raises money and contributes to candidates and the Democratic Party. USWA leaders appear before congressional hearings and serve on government task forces and commissions. The union organizes voter registration drives and educates its members on political issues. It also conducts training of political organizers. Internships available to rank-and-file members in the Washington office teach members how Washington works so that this knowledge can be shared back home with local union halls. The union also uses the legal system to reach its goals and has filed landmark lawsuits to uphold private pensions, affirmative action, and collective bargaining.

PROGRAMS

Conceding that the USWA will never be able to match the political spending of big business, the union's leadership launched the Rapid Response Program to defend union members' interests with "organized people power." Through fax links to the locals, the USWA is able to mount major grassroots campaigns on short notice. Issue fax alerts are sent out to local leaders and activists who in turn mobilize rank-and-file members to phone and write letters to congressional representatives and the White House. The goal is that four percent of each local's membership will be political activists who will each contact 20 or so union members personally and give them information on pressing issues. The program is also used to encourage members to support labor-friendly candidates during elections.

In 1998 USWA President George Becker observed of the union: "Our greatest challenge is organizing. Our ability to organize and grow the union bears directly on our effectiveness at the bargaining table and in the political arena." To offset membership losses due to corpo-

Wives of steelworkers picket city hall in 1937 during a violent strike in which over a dozen workers were killed. The United Steelworkers of America won a major victory that year when U.S. Steel the largest firm in the industry signed a contract guaranteeing a forty-hour week and a five dollar a day wage. (UPI/Corbis-Bettmann)

rate downsizing and international competition during the 1990s, the 1998 convention approved a special monthly dues payment to create the $40 million USWA Organizing Fund. Half of the money was earmarked for district and local union organizing and the other half was to be split between industry-wide organizing programs and organizer training. The goal of the union is to increase membership by 10 percent a year.

BUDGET INFORMATION

Not made available

HISTORY

The Amalgamated Association of Iron, Steel, and Tin Workers (AA) was founded in 1878 to organize skilled laborers in these industries. At this time a six-day week, 12-hour day, and child labor were standard practices, and there were virtually no occupational health or safety standards. The organization of workers into unions to combat the miserable working conditions was limited, however, by the opposition of employers who often threatened, fired, or physically assaulted budding union members. After some organizing successes the AA was virtually destroyed by what would become the U.S. Steel Corporation in the famous and bloody Homestead Steel Strike of 1892. Subsequent efforts to organize the steel industry over the decades that followed also failed, in large part due to antilabor laws and hostile courts and political officials.

The fortunes of organized labor changed with the election of Democratic President Franklin D. Roosevelt and the implementation of his "New Deal" programs designed to pull the country out of the Great Depression of the 1930s. The National Labor Relations Act of 1935 (NLRA) established workers' right to organize and bargain collectively with employers. Recognizing the opportunities offered by the law, several unions broke away from the conservative American Federation of Labor (AFL) to form the rival Congress of Industrial Organizations (CIO), dedicated to organizing both skilled and unskilled workers in mass-production industries such as steel and autos.

The CIO, led by the charismatic John L. Lewis, president of the United Mine Workers of America, reached an agreement in 1936 with the AA to form the Steel Workers Organizing Committee (SWOC) to launch a major organizing drive in the steel industry under the direction of Phillip Murray. Despite strong employer resistance, SWOC reached a membership of 125,000 by January of 1937. In March of that year the union won a major victory when U.S. Steel—the largest firm in the industry—signed a contract guaranteeing a 40-hour week and a five-dollar-a-day wage. After one of the most violent strikes of the period, in which over a dozen workers were killed, the union used provisions of the NLRA to force seven other companies known as "Little Steel" to the bargaining table in 1941 and 1942.

At the union's convention in 1942 the 700,000-member SWOC changed its name to the United Steelworkers of America and elected Murray its president. Murray was a firm supporter of Roosevelt and he cooperated with the administration by committing his union to a "no-strike" pledge during World War II (1939–45). In return the union was able to take its complaints before Roosevelt's National War Labor Board. The Board granted the USWA measures that helped it maintain its membership during the war and a wage increase that served as the pattern for all the mass production industries. During the war and its immediate aftermath, the USWA expanded into other metal industries and metal fabrication and it absorbed the Aluminum Workers of America. In the postwar period the USWA, through negotiations and strikes, won a pension plan and unemployment benefits for many of its members.

Postwar Years See Gradual Industry Downturn

Upon Murray's death in 1952, David J. McDonald assumed the presidency. Unemployment became a persistent problem following the longest strike in USWA history, which led to federal government intervention in 1959. Membership, which had reached 1.2 million in 1956, declined to 960,000. Discontent with McDonald's leadership resulted in the election of I. W. Abel as president in 1965. Abel opened up the union to rank-and-file participation and worked to eliminate racial discrimination in the union and the workplace. Because of U.S. involvement in the Vietnam War (1959–75), President Lyndon Johnson pressed the steel companies and the union to reach a settlement without a strike in the first round of negotiations under Abel, and the union won a sizable wage increase.

Organizing drives outside basic steel and mergers with other unions in the 1960s and early 1970s made the USWA the second largest union in the United States, even though employment in the steel industry was falling. The USWA contributed to a major legislative achievement in the passage of the Occupational Safety and Health Act in 1970 and contract negotiations with employers continued to produce gains for USWA members throughout the decade. Abel eventually was replaced by Lloyd McBride as president in a contested election upheld by the labor department.

The 1980s were a period of significant decline for the USWA. Foreign imports of steel, industrial restructuring, and economic recession shook up the industry and led to plant closings and employee layoffs. The union was forced to accept decreases in wages and benefits. By 1986 U.S. steel production bottomed out and over 200,000 steelworkers found themselves out of a job. The USWA, after losing 470,000 members in eight years, tried unsuccessfully to stem the loss of membership by organizing in other industries, bringing in a range of workers from shipyard employees to butchers.

Economic Upturn Benefits Union, Industry

Improvements in the general economy and in the steel industry in the 1990s reversed the USWA's decline. Union president, Lynn Williams, who assumed office following McBride's death, was an advocate of labor-management cooperation despite the union's historically adversarial relationship with employers. He led many locals into contracts that offered workers the opportunity to participate in management decisions and to help improve productivity and competitiveness. In many of the small steel firms workers became major stockholders.

In 1994 George Becker became president in an uncontested election. He restructured the union to cut administrative costs and make it more politically effective. In 1995 the 90,000-member United Rubber Workers merged with the USWA. In this same year Becker, seeking to improve the organization's clout in politics, collective bargaining, and organizing, committed the union to another merger, this one with the United Auto Workers (UAW) and the International Association of Machinists (IAM), to be completed by the year 2000. This merger would create the largest industrial union in North America.

CURRENT POLITICAL ISSUES

The USWA supports a range of policies designed to improve the standard of living for workers. It supports social welfare policies such as Social Security, Medicare, and Medicaid and has opposed recent efforts to privatize or cut back these government programs. The union supports reforms in the health care system that would offer more affordable health care and family-friendly policies such as greater government funding for public education and childcare. It has also been a strong advocate of occupational health and safety regulations and labor-law reform.

On the international level the USWA is committed to improving the rights and living standards of workers in other countries. It has been critical of the International Monetary Fund (IMF), an international agency that makes short-term loans to countries to help address financial crises that might threaten the world economy. In particular, the USWA has accused the IMF of placing the interests of investors and corporations above those of workers. The union suggests the IMF use its money and its clout to see that labor and human rights are enforced in the countries it aids. The USWA is also critical of the IMF's economic strategies in these countries, which the union claims, lead to a flood of cheap exports onto the world market. The USWA argues that a change in IMF policies will improve the lives of foreign workers and prevent the deterioration of living standards for U.S. workers who must compete with them in the global economy. Because the USWA has been severely hurt by international economic competition, it has also been very active in opposition to unrestricted free trade with other countries.

Case Study: USWA and Free Trade

Although the USWA considered Democratic President Bill Clinton an ally on many issues, it vigorously fought his effort to push through Congress the North American Free Trade Agreement (NAFTA) negotiated by President George Bush as a way to open trade between the United States, Canada, and Mexico. Organized labor was joined by environmentalists who argued that environmental and labor standards in Mexico—including lower wages and benefits, poorer working conditions, and limited or non-enforced worker protections—would either put the United States at an economic disadvantage or force it to lower its own standards. Ultimately, the USWA feared U.S. jobs would be lost to Mexico.

NAFTA supporters argued that good-paying jobs would be created in the United States and the bill would help raise Mexico's environmental and labor standards. Many high-technology companies supported NAFTA because it would simplify their efforts to sell their superior products abroad. Other businesses hoped to take advantage of the low-cost labor pool in Mexico. After an extensive lobbying effort on the part of the Clinton administration, NAFTA was passed by both the Senate and the House of Representatives in 1994.

In 1997 President Clinton, hoping to negotiate a similar agreement with South American countries, sought to obtain "fast-track authority" from Congress that would allow him a free hand in negotiating trade agreements, just as Bush had had in negotiating NAFTA. Under fast-track authority Congress can only vote to approve or reject a trade agreement; it cannot propose amendments to improve environmental or worker standards. The USWA and other labor unions claim they do not necessarily oppose all free trade agreements, but they want the opportunity to be able to shape them through lobbying Congress. Thus organized labor opposed the fast-track bill.

Still stung by its defeat on NAFTA, the USWA geared up for the battle over fast-track and launched one of the most significant lobbying efforts in its history in coordination with other unions and the AFL-CIO. Using its "Rapid Response" program of grassroots activism, the USWA turned out over 160,000 handwritten letters and thousands of phone calls from its members to Congress and the White House. The union also used rank-and-file members participating in its internship program to lobby congressional representatives on Capitol Hill. In the last days before the scheduled vote, USWA President Becker made back-to-back appointments with elected officials to plead his case. Over 600 steelworkers came to Washington to reinforce the lobbying effort.

To diffuse the opposition to fast-track in the final days of the struggle, President Clinton offered $750 million for training and assistance to workers displaced by economic competition. This proposal was termed by Becker as "too little, too late." Ultimately the Clinton administration withdrew the fast-track bill, convinced there were not enough votes to pass it. Many political analysts saw this as an unqualified victory for organized labor and a sign of the resurgence of unions as a political force.

In July of 1998 the USWA returned to the issue of NAFTA. Joining the Made-in-the-USA Foundation, an organization formed to encourage the consumption of U.S.-manufactured goods, the USWA filed a federal lawsuit challenging NAFTA's constitutionality. The two organizations argue that NAFTA was a treaty rather than an ordinary piece of legislation and therefore, according to the Constitution, it must be ratified by a two-thirds vote in the Senate rather than a simple majority. The USWA announced the lawsuit in a press conference where workers who had lost their jobs told emotional stories about the pain and dislocation caused by NAFTA. President Becker used the conference to highlight arguments against unrestricted free trade. He observed that even companies that decide to keep their production in the United States will often use the threat of moving to Mexico to scare their workers away from joining unions or asking for wage or benefit increases.

Public Impact

The economic effects of free trade are hotly debated. Opponents argue that free-trade agreements, without significant protections for workers' rights, ultimately reduce workers' bargaining power by throwing them into competition with each other. The short-term effect is the displacement of workers whose jobs were protected by tariffs or other government regulations before the agreement. The long-term effect is a lessening of the standard of living for workers in all countries involved. But proponents argue that free trade will create better jobs for workers in poor countries and will improve domestic workers' living standards by reducing prices and expanding demand for quality products.

FUTURE DIRECTIONS

Into the twenty-first century, the union will focus on the details of the proposed merger with the UAW and the IAM to be completed by 2000. The three unions will face the difficulty of merging different organizational cultures, constitutions, and officers. A conference of representatives of the three unions was held in February of 1999 in the hopes of addressing and resolving some of these difficulties. Future conferences were planned to be held as the date of unification approached.

GROUP RESOURCES

The USWA's Web site at http://www.uswa.org includes a brief history and time line, press releases and organizational news, backgrounds of the officers, and information from the various departments. For more information about the USWA, write the United Steelworkers of America, 5 Gateway Center, Pittsburgh, PA 15222, or call (412) 562-2400.

GROUP PUBLICATIONS

Steelabor, distributed to all members, is published six times a year. The USWA also distributes its "Message from Pittsburgh," a fax newsletter broadcast periodically by President George Becker's office to keep local leaders up to date. "BattleCry," another fax newsletter, is distributed to Rapid Response Program participants. Recent versions of both newsletters are available on the USWA's Web site. Information about USWA's

publications may also be obtained by writing the United Steelworkers of America.

BIBLIOGRAPHY

Baker, Stephen. "The Yelping over Labor's New Tactics." *Business Week*, 23 October 1995.

Bernstein, Aaron. "Working Capital: Labor's New Weapon?" *Business Week*, 29 September 1997.

———. "Rubber Workers with Nerves of Steel." *Business Week*, 18 December 1995.

Kelly, Nancy E. "The USWA Takes Aim at Republican Incumbents." *New Steel*, September 1996.

———. "USW Pushes for Fast-Track Defeat." *American Metal Market*, 7 November 1997.

Livingston, Sandra. "USW President Vows to Fight Trade Policies." *Plain Dealer*, October 1997.

McDermott, Michael. "Unions and Management: The Old Labels Don't Stick Anymore." *Journal of Business Strategy*, November/December 1994.

Robertson, Scott. "USW Pleads Case on Local TV." *American Metal Market*, 16 May 1997.

———. "USW Sets New Contract Goals." *American Metal Market*, 18 June 1998.

"Russo, Becker Testify about Korean Bailout." *New Steel*, March 1998.

"USW Unleashes People Power on Capitol Hill." *American Metal Market*, 8 January 1998.

United Transportation Union (UTU)

WHAT IS ITS MISSION?

Affiliated with the American Federation of Labor-Congress of Industrial Organizations (AFL-CIO), the United Transportation Union (UTU) represents approximately 140,000 active and retired railroad, bus, and mass transit workers throughout the United States and Canada. Considered one of the most powerful transportation labor unions in North America, the UTU "sets the pace in national and state legislative activity, collective bargaining, and in efforts to improve safety and working conditions on the railroads and in the bus and transit industries," according to the union's Web site.

The U.S. transportation industry boasts a long history of labor organizing as a means of improving working conditions and the UTU continues in this direction today. Providing a voice for transportation employees, the union often engages in face-to-face battles with industry representatives. Through the use of such strategies as well-timed strikes, collective bargaining, or pressure against key decision-makers, the UTU works to ensure that fair pay, workplace safety, and other conditions of employment are maintained for the benefit of its members.

ESTABLISHED: January 1, 1969
EMPLOYEES: 115
MEMBERS: 130,000 (U.S.); 10,000 (Canada)
PAC: Transportation Political Education League

Contact Information:

ADDRESS: 14600 Detroit Ave.
    Cleveland, OH 44107-4250
PHONE: (216) 228-9400
TOLL FREE: (800) 964-9464
FAX: (216) 228-5755
E-MAIL: utu@compuserve.com
URL: http://www.utu.org
INTERNATIONAL PRESIDENT: Charles Little

HOW IS IT STRUCTURED?

The UTU is headquartered in Cleveland, Ohio, with additional offices in Washington, D.C., and Ottawa, Canada. Overseeing the organization is a board including a president, assistant president, secretary/treasurer, national legislative directors representing both the United

States and Canada, and alternate legislative directors. Immediately beneath the board are 13 geographically representative vice-president positions. Two hundred general committees support the vice presidents, and under each committee are a number of related locals. For example, one committee might preside over all the local organizations of UTU members employed by Conrail.

UTU members participate in the organization through over 700 North American locals. Members are employed in the railroad, mass transit, or busing industries, with most from the rail and mass transit industries. Each local elects a delegate who attends a Union Convention held every four years. Members pay dues of $13.50 per month and a one-time membership fee of $50.00. Locals meet at least once monthly and are headed by 11 elected officers. Each local includes a legislative representative who meets regularly with UTU state or district legislative boards. Collectively, these legislative representatives comprise the UTU's Association of State Legislative Directors, which meets approximately every four years to plan legislative strategy and endorse political campaigns. Locals requiring assistance within the organization first report to their overseeing committee; the committee calls on the overseeing vice president if needed.

UTU International headquarters contains several departments, including the Legal Department which handles grievances and collective bargaining and also represents the Union in court or other legal situations; the Legislative Department which pursues legislative action and coordinates the efforts of state legislative directors; Membership Services, which coordinates member benefits; a research department that compiles information of interest to members; and departments that represent the specific interests of bus workers and rail yardmasters.

PRIMARY FUNCTIONS

The UTU's primary function is to advocate for its members in the rail, bus, and transit industries. As with all labor unions, one of the UTU's primary jobs is to represent its members in negotiations for jobs, wages, and benefits. Through collective bargaining the UTU attempts to secure higher wages and better working conditions for its members than they could have secured bargaining independently. At times negotiations are unsuccessful, in which case the UTU may call and organize a strike. Often even the threat of a strike is enough to force management to compromise. For example, in 1996 members of several unions, including the UTU, were able to avert a rail strike that would have shut down the nation's rail freight system. By some accounts, such a shutdown had the potential to cost U.S. freight rail users about $1 billion per day.

The UTU seeks to better the working conditions of its members through other means as well. For example,

the union pursues legislative activity at the state and national level. It monitors relevant legislation and informs members when their input is needed. The UTU also lobbies for or against specific policies that affect transportation workers. In 1996, for example, the union urged the House Transportation Committee to pressure the rail industry to install devices on trains that would prevent them from running away. A UTU official testified at congressional hearings that end-of-train devices designed for this purpose, and which have been required in Canada since 1987, would cost about $7,000 and that "most railroads could afford to install two-way end-of-train devices for about the cost of a CEO's salary."

In another example of union influence, this time in the non-legislative arena, in response to concerns over the 1997 Conrail Rail Company merger with CSX and Norfolk Southern, the UTU and other major unions joined under the umbrella of the AFL-CIO to approach the U.S. Surface Transportation Board. The unions cited safety concerns and threats to employee benefits.

In addition to policy and collective bargaining functions, the UTU handles member grievances at the local level. UTU's legal staff assists with grievances filed against management, and, in some cases, spearheads legal action involving the organization. The UTU also provides programs for members, among them substance abuse information and support services, and benefits such as insurance and retirement programs.

PROGRAMS

In addition to its collective bargaining and legislative work, the UTU operates a number of programs designed to improve the lives of transportation workers. For example, the UTU Insurance Association provides life, health, and annuity insurance options to UTU members. Additionally, the association sponsors a Volunteer of the Year award, and scholarship programs for members or their families. Another UTU scholarship program, Aid for Daughters of Railroaders, provides educational funds to eligible daughters of deceased railroad employees.

Operation Redblock is the UTU's drug- and alcohol-awareness and prevention program. The program provides support and information through union locals, insurance for treatment program expenses, and in some cases, can enlist the support of management.

The UTU Retiree Program serves retired members who, for reduced dues, can receive benefits including travel services and prescription discounts. And UTU's Income Security Program provides insurance to members who are unable to work for a short period of time, due to suspension or dismissal by management. Participants pay into the program and collect when unable to work.

BUDGET INFORMATION

Not made available.

HISTORY

Up until 1969 transportation workers were represented by various groups including the Brotherhood of Railroad Trainmen, the Brotherhood of Locomotive Firemen, the Switchmen's Union of North America, and the Order of Railway Conductors of America. The presidents of these four unions expressed an interest in merging as one representative union and began working toward that objective in 1968. The United Transportation Union was founded on January 1, 1969, and emerged with a combined membership of 200,000.

Each of the founding organizations had a history of advocating for better working conditions for members and protesting abuses such as long work hours and low pay, and some had existed for nearly a century prior to the conception of the UTU. Additional representative groups joined the UTU in subsequent years. The International Association of Railroad Employees, a group that advocated for African American rail workers, became part of the UTU in 1970. The Railroad Yardmasters of America, a group organized in 1918 to fight employer abuse, became affiliated with the UTU in 1985.

One of the more colorful union bosses at the UTU was Harold Pryor, who first became active in the 1940s under the Brotherhood of Railroad Trainmen. Between the mid-1950s and the 1970s Pryor organized several short but effective strikes of Long Island Rail Road (LIRR) workers. These strikes flummoxed commuters and made getting to work difficult—one strike was even called Christmas Eve as employees attempted to make it home for the holidays. Yet another was the first of its kind in winning a five-day workweek for LIRR employees when six to seven days was common for rail workers.

Rail labor issues in existence prior to the emergence of the UTU continued to affect members well into the 1970s and 1980s. For example, in 1973, after nearly 40 years of arguments with the industry, the UTU agreed to phase out the fireman job on diesel freight locomotives. Firemen on trains are responsible for servicing and maintaining the engine (as opposed to running it). This was a controversial topic because many families had come to rely on support from the now-defunct position of fireman.

Another long-running controversy surrounded "crew/consist" agreements, which determine how many employees are required to staff a train. The railroad industry claimed that crew/consist agreements in effect forced them to overstaff their trains; the UTU disagreed and refused to modify the agreements. The conflict came to a head in the early 1980s when cabooses were removed from most trains. This cut forced the two positions that

FAST FACTS

In Denver, commuters annually spend the equivalent of an entire workweek—40 hours—stuck in traffic jams.

(Source: Jillian Lloyd. "Selling Public Transportation to the American West." *Christian Science Monitor*, May 4, 1998.)

had previously occupied the caboose to share space in the front of the train, sometimes leading to conflict. In 1991 the federal government forced the UTU to accept new, much lower, crew/consist agreements. The resulting loss of jobs hit the union hard.

The deregulation of the railroads with the Staggers Rail Act of 1980 had a tremendous impact on transportation unions like the UTU. The Act changed the conditions of freight rail pricing, causing it to reflect expenses, revenue, and productivity. Not only did deregulation change routes—completely eliminating many that were deemed unprofitable—but according to a 1997 study, it removed 8,000 locomotives and 5,000 railroad cars from service, causing 300,000 rail employees to lose their jobs.

For the UTU and other transportation advocates, the formation of Amtrak—a nationwide, federally funded passenger rail system—in the early 1970s represented a major victory. Many passenger lines were forced out of business as highway and air travel became more widely available. This was an obvious concern for the union: with fewer passenger trains came fewer jobs for UTU members. The UTU, along with such groups as commuter alliances in the northeastern corridor (the line servicing Washington, D.C., and New York City) that represented heavy users of passenger trains, successfully lobbied the government to form a federally supported passenger rail system. The founding of the National Railroad Passenger Corporation (Amtrak's official name) solidified the relationship between the railroads and government.

CURRENT POLITICAL ISSUES

According to the UTU, many of the issues faced by members in the late 1990s are not much different from member concerns in the 1800s. The union continues its

The formation of Amtrak, a federally-supported passenger rail system formed in the 1970s, provided jobs for a large number of United Transportation Union members. Congress passed the Amtrak Reform and Accountability Act of 1997 to help the struggling passenger railroad and secure its future. (AP/Wide World Photos)

advocacy of safety on the job for transportation workers, a constant sticking point with management. For instance, a 1997 change in management at the Union Pacific Railroad threw train scheduling into turmoil and raised safety issues such as fatigued workers, poor training, and defective equipment. To respond to such issues the UTU puts pressure on transportation management by threatening walkouts and strikes, or encouraging members to report safety violations. However, employees are often intimidated into inaction. In 1996, shortly after a rail accident that killed two of its members, the UTU took a proactive stance on future safety issues by establishing the UTU Transportation Safety Team, which investigates accidents and evaluates safety standards and procedures.

The UTU remains concerned with obtaining fair pay for its members. To advocate for better pay, the UTU enters into collective bargaining with particular transportation companies, or organizes strikes if necessary. In 1994 the UTU organized a strike of conductors and trainmen of the Long Island Rail Road; the strike lasted for three days and won the employees an 8.7 percent pay increase for their next three-year contract. A more broad-ranging response was required of the union in 1993, when an effort to dismantle Amtrak funding nearly cost the union 2,500 jobs.

Case Study: The Fight for Reauthorization of Amtrak Funding

In 1993, when congressional authorization for Amtrak was up for reinstatement, opponents of the national passenger rail subsidy attempted to stall it in its tracks. The trucking and airline industries, with which Amtrak competes, consider federal support for passenger rails to be unfair.

Realizing that the demise of Amtrak could cost the union a number of jobs, the UTU legislative office used a multipronged approach to advocate for reauthorization of funding. In addition to lobbying for funding, the union endorsed and contributed to campaigns of politicians who supported the funding. It also formed coalitions with groups that would benefit from the continuance of Amtrak service, such as state governors (who had an interest in decreasing traffic congestion), environmentalists (who were convinced of the environmental advantages of riding the train), and Amtrak passengers themselves. The union emerged successful; funding for Amtrak was reinstated for fiscal year 1994. While the UTU did not get all their concessions met, the final authorization eliminated only five percent of jobs rather than the 75 percent predicted if reauthorization had not occurred.

Public Impact

While the Amtrak reauthorization clearly benefited the UTU and saved a number of jobs, the public, according to union officials, also benefited by not losing this transportation alternative. In densely populated East Coast regions, Amtrak commuter service provides an alternative for commuters who can't or don't wish to drive to work. In more rural areas of the country, Amtrak serves areas that may be hours from the nearest airport. For other consumers, Amtrak service may provide a less costly alternative to airplane travel.

FUTURE DIRECTIONS

In the late 1990s the UTU directed its sights toward exploring and solidifying a potential merger between itself and the Brotherhood of Locomotive Engineers (BLE). According to the UTU, such a merger would eliminate duplication and waste between the two transportation unions and provide strength in unity. The BLE, however, had shown resistance to the merger, citing a proud history and identity which they were reluctant to part with. Talks between the two groups were facilitated by a former AFL-CIO president. If the merger were successful, rail employees would all be represented by one union.

GROUP RESOURCES

The UTU provides a toll-free hot line at 1-800-964-9464 for members to report Union Pacific-related workplace problems. The organization provides toll-free assistance at 1-888-452-3729 for its Job Benefit/Income Security Program. The UTU maintains an extensive Web site at http://www.utu.org that includes a recap of organization programs, lists of officers, union news, and a record of awards in arbitration that the organization achieved.

GROUP PUBLICATIONS

The *UTU Daily News Digest* is available to the public on the union's Web site at http://www.utu.org. The *UTU News,* the union's monthly publication, is mailed to members or accessed on the Web site. Other publications include a Transportation Scrapbook and teaching aids such as coloring books. Call the UTU at (216) 228-9400 for more information.

BIBLIOGRAPHY

"A Bad Rail Merger Derailed?" *St. Louis Post-Dispatch,* 28 January 1997.

"All Aboard: French Rail Workers End Strike." *St. Louis Post-Dispatch,* 16 December 1995.

Chen, Edwin. "Senate Steers $5-Billion Bonus to Mass Transit." *Los Angeles Times,* 6 March 1998.

Fulmer, Melinda. "Union Pacific Still Seeing Big Delays in Southland Traffic." *Los Angeles Times,* 13 May 1998.

Gold, Russell. "Heavy Traffic Results in Train Wreck Dispatcher's Error; also Might Have Contributed to Fatal Collision in Texas." *Rocky Mountain News,* 20 July 1997.

Gonzalez, Erika. "Business Leaders Foresee Light Rail as 'Best Solution.'" *Rocky Mountain News,* 16 September 1997.

Melchionno, Rick, and Michael Sean Steinam. "The 1996-2006 Job Outlook in Brief." *Occupational Outlook Quarterly,* 22 March 1998.

Mulenga, Mildred. "AFL-CIO Condemns Rail Industry Raid on Pensions." *U.S. Newswire,* 16 December 1996.

Sims, John. "One Family's Finances: Running out of Track." *Money,* 1 September 1990.

"Threat of Amtrak Strike Ends." *Columbian,* 3 November 1997.

Veterans of Foreign Wars of the United States (VFW)

ESTABLISHED: 1899
EMPLOYEES: 290
MEMBERS: 2,151,845
PAC: VFW Political Action Committee (VFW-PAC)

Contact Information:

ADDRESS: 406 W. 34th St.
    Kansas City, MO 64111
PHONE: (816) 756-3390
FAX: (816) 968-1149
E-MAIL: info@vfw.org
URL: http://www.vfw.org
COMMANDER-IN-CHIEF: Thomas E. Pouliot
EXECUTIVE DIRECTOR: Kenneth Steadman

WHAT IS ITS MISSION?

The Veterans of Foreign Wars (VFW) endeavors to improve the conditions of living veterans through political activism and community service, preserve the memory of servicemen and women who sacrificed their lives in combat, and promote democratic and American ideals. According to a July 1998 VFW press release, "the VFW is the nation's oldest major veterans organization. Through a network of service officers it provides assistance to veterans and their families in obtaining entitlements. Through its legislative service it works with Congress in writing and passing veterans legislation. Other programs and projects provide a wide range of services, from college scholarships to community improvement."

HOW IS IT STRUCTURED?

The VFW is a veterans' advocacy group headquartered in Kansas City, Missouri. It also maintains a legislative arm out of offices located in Washington, D.C. A commander in chief leads the Missouri home base, while an executive director manages the Washington office. VFW service officers liaison with VFW members, helping with discharge services and veteran benefits. VFW field representatives provide the regulatory oversight of health care facilities, regional offices, and national cemeteries. Membership in the organization is available to all U.S. citizens who have been honorably discharged from the U.S. armed forces and have served overseas. Over half of the VFW membership is composed of World War II veterans. The VFW is affiliated with the

Ladies Auxiliary, which is an organization composed of 767,000 female relatives of veterans eligible for membership in the VFW.

PRIMARY FUNCTIONS

Each year the VFW puts forth a set of legislative objectives which correspond to the long and short term goals of the organization. The VFW subsequently commits considerable resources toward meeting these legislative objectives. For example some of the legislative goals for 1999 included encouraging a Department of Veterans' Affairs (VA) budget which accounts for veterans' health care; revising VA eligibility; fighting for a Cost of Living Adjustment for veterans and military retirees that corresponds to the consumer price index; and securing reasonable standards for veterans preference in public and private sector jobs.

The VFW works closely with the VA and congressional veterans' affairs committees providing research for legislative proposals, offering information for fiscal year budgets, and offering testimony at congressional hearings. For example the VFW is responsible for providing budgetary proposals on construction activities for the Independent Budget, the budget under which the Department of Veterans' Affairs operates. In a 1998 report to the House Budget Committee, VFW executive director Kenneth A. Steadman recommended an increase in appropriations for major and minor construction projects such as state extended-care facilities, infrastructure improvements for outpatient and inpatient facilities, and state veterans' cemeteries.

The VFW offers a variety of benefits to its members. Some of the programs offered include insurance, banking privileges, rebates on consumer products, a Visa card, travel services, and discounts on car rentals. The organization offers an array of different insurance plans such as cancer treatment, coronary care, burial cost coverage, life insurance, auto insurance, and home and travel accident insurance. For those members who have difficulty paying their deductibles and co-payments the VFW offers supplementary plans. The insurance plans are available to VFW members and their spouses and dependents. Over two million members participate in VFW-sponsored insurance plans.

PROGRAMS

The VFW advances a variety of national programs designed to promote the ideals of the organization. The VFW's Americanism program coordinates projects designed to promote civic responsibility, patriotism, and interest in U.S. history and traditions. The VFW is actively involved in community service programs that seek to improve education, the environment, health services, and overall community enhancement. Through its "Voice of Democracy" program, which is a national audio essay competition, the VFW promotes education by offering $2.7 million in college scholarships. The VFW also offer youth programs in conjunction with the Boy Scouts of America, the National Rifle Association, Reserve Officer Training Corps and safety programs which teach safety in the home, bicycle riding, and substance abuse awareness.

Possibly the most recognized of the VFW's community outreach programs is the "Buddy Poppy" program, which was established in 1922. Paper poppies are assembled by veterans in VA hospitals and are distributed in local communities to raise funds for disabled and needy veterans. Since its inception, the program has generated millions of dollars. In 1998 the VFW expanded the program by introducing Buddy Poppy Puppy, a white plush toy dog covered in red poppies. Sale of the the puppy is geared toward educating children about the role veterans have played in U.S. history.

The community service programs provided by the VFW extend beyond aid to veterans and their families. In 1997-98, through its Disaster Relief Fund, the VFW provided 12.6 million hours of service and donated $55 million to communities across the United States.

BUDGET INFORMATION

Not made available.

HISTORY

The origin of the VFW dates back to the Spanish-American War of 1898. Many injured servicemen returned from the war incapable of independently pursuing fulfilling lives. These veterans recognized the need to form an organization that would fight for the specific needs of veterans, and would include pension and health care benefits as well as employment assistance. The precursor to the VFW was founded in Columbus, Ohio in September 1899. The organization was called the American Veterans of Foreign Service. Other groups with similar objectives formed in Pennsylvania and Colorado. In 1913 these disparate groups decided to form a national organization and soon after decided on the name, the Veterans of Foreign Wars of the United States. The Ladies Auxiliary to the VFW was founded shortly thereafter.

During World War I (1914-18), many of the VFW members participated in the war effort; they volunteered to serve and to recruit men. Also during this time the VFW recognized that veterans of this war would be in the same predicament as members from twenty years before. It worked to get concessions from the federal gov-

FAST FACTS

Only one out of six veterans that are eligible currently belong to the VFW.

(Source: Lisa Brownlee. "VFW Fights for Respect With AD Blitz." *Wall Street Journal*, July 25, 1997.)

ernment in the form of job training for returning soldiers and benefits for their families. Membership in the VFW boomed following World War I and the VFW reorganized and built new headquarters in Kansas City, Missouri in 1930.

The Great Depression deeply affected American veterans and the VFW scrambled to aid its members. The redemption of bond certificates, given to veterans after World War I, was one of its major concerns. After a long legislative struggle by the VFW, veterans were able to borrow against those bond certificates in 1936, helping to ease some of the financial strain they were experiencing. VFW members also participated in community service activities that helped to keep the poor clothed and fed.

Despite the fact that the VFW argued for an isolationist approach to the events occurring in Europe and Asia during the late 1930s and early 1940s, when the United States did enter the World War II (1939-45) the organization was in firm support of its efforts. Members again volunteered for service. The VFW also lobbied for improved benefits for those serving overseas in the form of life insurance and the G.I. Bill of Rights. This bill allowed funds for education after the war, job training, and unemployment compensation.

The coming decades would be fraught with worry over the advance of communism. This was especially true as the United States became involved in two wars, the Korean War (1950-53) and the Vietnam War (1959-75) in which there was no clear victor and there was waning public support for U.S. action. In the face of this, the VFW wanted to make efforts to renew patriotism among the American people; to this end the organization established May 1 as Loyalty Day. The VFW also stood against those who chose to ignore draft call-ups as the organization felt that these "draft dodgers" were not performing their civic duty. Much to the VFW's dismay, in 1974 President Gerald Ford allowed draft dodgers to return from Canada.

In 1978, the VFW made an organizational decision that would forever change its make-up. Recognizing that

women were a vital part of every war effort, the VFW allowed women to join the organization after a vote during its annual convention.

The 1980s were marked by extreme budget cuts for many parts of the federal administration as President Ronald Reagan sought to reduce government spending. One of the main targets of this effort was the Veterans' Administration. Through stringent lobbying, the VFW was able to maintain most of the VA's funding, as well as to obtain the funds necessary for the creation of a Korean War memorial in 1987. Then, in 1989, the VFW achieved a great success with the upgrading of the VA to a cabinet-level department under President George Bush.

The 1990s began with a major disappointment for the VFW. By a 5 to 4 decision, the Supreme Court decided in 1990 that it was unconstitutional to disallow the desecration of the U.S. flag. Such a right, the court claimed, was protected under the First Amendment that guaranteed freedom of expression. The VFW was outraged and fought throughout the decade to have this decision reversed. After the Persian Gulf War (1991), the VFW's ranks were once again swelled by the return of veterans from the Middle East. The organization sought funding to address the particular needs of this group, some of whom suffered from a mysterious illness that may have been caused by their exposure to conditions in Kuwait and Iraq.

As the 1990s drew to a close, the VFW celebrated the passage of HR2400 in October of 1998; the bill included a provision to enhance the GI Bill Education rate and increase education benefits for the dependents of disabled or deceased veterans. The Veterans Benefits Improvement Act of 1998 also allowed for an increase in adaptive housing grants and automobile allowances. "These programs allow those [disabled] veterans to purchase homes adapted to their needs and to meet the rising cost of automobiles" said Bob Stump (R-Ariz.), chairman of the House Veterans Affairs Committee.

CURRENT POLITICAL ISSUES

One of the chief political initiatives of the VFW is making sure the U.S. government provides for those who have risked their lives in a foreign war or conflict. The VFW tracks legislation, lobbies for programs designed to benefit veterans, and cooperates with the Veterans' Affairs Department to meet the political goals of the organization.

For example, in recent years the VFW has co-authored the budget for the Department of Veterans' Affairs. The Department of Veterans' Affairs, established in 1989, is an executive Cabinet department that develops and implements federal programs for veterans. It is the second largest of the 14 Cabinet departments. In a 1998 report to the House of Representative's budget committee Kenneth A. Steadman, Executive Director of the VFW, argued for an increase in the Department of Veterans' Affairs' $17 billion health care appropriation. Mr. Steadman also argued for an increase in funds for cemeteries and appropriations for a Tampa, Florida, Spinal Cord Injury Center.

The VFW also puts forth efforts to locate the whereabouts and, if possible, recover the remains, of soldiers considered missing in action. According to VA reports, there are 2,050 soldiers missing in action in Southeast Asia, 8,100 missing from Korea, and 78,000 missing from WWII. One of highest priorities of the VFW is to account for missing soldiers and provide a respectful burial in honor of their tremendous sacrifice. The VFW encourages U.S. dignitaries to work with representatives from foreign nations that were once hostile to facilitate the recovery of MIAs.

Case Study: The VFW and the Search for POW/MIAs

In October of 1997 the United States reached a groundbreaking agreement with North Korea to cooperate in recovering the remains of U.S. solders who had died during the Korean War. One year later, VFW Executive Director Steadman accompanied members of four other veterans groups on a trip to North Korea to observe U.S.-North Korean efforts to recover the remains. The trip lasted four days during which two sets of remains were discovered at an excavation site. During a ceremony attended by Jane Bingham, National President of the Ladies Auxiliary, the remains were turned over to the United Nations command at Panmunjom on November 6. The remains are being examined for identification purposes at the U.S. Army's Central Identification Laboratory.

Since the joint operation began, 27 sets of remains have been recovered, all of whom are believed to be U.S. soldiers. Although the VFW is encouraged by the results, the organization is somewhat frustrated that more remains have not been discovered. According to Steadman, the VFW has tried to persuade North Korean authorities to search in areas that are more likely to contain a higher concentration of remains, such as former POW camps, however, North Korea has yet to comply. The VFW has made progress, however, in its efforts to continue and intensify the search. At the end of the 1997 search operation the North Koreans agreed to three searches in 1998. In large part due to the persistence of the VFW and other groups such as the American Legion, the Korean War Veterans Association, and the American Veterans Committee, the North Koreans were persuaded to increase the number of searches to five.

But the VFW and other interested parties may have intentions beyond the recovery of fallen soldiers' remains. Stirring beneath the tenuous diplomatic relations between the two countries lies disturbing reports that American POWs are still alive in North Korea. In 1979 a North Korean tour bus took a wrong turn and,

according to the driver, stumbled upon a farm in which ten Caucasian men were observed working in the fields. Several subsequent sightings have fueled speculation that U.S. POWs are still alive and being retained in North Korea against their will. A series of "live sightings" in 1996 led a Pentagon official to write in an internal memo that 10 to 15 Americans may still be alive in North Korea. North Korean officials deny there is any legitimacy to the reports.

An even more disturbing report came in 1996 when General Jan Sejina, a Czech defector, offered testimony at congressional hearings on the subject of POWs. Sejina contended that American POWs were used in medical experiments headed by Soviet military intelligence. Sejina testified that some POWs were used to practice amputation methods. Although the CIA and the Pentagon question the truthfulness of the testimony, Lt. Gen. James R. Clapper, Jr., former director of the Defense Intelligence Agency, reported not only that Sejina was a reliable source of information, but that no evidence of deception appeared on a polygraph test to which Sejina was subjected. The VFW continues to monitor all reports of POW/MIAs in the hopes that if any are still alive it will be able facilitate their safe return to the United States.

FUTURE DIRECTIONS

The VFW celebrated the 100th anniversary of its founding in 1999. On the legislative front the VFW plans to continue to secure sufficient funds for veterans programs provided by the Department of Veterans' Affairs. The VFW intends to push for a provision that will allow the VA to collect and retain Medicare payments for non-service-related health care services provided to veterans who qualify for Medicare. The VFW also plans to push for legislation that will provide Gulf War veterans compensation and health care for illnesses related to their service in the Middle East. Preserving and strengthening veterans' preference for public sector hiring practices will also top the initiatives list for the VFW in the coming years.

GROUP RESOURCES

The VFW provides an extensive Web site at http://www.vfw.org that contains up-to-date information about the organization. For more information about the VFW, write to the Veterans of Foreign Wars of the United States, 406 W. 34th St., Kansas City, Mo. 64111, call (816) 756-3390, or E-mail info@vfw.org.

GROUP PUBLICATIONS

The VFW has two major publications, the *VFW Magazine* and *Checkpoint*. *VFW Magazine* is a monthly magazine available to VFW members. Its circulation is over 2,000,000 and it is the 29th largest magazine in the United States. Recent issues of *VFW Magazine* can be viewed on-line at http://www.vfw.org/magazine/index.shtml. Information about subscriptions can be obtained by writing to the Veterans of Foreign Wars of the United States, 406 W. 34th St., Kansas City, Mo. 64111 or by calling (816) 756-3390. *Checkpoint* is published six times per year and is designed to provide information to VFW departments and posts that will allow members to improve job performance. It also provides information about the organization's activities.

BIBLIOGRAPHY

Bottoms, Bill. *The VFW: An Illustrated History of the Veterans of Foreign Wars of the United States*. Rockville, Md.: Woodbine House, 1991.

Brownlee, Lisa. "VFW Fights for Respect With AD Blitz." *Wall Street Journal*, 25 July 1997.

Dyhouse, Tim. "Progress Made on MIA Issue in North Korea." *Veterans of Foreign Wars Magazine*, 1 December 1998.

Dyhouse, Tim. "Veterans Benefits Expanded." *Veterans of Foreign Wars Magazine*, 1 November 1998.

Faces of Victory. Kansas City, Mo.: Addax Publishing Group, 1995.

Gardner, Jonathan. "Groups Seek End to VA Under-funding." *Modern Healthcare*, 11 January 1999.

Gugliotta, Guy. "Merchant Mariners Are Still Fighting for Inclusion." *Washington Post*, 26 March 1996.

Moon, John E. "Stiffing the Veterans to Pay for More Pork." *Wall Street Journal*, 9 June 1998.

Reza, H. G. "Vietnam Veterans are Considered Key to Increasing the Members, but Few Want to Join." *Los Angeles Times* 11 November 1998.

Steadman, Kenneth. Statement before the Budget Committee with Respect to the Independent Budget. 12 February 1998.

The Wilderness Society (TWS)

WHAT IS ITS MISSION?

According to the Web site of The Wilderness Society (TWS), its mission is "to protect America's wilderness and to develop a nation-wide network of wild lands through public education, scientific analysis and advocacy. Our goal is to ensure that future generations will enjoy the clean air and water, wildlife, beauty and opportunities for recreation and renewal that pristine forests, rivers, deserts and mountains provide."

HOW IS IT STRUCTURED?

TWS is led by a president who directs the organization's day-to-day operations. A board of directors led by a chairman helps to formulate policy and decide the organization's direction. TWS's national headquarters is in Washington, D.C., out of which most of its federal legislative lobbying efforts takes place. Its eight field offices are located in the following U.S. regions: Northeast, Southeast, California/Nevada, Alaska, Pacific Northwest, Northern Rockies, Four Corners, and Idaho.

TWS employees a staff of experts to provide the organization with research capabilities. For example, a staff under the Center for Landscape Analysis analyzes environmental data from satellites, aircraft observations, and computer-generated geographic data. TWS also relies heavily on its staff to give the organization the information it needs to plan its agenda.

Members contribute at least $30 annually to TWS for which they receive various membership benefits.

ESTABLISHED: 1935
EMPLOYEES: 98
MEMBERS: 270,000
PAC: None

Contact Information:
ADDRESS: 900 17th St. NW
    Washington, DC 20006-2596
PHONE: (202) 833-2300
FAX: (202) 429-3958
URL: http://www.tws.org
PRESIDENT: Bill Meadows
CHAIRMAN: Christopher J. Elliman

Members come from a wide range of backgrounds but are united behind their belief in TWS objectives.

PRIMARY FUNCTIONS

TWS works to accomplish its goals through two primary means: education and advocacy. TWS seeks to educate the U.S. public and the media about the importance of preserving the environment and the undeveloped areas of the country. It does so through a number of different programs as well as research and publications. Through its Center for Landscape Analysis, the TWS amasses data on logging, wildlife, and mineral resources and passes this information on to the public and media. TWS also publishes reports on such issues as how human advancement into undeveloped lands negatively affects the ecosystem.

TWS's primary means of activism in the area of wilderness preservation is through the grassroots actions of its members. It organizes its efforts through eight field offices, directing member energy into local concerns. The organization also presents its research and reports to Congress, supporting legislation that furthers its goals. Members are also encouraged to write letters to Congress.

PROGRAMS

TWS runs a variety of programs, most centering around the dissemination of information to the public. One of its most important is the Wild Alert! program. TWS invites interested individuals to sign up to receive a weekly E-mail that gives the most up-to date information in the organization's preservation efforts. These notices describe the situation in an endangered area and gives suggestions as to what action may be taken to prevent damage from being done.

In an effort to bring the knowledge of important preservation issues to as many people as possible, TWS has created the Kids Corner portion of its Web site. It contains several links that TWS hopes will both entertain and educate children. Kids Corner allows visitors to send an electronic postcard with a wilderness theme, print out a picture of an animal to color, or send in a personal story about the importance of the environment.

Finally, TWS offers an on-line store at http://www.tws.org/getinvolved/wildgifts. The organization welcomes the purchase of its t-shirts, hats, mugs, cards, and posters as asssistance in funding its preservation efforts.

BUDGET INFORMATION

TWS collects its revenue chiefly through member dues, but also via non-member subscriptions to *Wilder-ness* and various fund-raising efforts at all levels. Grants from over 100 foundations amounted to nearly 20 percent of TWS's total revenue for fiscal year 1994 (at just over $2 million). Total functioning expenses in 1994 reached nearly $11 million, with a reported surplus of nearly $1 million for the fiscal year. The breakdown of TWS expenditures for 1994 were as follows: program services, 74 percent; management salaries, rent and maintenance of offices, 11 percent; fund-raising, 10 percent; membership recruitment, 5 percent.

HISTORY

In 1934 four men, Benton Mac Kaye, Bernard Frank, Robert Marshall, and Harry Broome, who had been attending the annual convention of the American Forestry Association, took a drive to inspect a Civilian Conservation Corps work site. In the car, Marshall described his idea for a new conservation group that would be dedicated to preserving wilderness areas. The discussion became so intense that the men pulled off the road, got out, and spent the rest of the day hammering out the details of how to launch such an organization. Four more men, Harold Anderson, Aldo Leopold, Ernest Oberholtzer, and Robert Yard, were invited to join the founders to give the organization national scope. In January 1935, the eight men met in Washington, D.C., to adopt a platform and give the new organization a name, the Wilderness Society.

Robert Yard opened up an office in his home and for the next two years, the society operated through an executive committee of Yard, Marshall, and Anderson, the three members who lived in Washington. The founders agreed that the membership should be small and carefully limited to people who agreed with the society's principles. The primary concern of the society was reducing the number one threat to preserving the wilderness, the internal combustion engine in all its forms: airplanes, boats, and especially automobiles.

In 1937 Marshall proposed that the society incorporate and establish a new Governing Council and charge members $1 in annual dues. These recommendations were adopted to expand the group, broaden its sources of income, and increase its credibility with Congress. In 1939, Marshall died suddenly and while his death cost the society his invaluable leadership, Marshall ensured the society's survival by leaving a trust fund to provide annual income to TWS.

Robert Yard did most of the work of the society in the early years. He solicited and kept in contact with members, kept up correspondence with other conservation groups, and edited and supervised the production of the society's magazine, *The Living Wilderness*. When Yard passed away in 1945, his duties were assumed by two new staff members. Olaus Murie served as director, and later president of the society, and Howard Zahniser served as executive secretary, edited *The Living Wilderness*, monitored Congress, and tended to administrative matters. Together the two men guided the society for the next 20 years.

Cooperation and Success

Although the society had a well-defined purpose, Zahniser and Murie realized the benefits of cooperating with other conservation groups. In the late 1940s, the society successfully joined forces with the Sierra Club to save the San Gorgonio Primitive Area in southern California from development as a ski resort. The two groups also joined together to guarantee protection for Minnesota's Quetico-Superior Wilderness.

The major conservation battle of the 1950s was the fight against the Bureau of Reclamation's attempt to build a dam at Echo Park on the Colorado River in Dinosaur National Monument on the Utah-Colorado border. From 1950 to 1955, TWS led the efforts of an unprecedented coalition of national conservation groups to prevent the dam from being built and negatively impacting wilderness areas. Zahniser worked out a compromise, approved by Congress, that stipulated that any Colorado River projects could not violate any national park or monument.

Crowning Achievement

Flush with the Echo Park success, Zahniser felt the time had come for legislation that would give wilderness areas permanent legal protection. Rather than fight repetitive issues on a case-by-case basis, Zahniser drafted a bill in 1955 that called for the permanent protection of 163 wilderness areas covering over 50 million acres. No commercial intrusions, including mining and hydropower, would be allowed. The Wilderness Bill immediately drew strong opposition from timber, oil, mining, and grazing interests. These groups feared the bill would reduce their earning power and limit free enterprise.

For eight years, Zahniser tracked his bill though 18 hearings and 64 redraftings. TWS and other conservation groups worked tirelessly to convince the public and legislators of the necessity of protecting wilderness areas. Finally, the Wilderness Bill became law in the summer of 1964. The final bill guaranteed all established mining claims, permitted gas and oil leasing until 1983, and covered nine million acres as opposed to the proposed 50 million acres. Yet, despite these compromises, the Wilderness Act was the society's crowning achievement, guaranteeing protection for wilderness areas throughout the United States.

Years of Transition

When Murie and Zahniser passed away in the mid-1960s, TWS underwent a decade of administrative change. Although the society's membership and income

Because spotted owls reside only in old-growth forests, the Wilderness Society has sought to employ their declining numbers as a rallying point for lobbying federal and state legislators to suspend clear-cut logging of the forests. (Photograph by John & Karen Hollingsworth, U.S. Fish & Wildlife Service)

increased and it continued to work on issues such as implementing the Wilderness Act, federal land policy, and Alaskan wilderness preservation, the organization faced internal problems. An unsuccessful lawsuit against the Alaskan oil pipeline created a large budget deficit. Successive executive directors could not unify the board and the membership in determining the best long term course for the society.

When Bill Turnage took over the position of executive director in 1978, he brought professionalism to an organization in disarray. He recruited staff who were experts in their fields and brought in new financial advisers. Former Wisconsin Senator, Gaylord Nelson, also joined the society as its chairman. Nelson had compiled one of the best environmental voting records in the country and his support of the society's work and his political contacts and influence made him an invaluable asset.

Throughout the period of internal reorganization, the society refined and intensified its efforts over a broad range of concerns. These included studies of the effects of mining and oil leasing on wilderness areas, the Alaska National Interest Land Conservation Act, and the passage of the National Parkes Protection Act. The organization changed the name of its magazine to *Wilderness* and published a series of seven issues in 1981, setting forth a national conservation agenda.

Commitment to the Global Wilderness

In the 1980s and 1990s, TWS continued to work for the preservation of U.S. wilderness areas. But the society also began to play a role in growing international wilderness preservation efforts. The negative impact of rainforest destruction, mining the oceans, and Arctic exploration, led the society to endorse international efforts to preserve and protect wilderness areas all over the globe. In the twenty-first century, TWS will remain a powerful voice for preserving the few unspoiled wilderness areas that are rapidly disappearing from the planet.

CURRENT POLITICAL ISSUES

TWS advocates the conservation of wilderness lands throughout the United States. Particularly, the organization has focused on areas such as the Pacific Northwest, where the habitat of the spotted owl is being threatened by human encroachment and in Alaska, where the interests of oil companies have often taken precedent over environmental concerns.

Case Study: Old-Growth Forests

One of the issues of greatest concern for TWS is the encroachment of human activity on undeveloped land. This has especially been a concern in the few remaining old-growth forests that exist in the United States. TWS estimates that a mere five percent of old-growth forest is left across the country. The organization has worked diligently for decades to preserve these areas, primarily from logging companies interested in harvesting the valuable wood.

The threat from these logging companies increased greatly in the mid to late 1990s as they sought entrance from the U.S. Forest Service into virgin forests. The Forest Service has often been criticized by environmental groups as catering to the interests of the logging industry. TWS has unsuccessfully lobbied for tighter controls on the amount of forested land that the agency is able to designate for logging. However, a seeming victory was achieved in January of 1998 when Mike Dombeck, chief of the Forest Service, proposed an 18-month moratorium on the building of new roads into old-growth forests. A restriction on roads meant that logging companies would have difficulty reaching their targeted areas.

Despite this concession, TWS claimed that the measure was not enough of an impediment to determined logging companies. It stated that a number of easily exploited loopholes existed in the moratorium that essentially made it useless. The moratorium did not apply the road-building restrictions on almost 30 percent of the National Forests that contain old-growth trees and did not include any plans to study a permanent ban on road-building in these forests. Most importantly, it did not prevent logging companies from using roads adjacent to areas in which they were interested in logging.

Realizing that the Forest Service's actions were not effective enough, but that the timing might be right for policy reform, TWS joined with 26 other organizations in the release of *America's Forest Heritage at Risk*, a report detailing major timber sales that are planned to take place in 15 states as well as 24 areas that might be affected by the loopholes in the Forest Service's moratorium. While the Forest Service has not reversed its policies regarding the sale of old-growth trees to logging companies, the report may have had some effect. TWS was pleased to announce in December of 1998 that 300,000 acres of virgin forests in Maine, New Hampshire, Vermont, and New York had been preserved by the Northern Forest Alliance, which marks the largest interstate preservation purchase ever.

FUTURE DIRECTIONS

TWS has been advocating for preservation of the Arctic Circle habitat for decades; proposed legislation may succeed in accomplishing at least part of the organization's goals. The Morris K. Udall Wilderness Act of 1997, introduced to the House of Representatives in early 1999, would designate crucial avian nesting grounds as wilderness and protect them from development by oil rigs and drills. TWS plans to research the ramifications of the act, lobby Congress, and educate the public about the benefits of the act in its support of the act's passage.

GROUP RESOURCES

TWS maintains a Web site at http://www.tws.org, which gives basic information about the group, its activities, and its publications. For more information about the organization, write to The Wilderness Society, 900 17th St. NW, Washington, DC 20006, or call (202) 833-2300.

GROUP PUBLICATIONS

Publications available from TWS include *Wilderness*, a semiannual magazine featuring articles on wilderness issues and wildlife topics. In addition, the organization publishes a variety of reports, brochures, fact sheets, and alerts on conservation issues. Some of TWS's publications, including *Wilderness* magazine, are accessible via the World Wide Web at http://www.tws.org. For more information about the organization's publications, write to The Wilderness Society, 900 17th St. NW, Washington, DC 20006 or call (202) 833-2300.

BIBLIOGRAPHY

Byrnes, Patricia. "Rx for ESA." *Wilderness,* Winter 1995.

Crow, Patrick. "Sideshows on ANWR." *Oil and Gas Journal,* 25 September 1995.

"If a Tree Falls in the Wilderness." *Environmental Action,* Summer 1995.

Kriz, Margaret. "A Hands-On Conservationist Takes Charge." *National Journal,* 15 January 1994.

Line, Les. "A System Under Siege." *Wilderness,* fall 1995.

Watkins, T. H. "Doubling the Load." *Wilderness,* spring 1994.

Wilderness Society. *Wilderness Act Handbook.* Washington, D.C.: Wilderness Society, 1994.

The WISH List

ESTABLISHED: 1992
EMPLOYEES: 4
MEMBERS: 3,000
PAC: The WISH List

Contact Information:

ADDRESS: 3205 North St. NW
         Washington, DC 20007
PHONE: (202) 342-9111
FAX: (202) 342-9190
TOLL FREE: (800) 756-9474
URL: http://www.thewishlist.org
PRESIDENT: Patricia Goldman
EXECUTIVE DIRECTOR: Karen Raye

WHAT IS ITS MISSION?

According to the organization's Web site, The Women in the Senate and House (WISH) List "is a nationwide political donor network created to raise significant money for qualified Republican pro-choice women candidates. Our goal is to help more women take their rightful place as America's leaders." The structure and philosophy of The WISH List is modeled after the older political action committee (PAC) EMILY's List. An acronym for Early Money Is Like Yeast (it makes the dough rise), EMILY's List provides campaign aid to pro-choice Democratic women.

HOW IS IT STRUCTURED?

The WISH List is a PAC that supports Republican candidates, however due to its pro-choice mission it operates only as a satellite of the Republican Party. Because it is a new, small PAC, or perhaps it is a literal reflection of the Republican philosophy that less bureaucracy is better bureaucracy, The WISH List is a lean organization, with little administration and virtually no staff. It has two primary executives—a president and an executive director who are appointed by the organization's board of directors, a group of officers made up of donors, founders, and volunteers. The president and executive director recruit, select, and train WISH List candidates and are responsible for all facets of the PAC from political direction to day-to-day management. A small staff of assistants provides administrative support.

WISH List Membership

The 3,000 national "members" are donors to The WISH List and remain relatively silent partners in the organization. To become a regular member of The WISH List, a contributor must donate $100 annually to the organization and $100 to two WISH List candidates during a two-year election cycle. Corporations and organizations contributing a minimum of $500 annually to The WISH List are entitled to the same privileges as regular members.

A member of "Team 1000" presents The WISH List with a yearly gift of $1,000. The funds raised by "Team 1000" are dedicated specifically to recruiting and training WISH List candidates. Members at this level enjoy all benefits of membership including invitations to briefings, events, and receptions at the Republican National Convention. WISH List "Benefactors" receive all member benefits in exchange for an annual gift of $5,000. They are also provided with tickets to WISH List events across the country.

PRIMARY FUNCTIONS

The simplicity of The WISH List's organizational structure reflects the simplicity of its mission and operation. The WISH List contributes exclusively to candidates for governor, the U.S. Senate, and U.S. House of Representatives. The WISH List first identifies campaigns in which a pro-choice Republican woman is a candidate, then determines if the candidate is viable. The WISH List determines viability by examining the efficiency of a candidate's campaign organization, her record of service, and her chances of victory. If an office-seeker passes muster, she becomes a WISH List candidate and receives all the benefits of WISH List resources.

Bundling

Campaign finance laws prohibit organizations and individuals from donating more than $5,000 to any single candidate for any single election. The WISH List and similar PACs avoid these restrictions and raise great sums of money for their candidates through a process called "bundling." When a person or organization joins The WISH List, the PAC requires the prospective member to donate to two WISH List candidates as well. The member contributes $100 or more—although not more than $5,000—to The WISH List-sanctioned candidates of his or her choice. The donations are then "bundled" together and delivered to endorsed campaigns. Although there have been congressional efforts to limit bundling, it is still a very legal and very common practice.

The WISH List and the Republican Party

Many moderate, pro-choice Republican candidates were marginalized because they rejected the party's stri- dent pro-life position. The WISH List was created to provide alternative sources of campaign revenue for those pro choice Republican candidates. The dominant pro life wing of the party forces pro-choice organizations and candidates to exist on the fringes of the Republican party structure. Republicans for Choice and the National Republican Coalition for Choice are two PACs—like The WISH List—formed independently from the party structure and dedicated to electing pro-choice Republican candidates. These organizations combine with individuals and organizations like The WISH List to form a separate support group for pro-choice Republicans.

PROGRAMS

Perhaps because of its relative newness, The WISH List does not have the membership rolls of larger PACs. Its members cannot sustain long-term training programs, conduct voter polls, or provide campaign services to its candidates. It does hold fund raising events in the form of simple meetings or dinners with WISH list candidates and supporters. These events raise money and increase the visibility of The WISH List.

BUDGET INFORMATION

Not made available.

HISTORY

Although it was formed in 1992, the genesis of The WISH List can be traced to the Republican National Convention of 1980. At that time, Republicans known as the "New Right" were beginning to influence party policy. The New Right was a coalition of religious Republicans and social conservatives who believed that abortion was immoral and illegal. The New Right supported the candidacy of Ronald Reagan for president of the United States and when the Republican National Convention designated Reagan as its nominee, many New Right policies became Republican Party policies.

Since abortion was legalized by the Supreme Court in 1973, the Republican Party position on the issue had been one of "tolerance." That position was reversed at the 1980 convention. The Republican Party official platform on abortion then became "The unborn child has a fundamental right to life which cannot be infringed." In addition to the new stance on abortion, the coalition known as the New Right also forced the Republican Party to abandon its 40-year support for the Equal Rights Amendment (ERA).

Moderate Republicans who supported abortion rights and the ERA chafed under the new direction of their party. In election after election, pro-choice Republicans attempted to amend the party platform to include abortion rights. The pro-life agenda persisted as the New Right cemented its power within the party. Sporadic New Right attempts to pass anti-abortion legislation, however, were defeated by a Congress controlled by pro-choice Democrats.

In 1989, the Supreme Court's *Webster* ruling defended the state of Missouri's rights to limit public access to certain abortion services, thus giving states more power over abortion policy. Many pro-choice Republicans and Democrats viewed *Webster* as a first step toward the overturning of *Roe v. Wade*, the 1973 decision that legalized abortion. This perception was fueled by the fact that the three Supreme Court Justices appointed by pro-life President Ronald Reagan played key roles in the *Webster* ruling.

A rift began opening in the Republican Party: media polls conducted in 1989 showed that 65 percent of Republicans supported a woman's right to have an abortion; pro-choice Republican Holly Cork won a primary in South Carolina over two pro-life male candidates. In New York, the Republican Family Committee broke with Republican party leadership and refused to support any pro-life Republican candidates. Organizations such as Republicans for Choice, Pro-Choice America, and the National Republican Coalition for Choice began waging a sort of civil war. They did not leave the Republican Party, but instead attempted to change the party's positions and leadership from within. These independent groups began to have an impact immediately. Republican National Committee chairman Lee Atwater pleaded with his party to become a "big tent," where all Republican views could be accommodated.

Calling abortion rights ". . . basic, necessary, important, urgent, [and] critical," Candace Straight and Glenda Geenwald created The WISH List in 1992 because they, too, were concerned over the growing influence of the pro-life wing of the Republican Party. Greenwald, publisher of *Michigan Woman Magazine*, was a member of the organization EMILY's List, and a pro-choice activist. Greenwald believed that "the only way we can help ourselves is to elect pro-choice women legislators."

The WISH List was different from traditional pro-choice PACs because it provided substantial money to candidacies instead of focusing its activities on lobbying members of Congress on Capitol Hill. Greenwald used EMILY's List as the inspiration and model when she created The WISH List, mimicking its fund-raising methods and endorsement policies. Both organizations believe the fastest and most powerful way to support candidates (and therefore effect change) is to provide them with campaign funds. Although EMILY's List aims to be a larger, more comprehensive resource for Democratic women, The WISH List keeps its focus on fund raising.

The WISH List became a force within the Republican Party as soon as it was introduced, raising $180,000 from 250 members its first year. In 1993 Christine Todd Whitman became New Jersey's first woman governor with the help of The WISH List. The WISH List also supported her successful reelection campaign in 1997. The WISH List donated $55,000 to Kay Bailey Hutchinson in her effort to become the second Republican woman in the U.S. Senate. The Wish List marked it fourth election cycle in 1998 by supporting 14 incumbents and boasting over 3,000 active donors.

CURRENT POLITICAL ISSUES

Although the intense debate over abortion flares up in the public domain from time to time, it is an ongoing battle within the Republican Party. In 1996, several WISH List candidates demanded that a tolerance plank be added to the party platform. The request was denied. And the struggle by groups such as The Wish List to change party platform persists, especially when confronted by a powerful coalition such as the New Right. Christian conservatives, the base of the New Right, represent only 15 percent of all voters, but provide Republicans with three-fourths of their votes. Such polarity on a single issue continues to cause fragmentation within the Republican Party, fosters resentment among party candidates, and creates particular problems for The WISH List.

Case Study: Ryan vs. Dornan

Republican pro-life Representative Robert K. Dornan faced pro-choice Republican Judith Ryan in California's 1992 primary. Dornan was the incumbent, but some pro-choice Republicans enthusiastically supported Ryan. The *Los Angeles Times* incorrectly reported that The WISH List was among those who endorsed Ryan, even though the group makes clear it is not WISH List policy to challenge Republican incumbents. Dornan, unaware that the *Los Angeles Times* report was wrong, stormed a WISH List event, threatening the U.S. Representatives attending the function with challenges from anti-choice candidates in their primaries.

There was no just cause for the controversy, but Dornan's fight put a spotlight on The WISH List. In particular, detractors claim the policy of not challenging Republican incumbents dilutes The WISH List mission because it limits which pro-choice candidates get help. Eileen Padberg, who worked on Judith Ryan's losing primary battle against Bob Dornan, said "[The WISH List] is a worthless organization if they refuse to take on incumbents."

The fight further underscored the group's segregation from the Republican Party mainstream since the candidates the party endorses are not necessarily those The WISH List would like to endorse. In response to this difficulty, pro-choice Republican organizations, The WISH

List, and prominent pro-choice Republican officeholders such as New Jersey Governor Christine Todd Whitman and Governor Pete Wilson of California have formed a coalition of pro-choice Republicans. Their movement has had great impact on the party and the American public. The WISH List and similar organizations keep pro-choice Republicans in the party by providing them with candidates they will vote for, thus expanding the Republican Party's base of support.

This pro-choice coalition has grown in power but has failed to change the party's position. In the 1996 general election, former Kansas Senator Robert Dole approved the pro-life plank in his candidacy against President Bill Clinton. The Republican Party's pro-choice coalition fought the decision, but the pro-life plank stayed.

SUCCESSES AND FAILURES

The WISH List has been a significant contributor to pro-choice Republican women candidates. In 1994, it gave over $370,000 to 40 office-seekers. It has contributed to the successful campaigns of three Republican women senators and ten representatives. Aside from these tangible results, the greatest success of The WISH List and similar PACs has been to force a debate within the Republican Party over the party's position on abortion. In some instances the group has even affected policy. For instance, Republican leader Newt Gingrich intentionally omitted the pro-life agenda from the Contract With America, the to-do list agenda that followed the Republican victories in 1994. Another testimony to the growing power of groups like The WISH List, is that pro-life activists have begun their own grassroots networks. Susan B. Anthony's List and the Republican Network to Elect Women are PACs formed to raise money for pro-life candidates.

FUTURE DIRECTIONS

The WISH List continues development efforts to increase the size of its membership, an important goal because it does not have full support of its party. Although it enjoys independence, it does not enjoy the great resources the party could provide. Increased membership will build the organization's base of support and help it achieve its mission. The WISH List makes it explicit that its wants to balance the number of female Republican and Democratic U.S. Senators and U.S. Representatives.

GROUP RESOURCES

Persons interested in finding out more about The WISH List may call the organization toll free at 1-800-756-WISH, or send inquiries to: The WISH List, 3205 North St. NW, Washington, DC, 20007. The WISH List also maintains an informative Web site at http://wwwthewishlist.org. that includes biographies of its administrators, lists of its candidates, and updates on the organization.

GROUP PUBLICATIONS

The WISH List publishes a quarterly newsletter for members. Others may obtain the newsletter by calling (202) 342-9111.

BIBLIOGRAPHY

Ayres, B. Drummond. "GOP Moderates to Push Delegates for Abortion-Rights Plank." *New York Times,* 1 August 1996.

Bennett, William. "The Right's New Abortion Fight." *Harper's,* January 1996.

Freidman, Jon. "The Founding Mother." *New York Times Magazine,* 2 May 1993.

McDowell, Jeanne. "Turmoil Under the GOP Tent." *Time,* 4 May 1992.

Melich, Tanya. *The Republican War Against Women: An Insider's Report from Behind the Lines.* New York: Bantam Books, 1996.

———. "The Silent Republicans." *New York Times,* 7 March 1996.

———. "Warning to Republican Party: Listen to Women—or Lose." *Glamour,* July 1996.

Morris, Celia. "The Revolt of the Republican Women." *Vogue,* August 1992.

Rosenfield, Megan. "Insurgents in Pearls: Republican Women Who Are Pro-Choice." *Lears,* August 1992.

Rudy, Kathy. *Beyond Pro-Life and Pro-Choice: Moral Diversity in the Abortion Debate.* Boston: Beacon Press, 1996.

Seelye, Katherine. "GOP Moderates Vow to Revive Provision on Abortion Tolerance." *New York Times,* 7 August 1996.

Shin, Annys. "Our Side." *Ms,* May/June, 1995.

Summers, Anne. "Abortion: Election Turnaround?" *Ms,* September/October, 1990.

World Wildlife Fund (WWF)

ESTABLISHED: December 1961
EMPLOYEES: 300 to 400
MEMBERS: 1,200,000
PAC: None

Contact Information:

ADDRESS: 1250 24th St. NW
      Washington, DC 20037
PHONE: (202) 293-9211
TOLL FREE: (800) 225-5993
FAX: (202) 293-4800
E-MAIL: public.info@wwfus.org
URL: http://www.worldwildlife.org
PRESIDENT; CEO: Kathryn Scott Fuller

WHAT IS ITS MISSION?

According to the World Wildlife Fund (WWF), it is the largest private organization in the United States working to protect threatened wildlife populations and their habitats. "Our work," as the organization stated in its 1996 annual report, "is guided by three overarching priorities: to rescue species on the brink of extinction; to conserve the critical habitats upon which all life depends; and to change the international markets that drive the destruction of habitats and wildlife populations around the world."

HOW IS IT STRUCTURED?

The WWF is an affiliate of the World Wild Fund for Nature, an international organization with five million members and 28 national branches on every continent. The international president of the fund is Prince Philip, Duke of Edinburgh, who serves as a major patron of its activities; the administrative arm of the organization is based in Switzerland. The U.S. branch, known as WWF-U.S.A. to distinguish it from WWFs in other countries, is based in Washington, D.C., and is overseen by the national president.

The WWF executive board of directors has eight members. In addition, there is a board of directors consisting of 35 members, including executives, lawyers, and scholars mostly from the United States. Former chairman and founding member Russell E. Train, also a former head of the U.S. Environmental Protection Agency (EPA), is the long-time chairman emeritus. The board of directors elects the president and chief executive officer.

PRIMARY FUNCTIONS

WWF seeks to maintain the natural diversity of life on Earth. The organization is perhaps best known for its work protecting endangered species, including its symbol, the giant panda. Survival of China's giant pandas today can be credited in part to the role WWF has played since 1980 in leading international efforts to protect this highly endangered species. WWF works to educate the public on threats to endangered wildlife. It provides support for research on how best to preserve threatened species and habitats, as well as for antipoaching programs.

WWF also works to create national parks and reserves, with an eye toward slowing the rapid destruction of critical ecological systems on which life may ultimately depend. Relying on a worldwide network of support, the WWF has helped create nearly 450 national parks and reserves around the world, including Masai Mara in Kenya, Annapurna Conservation Area in Nepal, and Manu National Park in Peru.

WWF has placed a priority on developing political allies in the battle to—as the fund's literature proclaims—"save life on earth." The partnerships WWF has forged with local and federal governments, financial institutions, and other conservation organizations, have been the key to its long-standing success. Such alliances contributed to the protection of countless species from extinction, including the giant panda, humpback whale, and black rhino; and influenced aid and educational programs in developing countries such as Madagascar to promote conservation of its rich ecosystem. Not surprisingly, the WWF often finds itself at odds with other groups that range from small-time panda smugglers in China to giant oil corporations like Exxon.

WWF officials work hard to initiate political change at the national and international level that will lead to stricter wildlife protection measures, and more land and money devoted to conservation. WWF experts frequently make presentations on endangered species and the environment to organizations such as the U.S. Congress and the United Nations. In addition, WWF mobilizes its membership to contact government officials and make their support for wildlife conservation policies known.

PROGRAMS

The WWF attempts to work cooperatively with local governments and industries in finding innovative ways to preserve land, such as debt-for-nature agreements. Initiated in the mid-1980s with developing countries in Latin America, debt-for-nature programs allow the WWF to buy a country's foreign debt at a discounted price, and the proceeds from these sales are then used by the devel-

oping nation to buy land for conservation purposes. In 1989 when the program expanded to African countries, Madagascar reduced its debt burden by millions of dollars and used the money to develop parks for the endangered gorillas.

WWF's Wildlands and Human Needs Program helps indigenous people improve the quality of their lives without destroying their own natural resources. "In more than 20 developing nations," WWF membership literature states, "WWF field teams are teaching local people to use alternative fuels and practical methods of soil conservation, agro-forestry and animal husbandry, thus preserving millions of acres of productive forest and grazing lands."

WWF also devotes significant resources to educating the general public, as well as conservation professionals. The Train Education for Nature Program, established in 1994 and named after WWF's former chairman Russell E. Train, awards grants to promote the education and training of conservation leaders in developing countries. During its first two years, the program awarded more than 60 grants, totaling $500,000. One such grant was given to the guards who patrolled national park land in Rwanda in 1996. The guards risked their lives to successfully protect endangered mountain gorillas during the country's civil war.

WWF's trade monitoring program, TRAFFIC, takes an aggressive—and often confrontational—approach to conservation. TRAFFIC is largely responsible for tracking illegal trade of animals around the world. Undercover operations are organized, investigators deployed. In the early 1990s, an exposé on illicit trade of China's rare animals received considerable attention from the national press. "A grisly and illicit trade: an undercover investigator in China reveals a shocking black market in endangered species," read one *Time* magazine headline. The article documented the work of one WWF investigator, who discovered blackmarket sales of panda pelts, leopard skins, and tiger organs. More recently, TRAFFIC has monitored and reported on poaching activity threatening African and Asian elephants.

In 1996 WWF launched "Our Living Planet Campaign" to create and expand the public's preservation awareness as the millennium approached. Another prominent program is called "Windows on the Wild," which, with the help of a $2.5 million grant from the Eastman Kodak Company, seeks to educate children and adults through a mixture of multimedia products. The program is targeted and distributed to schools, zoos, aquariums, and natural history museums around the United States. "In all its public awareness activities," authors of WWF's 1996 annual report wrote, "WWF encourages people to become better stewards of the Earth's biological diversity simply by treading more lightly on the planet."

FAST FACTS

More than one-third of the world's oceans have become a permanent safe haven for whales, thanks in part to WWF's efforts to win approval from the international Whaling Commission for establishing the Southern Ocean Whale Sanctuary.

(Source: World Wildlife Fund Annual Report, 1996.)

BUDGET INFORMATION

WWF relies heavily on individual contributions ($29,389,569) and government grants ($28,242,654) to support the bulk of its operating expenses; endowments ($5,913,970) and long-term investments ($8,532,205) also help support WWF. In 1997 the organization's income was $93,129,564, while expenses totaled $82,629,722. The majority of the budget is spent on field and policy programs ($51,306,912), while public education accounts for $14,047,073 of expenses and membership programs run $7,720,949.

In 1997 as in previous years, WWF spent 8 percent on fund-raising and 4 percent on administrative support. Put another way, WWF spent 87.3 percent of its fund on programs. This streamlined budget won WWF recognition from both *Money* and *Smart Money* magazines as one of "America's best charities." In declaring WWF one of the top nonprofit organizations, *Smart Money* noted that WWF does "just what they say they do: put your money to work as efficiently as possible."

HISTORY

WWF-U.S.A. was established in December, 1961, by a small group of U.S. conservationists, including Russell Train. Despite the long history of conservation in the United States, no group had attempted to mount a global conservation effort. By affiliating itself with the international WWF, WWF-U.S.A. was able to strike off in new territory. The early goals of WWF revolved around saving animals and their habitat. In fact, the first fund-raising effort raised $33,000 for five projects designed to protect threatened species such as the giant panda, Bengal tiger, and humpback whale.

Changing Times

The 1980s marked a time of tremendous change for the organization. First, realizing it needed public support, WWF began accepting members in the early 1980s. In 1985 WWF-U.S.A. merged with The Conservation Foundation, a think tank devoted to research on environmental conditions and trends. This move was intended to combine the fund's experience with ecological and biological issues and the foundation's expertise in social science and policy analysis, as well as its knowledge of U.S. environmental policy. Finally, the arrival of Kathryn Fuller in 1989 as a successor for William Reilly, whom President George Bush had named to head the EPA, dramatically changed the shape of the organization.

Fuller, who gained experience working for the Justice Department's Land and Natural Resources Division, sought to strengthen the WWF's political clout. "We can do great work on the ground—saving tigers, getting parks established, and so on—but unless we can also influence opinion leaders, decisionmakers, those gains aren't consolidated for the long term," she told *Association Management* magazine. Seeking more political clout meant increasing membership; on that front, Fuller has made tremendous strides, doubling membership during her tenure, from 600,000 to 1.2 million. WWF's membership growth is all the more impressive considering that many U.S. environmental groups lost support during the early 1990s. The loss may have been due to a belief by the general public that President Bill Clinton and Vice President Al Gore would take care of the environment at the federal level and thus decreased the urgency of environmental action at the local level.

The Power of Partnerships

Strengthening WWF's political power has also come about through partnerships. WWF has joined forces with small local groups and foreign governments. "Beyond the community, you need effective advocate for the cause," Fuller explained to *Association Management* magazine, pointing to a successful alliance with the Nepalese government. "Along with a lot of Nepali champions, we got the government to remit 30 to 50 percent of proceeds from tourism directly back to the communities and parks themselves. Getting a government to relinquish money that would otherwise go into the central treasury is a real trick." In part, Fuller and WWF has had some help from powerful places, most notably the World Bank. Although the World Bank and WWF had joined forces for many projects over the years, the most significant venture emerged in 1997. At the time, the World Bank and WWF announced they would work together to "establish a network of protected areas covering at least 10 percent of the world's forest types by the year 2000," according to *Focus.*

As WWF chairman Roger Sant wrote in the 1996 annual report, which celebrated the fund's thirty-fifth anniversary: "WWF has long pioneered solutions as diverse as the challenges we face. Where species protection projects alone cannot suffice, we have also promoted the establishment of parks and protected areas. Where parks need more personnel, we have provided funds and professional training. Where key wildlife habitat is under threat from over exploitation, we have attempted to share local and international economic forces."

CURRENT POLITICAL ISSUES

WWF has become increasingly involved in preserving threatened ecosystems, whether they are wetlands or oceans or tropical rain forests. In this age of increased habitat destruction, the WWF has turned its attentions away from saving a single species to preserving life on Earth. As WWF has struggled to tackle larger global problems, it has sought to affect international policy governing issues such as wildlife trade, foreign aid to developing countries, toxic chemical use, and carbon dioxide reductions. WWF lobbied successfully for two highly visible issues in the United States: the strengthening of the Endangered Species Act and the acceptance of the Convention on Biological Diversity, an international treaty aimed at slowing the rate of plant and animal extinctions. WWF also contributes research to the growing collection of literature on the effects of greenhouse gases on animals and habitats.

In the late 1990s, the WWF (along with other conservation groups) put the devastation of the oceans high on their agenda of issues to address through action and legislation. Many studies showed the oceans to be in terrible condition, with fish populations dying out, and the plankton that form the basis of the marine food chain disappearing in some places. Some feared that the loss of plant life in the world's oceans would have a serious impact on the production of oxygen vital to life on earth.

Case Study: Overfishing

One cause of devastation to the oceans is overfishing. In 1998 WWF estimated that 70 percent of the world's fish species were being harvested faster than they reproduced. Continued over several years, such practices will drive species to extinction. As the global demand for seafood continues to exceed the supply, more and more large capacity boats chase fewer fish with more invasive and destructive methods. Many fishing boats have nets large enough to scoop up airplanes and trawl lines with up to 35,000 hooks that stretch more than 100 kilometers. Large nets gather up every living thing in their path and the sea life that has no market value is eventually thrown back into the water, too damaged to survive.

WWF responded to the crisis in the oceans with an all-out effort to create international agreements that address the problem of overfishing. Declaring 1998, "The

BUDGET:
1997 WWF Revenue

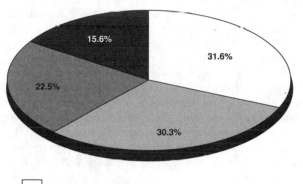

- 31.6%: Individual contributions
- 30.3%: Government grants
- 22.5%: Other
- 15.6%: Endowments and long-term investments

1997 WWF Expenses

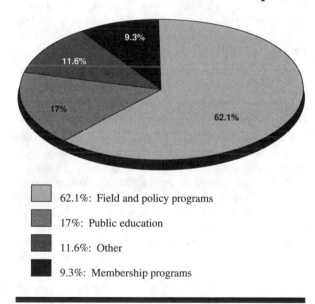

- 62.1%: Field and policy programs
- 17%: Public education
- 11.6%: Other
- 9.3%: Membership programs

Year of the Oceans," WWF conducted an international year-long campaign to educate citizens and governments about the dangers of overfishing and the need for worldwide cooperation to address the growing crisis. WWF also provided funding for research on the effects of overfishing on the ocean, and provided scientific data to policymakers in the United States and to other countries through the United Nations. A 1998 WWF study showed that the fishing power of many countries was five times higher than previously estimated and 155 percent greater than what marine life could support.

Partially due to WWF's urging for international plans to address the devastating effects of overfishing on the oceans, the United Nation's Food and Agriculture Organization (FAO) met in October 1998 to discuss options. In February 1999 the FAO adopted an International Plan of Action for the Management of Fishing Capacity. The action plan asks member nations to determine whether their fishing fleets are too big and to develop plans for reducing excessive fleets. Members must develop national plans to address fleet size and capacity preferably by 2003, and by no later than 2005. Countries will also be required to reduce government subsidies, or payments, to organizations that encourage overfishing.

Public Impact

The FAO resolutions represented a major step in the fight to save the oceans as they brought many countries together to respond to a truly global problem. While the plans represent a serious international intent to recognize and respond to the crisis of overfishing, it will be many years before the impact of the plans will be known. In the meantime, WWF continues its work to rescue the oceans by advocating for comprehensive management of fisheries and dealing with pirate vessels that ignore international regulations.

SUCCESSES AND FAILURES

Some of the WWF's greatest gains in recent years have come through its work with local governments, such as the Central African Republic. In the early 1980s, a WWF representative, biologist Richard Carroll, observed that the silverback gorilla habitat was being threatened by uncontrolled logging, population and agricultural encroachment, mining, and poaching. Development was being allowed by the indigenous hunter-gatherers, who wanted the benefits of modern society, such as medical care and education, even at the expense of their tropical rain forests. Carroll, however, was able to see another way to provide resources for the local people, while at the same time protecting their forests from development.

In collaboration with the BaAka, the local people, Carroll established a series of parks and reserves. In the parks, hunting wildlife was prohibited, while at the reserves local people could hunt and fish and commercial interests could pursue selective logging and tourism. Within two years, nearly 1,750 square miles of tropical forests were protected. And with the rise of ecotourism, where local guides and teachers lead tourists on plant collecting tours, the BaAka began reaping financial rewards for saving their land. "Today, 50 percent of the reserve's revenues are recycled back into park conservation, and 40 percent go toward community development," noted the WWF's 1996 annual report. "Decision-making authority has increasingly devolved to local organizations, and local wildlife are also reaping benefits. Improved enforcement efforts have helped make such a dent in elephant poaching that WWF is now working with villagers to test various tools, including electrified fences, to protect their crops from elephants who thrive in the area."

FUTURE DIRECTIONS

For WWF, the future holds only greater challenges as the pressures on existing ecosystems increase with, among other things, the explosion of the human population. WWF will continue to seek out animals on the brink of extinction, adding them to their growing list of projects, and mobilizing national and local efforts to establish protected reserves. One major new program is a conservation plan to protect the dwindling population of Asian tigers; launched at the beginning of 1998, the program coincided with the Chinese "Year of the Tiger." In part, relatively new satellite-mapping technology will help WWF to target the Asian tiger habitats most likely to offer long-term survival opportunity for tigers. As it moves toward the twenty-first century, WWF will continue to use high-tech tools in the fight to save endangered species.

GROUP RESOURCES

WWF maintains a Web page at http://www.wildlife. org documenting many of its conservation campaigns, as well as information about the organization's history and budget. The WWF offers educational resources such as the "Web of Life," a multimedia kit (geared toward grades seven through 10) and Vanishing Rainforests (geared toward grades two through six) that includes teacher manuals, posters, and videos. Pamphlets are also frequently published to educate members about specific new campaigns.

GROUP PUBLICATIONS

Focus, a bimonthly newsletter, is offered to all WWF members and provides in-depth updates on WWF projects and practical tips such as how to support a project by contacting the appropriate senators and representatives, donating money, or participating in the WWF travel program. WWF also publishes *Traffic,* a quarterly newsletter covering trends in wildlife trade.

In addition to its newsletters, the WWF publishes many books, including *Voice From Africa: Local Perspectives on Conservation, A Dictionary of Environmental Quotations,* and *A Guide to the Field of Environmental and Natural Resource Economics.* These and many other WWF publications can be ordered on-line at http://www.worldwildlife.org/pubs/index.htm. The WWF Publications office also takes orders by phone at (410) 516-6951, by fax at (410) 516-6998, or by mail at World Wildlife Fund Publications, PO Box 4866, Hampden Post Office, Baltimore, MD 21211.

BIBLIOGRAPHY

Bovet, Susan Fry. "Teaching Ecology: A New Generation Influences Environmental Policy." *Public Relations Journal,* April 1994.

Brown, Lester R., et al. *State of the World.* New York: W.W. Norton, 1990.

Colborn, Theo. *Our Stolen Future: Are We Threatening Our Fertility, Intelligence, and Survival?—A Scientific Detective Story.* E.P. Dutton, 1996.

Eckholm, Eik. *The Dispossessed of the Earth: Land Reform and Sustainable Development.* New York: W. W. Norton, 1978.

"A Fisherman's Tale: Overfishing is One Part Human Nature, and Two Parts Poor Management." *Economist,* 23 May 1998.

"Hook, Line, and Extinction." *Business Week,* 14 December 1998.

Postel, Sandra. *Altering the Earth's Chemistry: Assessing the Risks.* New York: W. W. Norton.

Raloff, Janet. "New Plan Drafted to Save Panda." *Science News,,* 14 March 1987.

Sachs, Andrea. "A Grisly and Illicit Trade: An Undercover Investigator in China Reveals a Shocking Black Market in Endangered Species." *Time,* 8 April 1991.

Glossary & Subject Index

Glossary

A

accession: The process by which a country becomes a member of an international agreement, such as the General Agreement on Tariffs and Trade (GATT) or the European Community.

accreditation: When official approval is given to an organization that has met certain standards of excellence.

acid rain: Rain that has increased amounts of acid. Caused by environmental factors and pollutants, such as industrial emissions and chemicals.

Acquired Immunodeficiency Syndrome: An incurable and lethal attack of the human immune system, commonly known as AIDS. Caused by infection with human immunodeficiency virus, or HIV, which is transmitted by humans through body fluids. HIV destroys T cells that enable the body to fight off illness and leaves patients vulnerable to many life threatening conditions.

ad hoc: Generally, for a specific purpose or task. Ad hoc committees are often formed to address a specific problem, without having long term or permanent responsibilities.

administration: The art or science of managing public affairs. Public administration is the function of the executive branch of government and is the procedure by which laws are carried out and enforced. In the United States, the president is the head of the executive branch, which includes an advisory staff and many agencies and departments.

admiral: The commander in chief of a navy or coast guard.

advocacy: The practice of supporting, defending, or working on behalf of a person, group, or cause.

affirmative action: The policy of affording special opportunities or advantages to members of groups that have been the historic victims of discrimination; taking positive steps to remedy past acts of discrimination.

agribusiness: An industry involved in farming operations on a large scale. May include producing, processing, storing, and distributing crops as well as manufacturing and distributing farm equipment.

AIDS: *See* Acquired Immunodeficiency Syndrome

alien: An individual who is not a citizen of the country in which he or she is living. In the United States, aliens may not hold public office or vote, but are provided with civil rights under the Constitution and do pay taxes. (*See also* citizen; naturalization)

Allies: Nations or states that form an association to further their common interests. The United States' partners against Germany during World War II (1939–45) are often known collectively as "The Allies" and include Great Britain and Russia. (*See also* Axis powers)

amalgamated local: Several small labor union groups in a specific region or city that have merged to form a single body.

ambassador: An official of a country or organization who formally represents that country or organization. In the United States, an ambassador is the top ranking diplomat and personal representative of the president, in other countries.

amendment: Changes or additions to an official document. In the United States government, constitutional amendments refer to changes in the Constitution. Such amendments are rare and may be proposed only by a two-thirds vote of both houses of Congress or by a convention called by Congress at the request of two-thirds of the state legislators.

amicus curiae: Literally, friend of the court. A person or organization who is not a party involved in a legal case, but is allowed by the court to provide information or advice.

amnesty: An act of government by which pardons are granted to individuals or groups who have violated a law. Generally, amnesty is a power exercised by the president of the United States when a federal law is violated, but Congress may also grant amnesties.

annuities: Investments or grants that pay money out yearly or at other regularly spaced intervals.

anti-abortion: The belief that abortion should be illegal. Often based on religious conviction that abortion is murder. (*See also* pro-choice; pro-life)

antidumping: A system of laws to remedy dumping, which is the sale of a commodity in a foreign market at less than fair value. (*See also* dumping)

antitrust (laws): Laws designed to prevent a company from completely dominating portions of the economy by the elimination of competitors through unethical business practices. Antitrust laws are designed to maintain competition in a market economy.

apartheid: The policy of political, social, and economic segregation and discrimination based on race. The political system in South Africa throughout most of the twentieth century.

appellate jurisdiction: The authority of a court to review the decisions of a lower court. In the federal court system the court of appeals and the Supreme Court have the power to review and reverse the decisions of district courts.

apportionment: The process by which a state's number of seats in the House of Representatives is determined. Each state is allotted one representative, then a formula based on population is used to determine how many additional seats a state is entitled to.

appropriations: Funds for specific government and public purposes as determined by legislation. (*See also* congressional appropriation)

arbitration: The process of submitting an issue to a person or committee for a decision. Arbitrators are often neutral third parties who decide disagreements between two involved parties such as an employer and an employee.

armistice: An agreement or truce that ends military conflict in anticipation of a peace treaty.

arms control: Reducing, eliminating, or otherwise restricting the production, use, or sale of weapons of war. During the Cold War the United States and the former Soviet Union developed numerous treaties to control such weapons as nuclear, biological, chemical, and space-based arms.

arms race: The effort by countries, particularly the United States and the former Soviet Union from the 1950s to the 1980s, to stockpile nuclear weapons faster than other countries and maintain military superiority.

Articles of Confederation: The compact made among the thirteen original colonies to form the basis of their government. Prepared in 1776, the Articles were adopted by all states in 1781 and replaced by the United States Constitution in 1789.

assimiliation: The process by which one culture or idea is absorbed by or blended with a larger culture or set of ideas.

assisted suicide: When one person, sometimes a doctor, helps another person to end their life by providing them with the means or the method. When a doctor is involved, the action is called physician assisted suicide.

atomic (weapons): Weapons of mass destruction with violent explosive power that results from the splitting of the nuclei of atoms (usually uranium or plutonium) by neutrons in a rapid chain reaction.

attach,: A representative of a government typically stationed at an embassy who serves the diplomatic staff in a support position.

attorney general: The chief legal officer of a state or nation. In the government of the United States, the attorney general is the legal adviser to the president and to all agencies of the executive branch and is the highest law enforcement officer in the country. The attorney general is also head of the Department of Justice and a member of the president's cabinet. (*See also* cabinet)

autonomy: Having the freedom to be self-governing and not be responsible to another body or authority.

Axis powers: The countries aligned against the Allied nations in World War II (1939–45). The term originally applied to Nazi Germany and Fascist Italy (Rome-Berlin Axis), and later extended to include Japan. (*See also* Allies)

B

baby boomer: Someone born between 1945 and the early 1960s. People of this generation are part of the huge number of babies born when World War II veterans returned home and started families.

ballot: Instrument used for casting a secret vote. It may be a paper or electronic system.

bicameral: A legislative body consisting of two chambers; an example is the U.S. Congress, which consists of the House of Representatives and the Senate.

bilateral negotiations: Discussions between, and problem solving efforts of, two parties or nations.

bill: A proposed law. In the United States bills may be drawn up by anyone, including the president or citizen groups, but they must be introduced in Congress by a senator or representative.

Bill of Rights: The first ten amendments to the Constitution of the United States that list the rights a person is entitled to that cannot be interfered with by the government, including freedom of speech and religion, and the due process of law.

biological warfare: Warfare that uses living organisms, such as diseases, germs, and their toxic products, as weapons.

bipartisan: Cooperation between the two major political parties; for example, Republican and Democratic. (*See also* partisan)

bond: A type of loan, such as savings bonds, issued by the government to finance public needs that cost more than existing funds can pay for. The government agrees to pay lenders back the initial cost of the bond, plus interest.

book banning: When a person, group, or organization refuses to allow a particular population access to books that are deemed immoral or politically subversive.

boycott: An organized refusal to buy certain goods or use certain services to express disapproval of a product, process, or organization. Boycotts are used as a tactic to bring about changes in products, processes, and organizations through economic and public pressure.

Brady Law: A federal law passed in 1993 that requires background checks on people buying guns to determine if there is a reason, such as a past criminal conviction, that would prevent them from purchasing a gun. The bill is named for gun control advocate, James Brady, who served as President Ronald Reagan's press secretary and was shot and paralyzed during the assassination attempt on Reagan in 1981.

budget deficit: Occurs when money spent by the government or other organization is more than money coming in.

budget surplus: Funds left over after all budgeted expenses have been paid for. A budget surplus occurs when money coming in to an organization, such as the federal government, exceeds the amount of money paid out for the organization's expenses.

bureau: A working unit of a department or agency with specific functions.

bureaucracy: An administrative system, especially of government agencies, that handles day-to-day business and carries out policies. Workers within a bureaucracy create and process forms, implement procedures, exist in chains of command, and establish routines that must be followed in order to get work accomplished.

C

cabinet: A group of advisers. In the federal government the cabinet is made up of advisers who offer assistance to the president. Each president determines the make up and role of their cabinets, although most include the heads of major departments such as State, Treasury, and Justice, and the vice president. (*See also* attorney general)

campaign: The organized activities of candidates seeking office to convince voters to vote for them, rather than their opponents. Campaigns raise money to pay for print and media messages to convince voters to support a particular candidate or cause.

campaign finance reform: A movement to improve the way political campaigns raise money to avoid financial contributors having too much influence on political candidates.

capitalism: An economic system based on private ownership of industries, and supply and demand, where suppliers sell products for profit and buyers determine which products they will purchase at what cost.

cartel: An organization of independent producers formed to regulate or fix the production, pricing, or marketing practices of its members in order to limit competition and maximize their market power.

caucus: The meeting of a political or other organized group in order to decide upon issues and policies or to choose a political candidate; also refers to the group itself.

censorship: When an individual or group in power determines what another individual or group may say, publish, view, or read based on what the group finds objectionable.

censure: A measure by which legislative bodies can discipline their own members with punishments ranging from withdrawal of privileges to expulsion.

census: An official counting of the inhabitants of a state or country; compiled data usually includes such details as gender, age, family size, and occupation.

Certiorari, writ of: The primary method by which cases reach the Supreme Court of the United States. The writ is discretionary and allows the Court to pick and choose which lower court cases it deems appropriate for a full hearing and possible decision.

charter school: A school established as an alternative to traditional public and parochial schools, that is recognized by the government as a valid educational institution.

checks and balances: A system, particularly in government, where equal branches must cooperate with each other, oversee each other, and enforce and support each others' decisions according to established rules. (*See also* separation of powers)

chief administrator: Person in charge of a particular agency or organization, and charged with ensuring that the group's responsibilities are carried out. In the federal government the chief administrator is the president.

chief executive: The head of a nation or state. In the United States the president is the chief executive who heads the government and formulates policies.

chief of state: The ceremonial head of government. In the United States the president is the chief of state whose duties include greeting foreign dignitaries, hosting state dinners, and many more symbolic events.

citizen: An individual who is a native or naturalized member of a nation or state and is entitled to all the protections and privileges of its laws. (*See also* alien; civil liberties; naturalization)

civilian: An individual who is not on active duty in the military.

civil disobedience: Refusal to obey the law on the grounds that the law is morally wrong. Civil disobedience may also encompass actions to change such laws.

civil law: The code that governs interactions between private persons as opposed to the code known as criminal law that governs individual conduct. Civil law provides a forum to settle disputes involving contracts, business dealings, and accidents. (*See also* criminal justice system)

civil liberties: Those recognized principles of American law that limit the powers of government and also guarantee the privileges of citizenship, such as voting and equality of treatment. (*See also* citizen)

civil rights: The privileges of all individuals to be treated as equals under the laws of their country; specifically, the rights given by certain amendments to the U.S. Constitution.

civil service: A term describing the system employing people in non-military government jobs. The system is based on merit classifications.

class action: A lawsuit in which one or more persons sue or are sued as representatives of a larger group such as a company or group of people with similar illnesses or grievances.

classified: Information or documents withheld from the public because their circulation could threaten national security. (*See also* declassify; secured document)

cloture: A parliamentary procedure used by a decision making body, such as Congress, to end discussion on a matter and move to a vote.

coalition: An alliance between political or special interest groups forged to pursue shared interests and agendas.

cold war: Conflict over ideological differences that is carried on by words and diplomatic actions, not by military action. The term is usually used to refer to the tension that existed between the United States and the USSR from the 1950s until the breakup of the USSR in 1991.

collective bargaining: The negotiations between workers who are members of a union and their employer for the purpose of deciding upon such as issues as fair wages and work-day hours.

commander in chief: The officer who is in command of a major armed force; the role of the president as the supreme commander of the nation's military forces and the national guard when it is called into federal service.

committee: A group of individuals charged by a higher authority with a specific purpose such as investigation, review, reporting, or determining action.

commonwealth: A free association of sovereign independent states that has no charter, treaty, or constitution. The association promotes cooperation, consultation, and mutual assistance among members.

communism; communist: A political, economic, and social theory that promotes common ownership of property for the use of all citizens. All profits are to be equally distributed and prices on goods and services are usually set by the state. Communism also refers directly to the official doctrine of the former USSR.

Communist bloc: Refers to a group of countries in Eastern Europe with Communist governments that supported and were influenced by the former Soviet Union. In the 1990s, many of these countries, such as Poland and Czechoslovakia overthrew Communist regimes and established democratic systems of government.

comptroller: An official who oversees spending to determine whether funds have or have not been spent on purchases they were intended for. The federal title is Comptroller General and the responsibility is to oversee funds to be spent according to legislative approval.

confederation: A unified group of independent states or nations where a central body makes decisions about matters of common concern but units make decisions affecting individuals.

confirmation: The process by which the Senate approves of presidential appointees to offices.

conflict of interest: When an individual's actions in a business or political situation are affected or motivated by their personal interest. Examples include politicians who vote on particular issues to gain financial support from like minded groups, or a federal official in charge of regulating an industry owning businesses in that industry.

conflict resolution: The process by which two or more opposing groups or individuals work out their differences non-violently through discussion, compromise, and mediation.

Congress: The term used to describe the combined Senate and House of Representatives. (*See also* House of Representatives; Senate)

congressional appropriation: Money that Congress approves for a specific purpose. (*See also* appropriations)

congressional district: The geographic area that a member of the House of Representatives is elected from and represents in Congress. Congressional districts are drawn up to include a nearly equal number of voters.

conscientious objector: A person who refuses to serve in the military because of personal beliefs. In the United States a person cannot refuse to serve, but Congress has allowed conscientious objectors to participate in non-combat duty or complete an exemption process on religious grounds. This exemption does not include objection for political, sociological, philosophical, or personal reasons, although the Supreme Court has upheld some requests for exemption based on these grounds if they are held with the fervor of religious beliefs.

conscription: The mandatory enlistment of citizens to serve in the military. (*See also* draft)

consensus: Agreement that is supported by all parties involved.

conservation: The preservation and protection of nature and natural resources.

conservative: In the United States, a political philosophy that generally favors state over federal action, and opposes regulation of the economy, extensive civil rights legislation, and federally funded social programs.

consortium: A group of business organizations that join together to achieve things they did not have the resources to accomplish individually.

constant-dollar: The dollar value after adjusting the inflation rate to a base value.

constituent; constituency: The registered voters in a governmental district; a group of people who support a position or a candidate.

constitution: Fundamental laws that establish government organization, determine the roles and duties of segments of government, and clarify the relationship between the people and their government. The United States Constitution, was created in 1787 and ratified in 1788.

consul: Officials sent to other countries to assist and provide support to citizens of the country the official represents. (*See also* consulate)

consulate: The official residence and place of business of a consul in a foreign country. (*See also* consul)

Consumer Price Index (CPI): The change in the cost of certain current goods and services used by the average consumer compared to the cost for the same goods and services in a chosen base year. Legislators use the CPI when considering wage and subsidy increases as well as other legislation affected by economic factors.

consumerism: The movement to achieve effective protection for consumers begun by Ralph Nader in the 1960s. Advocates of consumerism use the courts and lobby to increase consumer protection.

containment: Generally, the process of limiting or restraining something. Specifically, a policy adopted during President Harry Truman's administration (1945–53) to build up areas of U.S. military strength around the world to isolate and intimidate communist nations. The belief behind the policy was that communism would eventually collapse on its own if it was not allowed to spread and expand its power.

contingency fees: Payment to an attorney only after a case is decided in the client's favor. Contingency fees are often a percentage of the financial settlement an attorney secures for a client.

contraception: Methods used to prevent conception from taking place.

cooperatives: A business or organization that is owned by, and operated for, the benefit of members. For example, members pay dues to join a food cooperative and in return, they can buy groceries at lower prices because the food cooperative buys in bulk and does not operate to make a profit.

copyright: The exclusive right to own or use written documents or visual images. Copyrights are generally granted to the author or creator of a work by the Copyright Office of the Library of Congress for 28 years, with the option of renewing the copyright for another 28 years.

corporate welfare: An ironic phrase used to describe tax breaks and favorable laws the government creates for industry. The implication is that such supports are "charity" for big business. (*See also* welfare)

counterfeit: A copy or imitation of something valuable especially money, that is made with the intention of convincing people it is real.

counterinsurgency: Military force directed at a revolutionary group that tries to overthrow an established government.

CPI: *See* Consumer Price Index

criminal justice system: The United States court system that deals with criminal violations and punishment. Criminal law differs from civil law in that it regulates individual actions and not conduct between parties. (*See also* civil law)

customs: The fees imposed by a country on items imported and exported. In the United States, Customs can also apply to the agency that collects these fees.

D

declassify; declassification: The process of making previously secret information available to the public by removing or reducing its security classification. (*See also* classified; secured document)

decommission: When something is removed from active military service. Usually refers to military vessels such as ships and submarines.

deficit: The amount by which spending exceeds income over a given period.

demobilize: To disband or discharge military troops.

democracy: A form of government in which the power lies in the hands of the people, who can govern directly, or indirectly by electing representatives.

Democratic Party: One of the two major political parties in the United States that evolved from the Democratic-Republican group that supported Thomas Jefferson. In the twentieth century, the Democratic Party has generally stood for freer trade, more international commitments, greater government regulations, and social programs. Traditionally considered more liberal than the Republican Party.

demographic(s): Statistics about human populations including such categories as age, density, income, and distribution.

department: An administrative unit with responsibility for a broad area of an organization's operations. Federal departments include Labor, Interior, Health and Human Services, and Defense.

deposit insurance: Government-regulated protection for interest-bearing deposits, such as savings accounts, to protect the depositor from failure of the banking institution.

deregulation: The process of removing government restrictions and regulations.

diplomacy: The process by which nations carry out political relations with each other. In the United States, diplomacy is the primary responsibility of the Department of State.

diplomatic envoy: A person sent to represent their nation in dealings with another nation.

directorate: May refer to the office of a director, a board of directors, or the executive staff that works with a director.

discretionary program: A program or service that is not mandated by law or regulation. Federal discretionary programs are provided by the government only if Congress approves.

domestic policy: Policies that focus on issues internal to the United States. (*See also* foreign policy).

draft: The general term for the federal selective service system that allows a government to enlist individuals for service in the armed forces. (*See also* conscription)

due process: Protects the rights of individuals to life, liberty, and property by guaranteeing a fair system of justice. While due process of law is not specifically defined in government documents, it is understood that it limits the power of government over individuals through a series of laws that affect privacy and treatment of individuals suspected of crime.

dumping: The sale of a commodity in a foreign market at less than fair value. Dumping is generally recognized as unfair because the practice can disrupt markets and injure producers of competitive products in an importing country. (*See also* antidumping)

E

earned income credit: A federal tax credit for low income individuals that allows them to receive a refund on taxes that they have already paid or pay less federal tax during the calendar year.

economic forecast: Predictions about a country's economic future including projected revenues, employment statistics, and interest rates.

electoral college: The group of qualified voters chosen to represent their individual states, who ultimately elect the president and vice president of the United States. Their votes are based on the popular vote of their states and the number of voters is equal to the number of each state's congressional representatives. (*See also* popular vote)

electorate: The individuals who are qualified to vote in an election.

embargo: A legal restriction on commercial ships from entering a country's ports; any legal restriction of trade.

embassy: The office or residence of the ambassador of a foreign country; also collectively refers to an ambassador and his staff.

emigration: Leaving one's homeland or residence to live somewhere else.

endangered species: A particular animal, plant, or other living organism that is disappearing and may become extinct.

entitlement: A government program that guarantees benefits to qualified recipients. For example, citizens are guaranteed Social Security benefits when they reach age 65.

ethics: The principles and morals that govern an individual or group and clarify right behavior and wrong behavior.

eugenics: The science of improving hereditary qualities of a species or breed by controlling or altering genetic material.

euthanasia: The practice of killing or permitting the killing of terminally ill or hopelessly injured people in painless ways for merciful reasons.

excise tax: A tax or duty on the sale of specific commodities or groups of commodities; for instance, tobacco or liquor.

executive branch: In the United States, the branch of government charged with administering the laws and policies of the nation or state. In contrast, the legislative and judicial branches of government have the respective powers of creating and interpreting the laws. (*See also* judicial branch; legislative branch)

executive order: A rule or regulation issued by the president or a governor that has the effect of law. Executive orders are limited to those that implement provisions of the Constitution, treaties, and regulations governing administrative agencies.

executive privilege: The right of executive officials to keep information from or refuse to appear in front of a court or legislative body. In the United States only the president and officials designated by the president enjoy executive privilege.

export: Goods sold to foreign buyers; the act of selling goods to foreign buyers. (*See also* import)

extramural: Activities that take place outside of organized and recognized institutions. (*See also* intramural)

F

faction: Segment or group within an organization or government that is identified by its tendency to create dissension and disagree with the majority opinions.

fair housing laws: Group of laws that make discrimination in renting, purchasing, or selling housing, illegal.

fair labor practices: Group of laws that guarantee fair treatment of employees by employers including the right to unionize and the right to pursue grievances according to established personnel policies.

feasibility study: Process used by legislators (and others) to determine if proposed policies and programs are economically sound and capable of achieving desired results.

federal aid: Funds collected by the federal government (generally through taxes) and distributed to states for a variety of reasons including education and disaster relief.

federal budget: The annual financial plan of the United States government including all sources and amounts of income and items and amounts of expenditure. The federal budget must be approved by Congress and the president.

federal deposit libraries: Selected libraries throughout the United States where government publications are available.

federal government; federalism: The national system of government in the United States including the executive, legislative, and judicial branches.

federalist: A member of the Federalist political party, the first in America. The party developed during the later part of George Washington's (1789–96) administration that created national financial and economic programs.

federal poverty guidelines: Federal guidelines that define the maximum amount of income that families can earn to be considered living in poverty.

Federal Reserve notes: Currency issued by the Federal Reserve banks that is backed by government bonds and gold certificates.

felony: A serious criminal offense, usually punishable by a year in prison or more.

feminist: Someone who believes in the political, economic, and social equality of men and women.

fetal-alcohol syndrome: A variety of physical problems and defects experienced by infants born by women who drink alcohol during pregnancy. The syndrome can include mental retardation, stunted physical growth, and defects in the baby's face, skull, and brain.

filibuster: A tactic used in the Senate to defeat a bill by refusing to end discussion on an issue. The true purpose of a filibuster is to defeat proposed legislation by forcing the Senate to move on to other business, leaving the disputed measure unresolved.

fiscal: Relating to financial matters.

flat tax: A tax system wherein everyone pays the same percentage of their income in taxes.

flex time: Work schedules that allow employees to work their required hours on a flexible schedule throughout the work week rather than a set number of hours on specific days.

floor leader: Representatives and Senators who are selected by their party to carry out party decisions during legislative battles by influencing and working with undecided members.

FOI: *See* Freedom of Information Act

foreign aid: Funds provided by the United States government to assist other countries.

foreign policy: The plans and course of actions that the United States develops regarding other nations. (*See also* domestic policy)

foreign trade barrier: Government regulations and controls that limit or prevent free trade with other nations.

fraud: When one party deceives or lies to another party to gain something they want.

Freedom of Information Act (FOIA): A law established in 1966 that requires federal agencies to provide citizens with any public records they request. Some exceptions are national security materials, confidential personnel and financial data, and law enforcement files.

free enterprise system: The system of economics in which private business may be conducted with minimum interference by the government.

free market economy: An economic system that relies on the market, as opposed to government planners, to set the prices for wages and products.

free trade(rs): Trade between two entities, particularly the United States and another country, that is not limited by regulations and other restrictions.

friendly fire: When a military unit mistakenly fires or launches weapons at their own forces.

G

GDP: *See* Gross Domestic Product

gender bias: Discrimination against or favoritism toward someone because of his or her sex.

gene therapy: Treating, or attempting to prevent, hereditary diseases by altering the genetic materials that cause the disease.

general: A high ranking official in the army, marine corps, or air force.

gerrymandering: Apportionment of voters in such a way as to give unfair advantage to a political party or racial group.

glasnost: Policy of openness and freedom of expression. Embraced by Mikhail Gorbachev in the late 1980s as part of his attempt to reform the Soviet Communist system.

globalization: Expanding a policy or activity to apply worldwide.

global market(place): The buying and selling of products throughout the world, rather than limiting sales within a country or region.

Global Positioning System (GPS): A navigation network consisting of 24 satellites developed by the U.S. military. These satellites send signals that can be used for many purposes including time and date definition, and position locating.

global warming: Also called the greenhouse effect. The supposed gradual warming of the earth's climate as a result of various environmental factors including the burning of fossil fuels, the use of man-made chemicals, and deforestation.

GNP: *See* Gross National Product

government: The political and administrative system of a nation or state including legislative, executive, and judicial functions.

government securities: Certificates issued by the government as guarantees to repay loans.

GPS: *See* Global Positioning System

grand jury: A group of 12 to 23 people who hear evidence presented by a prosecuting attorney against someone accused of a serious crime and decide whether the person should be indicted, or charged with the crime.

grant: Money provided by a government or organization to an individual or group for a specific purpose. For example, the federal government makes education grants to students for college expenses and to states to improve schools.

grassroots: Political organizing at the most fundamental level of society—among the people.

Great Depression: Period in U.S. history from 1929 until the early 1940s when the economy was so poor that many banks and businesses failed and millions of people lost their jobs and their homes. The terrible business problems were combined with a severe drought that ruined many farms and contributed to the economic disaster.

Great Society: Term used by Lyndon Johnson during his presidential administration (1963–69) to describe his vision of the United States as a land without prejudice or poverty, that would be possible by implementing his series of social programs.

greenhouse effect: The warming of the Earth's surface and atmosphere caused by an increasing layer of pollution that traps gasses near the planet's surface and prevents their release and dispersion.

Gross Domestic Product (GDP): A measure of the market value of all goods and services produced within the boundaries of a nation, regardless of asset ownership. Unlike gross national product, GDP excludes receipts from that nation's business operations in foreign countries, as well as the share of reinvested earnings in foreign affiliates of domestic corporations.

Gross National Product (GNP): A measure of the market value of goods and services produced by the labor and property of a nation. Includes receipts from that nation's business operation in foreign countries, as well as the share of reinvested earnings in foreign affiliates of domestic corporations.

Gross State Product: The total value of goods and services produced within an individual state.

H

hate crimes: A crime, usually violence or vandalism directed at an individual or group because of their race, religion, or sexual preference.

health management organization (HMOs): Companies that provide health care services to enrolled individuals and families, by member physicians with limited referrals to specialists.

House of Representatives: One of the two bodies with specific functions that make up the legislative branch of the United States government. Each state is allocated representatives based on population. (*See also* Congress; Senate)

Human Immunodeficiency Virus (HIV): *See* Acquired Immunodeficiency Syndrome

humanitarian: A person who works for social reform and is concerned about the welfare of people.

I

ICBM: *See* intercontinental ballistic missile

illegal immigrant: A person who comes from another country to live in the United States without applying for entrance or completing the appropriate documents.

IMF: *See* International Monetary Fund

immigration: The process of leaving one's native country to live in another country.

impeach(ment): To charge someone with an offense that may lead to removal from the office they hold. In the United States, the House of Representatives has the power to bring charges and the Senate tries impeachment cases to determine the outcome.

implied powers: Authority granted to the federal government that is not specifically granted by the Constitution, but can be deduced from what is written in the Constitution.

import: Goods purchased from foreign suppliers; the act of purchasing goods from foreign suppliers. (*See also* export)

income tax: A tax levied on personal or corporate income, whether that income is in the form of wages or income from investments or property.

independent: A voter who does not belong to any political party and votes for individual candidates regardless of their party affiliation.

independent agency: A federal agency that is not part of a cabinet department. Such agencies include independent regulatory commissions, government corporations, or independent executive agencies.

indigenous: Native to or grown in, a particular place or environment.

inflation: An economic situation that occurs when prices increase to such a degree that the purchasing power of an average person decreases.

Information Superhighway: The name given to the ever increasing amount of knowledge and information available electronically via the Internet.

infrastructure: A basic system of public works such as roads, sewers, and power sources, and the people and resources needed to conduct activity.

intelligence: Gathering information on another country's military capabilities and political plans. In the United States, these operations are conducted by the Central Intelligence Agency, the National Security Agency, and military intelligence units.

intercontinental ballistic missile (ICBM): Missiles that are capable of traveling from one continent to another.

interest rate: A percentage of money borrowed that must be paid back in addition to the sum of the original loan for the privilege of being able to borrow.

intermodal (transportation): Using more than one kind of transportation during one journey.

International Monetary Fund (IMF): An agency of the United Nations that was created to promote international financial cooperation. The IMF loans money to member countries and stabilizes exchange rates.

interstate (commerce): Interstate commerce is business that is conducted between two or more states.

interstate highway system: The system of major highways built by the federal government that crisscross the country.

intramural: An activity conducted within the boundaries of, and limited to, the members of a particular institution. (*See also* extramural)

Iran-Contra affair: A scandal during the Reagan administration during which U.S. officials arranged for the sale of arms to Iran and funneled the profits to Nicaraguan guerillas (contras) to aide their struggle against the communist government in Nicaragua.

isolationism: A policy whereby one country refuses to become involved politically or economically with other countries.

J

joint committee: A committee composed of members from both the House of Representatives and the Senate to address an issue of mutual concern.

joint resolution: A measure that must be approved by the House of Representatives and the Senate and signed by the president to become law. However, if a joint resolution proposes an amendment to the Constitution, the president does not have to sign for the measure to become law.

Judeo-Christian: An idea, action, or value that has its roots in both Christian and Jewish traditions.

judicial branch: The segment of government that protects citizens against excessive use of power by the executive or legislature and provides an impartial setting for the settlement of civil and criminal cases. In the United States, the judiciary system is divided into state and federal courts with further divisions at those levels. State and federal courts are independent except that the Supreme Court of the United States may review state court decisions when a federal issue is involved. (*See also* executive branch; legislative branch)

jurisdiction: The right and authority of a court to hear and decide a case.

L

labor market: The people available for employment.

labor union: A group of organized workers who negotiate with management to secure or improve their rights, benefits, and working conditions as employees.

lame duck: An elected official who is not re-elected, serving out the portion of their term until the newly elected person is seated.

League of Nations: The forerunner of the United Nations, envisioned by its originator, Woodrow Wilson, as a forum where countries could resolve their differences without resorting to war. Formed in 1919, the League also promoted economic and social cooperation. Congress did not support President Wilson's plan and the United States did not join the League which contributed to its collapse in the late 1930s.

legal precedent: A court ruling that creates the basis for determining similar cases in the future.

legislation: Measures that are intended to become law after approval by legislative bodies.

legislative branch: The branch of government that makes or enacts laws. (*See also* executive branch; judicial branch)

liberal: A political philosophy that generally favors political, economic, or social change to benefit individuals. Liberals traditionally support federal action in the areas of civil rights, employment, and social programs.

line-item veto: The power of the president to disapprove a particular expense in the federal budget while approving the budget as a whole.

litigation: Disputes brought into court for legal decisions.

living will: A legal document that specifies what kind of medical treatments a person wishes to have administered if they become unconscious or are otherwise unable to direct their own medical care. Living wills often prohibit the administering of drastic measures, such as tubal feedings and ventilators for breathing, to extend life.

lobby, lobbies: A group of people who conduct activities designed to influence legislators to vote the way the lobby wants them to, or to convince legislators to introduce bills that are favorable to lobby interests. (*See also* lobbyist)

lobbyist: Someone who is paid to promote the interests of a particular group or industry in an attempt to influence the actions of legislators. (*See also* lobby)

M

macroeconomics: The study of the economy as a whole terms of income, employment, output, price levels, and rates of growth. (*See also* microeconomics)

major party: A political party that has many supporters and a great deal of power and influence.

mandate: Popular support for a political program or politician. Candidates espousing particular political plans are considered to be given a mandate by the people if they are elected, meaning that people agree with the candidates plans and want them to be implemented.

Mandus, writ of: A court order demanding an action. The court has the right to order an individual to perform an act that someone else has a legal right to expect, such as the fulfillment of a business contract.

Marshall Plan: Formally known as the European Recovery Program, a joint project between the United States and most Western European nations under which $12.5 billion in U.S. loans and grants was expended to aid European recovery after World War II (1939–45). Expenditures under the program, named for U.S. Secretary of State George C. Marshall, were made from fiscal years 1949 through 1952.

McCarthy Era: Period in American history from the late 1940s to the 1950s when Senator Joseph McCarthy of Wisconsin headed a committee investigating communist influence in the United States. Begun as a legitimate investigation, the committee began questioning individuals about their activities with little or no evidence that they had been involved in communist activities. The excesses of the committee and McCarthy created widespread suspicion and hysteria concerning national security. McCarthy was censured by the Senate in 1954 and the committee's activities were severely restricted.

media: Means of mass communication such as television, radio, newspapers, and magazines.

mediation: The intervention of an unbiased party to settle differences between two other disputing parties; any attempt to act as a go-between in order to reconcile a problem.

Medicaid: A federal program that provides health insurance to low-income families.

Medicare: A federal program that provides health insurance to the elderly.

merchant marine: The ships of a nation, whether privately or publicly owned, that are involved in commercial business. The term may also refer to someone who works on such ships.

metropolitan area: A large important city and the outlying suburbs that are connected to it geographically and economically.

microeconomics: The study of the economy of a particular unit such as a business, or of a specific activity such as pricing. (*See also* macroeconomics)

military intervention: When a government sends its armed forces into a situation to restore order or halt a conflict without a formal declaration of war.

military junta: The small military group in power of a country, especially after a coup.

military regime: Government conducted by a military force.

minimum wage: The wage established by law as the lowest amount to be paid to workers in particular jobs.

minor party: A small political party with little influence that is very often created around a single issue.

misappropriation: When public or private funds are used without authorization or for purposes not originally intended.

monopoly, monopolies The exclusive control of goods and services in a particular market, often leading to complete control over prices of those commodities.

moratorium: An emergency legislation allowing a delay in the payment of a debt; also an official delay or stoppage of some activity.

mortgage: A document held by a lender allowing them to take property if a borrower does not repay a loan.

most-favored-nation: A trading system in which all participants receive the same tax benefits. Although the term implies special treatment for one nation, it actually guarantees fair treatment of all trade participants.

multilateral negotiation: Discussions and meetings to resolve conflicts in which many countries participate.

multiparty system: Political system in which many political parties representing different viewpoints are participants. (*See also* two-party system)

N

NAFTA: *See* North American Free Trade Agreement

nation: A large group of people united by bonds of geography, language, customs, and shared collective experiences. Some nations that have developed governmental systems are also referred to as states. (*See also* state)

national debt: The public debt of the United States government. Whenever government expenses exceed revenue, the difference is added to the national debt.

National Income and Product Accounts (NIPA): Tracking system for a variety of statistics that give information about income and productivity.

national security: Ensuring that a country is protected from internal and external attacks.

national security adviser: A member of the National Security Council who consults with the president on matters of national security.

NATO: *See* North Atlantic Treaty Organization

naturalization: The legal process by which an alien becomes a citizen. An individual who is at least 18 may become a citizen after meeting certain qualifications including: residing in the United States for five years; reading, writing, and speaking English; and taking an oath of allegiance to the United States. (*See also* alien; citizen)

nepotism: Showing favoritism toward someone because they are related to you. For example, granting a family member a job only because he or she is a family member.

New Deal: The name given to Franklin Roosevelt's plan to save the nation from the devastating effects of the Great Depression. His programs included direct aid to citizens and a variety of employment and public works opportunities sponsored by the federal government.

NIPA: *See* National Income and Product Accounts

nongovernmental organizations (NGOs): Organizations that may lobby or advise the federal government, but are not officially part of or funded by the government.

nonpartisan: An action free from political party influence or undertaken by members of all political parties involved.

nonprofit: An organization which is not established for profit-making; all funds are spent on the organization's expenses and services.

nonproliferation: Stopping the increase in the number and spread of nuclear weapons. (*See also* proliferation)

North American Free Trade Agreement (NAFTA): An agreement between the United States, Canada, and Mexico that removes all trade barriers between the three countries. For purposes of trade, all boundaries disappear and the nations conduct business as if one country, rather than as foreign nations.

North Atlantic Treaty Organization (NATO): An organization formed in 1949 by countries bordering and near the north Atlantic Ocean. The purpose of NATO is to provide security to member nations that agree to come to each others defense if any member is attacked.

nuclear: Relating to radioactive materials that may be used for weapons, energy, or medicine.

nuclear waste: The toxic by-products created by the manufacture or use of radioactive materials.

O

ombudsmen: An appointed official who investigates private complaints against an organized group, such as a government.

omnibus: A term describing something that includes or involves many items. Used in government to describe bills that contain a variety of proposals.

Operation Desert Storm: The name of the military operation by the United States against Iraq, after Iraq invaded Kuwait in 1990–1991.

P

paramilitary: An organization created along military lines that is not part of any official military unit.

parliamentary: Related to a supreme legislative body made up of many representatives and similar to the British system of government.

partisan: An action or person that adheres to a political party's platform or opinion. (*See also* bipartisan)

patent: An official document granted by the federal government to an inventor of a product that gives the inventor the exclusive right to make, use, or sell the product. A patent also enables an inventor to pursue legal action against anyone who interferes with their exclusive rights.

peacekeeping: Describes military troops sent into conflict situations to keep the peace and restore order until a permanent resolution can be reached.

pension(s): Money given to an employee when they retire from a company. Pensions can be funded by the government, an employer, or through employee contributions.

per capita: Literally, per person; for each person counted.

plaintiff: A person or group that brings legal action in court.

pocket veto: A special veto wherein any bill passed by Congress but unsigned by the president when Con-

gress adjourns, dies. Unlike an ordinary presidential veto, which can be overridden, the pocket veto is absolute.

political action committee: A group that raises money to support the election of politicians that the group feels will support their interests.

political party: A group of individuals who organize for the purpose of nominating candidates for office, winning elections, operating government, and determining public policies.

political science: The academic study of political systems and theories.

politician: A person experienced in government as an appointed official or officeholder or someone involved in party politics. (*See also* politics)

politics: Relating to government or the conduct of government especially the making of government policies and organization. (*See also* politician)

popular vote: The actual vote of the population. (*See also* electoral college)

populism: A belief in the rights, wisdom, and virtues of average citizens. A political philosophy that advocates on behalf of common people as opposed to favoring the interests of industry.

pork barrel: Funds appropriated by Congress for local projects that are not critically needed. Members of Congress generally do not question other members' pork barrel legislation for fear their own local projects could be defeated.

post traumatic stress disorder: A condition characterized by depression, anxiety, nightmares, and the inability to function in normal life, that is the result of a traumatic event or series of events.

power of attorney: A document that allows someone to act legally on the signers behalf.

preferred provider organization (PPO): A company that provides health care services at reduced rates to members who voluntarily enroll in the program and use specific physicians and hospitals that have agreed to reduced fees.

press secretary: Assistant to the president who interacts regularly with the media on the president's behalf through press conferences and briefings. The press secretary provides information on the president's activities and plans.

price support: A program in which the federal government helps stabilize agricultural prices by buying up surplus products and granting loans.

primary: Election where voters choose one candidate to represent a political party in a race for an elected office.

private sector: The division of an economy in which production of goods and services is privately owned.

privatization: To change from public to private control or ownership.

pro bono: Providing professional services, particularly legal, to the people who could not afford them. Literally, "for the public good."

pro-choice: The belief that abortion should be legal and that the decision to have an abortion must be made by each individual woman considering the procedure. (*See also* anti-abortion; pro-life)

pro-life: A belief in the sanctity of all human life. Individuals who are pro-life usually believe that abortion should be illegal and that right-to-die legislation should not be enacted. (*See also* anti-abortion; pro-choice)

progressive tax: Any tax in which the tax rate increases as the amount to be taxed increases. For example, a progressive income tax might have a tax rate of 10% on the first $10,000 of income, a tax rate of 15% on the second $10,000, and a 20% tax rate on all income above $20,000.

Prohibition: The sale, manufacture, or transportation of alcoholic beverages was made illegal by constitutional provision between 1920 and 1933. The rapid repeal of this provision showed the unpopularity of this ban.

proliferation: The growth or expanse of something. Often refers to the increase in the number or spread of nuclear weapons. (*See also* nonproliferation)

proportional tax: Any tax wherein the tax rate remains the same no matter how much the amount to be taxed increases.

protectionist: Someone who supports restrictive government regulations on foreign products and companies to protect domestic producers.

pro tempore: Literally means "for the time being." The vice president is technically the head of the Senate, but a president pro tempore presides on a daily basis.

public corporation: Industries or businesses that are owned by the public through stock purchases or investments.

public debt: The entire debt of a government or nation.

public domain: Land owned by the federal government including national parks, forests, and grazing lands.

public interest: On behalf of the people, or for the good of the people.

public opinion: The combined opinions, attitudes, or beliefs of a large portion of a community that influences public policy and legislation.

public policy: A government plan of action for addressing issues that affect and involve the public.

public sector: The people of a country or community. Differs from the private sector which is made up of industries and organizations controlled by a few individuals, not the public as a whole.

public works: Facilities that are built or improved using government funds and benefit the general public. Parks, roads, hospitals, and harbors paid for by the government are all examples of public works.

Q

quorum: The minimum number of members that must be present for a decision making body to conduct business. The constitution states that "a majority of each (house) shall constitute a quorum to do business." This means 218 members must be present in the House of Representatives, and 51 in the Senate, to transact business.

quota system: A situation wherein only a certain predetermined number of individuals of a particular race or gender are admitted to a country, educational institution, or profession.

R

rank-and-file: Usually refers to the members of a labor union who do not hold offices or other positions of power.

ratification, ratified: The process by which constitutional amendments or treaties are formally approved. Amendments to the United States Constitution must be ratified by three-fourths of the states to become official. Treaties are approved in the Senate and by the president who officially ratifies a treaty in a signing ceremony with representatives of the treaty's other parties.

rearmament: To become armed again with new and better weapons.

recession: An economic slowdown of relatively short duration. During a recession, unemployment rises and purchasing power drops temporarily.

reconnaissance: A maneuver to gain information or explore territory. Often describes a military operation, when troops investigate enemy positions and plans.

Reconstruction: The period following the Civil War (1860–65), when the economy and infrastructure of the war-ravaged southern United States was rebuilt with the aid of the federal government.

regressive tax: Any tax in which the burden to pay falls relatively more heavily upon lower income groups than upon more wealthy taxpayers. Sales tax is an example of regressive tax because a larger portion of low income families wages are spent on necessary purchases, than that of higher earning families.

regulatory agency: A government office that makes rules for or concerning a particular product or service. For example, the Food and Drug Administration (FDA) determines which new foods and drugs will be made available to the public, and what quality standards products must meet to be sold in the United States.

regulatory reform: Attempts to streamline the processes of regulatory agencies because they are creating too many rules, rules that are too restricted, or taking too long to make decisions.

remediation: The process of pursuing legal action to prevent or reverse a wrong done to an individual.

representative: An elected member of the United States House of Representatives.

Republican Party: One of the two major political parties in the United States. The Republican Party emerged in the 1850s as an antislavery party. In the twentieth century, the Republican Party represents conservative fiscal and social policies and advocates a more limited role for federal government.

revenue: The total income collected by state or federal governments.

rider: A provision, unlikely to pass on its own merits, that is added to a bill so it will "ride" into passage. What may be considered an unrelated rider by one legislator, may be regarded as a legitimate amendment to a bill.

S

sanctions: A detrimental economic or military measure (such as stopping trade) taken by one country against another for the purpose of convincing that country to change its policies or practices.

secretary: In the federal government, secretary is the title of the head of an executive department.

secured document: An official document that is protected from general viewing due to high level security classification. (*See also* classified; declassify)

securities: Documents that prove debt or ownership such as a stock certificate or bond.

selective service: The program that determines which men will be selected for mandatory military service, also known as the draft.

Senate: One of the two bodies with specific functions that make up the legislative branch of the United States government. Each state is allocated two Senators. (*See also* Congress; House of Representatives)

Senator: An elected member of the United States Senate.

senatorial courtesy: An informal understanding among senators that the president will confer with senators of his party from a particular state before filling federal positions within that state. If there are no senators from the president's party in a state with openings, the president may consult state party leaders.

separation of powers: The cornerstone of U.S. government wherein power is divided among three branches of government—the executive, legislative, and judicial. Officials of each branch are selected differently, have different responsibilities, and serve different terms. The separation of power is not absolute, however, due to the system of checks and balances. (*See also* checks and balances)

social insurance: Benefits or subsidies provided to citizens fully or partially to prevent economic or health problems. Unemployment insurance and worker's compensation are examples.

socialized medicine: Medical and hospital services that are provided by state or federal agencies and paid for by taxes or donations.

Social Security: A public program that provides economic aid and social welfare for individuals and their families through social insurance or assistance. In the United States, Social Security was passed into law in 1935, as a life and disability insurance and old-age pension for workers. It is paid for by employers, employees, and the government.

sovereignty: The rule of a supreme political power, such as a king or queen; the complete independent authority of a governmental unit; also, freedom from external control.

special interest group: A group that organizes to influence legislation and government policies to further their specific interests. Special interest groups include the National Rifle Association, which advocates the right to own guns responsibly, and the Sierra Club, which promotes protecting the environment.

staggered term: System wherein only a portion of the Senate or House of Representatives is up for re-election at a time. This ensures that there are always experienced members at each session to guide new members through the legislative process.

stakeholder: Someone who holds shares of stock in a corporation or a personal or financial interest in the outcome of a situation or event.

state: A body of people, occupying a specific geographic location, that organize into a political unit. State can also refer to the smaller geographic and political units that make up a larger state. (*See also* nation)

statutory: Laws enacted by Congress or a state legislature. Statutes are public and private laws that are consecutively numbered during each session of Congress.

steering committee: Committees formed to direct the flow of work and the operations of a body. In legislative bodies, the steering committee determines in what order work will be addressed.

stewardship: The act of carefully managing and safeguarding something. In the United States government, the president not only has the right to administer the country, but the duty to protect the nation and its people.

stock market: A market where shares of stock, or certificates of ownership in a company, are bought and sold.

strike: When employees stop work until they get concessions from their employers on issues such as wages, hours, or working conditions.

subsidy, subsidies, subsidized: Money granted by one state to another or from a government to an individual or company for an activity that benefits the public.

suffrage: The right to vote.

Superfund: Special federal pool of money created to clean up and restore areas affected by toxic waste.

sustainable living: A lifestyle that promotes conservation of natural resources and replacing resources used. For example, sustainable homes are often powered by the wind and sun and use composts of household wastes to return nutrients to soil used for growing food.

sweatshops: Manufacturing facilities that deprive employees of decent wages, reasonable work schedules, and safe working conditions. Sweatshops exist in countries without labor laws or in violation of labor laws in countries such as the United States.

T

Taft-Hartley Act: A law passed in 1947 that was intended to limit the power of labor unions that they have since been given by the Wagner Act of 1935. Taft-Hartley outlawed jurisdictional strikes, secondary boycotts, political expenditures, and excessive dues. The Taft-Hartley Act is also known as the Labor-Management Relations Act of 1947. (*See also* Wagner Act)

tariff(s): Tax imposed on foreign products brought into the United States to protect domestic businesses from excessive competition.

tax: A charge, in the form of money, imposed on people or property by an authority and used for public purposes.

tax credits: Amounts that may be subtracted from one's total income and therefore reduce the amount of taxes owed. A specific dollar amount that can be subtracted for each minor child in a family is an example of a tax credit.

tax deductible: An expense or payment (such as a charitable contribution or mortgage interest) that can be subtracted from one's total income and therefore re-

duces the amount of income that taxes must be paid on.

tax shelter: An investment that is exempt from taxation and therefore decreases total tax owed.

telecommuting: Working from a location other than an employer's office (usually from home) but being connected to the office through telephone, fax, and computer.

Temperance Movement: A movement that grew in strength in the late 1800s and early 1900s and advocated abstinence from the use of alcohol. The Temperance Movement culminated in the passage of the Eighteenth Amendment to the U.S. Constitution in 1920 that outlawed alcoholic beverages. The Eighteenth Amendment was repealed in 1933 by the Twenty-First Amendment.

tenure: The right to hold a position or office without the possibility of arbitrary dismissal. Public employees in the civil service and teachers achieve tenure after serving a probationary period.

terrorism: Systematic acts of violence designed to frighten or intimidate.

think tank: An institute, corporation, or group that researches and studies technological or social problems.

third-world: A term used to describe less developed countries; as of the mid-1990s, it is being replaced by the United Nations designation less developed countries, or LDCs.

tort reform: Revising the branch of law that establishes rules for lawsuits involving acts that bring injury to persons, property, or reputation.

trade: The business of buying and selling goods and services.

trademark: A name or mark used by a manufacturer to identify a particular product or service the public. Trademarks are officially registered at and granted by the Patent Office.

trade sanction: A trade restriction imposed on another country by the United States to convince that country to reverse or amend a course of action that is unacceptable.

trade surplus: The extent by which a country's exports exceed its imports.

treaty: An agreement entered into by two or more nations that creates or limits mutual rights and responsibilities. In the United States all treaties are negotiated by the president and approved by the Senate.

two-party system: A political system dominated by two major political parties; for instance, the Democratic and Republican parties in the United States. (*See also* multiparty system)

U

unconstitutional: Acts or laws that violate the written or implied principles of a constitution.

unemployment insurance: Money paid into a fund by employers and paid out to employees for a limited time when the worker is laid off work.

union: An organization of workers that seek to improve the economic status of workers through collective bargaining and political action. Also known as labor union, or collectively as labor.

United Nations: Assembly organized in 1945 to find peaceful resolutions to international disputes and encourage cooperation in dealing with worldwide social and economic issues. Nations from all over the world are represented at the United Nations.

V

veteran: A person with long term experience in a skill or occupation. Veteran often refers to a former member of the armed services.

veto: When someone refuses to approve a measure or action. Particularly the power of the president to disapprove legislation.

voter referendum: A process by which voters in a state can disapprove a bill passed by state legislators. In states providing for referendums, a bill passed by the legislature does not take effect for a certain time period. During this period a bill may be suspended if the required number of voters sign a petition to do so. A suspended bill is then voted on by the public to determine whether or not it will go into effect.

voucher: A credit given to parents who choose to enroll their child in a school outside of the public school system, for all or part of the amount it would cost to educate the child in a public school. The credit, or voucher, can then be used to pay tuition and expenses at the school the parents choose.

W

Wagner Act: A major law passed in 1935 that guarantees workers the right to organize unions and bargain collectively through representatives of their own choosing. The act also established the National Labor Relations Board to administer its provisions and prevent employers from committing unfair labor practices. (*See also* Taft-Hartley Act)

watchdog: A government agency or special interest group that is responsible for ensuring that laws and regulations are followed. Such agencies often focus on specific activities such as trade and commerce.

welfare: The collective term to describe programs that give financial aid and provide necessities to people in need. (*See also* corporate welfare)

welfare reform: The process of dismantling the longstanding system of nearly unconditional, unlimited aid to the economically disadvantaged. Welfare reform establishes a system of aid that is conditional and aims to move recipients to self sufficiency as quickly as possibly.

white-collar crime: Non-violent crime involving violations of law that often take place in a business setting.

white paper: A detailed government report.

workfare: A collective term for programs that require people in need to work a certain number of hours in order to receive financial aid.

workers' compensation: An insurance program that provides money to workers injured in the workplace from a fund created by employer payments.

writ(s): A written order of a court commanding an individual or group to perform or cease a particular activity.

Z

zoning: The process of designating sections of a geographic area for specific purposes such as business or residential.

Subject Index

and gays in military, 137, 415
on global warming, 264
Gore Commission under, 464
government shutdowns under, 74–75
health care reform efforts by, 53, 93,
    148, 154, 155, 155, 347, 348,
    480–81, 576–77
highway funding under, 11
and Hispanic education issues, 561
historic preservation under, 648
impeachment proceedings against,
    530
John Birch Society opposition to,
    394
Kyoto Protocol signed by, 266, 304
labor support for, 371, 376
and land mine issue, 681, 763
and Monica Lewinsky political
    scandal, 685
and NAFTA, 384, 779
and National Governors'
    Association, 591
National Partnership Council
    established by, 75
NEA support for, 571
and needle-exchange programs, 17,
    260
and nursing facility industry, 103
Partial Birth Abortion Ban vetoed
    by, 254, 256, 322, 324, 325,
    398, 444, 445, 540, 541, 635,
    636, 699
Paula Jones harassment suit against,
    47, 713
on Pedro Zamora, 15
perceived environmentalism of, 802
political activity restrictions on
    federal employees relaxed by,
    476
post-Cold War defense policy of,
    290
Presidential Medal of Freedom
    awarded by, 540
pro-choice stance of, 635
and Puerto Rico, 733
Rainbow/PUSH Coalition support
    for, 708
social security proposal by, 75
speech at Hong Kong convention
    center by, *485*
Taxpayer Relief Act of 1997 signed
    by, 324
and Wall Street Project, 709
and welfare reform, 87–88, 609
and Whitewater investigation, 41–42
Clinton, Hillary Rodham, 411, 569
    and Children's Defense Fund, 212
    health care reform efforts by, 53,
        155, 348
Clinton administration, 328
    AIDS testing of treatments for
        children endorsed by, 99
    and airbag switches, 503
    campaign finance reform movement
        during, 773

consumer initiatives under, 270
and dolphin-chasing practices
    curtailment, 361
drug policy of, 604
and drug treatment programs, 567
firearms position of, 623
and global climate change treaty,
    758
Gulf War Syndrome review
    committee under, 300
habitat conservation plans approved
    under, 659
and health care reform efforts
    during, 718
and Internet access for schools, 572
labor relations during, 776
opposition to medical use of
    marijuana by, 48
and television rating system, 439
and welfare reform, 208
women elected to office during, 662
Clinton/Gore campaign
    charges of illegal campaign
        donations from Asian
        countries, 674
Clipper Chip proposal, 307, 308–309
Cloning, 713
    opposition to, 324
Clyburn, James, 257
CME. *See* Center for Media Education
CNBC, 604
CNN, 227, 490, 604
Coal industry subsidies, 771
Coalition against Consumer Fraud, 271
Coalition for Affordable Quality
    Healthcare, 347, 349
Coalition for Consumer Health and
    Safety, 268
Coalition for Consumer Protection and
    Quality in Health Care
    Reform, 271
Coalition for Health Insurance Choices,
    348
Coalition for Women's Appointments,
    662
Coalition of Medical Professionals, 333
Coal Miners' Political Action
    Committee (COMPAC), 754,
    755
Coal mining industry, 754–59
Coal usage, 757
Coastal Berry Co.
    and strawberry workers, 746
Coastal Berry Farm Workers
    Committee, 747
Coburn, Tom, 16, 17
Coca-Cola
    and boycotts, 707
Cocaine, 603
Cockfighting, 160, 358
COCO. *See* Conference on Consumer
    Organizations
Code of Conduct (weapons trade), 680
Code of Fair Competition for the Motor
    Vehicle Retailing Trade, 501

Cody, Cardinal, 540
Coia, Arthur A., 407, 410, 411
Coin programs, 35
Cold War, 170, 201, 394
    and censorship, 142
    end of, 186, 188, 245, 285
    peace activism during, 679
    and "peace dividend," 93
    U.S. defense policy following end
        of, 290
    U.S. foreign policy during, 290
Coleman, George, 280
Colgate-Palmolive
    testing on dogs by, 692
Collective bargaining, 84, 85, 86, 91,
    250, 777
    Chamber of Commerce support for,
        766
    by communications workers, 249,
        251
    early agreements for, 409
    by electrical industry workers, 373,
        374
    by farm workers, 742, 743, 744,
        745, 746
    by food and commercial workers,
        750
    guarantee for right to, 410
    by law enforcement officers, 327,
        328
    by letter carriers, 471, 472–73
    by machinists and aerospace
        workers, 368, 369
    by mine workers, 754, 755
    by nurses, 152, 154
    by service employees, 716
    by steelworkers, 775, 776, 778
    by teachers, 89, 92, 569
    through UAW, 736, 737
    by transportation workers, 728, 781,
        782, 784
    and union dues, 630
    and Wagner Act of 1935, 370
College Equal Suffrage League, 421
College Leadership Forum (NCLR), 560
Collier, John, 181, 545
Colloquia series (NAS), 449
Colonial Penn, 30
Colorado
    antigay rights referendum in, 587
    dust storm in (1930s), *68*
    school shootings in, 228
Colorado River
    dam building on, 793
Colston E. Warne program, 273
Colt Manufacturing
    "Smart Gun" technology from, 343
Columbia, 400
Columbia Broadcasting System (CBS),
    462
Columbian Squires, 398
Columbia River
    and stored nuclear waste, 547
Columbia University, 142
Columbus, Christopher, 399

W

Wagner, Robert, 86, 92
Wagner Act, 74, 249, 370, 410, 480, 746, 756
Wagner-Murray-Dingell bill
 AMA opposition to, 147
Walgreens drug stores
 boycotts against, 707
Walker, Robert J., 340
Walkouts, 784
Wallace, Henry A., 659
Walling, William English, 455
Wall Street Journal, 307
Wall Street Project (RPC)
 case study on, 708–709
Walt Disney Company, 436
 domestic partner benefits through, 417
 Mr. Magoo and National Federation of the Blind, 582
 See also Disney Corporation
Walter and May Reuther Family Education Center (Michigan), 737
Walters, Bishop Alexander, 455
War
 seeking abolition of, 677–82
War bonds, 766
War Charities Act, 280
War Department
 during Civil War, 449–50
Warehouse workers, 381
Warm Springs Reservation (Washington)
 radioactive waste released on, 546
Warner Brothers, 436
War of the Worlds, 462
"War on Drugs," 74, 601, 603
Washington (state)
 medical use of marijuana referenda in, 48
Washington, Booker T., 653
Washington Papers, 200
Washington Post, 227, 307
Washington Quarterly, 200, 203
Washington Times, 53
Washington Watch, 322, 325
Washington Weekly Report, 762, 763
Water
 military pollution of, 193
 safety standards for, 772
Watergate scandal, 51, 246, 530
 and Common Cause, 245
Water pollution, 207
 from industrial/toxic waste, 773
 from radioactive waste, 546
 and suburban sprawl, 469
Waters, Maxine, 260
Watsonville, California
 strawberry workers in, 746–47
Wattleton, Faye, 698
Watts, Glenn, 250
WEAF (radio)
 Roosevelt's "fireside chats" over, 462

Weapons
 children's use of, 228
 pollution from, 192–93
 trading of, 680
Weapons systems
 research and analysis of, 190, 191
WeatherCenter, 558
Weaver, Reginald, 568
"Web of Life" (ASPCA), 159
Webster, Noah, 402
Webster ruling, 798
Wednesday Group, 530
Welch, John, 619
Welch, Robert Henry Winborne, Jr., 392, 394, 395
Welch, William, 450
Welfare
 equal opportunity in, 651
 and restaurant industry, 620
Welfare Act (1996)
 impact of, on children, 214
Welfare reform, 321, 540
 AFSCME opposition to, 87
 and Asian-American community, 672, 674, 675
 and corporate welfare, 208
 and homelessness, 525
 impact on women and children, 609
 and National Governors' Association, 591
Welfare Reform Act of 1997, 699
WELL, 307
Wellcome Trust, 206
Wells, Orson, 462
Wells Fargo Bank, 575
Wetlands
 preservation of, 497, 803
 and suburban sprawl, 469
Wetlands Campaign, 494
Wetlands Citizen Education Program, 419
Whalers, 358
Whales, 802
 protection of, 338
Whaling industry
 and National Audubon Society efforts, 497
Wheelchair accessibility, 614
"When Justice Is Up To You," 175
Whistleblower protections
 for nursing profession, 153
Whiston, David A., 58, 59
White, Betty, 359
White, Lois Jean, 549, 551
White, Ryan, 15, *100*
White Cane Safety Day, 581
White Castle, 619
White Clover Program (AMVETS), 164
Whitehead, John, 711, 712, 713
White House, 194, 307
White House Climate Change Task Force
 and global temperature records, 264
White House Conference on Hate Crimes, 518, 519

White House Conference on Small Business, 639
White House Millennium Council, 649
White House Office of Policy Development, 323
White Ribbon Against Pornography Campaign (WRAP), 425
White rights movement, 401–406
Whites
 educational attainment among, 457
 in poverty, 458
Whitman, Christine Todd, 798, 799
Whittier, John Greenleaf, 495
Who Decides? A State-by-State Review of Abortion Rights, 443, 444, 446
Whole Earth Catalog, The, 305
WHOSE Death Is It, Anyway?, 216, 220
Who Stole Feminism? (Hoff-Sommers), 611
Why Women Pay More, 206
Wicker, Roger, 17
Widowed Persons Service (AARP), 29
Wilcox, Clyde, 663
Wild Alert! program (TWS), 792
Wild and Scenic Rivers Act
 and National Audubon Society efforts, 497
Wilderness
 protection of, 791–95
Wilderness, 792
Wilderness Act, 658, 723, 793
Wilderness Bill, 793
Wilderness magazine, 794
Wilderness Society, The (TWS), **791–95**
Wildlands and Human Needs Program (WWF), 801
Wildlife conservation, 357, 358, 360, 493–98, 656–60, 720–25, 800–805
Wildlife habitats
 and suburban sprawl, 469
Wildlife Land Trust, 358
Wildlife Productions, Inc., 657
Wildlife refuges, 358, 360
Wildmon, Donald E., 61, 63
Wilkerson, H. Dean, 429
William A. Schreyer Chair in Global Analysis (CSIS), 200
William E. Simon Chair in Political Economy (CSIS), 200
William M. Scholl Chair in International Business (CSIS), 200
Williams, Lynn, 778
Williams, Roy, 382
William W. Winpisinger Education and Technology Center, 369
Willingham, Clark, 509
Wilson, Arthur, 300
Wilson, Pete, 82, 251, 384, 604, 654, 799
Wilson, Richard, 115
Wilson, Woodrow, 81, 756, 766
 and Balfour Declaration, 131